*The Doubleday Roget's Thesaurus
in Dictionary Form*

THE DOUBLEDAY
ROGET'S THESAURUS
in Dictionary Form

✧

Sidney I. Landau

EDITOR IN CHIEF

Ronald J. Bogus   423

MANAGING EDITOR

Doubleday & Company, Inc., Garden City, New York

Library of Congress Cataloging in Publication Data

Main entry under title:
The Doubleday Roget's thesaurus
in dictionary form.

"Not based on any other thesaurus . . . Entries were selected from entries in the Doubleday dictionary, first published in 1975."
1. English language—Synonyms and antonyms.
2. English language—Dictionaries. 3. Americanisms.
I. Landau, Sidney I. II. Bogus, Ronald J. III. Title:
Thesaurus in dictionary form.
PE1591.D6   1977   423'.1
Library of Congress Catalog Card Number 76–7696
International Standard Book Number, Thumb-Index Edition 0-385-12379-5
International Standard Book Number, Regular Edition 0-385-01236-5

THESAURUS STAFF

Editor in Chief: Sidney I. Landau
Managing Editor: Ronald J. Bogus
Editors: Barbara Nolan, John S. Bowman,
Herbert Gilbert, Ruth Koenigsberg,
Helene MacLean, Kathleen D. Shafer

Contents

Preface

American thesauruses generally fall into two categories: the voluminous, subject-indexed variety and the brief, alphabetically arranged dictionary-style book. Many people find the subject-index thesaurus difficult to use because the breakdown of senses is overrefined and overlapping. One must often turn to two or three places to find synonyms for any one sense, and even so one frequently finds few apt synonyms and much redundancy, as well as a hodge-podge of antiquated clichés, phrases that are really brief definitions rather than synonyms, and words so artificially composed of Latin or Greek elements that it would be safe to say they have appeared nowhere else other than in thesauruses. On the other hand, the shorter, alphabetical thesauruses often give too few synonyms to be helpful. One is trapped between the Scylla of parsimony and the Charybdis of overabundance.

We hope to avoid this quandary by having a simple format with a comparatively full, but nevertheless selective, treatment of synonyms. *The Doubleday Roget's Thesaurus* is arranged in one alphabetical listing so that at the first reference one can find a sufficient number of apt synonyms for the term one is looking up. Synonyms for all the important meanings of the term can be found at the same place, without having to turn to a different section for each meaning.

As has been often observed, there are very few exact synonyms in English. To state the point more explicitly: very few words can be freely substituted for another word in a variety of contexts without changing the sense or making the statement unidiomatic or nonsensical. Any thesaurus that attempted to list only exact synonyms would be very short indeed, and not very useful; for one of the chief reasons for using a thesaurus is precisely to find words that are identical to the entry word in some contexts but not in others, or that differ in connotation or usage level, i.e., in the degree of formality or informality. The question is how far afield from the central core of meaning do we stray?

Our aim has been to provide the reader with words that closely reflect the particular meaning of the entry word—words that one can imagine being substituted for it in a fairly broad variety of contexts. Given this desired correspondence of meaning, we have tried to provide the reader with as wide a choice as possible. As a practical matter, we have usually limited the number of synonyms listed under any one meaning to twenty or fewer; to go much beyond this number would be likely to bury the reader in a plethora of words, many of them irrelevant. The essential criterion was always aptness; if the synonyms were apt, we would bend the rule to include as many as possible.

As a matter of policy, this thesaurus does not list types of things as synonyms. We do not, under *disease,* list kinds of diseases, nor under *doctor* do we list various specialties of medicine. Such lists are arbitrary—how many of the thousands of well-known kinds of insects should one list under *insect?*—and therefore too selective to be of any use; and they are not composed of synonyms. The alert reader will detect occasional contraventions of this policy, to which we freely admit; when we felt it was useful and not arbitrary to include terms of this kind, we have done so. The distinction between synonyms and words belonging to a sub-category is not always clear-cut, and in such cases we have tended to include these terms.

Very few thesauruses pay much attention to antonyms. We have paid a great deal of attention to them, believing that many readers find them useful in sharpening their appreciation of the range of meanings of the synonyms to which they apply. Although we have sought to avoid imposing antonyms on words which have no antonyms, we have even so found it necessary to be somewhat more flexible in selecting antonyms than in selecting synonyms. If there are few exact synonyms, there are even fewer exact antonyms. Antonyms have a way of meandering away from the basic meaning, so that the last word of a list of antonyms may have very little in common with the first. Yet at no point in the process is one aware of having made any quantum jumps in meaning. As with synonyms, so, more emphatically, with antonyms: too exacting a standard would rule out all but a few words, and the result would be a book of much diminished value.

One final word about how this book was written. *The Doubleday Roget's Thesaurus* is entirely new. None of it has been published before in any form. It is not based on any other thesaurus. Its entries were selected from the entries in *The Doubleday Dictionary,* first published in 1975, and the breakdown of meanings in this work is based, with many modifications, on the sense breakdowns in that dictionary. Since *The Doubleday Dictionary* is an extremely up-to-date work, we were assured that our entries would not neglect any important current terms. In spite of all our efforts, however, this book like any other new reference work is likely to have some omissions or errors, and for those we ask the reader's indulgence. We welcome any comments or criticisms that would help us correct these deficiencies.

SIDNEY I. LANDAU
Editor in Chief

Guide to the Use of This Thesaurus

Entry terms are arranged in a single alphabetical list and appear in large, bold type. Alphabetization is letter by letter, as in most dictionaries, rather than word by word. For example, *pitcher* precedes *pitch in*. Homographs such as *pit*[1] (cavity, hole) and *pit*[2] (stone, kernel) are entered separately and distinguished by superscript numbers.

The part-of-speech label follows the entry word. Part-of-speech labels are abbreviated as follows: *n.,* noun; *v.,* verb; *adj.,* adjective; *adv.,* adverb; *pron.,* pronoun; *prep.,* preposition. Phrases of two or more words are not labeled. If an entry has more than one part of speech—e.g., *run* is both a verb and a noun—successive parts of speech are introduced by a bold-faced dash. Different meanings under each part of speech are distinguished by numerals in bold type. To aid the reader in perceiving differences in meaning, the first few synonyms listed under each meaning are those that best distinguish it from other meanings. Within this limitation, synonyms are listed with commoner words first, followed by more specialized and less familiar terms. Occasionally, a brief definition or contextual reference is necessary to distinguish between different meanings, as in the case of *clever:*

> **clever** *adj.* **1** *physically skillful:* adroit,
> skillful, dexterous, nimble . . . **2**
> bright, keen, sharp, quick, ingenious,
> original, inventive . . .

Special attention has been given to slang words and terms, which are always labeled in this work. Slang synonyms are identified by the label (*Slang*) in parentheses. Slang entries are identified by the label *Slang* without parentheses. Terms that are chiefly British are labeled (*Brit.*). Words that are usually considered foreign are printed in italic type. It should be noted that many terms not labeled may be considered colloquial or informal in certain senses and contexts; but since a thesaurus must necessarily combine meanings that in a dictionary would be distinguished, it is not practicable to restrict the application of such terms.

Antonyms, keyed where appropriate to particular meanings, are listed following the synonym treatment, introduced by the abbreviation **ant.** In some cases, no antonyms are applicable.

Synonyms printed in small capital letters are cross-references. Thus:

plain-spoken *adj.* FRANK.

directs the reader to the entry *frank,* where a full list of synonyms that might be used for *plain-spoken* is to be found.

A

abandon v. desert, forsake, leave, quit, discontinue, desolate, drop, repudiate, reject, renounce, defect, jilt, be done with, be through with. —n. wantonness, unrestraint, wildness, imprudence, profligacy, libertinism, intemperance, self-indulgence, mindlessness, heedlessness, hedonism, abandonment.

ant. v. embrace, cling to, adhere to, stick by, remain with, stay with, continue. n. restraint, caution, prudence, self-control, mindfulness, deliberation.

abandoned adj. **1** deserted, forsaken, forlorn, desolate, discarded, rejected, jilted, cast off, solitary, marooned, friendless, left alone. **2** immoral, dissolute, wanton, unrestrained, wild, licentious, depraved, profligate, shameless, disreputable, degraded, unrepentant, wicked, loose.

ant. **1** cherished, befriended, cared for, accepted, loved. **2** moral, chaste, virtuous, respectable, repressed, priggish, puritanical.

abase v. humiliate, humble, belittle, shame, scorn, degrade, demean, cheapen, debase, dishonor, lower, bring down, deflate, put down (*Slang*).

ant. elevate, raise, uplift, exalt, honor, dignify.

abash v. confuse, disconcert, discompose, shame, embarrass, bewilder, discomfit, nonplus, discountenance, intimidate, put off, put out.

ant. relax, put at ease, comfort, nerve, hearten.

abate v. lessen, slacken, wane, diminish, slow down, weaken, dwindle, ease, ebb, recede, bate, calm down, decrease, taper off.

ant. increase, grow, intensify, strengthen, heighten, quicken.

abbreviate v. compress, condense, shorten, abridge, cut, contract, digest, lessen, curtail, diminish, reduce, epitomize.

ant. enlarge, expand, increase, lengthen, inflate, supplement.

abbreviation n. compression, shortening, reduction, contraction, abridgment, condensation, curtailment, diminution, epitome.

ant. expansion, enlargement, lengthening, increase, dilation, extension.

ABC's n. basics, fundamentals, essentials, rudiments, elementals, prerequisites, core, roots, grounding, groundwork.

abdicate v. renounce, give up, resign, relinquish, retire, vacate, abandon, quit, forego, waive, abjure.

abdomen n. BELLY.

abduct v. kidnap, carry off, make off with, shanghai, spirit away, take away, steal off with.

aberrant adj. ABNORMAL.

aberration n. deviation, oddity, nonconformity, abnormality, quirk, anomaly, irregularity, eccentricity, peculiarity, sport, freak, mutant, heteroclite, monstrosity, monster, oddity, curiosity, abortion.

ant. normality, normalcy, conformity, regularity, norm, standard.

abet v. encourage, support, second, assist, join with, connive, conspire, endorse, embolden, spur, further, sanction, advance, promote.

ant. discourage, deter, disapprove, undermine, check, frustrate.

abeyance n. inactivity, inaction, suspension, latency, cessation, recess, intermission, pause, quiescence, dormancy, remission, rest.

ant. continuity, continuation, incessancy, ceaselessness.

abhor *v.* loathe, detest, despise, abominate, hate, execrate, shrink from, recoil from, avoid, shun, scorn, disdain, reject.

abhorrent *adj.* detestable, horrible, despicable, loathsome, hateful, abominable, contemptible, nauseating, disgusting, offensive, foul, revolting, awful, terrible.

ability *n.* competence, talent, skill, aptitude, efficiency, effectiveness, proficiency, capacity, expertness, expertise, capability, flair, know-how.
ant. incompetence, ineptitude, weakness, inefficiency, ineffectiveness, inadequacy.

abject *adj.* **1** mean, base, sordid, contemptible, ignoble, infamous, debased, low. **2** miserable, wretched, helpless, hopeless, spiritless, resigned, servile, subservient, submissive, slavish, hangdog.

abjure *v.* renounce, forswear, retract, recant, disown, relinquish, abnegate, repudiate, discard, disclaim, disavow, revoke, renege, eat one's words.
ant. maintain, uphold, embrace, cling to, persist in, swear by.

able *adj.* **1** competent, fit, adequate, up to, efficient, trained, skilled, capable, practiced, grounded, qualified, versed in. **2** gifted, talented, superior, expert, creative, inventive, accomplished, masterful, outstanding, deft, apt, adroit.
ant. 1 incompetent, inadequate, unqualified, unfit, inefficient, weak. **2** ordinary, average, usual, run of the mill, untalented, ungifted.

able-bodied *adj.* ROBUST.

abloom *adj.* BLOOMING.

ablution *n.* BATH.

abnegate *v.* RENOUNCE.

abnegation *n.* renunciation, rejection, refusal, surrender, abandonment, abjuration, relinquishment, self-denial.

abnormal *adj.* unusual, unnatural, irregular, unexpected, extraordinary, freakish, odd, eccentric, weird,

anomalous, aberrant, atypical, deviant.
ant. normal, usual, standard, natural, ordinary, everyday, typical.

abode *n.* dwelling, home, residence, domicile, lodging, living quarters, habitation, habitat, haunt, address, place, headquarters, nest, pad (*Slang*).

abolish *v.* destroy, eradicate, erase, annul, end, put an end to, finish off, kill, do away with, exterminate, extirpate, wipe out, abrogate, crush, cancel, nullify.
ant. establish, build, create, inaugurate, institute.

abominable *adj.* loathsome, detestable, despicable, repulsive, hateful, disgusting, abhorrent, execrable, vile, evil, atrocious, contemptible, awful.

abominate *v.* HATE.

abomination *n.* loathing, detestation, horror, hatred, execration, abhorrence, disgust, repugnance, revulsion, aversion, antipathy.

aboriginal *adj.* PRIMITIVE.

abort *v.* miscarry, go awry, go wrong, come to nothing, come to naught, fail, fizzle, flop.

abortion *n.* **1** ABERRATION. **2** miscarriage, disaster, fiasco, disappointment, defeat, failure.

abortive *adj.* unfruitful, unproductive, failed, miscarried, vain, fruitless, unprofitable, unavailing, unsuccessful, unrewarding, misdirected, futile, idle, useless.
ant. effective, rewarding, successful, fruitful, profitable.

about *prep.* **1** all around, on all sides of, encircling, round about, on every side of. **2** approximately, nearly, around, almost, more or less, approximating, approaching, close to, circa. **3** referring to, concerning, anent, in reference to, in connection with, having to do with, regarding, touching on, re.

about-face *n.* change of heart, reversal, *volte-face*, backing out, backing down, recantation, shift, turnabout, switch.

aboveboard *adj.* honest, forthright, straightforward, frank, open, overt, trustworthy, candid, direct, unconcealed, guileless, clear-cut, plain.
ant. sneaky, underhand, covert, wily, devious, equivocal, ambiguous.

abracadabra *n.* spell, charm, incantation, magic, hocus-pocus, open-sesame, mumbo-jumbo, voodoo, sorcery, witchcraft, magic formula, invocation.

abrade *v.* RUB.

abrasion *n.* **1** wearing away, rubbing, friction, scraping, scratching, chafing, chapping. **2** roughness, excoriation, scrape, scratch, chafe, chap.

abrasive *adj.* irritating, annoying, nasty, cutting, unpleasant, hurtful, caustic, destructive, sharp, biting, galling, grating.
ant. soothing, mollifying, comforting, gentle, agreeable, pleasant.

abreast of BESIDE.

abridge *v.* condense, shorten, abbreviate, summarize, abstract, digest, sum up, recap, recapitulate, cut, reduce, telescope.
ant. expand, enlarge, lengthen, detail.

abridgment *n.* condensation, digest, abbreviation, summary, contraction, curtailment, recap, recapitulation, shortening, précis.
ant. enlargement, expansion, inflation, lengthening.

abrogate *v.* annul, repeal, abolish, cancel, nullify, rescind, countermand, override, withdraw, revoke, invalidate, set aside.

abrogation *n.* ANNULMENT.

abrupt *adj.* **1** sudden, unexpected, surprising, impulsive, precipitous, unanticipated, unforeseen. **2** curt, brusque, crisp, short, blunt, brisk, ungracious, unceremonious, snappish.
ant. **1** expected, anticipated, foreseen. **2** gracious, smooth, gentle, warm.

abscond *v.* flee, vanish, decamp, run off, steal away, take off, sneak off, escape, bolt, disappear, clear out, take flight, skip.

absence *n.* **1** nonexistence, inexistence, nonattendance, nonappearance. **2** lack, need, want, deficit, deficiency, inadequacy, incompleteness, imperfection, shortcoming, insufficiency, omission, defect.
ant. **1** presence, attendance, appearance, existence. **2** sufficiency, adequacy, completeness, abundance.

absent *adj.* **1** truant, missing, elsewhere, away, gone, unavailable, out, off the premises. **2** preoccupied, bemused, inattentive, absent-minded, abstracted, off in space, daydreaming, oblivious, unaware, out of it (*Slang*), tuned out (*Slang*).
ant. **1** present, at home, on the premises, available. **2** attentive, aware, alert, with it (*Slang*), tuned in (*Slang*).

absent-minded *adj.* inattentive, preoccupied, absorbed, absent, abstracted, forgetful, unreliable, undependable, distracted, distrait, oblivious, unaware, faraway, off in space, daydreaming, moony, bemused, remote.
ant. attentive, alert, observant, with it (*Slang*).

absolute *adj.* **1** unrestricted, unlimited, unconditional, unqualified, unhampered, unimpeded. **2** perfect, complete, ideal, consummate, unadulterated, pure, unmixed. **3** sheer, utter, unmitigated, out-and-out. **4** unquestionable, positive, unambiguous, unequivocal, certain, definite. **5** independent, autonomous, autocratic, absolutist, sovereign, dictatorial.
ant. **1** partial, limited, restricted, conditional. **2** imperfect, incomplete, fragmentary, diluted. **4** contingent, conjectural, provisional.

absolution. *n.* forgiveness, pardon, dispensation, exoneration, acquittal, remission, indulgence, mercy, amnesty, exculpation, clearance.

absolutism *n.* authoritarianism, dictatorship, autocracy, autarchy, despotism, tyranny, totalitarianism, Hitlerism, Stalinism, tsarism, Caesarism, Bonapartism.

absolve *v.* forgive, pardon, exonerate, acquit, remit, exculpate, clear, release, exempt, excuse, liberate, discharge, let off.
ant. accuse, blame, condemn, prosecute, convict.

absorb *v.* **1** drink in, suck up, blot up, take in, sponge up, incorporate, assimilate, ingest, digest, imbibe, embody, swallow, consume. **2** engross, captivate, preoccupy, fascinate, interest, occupy, engage, rivet, enthrall, entertain, attract, hold.
ant. 1 eliminate, discharge, give out, throw off. **2** bore, weary, tire, pall, cloy, repel.

absorbed *adj.* ENGROSSED.

absorbent *adj.* spongy, permeable, porous, penetrable, pervious, absorptive, assimilative.
ant. waterproof, water-repellent, nonabsorbent, moisture-proof, impermeable, impervious.

absorbing *adj.* engrossing, interesting, fascinating, entertaining, engaging, captivating, moving, exciting, thrilling, pleasing, engaging, intriguing.
ant. boring, dull, tiresome, tedious, uninteresting.

absorption *n.* ASSIMILATION.

abstain *v.* refrain, forbear, desist, hold back, avoid, forego, refuse, decline, deny oneself, resist, say no to, turn down.

abstemious *adj.* temperate, abstinent, continent, ascetic, sparing, judicious, self-disciplined, cautious, moderate, self-controlled, nonindulgent, sober, teetotal.
ant. excessive, indulgent, undisciplined, uncontrolled, abandoned.

abstinence *n.* continence, moderation, austerity, asceticism, abstention, sobriety, teetotalism, temperance, fasting, self-denial, self-discipline, self-control, self-restraint.

ant. indulgence, high living, dissipation, sybaritism, sensuality, abandon.

abstract *adj.* **1** general, theoretical, nonspecific, nonrepresentational, ideal, idealized, intangible, metaphysical, mathematical, philosophical, symbolic, generalized, ideational, conceptualized. **2** profound, abstruse, recondite, esoteric, arcane, deep, complex, subtle, transcendental, mysterious, impenetrable, difficult.
ant. 1 specific, concrete, practical, particular, particularized. **2** clear, obvious, simple, easy, uncomplicated.

abstracted *adj.* absent-minded, preoccupied, bemused, in a fog, off in space, remote, withdrawn, dreamy, daydreaming, woolgathering, inattentive, out of it (*Slang*).
ant. attentive, alert, responsive, mindful, with it (*Slang*).

abstraction *n.* idea, concept, symbol, formula, generalization, theory, thought, formulation, notion, theorem, conceptualization, idealization.

abstruse *adj.* esoteric, arcane, recondite, obscure, enigmatic, complicated, abstract, metaphysical, deep, subtle, refined, mandarin.
ant. simple, direct, straightforward, obvious, uncomplicated.

absurd *adj.* silly, ridiculous, irrational, foolish, preposterous, ludicrous, asinine, idiotic, screwy (*Slang*), crazy, kooky (*Slang*), incredible, meaningless, irrational, senseless.

absurdity *n.* nonsense, foolishness, joke, farce, travesty, paradox, folly, idiocy, drivel, babble, meaninglessness, irrationality, senselessness.

abundance *n.* **1** plenty, profusion, bounty, overflow, plenitude, sufficiency, amplitude, lavishness, glut, surplus. **2** wealth, affluence, riches, means, fortune.
ant. 1 scarcity, insufficiency, inadequacy, shortage, paucity. **2** poverty, want, privation, need.

abundant *adj.* ample, overflowing,

plentiful, rich, well-supplied, teeming, full, copious, lavish, luxuriant, profuse, bountiful, bounteous, superabundant.
ant. sparse, scarce, wanting, lacking, needful.

abuse *v.* **1** mistreat, harm, hurt, injure, damage, mar, maltreat, wrong, oppress, misuse, misapply. **2** curse, revile, malign, slander, vilify, smear, disparage, calumniate, inveigh, swear at, castigate, chew out (*Slang*). —*n.* **1** mistreatment, maltreatment, injury, harm, hurt, damage, oppression, ill-treatment, misuse, misapplication. **2** fault, wrong, offense, misconduct, wrongdoing, misdeed, sin, crime, delinquency.

abusive *adj.* hurtful, harmful, injurious, destructive, insulting, vituperative, slanderous, libelous, scathing, offensive, nasty, disparaging, derogatory, defamatory.
ant. helpful, supportive, respectful, laudatory, kind, complimentary.

abut *v.* border, touch, join, meet, verge on, impinge on, flank, connect with, neighbor.

abutment *n.* support, buttress, brace, strut, prop, pier, rampart, bulwark.

abysmal *adj.* profound, endless, infinite, immeasurable, incalculable, enormous, . boundless, stupendous, overwhelming, unbelievable, consummate, extreme, unparalleled, unimaginable.

abyss *n.* chasm, depth, pit, void, nothingness, emptiness, infinitude, endlessness, limbo, unknown, unknowable.

academic *adj.* **1** collegiate, campus, educational, professorial, scholarly, bookish, instructional, pedantic, curricular, lettered, erudite. **2** theoretical, conjectural, untested, moot, arguable, debatable, suppositional, presumptive, speculative, hypothetical, putative, undetermined.

accede *v.* consent, agree, assent, concur, grant, acquiesce, comply, accept, subscribe, yield, admit, endorse, go along with.
ant. disagree, balk at, dissent, oppose, differ.

accelerate *v.* hasten, hurry, speed, quicken, expedite, step up, rush, precipitate, spur, forward, advance, drive, prod, rev up.
ant. slow down, retard, brake, slacken, relax, decelerate, delay.

accent *n.* stress, emphasis, modulation, intonation, attack, tonality. —*v.* emphasize, stress, underline, call attention to, italicize, accentuate, feature, mark, hammer, drum, reiterate, dwell on.
ant. *v.* underplay, understate, minimize, pass over.

accentuate *v.* ACCENT.

accept *v.* **1** receive, take, acquire, get, gain, obtain, have. **2** acknowledge, affirm, admit, concur, accede, agree, approve, adopt, go along with, cooperate, buy (*Slang*), swallow, fall for (*Slang*). **3** submit, bow, yield, defer, capitulate.
ant. *v.* **1, 2** reject, turn down, refuse, have none of. **3** oppose, resist, struggle against, balk at.

acceptable *adj.* adequate, satisfactory, tolerable, admissible, passable, fair, unobjectionable, par, standard.
ant. substandard, below par, poor, unacceptable, inadmissible.

acceptance *n.* APPROVAL.

access *n.* approach, entrée, entrance, avenue, path, course, door, gateway, key, combination, technique, skill, means, wherewithal.

accessible *adj.* **1** within reach, nearby, at hand, attainable, possible, achievable, obtainable. **2** friendly, approachable, cordial, available, affable, accommodating, obliging, courteous, democratic.
ant. **1** unachievable, impossible, unobtainable, beyond reach, remote, distant. **2** forbidding, standoffish, aloof, unavailable, unapproachable, unfriendly.

accession *n.* SUCCESSION.

accessory *n.* addition, supplement, extra, plus, help, convenience, afterthought, trimming, adjunct, crutch, auxiliary, accompaniment, appendage. —*adj.* supplemental, supplementary, additional, extra, auxiliary, secondary, subordinate, helpful, contributory, ancillary, incidental.

accident *n.* **1** fortuity, inadvertence, random, fluke, freak, happenstance, the unexpected, the unforeseen. **2** misfortune, mishap, contretemps, misadventure, miscarriage, adversity, casualty, blunder, calamity, bad luck, catastrophe, crash, collision. **3** chance, fortune, luck, fate, hazard, act of God.

accidental *adj.* **1** fortuitous, unexpected, unforeseen, unanticipated, chance, freak, haphazard, random, adventitious, unpremeditated, unwitting, unintended, unintentional. **2** incidental, subordinate, secondary, nonessential, extraneous, collateral, accessory, supplementary, superfluous.

ant. 1 planned, intended, purposeful, foreseen, expected, anticipated. **2** essential, primary, basic, fundamental, intrinsic, inherent.

acclaim *v.* applaud, praise, welcome, hail, approve, laud, cheer, salute, extol, celebrate, congratulate. —*n.* applause, cheers, ovation, acclamation, enthusiasm.

ant. *v.* boo, hiss, heckle, catcall, razz (*Slang*). *n.* booing, hissing, heckling, razzing (*Slang*).

acclamation *n.* ACCLAIM.

acclimated *adj.* acclimatized, adapted, adjusted, habituated, accustomed, inured, acculturated, accommodated, seasoned, weathered, used to, reconciled.

acclimatized *adj.* ACCLIMATED.

accolade *n.* honor, praise, recognition, kudos, applause, acclaim, bouquet, medal, crown, laurel, testimonial, salute, tribute, acclaim, acclamation.

accommodate *v.* **1** oblige, help, assist,

cooperate, aid, serve, befriend, do for, lend a hand. **2** cater to, lodge, house, put up, quarter. **3** adapt, modify, adjust, acclimate, acclimatize, reconcile, habituate, accustom, get used to.

accommodating *adj.* helpful, obliging, cooperative, friendly, kind, willing, gracious, considerate, cordial, unselfish, sympathetic.

ant. uncooperative, selfish, disobliging, hostile, unfriendly.

accommodation *n.* **1** adaptation, adjustment, alteration, change, acclimatization, acclimation, habituation, transformation, capitulation, reorientation. **2** convenience, help, aid, advantage, benefit, boon, favor, service, kindness, courtesy.

ant. 1 rigidity, inflexibility, stubbornness. **2** disservice, inconvenience, hindrance, disadvantage.

accommodations *n.* lodging, housing, board, room, quarters, place, living space, bed and board, lodgment.

accompany *v.* go with, attend, escort, chaperon, squire, conduct, coexist, join, convoy, occur with, coincide, go hand in hand.

accomplice *n.* confederate, fellow-criminal, co-conspirator, accessory, partner-in-crime, henchman, co-defendant, tool, cat's-paw, aider and abettor.

accomplish *v.* perform, effect, do, finish, effectuate, complete, achieve, fulfill, produce, carry out, execute, discharge, bring about, conclude, terminate.

accomplished *adj.* skilled, proficient, able, gifted, talented, finished, polished, expert, skillful, well-trained, seasoned, masterly, cultivated, qualified.

ant. amateurish, unskilled, clumsy, inept, crude.

accomplishment *n.* achievement, attainment, acquisition, triumph, victory, skill, art, exploit, coup, masterstroke.

accord *v.* grant, concede, admit, allow,

award, yield, permit, give. —*n*. harmony, agreement, conformity, accordance, cooperation, friendship, unanimity, understanding, rapport, consent, uniformity.

ant. *n*. discord, disagreement, dissidence, argument, hostility.

accordance *n*. ACCORD.

accordingly *adv*. therefore, consequently, thus, as a result, hence, as a consequence, whereupon, and so, so, ergo.

accost *v*. address, speak to, hail, nab, salute, buttonhole, waylay.

accouchement *n*. BIRTH.

account *v*. consider, estimate, deem, reckon, classify, think, believe, judge, regard, look upon, rate, assess, evaluate, size up. —*n*. explanation, description, report, version, story, narrative, narration, summation, summary, view, opinion.

accountable *adj*. answerable, responsible, liable, chargeable, obligated, obliged, beholden, duty-bound, charged with.

account for *v*. explain, clarify, justify, rationalize, substantiate, validate, elucidate, illuminate, demonstrate, solve, answer.

accouter *v*. EQUIP.

accouterment *n*. EQUIPMENT.

accredit *v*. CERTIFY.

accredited *adj*. certified, recognized, official, qualified, authorized, commissioned, chartered, licensed, empowered, sanctioned, deputized, endorsed, approved, vouched for.

ant. unofficial, unlicensed, illicit, unauthorized, self-styled, so-called, *soi-disant*.

accretion *n*. addition, supplement, increase, accrual, enlargement, accumulation, augmentation, increment, extension.

ant. diminution, shrinkage, loss, lessening, reduction, decrease.

accrue *v*. ACCUMULATE.

accrued *adj*. totaled, accumulated, added, amassed, increased, expanded, enlarged.

acculturated *adj*. ACCLIMATED.

accumulate *v*. gather, amass, collect, heap, pile, cumulate, hoard, save, assemble, get together, accrue, store, garner.

ant. get rid of, spend, throw out, give away, distribute, dissipate.

accumulation *n*. collection, heap, pile, hoard, mass, store, aggregation, stockpile, stack, pile-up, lot.

accuracy *n*. PRECISION.

accurate *adj*. **1** correct, truthful, verifiable, actual, factual, unmistaken, faultless, right, just, unerring, on the mark, on target, authoritative, absolute, scientific. **2** careful, precise, rigorous, neat, punctilious, scrupulous, literal, meticulous, reliable.

ant. **1** incorrect, false, wrong, in error, mistaken. **2** sloppy, careless, unreliable, fanciful.

accursed *adj*. doomed, cursed, unfortunate, condemned, ill-fated, bedeviled, blasted, ruined, undone, hopeless, wretched.

ant. lucky, fortunate, blessed, hopeful.

accusation *n*. ALLEGATION.

accuse *v*. charge, blame, sue, prosecute, complain, indict, implicate, incriminate, inculpate, impeach, impute, denounce, censure, attack, recriminate.

accustomed *adj*. habitual, usual, everyday, ordinary, expected, conventional, familiar, common, customary, routine, fixed, regular.

ant. rare, unusual, special, extraordinary, alien.

ace *n*. star, champion, top, winner, headliner, king, queen, one and only, expert, master, head, superman.

acerbate *v*. IRRITATE.

acerbity *n*. sourness, bitterness, acidity, sharpness, severity, harshness, acridity, nastiness, unkindness, cruelty, hostility, unfriendliness, coldness, acrimony.

ant. gentleness, sweetness, kindness, warmth, tenderness.

ache *v*. **1** suffer, hurt, stab, pound,

twinge, throb. **2** suffer, agonize, sorrow, mourn, grieve, lament. **3** yearn, hunger, crave, hanker, desire, want, need, covet, long for. —*n.* pain, discomfort, twinge, throb, distress, soreness, irritation, inflammation, malaise.

achieve *v.* accomplish, fulfill, attain, reach, win, arrive, carry out, carry off, bring off, effect, effectuate, perform, realize.
ant. fail, miscarry, founder, falter, give up.

achievement *n.* **1** fulfillment, accomplishment, realization, attainment, completion, execution, fruition, production. **2** triumph, victory, exploit, feat, deed, success, coup, stroke, masterstroke.
ant. 2 failure, botch, mess, fiasco, abortion, miscarriage, dud, flop.

acid *adj.* **1** sour, tart, vinegary, citrous, sharp, acidulous. **2** sarcastic, acidulous, acrid, acerb, acrimonious, ill-tempered, biting, mordant, cutting, vitriolic, sardonic, derisive, scornful, nasty, snide.
ant. 1 sweet, sugary, honeyed, bland. **2** pleasant, agreeable, friendly, gentle, soothing.

acidity *n.* ACERBITY.

acidulous *adj.* ACID.

acknowledge *v.* **1** admit, confess, own, accept, concede, grant, allow, endorse, accede, approve, acquiesce, consent. **2** thank, appreciate, reward, requite, repay, recompense. **3** respond to, recognize, return, react to, take note of, notice.
ant. 1 disavow, refuse, refute, disallow, turn down. **2, 3** neglect, ignore, overlook.

acknowledgment *n.* ADMISSION.

acme *n.* summit, peak, top, zenith, high point, crown, pinnacle, apex, crest, culmination, maximum, optimum.
ant. bottom, nadir, base.

acolyte *n.* ASSISTANT.

acquaint *v.* familiarize, inform, advise, notify, tell, enlighten, disclose, reveal, announce, report, teach, edify, instruct, educate.

acquaintance *n.* awareness, information, knowledge, experience, cognizance, familiarity, training, consciousness, perception, enlightenment.
ant. ignorance, unawareness, unfamiliarity, inexperience, blindness.

acquiesce *v.* consent, concur, comply, assent, agree, accede, submit, yield, concede, conform, grant, capitulate, give in.
ant. disagree, argue, refuse, rebel, stand firm.

acquiescent *adj.* OBEDIENT.

acquire *v.* get, obtain, gain, buy, purchase, earn, win, contract, capture, attain, inherit, procure, realize, merit, reap, receive.
ant. lose, forfeit, give away, discard, get rid of.

acquirement *n.* skill, training, education, attainment, accomplishment, achievement, qualification, enlightenment, learning, information.

acquisition *n.* purchase, procurement, acquirement, obtainment, gift, gain, possession, proceeds, grant, property, prize.

acquisitive *adj.* avid, greedy, squirrelly, accumulative, hoarding, saving, covetous.

acquit *v.* **1** clear, free, exculpate, exonerate, absolve, vindicate, discharge, remit, reprieve, pardon, forgive. **2** unburden, relieve, liberate, excuse, let off, exempt.
ant. 1 convict, condemn, doom. **2** burden, saddle, weigh down.

acrid *adj.* **1** sharp, bitter, burning, smoky, pungent, stinging, biting, irritating. **2** ACID.

acridity *n.* ACERBITY.

acrimonious *adj.* sarcastic, sharp, cutting, biting, caustic, acerb, acidulous, stinging, waspish, harsh, testy, vitriolic, bitchy (*Slang*).
ant. kind, soft, gentle, soothing, pleasant, agreeable, sweet.

acrimony *n.* ACERBITY.

across-the-board *adj.* BLANKET.

act *v.* **1** impersonate, perform, play, enact, mimic, mime, represent, portray, personify, characterize. **2** feign, pretend, come on (*Slang*), behave, simulate, counterfeit, dissimulate, make believe, comport oneself, conduct oneself. —*n.* **1** deed, action, doing, feat, accomplishment, achievement, exploit, performance, execution. **2** edict, decree, enactment, statute, law, legislation, measure, order, ordinance, bill, mandate, judgment. **3** pose, posture, imposture, attitude, stance, performance, put-on (*Slang*), affectation, hypocrisy, airs, pretension, front, mask.

acting *adj.* substituting, officiating, delegated, deputy, substitute, surrogate, deputized, temporary, *pro tem.* **ant.** permanent, official, elected.

action *n.* **1** act, deed, performance, production, execution, accomplishment, achievement, deed, feat, exploit, exercise, exertion, perpetration. **2** working, functioning, movement, process, mechanics, motion, operation.

activate *v.* energize, mobilize, move, animate, start, stimulate, impel, stir, prompt, propel, push, nudge, motivate. **ant.** immobilize, paralyze, deaden, weaken, check, stop.

active *adj.* **1** busy, humming, bustling, bubbling, stirring, astir, alive, moving, vigorous, vibrant, jumping (*Slang*). **2** militant, aggressive, engaged, committed, activist, enterprising, zealous, forward, ambitious, energetic, assertive. **3** agile, lively, quick, spry, light, frisky, spirited, vital, animated, alive, vivacious, peppy, zippy. **ant.** **1** quiet, quiescent, dead, dormant, asleep. **2** nonchalant, detached, uninvolved, disengaged, uncommitted, degagé. **3** inert, sluggish, lethargic, logy, phlegmatic, slow.

activism *n.* agitation, confrontation, involvement, engagement, commitment, militancy, aggression, zeal, ardor, fervor. **ant.** inertia, disengagement, lethargy, passivity, detachment, fence-sitting.

activist *n.* doer, militant, enthusiast, partisan, champion, advocate. **ant.** neutral, fence-sitter.

activity *n.* **1** action, life, movement, mobility, operation, work, labor, exertion, enterprise. **2** stir, bustle, hum, ado, agitation, fuss, flurry, buzz, whirl, spirit, vitality, vigor, verve, liveliness, bounce. **3** project, pursuit, endeavor, job, assignment, doing, venture, undertaking, pastime, scheme, purpose, task. **ant.** **1** inactivity, immobility, torpor, stasis, inertia, stupor. **2** quiet, lull, stillness, calm, serenity.

actor *n.* **1** doer, agent, participant, participator, performer, executor, factor, perpetrator, operator, worker, practitioner, transactor, representative. **2** thespian, player, actress, performer, trouper, star, leading lady, leading man.

actual *adj.* real, factual, existent, de facto, present-day, current, live, living, present, authentic, verifiable, true, truthful, extant, tangible, genuine. **ant.** unreal, fictional, imaginary, imagined, absent, gone.

actuality *n.* REALITY.

actuate *v.* motivate, move, incite, activate, energize, effect, effectuate, stir, spur, quicken, rouse, drive, compel, force, promote. **ant.** deter, discourage, restrain, hinder, block.

act up *v.* **1** misbehave, make a scene, carry on, show off, rebel, cut up (*Slang*). **2** worsen, cause trouble, get worse, flare up, intensify, exacerbate.

acumen *n.* insight, discernment, acuteness, cleverness, shrewdness, perceptiveness, sharpness, sagacity, penetration, intelligence, perspicacity, perspicaciousness, astuteness.

acute *adj.* **1** keen, discerning, clever,

sharp, perceptive, aware, penetrating, sensitive, perspicacious, quick-witted, intuitive. **2** intense, piercing, sharp, severe, powerful, deep, racking, overpowering, overwhelming, poignant. **3** critical, crucial, severe, sudden, urgent, grave, serious, dangerous.

ant. 1 dull, stupid, unaware, insensitive, blind. **3** mild, unimportant, superficial.

adage *n.* proverb, saying, aphorism, precept, folk wisdom, maxim, truism, commonplace, bromide, old saw.

adamant *adj.* **1** adamantine, steely, stony, flinty, hard, impenetrable, rocky, unbreakable. **2** unyielding, unbending, resolute, fixed, inflexible, inexorable, rigid, unshakable, tough, unrelenting, intransigent, adamantine.

ant. 1 soft, pliable, fragile, frangible. **2** accommodating, yielding, flexible, irresolute.

adamantine *adj.* ADAMANT.

adapt *v.* alter, adjust, accommodate, acclimate, acclimatize, acculturate, compromise, change, transform, transmute, assimilate, modify, attune, convert.

adaptability *n.* RESILIENCE.

adaptable *adj.* adjustable, changeable, convertible, flexible, yielding, accommodating, compromising, pliable, tractable, malleable, realistic.

ant. rigid, inflexible, adamant, uncompromising, fixed, stubborn.

adaptation *n.* VERSION.

add *v.* **1** attach, affix, join, unite, annex, append, put on, tack on. **2** increase, augment, amplify, supplement, magnify, enlarge, raise, extend.

ant. 1 subtract, remove, withdraw, take away. **2** decrease, reduce, diminish, lessen.

addendum *n.* addition, supplement, augmentation, plus, extra, insertion, interpolation, affix, increment, extension, adjunct, appendage, postscript, afterthought.

addict *n.* junkie (*Slang*), head (*Slang*),

hophead (*Slang*), fiend, freak (*Slang*), devotee, fan, enthusiast, buff, nut (*Slang*).

addicted *adj.* devoted, disposed, inclined, fond, obsessed, absorbed, involved.

additional *adj.* supplementary, extra, more, appended, affixed, increased, auxiliary, further, spare, other, new, fresh.

ant. fewer, reduced, diminished, less.

addle *v.* CONFUSE.

addlebrained *adj.* SIMPLE-MINDED.

addlepated *adj.* SIMPLE-MINDED.

address *v.* **1** speak to, talk to, hail, salute, accost, say to, greet. **2** lecture, orate, discourse, speechify, harangue, declaim, spout, expatiate. **3** focus on, concentrate on, turn to, attend to, take care of, look to, undertake, engage in, concern oneself with, busy oneself with, take up, pitch into. —*n.* speech, lecture, talk, oration, discourse, sermon, disquisition, dissertation.

adduce *v.* CITE.

add up to AMOUNT TO.

adept *adj.* skillful, skilled, proficient, adroit, competent, talented, gifted, expert, masterful, clever, ingenious, apt, able. —*n.* expert, master, professional, pro, champion, old hand, trouble-shooter, genius, prodigy, whiz (*Slang*), hot shot (*Slang*), champ (*Slang*).

ant. *adj.* unskilled, inept, incompetent, maladroit, clumsy, klutzy (*Slang*). *n.* novice, beginner, neophyte, bungler, amateur, klutz (*Slang*).

adequate *adj.* **1** sufficient, suitable, enough, ample, right, satisfactory, fitting, effective, proportionate, commensurate, up to par, standard. **2** so-so, tolerable, fair, passable, mediocre, sparse, middling, not so hot (*Slang*), no great shakes (*Slang*).

ant. 1 insufficient, below, inadequate, wanting, substandard, below par.

adhere v. cling, cleave, cohere, stick, hold fast, merge, coalesce, consolidate, join, agglutinate, conglutinate. **ant.** separate, come apart, come unstuck, split, fall apart.

adherence n. DEVOTION.

adherent n. follower, devotee, believer, advocate, champion, disciple, member, supporter, upholder, ally, votary, backer. —adj. ADHESIVE. **ant.** detractor, critic, fault-finder, knocker.

adhesion n. ASSENT.

adhesive adj. sticky, gummy, clinging, adherent, gluey, mucilaginous.

adieu n. FAREWELL.

ad infinitum endlessly, infinitely, limitlessly, unendingly, unboundedly, everlastingly, unceasingly, interminably. **ant.** occasionally, temporarily, finitely.

adipose adj. FAT.

adjacent adj. near, close, next to, adjoining, abutting, contiguous, bordering, touching, neighboring, beside, contacting, juxtaposed, tangent. **ant.** remote, distant, removed, faraway.

adjoin v. BORDER.

adjoining adj. contiguous, touching, adjacent, tangent, joined to, continuous with, bordering, skirting, contacting, connected, joint. **ant.** separate, separated, disconnected, discontinuous.

adjourn v. put off, postpone, delay, defer, suspend, hold over, recess.

adjournment n. POSTPONEMENT.

adjudge v. adjudicate, decide, determine, pronounce, ordain, decree, rule, arbitrate, settle, referee.

adjudicate v. ADJUDGE.

adjunct n. supplement, auxiliary, appendage, appendix, subordinate, second, appendant, addendum, footnote, annex, assistant, aide, helper.

adjure v. ENTREAT.

adjust v. adapt, fit, true, correct, amend, regulate, regularize, condition, recondition, fix, compose, harmonize, settle, attune, correlate, compromise.

adjustment n. **1** ACCOMMODATION. **2** REGULATION.

ad-lib v. IMPROVISE.

administer v. **1** manage, boss, direct, oversee, control, superintend, supervise, execute, administrate, conduct, preside over. **2** provide, give, apply, treat, dispense, mete out, serve, hand out, supply, distribute, inflict, impose.

administrate v. ADMINISTER.

administration n. **1** management, direction, charge, responsibility, control, supervision, superintendence, execution, regulation, application, conduct, dispensation, distribution. **2** establishment, leadership, power structure, regime, authority, bureaucracy, policy-makers, hierarchy, office-holders, higher-ups, brass (Slang).

administrative adj. executive, managerial, supervisory, regulatory, directive, governmental, authoritative, bureaucratic, hierarchical.

administrator n. executive, boss, manager, head, supervisor, director, bureaucrat, official, overseer, wheel (Slang), big-shot (Slang).

admirable adj. praiseworthy, commendable, estimable, excellent, fine, rare, wonderful, superior, laudable, meritorious. **ant.** contemptible, despicable, worthless, lamentable, pitiful.

admirably adv. WELL.

admiration n. approval, awe, veneration, adulation, esteem, worship, hero-worship, regard, recognition, delight, wonder. **ant.** contempt, scorn, disrespect, disapproval.

admire v. **1** delight in, take pleasure in, approve of, be pleased by, love, like, enjoy, be fond of, appreciate, be taken with. **2** respect, esteem, venerate, adore, worship, look up to, idolize, honor, prize, praise. **ant. 1** dislike, disapprove of, despise, hate. **2** scorn, disrespect, disdain, deride.

admirer *n.* SUITOR.

admiring *adj.* RESPECTFUL.

admission *n.* **1** confession, acknowledgment, concession, allowance, avowal, profession, divulgence, disclosure, declaration, statement, announcement, revelation, confidence. **2** ENTRANCE.
ant. 1 concealment, withholding, dissimulation, silence.

admit *v.* **1** let in, receive, grant access, take in, accept, include. **2** concede, grant, acknowledge, confess, allow, avow, disclose, reveal, confide, announce, own up, come clean (*Slang*).
ant. 1 keep out, exclude, debar, shut out. **2** conceal, withhold, obscure, cloak.

admittance *n.* ENTRANCE.

admix *v.* MIX.

admixture *n.* MIXTURE.

admonish *v.* **1** scold, reprove, chastise, chide, reprimand, berate, disapprove, rebuke, censure, lecture, take to task, chew out (*Slang*). **2** warn, caution, alert, forewarn, counsel, advise, apprise, make aware, tip off.

admonition *n.* REPROOF.

ado *n.* fuss, to-do, trouble, bustle, stir, activity, bother, confusion, disturbance, commotion, excitement, agitation, fluster, goings on.
ant. peace, quiet, calm, inactivity, apathy.

adolescence *n.* YOUTH.

adolescent *n.* YOUTH.

Adonis *n.* god, Greek god, Apollo, charmer, he-man, matinee idol, looker (*Slang*).

adopt *v.* appropriate, take, use, employ, utilize, assume, copy, arrogate, affect, swipe (*Slang*).

adorable *adj.* attractive, charming, lovable, enchanting, precious, sweet, darling, winsome, lovely, fetching, cuddly, cute.
ant. unappealing, obnoxious, offensive, nasty.

adoration *n.* **1** WORSHIP. **2** LOVE.

adore *v.* **1** venerate, worship, revere, deify, apotheosize, honor. **2** love, cherish, dote on, idolize, idealize, admire, rejoice in, applaud.
ant. 1 curse, blaspheme, desecrate, execrate, profane. **2** loathe, detest, abominate, hate, dislike, scorn.

adorn *v.* ornament, beautify, decorate, embellish, dress up, trim, bedeck, grace, enrich, array, prettify, brighten, emblazon, trick out.

adornment *n.* **1** ORNAMENT. **2** ORNAMENTATION.

adroit *adj.* skillful, dextrous, dexterous, handy, clever, deft, apt, proficient, expert, nimble, able, practiced, slick.
ant. inept, clumsy, maladroit, incompetent, all thumbs, klutzy (*Slang*).

adroitness *n.* DEXTERITY.

adulate *v.* FLATTER.

adulation *n.* flattery, fawning, sycophancy, blandishment, bootlicking, fulsomeness, adoration, worship.

adult *adj.* MATURE.

adulterate *v.* debase, corrupt, degrade, worsen, pollute, spoil, contaminate, water down, weaken, devalue, cheapen, depreciate, attenuate, bastardize.
ant. purify, strengthen, upgrade, concentrate.

adumbrate *v.* SUGGEST.

advance *v.* **1** move forward, accelerate, proceed, go ahead, go on, go forward, move along, move ahead, speed, hasten, propel. **2** improve, upgrade, assist, strengthen, benefit, facilitate, quicken, foster, promote, further, expedite, boost. **3** propose, present, offer, suggest, submit, broach, proffer, propound, introduce, put, pose, recommend. —*n.* **1** acceleration, speedup, progression, propulsion. **2** improvement, progress, headway, betterment, strengthening, advancement, promotion, enhancement, melioration, amelioration, furtherance. **3** increase, climb, rise, ascent, escalation, elevation.
ant. v. 1 retreat, regress, retrogress,

ebb, slow down. **2** weaken, thwart, hold back, check, frustrate, hamper. *n.* **1** retreat, regression, retrogression, ebb. **2** reversal, relapse, reversion. **3** fall, drop, lowering, descent.

advanced *adj.* leading, precocious, foremost, avant-garde, progressive, pioneering.
ant. backward, retarded, reactionary, hindmost.

advancement *n.* **1** PROGRESSION. **2** PROMOTION.

advantage *n.* **1** benefit, gain, asset, boon, profit, help, plus, godsend, avail, improvement, use, blessing, good, service, windfall. **2** superiority, ascendancy, supremacy, edge, head start, power, lead, prestige, predominance, primacy, influence, pull, clout (*Slang*), drag (*Slang*).
ant. 1 hindrance, handicap, obstacle. **2** inferiority, weakness, helplessness, vulnerability.

advantaged *adj.* privileged, favored, influential, well off, affluent, ascendant, on top, fortunate, prosperous.
ant. disadvantaged, underprivileged, vulnerable, weak, neglected, unfortunate.

advantageous *adj.* beneficial, profitable, helpful, useful, valuable, expedient, favorable, fortunate, propitious, rewarding, gainful, availing, auspicious.
ant. adverse, untoward, unfavorable, disadvantageous, damaging, harmful.

advent *n.* arrival, appearance, occurrence, coming, onset, beginning.
ant. departure, end, conclusion, going, finish.

adventitious *adj.* accidental, extrinsic, incidental, supplemental, chance, superficial, fortuitous, unplanned, serendipitous.
ant. inherent, intrinsic, basic, built-in.

adventure *n.* escapade, lark, prank, caper, occurrence, incident, episode, happening, affair.

adventurer *n.* **1** hero, heroine, dare-devil, Don Quixote, giant-killer, wanderer, traveler, pioneer, dragon-slayer, romantic, vagabond, rogue, picaro, gambler, speculator. **2** fortune-hunter, social climber, mercenary, knave, charlatan, opportunist, careerist, gold digger.
ant. 1 stick-in-the-mud, homebody, stay-at-home.

adventuresome *adj.* ADVENTUROUS.

adventurous *adj.* venturesome, daring, devil-may-care, daredevil, thrill-seeking, enterprising, quixotic, audacious, rash, picaresque, curious, questing, romantic, adventuresome.
ant. cautious, conservative, timid, home-loving.

adversary *n.* opponent, antagonist, foe, enemy, rival, competitor, combatant.
ant. ally, confederate, collaborator, partner, colleague, friend.

adverse *adj.* **1** opposing, opposed, opposite, counter, contrary, conflicting, antagonistic, inimical, antithetical, contradictory, incompatible, hostile. **2** damaging, harmful, detrimental, destructive, pernicious, undermining, prejudicial, unpropitious, bad, injurious, grievous.
ant. 1 concurrent, joint, shared, common, mutual. **2** helpful, beneficial, fortunate, good, lucky.

adversity *n.* misfortune, ill luck, hardship, hard times, trial, suffering, affliction, tribulation, misery, trouble, vexation, heavy weather.
ant. good luck, felicity, smooth sailing.

advert *v.* **1** HEED. **2** REFER.

advertise *v.* publish, proclaim, announce, broadcast, tout, sell, publicize, push, promote, puff, air, feature, build up, spotlight, ballyhoo.

advertisement *n.* ad, notice, announcement, commercial, build-up, promotion, puffery, poster, come-on (*Slang*).

advice *n.* **1** counsel, suggestion, tip, hint, caution, guidance, tip-off, warning, admonishment, recommendation. **2** notification, information, news, report, communiqué, communication, intelligence, tidings, enlightenment.

advisable *adj.* recommended, suggested, expedient, wise, suitable, sensible, desirable, tried and true, practical, effective, fitting, prudent, discreet. **ant.** unwise, imprudent, improper, inappropriate, rash, outlandish.

advise *v.* counsel, recommend, guide, steer, tip off, suggest, admonish, urge, caution, preach, exhort, advocate.

advisement *n.* CONSIDERATION.

advise of *v.* inform, notify, enlighten, apprise, give notice, acquaint, make known, tell, send word, instruct, communicate, state, declare.

adviser *n.* counselor, guide, mentor, guru, teacher, instructor, director, tutor, consultant, pilot, *vade mecum.*

advocacy *n.* PROMOTION.

advocate *v.* favor, support, defend, uphold, back, champion, fight for, espouse, recommend, urge, promote, encourage, applaud. —*n.* **1** defender, supporter, champion, abettor, adherent, ally, backer, booster, subscriber, spokesman, proponent, propagandist, apologist, promoter, fan. **2** LAWYER. **ant.** *v.* oppose, discourage, counter, fight against. *n.* opponent, critic, enemy, adversary.

aegis *n.* auspices, sponsorship, patronage, support, backing, advocacy, favor, guardianship, protection, endorsement, wing, banner.

aerial *n.* ANTENNA.

aesthete *n.* CONNOISSEUR.

affability *n.* CORDIALITY.

affable *adj.* friendly, approachable, accessible, civil, courteous, genial, pleasant, gracious, cordial, agreeable, amiable, informal, folksy. **ant.** forbidding, standoffish, starchy, unfriendly, cold, unapproachable.

affair *n.* **1** business, doing, event, matter, concern, occasion, activity, happening, episode, undertaking, project, venture, case, prospect, shebang

(*Slang*). **2** party, social, do, get-together, gathering, ceremony, festivity, celebration, function, gala, shindig (*Slang*). **3** liaison, relationship, intrigue, romance, amour, intimacy.

affairs *n.* dealings, activities, concerns, problems, ups and downs, responsibilities, cares, finances, commitments, goings on.

affect[1] *v.* **1** act upon, change, alter, modify, adjust, influence, transform, moderate, incline, motivate, impel, prompt. **2** touch, perturb, stir, move, reach, soften, upset, trouble, grieve.

affect[2] *v.* imitate, counterfeit, adopt, sham, ape, mimic, put on, simulate, pretend, assume, feign, fake, come on (*Slang*).

affectation *n.* **1** pretense, fraud, show, display, counterfeiting, artificiality, simulation, fakery, sham, act, imitation, falsification, put-on (*Slang*). **2** airs, pretension, false front, facade, affectedness, ostentation, preciosity, phoniness (*Slang*), falseness, hypocrisy. **ant.** **1** authenticity, reliability, truthfulness, the real thing, the McCoy (*Slang*). **2** unaffectedness, spontaneity, sincerity, simplicity, naturalness.

affected[1] *adj.* moved, touched, stirred, influenced, impressed, disturbed, troubled, upset, distressed. **ant.** unmoved, unaffected, apathetic.

affected[2] *adj.* artificial, spurious, fake, contrived, fraudulent, sham, false, put-on (*Slang*), assumed, counterfeit, unnatural, mannered, stagy, unreal, show-off, phony (*Slang*). **ant.** spontaneous, real, natural, authentic, sincere, straightforward, unaffected.

affecting *adj.* moving, touching, stirring, disturbing, poignant, gripping, heart-rending.

affection *n.* **1** tenderness, regard, love, warmth, care, friendship, fellow-feeling, fondness, concern, attachment, devotion, solicitude. **2** disease, infection, illness, ailment, disorder, sickness, malady, complaint, discomfort, indisposition.

ant. 1 coolness, coldness, antipathy, dislike, detachment, unconcern.

affectionate *adj.* loving, tender, warm, fond, concerned, devoted, solicitous, cherishing, doting, demonstrative.

ant. cool, cold, uncaring, distant, unfeeling, apathetic.

affiliate *n.* BRANCH.

affiliate with *v.* **1** associate, merge, combine, ally, syndicate, amalgamate, confederate, unite, connect, consolidate. **2** enroll, enter, join, register, enlist.

ant. 1 break up, separate, secede, split up. **2** resign, quit, leave, retire, drop out.

affinity *n.* tendency, inclination, partiality, bias, liking, preference, propensity, proclivity, sympathy, predisposition, penchant, susceptibility, hankering, appetite.

ant. antipathy, hostility, dislike, disinclination.

affirm *v.* **1** assert, avow, propound, advance, asseverate, insist, maintain, claim, contend, allege, declare, aver, bear witness, profess, announce. **2** ratify, confirm, uphold, support, corroborate, endorse, approve, sustain.

ant. 2 veto, nullify, negate.

affirmation *n.* ASSERTION.

affirmative *adj.* corroborative, affirming, positive, concurring, agreeing, confirmatory, supportive, upholding.

ant. negative, nullifying, negating, contradictory.

affix *v.* **1** attach, fasten, fix, append, add, annex, tack on, adjoin, graft. **2** impute, attribute, ascribe, assign, charge, saddle with, burden, connect.

afflict *v.* plague, trouble, distress, upset, torment, burden, pain, grieve, oppress, weigh down, persecute, gall, aggrieve, beset, harass.

affliction *n.* **1** distress, pain, misery, torment, unhappiness, anguish, sorrow, oppression, grief, weariness, depres-

sion. **2** curse, plague, calamity, disaster, misfortune, catastrophe, blow, ordeal, hardship, adversity.

ant. 1 joy, comfort, happiness, elation, well-being, ease. **2** blessing, boon, windfall, godsend.

affluence *n.* wealth, riches, means, opulence, plenty, prosperity, resources, assets, substance, luxury, fortune, privilege.

ant. poverty, need, want, penury, insolvency.

affluent *adj.* wealthy, opulent, moneyed, rich, prosperous, privileged, fortunate, in the money, in the chips, well-fixed, well-off, well-to-do, well-heeled (*Slang*), loaded (*Slang*).

ant. poor, needy, insolvent, impoverished, underprivileged.

afford *v.* PROVIDE.

affray *n.* BRAWL.

affront *v.* insult, offend, outrage, anger, wound, provoke, irritate, annoy, vex, nettle, sting, pique, slap, put down (*Slang*). —*n.* insult, slight, slur, offense, barb, wound, injury, outrage, discourtesy, dig, provocation, incivility, put-down (*Slang*).

aficionado *n.* FAN.

afraid *adj.* frightened, fearful, apprehensive, scared, tense, jittery, anxious, nervous, alarmed, jumpy, worried, intimidated, uneasy, panicky, edgy, on edge, shaky.

ant. confident, dauntless, fearless, relaxed, self-confident.

afresh *adv.* AGAIN.

after *adv.* **1** afterward, later, then, subsequently, thereafter, consequently, eventually, ultimately. **2** behind, following, in back of, to the rear of, preceded by, last.

ant. 1 before, sooner, prior to, previous to, previously. **2** preceding, ahead, in front, first.

aftereffect *n.* EFFECT.

aftermath *n.* consequence, result, upshot, aftereffect, outcome, end, sequel, reward, finale, denouement, payoff.

ant. prelude, start, onset, beginning.

afterthought *n.* ADDENDUM.

afterward *adv.* AFTER.

again *adv.* once more, anew, again and again, over and over, time and again, time after time, persistently, afresh, repeatedly, more than once, often, bis.

age *n.* **1** lifetime, existence, duration, generation, era, years, epoch, life, times, extent, cycle, span. **2** stage, period, date, point, season, phase, time, year. —*v.* ripen, mellow, mature, grow, develop, foster, season, weather, wear.

aged *adj.* old, advanced, elderly, time-honored, venerable, ancient, superannuated, antique.
    ant. young, green, unseasoned, immature, new.

agency *n.* **1** power, force, means, medium, instrumentality, mechanism, action, function, intercession, support, effectiveness, doing, work. **2** organization, office, bureaucracy, establishment, operation, commission, setup, bureau.

agenda *n.* program, schedule, docket, order of business, timetable.

agent *n.* **1** doer, actor, executor, officer, arm, surrogate, deputy, aide, functionary, arm, performer, perpetrator, operator, worker. **2** power, force, means, medium, agency, factor, instrument, mechanism, machine, cause, provocation.

agglomeration *n.* **1** COLLECTION. **2** HEAP.

agglutinate *v.* ATTACH.

aggrandize *v.* enlarge, inflate, dilate, blow up, puff up, strengthen, extend, intensify, amplify, enrich, widen, maximize.
    ant. deflate, constrict, collapse, weaken, impoverish.

aggravate *v.* **1** worsen, exacerbate, intensify, exaggerate, heighten, emphasize, add to, deepen, magnify. **2** annoy, provoke, irritate, irk, bother, unsettle, disturb, nag, pester, exasperate, nettle, anger, vex, rile.
    ant. **1** relax, de-emphasize, pacify, ease.

aggravating *adj.* annoying, irritating, bothersome, troublesome, provoking, pesty, exasperating, vexing, irksome, obnoxious, unpleasant, unsettling, tiresome, nettling.
    ant. relaxing, soothing, calming, agreeable, pleasant.

aggravation *n.* ANNOYANCE.

aggregate *adj.* summed up, totaled, collected, cumulative, combined, collective, composite, amassed, assembled.
    ant. separate, individual, discrete, single.

aggregation *n.* COLLECTION.

aggress *v.* ATTACK.

aggression *n.* **1** assault, attack, invasion, offense, inroad, infringement, trespass, encroachment, raid, intrusion, sortie, siege, violation, rape. **2** violence, brutality, hostility, bellicosity, belligerence, combativeness, offensiveness, pugnacity, truculence, contentiousness.

aggressive *adj.* **1** hostile, belligerent, quarrelsome, contentious, argumentative, pugnacious, combative, angry, warlike, touchy. **2** energetic, forceful, vigorous, competitive, ambitious, hard-hitting, purposeful, dynamic, enterprising, persistent, self-assertive, militant, pushy, bold.
    ant. **1** peaceful, peace-loving, pacific, defensive, placatory. **2** timid, self-effacing, apathetic, sluggish, costive.

aggressiveness *n.* **1** self-assertion, ambition, competitiveness, get-up-and-go, energy, vigor, forcefulness, activism, militance. **2** AGGRESSION.
    ant. timidity, shyness, docility.

aggressor *n.* attacker, invader, belligerent, assailant, trespasser, raider, challenger.

aggrieve *v.* **1** DISTRESS. **2** AFFLICT.

aggrieved *adj.* sorrowful, grieving, sad, saddened, afflicted, beset, troubled, disturbed, grief-stricken, affronted, offended, hurt, wronged, wounded, stung.

aghast *adj.* shocked, stunned, horrified,

appalled, amazed, thunderstruck, terrified, dismayed, flabbergasted, panicky, dumbfounded, petrified, distressed.

agile *adj.* **1** nimble, spry, lithe, athletic, supple, fleet, quick, light-footed, acrobatic, graceful, active, volant, sprightly, spirited. **2** alert, quick-witted, quick, bright, clever, sharp, sparkling, incisive, apt, acute, perceptive, keen.
ant. **1** heavy, plodding, clumsy, inept, klutzy (*Slang*). **2** slow, slow-witted, dull, sluggish, oafish.

agility *n.* alacrity, celerity, legerity, dexterity, rapidity, speed, quickness, briskness, nimbleness, alertness, ease.
ant. slowness, sluggishness, ploddingness, languor, torpidity.

agitate *v.* **1** shake, move, jiggle, unsettle, disturb, ruffle, ripple, flutter, quiver, churn, quake, toss. **2** excite, stir up, impassion, foment, incite, arouse, inflame, instigate, provoke, spur, goad, ignite.
ant. **1, 2** calm down, soothe, quiet, still, allay, pacify.

agitation *n.* EXCITEMENT.

agitator *n.* rabble-rouser, troublemaker, inciter, instigator, provocateur, agent provocateur, demagogue, haranguer, firebrand, incendiary, revolutionary, malcontent, militant.

agnate *adj.* RELATED.

agnomen *n.* NICKNAME.

agog *adj.* expectant, excited, eager, enthusiastic, impatient, aquiver, atwitter, breathless, in suspense, anticipatory.
ant. uninterested, bored, cool, composed, apathetic.

agonize *v.* WORRY.

agony *n.* torment, anguish, suffering, pain, torture, distress, misery, affliction, sorrow, despair, hardship, laceration, martyrdom.
ant. comfort, bliss, happiness, joy, ease, pleasure.

agree *v.* **1** consent, accede, assent, acquiesce, grant, give in. **2** coincide, harmonize, accord, match, conform,

correspond, tally, suit, fit. **3** endorse, sanction, subscribe, affirm, support, second, accept, approve, concur.
ant. **1** negate, deny, contradict. **2** clash, conflict, diverge. **3** reject, veto, repudiate.

agreeable *adj.* **1** pleasing, pleasurable, enjoyable, gratifying, felicitous, welcome, delightful, comforting, satisfying, delectable, dulcet. **2** sympathetic, responsive, congenial, well-disposed, amenable, acquiescent.
ant. **1** displeasing, irritating, annoying, painful. **2** unsympathetic, obstinate, contrary, negative.

agreement *n.* understanding, pact, contract, arrangement, treaty, entente, compact, covenant, bargain, cartel, alliance, deal.

ahead *adv.* at the head, in front, out in front, onward, on, along, forward, in the lead, to the van, in the vanguard, in the foreground, frontward.
ant. behind, in the back, to the rear, trailing, following, backward.

aid *v.* help, assist, succor, serve, support, relieve, cooperate, advance, promote, oblige, accommodate, collaborate, abet, pitch in. —*n.* assistance, help, succor, support, avail, benefit, service, cooperation, encouragement, lift, boost, prop.
ant. *v.* hinder, impede, obstruct. *n.* hindrance, deterrent, impediment, obstacle.

aide *n.* ASSISTANT.

ail *v.* trouble, disturb, pain, bother, irritate, ache, distress, afflict, affect, sicken, upset.

ailing *adj.* ill, sick, unwell, under the weather, indisposed, enfeebled, debilitated, suffering, distressed, diseased, infirm, weak, laid up, bedridden.
ant. healthy, strong, sound, fit, recovering, cured, convalescent.

ailment *n.* discomfort, disturbance, complaint, sickness, pain, ache, sore, weakness, malady, disability, malaise.

aim *v.* **1** direct, point, slant, beam,

focus, level, draw a bead. **2** plan, intend, endeavor, propose, mean, have in mind, contemplate, purpose, aspire, resolve. —*n.* design, purpose, intention, plan, scheme, desire, wish, goal, target, aspiration, ambition, endeavor, end, desideratum.

aimless *adj.* purposeless, pointless, directionless, wayward, unfocused, undirected, unguided, vagrant, stray, erratic, frivolous, unpredictable, haphazard, chance.
ant. purposeful, intentional, destined, fated.

air *n.* **1** wind, breeze, current, draft, ventilation, blow, waft, gust. **2** aura, appearance, atmosphere, tone, impression, flavor, quality, mood, character, spirit, effect, ambiance. —*v.* display, exhibit, publicize, ventilate, broadcast, make known, reveal, expose, show, express, communicate.
ant. *v.* cover up, conceal, keep under wraps, hide.

airless *adj.* unventilated, close, stuffy, musty, stale, still, oppressive, heavy, suffocating, stifling.
ant. ventilated, airy, fresh, breezy.

airs *n.* mannerisms, pretensions, affectation, affectedness, artificiality, haughtiness, snobbishness, superciliousness, phoniness (*Slang*).
ant. simplicity, directness, spontaneity, matter-of-factness, naturalness.

airy *adj.* **1** breezy, ventilated, windy, gusty, drafty, blowy, fresh, open. **2** light, delicate, gossamer, ethereal, thin, wispy, lacy, filmy, gauzy, diaphanous, transparent, impalpable. **3** jaunty, debonair, nonchalant, flippant, vivacious, quick, breezy, perky, sprightly, bouncy, bubbly, lively.
ant. **1** airless, close, unventilated, stuffy, stifling. **2** heavy, thick, solid, weighty. **3** torpid, leaden, sluggish, grim, stolid, slow.

aisle *n.* passage, passageway, lane, path, avenue, walk, alley, clearing.

akin *adj.* **1** related, kin, kindred, consanguineous, cognate, agnate, inbred,

affiliated. **2** similar, alike, parallel, comparable, analogous, matching.
ant. **1** unrelated, unconnected. **2** unlike, different, dissimilar, disparate.

alacrity *n.* **1** eagerness, willingness, enthusiasm, zeal, readiness, heartiness, fervor, relish. **2** speed, quickness, readiness, dispatch, promptness, suddenness, swiftness.
ant. **1** distaste, unwillingness, reluctance, aversion. **2** delay, procrastination, sluggishness, torpidity.

alarm *n.* **1** fear, apprehension, trepidation, anxiety, foreboding, panic, perturbation, dread, uneasiness, dismay, nervousness. **2** alert, bell, warning, signal, siren, tocsin, SOS. —*v.* **1** frighten, affright, scare, perturb, startle, panic, terrify, unnerve. **2** warn, alert, signal.
ant. *n.* **1** fearlessness, confidence, intrepidity, assurance, enthusiasm. *v.* **1** allay, calm, reassure, encourage, nerve, embolden.

alarming *adj.* frightening, perturbing, scary, startling, disturbing, terrifying, ominous, threatening, inauspicious, disquieting, dire.
ant. reassuring, hopeful, optimistic, gratifying, heartening, encouraging.

alarmist *n.* scaremonger, prophet of doom, pessimist, Cassandra, Jeremiah, Chicken Little.

album *n.* scrapbook, memory book, notebook, portfolio, compendium, record, catalogue, memorabilia.

alcoholic *adj.* spiritous, vinous, distilled, fermented, hard.
ant. nonalcoholic, soft.

alcove *n.* recess, nook, cubicle, corner, bower, retreat, niche, compartment, cubbyhole, dressing room.

alert *adj.* **1** vigilant, watchful, wideawake, prepared, ready, at the ready, wary, on guard, cautious, on the *qui vive*, attentive, circumspect, on the lookout. **2** quick, perceptive, nimble, sharp, quick-witted, intelligent, lively, agile. —*n.* warning, siren, alarm, tocsin, signal, notice.
ant. *adj.* **1** napping, off guard, un-

mindful, unwary. **2** dull, slow, unperceptive, sluggish.

alertness *n.* READINESS.

alias *n.* assumed name, pseudonym, pen name, *nom de plume,* stage name.

alibi *n.* defense, explanation, excuse, plea, out, dodge, reason, justification, rationalization, pretext, claim, extenuating circumstance.

alien *adj.* foreign, strange, remote, distant, exotic, unfamiliar, bizarre. —*n.* foreigner, outsider, noncitizen, stranger, newcomer, outlander.
ant. *adj.* native, local, domestic, familiar, indigenous. *n.* native, citizen, countryman, compatriot, national, indigene.

alienate *v.* SEPARATE.

alienated *adj.* estranged, detached, indifferent, unfriendly, remote, withdrawn, disengaged, uninvolved, disaffected, separated, uncommitted, unrelated, anomic.
ant. close, akin, involved, attached, at home.

alien to contrary, opposed, inconsistent, foreign, contradictory, unnatural, uncongenial, unlike, strange, incongruous, counter, incompatible.
ant. natural, consistent, congenial, compatible.

alight *v.* settle, land, come down, come to rest, descend, dismount, light, perch, get down.

alight on *v.* chance on, happen on, hit on, come upon, find, discover, encounter, come across, run into.

alike *adj.* akin, analogous, like, paired, twin, corresponding, duplicate, identical, matched, kindred.
ant. unlike, dissimilar, different, opposite.

aliment *n.* FOOD.

alive *adj.* **1** living, existing, breathing, extant, present, animate. **2** lively, animated, active, alert, vivacious, spirited, energetic, sprightly, zestful, bouncy, bubbly, zippy, vigorous, brisk, snappy.
ant. 1 dead, gone, inanimate, nonex-

istent. **2** inert, phlegmatic, lethargic, torpid, slow.

alive with abounding in, teeming with, buzzing with, jumping, hopping, crawling, dense, packed, swarming, overrun, bristling.
ant. deserted, unoccupied, empty, void, desolate.

all *adj.* **1** entire, complete, undiminished, the whole of. **2** each, every, each and every, every single, all and sundry. —*n.* totality, everything, entirety, sum, aggregate, sum and substance, kit and caboodle, bag and baggage, body and soul.
ant. *adj.* **1** no, not one, not any. **2** some, selected, few, chosen. *n.* nothing, nil, zero.

all-around *adj.* VERSATILE.

allay *v.* mitigate, alleviate, calm, relieve, vitiate, pacify, soothe, hush, quiet, temper, ease, assuage, mollify, moderate.
ant. intensify, exacerbate, aggravate, heighten, excite, irritate.

allegation *n.* assertion, accusation, charge, claim, impugnment, statement, deposition, attack, complaint, indictment, impeachment, imputation, incrimination, aspersion.

allege *v.* assert, affirm, declare, charge, state, posit, indict, impeach, impute, incriminate, maintain, attribute, avow, profess, impugn.

alleged *adj.* HYPOTHETICAL.

allegiance *n.* loyalty, fealty, fidelity, faithfulness, adherence, constancy, homage, respect, obedience, deference.
ant. disloyalty, treachery, betrayal, perfidy, subversion.

allegory *n.* parable, fable, symbol, metaphor, representation, myth, folk tale, emblem, trope, image, icon, totem, abstraction, depiction, illustration.

allergic *adj.* sensitive, susceptible, hypersensitive, sensitized, anaphylactic.

alleviate *v.* lighten, ease, mitigate, soften, relieve, lessen, temper, allay, decrease, reduce, remedy, moderate, abate, lift.

ant. weigh down, worsen, aggravate, intensify, exacerbate, heighten.

alleviation *n.* RELIEF.

alley *n.* passageway, passage, dead end, cul-de-sac, aisle, lane, walk, avenue, path, way, pathway, promenade, esplanade.

alliance *n.* **1** treaty, pact, understanding, agreement, arrangement, accord, concordat, league, affiliation, merger, bloc, pool, cartel, union, marriage. **2** kinship, relationship, affinity, similarity, tie, connection, likeness, congruity.

ant. 2 uniqueness, dissimilarity, difference, disparity.

allied *adj.* affiliated, united, joined, joint, merged, connected, coordinated, amalgamated, federated, wed, bound.

ant. unconnected, disaffiliated, alone, single.

all-important *adj.* crucial, decisive, necessary, vital, critical, essential, overriding, indispensable, imperative, obligatory, pressing, fundamental, almighty, dominant, cardinal, chief.

ant. subsidiary, subordinate, secondary, unimportant, lesser, minor.

all in tired, wearied, weary, exhausted, fagged out, spent, frazzled, worn out, fatigued, enervated, beat, knocked out (*Slang*), pooped (*Slang*).

ant. energetic, vigorous, peppy (*Slang*), raring to go.

allocate *v.* earmark, designate, set apart, set aside, apportion, allot, allow, assign, mete, deal, distribute, divide, share, parcel out.

allocation *n.* ALLOTMENT.

allot *v.* ALLOCATE.

allotment *n.* portion, share, part, deal, fraction, parcel, percent, allowance, allocation, piece, ration, lot, measure, quota.

all-out *adj.* thorough, total, maximum, supreme, unstinted, unrestrained, undivided, unremitting, optimum,

thoroughgoing, full, unlimited, complete, utmost.

ant. partial, divided, casual, half-hearted.

all over finished, done with, ended, over, past and gone, dead, buried, at an end, *fini*, washed up (*Slang*).

ant. current, on, ongoing, in progress.

allow *v.* **1** permit, let, tolerate, suffer, authorize, entitle, give, vouchsafe, empower, license, put up with, submit, accede to, stand for. **2** confess, concede, admit, acknowledge, grant, own to, own up, declare, acquiesce. **3** ALLOCATE.

ant. 1 refuse, withhold, deny, disallow, disapprove, object to.

allowance *n.* allotment, share, stipend, income, ration, subsidy, quota, payment, dividend, annuity, dispensation, honorarium, fee, appropriation, dole, spending money, pocket money, pin money.

all-purpose *adj.* VERSATILE.

all right 1 satisfactory, adequate, passable, acceptable, okay, up to snuff, standard, up to par, average, unobjectionable. **2** correct, accurate, right, precise, authentic. **3** unharmed, uninjured, intact, sound, well, unhurt, unimpaired, undamaged, in one piece, unmarred.

ant. 1 unsatisfactory, inadequate, unacceptable, substandard, below par. **2** incorrect, wrong, mistaken, inaccurate, in error. **3** hurt, harmed, injured.

allude to hint, imply, insinuate, intimate, suggest, refer to, indicate, mention, speak of, point to, designate, touch on.

allure *n.* sex appeal, glamor, charm, attractiveness, magnetism, seductiveness, witchery, magic, desirability, fascination.

alluring *adj.* attractive, seductive, fascinating, charming, bewitching, enchanting, desirable, sexy, provocative, tempting, come-hither, enticing, captivating.

ant. unappealing, unappetizing, unattractive, repulsive.

allusion *n.* reference, mention, implication, insinuation, innuendo, suggestion, indication, hint, intimation, citation, quotation, attribution, illustration, instance.

ally *n.* partner, confederate, cooperator, collaborator, colleague, associate, friend, coworker, helper, assistant, upholder, supporter.

ant. enemy, adversary, foe, opponent, antagonist, rival, opposer.

almighty *adj.* omnipotent, all-powerful, invincible, supreme, sovereign, unrivaled, preeminent, unchallenged, transcendent, all-important.

almost *adv.* approximately, nearly, all but, well-nigh, mostly, practically, largely, not quite, close to, approaching, on the verge of.

alms *n.* charity, donation, gift, benefaction, dole, handout, offering, aid, contribution, assistance, relief.

alone *adj.* **1** lone, solitary, isolated, friendless, single, separate, unaccompanied, forsaken, deserted, desolate, abandoned. **2** unique, unequaled, unrivaled, unparalleled, sole, only, incomparable, peerless, singular, inimitable, nonpareil.

ant. 1 befriended, accompanied, escorted, together. **2** common, commonplace, ordinary, typical, usual, standard.

aloof *adj.* distant, forbidding, standoffish, cool, reserved, unfriendly, unapproachable, remote, offish, formal, chilly, starchy, unsociable, detached, unconcerned, disengaged.

ant. warm, friendly, enthusiastic, involved, participating.

aloud *adv.* audibly, distinctly, clearly, intelligibly, out loud, loudly, noisily, boisterously, clamorously, openly.

ant. silently, inaudibly.

already *adv.* by now, before now, before this time, just now, as of now, previously.

ant. not yet, eventually, in the future.

also *adv., conj.* **1** besides, and, too, in addition, plus, moreover, furthermore, to boot, along with, including. **2** likewise, ditto, similarly, correspondingly.

alter *v.* change, modify, moderate, transform, revise, transmute, permute, reshape, reform, remake, remodel, amend, accustom, adjust, convert, vary.

ant. maintain, continue, stet.

alteration *n.* modification, transformation, change, transmutation, permutation, transfiguration, emendation, variation, revision, conversion, mutation, metamorphosis, difference, departure, variance.

altercate *v.* **1** WRANGLE. **2** DISPUTE.

altercation *n.* quarrel, dispute, argument, controversy, clash, wrangle, remonstrance, fight, debate, bicker, falling-out, rhubarb (*Slang*).

ant. agreement, harmony, compatibility, concurrence.

alter ego 1 second self, double, twin, shadow, counterpart, simulacrum, *doppelgänger,* semblable. **2** mate, pal, buddy, crony, chum, comrade, confidante, sidekick (*Slang*).

alternate *v.* take turns, interchange, reciprocate, vary, oscillate. —*adj.* **1** reciprocal, rotating, back and forth, interchanging. **2** alternative, another, different, second, substitute, additional, further, other, surrogate, equivalent.

alternative *n.* choice, option, answer, preference, selection, solution, way out, substitute, replacement, equivalent, surrogate.

altogether *adv.* completely, entirely, wholly, totally, thoroughly, utterly, fully, absolutely, diametrically, undividedly, exhaustively, solidly, out and out, in every way, in toto.

ant. partially, partly, somewhat, moderately, rather, to a degree.

altruism *n.* PHILANTHROPY.

altruist *n.* benefactor, philanthropist, humanitarian, angel, patron, donor, subsidizer, Good Samaritan, Lady Bountiful, do-gooder, liberal.

ant. self-server, tightwad, Scrooge, cynic, misanthrope.

always *adv.* perpetually, eternally, endlessly, continually, infinitely, for all time, forever, ever, everlastingly, evermore, till doomsday.

ant. never, nevermore, never again, at no time.

amalgam *n.* mixture, combination, merger, union, bloc, amalgamation, compound, composite, blend, fusion, coalition, syndicate.

amalgamate *v.* compound, mix, combine, merge, unite, blend, fuse, commingle, federate, consolidate, ally, coalesce, integrate.

ant. separate, divide, part, split, disintegrate.

amalgamation *n.* AMALGAM.

amanuensis *n.* SECRETARY.

amass *v.* heap up, pile up, accumulate, collect, mass, gather, acquire, store up, assemble, garner, lay up, round up, compile, save, hoard.

ant. disperse, give away, spend, waste.

amateur *n.* **1** hobbyist, nonprofessional, layman, dilettante, dabbler, devotee, aficionado, buff, enthusiast, fan, freak (*Slang*). **2** novice, apprentice, beginner, incompetent, bungler, fumbler, rookie (*Slang*). —*adj.* AMATEURISH.

ant. 1, 2 professional, expert, master, authority, specialist, virtuoso.

amateurish *adj.* unprofessional, unskilled, unskillful, inept, incompetent, inexpert, bungling, clumsy, half-baked, unpolished, inadequate, substandard, amateur.

ant. professional, skillful, competent, expert, polished, finished.

amatory *adj.* passionate, impassioned, sexual, sexy, amorous, erotic, sensual, lascivious, libidinal, ardent, infatuated, romantic.

amaze *v.* ASTONISH.

amazement *n.* astonishment, wonder, surprise, awe, incredibility, bewilderment, stupefaction, incredulity, disbelief.

ant. unresponsiveness, boredom, apathy, indifference.

amazing *adj.* overwhelming, astonishing, surprising, startling, unanticipated, unexpected, astounding, unbelievable, electrifying, incredible, remarkable, miraculous, marvelous, bewildering, stunning, dazzling.

ant. ordinary, usual, normal, average, expected, familiar.

ambassador *n.* diplomat, legate, consul, deputy, agent, envoy, representative, intermediary, messenger, go-between, emissary, courier, factor, surrogate.

ambiance *n.* atmosphere, air, aura, character, quality, spirit, temper, tone, smell, odor, complexion, mood, tenor, flavor, vibrations (*Slang*), vibes (*Slang*).

ambidextrous *adj.* SKILLFUL.

ambiguous *adj.* equivocal, unclear, unprecise, uncertain, two-edged, double-edged, doubtful, unsure, foggy, hazy, vague, problematic, problematical, puzzling, misleading, inconclusive.

ant. clear, straightforward, definite, precise, unequivocal, unquestionable.

ambition *n.* **1** aspiration, purposefulness, will, determination, eagerness, appetite, get-up-and-go, dynamism, aggressiveness, push. **2** goal, purpose, aim, end, focus, target, intention, objective, desire, dream, wish, resolve, desideratum.

ant. 1 purposelessness, aimlessness, irresolution, apathy, inertia, laziness.

ambitious *adj.* **1** purposeful, aspiring, goal-oriented, determined, dynamic, energetic, hard-working, resolved, persevering, aggressive, pushing. **2** difficult, challenging, demanding, elaborate, grandiose, impressive, arduous, exacting.

ant. 1 purposeless, aimless, lethargic, idle, lazy, contented. **2** simple, easy, undemanding.

ambivalence *n.* conflict, indecision, irresolution, uncertainty, doubt, confusion, contradiction, inconclusiveness, incertitude, instability, fluctuation, vacillation, hesitancy, equivocation, tergiversation.

ant. determination, single-mindedness, certainty, decision, certitude, assurance, conviction.

ambivalent *adj.* undecided, unresolved, conflicting, mixed, unsettled, confused, contradictory, unfocused, inconclusive, unstable, debatable.

ant. definite, settled, resolved, clear, decided.

amble *v.* stroll, promenade, saunter, dawdle, meander, walk, ramble, drift, wander, gad.

ambrosial *adj.* DELICIOUS.

ambulate *v.* WALK.

ambuscade *n.* AMBUSH.

ambush *n.* **1** concealment, hiding, lurking, lying in wait, waylaying. **2** cover, blind, camouflage, shelter, retreat, screen, ambuscade, hideaway, hiding place, refuge.

ameliorate *v.* IMPROVE.

amelioration *n.* improvement, betterment, advancement, melioration, progress, reform, reformation, promotion, healing, assuagement, relief, mitigation, alleviation.

ant. deterioration, worsening, decadence, regression, decline, pejoration.

amenable *adj.* agreeable, tractable, cooperative, obedient, responsive, accessible, answerable, willing, docile, compliant, acquiescent, submissive, complaisant, decent, civil.

ant. refractory, stubborn, balky, unwilling.

amend *v.* **1** improve, correct, better, ameliorate, mend, remedy, strengthen, restore, redeem, relieve, doctor, rectify, reform. **2** transform, change, edit, alter, update, revise, rewrite, emendate, add, redact.

ant. 1 worsen, weaken, pollute, debase.

amendment *n.* **1** improvement, bettering, betterment, amelioration, correction, restoration, strengthening, reform, alteration, adjustment. **2**

clarification, revision, change, alteration, adaptation, updating, modification, addition, redaction.

ant. 1 weakening, worsening, debasement, erosion.

amends *n.* reparation, atonement, rectification, restoration, redress, recompense, relief, compensation, restitution, requital, indemnity, satisfaction, *quid pro quo.*

amenities *n.* manners, social graces, courtesy, civility, politeness, etiquette, protocol, gentility, pleasantries, social requirements, *politesse.*

amiability *n.* GENIALITY.

amiable *adj.* genial, warm, kind, pleasant, congenial, charming, lovable, obliging, good-hearted, outgoing, approachable.

ant. disagreeable, unpleasant, cold, unapproachable.

amicability *n.* AMITY.

amicable *adj.* peaceable, friendly, cooperative, well-disposed, neighborly, helpful, hospitable, sociable, benign.

ant. unfriendly, quarrelsome, hostile, antagonistic.

amid *prep.* amidst, midst, among, in, surrounded by, in the middle of.

amidst *prep.* AMID.

amigo *n.* FRIEND.

amiss *adj.* wrong, improper, out of order, awry, askew, confused, faulty, incorrect, inappropriate, haywire (*Slang*), snafu (*Slang*), screwed up (*Slang*), loused up (*Slang*), fouled up (*Slang*), kaput (*Slang*).

ant. okay, all right, in good shape.

amity *n.* friendship, cooperation, friendliness, amicability, accord, peace, understanding, good will, harmony, comradeship, fellowship, cordiality, tranquility.

ant. hostility, disharmony, ill will, discord, enmity.

ammunition *n.* **1** explosives, shot and shell, munitions, armaments, ordinance, arms, materiel. **2** resources, wherewithal, tools, material, support, means, supplies, capability, essentials, strength, influence, power, clout (*Slang*).

amnesty *n*. PARDON.

amok *adv*. madly, in a frenzy, wildly, destructively, insanely, uncontrollably, murderously, maniacally, ferociously, savagely, amuck, frenziedly.

amorous *adj*. amatory, concupiscent, lascivious, sexy, leering, ogling, erotic, passionate, provocative, lustful, lecherous, voluptuous, loving, seductive, adoring, romantic, comehither (*Slang*).

amorphous *adj*. shapeless, formless, unshaped, unformed, protoplasmic, undefined, undelineated, vague, indefinite, unsettled.
ant. structured, shaped, formed, defined, definite.

amount *n*. **1** sum, total, aggregate, addition, whole, entirety. **2** quantity, lot, pack, parcel, number, count, enumeration, volume, mass, bulk, extent, magnitude, expanse, estimation.

amount to 1 total, add up to, come to, sell for, go for, measure, be worth, number, cost. **2** equal, mean, indicate.

amour *n*. liaison, love affair, relationship, romance, intimacy, infatuation, dalliance.

amphitheater *n*. ARENA.

ample *adj*. **1** capacious, roomy, large, substantial, big, extensive, commodious, expansive, broad, voluminous, spacious. **2** abundant, sufficient, enough, adequate, full, plentiful, plenteous, lavish, unstinted.
ant. **1** cramped, tight, restricted, small, narrow. **2** sparse, scarce, insufficient, inadequate, stinted.

amplification *n*. ENLARGEMENT.

amplify *v*. **1** enlarge, extend, increase, broaden, widen, heighten, strengthen, raise, boost, fatten, augment. **2** detail, particularize, complete, footnote, expatiate, elaborate, illustrate, supplement, develop, beef up (*Slang*).

ant. **1** diminish, decrease, lower, weaken, restrict. **2** condense, summarize, shorten, abridge.

amputate *v*. cut off, remove, cut away, mutilate, dismember, sever.

amuck *adv*. AMOK.

amulet *n*. charm, talisman, fetish.

amuse *v*. **1** entertain, divert, charm, beguile, cheer, enliven, engage, interest, distract, regale. **2** tickle, convulse.
ant. **1** bore, weary, tire, annoy, irritate. **2** sadden, depress.

amusement *n*. **1** pleasure, fun, relaxation, recreation, laughter, mirth, merriment, enjoyment, gaiety, hilarity. **2** entertainment, comedy, hobby, avocation, diversion, sport, joke, lark, romp, prank, circus, picnic, spectacle, party.

amusing *adj*. **1** entertaining, diverting, relaxing, charming, cheering, enlivening, lively, beguiling, interesting, engaging, cheerful, joyous. **2** comical, funny, silly, clownish, facetious, witty, jocular, droll, ludicrous, hilarious, rib-tickling, zany.
ant. **1** boring, dull, uninteresting, tiresome. **2** sad, depressing, grim, tragic, funereal.

analgesic *n*. pain-killer, pain-reliever, anodyne, opiate, drug.

analogous *adj*. comparable, akin, similar, kindred, cognate, congenial, close, alike, corresponding, parallel, congruous, homologous.
ant. unlike, dissimilar, different, divergent, disparate.

analogy *n*. similarity, resemblance, parallel, likeness, correspondence, comparison, equivalence, homology, similitude.
ant. dissimilarity, disparity, difference, unlikeness.

analysis *n*. dissection, anatomization, resolution, sorting out, separation, division, assay, diagnosis, breakdown, reduction.

analytic *adj*. rational, logical, diagnostic, dissecting, atomistic, piecemeal, detailed, discrete, compartmentalized.

ant. synthetic, integrated, holistic.

analyze *v.* dissect, break down, simplify, resolve, sort out, decompose, diagnose, anatomize, assay, examine, study, consider, think through, evaluate, investigate.

anarchy *n.* CONFUSION.

anathema *n.* **1** curse, imprecation, condemnation, malediction, damnation, execration, denunciation, censure, vituperation. **2** abomination, enemy, pariah, *bête noire*, villain, foe, bane, outlaw, heretic, *persona non grata*.

ant. 1 blessing, approval, approbation, favor.

anathematize *v.* CURSE.

anatomize *v.* ANALYZE.

ancestor *n.* **1** forebear, progenitor, primogenitor, forefather, sire, procreator, parent. **2** precursor, forerunner, predecessor, originator, father, mother, begetter, antecedent, source, prototype, precedent.

ant. 1 descendant, heir, offspring, scion, child.

ancestry *n.* **1** forefathers, forebears, progenitors, ancestors, antecedents, family tree. **2** descent, lineage, extraction, parentage, origin, background, genealogy, stock, heredity, blood, pedigree.

anchor *n.* support, prop, security, protection, fastening, underpinning, safeguard, anchorage, mooring, mainstay, foundation, strong point, bulwark.

anchorage *n.* ANCHOR.

anchorite *n.* HERMIT.

ancient *adj.* **1** antique, prehistoric, antediluvian, classical, archaic, olden, primeval, primitive, immemorial. **2** old, aged, hoary, senile, moldering, fossilized, antique, superannuated, venerable, traditional.

ant. 1 modern, contemporary, recent, current. **2** young, new, novel.

ancillary *adj.* subordinate, subsidiary, secondary, accessory, supplemen-

tary, adjunct, assistant, extra, additional.

ant. principal, primary, main, central, chief, dominant, essential, leading.

androgynous *adj.* hermaphroditic, bisexual, unisexual, epicene, gynandrous.

anecdote *n.* tale, story, narrative, sketch, yarn, account, reminiscence, recounting, report.

anemic *adj.* PALE.

anent *prep.* ABOUT.

anesthetic *n.* analgesic, anodyne, painkiller, narcotic, opiate, soporific, sedative, nepenthe.

anew *adv.* AGAIN.

angel *n.* **1** spirit, cherub, seraph, archangel. **2** saint, ideal, paragon, darling, dear, beauty, dream, treasure. **3** benefactor, supporter, backer, patron, subsidizer, sponsor, endorser, guarantor, investor, underwriter.

angelic *adj.* saintly, virtuous, pure, perfect, ideal, lovely, beautiful, heavenly, divine, adorable, innocent, chaste, cherubic.

ant. impish, devilish, mischievous.

anger *n.* wrath, ire, fury, rage, indignation, irritation, annoyance, vexation, pique, petulance, resentment, umbrage, outrage, offense, dander, dudgeon, bile, spleen, choler, huff. —*v.* enrage, infuriate, vex, irk, inflame, incense, exasperate, madden, provoke, rile, gall, rankle, irritate, annoy, upset.

ant. *v.* soothe, pacify, mollify, tranquilize, please, placate, appease.

angle *n.* viewpoint, perspective, orientation, aspect, position, slant, frame of reference, point of view.

angle for solicit, wangle, cast about, fish, hunt, finagle, maneuver, contrive, scheme, seek.

angler *n.* fisherman, fisher, piscator.

angry *adj.* **1** wrathful, furious, irate, enraged, mad, infuriated, incensed, vexed, indignant, choleric, boiling, irritated, annoyed, upset, burnt up

(*Slang*), pissed off (*Slang*). **2** threatening, ominous, lowering, stormy, dark, turbulent, tempestuous, blusterous.

angst *n.* ANXIETY.

anguish *n.* agony, torment, torture, suffering, woe, pain, distress, sorrow, pang, grief, misery, heartbreak, despair, heartache.

angular *adj.* bony, gaunt, lanky, rawboned, lean, scrawny, skinny, spindly, skin and bones.
ant. plump, stout, fleshy, round, pudgy, stocky.

anile *adj.* INFIRM.

animadversion *n.* disapproval, censure, rebuke, criticism, condemnation, reproach, blame, reprimand, faultfinding, knock, pan, reflection, rap (*Slang*).
ant. praise, approval, commendation.

animadvert *v.* CRITICIZE.

animal *n.* creature, beast, brute, mammal, nonhuman.

animate *v.* **1** activate, quicken, vivify, energize, enliven, spark, galvanize, vitalize, invigorate, awaken. **2** incite, inspire, kindle, fire, spark, encourage, stimulate, arouse, spur.
ant. **1** kill, extinguish, destroy. **2** dampen, discourage, check.

animated *adj.* lively, spirited, vivacious, energetic, enthusiastic, vigorous, dynamic, vital, ebullient, buoyant, hearty.
ant. lethargic, sluggish, listless, spiritless, lifeless, torpid.

animation *n.* SPIRIT.

animosity *n.* hostility, animus, enmity, hatred, ill will, dislike, bitterness, rancor, bad blood, antipathy, strife, antagonism.
ant. friendship, harmony, good will, amity, amicability, affection.

animus *n.* ANIMOSITY.

annals *n.* chronicles, archives, chronologies, records, history, documents, journals, registers.

anneal *v.* temper, toughen, harden, steel, strengthen, indurate, caseharden.

annex *v.* add, append, attach, affix, connect, tack on, join, appose. —*n.* extension, addition, wing, branch, arm, attachment, ell.
ant. *v.* remove, disjoin, disconnect, separate.

annexation *n.* UNION.

annihilate *v.* demolish, wipe out, exterminate, kill, extinguish, eradicate, obliterate, do away with, destroy, abolish, erase, extirpate.

annihilation *n.* DESTRUCTION.

anniversary *n.* birthday, feast day, name day, fete, commemoration, holiday, jubilee.

annotate *v.* NOTE.

annotation *n.* NOTE.

announce *v.* proclaim, declare, report, reveal, tell, communicate, notify, divulge, promulgate, annunciate, signal, herald.

announcement *n.* declaration, proclamation, notice, bulletin, manifesto, statement, annunciation, decree, edict, disclosure.

announcer *n.* broadcaster, emcee, master of ceremonies, anchor man, commentator, newscaster, host, disc jockey.

annoy *v.* bother, vex, irk, irritate, harass, pester, heckle, bedevil, plague, trouble, disturb, tease, badger, get on one's nerves, pick on.

annoyance *n.* vexation, irritation, harassment, exasperation, aggravation, disturbance, bedevilment, trouble, nuisance, bother, botheration.

annoying *adj.* vexatious, troublesome, irritating, troubling, nagging, bothersome, irksome, exasperating, pestiferous, pesty, obnoxious, disturbing, aggravating, upsetting, disagreeable, unpleasant.
ant. pleasant, agreeable, comforting, soothing.

annual *adj.* yearly, yearlong, perennial.

annuity *n.* ALLOWANCE.

annul *v.* invalidate, nullify, cancel, repeal, abrogate, negate, void, rescind, revoke, abolish, vacate, overrule, dissolve.

annulment *n.* nullification, invalidation, repeal, revocation, abolition, cancellation, abrogation.

annunciate *v.* ANNOUNCE.

annunciation *n.* ANNOUNCEMENT.

anodyne *n.* ANALGESIC.

anoint *v.* consecrate, bless, sanctify, hallow, ordain, enthrone, crown, lay hands on.

anomalous *adj.* 1 ABNORMAL. 2 IRREGULAR.

anomaly *n.* 1 abnormality, deviation, irregularity, departure, aberration, eccentricity, inconsistency. 2 oddity, exception, peculiarity, miracle, freak, eccentric, deviate, deviation, abnormality, singularity.
   ant. 1 conformity, regularity, normalcy, consistency.

anomie *n.* ANXIETY.

anon *adv.* SOON.

anonym *n.* PSEUDONYM.

anonymous *adj.* nameless, unsigned, unknown, incognito, pseudonymous, uncredited, unidentified, unacknowleged, unnamed.
   ant. signed, credited, attributed, famous, well-known.

another *pron.* substitute, surrogate, replacement, proxy, variant, alternative.

answer *v.* 1 reply, respond, react, acknowledge, echo, rejoin, retort. 2 serve, do, suffice, work, pass, succeed, qualify, measure up, stand up, fill the bill, do the trick (*Slang*). 3 satisfy, serve, fulfill, suit, fit, meet, conform, correspond. —*n.* 1 reply, response, rejoinder, acknowledgment, rebuttal, retort, riposte, comeback (*Slang*). 2 reprisal, retaliation, retribution, reaction, reciprocation, exchange, backlash, reflex, requital, counterattack.
   ant. *v.* 1 ask, demand, inquire, query, question, quiz. *n.* 1 question, inquiry, query, quiz.

answerable *adj.* responsible, accountable, liable, amenable, subject, to blame.
   ant. exempt, excused, unaccountable, clear.

answer back contradict, rebut, refute, talk back, argue, disagree, contravene, countercharge, retort.

antagonism *n.* hostility, strife, bitterness, conflict, animosity, discord, rivalry, dissension, opposition, clash, feud.
   ant. friendship, good will, accord, harmony, agreement.

antagonist *n.* adversary, opponent, enemy, rival, competitor, foe, assailant, attacker, disputant.
   ant. ally, friend, supporter, helper.

antagonistic *adj.* opposed, hostile, conflicting, unfriendly, unsympathetic, inimical, clashing, incompatible, antithetical.
   ant. supportive, congenial, compatible, harmonious.

antagonize *v.* estrange, alienate, anger, offend, insult, disaffect, annoy, turn against, rub the wrong way, put off.
   ant. befriend, win over, ingratiate, please, charm.

ante *n., v.* STAKE.

antecedence *n.* PRECEDENCE.

antecedent *adj.* preceding, prior, anterior, earlier, previous, preliminary, precursory, former, first, foregoing. —*n.* ANCESTOR.
   ant. posterior, later, following, subsequent, succeeding, latter, ensuing.

antechamber *n.* FOYER.

antedate *v.* precede, antecede, forerun, forego, predate, preexist, anticipate.
   ant. follow, succeed, postdate.

antediluvian *adj.* PRIMITIVE.

antenna *n.* aerial, mast, tower, rabbit ears.

antennae *n.* feelers, appendages, tentacles, palpi, barbels, whiskers.

anterior *adj.* FORE.

anteroom *n.* FOYER.

anthem *n.* hymn, paean, psalm, chorale, chant, song.

antic *n.* prank, caper, trick, stunt, lark, escapade, shenanigan, practical joke, monkey business (*Slang*), monkeyshine (*Slang*), horse play. —*adj.* foolish, ludicrous, ridiculous, silly, incongruous, absurd, grotesque.

ant. *adj.* serious, dignified, sober, staid.

anticipate *v.* 1 foresee, expect, await, envision, contemplate, count on, look forward, hope, dread, apprehend. 2 precede, forerun, lead, pioneer, foreshadow, antedate. 3 forestall, preclude, intercept, prevent, avert, deter, obviate, rule out, head off, nip in the bud.

anticipation *n.* expectation, hope, premonition, presentiment, foreboding, apprehension, contemplation, preconception, foretaste, forethought.

anticlimax *n.* letdown, bathos, disappointment, comedown, fizzle.

antidote *n.* 1 counterpoison, mithridate, antivenin, antitoxin. 2 remedy, cure, countermeasure, neutralizer, counterbalance, offset.

antipathetic *adj.* AVERSE.

antipathy *n.* aversion, dislike, antagonism, hostility, abhorrence, loathing, repugnance, disgust, hatred, revulsion, animosity, animus.

ant. affection, liking, attraction, love, appeal.

antiphon *n.* CHANT.

antipode *n.* OPPOSITE.

antiquated *adj.* obsolete, old-fashioned, passé, superannuated, archaic, antediluvian, dated, outdated, outmoded, démodé, antique, outworn, shopworn, old hat (*Slang*).

ant. current, up-to-date, modern, new, fashionable.

antique *n.* relic, artifact, fossil, antiquity, memorabilia, museum piece. —*adj.* ANCIENT.

antiquity *n.* 1 olden days, prehistory, yore. 2 antique, relic, fossil, artifact, remains, ruins, monument.

antiseptic *adj.* aseptic, disinfectant, germicidal, bactericidal, sterile, sanitary, hygienic.

ant. septic, infected, putrid, contaminated.

antisocial 1 disruptive, rebellious, intractable, refractory, unmanageable, antiestablishment. 2 unsociable, alienated, estranged, reserved, anomic, hermitic, solitary.

ant. 1 docile, tractable, willing, cooperative. 2 sociable, genial, open, friendly, clubbable.

antithesis *n.* opposite, contrary, antipode, negation, contradiction, reverse, inverse, converse.

antithetical *adj.* OPPOSITE.

antitoxin *n.* ANTIDOTE.

anxiety *n.* apprehension, concern, misgiving, care, disquiet, foreboding, *angst*, anomie, qualm, fear, dread, worry, tension, nervousness, suspense.

ant. ease, confidence, assurance, equanimity, tranquility, peace of mind, security.

anxious *adj.* 1 worried, nervous, tense, taut, uneasy, distressed, apprehensive, fearful, concerned, jumpy, jittery, disturbed, ill at ease, afraid, uptight (*Slang*), anomic. 2 eager, keen, desirous, impatient, itching, yearning, enthusiastic.

ant. 1 calm, confident, secure, unafraid, relaxed, reassured. 2 indifferent, lukewarm, apathetic, unenthusiastic, loath, unwilling, reluctant.

anybody *pron.* anyone, someone, one, whoever, whosoever, no matter who.

anyhow *adv.* notwithstanding, however, in any case, anyway, nevertheless, regardless, nonetheless, at any rate.

anyone *pron.* ANYBODY.

A-OK *adj.* EXCELLENT.

A-one *adj.* EXCELLENT.

apace *adj.* FAST.

apart *adv.* 1 away, aloof, off, asunder, at arm's length. 2 separately, independently, singly, individually, severally, alone, piecemeal, in isolation, discretely.

ant. 2 together, collectively, mutually, in concert.

apart from aside from, besides, except for, excluding, save, but.

apartheid *n.* SEGREGATION.

apartment *n.* flat, tenement, suite, lodgings, digs, chambers, walk-up, pad (*Slang*).

apathetic *adj.* indifferent, unfeeling, unconcerned, uninterested, uncaring, unresponsive, emotionless, impassive, cool, half-hearted, lukewarm, lethargic, sluggish, listless, spiritless, phlegmatic.
   ant. concerned, caring, emotional, involved, sympathetic, moved, sensitive, alert.

apathy *n.* indifference, unconcern, impassivity, insensitivity, coldness, numbness, dispassion, disinterest, lethargy, listlessness, torpor, sluggishness.
   ant. sympathy, emotion, feeling, passion, warmth, spirit, enthusiasm, ardor.

ape *v.* mimic, imitate, emulate, copy, echo, mirror, parrot, counterfeit, mock, parody.

aperture *n.* opening, hole, crack, crevice, fissure, chink, peephole, breach, gap, interstice, cleft, rift, orifice, slot.

apex *n.* **1** top, tip, summit, pinnacle, peak, height, vertex, crest, crown, zenith, acme. **2** climax, culmination, acme, apogee, crest, peak.
   ant. 1 bottom, nadir, depth, low.

aphorism *n.* maxim, saying, epigram, adage, dictum, apothegm, proverb, truism, motto, slogan, saw, axiom.

aphrodisiac *adj.* erotic, amatory, erogenous, carnal, prurient, titillating, seductive, sexy.

aplomb *n.* poise, assurance, composure, self-confidence, self-assurance, self-possession, equanimity, coolness, balance, stability, serenity, imperturbability.
   ant. nervousness, self-doubt, instability, excitability, edginess.

apocalyptic *adj.* prophetic, oracular, revealed, mystical, farseeing, prescient.

apocryphal *adj.* spurious, dubious, fictitious, doubtful, unreliable, fake, unsubstantial, fabricated, mythical.

ant. factual, authenticated, genuine, verified, documented, authoritative, substantiated.

apogee *n.* APEX.

Apollo *n.* ADONIS.

apologetic *adj.* sorry, contrite, remorseful, repentant, regretful, penitent.
   ant. unrepentant, unremorseful, unregenerate, defiant, brazen.

apologia *n.* ARGUMENT.

apologist *n.* ADVOCATE.

apologize *v.* repent, beg pardon, confess, retract, acknowledge.

apology *n.* **1** confession, acknowledgment, regret, retraction, repentance, amends. **2** travesty, excuse, mockery, imitation, caricature, sham.

apoplectic *adj.* enraged, furious, overexcited, frenzied, seeing red, in a fit, beside oneself.

apostasy *n.* heresy, betrayal, desertion, disloyalty, renunciation, disavowal, defection, lapse, treachery, backsliding, heterodoxy.
   ant. loyalty, orthodoxy, faithfulness, steadfastness.

apostate *n.* heretic, traitor, renegade, defector, recreant, bolter, dissenter, dissident, revisionist.
   ant. loyalist, party-liner.

apostatize *v.* FORSAKE.

apostle *n.* **1** missionary, evangelist, preacher, proselytizer. **2** prophet, founder, pioneer, advocate, proponent, spokesman, reformer, propagandist.

apostrophe *n.* aside, digression, soliloquy, monologue.

apothecary *n.* druggist, pharmacist, pharmaceutist, chemist (*Brit.*)

apothegm *n.* APHORISM.

apotheosis *n.* deification, glorification, exaltation, enshrinement, enthronement, immortalization, elevation, ideal, essence, exemplification, paragon, quintessence, embodiment.

apotheosize *v.* DEIFY.

appall *v.* shock, horrify, frighten, terrify, stun, alarm, dismay, startle, unnerve, petrify, paralyze, distress.

appalling *adj.* shocking, frightful, horrifying, horrific, awful, dreadful, ghastly, horrible, terrible, dire, hideous, grim.

appanage *n.* RIGHT.

apparatus *n.* **1** machine, device, instrument, tool, appliance, utensil, implement, gadget, contraption, gizmo, widget (*Slang*). **2** machinery, equipment, gear, paraphernalia, outfit, plant, engines. **3** BUREAUCRACY.

apparel *n.* clothing, garments, dress, attire, garb, raiment, wardrobe, costume, vestments, robes, outfit, duds.

apparent *adj.* evident, obvious, manifest, clear, plain, patent, indubitable, unmistakable, visible, conspicuous, unequivocal, undeniable.
ant. doubtful, uncertain, questionable, obscure, hazy, hidden.

apparition *n.* specter, phantom, ghost, spirit, spook, wraith, shade, sprite.

appeal *n.* **1** entreaty, petition, plea, supplication, request, adjuration, solicitation, suit. **2** charm, attractiveness, charisma, fascination, interest, magnetism. —*v.* plead, entreat, supplicate, ask, request, beseech, beg, pray, implore, adjure, sue, invoke.

appealing *adj.* charming, attractive, desirable, engaging, inviting, tempting, captivating, enchanting, pleasing, winning, disarming.
ant. unappealing, repugnant, repulsive, unpleasant, disagreeable, distasteful.

appear *v.* **1** emerge, arise, materialize, show up, surface, arrive, turn up, come to light, issue, loom. **2** seem, look, feel, sound, strike one as.

appearance *n.* **1** emergence, materialization, manifestation, exposure, issuance, arrival, occurrence, reification. **2** exterior, facade, look, image, mien, demeanor, visage, air, bearing, form, semblance, aspect.

appease *v.* placate, pacify, mollify, calm, soothe, propitiate, conciliate, satisfy, allay, relieve, assuage, alleviate, quench, quell.
ant. irritate, exacerbate, antagonize, anger, aggravate, offend.

appellation *n.* name, title, label, designation, epithet, cognomen, nickname, sobriquet, handle (*Slang*), moniker (*Slang*).

append *v.* add, attach, affix, tack on, fasten, annex, connect, adjoin, supplement.
ant. detach, subtract, remove, cut off.

appendage *n.* attachment, addition, appurtenance, adjunct, offshoot, growth, protuberance, limb, arm, branch, tail, tentacle, knob.

appendant *n.* ADJUNCT.

appendix *n.* addition, addendum, supplement, codicil, rider, postscript, epilogue, follow-up.

appertain *v.* PERTAIN.

appetence *n.* **1** APPETITE. **2** PROPENSITY.

appetite *n.* **1** hunger, thirst, craving, voracity, stomach, ravenousness. **2** desire, yearning, drive, hankering, lust, yen, longing, craving, relish, taste, appetence, stomach, fondness.
ant. 2 aversion, revulsion, repugnance, distaste.

appetizing *adj.* tempting, inviting, alluring, appealing, enticing, tantalizing, desirable, beckoning, seductive.
ant. unappetizing, unattractive, distasteful, repugnant, repellent, unpalatable.

applaud *v.* **1** clap, cheer, hail, hurrah, give a hand. **2** acclaim, commend, praise, hail, extol, approve, compliment, eulogize, laud, exalt.
ant 1 boo, hiss, hoot, razz, catcall. **2** denigrate, denounce, condemn, criticize, knock, pan.

applause *n.* ovation, clapping, hand, cheer, salvo, acclaim, acclamation, accolade, plaudit, praise, commendation, kudos.
ant. denunciation, rejection, disapproval, condemnation, criticism.

apple polisher *Slang* FLATTERER.

applesauce *n. Slang* BUNK.

appliance *n.* apparatus, device, machine, implement, gadget, tool, contraption, fixture, instrument.

applicable *adj.* relevant, fitting, suitable, apt, pertinent, appropriate, germane, apposite, useful.
ant. irrelevant, unsuitable, inapplicable, inappropriate, useless.
application *n.* 1 salve, dressing, lotion, poultice, balm, emollient, ointment. 2 aptness, appropriateness, relevance, suitability, utility, fitness, bearing, pertinence.
apply *v.* 1 administer, lay on, spread, rub, pour, smear, place, anoint. 2 adapt, employ, utilize, harness, convert. 3 *of oneself:* devote, dedicate, engage, involve, concern, direct. 4 pertain, refer, regard, relate, fit, suit, involve, concern, deal with, have to do with, connect.
appoint *v.* designate, select, name, choose, hire, nominate, commission, assign, depute, deputize, engage, arrange, set, determine, establish.
appointed *adj.* equipped, outfitted, furnished, supplied, fitted, endowed, arrayed, provided, accoutered.
appointment *n.* 1 designation, selection, assignment, placement, employment, nomination, naming. 2 position, job, office, post, station, situation, commission, assignment, slot. 3 engagement, date, rendezvous, meeting, booking, assignation, tryst.
appointments *n.* accessories, equipment, furnishings, accouterments, appurtenances, fittings, trappings, paraphernalia.
apportion *v.* allot, parcel, allocate, ration, dispense, mete, dole, measure out, distribute, deal, share.
appose *v.* ANNEX.
apposite *adj.* appropriate, pertinent, apt, fitting, relevant, applicable, suitable, apropos, to the point, befitting.
ant. unsuitable, inapposite, inappropriate, ill-suited, irrelevant, beside the point.
appraisal *n.* evaluation, estimate, rating, assessment, assay, valuation, judgment, opinion.
appraise *v.* evaluate, assess, estimate,

judge, assay, price, value, rate, size up, gauge, calculate, figure.
appreciable *adj.* noticeable, discernible, perceptible, measurable, considerable, substantial, significant, estimable, material, pronounced.
ant. negligible, insignificant, trivial, inconsequential, unimportant.
appreciate *v.* 1 acknowledge, recognize, credit, thank. 2 value, prize, esteem, treasure, regard, admire, cherish, enjoy, savor, relish, like, dig (*Slang*). 3 gain, advance, grow, boost, raise, inflate, enhance, upgrade, soar.
ant. 2 dislike, disdain, disregard, disparage, underrate, deprecate, belittle. 3 cheapen, decline, depress, depreciate.
appreciation *n.* 1 esteem, regard, respect, admiration, enjoyment, delight, pleasure, understanding, awareness, sensitivity, responsiveness. 2 gratitude, acknowledgment, thankfulness, recognition. 3 growth, advance, bullishness, upswing, increase, gain, elevation.
ant. 1 disregard, disdain, contempt, rejection, dislike. 3 depreciation, decline, depression, bearishness.
appreciative *adj.* aware, pleased, cognizant, sympathetic, conscious, grateful, thankful, mindful, sensitive, responsive, hip (*Slang*).
ant. unappreciative, unaware, oblivious, indifferent, ungrateful, thankless.
apprehend *v.* 1 seize, arrest, capture, confine, incarcerate, imprison, jail, collar, nab, pinch (*Slang*). 2 comprehend, understand, grasp, perceive, know, discern, realize, appreciate, follow, recognize.
apprehensible *adj.* COMPREHENSIBLE.
apprehension *n.* 1 foreboding, premonition, anxiety, dread, fear, doubt, misgiving, disquiet, worry, uneasiness, suspicion, alarm. 2 seizure, arrest, capture, incarceration, collar (*Slang*).

ant. 1 security, tranquillity, serenity, confidence, assurance.

apprehensive *adj.* anxious, fearful, nervous, afraid, suspicious, uneasy, alarmed, disquieted, on edge, edgy, jumpy.

ant. calm, secure, relaxed, confident, fearless, unafraid, assured.

apprentice *n.* novice, neophyte, learner, beginner, tyro, student, freshman, greenhorn, recruit, rookie (*Slang*).

ant. expert, master, veteran, old hand.

apprise *v.* notify, inform, advise, tell, brief, warn, enlighten, disclose, acquaint, admonish.

approach *v.* **1** advance, near, gain on, converge, reach, bear down upon, meet, verge. **2** approximate, match, resemble, compare, meet, parallel. —*n.* method, means, procedure, system, measure, way, modus operandi. **ant.** *v.* **1** leave, depart, recede, diverge.

approachable *adj.* accessible, attainable, open, congenial, outgoing, friendly, communicative, cordial, receptive, affable.

ant. aloof, unfriendly, offish, distant, cold, hostile, unapproachable.

approbation *n.* approval, commendation, favor, praise, acceptance, support, sanction, endorsement.

ant. disapproval, criticism, disfavor, deprecation.

appropriate *adj.* proper, suitable, fitting, seemly, fit, becoming, meet, apt, apposite, appurtenant, relevant, right, applicable, germane, legitimate. —*v.* confiscate, seize, usurp, expropriate, take over, attach, adopt, annex, commandeer, assume, preempt.

ant. *adj.* inappropriate, unsuitable, improper, irrelevant, beside the point, outré.

appropriation *n.* **1** allocation, funds, allowance, budget, allotment, expenditure, stipend. **2** SEIZURE.

approval *n.* **1** sanction, approbation, endorsement, ratification, imprimatur, validation, assent, confirmation.

2 favor, acceptance, liking, approbation, appreciation, admiration, praise, commendation, compliment, applause, esteem, honor, acclaim.

ant. 1 denial, refusal, ban, prohibition, proscription, interdiction. **2** disapproval, dislike, disparagement, rebuke, opposition, displeasure, objection.

approve *v.* **1** commend, like, accept, praise, appreciate, esteem, admire, back, endorse. **2** sanction, authorize, license, validate, ratify, countenance, consent, permit, uphold, allow, rubber-stamp.

ant. 1 disapprove, frown on, repudiate, criticize, reject, reprove, condemn. **2** forbid, prohibit, refuse, turn down, reject, ban, deny, proscribe, outlaw.

approve of accept, allow, agree with, support, back, uphold, defend, condone, countenance, sanction.

ant. denounce, criticize, blast, attack, score, condemn, censure.

approximate *adj.* close, near, rough, proximate, approaching, comparable, verging on. —*v.* approach, near, meet, resemble, match, converge, reach, border on.

approximately *adv.* almost, nearly, about, around, more or less, in the neighborhood of, *circa.*

approximation *n.* approach, nearness, closeness, proximity, propinquity, similarity, correspondence, convergence, resemblance.

ant. divergence, difference, distance, separation.

appurtenances *n.* APPOINTMENTS.

appurtenant *adj.* APPROPRIATE.

apron *n.* pinafore, bib, smock, coverall, jumper.

apropos *adj.* germane, pertinent, relevant, appropriate, apt, suitable, apposite, applicable, to the point, on target.

ant. irrelevant, inappropriate, unsuitable, beside the point.

apt *adj.* **1** likely, liable, tending, inclined, prone, subject, disposed, given, susceptible. **2** *quick to learn:* quick, bright, clever, educable, teachable. **3** suitable, appropriate, fitting, pertinent, apropos, meet, seemly, timely, suited, relevant.

ant. 2 inapt, slow, difficult, ineducable. **3** unsuitable, inappropriate, irrelevant, ill-suited.

aptitude *n.* ability, endowment, talent, skill, finesse, virtuosity, faculty, knack, flair, gift, capability, potential.

arbiter *n.* **1** judge, referee, umpire, moderator, mediator, intermediary, arbitrator, go-between. **2** authority, expert, master, specialist, connoisseur.

arbitrary *adj.* **1** frivolous, capricious, whimsical, fanciful, erratic, random, unreliable, willful, peremptory. **2** absolute, despotic, tyrannical, autocratic, totalitarian, dictatorial, highhanded, overbearing, domineering, imperious.

ant. 1 responsible, lawful, reasoned, deliberated, consistent, considered.

arbitrate *v.* mediate, judge, referee, intercede, moderate, intervene, adjudicate, conciliate.

arbitrator *n.* ARBITER.

arc *n.* arch, curve, semicircle, bend, curl, convex, parabola.

arcade *n.* archway, gallery, cloister, colonnade, portico, vault, mall.

arcane *adj.* secret, hidden, esoteric, recondite, enigmatic, obscure, mysterious, cabalistic, occult, cryptic, abstruse, inscrutable.

ant. explicit, evident, obvious, public, plain, open, clear-cut, understandable.

arch[1] *n.* **1** vault, ogive. **2** curve, arc, bow, semicircle, parabola. —*v.* bend, curve, flex, curl, bow, camber, vault, span, bridge.

arch[2] *adj.* eminent, chief, principle, primary, main, top, greatest, highest, master, first-rate, first-class, number-one.

ant. minor, lesser, secondary, subordinate, lower.

archaic *adj.* ancient, antiquated, outdated, dated, *passé,* obsolete, obsolescent, old-fashioned, olden, old-hat.

ant. modern, recent, current, new, up-to-date, voguish, fashionable.

archenemy *n.* **1** nemesis, adversary, *bête noire,* foe, bugbear, scourge, archfoe. **2** DEVIL.

ant. 1 ally, friend, supporter, champion, defender.

archetypal *adj.* MODEL.

archetype *n.* prototype, example, ideal, paradigm, model, original, form, pattern, exemplar.

ant. copy, imitation, replica, instance.

archfiend *n.* **1** FIEND. **2** DEVIL.

archfoe *n.* ARCHENEMY.

architect *n.* **1** master builder, draftsman, home builder. **2** planner, creator, designer, inventor, author, originator, framer, engineer, founder, prime mover, pioneer.

archives *n.* records, documents, annals, papers, registry, minutes, chronicles, statistics, transactions.

arctic *adj.* frigid, frozen, ice-cold, icy, wintry, boreal, glacial, gelid.

ant. warm, temperate, mild, summery, tropical, torrid, hot.

ardent *adj.* passionate, zealous, eager, enthusiastic, fervid, fervent, vehement, intense, hot, earnest, devoted, impassioned, avid, zestful, warmblooded, hot-blooded.

ant. indifferent, apathetic, lukewarm, cool, lethargic, sluggish, torpid.

ardor *n.* eagerness, passion, zeal, fervor, warmth, enthusiasm, vehemence, devotion, gusto, zest, intenseness.

ant. apathy, coolness, indifference, reluctance, torpor.

arduous *adj.* difficult, laborious, heavy, strenuous, exhausting, grueling, onerous, toilsome, fatiguing, backbreaking, tough, rigorous, hard, wearisome, taxing, demanding, punishing, Herculean.

ant. easy, light, soft, effortless, low-pressure.

area *n.* **1** space, section, zone, field, stretch, expanse. **2** tract, region, parcel, territory, district, plot, lot, section, real estate, turf (*Slang*). **3** extent, scope, range, sphere, domain, breadth, width, compass.

arena *n.* **1** stadium, amphitheater, coliseum, pit, stage, ring, playing field, battleground. **2** sphere, area, realm, domain, sector, territory.

argot *n.* slang, jargon, cant, vernacular, lingo, dialect, patois.

argue *v.* **1** plead, maintain, assert, contend, hold, prove, indicate, convince, demonstrate, debate, show, refute, challenge. **2** dispute, disagree, feud, quarrel, bicker, fight, spat, debate, haggle, wrangle, contend.
ant. **2** agree, assent, concede, grant, accept.

argument *n.* **1** reason, evidence, case, grounds, proof, justification, defense, apologia. **2** demonstration, reasoning, logic, discussion, dialectic, persuasion. **3** dispute, disagreement, debate, controversy, polemic, quarrel, conflict, contention, disputation, schism, squabble, spat, altercation, feud, wrangle.
ant. **3** agreement, accord, concord, harmony, unanimity.

argumentation *n.* DISCUSSION.

argumentative *adj.* disputatious, contentious, quarrelsome, combative, polemic, scrappy, perverse, cantankerous, contrary, opinionated.
ant. conciliatory, compliant, tractable, amenable.

aria *n.* melody, air, song, tune, solo, number.

arid *adj.* **1** dry, parched, waterless, dehydrated, desiccated, barren, sterile. **2** dull, tedious, uninteresting, lifeless, spiritless, flat, dreary, sterile, jejune, colorless, vapid.
ant. **1** moist, humid, rainy, wet, damp, fertile, rich, lush. **2** exciting, fascinating, lively, spirited.

arise *v.* **1** stand up, sit up, get up. **2** as-cend, mount, climb, rise, lift, levitate, up. **3** originate, begin, occur, happen, commence, dawn, crop up, spring up, materialize, emerge, appear, well up.
ant. **1** sit down, lie down, recline. **2** descend, lower, fall, drop, sink, plunge, plummet. **3** subside, culminate, wind up.

arise from ensue, result, proceed, follow, issue, accrue, flow, eventuate, stem, come, attend.

aristocracy *n.* **1** nobility, gentry, peerage, upper class, upper crust, Four Hundred, *haut monde*. **2** elite, choice, pick, flower, best, cream of the crop, elect.
ant. **1** proletariat, working class, bourgeoisie, peasantry, folk, masses, hoi polloi, rabble, riffraff, scum of the earth. **2** cross section.

aristocrat *n.* nobleman, noblewoman, patrician, peer, gentleman, gentlewoman, blue blood, Brahmin, silk-stocking.
ant. plebeian, proletarian, peasant, commoner.

arm[1] *n.* branch, shoot, projection, appendage, offshoot, estuary, tributary, bough, limb, extension, spin-off, by-product.

arm[2] *n. of the military:* service, corps, force, unit, division, branch, wing, detachment, battalion, group. —*v.* **1** equip, supply, provide, outfit, gear, rig, furnish, accouter, mechanize, deck out. **2** strengthen, fortify, prepare, prime, mobilize, gird, brace.

armada *n.* fleet, squadron, flight, flotilla, navy.

armaments *n.* arms, weaponry, materiel, ammunition, munitions, ordnance, panoply.

armature *n.* ARMOR.

armed *adj.* equipped, fortified, supplied, furnished, geared, prepared, provided, ready.
ant. disarmed, stripped, unprepared, defenseless, unarmed, vulnerable.

armistice *n.* truce, cease-fire, peace, cessation, moratorium.

armor *n.* shield, protection, cover, bulwark, armature, helmet, mail, breastplate, plate.

armory *n.* ARSENAL.

armpit *n.* axilla, underarm.

arms *n.* **1** weaponry, armaments, munitions, ordnance, materiel, artillery, ammunition. **2** warfare, war, battle, conflict, hostilities, aggression.
ant. 2 peace, truce, conciliation, negotiation.

aroma *n.* fragrance, scent, perfume, redolence, bouquet, incense, savor, odor, smell.

aromatic *adj.* fragrant, spicy, odoriferous, savory, balmy, piquant, pungent, redolent.
ant. noisome, malodorous, fetid, rank, foul.

aromatize *v.* FLAVOR.

arouse *v.* **1** awaken, waken, awake, wake, rouse, revive, bestir. **2** excite, inflame, incite, provoke, stimulate, agitate, stir up, whip up, move, spur, goad, spark, instigate, pique.
ant. 2 dampen, deaden, quench, stifle, repress.

arraign *v.* accuse, charge, prosecute, call to account, indict, hold responsible, blame, incriminate.
ant. exculpate, exonerate, excuse, absolve, clear, acquit, dismiss, release.

arrange *v.* **1** order, rank, organize, align, tidy, straighten, form, design, position. **2** settle, work out, adjust, fix, resolve, straighten out, mediate. **3** plan, prepare, devise, draw up, plot, map out, organize, prearrange, set up.
ant. 1 disarrange, jumble, mix up, mess up, entangle.

arrangement *n.* **1** preparation, plan, setup, scheme, disposition, settlement, adjustment, resolution. **2** design, form, structure, system, pattern, style, manner, makeup, composition, organization, configuration.

arrant *adj.* egregious, flagrant, unspeakable, gross, glaring, complete, deplorable, notorious, disgraceful, despicable, base, unmitigated, rank.
ant. proper, decent, respectable, correct, acceptable, excusable.

array *n.* **1** order, neatness, orderliness, arrangement, marshaling, formation, disposition, lineup, alignment. **2** turnout, showing, gathering, assembly, crowd, parade, display, throng.
ant. 1 disarray, disorder, confusion, chaos, mess.

arrest *v.* **1** halt, stop, check, stay, hinder, inhibit, obstruct, interrupt, stall, suppress. **2** apprehend, capture, seize, catch, detain, nab, pinch (*Slang*), bust (*Slang*), collar, jail, imprison, incarcerate. **3** engage, attract, engross, absorb, fascinate, intrigue, grip, rivet, spellbind. —*n.* **1** halt, stoppage, cessation, interruption, suppression, blockage, inhibition. **2** detention, capture, apprehension, collar (*Slang*), incarceration.
ant. *v.* **1** continue, encourage, spur, promote, accelerate. **2** free, release, dismiss.

arresting *adj.* notable, striking, interesting, engaging, engrossing, fascinating, remarkable, intriguing, gripping.
ant. unexceptional, humdrum, ordinary, uninteresting, dull.

arrival *n.* **1** entrance, attainment, advent, coming, debarkation, landing, approach, return, access, homecoming, appearance. **2** newcomer, comer, entrant, caller, visitor, passenger.
ant. 1 departure, exit, leavetaking, parting, disappearance.

arrive *v.* **1** come, appear, return, attain, reach, enter, show up, land, disembark, debark. **2** succeed, prosper, make good, make one's mark, make the big time (*Slang*), hit the jackpot, go places.
ant. 1 depart, go, leave, take off, exit. **2** fail, flop, lose, miss.

arriviste *n.* parvenu, *nouveau riche*, upstart, social climber.

arrogance *n.* CONCEIT.

arrogant *adj.* haughty, overbearing, conceited, proud, disdainful, supercilious, high and mighty, uppish, snobbish, imperious, egotistic, presumptuous, assuming.

ant. modest, humble, self-effacing, unassuming, meek, diffident, servile.

arrogate *v.* assume, usurp, appropriate, presume, claim, demand, seize, take over, impute, ascribe, allege, blame.

arrogation *n.* SEIZURE.

arrow *n.* dart, spear, shaft, missile, projectile, bolt, streak, shot, pointer.

arsenal *n.* armory, depot, dump, magazine, depository, storehouse, stockpile, cache, pile, supply, stock, store, hoard.

art *n.* 1 skill, craft, knowledge, know-how, artistry, workmanship, knack, talent, dexterity, finesse, invention, virtuosity, trade, profession, science. 2 cunning, craft, artfulness, trickery, wile, deceit, guile, contrivance, artifice, duplicity, deception.

ant. 2 artlessness, ingenuousness, guilelessness.

artery *n.* CHANNEL.

artful *adj.* 1 crafty, cunning, tricky, sly, wily, clever, disingenuous, foxy, deceitful, designing, scheming, duplicitous, shrewd. 2 artificial, imitative, fake, contrived, simulated, false, counterfeit, synthetic, spurious. 3 skillful, adept, dexterous, ingenious, inventive, creative, imaginative, adroit, clever, resourceful.

ant. 1 artless, candid, sincere, open, naive, aboveboard, ingenuous, innocent. 2 genuine, real, natural, honest, authentic. 3 clumsy, inept, unimaginative, awkward, maladroit.

artfulness *n.* ARTIFICE.

article *n.* 1 object, item, thing, entity, commodity, element, piece, thing-amajig, doodad. 2 essay, composition, editorial, piece, tract, write-up, review, critique, feature. 3 proviso, clause, item, heading, division, stipulation, condition, paragraph, passage, section. 4 tenet, belief, canon, dogma, principle, doctrine, precept.

articulate *adj.* 1 fluent, verbal, eloquent, expressive, perspicuous, vocal,

voluble, glib, facile, smooth. 2 clear, coherent, intelligible, lucid, sensible, logical, comprehensible, understandable, rational. —*v.* enunciate, pronounce, utter, voice, verbalize, say, express.

ant. *adj.* 1 inarticulate, indistinct, hesitating, halting, mumbling. 2 confused, incoherent, incomprehensible, unintelligible, muddled, fuzzy.

articulation *n.* JOINT.

artifact *n.* invention, creation, fabrication, contrivance, construction, handiwork.

artifice *n.* 1 trickery, deception, cunning, craft, contrivance, guile, artfulness, fraud, duplicity, scheming, machination. 2 stratagem, expedient, maneuver, tactic, dodge, subterfuge, device, measure, means, ruse.

ant. 1 straightforwardness, honesty, sincerity, ingenuousness, candidness, openness.

artificial *adj.* 1 synthetic, manufactured, imitation, man-made, factitious, contrived, unnatural, simulated, made-up, counterfeit, fake, sham, mock, ersatz. 2 affected, unnatural, false, forced, mannered, stilted, studied, strained, put-on, unreal, phony (*Slang*).

ant. 1 natural, real, genuine, actual, authentic. 2 unstudied, natural, unaffected, down to earth.

artificiality *n.* AFFECTATION.

artisan *n.* craftsman, artist, technician, workman, mechanic, handicraftsman.

artist *n.* virtuoso, master, expert, genius, professional, pro.

artistic *adj.* aesthetic, tasteful, ornamental, decorative, attractive, beautiful, graceful, elegant, refined, sensitive.

ant. vulgar, tasteless, crude, gross, gauche.

artistry *n.* talent, skill, invention, genius, virtuosity, creativity, craftsmanship, mastery, style, polish, finesse, flair.

artless *adj.* 1 innocent, candid, open,

plain, direct, naive, ingenuous, child-like, unsophisticated, untutored, guileless, sincere, genuine, frank. **2** natural, simple, crude, plain, rude, homespun, unadorned, unpretentious, humble, primitive. **3** clumsy, inept, unskilled, incompetent, awkward, maladroit, bungling.

ant. 1 sophisticated, worldly, shrewd, sneaky, sly, scheming, calculating. **2** polished, slick, ornate, fancy. **3** skillful, expert, adept, handy, adroit, dexterous.

arty *adj.* pretentious, precious, overnice, bluestocking, highbrow.

ant. pedestrian, humdrum, modest.

ascend *v.* arise, climb, mount, rise, lift off, levitate, escalate, scale, slope up, slant up, incline.

ant. descend, fall, alight, dismount, drop.

ascendance *n.* ASCENDANCY.

ascendancy *n.* dominance, supremacy, dominion, rule, superiority, control, ascendance, power, sway, upper hand, authority, influence, predominance, preeminence.

ant. subjugation, subjection, subservience, subordination.

ascension *n.* ASCENT.

ascent *n.* rise, climb, mounting, ascension, levitation, escalation.

ant. descent, fall, drop, plunge.

ascertain *v.* determine, discover, learn, find out, establish, tell, certify, verify, see.

ascetic *adj.* austere, self-denying, self-abnegating, Spartan, abstinent, abstemious, frugal, puritanical, stern. —*n.* anchorite, hermit, recluse, holy man, solitary, monk.

ant. *adj.* epicurean, hedonistic, sybaritic, sensual, worldly, extravagant, voluptuous. *n.* sybarite, voluptuary, hedonist.

asceticism *n.* SELF-DENIAL.

ascribe *v.* attribute, credit, attach, assign, impute, charge to, arrogate, associate, connect, relate.

aseptic *adj.* ANTISEPTIC.

ashamed *adj.* embarrassed, mortified, abashed, humiliated, chagrined, shamed, shamefaced, sheepish, blushing, remorseful, sorry, disgraced, humbled, put-down (*Slang*).

ant. proud, boastful, brazen, shameless, unashamed, unabashed.

ashen *adj.* pale, ashy, pallid, white, wan, livid, pasty, blanched, anemic.

ant. ruddy, rosy, flushed, glowing, blooming.

ashes *n.* **1** residue, cinders, soot, scoria, embers. **2** corpse, cadaver, remains, body, bones, relics, dust, clay, carcass.

ashy *adj.* ASHEN.

aside *adv.* apart, away, beside, nearby, alongside, out, out of the way, sideward, sideways, laterally. —*n.* **1** apostrophe, soliloquy, monologue, stage whisper. **2** digression, tangent, excursion, departure, deviation, interposition, interjection, parenthesis, interpolation, elaboration, amplification.

aside from excepting, besides, excluding, barring, save, but, apart from, away from.

ant. including, together with.

asinine *adj.* silly, thoughtless, stupid, foolish, ridiculous, inane, nonsensical, absurd, senseless, moronic, fatuous, dumb.

ant. clever, witty, bright, intelligent, thoughtful, wise.

ask *v.* **1** question, query, interrogate, quiz, pose. **2** request, solicit, petition, seek, beg, plead, appeal, apply, supplicate, entreat, beseech, implore. **3** invite, summon, bid, send for, call.

ant. 1 answer, respond, reply, declare, assert, state. **3** exclude, reject, bar, snub, ignore, overlook.

askance *adv.* disdainfully, disapprovingly, critically, disparagingly, distrustfully, suspiciously, skeptically, incredulously.

ant. trustingly, approvingly, admiringly.

askew *adv.* aslant, obliquely, awry, crookedly, off center, sidelong, cockeyed (*Slang*).

aslant *adv.* ASKEW.

aspect *n.* **1** expression, air, visage, mien, manner, bearing, countenance, demeanor. **2** appearance, look, exterior, facade, image, shape, form, face, surface, mask, semblance. **3** interpretation, facet, side, factor, element, conception, impression. **4** phase, angle, orientation, point of view, position, prospect, exposure, direction, frame of reference.

asperity *n.* irritability, acrimony, surliness, crankiness, peevishness, crossness, irascibility, ill temper, acerbity, causticity, tartness, snappishness.
ant. good humor, affability, geniality, cheerfulness, warmth, amiability.

asperse *v.* SLANDER.

aspersion *n.* slander, defamation, libel, smear, slur, calumny, detraction, mudslinging, backbiting, discredit, reflection, attack, vilification, impugnment.

asphyxiate *v.* suffocate, smother, choke, drown, gas, stifle, strangle, throttle.

aspirant *n.* CANDIDATE.

aspiration *n.* hope, desire, ambition, yearning, longing, dream, expectation, goal, aim.

aspire *v.* strive, aim, wish, desire, hope, yearn.

ass *n.* fool, jackass, dolt, donkey, blockhead, numskull, nincompoop, dunce, fathead (*Slang*), jerk (*Slang*), boob (*Slang*).

assail *v.* attack, assault, set upon, lay into, abuse, sail into, flay, lash, berate, score, malign, revile.
ant. protect, defend, support, champion, stand up for.

assailant *n.* attacker, assaulter, mugger, aggressor, molester, waylayer.

assassin *n.* murderer, killer, slayer, thug, gunman, sniper, bravo, cutthroat, executioner, hit man (*Slang*).

assassinate *v.* KILL.

assassination *n.* murder, killing, slaying, extermination, homicide, liquidation, bloodshed, execution, dispatch.

assault *n.* **1** attack, ambush, violence, onslaught, attempt, mugging, rape, molestation, violation, outrage. **2** affront, insult, abuse, invective, diatribe, vituperation, offense, declamation, defamation.

assaulter *n.* ASSAILANT.

assay *n.* analysis, examination, test, trial, experiment, diagnosis, investigation, probe, inspection. —*v.* test, examine, evaluate, analyze, assess, diagnose, judge, weigh, inspect.

assemblage *n.* **1** ASSEMBLY. **2** COMBINATION.

assemble *v.* **1** congregate, convene, gather, collect, band, convoke, muster, meet, mass, flock, throng, crowd, aggregate, rally. **2** fit, piece, connect, erect, manufacture, compile, construct.
ant. **1** disperse, disband, scatter, break up. **2** dismantle, disassemble, disconnect, separate.

assembly *n.* **1** collection, convening, convocation, congregation, confluence, concourse, assemblage, union. **2** meeting, gathering, congregation, convention, rally, congress, throng, council, crowd, roundup, multitude, group.
ant. **1** dispersal, separation, disbanding.

assent *v.* agree, concur, consent, give in, go along, yield, concede, comply, accede, accept, approve, acquiesce. —*n.* concurrence, agreement, approval, consent, blessing, acceptance, accord, OK, acquiescence, adhesion, compliance.
ant. *v.* dissent, disagree, disapprove, oppose, protest, demur, take exception. *n.* denial, refusal, opposition, disagreement, challenge, objection.

assert *v.* affirm, declare, state, say, maintain, claim, aver, avow, allege, insist, swear, attest, contend, asseverate, profess.
ant. deny, contradict, negate, oppose, retract, disavow, disclaim, dis-

pute, gainsay, repudiate, eat one's words.

assertion *n.* declaration, statement, claim, allegation, affirmation, contention, word, profession, pronouncement.
ant. denial, negation, disclaimer, retraction, disavowal, contradiction, repudiation.

assertive *adj.* positive, decided, dogmatic, aggressive, emphatic, confident, strong-minded, sure, cocksure, sanguine, insistent, decisive, assured.
ant. timid, hesitant, tentative, uncertain, diffident, shy.

assess *v.* 1 charge, fine, tax, levy, impose, exact. 2 evaluate, weigh, take stock of, estimate, rate, value, appraise, calculate, consider.

assessment *n.* APPRAISAL.

asset *n.* qualification, talent, gift, treasure, resource, plus, advantage.
ant. liability, handicap, drawback, disadvantage.

assets *n.* property, wealth, effects, holdings, estate, belongings, goods, possessions, funds, capital, reserves, resources.

asseverate *v.* ASSERT.

assiduity *n.* DILIGENCE.

assiduous *adj.* diligent, industrious, energetic, attentive, hard-working, sedulous, persevering, dedicated, untiring, unflagging, indefatigable, tireless, busy.
ant. lazy, indolent, slothful, sluggish, idle, inactive, easygoing, lethargic.

assign *v.* 1 designate, appropriate, allocate, consign, earmark, reserve. 2 appoint, nominate, commission, name, delegate, place, send, choose, designate, select. 3 attribute, ascribe, apply, charge, pin, impute, project.

assignation *n.* tryst, rendezvous, appointment, engagement, meeting, date, affair, liaison.

assignment *n.* task, duty, chore, mission, job, instructions, lesson, drill, homework, exercise, obligation.

assimilate *v.* 1 incorporate, metabolize, digest, absorb. 2 integrate, internal-ize, adopt, embrace, mix, intermingle, naturalize, adapt, adjust, accommodate, coopt.
ant. 2 reject, isolate, separate, segregate.

assimilation *n.* ingestion, absorption, digestion, incorporation, perception, recognition, apperception, identification, reception.

assist *v.* 1 help, aid, support, succor, promote, further, back, benefit, relieve, boost. 2 serve, work for, tend, minister to, cooperate with, second, attend, wait on.
ant. 1 hinder, hamper, sabotage, foil, thwart. 2 supervise, command, take charge, manage, direct.

assistance *n.* help, aid, relief, support, succor, hand, lift, backing, cooperation, service.

assistant *n.* helper, aide, subordinate, underling, acolyte, attendant, apprentice, flunky, subaltern, attaché, adjunct.

associate *n.* companion, colleague, coworker, cohort, partner, confederate, accomplice, confrere, ally, bedfellow, comrade, consort. —*adj.* 1 united, allied, fellow, affiliated, related. 2 assistant, auxiliary, subordinate, secondary, adjunct, ancillary. —*v.* 1 affiliate, unite, merge, ally, confederate, amalgamate, combine, conjoin, connect. 2 *join mentally:* relate, connect, link, bracket, compare, group, lump.
ant. *adj.* 1 independent, separate, autonomous, unaffiliated. 2 principal, chief, primary, main, head, top. *v.* 1 dissociate, separate, divorce, divide, break off. 2 distinguish, discriminate.

association *n.* 1 fellowship, companionship, comradeship, friendship, partnership, alliance, affiliation. 2 organization, company, society, club, league, union, coalition, corporation, confederation, clique, syndicate. 3 *mental joining:* link, connection, relationship, comparison, correlation, juxtaposition, grouping.

assort *v.* CLASSIFY.

assorted *adj.* varied, miscellaneous, diverse, sundry, mixed, various, variegated, divers, heterogeneous.

ant. matching, similar, uniform, homogeneous.

assortment *n.* miscellany, mixture, variety, collection, aggregate, hodgepodge, heap, batch, pack, bunch, medley, potpourri.

assuage *v.* ease, allay, mitigate, moderate, soften, alleviate, relieve, soothe, palliate, calm, lull, pacify, mollify, tranquilize.

ant. irritate, exacerbate, aggravate, intensify, sharpen, worsen.

assume *v.* **1** adopt, embrace, take up, don, acquire. **2** undertake, embark on, take on, take over, usurp, appropriate, arrogate, seize, preempt. **3** suppose, presume, hypothesize, theorize, presuppose, posit, postulate, infer, believe, grant, admit, concede, take for granted.

ant. 1 renounce, abjure, forswear, abandon, shed.

assumed *adj.* pretended, fictitious, feigned, false, counterfeit, make-believe, fake, simulated, bogus, supposed, so-called.

ant. genuine, real, actual, authentic, bona fide.

assuming *adj.* PRESUMPTUOUS.

assumption *n.* supposition, conjecture, premise, hypothesis, theory, postulate, presupposition, guess, speculation, given, presumption.

assurance *n.* certainty, conviction, confidence, faith, trust, persuasion, positiveness, self-confidence, self-reliance, assuredness, security.

ant. doubt, hesitancy, misgiving, apprehension, distrust, insecurity, skepticism.

assure *v.* **1** establish, determine, confirm, verify, ascertain, find out, ensure. **2** convince, persuade, reassure, certify, affirm, attest, ensure, swear, pledge, promise, guarantee, vouch, give one's word.

ant. 1 disprove, raise doubts, question, refute.

assured *adj.* self-possessed, confident, secure, poised, certain, positive, assertive, sanguine, firm, complacent.

ant. nervous, insecure, uncertain, self-doubting.

astonish *v.* amaze, surprise, confound, astound, shock, daze, dazzle, stun, dumfound, stupefy, flabbergast, bedazzle, strike dumb.

astonishing *adj.* AMAZING.

astonishment *n.* surprise, amazement, wonder, bewilderment, wonderment, awe, consternation, stupefaction, bedazzlement.

astound *v.* stun, shock, astonish, startle, amaze, dumfound, confound, take aback, overwhelm, appall, stagger.

astounding *adj.* amazing, stunning, surprising, wondrous, overwhelming, incredible, unbelievable, remarkable, phenomenal, extraordinary, staggering.

ant. ordinary, expected, unexceptional, mundane.

astringent *adj.* **1** constrictive, contractile, styptic, binding, compressive. **2** harsh, stern, hard, austere, severe, stringent, strict, rigid, grim, rigorous, exacting.

ant. 2 lenient, easygoing, gentle, forbearing, indulgent, soft.

astute *adj.* clever, shrewd, intelligent, acute, sharp, sagacious, cunning, crafty, artful, canny, keen, able, perspicacious, quick, perceptive, knowing.

ant. obtuse, blind, dull, slow, naive, artless, ingenuous, gullible.

asunder *adj.* APART.

asylum *n.* refuge, shelter, haven, harbor, sanctuary, retreat, preserve, hide-out, hideaway.

atheist *n.* unbeliever, irreligionist, skeptic, doubter, agnostic, heathen, infidel, pagan.

ant. believer, theist, pietist, worshipper.

athirst *adj.* EAGER.

athletic *adj.* strong, robust, hearty, vigorous, strapping, husky, muscular, brawny, burly, beefy, sinewy, hefty, able-bodied.

ant. puny, feeble, frail, delicate, flabby, weak, soft, sickly.

atmosphere *n.* surroundings, environment, background, ambiance, aura, feeling, mood, climate.

atom *n.* iota, bit, jot, whit, shred, grain, speck, mite, crumb, scintilla, particle, corpuscle.

atomize *v.* pulverize, grind, disintegrate, vaporize, spray, volatilize, aerify.

atone *v.* repent, expiate, redress, make amends, pay, make up, do penance, confess.

atonement *n.* reparation, amends, compensation, repayment, expiation, redress, recompense, restitution, satisfaction.

atrabilious *adj.* 1 GLOOMY. 2 PEEVISH.

atrocious *adj.* monstrous, outrageous, wicked, heinous, horrible, fiendish, brutal, barbaric, savage, cruel, sadistic, criminal, vicious, inhuman, unspeakable.

ant. good, decent, kind, merciful, compassionate, benevolent, humane.

atrocity *n.* outrage, enormity, horror, crime, felony, brutality, inhumanity, savagery, cruelty.

atrophy *n.* degeneration, emaciation, decline, decay, consumption, deterioration, waste. —*v.* degenerate, decline, waste away, wither, wilt, shrivel, emaciate, dwindle, shrink, fade.

attach *v.* 1 fasten, append, affix, tack, pin, tie, secure, connect, cement, add, agglutinate, stick, link, hook, bind. 2 join, enlist, accompany, unite with, bind, connect, associate, latch on to (*Slang*). 3 attribute, ascribe, impute, assign, associate, connect, place, put.

ant. 1 detach, separate, loosen, untie, break off, disconnect, unfasten. 2 dissociate, quit, part.

attaché *n.* ASSISTANT.

attachment *n.* 1 connection, fastening, linkage, binding, joining, securing.

2 accessory, addition, device, fixture, apparatus, appurtenance, fitting. 3 affinity, affection, fondness, devotion, regard, attraction, friendship, bond, liking, predilection.

ant. 1 detachment, separation, unfastening, parting. 3 dislike, aversion, indifference, alienation.

attack *v.* 1 assault, set upon, assail, aggress, molest, waylay, invade, charge, storm, pitch into, strike, zap (*Slang*). 2 criticize, censure, assail, assault, denounce, berate, impugn, abuse, slander, malign, vituperate, vilify, rail at, tear into, scold. 3 tackle, undertake, plow into, tear into, apply oneself, buckle down, pitch in. —*n.* 1 assault, onslaught, offensive, charge, attempt, invasion, aggression, raid, incursion, strike. 2 seizure, stroke, fit, spell, bout, convulsion, spasm, paroxysm.

ant. *v.* 1 defend, ward off, protect, shield, repulse, resist. 2 praise, commend, applaud, uphold, defend, side with, support.

attacker *n.* ASSAILANT.

attain *v.* achieve, accomplish, reach, complete, secure, acquire, win, obtain, get, effect, procure, arrive at, score, make.

ant. fail, fall short, lose, forfeit, miss.

attainment *n.* accomplishment, acquisition, achievement, acquirement, success, realization, fulfillment, skill, knowledge, learning, qualification, technique.

attempt *v.* endeavor, try, essay, undertake, aim, strive, struggle, venture, seek. —*n.* effort, trial, endeavor, essay, undertaking, enterprise, venture, shot, crack, bid.

attend *v.* 1 minister to, serve, wait on, care for, assist, tend, look after, guard. 2 show up, arrive, frequent, haunt, appear, visit. 3 result in, follow from, await, accrue, accompany, go along, go hand in hand.

attendance *n.* PRESENCE.

attendant *n.* 1 servant, assistant, companion, aide, handmaid, valet, lackey, bodyguard, waiter, steward, stewardess, usher, acolyte. **2** participant, celebrater, onlooker, viewer, spectator.

attention *n.* **1** concentration, devotion, diligence, heedfulness, application, care, intentness, mindfulness, alertness, vigilance. **2** notice, observation, heed, regard, consideration, eye, spotlight, recognition, publicity.
ant. 1 forgetfulness, absent-mindedness, negligence, inattention, heedlessness, distraction, obliviousness. **2** neglect, disregard, slight.

attentions *n.* devotions, courtship, courtesies, favors, wooing, gallantries, amenities.

attentive *adj.* alert, careful, heedful, observant, conscientious, considerate, thoughtful, gracious, devoted, mindful, courteous, polite, deferential, respectful, gallant.
ant. negligent, heedless, thoughtless, unthinking, remiss, inconsiderate, discourteous.

attenuated *adj.* weakened, reduced, diminished, lessened, decreased, diluted, dilute, watered down, thinned, rarefied, drawn out.
ant. fortified, strengthened, amplified, intensified, thickened, compressed.

attest *v.* confirm, vouch for, affirm, assert, verify, authenticate, corroborate, bear out, support, testify, certify, substantiate.
ant. belie, negate, deny, refute, contradict, discredit, falsify.

attestation *n.* TESTIMONY.

attire *v.* dress, array, adorn, clothe, bedeck, deck, outfit, drape. —*n.* clothing, apparel, dress, raiment, garb, costume, wardrobe, garments, outfit, duds, finery.

attitude *n.* **1** posture, manner, bearing, pose, position, stance, carriage, mien. **2** mood, outlook, mind, disposition, response, frame, conduct, behavior, comportment, demeanor, temperament.

attitudinize *v.* POSE.

attorney *n.* advocate, lawyer, counsel, counselor, solicitor, barrister.

attract *v.* **1** draw, pull, lure, tempt, beckon, entice, invite. **2** allure, captivate, charm, magnetize, enchant, interest, fascinate, bewitch, appeal to.
ant. 1, 2 repel, repulse.

attraction *n.* affinity, appeal, allure, pull, magnetism, charm, fascination, interest, enticement, temptation, attractiveness, charisma.
ant. repulsion, aversion, revulsion, rejection.

attractive *adj.* inviting, appealing, alluring, enticing, tempting, magnetic, pleasing, winning, prepossessing, agreeable, fair, pretty, handsome, charming, well-favored, engaging, fetching.
ant. unattractive, repulsive, repellent, unappealing, ugly, distasteful.

attribute *v.* assign, impute, ascribe, credit, blame, charge, refer, arrogate, attach. —*n.* quality, characteristic, property, trait, feature, peculiarity, quirk, mark, point, aspect.

attrition *n.* weakening, erosion, attenuation, wearing down, disintegration, reduction, thinning out, decimation.
ant. reinforcement, buildup, accretion, fortification, strengthening.

attune *v.* HARMONIZE.

attuned *adj.* harmonious, concordant, consonant, adjusted, adapted, compatible, tuned, fitted, reconciled, conforming, according.
ant. discordant, clashing, dissonant, inharmonious, discrepant.

atypical *adj.* **1** UNUSUAL. **2** ABNORMAL.

au courant CONVERSANT.

audacious *adj.* **1** fearless, bold, intrepid, daring, venturesome, plucky, dauntless, hardy, brave. **2** brazen, insolent, impertinent, shameless, presumptuous, forward, impudent, assuming, fresh (*Slang*), disrespectful, cheeky.
ant. 1 timid, shy, fearful, apprehensive, cowardly. **2** courteous, po-

lite, respectful, humble, modest, circumspect, discreet.

audacity *n.* **1** BRAVERY. **2** PRESUMPTION.

audible *adj.* hearable, distinct, perceptible, clear, plain, recognizable, intelligible.
ant. inaudible, unintelligible, indistinct.

audience *n.* **1** assembly, congregation, gathering, spectators, onlookers, listeners, gallery, conference, hearing, interview, reception, consultation. **2** market, public, readership, constituency, following.

audit *v. of accounts:* check, examine, inspect, investigate, scrutinize, probe, certify, verify, balance, overhaul, oversee, monitor.

audition *n.* tryout, hearing, trial, interview, test, screening.

auditorium *n.* assembly hall, meeting place, lecture hall, concert hall.

augment *v.* enlarge, intensify, increase, expand, amplify, inflate, extend, magnify, swell, spread, add to, reinforce, aggrandize, build up, flesh out.
ant. diminish, decrease, reduce, lessen, contract, shrink, deflate.

augmentation *n.* **1** ENLARGEMENT. **2** INCREASE.

augur *n.* prophet, soothsayer, seer, diviner, diviness, fortuneteller, oracle, prognosticator. —*v.* herald, foreshadow, presage, portend, bode, anticipate, betoken, harbinger.

augury *n.* **1** divination, soothsaying, prophesy, prediction, forecasting, fortunetelling. **2** omen, portent, harbinger, herald, sign, auspice.

august *adj.* majestic, grand, imposing, venerable, glorious, exalted, dignified, stately, eminent, distinguished, illustrious, estimable, noble, weighty, considerable.
ant. lowly, humble, petty, small, common, vulgar.

aura *n.* ambiance, atmosphere, mood, feeling, air, aroma, emanation, spirit.

au revoir FAREWELL.

aurora *n.* DAWN.

auspices *n.* patronage, sponsorship, support, aegis, backing, promotion, guidance, supervision, protection, authority.

auspicious *adj.* propitious, favorable, hopeful, promising, encouraging, rosy, opportune, timely, successful, prosperous, fortunate, lucky, happy, felicitous, right.
ant. inauspicious, unpromising, unfavorable, ill-fated, doomed, unfortunate, unlucky, ill-starred.

austere *adj.* **1** severe, grave, stern, hard, harsh, forbidding, grim, stiff, formal, cold. **2** ascetic, abstemious, rigid, strict, self-denying, Spartan, simple, spare, unadorned, severe, chaste, plain, stark.
ant. **1** benign, cheerful, friendly, warm, relaxed, sunny. **2** extravagant, lavish, indulgent, ornate, luxurious, plush.

austerity *n.* **1** RIGOR. **2** ABSTINENCE. **3** ECONOMY.

authentic *adj.* genuine, real, actual, true, pure, veritable, factual, legitimate, bona fide, simon-pure.
ant. false, spurious, fictitious, fake, counterfeit, simulated, artificial, specious.

authenticate *v.* validate, certify, document, substantiate, confirm, prove, establish, vouch, corroborate, attest.
ant. falsify, discredit, belie, disprove, refute.

authenticity *n.* validity, legitimacy, truth, truthfulness, reality, genuineness, trustworthiness, authoritativeness, verity, factuality, factualness, creditability, believability.
ant. invalidity, illegitimacy, unreality, untruthfulness, untrustworthiness, sham, spuriousness, falsity.

author *n.* **1** writer, novelist, essayist, penman, playwright, dramatist, *litterateur*. **2** originator, creator, inventor, father, designer, framer, planner, architect, prime mover, founding father, founder. —*v.* WRITE.

authoritarian *adj.* strict, rigid, orthodox, dogmatic, autocratic, absolutistic, tyrannical, authoritative, dictatorial, domineering, imperious, arbitrary, totalitarian, despotic. —*n.* autocrat, absolutist, totalitarian, disciplinarian, dictator.

ant. *adj.* permissive, indulgent, tolerant, anarchic, heretical, heterodox.

authoritative *adj.* conclusive, authenticated, valid, reliable, sound, qualified, sanctioned, authorized, approved, confirmed, official.

ant. questionable, unreliable, apocryphal, disputed, dubious.

authorities *n.* officials, rulers, governors, magistrates, directors, administration, government, management, bureaucracy, officialdom, brass, the powers that be, the Establishment, City Hall.

authority *n.* **1** right, privilege, prerogative, command, charge, supremacy, jurisdiction, dominion, rule, control, sovereignty. **2** command, power, prestige, influence, credibility, esteem, respect, weight, clout (*Slang*). **3** expert, scholar, specialist, professional, master, judge, connoisseur.

authorization *n.* sanction, approval, permission, license, credentials, warrant, say-so.

authorize *v.* empower, commission, permit, license, charter, warrant, enable, invest, depute.

authorized *adj.* AUTHORITATIVE.

autocracy *n.* ABSOLUTISM.

autocrat *n.* tyrant, authoritarian, despot, overlord, totalitarian, dictator.

autograph *n.* **1** signature, handwriting, endorsement, inscription, John Hancock, moniker (*Slang*). **2** holograph, manuscript.

automatic *adj.* involuntary, reflex, instinctive, spontaneous, unconscious, impulsive, knee-jerk.

ant. deliberate, intentional, conscious, voluntary.

automaton *n.* **1** robot, android, computer. **2** *of persons:* machine, robot, zombie (*Slang*).

autonomous *adj.* free, independent, self-reliant, self-sufficient, self-determined, liberated.

ant. dependent, submissive, subject, bound.

autonomy *n.* independence, freedom, sovereignty, self-rule, self-determination, self-government.

ant. dependency, subjugation.

auxiliary *adj.* **1** assisting, supporting, supportive, aiding, helping, attending. **2** subsidiary, subordinate, ancillary, supplementary, additional, secondary, adjunct, accessory.

ant. 2 principal, main, major, primary, chief.

avail *n.* benefit, good, use, advantage, profit, gain, help, service, assistance. —*v.* assist, aid, profit, benefit, serve, help.

available *adj.* accessible, handy, ready, on hand, expendable, obtainable, on tap, in reserve.

ant. unavailable, inaccessible, tied up, frozen.

avalanche *n.* **1** landslide, snowslide, slide, quake. **2** cataclysm, deluge, downpour, storm, barrage, bombardment, groundswell.

avant-garde *n.* vanguard, pioneers, forefront, spearhead, modernists, innovators.

avarice *n.* GREED.

avaricious *adj.* greedy, covetous, grasping, acquisitive, rapacious, avid, hoggish, grabby, miserly, stingy, mercenary.

ant. generous, liberal, giving, charitable, munificent, philanthropic.

avenge *v.* punish, revenge, retaliate, repay, requite, reward, get even, get back at (*Slang*).

ant. forgive, excuse, pardon, overlook, forbear.

avenue *n.* **1** boulevard, thoroughfare, street, road, esplanade, highway, concourse, artery, freeway, expressway, turnpike, thruway, drive. **2** lane, approach, walk, entrance, drive, path. **3** *way of attaining something:* route, means, path, way, door, approach, access, entry, key, line.

aver *v.* affirm, attest, declare, swear, maintain, claim, insist, protest, asseverate, allege, contend, avow.

ant. deny, contradict, refute, disavow, dispute.

average *n.* norm, standard, rule, run, par. —*adj.* **1** mean, median, middle, center, medium. **2** normal, ordinary, common, standard, mediocre, typical, regular, run-of-the-mill, unexceptional, moderate, middling, fair, passable, so-so.

ant. *adj.* **2** extraordinary, outstanding, exceptional, atypical, excellent.

averse *adj.* opposed, unfavorable, antagonistic, hostile, disapproving, reluctant, loath, unwilling, disinclined, antipathetic, indisposed.

ant. agreeable, amenable, disposed, inclined, desirous, willing.

aversion *n.* repugnance, antipathy, hatred, hostility, odium, loathing, disgust, dislike, detestation, abhorrence, distaste, revulsion.

ant. fondness, attraction, liking, desire, taste, appetite, predilection.

avert *v.* turn away, deflect, shift, divert, sidetrack, prevent, preclude, forestall, deter, ward off, avoid.

ant. face, confront, meet, accept, welcome.

aviator *n.* pilot, flier, airman, aeronaut, ace.

avid *adj.* desirous, eager, enthusiastic, anxious, zealous, ardent, keen, greedy, voracious, avaricious, rapacious, insatiable.

ant. indifferent, apathetic, reluctant, cool, uninterested, halfhearted.

avidity *n.* **1** GREED. **2** ENTHUSIASM.

avocation *n.* hobby, sideline, diversion, pastime, pursuit.

avoid *v.* evade, shun, elude, escape, dodge, duck, steer clear of, shirk, avert.

ant. accept, welcome, meet, face, confront, pursue, seek.

avoidance *n.* EVASION.

avouch *v.* **1** VOUCH FOR. **2** AVOW.

avow *v.* declare, acknowledge, admit, own, confess, announce, allow, avouch, testify, profess, affirm, reveal, state.

ant. deny, disclaim, conceal, hide, disavow, repudiate, disallow.

avowal *n.* admission, acknowledgment, confession, declaration, affirmation, disclosure, revelation.

ant. denial, disclaimer, disavowal, repudiation.

avowed *adj.* acknowledged, admitted, confessed, declared, professed, open.

ant. secret, surreptitious, closet, private, unacknowledged, unadmitted.

await *v.* **1** expect, wait for, anticipate, abide, look forward to, watch for. **2** attend, threaten, impend, loom, approach, hover, hang.

awake *adj.* **1** wakeful, conscious, wide-awake. **2** alert, vigilant, watchful, attentive, on the lookout, on guard. —*v.* **1** waken, awaken, arouse, wake, wake up. **2** excite, spark, stimulate, bestir, arouse, agitate, spur, animate, incite, provoke, enkindle, inspire.

ant. *adj.* **1** asleep, unconscious, out, dozing, slumbering, napping. **2** inattentive, off guard. *v.* **2** dampen, repress, subdue, stifle, lull.

awaken *v.* AWAKE.

awakening *n.* stimulation, excitement, arousal, agitation, stirring, sparking, revival, renaissance, renascence, rebirth.

ant. ebbing, fading, decline, apathy.

award *v.* **1** grant, assign, accord, render, pay, compensate, settle, tender. **2** bestow, confer, present, reward, give, extend. —*n.* **1** settlement, verdict, judgment, decision, determination, finding. **2** prize, grant, compensation, restitution, damages, payment, settlement, indemnity.

aware *adj.* conscious, cognizant, knowing, informed, mindful, apprised, enlightened, sensible, conversant, appreciative, wise to, *au courant*, hip (*Slang*), tuned in (*Slang*).

ant. unaware, ignorant, oblivious, unconscious, uninformed.

awe *n.* wonder, solemnity, dread, fear, terror, amazement, astonishment, reverence, admiration, respect, veneration, worship, adoration.

ant. scorn, contempt, disrespect, irreverence, disdain, ridicule, derision.

awesome *adj.* formidable, redoubtable, solemn, impressive, intimidating, fearful, imposing, astonishing, overwhelming, awe-inspiring.

ant. insignificant, petty, trivial, mundane, frivolous, laughable, ridiculous.

awful *adj.* **1** disagreeable, unpleasant, disgusting, rotten, miserable, abominable, atrocious, offensive, objectionable, contemptible, despicable, obnoxious, lousy (*Slang*). **2** terrible, dreadful, appalling, horrendous, shocking, frightful, dire, calamitous, fearful, gruesome, horrible.

ant. **1** nice, pleasant, agreeable, charming, likable, passable, unobjectionable, good, delightful, lovely.

awkward *adj.* **1** ungraceful, ungainly, gawky, oafish, blundering, lumbering, stiff, graceless, gauche, inelegant, uncouth. **2** clumsy, inept, bungling, maladroit, unskillful, all thumbs, unhandy, artless. **3** embarrassing, disconcerting, delicate, perplexing, thorny, difficult, trying, compromising, sticky.

ant. **1** graceful, agile, supple, nimble, refined, elegant, polished. **2** adept, skillful, handy, deft, expert, dexterous, adroit.

awkwardness *n.* GAUCHERIE.

awning *n.* canopy, sunshade, marquee, cope, canvas, shade.

awry *adv.* **1** askew, aslant, obliquely, crookedly, lopsidedly. **2** amiss, astray, wrong, badly, erroneously, faultily, incorrectly, out of whack (*Slang*), out of kilter, off course, off target.

ant. **2** well, smoothly, correctly, accurately.

axiom *n.* truism, assumption, given, truth, postulate, theorem, principle, rule, law, precept, maxim, dictum.

axiomatic *adj.* **1** self-evident, assumed, understood, accepted, apodictic, indisputable, unquestioned, given, manifest. **2** aphoristic, epigrammatic, platitudinous.

ant. **1** dubious, questionable, unsound, uncertain.

axis *n.* **1** diameter. **2** coalition, alliance, affiliation, entente, bloc, league, union.

axle *n.* shaft, spindle, axis, arbor, mandrel.

B

babble *n.* **1** murmur, chatter, bubbling, burble, babel, confusion, tumult, clamor, noise, commotion, din. **2** prattle, gabble, blabber, burble, jabber, baby talk. —*v.* **1** murmur, chatter, bubble, burble, prattle, gabble, twaddle, prate, gibber, jabber. **2** blab, blurt, spill, divulge, reveal, gush, carry on, ooh and aah, blather, go on about, ramble, tattle, gas (*Slang*), natter (*Brit.*).

babe *n.* BABY.

babushka *n.* SCARF.

baby *n.* infant, babe, newborn, neonate, papoose. —*adj.* **1** tiny, small, teeny, diminutive, wee, teensy, midget, pygmy, little, minute, miniature, dwarf, undersized. **2** BABYISH. —*v.*

coddle, cosset, protect, cherish, hover, love, nurture, pet, pamper, indulge, fondle, spoil, mollycoddle, overprotect, mother, smother.

babyish *adj.* childish, infantile, baby, immature, whiny, petulant, spoiled, demanding, unreasonable, puerile, dependent, foolish.
ant. adult, mature, grown-up, reasonable, sensible, accommodating, self-reliant.

bacchanal *n.* ORGY.

bacchanalia *n.* ORGY.

back *n.* rear, posterior, tail end, hindquarters. —*v.* **1** support, assist, uphold, encourage, abet, help, aid, second, sanction, sponsor, subsidize, sustain, favor, endorse. **2** go backward, regress, retrogress, ebb, reverse, retreat, turn tail. —*adj.* **1** rear, posterior, hindmost, end, tail. **2** distant, remote, far, backwoods, isolated, secluded, undeveloped, removed, outermost, faraway, inaccessible, sequestered.
ant. *n.* front, anterior, face, head. *v.* **1** denounce, criticize, discourage, veto, challenge, undercut, undermine. **2** progress, advance, move forward, flow. *adj.* **1** front, anterior, leading, head. **2** close, near, accessible.

backbite *v.* SLANDER.

backbiting *n.* slander, gossip, malice, belittling, cattiness, abuse, denunciation, defamation, aspersion, disparagement, derogation, bitchiness (*Slang*), badmouthing (*Slang*).
ant. praise, compliments, approval, friendliness, loyalty.

backbone *n.* **1** spine, vertebrae, vertebral column, spinal column. **2** mainstay, support, prop, staff, pillar, foundation, basis, buttress, skeleton, framework. **3** courage, resolution, firmness, character, determination, fortitude, moral fiber, mettle, strength, stamina, toughness, guts (*Slang*), grit.
ant. 3 weakness, timidity, irresolution, spinelessness, cowardice.

backbreaking *adj.* fatiguing, exhausting, tiring, arduous, tough, demanding, wearying, laborious, difficult, hard, wearing.
ant. relaxing, light, slight, restful, easy, undemanding.

back down concede, give in, accede, submit, surrender, yield, acquiesce, be persuaded, give up, admit defeat, fink out (*Slang*), crap out (*Slang*), back out, renege, withdraw.
ant. stand firm, persevere, stand pat, insist.

backer *n.* patron, sponsor, supporter, angel, underwriter, investor, promoter, benefactor, subscriber, subsidizer, well-wisher, booster, Lady Bountiful.

backfire *v.* boomerang, fizzle, flop, fail, fall through, founder, crash, miss the boat, come to nothing, disappoint, miscarry.
ant. make it, come off, succeed, click (*Slang*).

background *n.* experience, training, culture, environment, upbringing, past, family, tradition, schooling, breeding, credentials, qualifications.

backing *n.* support, assistance, help, encouragement, patronage, sponsorship, money, funds, championship, subsidy, grant, defense, advocacy, endorsement, sympathy.
ant. detraction, ill-will, discouragement, criticism, faultfinding.

backlash *n.* REACTION.

backlog *n.* reserve, accumulation, stock, inventory, excess, hoard, amassment, supply, resources, means, savings, assets, nest egg, ace in the hole (*Slang*).

back out withdraw, renege, cancel, quit, forsake, jilt, go back on, recant, avoid, dodge, shirk, turn tail, disappoint, fink out (*Slang*).
ant. fulfill, carry out, show up, consummate.

backslide *v.* revert, relapse, regress, lapse, retrogress, return, recant, renege, retract, weaken, recidivate.
ant. stand pat, stick to one's guns.

back talk SASS.

backup *n., adj.* SUBSTITUTE.

backward *adj.* **1** shy, bashful, reticent, retiring, timid, self-effacing, diffident, deferential, unassuming, modest, demure, timorous. **2** retarded, slow, underdeveloped, childish, infantile, slow-witted, moronic, simple-minded, dull, stupid, subnormal, below average.

ant. 1 forward, bold, aggressive, self-confident, self-assertive, brazen. **2** precocious, advanced, quick, bright, above average.

backwash *n.* aftermath, consequence, wake, repercussion, upshot, outcome, aftereffect, backlash, reaction, payoff.

bad *adj.* **1** defective, inadequate, poor, lacking, unsatisfactory, incorrect, imperfect, inferior, substandard, below par. **2** unpleasant, disagreeable, offensive, displeasing, obnoxious, disgusting, revolting, repulsive, offputting, awful, rotten, terrible. **3** decayed, rancid, sour, rotted, decomposed, spoiled, contaminated, moldy, mildewed, putrid, putrescent. **4** immoral, corrupt, evil, debauched, sinful, wicked, naughty, obstreperous, outrageous, mischievous, devilish, disobedient, refractory, delinquent. **5** harmful, noxious, injurious, serious, acute, severe, inimical, baneful, critical, unfavorable, painful, dire, grave, unfortunate, detrimental.

ant. 1 good, superior, excellent, perfect, unflawed. **2** agreeable, attractive, pleasing, great. **3** fresh, new, sweet, uncontaminated, edible. **4** moral, upright, virtuous, compliant, well-behaved. **5** beneficial, healthful, favorable, fortunate.

badge *n.* **1** emblem, shield, insignia, medallion. **2** symbol, mark, distinction, hallmark, brand, label, tag, earmark, identification, sign, stamp, token, characteristic, attribute.

badger *v.* harass, nag, pester, importune, plague, torment, harry, chivy,

annoy, bother, hound, pursue, weary, hector, beset.

badinage *n.* banter, persiflage, wittiness, raillery, repartee, flippancy, jesting, teasing, joshing (*Slang*), kidding (*Slang*).

badly *adv.* **1** improperly, imperfectly, inadequately, incorrectly, ineptly, clumsily, poorly, unsatisfactorily, weakly, defectively, inefficiently, incompetently, stupidly, foolishly. **2** disagreeably, unpleasantly, nastily, annoyingly, obnoxiously, objectionably, disgustingly, repulsively. **3** disobediently, wickedly, naughtily, maliciously, mischievously, spitefully, shamefully, criminally, devilishly, fiendishly. **4** greatly, intensely, enormously, acutely, deeply, profoundly, keenly, severely, sharply, extremely, painfully, inordinately, a lot.

ant. 1 well, properly, adequately, correctly, adroitly, efficiently, skillfully. **2** pleasantly, nicely, agreeably, attractively, appealingly. **3** morally, obediently, virtuously, rightly. **4** superficially, slightly, somewhat, a little, not much.

bad-tempered *adj.* IRRITABLE.

baffle *v.* **1** confuse, perplex, bewilder, puzzle, mystify, confound, befuddle, nonplus, bemuse, elude, disorient, stymie, stump, throw. **2** fool, hoodwink, defeat, thwart, frustrate, hoax, bamboozle, outwit, contravene, checkmate, circumvent.

baffling *adj.* CONFUSING.

bag *n.* **1** sack, pouch, purse, sac, valise, suitcase, tote, carryall, grip, container, portmanteau, case, satchel. **2** *Slang* specialty, interest, field, job, skill, forte, profession, hobby, aptitude, talent, inclination, preference, thing (*Slang*), number (*Slang*), schtick (*Slang*). —*v.* **1** capture, take, shoot, kill, trap, net, hook, snare, carry off, acquire, get, take. **2** bulge, swell, blow up, inflate, belly, protrude, stick out, dilate, puff up, enlarge, expand, stretch, bloat.

bagatelle *n.* trifle, nothing, toy, bit,

gewgaw, triviality, foolishness, bauble, knickknack, little nothing, frippery, trinket, bibelot.

baggy *adj.* **1** loose, ill-fitting, oversize, ample, droopy, floppy, sagging, hanging, slack, roomy. **2** wrinkled, creased, pursy, puffy, bulgy, pouchy, swollen, inflated, blown up, bloated, distended.
ant. 1 close-fitting, well-tailored, neat, trim. **2** taut, flat, smooth, firm, unwrinkled.

bail *n.* security, bond, surety, deposit, guarantee, guaranty, pledge.

bailiwick *n.* domain, sphere, province, field, orbit, territory, neighborhood, place, beat, parish, base, home, center, turf (*Slang*).

bait *n.* attraction, lure, allurement, enticement, magnet, decoy, snare, temptation, inducement, bribe, come-on (*Slang*). —*v.* **1** harass, heckle, irritate, gall, provoke, annoy, tease, hound, fret, hector, worry, rile, irk, pique, anger. **2** lure, entice, attract, tempt, ensnare, trap, tantalize, fascinate, intrigue, bewitch, enthrall.
ant. *v.* **1** calm, soothe, pacify, please, lull. **2** repel, repulse, bore, disgust, revolt.

balance *n.* **1** equilibrium, equality, evenness, evenhandedness, equity, fairness, symmetry, equipoise, parity, equivalence, correspondence, stability. **2** sanity, poise, judiciousness, judgment, equanimity, self-control, steadiness, aplomb, imperturbability, unflappability, cool (*Slang*). —*v.* **1** equilibrate, poise, equalize, level, even, match, parallel, stabilize, steady. **2** compare, weigh, deliberate, ponder, consider, estimate, judge, calculate, think about, juxtapose, differentiate, discriminate.
ant. *n.* **1** imbalance, inequality, unevenness, lopsidedness, asymmetry, bias. **2** flightiness, instability, hotheadedness, irrationality.

balcony *n.* gallery, loggia, portico,

porch, extension, terrace, deck, overhang, platform, ledge, loge, lodge.

bald *adj.* **1** hairless, glabrous, shaven, depilated. **2** unadorned, plain, undecorated, unembellished, untrimmed, severe, stark, naked, basic, functional, uncluttered. **3** undisguised, overt, patent, clear, manifest, obvious, unconcealed, outright, flagrant, out-and-out, conspicuous, blunt, direct, unvarnished.
ant. 1 hairy, hirsute, shaggy. **2** ornate, fancy, decorated, rococo. **3** veiled, concealed, covert, disguised, masked, subtle.

balderdash *n.* NONSENSE.

baleful *adj.* hurtful, malignant, bad, pernicious, injurious, harmful, noxious, baneful, destructive, unwholesome, deleterious.
ant. beneficial, good, healthful, curative, advantageous, wholesome.

balk *v.* **1** thwart, frustrate, outwit, stymie, block, baffle, check, impede, circumvent, checkmate, outsmart, foil, disconcert, disappoint. **2** refuse, draw back, eschew, fight, dodge, shun, flinch, recoil, blench, demur, hang back, stick at, hesitate. —*n.* hindrance, disappointment, defeat, frustration, stymie, block, bar, check, impediment, obstruction, restraint, obstacle.
ant. *v.* **2** cooperate, help, assist, abet, aid, play along. *n.* success, achievement, progress, advancement.

balky *adj.* stubborn, intractable, unmanageable, uncooperative, unreliable, perverse, contrary, unpredictable, mulish, unruly, willful.
ant. cooperative, amenable, manageable, tractable.

ball *n.* sphere, globe, orb, round, bullet, globule.

ball game SITUATION.

balloon *v.* expand, swell, inflate, blow up, belly, bloat, puff, enlarge, distend, billow, increase, dilate, fill out, amplify, rise, go up, grow.
ant. deflate, shrink, lessen, contract, collapse, flatten.

ballpark *n.* STADIUM.

ballyhoo *n.* noise, babble, racket, hubbub, hue and cry, to-do, fuss, advertising, publicity, buildup, pitch, puffery, spiel (*Slang*), hoopla (*Slang*). —*v.* PROMOTE.

balm *n.* salve, emollient, comfort, anodyne, panacea, cure-all, assuagement, sedative, tranquilizer, narcotic. **ant.** irritant, abrasive, stimulant, excitant, nuisance.

balmy *adj.* **1** pleasant, mild, agreeable, temperate, soft, warm, fair, clement, gentle, refreshing. **2** soothing, comforting, salving, assuaging, sedative, narcotic. **3** *Slang* crazy, daft, daffy, eccentric, weird, bizarre, loony (*Slang*), cuckoo (*Slang*), goofy (*Slang*), nutty (*Slang*), kooky (*Slang*), off (*Slang*), barmy (*Brit. Slang*). **ant.** **1** inclement, disagreeable, stormy, unpleasant. **2** irritating, abrasive, chafing. **3** sensible, sane, practical, rational, sound, normal.

baloney *n.* NONSENSE.

bamboozle *v.* mislead, cheat, deceive, fool, hoodwink, trick, hoax, defraud, gyp, swindle, gull, dupe, take (*Slang*).

ban *v.* outlaw, prohibit, interdict, forbid, debar, disallow, circumscribe, proscribe, suppress, prevent, restrict, restrain. —*n.* prohibition, interdiction, disallowance, proscription, restriction, constraint, taboo, disapproval, rejection, suppression, censorship, embargo, boycott. **ant.** *v.* allow, let, permit, legalize, encourage. *n.* approval, permission, acceptance, encouragement, freedom, laissez-faire.

banal *adj.* commonplace, trite, ordinary, hackneyed, conventional, tired, prosaic, prosy, old hat, stock, bromidic, humdrum, vapid, stereotyped, platitudinous, stale, campy. **ant.** fresh, new, original, imaginative, unusual.

banality *n.* COMMONPLACE.

band[1] *n.* strip, stripe, binding, lacing, swath, belt, strap, ribbon, sash, cinch, bar, streak, length, fillet, tie. —*v.* bind, tie, swathe, belt, encircle, girdle, beribbon, festoon, lace, bandage, truss, swaddle.

band[2] *n.* group, league, gang, caucus, cabal, junta, association, fraternity, club, society, brotherhood, affiliation, fellowship, alliance, clique. —*v.* join, unite, affiliate, associate, incorporate, ally, group, federate, merge, consolidate. **ant.** *v.* break up, disagree, withdraw, fall out, go it alone.

bandanna *n.* HANDKERCHIEF.

bandit *n.* outlaw, criminal, robber, desperado, thug, brigand, hooligan, ruffian, hoodlum, gangster, racketeer, crook, public enemy, mobster (*Slang*).

bandy *v.* exchange, give and take, trade, swap, reciprocate, circulate, pass along, publish, broadcast, tell.

bane *n.* evil, harm, poison, venom, plague, pestilence, scourge, ruination, disaster, downfall, calamity, pollutant, pollution, curse. **ant.** good, benefit, cure, panacea, balm, blessing, boon.

baneful *adj.* injurious, deadly, ruinous, evil, harmful, noxious, poisonous, lethal, virulent, pestilential, disastrous, destructive, calamitous. **ant.** beneficial, good, helpful, curative, salutary, wholesome.

bang *n.* **1** whack, wallop, smack, thump, crack, clobber, chop, punch, clip, hit, wham, belt, sock (*Slang*). **2** explosion, detonation, thunder, clap, slam, din, boom, burst, clang, salvo, crash, peal, pop. **3** *Slang* thrill, excitement, pleasure, gratification, enjoyment, fun, amusement, entertainment, charge (*Slang*), kick (*Slang*). —*v.* **1** whack, smack, thwack, slam, wham, rap, knock, pound, pummel, lash. **2** explode, detonate, thunder, clap, boom, burst, clang, crash, peal, echo, drum, tattoo, resound, thump, stomp.

bang-up *adj.* *Slang* EXCELLENT.

banish *v.* **1** exile, deport, throw out, kick out, outlaw, extradite, excommunicate, expel. **2** eliminate, drive away, dismiss, dislodge, get rid of, drop, abandon, exclude, eradicate, discard, shake off.

bank[1] *n.* **1** mound, mass, heap, aggregation, accumulation, pile. **2** slope, rise, ridge, acclivity, ramp, grade, hill, ledge, reef, shelf, embankment, terrace. —*v.* **1** embank, dike, protect, abut, shore up, buttress, border, surround. **2** accumulate, pile, mound, amass, mass, heap, stack.

bank[2] *n.* line, tier, row, lineup, rank, series, range, string, succession, keyboard.

bank on depend on, rely on, count on, trust, lean on, hope for, anticipate, look forward to, assume, take for granted, look to.

bankrupt *adj.* insolvent, destitute, ruined, undone, broke, failed, pauperized, poverty-stricken, impoverished, wiped out, on the rocks, in the red, strapped, busted (*Slang*).
ant. solvent, flourishing, successful, in the black, in the money, in the chips (*Slang*).

bankruptcy *n.* FAILURE.

banner *n.* **1** device, motto, headline, advertisement, streamer, announcement, heading. **2** flag, pennant, standard, colors, ensign, streamer, pennon, banderole, bunting, oriflamme. —*adj.* leading, foremost, outstanding, champion, star, starring, red-letter, special, memorable, chief, principal, preeminent, main.

banquet *n.* FEAST.

bantam *adj.* **1** small, diminutive, undersized, runty, half-pint, pygmy, little, tiny, midget, immature, stunted, dwarf. **2** cocky, pugnacious, aggressive, self-assertive, pushy, quarrelsome, belligerent, feisty, strutting, self-important.
ant. **1** large, oversized, big, giant, mammoth, huge. **2** shy, retiring, timid, bashful, reticent.

banter *n.* badinage, raillery, chaffing,

teasing, persiflage, joking, repartee, kidding (*Slang*), joshing (*Slang*). —*v.* tease, joke, fool around, chaff, twit, quip, josh (*Slang*), kid (*Slang*), rib (*Slang*).

baptism *n.* initiation, introduction, trial, test, ritual, rite, launching, debut, ordeal, preparation, preliminary.

baptize *v.* **1** purify, cleanse, immerse, wash, purge. **2** initiate, admit, recruit, enroll, enlist, usher in, indoctrinate, instruct, qualify, prepare, take in, induct.

bar *n.* **1** barrier, obstruction, hindrance, impediment, obstacle, barricade, blockade, restriction, prohibition, constraint, taboo, ban, injunction, restraint. **2** court, courtroom, bench, seat of judgment, tribunal, courthouse, law court, judiciary, sessions, dock. **3** lawyers, attorneys, counsellors, attorneys-at-law, counsellors-at-law, advocates, legal fraternity, jurists, solicitors (*Brit.*), barristers (*Brit.*), mouthpieces (*Slang*). **4** stripe, band, streak, line, strip, blaze, striation, mark, wale. **5** SALOON. —*v.* **1** lock, fasten, secure, bolt, barricade, padlock, close. **2** confine, shut in, lock up, imprison, jail, immure, cloister, sequester, entomb, impound, incarcerate, pen, arrest. **3** obstruct, hinder, block, impede, thwart, check, restrict, blockade, prohibit, constrain, restrain, enjoin, outlaw, ban, interdict. **4** keep out, exclude, banish, eliminate, shut out, debar, spurn, blackball, blacklist, ostracize, isolate, segregate, cast out, leave out, boycott, forbid.
ant. *v.* **1** unlock, open, unfasten. **2** set free, let out, liberate. **4** invite, bid, include, accept, democratize, desegregate.

barb *n.* insult, affront, cut, slap, dig, jibe, rebuff, knock, bitchiness (*Slang*), putdown (*Slang*), rap (*Slang*).
ant. compliment, commendation, tribute, bouquet, buildup.

barbarian *n.* **1** savage, vandal, yahoo,

brute, animal, roughneck, redneck, lout, bully, hooligan, tough, hoodlum, cannibal, hood (*Slang*). **2** philistine, know-nothing, troglodyte, anti-intellectual, lowbrow, peasant, illiterate, boor, provincial, bigot. —*adj.* BARBAROUS.

barbaric *adj.* BARBAROUS.

barbarism *n.* **1** vulgarism, solecism, four-letter word, misuse, malapropism, slang, curseword, corruption. **2** savagery, cruelty, coarseness, vulgarity, brutishness, hooliganism, vandalism, depravity, crudity, offensiveness, barbarity.
ant. **1** standard speech, correct usage, the king's English. **2** civility, decency, kindness, humaneness.

barbarity *n.* **1** brutality, savagery, cruelty, animality, primitivism, heartlessness, cannibalism, dog-eat-dog. **2** BARBARISM.
ant. lawfulness, thoughtfulness, gentleness, philanthropy, fellow-feeling.

barbarous *adj.* **1** uncivilized, savage, primitive, wild, untamed, primeval, aboriginal, prehistoric, Stone-Age, barbaric, brutish. **2** rough, uncouth, vulgar, uncultivated, crude, coarse, gross, rude, philistine, ignorant, illiterate, uneducated, uncultivated, Neanderthal. **3** heartless, vicious, brutal, cruel, ferocious, sadistic, violent, unrestrained, fiendish, merciless, bloodthirsty, diabolical, monstrous, barbarian.
ant. **1** advanced, developed, enlightened, civilized. **2** cultivated, refined, fine, polished, cultured, worldly, urbane. **3** humane, kind, compassionate, merciful, charitable, reasonable.

barbed *adj.* **1** thorny, spiny, prickly, pointed, jagged, spiked, hooked, pronged, bristly, spurred, briary, brambly. **2** critical, nasty, acid, acidulous, hostile, hurtful, mean, unkind, insulting, cutting, catty, sharp-tongued, bitchy (*Slang*).
ant. **1** smooth, even, velvety, slick, satiny. **2** kind, thoughtful, considerate, flattering, complimentary.

bare *adj.* **1** naked, nude, unclothed, unclad, undressed, disrobed, stripped, stark, in the buff. **2** empty, unfurnished, barren, destitute, blank, hollow, vacant, wanting, lacking. **3** undisguised, unvarnished, unadorned, straightforward, bald, literal, plain, pure, simple, unembellished, basic, hard, cold.
ant. **1** clothed, dressed, clad, robed, covered. **2** full, well-supplied, furnished, filled, occupied. **3** disguised, embellished, masked, covered, colored.

barefaced *adj.* **1** unconcealed, open, manifest, naked, straightforward, forthright, unadorned, plain, simple, patent, obvious, clear, bare. **2** bold, impudent, brazen, brash, audacious, daring, shameless, rude, sassy, impertinent, forward, cheeky, snotty (*Slang*).
ant. **1** hidden, sneaky, devious, covert, concealed. **2** shy, timid, respectful, deferential, docile.

bargain *n.* agreement, understanding, pact, contract, deal, transaction, arrangement, pledge, promise, compact, entente. —*v.* agree, arrange, pledge, contract, stipulate, arrive at, promise, transact, negotiate, set terms, come to terms, do business, make a deal.

bargain for expect, count on, bank on, anticipate, foresee, envision, think likely, prevision, imagine, conceive, contemplate, suppose, believe.

barge in intrude, interrupt, impose oneself, infringe, horn in, butt in, crash, come uninvited, break in on, muscle in.

bark *n.* yelp, yip, yap, bell, cry, howl, growl, bow-wow, arf-arf. —*v.* **1** yelp, yap, yip, bay, cry, howl, growl. **2** bellow, shout, bawl, growl, yell, snap, threaten, menace, scold, bully, intimidate, bluster.

barmy *adj. Brit. Slang* BALMY.

baroque *adj.* ornate, overdecorated, rococo, florid, bizarre, fanciful, extravagant, showy, flashy, ostentatious, convoluted, outré.

ant. classical, pure, simple, functional, unadorned.

barrage *n.* **1** artillery, fire, shot, fusillade, bombardment, battery, shell, broadside, flak, ack-ack (*Slang*). **2** attack, assault, storm, hail, tempest, volley, burst, roar, blast, onslaught, eruption, torrent, pelting, rain.

barrel *n.* cask, tun, keg, tub, drum, hogshead, vat, butt, vessel, firkin.

barren *adj.* **1** sterile, infertile, impotent, infecund, childless, **2** unproductive, unfructuous, dry, arid, empty, void, desolate, treeless, bare. **3** dull, boring, uninteresting, flat, jejune, vapid, stale, unattractive, unimaginative, uninspired, poor.

ant. **1** child-bearing, fecund, fertile, generative, procreative. **2** arable, productive, yielding, fruitful, fructuous. **3** creative, imaginative, inventive, interesting, original.

barricade *v.* blockade, obstruct, bar, enclose, protect, hold off, defend, block off, fortify, shut off, stop up. —*n.* BARRIER.

barrier *n.* **1** fence, wall, barricade, moat, ditch, cordon, rampart, fortification, parapet, hedge, paling. **2** obstacle, stumbling block, impediment, block, bar, hurdle, difficulty, obstruction, hindrance, restraint, handicap, limitation.

barring *prep.* ASIDE FROM.

barrister *n.* LAWYER.

barter *n., v.* EXCHANGE.

basal *adj.* BASIC.

base[1] *n.* **1** bottom, foundation, foot, pedestal, support, plinth, substructure, groundwork, stand, underpinning, prop, bed, basement. **2** essential, fundamental, basis, root, source, origin, core, heart, backbone, *sine qua non*, indispensable, requisite, essence, starting point. **3** headquarters, point of origin, starting point, center, home, anchor, mooring, settlement, station, seat, post, bailiwick, turf. —*v.* build, establish, ground,

institute, hinge, depend, construct, proceed.

base[2] *adj.* **1** contemptible, vile, ignoble, sordid, debased, despicable, rotten, infamous, evil, immoral, brutish, sinister, wrong, corrupt, wicked. **2** menial, servile, miserable, wretched, poor, inferior, groveling, slavish, beggarly, subservient, shabby, lowly, abject, downtrodden.

ant. **1** noble, exalted, high, worthy, admirable. **2** commanding, important, superior, powerful.

baseless *adj.* UNFOUNDED.

bash *v.* smash, wallop, hit, strike, whack, punch, pommel, clip, trounce, whip, clobber (*Slang*), sock (*Slang*), belt. —*n.* *Slang* brawl (*Slang*), ball, party, carousal, revel, festivity, celebration, spree, saturnalia, wing-ding (*Slang*), clambake (*Slang*).

bashful *adj.* timid, shy, reticent, self-effacing, modest, reserved, diffident, demure, unassuming, coy, nervous, constrained, withdrawn.

ant. outgoing, friendly, forward, self-assertive, brash, cocky.

basic *adj.* essential, fundamental, indispensable, vital, key, cardinal, intrinsic, necessary, primary, prerequisite, elementary, basal.

ant. unnecessary, accessory, extra, supplementary, superfluous.

basics *n.* rudiments, ABC's, fundamentals, grounding, needs, basis, principles, axioms, prerequisites, essentials, necessaries, skills, training, core, facts.

basin *n.* **1** bowl, vessel, tub, pot, utensil, pan, container, tureen. **2** sink, washbowl, washbasin, lavatory, lavabo.

basis *n.* **1** base, support, foundation, bottom, ground, foot, bedrock, substructure. **2** basics, theory, premise, core, heart, essentials, root, key, cornerstone, prime cause, starting point, fundamentals, first principle, rudiments.

bask *v.* enjoy, relish, luxuriate, delight, revel, thrive, indulge oneself, savor, take pleasure, appreciate, eat up, lap up.

basket *n.* creel, pannier, hamper, wicker, wickerwork, bassinet, scuttle, dosser, punnet (*Brit.*).

bastard *adj.* BOGUS.

bastardize *v.* DEBASE.

baste *v.* BEAT.

bastion *n.* stronghold, mainstay, rock, prop, defense, support, bulwark, citadel, tower, pillar, staff, refuge, Gibraltar.

bat[1] *n.* club, stick, cudgel, mallet, racket, bludgeon, truncheon, billy, baton, blackjack, shillelagh, cane.

bat[2] *v.* FLUTTER.

batch *n.* group, crowd, bunch, lot, mass, aggregation, assortment, assemblage, collection, set, gathering, throng, cluster, pack.

bate *v.* ABATE.

bath *n.* wash, washing, tub, shower, douche, dip, ablution, cleansing, soaping.

bathe *v.* **1** immerse, dip, wet, dampen, irrigate, suffuse, cover, dunk, sop, soak, steep, ret. **2** wash, cleanse, soap, launder, shower, douche, lave, tub, scrub, sponge, deterge.

bathing suit swimsuit, maillot, beachwear, tank suit, bikini.

bathos *n.* sentimentality, mawkishness, melodrama, soppiness, mush, slush, corn (*Slang*), schmaltz (*Slang*), goo (*Slang*).

bathroom *n.* washroom, powder room, lavatory, bath, restroom, toilet, water closet, WC, latrine, loo (*Brit.*) john (*Slang*), head (*Slang*), can (*Slang*).

baton *n.* staff, stick, mace, scepter, rod, wand, billy, crosier, crook, caduceus, fasces.

battalion *n.* horde, army, mass, swarm, regiment, host, multitude, brigade, parade, gang, posse, drove, mob, throng, legion.

batten *v.* fatten, thrive, wax, flourish, grow, prosper, increase, bloom, succeed, boom, expand.

ant. weaken, decrease, fail, grow lean, go hungry.

batter *v.* strike, wallop, beat, bash, hit, lash, buffet, pommel, pound, assault, smash, clobber (*Slang*).

battery *n.* force, troop, army, legion, spearhead, guard, rally, pack, convoy, phalanx, muster, mobilization, band, team, brigade.

battle *n.* **1** combat, war, hostilities, engagement, skirmish, fray, action, attack, massacre, bloodshed, shootout, gang war, set-to, siege, gunfight. **2** dispute, argument, conflict, debate, disagreement, contest, controversy, quarrel, altercation, struggle, wrangle, litigation. —*v.* contend, struggle, dispute, argue, fight, vie, conflict, disagree, contest, feud, agitate, clamor, strive, war.

ant. *n.* **1, 2** peace, settlement, agreement, accord, harmony, truce, compromise. *v.* agree, accord, accept, comply, concur, reconcile.

battlement *n.* crenellation, parapet, breastwork, rampart, bulwark, bastion, stronghold, fort, fortification, escarpment, redoubt, ravelin.

batty *adj. Slang* CRAZY.

bauble *n.* trinket, trifle, gewgaw, tinsel, gimcrack, frippery, bagatelle, junk, trash, paste, knickknack.

bawd *n.* brothel-keeper, procuress, madam, prostitute, whore.

bawdy *adj.* obscene, indecent, improper, lewd, lascivious, salacious, immodest, vulgar, uncouth, off-color, raw, ribald, Rabelaisian, risqué, raunchy (*Slang*).

bawl *v.* **1** bellow, roar, shout, yell, holler, scream, bark, yowl, yammer, clamor, screech, shriek, halloo. **2** weep, sob, wail, cry, snivel, blubber, boohoo, whimper.

bawl out *Slang* tell off, scold, berate, reprimand, criticize, upbraid, chew out (*Slang*), censure, reprove, rebuke, admonish.

bay[1] *n.* inlet, cove, estuary, arm, strait, fiord, gulf, bayou, lagoon, harbor, basin, narrows, sound.

bay² *n.* compartment, nook, niche, cubicle, alcove, recess, space.

bay³ *v.* bark, bell, cry, howl, yelp, roar, hoot, bellow.

bazaar *n.* FAIR.

be *v.* **1** exist, live, inhabit, breathe. **2** happen, occur, take place, befall. **3** continue, stay, remain, abide, last, endure, survive, go on.

beach *n.* shore, strand, littoral, seacoast, seashore, seaboard, water's edge, sands.

beachcomber *n.* VAGRANT.

beacon *n.* signal, warning, guide, light, lighthouse, pharos, flare, smoke signal, pilot light, flash, alert, alarm, siren.

bead *n.* drop, globule, pellet, droplet, blob, spherule, pill.

beak *n.* bill, nose, neb, nib, proboscis, nozzle (*Slang*), schnozzle (*Slang*), schnozzola (*Slang*).

beam *n.* support, girder, plank, two-by-four, joist, transverse, rafter, spar.

beaming *adj.* radiant, bright, cheerful, sunny, happy, joyful, glowing, luminous, smiling, grinning. **ant.** gloomy, sullen, scowling, morose, threatening.

bear *v.* **1** support, hold up, prop up, sustain, brace, buttress. **2** carry, convey, transport, transfer, deliver, tote, bring, move. **3** suffer, endure, undergo, abide, tolerate, stand, withstand, take, weather, stomach, put up with, be subjected to. **4** give birth to, produce, generate, yield, engender, procreate, reproduce, breed, gestate, bring forth.

bearable *adj.* tolerable, supportable, endurable, sufferable, manageable. **ant.** intolerable, unbearable, excruciating, painful, awful, terrible.

bear down 1 approach, near, come close, draw close, move in, converge on, advance on, catch up with. **2** pressure, press, compel, urge, force, coerce, strong-arm, push, drive, constrain, exact, put the heat on (*Slang*), put the screws on (*Slang*).

bearer *n.* agent, messenger, porter, red-cap, conveyor, deliverer, carrier, deputy, servant, intermediary, runner, postman, errand boy.

bearing *n.* **1** conduct, comportment, carriage, manner, mien, presence, demeanor, attitude, posture, behavior, actions, movements, body language. **2** RELEVANCE.

bearings *n.* whereabouts, orientation, direction, course, location, position, compass reading, situation, latitude and longitude.

bear on refer to, relate to, concern, affect, touch on, pertain to, appertain to, have to do with, rest on, involve.

bear out confirm, justify, vindicate, prove, attest to, sustain, uphold, substantiate, corroborate, verify, check, endorse, authenticate. **ant.** negate, disprove, cancel, invalidate, discredit, refute.

beast *n.* **1** animal, quadruped, creature. **2** brute, savage, barbarian, murderer, killer, monster, ogre, demon, fiend, sadist, swine.

beastly *adj.* **1** brutish, brutal, savage, barbarous, murderous, monstrous, fiendish, swinish, sadistic, inhuman, cruel, feral, currish, depraved, vile, corrupt. **2** disagreeable, nasty, unpleasant, awful, foul, rotten, terrible, bum (*Slang*), lousy (*Slang*). **ant. 1** humane, civilized, refined, thoughtful, considerate, warmhearted, sympathetic. **2** agreeable, pleasant, enjoyable, fine, great, swell (*Slang*).

beat *v.* **1** pound, drum, tattoo, strike, hit, lay on, bang, cudgel, pommel, whip, wallop, lash, thrash, flail, truncheon, whale, larrup, collide, baste, shellac (*Slang*), lambaste (*Slang*), lam (*Slang*). **2** forge, shape, mold, hammer, fabricate, model, fashion. **3** defeat, outdo, triumph over, overcome, subdue, best, outstrip, overwhelm, conquer, master, vanquish, subjugate, lick, shellac (*Slang*). **4** flap, flutter, vibrate, tremble, throb, palpitate, thump, pulse, pulsate, quiver. —*n.* pulse, pulsation, flutter, quiver, throb, palpitation, tremor, shake, vibration, pounding, drumming. —*adj.* exhausted, tired, fatigued, knocked out, fagged out, bushed, frazzled, wearied, all in, spent, low.

ant. *adj.* energetic, lively, brisk, spirited, ambitious, zippy.

beat around the bush evade, equivocate, tergiversate, split hairs, avoid the issue, hedge, quibble, cavil, dodge, sidestep, beg the question, pussyfoot.

ant. come to the point, take a stand, face up to, come to grips, confront, face.

beaten *adj.* discouraged, disheartened, depressed, dejected, demoralized, hangdog, licked, hopeless, pessimistic, enervated, downcast, down.

ant. hopeful, forward-looking, cheerful, optimistic, eager, raring to go.

beatific *adj.* blissful, uplifted, elated, joyful, blessed, heavenly, happy, ecstatic, wonderful, glorious, divine, rapturous.

ant. hellish, awful, accursed, blighted, ill-fated, miserable, doomed.

beating *n.* **1** whipping, thrashing, flogging, caning, belting (*Slang*), shellacking (*Slang*), scourging, flagellation, drubbing, walloping, lashing, chastisement. **2** defeat, rout, overthrow, ruin, downfall, failure, debacle, subjugation, conquest, reversal, knockout.

beau *n.* suitor, lover, boyfriend, young man, admirer, swain, sweetheart, gentleman friend, man, guy.

beauteous *adj.* BEAUTIFUL.

beautiful *adj.* exquisite, attractive, lovely, good-looking, comely, handsome, enchanting, fair, gorgeous, radiant, shapely, beauteous, alluring.

ant. ugly, unsightly, misshapen, deformed, unattractive, grotesque.

beautify *v.* adorn, embellish, glamorize, pretty up, primp, paint, make up, bedeck, array, polish, do up, gussie up (*Slang*).

ant. spoil, distort, mar, deform, uglify.

beauty *n.* **1** belle, knockout (*Slang*), looker (*Slang*), eyeful (*Slang*), goddess, Venus. **2** pulchritude, attractiveness, bloom, allure, grace, charm, comeliness, shapeliness, loveliness, radiance.

ant. 1 eyesore (*Slang*), fright (*Slang*), horror (*Slang*), pig (*Slang*), dog (*Slang*). **2** ugliness, unattractiveness, homeliness, repulsiveness.

becalm *v.* quiet, calm, still, smooth, settle, hush, silence, compose, pacify, lull, soften, repose, sedate, tranquilize, narcotize.

ant. agitate, stir up, ruffle, trouble, roil, disquiet, upset.

because of on account of, by reason of, by dint of, as a result of, thanks to, in view of, as a consequence of.

beckon *v.* summon, call, signal, motion, gesture, invite, ask, bid, command, nod, wave, flag, hail.

becloud *v.* confuse, obfuscate, obscure, muddle, bemuse, befog, complicate, veil, screen, mix up, confound.

ant. clarify, illuminate, clear up, simplify, solve.

becoming *adj.* **1** appropriate, suitable, fitting, befitting, meet, proper, in accord with, seemly, in keeping with, compatible with, *comme il faut*. **2** attractive, flattering, enhancing, adorning, pleasing, beautifying, ornamental, tasteful, smart.

ant. 1 inappropriate, unsuitable, improper, incongruent, unexpected. **2** unflattering, unattractive, unbecoming, tasteless, ugly.

bedaub *v.* DAUB.

bedazzle *v.* **1** blind, dazzle, glare. **2** bewilder, stun, amaze, dumbfound, disorient, flabbergast, stupefy, awe, stagger, electrify, knock out.

bedeck *v.* adorn, deck, array, ornament, dress up, beautify, elaborate, trim, garnish, embellish, festoon, blazon, furbish, smarten, gussie up (*Slang*).

ant. denude, strip, simplify, divest, lay bare.

bedevil *v.* harass, worry, torment, plague, pester, annoy, fret, bully, tease, irritate, nettle, irk, torture, afflict, vex.

ant. becalm, soothe, please, mollify, pacify, gratify, delight.

bedew *v.* MOISTEN.

bedfellow *n.* ASSOCIATE.

bedim *v.* CLOUD.

bedlam *n.* uproar, confusion, hubbub, shambles, pandemonium, babel, racket, clamor, upheaval, riot, hullabaloo, madhouse.

bedraggled *adj.* muddy, dirty, disheveled, unkempt, sodden, dripping, soiled, messy, disordered, drenched, sloppy.

ant. clean, dry, neat, dapper, crisp, well-groomed.

bedridden *adj.* AILING.

bedrock *n.* **1** foundation, basis, basics, fundamentals, roots, starting point, grounds, ABC's, essentials, essence, core, origin. **2** bed, bottom, substructure, substratum, rock bottom, nadir.

ant. **1** superficialities, nonessentials, extras. **2** top, apex, dome, pinnacle.

bedroom *n.* bedchamber, chamber, boudoir, dormitory, nursery.

bed-wetting *n.* enuresis, incontinence.

beef *n.* *Slang* **1** heft, heftiness, brawn, muscles, strength, robustness, sinew, might, fitness, power, stamina, physique, huskiness. **2** gripe (*Slang*), complaint, criticism, objection, grumble, grouse, grievance, accusation, reproof, tirade, diatribe.

beef up *Slang* strengthen, reinforce, buttress, energize, vitalize, fortify, encourage, hearten, nerve, supplement, soup up (*Slang*), jazz up (*Slang*).

ant. weaken, sap, drain, enervate, tone down, water down.

beefy *adj.* BRAWNY.

beer and skittles *Brit.* PLEASURE.

befall *v.* happen, occur, betide, take place, come about, come to pass, materialize, eventuate, take effect, ensue, arrive, result.

befitting *adj.* FITTING.

befog *v.* **1** CLOUD. **2** OBSCURE.

before *adv.* **1** in front, ahead, in advance, first, forward, in the lead, to the fore, foremost. **2** previously, earlier, sooner, prior to, hitherto, heretofore, formerly, ere now, in the past.

ant. **1** after, following, behind, in back, in the rear, at the end. **2** later, afterward, then, latterly, subsequently.

befriend *v.* make friends, get acquainted, welcome, aid, encourage, cherish, stand by.

ant. avoid, shun, dislike, desert, part company.

befuddle *v.* confuse, addle, muddle, mix up, befog, stupefy, rattle, bewilder, intoxicate, disorient.

ant. straighten out, clear up, sober, bring to one's senses.

beg *v.* **1** panhandle, sponge, cadge, bum, scrounge (*Slang*), mooch (*Slang*), make a touch (*Slang*). **2** plead, implore, importune, entreat, supplicate, pray, beseech, clamor, petition.

beget *v.* **1** procreate, father, sire, breed, multiply, impregnate, reproduce, generate. **2** cause, lead to, occasion, result in, effect, effectuate, bring about, engender, produce, give rise to, yield.

ant. **2** prevent, exclude, obviate, avert, inhibit.

beggar *n.* **1** panhandler, vagrant, hobo, bum, tramp, mendicant, moocher (*Slang*), scrounger (*Slang*), clochard, schnorrer (*Slang*). **2** pauper, bankrupt, insolvent, down-and-outer, have-not. **3** person, individual, creature, fellow, guy, chap, customer.

beggarly *adj.* POOR.

begin *v.* **1** inaugurate, initiate, found, embark on, launch, create, pioneer, originate, introduce, usher in, present, set in motion, institute, undertake. **2** arise, start, commence, ap-

pear, emerge, come into being, dawn, crop up, spring up, happen.
ant. 2 conclude, stop, fade, wane, die, end, finish.

beginner *n.* novice, greenhorn, freshman, tyro, amateur, trainee, recruit, apprentice, neophyte, tenderfoot, student, rookie (*Slang*).
ant. old hand, expert, master, authority, veteran, specialist.

beginning *n.* **1** starting point, origin, outset, rise, dawn, outbreak, commencement, opening, debut, birth, inception, inauguration, launching, lead-off, founding, precedent. **2** seed, germ, egg, embryo, root, source, fountainhead, cause, spring.
ant. 1 finale, close, closing, conclusion, finish, end.

begrime *v.* dirty, muddy, soil, smirch, stain, splash, smear, spatter, splotch, tarnish.
ant. clean, cleanse, wash, launder, freshen.

begrudge *v.* **1** envy, resent, covet, crave. **2** grudge, withhold, stint, hold back, dole out, pinch.

begrudging *adj.* reluctant, hesitant, unwilling, resentful, grudging, loath, averse, disinclined, antipathetic, forced.
ant. eager, obliging, willing, spontaneous, quick, unhesitating.

beguile *v.* ENCHANT.

beguiling *adj.* bewitching, enchanting, alluring, attractive, interesting, charming, captivating, entertaining, diverting, enthralling, delightful, engaging, intriguing.
ant. dull, boring, tedious, uninteresting, unattractive, off-putting.

behalf *n.* interest, defense, sake, good, benefit, advantage, profit, account, support.

behave *v.* act, conduct oneself, comport oneself, demean oneself, deport oneself, function, react, acquit oneself, proceed, perform, cope, manage, operate.

behavior *n.* **1** conduct, comportment, deportment, demeanor, ways, actions, manner, address, bearing, style. **2** workings, operation, performance, action, functioning. **3** response, reaction, reflex, pattern, tendency.

behead *v.* decapitate, guillotine, execute, decollate.

behest *n.* order, command, mandate, dictate, decree, ruling, direction, demand, injunction, charge, instruction, say-so.

behind *adv.* **1** back, aback, in back, to the rear, rearward, backward, astern. **2** in the past, heretofore, gone by, formerly, erstwhile, once. —*n.* buttocks, fundament, seat, bottom, rump, posterior, ass (*Slang*), arse.
ant. *adv.* **1** in front, frontward, forward. **2** in the future, ahead, in time to come.

behold *v.* look at, notice, note, espy, glimpse, sight, catch sight of, see, observe, discern, view, survey, contemplate, perceive, get a load of (*Slang*).
ant. be blind to, fail to see, ignore, overlook.

beholden *adj.* OBLIGATED.

behoove *v.* befit, become, suit.

being *n.* **1** existence, actuality, life, mortality, living, existing, presence, reality, breath. **2** creature, entity, individual, organism, character, body, soul.
ant. 1 nonexistence, death, expiration.

belabor *v.* reiterate, repeat, go on about, explain, rehash, recapitulate, din, hammer away, pound, enlarge on, dwell on, expatiate, beat a dead horse.

belated *adj.* overdue, late, tardy, behind time, slow, delayed, behindhand, dilatory, remiss.
ant. prompt, well-timed, punctual, speedy, early.

belch *v.* **1** erupt, emit, disgorge, gush, spew forth, throw off, give off, spill over. **2** burp, bubble, eruct, eructate.

beleaguer *v.* HARASS.

beleaguered *adj.* annoyed, bothered, harassed, set upon, beset, badgered, put upon, persecuted, vexed, nagged, hectored, victimized, plagued, afflicted.

belie v. disguise, misrepresent, contradict, negate, confute, falsify, deceive, defy, gainsay, repudiate, counteract, give the lie to.

belief n. 1 acceptance, faith, credence, reliance, confidence, assumption, truth, credit, persuasion, certainty. 2 creed, credo, conviction, opinion, view, tenet, conclusion, judgment, construct, gospel, dogma, hypothesis, ideology, orthodoxy.
ant. 1 disbelief, distrust, suspicion, uncertainty, skepticism, incredulity.

believability n. CREDIBILITY.

believable adj. plausible, reasonable, acceptable, authentic, probable, likely, realistic, understandable, dependable, trustworthy, reliable, creditable.
ant. unlikely, implausible, farfetched, improbable, fantastic, inconceivable.

believe v. 1 hold, postulate, posit, maintain, think, opine, assume, deem, judge, know, be convinced, be sure, take for granted. 2 trust, have faith in, have confidence in, take the word of, count on, swear by, rely on, depend on.
ant. 1, 2 disbelieve, doubt, question, challenge, distrust, discredit.

believer n. follower, adherent, upholder, supporter, devotee, disciple, convert, proselyte, religionist, fanatic, zealot.
ant. critic, skeptic, doubter, scoffer, iconoclast.

belittle v. disparage, minimize, run down, put down, deride, ridicule, derogate, criticize, malign, scorn, sneer at, scoff at, depreciate, devalue, knock (Slang).
ant. build up, promote, upgrade, exalt, elevate, praise, glorify.

bell n. 1 ringing, pealing, tolling, signal, alarm, chime. 2 chimes, carillon, siren, gong, buzzer, tocsin.

bellicose adj. BELLIGERENT.

belligerence n. AGGRESSION.

belligerent adj. pugnacious, hostile, quarrelsome, contentious, bellicose, embattled, litigious, combative, aggressive, polemical, defiant, disputatious, argumentative, feisty, battling, warlike, warring.
ant. accommodating, easygoing, conciliatory, compromising, pacific, cool.

bellow v. roar, rage, bawl, blare, shout, clamor, yell, howl, holler, bark, trumpet, bluster, storm, thunder, boom. —n. roar, shout, yell, holler, howl, thunder, boom, rumble, explosion, blast, din, uproar.

bellwether n. pilot, leader, guide, shepherd, pacesetter, ringleader, chief, standard-bearer, boss.

belly n. abdomen, stomach, tummy, craw, maw, crop, insides, gut (Slang), bay window (Slang), paunch, corporation, pot, potbelly.

bellyache (Slang) v. COMPLAIN.

bellybutton n. navel, umbilicus, omphalos.

belonging n. relationship, community, attachment, loyalty, kinship, rapport, fellowship, acceptance, inclusion.

belongings n. possessions, assets, appurtenances, effects, property, chattels, worldly goods, paraphernalia, things, estate, bag and baggage.

beloved adj. cherished, adored, loved, dear, darling, precious, sweet, treasured, prized, valued, esteemed, revered.

below adv. lower, under, beneath, underneath, down.
ant. above, overhead, on top, atop, higher.

belt n. band, sash, girdle, cinch, strap, waistband, cummerbund, cincture. —v. wallop, smack, punch, hit, bang, whack, thwack, beat, clip, strike, clobber (Slang), sock (Slang).

belting n. BEATING.

bemoan v. mourn, lament, bewail, keen, sorrow, moan, grieve, sob, cry, deplore, complain, whine, regret, sigh, weep, rue, *kvetch* (*Slang*).

ant. rejoice, jubilate, celebrate, exult.

bemuse *v.* **1** muddle, stupefy, obscure, obfuscate, confound, mix up, confuse, addle, becloud, befuddle, daze, unhinge, unsettle, disorient. **2** engross, preoccupy, absorb, possess, arrest, engage, enthrall, fascinate, immerse, monopolize.

ant. 1 enlighten, illuminate, simplify, straighten out, clarify. **2** bore, repel, displease.

bemused *adj.* ABSENT-MINDED.

bench *n.* **1** seat, pew, settle, form. **2** judge, judges, jurists, justice, judgment, court, courtroom, bar, tribunal, judiciary.

benchmark *n.* reference, standard, model, prototype, norm, exemplar, archetype, guide, yardstick, precedent, principle, example, touchstone, paradigm.

bend *v.* curve, flex, deflect, turn, veer, deviate, arc, arch, deform, twist, snake, coil, distort, loop, buckle. —*n.* curve, crook, flex, curvature, bow, concavity, turn, loop, arch, arc, curl, coil, nod.

bender *Slang n.* SPREE.

beneath *adv.* BELOW.

benediction *n.* blessing, boon, benison, consecration, dedication, invocation, prayer, *benedictus*, orison.

ant. curse, malediction, execration, calumniation.

benefaction *n.* **1** liberality, benevolence, giving, charity, generosity, beneficence, philanthropy, largess. **2** alms, money, donation, gift, present, subsidy, endowment, gratuity, legacy, bequest, grant, handout.

benefactor *n.* patron, helper, supporter, contributor, donor, subsidizer, subscriber, promoter, backer, fairy godmother, Santa Claus, angel.

beneficence *n.* goodness, virtue, charity, altruism, benevolence, generosity, love, compassion, good will, helpfulness, sympathy, unselfishness, kindness, liberality.

ant. selfishness, malevolence, ill will, coldness, meanness, stinginess.

beneficial *adj.* helpful, advantageous, useful, salutary, profitable, rewarding, good, favorable, constructive, propitious, valuable, healthful, benign.

ant. harmful, hurtful, destructive, bad, baneful, disadvantageous, unprofitable.

beneficiary *n.* recipient, donee, receiver, inheritor, heir, heiress, pensioner, gainer, winner.

benefit *n.* profit, advantage, boon, blessing, help, reward, good, favor, value, asset, avail, gain, worth, service, aid, plus. —*v.* help, serve, assist, improve, better, succor, subsidize, support, avail, profit, ameliorate, advance, enhance, forward.

ant. *n.* loss, disadvantage, harm, disservice, handicap, drawback, detriment. *v.* harm, hinder, impair, undermine, retard, hamper, weaken.

benevolence *n.* good will, charity, generosity, kindness, fellow-feeling, sympathy, mercy, humaneness, beneficence, goodness, altruism, humanity.

ant. malevolence, ill will, ruthlessness, coldness, heartlessness, animosity, malice.

benevolent *adj.* kind, charitable, generous, warmhearted, merciful, humane, philanthropic, altruistic, helpful, beneficent, considerate, caring.

ant. malevolent, spiteful, nasty, hostile, cold, ruthless, misanthropic.

benighted *adj.* ignorant, unenlightened, uncivilized, primitive, backward, underprivileged, crude, illiterate, uncultivated, blind, obtuse.

ant. enlightened, educated, aware, cultivated, advanced, well-informed.

benign *adj.* **1** genial, kindly, well-disposed, sympathetic, generous, friendly, warm, amiable, benevolent, helpful, altruistic, affable. **2** mild, temperate, balmy, pleasant, serene, tranquil, clement, calm, soft. **3** beneficial, favorable, advantageous, healthful, curative, salutary, salubrious, wholesome, healing, bracing, benignant. **4** harmless, superficial, curable, limited, innocuous, slight, trivial, remediable. **ant. 1** cold, hostile, malign, nasty, mean. **2** stormy, violent, inclement, raging, tempestuous. **3** destructive, unhealthy, damaging. **4** malignant, serious, inoperable, unmanageable.

benignant *adj.* BENIGN.

benison *n.* BENEDICTION.

bent *n.* inclination, tendency, penchant, preference, impulse, talent, aptitude, knack, flair, propensity, proclivity, leaning, disposition, forte, humor, temperament.

bent on determined, set, fixed, insistent, disposed, inclined, directed, prone, partial.

benumbed *adj.* numb, deadened, immobilized, paralyzed, frozen, unresponsive, insensible, anesthetized, narcotized, dazed, stupefied, dulled, stunned. **ant.** aware, responsive, sensitive, lively.

bequeath *v.* bestow, hand down, leave, give, contribute, endow, impart, turn over, consign, render, entrust, commit, present.

bequest *n.* bequeathal, bequeathment, bestowal, gift, endowment, legacy, trust, estate, inheritance, settlement, dower, heritage, grant, subsidy, allotment, portion.

berate *v.* upbraid, castigate, revile, scold, yell at, censure, denounce, execrate, lash out at, rail, vituperate, bawl out (*Slang*), chew out (*Slang*).

bereaved *adj.* widowed, orphaned, in mourning, grief-stricken, desolate, inconsolable, anguished, brokenhearted, heavy-hearted.

bereft *adj.* deprived, wanting, lacking, cut off, minus, in need, destitute, unpossessed, shorn, devoid.

berserk *adj.* frenzied, manic, maniacal, out of control, uncontrollable, amok,

violent, wild, frantic, insane, crazy, dangerous, deranged, destructive. **ant.** calm, controlled, rational, reasonable, self-contained, self-controlled.

beseech *v.* beg, implore, entreat, importune, plead, supplicate, petition, press, adjure, clamor.

beset *v.* **1** plague, annoy, pester, bedevil, harass, badger, bother, nag, persecute, victimize, hector, harry, chafe, afflict, irk. **2** surround, besiege, attack, hem in, blockade, beleaguer, encircle, lay siege to, hedge in, encompass.

besetting *adj.* TROUBLESOME.

beside *prep.* close to, near, at the side of, next to, adjacent to, alongside, alongside of, abreast of.

beside oneself frantic, out of control, uncontrolled, deranged, demented, mad, insane, out of one's mind, crazed, maddened, unbalanced, unhinged. **ant.** controlled, self-contained, self-controlled, cool, sane, dispassionate.

besides *adv.* **1** in addition, as well, moreover, furthermore, too, also, further, what's more, aside from, to boot, along with. **2** otherwise, else, beyond, more, in addition.

besiege *v.* **1** beset, surround, attack, encircle, blockade, barricade, lay siege to, beleaguer, hem in. **2** crowd around, hem, hedge, fence, restrict, throng, block, hinder, enclose, obstruct, stall, stop.

besmirch *v.* taint, corrupt, stain, dishonor, debauch, smirch, soil, vilify, slander, smear, discredit, disgrace, degrade, defame. **ant.** exalt, honor, purify, ennoble, honor, respect.

besotted *adj.* drunk, drunken, intoxicated, inebriated, befuddled, bemused, stupefied, dazed, foolish, mindless, muddled, groggy, tipsy, confused, witless. **ant.** sober, clear-headed, steady, self-possessed.

bespatter *v.* SOIL.²

bespeak v. indicate, evince, betoken, foretell, foreshadow, presage, signify, suggest, testify to, display, show, augur, portend.
ant. belie, contradict, negate, contravene.

best v. defeat, outdo, triumph over, trounce, whip, conquer, subdue, lick, beat, surpass, outclass, humble.
ant. v. lose, be outdone, take a beating, succumb.

bestial adj. beastly, animalistic, brutish, savage, barbaric, feral, wild, inhuman, base, subhuman, swinish, disgusting.
ant. human, humane, benevolent, compassionate, gentle.

bestiality n. BRUTALITY.

bestir v. rouse, stir, move, provoke, agitate, get going, awaken, accelerate, quicken, prod, press, drive, stimulate, prompt, push, activate.

bestow upon present, confer, honor, award, accord, favor, bequeath, lavish, entrust, commit, deliver.

bestrew v. STREW.

bestride v. STRIDE.

bet n. wager, gamble, chance, risk, plunge, speculation, venture. —v. wager, stake, pledge, gamble, risk, speculate, lay money, hazard.

betake oneself v. GO.

bête noire BUGBEAR.

bethink v. REMEMBER.

betide v. BEFALL.

betoken v. indicate, portend, augur, signify, denote, bespeak, presage, bode, foreshadow, suggest, symbolize, mean, imply.

betray v. **1** deceive, abandon, jilt, run out on, defect, sell out, let down, break faith with, double-cross (*Slang*), two-time (*Slang*), rat on (*Slang*), fink (*Slang*). **2** reveal, disclose, show, manifest, evince, indicate, signalize, bespeak, betoken, let slip, give away, let drop, blurt out, squeal (*Slang*).
ant. 1 be faithful, adhere, support, cleave to.

betrayal n. TREACHERY.

betrayer n. TRAITOR.

betrothed adj. ENGAGED.

better adj. superior, preferable, finer, choicer, worthier, excelling, enhanced, surpassing.
ant. worse, poorer, inferior, lesser, second-rate.

betterment n. IMPROVEMENT.

better off advantaged, privileged, more comfortable, more fortunate, happier, richer.
ant. worse off, poorer, needier, disadvantaged, underprivileged.

between prep. mid, amidst, among, betwixt, halfway to, on the way to, midway.

beverage n. drink, liquid, potable, potation, potion, liquor, draft, refreshment, libation, sip, swallow, nip, dram.

bevy n. group, cluster, gathering, party, collection, knot, assemblage, clutch, bunch, covey, coterie, clique.

bewail v. bemoan, lament, cry, keen, sorrow, weep, wail, rue, regret, repent, be sorry, fret about, mourn, grieve.
ant. rejoice, smile, be happy about, take joy in.

beware v. avoid, shun, watch, mind, be wary of, look out for, give a wide berth to, be careful, take heed, steer clear of, refrain from.

bewilder v. confuse, addle, disorient, muddle, mix up, perplex, bemuse, daze, mystify, stump, puzzle, baffle, nonplus, confound.
ant. enlighten, inform, instruct, teach.

bewildered adj. DAZED.

bewildering adj. CONFUSING.

bewitch v. CHARM.

bewitching adj. captivating, charming, alluring, witching, enchanting, enthralling, irresistible, beguiling, magnetic, mesmerizing, fascinating, delightful, enticing, exciting.
ant. dull, uninteresting, boring, unattractive.

beyond prep. **1** farther than, on the far side of, outside of, away from, clear of, remote from, apart from. **2** after, later than, following, subsequent to, succeeding.

bias *n.* prejudice, inclination, preference, stand, slant, partiality, favoritism, one-sidedness, distortion, dogmatism, bigotry. —*v.* prejudice, slant, warp, twist, weight, influence, sway, indoctrinate, incline, predispose.

ant. *n.* even-handedness, detachment, impersonality, impartiality, fairness.

bibber *n.* DRUNK.

bibelot *n.* TRINKET.

bible *n.* handbook, manual, guide, guidebook, sourcebook, gospel, authority, scripture, *vade mecum*.

Bible *n.* Holy Scripture, Holy Writ, Old Testament, New Testament, Good Book, the Book, Gospel, the Law, Word of God.

bibulous *adj.* intemperate, alcoholic, tippling, guzzling, winebibbing, hard-drinking, toping, sottish, crapulous.

ant. temperate, abstemious, moderate, sober, on the wagon (*Slang*).

bicker *v.* wrangle, argue, cavil, squabble, scrap, fight, spat, haggle, contest, dispute, tiff, row.

ant. agree, get on, see eye to eye, go along with.

bid *v.* **1** order, command, instruct, direct, charge, ordain, require, dictate. **2** invite, ask, summon, call, solicit, appoint, name. —*n.* **1** offer, tender, proposal, proposition, price, amount, sum. **2** try, attempt, effort, endeavor, essay, exertion, striving, crack, venture, flier. **3** invitation, bidding, overture, summons.

biddable *adj.* DOCILE.

bidding *n.* command, behest, order, instruction, decree, request, invitation, summons, call, direction, desire, beck, solicitation, mandate, charge.

bide *v.* remain, wait, stay, tarry, abide, attend, linger.

biff *Slang n., v.* SMACK.[1]

bifurcate *v.* FORK.

big *adj.* **1** large, enormous, sizable, massive, great, appreciable, bulky,

ample, giant, gigantic, immense, extensive. **2** fully grown, mature, adult, grown up, full-sized, developed, complete, completed, ripe, ready. **3** important, consequential, momentous, weighty, significant, considerable, vital, powerful, prominent, outstanding, essential, influential, serious, special.

ant. **1** small, tiny, little, midget. **2** half-grown, immature, young. **3** trivial, petty, unimportant, picayune, inconsequential.

big-hearted *adj.* generous, charitable, open-handed, good-natured, magnanimous, unselfish, liberal, altruistic, benevolent, unstinting.

ant. mean, selfish, cold, ungenerous, uncharitable.

bigot *n.* FANATIC.

bigotry *n.* intolerance, prejudice, narrow-mindedness, sectarianism, unfairness, fanaticism, bias, dogmatism, provincialism, blindness, passion, mindlessness, ignorance.

ant. open-mindedness, acceptance, liberality, tolerance, fairness.

big-shot *Slang* wheel (*Slang*), brass hat (*Slang*), VIP, somebody, personage, name, bigwig, big gun (*Slang*), heavyweight, big wheel (*Slang*), wheeler-dealer (*Slang*).

ant. nobody, underling, nonentity, cipher, nebbish.

big wheel *Slang* BIG SHOT.

bigwig *n.* BIG SHOT.

bijou *n.* jewel, trinket, bauble, adornment, gem, ornament.

bile *n.* anger, peevishness, rancor, bitterness, spleen, crankiness, petulance, resentment, nastiness, ill humor, churlishness, irritability, irascibility, discontent.

ant. good humor, affability, geniality, pleasantness, cheerfulness.

bilge *n. Slang* nonsense, hogwash, foolishness, drivel, gibberish, bosh, twaddle, jabber, rubbish, hot air (*Slang*), bull (*Slang*), crap (*Slang*).

bilious *adj.* cross, petulant, ill-natured, crotchety, cranky, crabby, peevish, irritable, irascible, liverish, out of sorts, disagreeable.

ant. good-natured, agreeable, happy, contented, pleasant.

bilk *v.* cheat, swindle, defraud, bamboozle, trick, hoodwink, deceive, take (*Slang*), victimize, fleece, rook, gull, gyp, rip off (*Slang*).

bilker *n.* SWINDLER.

bill¹ *n.* 1 debt, charge, charges, fee, reckoning, account, invoice, tab, statement, debit, chit, IOU, tally. 2 program, list, itemization, schedule, agenda, roster, catalog, enumeration, inventory, listing. 3 handbill, poster, announcement, advertisement, placard, broadside, notice, bulletin, circular, affiche. —*v.* charge, debit, reckon, record, figure, invoice.

bill² *n.* beak, neb, nose, proboscis, snout, rostrum, schnozzle (*Slang*).

billet *n.* quarters, housing, berth, installation, lodging, barrack, shelter.

billingsgate *n.* cursing, swearing, abuse, vituperation, scurrility, vulgarity, profanity, foul language, gutter language.

billow *n.* swell, surge, wave, increase, intensification, rise, rush, deluge, flood, magnification, peaking, augmentation, expansion, amplification.

ant. decrease, lowering, diminution.

billy *n.* CLUB.¹

bin *n.* cubicle, cubbyhole, crate, container, closet, pantry, box, chest, coffer, crib, enclosure, receptacle, can.

bind *v.* 1 tie, secure, attach, fasten, enchain, tether, pin, solder, rope, shackle, connect, join, lace, knot. 2 bandage, encircle, swathe, belt, lash, girdle, truss, wrap, roll, swaddle, envelop. 3 glue, stick, wed, unite, cement, fix, amalgamate.

ant. 1 untie, unfasten, loose, disconnect, unlace. 3 pull apart, disjoin, separate, divorce, break.

binding *adj.* obligatory, compelling, mandatory, compulsory, imperative, necessary, unalterable, indissoluble,

unchangeable, hard-and-fast, unconditional, incumbent on.

ant. flexible, adjustable, changeable, elastic.

binge *n. Slang* spree, fling, orgy, carousal, toot (*Slang*), tear (*Slang*), jag (*Slang*) bender (*Slang*).

birth *n.* 1 delivery, parturition, accouchement, lying-in, confinement, childbirth, nativity. 2 beginning, start, commencement, opening, onset, appearance, arrival, genesis, emergence, inception, debut, embryo, infancy. 3 ancestry, descent, lineage, family, blood, pedigree, background, stock, line, genealogy, forebears, heredity, heritage, breed.

ant. 2 finish, end, decline, disappearance, death.

biscuit *n.* bread, bun, roll, muffin, cake, gem, scone, rusk, zwieback, hardtack.

bisexual *adj.* androgynous, hermaphroditic, gynandrous, AC-DC (*Slang*).

bistro *n.* RESTAURANT.

bit *n.* 1 piece, fragment, part, whit, portion, little, smidgen, fraction, crumb, morsel, drop, dram, segment, shard, cut. 2 second, moment, instant, little while, spell, period, interval, time.

bitch *v. Slang* COMPLAIN.

bitchy *adj. Slang* 1 shrewish, captious, critical, fault-finding, complaining, nagging, dissatisfied, disapproving, cranky, crabby, nit-picking. 2 malicious, spiteful, mean, nasty, rancorous, hostile, catty, venomous, vindictive, back-biting, begrudging, heartless, cruel.

ant. 1 easygoing, pleasant, uncritical, supportive, admiring. 2 kind, warm, friendly, trustworthy.

bite *v.* 1 gnaw, chew, nip, nibble, crunch, munch, champ, ruminate. 2 sting, prick, smart, prickle, cut, eat into, eat away, corrode, erode, wear away. —*n.* 1 sting, smarting, itch, prickle, lump, bump, swelling, puncture, hurt, lesion, tooth marks. 2

snack, refreshment, repast, pick-me-up, elevenses (*Brit.*).

biting *adj.* sharp, sarcastic, mordant, stinging, hurtful, catty, acidulous, caustic, cutting, acrimonious, incisive, trenchant, sharp-tongued, withering.
ant. kind, soothing, agreeable, pleasant, gentle.

bitter *adj.* **1** acrid, harsh, stinging, caustic. **2** galling, distressing, vexatious, painful, lamentable, unhappy, ruinous, rotten, wretched, grievous, discouraging. **3** hostile, rancorous, begrudging, resentful, spiteful, vindictive, acrimonious, nasty, truculent, mean, bitchy (*Slang*).
ant. 1 sweet, sugary, honeyed. **2** happy, heartening, joyous, gratifying. **3** well-disposed, amiable, friendly, warm, affectionate.

bizarre *adj.* outlandish, fantastic, grotesque, outré, freakish, freaky, eccentric, odd, unusual, strange, Kafkaesque, attention-getting, extraordinary, peculiar, crazy, kookie (*Slang*), kinky (*Slang*).
ant. inconspicuous, usual, ordinary, everyday, square (*Slang*).

blab *v.* **1** BLURT. **2** BLABBER. —*n.* BLABBERMOUTH.

blabber *v.* chatter, babble, blab, gab, gush, blather, reveal, divulge, let slip, spill (*Slang*), run off at the mouth (*Slang*). —*n.* BLABBERMOUTH.

blabbermouth *n.* gossip, tattletale, talebearer, rumormonger, gossipmonger, newsmonger, busybody, informer, bigmouth (*Slang*), blab, blabber.

black *adj.* **1** unlit, inky, dark, pitch-dark, pitch-black, unilluminated, sable, raven, ebony, jet, sooty, dingy, dim, sunless. **2** Negro, African, colored, dark-skinned, swart, swarthy, melanoid. **3** unlucky, dismal, disastrous, gloomy, morose, depressed, bitter, dire, ill-fated, grim, dreadful, melancholy, funereal. —*v.* BLACKEN.
ant. 1 bright, sunny, glowing, brilliant. **3** cheerful, happy, lucky, lighthearted, rosy.

black-and-blue *adj.* livid, discolored, bruised, contused, purple.

black art MAGIC.

blackball *v.* ban, exclude, ostracize, reject, turn down, blacklist, vote against, debar, snub, cold-shoulder, cut.
ant. invite, include, accept, ask, bid.

blacken *v.* **1** black, darken, ink, begrime, smudge, tar, besoot, ebonize, lacquer, tarnish, dull, dim. **2** slander, defame, vilify, calumniate, denigrate, discredit, defile, blemish, libel, stigmatize, sully, denounce.
ant. 1 brighten, whiten, shine, bleach, clean. **2** compliment, glorify, praise, honor, exalt.

blackguard *n.* scoundrel, villain, swine, fiend, evildoer, snake, rat (*Slang*), louse (*Slang*), SOB (*Slang*), bastard (*Slang*), heel (*Slang*), rotter (*Brit.*), cad (*Brit.*).

blackhearted *adj.* EVIL.

blackjack *n.* CLUB.[1]

blackleg *n.* SWINDLER.

black magic MAGIC.

blackmail *n.* extortion, bribe, bribery, coercion, threat, payment, hush money (*Slang*), shakedown (*Slang*), squeeze (*Slang*), screws (*Slang*).

blackout *n.* unconsciousness, loss of consciousness, faint, swoon, coma, insensibility, syncope, temporary amnesia, oblivion, stupor.

black out FAINT.

bladder *n.* sac, pouch, saccule, vesicle, utricle, pod, bag, bulb, pocket, vessel, container, cell, cyst, blister, sound.

blade *n.* knife, cutter, jacknife, sword, sabre, cutlass, scalpel, lancet, razor, chisel.

blah *adj.* *Slang* wishy-washy, lukewarm, stale, flat, vapid, insipid, bland, jejune, lifeless, tasteless, dull, commonplace, pedestrian, prosaic, dreary, tedious, uninteresting, char-

acterless, unimaginative. —*n.*
BLATHER.
ant. *adj.* animated, vibrant, stimulating, fascinating, spirited, vigorous.
blain *n.* BLISTER.
blamable *adj.* CULPABLE.
blame *v.* condemn, criticize, censure, reproach, admonish, complain, chide, scold, upbraid, disparage, castigate, denounce, rebuke, accuse, assign, ascribe, impute, attribute, saddle, incriminate, indict, impugn. —*n.* 1 responsibility, onus, liability, accountability, obligation, charge, attribution, imputation, incrimination. 2 censure, condemnation, accusation, admonition, reproof, rebuke, reproach, stricture, complaint, criticism.
blameless *adj.* innocent, irreproachable, unimpeachable, unoffending, unblemished, clear, guiltless, faultless, impeccable, sterling, upright, virtuous.
ant. guilty, culpable, blameworthy, faulty.
blameworthy *adj.* CULPABLE.
blanch *v.* 1 bleach, whiten, peroxide, decolorize, decolor, wash out, fade. 2 pale, whiten, fade, blench, dim, wan, dull.
blanched *adj.* PALE.[2]
bland *adj.* 1 suave, smooth, slick, glib, unctuous, smooth-tongued, ingratiating, deferential, courteous, politic, urbane, gracious. 2 mild, gentle, soft, weak, thin, soothing, mollifying, non-irritating, moderate, temperate, balmy. 3 insipid, vapid, jejune, flat, stale, tasteless, lackluster, dull, unexciting.
ant. 1 blunt, outspoken, gauche, impolitic, brusque. 2 sharp, biting, penetrating, piquant, pungent. 3 zestful, exciting, exhilarating, stimulating, provocative.
blandish *v.* FLATTER.
blandisher *n.* FLATTERER.
blandishment *n.* FLATTERY.
blank *adj.* 1 unmarked, bare, untouched, unadorned, unembellished,

uncompleted, unfilled, open, white, spotless, colorless. 2 lifeless, expressionless, dull, dead, vacant, empty, hollow, gaping, vacuous, bovine, inane, foolish. 3 complete, absolute, utter, thorough, outright, sheer, positive, perfect, consummate, stark, intense. —*n.* void, emptiness, vacancy, vacuum, nothingness, nullity, nihility, nil, zero, abyss, gulf, gap, lacuna, space.
ant. *n.* 1 marked, inscribed, filled-out, defaced. 2 animated, alert, glowing, vivacious.
blanket *n.* 1 cover, coverlet, comforter, robe, lap robe, quilt. 2 surface, covering, layer, cover, stratum, carpet, wrapper, envelope, padding, mantle, cloak, coat, housing. —*adj.* all-inclusive, wide-ranging, sweeping, over-all, comprehensive, across-the-board, omnibus, universal, encyclopedic, panoramic.
ant. *adj.* specific, detailed, precise, localized, limited, restricted.
blare *v.* blast, roar, resound, clamor, swell, peal, clang, jar, scream, bellow, trumpet, toot, hoot, honk.
blarney *n.* FLATTERY.
blasé *adj.* nonchalant, sophisticated, worldly-wise, insouciant, apathetic, casual, offhand, world-weary, bored, jaded, weary, satiated, sated, surfeited, glutted.
ant. naive, unaffected, ingenuous, candid, open, enthusiastic, eager.
blaspheme *v.* REVILE.
blasphemous *adj.* impious, irreverent, profane, irreligious, sacrilegious, disrespectful, disparaging, abusive, insolent, contemptuous.
ant. pious, reverent, religious, respectful, reverential.
blasphemy *n.* sacrilege, impiety, irreverence, profanation, desecration, execration, impiousness, cursing, swearing, disrespect, abuse, insolence, contempt.
ant. piousness, piety, devoutness, devotion, respect, reverence.
blast *v.* 1 burst, explode, blow up, shat-

ter, break up, demolish, destroy, ruin, wreck, raze, fell, level. **2** criticize, castigate, assail, attack, rail at, lash out at, slam, knock, rap (*Slang*), pan, flay, roast. —*n.* **1** wind, gust, flurry, burst, blow, whirlwind, storm, tempest, gale, blizzard, hurricane, tornado, cyclone, typhoon. **2** explosion, blowup, detonation, volley, discharge, salvo, burst, crash, bang, boom, crack, flash, flare.

blasted *adj.* withered, destroyed, ruined, blighted, decomposed, spoiled, rotten, desolated, ravaged, wasted, devastated.

blastoff *n.* launch, launching, shot, firing, ejection, expulsion, projection, discharge.

blatant *adj.* glaring, flagrant, conspicuous, brazen, prominent, pronounced, bold, bald, naked, overt, obvious, obtrusive.
ant. subtle, deft, devious, insidious.

blather *n.* drivel, twaddle, blabber, claptrap, gibberish, guff (*Slang*), hot air (*Slang*), bull (*Slang*), blah (*Slang*). —*v.* BLABBER.

blaze *v.* **1** emote, anger, get mad, bridle, bristle, flare up, flame up, ignite, explode. **2** shine, glow, flare, flash, glare, gleam, beam, beacon, radiate, bedazzle. —*n.* **1** fire, conflagration, bonfire, holocaust. **2** light, glare, flare, flash, glow, gleam, glitter, beam, radiance, luster, brilliance, refulgence, resplendence, flamboyance, splendor. **3** outburst, flare-up, outbreak, burst, flash, rush, eruption, upheaval, storm, fury.

blazon *v.* PROCLAIM.

bleach *v.* whiten, blench, blanch, decolor, lighten, wash out, pale, fade, dim, dull, tarnish.

bleak *adj.* **1** bare, gaunt, barren, desert, arid, raw, withered, destitute, desolate, exposed, windy, wind-swept. **2** dreary, dismal, cheerless, comfortless, disheartening, uninviting, somber, melancholy, gloomy, mournful, miserable, depressing.
ant. 1 verdant, lush, flourishing, lux-

uriant. **2** cheerful, bright, rosy, promising.

blear *adj.* BLEARY.

bleary *adj.* blurry, hazy, fuzzy, blurred, dim, blear, groggy, murky, misty, foggy, overcast, clouded, darkened.
ant. clear, distinct, vivid, clear-cut, precise.

blemish *n.* **1** mark, spot, stain, smudge, blot, blur, blotch, speck, taint, bruise, pock, mole. **2** fault, defect, flaw, taint, tarnish, smirch, blot, shortcoming, stigma, imperfection, eyesore.

blench¹ *v.* flinch, wince, cringe, shrink, recoil, weaken, hesitate, falter, quail, quiver, skulk, evade, elude.

blench² *v.* BLANCH.

blend *v.* mix, compound, merge, mingle, fuse, coalesce, amalgamate, harmonize, combine, unite. —*n.* mixture, mix, compound, combination, fusion, union, composite, concoction, preparation, brew, amalgam, alloy.
ant. *v.* separate, divide, split, set apart.

bless *v.* consecrate, sanctify, hallow, anoint, ordain, enshrine, devote, dedicate, celebrate, exalt, honor, glorify, extol, laud.

blessed *adj.* **1** consecrated, hallowed, sanctified, holy, sacred, sacrosanct, venerated, devoted, dedicated. **2** sainted, canonized, beatified, holy, venerable. **3** joyful, joyous, delighted, elated, blissful, rapturous.
ant. 3 sad, miserable, wretched, cheerless, dispirited.

blessing *n.* **1** benediction, grace, invocation, dedication, benison. **2** approval, approbation, sanction, favor, good wishes, compliment, congratulation, felicitation. **3** kindness, boon, favor, service, bounty, godsend, windfall, gift, advantage, benefit.
ant. 1 curse, malediction, denunciation, execration. **2** disapproval, condemnation, displeasure, rebuke. **3**

mishap, misfortune, adversity, calamity, affliction.

blight *n.* **1** affliction, contamination, pestilence, scourge, pest, bane, cancer, virus, poison, curse, woe, evil. **2** decay, rot, corruption, contamination, pollution. —*v.* decompose, decay, wither, taint, contaminate, shrivel, blast, spoil, ruin, mar, balk, dash, upset, thwart, frustrate, baffle, foil, disappoint.

blind *adj.* **1** sightless, unsighted, unseeing, visionless, eyeless, stone-blind. **2** obtuse, dense, mindless, senseless, myopic, shortsighted, heedless, negligent, imperceptive, unaware, undiscerning, unenlightened, purblind.

ant. 2 perceptive, discerning, alert, astute.

blink *v.* **1** wink, bat, twink, nictitate, squint, look askance, glance, glimpse, peer, spy. **2** twinkle, flicker, glitter, sparkle, glimmer, shimmer, waver, flutter, scintillate, flash, shine.

blip *v.* DELETE.

bliss *n.* rapture, delight, joy, happiness, pleasure, enchantment, elation, transport, paradise, ecstasy.

blissful *adj.* ecstatic, rapturous, enraptured, pleasurable, happy, enchanted, transported, elated, paradisiacal, joyous.

blister *n.* swelling, bleb, sore, inflammation, fester, welt, bubble, blob, sac, pimple, boil, canker, blain, lump, sty, abscess, pustule. —*v.* vesicate.

blithe *adj.* gay, carefree, merry, lighthearted, debonair, sprightly, buoyant, sparkling, animated, jaunty, spry, blithesome.

ant. morose, gloomy, grouchy, despondent, low-spirited.

blithesome *adj.* BLITHE.

blitz *n.* onslaught, attack, strike, assault, offensive, thrust, blitzkrieg, bombardment, raid, sally, foray, sortie, incursion, charge, drive, lunge.

blitzkrieg *n.* BLITZ.

blizzard *n.* **1** snowstorm, storm, snowfall, tempest, gale, blow, blast. **2**

rush, burst, swirl, torrent, deluge, cyclone, flurry, bustle.

bloat *v.* swell, inflate, distend, dilate, puff up, blow up, expand, enlarge, stretch, magnify, stuff, pack, cram, pad.

blob *n.* bubble, globule, drop, droplet, bulge, bleb, blister, bead, sphere, orb, pellet, particle.

bloc *n.* group, association, block, body, coalition, union, confederation, combination, league, entente, faction, axis, ring, cabal, clique.

block *n.* **1** piece, mass, lump, chunk, hunk, clump, wedge, nugget, cake. **2** engraving, cut, imprint, etching, intaglio, plate, copperplate, woodcut. **3** obstacle, impediment, obstruction, barrier, hindrance, interruption, bar, jam, pack, stoppage, snag. —*v.* obstruct, stop, bar, check, jam, blockade, barricade, curb, impede, hinder, arrest, restrict.

ant. *v.* advance, further, promote, facilitate.

blockade *n.* obstruction, barricade, obstacle, boundary, stoppage, closure, hurdle, impediment, restriction, barrier, hindrance.

blockhead *n.* dolt, dunce, fool, simpleton, booby, chump, dullard, clod, imbecile, idiot, sap (*Slang*), bonehead, ignoramus, numskull, woodenhead.

blockish *adj.* STUPID.

blocky *adj.* STOCKY.

bloke *n. Brit. Slang* GUY.

blood *n.* kinship, relationship, extraction, descent, ancestry, lineage, stock, strain, family, relations, relatives, kindred, kin.

blood bath BLOODSHED.

bloodcurdling *adj.* terrifying, frightening, chilling, hair-raising, alarming, startling, stunning, appalling, dreadful, fearful, horrendous, scary.

bloodless *adj.* spiritless, lifeless, passionless, torpid, dead, unemotional, insensible, dull, lackluster, drab, colorless, cold.

ant. vivacious, vital, animated, exuberant, passionate, ebullient.

bloodletting *n.* BLOODSHED.

bloodshed *n.* killing, murder, slaying, slaughter, carnage, massacre, blood bath, bloodiness, bloodletting, butchery, gore, warfare.

bloodthirsty *adj.* cruel, inhuman, brutal, savage, barbarous, bestial, ferocious, ruthless, murderous, homicidal, bloody.

bloody *adj.* BLOODTHIRSTY.

bloom *n.* 1 blossom, flowering, florescence. 2 peak, perfection, height, springtime, heyday, prime. 3 glow, flush, coloring, redness, blush, crimsoning, mantling, radiance, brilliance, loveliness, beauty. —*v.* 1 blossom, flower, effloresce, bud, sprout, germinate, burgeon, fructify, luxuriate, grow. 2 flourish, thrive, prosper, succeed, wax, blossom, flush, glow, flame, flare, blaze, incandesce.

ant. *v.* 2 wane, dwindle, decay, languish, waste away.

blooming *adj.* vigorous, fresh, vital, lively, healthy, green, flush, abloom, lusty, exuberant, flourishing, thriving, prosperous, booming, in clover.
ant. declining, flagging, withering, fading.

blooper *n. Slang* botch, blunder, bungle, fumble, fluff, muff, error, faux pas, gaffe, imprudence, indiscretion, goof (*Slang*), howler (*Slang*), booboo (*Slang*), boner (*Slang*).

blossom *n.* bloom, flower, floret, floweret, posy, inflorescence, bud, burgeon. —*v.* BLOOM.

blot *n.* 1 spot, speck, mark, stain, blotch, splotch, smudge, smear, daub, smirch. 2 fault, blemish, flaw, stain, tarnish, stigma, brand, reproach, disgrace, dishonor. —*v.* 1 blur, blotch, smear, stain, spot, smudge, smirch, spatter, soil, grease. 2 disgrace, dishonor, tarnish, sully, brand, taint, defame, debase.

blotch *n.* BLOT.

blot out 1 destroy, wipe out, obliterate,

annihilate, abolish, cancel, strike out, rub out, erase, delete, expunge, expurgate. 2 darken, obscure, black out, eclipse, shade, shadow, overshadow, overcast, cloud, adumbrate, obfuscate.

blow[1] *v.* 1 impel, propel, move, drive, waft, float, flow, stream. 2 emit, expel, exhale, breathe, puff. 3 sound, trumpet, blast, blare, whistle, hiss, toot, honk. —*n.* 1 exhaling, breathing, puffing, painting, gasping, blasting, sounding. 2 gale, wind, storm, gust, blast, tempest, flurry, squall, whirlwind, blizzard, hurricane, typhoon, cyclone, tornado, twister.

blow[2] *n.* 1 hit, punch, cuff, knock, stroke, thump, thwack, whack, wallop, buffet, bang, pat, rap, slug, smack, swipe. 2 misfortune, mishap, affliction, misadventure, setback, comedown, reversal, calamity, disaster, catastrophe.

blow over pass away, vanish, cease, finish, end, expire, lapse, run out.
ant. remain, persist, go on, continue.

blow up 1 inflate, fill, pump up, swell, bloat, enlarge, expand, distend. 2 explode, burst, blast, shatter, split, rupture, detonate, dynamite, torpedo, bomb.

blowzy *adj.* FROWZY.

blubber *v.* SOB.

bludgeon *n., v.* CLUB.

blue blood ARISTOCRAT.

blueprint *n.* plan, design, sketch, outline, prospectus, scheme, setup, layout, plot, chart, draft, proposal, project, conception.

blues *n.* depression, dumps, doldrums, dejection, melancholy, moodiness, glumness, despondency, moroseness, gloominess.

blue-sky *adj.* SPECULATIVE.

bluestocking *adj.* ARTY.

bluff[1] *v.* deceive, pretend, mislead, simulate, dissemble, delude, four-flush (*Slang*), fake, counterfeit, trick, hoax, dupe, bamboozle.

bluff[2] *n.* cliff, bank, slope, promontory, headland, ridge, knoll, height, peak, precipice, palisade, crag, escarpment, scarp, steep. —*adj.* rough, stern, gruff, crusty, blustering, plain-spoken, curt, frank, unceremonious, forthright, blunt, brusque.

ant. *adj.* suave, smooth, urbane, genteel.

blunder *n.* mistake, error, slip, slip-up, oversight, bungle, bobble, fumble, faux pas, false step, folly, omission, howler, boner (*Slang*), boo-boo (*Slang*), indiscretion. —*v.* bungle, botch, muff, goof (*Slang*), slip up, fudge, fumble, mix up, confuse, misjudge, miscalculate, miscarry.

blunt *adj.* **1** dull, thick, edgeless, unsharp, unpointed, unedged, unsharpened. **2** brusque, abrupt, short, candid, frank, plain-spoken, trenchant, curt, harsh, rough, rude, impolite, tactless, impudent. —*v.* deaden, dull, numb, weaken, dampen, cool, chill, soften, stifle, subdue, suppress, smother, stupefy, debilitate, anesthetize, deaden.

ant. *adj.* **1** sharp, edged, pointed, knifelike. **2** soft-spoken, gentle, tolerant, bland, conciliatory.

blur *n.* smudge, smear, stain, spot, daub, dab, blot, soil, splash. —*v.* **1** smudge, smear, daub, smirch, blotch, spot, blacken, stain, mar, deface. **2** obscure, conceal, hide, obfuscate, confuse, shroud, veil, overshadow, eclipse, becloud, befog, shade, darken.

ant. *v.* **2** delineate, define, clarify, illuminate.

blurt *v.* utter, exclaim, cry, sputter, snort, gush, blab, babble, tattle, spill.

blush *v.* flush, redden, color, crimson, glow, mantle.

bluster *n.* swagger, bravado, braggadocio, gasconade, bombast, boasting, crowing, bragging, gloating, raving, ranting, rodomontade. —*v.* **1** storm, rage, blow, huff, swirl, squall, brew, rampage. **2** crow, brag, gloat, rave, rant, boast, swagger, storm, blow, fulminate.

board *n.* **1** plank, length, piece, wood,

lumber, timber, beam, slab, stick, slat, stave, lath. **2** committee, body, council, directorate, executive, panel, commission, court, tribunal. —*v.* enter, mount, embark, entrain, enplane.

board up cover, enclose, screen, shield, sheathe, wall in, fence in.

boast *v.* brag, gloat, talk big, blow one's own horn, crow, puff, vaunt, exult, glory, bluster, flourish, swagger. —*n.* bragging, boasting, boastfulness, brag, bombast, gasconade, bravado, braggadocio, tall talk, hot air (*Slang*), gas (*Slang*), bunk (*Slang*), fish story.

boastful *adj.* bragging, inflated, swollen, vaunting, blustering, bombastic, cocky, proud, vain, egotistic, conceited, haughty, arrogant, overweening, pretentious, pompous.

ant. modest, retiring, diffident, self-effacing, humble.

boasting *n.* BOAST.

boat *n.* watercraft, vessel, craft, ship.

bob *v.* bounce, wobble, quiver, jerk, jog, twitch, waver, vibrate, oscillate, waggle, nod, weave, skip, duck.

bobble *n.* BLUNDER.

bob up appear, emerge, arise, turn up, pop up, spring up, break forth, burst forth, flare up, show up.

bode *v.* presage, portend, augur, prefigure, forebode, foreshadow, adumbrate, bespeak, signify, indicate, suggest, intimate, hint at, forewarn, threaten, foretell, predict, prophesy, prognosticate.

bodiless *adj.* incorporeal, discarnate, disembodied, immaterial, unsubstantial, spiritual, supernatural, spectral, ghostly.

ant. bodily, corporeal, physical, tangible, material.

bodily *adj.* corporeal, physical, fleshly, carnal, material, substantial, solid, concrete, tangible, actual, real, existent, factual.

ant. bodiless, incorporeal, discarnate, disembodied, immaterial.

body *n.* **1** physique, figure, form, build,

frame, shape, anatomy, cast, appearance. **2** corpse, cadaver, stiff (*Slang*), *corpus delicti*, deceased, remains, bones, skeleton, relics, mummy, carcass. **3** torso, trunk, midsection. **4** group, cluster, collection, association, combination, league, union, organization, division, bulk, mass, majority, gathering, band, circle, bloc, force, bunch, crowd, throng, horde. **5** PERSON.

bog *n.* marsh, mire, morass, swamp, swampland, slough, fen, mud, quicksand, quagmire.

bog down stall, stick, delay, mire, impede, bring to a halt, halt, slow down, slow up, come to a halt, grind to a halt.
ant. progress, advance, forge ahead, move, function.

boggle hesitate, pause, demur, shy, jib, shrink, recoil, reel, avoid, eschew, falter, waver, flounder, vacillate, shilly-shally.

boggy *adj.* swampy, marshy, miry, moory, fenny, spongy, splashy, oozy, soft, yielding, quaggy.

bogus *adj.* counterfeit, fake, spurious, sham, false, fraudulent, dummy, phony (*Slang*), pseudo, simulated, artificial, imitation.
ant. genuine, authentic, valid, real, actual.

bogy *n.* goblin, spirit, sprite, imp, specter, bugbear, bugaboo, boogyman, *bête noire*, nemesis, demon, fury.

Bohemian *adj.* unconventional, nonconformist, unorthodox, individualistic, offbeat, bizarre, exotic, arty, artistic, informal, loose, carefree, vagabond.
ant. conventional, straight, bourgeois, philistine, conformist.

boil[1] *v.* seethe, fume, throb, simmer, stew, churn, bristle, smolder, stir up, work up, tremble, quiver, shake, burn, rage, storm, fulminate.

boil[2] *n.* furuncle, pustule, bulla, blain, blister, bleb, fester, abscess, pimple, sore, swelling.

boil down condense, abridge, compress, reduce, shorten, abbreviate, cut, edit, capsulize, abstract.

boisterous *adj.* rowdy, obstreperous, rambunctious, tumultuous, turbulent, blustering, rollicking, knockabout, rough-and-tumble, unrestrained, noisy, loud, strident, shrill, clamorous.
ant. restrained, well-behaved, disciplined, orderly, quiet.

bold *adj.* **1** fearless, courageous, brave, valiant, audacious, intrepid, daring, stalwart, stout, resolute, adventurous, enterprising, defiant. **2** shameless, forward, unabashed, immodest, brassy, brazen, impudent, impertinent, insolent, cheeky, pert, saucy. **3** vigorous, strong, forceful, vivid, robust, lively, spirited, emphatic, striking, prominent, colorful, arresting, eye-catching.
ant. **1** timid, faint-hearted, irresolute, apprehensive. **2** humble, meek, demure, deferential. **3** pallid, vapid, jejune, weak, dull.

boloney *n. Slang* NONSENSE.

bolster *v.* support, maintain, sustain, back, prop up, brace, buttress, underpin, uphold, shore up, cradle, pillow.

bolt *n.* **1** lock, latch, catch, clinch, clamp, fastener, bar, rod, pin, screw, rivet. **2** lightning, thunderbolt, flash, sheet, brand, firebolt. —*v.* **1** rush, run, dash, fly, sprint, scoot, flit, spurt, hasten, hurry, spring, leap, jump, flee. **2** defect, secede, quit, break away, pull out, withdraw from, forsake, abandon, desert.

bomb *n.* **1** bombshell, missile, projectile, torpedo, mine, rocket, guided missile, blockbuster, depth bomb, depth charge, ash can (*Slang*), atom bomb, hydrogen bomb, MIRV. **2** *Slang* failure, flop, dud, bust (*Slang*), washout (*Slang*), mess, botch, fizzle, lemon (*Slang*), turkey (*Slang*), dog (*Slang*), fiasco. —*v.* **1** *Slang* fail, flop, blunder, flunk, abort, stumble, collapse. **2** BOMBARD.

ant. *n.* **2** success, hit, smash, triumph, wow (*Slang*). *v.* **1** triumph, succeed, overcome, prevail, win.

bombard *v.* **1** bomb, blitz, shell, barrage, cannonade, fusillade, pepper, strafe, rake, torpedo, shoot at, fire upon, open fire. **2** assail, attack, assault, snipe at, batter, unleash, press, beset.

bombast *n.* BOAST.

bombastic *adj.* extravagant, flamboyant, grandiose, highflown, inflated, swollen, turgid, fustian, flatulent, ranting, boastful, bragging, pompous, pretentious, wordy, verbose, prolix.
   ant. restrained, temperate, austere, elegant.

bombed *adj. Slang* DRUNK.

bond *n.* **1** binder, glue, band, cement, joint, link, fastener, knot, tie, coupling, connection, ligature, nexus, vinculum. **2** union, connection, link, tie, attachment, relation, liaison, adherence, allegiance, loyalty, fealty. **3** obligation, responsibility, pledge, promise, guarantee, agreement, compact, covenant, contract. —*v.* connect, link, fasten, bind, knot, tie, join, couple, glue, cement, weld, fuse, meld, merge, blend.
   ant. *v.* separate, sever, detach, disconnect, untie.

bondage *n.* servitude, subservience, dependence, subjugation, serfdom, thralldom, vassalage, peonage, enslavement, slavery, captivity, yoke.
   ant. freedom, liberty, independence, emancipation.

bonds *n.* shackles, chains, fetters, irons, manacles, handcuffs, cuffs, bracelets.

bonehead *n.* BLOCKHEAD.

boner *n. Slang* BLUNDER.

bone up *Slang* study, master, learn, relearn, read up, brush up, polish up, cram up, go over.

bon mot WITTICISM.

bonny *adj.* **1** PRETTY. **2** EXCELLENT.

bonus *n.* extra, bounty, premium, dividend, prize, honorarium, commission, reward, tip, gratuity.

bon vivant SYBARITE.

bony *adj.* lank, spare, lean, thin, skinny, lanky, angular, gaunt, scrawny, rawboned, fleshless, underweight, gangling, spindling.
   ant. fleshy, corpulent, plump, stout, fat.

boob *n. Slang* SIMPLETON.

boo-boo *n. Slang* BLUNDER.

booby *n.* DUNCE.

booby trap TRAP.

boodle *n. Slang* **1** BRIBE. **2** BOOTY. **3** PACK.

book *n.* volume, tome, publication, work, writing, opus, booklet. —*v.* engage, hire, sign on, retain, contract for, secure, reserve, line up, schedule, program, bill.

Book *n.* BIBLE.

bookish *adj.* pedantic, academic, didactic, inkhorn, scholarly, literary, esoteric, formalistic, sententious, stodgy.

boom[1] *n.* spar, pole, bar, beam, arm, shaft, timber, limb, lever.

boom[2] *v.* **1** roar, thunder, rumble, roll, crash, clap, bang, crack, resound, explode, reverberate, detonate. **2** thrive, flourish, prosper, succeed, grow, gain, increase, advance, strengthen, intensify, swell, mount, wax, rise, pyramid. —*n.* **1** roar, thunder, rumble, crash, clap, bang, reverberation, explosion, shot, cannonade. **2** growth, advance, increase, upswing, upturn, uptrend, expansion, gain, jump, leap, boost.
   ant. *v.* **2** fail, decline, collapse, dwindle. *n.* **2** failure, decline, collapse, downswing.

boomerang *v.* BACKFIRE.

booming *adj.* thriving, flourishing, prospering, blooming, mushrooming, bullish, vigorous, exuberant, well-off, prosperous.
   ant. failing, waning, declining, decaying, dying.

boon *n.* godsend, windfall, gift, favor, bounty, benefit, blessing, benefaction.

boondocks *n.* backwoods, sticks, Podunk, hinterland, provinces, backwater, nowhere.

boor *n.* oaf, lout, churl, vulgarian, guttersnipe, clown, bumpkin, clodhopper, rustic, yokel, hick, ruffian, rowdy.

boorish *adj.* loutish, lumpish, churlish, cloddish, rowdy, gross, coarse, crude, raw, rude, vulgar, uncouth, indelicate, unrefined.
ant. delicate, polite, sensitive, elegant, refined, sophisticated.

boost *v.* **1** raise, lift, hoist, heft, elevate, heighten, push, thrust, press. **2** promote, advance, plug (*Slang*), foster, abet, advocate, recommend, acclaim, extol, eulogize, hail, laud, praise, speak well of. **3** increase, raise, hike, up, inflate, jack up, advance. —*n.* **1** help, assistance, assist, support, aid, lift, leg up, encouragement, shot in the arm, hand. **2** increase, hike, rise, raise, addition, gain, upturn.
ant. *v.* **1** lower, drop, depress, submerge. **2** belittle, run down, disparage, knock, bad-mouth (*Slang*). *n.* **2** decrease, reduction, decline, downturn.

booster *n.* fan, rooter, supporter, follower, promoter, plugger (*Slang*), champion, partisan, backer.

boot *v.* **1** kick, punt, drop-kick. **2** expel, eject, throw out, oust, kick out. **3** *Slang* DISMISS.

booth *n.* stall, stand, counter, table, compartment, enclosure, cubby, cubbyhole.

bootless *adj.* useless, futile, fruitless, vain, unavailing, ineffective, unsuccessful, profitless.
ant. successful, profitable, favorable, prosperous, propitious.

bootlick *v.* TOADY.

bootlicker *n.* toady, fawner, spaniel, apple polisher (*Slang*), kowtower, yes-man, flunky, lackey, flatterer, truckler, sycophant.

booty *n.* plunder, loot, spoils, pillage, swag (*Slang*), haul, boodle (*Slang*), take, prize, winnings, gain.

booze *n.* liquor, drink, alcohol, spirits, hooch (*Slang*), lush (*Slang*), firewater, grog, beverage, intoxicant, inebriant.

boozy *adj.* DRUNK.

bop *v.* HIT.

border *n.* edge, margin, line, rim, brim, lip, brink, verge, skirt, borderline, boundary, frontier, borderland, bounds, limits, fringe, outskirt, marchland, pale, confines, enclosure, strip, hem, curb, hedge.

borderland *n.* BORDER.

borderline *adj.* indefinite, indeterminate, indefinable, unclassifiable, marginal, halfway, indecisive, ambivalent, equivocal, obscure, vague, unclear, inexact. —*n.* BOUNDARY.
ant. *adj.* definite, precise, emphatic, clear, absolute.

border on **1** approach, come close to, come near, approximate, resemble, match, parallel, echo. **2** touch, abut, impinge, contact, verge on, connect, adjoin, neighbor.

bore *v.* **1** auger, ream, gouge, penetrate, pierce, puncture, riddle, broach, lance, trepan, dig, burrow, tunnel, mine, dredge, quarry, excavate, sink. **2** tire, weary, wear on, annoy, irk, irritate, bother, trouble, pester. —*n.* **1** borehole, hole, perforation, opening, puncture, aperture, orifice, breach, hollow, tube, tunnel, burrow, pit, shaft. **2** pest, nuisance, annoyance, bother, headache, pain in the neck, wet blanket, drip (*Slang*), pill (*Slang*).

boreal *adj.* ARCTIC.

boredom *n.* tedium, monotony, ennui, dullness, humdrum, deadness, flatness, dreariness, stuffiness, weariness, tiredness, fatigue, discomfort, annoyance.
ant. excitement, stimulation, animation, enthusiasm, eagerness.

boring *adj.* tedious, monotonous, humdrum, uninteresting, unexciting, tiring, dull, flat, dead, wearisome, tiresome, long-winded, trite, stale, commonplace, prosaic.

ant. exciting, stimulating, thrilling, stirring, interesting.

born *adj.* NATURAL.

borrow *v.* **1** take a loan, raise money, touch (*Slang*), hit for (*Slang*). **2** adopt, take, copy, imitate, mirror, reflect, repeat, simulate, assume, appropriate, usurp, pirate, plagiarize.

ant. **1** lend, advance, credit, allow. **2** originate, initiate, invent, conceive, author.

bosh *n.* NONSENSE.

bosom *n.* **1** breast, bust, chest, mamma, teat, nipple, dug, udder. **2** emotions, feelings, affections, sentiments, sympathies, spirit, soul, breast, heart, heartstrings, passions. **3** center, core, heart, middle, interior, inner recess, nucleus, pith, marrow.

boss *n.* supervisor, superior, foreman, overseer, head, chief, leader, big cheese (*Slang*), big wheel (*Slang*), kingpin (*Slang*), superintendent, master, manager, director, administrator, executive, owner, employer. —*v.* control, command, run, direct, oversee, manage, conduct, lead, supervise, administrate.

ant. *n.* subordinate, worker, help, assistant, hand. *v.* work for, assist, help, aid, follow.

boss around domineer, press, overbear, oppress, push around, lord it over, throw one's weight around, tyrannize.

ant. submit, bow to, acquiesce, capitulate.

bossy *adj.* domineering, overbearing, imperious, lordly, arrogant, arbitrary, highhanded, despotic, dictatorial, tyrannical.

ant. easy-going, flexible, pliable, cooperative.

botch *v.* bungle, blunder, boggle, fumble, muff, foul up (*Slang*), goof (*Slang*), louse up (*Slang*), ruin, butcher (*Slang*), mar, spoil, mismanage, mishandle.

ant. realize, perform, carry out, bring off.

bother *v.* **1** annoy, pester, disturb, upset, vex, irritate, put out, inconvenience, trouble, distress, exasperate, agitate, pother. **2** confuse, fluster, excite, muddle, addle, flutter, flurry, baffle, divert, disconcert, perplex, bewilder. —*n.* annoyance, nuisance, trouble, pest, headache, irritation, worry, pother, vexation, aggravation, awkwardness, inconvenience.

botheration *n.* ANNOYANCE.

bothersome *adj.* annoying, irritating, exasperating, vexatious, troublesome, worrisome, distressing, disturbing.

bottle *n.* vessel, receptacle, container, jar, flask, carafe, decanter, ewer, flagon, vial, phial.

bottleneck *n.* obstruction, impediment, blockage, obstacle, block, barrier, bar, congestion, jam, detour.

bottom *n.* **1** base, foot, floor, ground, foundation. **2** nadir, zero, minimum, nothing, ebb, scratch.

ant. **1** top, tip, head, crown, roof. **2** zenith, acme, apex, summit, peak.

bough *n.* LIMB.

bounce *v.* **1** *Slang* throw out, kick out, boot out, heave out, turn out, oust, eject, expel. **2** BOUND.¹ **3** *Slang* DISMISS. —*n.* **1** BOUND.¹ **2** RESILIENCE.

bound¹ *v.* **1** rebound, bounce, spring back, ricochet, fly back, recoil, snap back. **2** leap, jump, spring, hop, bounce, vault, hurdle, pounce. —*n.* leap, jump, spring, hop, bounce, vault, hurdle, pounce.

bound² *v.* restrict, limit, confine, restrain, hem in, demarcate, circumscribe, encompass, enclose, encircle, surround, delimit, define, condition.

bound³ *adj.* **1** obligated, obliged, committed, engaged, liable, responsible, beholden, bounden, promised, indebted, answerable, accountable, pledged, contracted. **2** certain, sure, assured, decided, settled, determined, positive.

boundary *n.* border, frontier, borderland, bounds, limits, bourn, confines, borderline, edge, margin, fringe, brim, rim, hedge, hem, verge, brink.

bounden *adj.* BOUND.[3]

bounder *n.* SCOUNDREL.

boundless *adj.* endless, limitless, unbounded, inexhaustible, infinite, measureless, immeasurable, unfathomable, indeterminate, illimitable, perpetual, eternal, everlasting. **ant.** restricted, limited, narrow, confined.

bounteous *adj.* BOUNTIFUL.

bountiful *adj.* generous, liberal, unselfish, openhanded, lavish, munificent, princely, bounteous, abundant, plentiful, ample, copious, prolific, productive, fruitful, fertile, teeming, luxuriant, exuberant. **ant.** frugal, sparing, grudging, unproductive, unfertile.

bounty *n.* gifts, presents, largess, reward, bonus, benefit, aid, grant, premium, blessing, godsend.

bouquet *n.* **1** bunch, posy, corsage, buttonhole, boutonniere, nosegay, spray, garland, wreath. **2** aroma, fragrance, scent, odor, perfume, spirit, essence.

bourgeois *adj.* conventional, smug, middleclass, philistine, materialistic, square (*Slang*), rigid, correct, formal, traditional. **ant.** unconventional, Bohemian, uninhibited, eccentric, loose, informal.

bourn *n.* BOUNDARY.

bout *n.* **1** contest, match, encounter, competition, engagement, fight, scrap, tourney, joust, tilt, quarrel, squabble. **2** spell, period, stretch, turn, round, course, cycle, fit.

bow *v.* **1** bend, stoop, flex, arch, incline, nod, curtsy, make obeisance, genuflect, kneel, salaam. **2** submit, yield, capitulate, surrender, acquiesce, succumb, knuckle under, truckle, genuflect, kowtow, bow and scrape. —*n.* bending, bob, nod, inclination, curtsy, salaam, kowtow, obeisance, greeting, homage.

bowdlerize *v.* EXPURGATE.

bowels *n.* **1** intestines, entrails, guts, innards, viscera, vitals, stomach. **2** core, interior, insides, depths, deep, pit, abyss, hole, innards, guts.

bowl *n.* dish, container, pottery, ceramic, crockery, pot, plate, crock, vase, urn, jug.

bowl over 1 knock down, floor, fell, drop, bring down, dash down, mow down, lay out, overturn, overthrow, prostrate. **2** dumbfound, astound, stun, stagger, astonish, amaze, startle, shock, electrify, jar, jolt.

bow out withdraw, back out, give up, pull out, get out, retire, abandon, quit, resign, step down.

box[1] *n.* container, case, carton, crate, chest, trunk, bin, coffer, compartment, cell, stall, coffin, casket.

box[2] *v.* hit, cuff, strike, knock, rap, smack, buffet, beat, pound, thump, punch, belt, sock (*Slang*).

boxer *n.* fighter, prizefighter, pugilist, pug (*Slang*), sparrer, sparring partner.

box in trap, block, pen in, shut in, hem in, cage, coop up, isolate, surround, enclose, confine, impede.

boxing *n.* prizefighting, fisticuffs, pugilism, sparring, ring.

boy *n.* youth, youngster, lad, chap, kid, schoolboy, fellow, cub, sonny, junior, stripling.

boycott *v.* shut out, cut off, exclude, ban, bar, ostracize, blackball, reject, refuse, outlaw.

boy friend sweetheart, companion, steady (*Slang*), date, man, young man, fellow, beau, courter, suitor, lover, swain.

brace *v.* strengthen, fortify, reinforce, ready, prepare, support, sustain, hold, stay, prop, bolster, buttress, shore up, truss, bind, tie, lash. —*n.* support, reinforcement, backing, stay, prop, bar, arm, clasp, clamp, buttress, bulwark, strut, truss, fast, guy, lash, line, cable.

bracing *adj.* invigorating, refreshing, stimulating, exhilarating, regaling, vigorous, tonic, lively, fresh, brisk, chilly, cool.

ant. debilitating, languid, flaccid, enervating, enfeebling.

brackish *adj.* salty, saline, briny, foul, nasty, bitter, noxious, undrinkable, unpotable.

brag *v.* BOAST. —*n.* BRAGGART.

braggadocio *n.* **1** BOAST. **2** BRAGGART.

braggart *n.* boaster, blowhard (*Slang*), brag, blusterer, braggadocio, show-off, bluff, swaggerer, windbag (*Slang*), big deal (*Slang*).

bragging *n.* BOAST.

braid *v.* plait, plat, weave, interweave, twine, intertwine, twist, intertwist, raddle, lace, interlace, knot, wreathe.

brain *n.* intellect, genius, mastermind, wizard, prodigy, Einstein, thinker, pundit, sage, egghead (*Slang*), intellectual, highbrow, bookworm, scholar, savant.

brainless *adj.* senseless, unintelligent, unthinking, mindless, witless, thoughtless, irrational, shortsighted, inept, foolish, dumb, idiotic.
ant. sensible, level-headed, thoughtful, rational, reasonable, prudent.

brains *n.* mind, intellect, intelligence, sense, reason, sagacity, gray matter, wits, head, senses, faculties, capacities, parts.

brainy *adj.* intelligent, smart, bright, brilliant, quick-witted, alert, keen, clever, sharp.
ant. slow-witted, dumb, slow, thick, witless.

brake *v.* slow, slacken, decelerate, ease up, check, moderate, impede, clog, curb, hobble, stop.

brakes *n.* curb, stay, check, impediment, encumbrance, control, handicap, restraint, rein, bridle, leash.

branch *n.* **1** limb, bough, prong, offshoot, arm, stem, twig, spear, sprig, spray, shoot, runner, tendril. **2** subdivision, division, department, unit, part, office, bureau, desk, offshoot, arm, wing, group, affiliate, local, chapter.

branch out extend, spread out, expand, enlarge, develop, vary, diversify, multiply, proliferate.

brand *n.* **1** trademark, trade name, make, mark, label, seal, name, earmark, hallmark. **2** type, kind, sort, variety, ilk, species, genus, denomination, designation, stamp, cast, nature, character, persuasion. —*v.* stigmatize, censure, denounce, expose, characterize, mark, label, signal, accuse, gibbet.

brandish *v.* flourish, wield, flaunt, shake, display, exhibit, parade, emblazon, swing, wave, flap, flutter.

brand-new *adj.* NEW.

brash *adj.* **1** impetuous, rash, audacious, indiscreet, thoughtless, hotheaded, foolhardy, reckless, harebrained, hasty, imprudent, unwary. **2** disrespectful, impertinent, impudent, cheeky, cocky, sassy, brazen, saucy, flip, fresh (*Slang*), pert, bold, blunt, boorish.
ant. 1 cautious, prudent, wary, safe, thoughtful, farsighted. **2** modest, decorous, demure, reserved, humble, respectful.

brass *n.* cheek, gall, nerve (*Slang*), cockiness, rudeness, impudence, impertinence, audacity, presumption, effrontery, insolence, arrogance.

brassy *adj.* **1** blaring, piercing, sharp, trumpetlike, brazen, shrill, strident, jarring, cacophonous, raucous, harsh-sounding, grating, coarse. **2** flashy, showy, gaudy, splashy, jazzy (*Slang*), garish, blatant, loud, tawdry, meretricious, obtrusive, hard, vulgar. **3** BRAZEN.
ant. 1 muted, muffled, dampened, subdued, soft, gentle, delicate. **2** delicate, dainty, elegant, tasteful, subtle, refined.

bravado *n.* bluster, bluff, swagger, cockiness, boasting, bragging, bombast, braggadocio, fluster, ostentation, exhibitionism, bravura.

brave *adj.* courageous, fearless, valiant, bold, intrepid, heroic, gallant, lionhearted, resolute, unflinching, stalwart, stout, plucky, doughty, spunky, gritty. —*v.* confront, face, stand up to, endure, suffer, dare, brazen through, defy, challenge, flout, disregard, spurn, scorn.

ant. *adj.* cowardly, faint-hearted, craven, timorous, afraid.

bravery *n.* courage, valor, fearlessness, daring, heroism, gallantry, adventurousness, fortitude, boldness, hardihood, gameness, pluckiness, audacity.

ant. cowardice, timidity, fear, dread, funk.

bravo *n.* CUTTHROAT.

bravura *n.* virtuosity, dash, brilliance, spirit, animation, energy, vigor, drive, punch, splash, display, ostentation, exhibitionism, daring, audacity, chic, style.

ant. insipidness, mildness, wishy-washiness, lackluster, dullness.

brawl *n.* fight, row, scrap, fracas, ruckus, broil, set-to, imbroglio, quarrel, affray, dispute, squabble, commotion, disturbance. —*v.* fight, scrap, make a row, broil, roughhouse, rampage, wrangle, squabble, spat, tiff, quarrel, dispute.

brawn *n.* muscularity, muscles, burliness, beefiness, strength, power, vigor, potency, sturdiness, robustness, stamina.

brawny *adj.* muscular, well-built, rugged, powerful, strong, strapping, hefty, stout, sturdy, burly, beefy.

ant. frail, feeble, debilitated, emaciated, weak.

brazen *adj.* **1** bold, forward, brassy, brash, outspoken, cocky, sassy, barefaced, unblushing, shameless, impertinent, impudent, insolent, arrogant. **2** BRASSY.

ant. 1 diffident, reserved, retiring, shrinking, shy.

breach *n.* **1** violation, infringement, infraction, break, fault, defect, neglect, offense, infidelity, transgression, contravention. **2** gap, hole, break, crack, cleft, rift, fracture, rupture, split, fault, fissure, flaw. **3** estrangement, falling-out, alienation, disaffection, variance, division, divorce, split, rift, schism, rupture, break. —*v.* break

through, penetrate, pierce, broach, perforate, stab, stick, tap, rupture, break open, crack open, force open, pry open.

bread *n.* **1** food, foodstuffs, provisions, edibles, victuals, comestibles, provender, nourishment, nutriment, rations, groceries, grub (*Slang*), eats. **2** bread and butter, living, livelihood, necessities, subsistence, support, keep, sustenance, provisions, maintenance, nurture. **3** *Slang* dough (*Slang*), money, cash, bucks, change, dollars, funds, finances, gelt (*Slang*).

breadth *n.* **1** width, wideness, broadness, depth, span, latitude, beam, spread, stretch, amplitude, extent, expanse. **2** range, scope, extent, reach, compass, sweep, spread, capacity, scale, latitude, measure, volume.

break *v.* **1** fragment, shatter, splinter, burst, smash, split, rupture, crack, fracture, fissure, partition, separate, part, section, divide, pierce, chip. **2** ruin, destroy, wreck, smash, demolish, crush, crumble, mangle, mutilate, dismantle, tear apart, dismember, disassemble. **3** moderate, weaken, diminish, reduce, dilute, soften, cushion, discontinue, cut, interrupt, check, give up, abandon, stop. **4** violate, infringe, transgress, contravene, disregard, neglect, ignore, overlook, slight. **5** surpass, exceed, pass, top, excel, trump, beat, cap, outstrip, overrun, overshoot, outdo, eclipse, overshadow, transcend. —*n.* **1** crack, fracture, split, rent, rip, cut, breach, fault, rupture. **2** opening, gap, hole, crack, rift, cleft, crevice, fault, chasm, fissure. **3** pause, rest, recess, halt, breather, stay, lull, let-up, respite, interval, interlude, intermission, interruption, suspension, interim, caesura. **4** estrangement, falling-out, alienation, disaffection, divorce, division, separation, split, schism, rift, rupture, dissension, dispute. **5** opportunity, chance, possibility, advantage, opening, luck, stroke of luck, fortune, windfall, bonanza, fluke.

ant. *v.* **2** repair, service, fix, overhaul, maintain. **3** increase, intensify, exacerbate, accelerate. **4** observe, follow, obey, respect, comply with. **5** fall short, miss, fail, flounder.

breakdown *n.* **1** failure, collapse, crackup, downfall, wreck, debacle, decline, decay, disintegration, deterioration, debilitation. **2** ANALYSIS.

break down collapse, crack up, go to pieces, come apart, crumble, deteriorate, founder, decay, decline, disintegrate, fail.

breakthrough *n.* advance, advancement, development, gain, leap, improvement, growth, progress, furtherance, find, discovery, step forward.

breakup *n.* RIFT.

break up disperse, scatter, disband, dissipate, separate, part, divide, dissolve, end, stop, suspend, dismiss, recess, adjourn.

breast *n.* **1** chest, bosom, bust, torso. **2** bosom, bust, chest, thorax, brisket, mamma, teat, tit, nipple, dug, udder. **3** heart, soul, spirit, bosom, emotions, affections, sentiments, vitals, quick, depths, core, interior.

breastbone *n.* sternum.

breath *n.* air, wind, vapor, odor, pant, puff, sigh, gasp, whiff, wheeze, breathing, respiration, inhalation, exhalation, aspiration, inspiration.

breathe *v.* inhale, exhale, respire, sigh, pant, puff, gasp, wheeze, sniff, suck, draw in, inspire, expire, blow, expel, exhaust, emit.

breather *n.* pause, break, rest, respite, recess, stay, halt, let-up, spell, interlude, intermission, time out.

breathless *adj.* **1** gasping, winded, shortwinded, panting, choking, wheezing, asthmatic. **2** eager, fervent, avid, keen, ardent, fervid, impassioned, zealous, impatient, anxious, excited, tense.

ant. **2** listless, languid, lethargic, spiritless, indifferent, bored.

breathtaking *adj.* exciting, moving, stimulating, heart-stirring, overwhelming, astonishing, magnificent, impressive, stunning, thrilling, gorgeous.

breech *n.* BUTTOCKS.

breed *v.* **1** reproduce, generate, engender, procreate, propagate, proliferate, multiply, produce, bear, yield, bring forth, beget, sire, father, spawn, hatch, fructify. **2** cause, give rise to, produce, effect, occasion, induce, make, develop, bring about, generate, originate, create. **3** rear, raise, bring up, nurture, foster, cultivate, groom, inculcate, train, tutor, discipline, indoctrinate. —*n.* strain, variety, species, brood, race, tribe, group, type, sort, kind, ilk, nature, make, cast, stamp, brand, style, manner.

breeding *n.* upbringing, raising, rearing, nurture, development, cultivation, culture, refinement, gentility, polish, grooming, conditioning, training, discipline, manners.

breeze *n.* **1** wind, air, draft, current, puff, whiff, breath, zephyr, flurry, gust. **2** cinch (*Slang*), snap, pushover (*Slang*), child's play, picnic (*Slang*), pie (*Slang*), setup, duck soup (*Slang*).

breezy *adj.* **1** windy, gusty, blustery, windblown, brisk, fresh, airy, drafty, blowy, squally, stormy. **2** jaunty, easygoing, casual, informal, airy, vague, carefree, lighthearted, debonair.

ant. **1** calm, still, motionless, becalmed, unruffled. **2** formal, rigid, punctilious, stiff, uptight (*Slang*).

brevity *n.* conciseness, succinctness, briefness, economy, crispness, curtness, pithiness, terseness, trenchancy, reticence, taciturnity, laconism, shortness.

ant. verbosity, garrulity, loquacity, prolixity, long-windedness.

brew *v.* concoct, devise, cook up, contrive, invent, hatch, engineer, arrange, maneuver, scheme, connive.

bribe *n.* **1** payoff (*Slang*), graft, sop, soap (*Slang*), hush money, boodle (*Slang*), payola (*Slang*). **2** inducement, incentive, incitement, invitation, persuasion, spur, stimulus, allure, seduction. —*v.* pay off (*Slang*), corrupt, buy off, suborn, grease (*Slang*), grease the hand (*Slang*), grease the palm (*Slang*).

bric-a-brac *n.* knickknacks, knacks, gewgaws, trinkets, curios, baubles, bibelots, objets d'art, virtu.

bridge *n.* **1** span, overpass, viaduct, arch, passageway. **2** connection, connector, tie, link, coupling, bond, band, nexus, joint. —*v.* span, arch over, extend over, connect, link, join, couple, yoke, attach, unite.

bridle *v.* check, curb, rein, restrain, constrain, hold in, keep in check, inhibit, control, govern, arrest, shackle, fetter, muzzle, gag.

brief *adj.* **1** short, little, small, quick, brisk, short-term, momentary, swift, fast, transitory, ephemeral, fleeting. **2** concise, compact, succinct, short, summary, thumbnail, compressed, condensed, abridged, abbreviated, pithy, crisp, trenchant, terse, laconic, pointed, curt. **3** BRUSQUE. —*n.* summary, synopsis, précis, digest, abstract, epitome, abridgment, condensation, capsule, conspectus.

ant. *adj.* **1** long, extended, elongated, prolonged, sustained. **2** long-winded, drawn-out, verbose, garrulous, digressive, rambling, inflated.

briefing *n.* instructions, directions, preparation, priming, cramming, conditioning, indoctrination, drill, rundown, orders.

brig *n.* JAIL.

brigade *n.* crew, group, band, body, company, party, outfit, unit, gang, pack, force, squad, team, troop, corps, detail.

brigand *n.* bandit, outlaw, robber, highwayman, rover, marauder, freebooter, plunderer, pillager, looter, spoiler, pirate, corsair, privateer.

bright *adj.* **1** light, shiny, shining, gleaming, glowing, luminous, radiant, effulgent, dazzling, sparkling, resplendent, brilliant, colorful, florid, vivid, intense, rich. **2** intelligent, smart, brainy, sensible, reasonable, alert, astute, keen, quick-witted, sharp, clever. **3** cheerful, gay, cheery, happy, pleasant, sunny, blithe, buoyant, genial, radiant. **4** promising, hopeful, encouraging, rosy, palmy, optimistic, golden, sunny, sanguine, favorable, auspicious, propitious.

ant. **1** dark, dim, unilluminated, dull, pale, faded, pallid. **2** slow-witted, dull, dumb, thick, simple-minded, obtuse. **3** glum, downcast, morose, dispirited, depressed. **4** inauspicious, ominous, unpromising, poor, bad.

brighten *v.* **1** illuminate, light up, shine, glow, beam, radiate, gleam, glare, sparkle, burn, blaze. **2** cheer up, buoy up, boost, give a lift, buck up, perk up, gladden, hearten, encourage, animate, enliven, invigorate, inspire, elate.

ant. **1** darken, blacken, dim, shade, shadow, obscure. **2** depress, dishearten, dampen, chill, oppress.

brilliant *adj.* **1** radiant, shining, gleaming, glaring, luminous, resplendent, dazzling, glittering, sparkling, scintillating, vivid, intense, glossy. **2** splendid, glorious, dazzling, stunning, ravishing, devastating, flamboyant, virtuoso, bravura, fantastic. **3** intelligent, brainy, intellectual, quick-witted, sharp-witted, clever, bright, smart, gifted, accomplished, skilled, proficient, talented, masterly, expert.

ant. **1** tarnished, dull, lusterless, matte, murky, opaque. **2** lackluster, lifeless, uninspired, perfunctory, mediocre, undistinctive. **3** unintelligent, dull, second-rate, untalented, clumsy.

brim *n.* rim, edge, lip, border, verge, margin, fringe, ledge, brink, hem, curb.

brimful *adj.* PACKED.

brim over overflow, run over, flow over, well over, spill, dribble, drip, trickle, stream, slop, slosh, flood, cascade, inundate.

brine *n.* SEA.

bring *v.* **1** convey, take, bear, transport, haul, pack, move, deliver, accompany, conduct, lead, carry, lift, fetch, retrieve. **2** cause, effect, result in, produce, give rise to, occasion, create, make, contribute to, inflict, wreak. **3** persuade, induce, prompt, move, influence, sway, incline, dispose, urge, compel, force.

bring about cause, bring to pass, produce, effect, effectuate, give rise to, generate, originate, create, occasion, perform.

bring down fell, overturn, upset, overthrow, drop, knock over, cut down, floor, pull down, level, raze.

bring forth PRODUCE.

bring off accomplish, achieve, execute, perform, discharge, dispatch, carry out, carry off, succeed, prevail, bring to pass, put into practice, make a go of, put through, translate into action, pull off.

bring up 1 rear, raise, train, nurture, groom, breed. **2** introduce, mention, submit, propose, broach, move, put forward, advance, face with, put before, confront with.

brink *n.* edge, verge, brim, rim, margin, fringe, lip, skirt, hem, brow, curb, border, boundary, line, limit.

brisk *adj.* spirited, vigorous, energetic, quick, dynamic, strenuous, forceful, peppy (*Slang*), snappy, spanking, smacking, keen, biting, sharp, zestful, stimulating, animated, intense, active, lively.

ant. limp, slack, lethargic, enervated, slow, lifeless.

bristle *v.* anger, flare up, seethe, rage, bridle, lose one's temper, get mad, get sore, get one's dander up, see red.

brittle *adj.* **1** fragile, frail, delicate, frangible, breakable, shatterable, crushable, friable, splintery, crisp. **2**

stiff, stilted, tense, strict, prim, precise, punctilious, rigid, inflexible, unyielding.

ant. 1 hard, tough, solid, unbreakable. **2** relaxed, mellow, easygoing, nonchalant.

broach *v.* introduce, bring up, inaugurate, usher in, set afoot, open up, institute, start, launch, mention, submit, advance.

broad *adj.* **1** wide, deep, extensive, large, voluminous, roomy, spacious, capacious, commodious, ample, diffuse, widespread, expansive, generous. **2** comprehensive, all-inclusive, wide-ranging, far-flung, sweeping, extensive, blanket, omnibus, universal, panoramic, encyclopedic. **3** general, nonspecific, undetailed, undefined, loose, approximate, surface, vague, superficial. **4** BROAD-MINDED.

ant. 1 narrow, slim, slender, tight, cramped, pinched. **2** specialized, limited, narrow, focused. **3** detailed, specific, particular, precise.

broadcast *v.* disseminate, spread, diffuse, circulate, promulgate, propagate, make public, publicize, report, proclaim, announce, publish, advertise, hawk, bandy about.

broaden *v.* widen, spread, amplify, stretch, expand, extend, enlarge, deepen, augment, add to, increase, magnify.

ant. narrow, tighten, straiten, confine, constrict.

broad-minded *adj.* tolerant, open-minded, receptive, accessible, responsive, liberal, catholic, cosmopolitan, free-thinking, undogmatic, unbigoted, detached, impartial, indulgent, permissive, broad.

ant. narrow-minded, petty, insular, parochial, opinionated, bigoted, dogmatic.

broadside *n.* **1** DENUNICATION. **2** VOLLEY.

brochure *n.* pamphlet, booklet, leaflet, flier, folder, circular, mailing, tract, handbill, throwaway.

broil *v.* heat, cook, burn, bake, roast,

grill, fire, scorch, toast, sear, singe, fry, parch, blister.

broke *adj.* IMPOVERISHED.

broken *adj.* **1** split, severed, cracked, rent, separated, fractured, ruptured, apart, burst, splintered, shattered, fragmented. **2** out of order, nonfunctioning, run-down, damaged, disconnected, impaired, spoiled, ruined, busted (*Slang*), dilapidated, ramshackle. **3** humbled, crushed, oppressed, subdued, abused, subjugated, reduced, browbeaten. **ant. 1** whole, intact, flawless, sound. **2** working, functioning, operating, in repair. **3** undaunted, unbowed, invincible, intrepid, resolute, indomitable.

broken-hearted *adj.* GRIEF-STRICKEN.

bromide *n.* platitude, cliché, banality, commonplace, sterotype, old saw, chestnut, corn (*Slang*), slogan, motto, maxim, proverb.

brooch *n.* pin, clasp, broach, breastpin, fibula, buckle, cameo, chatelaine.

brood *n.* hatch, clutch, offspring, chicks, babes, young, litter, farrow, spawn, spat, fry, seed, fruit, issue, progeny, kind, family, infants, children. —*v.* fret, mope, pine, agonize, muse, ponder, ruminate, think over, weigh, reflect, deliberate, consider, meditate, contemplate, speculate.

broody *adj.* MOODY.

brook[1] *n.* stream, creek, streamlet, rivulet, rill, watercourse, run, kill, branch, fork, tributary.

brook[2] *v.* tolerate, condone, put up with, countenance, accept, support, abide, stand, bear, endure, suffer.

brothel *n.* whorehouse, bordello, house, house of prostitution, house of ill repute, bawdyhouse, cathouse (*Slang*), stew.

brotherhood *n.* fellowship, fraternity, fraternalism, confraternity, comradeship, sodality, community, alliance, connection, affiliation, ties, kinship, chumminess.

brotherly *adj.* fraternal, affectionate, sympathetic, cordial, benevolent, humane, philanthropic, altruistic, neighborly, communal, kindred.

browbeat *v.* intimidate, domineer, lord it over, overbear, bully, bulldoze (*Slang*), cow, henpeck, hector, harass, grind, oppress, tyrannize.

brown study reverie, abstraction, meditation, contemplation, musing, trance, absorption, thoughtfulness, rumination, reflection, deliberation, self-communion.

browse *v.* scan, skim, glance at, dip into, look through, flip through, thumb through, leaf through, skip through, run over.

bruise *v.* wound, injure, hurt, offend, insult, displease, distress, pain, grieve, chafe, prick, sting. —*n.* contusion, discoloration, abrasion, black-and-blue mark, scrape, injury, hurt, sore, pain, inflammation, swelling, lesion.

bruiser *n.* FIGHTER.

bruit about 1 REPORT. **2** PUBLICIZE.

brunt *n.* impact, force, shock, thrust, pressure, stress, strain, burden, severity, oppression.

brush[1] *n.* **1** broom, besom, whisk, whisk broom. **2** touch, contact, glance, grazing, swish, rustle, whisper, breath, caress, kiss, rub, scrape, stroke. **3** skirmish, fracas, fray, clash, run-in, melee, scrap, scuffle, tussle, set-to, fight, battle, conflict. —*v.* **1** paint, coat, cover, dab, daub, smear, sweep, whisk, broom, swish, swab, dust, clean, wipe, polish, smooth, tend, rub down, groom, curry. **2** touch, contact, graze, glance, rub, scrape, skim, sweep, stroke, caress, kiss, lick, lap, nuzzle.

brush[2] *n.* thicket, bush, growth, shrubbery, shrubs, underbrush, undergrowth, scrub, coppice, copse, bracken, maquis, stand, trees, timber, woods, forest.

brush-off *n.* cold shoulder, dismissal, denial, slight, snub, rebuff, cut, go-by, refusal, rejection, turndown, repudiation, kiss-off (*Slang*).

brush off dismiss, reject, slight, snub,

cut, cold-shoulder, scorn, spurn, rebuff, refuse, disregard, repudiate, disown, disclaim, deny, ignore, disdain, turn down, kiss off (*Slang*).

brush up BONE UP.

brusque *adj.* blunt, abrupt, curt, short, sharp, harsh, severe, brash, churlish, surly, crusty, gruff, bluff.
ant. genial, cordial, affable, sociable, warm, friendly.

brutal *adj.* **1** cruel, fierce, vicious, wild, savage, ferocious, feral, bestial, animalistic, brute, bloodthirsty, inhuman, bloody, barbarous, primitive, inhumane, unfeeling. **2** harsh, agonizing, punishing, racking, tortuous, excruciating, harrowing, ruthless, intolerable, unbearable, insufferable, unendurable.
ant. **1** gentle, humane, compassionate, good, merciful, sympathetic, tender.

brutality *n.* cruelty, viciousness, barbarity, ferociousness, bloodthirstiness, ruthlessness, inhumanity, savagery, bestiality, cannibalism.
ant. humaneness, compassion, mercy, tenderness, benevolence.

brute *n.* **1** animal, beast, creature. **2** bully, monster, beast, savage, fiend, devil, villain, wretch, troglodyte, scoundrel, thug, hoodlum. —*adj.* BRUTAL.

brutish *adj.* gross, crude, coarse, crass, boorish, swinish, beastly, bestial, cruel-hearted, uncouth, vulgar, offensive, carnal, lustful, lewd.
ant. refined, decorous, delicate, cultivated, genteel.

bubble *n.* **1** globule, sphere, ball, orb, drop, droplet, bead, foam, froth, spume, burble, trickle, dribble, bulge, bulb, blister. **2** illusion, fantasy, fancy, phantom, froth, trifle, dream, figment, will-o'-the-wisp, chimera. —*v.* burble, dribble, ripple, trickle, drip, lap, splash, slosh, gurgle, trill, purl, murmur, babble.

buccaneer *n.* PIRATE.

buck *n.* playboy, dude, gay blade, lover, cavalier, beau, lady's man, gallant, dandy, spark. —*v.* **1** leap, jump, spring, start, bound, vault, skip, jolt, jerk, hop, prance, caper. **2** oppose, resist, contest, battle, fight, combat, struggle against, contend against, grapple with, confront, challenge, defy.
ant. *v.* **2** conform, submit, acquiesce, accept, accede.

bucket *n.* pail, container, receptacle, can, scuttle, hod, bail, piggin.

buck for *Slang* strive, struggle, strain, exert oneself, work, labor, persist, push, spare no effort, try hard, knock oneself out.

buckle[1] *n.* clasp, clip, hitch, catch, clamp, grip, snap, fastener, hook and eye, hasp. —*v.* clasp, clip, clinch, clamp, hitch, hook, latch, snap, fasten, join, connect, attach, fix, link, unite, secure.
ant. *v.* unbuckle, unhitch, release, disengage, open.

buckle[2] *v.* **1** bend, twist, crimp, crinkle, crook, wrench, crumple, warp, contort, distort, deform. **2** collapse, give way, cave in, fall through, break down, fold, founder, topple, break.

buckle down work, labor, sweat, slave, apply oneself, pitch in, fall to, set to, exert oneself, launch into, get to it, knuckle down.
ant. dawdle, procrastinate, malinger, goof off (*Slang*), slack, slow down.

buck up brace up, perk up, cheer up, brighten up, refresh, revive, fortify, invigorate, hearten, encourage, embolden, assure, inspire.
ant. discourage, dishearten, dampen, disenchant, depress.

bucolic *adj.* RUSTIC.

bud *v.* **1** sprout, gemmate, shoot, burgeon, vegetate, germinate, bloom, blossom, flower, leaf. **2** BURGEON.

buddy *n.* pal, chum, crony, mate, sidekick, fellow, friend, comrade, partner, brother, companion, intimate.

budge *v.* move, go, shift, stir, proceed, propel, push, impel, displace, dislodge, dislocate, unseat.

budget *n.* APPROPRIATION.

buff *n.* fan, admirer, enthusiast, nut (*Slang*), freak (*Slang*), bug (*Slang*), bum, faddist, fancier, follower, maven, connoisseur, devotee, votary, zealot.

buffer *n.* absorber, cushion, mattress, pillow, intermediate, alleviator, moderator, guard, bumper, fender, backstop.

buffet *v.* strike, hit, pound, beat, knock, box, cuff, smack, slap, whack, thump, knock about, belabor, batter, clobber (*Slang*), pummel, drub, thrash.

buffoon *n.* fool, clown, zany, jokester, comedian, jester, *buffo*, punchinello, harlequin, booby, chump, dolt, ʻblockhead, lout, boor.

bug *n.* defect, fault, catch, hitch, snag, snarl, rub, drawback, failing, flaw, weakness, blemish. —*v.* 1 wiretap, tap, listen in, eavesdrop. 2 annoy, bother, pester, irk, harass, hector, badger, nettle, nag, pique, vex, disturb, irritate.

bugaboo *n.* BUGBEAR.

bugbear *n.* specter, bogy, boogy, goblin, bugaboo, demon, fiend, devil, nemesis, bête noire.

buggy *adj. Slang* CRAZY.

build *v.* 1 construct, make, erect, put up, set up, raise, frame, fabricate, form, fashion, assemble, forge, produce, manufacture. 2 start, begin, establish, found, institute, set up, base, originate, ground, create, develop. —*n.* physique, figure, body, shape, frame, form, stature, appearance.
ant. *v.* 1 demolish, tear down, wreck, raze, destroy, disassemble.

building *n.* structure, construction, edifice, erection.

buildup *n.* 1 increase, gain, growth, enlargement, expansion, accumulation, accretion, upswing, uptrend, jump, leap, boom. 2 praise, compliment, tribute, commendation, endorsement, testimonial, promotion, publicity, puff, plug, ballyhoo, blurb.
ant. 1 decrease, reduction, decline, retrenchment.

build up 1 increase, intensify, augment, heighten, deepen, amplify, expand, extend, add to, advance, pyramid, reinforce, strengthen, boost, stimulate, enhance, improve, fortify. 2 promote, publicize, plug, boost, advertise, ballyhoo, spotlight.
ant. 1 decrease, slacken, lessen, weaken.

bulb *n.* BULGE.

bulge *v.* swell, distend, protrude, stick out, expand, puff out, inflate, project, rise, dilate. —*n.* swelling, lump, protrusion, protuberance, projection, bump, bulb, knob, boss, knot, gnarl, node, nodule.
ant. *v.* contract, shrink, deflate, shrivel, dwindle. *n.* cavity, dent, indentation, dip, hole.

bulk *n.* 1 mass, volume, substance, body, weight, size, amount, measure, portion, batch, quantity, sum, number. 2 majority, most, preponderance, plurality, main part, generality, mass.

bulky *adj.* 1 large, big, sizable, massive, huge, ample, considerable, vast, monumental, immense, enormous, great. 2 massy, heavy, weighty, ponderous, cumbrous, hulky, unwieldy, ungainly, clumsy.
ant. 1 small, little, miniature, minute, infinitesimal. 2 compact, concentrated, condensed, economical.

bull *v.* force, push, press, drive, thrust, crowd, propel, elbow, shoulder, jostle, shove, bump, bulldoze.

bulldoze *v. Slang* 1 bully, cow, browbeat, hector, coerce, intimidate. 2 force, shove, thrust, push, drive, propel, bump.

bullet *n.* shell, shot, slug, cartridge, pellet, ball, dumdum, projectile, missile.

bulletin *n.* report, account, dispatch, message, communication, article, item, note, statement, entry, record, memorandum.

bullheaded *adj.* stubborn, dogged, mulish, pigheaded, stiff-necked, unyielding, obstinate, inflexible, rigid, tenacious, obdurate, willful.

ant. submissive, docile, compliant, adaptable, flexible.

bullish *adj.* CONFIDENT.

bully *adj.* excellent, admirable, first-rate, splendid, superb, fine, wonderful, capital, good, great, grand, swell (*Slang*), nifty (*Slang*). —*v.* coerce, intimidate, domineer, bluster, abuse, bulldoze (*Slang*), browbeat, hector, harass, frighten, terrorize.

bulwark *n.* **1** rampart, wall, abutment, parapet, embankment, bastion, bank, earthwork, shoulder, dam, safeguard, bumper, screen, reinforcement. **2** support, backing, mainstay, sustainer, maintainer, reinforcement, brace, prop, staff, crutch, backbone, champion, advocate.

bum *n.* loafer, idler, dawdler, ne'er-do-well, good-for-nothing, beggar, panhandler, drifter, hobo, tramp, vagabond, vagrant, derelict, wretch.

bumbling *adj.* awkward, clumsy, inept, incompetent, bungling, blundering, gauche, maladroit, inefficient, ungainly, lumbering.
ant. dexterous, facile, proficient, nimble, handy.

bump *v.* **1** hit, strike, knock, bang, jolt, jog, clash, collide, sideswipe, graze, carom, prod, shove. **2** displace, dislodge, depose, unseat, move, remove, do away with, discharge, demote, bust (*Slang*), bounce (*Slang*). —*n.* **1** jolt, bang, clash, crash, thud, thump, butt, knock, blow, jar, jostle, bounce, swipe, shock, collision, impact. **2** lump, bulge, swelling, protuberance, swollenness, knot, knob, pimple, welt, tumor, tumescence, node, hump, rising, ridge, roughness, irregularity, unsmoothness, corrugation.

bumpkin *n.* yokel, hick, hayseed (*Slang*), rube (*Slang*), rustic, farmer, clodhopper, lumpkin, yahoo.

bumptious *adj.* conceited, arrogant, self-assertive, overbearing, forward, swaggering, insolent, impertinent, blustering, boastful, presumptuous, obtrusive, pushy.

ant. self-effacing, unobtrusive, retiring, diffident, sheepish, shrinking.

bumpy *adj.* rough, uneven, bouncy, irregular, choppy, jolting, jarring, rugged, ragged, jagged, rocky, craggy, gnarled, knotty, coarse, granulated.
ant. smooth, flat, level, polished, flush.

bunch *n.* group, cluster, knot, clump, mass, batch, heap, lot, quantity, number, collection, pack, multitude, body, company, band, party, gang, crew, troop, outfit, crowd, throng, herd, swarm, flock, gathering, assembly, congregation.

buncombe *n.* BUNK.

bundle *n.* **1** mass, quantity, bulk, assortment, lot, collection, accumulation, pack, batch, bunch, stack, heap, sheaf, pile. **2** package, packet, pack, parcel, box, bale, bag, carton, hamper.

bungalow *n.* cottage, cabin, summer house, ranch house, lodge, villa, chalet, cabana.

bungle *v.* botch, boggle, mess up, foul up (*Slang*), louse up (*Slang*), gum up (*Slang*), goof (*Slang*), muff, fudge, blunder, spoil, mar, misdo, mismanage, butcher (*Slang*).

bungling *adj.* INCOMPETENT.

bunk *n.* *Slang* buncombe, bunkum, baloney (*Slang*), rubbish, bosh, nonsense, hokum (*Slang*), hooey (*Slang*), malarky (*Slang*), applesauce (*Slang*), balderdash, claptrap, humbug, hot air (*Slang*), bombast.

buoyancy *n.* **1** GAIETY. **2** RESILENCE.

buoyant *adj.* jaunty, lighthearted, debonair, blithe, breezy, cheerful, gay, chipper, vivacious, carefree, enthusiastic, hopeful, optimistic, sanguine.
ant. depressed, downcast, low, somber, pessimistic.

burble *v.* BUBBLE.

burden *n.* **1** load, weight, contents, substance, pack, charge, cargo, freight, loading, lading. **2** responsibility, obligation, charge, onus, pressure, encumbrance, millstone, cross, trouble,

worry, concern, affliction, suffering.
—*v.* **1** overload, strain, exert, stuff,
cram, choke, crowd, lumber, saddle,
encumber, lade, handicap, hamper.
2 oppress, strain, worry, bother, disturb, weigh down, overwork, drive,
tax.

burdensome *adj.* oppressive, arduous,
onerous, strenuous, cumbersome, irksome, troublesome, bothersome, trying, difficult, tough, hard.
ant. effortless, easy, unexacting, light,
simple.

bureau *n.* **1** dresser, chest of drawers,
chest, commode, chiffonier. **2** department, division, subdivision,
agency, office, branch.

bureaucracy *n.* **1** civil service, officials,
apparat, apparatus, authorities, administration, government, officialdom, bureaucratism. **2** red tape, regulations, directions, officialism, beadledom, Bumbledom.

bureaucrat *n.* functionary, civil servant, official, clerk, penpusher, rubber stamp, apparatchik, officeholder,
public servant, politician.

burgeon *v.* **1** flourish, thrive, burst
forth, shoot up, mushroom, expand,
enlarge, wax, increase, develop,
grow. **2** BUD.
ant. 1 diminish, shrink, dwindle, collapse, fail.

burial *n.* interment, burying, inhumation, entombment, sepulture, funeral,
last rites, obsequies.

burlesque *n.* parody, takeoff, travesty,
mockery, caricature, satire, farce,
slapstick, mock-heroic, send-up
(*Brit. Slang*). —*v.* parody, take off
on, travesty, mock, caricature, satirize, send up (*Brit. Slang*), ridicule,
deride, taunt, twit, poke fun at.

burly *adj.* hefty, thickset, brawny,
heavy-set, stocky, bulky, strapping,
hulking, stout, beefy, portly.
ant. slim, slight, slender, skinny,
spare.

burn *v.* **1** incinerate, reduce to ashes,
go up in smoke, consume, cremate,
conflagrate, scorch, roast, toast,

char, carbonize, blister, singe, sear,
brand, cauterize. **2** ignite, light, fire,
set fire to, set on fire, touch off, kindle, enkindle. **3** tremble, thrill,
quiver, tingle, seethe, chafe, fret,
simmer, smolder, fume, flame, flare
up.

burning *adj.* important, significant, crucial, vital, critical, dominant, compelling, urgent, pressing, controversial,
provocative.
ant. trivial, inconsequential, piddling, petty, subordinate, minor.

burnish *v.* polish, shine, gloss, brighten,
luster, furbish, glaze, buff, rub, wax.

burp *v.* BELCH.

burrow *n.* hole, tunnel, dugout, covert,
cavity, cave, grotto, cavern, nook,
den, lair, lodge, excavation. —*v.* tunnel, dig, root out, scoop, gouge, furrow, grub, dredge, mine, quarry, excavate.

burst *v.* **1** explode, blow out, erupt,
break open, rupture, come apart,
tear, rip, rend, breach, bust (*Slang*),
shatter, disintegrate, blast. **2** rush,
barge, pop, spring, run, dart, leap,
jump, tear. —*n.* explosion, outburst,
eruption, fit, outbreak, outpouring,
discharge, spurt, surge, rush, gush,
gust.

bury *v.* **1** inter, inhume, entomb, lay to
rest, sepulcher, sepulture. **2** secrete,
conceal, cover, hide, cache, screen,
cloak, veil, immerse, submerge.
ant. 2 expose, disclose, reveal, unveil, air.

bush *n.* **1** shrub, scrub, plant, sapling,
clump, bramble, brier. **2** scrubland,
scrub, brush, heath (*Brit.*), woods,
barrens, veld, maquis, garigue.
—*adj. Slang* BUSH-LEAGUE.

bushed *adj.* exhausted, worn-out, beat,
dog-tired, fagged, played out,
pooped (*Slang*), spent, tuckered out,
fatigued, weary, breathless.
ant. energetic, vigorous, spry, spirited, lively.

bush-league *adj. Slang* second-rate, mediocre, minor, unimportant, insignificant, inconsequential, inferior, small-time, small-fry, bush (*Slang*).

business *n.* **1** occupation, employment, job, work, line, situation, position, practice, pursuit, specialty, assignment, station, career, vocation, calling, profession, trade. **2** function, role, capacity, duty, mission, commission, policy, concern, interest, affair, office, province, sphere, field, department, beat, lookout. **3** commerce, enterprise, trade, dealings, marketing, merchandising, industry, manufacturing. **4** company, firm, office, concern, house, business establishment, enterprise, organization, corporation.

businesslike *adj.* methodical, orderly, in order, well-ordered, systematic, shipshape, thorough, efficient, functional, practical, workaday, regular.

buss *n.* KISS.

bust[1] *n.* chest, breast, bosom, mamma, thorax, torso.

bust[2] *Slang v.* **1** demote, downgrade, reduce, drop, bump, break, lower, depose, displace. **2** hit, strike, knock, belt, jab, paste (*Slang*), poke, punch, slug, smack, sock (*Slang*), whack. **3** BURST. **4** ARREST. —*n.* **1** failure, fiasco, flop, fizzle, dud, washout (*Slang*), turkey (*Slang*). **2** ARREST.

bustle *n.* commotion, stir, fuss, flurry, hubbub, uproar, hurly-burly, tumult, ado, unrest, ferment, agitation. —*v.* hustle, fuss, stir, hasten, hurry, rush, tear around, scramble, scurry, scamper, flutter, fidget.

ant. *n.* calmness, serenity, tranquillity, peacefulness, composure.

bustling *adj.* ACTIVE.

busy *adj.* **1** active, lively, bustling, on the go, energetic, hard at it, industrious, hard-working, indefatigable, enterprising. **2** employed, engaged, occupied, engrossed, working.

ant. **1** slow, easy-going, sluggish, listless, languid, lackadaisical. **2** lazy, idle, indolent, loafing.

busybody *n.* meddler, intruder, backseat driver, kibitzer, gossip, eaves-dropper, snoop, trespasser, interloper, interferer.

butcher *v.* **1** slaughter, massacre, liquidate, exterminate, assassinate, murder, slay, kill, fell, destroy. **2** *Slang* BOTCH.

butt[1] *v.* ram, bump, buck, bunt, knock, strike, jam, push, shove, drive. —*n.* stroke, blow, bunt, prod, punch, poke, push, shove, thrust, propulsion.

butt[2] *n.* target, goal, object, subject, victim, laughingstock, easy mark, fair game, dupe, gull, sucker (*Slang*), chump, fool, scapegoat.

butt[3] *n.* end, stock, stub, stump, base, foot, fundament, tail, extremity.

butter up flatter, soft-soap, oil, honey, puff up, blarney, fawn upon, cajole, wheedle, praise.

buttocks *n.* rump, hind end, posterior, haunches, behind, backside, derriere, rear, bottom, butt (*Slang*), breech, seat, tail, stern, prat (*Slang*).

buttonhole *v.* ACCOST.

buttress *n.* brace, support, stay, prop, bulwark, frame, arch, reinforcement, mainstay, backing, rampart, abutment. —*v.* encourage, sustain, support, reassure, strengthen, reinforce, buoy up, bolster, boost, steel.

buxom *adj.* chesty, well-developed, full-figured, fleshy, ample, plump, chubby, lush, voluptuous.

buy *v.* **1** purchase, procure, get, obtain, acquire. **2** *Slang* ACCEPT. —*n.* bargain, sale, steal, find, money's worth, bonanza, discovery, purchase.

buy off BRIBE.

buzz *v.* hum, drone, whir, thrum, burr, whiz. —*n.* hum, drone, whir, thrum, whiz, burr.

bygone *adj.* former, previous, earlier, older, past, bypast, onetime, sometime, erstwhile, elapsed, forgotten, lost, extinct.

ant. present, immediate, current, existent, modern.

bypass *v.* detour around, deviate from, circumvent, go around, get around, pass around, depart from, avoid, neglect, ignore, outflank.

byproduct *n.* spin-off, offshoot, outgrowth, extra, effect, result, aftereffect, bonus, side effect, appendage, side issue, supplement, adjunct, rider, extension.

bystander *n.* onlooker, passerby, looker-on, watcher, observer, viewer, spectator, witness, eyewitness, kibitzer.

byword *n.* proverb, saw, adage, saying, maxim, catchword, commonplace, truism, dictum, motto, slogan, watchword, axiom, aphorism, apothegm, shibboleth.

C

cabal *n.* **1** CONSPIRACY. **2** CLIQUE.

caballer *n.* TRAITOR.

caballero *n.* CAVALIER.

cabana *n.* CABIN.

cabaret *n.* SALOON.

cabin *n.* hut, shack, shed, shelter, cottage, cot, shanty, hovel, lodge, bungalow, hideout, hostel, chalet, cabana.

cabinet *n.* case, chest, cupboard, closet, locker, whatnot, dresser, commode, trunk, file, repository.

caboodle *n.* PACK.

cache *n.* **1** storehouse, hide-out, hideaway, repository, covert, store, storehouse, locker. **2** hoard, store, stock, stockpile, reserve, accumulation, heap.

cachet *n.* **1** CHARACTERISTIC. **2** MARK.

cachinnate *v.* GUFFAW.

cackle *v.* **1** cluck, gabble, quack, gobble. **2** chuckle, chortle, giggle, jabber, prattle, prate, clack. —*n.* **1** cluck, quack, gabble, gobble. **2** prattle, chortle, giggle, titter, clack, chuckle, laugh.

cad *n.* boor, vulgarian, bounder, clod, churl, lout, clown, yokel, peasant, barbarian, rotter (*Slang*).

cadaver *n.* corpse, remains, body, carcass, deceased, dead, specimen, subject, stiff (*Slang*), bones.

cadaverous *adj.* corpselike, pale, ghastly, gaunt, grim, hideous, deathly, wasted, pallid, livid, ashen.

ant. blooming, robust, rosy, hale, lively, glowing.

cadence *n.* rhythm, beat, meter, measure, tempo, fall, time, lilt, swing, movement.

cadre *n.* core, nucleus, skeleton, framework, infrastructure, cell.

café *n.* RESTAURANT.

cafeteria *n.* RESTAURANT.

caftan *n.* ROBE.

cage *n.* enclosure, coop, pen, cell, mew, fold, box, receptacle, pound, trap, pinfold. —*v.* confine, imprison, shut in, box up, trap, cloister, mew, impound, keep in, restrain, hem in, fence in.

ant. v. release, set free, liberate, let go, uncage, let out.

cagey *adj.* shrewd, wary, leery, sly, cautious, wily, vigilant, suspicious, hesitant, noncommittal, shifty, cunning, alert.

ant. trusting, unguarded, open, careless, innocent, imprudent.

cahoots *n.* partnership, collusion, league, connivance, cooperation, concert, tandem, conspiracy, alliance, conjunction, association.

caitiff *n.* coward.

cajole *v.* coax, wheedle, flatter, butter up, beguile, entice, inveigle, jolly, blandish, lure, delude, induce.

cajolery *n.* FLATTERY.

cake *n.* loaf, pastry, torte, sweet.

cakes and ale PLEASURE.

calaboose *n. Slang* JAIL.

calamitous *adj.* disastrous, catastrophic, ruinous, devastating, dire, cataclysmic, grievous, baleful, pernicious, fatal, mortal, deadly.

ant. advantageous, beneficial, providential, heaven-sent, propitious, favorable.

calamity *n.* disaster, cataclysm, catastrophe, affliction, scourge, stroke, blow, misfortune, tragedy, fatality, ruin, hardship.

ant. blessing, benison, boon, fortune, luck, windfall.

calculate *v.* compute, figure, reckon, determine, estimate, gauge, ascertain, conjecture, predict, surmise, presume.

calculated *adj.* INTENTIONAL.

calculating *adj.* scheming, crafty, shrewd, sly, artful, devious, manipulative, contriving, designing, tricky, sharp, self-interested.

ant. straightforward, candid, aboveboard, honest, simple, artless.

calculation *n.* THOUGHT.

caldron *n.* KETTLE.

caliber *n.* quality, rating, stature, merit, ability, importance, capability, power, scope, talent, capacity, potency.

calibrate *v.* GRADUATE.

call *v.* **1** shout, roar, bawl, exclaim, clamor, yell, scream, trumpet. **2** summon, hail, address, appeal to, telephone, inform, speak to, page. **3** convoke, convene, assemble, summon, gather, muster, draft. **4** name, designate, dub, title, term, denominate. —*n.* **1** shout, cry, yell, note, scream, roar, signal. **2** appeal, summons, command, request, supplication, entreaty, notice. **3** demand, need, claim, requirement, want, request, market.

caller *n.* VISITOR.

call for require, demand, order, request, necessitate, occasion, entail, want, crave, need, suggest.

call girl PROSTITUTE.

calling *n.* occupation, vocation, profession, mission, métier, pursuit, business, craft, line, forte, specialty, work, trade.

call off cancel, countermand, revoke, recall, repeal, annul, abolish, give up, quash, retract.

call on visit, look in on, drop in on, look up, see.

callous *adj.* **1** horny, indurated, thickened, hardened, crusty, tough. **2** unfeeling, cold, insensitive, cruel, hard, heartless, hardhearted, thick-skinned, casehardened.

ant. 2 sympathetic, kind, affectionate, warm, solicitous, tender.

callow *adj.* inexperienced, youthful, unseasoned, immature, green, juvenile, unfledged, raw, untrained, crude, unsophisticated.

ant. experienced, practiced, adult, mature, ripe, worldly-wise.

calm *adj.* **1** unruffled, composed, relaxed, cool, equable, unperturbed, undisturbed, unshaken, impassive, collected, staid, sedate, serene. **2** quiet, still, windless, halcyon, motionless, tranquil, smooth, placid, peaceful, restful.

ant. 1 tense, agitated, roiled, worked up, disturbed, roused. **2** turbulent, rough, stormy, windy, inclement, seething.

calumniate *v.* SLANDER.

calumnious *adj.* SLANDEROUS.

calumny *n.* defamation, obloquy, slander, scurrility, denigration, libel, abuse, aspersion, imputation, revilement, backbiting, scandal.

ant. praise, approval, testimonial, acclaim, glorification, puffery.

camaraderie *n.* comradeship, brotherhood, friendliness, good will, fellowship, companionship, bonhomie, geniality, fraternization, familiarity, solidarity.

camarilla *n.* CLIQUE.

camber *v.* ARCH.[1]

camouflage *n.* disguise, masquerade, pretense, mask, cover, cloak, screen, cover-up, smoke screen, front, mimicry. —*v.* disguise, obfuscate, cover up, gloss over, simulate, falsify, misrepresent, counterfeit, feign, hide, obscure.

camp *n.* **1** bivouac, encampment, cantonment, campsite, campground, settlement, position, camp meeting, gathering, stopover. **2** clique, faction, party, persuasion, circle, sect, group, league, alliance, community, lodge. —*v.* bivouac, quarter, stop over, lodge, tent, pitch camp, rough it, shelter, station.

campaign *n.* crusade, drive, movement, push, bid, program, project, action, attack, war, jihad.

campanile *n.* TOWER.

camp follower PROSTITUTE.

campy *adj.* BANAL.

can *n.* container, jar, tin, receptacle, bottle, vessel, pot, package, unit, pack, carton.

canaille *n.* RABBLE.

canal *n.* duct, tube, groove, passage, channel, vas, pipe, conduit, gut, tubule, foramen, fistula.

canard *n.* RUMOR.

cancel *v.* **1** strike out, cross off, delete, void, blue-pencil, erase, x, nullify, obliterate, expunge. **2** countermand, call off, repeal, revoke, rescind, repudiate, quash, invalidate, annul, set aside, forgive. **3** counterbalance, make up for, offset, counteract, expiate, atone for, redeem, repay, compensate for.

cancellation *n.* REPEAL.

cancer *n.* canker, blight, corruption, pestilence, rot, bane, curse, plague, infection, poison, evil, malignancy.

candid *adj.* **1** frank, open, sincere, free, ingenuous, straightforward, blunt, plain-spoken. **2** impartial, fair, unbiased, truthful, sincere, honest, just.

ant. **1** disingenuous, artful, veiled, misleading, underhand. **2** double-dealing, deceitful, biased, prejudiced, unfair.

candidate *n.* aspirant, office-seeker, nominee, contender, contestant, applicant.

candor *n.* **1** openness, frankness, forthrightness, simplicity, artlessness, guilelessness, outspokenness. **2** impartiality, fairness, honesty, sincerity, truthfulness, veracity, justice.

ant. **1** reserve, duplicity, guile, double talk, cunning. **2** prejudice, bias, deceit, injustice, dishonesty.

candy *n.* confection, sweet, sweetmeat, confectionery, comfit.

cane *n.* stick, walking stick, staff, club, cudgel, alpenstock, rod, crook, shillelagh, crutch, prop.

canker *n.* ulcer, sore, lesion, blister, inflammation.

cannon *n.* gun, fieldpiece, artillery, weapon, arm, ordnance, mortar, howitzer.

canny *adj.* shrewd, astute, clever, sharp, smart, wise, knowing, sagacious, cunning, artful, worldly-wise, practical.

ant. simple, artless, guileless, ingenuous, slow, naive.

canon[1] *n.* law, rule, principle, standard, criterion, maxim, precept, formula, yardstick, touchstone, test, norm, model.

canon[2] *n.* CLERGYMAN.

canopy *n.* awning, covering, marquee, shade, hood, tilt, sunshade, baldachin.

cant[1] *n.* slant, slope, tilt, pitch, list, rake, incline, rise, tip, ramp. —*v.* **1** tilt, tip, slant, incline, slope, lean, list, rake. **2** swerve, veer, turn, tack, zigzag, careen, angle.

cant[2] *n.* **1** hypocrisy, pretense, humbug, lip service, mummery, religiosity, sanctimony. **2** jargon, lingo, argot, dialect, vernacular, slang.

cantankerous *adj.* bad-tempered, quarrelsome, fractious, crotchety, peevish, cranky, irritable, cross, irascible, choleric, contrary, perverse.

ant. equable, serene, debonair, good-humored, affable, pleasant.

canteen *n.* flask, bottle, thermos, jug, can, skin.

canter *n.* amble, lope, trot, run, gallop, dogtrot.

canticle *n.* HYMN.

canto *n.* VERSE.

canvass *v.* examine, discuss, survey, scrutinize, consider, investigate, explore, contemplate, analyze, ventilate, dispute, sift. —*n.* survey, poll, examination, scrutiny, inquiry, overview, investigation, evaluation, enumeration, tally.

canyon *n.* gorge, ravine, gulch, chasm, cut, pass, valley, glen, gap, gully, arroyo.

cap *n.* **1** headdress, headgear, beret, beanie, skullcap, tam-o'-shanter, tuque, yarmulke. **2** top, lid, cover, dome, cowling, cowl, crown. —*v.* surpass, top off, crown, outdo, top, defeat, eclipse, outstrip, excel.

capability *n.* ability, capacity, competence, possibility, wherewithal, means, power, potentiality, potency, facility, proficiency.

capable *adj.* competent, able, qualified, fit, adequate, adroit, efficient, accomplished, suitable, skillful, adapted, gifted, fitted.
ant. maladroit, inept, inadequate, clumsy, ineffectual, incapable.

capacious *adj.* ROOMY.

capacitate *v.* QUALIFY.

capacity *n.* **1** volume, size, magnitude, compass, scope, range, extent, caliber. **2** power, aptitude, ability, capability, competence, potentiality, endowment, quality. **3** position, role, office, character, guise, function, post.

cape[1] *n.* point, promontory, ness, headland, spit, tongue, peninsula, chersonese.

cape[2] *n.* mantle, cloak, wrap, capote, poncho, pelisse, shawl, cover, blanket.

caper *n.* **1** skip, jump, leap, spring, gambol, prance, hop, caracole, romp, frisk, trip, bound. **2** prank, antic, escapade, adventure, dido, lark, frolic, capriccio, jape, trick, joke, revel, spree.

capital *n.* property, wealth, resources, principal, riches, money, assets, savings, reserves, funds. —*adj.* **1** chief, principal, foremost, prime, main, central, key, uppermost, predominant, major, leading. **2** excellent, first-rate, unequaled, superb, fine, choice, superior, perfect, supreme, matchless.

capitalist *n.* PLUTOCRAT.

capitalize on profit by, take advantage of, exploit, utilize, avail oneself of, turn to account, make capital of, trade on, cash in on, make hay with.

capitation *n.* TAX.

capitulate *v.* surrender, give in, yield, submit, acquiesce, give ground, comply, accede, relent, succumb, cede, defer, bow, quit, say uncle (*Slang*).

capitulation *n.* SURRENDER.

capriccio *n.* CAPER.

caprice *n.* impulse, whim, notion, conceit, crotchet, quirk, kink, peculiarity, vagary, fad, craze, humor, brain wave.

capricious *adj.* fickle, erratic, changeable, crotchety, inconstant, mercurial, skittish, giddy, fitful, frivolous, volatile, unstable, irresponsible, irresolute.
ant. steadfast, reliable, constant, unchanging, firm, regular.

capsize *v.* upset, overturn, keel over, tip, tip over, overset, upturn, turn turtle, roll, invert.

capsule *n.* pill, lozenge, troche, tablet, pellet, bolus, tabloid.

captain *n.* chief, leader, master, commander, head, principal, manager, skipper, governor, boss, foreman, chieftain. —*v.* command, lead, direct, control, supervise, manage, govern, head, administer, boss.

caption *n.* heading, title, head, superscription, legend, inscription, rubric.

captious *adj.* faultfinding, critical, censorious, carping, deprecating, nagging, caviling, disparaging, disapproving, querulous, hypercritical, biting, severe, nit-picking.
ant. appreciative, laudatory, complimentary, flattering, uncritical, approving.

captivate *v.* CHARM.

captivating *adj.* charming, fascinating, bewitching, seductive, taking, alluring, enthralling, enchanting, irresistible, attractive.
ant. unpleasant, repellent, off-putting, offensive, repulsive, disgusting.
captive *n.* prisoner, internee, bondman, thrall, hostage, convict, jailbird.
captivity *n.* RESTRAINT.
captor *n.* JAILER.
capture *v.* 1 seize, catch, grasp, arrest, apprehend, corner, snare, trap, take, collar. 2 attain, earn, gain, acquire, get, procure, secure, make, win. —*n.* possession, seizure, taking, catch, winning, apprehension, appropriation, arrest, occupation.
car *n.* 1 automobile, motorcar, motor, machine, limousine, jitney, jalopy. 2 coach, train, trolley, tram, streetcar, carriage (*Brit.*), rolling stock.
caravan *n.* company, procession, cavalcade, motorcade, train, wagon train, band, column, line, string.
caravansary *n.* INN.
carbon copy duplicate, facsimile, echo, match, twin, mirror image, counterpart, reflection, isomorph, homologue, spitting image, ringer (*Slang*).
ant. original, archetype, rarity, oddity, singularity, opposite.
carbonize *v.* BURN.
carcass *n.* corpse, cadaver, body.
card *n.* slip, pasteboard, credential, identification, certificate, record, ticket, calling card.
cardinal *adj.* prime, essential, principal, fundamental, vital, basic, key, intrinsic, chief, predominant, paramount, foremost, main, central.
ant. extraneous, secondary, insignificant, trivial, immaterial, irrelevant.
care *v.* be concerned, have regard, mind, heed. —*n.* 1 anxiety, concern, worry, solicitude, perplexity, trouble, apprehension, pressure, stress, burden. 2 attention, heed, regard, watchfulness, vigilance, interest, caution, carefulness. 3 charge, custody, keep, control, protection, ministra-

tion, management, supervision, responsibility.
careen *v.* lurch, sway, totter, reel, stumble, stagger, pitch, twist, yaw, cant.
career *n.* 1 lifework, profession, livelihood, métier, pursuit, occupation, calling, vocation, work, job. 2 course, passage, progress, orbit, development, march, advancement, ambit. —*v.* rush, run, speed, bolt, move, scramble, dash, sprint, course, race.
care for 1 protect, provide for, watch over, tend, look after, mind, guard, attend, foster. 2 love, be fond of, cherish, adore, prize, treasure, respect, like.
carefree *adj.* light-hearted, untroubled, secure, buoyant, jaunty, debonair, breezy, blithe, cheerful, lightsome, joyous, happy.
ant. heavy-hearted, careworn, harassed, gloomy, worried, melancholy.
careful *adj.* attentive, heedful, circumspect, cautious, alert, observant, guarded, prudent, scrupulous, thoughtful, painstaking, particular, meticulous, precise, accurate.
ant. careless, heedless, perfunctory, forgetful, reckless, neglectful.
careless *adj.* 1 untidy, slap-dash, slipshod, sloppy, slovenly, negligent, offhand, inaccurate. 2 unconcerned, rash, lax, irresponsible, inconsiderate, remiss, slack, forgetful, unheedful, unheeding, negligent.
ant. 1 neat, precise, careful, exact, accurate. 2 prudent, careful, wary, cautious, attentive.
caress *n.* pat, embrace, stroke, kiss, fondling, blandishment, stroking, squeeze, cuddle, buss, chuck. —*v.* fondle, embrace, cuddle, hug, squeeze, enfold, clasp, squeeze, pat, pet, buss, kiss, stroke.
caretaker *n.* custodian, watchman, super, supervisor, superintendent, janitor, handyman, maintenance man, concierge, attendant, guard, curator, steward, doorkeeper.

careworn *adj.* harassed, worried, weary, toilworn, haggard, dispirited, woebegone, dejected, troubled, bleak, tired.
ant. untroubled, carefree, sunny, vivacious, happy, cheerful.

cargo *n.* freight, lading, load, goods, shipment, consignment, payload, burden.

caricature *n.* travesty, parody, distortion, cartoon, takeoff, mockery, burlesque, satire, farce, lampoon. —*v.* travesty, ridicule, mock, take off, exaggerate, burlesque, parody, distort, satirize, lampoon.

carnage *n.* massacre, slaughter, holocaust, blood bath, butchery, pogrom, decimation, savagery, shambles, genocide, mass murder.

carnal *adj.* sensual, bodily, fleshly, sexual, animal, physical, corporeal, voluptuous, lustful, libidinous, worldly, mundane, profane.
ant. spiritual, intellectual, austere, ascetic, virginal, moral.

carnival *n.* festival, celebration, jamboree, festivity, revelry, kermess, field day, merrymaking, saturnalia, jubilee, feast.

carol *v.* warble, sing, trill, pipe, intone, descant, chirrup, croon. —*n.* song, ballad, noel, canticle, hymn, paean, motet.

carom *v.* GLANCE.

carousal *n.* CELEBRATION.

carouse *v.* revel, make merry, roister, wassail, skylark, celebrate, overindulge, drink, guzzle, quaff, tipple. —*n.* CELEBRATION.

carp *v.* nag, find fault, pick at, scold, complain, cavil, grumble, deplore, disparage, reproach, censure, fault.

carpet *n.* rug, mat, carpeting, matting, covering, padding, blanket. —*v.* cover, blanket, overlay, pad, shroud.

carping *adj.* CAPTIOUS.

carriage *n.* **1** conveyance, vehicle, rig, coach. **2** posture, bearing, air, stance, presence, deportment, demeanor, gait, comportment.

carry *v.* **1** transport, convey, bear, tote, haul, move, take, transmit, transfer, bring, schlep (*Slang*). **2** bear up, hold up, support, sustain, maintain, stand, suffer.

carry off ACHIEVE.

carry on continue, keep going, maintain, persevere, persist, endure, strive, retain, perpetuate, preserve, proceed.
ant. discontinue, terminate, give up, interrupt, cease, abandon.

carry out accomplish, carry through, complete, consummate, realize, achieve, fulfill, effect, see through, discharge, execute, perform.

cart *n.* wagon, truck, barrow, dray, pushcart, tumbrel, vehicle.

carte blanche discretion, blank check, free rein, free hand, liberty, authority, license, freedom.

carton *n.* container, box, case, package, casket, pack, chest.

cartoon *n.* caricature, sketch, takeoff, drawing, parody, travesty, funnies, comic strip.

carve *v.* cut, chisel, hew, sculpture, form, shape, fashion, whittle, tool, grave, engrave, incise, sculpt, chip.

cascade *n.* waterfall, cataract, fall, chute, torrent, rapids, outpouring, fountain, flood, flume. —*v.* tumble, plunge, descend, fall, pour, overflow, pitch, flood, spill.

case[1] *n.* **1** instance, example, question, dilemma, illustration, representation, exemplification, specimen, sample. **2** facts, situation, circumstance, position, argument, context. **3** patient, client, victim, applicant, problem, illness. **4** lawsuit, proceeding, dispute, cause, action, suit.

case[2] *n.* box, sheath, receptacle, holder, caddy, container, cover, capsule, casing, crate, trunk, chest, carton. —*v.* **1** encase, put away, pack, sheath, cover, stow, box, crate. **2** *Slang* look over, inspect, reconnoiter, investigate, size up, examine, survey.

case-hardened *adj.* CALLOUS.

case history RECORD.

cash *n.* currency, money, legal tender, coinage, funds, change, coin, specie.

cashier *v.* dismiss, discharge, drum out, expel, oust, remove, turn out, let go, release, bust (*Slang*).

cash in on GAIN.

casing *n.* cover, wrapper, jacket, sheath, envelope, covering, sheathing, coating, case, cocoon, coat, skin.

cask *n.* barrel, keg, vat, firkin, hogshead, butt, tub, puncheon, vessel, drum.

casket *n.* **1** coffin, sarcophagus, box, crate, receptacle. **2** container, case, caddy, canister, coffer, box, crate, receptacle.

Cassandra *n.* ALARMIST.

cast *v.* **1** throw, fling, hurl, dash, pitch, toss, heave, strew, sling, propel. **2** formulate, draw up, frame, embody, organize, express, materialize, devise, systematize, marshal. —*n.* **1** hurl, toss, fling, pitch, dash, heave, propulsion, projection, strewing. **2** mold, impression, pattern, shape, form, embodiment, replica, casting. **3** tinge, shade, complexion, air, appearance, semblance, look. **4** company, actors, players, troupe, performers, characters, dramatis personae.

cast about SEEK.

castaway *n.* outcast, pariah, derelict, beachcomber, deportee, exile, leper, stray, vagrant, vagabond, hobo, outlaw, renegade.

cast away discard, reject, dispose of, throw out, refuse, repulse, eject, oust, forswear, disclaim, jettison, scrap, shed, get rid of.

caste *n.* class, station, status, rank, standing, prestige, stratum, lineage, sphere, grade, position, condition, estate.

castigate *v.* punish, chastise, berate, chasten, scold, correct, censure, admonish, reprimand, discipline, scourge, smite. —**ant.** excuse, pardon, indulge, condone, absolve, spare.

castle *n.* palace, mansion, stronghold, citadel, villa, chateau, manor, alcazar, keep.

castoff *n.* reject, discard, refuse, debris, jetsam, detritus, scrap, trash, rubbish, garbage, leavings, flotsam, redundancy.

cast off shed, get rid of, discard, jettison, throw out, cast away, reject, dispose of, oust, eject, disclaim, repulse.

castrate *v.* **1** geld, emasculate, eunuchize, unsex, unman, caponize. **2** spay, unsex. **3** devitalize, weaken, emasculate, incapacitate, eviscerate, unman, disable, debilitate, enfeeble.

casual *adj.* **1** chance, accidental, fortuitous, involuntary, unexpected, haphazard, random. **2** irregular, informal, occasional, careless, haphazard, offhand. **3** nonchalant, unconcerned, cool, calm, blasé, careless, indiferent, apathetic. —**ant.** **1** intentional, planned, predetermined, ordained, ordered. **2** formal, ceremonious, precise, orderly, punctilious. **3** involved, concerned, interested, engaged, active.

casualty *n.* victim, sufferer, loss, fatality, martyr.

cataclysm *n.* upheaval, disaster, convulsion, calamity, catastrophe, blow, misfortune, scourge, debacle, deluge, destruction, devastation.

catalog *n.* list, index, register, inventory, roster, roll, schedule, directory, record, bulletin, syllabus, calendar. —*v.* list, index, record, post, tabulate, enumerate, enter, register, note, schedule, classify, order, file, inventory.

catalogue *n.*, *v.* CATALOG.

catalyst *n.* stimulus, spur, trigger, sparkplug, fuel, goad, impetus, instigator, accelerator, activator.

catapult *v.* hurtle, plunge, pitch, fling, propel, hurl, toss, throw, rush, fly, spin.

catastrophe *n.* misfortune, disaster, calamity, debacle, mishap, blow, distress, scourge, hardship, ruin, reverse, cataclysm, tragedy.

catcall *n.* boo, hoot, heckling, whistle, howl, hiss, jeer, gibe, Bronx cheer (*Slang*), raspberry (*Slang*).

catch *v.* **1** take, seize, capture, entrap, ensnare, grasp, clench, grab, arrest. **2** see, apprehend, perceive, grasp, understand, take in, follow. **3** surprise, detect, discover, find out, disclose, expose, reveal, unmask. **4** contract, incur, acquire, come down with, get, develop. —*n.* **1** seizure, capture, apprehension, hold, grasp, grab, clutch. **2** prize, bag, take, booty, reward, gain, spoils, pickings, haul, plunder. **3** snag, gimmick, joker, ruse, trick, hoax, irony, kicker (*Slang*).

catching *adj.* infectious, contagious, communicable, taking, pestilential, inoculable, infective.

catch on understand, see, grasp, fathom, see through, comprehend, find out, figure out, apprehend, solve, wise up (*Slang*).

catch up overtake, gain on, overhaul, come up to, approach, run down, reach, attain.
   ant. fall behind, lose ground.

catchword *n.* shibboleth, formula, slogan, refrain, byword, battle cry, tag, watchword, password, cliché.

catchy *adj.* interesting, infectious, beguiling, captivating, catching, provocative, attractive, enchanting, fascinating, fetching, haunting, obsessive.
   ant. dull, vapid, ordinary, neutral, common, unremarkable.

catechize *v.* **1** INSTRUCT. **2** QUESTION.

categorical *adj.* absolute, unequivocal, unqualified, independent, unmitigated, implicit, positive, unconditional, unmistakable, inalienable, ineluctable.
   ant. arguable, nonessential, contingent, adventitious, dependent, qualified.

categorize *v.* classify, denominate, designate, catalog, pigeonhole, class, assign, rank, brand, tag, describe, name.

category *n.* class, division, group, department, rank, denomination, kind, sort, grade, grouping, heading, classification, order.

cater *v.* **1** provision, victual, purvey, feed, provide for, arrange, organize. **2** pander, indulge, gratify, humor, pamper, coddle, wait on, minister.

caterwaul *v.* screech, squawk, mewl, yowl, cry, meow, squeal, shriek, scream, hoot, yell, holler, whine.

catharsis *n.* purification, lustration, cleansing, renewal, release, purging, purgation, outlet, abreaction.

catholic *adj.* universal, general, broadminded, eclectic, comprehensive, all-inclusive, liberal, broad, impartial, indulgent.
   ant. sectarian, narrow-minded, restricted, circumscribed, exclusive, cliquish.

catnap *n.*, *v.* DOZE.

cat's-paw *n.* ACCOMPLICE.

catty *adj.* malicious, spiteful, mischievous, nasty, ill-disposed, ill-natured, treacherous, invidious, rancorous, venomous, virulent.
   ant. amiable, generous, well-intentioned, benevolent, charitable, kindly.

caucus *n.* conclave, powwow, conference, hearing, council, parley, synod, deliberations, consultation, get-together, meeting, assembly.

causal *adj.* teleological, etiological, formative, germinal, causative, generative, determinative, determinantal, creative, originative, productive, conducive.

causation *n.* CAUSE.

cause *n.* **1** antecedent, root, origin, mainspring, determinant, genesis, inducement, stimulus, etiology, causation. **2** aim, motive, purpose, reason, objective, object, motivation, teleology. **3** principle, enterprise, movement, justification, inspiration, tenet, aim. —*v.* effect, bring about, produce, create, give rise to, generate, lead to, result in, compel, induce, evoke.

caustic *adj.* **1.** corrosive, gnawing, destructive, mordant, erosive, acrid, wasting. **2** sarcastic, biting, brusque, scathing, harsh, acrimonious, stinging, sardonic, bitter.

ant. 1 neutral, inactive, inert. **2** mild, gentle, soothing, bland, suave.

caution *n.* **1** care, prudence, wariness, heed, watchfulness, vigilance, circumspection, concern, attention, thought. **2** admonition, warning, caveat, alert, alarm, tip-off. —*v.* warn, alert, forewarn, admonish, alarm, exhort, forebode, portend, tip off.

ant. *n.* **1** neglect, negligence, indiscretion, rashness, imprudence, carelessness. *v.* lull, soothe, calm, pacify tranquilize.

cautious *adj.* wary, prudent, careful, discreet, circumspect, heedful, chary, guarded, alert, watchful, vigilant, attentive, deliberate.

ant. heedless, rash, negligent, careless, daring, reckless.

cavalcade *n.* procession, parade, march-past, cortege, caravan, file, train, column, retinue, company.

cavalier *adj.* offhand, informal, free and easy, unconstrained, unconcerned, curt, grand, arrogant, lordly, disdainful, haughty, lofty, supercilious. —*n.* horseman, knight, trooper, rider, cavalryman, caballero.

ant. *adj.* attentive, obliging, courteous, unpretentious, considerate, humble.

cave *n.* grotto, cavern, chamber, tunnel, pit, cavity, hole, hollow.

caveat *n.* CAUTION.

cave-in *n.* collapse, falling in, subsidence, crash, breakdown, rockfall, landslide, implosion.

cave in 1 collapse, fall in, crumple, tumble, give way, implode. **2** give up, yield, retreat, break down, go to pieces, fall apart.

ant. 2 resist, fight, bear up, recover, make a stand, rally.

cavernous *adj.* spacious, hollow, yawning, vast, roomy, huge, sunken, cavelike, abysmal, profound.

cavil *v.* quibble, peck at, pick, carp, belittle, nit-pick, jibe, nag, object, complain, find fault, disparage, discredit.

cavity *n.* hollow, depression, crater, burrow, pocket, dent, hole, niche, space, gap, void, vacuole.

cavort *v.* **1** *of humans:* act up, frolic, romp, horse around, carry on, cut up (*Slang*). **2** *of horses:* prance, paw, caper, caracole, bound, frisk, buck.

cease *v.* leave off, discontinue, stop, end, break off, desist, conclude, terminate, finish, quit, halt, abstain, refrain.

ant. start, begin, continue, carry on, resume, persist.

cease-fire *n.* truce, suspension, remission, lull, stay, respite, intermission, interruption, pause, halt, breather, white flag.

ceaseless *adj.* unending, continuous, perpetual, unceasing, everlasting, eternal, endless, constant, incessant, unremitting, unrelenting, interminable, protracted, enduring.

ant. spasmodic, fitful, fleeting, ephemeral, transitory, temporary.

cede *v.* yield, give up, surrender, hand over, transfer, renounce, resign, vouchsafe, give in, capitulate, concede.

ceiling *n.* maximum, limit, top, control, check, damper, restraint, restriction.

celebrate *v.* **1** observe, commemorate, keep, remember, solemnize. **2** extol, honor, praise, eulogize, glorify, exalt, drink to, toast.

celebrated *adj.* famous, renowned, prominent, popular, honored, eminent, illustrious, notable, distinguished, outstanding, noted, lionized, well-known, important.

ant. unknown, obscure, insignificant, unimportant, nondescript, inglorious.

celebration *n.* **1** observance, commemoration, solemnization, remembrance, keeping. **2** ceremony, spectacle, pageant, jubilee, festival, gala, festivities, rites, party, revel, revelry, carouse, carousal.

celebrity *n.* **1** star, notable, personage, personality, bigwig, name, lion, luminary. **2** renown, fame, note, eminence, prominence, distinction, prestige, popularity, standing.
ant. 2 obscurity, discredit, oblivion, disgrace, disregard, privacy.

celerity *n.* speed, rapidity, quickness, fleetness, dispatch, haste, alacrity, swiftness, briskness, expedition, velocity.
ant. sloth, leisureliness, sluggishness, deliberation, dawdling, indolence.

celestial *adj.* heavenly, divine, ethereal, empyrean, sublime, angelic, otherworldly, godlike, supernal, Elysian, paradisaic.

celibate *adj.* unmarried, abstinent, chaste, virginal, continent, unwed, single, pure, virtuous, virgin.
ant. profligate, dissolute, promiscuous, wanton.

cell *n.* compartment, niche, chamber, nook, den, stall, closet, crib, booth, box, manger.

cellar *n.* basement, vault, storeroom.

cement *v.* seal, strengthen, weld, bind, fuse, fix, solidify, set, stabilize, merge, unite, join.
ant. dissolve, separate, liquidate, loosen, tear apart, destroy.

cemetery *n.* graveyard, churchyard, potter's field, necropolis, catacomb.

censor *v.* expurgate, bowdlerize, blue-pencil, excise, veto, suppress, delete, erase, black out, blip.

censorious *adj.* critical, carping, disparaging, abusive, complaining, hypercritical, faultfinding, derogatory, querulous, severe, captious, condemnatory.
ant. uncritical, laudatory, encouraging, endorsing, praising, flattering.

censurable *adj.* DISGRACEFUL.

censure *n.* condemnation, blame, disapproval, admonition, rebuke, reproach, stricture, invective, reprimand, castigation, criticism. —*v.* condemn, rebuke, denounce, criticize, judge, castigate, admonish, reprove, chide, blame, reprimand, reproach, upbraid.
ant. *n.* praise, approval, endorsement, sanction, admiration, support. *v.* praise, approve, encourage, support, admire, confirm.

center *n.* **1** middle, midpoint, pivot, axis, focus, focal point, median. **2** heart, nucleus, kernel, core, hub, focus, pith, marrow. **3** middle-of-the-roader, moderate, centrist. —*v.* concentrate, focus, collect, converge, gather, unite, meet, cluster, congregate.

centerpiece *n.* feature, highlight, keynote, exhibit, attraction, drawing-card, spectacle, display, focus, cynosure, pivot.

central *adj.* **1** middle, interior, axial, pivotal, focal, mid, median, mean, halfway. **2** dominant, essential, crucial, key, fundamental, primary, basic, principal.
ant. 1 peripheral, outer, external, extraneous, terminal, marginal, distal. **2** ancillary, secondary, inferior, subordinate, peripheral, subsidiary.

centralize *v.* consolidate, focus, concentrate, amalgamate, coalesce, condense, center, focalize, converge, join, meet.
ant. scatter, dispel, disperse, separate, diverge.

cerebral *adj.* intellectual, intelligent, thoughtful, reflective, contemplative, highbrow, mental, brainy, scholarly, thinking, speculative, analytical.

cerebrate *v.* THINK.

ceremonial *adj.* ritual, formal, ceremonious, solemn, stately, punctilious, ritualistic, pompous, stereotyped, lofty, conventional, routine.

ceremonious *adj.* formal, polite, ceremonial, ritual, meticulous, punctilious, stiff, correct, precise, starchy, prim, affected, conventional.
ant. informal, negligent, familiar, irregular, rude, careless.

ceremony *n.* **1** rite, observance, celebration, ceremonial, pageant, solemnity, function, service, form. **2** formality, civility, propriety, punctilio, preciseness, decorum, conformity, nicety.

certain *adj.* **1** true, unquestionable, conclusive, undoubted, authoritative, incontrovertible, unmistakable, indubitable, definite. **2** convinced, sure, confident, assured, undoubting, satisfied, positive, determined, fixed. **ant. 1** false, doubtful, questionable, inconclusive. **2** skeptical, undecided, unconvinced, open.

certainly *adv.* surely, doubtless, indeed, really, assuredly, positively, unquestionably, decidedly, categorically, absolutely, definitely, inescapably, verily, exactly.

certainty *n.* **1** certitude, conviction, confidence, faith, trust, belief, assurance, knowledge. **2** fact, reality, actuality, verity, truth, datum. **ant. 1** doubt, skepticism, reservation, disbelief. **2** illusion, dream, hallucination, fancy, chimera.

certificate *n.* document, permit, validation, authorization, instrument, credential, warranty, testimonial, affidavit, deed, warrant, voucher, diploma.

certify *v.* guarantee, vouch for, attest, authenticate, witness, notarize, endorse, validate, confirm, approve, sanction, accredit.

certitude *n.* CERTAINTY.

cessation *n.* ceasing, stop, pause, interruption, standstill, suspension, hiatus, arrest, stay, blockage, termination, hitch, completion, quietus. **ant.** continuation, extension, persistence, protraction, prolongation, perpetuation.

cession *n.* SURRENDER.

cesspool *n.* sewer, sink, sump, cloaca, drain, conduit, main, dump, septic tank, sewerage.

chafe *v.* **1** abrade, inflame, excoriate, scrape, scratch, scrub, fray. **2** irritate, annoy, harass, irk, aggravate, exasperate, nettle, gall, torment, molest.

chaff[1] *n.* refuse, rubbish, waste, debris, sweepings, junk, leavings, trash, rubble, litter, dross, shoddy.

chaff[2] *v.* RIDICULE.

chaffer *v.* haggle, bargain, negotiate, dicker, horse-trade, deal, wrangle, barter, trade, truck, cavil, stickle.

chafing *adj.* GALLING.

chagrin *n.* distress, embarrassment, mortification, dismay, resentment, vexation, frustration, confusion, shame, humiliation, disgruntlement, despair. **ant.** contentment, satisfaction, gladness, gratification, delight, triumph.

chagrined *adj.* mortified, embarrassed, humiliated, disconcerted, confused, dismayed, vexed, abashed, discountenanced, put out. **ant.** delighted, flattered, proud, pleased, glad, undismayed.

chain *n.* **1** links, fob, braid, cable, rope, string, tie, lace, leash. **2** series, train, sequence, succession, suite, row, string, catena. —*v.* fasten, shackle, fetter, bind, enchain, leash, strap, hamper.

chains *n.* **1** bondage, captivity, servitude, slavery, thralldom, subjugation, duress, yoke. **2** shackles, fetters, trammels, irons, manacles, bonds, gyves, handcuffs.

chair *n.* **1** seat, stool, throne, bench. **2** office, professorship, chairmanship, appointment, installation. —*v.* **1** install, seat, inaugurate, induct, enthrone. **2** preside, moderate, guide, manage, direct, lead.

chairman *n.* speaker, moderator, chair, master of ceremonies, director, supervisor, executive, manager, administrator, arbiter, chairwoman, chairperson.

chairperson *n.* CHAIRMAN.

chalk up score, attain, achieve, record, note, tally, log, register, obtain, gain, get, earn, win.

chalky *adj.* **1** cretaceous, crumbly, friable, dusty, powdery. **2** pale, wan, ashen, white, bleached, pallid.

challenge *v.* **1** dare, confront, defy, threaten, accost, beard. **2** question, dispute, object to, query, contest, doubt, impugn. **3** stimulate, excite, arouse, animate, spur, stir. —*n.* **1** dare, defiance, confrontation, threat, summons, gauntlet. **2** objection, protest, charge, demurrer, countercharge, denunciation. **3** stimulus, spur, provocation, lure, impetus, incentive.

chamber *n.* room, bedroom, boudoir, bedchamber, cubicle, alcove, cell, anteroom, nook, apartment, closet.

champ *v.* munch, chew, crunch, gnaw, gnash, nibble, grind, ruminate, browse, bite.

champion *n.* **1** victor, winner, conqueror, leader, master, paragon, laureate, nonpareil. **2** defender, protector, guardian, backer, advocate, patron, protagonist, supporter. —*v.* defend, stand up for, advocate, plead for, uphold, sustain, justify, guard, assist, support, back up.

championship *n.* **1** SUPREMACY. **2** PROMOTION.

chance *n.* **1** luck, providence, fortune, cast, fate, toss-up. **2** probability, likelihood, odds, possibility, tendency. **3** accident, contingency, fortuity, hap, happenstance. **4** opportunity, occasion, opening, scope, liberty. **5** risk, hazard, peril, jeopardy, danger. —*v.* **1** happen, occur, transpire, befall, arrive, take place, result. **2** risk, wager, hazard, speculate, gamble, dare, venture, bet. —*adj.* accidental, random, unforeseen, casual, fortuitous, incidental.

chancy *adj.* risky, dicey, uncertain, speculative, iffy, venturesome, problematical, unreliable, mutable, precarious, dangerous, hazardous. **ant.** certain, sure, infallible, inevitable, cut-and-dried, fixed.

change *v.* **1** alter, vary, transform, modify, diversify, modulate, mutate, metamorphose. **2** exchange, substitute, replace, interchange, alternate, trade, swap, convert. —*n.* **1** alteration, modification, metamorphosis, transition, transposition, shift, inno-

vation, mutation. **2** novelty, switch, turnabout, difference, variation, surprise, diversion, break, variety.

changeable *adj.* inconstant, unsteady, wavering, uncertain, variable, vacilating, mercurial, temperamental, protean, labile, capricious, skittish, erratic, fickle, fitful. **ant.** stable, reliable, constant, inflexible, steady, persistent.

changeless *adj.* CONSTANT.

change of life climacteric, menopause.

channel *n.* groove, tube, passage, trench, furrow, artery, duct, conduit, canal, race, sluice. —*v.* convey, conduct, pipe, direct, steer, lead, siphon, funnel.

chant *n.* song, recitative, plainsong, hymn, antiphon, melody, tune, trill, lilt, croon, warble. —*v.* intone, sing, cantillate, vocalize, hymn, descant.

chaos *n.* disorder, confusion, turmoil, pandemonium, tumult, disorganization, uproar, ferment, agitation, commotion, furor. **ant.** order, harmony, concord, system, calm, tranquillity.

chaotic *adj.* disordered, deranged, tempestuous, confused, tumultuous, turbulent, upset, muddled, formless, turbid, topsy-turvy, anarchic, riotous, raging. **ant.** orderly, tranquil, methodical, systematic, neat, harmonious.

chap[1] *n.* fellow, lad, man, person, guy, individual, customer, character, brother, boy, gink (*Slang*), cove (*Brit. Slang*).

chap[2] *v.* redden, roughen, chafe, crack, split, fissure, break, gash, slit open, craze.

chaperon *n.* matron, duenna, escort, attendant, companion, guardian, governess. —*v.* escort, attend, guard, shepherd, safeguard, protect, accompany, care for, watch over.

chapter *n.* **1** division, section, passage, part, sequence, topic. **2** episode, phase, stage, period, era, age.

char *v.* BURN.

character *n.* **1** type, nature, makeup,

flavor, quality, composition, personality, temperament, essence. 2 trait, characteristic, feature, attribute, property. 3 reputation, status, repute, prestige, integrity, position, standing. 4 fellow, person, man, guy, clown, eccentric. 5 figure, mark, sign, cipher, emblem, insignia, letter, logo.

characteristic *adj.* typical, distinguishing, peculiar, distinctive, illustrative, singular, idiosyncratic, individual, special, specific. —*n.* feature, trait, idiosyncrasy, peculiarity, singularity, quality, attribute, mark, lineament, property, cachet.

ant. *adj.* atypical, aberrant, deviant, unusual, exceptional, anomalous.

characterize *v.* 1 describe, portray, label, tag, name, depict, represent, delineate. 2 distinguish, mark, differentiate, identify, specify, signalize.

charade *n.* PRETENSE.

charge *v.* 1 load, burden, encumber, oppress, afflict, tax. 2 accuse, indict, blame, reproach, impeach, incriminate. 3 attack, assault, assail, set on, strike, close in on. —*n.* 1 care, custody, concern, responsibility, ward, encumbrance, management. 2 instruction, command, order, bidding, direction, regulation, demand. 3 accusation, complaint, reproach, indictment, blame, tirade. 4 price, cost, expense, value, expenditure, amount.

charisma *n.* magnetism, glamor, presence, allure, personality, fascination, interest, attractiveness, elegance, charm, polish, color.

charismatic *adj.* MAGNETIC.

charitable *adj.* 1 generous, bountiful, benevolent, liberal, open-handed, unstinting, eleemosynary, philanthropic. 2 tolerant, forgiving, benevolent, kindly, magnanimous, indulgent, lenient, humane.

ant. 1 mean, stingy, close, miserly, niggardly, penurious. 2 intolerant, malevolent, cruel, harsh, stern, unkind.

charity *n.* 1 alms, assistance, hand-out, offering, donation, welfare, dole, relief, grant. 2 kindness, good will, altruism, generosity, grace, favor, mitzvah, philanthropy. 3 tolerance, leniency, compassion, humanity, mercy, sufferance, clemency.

charlatan *n.* quack, humbug, fraud, mountebank, fake, trickster, cheat, confidence man, impostor, deceiver, swindler, hypocrite.

charm *v.* attract, delight, enchant, bewitch, bemuse, allure, fascinate, captivate, magnetize, transport, entice, enamor, please, catch. —*n.* 1 enchantment, attraction, magnetism, fascination, allurement, delightfulness. 2 spell, magic, witchery, incantation, sorcery.

ant. *v.* frighten, repulse, irritate, repel, anger, offend.

charming *adj.* enchanting, fascinating, bewitching, entrancing, captivating, delightful, winsome, engaging, alluring, lovely, attractive, pleasant, charismatic.

ant. repellent, unpleasant, ugly, offensive, uncouth, unattractive.

charred *adj.* scorched, carbonized, blackened, singed, seared, burned, calcined, incinerated.

chart *n.* figure, diagram, table, graph, plan, blueprint, sketch, tabulation, outline, visual aid. —*v.* outline, tabulate, plot, draft, draw up, map out, plan, shape, design, sketch.

charter *n.* permit, license, franchise, authority, document, instrument, compact, covenant. —*v.* hire, rent, lease, engage, let, employ, commission.

chary *adj.* 1 cautious, wary, prudent, careful, uneasy, shrewd, suspicious, circumspect. 2 thrifty, sparing, careful, parsimonious, stingy, frugal, niggardly, close-fisted, close.

ant. 1 reckless, heedless, negligent, precipitate, rash. 2 liberal, open-handed, generous, bountiful, wasteful.

chase *v.* 1 pursue, hunt, follow, trail,

course, run after, shadow, seek, track, dog. **2** drive away, dispel, repulse, disperse, repel, scatter, beat back, evict, cast out. —*n.* **1** pursuit, race, search, quest, trail, striving, following. **2** prey, game, quarry, victim.

chasm *n.* **1** gorge, gap, void, abyss, crater, pit, gulch, ravine, fissure, cleft. **2** difference, divergence, disagreement, separation, alienation, rift, split.

chaste *adj.* **1** celibate, abstinent, virginal, abstemious, continent, vestal, virtuous. **2** pure, modest, decent, innocent, wholesome, righteous.

ant. 1 lewd, wanton, immoral, profligate, promiscuous. **2** indecorous, immodest, corrupt, depraved, shameless.

chasten *v.* **1** discipline, chastise, punish, penalize, castigate, scourge, rebuke, correct. **2** moderate, soften, temper, restrain.

ant. 1 gratify, pamper, humor, mollycoddle, indulge, cater to.

chastise *v.* punish, scold, whip, lash, castigate, rebuke, upbraid, berate, discipline, chasten.

chastity *n.* virtue, abstinence, virginity, abstention, continence, purity, modesty, sinlessness, innocence, celibacy, restraint.

ant. lewdness, license, lust, lechery, adultery, fornication.

chat *v.* converse, prate, chatter, gossip, palaver, visit, confabulate, confab, babble, prattle, chin, chew the fat (*Slang*), chew the rag (*Slang*). —*n.* talk, conversation, tête-à-tête, prattle, gossip, chit-chat, visit, babble, confab, chatter, palaver.

chateau *n.* CASTLE.

chattel *n.* possession, effect, belonging, asset, holding, property, equipment, accoutrement.

chatter *v.* prattle, babble, prate, gossip, jabber, confabulate, gabble, blabber, blather, ramble, blab.

chatterbox *n.* GOSSIP.

chatty *adj.* TALKATIVE.

cheap *adj.* **1** inexpensive, cut-rate, low-priced, reasonable, moderate, reduced, dirt-cheap. **2** easy, effortless, unearned, facile, undeserved. **3** shoddy, inferior, spurious, tawdry, sham, imitation, specious, two-bit (*Slang*). **4** vulgar, low, contemptible, despicable, scurvy, sordid. **5** stingy, tight, mean, close, miserly, grudging.

ant. 1 costly, dear, expensive, high-priced. **2** hard-won, difficult, costly. **3** first-rate, excellent, superior, quality. **4** elegant, polished, refined. **5** generous, liberal, bountiful.

cheapen *v.* DEPRECIATE.

cheapskate *n. Slang* MISER.

cheat *v.* defraud, deceive, delude, trick, cozen, swindle, bilk, overreach, victimize, hoodwink, rook, shortchange, bamboozle, mislead, fleece, skin, take (*Slang*). —*n.* **1** swindle, hoax, deception, stratagem, imposture, trick, fraud, sham. **2** trickster, pretender, bilk, swindler, rogue, deceiver, sharper, impostor, spiv (*Brit.*).

check *n.* **1** stop, halt, block, barrier, stopper, hindrance, obstacle, checkmate. **2** control, restraint, curb, damper, rein, harness, clog. **3** test, audit, examination, inquiry, review, scrutiny. —*v.* **1** restrain, stop, curb, stanch, control, obstruct, rebuke, rebuff. **2** investigate, test, scrutinize, look into, examine, verify. **3** mark, tally, tick off, record, score, notch, note, register. **4** accord, agree, correspond, tally, fit, conform.

checkered *adj.* varied, diversified, variegated, irregular, changeful, fluctuating, mutable, unsettled, uneven, many-sided.

ant. uniform, limited, even-tenored, monotonous, unvaried, uneventful.

check in register, enroll, enter, arrive, report, punch in, start, begin, sign in.

check into investigate, scrutinize, follow up, inspect, probe, explore, sift, research, pursue, examine, query.

checkmate *n.* CHECK.

check out LOOK INTO.

cheek *n.* INSOLENCE.

cheeky *adj.* impudent, brazen, saucy, bold, pert, forward, rude, impertinent, insolent, insulting, flippant, audacious.
  ant. mannerly, modest, retiring, respectful, decorous, meek.

cheer *n.* **1** shout, applause, plaudit, acclamation, hurrah, huzza, encouragement, yell, bravo. **2** cheerfulness, geniality, gaiety, animation, jollity, vivacity, merriment, liveliness. —*v.* **1** comfort, solace, invigorate, encourage, gladden, cheer up. **2** applaud, salute, hail, acclaim, laud.
  ant. *n.* **1** catcall, hoot, boo, heckling, raspberry (*Slang*). **2** gloom, dejection, dullness, sadness, gravity, seriousness. *v.* **1** depress, dishearten, sadden, oppress.

cheerful *adj.* joyous, happy, cheery, sprightly, merry, blithe, buoyant, gay, joyful, lighthearted, sunny, glad, spirited, optimistic.
  ant. glum, dour, gloomy, morose, pessimistic, dejected.

cheerless *adj.* bleak, gloomy, dismal, melancholy, miserable, joyless, desolate, mournful, sad, cold, austere, grim.
  ant. cheerful, lighthearted, sunny, bright, warm, joyous.

cheer up revive, rally, enliven, encourage, exhilarate, brighten, jolly, elate, comfort, gladden, take heart, cheer.
  ant. depress, deject, sadden, weary, oppress, dishearten.

cheery *adj.* CHEERFUL.

cheesy *adj.* SHODDY.

chef-d'oeuvre *n.* MASTERPIECE.

chemistry *n.* PROCESS.

cherish *v.* care for, hold dear, nurture, value, foster, treasure, prize, sustain, protect, support, appreciate, indulge.
  ant. neglect, slight, despise, spurn, forsake, abandon.

cherubic *adj.* ANGELIC.

chest *n.* **1** thorax, breast, trunk, bosom, bust. **2** box, casket, crate, case, carton, cabinet, bureau, container, bin, coffer.

chestnut *n.* CLICHÉ

chesty *adj.* COCKY.

chew *v.* masticate, crunch, gnaw, ruminate, munch, champ, grind, nibble, chaw.

chew out *Slang* scold, reprimand, dress down, berate, censure, chide, upbraid, rebuke, reprehend, admonish, blame, reproach, reprove.

chew the fat *Slang* CHAT.

chew the rag *Slang* CHAT.

chic *adj.* STYLISH.

chicanery *n.* trickery, deception, trick, dodge, fraud, subterfuge, sophistry, cunning, guile, feint, hocus-pocus, fake.

chichi *adj.* STYLISH.

chicken *n., adj.* SISSY.

chicken-hearted *adj.* timid, cowardly, faint-hearted, pusillanimous, craven, timorous, retiring, weak, afraid, apprehensive, fearful, diffident.
  ant. bold, plucky, courageous, brave, stout-hearted, daring.

chide *v.* scold, reprove, reprimand, admonish, criticize, censure, berate, upbraid, reproach, rebuke, castigate, blame, find fault, condemn.

chief *n.* leader, ruler, head, director, principal, manager, master, captain, commander, boss. —*adj.* principal, highest, paramount, prime, supreme, top-level, foremost, central, greatest, first, number-one, cardinal, main.
  ant. *n.* subordinate, servant, underling, follower. *adj.* lowest, least, last, smallest, slightest.

chiefly *adv.* generally, mostly, mainly, primarily, principally, especially, foremost, above all, eminently, peculiarly, preeminently, first.
  ant. slightly, minimally, secondarily, partially, least, lastly.

chieftain *n.* leader, chief, ruler, headman, potentate, lord, monarch, hetman, godfather, bellwether.

child *n.* **1** youngster, minor, juvenile, toddler, tot, tyke, kid, kiddy, moppet, baby, girl, boy, tad, offspring. **2** innocent, ingenue, naif, natural, retardate.

childbirth *n.* BIRTH.

childhood *n.* YOUTH.

childish *adj.* immature, petty, puerile, babyish, infantile, juvenile, foolish, trivial, silly, senseless, stupid.
ant. mature, adult, grown-up, sensible, wise.

childlike *adj.* innocent, naive, artless, unfledged, simple, trustful, tender, dependent, credulous, inexperienced.
ant. sophisticated, worldly-wise, experienced, independent.

chill *n.* **1** coldness, chilliness, frigidity, shivers, coolness. **2** discouragement, depression, hopelessness, despondency, damping, despair, wet blanket.

chilly *adj.* **1** cold, frigid, clammy, wintry, gelid, icy, nippy, sharp, cool. **2** unfriendly, haughty, hostile, cool, stiff, condescending, forbidding, indifferent.
ant. 1 warm, summery, balmy, clement, sultry. **2** friendly, cordial, hospitable, warm-hearted, generous.

chime *v.* ring, sound, peal, jingle, strike, tinkle, toll, bong, ting, clang, clangor.

chime in 1 harmonize, agree, jibe, match, coincide, blend, correspond, accord, fit in with, concur, cooperate, square, reciprocate, reinforce. **2** interject, interrupt, interpose, break in, interpolate.
ant. 1 contradict, be at odds with, diverge, conflict, disagree, differ from.

chimera *n.* fancy, dream, will-o'-the-wisp, phantasmagoria, delusion, vagary, fantasy, ignis fatuus, illusion, daydream, specter, snare.

chimes *n.* **1** carillon, bells, gong, tocsin, peal. **2** ringing, dingdong, peal, change, tocsin, angelus.

chin *v.* CHAT.

china *n.* porcelain, chinaware, dishes, crockery, pottery, earthenware, ceramics.

chink *n.* crack, crevice, cleft, fissure, hole, aperture, cranny, cut, gap, break, slit, fault, flaw.

chintzy *adj.* tacky, cheap, dowdy, frumpy, sleazy, shabby, frowzy, unstylish, seedy, tawdry, meretricious, schlock (*Slang*).
ant. elegant, fashionable, stylish, chic, expensive, smashing.

chip *n.* **1** fragment, piece, scrap, shard, cut, crack, break, fracture, flake, flaw, fault, sliver, bit, mark, dent. **2** disk, counter, wafer, token, coin.
—*v.* crack, break, fracture, cut, sliver, slice, pare, shatter, fragment, whittle, nick, notch, splinter, damage.

chip in contribute, participate, share, go halves, go Dutch, subscribe, donate, ante (*Slang*).

chipper *adj.* cheerful, brisk, lively, jaunty, carefree, sprightly, energetic, lighthearted, zippy, high-spirited, frisky, spry, breezy, peppy (*Slang*), up (*Slang*).
ant. lethargic, sluggish, low, careworn, exhausted, downhearted, sad.

chirography *n.* PENMANSHIP.

chirp *v.* tweet, trill, warble, cheep, chirrup, sing, peep, lilt, pipe.

chirrup *v.* CHIRP.

chisel *v.* **1** cut, engrave, carve, hew, shape, incise, model, delineate, sculpt, form, fashion, contrive, tool, groove. **2** cheat, swindle, finagle, cadge, sponge, freeload, fleece, rook, mulct, gyp, defraud.

chit-chat *n.* chat, gossip, gab, talk, chatter, small talk, prattle, tête-à-tête, causerie, conversation, kaffeeklatsch, yak (*Slang*).

chivalrous *adj.* gallant, courteous, courtly, brave, honorable, heroic, valorous, romantic, quixotic, adventurous, noble, well-bred.
ant. churlish, rude, cowardly, dishonorable, timid.

chivalry *n.* GALLANTRY.

chivy *v.* harass, hound, harry, torment, haze, rag, bully, pester, badger, bother, vex, irritate, irk, chafe, fret, annoy.
ant. soothe, calm, gratify, appease, please.

chock-a-block *adj.* PACKED.

chock-full *adj.* brimming, overflowing, replete, luxuriant, crammed, stuffed, packed, abundant, plentiful, loaded, bursting, copious, teeming, solid, dense, chock-a-block, laden.
ant. sparse, thin, inadequate, wanting, devoid.

choice *n.* 1 selection, pick, preference, alternative, culling, choosing, discrimination. 2 *the right to choose:* option, alternative, possibility, vote, election, decision, selectivity. —*adj.* excellent, select, elite, special, prime, superior, A-one, uncommon, best, preferred, first-rate, first-class, exceptional, top-drawer.
ant. *adj.* common, ordinary, everyday, usual, average, mediocre, run-of-the-mill.

choke *v.* 1 strangle, garrote, throttle, smother, suffocate, stifle, asphyxiate, gag. 2 suppress, repress, obstruct, close up, retard, dam, clog, glut, overfill, gorge, flood, check, constrict, occlude, cramp.
ant. 2 open, unstop, ease, clear, stimulate.

choke up falter, stammer, gasp, sob, sputter, splutter, tremble, fumble, mumble.

choler *n.* ANGER.

choleric *adj.* ANGRY.

choose *v.* 1 select, pick, elect, nominate, fancy, espouse, embrace, point to, single out, separate, settle upon, eliminate, isolate, sort out. 2 wish, want, prefer, desire, opt, resolve, intend, mean, plan, see fit.

choosy *adj.* particular, fastidious, fussy, picky, discriminating, finicky, dainty, selective, exacting, meticulous, critical, demanding, persnickety.
ant. undiscriminating, uncritical, accepting.

chop *v.* hew, cut, hack, clip, fell, rend, gash, lop, shear, slash, crop, mince, hash, dice. —*n.* whack, blow, thwack, punch, crack, uppercut,

wham, rap, swipe, clout, cuff, jab, sock (*Slang*), bust (*Slang*).

choppy *adj.* 1 stormy, rough, wind-lashed, windswept, ruffled, squally. 2 jerky, irregular, shifting, discontinuous, spasmodic, spastic, uneven, changeable, unstable, broken, bumpy, jagged.
ant. 1 glassy, calm, unruffled, smooth, mirrorlike. 2 flowing, regular, even, smooth, continuous, unbroken.

chorale *n.* hymn, paean, canticle, anthem, psalm, offertory, prayer, motet, musical offering, chant.

chore *n.* task, job, responsibility, duty, assignment, stint, routine, charge, concern, nuisance, burden, care, trouble, bother, inconvenience.
ant. pleasure, indulgence, delight, breeze, snap.

chortle *v.* chuckle, cackle, laugh, giggle, crow, snort, gloat, rejoice.

chorus *n.* 1 glee club, choir, ensemble, choristers, vocalists, singers. 2 group, unison, consensus, accord, unanimity, concert, concordance, concord, one voice.
ant. 2 disunity, disharmony, disagreement, difference, squabble.

chosen *adj.* elite, elected, designated, selected, special, named, distinguished, preferred, appointed, favored.
ant. neglected, ignored, passed over, left out.

chow *n. Slang* FOOD.

christen *v.* name, baptize, call, designate, dub, term, title, label, launch, dedicate, tab.

chronic *adj.* 1 long-lasting, continuing, prolonged, lingering, ongoing, ineradicable, incurable, protracted, persistent. 2 habitual, inveterate, constant, perennial, everlasting, incessant, ceaseless, frequent, confirmed, perpetual.
ant. 1 temporary, brief, acute, transitory, short, curable. 2 occasional, intermittent, fitful, rare.

chronicle *n.* history, archives, record,

annals, journal, log, diary, minutes, transactions, calendar, biography. —*v.* record, keep track of, log, calendar, register, document, report, recount, write about, describe, narrate.

chronological *adj.* sequential, in sequence, in order, temporal, dated, consecutive, serial, ordered, progressive, successive.

chubby *adj.* plump, pudgy, overweight, rotund, stocky, thickset, fat, heavy, chunky, tubby, overfed, oversized, buxom, portly, zaftig (*Slang*).
ant. skinny, bony, lean, thin, angular, spare, underweight.

chuck *v.* **1** pat, tap, stroke, tickle, caress, flick, fondle, pet. **2** throw, toss, hurl, flip, sling, pitch, cast. **3** get rid of, throw away, toss out, throw out, dispose of, eliminate, evict, turn out, expel, oust, remove.

chuckle *v.* laugh, chortle, cackle, giggle, smile. —*n.* laugh, chortle, cackle, giggle, smile.

chucklehead *n.* FOOL.

chum *n.* pal, buddy, friend, companion, crony, comrade, mate, partner, *amigo*, sidekick (*Slang*).

chummy *adj.* friendly, close, intimate, congenial, companionable, familiar, fond, devoted, inseparable, palsy-walsy (*Slang*), matey (*Brit.*).
ant. distant, uncongenial, unfriendly, formal.

chump *n.* fool, dupe, butt, ninny, jackass, pushover (*Slang*), schnook (*Slang*), schlemiel (*Slang*), nebbish (*Slang*), sucker (*Slang*), sap (*Slang*), fall guy (*Slang*).
ant. wiseacre, smart aleck, know-it-all, wise guy (*Slang*).

chunk *n.* hunk, lump, slab, piece, wad, gob, batch.

chunky *adj.* stocky, chubby, thickset, stubby, lumpy, plump, heavyset, stout, pudgy, dumpy, strapping, beefy.
ant. slim, slender, lithe, willowy, scrawny, lanky, gangling.

church *n.* **1** temple, house of worship, cathedral, chapel. **2** clergy, ministry,

priesthood, the cloth, preachers, ecclesiastics, the pulpit.

churchman *n.* CLERGYMAN.

churl *n.* BOOR.

churlish *adj.* boorish, vulgar, surly, loutish, oafish, rude, unmannerly, impolite, uncivilized, cranky, brusque, uncouth, obnoxious, quarrelsome.
ant. civil, mannerly, polite, civilized, pleasant, agreeable, cultivated.

churn *v.* stir, agitate, whip, shake, whisk, beat, toss, foam, surge, swirl, convulse, eddy.

chute *n.* trough, slide, passageway, incline, ramp, sluice, duct, trench, channel, runway.

chutzpah *n.* GALL.

cicatrix *n.* SCAR.

cicerone *n.* GUIDE.

cinch *n.* **1** *Slang* snap, breeze, sure thing, pushover (*Slang*), duck soup (*Slang*), setup, natural, winner, child's play. **2** GIRDLE.
ant. 1 tough nut (*Slang*), backbreaker (*Slang*), sweat, murder, drag (*Slang*).

cincture *n.* BELT.

cinders *n.* ASHES.

cinema *n.* motion pictures, movies, moving pictures, film, films, film-making, movie-making, screen, cinematography, flicks (*Slang*).

cipher *n.* **1** zero, naught, aught, nothing, goose egg (*Slang*). **2** nobody, nothing, nullity, dummy, dud, mediocrity.
ant. 2 somebody, personage, mensch (*Slang*), figure, name, big shot (*Slang*), VIP.

circa *adv.* APPROXIMATELY.

circle *n.* **1** ring, orb, band, circlet, wheel, disk, ball, globe, circumference, round, cylinder, roundel, ringlet, loop, coil. **2** cycle, series, course, circuit, revolution, curl. **3** clique, set, group, coterie, crowd, sphere, orbit, area, domain, dominion, territory, scene, realm, bailiwick. —*v.* encircle, ring, compass, encompass, girdle, loop, enclose, coil, belt, envelop, circumscribe, enfold.

circuit *n.* **1** route, course, ambit, round, beat, tour, routine, journey, trip, run, itinerary, path, orbit, lap, sphere. **2** conference, league, association, district, division, group, wing, fellowship, meet. **3** CIRCLE.

circuitous *adj.* roundabout, indirect, devious, overcomplicated, labyrinthine, serpentine, meandering, time-wasting, discursive, circumlocutory, oblique, digressive.
ant. direct, straightforward, simple, straight, short, uncomplicated, undeviating.

circuitousness *n.* INDIRECTION.

circuity *n.* INDIRECTION.

circular *adj.* round, curved, arched, coiled, globular, spherical, spheroid, cupped, cylindrical, orbital, helical, hollow, concave, looped, spiral. —*n.* leaflet, handbill, pamphlet, notice, throwaway, petition, appeal, advertisement, ad, announcement, flier, bulletin, brochure, statement, mailing piece, come-on (*Slang*).

circulate *v.* travel, course, revolve, rotate, gyrate, spin, move around, get around, peregrinate, journey, tour, circumnavigate, perambulate, meander, flow, encompass.

circulation *n.* rotation, revolution, ambit, circuit, orbit, spin, gyration, dissemination, distribution, spread, transmission, broadcast, flow, diffusion.

circumference *n.* girth, periphery, perimeter, bound, compass, boundary, scope, ambit.

circumlocution *n.* indirection, periphrasis, wordiness, circuitousness, deviousness, verbiage, digression, diffuseness, redundance, redundancy, verbosity, prolixity, long-windedness, fustian, bombast, gobbledygook, pleonasm, rigmarole, euphemism.
ant. terseness, directness, pithiness, rigor, brevity, conciseness.

circumscribe *v.* **1** encircle, encompass, ring, gird, girdle, hoop, belt, **2** confine, limit, restrict, bind, restrain, corset, proscribe, define, curb, hem in, hinder, impede, demarcate, contain.

circumspect *adj.* cautious, careful, prudent, wary, heedful, watchful, attentive, discreet, judicious, vigilant, alert, chary, politic, guarded.
ant. daring, bold, heedless, venturesome, unwary, careless, spontaneous.

circumstance *n.* condition, occurrence, fact, event, matter, state, factor, happening, episode, affair, particular, item, phenomenon, incident, happenstance.

circumstances *n.* standing, position, status, situation, station, income, life style, footing, finances, lot, estate, resources, place.

circumstantial *adj.* **1** provisional, iffy, uncertain, contingent, unsure, unpredictable, tentative, variable, conjectural, open, unsettled, conditional. **2** incidental, inessential, superficial, extrinsic, supplemental, collateral, external, accessory, ancillary.
ant. **1** definite, fixed, settled, immutable, predictable. **2** intrinsic, inherent, inner, fundamental, characteristic.

circumvent *v.* avoid, bypass, evade, ward off, steer clear of, eschew, escape, shun, detour, go around, get away from, dodge, sidestep, outflank.
ant. face, confront, deal with, cope with, meet head on.

circus *n.* **1** big top, spectacle, side show, carnival. **2** lark, romp, carousal, high old time, high jinks, saturnalia, ball (*Slang*), howl (*Slang*), gas (*Slang*).
ant. **2** dud, bore, washout, funeral.

cistern *n.* TANK.

citadel *n.* **1** fortress, fort, fortification, castle, palisade, stockade, rampart, battlement. **2** haven, safeguard, stronghold, bastion, protection, defense, barricade, barrier, buttress, wall, guard.

citation *n.* **1** quotation, quote, source, passage, mention, extract, excerpt, il-

lustration, text, reference, allusion.
2 honorable mention, commendation, award, honor, eulogy, praise, recognition, acclaim, kudos, homage.
3 summons, writ, subpoena, command, order, charge, call, injunction, warrant.

cite *v*. quote, refer to, mention, adduce, illustrate, substantiate, allude to, commend, honor, recognize, specify, point out, indicate.

citified *adj*. URBAN.

citizen *n*. native, national, resident, subject, inhabitant, voter, countryman, compatriot.
 ant. foreigner, alien, outsider, outlander, immigrant, visitor, transient.

city *n*. municipality, metropolis, metropolitan area, megalopolis, town, polity, burg (*Slang*).

civic *adj*. CIVIL.

civil *adj*. **1** civic, civilian, secular, municipal, political, urban, communal, metropolitan, popular, governmental, state, public, societal, social. **2** polite, decent, courteous, mannerly, well-bred, civilized, well-mannered, cordial, neighborly, well-behaved.
 ant. **2** rude, boorish, churlish, impolite, nasty, hostile.

civility *n*. courtesy, politeness, mannerliness, breeding, decency, cordiality, cultivation, good manners, refinement, tact, graciousness, affability.
 ant. rudeness, boorishness, bad manners, impoliteness, hostility, coarseness, insolence.

civilization *n*. cultivation, education, refinement, development, advancement, culture, enlightenment, edification, humanization, progress.
 ant. savagery, backwardness, wilderness, darkness, barbarousness, ignorance.

civilize *v*. EDUCATE.

civilized *adj*. cultivated, refined, educated, cultured, advanced, humanized, enlightened, tolerant, civil, humane.

 ant. savage, brutish, backward, wild, coarse, unenlightened, provincial.

clabber *v*. CURDLE.

clack *n*., *v*. CLICK.

claim *v*. **1** demand, deserve, require, assert, insist on, ask for, clamor, merit, warrant, seek, exact, petition, compel, appeal. **2** believe, think, hold, maintain, know, accept, contend, profess, put forward, defend, justify.

clairvoyant *adj*. prescient, telepathic, psychic, precognitive, mediumistic, prophetic, oracular, sibylline, extrasensory, divining.

clambake *n*. *Slang* BASH.

clamber *v*. CLIMB.

clammy *adj*. damp, dank, sticky, moist, slimy, mucoid, cool, sweaty, perspiring, pasty, viscid, gluey.
 ant. dry, warm, smooth, velvety.

clamor *n*. **1** noise, din, outcry, uproar, tumult, hullaballoo, hubbub, stir, brouhaha, commotion, racket, babel, to-do, bedlam, chaos. **2** agitation, protest, demand, insistence, vociferation, vehemence, storm, ferment, challenge, dissension, denunciation.
 ant. **1**, **2** quiet, silence, calm, serenity, tranquillity, peace.

clamorous *adj*. noisy, tumultuous, rackety, loud, vociferous, insistent, vehement, tumultuous, turbulent, loudmouthed, boisterous.
 ant. quiet, peaceful, calm, tranquil, reposed.

clamp *n*. vise, grip, bracket, brace, clasp, hold.

clan *n*. tribe, family, kin, sect, sept, group, commune, fraternity, line, clique, set, coterie, gang, faction.

clandestine *adj*. surreptitious, secret, undercover, underground, covert, hidden, concealed, furtive, stealthy, disguised, unrevealed, undisclosed, conspiratorial.
 ant. forthright, aboveboard, open, overt, manifest, unconcealed, public.

clang *v*. clank, ring, resound, reverberate, bong, toll, jangle, clash, peal.

clannish *adj*. narrow, sectarian, provincial, exclusive, cliquish, parochial, limited, intolerant, unfriendly, snobbish, insular, illiberal.

ant. worldly, sophisticated, open-minded, tolerant, friendly, neighborly.

clap *v.* **1** applaud, approve, appreciate, acclaim, commend, support. **2** smack, hit, strike, whack, box, thwack, wallop, rap, slam, bang, cuff, clip. **3** thrust, throw, toss, rush, cast, shove, pitch, propel. —*n.* **1** bang, peal, crash, thunder, burst, salvo, detonation, shot, boom, report, clang. **2** slap, whack, thwack, wallop, bang, rap, cuff, smack, box.

ant. *v.* **1** hiss, boo, catcall, disapprove, heckle, razz (*Slang*).

claptrap *n.* false front, pretentiousness, sham, staginess, speciousness, gaudiness, tomfoolery, nonsense, fustian, frippery, affectation, tawdriness, tinsel, veneer.

claque *n.* CLIQUE.

clarify *v.* explain, elucidate, illuminate, untangle, explicate, decipher, simplify, clear up, account for, define, interpret, solve, footnote.

ant. obscure, muddle, tangle, conceal, obfuscate, veil.

clarity *n.* lucidity, distinctness, definition, specificity, intelligibility, understanding, comprehensibility, transparency, obviousness, straightforwardness, explicitness, sharpness, delineation, perspicuity, precision, keenness.

ant. obscurity, obfuscation, muddle, impenetrability, fuzziness, unintelligibility.

clash *v.* **1** crash, clang, clank, clatter, jangle, rattle, bang. **2** conflict, fight, war, battle, argue, contend, combat, wrangle, quarrel, dispute, collide, differ, feud, squabble. —*n.* **1** crash, clang, clank, clatter, jangle, rattle, bang, cacophony, din. **2** *of colors, etc.*: disharmony, discordance, unsuitability, incongruity, uncongeniality, disagreement, clash.

ant. *v.* **2** agree, concur, harmonize,

coincide, correspond. *n.* **2** harmony, compatibility, suitability, congruence.

clasp *n.* **1** fastener, hook, pin, hasp, clip, catch, buckle, snap, clamp, closing. **2** grasp, embrace, hold, grip, clutch, grab, pressure, hug, squeeze. —*v.* **1** embrace, hug, enfold, encircle, envelop. **2** grab, snatch, grasp, hold, grip, squeeze, clutch, press, wrest, seize.

class *n.* **1** group, grouping, category, sort, order, division, department, breed, stripe, kind, type. **2** rating, rank, status, standing, pedigree, prestige, lineage, quality, estate, caste, station, sphere, stratum. **3** *Slang* elegance, flair, pizzazz (*Slang*), tone, smartness, chic, style, excellence, superiority. —*v.* classify, sort, order, categorize, departmentalize, type, name, designate, arrange, assort, catalogue, codify, organize.

classic *adj.* **1** exemplary, ideal, classical, model, paradigmatic, standard, masterly. **2** formal, regular, controlled, stylized, traditional, established, polished, symmetrical, balanced, proportioned, restrained, elegant. —*n.* touchstone, cornerstone, standard, paradigm, ideal, model, exemplar, masterpiece, masterwork, criterion, high point, achievement.

ant. *adj.* **2** subjective, free, formless, romantic, impressionistic, undisciplined, impassioned.

classical *adj.* CLASSIC.

classification *n.* **1** organization, labeling, categorization, denomination, arrangement, assortment, separation, division, grouping, codification, system, file, taxonomy, hierarchy. **2** category, grade, sort, class, label, rank, status, standing, group, kind, type, ilk, brand, bracket.

classified *adj.* CONFIDENTIAL.

classify *v.* systematize, categorize, assort, arrange, departmentalize, denominate, group, bracket, label, rank, catalogue, grade, methodize, codify, tag.

classy *adj. Slang* elegant, smart, nifty (*Slang*), swell, de luxe, superior, aristocratic, high-class, gilt-edged, ritzy (*Slang*), posh, swank. **ant.** chintzy, shabby, ordinary, common, cheap, mediocre, low-class.

clatter *v.* rattle, bang, clank, clang, crash, bang, jangle, click, clack.

clause *n.* ARTICLE.

claw *n.* talon, nail, spur, hook, unguis, pincer. —*v.* scratch, tear, pull, hook, gouge, spur, mangle, lacerate, scrape, gash, slash, pierce, grip, maul, cut, bloody, graze.

clay *n.* earth, dirt, soil, marl, dust, ashes, loam, sod, turf, mud.

clean *adj.* **1** unstained, spotless, neat, tidy, cleanly, immaculate, scrubbed, cleansed, purified, sanitary, antiseptic, hygienic, washed, laundered, bathed. **2** pure, faultless, untainted, undefiled, virginal, virtuous, innocent, chaste. **3** complete, thorough, entire, total, regular. **4** sportsmanlike, fair, even-handed, equitable, just, judicious, upright, sporting, square-shooting, impartial, open and aboveboard, straight. —*v.* cleanse, purify, bathe, wash, purge, scrub, launder, deterge, decontaminate, sanitize, scour, neaten, tidy, sterilize, disinfect. **ant.** *adj.* **1** stained, spotted, dirty, messy, filthy. **2** defiled, wicked, vulgar, tainted, debauched. **3** partial, halfway, uneven, irregular. **4** underhand, prejudiced, unfair, crooked. *v.* dirty, pollute, stain, spot, soil, mess, contaminate.

clean-cut *adj.* **1** delineated, defined, chiseled, etched, incised, outlined, demarcated, clear, distinct, precise, sharp, sharp-edged, unambiguous, evident. **2** neat, trim, spruce, dapper, tidy, proper, wholesome, conventional, square (*Slang*). **ant. 1** hazy, fuzzy, ill-defined, vague, unclear, indistinct, smudged. **2** messy, sloppy, untidy, unwashed, unkempt.

cleanly *adj.* CLEAN.

cleanse *v.* CLEAN.

cleanup *n.* KILLING.

clean up NET.[2]

clear *adj.* **1** distinct, obvious, plain, evident, patent, manifest, understandable, unambiguous, unequivocal, comprehensible, lucid, limpid. **2** unhindered, unhampered, unobstructed, unfettered, unclogged, rid, free, liberated, disentangled, open, relieved, divested. **3** transparent, limpid, glass, see-through, diaphanous, crystalline. —*v.* **1** brighten, shine, lighten, illuminate. **2** wash, clean, cleanse, purify, free, liberate, open, emancipate, release, disengage, ease, rid. **3** exonerate, exculpate, absolve, pardon, discharge, acquit, excuse, remit, reprieve. **4** clarify, elucidate, define, delineate, explicate, disentangle, illuminate, simplify, explain. **5** NET.

ant. *adj.* **1** fuzzy, indistinct, blurred, unintelligible, incomprehensible, hazy, foggy. **2** obstructed, clogged, snarled, jammed, closed, hindered, barred. **3** opaque, filmy, cloudy, smoky, turbid, murky, frosted. *v.* **1** dim, darken, cloud, haze. **2** soil, pollute, hinder, obstruct, close, bar, clog. **3** implicate, charge, accuse, indict, incriminate. **4** confuse, muddy, becloud, obfuscate, obscure.

clearance *n.* GREEN LIGHT.

clear-cut *adj.* definite, plain, obvious, unambiguous, sure, unquestionable, indubitable, specific, incontrovertible, unarguable, unmistakable, concise, explicit, unequivocal. **ant.** vague, ambiguous, indefinite, doubtful, unclear, questionable.

clear-headed *adj.* sensible, rational, practical, realistic, lucid, clearsighted, judicious, perceptive, perspicacious, unerring, logical, dependable, discerning, astute, sober. **ant.** foolish, unrealistic, impractical, confused, irrational, dense, stupid.

clearly *adv.* plainly, obviously, patently, manifestly, doubtlessly, undoubtedly, unquestionably, indubitably, undeniably, evidently, unmistakably.

ant. maybe, perhaps, possibly, perchance.

clear out take off, push off, vacate, decamp, exit, leave, go, depart, quit, withdraw, scram (*Slang*), bug off (*Slang*).

clear-sighted *adj.* CLEAR-HEADED.

clear up solve, straighten out, disentangle, explain, resolve, elucidate, unravel, clarify, answer.

ant. confuse, obscure, hide, conceal, tangle.

cleavage *n.* cleft, split, division, schism, break, fracture, breach, fissure, separation, part, parting, discontinuity, rift, divorce.

ant. solidarity, smoothness, unity, wedding, welding.

cleave[1] *v.* split, sunder, cut, break, fracture, divide, separate, part, sever, rive, disunite, crack.

ant. join, unite, wed, weld, unify, solidify.

cleave[2] *v.* adhere, abide, stick to, cling, embrace, hold fast, cherish, stand by, support, uphold, follow, adhere, espouse.

ant. desert, abandon, divorce, forsake, defect.

cleft *n.* crack, split, fissure, crevice, divide, cleavage, division, cut, gap, rift, slit, separation, dimple.

clemency *n.* leniency, mercy, charity, humaneness, compassion, forbearance, amnesty, tolerance, understanding, forgiveness, good will, fellow-feeling, sympathy, benevolence.

ant. vengefulness, vindictiveness, brutality, cruelty, intolerance, ill-will, ruthlessness.

clement *adj.* **1** MERCIFUL. **2** MILD.

clench *v.* grasp, grip, close, lock, tighten, tense, contract, constrict, grit.

ant. loosen, open, free, let go, relax.

clergy *n.* ministry, priesthood, the cloth, ecclesiastics, the church, the pulpit, churchmen, preachers, pastors, prelates, the first estate.

ant. laity, populace, body politic, laymen.

clergyman *n.* minister, priest, rabbi, cleric, father, churchman, pastor, divine, parson, preacher, reverend, prelate, curate, canon.

cleric *n.* CLERGYMAN.

clerical *adj.* priestly, churchly, ecclesiastical, sacerdotal, pastoral, religious, hierarchical, ministerial, canonical.

ant. secular, lay, temporal, worldly.

clever *adj.* **1** *physically skillful:* adroit, skillful, dexterous, nimble, handy, deft, capable, competent, efficient, expert. **2** bright, keen, sharp, quick, ingenious, original, inventive, innovative, intelligent, alert, quick-witted, resourceful, perceptive, shrewd, astute, smart, canny.

ant. **1** clumsy, awkward, maladroit, fumbling, inept, incompetent, klutzy (*Slang*). **2** stupid, dense, obtuse, slow, dull, slow-witted, unresourceful, dumb.

cliché *n.* platitude, commonplace, bromide, old saw, truism, banality, stereotype, chestnut. —*adj.* HACKNEYED.

clichéd *adj.* HACKNEYED.

click *v.* **1** snap, clink, clack, chink, flick, tap, cluck. **2** *Slang* succeed, make it (*Slang*), come off (*Slang*), catch on, go over, score, make the grade.

ant. **2** flop, fail, fizzle, lay an egg (*Slang*), fold (*Slang*), bomb (*Slang*).

client *n.* patron, customer, buyer, patronizer, shopper.

clientele *n.* clients, following, followers, custom, patronage, customers, business, trade, market, retainers.

cliff *n.* precipice, bluff, tor, crag, overhang, escarpment, eminence, peak, ledge, palisade, promontory, overlook, steep.

climactic *adj.* crucial, critical, decisive, peak, climacteric, major, crowning, supreme, dominant, paramount, maximal, orgasmic.

climate *n.* trend, atmosphere, mood, clime, tendency, character, condition, state, direction, drift, disposition, nature, quality, coloration, temperature, pulse.

climax *n.* **1** peak, summit, apex, zenith, culmination, high point, top, crisis, crown, limit, maximum, turning point, flood tide, crest, utmost. **2** orgasm, fulfillment, satisfaction.
ant. 1 low point, nadir, ebb, bottom, minimum, beginning.

climb *v.* **1** ascend, clamber, scale, mount, shin, creep, scramble, descend, go down, alight, shinny. **2** succeed, advance, progress, aspire, achieve, rise, get ahead, make headway, flourish, excel, compete, make it (*Slang*).

clime *n.* CLIMATE.

clinch *v.* **1** secure, fasten, nail down, rivet, clamp, set, fix, pinion. **2** confirm, settle, decide, determine, set, fix, conclude, establish, wind up, culminate, bind, nail down, ice (*Slang*). —*n. Slang* embrace, hug, cuddle, clutch, squeeze, clasp.

cling *v.* adhere, stick, grasp, hold, clasp, embrace, stay, remain, cleave, linger, last, cherish.
ant. let go, leave, abandon, forsake, depart.

clinical *adj.* scientific, impersonal, detached, objective, experimental, analytic, dispassionate, unprejudiced, unbiased, open-minded, disinterested.
ant. subjective, personal, biased, opinionated, bigoted, close-minded, impassioned.

clink[1] *v.* clang, ring, clank, rattle, clack, jangle, tink, tinkle, jingle.

clink[2] *n. Slang* PRISON.

clinker *n. Slang* MISTAKE.

clip[1] *n.* clasp, pin, grip, clamp, fastener, binder, brace, hasp, hook, vise. —*v.* grip, fasten, hold, pin, clamp, bind, brace, hook, clench, couple, attach, buckle.

clip[2] *v.* **1** cut, crop, bob, shear, scissor, trim, mow, snip, pare, fleece, shorten, shave, nip. **2** check, reduce, abridge, curtail, cut short, stunt, constrict, cramp, diminish, abbreviate, condense, elide, abort. **3** strike, hit, smack, punch, wallop, clap, slug, clout, whack, jab, sock (*Slang*). —*n.* gallop, run, trot, stride, high gear, hurry, speed-up, dash, rush, dart.
ant. *v.* **2** lengthen, inflate, encourage, add to, increase, maximize. *n.* dawdle, saunter, slouch, drag.

clique *n.* set, coterie, clan, tribe, group, gang, caucus, conclave, cabal, camarilla, sect, cult, following, adherents, devotees, admirers, claque, supporters.

cliquish *adj.* clannish, exclusive, snobbish, unfriendly, sectarian, provincial, partisan, narrow, prejudiced, insular, secretive, parochial.
ant. bluff, approachable, openhearted.

cloak *n.* **1** cape, wrap, coat, mantle, manteau, robe, overcoat, capote. **2** disguise, pretext, veil, mask, decoy, cover, blind, dodge, excuse, subterfuge, veneer, artifice, camouflage, misrepresentation, pretense, dissimulation. —*v.* disguise, conceal, mask, veil, cover, camouflage, pretend, dissimulate, misrepresent, falsify, screen, deceive.
ant. *v.* reveal, lay bare, unmask, uncover, come clean.

clobber *v. Slang* sock (*Slang*), wallop, beat up, hit, strike, punch, thrash, whack, lick, clout, slug (*Slang*), belt (*Slang*).

clod *n.* **1** lump, mass, clot, wad, chunk, fragment, hunk, piece, gob, morsel, nugget, batch. **2** oaf, lout, dimwit, halfwit, bumpkin, yokel, dolt, dunce, peasant, simpleton, moron, fathead (*Slang*).

clodhopper *n.* HICK.

clog *n.* occlusion, clot, impedance, hindrance, obstruction, block, bar, jam, embolism, encumbrance, drag, bottleneck, trammel, hobble, handicap, curb, drawback. —*v.* **1** obstruct, choke, hinder, occlude, jam, block, bar, close, brake, trammel, impede, restrict. **2** coagulate, coalesce, clot, solidify, thicken, conglomerate, congeal, cake, condense, agglutinate, mass.

ant. *v.* **2** melt, flow, loosen, liquefy, dissolve.

cloister *n.* courtyard, colonnade, arcade, walk, walkway, portico, gallery, corridor, stoa, promenade. —*v.* seclude, confine, isolate, immure, shelter, sequester, closet, withdraw, remove, segregate, enclose, coop up.

cloistered *adj.* **1** SECURE. **2** INSULAR.

close *adj.* **1** near, proximal, approximate, next to, following, adjoining, adjacent, neighboring, approaching, tangential, contiguous, touching, impending. **2** compact, dense, serried, compressed, tight, congested, crowded, packed, pressed, clogged, clotted, thick. **3** intimate, friendly, allied, affectionate, warm, attached, firm, loyal, loving, dear, cherished. **4** accurate, exact, literal, true, verbatim, thorough, all-out, thoroughgoing, careful, detailed, painstaking, strict, rigorous, intense, searching, intent. **5** secretive, reticent, closemouthed, taciturn, uncommunicative, silent, cryptic, laconic, brief, concise, unrevealing, cautious. **6** airless, ill-ventilated, warm, stifling, musty, stale, stuffy, unventilated, muggy, dank, suffocating, uncomfortable. —*v.* **1** shut, lock, secure, bolt, seal, bar. **2** obstruct, fill up, clog, enclose, imprison, cage, bar, choke, dam, hinder, hamper. **3** unite, join, coalesce, ally, federate, merge, connect, consolidate, integrate, unify, couple. **4** terminate, conclude, end, cease, finish, accomplish, achieve, fulfill, satisfy, stop, discontinue. —*n.* end, conclusion, finish, termination, stop, settlement, achievement, fulfillment, consummation, expiration, denouement, twilight, death.

ant. *adj.* **1** distant, far, faraway, remote. **2** sparse, thin, roomy, loose, uncongested. **3** cool, unsympathetic, alien, estranged, hostile. **4** superficial, casual, hit-or-miss, careless, surface. **5** open, talkative, communicative, gabby, revealing, outgoing. **6** airy, breezy, drafty, fresh. *v.* **1** open, unlock, unseal, unbolt. **3** separate, sever, divide, disunite, fragment. **4** begin, start, commence, inaugurate, initiate. *n.* beginning, opening, start, birth, dawn, inception.

closefisted *adj.* STINGY.

closemouthed *adj.* taciturn, uncommunicative, close, laconic, terse, tight-lipped, distant, unrevealing, silent, mute, curt, sullen, reserved, secretive, cautious, suspicious, untrusting.

ant. talkative, communicative, outgoing, outspoken, forthright, confiding.

closet *n.* storeroom, recess, cupboard, cabinet, depository, larder, compartment, wardrobe, cubicle, armoire. —*adj.* concealed, hidden, unrevealed, covert, confidential, private, secret, intimate, personal, restricted, undisclosed, undercover.

ant. *adj.* overt, public, forthright, revealed, outspoken, exposed.

clot *n.* mass, lump, coagulation, occlusion, embolism, gob, coalescence, curd. —*v.* coagulate, coalesce, clog, curdle, thicken, solidify, cake, condense, congeal, inspissate.

ant. flow, run, bleed, liquefy, pour.

cloth *n.* fabric, material, goods, yardage, yard goods, textiles, dry goods, stuff, covering, drape, hanging, drop.

clothe *v.* dress, attire, garb, cover, array, cloak, bedeck, deck, drape, put on, don, costume, accouter, outfit, adorn, rig out, tog, robe.

ant. undress, disrobe, unclothe, denude, take off, uncover.

clothes *n.* CLOTHING.

clothing *n.* clothes, apparel, attire, garments, raiment, habiliments, dress, wearing apparel, wear, array, outfit, togs, toggery, vestments, garb, couture, wardrobe, getup, uniform, vesture, duds, rags (*Slang*).

cloud *n.* **1** vapor, film, haze, mist, steam, fog, smoke, flock, swarm, shower, puff, jet. **2** shadow, pall, stain, taint, wet blanket, blotch, eclipse, sorrow, grief, shroud, curse, misfortune, evil. —*v.* **1** dim, darken, obscure, film, cover, bedim, befog, eclipse, obfuscate, overcast, overshadow, lower, conceal, hide, veil, screen. **2** threaten, depress, desolate, deject, sadden, dull, discourage, trouble, mar, sully, detract from, daunt, taint, stain, smirch, discredit.

ant. *v.* **1** lighten, clear up, elucidate, brighten, reveal, lay bare, spotlight. **2** hearten, gladden, cheer up, elate, uplift, exalt, praise.

cloudy *adj.* **1** overcast, gray, misty, foggy, smoggy, smoky, hazy, vaporous, lowering, leaden, sunless, murky, soupy. **2** vague, obscure, nebulous, unclear, confused, uncertain, faint, muddy, ill-defined, impenetrable, doubtful, unsure, indistinct, fuzzy, baffling, perplexing. **3** troubled, gloomy, depressing, dismal, dreary, cheerless, joyless, unhappy, downcast, depressed, glum, morose, downhearted.

ant. 1 bright, sunny, clear, cloudless, azure. **2** distinct, precise, definite, lucid, well-defined, certain. **3** cheerful, happy, untroubled, halcyon, smiling.

clout *n.* **1** wallop, blow, cuff, whack, slap, punch, clobber (*Slang*), thwack, clip, wham, jab, sock (*Slang*), biff (*Slang*). **2** *Slang* pull, influence, power, drag (*Slang*), prestige, persuasiveness, weight, authority, importance, standing.

clown *n.* buffoon, jester, jokester, wit, comedian, comedienne, comic, zany, fool, wag, harlequin, merry-andrew, card, mime.

clownish *adj.* comical, comic, funny, amusing, diverting, zany, foolish,

waggish, witty, droll, antic, prankish, entertaining, nonsensical, slapstick, Chaplinesque.

ant. staid, sober, somber, serious, grave, sedate.

cloy *v.* sate, satiate, surfeit, glut, overfeed, gorge, stuff, cram, choke, sicken, nauseate.

ant. starve, deprive.

cloying *adj.* EXCESSIVE.

club[1] *n.* stick, staff, cudgel, bludgeon, billy, blackjack, truncheon, mace, shillelagh. —*v.* beat, bludgeon, hit, slug, whack, thwack, wallop, blackjack, pommel, bash, flail, hammer, bang, buffet, clout, clobber (*Slang*).

club[2] *n.* society, fraternity, sorority, federation, organization, group, fellowship, brotherhood, sisterhood, sodality, guild, gang, clique, coterie.

clubby *adj.* FRIENDLY.

cluck *n.* CLICK.

clue *n.* sign, hint, inkling, lead, scent, trail, tip-off, tip, cue, key, intimation, suggestion, indication, glimmer, evidence, fact, token, trace, spoor, blaze.

clue in inform, divulge, reveal, tip off, spill, open up, enlighten, make known, advise, report, tell, communicate, explain, describe.

clump *n.* **1** cluster, bunch, lump, mass, wad, clod, clot, dollop, bundle, pack, collection, node, knob, protuberance. **2** bang, knock, thud, plunk, stomp, tramp, stamp. —*v.* thud, stomp, march, stump, thump, bang, tramp, bumble.

clumsy *adj.* **1** awkward, bumbling, maladroit, ungainly, unhandy, fumbling, left-handed, ungraceful, inept, gauche, klutzy (*Slang*), all thumbs. **2** unwieldy, cumbersome, bulky, makeshift, inconvenient, cumbrous, troublesome, unmanageable. **3** *of language or manners:* awkward, sloppy, slovenly, bumbling, bungled, rude, tactless, ill-considered, insensitive, oafish, inelegant, uncouth, doltish.

ant. 1 deft, adroit, graceful, nimble,

skilled, expert. **3** elegant, polished, smooth, suave, dainty.

cluster *n.* group, bunch, bouquet, clump, collection, grouping, clutch, assembly, assemblage, coterie, set, clique, bevy, swarm, crowd, ring, circle.

clutch[1] *v.* snatch, grasp, grab, hold, hang on to, cling, seize, grip, cleave, adhere, catch, wrest.

ant. release, let go, relinquish, drop, unhand.

clutch[2] *n.* CLUSTER.

clutches *n.* power, sway, control, hands, influence, grasp, mastery, dominion, disposition, rule, supervision, command, grip.

clutter *n.* disorder, mess, litter, disorderliness, sloppiness, disarray, confusion, jumble, tangle, hodgepodge, dishevelment. —*v.* disorder, litter, mess, strew about.

ant. *n.* neatness, tidiness, orderliness. *v.* neaten, tidy, simplify, untangle, straighten up.

coach *n.* trainer, tutor, director, teacher, mentor, adviser, instructor, guide. —*v.* train, tutor, teach, instruct, prepare, cram, advise, guide, drill, direct, exercise, work out.

coagulate *v.* clot, solidify, jell, congeal, form, thicken, harden, set, curdle, condense, mass, gelatinize, inspissate.

ant. liquefy, melt, run, flow, thin out, bleed.

coalesce *v.* fuse, blend, weld, consolidate, integrate, merge, unify, combine, amalgamate, agglutinate, mingle, intermingle, mix.

ant. separate, divide, split, sever, cleave, fragment, break up, disintegrate.

coalition *n.* alliance, bloc, merger, fusion, union, federation, combination, faction, caucus, agreement, entente, partnership, league, amalgam, cooperative.

ant. split, schism, separation, severance, disagreement, enmity, antagonism.

coarse *adj.* **1** gritty, rough, sandy, grainy, mealy, pebbly, ridged, nubby, scratchy, bumpy, lumpy, unfinished, crude, unrefined, homespun, rough-hewn. **2** vulgar, indelicate, gross, boorish, coarse-grained, insensitive, loutish, foul-mouthed, smutty, earthy, lewd, obscene, offensive, dirty, ribald, off-color.

ant. **1** smooth, finished, elegant, silken, fine, refined. **2** polite, mannerly, delicate, prim.

coarse-grained *adj.* COARSE.

coast *n.* seacoast, seashore, strand, beach, seaboard, littoral, seaside, waterside, shore. —*v.* sail, glide, slide, ride, descend, get by, skim, sweep, drift, float, cruise, roll, course.

coat *n.* **1** overcoat, jacket, mantle, wrap, cloak, tunic, blazer, topcoat. **2** covering, pelt, hide, skin, fur, fleece, hair, wool, shell, bark, crust, rind, coating, outside, exterior, surface.

coating *n.* coat, layer, lamination, crust, film, membrane, covering, polish, lacquer, envelope, veneer, patina, leaf, overlay, varnish, protection.

coax *v.* wheedle, cajole, urge, beg, insist, nudge, inveigle, manipulate, beguile, flatter, humor, persuade, prevail upon, importune, enjoin, appeal to.

cock *n.* **1** rooster, chanticleer, cockerel. **2** champion, leader, winner, star, king, expert, victor, hero, master, chief, boss, champ (*Slang*).

cockeyed *adj.* *Slang* **1** askew, awry, off, lopsided, crooked, distorted, out of whack (*Slang*), uneven, unbalanced, irregular, off-center, twisted, asymmetrical. **2** absurd, preposterous, cuckoo (*Slang*), goofy (*Slang*), nutty (*Slang*), wild (*Slang*), fishy, improbable, ridiculous, nonsensical, unbelievable, crazy, mad.

ant. **1** straight, even, balanced, centered, symmetrical. **2** sensible, reasonable, believable.

cocksure *adj.* **1** SURE. **2** COCKY.

cocky *adj.* conceited, swaggering, over-confident, aggressive, arrogant, swell-headed, smug, opinionated, brash, strutting, chesty, lordly, vain, overbearing, bumptious, cocksure, self-satisfied.
ant. deferential, shy, timid, humble, self-effacing.

coddle *v.* pamper, baby, cosset, cater to, indulge, mollycoddle, humor, dote on, overindulge, spoil.

code *n.* system, rules, regulations, standard, ethic, ethos, manners, beliefs, morality, etiquette.

codger *n.* character, eccentric, oddball, old bird, crank, sourpuss (*Slang*), fuddy-duddy, geezer (*Slang*).

codicil *n.* APPENDIX.

codify *v.* systematize, organize, rationalize, methodize, classify, arrange, tabulate, catalog, label, coördinate.

coerce *v.* force, compel, constrain, make, bully, intimidate, press, drive, impel, command, strong-arm, dragoon, overpower, exact, oblige.

coercion *n.* force, duress, constraint, exaction, bullying, overpowering, compulsion, violence, control, bondage, arrest.

coercive *adj.* threatening, menacing, aggressive, constraining, forceful, bullying, compelling, violent, powerful, demanding, high-pressure, strong-arm.

coeval *adj.* CONTEMPORARY.

coffer *n.* safe, strongbox, chest, bank, depository, repository, hold, locker, vault, till, money box, cash box.

coffers *n.* funds, cash, reserves, savings, assets, money, finances, means, capital, wherewithal.

coffin *n.* casket, box, chest, case, sarcophagus.

cog *n.* **1** tooth, projection, gear, serration, ratchet, tenon, sprocket. **2** bureaucrat, apparatchik, pencil pusher, small fry, wage slave, menial, underling, subordinate, minion.
ant. 2 big wheel (*Slang*), decision-maker, boss, overlord, dictator.

cogency *n.* FORCE.

cogent *adj.* forceful, compelling, trenchant, weighty, persuasive, convincing, undeniable, sound, rational, inescapable, incontrovertible, effective, potent, powerful.
ant. weak, ineffective, unconvincing, foolish, irrelevant.

cogitate *v.* PONDER.

cogitation *n.* thought, consideration, reflection, meditation, mulling, pondering, contemplation, examination, review, deliberation, musing, rumination, lucubration.

cognate *adj.* kindred, allied, related, akin, affiliated, family, associated, collateral, generic, similar, close, matching, parallel, analogous.
ant. unrelated, dissimilar, different, alien, distant.

cognition *n.* COGNIZANCE.

cognizance *n.* awareness, perception, apprehension, comprehension, knowledge, sentience, grasp, ken, insight, imagination, intelligence, recognition, cognition.
ant. unawareness, blindness, incomprehension, ignorance.

cognizant *adj.* aware, informed, knowing, understanding, recognizing, conversant, conscious, familiar, sensible, versed, on to, hip (*Slang*).
ant. unaware, uninformed, ignorant, blind, unconscious, in the dark.

cognomen *n.* NICKNAME.

cohere *v.* **1** stick, adhere, cling, cleave, condense, consolidate, hold fast. **2** hang together, make sense, square with, hold water.

coherence *n.* consistency, intelligibility, rationality, meaning, reason, logic, harmony, identity, congruity, clarity, connection, unity.
ant. incoherence, confusion, inconsistency, inconsequence, absurdity, disjunction.

coherent *adj.* **1** cleaving, holding fast, adhering, sticky, compact, integrated, united, connected, agglutinated. **2** logical, intelligible, articulate, consistent, rational, cohesive, organized, systematic, orderly.

ant. 2 incoherent, confused, mixed up, jumbled, disorganized.

cohesion *n.* stickiness, tenacity, attraction, coherence, blending, fusion, solidification, consolidation, agglutination, union, consistency, toughness, stability.

ant. repulsion, dissipation, scattering, dispersal, antagonism, separation.

cohesive *adj.* consistent, coherent, agglomerative, sticky, agglutinating, flocculent, coagulative, fused, coalescent, adhesive.

cohort *n.* **1** companion, colleague, follower, supporter, accomplice, peer, associate, fellow, mate, buddy, pal, chum. **2** class, set, group, peer group, band.

coil *n.* ring, spiral, loop, helix, volute, convolution, whorl, curlicue, corkscrew, roll. —*v.* wind, twist, turn, spiral, sinuate, reel, snake, loop, twirl, convolve.

coin *v.* **1** mint, issue, stamp, monetize. **2** originate, invent, devise, create, compose, conceive, concoct, frame.

coinage *n.* creation, fabrication, origination, innovation, neologism, invention, conception, contrivance, concoction, composition, device.

coincide *v.* **1** agree, square, tally, fit, correspond, accord, meet, harmonize, equal, dovetail. **2** coexist, synchronize, concur, attend, accompany.

ant. 1 differ, disagree, diverge, clash, depart from, conflict.

coincidence *n.* correspondence, concurrence, conjunction, concord, correlation, congruency, synchronism, contemporaneousness, agreement, coherence, accord, parallelism.

coincident *adj.* concurrent, concomitant, corresponding, coincidental, synchronous, accompanying, coinciding, simultaneous.

coincidental *adj.* **1** fortuitous, accidental, unintentional, circumstantial, chance, lucky, serendipitous. **2** CO-INCIDENT.

ant. 1 deliberate, planned, scheduled, determined, fated, predestined.

coitus *n.* sexual intercourse, copulation, fornication, union, congress, conjugation, consummation.

cold *adj.* **1** frigid, frozen, intemperate, inclement, freezing, wintry, arctic. **2** shivery, piercing, biting, chilly. **3** coldhearted, unmoved, indifferent, distant, removed, unfriendly, haughty, aloof, icy, glacial, unapproachable, reserved. **4** depressing, discouraging, dreary, somber, sullen, bleak. —*n.* frigidity, glaciation, iciness, frostiness, severity, rigor, chill, rawness, inclemency, chilliness.

ant. *adj.* **1** warm, hot, torrid, tropical, balmy. **2** feverish, oppressive, fiery, burning, warm. **3** friendly, cordial, involved, sympathetic, hospitable. **4** cheerful, bright, cozy, sunny, pleasant. *n.* warmth, heat, incandescence, sultriness, glow, temperature.

coldblooded *adj.* cruel, heartless, implacable, merciless, ruthless, brutal, unfeeling, pitiless, barbarous, callous, grim, inhuman, savage, fell.

ant. warm-hearted, humane, tender, compassionate, sympathetic, kind.

coldhearted *adj.* unfeeling, pitiless, indifferent, callous, heartless, apathetic, phlegmatic, impassive, unsympathetic, frigid, inhuman.

ant. sympathetic, understanding, affectionate, kind, warm-hearted, humane.

coliseum *n.* ARENA.

collaborate *v.* cooperate, coauthor, combine, associate, affiliate, concur, join, coact, assist, aid.

collaboration *n.* cooperation, teamwork, affiliation, association, partnership, alliance, synergism, coaction, assistance, aid.

collaborationist *n.* collaborator, quisling, traitor, turncoat, fraternizer, fifth columnist, renegade, timeserver, opportunist.

collapse *v.* **1** give way, cave in, crumple, disintegrate, fall, tumble, topple.

2 fail, crash, fold, flounder, plump. **3** succumb, fall ill, be stricken, break down. —*n.* **1** cave-in, breakdown, tumble, disintegration, downfall, plunge. **2** failure, ruin, downfall, fiasco, depression. **3** prostration, exhaustion, debility, breakdown, seizure, stroke.

collar *v.* CAPTURE.

collateral *adj.* **1** subordinate, secondary, ancillary, adjunct, concomitant. **2** corroborating, confirming, confirmatory, substantiating, supportive, validating, warranting. **3** guaranteed, secured, warranted, endorsed, bonded, authenticated. —*n.* security, bond, warranty, deposit, guarantee, pledge, surety.

collation *n.* SNACK.

colleague *n.* associate, cohort, confrere, collaborator, compeer, co-worker, confederate, fellow, teammate, partner, ally, companion, comrade.

collect *v.* **1** assemble, congregate, gather, meet, bring together, concentrate, sheave. **2** obtain, acquire, raise, amass, accumulate, solicit. **3** control, muster, command, summon, recover, marshal.

collected *adj.* **1** assembled, gathered, amassed, concentrated, mustered, garnered, heaped. **2** composed, self-possessed, unruffled, nonchalant, cool, imperturbable, level-headed, calm.
ant. 1 dispersed, scattered, far-flung. **2** distracted, agitated, distraught, upset.

collection *n.* **1** gathering, mobilization, concentration, compilation, convocation, convergence, muster. **2** store, mass, aggregation, hoard, accumulation, group, assembly, pile, congeries, cluster, agglomerate, corpus.

collective *adj.* **1** cumulative, composite, aggregated, total, comprehensive, representative. **2** joint, shared, common, cooperative, mutual, united.

college *n.* body, company, association, group, institute, organization, league,

society, establishment, school, institution, council, committee, guild, collegium, junta.

collide *v.* **1** crash, smash, bump, strike, run into, hit, beat, bang. **2** conflict, interfere, oppose, obstruct, counter, clash.

collision *n.* **1** impact, crash, smash-up, shock, concussion, impingement, contact, accident. **2** conflict, encounter, struggle, interference, clash, disagreement, confrontation, challenge.

colloquial *adj.* conversational, informal, familiar, everyday, ordinary, usual, demotic, common, casual, idiomatic, vernacular.
ant. literary, formal, correct, classic, standard, literate.

colloquy *n.* conversation, conference, dialogue, talk, discussion, council, parley, exchange, caucus, session, congress, discourse.

collude *v.* CONNIVE.

collusion *n.* conspiracy, intrigue, connivance, complicity, machination, plot, trickery, fraud, deceit, cabal, scheming.

colonist *n.* colonizer, colonial, settler, immigrant, emigrant, pioneer, frontiersman, squatter, outlander, foreigner, invader.
ant. native, indigene, aborigine, autochthon.

colonize *v.* SETTLE.

colonnade *n.* ARCADE.

colony *n.* **1** community, society, outpost, settlement. **2** clump, body, flock, swarm, band, group, set, clique.

color *n.* **1** hue, tone, cast, tint, coloration, coloring. **2** pigment, dye, paint, coloring, stain. **3** semblance, appearance, show, cast, look, aspect, effect, intent. **4** animation, vividness, éclat, brilliance, richness, liveliness. —*v.* **1** paint, dye, stain, tint, tinge. **2** misrepresent, exaggerate, distort, prejudice, slant, cast, tilt, falsify, embroider, embellish. **3** blush, flush, mantle, redden, brighten, ripen.

colorable *adj.* DECEPTIVE.

coloration n. COLOR.

colored adj. exaggerated, prejudiced, influenced, shaped, determined, molded, affected, slanted, biased, embroidered, highlighted, distorted, misrepresented.

ant. disinterested, unbiased, detached, straight, honest.

colorful adj. interesting, picturesque, eventful, varied, diversified, adventurous, vivid, brilliant, lively, variegated, stimulating.

ant. humdrum, lackluster, drab, uniform, dull, nondescript.

coloring n. COLOR.

colorless adj. **1** pale, ashen, pallid, washed-out, faded, blanched, bleached, white. **2** dull, uninteresting, insipid, tame, neutral, characterless, monotonous, vapid, vacant, vacuous.

ant. **1** colored, painted, tinted, stained, dyed. **2** colorful, vivid, piquant, interesting, zesty.

colors n. **1** flag, banner, pennant, standard, ensign, pennon, bunting. **2** insignia, identification, badge, mark, identity, livery, silks.

colossal adj. **1** enormous, huge, gigantic, vast, giant, mammoth, stupendous, prodigious, Brobdingnagian. **2** unbelievable, extraordinary, unqualified, extreme, unmitigated, downright, egregious, incredible.

ant. **1** tiny, Lilliputian, miniature, diminutive, slight.

colossus n. giant, titan, prodigy, behemoth, leviathan, mountain, mammoth, whopper, whale, monster.

ant. pygmy, midget, shrimp, runt, dwarf, peewee.

colt n. NOVICE.

column n. **1** shaft, pillar, pilaster, tower, pier, pole, post, cylinder. **2** line, file, row, string, procession, group, force.

coma n. stupor, lethargy, torpor, apathy, drowsiness, dullness, sluggishness, listlessness, somnolence, insensibility, oblivion, unconsciousness, swoon.

comb v. search, ransack, scour, rummage, rifle, sift, rake, screen, beat the bushes.

combat n. battle, fight, struggle, conflict, resistance, strife, opposition, contest, antagonism, war. —v. resist, oppose, withstand, defy, challenge, counteract, antagonize, negate, foil, struggle, fight.

ant. n. peace, harmony, cooperation, teamwork, detente, agreement, synergy.

combatant n. contender, contestant, fighter, champion, warrior, assailant, battler, adversary, opposition, antagonist, enemy, belligerent, foe. —adj. fighting, battling, belligerent, contending, opposing, assailant, militant, conflicting, warring, clashing.

combative adj. pugnacious, warlike, bellicose, belligerent, hostile, aggressive, truculent, scrappy, contentious, competitive, quarrelsome, militant, offensive.

ant. peaceable, cooperative, pacific, irenic, retiring, self-effacing.

combination n. **1** joining, association, union, unity, conjunction, connection, assemblage, amalgamation, composition. **2** alliance, compound, complex, mixture, blend, league, party, faction, cabal.

combine v. join, unite, blend, merge, intermix, commingle, associate, connect, link, wed, synthesize. —n. association, cartel, alliance, syndicate, junta, trust, league, pool, gang, coterie, conspiracy.

ant. v. separate, disjoin, sunder, divorce, part, analyze.

combustible adj. flammable, inflammable, burnable, ignitable.

ant. nonflammable, inert.

combustion n. burning, incineration, blazing, fire, blaze, flame, conflagration, ignition, kindling, oxidation, consuming.

come v. **1** approach, move toward, near, advance, go to, approximate. **2** arrive, develop, attain, reach, touch, appear, materialize. **3** come about, happen, arise, proceed, turn out, emerge, end up, result, follow, depend, ensue, befall, betide, chance, take place.

ant. 1 go, depart, leave, exit, move off.

come about occur, befall, arise, eventuate, come to pass, happen, come up.

come across happen upon, meet, encounter, stumble upon, come upon, discover, unearth, hit upon, dig up.

comeback *n.* **1** recovery, return, revival, resurgence, regeneration, renewal, renascence, rally. **2** *Slang* retort, riposte, crack, witticism, back talk, response, answer, reply.

comedian *n.* comic, comedienne, clown, funnyman, mountebank, jester, humorist, joker, entertainer, wag, buffoon.

comedown *n.* descent, downfall, debasement, lowering, decline, demotion, reverse, fall, drop, comeuppance, mortification, humiliation.

comedy *n.* farce, joke, jest, gag, riot, fun, sport, pleasantry, banter, slapstick, travesty, burlesque.

come-hither *adj.* ALLURING.

comely *adj.* attractive, pleasing, personable, pretty, handsome, good-looking, winsome, bonny, fair, cute, lovely, beautiful, sightly.

ant. homely, unattractive, plain, ordinary, unlovely, ill-favored.

come off SUCCEED.

come-on *n. Slang* LURE.

comestible *adj.* EDIBLE.

come through measure up, perform, accommodate, pull it off, accomplish, see through, make the grade, succeed, survive, handle, manage, hack it (*Slang*).

ant. fail, go under, flunk, lose out.

come up COME ABOUT.

come upon COME ACROSS.

comeuppance *n.* DESERTS.

come up with suggest, propose, produce, present, create, engender, initiate, sponsor, set up, put forward, work up, plan.

comfit *n.* CONFECTION.

comfort *n.* **1** well-being, contentment, ease, coziness, satisfaction, snugness, opulence. **2** relief, encouragement, support, consolation, solace, succor, cheer. —*v.* console, solace, soothe, calm, hearten, sustain, reassure, gratify, stroke, refresh.

ant. *n.* **1** discomfort, misery, twinge, hurt. **2** discouragement, trouble, bother, alarm. *v.* worry, trouble, disquiet, afflict, bother, grieve.

comfortable *adj.* **1** cozy, snug, restful, easy, agreeable, sheltered, pleasant. **2** contented, cheerful, relaxed, easy, serene, flourishing, genial. **3** affluent, ample, well-to-do, prosperous, sufficient.

ant. 1 uncomfortable, forsaken, neglected, abject. **2** miserable, unhappy, discontented, cheerless. **3** wretched, squalid, destitute.

comforter *n.* **1** sympathizer, solace, pacifier, mollifier, support, consoler, palliative. **2** quilt, coverlet, bedcover, blanket, throw, eiderdown.

comforting *adj.* soothing, supportive, encouraging, reassuring, consoling, solacing, relieving, heartening, bolstering, succoring, cheerful, consolatory.

ant. annoying, troubling, afflicting, bothering, worrying, grievous.

comic *n.* comedian, clown, humorist, funnyman, wit, zany, jester, joker, buffoon, wag. —*adj.* COMICAL.

comical *adj.* funny, ludicrous, amusing, laughable, humorous, droll, comic, risible, whimsical, waggish, absurd, ridiculous, diverting, farcical.

ant. serious, solemn, grave, sober, tragic, pathetic.

coming *adj.* **1** approaching, next, forthcoming, imminent, impending, prospective, nearing, proximate. **2** promising, ambitious, striving, future, advancing, progressing. —*n.* arrival, advent, approach, accession, appearance, birth, proximity, nearing, reaching, visit.

comity *n.* COURTESY.

command *v.* **1** order, require, enjoin, ordain, decree, summon, grant. **2** control, direct, rule, guide, govern, reign, compel, manage. **3** exact, levy, impose, elicit, evoke, request. —*n.* **1** authority, power, control, domination, upper hand, sway, supremacy. **2** injunction, order, fiat, commandment, charge, behest, direction.

commandant *n.* COMMANDER.

commandeer *v.* **1** conscript, draft, constrain, impress, press, shanghai. **2** confiscate, take over, appropriate, requisition, expropriate, usurp, hijack.

commander *n.* leader, chief, manager, director, master, commandant, superior, dictator, chieftain, captain, boss.

commanding *adj.* **1** governing, in charge, powerful, authoritative, decisive, domineering, dictatorial, imperative, autocratic, masterful. **2** impressive, imposing, eminent, authoritative, dignified, significant, influential, masterly.

commandment *n.* LAW.

commemorate *v.* celebrate, memorialize, immortalize, honor, remember, salute, mark, observe, keep, solemnize.

commemoration *n.* celebration, jubilee, anniversary, observance, memorialization, remembrance, honoring, perpetuation, recognition, keeping, solemnization, salutation.

commence *v.* begin, initiate, start, enter upon, undertake, broach, launch, inaugurate, originate, introduce, spring up, set in, open.

ant. end, terminate, close, conclude, cease, finish.

commencement *n.* BEGINNING.

commend *v.* **1** praise, applaud, extol, acclaim, eulogize. **2** recommend, boost, endorse, certify, approve. **3** entrust, commit, confide, yield, deliver.

ant. 1, 2 censure, disparage, condemn, discredit, denounce, decry.

commendable *adj.* praiseworthy, creditable, exemplary, laudable, meritorious, estimable, admirable, commendatory, deserving, signal, notable.

ant. blameworthy, inferior, contemptible, culpable, faulty, execrable.

commendation *n.* approbation, approval, eulogy, praise, citation, endorsement, acclaim, recommendation, panegyric, encomium, applause, award.

ant. censure, blame, incrimination, disapproval, blackball, criticism.

commendatory *adj.* COMMENDABLE.

commensurable *adj.* COMMENSURATE.

commensurate *adj.* proportionate, equivalent, appropriate, due, corresponding, suitable, adequate, coextensive, comparable, commeasurable, commensurable, in keeping with, coterminous.

ant. disproportionate, unsuitable, inappropriate, inapplicable, different, divergent.

comment *n.* **1** note, explanation, remark, opinion, criticism, observation, reflection, clarification, gloss. **2** talk, conversation, gossip, remark. —*v.* remark, say, observe, explain, note, mention, touch on, criticize, opine.

commentary *n.* **1** exposition, critique, review, exegesis, comment, interpretation, notes, treatise, scholium. **2** illustration, clarification, illumination, observation, criticism, reflection, note, example.

commentator *n.* discussant, critic, editorialist, interpreter, reporter, journalist, analyst, reviewer, panelist.

commerce *n.* **1** trade, traffic, business, merchandising, dealing, barter, economy. **2** communication, give-and-take, fraternization, sociability, socializing, intercourse, relation.

commercial *adj.* **1** mercantile, trade, business, trading, market, economic. **2** mercenary, venal, material, materialistic, entrepreneurial, profiteering, exploitative, monetary. **3** salable, marketable, vendible, merchantable, popular, desirable, acceptable, in demand, wanted, hot.

commingle *v.* MINGLE.

comminute *v.* PULVERIZE.

commiseration *n.* SYMPATHY.

commission *n.* **1** entrusting, relegation, authorization, assignment, instruction. **2** board, committee, council, agency, delegation. **3** fee, compensation, allowance, stipend, pay, honorarium, percentage. —*v.* **1** appoint, delegate, authorize, accredit, assign. **2** hire, engage, charter, order, requisition, demand.

commit *v.* **1** do, perpetrate, practice, carry on, enact, effect. **2** incarcerate, confine, intern, immure, imprison. **3** entrust, depute, consign, confide, engage, relegate. **4** devote, pledge, promise, vow, obligate, dedicate, bind.

commitment *n.* **1** consignment, delivery, placement, transfer, surrendering, relegation, disposal. **2** pledge, promise, word, compact, obligation, guarantee, warrant. **3** involvement, adherence, devotion, dedication, espousal, engagement.

commode *n.* TOILET.

commodious *adj.* spacious, roomy, ample, large, big, extensive, comfortable, luxurious, capacious, convenient.

ant. cramped, narrow, constricted, confining, strait, close.

commodity *n.* goods, wares, thing, object, article, item, product, chattel, merchandise, vendible, property, stock.

common *adj.* **1** ordinary, commonplace, usual, regular, plain, middling. **2** communal, public, collective, popular, social, societal. **3** widespread, general, prevalent, extensive, prevailing, pervasive, familiar. **4** coarse, vulgar, low, inferior, cheap, shoddy, second-rate, despicable.

ant. 1 unusual, strange, peculiar, unique. **2** private, individual, personal. **3** infrequent, scarce, rare. **4** choice, superior, high-class, first-rate, refined, tasteful.

commonalty *n.* MASSES.

commonly *adv.* usually, normally, generally, ordinarily, routinely, of course, as a rule, often, repeatedly, habitually, customarily.

ant. seldom, exceptionally, hardly, scarcely, rarely, now and then.

commonplace *adj.* ordinary, routine, common, familiar, everyday, trivial, hackneyed, trite, stale, jejune. —*n.* platitude, truism, cliché, triviality, bromide, banality, maxim, axiom, saying, adage.

ant. adj. remarkable, unusual, rare, original, new, fresh.

common-sense *adj.* practical, sensible, thoughtful, reasonable, down-to-earth, plausible, realistic, sagacious, matter-of-fact, sound, evident, untutored, obvious, accepted, conventional.

ant. foolish, rash, outré, impractical, far-fetched, fantastic.

common sense judgment, sense, practicality, discernment, intelligence, judiciousness, level-headedness, mother wit, horse sense, prudence, understanding, sobriety, moderation.

ant. impulsiveness, extremism, imprudence, extravagance, hot-headedness, rashness.

commotion *n.* **1** disturbance, ado, fuss, pother, to-do, flurry, ferment, stir, bustle, excitement. **2** agitation, tumult, uproar, convulsion, tempest, confusion, noise, upheaval, rumpus, ruckus (*Slang*).

ant. 1, 2 tranquillity, calm, placidity, peace, serenity, quiet.

communal *adj.* common, public, collective, general, shared, joint, social, popular, societal.

ant. private, individual, personal, exclusive, restricted, privy.

commune *v.* contemplate, ponder, get close to, converse, parley, dialogue, discourse, reflect, muse, communicate.

communicable *adj.* transmittable, contagious, infectious, taking, catching, transferable.

communicate *v.* **1** impart, transmit, convey, give, instill, submit. **2** declare, divulge, disclose, tell, announce, inform. **3** join, link, connect, abut, touch, adjoin.

communication *n.* **1** conveyance, exchange, dissemination, disclosure, notification, expression, mention, intelligence, intercourse, participation. **2** rapport, harmony, accord, communion, fellowship, concord, liaison.

communicative *adj.* frank, talkative, forthright, free, informative, open, forthcoming, candid, fluent, voluble, wordy, loquacious.
ant. close-mouthed, taciturn, secretive, reserved, terse, laconic.

communion *n.* **1** communication, association, sharing, communing, intermingling, participation. **2** closeness, affinity, tête-à-tête, intimacy, sympathy, concord, harmony, agreement.

community *n.* **1** public, society, commonwealth, commonalty, state, population. **2** sharing, participation, collectivism, communion, cooperation. **3** similarity, likeness, affinity, resemblance, fellowship, rapport.
ant. **3** polarity, difference, duality, contrariety, antagonism, diversity.

commutation *n.* substitution, reduction, replacement, palliation, remission, respite, compromise, extenuation, relaxation, easement, amnesty, exchange, trade.

commute *v.* exchange, alter, reverse, modify, mitigate, remit, extenuate, alleviate, diminish, adjust, change, soften, supersede.

compact[1] *adj.* **1** solid, dense, close, well-knit, thick, firm, thickset. **2** condensed, brief, terse, succinct, short, laconic. —*v.* condense, pack, compress, tamp, concentrate, squeeze, cram, constrict, solidify.
ant. *adj.* **1** spongy, flimsy, inflated, light, gossamer, foamy. **2** dispersed, prolonged, long-drawn, discursive. *v.* expand, disperse, blow up, inflate.

compact[2] *n.* covenant, agreement, contract, bargain, settlement, engagement, undertaking, arrangement, understanding, treaty, deal, alliance, coalition.

companion *n.* **1** partner, associate, attendant, comrade, fellow, friend, escort, colleague. **2** counterpart, mate, complement, twin, match, analogue, double, mirror image, doppelganger.

companionable *adj.* friendly, sociable, gregarious, affable, cordial, ingratiating, amicable, accessible, convivial, genial, well-disposed, gracious.
ant. reserved, distant, unsociable, unfriendly, aloof, haughty.

company *n.* **1** companionship, society, fellowship, presence, association. **2** firm, association, partnership, corporation, syndicate, concern, house, congregation, assembly. **3** troupe, body, band, party, unit, repertory, assemblage.

comparable *adj.* similar, akin, like, matching, approaching, cognate, homologous, analogous, corresponding, tantamount, commensurate, equivalent, consonant.
ant. dissimilar, unrelated, disparate, heterogeneous, diversified, unique.

comparative *adj.* relative, parallel, contingent, similar, approximate, provisional, like, comparable, conditional, modified, figurative.
ant. total, absolute, unconditional, categorical, positive, definite.

comparatively *adv.* PARTLY.

compare *v.* equate, liken, collate, match, juxtapose, contrast, correlate, balance. —*n.* COMPARISON.

compare with equal, parallel, match, correspond, resemble, approximate, vie.

comparison *n.* **1** matching, equation, correlation, simile, distinction, analogy, ranking, rating, collating, crosscheck, likening. **2** similarity, resemblance, comparability, identity, likeness, equivalence, analogousness, homogeneity, consonance, parity, relationship.

compartment *n.* **1** cell, niche, section, nook, stall, corner, booth, cubicle, hole. **2** category, division, section, department, subdivision, form.

compass *n.* **1** area, expanse, field, zone, realm, sphere. **2** limit, boundary, perimeter, circuit, circumference. **3** scope, range, reach, extent, gamut, purview. —*v.* **1** go around, encircle, engird, embrace, encompass, environ, enclose. **2** hem in, besiege, blockade, invest. **3** grasp, comprehend, perceive, realize, penetrate.

compassion *n.* mercy, commiseration, empathy, clemency, charity, sympathy, pity, ruth, heart, humanity, gentleness, kindness, grace.
ant. severity, harshness, antipathy, savagery, cruelty, aversion.

compassionate *adj.* sympathetic, tender-hearted, charitable, magnanimous, merciful, lenient, clement, benevolent, gentle, tender, indulgent, benign.
ant. harsh, ruthless, unfeeling, merciless, heartless, vindictive.

compatible *adj.* congenial, congruous, harmonious, sympathetic, agreeable, cooperative, adaptable, consonant, consistent, conformable, suitable, in keeping.
ant. incompatible, divergent, incongruous, discordant, inconsistent, antagonistic.

compeer *n.* **1** COLLEAGUE. **2** PEER.

compel *v.* **1** oblige, constrain, drive, urge, insist, domineer, subdue, control. **2** force, coerce, overpower, enforce, oppress, tyrannize.

compelling *adj.* convincing, cogent, persuasive, telling, valid, forceful, unanswerable, irrefutable, conclusive, well-taken, inescapable, sound, powerful.
ant. unconvincing, inconclusive, lame, invalid, indecisive, feeble.

compendious *adj.* LACONIC.

compendium *n.* abridgment, summary, synopsis, digest, abstract, précis, outline, résumé, epitome, syllabus, review, brief.

compensate *v.* **1** remunerate, pay, recompense, reimburse, reward, satisfy, indemnify, repay. **2** offset, counteract, balance, make up for, cancel, redress, countervail.

compensation *n.* **1** remuneration, payment, settlement, indemnification, satisfaction, atonement, equalization. **2** wages, reward, earnings, profit, benefit, gain, deserts.

compete *v.* vie, contend, rival, emulate, contest, strive, oppose, dispute, cope, encounter, struggle.

competence *n.* fitness, sufficiency, adequacy, ability, proficiency, competency, capacity, capability, efficiency, qualification, skill, expertise, know-how.
ant. incompetence, inability, ineptitude, insufficiency, inadequacy, lack, shortcoming.

competency *n.* COMPETENCE.

competent *adj.* **1** able, capable, fit, endowed, proficient, qualified, efficient. **2** sufficient, adequate, apt, enough, fitting, plenty, appreciable.
ant. 1 incompetent, inept, unskilled, inexpert. **2** inadequate, lacking, deficient, short.

competition *n.* **1** rivalry, emulation, opposition, conflict, contention, jousting, battling. **2** competitor, rival, opponent, contender, adversary, opposition, contestant. **3** match, bout, race, contest, encounter, struggle.

competitive *adj.* rivaling, emulative, vying, striving, opposing, combative, rival, emulous, competing, struggling, at odds, adversary.
ant. cooperative, collaborative, confederate, aiding, helpful, concerted.

competitor *n.* rival, contestant, aspirant, emulator, opponent, contender, antagonist, adversary, foe, entrant, participant, competition.

compilation *n.* COLLECTION.

compile *v.* collect, gather, assemble, amass, anthologize, combine, organize, arrange, make, compose, draw up, group.

complacency *n.* **1** self-satisfaction,

complacence, smugness, contentment, gratification, conceit. **2** equanimity, composure, unconcern, calmness, serenity, repose, self-possession, tranquillity.

complacent *adj.* smug, self-satisfied, serene, imperturbable, gratified, contented, pleased, composed, unconcerned, at ease.

ant. concerned, bothered, uneasy, agitated, perturbed, upset.

complain *v.* protest, object, criticize, murmur, grumble, deplore, lament, whine, bewail, repine, gripe, rail, remonstrate, bitch (*Slang*), squawk (*Slang*), bellyache (*Slang*).

complaint *n.* **1** lament, protest, jeremiad, objection, plaint, petition, litany. **2** grievance, injustice, hurt, hardship, wrong, trouble, bitch (*Slang*), squawk (*Slang*). **3** ailment, illness, disease, malady, sickness, affliction.

complaisance *n.* DEFERENCE.

complaisant *adj.* obliging, agreeable, gracious, deferential, amiable, compliant, good-natured, conciliatory, considerate, respectful, obedient.

ant. contrary, obstinate, self-willed, wayward, perverse, fractious.

complement *n.* **1** balance, remainder, supplement, residue, rest, reserve. **2** totality, entirety, aggregate, quota, limit, maximum, gross, completeness. **3** counterpart, equivalent, parallel, match, obverse. —*v.* supplement, complete, fulfill, make up, round out, consummate, satisfy.

complementary *adj.* completing, reciprocal, compensatory, corresponding, reciprocating, mutual, correlative, interdependent, integral, parallel, interrelating.

complete *adj.* **1** entire, whole, plenary, integral, total, full, unabridged. **2** finished, fulfilled, accomplished, concluded, ended, mature, ripe. **3** perfect, thorough, consummate, total, absolute, dyed-in-the-wool. —*v.* **1** perfect, round out, consummate, crown, cap, realize, mature. **2** finish,

end, perform, fulfill, conclude, carry out.

ant. *adj.* **1** lacking, wanting, deficient, partial. **2** immature, premature, unfinished, half-baked. **3** second-rate, imperfect, partial, incompetent.

completion *n.* accomplishment, fulfillment, fruition, conclusion, execution, realization, attainment, discharge, finish, consummation, satisfaction, finale, capstone, crown.

complex *adj.* **1** composite, compound, multiplex, manifold, synthesized. **2** complicated, intricate, involved, elaborate, knotty, difficult. —*n.* maze, network, conglomerate, compound, composite, complexity, reticulum, ensemble, synthesis.

ant. *adj.* **1** elemental, integral, simple. **2** simple, clear, plain, easy.

complexion *n.* **1** color, hue, coloration, tone, skin, coloring. **2** aspect, character, quality, nature, guise, makeup, appearance, mien.

complexity *n.* **1** involvement, entanglement, complication, intricacy, multiplication, elaboration, difficulty. **2** maze, tangle, snarl, complex, puzzle, network, knot, labyrinth.

ant. 1 simplicity, unity, integrity, easiness.

complexity *n.* **1** involvement, ence, assent, yielding, concession, agreement. **2** affability, docility, obligingness, flexibility, pliability, complaisance, tractability, meekness, willingness.

ant. 1 defiance, resistance, denial. **2** surliness, insolence, obstinacy.

compliant *adj.* COMPLAISANT.

complicate *v.* confound, confuse, muddle, embroil, compound, involve, entangle, mix up, snarl, hamper, knot, foul, snag.

ant. simplify, disentangle, clarify, extricate, unravel, clear up.

complicated *adj.* **1** intricate, complex, involved, elaborate, manifold, multiplex, mazy, knotty. **2** difficult, abstruse, recondite, obscure, puzzling, involute, problematic.

ant. 1 plain, uniform, simplex. **2** easy, straightforward, obvious, evident.

complication *n.* **1** variation, obstruction, involvement, puzzlement, intricacy, entanglement, embarrassment, confusion. **2** problem, difficulty, snag, obstacle, handicap, addition, factor, web.

compliment *n.* praise, encomium, admiration, tribute, kudos, eulogy, commendation, panegyric. —*v.* **1** flatter, praise, eulogize, applaud, extol, commend, acclaim. **2** congratulate, felicitate, hail, salute, greet, welcome, toast.

complimentary *adj.* **1** flattering, congratulatory, favorable, commendatory, laudatory, praising, approving, adulatory. **2** free, gratis, honorary, gratuitous, voluntary, donated.

ant. 1 adverse, critical, severe, disparaging, censorious, insulting.

compliments *n.* greetings, regards, remembrances, welcome, salutation.

comply *v.* conform, obey, consent, defer, yield, accommodate, submit, adapt, observe, respect, discharge, concur.

ant. resist, demur, oppose, object, defy, disagree.

component *n.* constituent, ingredient, element, part, module, member, factor, segment, item. —*adj.* constituent, underlying, constituting, partial, basic, essential, modular, fundamental, inherent, intrinsic.

comport *v.* **1** behave, conduct, act, deport, bear, carry, acquit. **2** agree, square, correspond, concur, tally, conform, accord, harmonize.

ant. 2 disagree, differ, mismatch, contrast, clash, diverge.

comportment *n.* BEHAVIOR.

compose *v.* **1** constitute, make up, form, fashion, compound, construct. **2** tranquilize, calm, quiet, soothe, pacify, placate, still. **3** reconcile, arrange, settle, adjust, resolve, com-

promise. **4** create, frame, formulate, conceive, write, produce.

ant. 1 tear down, destroy, take apart. **2** agitate, trouble, excite. **3** aggravate, stir up, antagonize.

composed *adj.* calm, tranquil, quiet, self-possessed, cool, unruffled, nonchalant, level-headed, imperturbable, temperate, collected, unflappable.

ant. agitated, distraught, uneasy, nervous, disconcerted, uptight (*Slang*).

composite *adj.* compound, manifold, multiform, complex, mixed, mingled, varied, heterogeneous. —*n.* compound, amalgam, combination, fusion, complex, synthesis, concoction, accumulation.

ant. *adj.* simple, elementary, primary, unmixed, unalloyed, single.

composition *n.* **1** invention, creation, shaping, synthesis, fashioning. **2** opus, essay, creation, work, etude. **3** arrangement, construction, organization, formulation, formation, structure, makeup, constitution, nature, content.

composure *n.* tranquillity, calmness, serenity, self-possession, equanimity, aplomb, coolness, *sang-froid*, placidity, sedateness, quiet.

ant. agitation, disquiet, embarrassment, discomfiture, perturbation, excitement.

compound *n.* combination, mixture, composite, complex, blend, amalgam, fusion, mélange, medley, concoction. —*v.* **1** combine, mix, blend, prepare, make up, mingle, fuse, alloy, concoct. **2** complicate, augment, increase, intensify, add to, aggravate, worsen. —*adj.* multiple, manifold, composite, complex, variegated, mingled, miscellaneous, complicated, conglomerate.

ant. *adj.* simple, elemental, single, homogeneous, pure, unmixed.

comprehend *v.* **1** grasp, understand, appreciate, perceive, discern, apprehend, conceive. **2** include, comprise, take in, embrace, involve, contain, embody.

ant. 2 exclude, omit, except, reject, bar.

comprehensible *adj.* understandable, intelligible, plain, distinct, decipherable, clear, clear-cut, knowable, apprehensible, lucid, obvious, conceivable.

ant. unfathomable, puzzling, incomprehensible, abstruse, ambiguous, garbled.

comprehension *n.* **1** perception, realization, understanding, recognition, assimilation, apprehension. **2** grasp, capacity, scope, insight, understanding, range, cognition.

comprehensive *adj.* **1** inclusive, far-reaching, wide, extensive, universal, all-embracing, exhaustive, catholic, broad. **2** understanding, perceptive, penetrating, keen, discerning.

ant. 1 exclusive, narrow, limited, restricted, strait, confined.

compress *v.* compact, squeeze, press, contract, condense, reduce, constrict, deflate, shrink, crowd, force.

ant. stretch, spread, expand, enlarge, dilate, inflate.

compression *n.* contraction, pressure, condensation, constriction, squeezing, shrinkage, crowding, density, reduction, deflation.

ant. stretching, spreading, dilation, inflation, expansion, enlargement.

comprise *v.* include, consist of, contain, encompass, take in, embody, embrace, subsume, involve, enclose, comprehend, cover.

compromise *n.* **1** arrangement, conciliation, reconciliation, concession, settlement, agreement, accord. **2** balance, mean, middle ground, medium, settlement, give-and-take, accommodation, adjustment, trade-off. —*v.* **1** adjust, settle, meet halfway, arbitrate, compose, agree. **2** imperil, risk, jeopardize, prejudice, discredit, disgrace, surrender.

compulsion *n.* **1** coercion, constraint, imposition, obligation, domination,

compelling, forcing. **2** need, drive, urge, impulse, necessity, addiction, stress, urgency.

ant. 1 election, choice, freedom.

compulsive *adj.* OBSESSIVE.

compulsory *adj.* **1** coercive, compelling, inescapable, necessary, exigent, unavoidable, ineluctable, forcible, constraining, involuntary, imperious. **2** obligatory, mandatory, binding, prescriptive, enforced, required, constrained.

ant. 2 optional, voluntary, free, elective, permissive, discretionary, facultative.

compunction *n.* guilt, self-reproach, scruple, qualm, demur, misgiving, repentance, contrition, regret, remorse, shame, penitence.

computation *n.* calculation, numeration, reckoning, estimation, estimate, account, score, tally, compute, gauge, figuring, assessment.

compute *v.* estimate, calculate, determine, reckon, figure, score, cipher, tally, gauge, count, valuate, appraise, work out, solve.

comrade *n.* companion, friend, *confrère*, associate, ally, partner, colleague, co-worker, confederate, attendant, fellow, pal, chum, buddy.

con *Slang v.* **1** defraud, swindle, cheat, trick, bilk, gull, deceive, dupe, rook, overreach, rip off (*Slang*). **2** persuade, mislead, inveigle, outwit, outfox, cajole, take in, beguile, cozen, psych (*Slang*).

concatenate *v.* LINK.

conceal *v.* hide, secrete, camouflage, cover, mask, screen, shield, bury, disguise, becloud, obscure, obfuscate.

ant. reveal, display, expose, disclose, uncover, show.

concealment *n.* **1** hiding, obfuscation, stealth, secrecy, cover-up, camouflage, veiling. **2** hideaway, hide-out, ambush, cover, disguise, blind, refuge, smoke screen.

concede *v.* grant, acknowledge, admit,

allow, agree, accept, acquiesce, assent, avow.

ant. deny, resist, contradict, disavow, renege.

conceit *n.* **1** egotism, vanity, vainglory, self-importance, arrogance, complacency, swagger, narcissism, smugness, complacency, fanfaronade. **2** notion, fancy, caprice, whim, fantasy, whimsy, crotchet, vagary.

ant. 1 modesty, humility, diffidence.

conceited *adj.* vain, self-important, cocky, smug, self-satisfied, vainglorious, arrogant, haughty, pompous, self-important, immodest, egotistical, proud, narcissistic, complacent, bombastic.

ant. modest, humble, unassuming, meek, diffident, retiring.

conceivable *adj.* **1** believable, credible, reasonable, tenable, plausible. **2** possible, thinkable, understandable, imaginable, supposable, comprehensible.

ant. 1 questionable, doubtful, incredible. **2** inconceivable, ineffable, unthinkable.

conceive *v.* **1** originate, start, begin, initiate, create, invent, think of, envision, imagine, consider. **2** believe, suppose, appreciate, assume, realize, guess, reckon. **3** phrase, compose, coin, utter, declare, voice.

concentrate *v.* **1** center, converge, focus, cluster, centralize, close in, hem in. **2** attend, heed, pay attention, regard. **3** collect, assemble, gather, converge, congregate, meet.

ant. 1, 3 disperse, scatter, dissipate, disband, dissolve, separate.

concentration *n.* **1** centralization, convergence, focus, condensation, consolidation, compression. **2** intentness, attention, single-mindedness, application, absorption, regard, engrossment, study, heed, lucubration. **3** mass, assemblage, gathering, heap, pile, throng, cluster, swarm, horde, agglomerate, collection, congeries.

ant. 1 scattering, rarefaction, expansion, explosion. **2** inattention, wandering, diversion, absent-mindedness.

concept *n.* idea, thought, opinion, notion, conception, view, impression, image, construct, reification, conjecture, conviction, consideration, view, supposition, precept.

conception *n.* **1** formulation, ideation, speculation, imagination, origination, visualization, meditation. **2** idea, thought, notion, concept, impression, inkling, fancy, conceit, view, apperception, viewpoint.

conceptual *adj.* THOUGHTFUL.

concern *v.* **1** involve, affect, bear on, pertain to, implicate, influence, interest. **2** worry, vex, disquiet, trouble, distress, bother, put out, discountenance, disconcert. —*n.* **1** affair, interest, business, mission, matter, occupation. **2** reference, relation, regard, interest, attention, consideration. **3** worry, anxiety, distress, disquietude, solicitude, apprehension. **4** organization, establishment, company, firm, house, business.

concerned *adj.* **1** involved, implicated, privy, interested, mixed up, connected, related. **2** anxious, uneasy, distressed, worried, disturbed, perturbed, bothered, exercised, upset, edgy, on edge.

ant. 1 free, clear, clean, innocent. **2** nonchalant, relaxed, unconcerned, tranquil, easy.

concerning *prep.* regarding, about, as to, respecting, touching, apropos of, re, pertaining to, anent, with reference to.

concert *n.* harmony, unity, accord, teamwork, collaboration, association, cooperation, complicity, unanimity, agreement, union, concord.

ant. discord, disunity, cross-purpose, opposition, schism, scission, disruption.

concerted *adj.* collaborative, cooperative, contrived, conjoint, coactive, united, joint, collusive, synergetic, agreed on.

concession *n.* yielding, compromise, allowance, admission, acknowledgment, compliance, assent, adjustment, grant, permit, indulgence.

conciliate *v.* **1** placate, appease, mollify, disarm, soothe, pacify, arbitrate. **2** beguile, persuade, win over, reconcile, propitiate, ingratiate, secure.
ant. 1 antagonize, arouse, stir up.

conciliation *n.* PEACE.

conciliatory *adj.* compromising, placatory, pacific, irenic, peaceable, appeasing, amicable, reassuring, reconciling, soothing, winning, friendly, affable.
ant. acrimonious, antagonistic, hostile, belligerent, implacable, acerb, hard-nosed (*Slang*).

concise *adj.* brief, terse, pithy, short, compact, summary, succinct, compendious, trenchant, laconic, epigrammatic, sparing.
ant. wordy, verbose, prolix, long-winded, redundant, profuse.

conclude *v.* **1** decide, determine, fix, resolve, decree, establish. **2** infer, deduce, reason, judge, gather, reckon, suppose. **3** settle, effect, end, terminate, finish, consummate, close, resolve, wind up.

conclusion *n.* **1** termination, end, finish, stoppage, surcease, cessation, closing, wind-up, phase-out. **2** inference, deduction, judgment, conviction, summation. **3** outcome, result, culmination, end, last, finale, upshot, denouement, event, fruit, omega, terminus.
ant. 1, 3 beginning, introduction, commencement, alpha, start, continuation.

conclusive *adj.* **1** decisive, definitive, irrefutable, convincing, definite, determinative, telling, incontrovertible, unarguable. **2** final, terminal, ultimate, eventual, last, concluding.
ant. 1 inconclusive, tentative, unconvincing, questionable, invalid, doubtful. **2** early, beginning, initial, first, opening.

concoct *v.* **1** mix, blend, brew, compound, prepare. **2** contrive, devise, hatch, cook up, invent, fabricate, project.

concoction *n.* mixture, preparation, composition, blend, brew, compound, creation, synthesis, mixture, potpourri, medley, jumble.

concomitant *adj.* attendant, concurrent, accompanying, accessory, simultaneous, collateral, supplementary, synchronous, coincidental. —*n.* incidental, appendage, accompaniment, adjunct, accessory, complement, addition, episode.

concord *n.* **1** agreement, accord, unity, harmony, concordance, compatibility, communion, rapport, peace, detente. **2** treaty, compact, concordat, contract, agreement, covenant, truce.
ant. 1 discord, dissent, disagreement, antipathy, odds, hostility.

concordance *n.* CONCORD.

concordant *adj.* HARMONIOUS.

concordat *n.* CONCORD.

concourse *n.* **1** assembling, convergence, confluence, congregation, meeting, junction, concentration, aggregation. **2** assembly, throng, crowd, host, legion, group, press, attendance.

concrete *adj.* **1** specific, explicit, definite, particular, precise, distinct. **2** real, material, actual, sensible, tangible, factual. **3** solid, massive, substantial, firm, stony, dense. —*v.* unite, solidify, petrify, congeal, weld, condense, harden, set, coalesce.
ant. adj. 1 abstract, general, vague. **2** imaginary, immaterial, intangible. **3** gossamer, wispy, soft, diaphanous.

concretion *n.* **1** agglomeration, consolidation, condensation, accretion, aggregation, solidification, conglomeration, fusion. **2** mass, ball, cluster, lump, rock, conglomerate, aggregate, agglomerate.

concupiscence *n.* LUST.

concur *v.* **1** agree, assent, acquiesce, accede, consent, approve. **2** coexist, coincide, meet, come together, accompany.

ant. 1 contend, object, dissent, deny, diverge, differ.

concurrent *adj.* **1** coexistent, concomitant, conjoined, concerted, simultaneous, associated, attendant, coincident, contemporary. **2** parallel, compatible, agreeing, consistent, conformable, collaborative, harmonious, agreeable.

ant. 2 contrasting, opposite, contradictory, antithetical, counter, reverse.

concussion *n.* shock, shaking, jolt, impact, bump, crash, jar, jounce, agitation, clash, bang, collision.

condemn *v.* **1** censure, blame, denounce, vilify, attack, scold, pillory, reprehend, criticize, rebuke, reprobate. **2** doom, sentence, convict, adjudge, damn.

ant. 1 praise, approve, glorify. **2** absolve, pardon, remit.

condemnation *n.* censure, judgment, denunciation, blame, stricture, conviction, reprobation, criticism, reprehension, sentence, reproof.

ant. commendation, acquittal, absolution, exoneration, pardon, approval.

condensation *n.* **1** compression, liquefaction, precipitation, solidification, consolidation, curtailment, reduction, abbreviation. **2** condensate, moisture, liquid, precipitation, precipitate, solid. **3** digest, summary, brief, précis, abridgment, epitome.

condense *v.* **1** compress, concentrate, decoct, thicken, compact, consolidate, solidify, constrict, **2** abridge, shorten, abbreviate, digest, reduce, contract.

ant. 1 rarefy, attenuate, inflate. **2** amplify, expand, lengthen, expatiate.

condescend *v.* deign, patronize, unbend, vouchsafe, stoop, lower oneself, see fit, grant, indulge.

condescending *adj.* patronizing, haughty, lofty, lordly, pretentious, pompous, stilted, snobbish, superior, stiff.

ant. unassuming, simple, modest, unpretentious.

condign *adj.* DESERVED.

condition *n.* **1** state, circumstance, case, aspect, situation, mode, phase. **2** health, fitness, trim, fettle, tone. **3** stipulation, specification, proviso, premise, requisite. **4** status, position, rank, footing, class, place. —*v.* train, prepare, ready, adapt, modify, mold, accustom, habituate.

conditional *adj.* indefinite, uncertain, contingent, qualified, provisional, indeterminate, restricted, limited, tentative, dependent.

ant. definite, certain, categorical, independent, absolute, sure.

condole *v.* SYMPATHIZE.

condolence *n.* sympathy, commiseration, solace, consolation, comfort, pity, compassion.

condone *v.* forgive, excuse, overlook, pardon, wink at, remit, justify, extenuate, blink at, absolve, ignore, disregard, let pass.

ant. condemn, punish, deplore, judge, discountenance.

conduce to LEAD TO.

conducive *adj.* contributing, helping, tending, promoting, instrumental, contributive, furthering, expeditious, ancillary, productive, subservient, calculated.

ant. inimical, adverse, obstructive, counter, hindering, preventive.

conduct *v.* **1** guide, escort, usher, convoy, marshal, pilot. **2** manage, control, direct, lead, supervise, regulate. **3** act, behave, comport, acquit, deport. —*n.* **1** behavior, comportment, bearing, demeanor, manner, attitude, ways. **2** direction, control, management, leadership, supervision.

conductor *n.* leader, guide, pilot, escort, usher, adviser, director, chief, manager, mentor.

conduit *n.* duct, channel, artery, passage, canal, course, main, tube, pipe, flume.

confab *v., n.* CHAT.

confabulate *v.* CHAT.

confection *n.* sweet, candy, tidbit, sweetmeat, comfit, bonbon, confectionary, dainty, delicacy.

confederacy *n.* **1** league, confederation, alliance, association, organization, society, bloc. **2** conspiracy, cabal, syndicate, ring, gang.

confederate *n.* associate, accomplice, colleague, abettor, accessory, partisan, adherent, ally, consort, tool. —*v.* unite, federate, band together, combine, league, merge, amalgamate, consolidate, join, incorporate, associate.

ant. *v.* split apart, secede, disjoin, withdraw.

confederation *n.* **1** joining, association, alliance, union, coalition, incorporation, consolidation, combination, merging, federation, partnership. **2** CONFEDERACY.

ant. **1** secession, withdrawal, departure, dissolution.

confer *v.* **1** give, grant, bestow, present, award, donate, afford. **2** consult, converse, parley, discuss, deliberate, discourse, advise, talk.

conference *n.* **1** meeting, seminar, convocation, assembly, symposium, colloquium, discussion, consultation, argument, talk, parley, tête-à-tête. **2** league, association, organization, assembly, synod, body, division.

confess *v.* **1** acknowledge, admit, concede, own, confide, avow, expose. **2** profess, disclose, attest, manifest, show, evince, reveal, declare.

ant. **1, 2** deny, conceal, cover, disavow, repudiate, hide.

confession *n.* **1** admission, acknowledgment, avowal, divulgence, concession, revelation, exposé. **2** credo, declaration, confirmation, creed, exposition.

confidant *n.* INTIMATE.[1]

confide *v.* **1** divulge, tip off, tell, whisper, breathe, inform, confess. **2** entrust, depute, commit, consign, commend, delegate, trust.

confidence *n.* **1** trust, reliance, faith, credence, belief, assurance, certitude, conviction, persuasion, certainty. **2** self-reliance, boldness, aplomb, self-confidence, assurance, self-possession.

ant. **1** distrust, suspicion, skepticism, doubt, uncertainty, irresolution. **2** diffidence, timidity, reserve, self-doubt.

confident *adj.* assured, self-confident, self-assured, cocksure, cocky, certain, convinced, positive, bullish, sure, secure, expectant, self-reliant, undaunted, bold.

ant. dubious, diffident, uncertain, timorous, apprehensive, despondent.

confidential *adj.* **1** trustworthy, honest, faithful, honorable, discreet, familiar. **2** secret, restricted, classified, privy, private, privileged, tête-à-tête.

ant. **1** suspect, indiscreet, disloyal. **2** public, unrestricted.

configuration *n.* arrangement, conformation, contour, form, structure, build, formation, cast, set, disposition, figuration, interrelationship.

confine *v.* **1** imprison, intern, detain, incarcerate, shut up. **2** tie, restrain, bind, limit, restrict, cramp, straitjacket. —*n.* boundary, limit, margin, border, pale, verge, edge, frontier.

ant. *v.* **1, 2** release, free, liberate, set loose, emancipate.

confinement *n.* **1** imprisonment, incarceration, house arrest, captivity, custody, detention, immurement. **2** constraint, limitation, restriction, restraint, circumscription, duress. **3** childbirth, parturition, labor, lying-in, accouchement, delivery.

ant. **1, 2** release, freedom, liberty.

confirm *v.* **1** assure, verify, prove, establish, certify, bear out, validate, authenticate. **2** strengthen, augment, corroborate, bear out, support, substantiate, increase, **3** ratify, approve, sanction, attest, endorse.

ant. **1** deny, contradict, disprove. **2** nullify, overthrow, weaken, contradict, shatter. **3** void, cancel, annul.

confirmation *n.* **1** verification, corroboration, affirmation, authentication, substantiation. **2** ratification, approval, enactment, passage, validation. **3** proof, evidence, grounds, testimony.

ant. 1 contradiction, refutation, negation. **2** interdiction, veto, prohibition.

confirmatory *adj.* AFFIRMATIVE.

confirmed *adj.* inveterate, established, addicted, habituated, chronic, inured, habitual, battle-scarred, experienced.

ant. green, unaccustomed, new.

confiscate *v.* appropriate, preempt, seize, possess, sequester, impound, expropriate, dispossess, usurp, mulct, commandeer, arrogate, hijack.

confiscation *n.* SEIZURE.

conflagration *n.* wildfire, holocaust, firestorm, blaze, inferno, bonfire.

conflict *n.* **1** struggle, battle, combat, fight, war, dispute, fray, encounter. **2** antagonism, discord, dissension, collision, opposition, disagreement, difference, confrontation, variance. —*v.* **1** oppose, clash, disagree, diverge, jar, collide. **2** battle, struggle, quarrel, wrestle, fight, contend, vie, combat.

ant. *n.* **1** peace, amity, accord. **2** harmony, agreement, entente, concord. *v.* **1** go together, harmonize, blend, match.

conflicting *adj.* CONTRADICTORY.

confluence *n.* **1** convergence, juncture, union, conflux, junction, meeting. **2** throng, congregation, gathering, congress, assembly, concourse, multitude, swarm.

confluent *adj.* convergent, mingling, coalescing, meeting, joining, commingling, coinciding, blending, concurrent, uniting.

ant. divergent, dividing, ramifying.

conflux *n.* CONFLUENCE.

conform *v.* **1** reconcile, fit, adapt, square, correspond, harmonize. **2** comply, comport, adjust, agree, accord, acquiesce, submit.

ant. 1, 2 oppose, diverge, differ, deviate, disagree.

conformable *adj.* **1** similar, suited, adapted, fitting, congruent, resembling, like. **2** obedient, submissive, docile, compliant, amenable, compatible.

ant. 1 different, dissonant, incongruous. **2** refractory, defiant, rebellious, dissident.

conformance *n.* CONFORMITY.

conformation *n.* **1** structure, form, figure, shape, arrangement, configuration, build, topology, outline, pattern. **2** adaptation, compliance, conformity, agreement, flexibility, accordance.

ant. 2 opposition, resistance, contrariety, disagreement, noncompliance, dissent.

conformist *n.* philistine, follower, yesman, Babbitt, conventionalist, standpatter, stick-in-the-mud, formalist, imitator, copycat.

ant. rebel, heretic, dissident, dissenter, avant-gardist, innovator.

conformity *n.* **1** conformance, harmony, correspondence, accord, likeness, congruity, affinity, resemblance. **2** acquiescence, compliance, yielding, submission, obedience, observance, conventionality.

confound *v.* **1** amaze, puzzle, perplex, bewilder, flabbergast, dumbfound, confuse. **2** mix up, mistake, confuse, jumble, tangle, mingle.

ant. 2 recognize, differentiate, distinguish, discriminate, tell.

confounding *adj.* CONFUSING.

confront *v.* **1** withstand, oppose, face up to, resist, defy, beard, challenge, cope. **2** face, encounter, meet, contemplate, loom.

ant. 1, 2 avoid, shun, evade, give way, dodge.

confrontation *n.* **1** meeting, encounter, opposition, facing, withstanding, counteraction, grappling. **2** challenge, crisis, conflict, dare, defiance, contest, battle.

ant. 1, 2 avoidance, flight, evasion, forbearance, retreat.

confront with defy, challenge, face

with, dare, accuse, bring face to face with, put before.

confuse *v.* **1** perplex, confound, bewilder, baffle, puzzle, defeat, stump, bemuse, stupefy, mix up, frustrate. **2** jumble, disorder, tangle, derange, entangle, bungle, bumble. **3** disconcert, embarrass, upset, fluster, unsettle, discomfit, discountenance, rattle, addle, perturb, discompose.
ant. 2 tidy, straighten, order, disentangle, set right.

confused *adj.* DAZED.

confusing *adj.* perplexing, bewildering, puzzling, contradictory, inconsistent, complicated, misleading, mystifying, baffling, unclear, ambiguous, befuddling, confounding, muddled, fuzzy, muddy, unfathomable.
ant. clarifying, simple, clear, plain, reassuring.

confusion *n.* **1** puzzlement, bewilderment, bafflement, mystification, quandary, perplexity, befuddlement, muddle, complication, distraction, embarrassment, discomfiture, stupefaction, disorientation, daze. **2** disorder, tumult, disorganization, turmoil, uproar, bustle, mess, chaos, anarchy, fluster, to-do, hubbub, pandemonium, hugger-mugger, hodge-podge, jumble, maze, blur, tangle, mix-up, mistake, error, foul-up (*Slang*), bungle.
ant. 1 clarity, lucidity, simplicity, plainness. **2** order, organization, system, neatness, tidiness.

confute *v.* **1** refute, disprove, controvert, negate, invalidate. **2** vanquish, squelch, demolish, show up, contradict, rebut.
ant. 1, 2 support, confirm, verify, prove, demonstrate.

congeal *v.* **1** solidify, stiffen, set, freeze, harden. **2** curdle, coagulate, thicken, clot, condense.
ant. 1 melt, liquefy, fuse, soften, deliquesce.

congenial *adj.* **1** kindred, compatible, like, congruous, consistent, sympathetic. **2** agreeable, gratifying, pleasant, amenable, cordial, likable.
ant. 1, 2 alien, antipathetic, uncongenial, unpleasant, disagreeable, cold.

congenital *adj.* natal, connate, inherent, ingrained, innate, inborn, inbred, intrinsic, hereditary, constitutional, natural.
ant. acquired, learned, extrinsic, superimposed, conditioned, accidental.

congest *v.* crowd, clog, jam, glut, overburden, accumulate, pile up, choke, pack, distend, press, cram, fill.

congested *adj.* PACKED.

congestion *n.* crowding, fullness, profusion, surfeit, repletion, obstruction, bottleneck, clogging, jam, swelling, plethora.

conglomerate *adj.* massed, clustered, agglomerate, bunched, coalescent, complex, composite, mixed, heterogeneous. —*v.* accumulate, aggregate, mass, cluster, gather, coalesce, cohere, ball, snowball.

conglomeration *n.* assortment, accumulation, composite, congeries, conglomerate, mass, jumble, hodgepodge, potpourri, medley, olio, acervation.

conglutinate *v.* ADHERE.

congregate *v.* assemble, get together, forgather, muster, collect, convene, gather, flock, throng, convoke, cluster, rally, meet, swarm, mass, concentrate.
ant. disperse, scatter, spread out, separate, part.

congregation *n.* assembly, group, swarm, throng, host, multitude, crowd, flock, gathering, mass.

congress *n.* **1** assembly, council, caucus, parliament, senate, diet, conference, congregation. **2** concourse, conflux, union, collection, muster, meeting, gathering, convocation.

congruence *n.* harmony, conformity, agreement, consistency, congruity, concurrence, coincidence, accord, identity, correspondence.

ant. disparity, difference, incongruity, nonconcurrence, discord.

congruent *adj.* superposable, parallel, congruous, conformable, agreeing, identical, similar, alike, accordant, correspondent, consonant, suitable.
ant. divergent, disagreeing, contrary, conflicting, different.

congruity *n.* agreement, harmoniousness, consonance, fitness, concord, correspondence, suitability, compatibility, conformity, consistency, pertinence.
ant. disparity, incongruity, deviation, divergence, contrast, discrepancy.

congruous *adj.* CONGRUENT.

conic *adj.* conical, conoid, cone-shaped, coniform, funnel-shaped, infundibular, infundibuliform, tapering.

conjectural *adj.* speculative, hypothetical, supposed, presumptive, suppositional, theoretical, inferential, tentative, doubtful, uncertain, surmised, alleged.
ant. factual, actual, certain, empirical, evidential.

conjecture *v.* guess, estimate, assume, suppose, speculate, hypothesize, suspect, surmise, theorize, imagine. —*n.* guess, supposition, presumption, assumption, surmise, inference, speculation, conception, theory, fancy, hypothesis, guesstimate (*Slang*).
ant. *n.* certainty, knowledge, fact, truth, reality.

conjoin *v.* associate, connect, unite, combine, league, yoke, band, merge, incorporate, consolidate.
ant. part, separate, dissolve, disband, disjoin.

conjoint *adj.* associated, conjoined, connected, united, combined, attached, mutual, joint, common, corporate, pooled, indivisible.
ant. competing, antagonistic, separate, individual, disjoined, distinct.

conjugal *adj.* matrimonial, connubial, hymeneal, marital, nuptial, spousal, wedded, mated, married, united, paired.

ant. celibate, spouseless, single, unwed, unmarried.

conjugation *n.* CONJUNCTION.

conjunction *n.* union, association, combination, connection, alliance, concatenation, meeting, intercourse, conjugation, coincidence, league, assemblage, concourse.
ant. division, cleavage, separation, disjunction, breach, split.

conjunctive *adj.* CONNECTIVE.

conjuncture *n.* **1** pass, concatenation, case, juncture, condition, point, stage, predicament. **2** CONNECTION.

conjuration *n.* incantation, enchantment, spell, mumbo jumbo, abracadabra, hocus-pocus, magic, sorcery, legerdemain, pass.

conjure *v.* **1** beg, appeal, beseech, implore, supplicate, adjure, entreat, pray. **2** enchant, bewitch, ensorcell, charm, fascinate, bedevil, voodoo, hex, jinx.

connect *v.* join, combine, unite, link, hinge, articulate, depend, couple, associate, relate, adjoin, bind, conjoin, amalgamate, continue, relate.
ant. detach, separate, uncouple, disconnect, dissociate.

connection *n.* **1** juncture, union, joint, link, bond, nexus, couple, coupling, conjunction, combination, conjuncture, jointure, association, splice, amalgam, blend, relationship, togetherness, coherence, continuity, alliance. **2** friend, associate, relative, acquaintance, ally, entrée, sponsor, in.
ant. **1** separation, disjunction, severance, alienation, distance, hiatus.

connective *adj.* joining, binding, conjunctive, unitive, combinative, coalescent, conjunct, conjugate, conjoined, combined, united.
ant. separate, discrete, discontinuous, disjoined, unconnected, disparate.

conniption *n.* FIT.

connivance *n.* COLLUSION.

connive *v.* conspire, cabal, scheme, collude, plot, cook up, contrive, intrigue, concert, complot.

connoisseur *n.* expert, authority, judge,

arbiter, cognoscente, critic, savant, aesthete, maven, adept.
ant. ignoramus, novice, greenhorn, duffer, tyro.
connotation *n.* implication, significance, denotation, intension, import, drift, intent, sense, meaning, force, essence, reference, substance, definiens.
connote *v.* imply, suggest, insinuate, convey, betoken, mean, signify, indicate, intimate, hint, allude, involve.
connubial *adj.* conjugal, matrimonial, nuptial, marital, hymeneal, married, wedded, mated, bridal, spousal.
ant. celibate, unmated, single, unmarried, spouseless, unwed.
conquer *v.* overcome, subdue, subjugate, master, prevail, triumph, surmount, succeed, vanquish, defeat, beat, quell, overpower.
ant. lose, fail, succumb, fall, give up.
conqueror *n.* victor, lord, champion, master, vanquisher, subduer, conquistador, winner, ace.
ant. slave, liege, subject, victim, failure, loser.
conquest *n.* victory, triumph, overthrow, defeat, invasion, domination, subjugation, occupation, subjection, subversion, ascendancy, overcoming, win.
conquistador *n.* CONQUEROR.
consanguineous *adj.* RELATED.
conscientious *adj.* **1** scrupulous, honest, principled, conscionable, upright, just, honorable, ethical, moral, righteous. **2** careful, thorough, meticulous, exacting, precise, attentive, painstaking, particular.
ant. **1** corrupt, unscrupulous, immoral, dishonest, dishonorable. **2** careless, slovenly, sloppy, hasty, heedless.
conscionable *adj.* CONSCIENTIOUS.
conscious *adj.* **1** cognizant, sentient, aware, awake, alert, sensible, alive, apprehending, perceiving, responsive. **2** deliberate, premeditated, intentional, studied, calculated, knowing, responsible.

ant. **1** unconscious, asleep, insensible, unaware, dead. **2** unwitting, automatic, chance, inadvertent, unintentional.
consciousness *n.* awareness, knowledge, concern, recognition, sensibility, feeling, intelligence, apperception, understanding, apprehension, sense, mind, thought, psyche.
ant. insensibility, ignorance, impassivity, unconsciousness, unawareness.
consecrate *v.* **1** hallow, bless, purify, sanctify, exalt, anoint, baptize, cleanse. **2** devote, dedicate, give over, set apart, ordain, destine, surrender, commit.
ant. **1** desecrate, profane, taint, pollute, violate.
consecutive *adj.* successive, sequential, serial, uninterrupted, subsequent, ensuing, next, sequent, succeeding, following, continuous.
ant. interrupted, irregular, intermittent, discontinuous, unconnected, simultaneous.
consensus *n.* agreement, unanimity, consent, concord, unison, concurrence, concordance, accord, affirmation, harmony.
ant. disagreement, strife, discord, dissension, contradiction, protest.
consent *v.* agree, yield, accede, acquiesce, permit, assent, concur, accept, approve, subscribe. —*n.* agreement, acquiescence, concurrence, yielding, assent, compliance, acceptance, permission, approval, subscription, approbation, accord, harmony, consensus.
ant. *v.* dissent, object, demur, deny, oppose. *n.* disagreement, dissent, denial, disavowal, veto, refusal.
consequence *n.* **1** result, event, outcome, upshot, sequel, effect, aftermath, development, issue. **2** distinction, note, importance, significance, moment, weight, import.
ant. **1** antecedent, cause, origin, preliminary, precursor, source. **2** unimportance, insignificance, obscurity, nullity, trashiness, paltriness.

consequent *adj.* SUBSEQUENT.

consequential *adj.* important, weighty, memorable, momentous, striking, notable, eventful, signal, far-reaching, noteworthy, grave, serious.
ant. inconsequential, trivial, slight, insignificant, worthless.

consequently *adv.* therefore, hence, accordingly, thus, so, ergo, necessarily, inevitably, unavoidably, wherefore.

conservation *n.* protection, preservation, safekeeping, maintenance, safeguarding, upkeep, support, saving, salvation, custody, defense.
ant. negligence, impairment, consumption, deterioration, loss, destruction.

conservative *adj.* traditional, unchanging, moderate, cautious, guarded, prudent, tory, die-hard, conventional, hidebound, reactionary, middle-of-the-road, right-wing, standpat.
ant. progressive, modern, innovative, avant-garde, new-fangled, revolutionary.

conserve *v.* save, preserve, protect, sustain, maintain, uphold, keep, safeguard, spare, husband, nurse, horde.
ant. spend, consume, exhaust, deplete, use up, neglect.

consider *v.* **1** think, regard, reflect, deliberate, study, contemplate, ponder, mull over. **2** *take into account:* remember, allow for, bear in mind, heed, note, count, weigh.
ant. 2 ignore, omit, forget, leave out, pass over, disregard.

considerable *adj.* **1** sizable, large, goodly, tidy, ample, extensive, substantial, marked, reasonable, tolerable, comfortable. **2** significant, important, influential, notable, noticeable, noteworthy, meritorious, respectable, conspicuous.
ant. 1 trifling, minuscule, scanty, small, insignificant. **2** humble, insignificant, nondescript, unimportant, contemptible.

considerate *adj.* thoughtful, mindful, tactful, attentive, patient, kind, deliberate, prudent, serious, sober, discreet, judicious, sensitive.
ant. inconsiderate, thoughtless, unfeeling, heedless, harsh, unkind.

consideration *n.* **1** thinking, reflection, deliberation, study, thought, contemplation, advisement, cogitation, judgment. **2** thoughtfulness, regard, tact, considerateness, kindness, friendliness, attention. **3** reason, motive, ground, score, sake, cause, circumstance, inducement, account. **4** fee, recompense, remuneration, compensation, pay, payment, commission, percentage, stipend.
ant. 2 disregard, neglect, carelessness, thoughtlessness, default.

consign *v.* **1** entrust, confide, delegate, commit, make over, relegate, refer. **2** forward, send, transmit, dispatch, convey, ship.

consignment *n.* sending, transmittal, dispatch, allocation, shipment, transmission, conveyance, relegation, commitment, committal, distribution, delivery.

consistency *n.* compatibility, harmony, consonance, correspondence, congruity, agreement, conformity, coherence, similarity, uniformity.
ant. contradiction, incongruity, inconsistency, disagreement, variance, difference.

consistent *adj.* consonant, homogeneous, congruous, harmonious, correspondent, compatible, conformable, congenial, agreeing, suitable, sympathetic.
ant. inconsistent, inconsonant, incoherent, illogical, incompatible, unsuitable.

consist in inhere, lie, pertain, enter into, appertain, reside, belong.

consist of comprise, amount to, include, incorporate, involve, contain.

consolation *n.* solace, comfort, cheer, succor, condolence, encouragement, reassurance, sympathy, easement, relief.
ant. aggravation, harassment, provo-

cation, discouragement, discomfort, irritation.

consolatory *adj.* COMFORTING.

console *v.* comfort, solace, cheer, soothe, ease, support, gladden, assuage, alleviate, relieve, calm, encourage, sympathize.
ant. afflict, grieve, dishearten, aggravate, depress, trouble.

consolidate *v.* **1** solidify, secure, strengthen, concentrate, condense, compact, compress. **2** unite, merge, combine, federate, organize, incorporate, amalgamate, centralize.
ant. **1** weaken, dilute, thin, rarefy, vaporize. **2** diversify, disband, disorganize, dissociate, separate, disperse.

consonance *n.* agreement, harmony, accord, consistency, congruence, congruity, unison, concord, attunement, accordance, consonancy, correspondence.
ant. dissonance, opposition, disparity, conflict, divergence, disagreement.

consonant *adj.* consistent, concordant, compatible, harmonious, congenial, sympathetic, apt, fit, corresponding, congruous, like, agreeable, suitable, accordant.
ant. inconsonant, discordant, inconsistent, opposed, divergent, contrary.

consort *n.* companion, associate, partner, colleague, helper, alter ego, sidekick (*Slang*). —*v.* **1** harmonize, conform, agree, accord, jibe, tally, square. **2** associate, join, companion, fraternize, unite, mingle.
ant. *v.* **1** disagree, oppose, contend, diverge, clash. **2** disassociate, shun, leave, avoid, hold aloof.

conspicuous *adj.* **1** *to the senses:* noticeable, visible, apparent, plain, patent, obvious, prominent, salient, evident, clear. **2** *to judgment:* unusual, striking, notable, remarkable, eminent, egregious, flagrant, prominent, brilliant, illustrious, flashy.
ant. **1** inconspicuous, indistinct, hidden, shrouded, indistinguishable.

2 insignificant, unobtrusive, obscure, low-key, cryptic.

conspiracy *n.* connivance, collusion, machination, plot, cabal, intrigue, racket, scheme, compact, complot, plan, frame-up, combination, scenario.

conspirator *n.* TRAITOR.

conspire *v.* **1** plot, contrive, scheme, cabal, devise, intrigue. **2** concur, combine, cooperate, conduce, tend, contribute.

constant *adj.* **1** steady, resolute, persevering, firm, stalwart, determined, unflagging, persistent, diligent, assiduous, tough, uncompromising, dogged, hard-nosed (*Slang*). **2** faithful, loyal, true, staunch, devoted, trustworthy, dedicated, steadfast, trusty. **3** invariable, unchanging, changeless, continual, uniform, even, incessant, continuous, regular.
ant. **1** inconstant, irresolute, vacillating, faltering, uncertain. **2** fickle, inconstant, faithless, treacherous, disloyal. **3** variable, uneven, fitful, intermittent, irregular.

constellation *n.* array, assemblage, collection, group, gathering, cluster, configuration, arrangement, muster, pattern, galaxy.

consternation *n.* amazement, confusion, dismay, shock, astonishment, distraction, bewilderment, stupefaction, awe, alarm, trepidation, indignation, horror.
ant. composure, equanimity, tranquillity, repose, calm, quietude.

constituent *adj.* component, intrinsic, constituting, composing, elementary, basic, integral, inherent, fundamental, elemental. —*n.* component, element, ingredient, rudiment, part, factor, essential, module, unit.
ant. *adj.* adventitious, extrinsic, supplemental, alien, external, superadded.

constitute *v.* **1** form, make up, compose, frame, compound, produce, concoct. **2** establish, found, institute, fix, set up, create, determine. **3** ordain, name, appoint, authorize, depute, install, empower, relegate.

constitution *n.* COMPOSITION.

constrain *v.* **1** compel, oblige, necessitate, coerce, force, press, drive, urge. **2** confine, curb, restrain, prevent, check, repress, bind, enthrall.
ant. 1 plead, coax, implore, beg, request. **2** free, release, liberate, loose, let go.

constrained *adj.* COMPULSORY.

constraint *n.* **1** compulsion, necessity, obligation, force, coercion, pressure, duress. **2** embarrassment, diffidence, modesty, bashfulness, shame, inhibition, shyness. **3** curb, check, rein, damper, ban, obstacle, obstruction, hindrance, roadblock, proscription, hang-up (*Slang*).

constrict *v.* compress, bind, squeeze, contract, narrow, shrink, condense, clench, cramp, tighten, pinch, strangulate.
ant. expand, widen, stretch, dilate, distend, open.

constriction *n.* **1** contraction, narrowing, strangulation, compression, clenching, squeezing, narrowness, stenosis, coarctation. **2** bottleneck, stricture, constraint, squeeze, bind, restraint, pressure, cramp.

construct *v.* build, fabricate, erect, constitute, put up, make, invent, frame, shape, arrange, set up, found, raise, produce, create, form, engineer.
ant. raze, dismantle, demolish, topple, destroy, overthrow.

construction *n.* **1** building, erection, fabrication, organization, manufacture, formation, creation, invention, composition, configuration. **2** interpretation, meaning, exegesis, explanation, explication, reading, rendering.

constructive *adj.* affirmative, positive, helpful, useful, advantageous, favorable, valuable, productive, practical, beneficial.
ant. destructive, negative, adverse, inimical, contrary.

construe *v.* explain, interpret, understand, decipher, explicate, spell out, take, read, infer, analyze, translate, expound, render.

consult *v.* discuss, confer, deliberate, parley, inquire, counsel, palaver, talk, meet, consider, rap (*Slang*).

consultation *n.* consulting, conference, discussion, deliberation, advisement, argument, council, counsel, colloquy, parley, session, hearing, interview, meeting, palaver.

consume *v.* **1** destroy, demolish, annihilate, ravage, lay waste, devastate, sack. **2** squander, exhaust, expend, waste, dissipate, use up, deplete. **3** engross, interest, preoccupy, absorb, monopolize, dominate, spellbind.
ant. 2 amass, collect, restore, hoard, accumulate.

consummate *v.* achieve, perfect, effect, accomplish, complete, crown, finish, compass, carry out, fulfill, execute, perform. —*adj.* perfect, absolute, supreme, thorough, utter, unqualified, unmitigated, complete, accomplished, conspicuous, excellent.
ant. *adj.* mediocre, indifferent, amateurish, unskilled, poor, insignificant.

consummation *n.* completion, fulfillment, capstone, realization, achievement, attainment, accomplishment, culmination, perfection, crown, acme, end, close.

consumption *n.* consuming, utilization, use, exploitation, assimilation, depletion, expenditure, exhaustion, dissipation, diminution, decrement, destruction, wastage.
ant. saving, conservation, preservation, husbandry, maintenance, restoration.

contact *n.* **1** meeting, collision, union, junction, juncture, touching, touch. **2** proximity, association, closeness, connection, communication, contiguity, relationship. —*v.* **1** touch, meet, graze, impinge, brush, scrape, swipe. **2** communicate with, approach, see, meet, reach, look up, seek out.

contagion *n.* communication, circulation, transference, transmission, dispersion, propagation, insinuation, suggestion, passage.

contagious *adj.* transmissible, communicable, catching, infectious, spreading, inoculable.

contain *v.* **1** hold, carry, accommodate, bear, enclose, surround. **2** comprise, include, comprehend, involve, embrace, embody, subsume. **3** restrain, control, hold back, repress, check, halt, stifle, limit, bind.

contaminate *v.* taint, defile, pollute, adulterate, corrupt, debase, vitiate, infect, besmirch, tarnish, soil, stain, sully, befoul, poison.
ant. purify, decontaminate, cleanse, purge, ameliorate, freshen.

contamination *n.* adulteration, defilement, pollution, impurity, taint, stain, degradation, debasement, corruption, vitiation, infection.

contemn *v.* DESPISE.

contemplate *v.* **1** gaze, survey, eye, view, behold, peer, look on, stare. **2** ponder, consider, meditate, ruminate, study, muse, reflect, think about, mull over, deliberate. **3** intend, plan, propose, consider, anticipate, look forward to, expect, foresee.

contemplation *n.* rumination, thought, consideration, meditation, reflection, speculation, study, deliberation, cogitation, reverie, musing, pondering.

contemplative *adj.* meditative, thoughtful, studious, reflective, pensive, ruminative, speculative, thinking, musing, rapt, engrossed, sober, deliberative.
ant. unreflective, scatterbrained, impulsive, impetuous, thoughtless, active.

contemporaneous *adj.* CONTEMPORARY.

contemporary *adj.* **1** contemporaneous, simultaneous, synchronous, coeval, coincident, coexistent, concurrent. **2** modern, up-to-date, current, latter-

day, living, present, recent, now, with-it (*Slang*).
ant. **2** historical, out-of-date, former, past, ancient, old-fashioned.

contempt *n.* **1** disdain, scorn, ridicule, mockery, derision, despite, contumely, condescension, arrogance. **2** shame, disgrace, dishonor, humiliation, abasement.
ant. **1, 2** respect, reverence, admiration, approval, regard, honor.

contemptible *adj.* despicable, vile, disreputable, scurvy, ignominious, wretched, abject, sorry, beggarly, base, mean, mean-spirited, worthless, petty, little, small-minded.
ant. admirable, respectable, worthy, excellent, estimable, decent.

contemptuous *adj.* disdainful, scornful, supercilious, sneering, derisive, mocking, impertinent, insulting, haughty, insolent, condescending, arrogant, imperious, high and mighty.
ant. respectful, deferential, humble, admiring, approving, obsequious.

contend *v.* **1** maintain, assert, declare, state, affirm, argue, debate, dispute, discuss, quarrel, oppose. **2** strive, vie, compete, emulate, contest, rival, fight, struggle, battle, engage, resist, clash.

contender *n.* CONTESTANT.

content[1] *n.* **1** significance, meaning, burden, gist, nub, heart, core, essence, intent, purport, substance, text. **2** capacity, size, volume, compass, measure.

content[2] *v.* satisfy, appease, gratify, mollify, beguile, win over, quiet, cheer, reconcile, please. —*adj.* CONTENTED. —*n.* CONTENTMENT.
ant. dissatisfy, disturb, offend, trouble, distract.

contented *adj.* satisfied, content, complacent, gratified, carefree, comfortable, serene, appeased, mollified, happy, pleased, cheerful, glad, tranquil, easygoing, at peace, snug, cozy, relaxed.
ant. dissatisfied, discontented, fret-

ful, uneasy, disgruntled, troubled, malcontent.

contention *n.* **1** strife, conflict, struggle, dispute, argument, dissension, discord, feud, wrangling, confrontation, enmity, rivalry. **2** assertion, claim, declaration, argument, thesis, position, point, view, opinion, viewpoint, point of view, idea.
ant. 1 agreement, peace, harmony, friendship, accord, cooperation.

contentious *adj.* quarrelsome, belligerent, combative, fractious, bellicose, disputatious, petulant, obstinate, stubborn, embattled, recalcitrant, captious.
ant. peaceable, harmonious, serene, amicable, orderly, calm.

contentment *n.* satisfaction, content, gratification, fulfillment, happiness, felicity, complacency, gladness, pleasure, joy, repletion, ease, comfort, *Gemütlichkeit*.
ant. discontent, misery, dissatisfaction, vexation, uneasiness, craving.

contest *n.* struggle, conflict, controversy, encounter, challenge, match, competition, dispute, argument, struggle, battle, fight, quarrel, confrontation, contention. —*v.* contend, strive, compete, vie, fight over, struggle, dispute, debate, challenge.

contestant *n.* competitor, entry, entrant, participant, contender, aspirant, combatant, opponent, rival.

context *n.* situation, circumstance, milieu, ambience, setting, framework, environment, case, background, frame of reference, contingency, relationship, orientation.

contiguous *adj.* touching, next, adjoining, abutting, proximate, immediate, conterminous, adjacent, near, neighboring, close, nearby, handy, propinquant.
ant. distant, far, remote, removed, separate, detached.

continence *n.* **1** self-restraint, self-control. **2** chastity, moderation, abstemiousness, purity, virtue, forbearance, temperance, sobriety.

ant. 1 incontinence. **2** licentiousness, carnality, excess, dissipation, debauchery, lechery.

continent *adj.* self-restrained, abstinent, chaste, temperate, moderate, self-controlled, restrained, austere, abstemious, sober, Spartan.
ant. licentious, unrestrained, incontinent, dissolute, wanton, prurient, impassioned.

contingency *n.* **1** chance, uncertainty, possibility, likelihood, probability, liability, eventuality, exigency. **2** juncture, emergency, pinch, crisis, accident, incidental, chance, strait, stroke.

contingent *adj.* uncertain, fortuitous, accidental, provisional, conditional, possible, chance, unexpected, random, unforeseen, casual, serendipitous. —*n.* group, body, deputation, delegation, quota, quorum, mission, task force.
ant. *adj.* planned, arranged, contrived, necessary, predetermined, foreseen.

continual *adj.* perpetual, repeated, repetitive, unending, repetitious, incessant, recurrent, recurring, continued, continuous, eternal, everlasting.
ant. sporadic, temporary, infrequent, intermittent, scattered, isolated.

continually *adv.* repeatedly, perpetually, constantly, incessantly, continuously, eternally, persistently, forever, always, ceaselessly, endlessly, interminably, perennially.
ant. occasionally, irregularly, fitfully, randomly, spasmodically, sometimes.

continuance *n.* **1** duration, prolongation, continuation, period, term, interval, time. **2** CONTINUITY.

continuation *n.* **1** continuance, continuity, persistence, endurance, duration, maintenance, recurrence, retention, perpetuation. **2** extension, prolongation, furtherance, advancement, resumption, addition, supplement, extra, addendum, postscript.

ant. **1**, **2** curtailment, retraction, pull-back, stoppage, termination, interruption, cessation.

continue v. **1** *extend in space:* extend, protract, stick out, abut, project, outreach, lie. **2** *extend in time:* prolong, protract, extend, maintain, preserve, perpetuate, last, persist, remain, go on, postpone, perdure, endure. **3** keep on, persist, persevere, hold out, stick at, pursue, remain, abide, endure, last, stay, tolerate, suffer, resist. ant. **1** retract. **2** terminate, cut short, end, leave off, finish, desist, cease. **3** give up, desist, surrender, weaken, flag, fail.

continuity n. continuation, extension, continuance, coherence, persistence, duration, progression, prolongation, perpetuation, succession, endurance, sequence. ant. cessation, stoppage, interruption, termination, suspension.

continuous adj. connected, extended, prolonged, unbroken, entire, whole, continuing, uninterrupted, unchanging, unremitting, intact, undivided, endless. ant. discontinuous, interrupted, suspended, broken, sporadic, divided, periodic.

contort v. twist, wrench, bend, buckle, deform, distort, warp, misshape, gnarl, knot, writhe, convolute. ant. straighten, smooth, compose, align, rectify, untangle.

contour n. outline, profile, silhouette, shape, form, figure, curve, slope, topography, relief.

contraband adj. forbidden, excluded, illicit, illegal, unlawful, unlicensed, bootleg, smuggled, prohibited, taboo.

contract v. **1** reduce, shrink, narrow, constrict, decrease, compress, shorten, condense, diminish, lessen, dwindle, reduce, abate. **2** agree, pledge, undertake, engage, covenant, bargain. —*n.* agreement, covenant, deal, commitment, compact, lease, arrangement, obligation, promise,

transaction, treaty, pact, commission. ant. *v.* **1** expand, enlarge, widen, lengthen, swell, magnify, increase.

contraction n. shortening, diminution, lessening, shrinkage, reduction, compression, condensation, abridgment, abbreviation, constriction, narrowing, decrease, abatement, lessening. ant. expression, increase, lengthening, augmentation, amplification.

contradict v. **1** deny, disagree, gainsay, rebut, refute, dispute, controvert, impugn, belie. **2** contravene, counteract, annul, abrogate, negate, thwart, obstruct, counter, combat, cancel out. ant. **1** agree, endorse, confirm, corroborate, second. **2** support, bear out, uphold, authenticate, verify.

contradictory adj. contrary, opposed, opposing, opposite, antithetical, antagonistic, conflicting, inconsistent, paradoxical, negative. ant. corroborative, confirmatory, consistent, compatible, like.

contraption n. contrivance, gadget, device, mechanism, construction, appliance, rig, invention, creation, gimmick.

contrary adj. **1** *of behavior:* perverse, wayward, froward, balky, restive, ornery, obstinate, fractious, cantankerous, unpredictable. **2** *of facts or opinions:* opposed, opposite, antagonistic, other, alternate, different, antithetical, complementary, contradictory, alternative, reverse, inconsistent. ant. **2** identical, parallel, similar, consistent.

contrast v. **1** compare, differentiate, distinguish, discriminate, collate. **2** differ, vary, diverge, deviate, mismatch, oppose. —*n.* difference, dissimilarity, disparity, antithesis, foil, counterpart, contradiction, distinction, divergence. ant. *n.* similarity, identity, affinity, sameness, agreement, coincidence.

contravene v. **1** act against, infringe on,

transgress, violate, negative, disobey, break, overreach. **2** contradict, deny, gainsay, disagree, negative, impugn, object, contend.

ant. 1 uphold, observe, comply, adhere to, satisfy. **2** affirm, agree, corroborate, sustain, support.

contretemps *n.* ACCIDENT.

contribute *v.* donate, furnish, give, supply, present, offer, bestow, dispense, subscribe, volunteer, cooperate, add to, chip in, supplement.

contribution *n.* grant, gift, subsidy, gratuity, award, offering, donation, present, allowance, dispensation, bestowal, endowment, payment, input.

contrite *adj.* remorseful, penitent, sorry, rueful, regretful, conscience-stricken, repentant, chastened, apologetic, compunctious.

ant. unrepentant, irreclaimable, hardened, impenitent, callous.

contrition *n.* REMORSE.

contrivance *n.* **1** scheme, invention, stratagem, design, artifice, ingenuity, inventiveness. **2** device, tool, gadget, apparatus, appliance, contraption, implement, artifact, gimmick.

contrive *v.* **1** scheme, plan, devise, plot, conspire, hatch, complot, intrigue. **2** improvise, invent, create, frame, design, form, make, manage.

ant. 2 destroy, demolish, smash, ruin, waste.

contrived *adj.* artificial, labored, strained, unnatural, affected, forced, overdone, elaborate, ingenious, meretricious, arty, recherché.

ant. artless, simple, natural, straightforward, unaffected, plain.

control *v.* restrain, curb, guide, govern, master, dominate, manipulate, determine, conduct, manage, command, supervise, steer, regulate, direct, pilot, oversee, prescribe. —*n.* management, guidance, restraint, mastery, sway, rule, government, supervision, authority, subjection, command.

controversial *adj.* debatable, disputatious, arguable, controvertible, disputable, contestable, sensitive, delicate, questionable, doubtful, argumentative, polemical, moot.

controversy *n.* debate, disputation, quarrel, dispute, conflict, argument, contention, altercation, wrangling, disagreement, polemics, confrontation, discord.

ant. agreement, consensus, harmony, accord, conformity, concord.

controvert *v.* deny, oppose, confute, contradict, dispute, refute, rebut, disprove.

ant. prove, demonstrate, verify, affirm, maintain, corroborate.

controvertible *adj.* transformable, transmutable, mutable, changeable, alterable, variable.

ant. fixed, immutable, invariable, stable, unchanging.

contumacy *n.* insubordination, lawlessness, disorderliness, disrespect, insolence, rebelliousness, disobedience, obstinacy, impertinence, delinquency, revolt.

ant. obedience, respectfulness, tractability, docility, civility, orderliness.

contumely *n.* rudeness, insolence, abuse, scorn, contempt, disdain, obloquy, arrogance, reproach, opprobrium, impertinence, superciliousness.

ant. politeness, esteem, civility, respect, regard, courtesy.

contusion *n.* BRUISE.

conundrum *n.* puzzle, mystery, enigma, riddle, paradox, poser, problem, charade, arcanum, sphinx.

convalesce *v.* RECUPERATE.

convalescence *n.* recuperation, rehabilitation, recovery, improvement, rally, restoration, rejuvenation, renascence, cure, remission.

convene *v.* convoke, assemble, summon, call, muster, rally, gather, bring together, meet, congregate, cite.

ant. dismiss, dissolve, adjourn, disperse, disband, recess.

convenience *n.* serviceability, handiness, suitability, adaptability, usefulness, utility, fitness, satisfaction, benefit, service, ease, comfort.

ant. inconvenience, disadvantage, nuisance, discomfort, awkwardness, embarrassment.

convenient *adj.* **1** serviceable, handy, manageable, advantageous, suited, adapted, comfortable, easy, commodious, beneficial. **2** nearby, near, accessible, adjacent, available, attainable, reachable, close by, at hand, proximate.

ant. 1 inconvenient, awkward, unsuitable, unwieldy, inopportune, unmanageable. **2** remote, out-of-the-way, unavailable, inaccessible, distant.

convention *n.* **1** meeting, assemblage, gathering, congregation, caucus, convocation, synod, parley. **2** custom, practice, formality, tradition, conventionality, usage, agreement, understanding, practice, code, protocol.

conventional *adj.* **1** customary, habitual, normal, traditional, prescriptive, ceremonial, ceremonious, formal, ritual. **2** commonplace, trite, banal, routine, ordinary, undistinguished, pedestrian, unimaginative, stereotyped, mechanical, usual.

ant. 1 innovative, avant-garde, extempore, improvisational. **2** spontaneous, original, unusual, imaginative.

conventionality *n.* CONVENTION.

converge *v.* **1** join, meet, unite, link, conjoin, combine, connect, close in upon, center, focus, focalize, funnel. **2** focus, concur, conduce, conspire, concide, agree.

ant. 1 separate, disperse, scatter, spread, disassemble, disconnect.

convergence *n.* conflux, confluence, concourse, concurrence, conjunction, concentration, focalization, meeting, encounter.

ant. separation, dispersion, segregation, dissolution, segmentation.

conversant *adj.* familiar, acquainted, versed, proficient, *au fait,* capable, skilled, practiced, tutored, learned,

erudite, well-informed, up on, *au courant,* up-to-date.

ant. unfamiliar, ignorant, uninformed, unskilled, incapable, unversed.

conversation *n.* talk, communication, chat, dialogue, discussion, colloquy, discourse, conference, converse, tête-à-tête, interlocution, palaver, chitchat, gab, rap (*Slang*).

conversationalist *n.* speaker, talker, interlocutor, discourser, colloquist, gossip.

converse[1] *v.* speak, talk, communicate, chat, discuss, confabulate, discourse, parley, confer, colloque, palaver, chin, chew the rag (*Slang*), gossip, chitchat, gab. —*n.* CONVERSATION.

converse[2] *adj.* transposed, reversed, opposite, counter, inverse, obverse, contrary. —*n.* opposite, reverse, obverse, contrary, antithesis.

conversion *n.* change, transformation, modification, changeover, adaptation, alteration, revision, inversion, transmutation, transfiguration, metamorphosis, transmogrification.

convert *v.* **1** change, transform, transmute, alter, vary, metamorphose, transfigure, translate. **2** modify, retool, reform, revise, reorganize, invert, divert, adapt. —*n.* proselyte.

convertible *adj.* ADAPTABLE.

convey *v.* **1** transport, carry, bear, bring, transmit, lead, conduct, fetch, move, guide, send, forward, dispatch, remit, consign. **2** communicate, impart, tell, inform, relate, disclose, reveal, divulge, confide.

conveyance *n.* transference, movement, transmission, conduction, guidance, consignment, communication, disclosure, revelation.

convict *n.* criminal, prisoner, felon, inmate, delinquent, malefactor, culprit, jailbird, con (*Slang*), captive.

conviction *n.* belief, faith, persuasion, view, viewpoint, opinion, *idée fixe,* position, conclusion, credence, tenet, doctrine, dogma.

ant. unbelief, doubt, disbelief, uncertainty, skepticism, incredulity.

convince *v.* persuade, satisfy, influence, win over, bring round, sway, impress, assure, prevail upon.

ant. dissuade, discourage, deter, divert.

convincing *adj.* persuasive, plausible, telling, cogent, valid, sound, solid, potent, logical, powerful, impressive, conclusive, effective, incontrovertible.

ant. unconvincing, implausible, invalid, fallacious, unimpressive, dubious, unsound.

convivial *adj.* festive, jovial, gay, joyous, genial, sociable, cordial, vivacious, merry, jolly, hilarious, lively, affable.

ant. staid, reserved, reticent, unsociable, dour, taciturn, sober.

conviviality *n.* festivity, joviality, joyousness, geniality, sociability, cordiality, vivaciousness, jollity, mirth, hilarity, liveliness, affability, gaiety.

ant. unsociability, joylessness, sobriety, staidness, reticence, taciturnity, dourness.

convocation *n.* assembly, assemblage, congregation, gathering, ingathering, convention, conclave, congress, concourse, forgathering, council.

convoke *v.* summon, assemble, gather, muster, call, convene, collect, congregate.

ant. adjourn, dismiss, recess, terminate.

convolution *n.* fold, coil, twist, roll, buckle, volute, spiral, curlicue, helix, scroll, worm.

convoy *n.* escort, guard, safeguard, bodyguard, protection. —*v.* accompany, escort, chaperon, lead, usher, attend, guard, protect, watch.

ant. *v.* desert, abandon, forsake.

convulsion *n.* spasm, fit, paroxysm, throe, tremor, pang, twinge, throb, tic, twitch.

convulsive *adj.* fitful, spasmodic, agitative, sporadic, jerky, violent, turbulent, volcanic, explosive.

cook up concoct, improvise, invent, devise, brew, falsify, fabricate, scheme, contrive.

cool *adj.* **1** chilly, cold, icy, gelid, unheated. **2** self-controlled, self-possessed, composed, calm, collected, unruffled, placid, sedate, imperturbable, unflappable, dispassionate, undisturbed, unimpassioned, deliberate. **3** unfriendly, chilling, cold-blooded, frigid, distant, indifferent, unconcerned, superior, apathetic, detached, standoffish, aloof, nonchalant. —*v.* **1** chill, refrigerate, freeze, ice. **2** allay, calm, moderate, quiet, temper, assuage, abate, dampen, mitigate, calm down, cool off, blunt. —*n.* *Slang* self-possession, self-control, imperturbability, self-containment, self-reliance, dignity, confidence, temperateness, self-discipline, self-mastery, placidity, calmness, poise.

ant. *adj.* **1** warm, heated. **2** agitated, ruffled, excited, disturbed, passionate, impassioned, perturbed. **3** friendly, warm, approachable, concerned, committed. *v.* **1** heat, warm up, melt. **2** aggravate, intensify, inflame, ruffle, exasperate.

coop *n.* **1** enclosure, pen, cage, confine, fold, pound, hutch, compound, paddock. **2** *Slang* JAIL. —*v.* confine, shut up, fence, pen, impound, cage, intern, jail, imprison, confine, lock up, incarcerate.

cooperate *v.* collaborate, unite, pool, coordinate, coact, combine, help, pitch in, contribute, conjoin, join, band, play ball, collude, conspire.

cooperation *n.* unity, concert, coaction, concurrence, participation, union, collaboration, complicity, association, confederation, compliance, helpfulness, combination, collusion, coordination, detente.

cooperative *adj.* concerted, participatory, joint, united, unified, supportive, helpful, coactive, harmonious, contributive, collusive.

ant. uncooperative, aloof, destructive, separate, autonomous, individual.

coopt v. appropriate, preempt, assimilate, absorb, persuade, influence, monopolize, usurp, assume, expropriate.

coordinate adj. equal, coequal, equivalent, alike, parallel, tantamount, synonymous, analogous, correlative. —v. harmonize, organize, adjust, regulate, systematize, synchronize, correlate, methodize, arrange, equalize, adapt, agree, marshal.

coordination n. harmony, cooperation, synchronization, equalization, participation, concordance, unity, agreement, correspondence, correlation, accordance, conformity, partnership.

cope v. manage, make do, control, weather, work out, deal with, contend, handle, succeed, accomplish, persevere, carry on, hack it (*Slang*).

copious adj. ample, abundant superabundant, plentiful, plenteous, bountiful, replete, luxuriant, chock-full, overflowing, surplus, large, rich, full, liberal.
ant. scanty, scant, meager, insufficient, sparse, paltry, spare.

cop-out n. *Slang* pretext, excuse, pretense, alibi, justification, story, gimmick, device.

cop out *Slang* 1 renege, renounce, deny, revoke, disavow. 2 quit, give up, abandon, withdraw, forgo, desert, forsake, skip.

copse n. thicket, grove, scrub, scrubwood, brush, brushwood, covert, wood, stand.

copulation n. sexual intercourse, sexual union, lovemaking, coition, coitus, coupling, mating, congress, fornication, commerce, carnal knowledge.

copy n. reproduction, imitation, facsimile, duplicate, replica, carbon, likeness, example, representation, counterfeit. —v. 1 reproduce, duplicate, reduplicate, replicate, counterfeit. 2 imitate, model, pattern, simulate, mimic, ape, mock, impersonate, parody, burlesque, caricature.

ant. n. original, archetype, prototype, type, pattern, model.

coquet v. 1 flirt, philander, trifle, dally, wanton, tease, pet. 2 trifle, dally, dillydally, toy, dawdle, play, loiter, delay, procrastinate, idle, putter, fiddle, lag, linger.
ant. 2 hasten, speed, expedite, rush, quicken, accelerate.

coquette n. FLIRT.

coquettish adj. flirtatious, flirty, wanton, dallying, coy, fast, loose, inviting.
ant. standoffish, proper, staid, distant, cool.

cord n. bond, bind, tie, link, connection, hold, nexus, union, yoke, coupling, umbilical cord.

cordial adj. warm, sincere, hearty, heartfelt, genial, sociable, friendly, ardent, affectionate, gracious, amiable, amicable, responsive, outgoing.
ant. cool, cold, unfriendly, hostile, indifferent, withdrawn.

cordiality n. warmth, sincerity, heartiness, geniality, friendliness, affability, earnestness, amiability, amicability, graciousness.
ant. coldness, insincerity, cheerlessness, severity, disagreeableness.

cordon n. line, circle, barrier, girdle, ring, picket, guard. —v. enclose, isolate, fence, separate, surround, guard, pen, hem, quarantine.

core n. center, middle, hub, nucleus, kernel, heart, focus, substance, gist, nitty-gritty (*Slang*), meat, pith, nub, essence, quintessence.
ant. shell, covering, skin, exterior.

cork v. stop, stopper, restrain, check, curb, plug, halt, arrest, repress, bridle, curtain, obstruct, block, hinder, control.
ant. uncork, release, unbridle, let go.

corker n. *Slang* WONDER.

corking adj. *Slang* EXCELLENT.

corner v. TRAP.

cornerstone n. BASIS.

corny adj. *Slang* trite, banal, hackneyed, unsophisticated, square, old-fashioned, stale, commonplace, sen-

timental, maudlin, ordinary, stereotyped.
ant. fresh, original, unusual, sophisticated, extraordinary, remarkable.

corollary *n.* inference, deduction, conclusion, result, resultant, upshot, outcome, denouement, effect, consequence, end, product, fruit, aftermath.

corporal *adj.* bodily, physical, material,
corporeal, carnal, fleshly, incarnate,
somatic, anatomical.

corporate *adj.* combined, collective,
joint, united, unified, shared, pooled,
federated, merged, allied, cooperative, collaborative, communal, several.

corporeal *adj.* **1** substantial, material,
tangible, solid, palpable, physical, somatic, animal, real, embodied. **2**
CORPORAL.
ant. incorporeal, spiritual, intangible, insubstantial, ethereal.

corps *n.* body, group, band, team, organization, squad, crew, troupe, set,
circle, party, force, detachment,
outfit, company.

corpse *n.* body, cadaver, carcass, corpus, zombie, stiff (*Slang*).

corpulence *n.* stoutness, obesity,
fleshiness, fatness, fattiness, portliness, chubbiness, plumpness, pudginess, tubbiness, blubber, bulkiness.
ant. thinness, skinniness, leanness,
slenderness, lankness.

corpulent *adj.* fat, obese, fleshy, stout,
portly, rotund, chubby, fatty, fattish,
plump, pudgy, podgy, tubby, blub-
bery, bulky, bloated, roly-poly, overweight.
ant. thin, skinny, gaunt, lean, slender, lank, emaciated.

corpus *n.* **1** COLLECTION. **2** CORPSE.

corral *v.* **1** enclose, mass, gather, collect, fence in, round up, cluster,
bunch, rein in, paddock, herd, drive.
2 seize, capture, secure, collar, grab,
arrest, detain, hold, nab, pinch, fetter, trap, apprehend.

correct *v.* **1** rectify, adjust, remedy,
right, set right, redress, improve,
emend, amend, doctor, touch up, reform, mend, repair, regulate, fix,
cure, restore, recondition. **2** rebuke,
chasten, scold, admonish, discipline,
reprove, reprimand, chide, chastise,
castigate, censure, instruct. —*adj.* **1**
accurate, precise, right, true, faultless, errorless, exact, factual, strict,
perfect, unerring, unmistaken, infallible, all right, OK. **2** proper, acceptable, appropriate, fit, fitting, suitable,
standard, regular, expected, suited,
befitting, right, becoming, meet, diplomatic, seemly, kosher (*Slang*).
ant. *v.* **1** ruin, spoil, destroy, mar, impair, harm. **2** coddle, pet, pamper,
indulge, cherish, spoil. *adj.* **1** incorrect, faulty, imprecise, untrue, false,
wrong. **2** improper, unacceptable,
unsuitable, unseemly, unbecoming,
inappropriate, ill-chosen.

correctable *adj.* REPARABLE.

correction *n.* **1** rectification, improvement, emendation, amendment,
righting, reparation, indemnification,
redress, remediation. **2** remedy, repair, restorative, curative, antidote,
corrective, relief, righting. **3** chastisement, punishment, chastening,
reproof, discipline, castigation, admonishment, admonition, instruction.

corrective *adj.* remedial, improving,
rectifying, rehabilitative, amenda-
tory, restorative, curative, healing,
palliative, educative therapeutic,
punitive, penal, disciplinary. —*n.*
remedy, curative, antidote, relief,
remediation, palliative, reparation,
restorative.

correlate *n.* COORDINATE.

correlation *n.* reciprocation, reciprocity, interdependence, correspondence, mutuality, alternation,
equivalence, give-and-take, *quid pro
quo*, interchange, trade-off.

correspond *v.* agree, conform, harmonize, accord, match, correlate, tally,
concur, coincide, complement, fit,
suit, converge, unite.

ant. differ, diverge, disagree, vary, deviate.

correspondence *n.* agreement, conformity, harmony, accordance, concurrence, congruity, consonance, correlation, coherence, coincidence, receptivity, uniformity, similarity, comparability, analogy.
ant. incongruity, dissimilarity, discordancy, incoherence.

correspondent *adj.* CORRESPONDING.

corresponding *adj.* reciprocal, analogous, equivalent, correspondent, correlative, interchangeable, complementary, mutual, interrelated, common.

corridor *n.* hall, hallway, passage, passageway, gallery, arcade, aisle, lobby, cloister.

corrigible *adj.* REPARABLE.

corroborate *v.* CONFIRM.

corroboration *n.* proof, confirmation, verification, substantiation, affirmation, certification, support, validation, evidence, testimony, authentication, attestation, vindication, endorsement.

corroborative *adj.* AFFIRMATIVE.

corrosive *adj.* caustic, scathing, venomous, poisonous, deadly, virulent, harsh, sarcastic, mordant, trenchant, biting, cutting, sharp, brutal, cruel.
ant. gentle, soothing, pleasant, courteous, kind, soft-spoken.

corrugated *adj.* ridged, furrowed, fluted, grooved, wrinkled, serrated, crinkled, channeled, troughed, ribbed, creased, uneven, scored, crenellated, rough.
ant. smooth, flat, level, even.

corrupt *adj.* **1** immoral, depraved, debased, sinful, base, wicked, perverted, vicious, evil, iniquitous, degenerate, dissolute, debauched, reprobate, wanton, perverse, fallen. **2** dishonest, dishonorable, unprincipled, unscrupulous, venal, untrustworthy, knavish, bribable, sordid, fraudulent, crooked, shady, rotten. **3** altered, adulterated, doctored, distorted, bowdlerized, falsified, expur-

gated, changed, perverted. —*v.* entice, lure, suborn, demoralize, deprave, debase, debauch, vitiate, pervert, dishonor, disgrace, defraud, abuse, debase, taint, defile, infect.
ant. **1** pure, upright, chaste, noble, moral, good, righteous. **2** principled, honest, honorable, incorruptible. **3** complete, whole, unaltered, unchanged, uncut.

corruptible *adj.* VENAL.

corruption *n.* **1** immorality, depravity, debasement, sinfulness, wickedness, perversion, viciousness, evil, vice, iniquity, baseness, degeneration, dissolution, debauchery, wantonness, perversity. **2** dishonesty, bribery, venality, crookedness, shadiness, unscrupulousness, knavery, malfeasance, fraudulence. **3** adulteration, falsification, perversion, distortion, alteration, expurgation, bowdlerization.
ant. **1** morality, purity, goodness, righteousness, justice.

cortege *n.* train, retinue, entourage, suite, staff, court, escort, procession, company.

coruscate *v.* sparkle, glitter, flash, shine, gleam, glare, beam, glisten, glister, blaze, glow, scintillate, twinkle, flicker.

cosmic *adj.* immense, vast, enormous, huge, great, extensive, large, gigantic, colossal, mammoth, boundless, unlimited, measureless, infinite, monstrous.
ant. tiny, small, minuscule, infinitesimal, microscopic, limited.

cosmopolitan *adj.* international, urban, urbane, metropolitan, universal, sophisticated, catholic, unprovincial, worldly, worldly-wise, well-traveled.
ant. provincial, local, small-town, narrow, parochial.

cosmos *n.* UNIVERSE.

cosset *v.* pamper, coddle, indulge, mollycoddle, pet, caress, cuddle, pat, cocker, humor, baby, cater, spoil, gratify.
ant. chasten, discipline, punish, chide, scold, rebuke, restrain.

cost *n.* **1** price, charge, expense, expenditure, outlay, rate, figure, amount, damage, tab, sum. **2** loss, suffering, detriment, penalty, expense, damage, pain, sacrifice.

costly *adj.* **1** expensive, dear, high-priced, valuable, precious, steep, stiff, priceless, inestimable, exorbitant, extortionate. **2** splendid, sumptuous, opulent, rich, priceless, precious, luxurious, magnificent, grand, elegant, exquisite, superb, fine, excellent.
ant. 1 inexpensive, cheap, low-priced, reasonable, economical. **2** poor, sordid, squalid, tawdry, inferior, ordinary.

costume *n.* clothing, clothes, ensemble, outfit, rig, get-up, uniform, habit, garb, attire, apparel, garment, gown, dress. —*v.* clothe, dress, outfit, garb, attire, rig, robe, don, array, deck, gown.
ant. *v.* undress, disrobe, doff, strip.

cosy *adj.* COZY.

coterie *n.* group, set, circle, society, association, clique, club, company, brotherhood, fraternity.

cotillion *n.* DANCE.

cottage *n.* cabin, bungalow, chalet, croft, shack, hut, cot, lodge, shed, hovel, *pied-à-terre*.
ant. palace, castle, chateau, mansion.

cotton to befriend, like, embrace, help, receive, succor, stand by, support, favor, incline toward, take up with, hit it off.

cotton up to FLATTER.

couch *v.* phrase, express, voice, word, utter, frame, set forth, verbalize.

cough up *Slang* deliver, surrender, hand over, give up, fork over (*Slang*), come across, plunk down, ante up (*Slang*), shell out.

council *n.* **1** assembly, meeting, convocation, conclave, convention, conference, synod, gathering, session, caucus, parley, congress, colloquy. **2** COUNSEL.

counsel *n.* **1** consultation, deliberation, consideration, advisement, conference, parley, council, powwow, session, palaver. **2** advice, opinion, recommendation, instruction, finding, suggestion, caution, warning, forewarning, admonition, forethought, guidance. **3** lawyer, attorney, counselor, advisor, advocate, jurist, barrister (*Brit.*), solicitor (*Brit.*). —*v.* **1** recommend, advise, favor, urge, prompt, instruct, charge, advocate, exhort, caution, warn. **2** confer, talk, deliberate, convene, meet, assemble, gather, caucus, powwow, parley, consult, discourse.

counselor *n.* **1** ADVISOR. **2** COUNSEL.

count *v.* **1** number, enumerate, numerate, tally, total, score, figure, estimate, reckon, compute, calculate, list, call off, account. **2** consider, regard, think, look upon, judge, adjudge, deem, hold. **3** rely, depend, bank, hinge, lean, reckon, pin faith, put faith. —*n.* **1** enumeration, calculation, reckoning, computation, numbering, numeration, estimation, accounting, summation. **2** sum, lump, result, total, totality, tally, quantity, amount, aggregate, summation, addition.

countenance *n.* **1** face, features, visage, physiognomy, lines, profile, outline, silhouette, traits, contour. **2** expression, appearance, aspect, look, mien, semblance, air, cast, image, presence. **3** approval, support, sanction, favor, encouragement, air, assistance, patronage, approbation, succor, good will. —*v.* approve, support, sanction, tolerate, favor, endorse, abet, encourage, aid, assist, succor, patronize, facilitate.
ant. *n.* **3** disapproval, disfavor, hindrance, obstruction. *v.* condemn, disapprove, prohibit, inhibit, disfavor, impede, proscribe.

counter *adv.* contrary, contrarily, contrariwise, inversely, vice versa, conversely, over against, versus, contra, athwart. —*adj.* opposing, opposite, contrary, antithetical, contradictory, contrasting, inverse, obverse, adverse. —*v.* **1** oppose, check, counteract, neutralize, offset, counterbalance, countervail, counterpoise, contravene, thwart, annul. **2** parry, counterattack, riposte, check, counterpunch, respond, return, ward off, hit back.

counteract *v.* oppose, resist, offset, check, thwart, neutralize, annul, counterbalance, counterattack, countervail, contravene, frustrate.

counterbalance *v.* COUNTERPOISE.

counterfeit *v.* **1** pretend, feign, simulate, sham, fake, dissemble, dissimulate, deceive, fabricate, assume. **2** imitate, forge, copy, fake, falsify, mimic, ape, model. —*n.* imitation, forgery, copy, phony, slug, dummy, fake, reproduction, duplicate, double, facsimile, replica, ersatz, substitute. —*adj.* **1** false, spurious, fake, bogus, fraudulent, forged, ersatz, phony, substitute, pseudo, make-believe. **2** pretended, feigned, sham, simulated, fraudulent, false, mock, fake, unreal, artificial, deceptive, hypocritical, put-on.
ant. *adj.* **1** genuine, authentic, real, original, true, actual. **2** honest, open, unconcealed, genuine, felt.

countermand *v.* cancel, revoke, recall, rescind, abrogate, repeal, retract, reverse, override, set aside, annul, nullify, abolish, void.

counterpart *n.* parallel, analogue, correlate, complement, supplement, likeness, similarity, double, replica, copy, duplicate, reproduction, facsimile, *doppelgänger*.
ant. antithesis, opposite, contradictory, contrary, antipodes, antonym.

counterpoint *n.* contrast, foil, complement, balance, counterbalance, setoff, antithesis, counterpoise.

counterpoise *v.* offset, compensate, counterbalance, counteract, balance, countervail, equalize, neutralize, allow for, make up for.

countersign *n.* password, watchword, signal, sign, code, cue, shibboleth, identification.

count in INVOLVE.

countless *adj.* innumerable, numberless, uncounted, unnumbered, many, numerous, incalculable, infinite, myriad, multitudinous, untold, legion, limitless.
ant. few, minute, finite.

count on EXPECT.

count out EXCLUDE.

countrified *adj.* rural, rustic, agrarian, bucolic, pastoral, agricultural, provincial, sylvan, arcadian.
ant. urban, citified, metropolitan, cosmopolitan, sophisticated.

coup *n.* masterstroke, stroke, feat, stunt, maneuver, blow, *coup de main, tour de force*, achievement, accomplishment.

couple *v.* join, link, unite, fasten, associate, pair, conjoin, connect, attach, combine, bind, bond, yoke, amalgamate.
ant. separate, unfasten, disjoin, disconnect, divide, sever.

courage *n.* bravery, fearlessness, intrepidity, valor, dauntlessness, fortitude, pluck, heroism, daring, hardihood, mettle, backbone, gallantry, chivalry, audacity, derring-do, grit, guts (*Slang*).
ant. cowardice, timidity, cravenness, baseness, faintheartedness.

courageous *adj.* brave, fearless, intrepid, valorous, valiant, stout, gallant, spirited, stouthearted, resolute, bold, rugged, dashing, doughty, mettlesome, manly, chivalrous, indomitable, dogged.
ant. cowardly, craven, timid, fainthearted, fearful, skittish.

courier *n.* messenger, runner, bearer, carrier, envoy, emissary, herald.

course *n.* **1** progression, progress, passage, march, speed, movement, headway, advancement, way. **2** path, way, route, trail, track, channel, road, passage, pass, artery. **3** policy, conduct, program, behavior, deportment, method, mode, procedure. **4** sequence, succession, order, turn, progression, regularity, rotation, series, line, set. —*v.* **1** run, race, hurry, rush, speed, gallop, fly, scamper, hasten, bolt, dart, dash, move apace, sprint, traverse. **2** hunt, chase, follow, pursue, track, stalk, trail, ride.

ant. *v.* **1** delay, slow, stroll, straggle, lag.

court *n.* **1** courtyard, quadrangle, patio, areaway, piazza, cloister, plaza, square. **2** palace, castle, chateau, *palazzo, palais.* —*v.* **1** woo, pay suit, sue, wheedle, flirt, spoon, coo, spark, make eyes. **2** fawn, curry favor, kowtow, flatter, ingratiate, grovel, toady, truckle, cringe, cajole, pander, softsoap, cultivate. **3** invite, solicit, tempt, lure, incite, provoke, attract, entice.

ant. 2, 3 shun, put off, turn away, snub, cold-shoulder.

courteous *adj.* polite, respectful, civil, well-mannered, well-bred, urbane, debonair, affable, gracious, courtly, obliging, genteel, deferential, gallant, decent.

ant. discourteous, rude, impolite, ill-mannered, curt, brusque.

courtesan *n.* prostitute, mistress, paramour, concubine, call girl, demimondaine, hetaera, whore.

courtesy *n.* **1** graciousness, politeness, respect, civility, breeding, urbanity, comity, gentility, cultivation, polish, gallantry, consideration, refinement, affability. **2** consideration, generosity, respect, regard, deference, honor, munificence, benevolence, good will, hospitality, benefaction.

ant. 1 discourtesy, impoliteness, ill-breeding, rudeness, boorishness.

courtliness *n.* gallantry, chivalry, grace, elegance, civility, breeding, decorum, gentility, etiquette, politeness.

ant. boorishness, impoliteness, ill breeding, rudeness, barbarism, incivility.

courtly *adj.* ceremonious, ceremonial, decorous, dignified, stately, formal, august, aristocratic, elegant, polished, high-bred, graceful, polite, refined, stylish, genteel.

ant. unrefined, coarse, vulgar, graceless, crude, churlish.

covenant *n.* compact, agreement, contract, promise, pledge, bargain, arrangement, understanding, pact, treaty. —*v.* promise, agree, contract, pledge, undertake, stipulate, bargain, engage.

cover *v.* **1** spread, overspread, overlay, superimpose, extend over, mantle, shroud, envelop, coat, enwrap, clothe, invest. **2** hide, conceal, cover up, secrete, curtain, veil, cloak, shroud, enshroud, screen, disguise, mask, hood, camouflage, sleek. **3** include, comprise, comprehend, embrace, embody, contain, take in, provide for, subsume, absorb. **4** report, detail, write up, describe, tell, chronicle. **5** substitute for, stand in, double, alternate, back up, fill in, pinch-hit, sub. —*n.* **1** disguise, mantle, shroud, curtain, cloak, veil, screen, mask, lid, coat, hood. **2** shelter, protection, covering, asylum, refuge, concealment, defense, guard, safeguard, sanctuary. **3** mask, concealment, camouflage, subterfuge, disguise, deception, straw man.

ant. *v.* **2** uncover, reveal, strip, unmask, expose.

covering *n.* COVER.

covert *adj.* **1** concealed, secret, hidden, clouded, unseen, unknown, unsuspected, clandestine, *sub rosa*, surreptitious, privy, dissembled. **2** sheltered, protected, covered, concealed, disguised, screened, shielded. —*n.* shelter, hut, blind, thicket, copse, shade, grove, camouflage, ambush.

ant. *adj.* **1** overt, open, revealed, unconcealed, candid, apparent. **2** exposed, vulnerable.

cover-up *n.* CAMOUFLAGE.

cover up COVER.

covet *v.* desire, lust, envy, long for, wish, yearn, fancy, begrudge, aspire, hanker, crave, thirst, burn, hunger.

ant. relinquish, renounce, reject, forswear, forsake.

covetous *adj.* greedy, acquisitive,

grasping, lustful, avaricious, rapacious, selfish, stingy, mercenary, venal, longing, yearning.

ant. generous, unselfish, liberal, charitable, benevolent.

covey *n.* band, clique, set, group, coterie, flock, cluster, party, company.

cow *v.* intimidate, daunt, dismay, horrify, appall, unnerve, subdue, frighten, terrify, bully, threaten.

ant. embolden, hearten, inspirit.

coward *n.* poltroon, milksop, recreant, quitter, cad, dastard, caitiff, craven, mollycoddle, flincher, cur, sissy, weak sister, milquetoast.

ant. hero, daredevil, lion.

cowardice *n.* fearfulness, poltroonery, dastardliness, timidity, pusillanimity, baseness, faintheartedness.

ant. bravery, temerity, boldness, intrepidity, audacity.

cowardly *adj.* fearful, craven, timid, dastardly, pusillanimous, recreant, timorous, fainthearted, chickenhearted, lily-livered, yellow, scared, sissy, weak-hearted, weak-kneed, spineless.

ant. brave, bold, valiant, courageous, dauntless, stouthearted.

cower *v.* cringe, quail, shrink, grovel, flinch, skulk, wince, recoil, shy, sneak, fawn.

ant. strut, flaunt, swagger.

co-worker *n.* ASSOCIATE.

coxcomb *n.* fop, dandy, dude, exquisite, beau, swell, peacock, Beau Brummell, popinjay, jackanapes, Teddy Boy (*Slang*).

coy *adj.* shy, diffident, retiring, self-effacing, bashful, modest, shrinking, sheepish, abashed, reserved, skittish.

ant. bold, pert, saucy, brazen, forward, arch.

cozen *v.* cheat, deceive, delude, hoodwink, defraud, swindle, trick, gyp, spoof, overreach, hoax, dupe, bilk.

cozy *adj.* snug, comfortable, warm, safe, secure, sheltered, homey, restful, friendly, comfy.

ant. uncomfortable, cold, unfriendly, unsafe, unpleasant.

crab *v.* **1** complain, grumble, carp, grouse, bitch (*Slang*), murmur, whine, moan, bewail, lament, nag, fault, criticize. **2** ruin, spoil, frustrate, interfere, mess up, thwart, baffle, balk, complicate, intrude. —*n.* CRANK.

crabbed *adj.* **1** abstruse, recondite, obscure, garbled, complicated, abstract, difficult, vague, blurred, ambiguous, covert, enigmatic, concealed, puzzling. **2** CRABBY.

ant. clear, straightforward, precise, transparent, obvious, distinct.

crabby *adj.* cross, ill-natured, crabbed, bad-tempered, sour, testy, petulant, ill-humored, sulky, snappish, peevish, moody, cantankerous, grouchy.

ant. even-tempered, good-natured, genial, pleasant, sweet.

crack *v.* **1** break, split, cut, sever, fracture, chip, splinter, rip, slash, chop, cleave, rend, tear, rive. **2** crush, destroy, smash, obliterate, crumble, grind, crumple, shatter, wreck, pulverize, devastate. **3** *strike sharply:* strike, clip, punch, hit, beat, sock, slap. **4** *make a sharp sound:* snap, clap, clout, slap, bang, whack, thump, crackle, pop, crunch. —*n.* **1** fissure, opening, separation, flaw, gap, fracture, rupture, break, cleft, chink, breach, cranny, interstice, rent, rift, breach. **2** report, snap, clap, pop, burst, explosion, shot, volley, salvo, whop. **3** *resounding blow:* snap, slap, clout, blow, smack, slam, bang, whack, thump, thwack, clout, pelt, pound, pop. —*adj.* superior, excellent, par excellence, preeminent, choice, first-class, prime, first-rate, tops (*Slang*).

crackbrain *n.* CRACKPOT.

crackbrained *adj.* CRACKED.

crackdown *n.* DISCIPLINE.

crack down DISCIPLINE.

cracked *adj.* **1** broken, split, fissured, crazed, fractured, crannied, damaged, faulty, defective, chinky, rent. **2** hoarse, husky, shrill, raspy, throaty, croaking, creaky, dry, whispery, scratchy, harsh, rough. **3** crazy, insane, unsound, demented, deranged, nuts (*Slang*), nutty (*Slang*), mad, berserk, crazed, touched, crackpot, crackbrained, lunatic, loony (*Slang*).

ant. 2 smooth, clear, mellow, dulcet, ringing, mellifluous. **3** sane, lucid, rational, sound, level-headed.

crackerjack *adj.* outstanding, excellent, first-class, expert, superior, topflight, preeminent, tops (*Slang*), superb, leading, top-drawer, supreme, distinguished, notable, exceptional, extraordinary. —*n.* genius, prodigy, past master, wizard, savant, colossus, master, expert.

ant. *adj.* inferior, undistinguished, unexceptional, unimpressive, mediocre, ordinary.

crackle *v.* crack, crepitate, snap, pop.

crackpot *n.* eccentric, crackbrain, crank, maniac, monomaniac, madman, fool, character, nut (*Slang*), screwball (*Slang*), kook (*Slang*), freak (*Slang*). —*adj.* eccentric, foolish, insane, erratic, odd, queer, impractical, cracked, crackbrained, nuts (*Slang*), nutty (*Slang*), balmy (*Slang*), cuckoo (*Slang*), kooky (*Slang*), kinky (*Slang*).

ant. *adj.* sane, lucid, rational, sound, conventional.

crackup *n.* **1** crash, accident, wreck, collision, smash-up, pile-up, disaster, catastrophe, mishap. **2** breakdown, nervous breakdown, collapse, prostration, exhaustion, fatigue.

cradle *n.* birthplace, origin, source, spring, springhead, fountain, fountainhead, fount, well, wellspring. —*v.* support, protect, defend, shield, secure, watch over, nurture, foster, nurse, train.

craft *n.* **1** skill, art, ingenuity, ability, dexterity, specialty, aptitude, expertise, expertness, artistry, mastery, facility. **2** business, job, vocation, employment, métier, calling, handicraft, handiwork, trade, line, skill. **3** guile, cunning, trickery, artfulness, deceit,

craftiness, artifice, duplicity, double-dealing, hypocrisy, underhandedness, treachery, perfidy.

ant. trust, honesty, sincerity, dependableness, reliability, open-handedness.

craftsman *n.* ARTISAN.

craftsmanship *n.* ARTISTRY.

crafty *adj.* guileful, deceitful, duplicitous, artful, cunning, sly, double-dealing, hypocritical, treacherous, two-faced, perfidious, underhanded.

ant. guileless, honest, sincere, straightforward, frank, artless.

crag *n.* precipice, cliff, bluff, escarpment, scarp, palisade, aiguille.

craggy *adj.* rocky, precipitous, rugged, stony, rock-ribbed, rock-bound, scraggy, jagged, broken, rough.

cram *v.* press, pack, crowd, stuff, jam, ram, choke, fill, compress, squeeze, overcrowd, force, satiate, sate, overindulge, gorge, glut, surfeit, saturate.

cramp[1] *n.* **1** clamp, clasp, brace, fastener, band, yoke. **2** restraint, obstruction, hindrance, crimp, check, hold, stoppage, encumbrance, snag, stint, damper, control, bar, dam, shackle. —*v.* hinder, prevent, restrain, confine, crimp, secure, hold, constrain, control, constrict, limit, restrict, check, shackle, clamp, bar, dam, rein in, circumscribe.

cramp[2] *n.* contraction, spasm, seizure, charley horse, twinge, convulsion, twitch, crick, pang, kink.

crank *n.* **1** eccentric, oddball, crackpot, nut (*Slang*), freak (*Slang*), weirdo (*Slang*), character, oddity. **2** grouch, crab, scold, curmudgeon, grump, sourpuss (*Slang*), killjoy, crosspatch, sorehead.

cranky *adj.* cross, testy, sulky, choleric, splenetic, irascible, touchy, ill-tempered, crotchety, cantankerous, snappish, crabby, petulant, peevish, sour, captious.

ant. calm, placid, tranquil, serene, even-tempered, good-natured.

cranny *n.* opening, fissure, gap, crack, crevice, chink, aperture, orifice, cleft, interstice, breach, rift, cavity, break, rent, gash.

crap *n.* EXCREMENT.

crapulous *adj.* drunk, intoxicated, inebriated, sottish, bibulous, tipsy, boozy, plastered (*Slang*), intemperate, gluttonous, voracious, piggish, hoggish.

ant. temperate, moderate, sober, self-restrained, abstemious.

crash *v.* **1** smash, demolish, shatter, disintegrate, dash, splatter, splinter, shiver, break, sever, obliterate, crush, blow up, crumble, crumple, split. **2** totter, topple, collapse, crack up, collide, clash, smash, shatter, wreck, devastate. **3** clash, bang, rumble, boom, thunder, clatter, roar. —*n.* **1** clash, bang, crack, din, boom, racket, blast, rending, clatter, clap, burst, split, rend. **2** collision, crash, smash-up, crackup, clash, wreck, devastation, pile-up, accident, impact. **3** collapse, ruin, failure, depression, fall, breakdown, debacle, crisis.

crass *adj.* **1** coarse, unrefined, gross, rough, crude, indelicate, rude, vulgar, lowbrow, philistine, insensitive, unpolished, boorish, churlish, mean. **2** dull, dull-witted, stupid, dumb, obtuse, stolid, doltish, ignorant, simple, insensitive, thick-headed, foolish, lumpish, half-witted, witless, sottish, asinine, dense.

ant. **1** fine, refined, sensitive, delicate, cultivated, polished. **2** brilliant, bright, intelligent, clever, shrewd.

crassness *n.* **1** coarseness, grossness, crudeness, vulgarity, indelicacy, insensitivity, rudeness, crudity, roughness, earthiness, boorishness, meanness, churlishness, unrefinement. **2** dullness, stupidity, ignorance, simplicity, doltishness, witlessness, simple-mindedness, oafishness, sottishness, asininity, lumpishness, obtuseness, denseness, stolidity.

ant. **1** refinement, sensitivity, delicacy, cultivation. **2** intelligence, brilliance, wit, astuteness, quickness, brightness.

crate *n.* box, framework, kit, barrel, cage, hamper, pannier, basket. —*v.* pack, store, encase, case, box, stow, enclose, carry, transport, haul, cart, ship, freight.

crave *v.* **1** beg for, ask, solicit, seek, request, beseech, petition, implore, plead for, entreat, supplicate, pray for. **2** long for, desire, yearn for, wish for, want, hanker after, pine for, hunger for, thirst for, covet, lust for, lust after.

ant. **1** relinquish, renounce, cede, yield, forswear, waive, reject.

craven *adj.* cowardly, dastardly, pusillanimous, yellow, fearful, timid, timorous, sneaking, base.

ant. bold, daring, brave, intrepid, fearless.

craving *n.* desire, lust, longing, yearning, wish, hankering, hunger, thirst, need, requirement.

crawl *v.* CREEP.

craze *v.* madden, dement, derange, unsettle, unbalance, crack, unhinge. —*n.* fad, rage, enthusiasm, mania, distemper, fashion, last word, mode, fancy, whim, furor, *dernier cri*, passion.

crazy *adj.* **1** insane, mad, demented, deranged, lunatic, potty, daft, daffy, pixilated, berserk, unbalanced, incompetent, buggy (*Slang*), touched, cracked, raving, rabid, unhinged, maniacal, nuts (*Slang*), batty (*Slang*). **2** infuriated, enraged, wild, delirious, hysterical, inflamed, furious, beside oneself, at one's wit's end, maddened. **3** impractical, illogical, absurd, foolish, wild, quixotic, potty, (*Brit.*), fantastical, visionary, unworkable, shaky. **4** enthusiastic, wild, eager, zealous, rabid, ardent, fervent, excited, devoted, passionate, fanatical.

ant. **1** sane, well-balanced, rational, lucid, sound. **2** calm, serene, level-headed, controlled. **3** practical, workable, useful, down-to-earth, sensible.

4 apathetic, indifferent, cool, unconcerned, impassive.

creak *n.* squeak, grate, scrape, grind, rasp, stridulation, scratch. —*v.* squeak, rasp, grind, grate, screech, grit, scratch, stridulate, scrape.

creaky *adj.* squeaky, screechy, raspy, rasping, grating, strident, sharp, acute, piercing, penetrating, unoiled, rusty, stridulous, stridulant.

cream *v. Slang* DEFEAT.

crease *n.* wrinkle, fold, pleat, rumple, ridge, ruffle, crimp, crimple, double. —*v.* wrinkle, fold, double, ply, ruffle, rumple, crimp, crimple, muss.

create *v.* **1** originate, make, cause, occasion, constitute, produce, procreate. **2** design, fashion, conceive, form, invent, discover, evolve, dream up, coin, devise, hatch, contrive, mold, shape, construct, build.

creation *n.* birth, nativity, nascency, procreation, genesis, formation, fabrication, imagination, formulation, conception.

creative *adj.* **1** productive, prolific, fertile, fecund, propagative, fruitful, progenitive, pregnant, reproductive, procreative. **2** inventive, original, ingenious, imaginative, resourceful, gifted, artistic, talented, endowed, clever, demiurgic. **ant. 1** barren, sterile, impotent, effete, arid, unproductive. **2** unimaginative, unresourceful, plodding.

creativity *n.* inventiveness, originality, ingenuity, talent, art, endowment, cleverness, productivity, fertility, fecundity. **ant.** sterility, barrenness, impotence, inanition.

creator *n.* maker, author, originator, generator, inventor, framer, producer, designer, fashioner, founder, architect, builder, artist, artisan.

creature *n.* **1** being, animal, beast, lower animal, critter, brute. **2** human being, being, man, mankind, person, homo sapiens, mortal, individual, personage, somebody, body, someone, one, living soul, earthling.

credence *n.* belief, assurance, reliance, credit, trust, confidence, faith, trustworthiness, dependence, certitude, certainty. **ant.** distrust, mistrust, disbelief, doubt, incredulity.

credentials *n.* AUTHORIZATION.

credibility *n.* trustworthiness, believability, likelihood, plausibility, prospect, veracity, verisimilitude, reasonableness, tenability. **ant.** implausibility, unlikelihood, improbability, untenability.

credible *adj.* reliable, believable, trustworthy, plausible, probable, ostensible, tenable, acceptable, possible, likely, feasible, persuasive, reasonable, unquestionable. **ant.** unbelievable, unreliable, incredible, implausible, unlikely, dubious, questionable.

credit *n.* **1** belief, trust, confidence, faith, reliance, credence, trustworthiness, credibility. **2** character, repute, estimation, name, esteem, regard, standing, position, rank, prestige, renown. **3** approval, praise, commendation, honor, merit, acknowledgment, regard, esteem. —*v.* **1** recognize, acknowledge, accept, vouchsafe, notice, identify, realize, concede, grant, endorse. **2** trust, rely upon, depend on, confide in, swear by, count on, bank on, lean on. **3** ascribe, impute, attribute, assign, refer, charge to, accredit, lay to, trace to, saddle with, blame on, arrogate. **ant.** *n.* **1** mistrust, disbelief, skepticism, doubt. **3** disapproval, dispraise, disesteem. *v.* **1** ignore, disregard, overlook. **2** mistrust, doubt, disbelieve.

creditable *adj.* praiseworthy, meritorious, estimable, respectable, deserving, worthy, honorable, exemplary, noble, fine. **ant.** unworthy, undeserving, disreputable, disgraceful.

credo *n.* CREED.

credulity *n.* TRUST.

credulous *adj.* believing, trusting, trustful, gullible, unsuspecting, overtrustful, unwary, ingenuous, green, naive, innocent.

ant. incredulous, wary, alert, cautious, watchful, shrewd.

creed *n.* credo, confession, formula, profession, belief, tenet, doctrine, persuasion, dogma, faith, conviction.

creek *n.* stream, streamlet, run, rivulet, rill, freshet, spring, bayou, runnel, runlet, brooklet.

creep *v.* **1** crawl, wriggle, writhe, worm, squirm, drag, snake, wind, sneak, steal, tiptoe, dawdle, glide. **2** cringe, cower, quail, shrink, squirm, grovel, wince, skulk, flinch, crouch, toady, truckle, bow, scrape.

creepy *adj.* disgusting, revolting, repugnant, awful, unpleasant, frightening, dreadful, jittery, eerie, weird, sinister, direful, ominous.

crescent *adj.* increasing, growing, waxing, enlarging, swelling, lengthening, multiplying.

ant. decreasing, waning, diminishing, subsiding.

crest *n.* **1** comb, cockscomb, tuft, plume, plumage, topknot, mane, crown, headpiece, panache, pompon, feather, aigrette. **2** top, summit, crown, ridge, tip, height, cap, pinnacle, peak, apex, vertex. **3** zenith, climax, culmination, acme, high tide, heyday, prime, height, flower, bloom, pinnacle, peak, apex. —*v.* cap, top, crown, peak, tip.

ant. *n.* **3** nadir, ebb, bottom.

crestfallen *adj.* dejected, depressed, discouraged, downhearted, sad, dispirited, disheartened, despondent, cast down, downcast, morose, melancholy, gloomy, woebegone, blue, oppressed, unhappy.

ant. happy, cheerful, delighted, satisfied, glad.

cretaceous *adj.* CHALKY.

crevice *n.* fissure, crack, split, rift, cleft, cranny, chink, scissure, rent, slit, breach, gap, break, lacuna, hole.

crew *n.* group, squad, gang, team, company, band, troupe, clique, party, set, crowd, horde, force, host, mob, bunch.

crib *v.* plagiarize, cheat, copy, pirate, steal, rob, take, swipe, lift, purloin, filch, pinch, shoplift, rook, poach, rip off (*Slang*).

crick *n.* spasm, convulsion, contraction, cramp, twitch, twinge, kink, ache, pang.

crime *n.* **1** felony, offense, misdemeanor, tort, infraction, malefaction, illegality. **2** transgression, violation, wrong, wrongdoing, misconduct, delinquency, iniquity, sin, wickedness, unrighteousness, dereliction, villainy, trespass, malefaction, vice, outrage.

criminal *adj.* **1** guilty, culpable, felonious, condemnable, blameworthy, censurable, reprehensible, reproachable, indictable, chargeable, peccant. **2** disgraceful, regrettable, shameful, wicked, vile, immoral, abominable, wrong, unlawful, sinful, iniquitous, delinquent, outrageous, vicious. —*n.* felon, convict, culprit, offender, delinquent, malefactor, prisoner, inmate.

ant. *adj.* **1** guiltless, blameless, innocent, faultless. **2** upright, moral, good, innocent, virtuous.

crimp *v.* **1** plait, flute, corrugate, fold, crease, crimple, twist, wrinkle, buckle, coil, roll, scallop, goffer. **2** curl, wave, friz, frizzle, crisp, ripple, shape, twirl, roll, pat, primp. **3** hinder, cramp, obstruct, bar, thwart, prevent, block, trammel, check, encumber, retard, impede, restrain, hobble. —*n.* **1** pleat, flute, fold, crease, wrinkle, coil, goffer. **2** obstruction, hindrance, bar, block, barrier, check, encumbrance, impediment, deterrent, restraint, hobble, obstacle, pall, wet blanket.

cringe *v.* **1** draw back, flinch, shrink, cower, quail, shy, recoil, stoop, duck, skulk. **2** truckle, fawn, crawl, grovel, flatter, toady, gratify, bow, scrape, bootlick.

crinkle *v.* **1** wrinkle, crumple, twist,

twirl, crimp, crimple, rumple, pucker, kink, wave, undulate, muss, ruffle. **2** crackle, rustle, swish, murmur, hum, whisper, whir, stir. —*n.* wrinkle, ruffle, crimple, kink, ripple, wave, undulation.

ant. *v.* **1** smooth, straighten, flatten, iron, level.

cripple *v.* **1** maim, lame, paralyze, mangle, injure, wound, disable, mutilate, lacerate, hamstring, hock, amputate. **2** impair, disable, weaken, paralyze, ruin, destroy, harm, enfeeble, wound, incapacitate, emasculate.

ant. 2 repair, rebuild, strengthen, restore, cure.

crisis *n.* turning point, emergency, climax, exigency, strait, pinch, rub, crux, dilemma, predicament, plight, trial, quandary, confrontation, crunch (*Slang*).

crisp *adj.* **1** brittle, crumbly, friable, fragile, frangible, breakable. **2** clean, neat, tidy, done up, clean-cut, trim, spruce, orderly, ordered, smart. **3** terse, pithy, trenchant, plain-spoken, piquant, scintillating, sprightly, sharp, brilliant, witty, lively. **4** bracing, invigorating, stimulating, refreshing, tonic, cool, brisk, chilly.

ant. 2 sloppy, untidy, disorderly, dirty, slovenly, slipshod. **3** prolix, wordy, diffuse, verbose, tedious, witless, vapid.

criterion *n.* standard, rule, test, yardstick, principle, guideline, guidepost, measure, parameter, proof, touchstone, fact, law, model, norm, canon, gauge, scale, example.

critic *n.* judge, connoisseur, cognoscente, adept, aesthetician, dilettante, virtuoso, arbiter, expert.

critical *adj.* **1** faultfinding, censorious, condemnatory, captious, carping, disapproving, caviling, severe, disparaging, unflattering, derogatory, hypercritical, cutting. **2** discriminating, judicious, tasteful, exact, precise, fastidious, nice, fine, analytical, acute, discerning, perspicacious,

scrupulous. **3** risky, perilous, dangerous, suspenseful, hazardous, precarious, ticklish, slippery, uncertain, touch-and-go, chancy, harrowing, hairy (*Slang*). **4** decisive, grave, serious, urgent, pressing, important, vital, essential, weighty, determining, crucial, sensitive, telling.

ant. 1 commendatory, supportive, approving, helpful. **2** undiscriminating, injudicious, loose, lax. **3** safe, certain, sound, sure, assured.

criticism *n.* **1** evaluation, judgment, appreciation, appraisal, assessment, analysis, estimate, discernment, discrimination, reflection. **2** censure, stricture, animadversion, pan, knock, diatribe, hatchet job, reproof, sarcasm, condemnation, slam, rap (*Slang*). **3** review, critique, comment, commentary, write-up, editorial, article, dissertation, treatise, study, notice, analysis, descant.

ant. 2 approval, praise, rave, acclaim, accolade, commendation.

criticize *v.* **1** judge, evaluate, examine, appraise, dissect, review, treat, analyze, investigate, survey, scan, probe. **2** censure, fault, blame, flay, denounce, ridicule, condemn, pillory, damn, slam, animadvert, score, excoriate, oppugn, pan, reprehend, roast, rake, scarify, scathe, scorch, rap (*Slang*).

ant. 2 praise, commend, acclaim, approve, laud, extol, applaud.

critique *n.* review, examination, commentary, comment, write-up, article, notice, editorial, remark, discussion, appreciation, assessment.

critter *n.* CREATURE.

croak *v. Slang* DIE.

crony *n.* friend, buddy, chum, companion, pal, comrade, mate, colleague, sidekick (*Slang*), bedfellow, roommate, partner, *ami, amigo.*

crook *n.* **1** bend, curve, curvature, angle, arc, turn, hook, bow, flexure, inflection, fold. **2** criminal, felon, shyster, thief.

crooked *adj.* **1** bent, angled, angular,

winding, wavy, curved, bowed, sinuous, devious, zigzag, tortuous, twisted, hooked, serpentine, spiral, oblique. **2** tricky, dishonest, thievish, unscrupulous, fraudulent, unprincipled, deceptive, underhanded, crafty, cunning, unfair, insidious. **ant. 1** straight, smooth, flat, level, even. **2** honest, straight, scrupulous, open-handed, trustworthy, fair.

crop *v.* trim, cut, clip, top, lop, snip, mow, shear, barber, pare, prune.

crop up ARISE.

cross *n.* **1** crucifix, rood, holy rood. **2** trouble, suffering, misfortune, trial, tribulation, misery, burden, difficulty, distress, affliction, calamity, adversity, woe, sorrow. —*v.* **1** traverse, pass over, ford, cut across, overpass, go across, ply, travel over, transit. **2** intersect, crisscross, lace, intertwine, intertwist, interweave, interlink, entwine, twist, braid, entangle. **3** oppose, thwart, frustrate, baffle, contradict, foil, deny, resist, hinder, check, prevent, interfere, confront. **4** interbreed, hybridize, mongrelize, crossbreed, mix, blend, cross-fertilize, cross-pollinate. —*adj.* **1** contrary, opposed, opposing, adverse, unfavorable, opposite, contradictory, counter, antithetical, reverse, antagonistic. **2** ill-tempered, peevish, petulant, waspish, crabbed, crabby, cranky, churlish, sulky, cantankerous, sullen, complaining, snappish, fretful, moody, testy. **ant.** *v.* **3** support, assist, help, sustain. *adj.* **1** obliging, compliant, tractable, favorable, consenting. **2** agreeable, pleasant, amiable, serene.

cross-examine *v.* EXAMINE.

cross-eye *n.* strabismus, squint, walleye, exotropia.

cross-grained *adj.* STUBBORN.

crosspatch *n.* CRANK.

crotchet *n.* eccentricity, whimsy, whim, vagary, quirk, caprice, freakishness, peculiarity, idiosyncrasy, irregularity, oddity.

crotchety *adj.* eccentric, perverse, cantankerous, erratic, flighty, freakish, whimsical, capricious, quirky, odd, unpredictable, peculiar, bizarre, fey. **ant.** steadfast, constant, steady, predictable, undistracted, normal.

crouch *v.* **1** stoop, bend, squat, bow, kneel. **2** cringe, cower, grovel, quail, crawl, truckle, fawn, flatter, toady, bootlick, kowtow, wheedle. —*n.* crouch, stoop, squat, bend, kneel.

crow *v.* exult, boast, jubilate, gloat, rejoice, vaunt, brag, bluster, triumph, swagger, strut. **ant.** depreciate, belittle, disparage, discredit, minimize.

crowd *n.* **1** throng, multitude, host, company, herd, swarm, horde, gang, flock, array, crush, troop. **2** masses, people, populace, proletariat, plebeians, rabble, mob, hoi polloi, grass roots, riffraff, rank and file. **3** clique, coterie, set, circle, party, knot, clan, cabal, class, ring, gang, junta, body, faction. —*v.* **1** shove, push, press, jostle, shoulder, elbow, jolt, force, joggle, butt, batter. **2** cram, pack, press, jam, squeeze, cramp, force, congest, compress, lump, bunch, bundle. **3** assemble, throng, swarm, flock, gather, herd, huddle, congregate, collect, muster, surge, cluster, mass, stream, concentrate. **ant.** *v.* **3** disperse, separate, scatter, break up, dissolve.

crowded *adj.* PACKED.

crown *n.* **1** sovereign, monarch, ruler, king, queen, emperor, empress. **2** crest, summit, peak, pinnacle, top, tip, apex, acme. —*v.* **1** cap, surmount, head. **2** climax, complete, consummate, finish, cap, perfect, fulfill, round out, terminate, compass, top. **ant.** *n.* **2** pit, nadir, depth, underpinning, base.

crucial *adj.* **1** critical, final, grave, serious, pivotal, decisive, weighty, far-reaching, urgent, pressing, vital, essential, central, determining, sensitive. **2** trying, difficult, severe, grave, acute, knotty, tough, formidable, complicated, intricate, ticklish, pains-taking, onerous, toilsome.

ant. 2 easy, simple, uncomplicated, effortless.

crucible *n.* TEST.

crucify *v.* torture, torment, rack, perse-cute, wring, harrow, convulse, ago-nize, distress, brutalize, trouble, mis-treat, annoy, tease.

ant. soothe, comfort, console, tran-quilize, pacify, assuage.

crude *adj.* **1** *lacking refinement:* unrefined, coarse, gross, ill-man-nered, brutish, churlish, tactless, heavy, uncouth, awkward, crass, clumsy, vulgar, primitive, inartistic, uncultured. **2** *rough in workman-ship:* coarse, unpolished, incomplete, unrefined, sketchy, rough, rude, makeshift, inferior, primitive, func-tional, unadorned, rough-hewn, jerry-built, schlocky (*Slang*). **3** un-disguised, bold, blunt, bare, frank, abrupt, brusque, harsh, direct, rough, candid, unvarnished, stark, exposed.

ant. 1 refined, polished, well-man-nered, suave, civilized, gracious. **2** fine, quality, elegant, finished, pol-ished. **3** subtle, indirect, disguised, veiled, cloaked, camouflaged.

cruel *adj.* **1** barbarous, savage, brutal, brutish, sanguinary, ferocious, blood-thirsty, vicious, merciless, unmerci-ful, relentless, unpitying, pitiless, sadistic, ruthless, hardhearted, in-human, unmoved, truculent, unfeel-ing, harsh. **2** severe, bitter, hard, cold, harsh, sharp, biting, acute, raw, poignant, torturous, excruciating, painful, stinging.

ant. 1 kind, merciful, forgiving, be-nevolent, charitable, compassionate. **2** warming, soothing, smooth, pleas-ing, beneficial, feeling.

cruelty *n.* barbarity, brutality, ruthless-ness, harshness, inhumanity, atroc-ity, ferocity, savagery, fiendishness, sadism, bloodthirstiness, tyranny, torment, persecution, hardhearted-ness, viciousness.

ant. kindness, mercy, benevolence, tenderness, sympathy, charity.

crumb *n.* morsel, piece, bit, bite, scrap, fragment, grain, sliver, shred, slip, snip, splinter, snatch, nip, pinch, dash, speck, dab, soupçon.

crumble *v.* disintegrate, degenerate, ret-rograde, decline, perish, collapse, decay, molder, decompose, break up, break down, tumble, fade away.

crummy *adj.* shoddy, inferior, cheap, trashy, worthless, crude, useless, sham, trivial, jerry-built, schlocky (*Slang*), contemptible.

ant. superior, expensive, superb, well-made, quality.

crumple *v.* **1** rumple, wrinkle, ruffle, crinkle, crisp, corrugate, pucker, crimple, twill, frizzle, crease, ripple, rimple. **2** collapse, give way, fall, cave in, break, topple, tumble, go to pieces, smash.

crunch *n.* *Slang* CRISIS.

crusade *n.* CAMPAIGN.

crush *v.* **1** mash, smash, grind, break, pound, shatter, crunch, pulverize, granulate, powder, crumple, crum-ble, disintegrate. **2** crowd, press, squeeze, compress, force, push, shove, wedge, cram, cramp, pack, stuff, jam. **3** subdue, overwhelm, put down, suppress, quell, overpower, overcome, quash, quench, overrun, vanquish, blot out, stamp out. **4** oppress, conquer, maltreat, perse-cute, wrong, depress, burden, weigh down, subjugate, enslave, reduce, humiliate. —*n.* jam, jam-up, cram, crowd, huddle, squeeze, press, pile-up.

ant. *v.* **3**, **4** liberate, free, disencum-ber, unburden, release, emancipate, rescue.

crust *n.* **1** cake, coating, rind, shell, hull, skin, incrustation, integument, layer, cover, cortex, husk, exterior, casing, scab, patina. **2** *Slang* inso-lence, impertinence, curtness, sur-liness, impudence, effrontery, bra-zenness, freshness, cheekiness, nerve, rudeness, sauciness, discourtesy.

ant. 1 interior, filling, inside, core, contents, kernel, pith, crumb, meat. **2** courtesy, courtliness, patience, humility.

crusty *adj.* surly, peevish, ill-tempered, curt, gruff, blunt, brusque, choleric, waspish, snappish, crabby, testy, splenetic, cranky, sullen, short-tempered.

ant. patient, unruffled, even-tempered.

crutch *n.* prop, stay, support, aid, upholder, buttress, staff, arm, brace, mainstay, backbone, bulwark, underpinning, strut.

crux *n.* heart, essence, core, body, *sine qua non,* hinge, pivot, axis, nub, fundamental, root, key, cornerstone, landmark, gist, pith.

cry *v.* **1** shout, exclaim, proclaim, announce, broadcast, call, yell, bellow, roar, vociferate, scream, squawk, clamor, pipe, thunder, sing out. **2** weep, sob, wail, bewail, lament, grieve, bawl, squeal, yowl, whimper, mewl, bemoan, blubber, whine, snivel, pule. —*n.* **1** shout, exclamation, yell, call, bellow, scream, announcement. **2** weeping, wailing, sobbing, lamentation, tears, sniveling, puling. **3** appeal, entreaty, pleading, clamor, plaint, solicitation, supplication, request, plea, prayer, orison, petition, adjuration. **4** outcry, tumult, protest, exclamation, ejaculation, hullabaloo, hubbub, chorus, uproar, vociferation, hue and cry, whoop, alarm, upheaval.

crying *adj.* PRESSING.

crypt *n.* vault, tomb, recess, catacomb, sepulcher, pit, grave, mausoleum, chamber.

cryptic *adj.* puzzling, ambiguous, mysterious, vague, perplexing, latent, equivocal, apocryphal, obscure, covert, secret, arcane, dark, hidden, occult, mystic, recondite, enigmatic, cabalistic, oracular.

ant. lucid, open, obvious, overt, clear, distinct.

crystallize *v.* FORM.

cub *n.* **1** puppy, pup, whelp, offspring, baby, suckling. **2** beginner, novice, learner, tyro, amateur, neophyte, junior, fledgling, recruit, dilettante, whippersnapper, babe, freshman, greenhorn, tenderfoot. —*adj.* young, inexperienced, callow, green, immature, budding, unsophisticated.

ant. *n.* **2** professional, expert, veteran, master, authority, specialist. *adj.* mature, experienced, senior, skilled, advanced, qualified, trained.

cubbyhole *n.* NICHE.

cuckoo *adj. Slang* CRACKPOT.

cuddle *v.* caress, embrace, hug, nestle, fondle, cling to, clasp, nuzzle, kiss, stroke, pet, pat, coddle, dandle, snuggle, pamper.

cuddly *adj.* LOVABLE.

cudgel *v.* BEAT. —*n.* CLUB[1].

cue *n.* hint, suggestion, sign, signal, clue, intimation, catchword, password, nod, wink, innuendo, insinuation, inkling, key.

cuff *v.* slap, buffet, clap, beat, pommel, box, smite, knock, blow, tap, whack, clobber, biff, clout, belt, punch. —*n.* blow, smack, slap, box, buffet, stroke, clap, rap, knock, tap, whack, lick, clout, belt, punch.

cul-de-sac *n.* ALLEY.

cull *v.* collect, select, sort out, pick, choose, single out, elect, excerpt, winnow, sift, separate, glean, gather, garner.

ant. disperse, scatter, strew, diffuse, mix.

culminate *v.* ripen, climax, end, finish, result, consummate, perfect, crown, complete, accomplish, fulfill, cap, achieve, wind up.

ant. commence, begin, start, originate, undertake, initiate, venture.

culmination *n.* summit, zenith, apogee, apex, pinnacle, acme, cap, crest, peak, crown, utmost, *ne plus ultra,* maximum, limit, tip-top, pink, quintessence, extremity.

culpability *n.* guilt, blame, blameworthiness, blot, peccability, faultiness, criminality, impeachability.

ant. impeccability, blamelessness, faultlessness, innocence, unimpeachability.

culpable *adj.* blameworthy, blamable, censurable, guilty, reprehensible, peccable, faulty, at fault, reprovable, reproachable, answerable, chargeable, impeachable, wrong.

ant. blameless, guiltless, inculpable, innocent, impeccable, faultless, taintless.

culprit *n.* offender, criminal, felon, convict, prisoner, malefactor, delinquent, transgressor, miscreant, lawbreaker, wrongdoer, evildoer, rascal, sinner.

cult *n.* **1** CLIQUE. **2** WORSHIP. **3** DEVOTION.

cultivate *v.* **1** train, develop, improve, refine, discipline, educate, instruct, civilize, better, lift, elevate, ameliorate, enrich, nurture, enhance, liberalize, humanize. **2** encourage, further, advance, progress, expand, foster, promote, forward, strengthen, elevate. **3** befriend, ingratiate, play up to, curry favor with, court, cherish, patronize, associate with, entertain, consort with, succor.

ant. **1** stunt, stultify, atrophy. **2, 3** neglect, ignore, disregard, slight, impair, discourage.

cultivation *n.* **1** enhancement, improvement, elevation, advancement, amelioration, enrichment, betterment, nurture, instruction, training, education, enlightenment. **2** refinement, culture, breeding, civility, manners, civilization, education, learning, erudition, scholarship, knowledge, letters.

ant. **1** degeneration, decline, decadence, deterioration, worsening. **2** grossness, boorishness, incivility, ignorance, crassness.

culture *n.* **1** civilization, enlightenment, acquirements, attainments, accomplishments, refinement, society, *kultur,* experience, education, learning, knowledge, art. **2** breeding, cultiva-

tion, refinement, urbanity, manners, taste, polish, suavity, elegance, gentility, chivalry, civility, gallantry, courtliness. **3** betterment, elevation, advancement, improvement, enrichment, knowledge,

ant. **2** incivility, tastelessness, boorishness, vulgarity, ill-breeding, awkwardness. **3** decadence, decline, degeneration, stultification, worsening.

cultured *adj.* civilized, refined, polished, enlightened, learned, advanced, educated.

ant. uncultured, backward, primitive, unenlightened.

cumbersome *adj.* clumsy, unwieldy, heavy, awkward, cumbrous, burdensome, massive, ponderous, weighty, hefty, hulking, bulky, unmanageable, inconvenient, incommodious, ungainly.

ant. wieldy, light, manageable, compact, easy, facile.

cumbrance *n.* ENCUMBRANCE.

cumbrous *adj.* CUMBERSOME.

cumulate *v.* ACCUMULATE.

cunning *n.* **1** guile, artifice, craftiness, cleverness, wiliness, trickery, slyness, artfulness, diplomacy, subtlety, scheming, duplicity, knavery, deception, chicanery. **2** proficiency, skill, ability, dexterity, talent, art, craft, deftness, adeptness, adroitness, ingenuity, ingeniousness, cleverness, knack. —*adj.* **1** crafty, tricky, artful, guileful, sly, foxy, wily, devious, crooked, oblique, shrewd, knowing, smart, sharp, canny. **2** appealing, attractive, pretty, cute, charming, lovable, sweet, dainty, quaint, petite, darling, winning. **3** ingenious, clever, adroit, skillful, skilled, adept, proficient, expert, masterly, deft, talented, able.

ant. *n.* **1** candidness, honesty, sincerity, guilelessness, veracity. **2** ingenuousness, artlessness, unskillfulness, inability. *adj.* **1** honest, straightforward, direct, open, artless, natural. **2** unappealing, unattractive, ugly, repulsive, plain. **3** ingenuous, naive, unsophisticated, stupid.

cupidity *n.* avarice, greed, rapacity, insatiability, covetousness, acquisitiveness, avidity, voracity, ravenousness, craving, grasping, longing, concupiscence, parsimony, niggardliness.
ant. generosity, unselfishness, open-handedness, charity.

cur *n.* scoundrel, blackguard, rascal, cad, good-for-nothing, mountebank, villain, miscreant, knave, rogue, varlet, varmint, wretch, viper, serpent, reptile, coward, cheat.

curate *n.* CLERGYMAN.

curb *n.* restraint, check, control, bridle, rein, cramp, crimp, deterrent, harness, deterrence. —*v.* restrain, check, subdue, repress, manage, inhibit, cramp, crimp, limit, bridle, constrain, retard, restrict, tame, compel, rein, muzzle, leash, tether.
ant. encourage, further, foster, help, aid, assist.

curd *v.* CURDLE.

curdle *v.* **1** thicken, congeal, coagulate, cohere, stiffen, curd, clabber, jell, solidify, harden, set, clot, consolidate, condense. **2** sour, embitter, envenom, inflame, disgruntle, chafe, irritate, peeve, vex, nettle, provoke, annoy, mortify.
ant. 1 dilute, thin, water down, weaken, reduce, rarefy. **2** please, satisfy, content, comfort, gladden, cheer, pacify.

cure *n.* **1** remedy, treatment, antidote, medicine, medication, regimen, potion, nostrum, drug, dose, stimulant, analeptic, balm. **2** restoration, healing, recovery, recuperation, regeneration, rehabilitation, convalescence, rally, comeback, instauration. —*v.* heal, restore, remedy, mend, correct, repair, relieve.

cure-all *n.* panacea, elixir, *elixir vitae,* nostrum, catholicon.

curio *n.* CURIOSITY.

curiosity *n.* **1** inquisitiveness, interest, nosiness. **2** curio, novelty, knick-knack, trifle, trinket, bibelot, memento. **3** rarity, marvel, wonder, phenomenon, sight, freak, oddity, spectacle.
ant. 1 indifference, disinterestedness, detachment, aloofness.

curious *adj.* **1** inquiring, inquisitive, questioning, interested, examining, scrutinizing. **2** prying, snoopy, nosy, meddling, intrusive, interrogatory, inquisitorial. **3** novel, odd, strange, mysterious, unusual, rare, singular, unique, queer, foreign, exotic, extraordinary, special, remarkable.
ant. 1 blasé, indifferent, world-weary, detached, unconcerned, aloof. **3** common, commonplace, customary, usual, ordinary, pedestrian.

curl *v.* twist, coil, wind, wave, spiral, writhe, ripple, wreathe, buckle, twine, wrinkle, contort, fold, convolute, involute, roll, undulate. —*n.* coil, spiral, twist, roll, wave, volute, corkscrew, helix, worm, kink, tendril, scroll, convolution.

curmudgeon *n.* GROUCH.

current *adj.* **1** present, prevalent, prevailing, general, widespread, present-day, circulating, common, contemporaneous, rife, ubiquitous. **2** accepted, acknowledged, voguish, stylish, fashionable, up-to-date, *à la mode,* in, popular, conventional, approved, standard, orthodox.
ant. 1 previous, bygone, past, historical, former. **2** outmoded, out-of-date, unpopular, unfashionable, outré.

currish *adj.* BEASTLY.

curse *v.* **1** damn, excoriate, maledict, doom, condemn, blight, denounce, fulminate, blaspheme, anathematize, revile, swear, cuss, blast, ban. **2** plague, doom, scourge, afflict, torture, destroy, trouble, vex, annoy, harass, injure, molest, bother. —*n.* **1** blasphemy, profanity, sacrilege, irreverence, swearing, invective, impiety. **2** malediction, imprecation, execration, damnation, denunciation, excommunication, fulmination, commination, condemnation, cuss. **3** evil, misfortune, affliction, trouble, hardship, tribulation, calamity, vexation, torment, bane, bitter pill, scourge, plague, thorn, woe.

ant. *v.* **1** bless, sanction, favor, approbate, approve, ratify. *n.* **3** blessing, benefaction, mercy, grace, favor.

cursed *adj.* **1** damned, accursed, blighted, banned, doomed, foredoomed, fated, cast out, confounded, plagued, excommunicated. **2** hateful, detestable, revolting, vile, abominable, loathsome, disgusting, execrable, wretched, damnable, odious, diabolic, hellish, villainous, infernal.

ant. 2 praiseworthy, laudatory, commendatory, estimable, deserving.

cursory *adj.* hurried, hasty, rapid, slapdash, perfunctory.

ant. painstaking, comprehensive, detailed, heedful, thorough, diligent.

curt *adj.* **1** concise, brief, terse, succinct, short, shortened, abbreviated, laconic, pithy, summary, crisp, condensed, compact, compendious. **2** brusque, short, abrupt, sharp, rude, snappish, snappy, tart, blunt, taciturn, unceremonious, direct.

ant. 1 long, extended, drawn-out, lengthy. **2** courteous, courtly, civil, cordial, polite, patient.

curtail *v.* abbreviate, cut, lessen, reduce, abridge, diminish, decrease, shorten, prune, trim, pare, blunt, dock, contract, truncate.

ant. expand, extend, lengthen, draw out, enlarge, prolong.

curtain *v.* conceal, cover, hide, shade, screen, veil, cloak, shutter, shroud, camouflage, drape, block, mask, shield, wall, shut off.

ant. expose, uncover, unmask, disclose, unveil.

curvaceous *adj.* SHAPELY.

curve *v.* bend, turn, twist, swerve, crook, coil, wind, swing, hook, bow, round, arch, deflect, spiral, encircle, wreathe.

cushion *n.* pillow, hassock, seat, pad, padding, mat, buffer, prop, bolster, way, rest, pillion, lining, reinforcement, support, headrest. —*v.* absorb, check, slow, pillow, assimilate, neutralize, offset, cradle, buttress, reinforce, muffle, dull, dampen, deaden, soften.

cushy *adj.* *Slang* comfortable, agreeable, easy, effortless, facile, soft, simple, carefree, posh.

ant. difficult, uncomfortable, disagreeable, hard.

cuss *n., v.* CURSE.

custodian *n.* guardian, guard, caretaker, janitor, porter, concierge, keeper, warden, warder, doorkeeper, attendant.

custody *n.* **1** keeping, safekeeping, guardianship, custodianship, care, charge, watch, preserving, preservation, protection, wardship. **2** detention, house arrest, imprisonment, confinement, incarceration, quarantine, durance.

custom *n.* **1** habit, practice, procedure, usage, use, rule, wont, fashion, manner, routine, convention, precedent, habitude. **2** rule, convention, form, observance, formality, prescription, beaten path, conventionalism, etiquette. **3** tariff, duty, impost, tribute, toll, levy.

ant. 1, 2 irregularity, divergence, deviation, departure, difference.

customary *adj.* habitual, usual, conventional, common, regular, wonted, familiar, ordinary, accustomed, general, normal, acknowledged, everyday, traditional, popular.

ant. irregular, unusual, rare, uncommon, unaccustomed.

customer *n.* purchaser, patron, buyer, user, client, patronizer, shopper, prospect, consumer, regular, vendee.

ant. seller, vendor, merchant, merchandiser, salesman, trader.

cut *v.* **1** pierce, gash, slash, slit, lance, penetrate, incise, wound, nick. **2** insult, hurt, wound, sting, touch, slight, ignore, snub, cold-shoulder, freeze out. **3** segment, sever, part, divide, slice, separate, split, carve, cleave, sunder, rive, bisect, chip. **4** fell, mow, hew, hack, lop off, topple, crop, harvest, trim, shear, pare, clip, prune, shave. **5** edit out, excise, delete, contract, reduce, condense, abridge, abbreviate, crop, reduce, curtail, diminish, lower, lessen, shorten. —*n.* **1** incision, wound, slash, gash, slit, groove, nick, cleft, division, opening, indentation. **2** channel, passage, passageway, strait, course, canal, groove, furrow, trough, route, pass, path, trench. **3** segment, part, section, slice, division, piece, chop. **4** reduction, decrement, decrease, diminution, excision, deletion, elision, omission, abbreviation.

cutback *n.* reduction, contraction, decrease, abridgment, curtailment, retrenchment, compression, shrinkage, sag, falling off, sinkage, slash, drop, fall, plunge, cessation, discontinuance, stop.
ant. increase, expansion, extension, boost, step-up.

cute *adj.* **1** dainty, pretty, attractive, charming, delicate, adorable, delightful, cunning, sweet, angelic. **2** clever, sharp, smart, shrewd, cagey, canny, cunning, keen, discerning, slick, wily, calculating. **3** artificial, affected, precious, synthetic, contrived, ersatz, factitious, unnatural, sham, imitation.
ant. 1 ugly, unattractive, gross, plain. **2** naive, unknowing, dull, dumb. **3** genuine, real, authentic, actual, natural, bona fide.

cutoff *n.* termination, cessation, ceasing, halt, arrestment, conclusion, stoppage, stop, stay, discontinuance, pause, cloture, closure, suspension.

cutthroat *adj.* **1** murderous, cruel, harsh, severe, ferocious, savage, barbarous. **2** merciless, ruthless, unprincipled, pitiless, unpitying, unmerci-

ful, hard-hearted, unrelenting, truculent, inhuman. —*n.* murderer, killer, assassin, slayer, homicide, hatchet man (*Slang*), trigger man (*Slang*), butcher, gunman, slaughterer, bravo.
ant. 1, 2 merciful, compassionate, humane, principled, cooperative, relenting.

cutting *adj.* **1** sharp, edged, honed, sharpened, keen, razor-sharp, pointed. **2** piercing, penetrating, chilling, freezing, raw, biting, numbing, stinging, sharp. **3** sarcastic, bitter, sardonic, biting, stinging, caustic, offensive, insulting, outrageous, mean, severe, harsh, mordant, malicious, pointed, poignant.
ant. 1 dull, blunt, rounded, thick, flat.

cycle *n.* eon, age, period, epoch, era.

cyclone *n.* windstorm, storm, tornado, twister, hurricane, tempest, whirlwind, typhoon, monsoon, sirocco, gale, gust, squall, blast.

cynic *n.* skeptic, pessimist, misanthrope, scoffer, faultfinder, sneerer, critic, detractor, censurer, carper, caviler, castigator, traducer.
ant. optimist, enthusiast, utopian, supporter.

cynical *adj.* skeptical, pessimistic, distrustful, disbelieving, misanthropic, ridiculing, censorious, captious, carping, scoffing, mocking, sarcastic, sardonic, scornful, contemptuous, derisive, cutting.
ant. optimistic, trustful, hopeful, enthusiastic, confident, sanguine.

cynicism *n.* skepticism, pessimism, misanthropy, sullenness, moroseness, acrimony, asperity, acerbity, morbidity, despair, satire, castigation, vituperation, mordancy.
ant. optimism, hope, trust, faith, confidence, belief, assurance.

czar *n.* autocrat, overlord, ruler, tyrant, tsar, tzar, dictator, boss, chief, master, leader, potentate, plutocrat, captain.

D

dab *n.* **1** pat, touch, daub, stroke, flick, swat, bat, peck. **2** morsel, bit, dollop, scrap, pat, piece, pinch, crumb, dash, smidgen, soupçon. —*v.* tap, poke, pat, daub, touch, flick, swat, paint, swab.

dabbler *n.* dilettante, amateur, tinkerer, piddler, trifler, sciolist.
ant. expert, authority, specialist, professional, master, scholar, maven (*Slang*).

daffy *adj.* CRAZY.

daft *adj.* CRAZY.

dagger *n.* dirk, poniard, knife, stiletto, blade, shiv (*Slang*).

daily *adj.* everyday, quotidian, diurnal, per diem.

dainty *adj.* **1** delicate, pretty, charming, graceful, petite, appealing, attractive, pleasing. **2** refined, cultivated, fine, elegant, exquisite, fussy, finicky, picky, mincing, precious, subtle.
ant. **1** gross, clumsy, awkward, oafish, unappealing, klutzy (*Slang*). **2** crude, uncouth, robust, hearty.

dais *n.* PLATFORM.

dale *n.* VALLEY.

dalliance *n.* AMOUR.

dally *v.* **1** trifle, flirt, coquet, toy, philander, frolic, play, sport, tease. **2** dawdle, loiter, tarry, linger, fool around, hang about, idle, putter, poke, boondoggle, diddle.
ant. **2** dash, rush, hurry, bustle, get going, move along.

dam *v.* restrain, obstruct, inhibit, repress, check, bridle, rein, leash, hinder, impede, hold in, bar, block.
ant. release, loose, free, let out, unleash.

damage *n.* injury, harm, hurt, destruction, defacement, defilement, disfigurement, deterioration, mutilation, spoliation, impairment, loss, ruin. —*v.* harm, hurt, impair, injure, deface, defile, disfigure, spoil, mutilate, ravage, wreck, vandalize, sabotage, ruin.

damn *v.* **1** condemn, denounce, criticize, censure, blame, reprove, rebuke, descry, disparage, impugn, upbraid, blacklist, blackball. **2** curse, swear at, execrate, doom, anathematize, fulminate, vilify, excoriate.
ant. **1** commend, praise, applaud, accept, approve. **2** bless, glorify, honor, consecrate.

damnable *adj.* detestable, outrageous, horrible, offensive, execrable, atrocious, culpable, blameworthy, despicable, hateful, evil, accursed, bad, sinful.
ant. commendable, meritorious, praiseworthy, good, admirable, worthy.

damnation *n.* **1** ANATHEMA. **2** CURSE.

damp *n.* moisture, humidity, mist, fog, drizzle, vapor, dew, sogginess, wetness. —*adj.* moist, humid, dewy, misty, soggy, foggy, drizzly, vaporous, dank, clammy.

dampen *v.* **1** moisten, humidify, vaporize, moisturize, bedew, sprinkle, wet, spray, hose, sponge, dab. **2** reduce, lower, lessen, muffle, moderate, check, discourage, modulate, diminish, temper, subdue, smother, weaken, dash, spoil.
ant. **1** dry, dehumidify, dehydrate, parch. **2** increase, heighten, intensify, encourage, inflame.

damsel *n.* MAIDEN.

dance *v.* prance, sway, glide, bob, flutter, flit, bounce, skip, spring, leap, bound, cavort, caper, frisk. —*n.*

party, ball, hop, prom, cotillion, shindig (*Slang*).

dander *n.* ANGER.

dandle *v.* bounce, jounce, jiggle, joggle, caress, cuddle, nestle, nuzzle, pet, fondle.

dandy *n.* fop, clotheshorse, fashion plate, peacock, beau, dude, coxcomb, swell, popinjay, Beau Brummell, toff (*Brit.*), nob (*Brit.*). —*adj.* terrific, great, fine, excellent, first-rate, wonderful, topnotch, swell (*Slang*), nifty (*Slang*), cool (*Slang*), super (*Slang*), groovy (*Slang*).
ant. *adj.* awful, terrible, rotten, miserable.

danger *n.* risk, peril, jeopardy, hazard, pitfall, threat, menace, endangerment, insecurity, precariousness, booby trap.
ant. safety, security, certainty, protection, safeguard, invulnerability.

dangerous *adj.* unsafe, harmful, perilous, injurious, hazardous, threatening, menacing, risky, vulnerable, ominous, untrustworthy, unreliable, shaky, sticky, hairy (*Slang*).
ant. safe, harmless, solid, protected, reliable, innocuous, trustworthy.

dangle *v.* flap, swing, hang, wave, oscillate, flutter, suspend, depend, swish, sway, dip.

dank *adj.* clammy, chilly, damp, wet, moist, soggy, humid.

dapper *adj.* jaunty, trim, spruce, debonair, dashing, natty, sporty, smart, well-groomed, neat, well-tailored, stylish, spiffy (*Slang*), foppish.
ant. sloppy, untidy, messy, slovenly, unkempt, shabby.

dappled *adj.* flecked, spotted, variegated, pied, piebald, brindled, mottled, checkered, dotted, stippled, speckled.
ant. solid, uniform, unvaried, homogeneous.

dare *v.* **1** venture, risk, brave, confront, face, hazard, presume, gamble, plunge, speculate. **2** defy, challenge, oppose, provoke, dispute, object,

contradict, goad, resist, flout, scorn, taunt.

daredevil *n.* thrill-seeker, adventurer, death-defier, showoff, madcap, desperado, exhibitionist, lunatic, hotshot (*Slang*).

daring *adj.* bold, courageous, imprudent, rash, adventurous, fearless, intrepid, valorous, gallant, audacious, venturesome, reckless, devil-may-care, aggressive, gutsy (*Slang*). —*n.* courage, boldness, imprudence, rashness, intrepidity, audacity, recklessness, heedlessness, valor, heroism, grit, nerve, guts (*Slang*).
ant. *adj.* timid, prudent, cautious, careful, fearful. *n.* caution, prudence, heed, mindfulness, discretion, circumspection, timidity.

dark *adj.* somber, dusky, shadowy, deep, inky, unlit, black, raven, charcoal, ebon, brunette, pitch-dark, pitchy.
ant. light, bright, brilliant, colorful, pale, pastel.

darken *v.* CLOUD.

darkling *adj.* DIM.

darling *adj.* beloved, cherished, dear, treasured, precious, lovable, adorable, lovely, winsome, pet, prized, sweet, endearing, enchanting.
ant. unlovable, unpleasant, disagreeable, uncherished, rejected, forlorn.

dart *v.* dash, spurt, leap, flit, skitter, thrust, pitch, shoot, spring, bound, fly, dartle, scoot, sprint, career, careen, skim, zip.

dartle *v.* DART.

dash *v.* **1** hit, strike, throw, thrust, knock, whack, thwack, wallop, smash, shatter, break, bruise, ram, hurl, cast, slam. **2** frustrate, discourage, daunt, confound, dispirit, thwart, depress, dishearten, dampen, sadden, disappoint, foil, blight, overthrow. **3** hurry, rush, leap, bound, speed, race, hasten, spurt, spring, flash, dart, zip.
ant. 2 encourage, hearten, inspirit, support, aid, nourish.

dashing *adj.* debonair, dapper, stylish, jaunty, spirited, energetic, lively, animated, smart, bright, brilliant, colorful, zippy, snappy, dashy.

ant. dull, lethargic, colorless, lifeless, shabby.

dashy *adj.* DASHING.

dastard *n.* COWARD.

dastardly *adj.* cowardly, craven, mean, base, low, sneaky, mean-spirited, dishonorable, lily-livered, weak-kneed, contemptible, villainous, rotten, yellow.

ant. brave, heroic, honorable, admirable, courageous, high-minded.

date *n.* appointment, engagement, rendezvous, tryst, commitment, assignation, interview, session, meeting. —*v.* meet, arrange, schedule, take out, entertain, regale, wine and dine.

dated *adj.* old-fashioned, passé, antiquated, outmoded, obsolete, archaic, out of date, stale, tired, antediluvian, moth-eaten, out, old-fogeyish, old hat (*Slang*), démodé.

ant. new, current, latest, now, fashionable, à la mode, in, hot, *au courant*.

datum *n.* FACT.

daub *v.* smear, dab, cover, plaster, smirch, bedaub, mess, dabble, smudge, spatter, splash, brush.

dauber *n.* PAINTER.

daunt *v.* DISHEARTEN.

dauntless *adj.* fearless, courageous, heroic, brave, daring, intrepid, bold, stout-hearted, unflinching, valiant, stalwart, gritty, gutsy (*Slang*).

ant. fearful, cowardly, craven, scared, yellow, chicken (*Slang*).

dawdle *v.* loiter, linger, malinger, trifle, dally, diddle, fritter, poke, fiddle, dillydally, loaf, fool around, shirk, goldbrick.

ant. hurry, rush, get going, move along, hustle, bustle.

dawn *n.* **1** daybreak, sunup, sunrise, daylight, morning, aurora. **2** beginning, start, opening, commencement, awakening, first blush, birth, rise,

spring, emergence, inception, origin, inauguration.

ant. *n.* **1** sunset, twilight, evening, eventide, dusk, crepuscule. **2** end, finish, close, last gasp, decline, fall, swan song.

day *n.* period, age, stage, time, epoch, point, years, generation, lifetime.

daybreak *n.* DAWN.

daydream *n.* reverie, fantasy, phantasm, fancy, fond hope, wish, longing, imagining, musing, vision, pipe dream, stargazing, illusion, aspiration.

daydreamer *n.* visionary, illusionist, fantasist, wool-gatherer, wishful thinker, romancer, Walter Mitty.

ant. realist, activist, doer, pragmatist.

daze *v.* BEWILDER.

dazed *adj.* bewildered, stunned, stupefied, shocked, perplexed, numbed, nonplussed, disoriented, muddled, confused, disconcerted, baffled, rattled, raddled, confounded, staggered, dizzy, lightheaded, flabbergasted, punch-drunk, groggy, foggy, out of it (*Slang*), woozy (*Slang*), dopey (*Slang*).

ant. clear-headed, lucid, alert, on the beam, with it (*Slang*).

dazzle *v.* **1** blind, blur, bedim, befog, daze, confuse, dizzy, obscure. **2** enchant, hypnotize, charm, enthrall, bewitch, bewilder, overpower, overwhelm, astonish, awe, intoxicate, fascinate, knock for a loop (*Slang*), kill (*Slang*).

dazzling *adj.* BRILLIANT.

dead *adj.* **1** deceased, lifeless, defunct, gone, expired, nonexistent, passed away, finished. **2** unresponsive, insensible, deathly, inert, unconscious, motionless, frozen, torpid, immobile, unfeeling, numb, paralyzed, exhausted, beat (*Slang*). **3** boring, dull, tiresome, vapid, uninteresting, flat, devitalized, ineffectual, deadened, smothered, stale. **4** unproductive, extinguished, sterile, impotent, inoperative, inflexible, rigid. **5** complete, absolute, utter, total, sure, unfailing, certain, unerring, entire, exact, direct, unqualified, out-and-out, downright, thorough.

ant. 1 alive, living, animate, existing, quick. **2** conscious, aware, lively, animated, sensate, responsive, cognizant. **3** interesting, vital, bright, colorful, sharp, bubbly. **4** viable, live, productive, operative, effective, potent.

deaden *v.* muffle, mute, diminish, weaken, subdue, sap, lessen, enfeeble, soften, devitalize, stifle, hush, choke, suppress, soft-pedal.

ant. amplify, enliven, brighten, enlarge, strengthen.

deadhead *n.* DUNCE.

dead heat STALEMATE.

deadlock *n.* STALEMATE.

deadly *adj.* **1** fatal, lethal, noxious, toxic, poisonous, death-dealing, deathly, venomous, suicidal, killing, murderous, virulent. **2** implacable, unrelenting, mortal, relentless, cruel, savage, vicious, ruthless, bloodthirsty, homicidal, ferocious, inhuman, cold-hearted. **3** effective, accurate, unerring, unfailing, exact, sure.

ant. 1 harmless, benign, safe, innocuous, nontoxic. **2** kind, humane, conciliatory, peaceable, warm. **3** hit-or-miss, ineffectual, ordinary, sloppy, casual.

deal *v.* **1** distribute, give out, hand out, deliver, mete out, disseminate, bestow, administer, inflict, issue, convey, disperse, broadcast. **2** behave, act, conduct oneself, comport oneself, treat, handle, cope, manage, proceed, react, function, meet. **3** trade, negotiate, transact, haggle, traffic, barter, patronize. —*n.* **1** quantity, amount, extent, degree, portion, lot, measure, number, share, batch, bunch, allotment. **2** transaction, arrangement, maneuver, ploy, stratagem, tactic, setup, compact, contract, understanding, pact, entente, accommodation, scheme.

dealings *n.* negotiation, transaction, arrangement, traffic, trade, conduct,

procedure, behavior, policy, practice, commerce, business, affairs, truck.

dean *n.* senior, veteran, elder statesman, grand old man, leader, doyen, first, foremost, elder, chief, *éminence grise,* big wheel (*Slang*).

dear *adj.* **1** beloved, precious, darling, cherished, priceless, irreplaceable, treasured, prized, loved, pet. **2** expensive, high-priced, costly, high, de luxe, overpriced, exorbitant, extravagant, lavish, extortionate. —*n.* beloved, precious, darling, pet, treasure, sweetheart, angel, honey, sugar (*Slang*).

ant. *adj.* **2** cheap, inexpensive, low-priced, reasonable, nominal.

dearth *n.* scarcity, lack, famine, shortage, paucity, need, want, absence, insufficiency, inadequacy, deficiency, scantiness, poverty, privation, meagerness, skimpiness.

ant. abundance, overflow, plenty, oversupply, wealth, fullness, plethora.

death *n.* **1** decease, demise, departure, exit, end, expiration, passing, quietus, rigor mortis. **2** destruction, annihilation, downfall, extinction, demolition, extermination, eradication, finish, ruin, undoing, immolation, obliteration, ruination, extirpation.

ant. 1 life, existence, being, consciousness. **2** birth, genesis, beginning, inception, creation, construction, start.

deathless *adj.* immortal, eternal, imperishable, limitless, perpetual, undying, everlasting, unceasing, endless, unfading, indestructible, inextinguishable.

ant. mortal, finite, transitory, perishable, fleeting, temporal, ephemeral.

deathly *adj.* DEADLY.

debacle *n.* disaster, collapse, downfall, ruin, overthrow, bankruptcy, cataclysm, catastrophe, deluge, dissolution, havoc, ruination, crash, wreck, devastation.

debar *v.* EXCLUDE.

debark v. ARRIVE.

debarkation n. ARRIVAL.

debase v. degrade, devalue, depreciate, demean, defile, depress, cheapen, adulterate, weaken, deprave, corrupt, pollute, vitiate, prostitute, bastardize, dishonor, disgrace.
  ant. enhance, enrich, elevate, raise, promote, improve, uplift.

debatable adj. DUBIOUS.

debate v. **1** argue, dispute, discuss, contend, contest, moot, squabble, quarrel, wrangle, hassle, controvert. **2** think, reflect, deliberate, consider, cogitate, ponder, ruminate, mull over, meditate. —n. discussion, dispute, moot, disputation, argument, disagreement, controversy, contest, contention, altercation, hassle, squabble, palaver, talk, polemics, rap session (*Slang*).

debauch v. CORRUPT.

debauched adj. depraved, corrupt, dissolute, dissipated, immoral, wanton, licentious, shameless, debased, profligate, degenerate, perverted, degraded, reprobate.
  ant. pure, undefiled, virtuous, good, high-minded, moral, righteous.

debauchery n. DEPRAVITY.

debilitate v. ENFEEBLE.

debility n. weakness, feebleness, exhaustion, infirmity, frailty, frailness, prostration, enervation, asthenia, decrepitude, delicacy, invalidism.
  ant. strength, vigor, energy, robustness, vim, heartiness.

debit n. DEBT.

debonair adj. affable, smooth, suave, gallant, carefree, insouciant, dapper, dashing, jaunty, blithe, lighthearted, breezy, animated, sprightly, high-spirited.
  ant. gloomy, sad, sluggish, melancholy, shy, self-conscious.

debouch v. EMERGE.

debris n. rubble, rubbish, wreckage, ruins, trash, junk, waste, dregs, dross, shards, litter, sweepings, detritus, crap (*Slang*), crud (*Slang*).

debt n. **1** debit, indebtedness, liability,

arrears, deficit, claim, encumbrance, lien. **2** obligation, duty, commitment, responsibility, pledge, covenant, promise, due, burden, onus.

debunk v. expose, show up, muckrake, criticize, uncover, strip, bare, air, disparage, deflate, mock, lampoon, ridicule, satirize.

debut n. launching, beginning, premiere, entrance, initiation, inauguration, introduction, coming-out, presentation, unveiling, bow.
  ant. goodbye, farewell, finis, swan song, last hurrah.

decadence n. decay, decline, deterioration, degeneration, fall, debasement, waning, ebb, degradation, debauchery, degeneracy, falling-off, devitalization, effeteness, enervation.
  ant. flowering, blossoming, bloom, rise, high noon, vigor, health.

decadent adj. debased, declining, degenerate, decayed, withered, effete, enervated, tainted, devitalized, artificial, corrupted, debauched, mannered, unwholesome, unsound.
  ant. robust, hearty, vigorous, blooming, young, spontaneous, sound.

decamp v. ESCAPE.

decapitate v. BEHEAD.

decay v. **1** decline, degenerate, deteriorate, shrivel, wither, fail, fall, ebb, wane, debase, weaken, waste, molder, atrophy, fade, sicken. **2** putrefy, decompose, disintegrate, gangrene, perish, die. —n. decline, deterioration, decomposition, impairment, weakening, disintegration, rottenness, dilapidation, enfeeblement, ruin, decadence, degeneration, disrepair, collapse, downfall.
  ant. v. **1, 2** strengthen, heal, flower, grow, bloom. n. rise, growth, development, strength, health, vigor, bloom.

decease v. DIE.

deceased adj. dead, expired, lifeless, defunct, gone, departed, late, lost, finished.
  ant. alive, living.

deceit n. fraud, deception, fraudulence,

deceptiveness, sham, counterfeit, imposture, falseness, hypocrisy, duplicity, underhandedness, cunning, double-dealing, treachery, treason, betrayal.

ant. honesty, truth, truthfulness, straightforwardness, openness, candor, authenticity.

deceitful *adj.* dishonest, false, lying, fraudulent, tricky, two-faced, double-dealing, underhanded, dissembling, wily, Janus-faced, duplicitous, insincere, cunning, foxy, treacherous, untrustworthy.

ant. honest, truthful, straightforward, open, candid, forthright.

deceive *v.* mislead, delude, misinform, defraud, cheat, fool, take in, hoax, bamboozle, lie, hoodwink, swindle, dupe, gull, seduce, con (*Slang*), put on (*Slang*), hype (*Slang*).

decency *n.* propriety, decorum, seemliness, civility, etiquette, good form, good manners, suitability, respectability, acceptability, correctness, pleasantness.

ant. impropriety, bad form, rudeness, outrageousness, shamefulness, indecency.

decent *adj.* **1** respectable, proper, chaste, modest, suitable, appropriate, decorous, mannerly, correct, civil, virtuous, moral, right. **2** adequate, fair, normal, average, satisfactory, standard, usual, acceptable, so-so, par. **3** generous, considerate, kind, thoughtful, understanding, humane, sympathetic, warmhearted, unselfish, civilized.

ant. 1 shocking, disreputable, shameful, immodest, indecent, outrageous. **2** substandard, inadequate, subnormal, below par, poor, low. **3** selfish, thoughtless, unsympathetic, inconsiderate.

deception *n.* delusion, illusion, fraud, lie, sham, hoax, facade, bluff, fiction, mask, legerdemain, hocus-pocus, masquerade, put-on (*Slang*).

ant. truth, fact, authenticity, reality, actuality, accuracy.

deceptive *adj.* misleading, false, delusive, fraudulent, deceitful, mock, fake, spurious, specious, illusory, colorable, bogus, tricky, treacherous, phony (*Slang*).

ant. genuine, real, authentic, true, accurate, undisguised, verifiable.

decide *v.* determine, settle, arbitrate, rule, conclude, fix, adjudicate, resolve, establish, regulate, arrange, stipulate, umpire, decree, referee.

ant. waver, vacillate, stall, hang fire, hem and haw.

decided *adj.* fixed, settled, unequivocal, certain, definite, defined, determined, resolute, emphatic, unambiguous, firm, unfaltering, unwavering.

ant. vague, indefinite, unsure, uncertain, questionable, wavering, weak.

decimate *v.* DESTROY.

decipher *v.* decode, figure out, translate, read, interpret, construe, solve, unravel, explain, untangle, deduce.

decision *n.* **1** determination, resolve, decisiveness, resolution, conviction, firmness, strength, will, certainty, assertiveness, willfulness, perseverance. **2** result, answer, judgment, decree, conclusion, settlement, outcome, finding, opinion, verdict.

ant. weakness, uncertainty, vacillation, vagueness, evasion, indecisiveness.

decisive *adj.* conclusive, peremptory, obligatory, binding, unalterable, crucial, critical, momentous, fateful, historic, weighty, far-reaching, consequential, determinative, definitive, final, determinant.

ant. inconclusive, unimportant, minor, moot, questionable, inconsequential.

deck *v.* adorn, array, dress, clothe, ornament, decorate, festoon, embellish, enhance, trim, enrich, beautify, furbish, accouter.

declaim *v.* orate, harangue, lecture, perorate, proclaim, hold forth, sermonize, address, preach, pontificate, speechify.

declamatory *adj.* ORATORICAL.

declaration *n.* statement, proposal, proposition, assertion, utterance, deposition, avowal, presentation, disclosure, expression, recital, speech, recitation.

declare *v.* assert, avow, announce, state, propose, disclose, express, affirm, aver, pronounce, proclaim, expound, enunciate, avouch, profess, propound, asseverate.

declination *n.* DENIAL.

decline *v.* **1** refuse, turn down, reject, forgo, eschew, avoid. **2** weaken, wane, ebb, lessen, fail, sink, flag, recede, diminish, worsen, deteriorate, wither, waste, decay, droop. **3** slope, bend, slant, angle, incline, descend, dip, rake, pitch, tilt, list. —*n.* deterioration, decay, enfeeblement, degeneration, waning, dwindling, withering, erosion, drop, waste, diminution, downturn, failure, aging, downfall.

ant. *v.* **1** accept, take, agree to, comply with. **2** strengthen, improve, better, bloom, grow, wax, blossom. *n.* improvement, increase, strengthening, vitalization, growth, escalation, betterment.

declivity *n.* SLOPE.

decoct *v.* CONDENSE.

decompose *v.* DECAY.

décor *n.* DECORATION.

decorate *v.* adorn, ornament, embellish, trim, dress up, beautify, deck, bedeck, brighten, furbish, grace, drape, array, garnish, festoon.

decoration *n.* **1** adornment, ornamentation, embellishment, trimming, beautification, ornament, décor, flourish, curlicue, frill, display, enrichment, garnish. **2** medal, badge, emblem, award, insignia, ribbon, honor, citation, recognition.

decorative *adj.* ornamental, festive, embellishing, adorning, colorful, enhancing, beautifying.

decorous *adj.* well-behaved, proper, polite, mannerly, suitable, seemly,

demure, fitting, conventional, becoming, *comme il faut.*

ant. crude, unmannerly, loud, boisterous, aggressive, rude.

decorum *n.* propriety, etiquette, mannerliness, seemliness, decency, civility, respectability conformity, conventionality, good form.

ant. boorishness, bad manners, indecency, outlandishness, rudeness.

decoy *n.* lure, snare, bait, allurement, trap, enticement, hook, pitfall, seducer, inducement, shill (*Slang*), plant (*Slang*), come-on (*Slang*). —*v.* lure, snare, bait, trap, entice, hook, induce, lead on, seduce, beguile, enmesh.

decrease *v.* diminish, lessen, abate, reduce, wane, decline, fall off, shrink, curtail, abbreviate, drop, sink, plummet, plunge, shorten, weaken, contract, compress, dwindle, de-escalate. —*n.* reduction, lessening, decline, abbreviation, shortening, contraction, drop, falling off, compression, ebb, diminution, retrenchment, depreciation, deflation, decrement.

ant. *v.* increase, grow, rise, soar, escalate, strengthen, expand, burgeon. *n.* increase, growth, rise, inflation, strengthening, enlargement, escalation.

decree *n.* edict, order, ordinance, statute, pronouncement, proclamation, manifesto, mandate, fiat, ruling, ukase, pronunciamento, canon, law. —*v.* ordain, order, proclaim, enact, command, pronounce, authorize, regulate, dictate, rule, prescribe, decide.

decrement *n.* DECREASE.

decrepit *adj.* weak, weakened, feeble, broken down, worn out, falling apart, dilapidated, infirm, invalid, battered, debilitated, incapacitated, rickety, doddering, shaky.

ant. strong, robust, stout, serviceable, in good shape.

decrepitude *n.* DEBILITY.

decry *v.* condemn, disparage, criticize, censure, blame, fault, belittle, depreciate, denounce, damn, vilify, rail against, berate, reproach, vituperate, attack, degrade, deprecate.

ant. approve, uphold, praise, support, commend, applaud.

dedicate *v.* consecrate, set apart, sanctify, enshrine, hallow, bless, glorify, celebrate.

dedication *n.* **1** consecration, sanctification, enshrinement, hallowing, celebration, glorification, application, devotion, loyalty, absorption, calling, vocation, commitment. **2** inscription, message, address, memento, memorial.

deduce *v.* infer, conclude, derive, assume, reason, analyze, presume, interpret, gather, glean, suppose, reckon, calculate, comprehend, understand, surmise, guess.

deduct *v.* subtract, diminish, take away, lessen, remove, rebate, curtail, shorten, pare down, eliminate, retrench.

ant. add, increase, annex, affix, amplify, extend.

deduction *n.* inference, conclusion, assumption, derivation, presumption, analysis, interpretation, finding, supposition, understanding, reasoning, calculation, reckoning, comprehension.

deed *n.* act, action, event, achievement, performance, feat, gesture, exploit, accomplishment, move, stroke, *fait accompli*, work, operation.

deem *v.* judge, think, regard, hold, believe, reckon, suppose, consider, view, estimate, surmise, feel, look upon, view, fancy.

deep *adj.* **1** profound, penetrating, abstruse, esoteric, subtle, arcane, complex, mysterious, mystifying, recondite, unfathomable. **2** heartfelt, earnest, sincere, hearty, ardent, fervent, wholehearted, profound, unalloyed, intense, warm. **3** severe, acute, grave, critical, great, unusual, extraordinary. **4** scheming, sly, wily, artful, designing, calculating, covert, shrewd, insidious, Machiavellian, tricky.

ant. 1 shallow, superficial, obvious, simple, external. **2** casual, offhand, halfhearted, nonchalant, indifferent. **3** mild, light, ordinary, usual, unimportant. **4** straightforward, ingenuous, open, direct, forthright.

deep-rooted *adj.* DEEP-SEATED.

deep-seated *adj.* ingrained, deep-rooted, inherent, invererate, ineradicable, inalienable, buried, fixed, intrinsic, fundamental, repressed, unconscious.

ant. superficial, skin-deep, shallow, alterable, changeable, eradicable.

de-escalate *v.* DECREASE.

deface *v.* mar, disfigure, mutilate, deform, damage, scratch, spoil, soil, mark, maim, scar, blotch, ruin.

de facto ACTUAL.

defalcate *v.* STEAL.

defamation *n.* SLANDER.

defamatory *adj.* slanderous, libelous, denigrating, stigmatizing, derogatory, vituperative, disparaging, insulting, calumnious, damaging, denunciatory, compromising.

ant. complimentary, flattering, laudatory, eulogistic, approving, congratulatory.

defame *v.* slander, libel, malign, traduce, stigmatize, disparage, belittle, depreciate, vilify, blacken, insult, derogate, revile, denigrate, calumniate.

ant. compliment, flatter, boost, laud, applaud.

default *v.* shirk, evade, dodge, fail, neglect, swindle, defraud, welsh (*Slang*), fink out (*Slang*), crap out (*Slang*).

ant. pay up, fulfill, satisfy, comply with.

defeat *v.* overcome, vanquish, best, win, trounce, beat, overpower, overwhelm, prevail, overthrow, overturn, put down, crush, subdue, suppress, conquer, shellac (*Slang*), cream (*Slang*). —*n.* loss, setback, rout, upset, downfall, debacle, disaster, conquest, beating, trouncing, shellacking (*Slang*), Waterloo.

ant. *n.* victory, triumph, success, killing.

defeated *adj.* thwarted, overpowered, conquered, frustrated, beaten, crushed, vanquished, overwhelmed, subdued, checkmated, put down, licked.

ant. triumphant, successful, victorious, undefeated, unconquered, on top.

defeatist *n.* QUITTER.

defect *n.* failing, fault, imperfection, peccadillo, deficiency, foible, shortcoming, minus, weakness, drawback, lack, infirmity, blemish. —*v.* desert, abandon, revolt, secede, withdraw, forsake, quit, leave.

ant. *n.* strength, forte, plus, asset.

defection *n.* desertion, abandonment, disloyalty, treason, apostasy, revolt, rebellion, unfaithfulness, betrayal, double-cross (*Slang*).

ant. loyalty, fealty, allegiance, commitment.

defective *adj.* imperfect, marred, flawed, faulty, subnormal, substandard, subpar, broken, poor, inadequate, inoperative, out of order.

ant. intact, whole, perfect, operative, functional, normal.

defector *n.* TRAITOR.

defend *v.* **1** protect, fortify, safeguard, arm, man, secure, cover, watch over, preserve, guard, shelter, armor, bulwark. **2** justify, vindicate, support, uphold, sustain, rally to, aid, assist, hold forth, corroborate, abet, champion, preserve.

ant. 1, 2 attack, assail, subvert, undermine, destroy.

defense *n.* protection, justification, vindication, support, bastion, bulwark, assistance, preservation, guard, cover, security.

defenseless *adj.* powerless, vulnerable, unarmed, naked, weak, endangered, unguarded, exposed, disabled, imperiled.

ant. fortified, armed, protected, invincible, invulnerable, shielded.

defensible *adj.* JUSTIFIABLE.

defer[1] *v.* delay, postpone, put off, table, shelve, pigeonhole, retard, stall, suspend, adjourn, procrastinate, temporize.

defer[2] *v.* SUBMIT.

deference *n.* respect, regard, esteem, consideration, homage, courtesy, civility, graciousness, politeness, complaisance, obeisance.

ant. impertinence, self-assertion, disrespect, rudeness, presumption, aggressiveness.

deferential *adj.* respectful, considerate, polite, gracious, obeisant, mannerly, ceremonious, regardful, gallant, courtly, courteous.

ant. rude, impolite, inconsiderate, boorish, unmannerly, pushy.

defiance *n.* HOSTILITY.

defiant *adj.* rebellious, mutinous, disobedient, refractory, fractious, stubborn, recalcitrant, ungovernable, lawless, headstrong, willful, reckless, audacious, bold.

ant. submissive, obedient, docile, timid, dutiful, compliant.

deficiency *n.* lack, need, want, scarcity, insufficiency, inadequacy, shortage, shortcoming, weakness, absence, dearth, deficit, fault, flaw, defect, scantiness.

ant. excess, surplus, overflow, oversupply, glut, plethora.

deficient *adj.* **1** insufficient, inadequate, short, wanting, needful, scant, scanty, lacking, lean, meager, sparing, exiguous. **2** defective, incomplete, subnormal, substandard, subpar, faulty, inferior, second-rate, malfunctioning, poor.

ant. 1 enough, adequate, plentiful, bountiful, rich. **2** whole, working, regular, standard, normal.

defile *v.* corrupt, befoul, besmirch, dirty, pollute, sully, profane, infect, taint, soil, vitiate, smear, contaminate, degrade, dishonor, debauch.

ant. cleanse, purify, uplift, honor, better, decontaminate.

define *v.* explain, describe, delimit, determine, specify, clarify, spell out, construe, interpret, fix, detail, designate, characterize.

definite *adj.* **1** clear, precise, exact, delimited, determined, fixed, set, settled, specific, specified, delineated, circumscribed, concrete, particular. **2** certain, sure, positive, incontrovertible, inevitable, unchangeable, unquestionable, absolute, inescapable, invariable, inexorable.
ant. 1 indistinct, vague, unclear, blurred, ambiguous. **2** uncertain, unsure, doubtful, chancy, iffy, possible.

definitely *adv.* certainly, surely, unquestionably, without doubt, doubtless, positively, indubitably, unequivocally, inescapably, unavoidably, assuredly, incontrovertibly.
ant. possibly, perhaps, maybe.

definition *n.* **1** meaning, sense, definiens, denotation, connotation, clarification, explanation, particularization, description, characterization, designation, concretization. **2** precision, distinctness, clarity, sharpness, character, design, outline, focus, definiteness, specificity, particularity, concreteness, discreteness.
ant. 2 vagueness, blur, imprecision, ambiguity, fuzziness, amorphousness, indistinctness.

definitive *adj.* decisive, final, absolute, conclusive, complete, thorough, thoroughgoing, comprehensive, exhaustive, consummate, unconditional, allout.
ant. partial, inconclusive, incomplete, indefinite, open, questionable.

deflate *v.* **1** collapse, empty, flatten, exhaust, shrink, contract, crumple. **2** humble, humiliate, put down (*Slang*), abase, lower, chagrin, mortify, depreciate, belittle, chasten, needle, debunk.
ant. 1 inflate, aerate, swell, enlarge, expand, dilate, puff up. **2** compliment, flatter, applaud, soft-soap, butter up.

deflect *v.* swerve, veer, turn aside, deviate, bend, divert, shift, switch, diverge, tack, shy, sidetrack.

deform *v.* DISTORT.

deformed *adj.* misshapen, warped, distorted, malformed, awry, bent, askew, unshapely, crooked, unsightly, crippled, disfigured, twisted, unattractive, ugly, grotesque, unnatural.
ant. natural, sound, shapely, attractive, normal, perfect.

deformity *n.* malformation, distortion, disfigurement, crookedness, deformation, irregularity, abnormality.

defraud *v.* cheat, swindle, trick, fleece, bamboozle, rook, skin, dupe, gull, victimize, gyp, take (*Slang*), con (*Slang*), rip off (*Slang*).

defray *v.* PAY.

deft *adj.* adroit, dexterous, skillful, handy, nimble, expert, able, facile, adept, proficient, ingenious, quick.
ant. clumsy, heavy-handed, maladroit, awkward, bumbling, bungling.

defunct *adj.* nonexistent, gone, inoperative, dead, out of commission, extinct, obsolete, finished, done with, discarded, kaput (*Slang*).
ant. active, operative, functioning, living, in use, in circulation.

defy *v.* **1** resist, rebel, mutiny, challenge, dare, scorn, spurn, brave, mock, outface, flout. **2** resist, obstruct, withstand, impede, frustrate, foil, repel, repulse, thwart, prevent, defeat, baffle, hinder.
ant. 1 cooperate, agree, submit, obey, yield, comply.

degeneracy *n.* DEPRAVITY.

degenerate *v.* deteriorate, decay, rot, worsen, disintegrate, decline, sink, regress, retrogress, retrograde, fail, crumble, shrink. —*adj.* dissolute, debased, depraved, rotten, decadent, perverted, profligate, immoral, debauched, dissipated, degraded, retrograde, ignoble, base, fallen. —*n.* pervert, debauchee, rake, profligate, roué, lecher, scoundrel, good-fornothing, rotter (*Brit.*).
ant. *v.* improve, flourish, progress, bloom. *adj.* wholesome, healthy, sound, moral, decent.

degradation *n.* DISHONOR.

degrade *v.* debase, debauch, defile, dishonor, humble, demean, corrupt, sully, pollute, disgrace.
ant. honor, elevate, uplift.

degrading *adj.* debasing, humiliating, demeaning, unworthy, lowering, shameful, disgraceful, contemptible, dishonorable, undignified, *infra dig.*
ant. self-respecting, honorable, worthy, dignified, uplifting.

degree *n.* 1 stage, grade, step, status, position, rank, level, worth, dignity, merit, value, station, class, sphere, order, situation. 2 intensity, extent, severity, measure, scope, level, range.

dehydrated *adj.* ARID.

deification *n.* APOTHEOSIS.

deify *v.* 1 glorify, exalt, apotheosize, extol, ennoble, elevate, dignify, enshrine, beatify, sanctify. 2 worship, adore, venerate, idolize, revere, honor, celebrate.

deity *n.* god, goddess, idol, divinity, immortal, godhead, supreme being, divine being.

deject *v.* DEPRESS.

dejected *adj.* depressed, disheartened, dispirited, discouraged, hopeless, forlorn, melancholy, heavy-hearted, despondent, downhearted, downcast, brooding, sad, down, blue.
ant. cheerful, happy, hopeful, merry, lighthearted, joyful, carefree.

de jure LEGAL.

delay *v.* 1 postpone, defer, put off, procrastinate, shelve, stay, linger, wait, prolong, tarry, stall, filibuster, loiter. 2 hold up, detain, impede, retard, arrest, deter, hamper, check, restrain, obstruct, inhibit, restrict, clog. —*n.* postponement, deferment, stop, stay, procrastination, wait, arrest, filibuster, retardation, prolongation, protraction.
ant. *v.* 1 speed, hurry, rush, hasten. 2 advance, promote, precipitate, expedite, stimulate. *n.* advancement, stimulation, speed, hurry, rush, precipitation, promotion.

delectable *adj.* delightful, charming, pleasing, delicious, dainty, appealing, appetizing, savory, toothsome, tasty, inviting, enticing, pleasurable.
ant. unappealing, disagreeable, tasteless, unappetizing.

delectation *n.* DELIGHT.

delegate *n.* deputy, representative, agent, envoy, proxy, ambassador, alternate, substitute, surrogate, factor, commissioner, vicar, intermediary, go-between. —*v.* charge, instruct, empower, authorize, depute, deputize, nominate, accredit, consign, commission, entitle, entrust.

delegation *n.* embassy, deputation, agency, legation, mission, representation, commission, convention, contingent.

delete *v.* take out, omit, cancel, strike out, erase, eradicate, expunge, censor, expurgate, obliterate, dele, abridge, elide, abbreviate, blip.
ant. insert, interpolate, add, put in, set in.

deleterious *adj.* injurious, harmful, destructive, detrimental, baneful, pernicious, hurtful, malignant, unwholesome, damaging, bad, ruinous, inimical, corrupting.
ant. beneficial, healthy, wholesome, good, curative, favorable.

deliberate *v.* consider, weigh, think about, ponder, reflect, contemplate, cogitate, cerebrate, reason, examine, speculate, study, pore over, mull over. —*adj.* considered, careful, thoughtful, intentional, slow, ponderous, thorough, painstaking, unhurried, prudent, studied, circumspect, premeditated, calculated, leisurely.
ant. *adj.* spontaneous, thoughtless, careless, hasty, rash, superficial.

deliberation *n.* thought, consideration, thoughtfulness, care, reflection, contemplation, examination, prudence, judiciousness, cogitation, study, analysis, thoroughness.
ant. haste, rashness, thoughtlessness, imprudence, carelessness, superficiality.

deliberative *adj.* THOUGHTFUL.

delicacy *n.* **1** sensitivity, sensibility, discrimination, tact, savoir faire, consideration, diplomacy, responsiveness, finesse, refinement, fastidiousness, awareness, cultivation, subtlety, skill. **2** tidbit, dainty, morsel, treat, goody, confection.
ant. 1 bluntness, toughness, crassness, crudity, grossness, insensitivity, tactlessness.

delicate *adj.* **1** *of quality or style:* precise, subtle, fine, sensitive, nice, elegant, exquisite, refined, cultivated, sophisticated, deft, skillful, accurate. **2** *of feeling or manner:* considerate, tactful, sensitive, subtle, diplomatic, tender, regardful, caring, careful, responsive. **3** frail, dainty, fragile, vulnerable, feeble, weak, ailing, susceptible, tender, precarious, tenuous, shaky, insecure.
ant. 1 rough, crude, unrefined, blatant. **2** heavy-handed, tactless, blunt, insensitive, boorish. **3** hearty, robust, fit, strong.

delicious *adj.* delectable, tasty, savory, appetizing, mouth-watering, delightful, enjoyable, luscious, refreshing, ambrosial.
ant. unpalatable, tasteless, inedible, unpleasant.

delight *n.* pleasure, joy, gratification, happiness, felicity, gladness, enchantment, delectation, well-being, elation, exhilaration, rapture.
ant. disgust, displeasure, dissatisfaction, distaste, bore, drag (*Slang*).

delightful *adj.* pleasurable, charming, pleasant, delectable, enjoyable, agreeable, winning, pleasing, captivating, congenial, enchanting, happy, lovely, peachy (*Slang*), ducky (*Slang*).
ant. unpleasant, distasteful, repulsive, depressing.

delight in enjoy, relish, like, love, rejoice, appreciate, bask, revel, savor, fancy, thrill to.
ant. avoid, shun, scorn, object to, dislike.

delimit *v.* BOUND.

delineate *v.* **1** outline, trace, silhouette,

draw, pen, limn, diagram, define, draft, blueprint. **2** portray, depict, contour, limn, describe, specify, detail, characterize, sketch.

delineation *n.* PICTURE.

delinquency *n.* offense, fault, neglect, illegality, immorality, dereliction, misdeed, misconduct, transgression, wrong, sin, crime, violation, default, breach.

delinquent *adj.* remiss, neglectful, derelict, faulty, negligent, culpable, reprehensible, blameworthy, in the wrong. —*n.* law-breaker, offender, wrongdoer, miscreant, culprit, violator, malefactor, perpetrator, scapegrace, hoodlum, hood (*Slang*).

delirious *adj.* hallucinating, fantasizing, feverish, frenzied, manic, maniacal, intoxicated, demented, deranged, unhinged, disordered, raving, mad, incoherent.
ant. lucid, reasonable, rational, cool-headed, sane, self-controlled.

delirium *n.* FRENZY.

deliver *v.* **1** hand over, transfer, carry, distribute, pass to, bring, turn over, convey, impart, remit, bequeath, surrender, consign, grant. **2** rescue, redeem, liberate, release, extricate, unbind, unfetter, loose, ransom, succor, save, emancipate, recover. **3** throw, pitch, send, administer, give, strike, discharge, emit, toss off, hurl, project, cast, launch, fire, shoot.
ant. 1 keep, retain, hold, hoard, conserve, guard. **2** detain, subjugate, dominate, imprison, enslave, kidnap, bind.

delivery *n.* distribution, transfer, conveyance, bequest, bequeathal, transmission, surrender, passage, consignment.

dell *n.* VALLEY.

delude *v.* deceive, mislead, trick, fool, hoax, gull, hoodwink, cheat, take in, outwit, dupe, misinform, misrepresent, ensnare, seduce, put on (*Slang*), con (*Slang*).

deluge *v.* **1** flood, inundate, drown, engulf, submerge, swamp, drench, flow over, immerse. **2** overwhelm, surfeit, overload, glut, swamp. —*n.* **1** flood, inundation, torrent, downpour. **2** spate, onrush, cataract, overflow, superabundance, ocean, wave, tide.

delusion *n.* hallucination, fantasy, phantasm, unreality, mirage, misconception, misapprehension, self-deception, aberration, obsession, delirium, madness, insanity, irrationality, lunacy.

ant. actuality, fact, reality.

delusive *adj.* MISLEADING.

de luxe luxurious, choice, select, prime, elite, costly, splendid, sumptuous, elegant, special, expensive, rich, exclusive, high-class, grand, posh (*Slang*), classy (*Slang*).

ant. common, ordinary, mediocre, cheap, run of the mill, everyday.

demagogue *n.* rabble-rouser, haranguer, malcontent, opportunist, soapbox orator, fomenter, agitator.

demand *v.* **1** insist on, claim, petition, urge, press for, appeal for, solicit, seek, sue, adjure, requisition, enjoin, exact, importune, order. **2** need, require, want, necessitate, call for, lack. —*n.* claim, ultimatum, injunction, requisition, stipulation, exhortation, exaction, call, order, appeal, extortion, objective, suit.

demanding *adj.* exacting, pressing, insistent, imperious, exigent, difficult, exhausting, tedious, wearisome, taxing, hard, inconsiderate, unsparing, burdensome, trying, nagging.

ant. soft, easy, leisurely.

demarcate *v.* MARK.

demarcation *n.* boundary, limit, line, border, frontier, margin, edge, rim, periphery, outside, end, separation.

demean *v.* degrade, debase, lower, abase, abash, shame, humiliate, humble, reduce, demote, discredit, embarrass, disgrace, dishonor.

ant. uplift, raise, honor, exalt, promote, upgrade, inflate.

demean oneself BEHAVE.

demeanor *n.* behavior, manner, deport-

ment, comportment, appearance, mien, conduct, actions, style, bearing, carriage, air, expression, presence.

demented *adj.* insane, crazed, crazy, lunatic, irrational, unhinged, mad, delirious, psychotic, psychopathic, cracked, daft, cuckoo (*Slang*), nuts (*Slang*).

ant. sane, rational, reasonable, sensible, self-controlled, clear-headed.

demise *n.* death, finish, end, decease, cessation, departure, expiration, extinction, downfall, ruin, annihilation, extermination, temination.

ant. beginning, birth, commencement, start, origin, unfolding.

democratic *adj.* **1** self-governing, self-ruling, autonomous, self-determining, egalitarian, populist, elective, republican. **2** tolerant, liberal, informal, relaxed, broadminded, folksy, free and easy, casual, unsnobbish.

ant. **1** authoritarian, dictatorial, autocratic, absolutist, despotic. **2** snobbish, exclusive, haughty, aristocratic, highfalutin, snooty.

démodé *adj.* OLD-FASHIONED.

demolish *v.* **1** raze, tear down, level, fell, wreck, pulverize, devastate, dismantle, atomize, disassemble, flatten, total (*Slang*). **2** overthrow, annihilate, exterminate, wipe out, ruin, destroy, ravage, shatter, smash, break, crush, undo, trash (*Slang*).

ant. **1**, **2** restore, repair, build, erect, construct.

demolition *n.* DESTRUCTION.

demon *n.* **1** devil, fiend, imp, goblin. **2** brute, beast, monster, sadist, torturer, hellcat, evil-doer, ghoul, viper, snake, witch. **3** master, whiz (*Slang*), wizard, past master, fiend, fanatic, expert, pro, maniac (*Slang*), nut (*Slang*), addict, buff, devotee, aficionado, maven (*Slang*).

ant. **1**, **2** angel, saint, cherub, paragon. **3** tyro, beginner, learner, bungler.

demoniac *adj.* fiendish, devilish, hellish,

frenzied, demoniacal, demonic, diabolic, satanic, Mephistophelian, ghoulish, infernal, monstrous, evil, vicious, manic, maniacal, Dionysian. **ant.** angelic, seraphic, saintly, good, kind, humane, virtuous, Apollonian.

demonic *adj.* DEMONIAC.

demonstrable *adj.* EVIDENT.

demonstrate *v.* 1 explain, describe, tell, show, display, bespeak, indicate, illustrate, present, exhibit, exemplify, evince, manifest, express, denote. 2 prove, substantiate, sustain, attest, establish, certify, evidence, argue, confirm, affirm, support, corroborate, verify, illustrate, justify, document, validate.

demonstration *n.* 1 proof, evidence, testimony, justification, substantiation, vindication, verification, attestation, corroboration, certification, validation, support. 2 exhibit, show, display, illustration, presentation, performance, explanation, description, trial, test, exposition, manifestation, exhibition. 3 mass meeting, protest, rally, assembly, mobilization, meet, reunion, convocation, caucus, convention.

demonstrative *adj.* expansive, effusive, outgoing, gushing, emotional, unrestrained, expressive, dramatic, histrionic, affectionate, warm, unconstrained, physical, relaxed, open, free. **ant.** reserved, inhibited, restrained, reticent, cerebral, repressed, undemonstrative, uptight (*Slang*).

demoralize *v.* undermine, discourage, dishearten, dispirit, unnerve, weaken, discomfit, incapacitate, enfeeble, devitalize, cripple, shake, sap, psych out (*Slang*). **ant.** encourage, hearten, steel, nerve, strengthen, support, abet.

demote *v.* LOWER.

demulcent *adj.* SOOTHING.

demur *v.* object, disagree, decline, refute, hesitate, delay, stall, postpone, waver, pause, hedge, duck, balk, temporize, disapprove, cavil, wrangle, dissent. **ant.** concur, acquiesce, consent, accept, agree.

demure *adj.* sedate, shy, modest, retiring, timid, self-effacing, bashful, coy, prim, prudish, priggish, stiff, straitlaced, prissy, proper. **ant.** brash, bold, aggressive, impudent, brazen, saucy, vulgar.

demurrer *n.* OBJECTION.

den *n.* 1 cavern, cave, lair, hollow, hole, hideout, covert, shelter, burrow, dugout, tunnel, haunt. 2 study, retreat, sanctuary, hideaway, snuggery, cloister, nest, sanctum.

denial *n.* refusal, rejection, disallowance, rebuff, declination, withholding, forbidding, no, negation, veto, disapproval, repulsion, prohibition, thumbs down. **ant.** approval, acceptance, affirmation, permission, allowance, yes, okay.

denigrate *v.* slander, defame, blacken, besmirch, soil, vilify, abuse, malign, disparage, downgrade, stigmatize, calumniate. **ant.** whitewash, exculpate, excuse, absolve, upgrade.

denigration *n.* SLANDER.

denizen *n.* 1 resident, inhabitant, native, dweller, occupant, tenant, indigene, addressee. 2 frequenter, habitué, regular, devotee, patron, follower, member. **ant.** 1, 2 outsider, alien, foreigner, stranger.

denominate *v.* NAME.

denomination *n.* 1 name, designation, title, appellation, term, specification, nomenclature, type, sort, category, grouping, heading, rubric, brand. 2 sect, group, faction, school, persuasion, affiliation, clan, brotherhood, fellowship, society, cult, order.

denotation *n.* MEANING.

denote *v.* point out, mark, make known, signify, indicate, mean, designate, import, betoken, show, express, imply, convey, suggest, intimate, connote.

denouement *n.* OUTCOME.

denounce *v.* condemn, inveigh, upbraid, impugn, vilify, revile, brand, stigmatize, castigate, vituperate, curse, damn, boycott, blacklist, denunciate.

ant. praise, approve, uphold, applaud, extol, commend, laud.

dense *adj.* **1** compact, crowded, close, compressed, thick, condensed, serried, solid, concentrated, sclerotic, massed, firm, teeming, full. **2** stupid, dull, unintelligent, slow, cloddish, dimwitted, thick, thickheaded, obtuse, slow-witted, unaware, unperceptive.

ant. **1** sparse, thin, meager, spaced, scattered, scanty. **2** quick, alert, sensitive, perceptive, aware, responsive, hip (*Slang*).

dent *n.* nick, notch, hollow, groove, indentation, depression, concavity, pit, dimple, relief, intaglio.

ant. bump, lump, nodule, protuberance, knob, convexity.

denude *v.* STRIP.

denunciate *v.* DENOUNCE.

denunciation *n.* condemnation, invective, fulmination, stigmatization, execration, curse, diatribe, warning, tirade, philippic, screed, harangue, broadside, reprimand, scolding, chewing out (*Slang*).

ant. eulogy, panegyric, encomium, commendation, homage, acclaim, kudos.

deny *v.* **1** contradict, gainsay, nullify, negate, negative, controvert, disaffirm, dispute, protest, rebut, refute, repudiate, disavow, disown, disclaim. **2** withhold, refuse, begrudge, turn down, veto, prohibit, forbid, repulse.

ant. **1** affirm, acquiesce, concede, avow, believe. **2** allow, let, permit, give, offer, provide.

depart *v.* **1** leave, go, quit, abandon, exit, withdraw, disappear, vanish, recede, retire, retreat, escape, vacate, light out (*Slang*). **2** deviate, differ,

vary, diverge, digress, swerve, veer, deflect, turn, bend, stray, drift, err, wander.

ant. **1, 2** remain, rest, adhere, abide.

department *n.* division, section, subdivision, unit, office, dominion, category, specialty, area, domain, realm, sphere, line, bureau, sector.

departure *n.* **1** exit, withdrawal, leave, going, disappearance, abandonment, leavetaking, embarkation, farewell, goodbye, retreat, escape, retirement, parting, exodus. **2** deviation, divergence, variance, digression, deflection, turn, bend, divagation, aberration, error.

ant. **1** arrival, entrance, coming, onset, appearance, stay. **2** loyalty, devotion, rigidity, conformity, adherence.

depend *v.* **1** trust, rely on, put faith in, count on, bank on, lean on, believe in. **2** require, need, hinge on, ride on, rest on, revolve around.

dependable *adj.* reliable, trustworthy, stable, unfailing, faithful, steady, true, stalwart, reliable, sure, fixed, invariable, established, authoritative, scrupulous.

ant. changeable, variable, mercurial, unreliable, unstable, shaky, undependable.

dependence *n.* reliance, need, dependency, contingency, expectation, credence, faith, interconnection, symbiosis, parasitism.

ant. independence, autonomy, control, self-sufficiency.

dependency *n.* DEPENDENCE.

dependent *adj.* contingent, reliant, trusting, expectant, requiring, needful, subject to, weak, clinging, subordinate, parasitic, immature.

ant. independent, autonomous, self-sufficient, self-supporting, strong, mature.

depict *v.* **1** portray, paint, picture, draw, delineate, sculpt, model, figure, contour, sketch, outline, limn, blueprint, lay out, form, carve. **2** describe, narrate, tell, dramatize, fictionalize, characterize, verbalize, detail, set forth, illustrate, show, relate, recount, chronicle.

depiction *n*. PICTURE.

deplete *v*. exhaust, use up, empty, reduce, lessen, waste, drain, decrease, spend, weaken, impoverish, wear out, consume, expend.

ant. fill, increase, enlarge, replenish, add, enrich.

depletion *n*. REDUCTION.

deplorable *adj*. regrettable, lamentable, unfortunate, distressing, miserable, sad, unhappy, grievous, sorry, disastrous, calamitous, ill-fated.

ant. fortunate, happy, felicitous, agreeable, cheering, gratifying, pleasant.

deplore *v*. regret, lament, grieve, rue, mourn, bewail, bemoan.

ant. celebrate, rejoice, exult.

deploy *v*. use, utilize, set up, arrange, set out, position.

deport *v*. expel, banish, exile, cast out, expatriate, outlaw, ban, exclude.

deportment *n*. conduct, behavior, demeanor, manner, style, bearing, carriage, comportment, look, manners, etiquette.

deport oneself BEHAVE.

depose *v*. unseat, oust, dismiss, displace, dethrone, expel, throw out, discharge, cashier, degrade, divest, unfrock, demote, remove, fire, sack (*Slang*), can (*Slang*).

ant. install, enthrone, empower, seat, crown.

deposit *v*. entrust, consign. —*n*. money, assets, savings, security, cash, down payment, pledge, collateral, retainer, warranty.

depot *n*. 1 warehouse, storehouse, arsenal, repository, station, magazine, supply center, armory, commissariat, commissary, *entrepôt*. 2 terminal, terminus, station.

deprave *v*. CORRUPT.

depraved *adj*. corrupt, debased, debauched, immoral, wicked, sinful, evil, vicious, lecherous, degenerate, base, low, shameless, besotted, degraded, dissolute, fallen, perverted.

ant. pure, wholesome, virtuous, high-minded, moral, unspoiled.

depravity *n*. debauchery, degeneracy, wickedness, sinfulness, corruption, debasement, viciousness, lechery, vice, evil, lewdness, shamelessness, sinfulness, immorality.

ant. morality, high-mindedness, purity, goodness, virtue, decency, wholesomeness.

deprecate *v*. regret, disapprove, condemn, belittle, deplore, disfavor, object to, take exception to, frown on, disparage, take a dim view of.

ant. condone, commend, approve, accept, favor.

deprecatory *adj*. belittling, disparaging, apologetic, disapproving, condemnatory, condescending, patronizing, derogatory.

ant. complimentary, approving, respectful, deferential, congratulatory.

depreciate *v*. 1 devalue, lessen, lower, cheapen, drop, fall, wane, decline, diminish, sink, ebb, slump, sag, tumble, plunge. 2 look down on, belittle, denigrate, disparage, sneer, slight, scorn, condescend, derogate, slur, scoff, ridicule.

ant. 1 rise, grow, go up, climb, wax, increase, escalate. 2 respect, prize, esteem, value, look up to, honor.

depreciation *n*. devaluation, drop, fall, decline, depression, slump, sag, bearishness.

ant. appreciation, increase, rise, jump, bullishness.

depredate *v*. PLUNDER.

depress *v*. 1 sadden, discourage, dispirit, enervate, slow up, devitalize, dishearten, deject, sap. 2 cheapen, debase, degrade, depreciate, devalue, reduce. 3 press down, push down, dent, hollow, flatten, level, deepen, dimple, sink.

ant. 1 gladden, encourage, uplift, elate, enliven, invigorate, energize. 2 upgrade, appreciate, raise, heighten.

depressed *adj*. dejected, sad, low, dispirited, morose, unhappy, glum, melancholy, down, blue, gloomy, apathetic, sullen, grim, cheerless, despondent, low-spirited, downhearted, moody, hopeless, forlorn.

ant. cheerful, happy, energetic, animated, lively, optimistic, upbeat.

depression *n.* **1** dejection, sadness, melancholy, despair, hopelessness, pessimism, despondency, gloominess, discouragement, downheartedness, torpor, sluggishness, lassitude, ennui, acedia, the blues. **2** dent, hollow, concavity, pit, dimple, impression, groove, furrow, dip, rut, fissure, cranny, chink, bed.

ant. 1 cheerfulness, high spirits, lightheartedness, optimism, animation, hopefulness. **2** rise, bump, ridge, node, convexity.

deprivation *n.* LOSS.

deprive *v.* divest, take away, expropriate, keep from, dispossess, wrest, denude, rob, confiscate, debar, exclude, bereave, curtail, estop, cut off, strip, except, hinder, prohibit.

depth *n.* pit, bottom, heart, core, soul, center, abyss, bowels, profundity, intensity, density, exhaustiveness, penetration, comprehensiveness, complexity, abstruseness.

ant. surface, superficiality, appearance, facade.

deputation *n.* DELEGATION.

depute *v.* APPOINT.

deputize *v.* APPOINT.

deputy *n.* agent, representative, aide, proxy, second, substitute, surrogate, delegate, alternate, vicar, lieutenant, assistant, envoy, emissary, intermediary, ambassador, go-between.

derange *v.* DISORDER.

deranged *adj.* demented, crazed, maddened, frenzied, berserk, frantic, delirious, unhinged, lunatic, irrational, eccentric, crazy, mad, psychotic, daft, cuckoo (*Slang*), nuts (*Slang*).

ant. sane, rational, lucid, clearheaded, calm, sensible.

derelict *adj.* negligent, neglectful, remiss, lax, careless, delinquent, un-

mindful, thoughtless, irresponsible, shiftless, laggard, slipshod. —*n.* vagrant, outcast, drifter, tramp, hobo, pariah, loafer, bum, wreck, good-for-nothing.

ant. *adj.* dutiful, mindful, responsible, careful, meticulous.

dereliction *n.* NEGLECT.

deride *v.* ridicule, mock, jeer, sneer, taunt, scoff, jibe, laugh at, heckle, make fun of, lampoon, satirize, burlesque, rag (*Slang*), razz (*Slang*).

de rigueur NECESSARY.

derision *n.* ridicule, scorn, mockery, contempt, contumely, disdain, heckling, sneering, satire, disparagement, disrespect, hissing, booing, razzing (*Slang*), Bronx cheer (*Slang*).

ant. esteem, respect, admiration, applause, approval, commendation, kudos.

derisive *adj.* **1** SCORNFUL. **2** RIDICULOUS.

derivation *n.* origin, source, font, fountainhead, cradle, seed, germ, root, spring, wellspring, cause, ancestry, beginning, commencement, foundation, basis.

derivative *adj.* unoriginal, derived, imitative, superficial, secondary, copied, uninventive, eclectic, trite, secondhand, plagiaristic, old hat.

ant. original, basic, primary, fresh, firsthand, new.

derive *v.* deduce, draw, receive, conclude, obtain, get, secure, procure, glean, gain, profit from, enjoy, take in, benefit.

derogate *v.* BELITTLE.

derogative *adj.* DEROGATORY.

derogatory *adj.* disparaging, deprecatory, belittling, derogative, harmful, slanderous, contemptuous, defamatory, unflattering, injurious, discrediting, calumnious, humiliating, hurtful, damaging.

ant. flattering, complimentary, respectful, appreciative, congratulatory, eulogistic, kind.

derriere *n.* BUTTOCKS.

derring-do *n.* COURAGE.

descend v. **1** go down, move down, slope, incline, drop, fall, dip, sink, gravitate, plummet, plunge, tumble. **2** lower oneself, stoop, demean oneself, abase oneself, condescend, grovel, kneel, humble oneself.
  ant. 1 ascend, rise, soar, climb, mount.

descendant n. offspring, son, daughter, child, progeny, posterity, heir, heiress, offshoot, derivative, by-product, consequence, outcome, outgrowth, result, product, effect.
  ant. parent, progenitor, ancestor, forebear, root, source, cause.

descent n. **1** fall, drop, dip, droop, downrush, decrease, decline, gravitation, plunge, tumble. **2** slope, declivity, ramp, pitch, grade, incline, inclination, slide, declination. **3** deterioration, decline, degeneration, downgrading, debasement, lowering, waning, weakening, ebbing, loss, depreciation, decadence. **4** ancestry, lineage, line, forefathers, source, origin, seed, pedigree, stock, heredity, parentage, family tree.
  ant. 1 ascent, climb, mount, rise. **3** improvement, upgrading, betterment, strengthening, regeneration, gain, increase, amelioration.

describe v. speak of, narrate, relate, recount, portray, characterize, depict, tell of, detail, set forth, chronicle, specify, recite, explain, express, articulate, verbalize, report.

description n. account, report, statement, recounting, portrayal, depiction, characterization, chronicle, recital, explanation, delineation, illustration, picture, verbalization, definition, sketch, outline.

descriptive adj. explanatory, illustrative, detailed, graphic, vivid, pictorial, colorful, clear, picturesque, imaginative, lifelike, real, particularized.
  ant. vague, abstract, unclear, general, nondescript.

descry v. DISCERN.

desecrate v. profane, pervert, prostitute, contaminate, defile, secularize, taint, debase, pollute, abuse, maltreat, cheapen.
  ant. consecrate, hallow, sanctify, purify, enshrine, glorify, exalt.

desert[1] n. wasteland, waste, Sahara, barren, wilderness, tundra, moor, bush, steppe, no man's land, veldt, dustbowl, plain, prairie.
  ant. garden, civilization, Eden, land of milk and honey.

desert[2] v. forsake, abandon, quit, leave, strand, flee, betray, maroon, run away, cast off, renounce, repudiate, reject, disclaim, bug out (*Slang*).
  ant. remain, abide, fulfill, stand firm, adhere.

deserter n. TRAITOR.

deserts n. reward, compensation, payment, recompense, retribution, due, worth, requital, retaliation, pay, return, punishment, comeuppance, chastening, penalty.

deserve v. earn, merit, be worthy of, be entitled to, rate, warrant, justify, qualify.

deserved adj. merited, warranted, just, earned, rightful, justified, justifiable, fair, evenhanded, proper, due, condign, fit, fitting, appropriate.
  ant. unwarranted, unfair, unjust, unjustified.

deserving adj. WORTHY.

desiccated adj. DRY.

desideratum n. AIM.

design v. **1** draw, sketch, outline, lay out, prepare, make, fashion, style, blueprint, detail, specify, delineate, model, structure, draft, program, flesh out, build. **2** invent, create, originate, plan, conceive, project, contrive, scheme, concoct, cook up, think up, dream up, hatch, nurture. —n. **1** plan, sketch, pattern, arrangement, layout, mockup, model, blueprint, outline, drawing, paste-up. **2** purpose, meaning, structure, explanation, logic, unity, causation, theme, *telos*. **3** objective, undertaking, scheme, enterprise, project, venture, prospect, ambition, experiment, proposal.

ant. *n.* **2** chaos, anarchy, disorder, chance, purposelessness.

designate *v.* **1** indicate, name, characterize, signify, specify, denote, particularize, call, dub, describe, distinguish, signalize, point to, individualize, mention, earmark, label. **2** nominate, appoint, name, elect, select, choose, assign, commission, delegate, deputize, propose, authorize, ordain, bid.

designation *n.* **1** appointment, nomination, election, selection, assignment, delegation, authorization, bid. **2** title, label, description, mark, earmark, cachet, brand, trademark, appellation, signature, identification, individualization, distinction.

designing *adj.* scheming, plotting, artful, guileful, contriving, foxy, calculating, conniving, conspiratorial, underhand, covert, cunning, clever, subtle, deep.

ant. guileless, ingenuous, open, spontaneous, forthright, direct.

desirable *adj.* **1** worthwhile, beneficial, good, gratifying, welcome, pleasant, advantageous, gainful, profitable, useful, enjoyable. **2** alluring, provocative, seductive, tantalizing, fetching, exciting, tempting, captivating, sexy.

ant. 1 injurious, damaging, useless, unpleasant, unwanted, unnecessary, deplorable.

desire *v.* long for, want, crave, wish for, ask for, request, aspire to, require, hanker after, need, hunger for, thirst for, ache for, yearn for, covet. —*n.* **1** longing, craving, hankering, yearning, wish, need, aspiration, hope, hunger, thirst, covetousness, ache, want. **2** lust, passion, appetite, concupiscence, lechery, yen, libidinousness, sexuality, ardor, amorousness, carnality.

desirous *adj.* longing, needful, craving, yearning, aspiring, wanting, hungry,

aching, wishful, hopeful, eager, ambitious, wistful.

desist *v.* cease, stop, discontinue, leave off, abstain, avoid, forbear, refrain, suspend, put off, postpone, halt, quit, end, conclude, drop, lay off (*Slang*).

ant. continue, persist, go on, persevere.

desolate *adj.* **1** deserted, uninhabited, solitary, isolated, lonely, depopulated, bleak, empty, abandoned, unoccupied, barren, cheerless. **2** friendless, forlorn, forsaken, sorrowful, abject, dejected, downcast, pitiable, despondent, lonesome, alone, bereft, wretched, miserable.

ant. 1 inhabited, populated, bustling, humming, lively. **2** befriended, popular, well-liked, cheerful.

despair *v.* lose heart, lose hope, give up, despond. —*n.* hopelessness, discouragement, depression, alienation, desperation, disillusion, melancholy, defeatism, bitterness, pessimism, wretchedness, disaffection, misery.

ant. *v.* hope, expect, aspire, look forward to, anticipate. *n.* hope, courage, spirit, anticipation, optimism, cheerfulness.

despatch *v.* DISPATCH.

desperado *n.* outlaw, criminal, escapee, brigand, jailbird, gunman, gangster, marauder, lawbreaker, bandit, fugitive, ruffian.

desperate *adj.* **1** reckless, heedless, mindless, uncaring, rash, unmindful, death-defying, devil-may-care, frantic, wild, headlong, imprudent, foolhardy. **2** critical, crucial, drastic, last-ditch, all-out, decisive, supreme, final, violent, extreme, urgent, pressing, exigent.

ant. 1 cautious, prudent, careful, self-protective, sensible. **2** casual, ordinary, effortless, routine.

desperation *n.* recklessness, heedlessness, foolhardiness, imprudence, frenzy, daring, defiance, extremity, risk, precipitateness, rashness.

ant. caution, prudence, sense, wariness, circumspection, thought, consideration.

despicable *adj.* contemptible, hateful, loathsome, mean, vile, low, ignominious, base, infamous, disgraceful, shameful, detestable, reprehensible, wretched, worthless, disreputable.
ant. admirable, commendable, meritorious, praiseworthy, respectable.

despise *v.* scorn, spurn, disdain, contemn, look down on, misprize, sneer at, loathe, detest, deride, revile.
ant. respect, esteem, admire, value, commend, praise, look up to.

despite *n.* **1** CONTEMPT. **2** SPITE.

despoil *v.* PLUNDER.

despond *v.* DESPAIR.

despondency *n.* despair, dejection, discouragement, desperation, hopelessness, dispiritedness, depression, pessimism, melancholy, defeatism, unhappiness, wretchedness, misery, funk, the blues.
ant. cheerfulness, courage, spirit, lightheartedness, optimism, elation.

despondent *adj.* dejected, depressed, disheartened, downhearted, dispirited, discouraged, disconsolate, forlorn, desolate, melancholy, sad, glum, morose, wretched, unhappy, miserable, blue, down (*Slang*).
ant. cheerful, spirited, optimistic, hopeful, buoyant, happy, up (*Slang*).

despot *n.* autocrat, tyrant, oppressor, dictator, authoritarian, fascist, inquisitor, martinet, bully, Simon Legree, slavedriver, taskmaster.
ant. democrat, egalitarian, humanitarian, leveler.

despotic *adj.* tyrannical, autocratic, oppressive, dictatorial, authoritarian, fascist, inquisitorial, bullying, arbitrary, unyielding, imperious, inhumane, merciless, unreasonable, Draconian.
ant. democratic, egalitarian, flexible, yielding, lax, liberal, humane.

desiccated *adj.* DRY.

despotism *n.* TYRANNY.

destination *n.* **1** terminal, terminus, ad-

dress, resting place, journey's end, haven, port, harbor, home, anchorage, stop, station. **2** goal, purpose, aim, end, aspiration, intention, design, object, ambition, target, hope, wish, desire.

destine *v.* DETERMINE.

destiny *n.* fate, lot, inevitability, fortune, portion, providence, doom, star, karma, kismet.

destitute *adj.* **1** lacking, depleted, devoid, used up, exhausted, empty, deficient, void, inadequate, low, short, wanting, vacant. **2** poverty-stricken, needy, badly off, poor, hard up, insolvent, indigent, impoverished, in want, penniless, broke, stone-broke, strapped, pauperized, busted (*Slang*).
ant. **1** full, replete, plentiful, well-supplied, abundant. **2** well off, affluent, rich, flush, loaded (*Slang*), well-heeled (*Slang*).

destroy *v.* **1** annihilate, exterminate, extinguish, consume, quench, undo, ruin, obliterate, efface, eradicate, decimate, wipe out, erase, remove, extirpate, cancel, expunge, end, trash (*Slang*), shipwreck. **2** tear down, raze, demolish, pull down, wreck, shatter, blast, gut, devastate, break.
ant. **1, 2** create, make, construct, erect, raise.

destruction *n.* havoc, ruin, annihilation, extermination, undoing, obliteration, removal, demolition, overthrow, subversion, slaughter, fall, end, wreck.
ant. construction, creation, birth, restoration, renewal, recovery.

destructive *adj.* hurtful, harmful, injurious, damaging, negative, deleterious, bad, discouraging, undermining, disheartening, detrimental, disruptive, subversive, baneful.
ant. constructive, beneficial, helpful, positive, wholesome, good.

desultory *adj.* aimless, unmethodical, changeable, discontinuous, casual, wandering, spasmodic, off and on, irregular, capricious, discursive, cursory, undirected, episodic, purposeless, erratic, nonchalant.

ant. methodical, purposeful, focused, steady, regular, pointed.

detach *v.* separate, disconnect, unfasten, sever, disengage, loosen, divide, sunder, part, free, isolate, cut, withdraw, undo, disjoin, divorce.

ant. connect, combine, fasten, attach, weld, knit, join.

detached *adj.* **1** separated, disconnected, severed, sundered, divided, free, discrete, isolated, disjointed, segregated, divorced, cut, parted. **2** impartial, unbiased, disinterested, objective, uncommitted, fairminded, just, nonpartisan, impersonal, unprejudiced, dispassionate, disengaged, neutral.

ant. 1 connected, unified, united, welded, joined. **2** partisan, concerned, prejudiced, biased, involved, impassioned.

detachment *n.* impartiality, objectivity, disinterestedness, indifference, aloofness, dispassion, nonpartisanship, unconcern, coolness, neutrality, fairmindedness, justice, remoteness, disengagement.

ant. partiality, bias, prejudice, partisanship, devotion, involvement, vested interest.

detail *n.* part, item, particular, iota, datum, specific, particularity, feature, itemization, particularization, triviality.

ant. whole, entirety, totality, summary, overview.

detailed *adj.* SPECIFIC.

detain *v.* restrain, stop, arrest, delay, hold, retard, hinder, impede, confine, lock up, kidnap, jail, imprison.

ant. let free, loose, liberate, speed, hasten, dispatch, advance.

detect *v.* discover, uncover, expose, reveal, make known, find, catch, espy, see, disclose, notice, unmask, unveil, air, observe.

ant. overlook, miss, disregard, neglect, ignore.

detection *n.* discovery, revelation, exposure, disclosure, unmasking, exposé, learning, unearthing, uncovering, ferreting out.

detective *n.* sleuth, operative, G-man, investigator, private eye, plainclothes man, secret agent, gumshoe (*Slang*), dick (*Slang*), bloodhound (*Brit.*), undercover agent.

detention *n.* restraint, confinement, arrest, house arrest, delay, hindrance, incarceration, imprisonment, kidnaping, jailing, duress, bondage.

ant. freedom, liberation, liberty, unconstraint.

deter *v.* dissuade, discourage, restrain, warn, hold back, prevent, check, dishearten, dampen, divert, cool, disincline, curb, undermine, unnerve, daunt, hinder, stop.

ant. encourage, hearten, spur, stimulate, embolden.

deterge *v.* CLEAN.

deteriorate *v.* degenerate, decay, worsen, decline, ebb, wane, weaken, disintegrate, degrade, devalue, damage, retrogress.

ant. improve, ameliorate, enhance, strengthen, wax, bloom.

determinate *adj.* SPECIFIC.

determination *n.* **1** decision, settlement, finding, arbitration, ascertainment, conclusion, judgment, opinion, resolution, adjudication, verdict, verification, confirmation, corroboration, authentication. **2** willpower, resolve, firmness, steadfastness, purposefulness, dedication, tenacity, singlemindedness, strength, stamina, courage, backbone, grit, pluck, perseverance, stick-to-itiveness.

ant. 2 vacillation, uncertainty, irresolution, hesitation, indecision, spinelessness.

determine *v.* **1** settle, decide, arbitrate, ordain, foreordain, destine, ascertain, conclude, judge, resolve, adjudicate, verify, confirm, substantiate, corroborate, authenticate, fix. **2** influence, affect, sway, regulate, control, govern, condition, define, shape, mold, guide.

determined *adj.* settled, resolved, resolute, fixed, purposeful, firm, tenacious, perseverant, persistent, devoted, set, dedicated, unwavering, steadfast, strong-willed, plucky.
ant. uncertain, dubious, wavering, undecided, vacillating, spineless.

deterrent *n.* DISCOURAGEMENT.

detest *v.* hate, despise, abhor, abominate, loathe, execrate, contemn, recoil from, dislike, disdain.
ant. like, care for, value, admire, treasure, love.

detestable *adj.* hateful, abhorrent, loathsome, abominable, odious, execrable, contemptible, disgusting, repulsive, revolting, obnoxious, offensive, vile, awful.
ant. likable, congenial, pleasant, pleasing, appealing, admirable.

detestation *n.* HATRED.

dethrone *v.* DEPOSE.

detonate *v.* EXPLODE.

detour *n.* bypass, byroad, divergence, deviation, branch, offshoot, circumvention, divagation, spur, short cut, roundabout way, zigzag.

detriment *n.* harm, hurt, injury, disservice, prejudice, impairment, loss, damage, mishap, misfortune, disadvantage.
ant. benefit, good, advantage, boon, help, gain.

detrimental *adj.* harmful, hurtful, injurious, prejudicial, damaging, unfortunate, disadvantageous, bad, destructive, deleterious, inimical, noxious.
ant. beneficial, advantageous, good, helpful, favorable, positive.

detritus *n.* DEBRIS.

devastate *v.* lay waste, waste, crush, overwhelm, wipe out, strip, ravage, pillage, destroy, level, desolate, sack, ruin, plunder, demolish, raze, gut.

devastating *adj.* overwhelming, crushing, definitive, murderous, savage, utter, withering, ruinous, cruel, total, entire, destructive, unconscionable.

develop *v.* **1** mature, ripen, grow up, age, mellow, blossom, burgeon, maturate. **2** progress, evolve, unfold, grow, advance, educate, train, cultivate, promote. **3** amplify, enlarge upon, augment, expand, broaden, dilate upon, enrich, further, extend, flesh out, perfect, heighten, pad, blow up, expound. **4** intensify, step up, escalate, exercise, emphasize, stress, reinforce, harden, energize, fortify, buttress, invigorate, rejuvenate.
ant. 1 stunt, stifle, shrivel. **2** regress, retrogress, recede, backslide. **4** slight, minimize, de-emphasize, relax, soften.

development *n.* **1** evolution, growth, rise, increase, expansion, escalation, progress, advancement, maturation, ripening, promotion, propagation, flowering, burgeoning, coming of age. **2** event, happening, occurrence, episode, outcome, upshot, result, circumstance, issue, aftermath, incident, phenomenon, situation.
ant. 1 decrease, decline, retrogression, weakening, withering, decadence, decay.

deviate *v.* diverge, differ, swerve, veer, stray, err, wander, turn, bend, vary, depart, tack, ramble, sidetrack, digress, divagate, desert, defect.
ant. adhere, follow, conform, comply, cling to.

deviation *n.* DIVERGENCE.

device *n.* **1** contrivance, tool, implement, invention, appliance, apparatus, contraption, gadget, mechanism, utensil. **2** plot, scheme, plan, design, trick, artifice, stratagem, means, way, ruse, ploy, gimmick, stunt, twist, improvisation, angle, dodge, *deus ex machina.*

devil *n.* **1** Satan, Lucifer, Mephistopheles, Old Nick, Beelzebub, Archfiend, Archenemy, Evil One, Serpent, Prince of Darkness, Spirit of Evil, Tempter, Adversary. **2** fiend, demon, terror, monster, ogre, evildoer, villain, brute, beast, savage, hellcat, hellion, imp, troublemaker, rogue, scoundrel. —*v.* harass, bedevil, tease, badger, provoke, victimize, bully, plague, beset, afflict, annoy, persecute, vex, trouble, hound. **ant.** *n.* **2** angel, saint, paragon, ideal, doll (*Slang*).

devilish *adj.* **1** challenging, difficult, complex, convoluted, subtle, devious, provocative, provoking, intriguing, profound, penetrating, complicated, intricate. **2** mischievous, impish, naughty, puckish, troublesome, fiendish, willful, disobedient, refractory, rebellious, disrespectful, self-assertive, impudent.

ant. 1 simple, obvious, easy, boring, unchallenging. **2** well-behaved, angelic, good, obedient, submissive, respectful.

devil-may-care *adj.* RECKLESS.

devilment *n.* MISCHIEF.

devious *adj.* roundabout, wily, foxy, sly, evasive, crooked, underhand, covert, circuitous, dishonest, sneaky, tricky, deceitful, treacherous, slippery, shifty. **ant.** straightforward, honest, direct, bluff, forthright, truthful, reliable.

devise *v.* invent, contrive, create, form, plan, fashion, concoct, think up, frame, prepare, conceive, imagine, dream up, originate, establish, found, pioneer, map out.

devitalize *v.* WEAKEN.

devoid *adj.* destitute, empty, depleted, lacking, wanting, bereft, stripped, bare, denuded, emptied, out of, short of, missing, free, divested. **ant.** full, replete, filled, laden, fraught.

devoir *n.* DUTY.

devote *v.* give, consign, dedicate, allot, apply, concentrate, apportion, invest, attend, do, undertake, concern oneself, occupy oneself.

devoted *adj.* faithful, loyal, ardent, devout, concerned, caring, dedicated, committed, involved, consecrated, affectionate, warm, loving, close, dependable, attached, fond. **ant.** cool, inimical, distant, detached, unconcerned.

devotee *n.* fan, admirer, follower, enthusiast, adherent, disciple, demon, addict, buff, fanatic, expert, aficionado, nut (*Slang*).

devotion *n.* **1** dedication, application, attachment, affection, loyalty, adherence, cult, faithfulness, warmth, ardor, love, fondness, concern, closeness, commitment, involvement. **2** piety, religiosity, consecration, holiness, prayer, worshipfulness, devoutness, reverence, sanctity, faith, humility, spirituality. **ant. 1** apathy, coolness, detachment, aloofness. **2** godlessness, disbelief, impiety, irreverence.

devour *v.* **1** gobble up, consume, gorge, eat, bolt, gulp, wolf, stuff, raven, guzzle. **2** be engrossed by, absorb, go through, soak up, delight in, drink in, enjoy, revel in, feast on, relish, appreciate.

devout *adj.* **1** pious, religious, reverent, worshipful, godly, holy, consecrated, devoted, spiritual, believing, orthodox, pietistic. **2** heartfelt, sincere, earnest, ardent, intense, profound, impassioned, fervent, keen, wholehearted, deep, genuine, unalloyed. **ant. 1** irreligious, impious, worldly, atheistic, godless. **2** superficial, casual, hypocritical, halfhearted, insincere.

dewy *adj.* MOIST.

dexterity *n.* adroitness, skill, agility, facility, handiness, touch, mastery, skillfulness, aptitude, knack, proficiency, expertise. **ant.** clumsiness, ineptitude, maladroitness, awkwardness, incompetence, heavy-handedness.

dexterous *adj.* ADROIT.

diabolic *adj.* devilish, satanic, fiendish, demonic, Mephistophelean, wicked, cruel, evil, malevolent, baleful, malefic, infernal, hellish, vicious, atrocious, monstrous. **ant.** angelic, saintly, virtuous, pure, good, humane, benevolent.

diabolism *n.* SORCERY.

diagnose *v.* ANALYZE.

diagnosis *n*. ANALYSIS.

dial *n*. indicator, pointer, gnomon, calibrator, face, hand, timer, clock, watch, sundial, gauge, meter.

dialect *n*. jargon, vernacular, cant, argot, patois, colloquialism, idiom, parlance, localism, provincialism, regionalism, diction, lingo, slang.

dialectic *n*. ARGUMENT.

dialogue *n*. **1** conversation, chat, repartee, exchange, causerie, tête-à-tête. **2** conference, colloquium, interview, colloquy, discourse, discussion, parley, palaver, consultation, debate, bull session, rap session (*Slang*), give-and-take, meeting, conclave, huddle.

diametrical *adj*. opposite, contrary, mutually exclusive, different, antipodal, opposed, counter, antithetical, contrasting, conflicting, counterposed, antagonistic, inimical. **ant**. similar, alike, corresponding, comparable, equivalent, parallel.

diametrically *adv*. ALTOGETHER.

diaphanous *adj*. transparent, sheer, filmy, lacy, flimsy, cobwebby, translucent, gauzy, chiffon, thin, delicate, gossamer, peekaboo, see-through (*Slang*). **ant**. opaque, solid, dense.

diatribe *n*. INVECTIVE.

dicey *adj*. RISKY.

dicker *v*. haggle, bargain, barter, trade, cavil, negotiate, deal, quibble, wrangle.

dictate *v*. **1** read aloud, transmit, communicate, compose, draft, say, utter, speak, pronounce. **2** command, authorize, order, rule, enjoin, direct, decree, ordain, demand, require, charge, compel, impose. —*n*. law, order, ordinance, rule, decree, commandment, authorization, injunction, statute, ultimatum, direction, fiat, edict, regulation.

dictator *n*. authoritarian, despot, tyrant, absolutist, autocrat, totalitarian, oppressor, Hitler, Führer, czar.

dictatorial *adj*. autocratic, despotic, tyrranical, overbearing, imperious, bossy, oppressive, dogmatic, arbitrary, arrogant, supercilious, opinionated, tough, unyielding, rigid, unreasonable. **ant**. open-minded, liberal, democratic, reasonable, flexible, tolerant.

dictionary *n*. lexicon, wordbook, thesaurus, glossary, vocabulary, concordance.

dictum *n*. pronouncement, pronunciamento, edict, command, commandment, fiat, order, decree, assertion, decision, verdict, declaration, manifesto.

didactic *adj*. informative, edifying, enlightening, instructive, educational, heuristic, expository, exegetical, preceptive, pedantic, pedagogical, preachy.

didactics *n*. PEDAGOGY.

diddle *v*. DAWDLE.

dido *n*. CAPER.

die *v*. **1** expire, perish, pass away, succumb, decease, croak (*Slang*). **2** fade, weaken, wither, ebb, wane, dwindle, peter out, lapse, decay, disappear, vanish, go, depart, leave. **3** pine for, languish, swoon, ache, aspire, hunger, yearn. **ant**. **1** exist, live, be, breathe. **2** grow, strengthen, blossom, increase, rise, brighten.

die-hard *n*. reactionary, old fogy, bitter-ender, standpatter, stick-in-the-mud, Tory, zealot, crank, blimp (*Brit.*). **ant**. progressive, liberal, meliorist, reformer, radical.

diet *n*. nourishment, sustenance, meals, food and drink, nutrition, nutriments, fare, provisions, nurture, victuals, foodstuffs, edibles, eats, grub (*Slang*).

differ *v*. **1** vary, contrast, stand apart. **2** dispute, oppose, contest, disagree, dissent, contend, diverge, deviate, clash, conflict, jar, war, contradict. **ant**. **1** match, correspond, tally, equal, coincide. **2** consent, accede, concur, agree, cooperate.

difference *n.* **1** dissimilarity, distinctness, discreteness, separateness, discrepancy, conspicuousness, variety, individuality, unusualness, differentiation, contrast, antithesis, originality, discrimination. **2** distinction, variation, mark, nuance, eccentricity, divergence, deviation, mutation. **3** quarrel, controversy, disagreement, incompatibility, discord, dissension, variance, dissonance, opposition, clash, argument, dispute, spat, confrontation. —*v.* DISTINGUISH.
ant. 1 correspondence, sameness, oneness, resemblance, accord. **3** agreement, accord, peace, compatibility, concurrence, unanimity.

different *adj.* **1** distinct, other, separate, various, diverse, discrete, delineated, differentiated, characteristic, individual, unique. **2** dissimilar, antithetical, incongruous, incompatible, unalike, contrasting, divergent, disparate, uncongenial, discordant, clashing, opposed, deviating, at odds, at variance. **3** unusual, extraordinary, atypical, nonpareil, strange, odd, aberrant, eccentric, distinctive, distinguished, outstanding, *sui generis*, special, individual, singular, unique, one of a kind. **4** assorted, various, varied, many, divers, multiple, several, heterogeneous, miscellaneous, diverse, sundry, manifold, mixed.
ant. 1 unified, connected, joined, together, whole. **2** same, similar, alike, corresponding, congruous, harmonizing. **3** ordinary, usual, typical, average, run-of-the-mill. **4** homogeneous, uniform, pure, identical, unvaried.

differentiate *v.* mark off, distinguish, separate, set apart, earmark, discern, divide, designate, judge, characterize, classify, sort out, assort.
ant. lump together, homogenize, combine, mix.

differentiation *n.* DIFFERENCE.

difficult *adj.* **1** laborious, demanding, arduous, hard, exhausting, onerous, burdensome, irksome, wearisome, troublesome, fatiguing, strenuous, Herculean. **2** perplexing, puzzling, complicated, impenetrable, tough, challenging, intricate, involved, problematical, baffling, enigmatic, abstruse, thorny, hairy (*Slang*). **3** uncontrollable, willful, stubborn, trying, perverse, unruly, rambunctious, refractory, unmanageable, tiresome, unyielding, wild, contrary, cranky, fussy.
ant. 1 easy, undemanding, painless. **2** obvious, simple, clear. **3** docile, tractable, complaisant, accommodating.

difficulty *n.* problem, obstacle, objection, hindrance, puzzle, enigma, maze, trap, complication, embarrassment, involvement, snag, contretemps, pitfall, predicament, worry, concern, mess, jam.

diffidence *n.* SHYNESS.

diffident *adj.* timid, shy, self-effacing, retiring, anxious, unsure, uncertain, unaggressive, timorous, unassuming, bashful, humble, constrained, hesitant, modest, recalcitrant.
ant. assured, poised, confident, forward, presumptuous, bold, aggressive.

diffuse *v.* spread, disseminate, permeate, suffuse, disperse, strew, broadcast, scatter, distribute, pervade, percolate, penetrate. —*adj.* **1** wordy, verbose, prolix, garrulous, long-winded, discursive, unfocused, rambling, circumlocutory, extended, meandering, fustian, prolonged, pointless, oblique. **2** widespread, spread out, prevalent, pervasive, broad, swarming, universal, general, scattered, extended, far-ranging, unconcentrated, dispersed, diffusive, distributed, extensive, sweeping.
ant. *v.* concentrate, distill, focus, localize, confine, limit, narrow. *adj.* **1** terse, laconic, brief, crisp, pithy, succinct, condensed. **2** localized, confined, limited, narrow, concentrated.

diffusion *n.* SPREAD.

diffusive *adj.* DIFFUSE.

dig v. *Slang* understand, see, get, like, follow, grasp, catch on, perceive, comprehend, fathom, digest, assimilate, grasp, prefer, be on to (*Slang*). —n. *sarcastic remark:* crack, slur, knock, cut, taunt, reproach, slight, put-down (*Slang*), insult, snub.

ant. n. boost, bouquet, praise, compliment, pat on the back.

digest v. 1 take in, understand, comprehend, assimilate, absorb, know, master, fathom, get, savvy (*Slang*), incorporate, grasp, dig (*Slang*). 2 shorten, condense, compress, abridge, abstract, systematize, summarize, recap, recapitulate, methodize, codify. —n. abridgment, shortening, précis, recap, recapitulation, condensation, abstract, summary, outline, brief, résumé, draft, syllabus.

digestion n. ASSIMILATION.

diggings n. LODGING.

digit. n. NUMBER.

dignified *adj.* stately, noble, lofty, grand, worthy, elevated, exalted, magnificent, august, solemn, imposing, distinguished, weighty, lordly, honored, *distingué*.

ant. lowly, unimposing, humble, mean, undignified, informal.

dignify v. elevate, ennoble, exalt, honor, distinguish, glorify, crown, enthrone, advance, promote, better, raise, uplift, aggrandize, meliorate.

ant. humble, abase, humiliate, bring down, demean, degrade.

dignitary n. notable, somebody, name, worthy, VIP, lion, personage, functionary, big shot (*Slang*), big wheel (*Slang*), brass (*Slang*).

ant. nonentity, nobody, cipher, unperson.

dignity n. 1 stateliness, loftiness, gravity, courtliness, worthiness, honor, excellence, worth, grandeur, solemnity. 2 rank, title, distinction, station, honor, merit, status, importance, standing, repute, prominence, prestige, eminence, worth. 3 self-respect,

pride, self-esteem, self-regard, *amour propre*.

ant. 1, 2 unimportance, disrepute, humility, ignobility, lowness, baseness. **3** self-disgust, self-hatred, self-abnegation, shame, guilt, self-abasement.

digress v. RAMBLE.

digression n. deviation, divagation, side issue, departure, footnote, ramification, parenthesis, apostrophe, aside, irrelevancy, detour, bypath.

digressive *adj.* DISCURSIVE.

dig up v. uncover, excavate, exhume, disinter, reveal, find, come upon, expose, unearth, detect, bring to light.

ant. bury, hide, conceal, cover, inter, shroud.

dike n. embankment, bank, obstruction, barrier, wall, dam, obstacle, levee, breakwater, rampart, bulwark, pier.

dilapidated *adj.* decaying, falling apart, run-down, ramshackle, time-worn, rickety, tumble-down, disintegrating, decrepit, ruined, raddled, deteriorated, shaky, crumbling.

ant. solid, firm, strong, well-built, sturdy, in good shape.

dilate v. widen, enlarge, expand, distend, grow, spread, broaden, swell, inflate, amplify, stretch, puff out, extend, blow up, wax.

ant. contract, compress, reduce, condense, lessen, shrink, wane.

dilation n. SWELLING.

dilatory *adj.* slow, tardy, flagging, sluggish, laggard, lingering, procrastinating, behindhand, phlegmatic, dawdling, languid, inert, torpid, slothful.

ant. quick, brisk, active, eager, prompt, energetic, dynamic.

dilemma n. quandary, strait, plight, bind, puzzle, perplexity, impasse, fix, predicament, embarrassment, confusion, Hobson's choice, crunch (*Slang*).

dilettante n. amateur, nonprofessional, dabbler, hobbyist, tyro, eclectic.

ant. professional, specialist, master, expert, scholar, authority.

diligence *n.* application, industry, assiduity, industriousness, meticulousness, perseverance, persistence, vigor, constancy, intentness, earnestness, zeal, effort, stick-to-itiveness, doggedness.

ant. laziness, sloth, carelessness, lethargy, indifference, indolence.

diligent *n.* industrious, hard-working, painstaking, assiduous, meticulous, persevering, zealous, dogged, plodding, businesslike.

ant. lazy, slothful, indolent, indifferent.

dillydally *v.* hem and haw, waver, vacillate, trifle, dally, delay, pause, piddle, dawdle, linger, fiddle, procrastinate, shilly-shally, poke, hesitate.

ant. decide, conclude, choose, resolve, hurry, move, get going.

dilute *v.* weaken, thin, adulterate, water down, attenuate, reduce, diminish, rarefy, contaminate, pollute, debase, doctor, cut. —*adj.* DILUTED.

ant. strengthen, concentrate, purify, distill, condense, cleanse.

diluted *adj.* watered down, weakened, thinned, dilute, adulterated, attenuated, reduced, diminished, emasculated, simplified, wishy-washy.

ant. strengthened, concentrated, distilled, powerful, strong.

dim *adj.* **1** poorly lit, faint, obscure, murky, dark, indistinct, shadowy, dusky, blurry, misty, hazy, opaque, nocturnal, darkling, gray, vague, matte. **2** dense, dull, obtuse, dimwitted (*Slang*), dull-witted, lackluster, lusterless, doltish, stupid, dingy. **3** discouraging, gloomy, ominous, somber, unpromising, portentous, depressing, dashing, daunting, hopeless.

ant. 1, 2 bright, sharp, brilliant, sparkling. 3 rosy, glowing, hopeful, encouraging, promising.

dimension *n.* extent, magnitude, size, amplitude, expanse, extension, meas-ure, caliber, scope, range, bulk, proportion, scale.

diminution *n.* lessening, reduction, curtailment, decrease, shrinkage, abatement, alleviation, ebb, decline, weakening, let-up.

ant. increase, enlargement, addition, aggrandizement, inflation.

diminutive *adj.* tiny, petite, dainty, small, little, wee, teeny, dwarfed, miniature, undersized, Lilliputian, pocket-size, half-pint (*Slang*).

ant. large, big, gross, enormous, gigantic, oversize, giant.

dimwit *n.* DUNCE.

din *n.* clamor, riot, to-do, racket, commotion, noise, hullabaloo, tumult. —*v.* **1** clatter, crash, bang, blast, rumble, shriek, boom, thunder, resound, peal, ring, deafen. **2** argue, protest, press, insist, urge, reiterate, repeat, nag, pound, hammer, drum, vociferate, agitate, shout.

dine *v.* eat, consume, partake, sup, feed, fare, board, fall to, break bread, taste, gourmandize, feast, banquet.

ant. fast, abstain.

diner *n.* RESTAURANT.

dingy *adj.* drab, dull, shabby, grimy, bleak, dim, lackluster, somber, dirty, soiled, tarnished, faded, murky, colorless.

ant. bright, shiny, clean, new, sparkling, colorful, flamboyant.

dining room RESTAURANT.

dinky *adj.* LITTLE.

dinner *n.* feast, banquet, spread, festivity, regalement, blowout (*Slang*).

dint *n.* EFFORT.

dip *v.* **1** immerse, submerge, soak, scoop, bale, ladle, wet, moisten, bathe, plunge, dunk, duck, bow, bend, bob, nod. **2** slope, decline, subside, droop, sag, settle, sink, set, descend, drop, fall, plunge.

ant. 2 rise, ascend, climb, float, soar.

diplomat *n.* moderator, compromiser, politician, negotiator, arbitrator, referee, go-between, tactician, strategist.

diplomatic *adj.* tactful, discreet, artful, adept, delicate, subtle, sensitive, thoughtful, polite, suave, urbane, cautious, politic, expedient, intriguing.

ant. tactless, rude, bluff, abrupt, plain-spoken, unceremonious.

dire *adj.* **1** dreadful, terrible, fearful, horrid, horrible, shocking, disastrous, calamitous, appalling, grim, awful, dismal, gloomy, woeful. **2** urgent, drastic, exigent, immoderate, extreme.

ant. 1 happy, pleasant, successful, favorable, advantageous, wonderful.

direct *v.* **1** control, manage, conduct, lead, administer, supervise, handle, run, mastermind, sway, influence, guide, advise, instruct, regulate, rule, govern, command, order. **2** point, aim, guide, show, lead, orient, usher, turn, focus, level, train, slant, fix. **3** address, intend, mean, aim, level, cast, point. —*adj.* **1** straight, short, near, point-blank, undeviating, unswerving, even, true. **2** firsthand, personal, immediate, head-on. **3** complete, total, absolute, categorical, express, exact, positive, unequivocal, unambiguous. **4** candid, plain, open, sincere, outspoken, honest, straightforward, blunt, frank, bald, downright.

ant. *v.* **1** follow, obey, comply, conform. **2** mislead, misguide, divert, disorient. *adj.* **1** roundabout, crooked, winding, long. **2** secondhand, rumored, circumstantial, abstract. **4** guarded, cultivated, ambiguous, devious, sly.

direction *n.* **1** leadership, management, supervision, administration, control, conduct, care, surveillance, guidance, instruction. **2** command, order, charge, injunction, regulation, prescription, instruction, briefing. **3** tendency, trend, way, course, drift, bent, inclination, bearing, aim, end, tenor, fashion.

directive *n.* order, regulation, direction, instruction, injunction, ruling, notice, mandate, decree, command, ordinance, directorial, edict, proclamation.

directly *adv.* immediately, at once, instantly, straightaway, forthwith, presently, quickly, speedily, promptly, shortly, soon.

ant. later, afterwards, eventually, thereafter, next.

directness *n.* frankness, forthrightness, outspokenness, bluntness, brusqueness, candor, sincerity, honesty, openness.

ant. vagueness, obscurity, ambiguity, deviousness.

director *n.* leader, manager, organizer, head, chief, boss, superintendent, supervisor, overseer, administrator, commander, master.

directorial *n.* DIRECTIVE.

directory *n.* LIST.

direful *adj.* dreadful, terrible, fearful, horrible, horrid, dire, awful, appalling, shocking, ghastly.

dirk *n.* DAGGER.

dirt *n.* **1** filth, grime, muck, mire, slime, mud, dust, soot, smudge, stain. **2** earth, soil, land, ground, loam, sod, mud, dust. **3** obscenity, pornography, filth, smut, indecency, ribaldry, bawdiness. **4** scandal, gossip, tattle, rumor, talk, grapevine, scuttlebutt, slander.

dirt-cheap *adj.* CHEAP.

dirty *adj.* **1** soiled, unclean, unwashed, begrimed, grimy, grubby, stained, filthy, foul, contaminated, unsterile, unsterilized, polluted. **2** obscene, pornographic, indecent, risqué, filthy, smutty, lewd, lascivious, salacious, lecherous, prurient. **3** unfair, unsportsmanlike, foul, mean, vile, low, base, sordid, ignoble, despicable, contemptible, corrupt, crooked, treacherous, —*v.* soil, foul, spot, stain, smudge, muddy, begrime, defile, sully, contaminate, pollute.

ant. *adj.* **1** clean, spotless, snowy, immaculate. **3** sportsmanlike, fair, admirable, honorable, honest.

disability *n.* infirmity, handicap, impairment, affliction, complaint, disorder, ailment, malady.

disable *v.* CRIPPLE.

disabled *adj.* incapacitated, crippled, handicapped, infirm, weak, enfeebled, frail, failing, debilitated, invalid, confined, bedridden.

ant. healthy, strong, sound, vigorous, active, rehabilitated.

disabuse *v.* undeceive, disenchant, disillusion, unbeguile, enlighten, set straight, correct.

ant. deceive, hoodwink, lead astray, bamboozle.

disadvantage *n.* drawback, hindrance, encumbrance, liability, handicap, inconvenience, nuisance, embarrassment, disservice, detriment.

ant. help, advantage, service, aid, asset.

disadvantaged *adj.* underprivileged, deprived, handicapped, underdeveloped, emerging, emergent.

ant. privileged, advantaged, favored, developed, affluent.

disadvantageous *adj.* unfavorable, detrimental, adverse, troublesome, objectionable, inconvenient, ill-timed, inopportune, inexpedient, discommodious.

ant. favorable, helpful, advantageous, valuable, opportune.

disaffect *v.* SEPARATE.

disaffected *adj.* alienated, estranged, withdrawn, dissatisfied, discontented, uncompliant, unsubmissive, unfriendly, inimical, antagonistic, hostile, turned off (*Slang*).

ant. contented, compliant, cooperative, conformist.

disagree *v.* differ, dissent, vary, contradict, dispute, argue, contend, contest, conflict, oppose, quarrel, clash, bicker.

ant. agree, concur, subscribe, acquiesce, reconcile, compromise.

disagreeable *adj.* **1** offensive, repugnant, repellent, repulsive, displeasing, unpleasant, distasteful, uninviting, unpalatable, disgusting, nasty, obnoxious. **2** bad-tempered, ill-tem-

pered, ill-humored, ill-natured, unpleasant, unlikable, irritable, grouchy, gruff, testy, petulant.

ant. 1 attractive, delicious, tasty, palatable. **2** good-natured, amiable, gracious, genial.

disagreement *n.* quarrel, dispute, conflict, difference, dissension, incompatibility, discord, rift, rupture, split, clash, strife, altercation, wrangle, squabble.

disallow *v.* REJECT.

disallowance *n.* DENIAL.

disappear *v.* **1** recede, fade away, pass, go, depart, withdraw, retire, exit, vanish, wane, ebb, fly, flee, escape. **2** stop, cease, end, perish, expire, vanish, evaporate, dissolve.

ant. 1 appear, arrive, show, dawn, loom.

disappearance *n.* DEPARTURE.

disappoint *v.* **1** fail, let down, miscarry, flounder, abort, dash, delude, disillusion, disenchant, dissatisfy, discourage. **2** frustrate, prevent, balk, foil, hinder, baffle, mislead, disconcert, thwart.

ant. 1 please, satisfy, gratify, delight, come through.

disappointing *adj.* sorry, sad, unsatisfactory, unworthy, scant, inadequate, defective, unfulfilling, pathetic.

ant. satisfying, gratifying, successful, appropriate.

disappointment *n.* **1** dissatisfaction, discontent, frustration, regret, chagrin, disillusionment, disenchantment. **2** letdown, frustration, failure, defeat, dud, washout (*Slang*), bomb (*Slang*), fiasco, fizzle, cop-out (*Slang*).

ant. 1 satisfaction, contentment, happiness, fulfillment, success.

disapproval *n.* CENSURE.

disapprove *v.* censure, criticize, object to, frown upon, dislike, deprecate, disparage, condemn, rebuke, admonish, disfavor.

ant. approve, commend, praise, appreciate, encourage.

disarm *v.* WIN OVER.

disarming *adj.* charming, winning, ingenuous, encouraging, diverting, enticing, tempting, likable, irresistible, bewitching, seductive.
ant. abrasive, offensive, unpleasant, repugnant.

disarrange *v.* DISORDER.

disarray *n.* disorder, untidiness, jumble, clutter, mix-up, scramble, upset, confusion, dislocation, disorganization, disarrangement.

disassemble *v.* PART.

disaster *n.* calamity, catastrophe, cataclysm, tragedy, ruin, reverse, blow, stroke, mishap, misfortune, accident, adversity.

disastrous *adj.* ruinous, dreadful, calamitous, catastrophic, tragic, hapless, destructive, adverse, portentous, dire.

disavow *v.* repudiate, disown, disclaim, deny, disallow, reject, renounce, retract, recant, abjure.

disband *v.* break up, disperse, scatter, separate, dismiss, disorganize, dissolve, adjourn.
ant. organize, unite, consolidate, coordinate, merge.

disbelief *n.* doubt, incredulity, distrust, rejection, unbelief, dissent, skepticism, nihilism, agnosticism.
ant. credulity, credence, trustfulness, faith.

disburse *v.* EXPEND.

disbursement *n.* expenditure, outlay, payment, spending, expense, cost, charge, price, amount, tariff, toll, fee, bill.

discard *v.* reject, eliminate, dispense with, throw out, abandon, relinquish, expel, repudiate, forsake, shed, cast off, do away with, scrap, junk, doff.
ant. retain, keep, adopt, embrace, save.

discern *v.* apprehend, understand, perceive, ascertain, recognize, discover, observe, notice, note, see, behold, descry.
ant. disregard, neglect, overlook, slight.

discerning *adj.* discriminating, perceptive, sensitive, subtle, knowing, insightful, critical, penetrating, acute, astute, perspicacious, judicious.
ant. unobservant, insensitive, unaware, inattentive, dull, obtuse.

discernment *n.* ACUMEN.

discharge *v.* **1** unload, remove, send forth, unburden, disburden, debark, disembark. **2** excrete, emit, expel, eject, exude, project, leak, ooze, gush. **3** shoot, fire, set off, detonate, explode, burst. **4** dismiss, lay off, fire, suspend, give notice, remove, oust, sack (*Slang*), cashier, exempt, release, relieve, liberate. **5** fulfill, perform, execute, accomplish, achieve, effect, observe, meet, carry out, honor, settle, square. —*n.* **1** release, exemption, remittance, clearance, liberation, manumission. **2** excretion, emission, exudation, flow, pus, ooze, ejection, expulsion.
ant. **1** load, pack, take on, fill, stow. **4** keep, hold, maintain, sign on, hire, detain.

disciple *n.* follower, supporter, adherent, devotee, partisan, satellite, votary, proselyte, apostle, student, pupil.

disciplinarian *n.* AUTHORITARIAN.

discipline *n.* **1** self-control, self-restraint, diligence, drill, exercise, practice, training, method, order. **2** punishment, correction, control, penalty, reproof, reprimand, chastisement, crackdown, castigation. **3** field, area, subject, branch, course, curriculum, elements, teaching, doctrine. —*v.* **1** instruct, train, teach, educate, school, tutor, prepare, ground, drill, practice, exercise. **2** punish, reprimand, penalize, chastise, chasten, castigate, reprove, crack down, correct, criticize.

disclaim *v.* deny, decline, reject, disown, repudiate, disavow, renounce, discountenance, abnegate.
ant. affirm, accept, claim, consent, approve, acknowledge.

disclose *v.* divulge, reveal, show, tell,

make known, communicate, impart, inform, explain, clarify, betray, spill. **ant.** withhold, conceal, hide, deceive, misrepresent.

disclosure *n.* announcement, declaration, acknowledgment, admission, discovery, revelation, uncovering, exposure, leak.

discolor *n.* STAIN.

discomfit *v.* **1** frustrate, disconcert, confound, baffle, upset, balk, foil, hamstring, defeat. **2** embarrass, fluster, unsettle, abash, disconcert, confuse, rattle, faze, daunt. **ant. 1, 2** help, support, assure, ease, expedite, encourage.

discomfort *n.* **1** uneasiness, annoyance, displeasure, unpleasantness, ache, distress, malaise, pain, suffering, soreness, anguish. **2** nuisance, inconvenience, awkwardness, trouble, irritation, ache, pain.

discommode *v.* INCONVENIENCE.

discompose *v.* DISTURB.

disconcert *v.* upset, confuse, baffle, confound, perplex, embarrass, discountenance, put off, bewilder, discomfit, rattle, shake up (*Slang*). **ant.** reassure, comfort, pacify, calm.

disconcerted *adj.* UPSET.

disconcerting *adj.* confusing, upsetting, distracting, awkward, frustrating, bewildering, disturbing, perplexing. **ant.** reassuring, comforting.

disconnect *v.* detach, separate, disengage, sever, part, divide, unlink, uncouple, sunder, cleave, rend. **ant.** connect, fasten, join, link, couple.

disconnected *adj.* incoherent, rambling, wandering, episodic, discontinuous, jumbled, aimless, desultory, inconsistent, distracted, distraught, babbling, irrational. **ant.** coherent, organized, methodical, consistent, systematic.

disconsolate *adj.* heartbroken, distressed, dejected, dispirited, forlorn, melancholy, desolate, cheerless, sorrowful, miserable, inconsolable, despairing.

ant. cheerful, joyous, elated, buoyant, vivacious, optimistic.

discontent *n.* dissatisfaction, displeasure, uneasiness, restlessness, frustration, regret, unhappiness, misery. **ant.** contentedness, satisfaction, placidity, complacency, smugness.

discontented *adj.* dissatisfied, frustrated, disaffected, disgruntled, displeased, unhappy, maladjusted, alienated, miserable. **ant.** grateful, contented, satisfied, complacent.

discontinuance *n.* TERMINATION.

discontinuation *n.* TERMINATION.

discontinue *v.* stop, cease, end, drop, terminate, quit, desist, break off, leave off, interrupt, hold off, postpone, put off, withhold. **ant.** continue, carry on, maintain, prolong, sustain.

discontinuity *n.* GAP.

discord *n.* disagreement, disturbance, dissension, dissonance, difference, quarreling, conflict, contention, disharmony, dispute, rupture, clash, strife. **ant.** harmony, amity, agreeableness, tranquillity.

discordant *adj.* **1** incompatible, contradictory, conflicting, inconsistent, contrary, discrepant, disagreeing, contentious, fractious, quarrelsome. **2** dissonant, unharmonious, unmelodious, jangling, jarring, grating, shrill, harsh, clashing, strident, cacophonous. **ant. 1** compatible, coincident, mutual, allied, congenial. **2** harmonious, euphonious, attuned, mellifluous, pleasing.

discountenance *v.* DISCONCERT.

discourage *v.* **1** dishearten, dispirit, deject, cast down, depress, dismay, blunt, unnerve, daunt. **2** dampen, cool, chill, disfavor, disparage, deprecate, downgrade, belittle, depreciate. **ant. 1, 2** encourage, hearten, embolden, stimulate, prompt, foster, favor.

discouraged *adj.* DISPIRITED.

discouragement *n.* **1** dejection, despondency, weariness, hopelessness, disappointment, frustration, discomfiture, depression, melancholy, gloom, moroseness, pessimism, despair. **2** constraint, restraint, deterrent, curb, check, hindrance, impediment, obstacle, disincentive, damper, wet blanket, cold water.
ant. 1 joy, cheerfulness, enthusiasm, elation, exultation, fulfillment, satisfaction. **2** stimulus, incentive, lift, reassurance, inspiration.

discouraging *adj.* disheartening, dispiriting, wearying, frustrating, disappointing, depressing, unsettling, daunting, intimidating, off-putting.
ant. encouraging, comforting, reassuring, inspiring, rewarding.

discourse *n.* conversation, talk, communication, converse, colloquy, intercourse, speech, address, disquisition, dissertation, oration, monologue, chat, gab. —*v.* speak, talk, hold forth, harangue, lecture, declaim, expatiate, sermonize, discuss, debate, argue, confer, converse, parley, palaver, chat.

discourteous *adj.* impolite, ungracious, unmannerly, ill-mannered, uncivil, disrespectful, impudent, rude, ill-bred, brusque, boorish, insolent, surly, cheeky, fresh.
ant. polite, civil, courteous, gallant, gracious, thoughtful.

discourtesy *n.* impoliteness, incivility, rudeness, ill-breeding, brusqueness, impudence, insolence, surliness, boorishness.
ant. politeness, civility, refinement, graciousness.

discover *v.* unearth, notice, discern, ascertain, distinguish, uncover, find out, determine, solve, detect, learn of, reveal, disclose, realize, understand, recognize, perceive.
ant. overlook, miss, pass over, lose sight of.

discoverer *n.* inventor, originator, initi-

ator, founder, pioneer, author, architect, producer.

discovery *n.* **1** disclosure, revelation, finding, exposure, unearthing, detection, espial, discernment, perception, ascertainment. **2** find, invention, coup, breakthrough, secret, acquisition, bonanza, godsend, catch.

discredit *v.* disparage, demean, degrade, debase, humble, depreciate, defame, slur, slander, disgrace, dishonor, blame, censure.

discreditable *adj.* disreputable, disgraceful, shameful, derogatory, dishonorable, unworthy, blameworthy, reprehensible, pejorative, infamous, ignominious, opprobrious, scandalous, humiliating.
ant. admirable, laudable, reputable, worthy, honorable.

discreet *adj.* tactful, sensitive, diplomatic, politic, judicious, considerate, attentive, circumspect, thoughtful, prudent, guarded, cautious, careful, wary.
ant. indiscreet, insensitive, inconsiderate, careless, reckless, precipitate.

discrepancy *n.* difference, gap, disparity, margin, variance, hiatus, deviation, divergence, inconsistency, disagreement, incongruity, discordance.
ant. similarity, agreement, consistency, unity.

discrepant *adj.* DISCORDANT.

discrete *adj.* distinct, separate, several, disconnected, discontinuous, detached, disjunctive, segregated, individual, unattached, unassociated, apart.
ant. combined, merged, connected, linked, united, one.

discretion *n.* **1** diplomacy, circumspection, thoughtfulness, tact, caution, prudence, foresight, sagacity, responsibility, maturity. **2** freedom, liberty, pleasure, choice, preference, wish, desire, will, option, license, purpose, intent, responsibility.

discriminate *v.* **1** favor, prejudge, show bias, disfranchise. **2** differentiate, separate, set apart, compare, distinguish, segregate, sift, discern, evaluate, assess, estimate, criticize.

discriminating *adj.* sensitive, acute, keen, critical, particular, nice, fastidious, refined, discerning, astute, discriminative, cultivated, tasteful, finical.

ant. indiscriminating, undiscerning, unperceptive, uninformed, dull, vulgar.

discrimination *n.* **1** perception, discernment, astuteness, sagacity, acumen, keenness, care, sensitivity, tact, wisdom, diplomacy, foresight, prudence, vigilance. **2** bias, prejudice, partisanship, favoritism, bigotry, intolerance, inequity, injustice.

ant. 1 insensitivity, dullness, obtuseness, carelessness. **2** impartiality, equity, fairness, justice, disinterestedness.

discriminative *adj.* DISCRIMINATING.

discursive *adj.* digressive, circuitous, diffuse, prolix, wandering, rambling, meandering, episodic, anecdotal, maundering, roundabout, tortuous, fustian.

ant. organized, focused, direct, unambiguous, straightforward.

discuss *v.* talk over, converse, confer, deliberate, consider, speak of, examine, reason, parley, canvass, ventilate, debate, argue, dispute, negotiate.

discussion *n.* conversation, deliberation, conference, colloquy, examination, consideration, consultation, parley, inquiry, symposium, debate, argument, argumentation, disputation, confrontation.

disdain *n.* scorn, contempt, insolence, contumely, arrogance, haughtiness, snobbishness, hauteur, superciliousness, pride.

ant. tolerance, respect, humility.

disdainful *adj.* scornful, contemptuous, insolent, arrogant, haughty, imperious, lordly, proud, aloof, supercilious, cavalier, snobbish, pompous, highfalutin.

ant. respectful, courteous, deferential, humble.

disease *n.* **1** illness, sickness, ailment, malady, affliction, indisposition, upset, infirmity, distemper, disorder. **2** disturbance, disorder, unsoundness, derangement, contamination, corruption, malady, breakdown, plague, cancer, crackup, collapse.

ant. 1, 2 healthiness, well-being, soundness, strength, vitality, vigor.

diseased *adj.* ill, sick, ailing, unwell, indisposed, afflicted, poorly, unhealthy, laid up, under the weather.

ant. healthy, sound, well, hale, robust.

disembodied *adj.* intangible, unreal, ethereal, spiritual, airy, bodiless, unearthly, ghostly, incorporeal.

disembowel *v.* eviscerate, embowel, gut, draw.

disenchanted *adj.* disillusioned, undeceived, disabused, disappointed, blasé, cynical.

ant. credulous, gullible, naive, trusting.

disencumber *v.* EXTRICATE.

disengage *v.* EXTRICATE.

disentangle *v.* EXTRICATE.

disfavor *n.* DISGRACE.

disfigure *v.* injure, mar, deform, deface, spoil, damage, vandalize, mutilate, blemish, bruise, scar, sully, impair, disfeature.

disgorge *v.* VOMIT.

disgrace *v.* dishonor, discredit, defame, shame, humiliate, debase, degrade, tarnish, stain, taint, sully. —*n.* dishonor, disfavor, disrepute, discredit, odium, shame, infamy, degradation, ignominy, opprobrium, obloquy.

ant. *n.* honor, credit, pride, glory, reverence.

disgraceful *adj.* shameful, disreputable, infamous, outrageous, ignoble, ignominious, inglorious, notorious, blameworthy, scandalous, censurable, degrading, odious, vile, contemptible, reprehensible.

ant. admirable, commendable, worthy, excellent, glorious.

disgruntled *adj.* DISCONTENTED.

disguise *v.* conceal, hide, camouflage, muffle, mask, cloak, veil, shroud, dissimulate, feign, pretend, misrepresent, gloss over, varnish, dress up. —*n.* mask, cover, veneer, camouflage, concealment, dress, veil, costume, cloak.

ant. *v.* reveal, disclose, show, bare, expose, uncover, unveil.

disgust *v.* offend, displease, irritate, incense, irk, anger, repel, repulse, revolt, sicken, nauseate. —*n.* repulsion, aversion, loathing, abhorrence, repugnance, nausea, distaste, contempt, detestation, antipathy.

disgusting *adj.* offensive, distasteful, repulsive, repugnant, revolting, loathsome, repellent, abominable, vile, nauseous, sickening, odious, foul, hateful.

ant. attractive, delightful, alluring, captivating, delectable.

dish *n.* vessel, bowl, receptacle, container, utensil, tableware, plate, saucer, platter, crock, tureen.

disharmony *n.* DISCORD.

dishearten *v.* discourage, dispirit, dampen, disappoint, displease, deject, daunt, deter, faze, dash, cow, crush, depress, appall, indispose, disincline.

ant. encourage, animate, enliven, embolden, cheer, inspire.

disheartened *adj.* DISPIRITED.

disheveled *adj.* untidy, disorderly, unkempt, disarranged, disarrayed, slovenly, slatternly, rumpled, tousled, frowzy, frumpy, mussed, dowdy.

ant. neat, trim, tidy, orderly, well-kept, spruce.

dishonest *adj.* untrustworthy, deceitful, unscrupulous, perfidious, false, shady, conniving, corrupt, fraudulent, lying, crooked.

ant. honest, scrupulous, trustworthy, upright.

dishonor *v.* disgrace, discredit, degrade, debase, humiliate, insult, affront, shame, outrage. —*n.* disgrace, degradation, discredit, disrepute, disrespect, disparagement, derogation, reproach, shame, ignominy, obloquy, opprobrium.

dishonorable *adj.* disgraceful, ignoble, discreditable, corrupt, venal, unscrupulous, infamous, shameless, untrustworthy, scandalous, notorious, unprincipled, roguish.

ant. admirable, praiseworthy, reputable, scrupulous, high-minded.

disillusion *v.* disenchant, disabuse, undeceive, disenthrall, disappoint, embitter, clue in, wise up (*Slang*).

disincentive *n.* DISCOURAGEMENT.

disinclined *adj.* reluctant, hesitant, indisposed, grudging, loath, backward, unwilling, antipathetic, averse.

ant. disposed, desirous, willing, eager, anxious.

disinfect *v.* sterilize, purify, sanitize, clean, deodorize, fumigate, pasteurize.

disinfectant *adj.* ANTISEPTIC.

disingenuous *adj.* ARTFUL.

disintegrate *v.* break up, fall apart, separate, crumble, decompose, decay, dissolve, erode, rot, pulverize.

disinterest *n.* **1** indifference, unconcern, lethargy, boredom, apathy, ennui, tedium, disregard, nonchalance, dispassion. **2** impartiality, detachment, neutrality, fairness, equity, justice.

disinterested *adj.* **1** impartial, unbiased, unprejudiced, evenhanded, detached, neutral, equitable, fair, just, unselfish, fair-minded, impersonal. **2** indifferent, uninterested, incurious, unconcerned, apathetic, bored, dispassionate, aloof, careless, perfunctory, lackadaisical.

ant. **1** biased, partial, prejudiced, unfair, inequitable. **2** concerned, occupied, engrossed, curious, engaged, enthusiastic.

disjoin *v.* SEPARATE.

disjointed *adj.* incoherent, rambling, episodic, disorganized, loose, irregular, desultory, spasmodic, fitful, irrational, disconnected, discontinuous, disjunct.

ant. coherent, consistent, comprehensible, logical, rational.

disk *n.* discus, circle, orb, plate, dish, saucer, roundel, paten.

dislike *v.* disapprove, disfavor, mislike, be averse, resent, shun, scorn, hate, abhor, despise, detest, loathe. —*n.* distaste, displeasure, contempt, hostility, dissatisfaction, objection, repugnance, aversion, animosity, disgust, loathing, antipathy, antagonism, repulsion.

ant. *v.* like, enjoy, admire, fancy, relish. *n.* delight, pleasure, satisfaction, attraction.

disloyal *adj.* unfaithful, untrustworthy, faithless, false, disaffected, treacherous, perfidious, traitorous, treasonous, two-faced, apostate.

ant. loyal, faithful, true, honest, trustworthy.

dismal *adj.* dreary, drab, dingy, bleak, dark, gloomy, cheerless, somber, downcast, depressing, sorrowful, sad, doleful, mournful.

ant. pleasing, cheerful, joyful, exhilarating, promising.

dismay *v.* appall, abash, intimidate, alarm, scare, terrify, dishearten, dispirit, daunt, cow, discourage, unnerve. —*n.* anxiety, apprehension, consternation, alarm, awe, dread, fear, fright, terror, horror.

dismiss *v.* 1 fire, discharge, suspend, lay off, boot (*Slang*), send packing, give notice, remove, oust, bounce (*Slang*), cashier, drum out, depose, unseat. 2 release, let go, send off, send away, evict, eject, expel, oust, dispossess, disperse, dissolve, adjourn. 3 reject, spurn, set aside, refuse, decline, disdain, discard, repel, disclaim, relegate, drop, shelve.

ant. 1 hire, sign on, employ, keep, maintain. 2 hold, detain, confine, restrict. 3 accept, receive, consider, allow, consent, approve.

dismissal *n.* discharge, removal, ousting, deposal, laying off, release, cashiering, notice, suspension, walking papers.

disobedience *n.* insubordination, unruliness, recalcitrance, defiance, indiscipline, insurgence, mutiny.

disobedient *adj.* insubordinate, unruly, unmanageable, unyielding, obstinate, stubborn, ungovernable, fractious, contumacious, refractory, defiant, recalcitrant, rebellious, mutinous.

ant. obedient, deferential, compliant, governable, dutiful, law-abiding.

disobey *v.* defy, violate, infringe, transgress, contravene, disregard, ignore, resist, rebel.

ant. obey, comply, observe, respect, satisfy, conform to.

disoblige *v.* 1 DISTURB. 2 OFFEND.

disorder *n.* 1 untidiness, disarray, clutter, mess, jumble, confusion, topsy-turvy, disarrangement, neglect, disorganization. 2 commotion, turmoil, disturbance, unrest, distemper, turbulence, clamor, tumult, uproar, brawl, riot. 3 disease, illness, malady, ailment, infirmity, affliction, disturbance, derangement. —*v.* disarrange, disorganize, mess up, scatter, shuffle, disturb, derange, unsettle, upset, confuse, confound.

ant. *n.* 1 order, form, method, neatness, tidiness. 3 soundness, vigor, vitality, well-being, health, balance, sanity.

disorderly *adj.* 1 untidy, messy, topsy-turvy, chaotic, disorganized, confused, irregular, unmethodical, helter-skelter, pell-mell, higgledy-piggledy. 2 unruly, unrestrained, unmanageable, ungovernable, turbulent, rough-and-tumble, tumultuous, lawless, rebellious, riotous, abandoned.

ant. 1 tidy, trim, neat, organized, meticulous, fastidious. 2 well-behaved, civil, restrained, peaceable, quiet.

disorient *v.* confuse, upset, divert, deflect, sidetrack, shift, turn aside, switch, turn, shunt.

disoriented *adj.* DAZED.

disown *v.* renounce, repudiate, disavow, disclaim, deny, abnegate, reject.

ant. consent, assent to, accede to, accept, admit, claim, avow.

disparage *v.* demean, belittle, discredit, minimize, depreciate, deprecate, run down, criticize, underrate, undervalue, dispraise, underpraise, underestimate, disdain, dismiss, put down (*Slang*).

ant. esteem, appreciate, value, praise, acclaim, cherish.

disparate *adj.* DISSIMILAR.

disparity *n.* difference, gap, inconsistency, incongruity, divergence, disproportion, inequality, dissimilarity, disagreement, contradiction.

ant. accord, conformity, concurrence, correspondence, unity, harmony.

dispassionate *adj.* **1** unexcitable, imperturbable, unruffled, composed, collected, temperate, serene, sober, cool, cold-blooded. **2** impersonal, detached, impartial, disinterested, unbiased, unprejudiced, objective, equitable, fair, just.

ant. **1** excitable, temperamental, emotional, demonstrative, irrepressible. **2** committed, devoted, zealous, fanatical, enthusiastic, subjective, partisan, prejudiced.

dispatch *v.* **1** expedite, dispose of, finish, press, push, hasten, settle, conclude, finalize, wrap up. **2** kill, slay, murder, execute, assassinate, finish off, shoot, dispose of, slaughter, butcher. —*n.* **1** sending, forwarding, discharge, dismissal, consignment, expediting, posting. **2** story, news, communiqué, account, report, message, word, note, bulletin, article, comment, item, letter. **3** speed, haste, hurry, quickness, promptness, alacrity, expedition, precipitateness.

ant. *v.* **1** stall, dally, temporize, delay, hamper, retard. *n.* **3** stalling, tardiness, dawdling, procrastination.

dispel *v.* drive away, send away, disperse, dismiss, banish, rout, dissi-

pate, diffuse, scatter, spread, strew, disseminate.

ant. assemble, collect, gather, amass, accumulate.

dispensable *adj.* UNNECESSARY.

dispensation *n.* **1** distribution, dispersion, dissemination, spread, scattering, consignment, allotment, apportionment, diffusion, partition, division. **2** share, portion, allotment, dole, interest, part, consignment, appropriation, parcel, award, proportion, quota, percentage, cut. **3** exemption, exception, remission, relinquishment, relief, relaxation, release, privilege, permission, freedom, license.

dispense *v.* distribute, deal, parcel out, assign, award, mete, share, dole, allot, allocate, divide, apportion.

dispense with do without, give up, relinquish, forgo, omit, set aside, suspend, waive, abstain, spare, forbear.

disperse *v.* scatter, dissipate, break up, separate, spread, strew, disband, disseminate, diffuse, dissolve, dispel.

dispirited *adj.* dejected, despondent, gloomy, sad, glum, morose, melancholy, depressed, disheartened, discouraged, downcast, crestfallen, moody, out of sorts.

ant. ebullient, lighthearted, cheerful, gay, joyful, elated.

displace *v.* **1** move, disturb, unsettle, shift, transpose, remove, derange, disarrange, dislodge, transfer, dislocate, prolapse, uproot. **2** replace, supplant, substitute, supersede, succeed, depose, unseat, force out, oust, bump.

display *v.* exhibit, show, present, demonstrate, feature, manifest, evidence, evince, reveal, unfurl, parade, flaunt, expose. —*n.* exhibition, exhibit, show, demonstration, exposition, manifestation, array, panorama, pageant, flourish, pomp, exposure.

ant. hide, conceal, cover, obscure, screen.

displease *v.* upset, disturb, annoy, disappoint, irritate, dissatisfy, vex, rile, chafe, pique, irk, provoke, offend, affront, incense.

ant. gratify, gladden, delight, charm, enrapture.

displeasure *n.* annoyance, vexation, irritation, dislike, distaste, disappointment, resentment, dissatisfaction, disapproval, dudgeon.

ant. enjoyment, delight, enchantment, comfort, satisfaction, approval.

disport *v.* play, frolic, romp, sport, gambol, frisk, caper, carouse, revel.

disposal *n.* **1** arrangement, grouping, order, array, pattern, distribution, disposition, configuration, juxtaposition, method, adjustment. **2** settlement, assignment, transference, transfer, bestowal, dispensation, gift, sale, bequest. **3** control, power, management, direction, command, regulation, determination, government, responsibility, supervision, aegis, sponsorship, authority.

dispose *v.* **1** arrange, place, put, order, set, organize, adjust, distribute, marshal, group, range, classify. **2** influence, affect, induce, actuate, prompt, lead, move, incline, predispose, prejudice, bias.

ant. **1** disarrange, scramble, upset, mix, disturb. **2** deter, dissuade, discourage, repel.

disposed *adj.* INCLINED.

dispose of **1** settle, finish, conclude, expedite, abolish, finalize, resolve, determine, eliminate, remove. **2** throw away, discard, get rid of, remove, eliminate, unload, scrap, junk, dump, deep-six (*Slang*).

disposition *n.* **1** placement, arrangement, grouping, disposal, pattern, configuration, location, distribution, assignment, order, array, organization, classification. **2** direction, settlement, conclusion, handling, management, administration, regulation, control, power, authority, sponsorship. **3** temperament, temper, nature, make-up, character, humor,

spirit, soul, tendency, bent, propensity, inclination, proclivity.

dispraise *v.* DISPARAGE.

disproof *n.* refutation, confutation, invalidation, rebuttal, counterargument, negation.

ant. substantiation, corroboration, confirmation, verification, affirmation.

disprove *v.* refute, confute, rebut, controvert, contradict, belie, subvert, expose, oppose, negate, deny.

ant. sustain, support, uphold, confirm, attest, corroborate, verify.

disputable *adj.* DUBIOUS.

disputant *n.* ANTAGONIST.

disputation *n.* CONTROVERSY.

disputatious *adj.* ARGUMENTATIVE.

dispute *v.* **1** argue, debate, contend, quarrel, squabble, altercate, wrangle, bicker, brawl, clash. **2** question, differ, disagree, challenge, contradict, deny, controvert, impugn. —*n.* disagreement, difference, discussion, debate, argument, controversy, contest, quarrel, polemic, feud, wrangle, bickering, squabble.

ant. *v.* **2** concede, yield, acquiesce, assent, acknowledge, agree. *n.* accord, unison, harmony, concord.

disquiet *n.* restlessness, uneasiness, disquietude, discomposure, vexation, anxiety, disturbance, turmoil.

ant. calm, composure, relaxation, tranquillity.

disquietude *n.* DISQUIET.

disquisition *n.* dissertation, treatise, discourse, lecture, speech, commentary, harangue, sermon, thesis, theme, essay, study, inquiry, tract.

disregard *v.* ignore, neglect, pass over, miss, skip, omit, overlook, forget, minimize, slight, disdain, snub, disobey, transgress, defy.

ant. observe, follow, respect, acknowledge, conform to, obey.

disrepair *n.* DECAY.

disreputable *adj.* disgraceful, shameful, unworthy, ignoble, dishonorable, infamous, scandalous, notorious, opprobrious, low, base, vulgar, wicked, evil.

ant. respectable, admirable, estimable, high-principled, scrupulous.

disrepute *n.* disgrace, ill repute, shame, discredit, dishonor, disesteem, humiliation, obloquy, opprobrium, reproach, ignominy, degradation.

ant. respect, prestige, renown, eminence, honor, distinction, respectability.

disrespect *n.* discourtesy, incivility, impoliteness, irreverence, affront, neglect, indignity, insolence, rudeness, slight, snub.

ant. deference, regard, consideration, civility, courtesy.

disrespectful *adj.* impolite, discourteous, uncivil, rude, impertinent, impudent, irreverent, disparaging, slighting, derisive, insulting, contemptuous.

ant. deferential, obliging, complaisant, courteous, awed.

disrobe *v.* undress, uncover, divest, take off, denude, bare, shed, doff, strip.

ant. clothe, dress, garb, drape, costume, mantle, attire.

disrupt *v.* interrupt, break up, interfere, interject, interpose, upset, disorganize, spoil, agitate, convulse.

disruption *n.* INTERRUPTION.

disruptive *adj.* unsettling, upsetting, troublesome, confusing, distracting, disorderly, unruly, troublemaking, obstreperous.

ant. calming, quieting, tranquilizing, settling, soothing.

dissatisfaction *n.* **1** discontent, disappointment, regret, disaffection, uneasiness, discomfort, dismay, dislike, displeasure, disapproval. **2** disappointment, unpleasantness, objection, frustration, irritation, annoyance, sore point, pet peeve.

ant. **1** contentment, satisfaction, comfort, happiness, well-being.

dissatisfactory *adj.* UNSATISFACTORY.

dissatisfied *adj.* discontented, frustrated, disappointed, disaffected, un-

fulfilled, ungratified, disgruntled, frustrated, displeased, unhappy, malcontent.

ant. contented, complacent, serene, carefree, easygoing.

dissatisfy *v.* DISPLEASE.

dissemble *v.* pretend, feign, simulate, dissimulate, affect, counterfeit, sham, falsify, conceal, hide, camouflage, mask, disguise.

disseminate *v.* circulate, promulgate, propagate, spread, disperse, distribute, diffuse, scatter, sow, broadcast.

dissemination *n.* SPREAD.

dissension *n.* discord, friction, trouble, dispute, strife, conflict, quarrel, contention, dissent, disagreement, difference, variance, factionalism, heresy.

ant. unity, consensus, agreement, concurrence, conformity.

dissent *v.* disagree, differ, dispute, contradict, object, oppose, contend, decline, deny, disapprove. —*n.* disagreement, opposition, resistance, dissidence, nonconformity, heterodoxy, objection.

ant. *v.* assent, concur, acquiesce, comply, conform with. *n.* compliance, conformity, concurrence, submission, obedience.

dissertation *n.* thesis, treatise, study, disquisition, composition, exposition, critique, commentary, tract, essay, discussion, discourse, speech, lecture.

disservice *n.* HARM.

dissever *v.* PART.

dissidence *n.* DISSENT.

dissident *n.* dissenter, protestor, agitator, individualist, iconoclast, maverick, nonconformist, sectarian, recusant.

dissimilar *adj.* unlike, different, distinct, disparate, unrelated, opposite, polar, contrary, divergent, diverse, various, heterogeneous, mismatched, mismated.

ant. similar, like, corresponding, comparable, equivalent, kindred, paired.

dissimilarity *n.* DIFFERENCE.

dissimulate *v.* DISSEMBLE.

dissipate *v.* **1** scatter, drive away, disperse, disseminate, dispel, spread, diffuse, broadcast, strew, sow. **2** disappear, vanish, disintegrate, dissolve, spill, ebb, leak, deplete, exhaust, consume, waste, squander, lavish, fritter.

ant. 2 preserve, conserve, save, keep, maintain.

dissipated *adj.* DISSOLUTE.

dissipation *n.* self-indulgence, dissoluteness, profligacy, debauchery, sensuality, excess, waste, extravagance, distraction, diversion, gratification, amusement.

dissociate *v.* SEPARATE.

dissociation *n.* SEPARATION.

dissolute *adj.* dissipated, profligate, depraved, rakish, licentious, abandoned, libertine, loose, lax, wanton, lewd, debauched, immoral, impure, degenerate, corrupt.

ant. virtuous, chaste, upstanding, rigorous, austere, prim, puritanical.

dissolve *v.* **1** melt, liquefy, deliquesce, evaporate, disintegrate, thaw, render, fuse, soften, macerate. **2** end, conclude, finish, terminate, break up, destroy, sever, disunite, loosen, free, disperse, dismiss, disband, recess, adjourn, prorogue. **3** fade, dwindle, melt, scatter, decompose, disintegrate, crumble, evanesce, dematerialize, vanish, disappear.

ant. 1 solidify, thicken, congeal, crystallize, petrify, harden, set. **2** unite, join, link, consolidate, collect, summon, convene, convoke.

dissonance *n.* DISCORD.

dissonant *adj.* **1** grating, harsh, jarring, clashing, jangling, raucous, strident, discordant, unharmonious, unmelodious, cacophonous. **2** incompatible, disagreeing, inconsistent, discrepant, incongruous, contradictory, inapposite, opposite, irreconcilable, hostile, warring, clashing.

ant. 1 harmonious, melodious, euphonious, tuneful, agreeable, pleas-

ant. **2** compatible, congruent, consonant, suitable, uniform.

dissuade *v.* discourage, disincline, dampen, caution, avert, warn, remonstrate, expostulate, turn, divert, deter, restrain.

ant. encourage, embolden, assure, inspire.

distance *n.* space, length, extent, remove, farness, span, reach, range, stretch, remove, gap, interval, period, margin, lapse.

distant *adj.* **1** far, far-off, faraway, remote, outlying, apart, removed, separated, distinct, unrelated. **2** reserved, unapproachable, aloof, standoffish, cool, cold, haughty, unfriendly, uncordial, stiff, formal, detached, diffident.

ant. 1 near, close, adjacent, immediate, neighboring, proximate. **2** accessible, obliging, affable, cordial, warm, familiar.

distaste *n.* dislike, aversion, repugnance, disgust, displeasure, disinclination.

ant. liking, taste, relish, preference, propensity.

distasteful *adj.* offensive, disgusting, repugnant, repellent, abhorrent, repulsive, loathsome, disagreeable, unpleasant, displeasing, unsavory, unpalatable, obnoxious, nauseating.

ant. attractive, appealing, appropriate, decorous, polished, refined.

distemper *n.* **1** DISORDER. **2** CRAZE.

distend *v.* DILATE.

distended *adj.* expanded, enlarged, stretched, swollen, dilated, inflated, bloated, puffy, tumescent.

ant. shrunken, reduced, contracted, shriveled, withered.

distill *v.* extract, separate, press out, squeeze out, expel, express, compress, condense, refine, clarify, rarefy, brew.

distillation *n.* essence, quintessence, spirit, substance, extract, heart, essential, elixir, epitome, nub, core, pith, gist.

distinct *adj.* **1** clear, plain, definite,

well-defined, clear-cut, unmistakable, obvious, evident, manifest, transparent. **2** separate, different, dissimilar, unlike, individual, discrete, unattached, unconnected, disjunctive.

ant. 1 indistinct, confusing, muddled, vague, obscure. **2** linked, attached, merged, united, associated, consolidated.

distinction *n.* **1** characteristic, difference, particularity, individuality, peculiarity, mark, sign, feature, cachet, stamp, imprint, signature. **2** eminence, honor, excellence, importance, superiority, credit, note, account, repute, reputation, renown, fame, celebrity.

ant. 1 anonymity.

distinctive *adj.* particular, special, peculiar, unique, individual, characteristic, differentiating, distinguishing, personalized, unusual, extraordinary.
ant. anonymous, common, ordinary, prevailing, expected, familiar, conventional.

distingué *adj.* DISTINGUISHED.

distinguish *v.* **1** differentiate, single out, isolate, separate, divide, demarcate, discriminate, designate, mark, characterize, individualize, define, classify, categorize, difference. **2** perceive, discern, apprehend, observe, recognize, know, tell, note, descry.

distinguished *adj.* eminent, notable, noted, acclaimed, illustrious, renowned, famed, famous, celebrated, distingué, outstanding, extraordinary, superior, dignified, heralded, imposing, grand, majestic.
ant. undistinguished, unsuccessful, mediocre, second-rate, indifferent, commonplace, ordinary.

distort *v.* **1** deform, misshape, disfigure, contort, warp, twist, bend, torture. **2** misrepresent, mislead, misconstrue, misstate, deceive, misinterpret, misquote, pervert, falsify, twist, dissimulate, angle, slant, color, garble, mangle.

distortion *n.* misrepresentation, misstatement, evasion, exaggeration, deception, perversion, falsification, inaccuracy, dissimulation, lie, prevarication.

distract *v.* **1** divert, turn aside, interrupt, interfere with, disturb, tempt, beguile, amuse, entertain. **2** bewilder, disconcert, fluster, flurry, befuddle, confuse, perplex, confound, muddle, discompose, disturb, annoy, agitate, harass.

distracted *adj.* **1** bewildered, perplexed, confused, confounded, bemused, puzzled, mystified, harassed. **2** mad, deranged, demented, disturbed, insane, troubled, frantic, raving, crazy, delirious, beside oneself.

ant. 1 composed, steady, coolheaded, collected, self-possessed. **2** sane, sound, rational, lucid, reasonable.

distraction *n.* **1** distress, agitation, consternation, perturbation, disturbance, turmoil, discord, confusion, perplexity, befuddlement, discomposure, quandary, mystification. **2** pastime, amusement, diversion, entertainment, beguilement. **3** interruption, interference, annoyance, commotion, to-do, bother.

distrait *adj.* ABSENT-MINDED.

distraught *adj.* anxious, upset, distracted, distressed, agitated, overwrought, frantic, feverish, delirious, frenzied, raving, raging, mad, wild, crazed, beside oneself.

ant. calm, composed, serene, tranquil, placid.

distress *v.* bother, trouble, upset, worry, annoy, perturb, vex, disturb, afflict, harrow, oppress, pain, sadden, aggrieve. —*n.* worry, trouble, concern, malaise, anxiety, discomfort, suffering, pain, misery, agony, anguish, grief, sorrow, woe.

ant. *v.* comfort, console, solace, sustain, assuage.

distressed *adj.* DISTRAUGHT.

distressing *adj.* GALLING.

distribute *v.* parcel, deal out, dispense, dole out, share, mete, assign, divide, apportion, allot, allocate, scatter, spread, strew, disseminate, diffuse, broadcast.

ant. collect, gather, accumulate, amass.

distribution *n.* **1** dispersion, spread, dispensation, consignment, sharing, partition, division, apportionment, allotment, allocation. **2** placement, location, situation, disposition, disposal, grouping, arrangement, order, pattern, assignment, division, apportionment.

district *n.* region, area, section, space, tract, domain, sphere, precinct, division, quarter, locality, place, neighborhood, ward, department, province.

distrust *v.* mistrust, doubt, disbelieve, question, suspect, query, demur, challenge, dispute, misgive. —*n.* suspicion, mistrust, misgiving, apprehension, uncertainty, hesitation, qualm, skepticism, dubiousness, doubt, disbelief.

ant. *v.* trust, believe, credit, accept. *n.* confidence, credence, faith, assurance.

distrustful *adj.* SUSPICIOUS.

disturb *v.* **1** interrupt, interfere with, rouse, discompose, bother, trouble, distract, disrupt, discommode, incommode, disoblige, inconvenience, disarrange, annoy, upset, stir, agitate, perturb. **2** distress, upset, unsettle, ruffle, bewilder, fluster, confuse, confound, annoy, trouble, bother, vex, perturb, alarm.

disturbance *n.* commotion, disorder, row, altercation, hubbub, uproar, tumult, ruckus, turmoil, outbreak, fracas, fray, brawl, riot.

disturbed *adj.* DISTRACTED.

disunite *v.* SEPARATE.

ditch *n.* trench, channel, drain, trough, excavation, gully, hollow, passage, watercourse, canal, gutter, duct, moat, fosse. —*v.* **1** dig, channel, furrow, excavate, trough, tunnel, gash, carve, gouge, scratch, score. **2** *Slang* abandon, get rid of, drop, discard,

reject, dispose of, cast off, scrap, junk, dump, unload.

dither *n.* FLAP.

diurnal *adj.* DAILY.

dive *v.* plunge, plummet, descend, leap, drop, pitch, fall, swoop, pounce, submerge, submerse, immerse, engulf, inundate, sink, dip, duck, dunk, douse. —*n.* **1** plunge, descent, drop, fall, pitch, swoop, pounce, header, submergence, submersion, immersion, duck, dip. **2** *disreputable resort:* joint (*Slang*), hole, den, honky-tonk (*Slang*), hangout (*Slang*), dump (*Slang*), bar, tavern, speak-easy.

diverge *v.* DIFFER.

divergence *n.* deviation, digression, branch, fork, departure, excursion, declination, divagation, inclination, discrepancy, disparity, incongruity, inconsistency, difference, distinction.

ant. convergence, confluence, union, congruence, correspondence, similarity.

divers *adj.* SUNDRY.

diverse *adj.* distinct, separate, particular, individual, various, dissimilar, differing, several, different, discrete, divers, unlike.

ant. similar, parallel, identical, like, corresponding, common.

diversify *v.* vary, mix, assort, variegate, change, modify, alter, branch out.

diversion *n.* amusement, entertainment, fun, divertissement, pleasure, relaxation, recreation, distraction, play, sport, beguilement, avocation.

diversity *n.* difference, distinctiveness, dissimilitude, variety, heterogeneity.

ant. uniformity, regularity, homogeneity, monotony, repetition, routine.

divert *v.* **1** DEFLECT. **2** DISTRACT.

diverting *adj.* amusing, entertaining, enjoyable, pleasant, humorous, playful, whimsical, sportive, beguiling, festive, fun.

ant. serious, earnest, solemn, intense, profound.

divest *v.* deprive, dispossess, remove, strip, confiscate, expropriate, debar.

ant. empower, confer, commission, sanction.

divide *v.* **1** separate, part, partition, disjoin, divorce, detach, rend, dissolve, sunder, cut, cleave, ramify, shear, distinguish, categorize, classify, arrange, sort. **2** distribute, deal out, dispense, dole, mete, assign, share, allot, apportion, divvy up (*Slang*).
ant. 1 unite, link, splice, fuse, cement, bridge.

divination *n.* **1** prophesying, foretelling, augury, divining, soothsaying, prescience, fortunetelling, clairvoyance. **2** prophecy, forecast, prediction, augury, premonition, surmise, horoscope, conjecture, guess.

divine *adj.* sacred, holy, religious, godlike, godly, sanctified, consecrated, sainted, superhuman, heavenly, celestial —*v.* predict, foretell, forecast, prophesy, prognosticate, presage, foresee, foreknow, anticipate, surmise, conjecture, suspect, guess.
ant. *adj.* profane, secular, earthly, worldly.

division *n.* **1** part, section, portion, element, partition, compartment, category, segment, component, member, piece. **2** disagreement, dissension, discord, difference, variance, break, breach, rift, dissent, opposition, rupture, feud, estrangement, alienation.
ant. 2 unity, harmony, agreement, accord, cooperation.

divisive *adj.* disruptive, discordant, unsettling, inharmonious, troublesome, provocative, damaging, estranging, alienating, inflammatory, pernicious, detrimental, mischievous.
ant. conciliatory, concordant, accommodative, gracious, tactful, winning.

divorce *n.* separation, rupture, severance, break, disunion, dissolution, repudiation. —*v.* separate, sever, split, dissolve, sunder, isolate, segregate, repudiate, detach.
ant. *n.* union, unification, fusion, harmony, accord, agreement. *v.* join, link, merge, converge, consolidate.

divulge *v.* disclose, reveal, confide, confess, bare, leak, expose, publish, broadcast, report, announce, inform, declare, relate, tell, give away, spill.
ant. conceal, hide, cloak, secrete, dissemble.

divvy *n.* SHARE.

divvy up DIVIDE.

dizzy *adj.* **1** giddy, lightheaded, unsteady, reeling, wheeling, swimming, bewildered, confused, vertiginous. **2** silly, frivolous, flighty, lightheaded, frothy, fickle, capricious, confused, thoughtless, foolish, crazy, harebrained.
ant. 2 prudent, thoughtful, stable, level-headed.

do *v.* **1** perform, carry out, bring about, engage in, act, undertake, conduct, transact, wage, render, dispatch, effect, execute, expedite, produce, cause. **2** finish, complete, end, conclude, terminate, fulfill, settle, consummate, wind up, see through, accomplish, achieve, succeed. **3** solve, work out, resolve, figure out, clear up, unravel, disentangle, puzzle out. **4** suffice, serve, satisfy, suit, avail, fit, pass, answer, work.
ant. 1 neglect, fail. **2** leave off, abandon, quit. **4** fall short, disappoint, miss.

do away with 1 DISCARD. **2** KILL.

docile *adj.* tractable, manageable, submissive, compliant, complaisant, obedient, biddable, gentle, meek, humble, amenable, orderly, pliant, teachable.
ant. unruly, restive, refractory, defiant, rebellious.

dock *n.* pier, wharf, landing, quay, marina.

docket *n.* AGENDA.

doctor *v.* alter, modify, manipulate, fabricate, tamper with, disguise, falsify, contaminate, adulterate, debase.

doctrinaire *adj.* dogmatic, rigid, absolute, arbitrary, inflexible, opinionated, ideological, academic, speculative, abstract, ideal, pure, theoretical, impractical, visionary.

ant. sensible, reasonable, moderate, temperate, humane, realistic.

doctrine *n.* belief, precept, tenet, dogma, thesis, principle, rule, creed, gospel, faith, conviction.

document *n.* record, paper, writing, certificate, instrument, credential, deed, evidence, proof. —*v.* corroborate, authenticate, prove, certify, validate, substantiate, sustain, support, detail, cite, instance, particularize, back up.

dodder *v.* totter, potter, tremble, stagger, quiver, quaver, dither, shake, falter.

dodge *v.* **1** duck, swerve, shift, turn aside, twist, sidestep, sheer off, jib, start, lurch, evade, avoid. **2** avoid, evade, elude, parry, hedge, shuffle, fudge, quibble, equivocate, prevaricate, trick, deceive. —*n.* twisting, turning, sidestep, swerving, maneuver, deviation, evasion, device, wile, artifice, subterfuge, ruse, trick, deceit.

ant. *v.* **2** confront, face, meet, brave, withstand.

doer *n.* ACTIVIST.

doff *v.* DISCARD.

dog *n.* SCOUNDREL. —*v.* HOUND.

dogfight *n.* FIGHT.

dogged *adj.* stubborn, obstinate, tenacious, unyielding, resolute, persistent, determined, perseverant, steadfast, rigid, inflexible, plodding, dogmatic, mulish.

ant. irresolute, undecided, ambivalent, uncertain.

doggedness *n.* OBSTINACY.

doggish *adj.* STYLISH.

dogma *n.* tenet, doctrine, creed, proposition, principle, conviction, maxim, precept, credo, gospel, belief.

dogmatic *adj.* opinionated, doctrinaire, intolerant, one-sided, categorical, convinced, settled, close-minded, fanatical, authoritative, domineering, overbearing, assertive, arrogant, dictatorial.

ant. indecisive, vacillating, equivo-

cal, ambiguous, uncertain, reasonable.

doings *n.* actions, acts, events, affairs, proceedings, transactions, goings on, deeds, works, circumstances, accomplishments, conduct, behavior.

doldrums *n.* dullness, boredom, tedium, inertia, malaise, ennui, apathy, lassitude, listlessness, dumps, blues, depression, melancholy.

dole *n.* ALLOWANCE. —*v.* APPORTION.

doleful *adj.* dismal, gloomy, cheerless, sad, sorrowful, baleful, woeful, melancholy, lugubrious, mournful, grief-stricken.

ant. cheerful, gay, blithe, bright, sunny, happy.

dole out distribute, dispense, deal out, parcel out, hand out, mete, apportion, partition, allot, assign, divide, share, disseminate.

dolor *n.* SORROW.

dolorous *adj.* sorrowful, woebegone, anguished, pitiable, pathetic, lugubrious, mournful, miserable, wretched, painful, cheerless, sad.

ant. happy, cheerful, lighthearted, carefree, elated.

dolt *n.* simpleton, dunce, blockhead, fool, idiot, dimwit, nitwit, dullard, loon, numskull, jackass, lout, clod.

domain *n.* **1** work, discipline, job, position, branch, department, area, field, province, realm, sphere. **2** property, land, estate, grounds, acres, acreage, realty, demesne.

dome *n.* cupola, vault, vaulting, roof, ceiling, span, canopy, cup, hemisphere, arch, arcade, rotunda.

domestic *adj.* **1** domesticated, home-loving, house-proud, stay-at-home, household, family, familial. **2** native, autochthonous, endemic, indigenous.

ant. 2 foreign, exotic, alien.

domesticate *v.* TAME.

domesticated *adj.* TAME.

domicile *n.* home, house, residence, dwelling, habitation, abode, accommodations, quarters, rooms, lodging, mansion, apartment, flat, roost, perch, pad (*Slang*), digs.

dominance *n.* power, command, mastery, rule, government, control, domination, supremacy, sway, ascendancy, authority.

dominant *adj.* superior, major, chief, supreme, main, foremost, prime, paramount, leading, preponderant, predominant, preeminent, prevailing, controlling, governing, ruling, sovereign.
    ant. subordinate, secondary, minor, lesser, inferior.

dominate *v.* control, direct, predominate, monopolize, master, lead, govern, rule, subjugate, overpower, tyrannize, domineer, overbear.

domineer *v.* BULLY.

domineering *adj.* overbearing, oppressive, imperious, bossy, dictatorial, tyrannical, arrogant, despotic, highhanded, arbitrary, doctrinaire, masterful, authoritative.
    ant. subservient, docile, servile, obsequious, tractable.

dominion *n.* authority, sovereignty, government, jurisdiction, supremacy, sway, mastery, command, control, power.

donate *v.* contribute, give, subscribe, bestow, grant, present, award, accord, confer, consign.

donation *n.* giving, granting, presentation, charity, philanthropy, relief, munificence, offering, benefaction, subscription, largess, contribution, gift, present, grant, award, alms, gratuity.

done *adj.* completed, finished, concluded, terminated, ended, over, through, settled, accomplished, effected, executed, realized, rendered, performed, achieved, fulfilled.
    ant. undone, unfinished, incomplete, up in the air, in limbo.

done for ruined, destroyed, defeated, wrecked, lost, disabled, spoiled, frustrated, dashed, shelved, fruitless, hopeless, doomed, kaput (*Slang*).

ant. viable, surviving, enduring, flourishing.

donkey *n.* ASS.

donnish *adj.* PEDANTIC.

donor *n.* contributor, giver, donator, benefactor, bestower, grantor, subscriber, almsgiver, almoner, philanthropist.

do-nothing *n.* idler, shirker, drone, dawdler, loafer, malingerer, sluggard, lounger, loller, loiterer, goldbrick.

doodad *n.* DOOHICKEY.

doohickey *n.* doodad, thingumajig, thingumabob, widget, gizmo, whatchamacallit, gimmick, gadget, device, contrivance, object, thing.

doom *v.* condemn, damn, threaten, predetermine, predestine, foreordain, consign, decree, adjudge. —*n.* ruin, death, destruction, catastrophe, downfall, end, finish, fate, destiny, lot.

doorway *n.* access, gateway, threshold, portal, door, path, pathway, avenue, route, course, means.

dope *Slang n.* **1** drug, narcotic, opiate, heroin. **2** facts, info, scoop, tip, report, account, data, information, warning, forecast, prediction. **3** jerk (*Slang*), drip (*Slang*), creep (*Slang*), fool, idiot, dumbbell, dunce, simpleton, dolt, dimwit. —*v.* drug, narcotize, sedate, stupefy, deaden, desensitize, numb, anesthetize, knock out, stun, spike, fortify, exhilarate, stimulate.

dope out *Slang* solve, figure out, resolve, calculate, compute, estimate, reckon, plan, explain, unravel, get to the bottom of.

dopey *adj.* STUPID.

doppelgänger *n.* ALTER EGO.

dormant *adj.* **1** quiet, motionless, inert, immobile, static, passive, latent, suspended, oblivious, unconscious, comatose, slumbering, asleep, sleeping. **2** inactive, unused, standing, immobile, unemployed, inoperative, disengaged, suspended, potential.

ant. 1 wide-awake, vigorous, alert, lively. **2** functioning, serviceable, operative, working.

dose *n*. PORTION.

dot *n*. point, circle, spot, speck, jot, mote, blotch, fleck, mark, particle.

dotage *n*. senility, decrepitude, feebleness.

dote on TREASURE.

doting *adj*. adoring, fond, loving, devoted, affectionate, demonstrative, lovesick, lovelorn, languishing, sentimental, romantic.

dotty *adj*. ECCENTRIC.

double-cross *v*. BETRAY.

double-dealer *n*. TRAITOR.

double-dealing *adj*. TREACHEROUS. —*n*. TREACHERY.

double-faced *adj*. HYPOCRITICAL.

doubt *v*. **1** question, query, challenge, dispute, object, disbelieve, demur, scruple, discredit. **2** mistrust, distrust, suspect, fear. —*n*. **1** uncertainty, indecision, irresolution, mistrust, faltering, vacillation, hesitancy, apprehension, perplexity, quandary, ambiguity. **2** misgiving, qualm, scruple, question, suspicion, dubiety, dissent, objection, caution, caveat.

ant. *v*. **1, 2** believe, trust, credit, accept, put faith in, rely on. *n*. **1** certitude, certainty, trust, belief, conviction, assurance.

doubter *n*. skeptic, disbeliever, freethinker, iconoclast, heretic, agnostic. **ant.** believer.

doubtful *adj*. **1** undecided, uncertain, indefinite, unconfirmed, indeterminate, erratic, variable, unresolved, speculative, undemonstrated, tentative. **2** unlikely, problematical, disputable, quesionable, dubious, controvertible, far-fetched, equivocal, precarious, indistinct, vague, obscure, ambiguous.

ant. 1 determined, decisive, unhesitating, firm, positive, definite, resolute. **2** probable, likely, unquestionable, stable.

doubtless *adv*. **1** absolutely, positively, definitely, certainly, surely, assur-

edly, unquestionably, incontestably, indisputably, indubitably. **2** probably, most likely, apparently, presumably, seemingly, supposedly, plausibly, conceivably, ostensibly.

ant. 1 disputably, arguably, questionably. **2** unlikely, improbably, hardly, scarcely.

dough *n*. *Slang* money, cash, funds, change, currency, bucks (*Slang*), bread (*Slang*), jack (*Slang*).

doughty *adj*. BRAVE.

dour *adj*. **1** gloomy, sullen, grim, glum, sour, pessimistic, dreary, dismal, cheerless, morose, melancholy, depressed, bitter, misanthropic. **2** aloof, stern, severe, forbidding, austere, strict, rigid, inflexible, unyielding.

ant. 1 cheerful, sunny, bright, warm, sweet. **2** open, accessible, easy, genial, cordial.

douse *v*. immerse, submerge, sink, inundate, drown, plunge, steep, dip, duck, dunk, drench, dowse, soak, saturate, souse, slosh, splash, bathe, sprinkle.

dowdy *adj*. shabby, seedy, poky, tacky, frumpish, frumpy, down-at-the-heels, unfashionable, bedraggled, disheveled, sloppy, untidy, slovenly, slatternly. —*n*. SLATTERN.

ant. *adj*. stylish, chic, smart, elegant, modish, well-groomed.

down *adj*. dejected, discouraged, disheartened, low-spirited, downcast, crestfallen, gloomy, depressed, despondent, melancholy. —*v*. fell, drop, overthrow, floor, bowl over, subdue, tackle, prostrate, level, raze. —*n*. descent, dropping, drop, fall, falling, decline, downrush.

ant. *adj*. jaunty, carefree, exuberant, up.

downcast *adj*. DESPONDENT.

downfall *n*. comedown, overthrow, upset, collapse, nosedive, tailspin, upheaval, debacle, fall, ruin, disgrace, comeuppance.

downhearted *adj*. dejected, discouraged, disheartened, dispirited, downcast, low-spirited, despondent, blue. **ant.** elated, exultant, flushed, jubilant.

downright *adj.* absolute, thorough, total, outright, utter, exhaustive, unqualified, sheer, complete, blatant, perfect, pure, plain. **ant.** qualified, partial, conditional.

down to earth practical, no-nonsense, matter-of-fact, pragmatic, realistic, hard-headed, sensible, sane, unsentimental, plain-spoken, earthy, coarse, crass. **ant.** pretentious, puffed up, highfalutin, inflated, extravagant, impractical, romantic.

downtrodden *adj.* OPPRESSED.

downturn *n.* DECLINE.

downy *adj.* soft, soothing, fluffy, fleecy, woolly, fuzzy, flossy, feathery, velvety. **ant.** rough, scratchy, bristling, coarse, abrasive.

dowse *v.* DOUSE.

doze *v.* nap, drowse, snooze, catnap, nod, slumber, sleep. —*n.* nap, snooze, drowse, catnap, forty winks, siesta.

dozy *adj.* DROWSY.

drab[1] *adj.* dull, colorless, lackluster, dreary, dingy, somber, leaden, bleak, lifeless, unexciting, barren, vapid, flat, insipid, humdrum, commonplace. **ant.** bright, vivid, rich, sparkling, vibrant, animated.

drab[2] *n.* SLATTERN.

Draconian *adj.* SEVERE.

draft *n.* **1** wind, breeze, air, breath, current, waft, stream, flow, undercurrent, inhalation, flatus. **2** drink, potion, sip, drop, nip, swig, quaff, draught, guzzle, libation. **3** sketch, outline, rough, plan, projection, conspectus, synopsis, skeleton, profile, version, drawing, tracing, blueprint, mockup, model, diagram. —*v.* **1** sketch, outline, delineate, describe, project, plot, brief, block in, rough in, trace, diagram, chart. **2** induct,

conscript, select, call up, muster, mobilize, levy, press, impress, sign up, enlist, enroll, recruit.

drafty *adj.* breezy, windy, airy, blowy, gusty, chilly, cool. **ant.** close, stuffy, airless, warm.

drag *v.* pull, haul, draw, tow, tug, trail, hale, lug. —*n.* **1** curb, brake, check, governor, clog, friction, interference, impediment. **2** *Slang* pull (*Slang*), in (*Slang*), influence, connections, inside track, favor, clout (*Slang*). **3** *Slang* bore, pest, stiff, wet blanket, nuisance, headache, drip (*Slang*), pain (*Slang*). **ant.** *v.* push, shove, thrust, impel, propel.

dragoon *v.* COERCE.

drain *v.* **1** draw off, tap, pump out, siphon off, sluice, milk, broach, decant, discharge, release, withdraw, remove, divert. **2** empty, exhaust, use up, spend, deplete, impoverish, sap, bleed, tax, consume, eat up, wear, strain, reduce, ruin. **ant. 2** energize, replenish, fill, stimulate, enliven.

dram *n.* BIT.

drama *n.* **1** play, show, representation, piece, vehicle, spectacle, extravaganza, pageant, tragedy, comedy, melodrama. **2** theater, dramaturgy, stagecraft, histrionics, playwrighting, theatricals, stage, showmanship, show business, Broadway, show biz (*Slang*). **3** excitement, emotion, turmoil, spectacle, theatrics, histrionics, staginess, crisis, expectancy, tension.

dramatic *adj.* **1** theatrical, histrionic, Thespian, scenic, spectacular, stagy, make-believe, dramaturgic. **2** vivid, intense, striking, impressive, thrilling, sensational, melodramatic, climactic, spectacular, remarkable. **ant. 2** flat, commonplace, everyday, mundane, prosaic.

dramatize *v.* exaggerate, intensify, play up, embellish, embroider, highlight, color, punctuate, interpret, overdo, emote, spout, rant.

ant. understate, play down, minimize.

drastic *adj.* extreme, radical, intense, forceful, powerful, strong, rigorous, dynamic, harsh, all-out, severe, Draconian.

ant. moderate, lenient, mild, compromising.

draught *n.,v.* DRAFT.

draw *v.* **1** pull, haul, drag, tow, hale, lead, trail, tug, yank. **2** *cause to come forth or happen:* elicit, induce, earn, bring forth, attract, solicit. **3** attract, allure, entice, move, rouse, charm, fascinate. **4** inhale, breathe in, inspire, suck in, puff, pull. **5** depict, delineate, sketch, portray, trace, diagram, define, outline, describe, limn.

ant. 1 push, shove, thrust. **3** repel, dispel, repulse, disperse. **4** exhale, breathe out, expire, blow out.

drawback *n.* disadvantage, deficiency, defect, handicap, hitch, snag, difficulty, impediment, hindrance, check, setback, nuisance, obstacle, liability, trouble.

ant. advantage, benefit, gain, compensation, windfall.

drawing *n.* **1** draftsmanship, art, sketching, design. **2** picture, sketch, study, illustration, delineation, composition, cartoon, draft, tracing, outline, silhouette, design, plan, diagram.

drawn *adj.* haggard, strained, taut, harrowed, tense, tired, fatigued, weary, exhausted, sapped, spent, wan.

ant. relaxed, rested, fresh, energetic, primed.

draw out prolong, protract, drag out, string out, extend, stretch, lengthen, continue, sustain, persist.

ant. curtail, reduce, abridge, shorten, conclude, tighten.

draw up 1 write out, draft, prepare, formulate, compose, frame, indite. **2** halt, stop, pull up, stop short, stay, brake, wait, rest, pause.

dread *v.* fear, worry, cower, tremble, falter, shudder, shrink, quail, quiver.

—*n.* fright, terror, horror, fearfulness, trepidation, aversion, dismay, anxiety, worry, misgiving, apprehension, suspicion.

dreadful *adj.* terrible, frightful, horrid, ghastly, awful, grim, appalling, shocking, calamitous, awesome, portentous, dire, direful.

dream *n.* **1** reverie, daydream, fancy, fantasy, vagary, conceit, vision, apparition, hallucination, trance, delusion, illusion. **2** delight, joy, treasure, gem, marvel, beauty. —*v.* muse, daydream, imagine, suppose, conceive, idealize.

dreamer *n.* VISIONARY.

dream up concoct, cook up, think up, spin, brew, hatch, create, originate, imagine, elaborate, contrive, devise, fabricate, trump up.

dreamy *adj.* VISIONARY.

drear *adj.* DREARY.

dreary *adj.* **1** gloomy, dismal, bleak, joyless, forlorn, drear, doleful, sad, melancholy, depressing, mournful. **2** drab, dull, uninteresting, lifeless, humdrum, monotonous, tedious, wearisome, tiresome, colorless.

ant. 1 cheerful, pleasant, gay, lively, heartening, joyful. **2** exciting, challenging, vibrant, compelling.

dregs *n.* outcasts, riffraff, rabble, scum, trash, leftovers, settlings, flotsam, jetsam, debris, dross, residue, remains, refuse.

drench *v.* soak, saturate, wet, souse, douse, dip, dunk, duck, drown, immerse, submerge, inundate.

dress *v.* **1** clothe, attire, garb, apparel, array, accouter, robe, gown, drape, titivate, rig, don, trick out. **2** decorate, adorn, trim, ornament, array, deck, garnish, drape, enrich, embellish, beautify, festoon, spruce up. —*n.* **1** clothes, garments, clothing, apparel, attire, garb, raiment, wear, wardrobe, array, vesture, toilet, togs, duds. **2** gown, robe, frock, costume, shirtdress, sheath, pinafore, jumper, muu-muu, sari.

ant. *v.* **1** undress, disrobe, divest, take off, shed, doff.

dresser[1] *n.* clotheshorse (*Slang*), fashion plate, dude, dandy, fop, dapper Dan.

dresser[2] *n.* chest, chest of drawers, bureau, chiffonier, drawers.

dressing-down *n.* REPRIMAND.

dressy *adj.* showy, flashy, splashy, dapper, foppish, ritzy, classy, fancy, sporty, swank, sharp, stylish, spruce, smart, chic, neat, trim, elegant.
ant. drab, dowdy, shabby, frumpy, tacky.

dribble *v.* **1** drip, trickle, fall, leak, run, seep, ooze, filter, percolate, squirt, spurt. **2** drool, slobber, drivel, slaver, spit.

drift *n.* **1** mass, heap, bank, pile, mound, pack, lump, hill, dune. **2** tendency, trend, tenor, tone, vein, bent, bias, propensity, import, sense, intention, meaning. —*v.* **1** float, waft, skim, ride, carry along, bear, gravitate. **2** pile up, accumulate, mound, agglomerate, stack, heap up, collect, mass, bank up. **3** wander, roam, rove, meander, tramp, knock about, traipse, ramble, prowl, peregrinate, perambulate.

drifter *n.* vagabond, wanderer, rover, vagrant, hippie, gypsy, itinerant, beachcomber, tramp, hobo, nomad.

drill *n.* exercise, practice, discipline, regimen, routine, instruction, indoctrination, rehearsal, repetition. —*v.* **1** bore, auger, ream, tap, puncture, pierce, penetrate. **2** exercise, practice, discipline, rehearse, train, instruct, teach, school, ground, inculcate, drum in.

drink *v.* swallow, sip, sup, gulp, suck, lap, quaff, bolt, swig, guzzle, imbibe, ingest. —*n.* **1** beverage, potion, liquid, refreshment, potation, libation, juice, draft, brew. **2** alcohol, liquor, spirits, cocktail, booze, nip, shot, hooker, toddy, moonshine, firewater, grog, intoxicant, inebriant.

drink in ABSORB.

drip *n.* **1** dribble, drop, trickle, dripping, leak, gurgle, burble, ripple. **2** *Slang* nuisance, pill, pest, jerk (*Slang*), drag (*Slang*), bore, schlemiel (*Slang*), schlep (*Slang*). —*v.* dribble, trickle, drop, leak, sprinkle, splash, ooze, gurgle, run, issue, percolate.

drive *v.* **1** hit, strike, knock, propel, bat, clout, belt, pound, pole, tap, bunt, hurl, shoot, aim, move, force, impel, push, press, shove, thrust, advance, accelerate. **2** compel, spur, stimulate, actuate, animate, incite, move, force, impel, instigate, promote, encourage, oblige, motivate, urge, hustle, hurry, quicken. **3** control, pilot, operate, steer, ride, motor, travel, tour, convey, guide, conduct, lead. —*n.* **1** ride, excursion, outing, spin, whirl, jaunt, trip, tour, journey, circuit. **2** energy, vitality, vigor, vim, pep, verve, intensity, concentration, push, hustle, get-up-and-go, ambition, aggressiveness, enterprise, initiative. **3** campaign, canvass, solicitation, appeal, crusade, cause, action, effort. **4** stroke, thrust, motion, impulse, force, pressure.

drivel *n.* **1** drool, dribble, slaver, slobber, spittle, spit, saliva, sputum, expectoration. **2** nonsense, rubbish, blather, blah (*Slang*), bosh, bull (*Slang*), twaddle, prattle, babble, balderdash, poppycock, gibberish.

driver *n.* operator, motorist, chauffeur, motorman, trucker, teamster, coachman, pilot.

droll *adj.* humorous, comic, funny, amusing, entertaining, diverting, waggish, whimsical, fantastic, curious, odd, quaint, queer, eccentric, bizarre, pixilated.

drone *v.* **1** hum, buzz, thrum, purr, whir. **2** drawl, intone, croon, chant, singsong. —*n.* hum, buzz, thrum, purr, whir, noise, monotone, tone, note, drawl, singsong.

drool *v.* **1** drivel, dribble, slaver, slobber, salivate, spit. **2** prattle, babble, jabber, gibber, slaver, blather, gabble, twaddle.

droop *v.* **1** sag, sink down, slump, dangle, wilt, flap, flop, bend, hang, slouch, drag, trail, sink, founder, depend, collapse. **2** weary, languish, pine, faint, flag, tire, weaken, fade, fail, wilt, wither, sink, decline, dwindle, waste away.

ant. 1 stand, rise, tower, extend, stiffen, harden. **2** persist, endure, persevere, sustain, weather, stomach, resist.

drop *n.* **1** globule, droplet, drip, drible, trickle, blob, tear, bead, pearl, sphere. **2** particle, bit, speck, driblet, mite, dab, lick, dash, trace, touch, smidgen, dram, whit. **3** fall, plunge, dive, pitch, dip, descent, decline, precipice, downgrade, slope, inclination, gradient. —*v.* **1** drip, trickle, dribble, leak, sprinkle, burble, ripple, filter, percolate, distill, shed. **2** release, let fall, let go, lower, dump. **3** stop, give up, cease, have done with, desist, abandon, dismiss, relinquish, cede, yield, forgo, surrender, renounce, abjure. **4** deliver, leave off, hand over, deposit, place, put, consign, bring, convey. **5** dismiss, fire, discharge, let go, lay off, release, cashier, sack (*Slang*), can (*Slang*), bounce (*Slang*). **6** collapse, fall down, topple, tumble, sprawl, stumble, lurch, pitch, founder, faint, swoon, flag, wilt, weary.

ant. *n.* **3** ascent, ascension, rise, upgrade, climb, incline. *v.* **3** continue, sustain, follow, engage in, undertake, assume. **4** collect, pick up, gather, take away.

droplet *n.* DROP.

dropout *n.* QUITTER.

drop out withdraw, back out, abandon, leave, forsake, stop, renege, give up, quit.

droppings *n.* dung, excrement, feces, ordure, manure, waste, chips, guano.

dross *n.* impurity, dregs, residue, leavings, leftovers, refuse, remains, debris, junk, rubbish.

drown *v.* **1** submerge, immerse, engulf, flood, deluge, inundate, sink, over-

flow. **2** overpower, overwhelm, deaden, muffle, stifle, smother, quash, quench, suppress, extinguish, wipe out, obliterate.

drowse *v.* doze, snooze, nap, catnap, nod, drop off, rest, slumber, sleep, repose.

drowsy *adj.* sleepy, dozy, half-asleep, nodding, dozing, comatose, dormant, lethargic, languid, torpid, sluggish, dull, soporific, soothing, lulling, restful, calming, dreamy.

ant. awake, alert, acute, sharp, keen, on the qui vive.

drub *v.* **1** thump, thrash, beat, pound, pummel, trounce, wallop, belabor, buffet, flog, cudgel, cane, birch. **2** defeat, beat, vanquish, overcome, trounce, rout, lick, put to rout, whip, thrash, outplay, outclass.

drubbing *n.* **1** beating, pounding, thrashing, walloping, pommeling, thwacking, cudgeling, flogging. **2** defeat, licking, beating, rout, trouncing, clobbering, shellacking (*Slang*), shutout.

drudge *v.* slave, grind, toil, sweat, grub, scrub, hack, labor, work. —*n.* menial, slave, servant, grind, plodder, hack, flunky, work horse, toiler, laborer, factotum, slavey (*Brit.*).

drudgery *n.* toil, grind, chore, labor, hackwork, exertion, travail, slavery, servility, serfdom, bondage, oppression.

drug *n.* **1** medicine, medication, medicament, prescription, remedy, compound, palliative, dose. **2** narcotic, dope (*Slang*), opiate.

druggist *n.* pharmacist, apothecary, pharmacologist, chemist (*Brit.*).

drunk *adj.* intoxicated, inebriated, drunken, high, tipsy, under the influence, tight (*Slang*), muddled, boozy, plastered (*Slang*), potted (*Slang*), stewed (*Slang*), stoned (*Slang*), bombed (*Slang*), pickled (*Slang*), under the weather, looped (*Slang*), besotted, smashed (*Slang*). —*n.* **1** drunkard, alcoholic, sot, sponge (*Slang*), lush (*Slang*), soak

(*Slang*), souse (*Slang*), bibber, wino (*Slang*), bum, dipsomaniac. **2** binge (*Slang*), spree, bender (*Slang*), bat (*Slang*), bust, toot (*Slang*), tear (*Slang*), carousal.

drunkard *n.* alcoholic, sot, drunk, tippler, toper, boozehound (*Slang*), wino (*Slang*), barfly, lush (*Slang*), sponge (*Slang*), soak (*Slang*), rummy (*Slang*), inebriate, dipsomaniac.

drunken *adj.* DRUNK.

dry *adj.* **1** arid, parched, waterless, evaporated, anhydrous, barren, baked, desiccated, withered, shriveled, sear, blasted. **2** dull, uninteresting, lifeless, unimaginative, sterile, barren, vapid, insipid, jejune, bare, plain, prosaic, boring. **3** understated, subtle, low-keyed, subdued, droll, jocose, humorous, sly, canny, shrewd, astute, satirical, sarcastic. **4** aloof, remote, impersonal, unemotional, distant, indifferent, cold, forbidding, severe, staid, stuffy, stodgy, unapproachable.

ant. 1 wet, damp, moist, humid, dank, soaked. **2** exciting, stimulating, engaging, vivacious, interesting, absorbing. **3** blatant, heavy-handed, bluff, obvious, gross. **4** genial, cordial, affectionate, affable, approachable.

dry run TRYOUT.

dub *v.* name, nickname, call, christen, baptize, term, style, characterize, label, tag, designate, denominate, entitle, bestow, confer.

dubiety *n.* DOUBT.

dubious *adj.* **1** uncertain, unsure, doubtful, undecided, unsettled, indefinite, vague, unpredictable, indecisive, hesitant, irresolute, disputable, debatable, problematic, ambiguous, equivocal, spurious, inauthentic. **2** suspect, unreliable, questionable, puzzling, mysterious, untrustworthy.

ant. 1 fixed, decided, definite, irrefutable, unquestionable, genuine, authentic. **2** sound, reliable, trustworthy, top-drawer.

duck *v.* **1** submerse, immerse, submerge, dip, dunk, douse, drench, souse, wet, plunge, sink, engulf, baptize. **2** bob, lower, bow, stoop. **3** dodge, sidestep, avoid, shun, evade, elude, hedge, shy, quail, steer clear of, swerve, jib, skip, ditch (*Slang*), retreat, parry, recoil, shrink, shirk, demur.

ant. 2 lift up, raise, elevate, straighten up. **3** confront, face, cope with, undertake, face up to, assume, welcome, embrace.

ducky *adj. Slang* DELIGHTFUL.

duct *n.* passage, tube, pipe, channel, conduit, artery, vein, canal, trough, gutter, main, flue, chimney, funnel.

ductility *n.* RESILIENCE.

dud *n.* FAILURE.

dude *n.* fop, dandy, dapper Dan, Beau Brummell, sport, swell, clotheshorse (*Slang*).

dudgeon *n.* DISPLEASURE.

duds *n.* CLOTHING.

due *adj.* **1** payable, owed, owing, demandable, unpaid, in arrears, outstanding, mature, accrued, redeemable. **2** appropriate, fitting, suitable, becoming, satisfactory, sufficient, ample, adequate, merited, deserved, correct, rightful, lawful. **3** scheduled, listed, slated, booked, billed, promised, appointed, expected, anticipated, awaited, looked for, coming, imminent.

ant. 2 unsuitable, unbecoming, undeserved, inapt, inappropriate, wrong.

duel *n.* contest, competition, rivalry, encounter, engagement, struggle, fight, strife, combat, battle, conflict, clash. —*v.* contest, contend, compete, battle, vie with, rival, dispute, fence, joust, tilt, war, struggle, strive, collide, clash, fight, combat.

dues *n.* fee, assessment, levy, contribution, charge, price, cost, admission, fare, demand, toll.

duffer *n.* slouch, bungler, blunderer,

amateur, tyro, novice, fumbler, butterfingers, incompetent, lummox, oaf, clod, dub (*Slang*), schlemiel (*Slang*).

ant. expert, pro, master, virtuoso.

dulcet *adj.* AGREEABLE.

dull *adj.* **1** subdued, moderate, mild, softened, faded, muted, muffled, matte, diffuse, indistinct, feeble. **2** slow-witted, thick-headed, stolid, dense, vacuous, slow, obtuse, crass, insensitive, imperceptive, undiscerning. **3** boring, tedious, insipid, vapid, spiritless, unimpassioned, lackluster, unimaginative, ordinary.

ant. 1 intense, acute, keen, penetrating, piercing, **2** astute, keen, sharp, quick, discriminating. **3** exciting, stimulating, engaging, lively, stirring, spirited.

dullard *n.* clod, dolt, simpleton, blockhead, dimwit, numskull, dumbbell (*Slang*), fool, dunce, moron.

dumb *adj.* **1** silent, still, mute, mum, speechless, wordless, soundless, taciturn, reticent. **2** stupid, slow-witted, doltish, dull, featherbrained, foolish, senseless, irresponsible, thoughtless.

ant. 1 garrulous, voluble, verbose, loquacious. **2** brainy, intelligent, ingenious, clever, shrewd.

dumbbell *n.* DUNCE.

dumbfound *v.* stun, stupefy, stagger, flabbergast, nonplus, overwhelm, confound, astonish, startle, amaze, surprise, bewilder, confuse.

dumbfounded *adj.* FLABBERGASTED.

dummy *n.* **1** dolt, dimwit, simpleton, blockhead, dullard, dunce, dumbbell (*Slang*), jerk (*Slang*). **2** model, manikin, mannequin, mock-up, figure, image, likeness, stand-in, double, waxwork, puppet, doll. —*adj.* phony, fake, false, sham, bogus, counterfeit, spurious, imitation.

ant. *adj.* genuine, authentic, real, legitimate, true, right, valid.

dump *v.* **1** drop, throw down, fling down, expel, cast off, jettison, heap, leave, deposit. **2** empty, clear out, void, tipple, dispose of, unload, dis-

charge, upset, overturn. **3** discard, get rid of, reject, dispense with, relinquish, abandon, dismiss. —*n.* **1** wasteyard, junkyard, rubbish heap. **2** *Slang* hovel, hole, shack, pigpen, sty, den, dive, joint (*Slang*).

ant. *v.* **2** fill, load, pack, replenish. **3** keep, hold, save, store, hoard.

dumps *n.* MELANCHOLY.

dumpy[1] *adj.* stocky, stubby, stumpy, chunky, chubby, pudgy, squat, short, thickset.

ant. slender, slim, lean, trim, sleek.

dumpy[2] *adj.* GLOOMY.

dunce *n.* ignoramus, simpleton, numskull, thickhead, deadhead, blockhead, booby, nitwit, dimwit, fool, clown, noddy, dumbbell (*Slang*), dullard, idiot, imbecile, moron.

dung *n.* manure, droppings, ordure, excrement, feces, cow chips, guano.

dungeon *n.* PRISON.

dunk *v.* dip, sop, duck, douse.

dupe *n.* victim, sucker (*Slang*), fall guy (*Slang*), patsy (*Slang*), gull, pigeon (*Slang*), easy mark, soft touch, softy, pushover (*Slang*), schlemiel (*Slang*), chump, fool, puppet, greenhorn. —*v.* trick, cheat, hoodwink, bamboozle, fool, deceive, defraud, swindle, hoax, victimize, put on (*Slang*), rip off (*Slang*).

duplicate *adj.* identical, like, alike, similar, matching, resembling, equivalent, double, twin, dual, twofold. —*n.* facsimile, copy, replica, reproduction, imitation, likeness, transfer, transcript, reprint, offprint, carbon, photocopy, Xerox, photostat, counterfeit, counterpart, double, twin, second, match, mate, fellow. —*v.* copy, reproduce, replicate, transcribe, photocopy, Xerox, imitate, repeat, double, echo.

duplicity *n.* deception, double-dealing, deceitfulness, dissimulation, hypocrisy, cant, insincerity, guile, artifice.

ant. straightforwardness, genuineness, artlessness, openness, candor.

durability *n.* ENDURANCE.

durable *adj.* sturdy, solid, strong,

sound, substantial, firm, resistant, enduring, lasting, abiding, immutable, constant, permanent.

ant. shoddy, cheap, gimcrack, perishable.

duration *n.* period, time, term, stretch, space, spell, stage, while, extent, date, season, era, eon, epoch, interval, interim.

duress *n.* compulsion, obligation, coercion, constraint, force, pressure, urgency, demand, emergency, necessity, exigency.

dusk *n.* TWILIGHT.

dusky *adj.* **1** dark, swarthy, darkish, tawny, sable, black. **2** shadowy, twilight, crepuscular, nocturnal, shady, murky, gloomy, misty, overcast, opaque, obscure.

ant. 1 fair, light, blond, pale, white. **2** sunny, bright, light, shining, clear.

dusty *adj.* **1** dirty, unclean, unswept, grimy, messy, musty, sooty, grubby, filthy. **2** powdery, crumbly, pulverized, friable, disintegrated, chalky, granular, sandy.

ant. 1 clean, polished, shiny, immaculate.

duteous *adj.* DUTIFUL.

dutiful *adj.* obedient, submissive, conscientious, punctilious, compliant, duteous, respectful, deferential, filial.

ant. negligent, careless, disobedient, fractious, unruly.

duty *n.* **1** obligation, responsibility, trust, liability, commission, charge, onus, task, service, devoir, debt, function, office, province. **2** tax, tariff, customs, excise, impost, toll, levy, assessment, rate, fee, charge, due.

dwarf *n.* midget, pygmy, bantam, runt, shrimp, tot, doll, manikin, mannikin, elf, gnome, Lilliputian, homunculus.
—*v.* overshadow, tower over, over-

power, surpass, excel, exceed, top, trump.

ant. *n.* giant, colossus, mammoth, monster, Brobdingnagian.

dwarfish *adj.* SMALL.

dwell *v.* reside, live, inhabit, domicile, quarter, stay, remain, settle, roost, occupy, room, bunk.

dwelling *n.* house, home, residence, habitation, domicile, abode, lodging, quarters, haunt, place, establishment, den, castle.

dwell on linger over, emphasize, insist upon, harp on, thrash over, expatiate, elaborate, repeat.

ant. neglect, disregard, skip, gloss over, skim over.

dwindle *v.* decrease, diminish, lessen, fade, de-escalate, subside, wane, ebb, contract, shrivel, peter out, decline, degenerate.

ant. increase, enlarge, multiply, augment, strengthen.

dyed-in-the-wool *adj.* COMPLETE.

dying *adj.* **1** moribund, expiring, passing, ebbing, failing, waning, final, mortal. **2** disappearing, vanishing, diminishing, declining, dwindling, ebbing, waning, passing, receding, retiring, retreating.

ant. 2 thriving, flourishing, vigorous, booming.

dynamic *adj.* **1** kinetic, motive, active, driving, oscillating, propulsive, impelling. **2** energetic, forceful, active, intense, vigorous, potent, high-powered, aggressive, capable, magnetic, charismatic, galvanic, vibrant.

ant. 1 stable, fixed, inert, still, dead. **2** passive, weak, enervated, impotent, ineffectual, uninspiring.

dynamism *n.* ENERGY.
dynamite *n.* WONDER.
dynamo *n.* WONDER.
dynast *n.* RULER.

E

eager *adj.* avid, enthusiastic, keen, desirous, zealous, anxious, impatient, longing, yearning, athirst, greedy, agog, impetuous, raring.
    ant. apathetic, impassive, inert, dull, listless, lethargic, cold, sluggish, indifferent.

eagerness *n.* ARDOR.

early *adj.* first, opportune, timely, prompt, forward, advanced, precocious, premature.
    ant. late, retarded, tardy, delayed, backward.

earmark *n.* characteristic, peculiarity, trait, feature, brand, sign, stamp, token, signature, trademark.

earn *v.* **1** gain, receive, make, draw, win, obtain. **2** merit, deserve, reap, call for, rate.

earnest *adj.* intent, sincere, serious, direct, zealous, heartfelt, ardent, fervent, impassioned, purposeful, devoted.
    ant. frivolous, superficial, giddy, flighty, flippant, light-headed, shallow, insincere.

earnings *n.* wages, salary, pay, compensation, stipend, income, proceeds, profits, gain, emolument, return.

earth *n.* land, ground, soil, dirt, loam, humus, turf.

earthiness *n.* SPICE.

earthly *adj.* **1** terrestrial, terrene. **2** worldly, mundane, secular, temporal, profane, material, sensual, base.
    ant. 2 spiritual, heavenly, celestial, other-worldly, sacred, divine, holy.

earthy *adj.* coarse, robust, lusty, simple, natural, unrefined, crude, rough, ribald, raunchy (*Slang*), funky (*Slang*).
    ant. refined, polished, genteel, courtly, rarefied, elegant, dainty.

ease *n.* comfort, tranquillity, naturalness, facility, readiness, freedom, leisure, unconstraint, liberty, relief.
    —*v.* relieve, comfort, lessen, alleviate, pacify, assuage, soothe, moderate.

easily *adv.* **1** effortlessly, readily, smoothly, facilely, lightly, gracefully, naturally. **2** unquestionably, doubtlessly, far and away.
    ant. 1 laboriously, painfully, painstakingly, ardously. **2** hardly.

easiness *n.* **1** comfort, contentment, tranquillity, satisfaction, repose, leisure, liberty. **2** simplicity, lightness, convenience, facility.
    ant. 1 discomfort, poverty, penury, misery, torment, unrest. **2** difficulty, hardness, arduousness, laboriousness.

easy *adj.* **1** light, painless, comfortable, effortless. **2** comfortable, pleasant, relaxed, undemanding, reasonable, gentle, moderate, lenient, indulgent, friendly, unpretentious, informal, flexible, pliant, unexacting.
    ant. 1 difficult, painful, laborious, arduous, wearisome, irksome, fatiguing. **2** harsh, stern, unfriendly, demanding, exacting, strict, tense, constrained, unbending, stiff, formal.

easygoing *adj.* relaxed, unconcerned, unhurried, complacent, calm, carefree, nonchalant, insouciant, cheerful, placid, serene, mild, uncritical.
    ant. demanding, stern, harsh, exacting, severe, rigorous, critical, strict, peremptory.

easy mark DUPE.

eat *v.* **1** ingest, consume, devour, swallow, gulp, wolf. **2** corrode, consume, waste, wear away, erode, rust.

eats *n.* FOOD.

eavesdrop *v.* listen, spy, overhear, monitor, snoop, wiretap.

eavesdropper *n.* listener, monitor, wiretapper, snoop, spy.

ebb *v.* decline, recede, fall, lessen, diminish, shrink, wane, dwindle, sink, decrease, weaken.
   ant. grow, increase, wax, thrive, prosper, enlarge, swell.

ebullience *n.* ENTHUSIASM.

ebullient *adj.* bubbling, sparkling, enthusiastic, excited, effervescent, exhilarated, effusive, elated.
   ant. apathetic, lethargic, indifferent, cold, unmoved, impassive.

eccentric *adj.* unconventional, odd, strange, bizarre, weird, queer, fey, erratic, outlandish, idiosyncratic, peculiar, whimsical, dotty, quirky, cranky, screwy (*Slang*). —*n.* crank, nonconformist, misfit, nut (*Slang*), crackpot (*Slang*), oddball (*Slang*), weirdo (*Slang*), kook (*Slang*), screwball (*Slang*).
   ant. *adj.* conventional, ordinary, regular, normal.

eccentricity *n.* **1** caprice, whim, freak, quirk, kink, foible, idiosyncracy, oddity. **2** strangeness, oddness, oddity, irregularity, singularity, aberration.
   ant. **2** conventionality, normality, regularity, ordinariness.

ecclesiastical *adj.* churchly, religious, priestly, clerical.
   ant. secular, mundane, worldly.

echelon *n.* level, rank, hierarchy, grade, status, position, place.

echo *n.* **1** REVERBERATION. **2** imitation, reaction, response, repetition, reflection. **3** trace, suggestion, reminder, hint, allusion, intimation. —*v.* repeat, imitate, second, copy, mimic, reiterate, parrot.

echoic *adj.* IMITATIVE.

éclat *n.* SPLENDOR.

eclectic *adj.* diverse, selective, broad, comprehensive, liberal, catholic, general, dilettantish.
   ant. narrow, rigid, specialized, confined, limited.

eclipse *v.* **1** obscure, darken, dim, blot out, erase, hide, conceal, extinguish. **2** overshadow, surpass, excel, outdo, outshine, outstrip, transcend.

economical *adj.* **1** frugal, thrifty, spare, saving, chary, prudent. **2** terse, concise, unadorned, spare, austere, severe.
   ant. **1** prodigal, extravagant, spendthrift, lavish, improvident. **2** expansive, ample, elaborate.

economy *n.* frugality, thrift, husbandry, care, prudence, austerity.
   ant. extravagance, wastefulness, lavishness, prodigality.

ecstasy *n.* joy, exaltation, rapture, delight, bliss, exhilaration, rejoicing, transport, ravishment, elation, jubilation, ebullience.
   ant. gloom, misery, depression, sadness, despondency, sorrow, despair, woe.

ecstatic *adj.* overjoyed, rapturous, delighted, happy, exultant, enraptured, entranced, beatific, elated, blissful, radiant, delirious, ebullient.
   ant. gloomy, sullen, despondent, sad, unhappy, depressed, morose, sorrowful.

eddy *n.* current, whirlpool, vortex, maelstrom.

edge *n.* **1** keenness, sharpness, bite, incisiveness, acuteness, pungency, asperity. **2** border, margin, boundary, verge, brink, limit, outline, contour. **3** advantage, superiority, lead.

edgy *adj.* nervous, irritable, apprehensive, fearful, anxious, jumpy, on edge.
   ant. relaxed, calm, serene, unruffled, complacent, placid.

edible *adj.* eatable, comestible, esculent.

edict *n.* decree, law, proclamation, command, ordinance, fiat, order, manifesto, ukase.

edification *n.* instruction, information, education, enlightenment, improvement, teaching, guidance.

edifice *n.* BUILDING.

edify *v.* EDUCATE.

edifying *adj.* enlightening, instructive, educational, informative, helpful, uplifting, stimulating, heuristic, educative.

ant. unedifying, mystifying, baffling.

edit *v.* revise, correct, emend, adapt, polish, redact, condense, annotate, blue-pencil.

educate *v.* train, school, develop, instruct, teach, enlighten, edify, inform, nurture, indoctrinate, discipline, cultivate, civilize.

educated *adj.* trained, informed, cultivated, tutored, cultured, enlightened, lettered, polished, well-bred, refined. **ant.** untrained, ignorant, uninformed, crude, unlettered, illiterate.

education *n.* schooling, training, instruction, learning, edification, enlightenment, development, discipline, skill, craft, cultivation, nurture, breeding.

educational *adj.* instructive, informative, heuristic, edifying, scholastic, didactic, pedagogic.

educative *adj.* EDIFYING.

educator *n.* teacher, instructor, tutor, trainer, mentor, pedagogue.

educe *v.* EVOKE.

eerie *adj.* weird, strange, frightening, unearthly, spectral, bizarre, odd, spooky, uncanny, ghostly, mysterious, ominous, portentous, outlandish.

efface *v.* erase, cancel, obliterate, destroy, delete, blot out, expunge, eradicate, excise.

effect *n.* **1** result, consequence, upshot, outcome, aftermath, conclusion, impression, reaction, repercussion, aftereffect, issue, event. **2** power, capacity, efficacy, potential, energy, clout (*Slang*). **3** force, operation, action, execution. —*v.* cause, bring about, actuate, effectuate, accomplish, produce, create, initiate.

effective *adj.* **1** effectual, adequate, sufficient, competent, active, efficacious. **2** impressive, striking, emphatic, powerful, cogent, telling, successful.

ant. **1, 2** weak, inadequate, ineffective, powerless, impotent, ineffectual, negligible, inconsequential.

effectiveness *n.* force, potency, capability, cogency, effect, efficacy, success, strength, power, efficiency, validity.

effects *n.* goods, possessions, belongings, property, movables, chattels, trappings, luggage, baggage.

effectual *adj.* EFFECTIVE.

effectuate *v.* EFFECT.

effeminate *adj.* womanish, unmanly, soft, weak, sissyish.

effete *adj.* **1** barren, sterile, exhausted, worn-out, unproductive, sere. **2** weak, spent, decayed, decadent, spoiled, self-indulgent, sybaritic, deteriorated.

ant. **1** fruitful, prolific, inventive, creative, teeming. **2** strong, vigorous, youthful, energetic, vital.

efficacious *adj.* EFFECTIVE.

efficacy *n.* EFFECTIVENESS.

efficiency *n.* effectiveness, efficacy, potency, ability, capability, skill, deftness, facility, proficiency, adroitness, dexterity, know-how.

efficient *adj.* effective, active, potent, effectual, economical, skillful, deft, able, capable, competent, proficient, efficacious.

ant. wasteful, unproductive, haphazard, slipshod.

effort *n.* **1** exertion, struggle, strain, stress, labor, application, dint. **2** endeavor, attempt, trial, essay, try, venture. **3** achievement, product, feat, production, brainchild, accomplishment.

effortless *adj.* easy, facile, offhand, casual, smooth, graceful.

ant. laborious, painful, painstaking, labored.

effrontery *n.* audacity, insolence, impudence, boldness, arrogance, presumptuousness, hardihood, cheek, chutzpah, assurance, shamelessness, nerve, gall, brass.

ant. timidity, meekness, shyness, diffidence, bashfulness.

effulgence *n.* radiance, brightness, brilliance, luster, splendor.

ant. dullness, drabness, monotony, somberness.

effulgent *adj.* radiant, brilliant, luminous, lustrous, resplendent, beaming.

ant. dull, colorless, drab, opaque, somber, monotonous, dingy.

effuse *v.* EXUDE.

effusion *n.* OUTPOURING.

effusive *adj.* overflowing, gushing, sentimental, demonstrative, expansive, ebullient, lavish, profuse, unrestrained, fulsome.

ant. reticent, restrained, cool, aloof, guarded, taciturn.

effusiveness *n.* GARRULITY.

egalitarian *adj.* EQUAL.

egg *n.* ovum, ovule, embryo.

egghead *n. Slang* INTELLECTUAL.

egg on INCITE.

ego *n.* **1** SELF. **2** EGOTISM.

egocentric *adj.* EGOTISTIC.

egoism *n.* EGOTISM.

egomania *n.* EGOTISM.

egotism *n.* self-centeredness, conceit, vanity, egoism, egocentricity, ego, egomania, self-importance, selfishness, self-love, narcissism, vainglory.

egotist *n.* egoist, boaster, braggart, coxcomb, swaggerer, narcissist, peacock.

egotistic *adj.* selfish, self-centered, egocentric, egoistic, vain, conceited, narcissistic, self-important, proud, boastful, bragging, overweening, arrogant, vainglorious, pompous.

ant. unselfish, modest, humble, reserved.

egregious *adj.* flagrant, glaring, notorious, rank, gross, monstrous, arrant, blatant, obvious, excessive, extreme, huge, prodigious.

ant. moderate, restrained, measured, proportionate, just.

egress *n.* EXIT.

ejaculate *v.* utter, cry, exclaim, shout, blurt.

ejaculation *n.* EXCLAMATION.

eject *v.* throw out, expel, oust, dislodge, dismiss, dispossess, discharge, remove, banish, get rid of, turn out, bounce (*Slang*).

ejection *n.* EXPULSION.

elaborate *v.* work out, develop, devise, construct, build, fashion, embellish, improve, adorn, polish, enrich, enhance, refine. —*adj.* complicated, detailed, ornate, intricate, painstaking, careful, thorough, skillful, minute, ostentatious, showy, extravagant, fancy.

ant. *adj.* simple, plain, basic, natural, artless, chaste.

élan *n.* VERVE.

elapse *v.* pass, slip by, expire, intervene, lapse, glide.

elastic *adj.* adaptable, resilient, supple, springy, pliant, buoyant, flexible, accommodating, yielding, responsive, complaisant, adjustable.

ant. brittle, refractory, hard, stubborn, obstinate, obdurate, inflexible, rigid, tense, perverse.

elasticity *n.* RESILIENCE.

elate *v.* EXCITE.

elated *adj.* joyful, exultant, triumphant, exhilarated, jubilant, excited, happy, rejoicing, gleeful, ebullient, overjoyed.

ant. sad, gloomy, depressed, low-spirited, mournful, sullen.

elation *n.* exaltation, joy, excitement, happiness, rapture, ecstasy, bliss, jubilation, triumph, exultation, delight.

ant. gloom, depression, sadness, melancholy, misery.

elbow *v.* push, jostle, crowd, shoulder, hustle, nudge, bump, shove.

elder *adj.* senior, older, earlier, prior, former. —*n.* senior, veteran, dignitary, father, counselor, old-timer.

ant. *adj.* later, younger, junior, newer.

elderly *adj.* OLD.

elect *v.* choose, select, pick out, vote, prefer, settle, decide upon, opt for. —*adj.* selected, chosen, preferred, picked out, choice, exclusive, elite. —*n.* ELITE.

election *n.* choice, selection, determination, decision, discrimination, judgment, preference, vote.

elective *adj.* electoral, chosen, optional, discretionary.

ant. required, imperative, prescribed, appointed, determined.

electric *adj.* dynamic, exciting, thrilling, electrifying, stirring, inspiring, charged, stimulating, galvanizing, startling, tense, expectant.

electricity *n.* EXCITEMENT.

electrify *v.* arouse, thrill, startle, excite, rouse, stir, inspire, animate, fascinate, astonish, astound, amaze, confound.

electrifying *adj.* AMAZING.

elegance *n.* refinement, dignity, opulence, richness, taste, style, distinction, propriety, symmetry, fineness, politeness, gentility, courtliness, polish, class (*Slang*).

elegant *adj.* refined, dignified, graceful, tasteful, rich, exquisite, opulent, polished, polite, courtly, genteel, well-bred, stylish, classy (*Slang*).

ant. coarse, uncouth, rude, boorish, tasteless, garish, gaudy, tacky.

elegiac *adj.* sad, mournful, lamenting, plaintive, melancholy, meditative, reflective, nostalgic, valedictory.

element *n.* component, part, factor, constituent, ingredient, member, feature, characteristic, quality, property, material, substance.

elemental *adj.* ELEMENTARY.

elementary *adj.* **1** basic, fundamental, rudimentary, elemental, primary, initial, original. **2** simple, easy, plain, clear, understandable, intelligible.

ant. **1** complicated, complex, involved, advanced. **2** difficult, tortuous, labyrinthine.

elephantine *adj.* HUGE.

elevate *v.* **1** raise, lift, hoist, erect, mount, upraise, uplift, rear. **2** promote, advance, exalt, honor, improve, aggrandize, enhance, strengthen.

ant. **2** debase, degrade, belittle, depreciate, reduce, impair, weaken.

elevated *adj.* exalted, lofty, noble,

dignified, grand, eminent, high-minded, majestic, stately, Olympian.

ant. banal, mundane, pedestrian, mediocre, trivial.

elevation *n.* height, altitude, lift, prominence, eminence, ascent, superiority, loftiness, distinction, grandeur, nobility, majesty, exaltation, improvement, advancement.

elf *n.* **1** fairy, pixy, sprite, dwarf, gnome, brownie, leprechaun. **2** imp, rascal, urchin, gamin.

elfin *adj.* mischievous, prankish, playful, elfish, frolicsome, dainty, diminutive, fragile, fleeting, elusive.

elfish *adj.* ELFIN.

elicit *v.* draw, extract, derive, deduce, develop, extort, wrest.

elide *v.* OMIT.

eligible *adj.* suitable, proper, acceptable, desirable, fitting, worthy.

eliminate *v.* **1** get rid of, remove, eject, expel, exclude, discharge, erase, eradicate, extirpate, exterminate, annihilate, rub out (*Slang*). **2** omit, leave out, disregard, exclude, ignore, suppress, drop, delete, cancel.

elimination *n.* removal, expulsion, rejection, exclusion, suppression, cancellation, deletion.

elite *n.* aristocracy, gentry, nobility, flower, elect, cream of the crop, the privileged, upper class, oligarchy, meritocracy, clique, coterie, cabal.

elitist *n.* snob, oligarch, meritocrat.

elixir *n.* **1** essence, embodiment, quintessence, basis, concentrate, extract. **2** panacea, cure-all, potion, nostrum, snake oil.

elocution *n.* **1** oratory, declamation, recitation, delivery, speech-making, rhetoric. **2** diction, enunciation, articulation, style, phraseology, eloquence, fluency, locution.

elongate *v.* lengthen, stretch, extend, prolong, protract, draw out.

ant. curtail, shorten, reduce, cut, abridge, diminish, decrease.

elongated *adj.* stretched, lengthened, drawn-out, slender, attenuated, extended, distended, protracted.

ant. shortened, curtailed, cut-off, trimmed, reduced, contracted, compressed.

eloquence *n.* fluency, expression, appeal, persuasion, oratory, rhetoric.

eloquent *adj.* **1** articulate, fluent, graceful, well-expressed, persuasive, cogent, inspired, ringing. **2** expressive, meaningful, significant, affecting, moving, telling, pregnant.

ant. **1** inarticulate, hesitant, clumsy, dull, tongue-tied. **2** empty, vapid, inexpressive, enigmatic.

elucidate *v.* clarify, explain, illuminate, interpret, unfold, clear up, explicate.

ant. confuse, obfuscate, cloud, muddle, bewilder, perplex.

elucidation *n.* EXPLANATION.

elude *v.* **1** escape, evade, outrun, shun, avoid, flee, get away. **2** baffle, thwart, frustrate, circumvent, slip by.

elusive *adj.* **1** evasive, slippery, fleeting, transient, transitory, shifty. **2** subtle, baffling, mysterious, abstruse, complicated, difficult.

emaciated *adj.* scrawny, wasted, thin, gaunt, weedy, famished, starved, pinched, haggard, frail, slight, wizened, skeletal, atrophied.

ant. fat, plump, well-fed, corpulent, obese.

emanate *v.* issue, flow, proceed, arise, originate, discharge, exude, debouch.

emancipate *v.* free, liberate, release, deliver, unchain, manumit, disencumber, disburden.

ant. enslave, oppress, subjugate, dominate, subdue.

emancipation *n.* RELEASE.

emasculate *v.* **1** castrate, geld, unman, caponize, eunuchize. **2** weaken, debilitate, soften, enervate, censor, expurgate, bowdlerize.

embargo *n.* stoppage, restraint, prohibition, ban, proscription, impediment, hindrance, blockage, barrier, interdiction, quarantine. —*v.* prohibit, block, bar, impede, check, interdict, proscribe, ban, quarantine.

embark *v.* **1** board, set sail, ship out. **2** begin, venture, undertake, launch, institute, enter, initiate, engage, assume, broach, set out.

ant. **1** disembark, land, debark, put in. **2** cease, stop, break off, halt, quit, desist.

embarkation *n.* DEPARTURE.

embarrass *v.* disconcert, abash, mortify, shame, chagrin, upset, fluster, agitate, confuse, discountenance, distract, discompose, perplex, rattle.

embarrassing *adj.* mortifying, disconcerting, sensitive, tricky, touchy, compromising, humiliating, awkward.

embarrassment *n.* DIFFICULTY.

embed *v.* SET.

embellish *v.* adorn, ornament, enrich, garnish, enhance, exaggerate, embroider.

embellishment *n.* decoration, ornamentation, enrichment, beautification, trimming, frill.

embers *n.* ASHES.

embezzle *v.* STEAL.

embittered *adj.* resentful, rancorous, angry, hostile, envenomed, spiteful, hateful, disillusioned, cynical.

emblazon *v.* ADORN.

emblem *n.* symbol, badge, representation, insignia, mark, token, image, device, model, example.

emblematic *adj.* symbolic, representative, figurative, typical, indicative, suggestive, allegorical, metaphorical.

embodiment *n.* incarnation, personification, image, representation, realization, manifestation, expression, example, incorporation, exemplification.

embody *v.* **1** incorporate, incarnate, concretize, materialize, verify, externalize, integrate, substantiate, concentrate, consolidate, reify. **2** personify, represent, manifest, express, exhibit, stand for, typify, symbolize.

embolden *v.* encourage, hearten, cheer, strengthen, inspirit, stimulate, rouse, invigorate, reassure, nerve.

ant. intimidate, scare, frighten, cow, daunt, unnerve, subdue, terrorize.

embosom *v.* EMBRACE.

embrace *v.* **1** hug, clasp, squeeze, cuddle, hold, clutch, enfold, infold, embosom, snuggle, caress. **2** accept, adopt, espouse, endorse, receive, choose. **3** comprehend, include, cover, contain, comprise, take in, survey, subsume, implicate, involve. —*n.* clasp, hug, caress, squeeze.

embroider *v.* embellish, elaborate, exaggerate, stretch, adorn, color, dress up, fabricate.

embroil *v.* implicate, entangle, ensnare, snarl, enmesh, confuse, disturb, distract, discompose, muddle.

embryo *n.* nucleus, seed, beginning, origin, start, commencement, incipience, germ, rudiment.

embryonic *adj.* undeveloped, unfinished, rudimentary, incipient, immature, primary, imperfect, inchoate.
ant. mature, complete, finished, fulfilled, ripe.

emcee *n.* MASTER OF CEREMONIES.

emend *v.* CORRECT.

emendation *n.* correction, alteration, revision, editing, redaction, improvement, amendment, amelioration.

emerge *v.* arise, appear, come forth, issue, debouch, rise, proceed, emanate, transpire, escape, crop up.

emergence *n.* APPEARANCE.

emergency *n.* crisis, extremity, exigency, difficulty, predicament, contingency, scrape, fix, hole, jam, pickle.

emeritus *adj.* RETIRED.

emetic *adj.* NAUSEOUS.

eminence *n.* **1** rank, standing, station, importance, renown, repute, honor, greatness, grandeur, dignity, distinction, excellence, fame, note, celebrity, purple. **2** height, elevation, hill, rise, bluff, cliff, peak, promontory.

eminent *adj.* outstanding, excellent, foremost, renowned, distinguished, conspicuous, noteworthy, notable, honored, esteemed, famous, celebrated, illustrious, noted, laureate, paramount, preeminent, topping.

ant. undistinguished, obscure, unknown, humble, mediocre.

emissary *n.* agent, messenger, ambassador, envoy, courier, representative, minister, herald, scout, spy, informer.

emission *n.* radiation, emanation, discharge, ejection, diffusion, projection, exhalation, extrusion, excretion.

emit *v.* discharge, give out, radiate, diffuse, send, expel, secrete, excrete, exhale, utter.

emollient *adj.* SOOTHING.

emolument *n.* compensation, gain, profit, recompense, remuneration, payment, earnings, wages, stipend, income, revenue, reward, return.

emotion *n.* feeling, passion, sentiment, excitement, reaction, affect.

emotional *adj.* **1** feeling, sensitive, susceptible, demonstrative, excitable, warm, enthusiastic, impulsive, responsive, fervent, ardent, fiery, hot-blooded. **2** stirring, impassioned, exciting, thrilling, dramatic, sensational, poignant, emotive, pathetic, heart-rending, tear-jerking (*Slang*).
ant. **1** cold, unfeeling, unmoved, hard-hearted, cool, impassive, apathetic.

emotive *adj.* EMOTIONAL.

empathy *n.* SYMPATHY.

emperor *n.* sovereign, monarch, czar, autocrat, dictator, kaiser.

emphasis *n.* stress, importance, weight, accent, significance, prominence, attention, insistence.

emphasize *v.* stress, feature, accentuate, underscore, underline, italicize, intensify.
ant. belittle, underplay, de-emphasize, neglect, minimize.

emphatic *adj.* forceful, decisive, marked, strong, distinct, pointed, intense, prominent, vigorous, definitive, powerful, conspicuous, assertive, stressed, decided.
ant. doubtful, indefinite, indecisive, vague, noncommittal, hesitant, wishy-washy.

empirical *adj.* experiential, pragmatic, provisional, tentative, hypothetical, practical.

emplacement *n.* position, location, station, situation, establishment, lodgement, site.

employ *v.* **1** hire, engage, enlist, retain, commission. **2** use, devote, apply, utilize, exercise, operate, wield, ply, handle, manipulate.

employee *n.* worker, wage-earner, jobholder, aide, hand, agent, assistant, underling, hireling.

employer *n.* boss, owner, proprietor, hirer, contractor, manager.

employment *n.* **1** use, application, utilization, exercise, operation, service, recourse, resort. **2** occupation, work, trade, business, job, profession, craft, position, vocation, pursuit, situation, function, station, duty.

emporium *n.* STORE.

empower *v.* enable, permit, authorize, commission, license, warrant, sanction, entitle, allow, delegate, depute, accredit, ratify.

emptiness *n.* VOID.

empty *adj.* **1** vacant, void, unoccupied, bare, blank, clear, hollow. **2** vain, insincere, vacuous, meaningless, unsubstantial, senseless, frivolous, shallow, silly, witless, inane, worthless, futile. —*v.* drain, deplete, exhaust, evacuate, sweep, clear, gut. **ant.** *adj.* **1** full, stuffed, stocked, replete, abundant. —*v.* fill, stock, stuff, pack, cram, replenish.

empty-headed *adj.* FOOLISH.

empyreal *adj.* HEAVENLY.

emulate *v.* rival, imitate, copy, challenge, mimic, contend, compete.

enable *v.* empower, facilitate, authorize, license, permit, sanction, warrant, qualify, capacitate, delegate, depute.

enact *v.* legislate, decree, pass, establish, ordain, institute, sanction, execute, prescribe, ratify, effect.

enactment *n.* law, statute, act, decree, measure, ordinance, regulation, provision, mandate.

enamored *adj.* in love, captivated, entranced, bewitched, charmed, fascinated, enthralled, infatuated, taken.

encapsulate *v.* summarize, condense, sum up, abbreviate, epitomize, abridge, digest, compress.

encapsulation *n.* SUMMARY.

encase *v.* ENCLOSE.

enchain *v.* BIND.

enchant *v.* **1** bewitch, ensorcel, hypnotize, mesmerize, charm. **2** delight, fascinate, charm, win, beguile, captivate, enrapture, ravish.

enchanting *adj.* charming, fascinating, delightful, beguiling, captivating, ravishing, bewitching, alluring, seductive, engaging, entrancing, winning.

enchantment *n.* magic, sorcery, witchcraft, wizardry, conjuration, thaumaturgy.

encircle *v.* surround, gird, encompass, enclose, hem in, confine, circumscribe, envelop, embrace, invest, beset, besiege.

enclose *v.* **1** fence, surround, shut in, encircle, hem in, encase, circumscribe, engird, bound, encompass. **2** insert, add, append, wrap, contain, surround, hold, embrace, comprehend, include, incorporate.

encomium *n.* EULOGY.

encompass *v.* include, embrace, admit, comprise, contain, comprehend, involve, cover, take in, circumscribe, subsume. **ant.** exclude, omit, except, preclude, leave out.

encounter *n.* meeting, conjunction, gathering, confrontation. —*v.* meet, come upon, face, confront, run into, happen upon, see.

encourage *v.* hearten, inspire, embolden, help, rally, foster, abet, favor, inspirit, stimulate, spur, promote, advance, support, advocate, boost, succor. **ant.** discourage, deter, dissuade, dishearten, daunt.

encouragement *n.* help, stimulus, hope, cheer, assurance, favor, support, incentive, aid, succor, assistance, backing, inspiration, promotion, prompting, comfort.

ant. hindrance, dissuasion, restriction, constraint, obstruction, impediment.

encouraging *adj.* HOPEFUL.

encroach *v.* intrude, trespass, infringe, usurp, invade, appropriate, impinge, crowd, obtrude, arrogate, overstep.

encroachment *n.* trespass, intrusion, invasion, incursion, infringement, imposition, assumption, inroad, usurpation, infraction.

encumber *v.* burden, obstruct, impede, hinder, block, clog, overload, hamper, check, charge, trammel, handicap, oppress, cramp, incommode.

ant. free, lighten, liberate, disburden, release, ease, facilitate.

encumbrance *n,* burden, impediment, obstruction, hindrance, obstacle, cumbrance, difficulty, clog, block, millstone, deadwood.

encyclopedic *adj.* comprehensive, broad, universal, erudite, polymath, inclusive, exhaustive, wide-ranging, omniscient.

ant. limited, specialized, confined, specific.

end *n.* **1** terminus, extremity, limit, edge, boundary, tip, point, bourne, termination. **2** finish, ending, conclusion, close, finale, finis, stop, cessation, surcease, expiration, completion, consummation, fulfillment, resolution, denouement, aftermath. **3** purpose, intention, aim, goal, cause, objective, destination, intent, object. **4** result, consequence, outcome, upshot, issue, event, settlement, fruit.

—*v.* finish, conclude, cease, stop, terminate, surcease, discontinue, quit, desist, expire, complete, wind up.

ant. *n.* **2** beginning, commencement, incipience, origin, source, outset, start, infancy, inception. —*v.* begin, start, commence, initiate, arise, spring, open.

endanger *v.* imperil, jeopardize, haz-

ard, risk, expose, commit, compromise.

ant. protect, shield, safeguard, defend, shelter, screen.

endangerment *n.* MENACE.

endearing *adj.* lovable, charming, attractive, affecting, amiable, sweet, winning, engaging, adorable.

endeavor *n.* attempt, effort, try, essay, venture, striving, undertaking, trial, aim, exertion, struggle, crack, go. —*v.* try, attempt, strive, venture, essay, undertake, tackle, struggle.

ending *n.* END.

endless *adj.* boundless, eternal, infinite, everlasting, unending, incessant, interminable, ceaseless, continuous, constant, perpetual, immortal, illimitable, limitless.

ant. finite, limited, defined, bounded, restricted, measured.

endorse *v.* support, back, ratify, guarantee, sustain, favor, recommend, approve, advocate, sanction.

endorsement *n.* backing, support, approval, approbation, ratification, advocacy, confirmation, commendation, acceptance.

endow *v.* **1** fund, bestow, supply, grant, award, settle, vest, donate, bequeath, contribute, subsidize. **2** furnish, equip, confer, gift, grace, favor, provide, endue.

endowment *n.* **1** donation, grant, gift, fund, bequest, subsidy, benefaction, legacy. **2** attribute, talent, gift, aptitude, resource, ability, asset, faculty, capability, flair.

endue *v.* ENDOW.

endurance *n.* stamina, fortitude, stability, durability, toughness, permanence, sturdiness, ruggedness, hardihood, hardiness, tolerance, staying power.

endure *v.* **1** bear, tolerate, undergo, sustain, withstand, bear up, support, brook, abide, suffer, stand, weather, cope with. **2** last, continue, abide, remain, persist, hold, stand, wear, survive, stay.

ant. 1 collapse, fall, break down, fail, buckle, give way.

enduring *adj*. lasting, permanent, continuing, durable, perennial, persisting, surviving, extant, existing, living, thriving, imperishable.

ant. ephemeral, transient, transitory, fleeting, impermanent, temporary, extinct.

enemy *n*. foe, opponent, adversary, antagonist, assailant, rival, competitor, nemesis.

ant. friend, ally, supporter, advocate, helper, partner, adherent, partisan.

energetic *adj*. vigorous, active, forceful, strenuous, brisk, dynamic, lively, animated, robust, hearty, zippy, spirited, enterprising, tireless.

ant. lazy, torpid, slothful, indolent, sluggish, lackadaisical, languid, shiftless, phlegmatic.

energize *v*. ACTIVATE.

energy *n*. vigor, force, drive, animation, fervor, vitality, dynamism, fire, verve, élan, punch, intensity, pep, zip, vim.

enervate *v*. weaken, debilitate, enfeeble, wear out, tire, sap, paralyze, exhaust, prostrate, attenuate, incapacitate, disable.

ant. invigorate, inspirit, stimulate, animate, fortify, strengthen, vivify, brace.

enervated *adj*. WEAK.

enfeeble *v*. weaken, exhaust, deplete, enervate, debilitate, impair, cripple, invalidate, diminish, disable, undermine.

ant. strengthen, aid, reinforce, sustain, fortify, invigorate.

enfold *v*. EMBRACE.

enforce *v*. compel, impose, require, exact, oblige, constrain, enjoin, coerce, necessitate, press, execute, carry out.

enforcement *n*. execution, obligation, compulsion, constraint, coercion, pressure, insistence, duress.

engage *v*. **1** bind, pledge, contract, commit, promise, obligate, indenture, undertake. **2** hire, lease, char-

ter, rent, reserve, book, retain, commission, appoint. **3** occupy, engross, preoccupy, interest, involve, absorb, busy, concern, grip. **4** mesh, interlock, interconnect, interact, join, dovetail.

engaged *adj*. **1** betrothed, affianced, promised, pledged. **2** occupied, busy, in use, employed, tied up, involved, working, unavailable.

ant. 2 free, available, at large, at liberty, idle.

engagement *n*. **1** appointment, obligation, promise, agreement, pledge, assurance, guarantee, commitment. **2** betrothal, troth, banns, pledge, promise. **3** encounter, conflict, battle, contest, combat, fight, skirmish, scuffle, struggle, fray, collision.

engaging *adj*. charming, winning, delightful, pleasing, attractive, winsome, captivating, enchanting, inviting, interesting, appealing, fetching, fascinating.

ant. unattractive, unappealing, uninviting, dull, boring.

engender *v*. cause, produce, generate, create, instigate, incite, foment, spawn, breed, beget, initiate, originate, bring forth.

engine *n*. motor, turbine, machine, mechanism, dynamo, generator.

engineer *n*. manager, inventor, plotter, director, planner, manipulator, operator, schemer. —*v*. devise, plot, mastermind, scheme, maneuver, machinate, intrigue, concoct, connive, finagle.

engorged *adj*. swollen, bloated, distended, tumid, congested, stuffed, satiated, glutted.

engrave *v*. **1** etch, carve, cut, scratch, chisel, inscribe, mark, print. **2** *fix in mind:* ingrain, imprint, impress, embed.

implant, inculcate, establish, stamp,

engross *v*. ABSORB.

engrossed *adj*. absorbed, involved, rapt, intrigued, fascinated, immersed, lost, occupied, engaged, busy, preoccupied.

engrossing *adj.* absorbing, fascinating, intriguing, engaging, gripping, captivating, interesting, compelling, preoccupying.
ant. boring, tedious, dull, dreary, tiresome, humdrum.

engulf *v.* envelop, overwhelm, absorb, overcome, bury, swallow, surround, submerge, deluge, swamp, cover.

enhance *v.* improve, heighten, better, intensify, strengthen, fortify, reinforce, magnify, augment, aggrandize, exalt, elevate, escalate, expand, enlarge.
ant. detract, diminish, weaken, worsen, undermine.

enigma *n.* puzzle, riddle, mystery, problem, conundrum.

enigmatic *adj.* ambiguous, puzzling, perplexing, baffling, cryptic, mystifying, obscure, inscrutable, inexplicable, confusing, bewildering, mysterious, unfathomable, incomprehensible.
ant. explicit, clear, straightforward, obvious, evident, manifest.

enjoin *v.* **1** order, direct, demand, decree, command, require, prescribe, ordain, charge, jawbone (*Slang*). **2** forbid, ban, prohibit, interdict, proscribe, prevent, bar.
ant. **2** let, permit, allow, grant, sanction, approve.

enjoy *v.* **1** savor, relish, delight in, like, revel. **2** use, possess, partake, have, own, hold, benefit, profit, utilize.

enjoyable *adj.* pleasurable, agreeable, satisfying, delightful, gratifying, fun, pleasant, nice.
ant. disagreeable, unpleasant, dissatisfying.

enjoyment *n.* pleasure, satisfaction, gratification, amusement, delectation, recreation, entertainment, fun, relish, gusto, zest.

enkindle *v.* **1** kindle, light, ignite, fire, inflame. **2** excite, inflame, stir up, arouse, awake, impassion, incite, provoke, foment, instigate.
ant. **1** douse, dampen, extinguish, quench.

enlace *v.* ENTANGLE.

enlarge *v.* increase, expand, magnify, grow, widen, broaden, augment, multiply, extend, amplify, pad, inflate, swell, distend, dilate, escalate.
ant. diminish, shrink, decrease, dwindle, contract, shorten, lessen, condense.

enlargement *n.* magnification, blowup, expansion, growth, augmentation, extension, amplification, increase.

enlighten *v.* inform, instruct, teach, educate, edify, illuminate, clarify, clear up, apprise, wise up (*Slang*).
ant. confuse, delude, confound, mislead, deceive, obfuscate.

enlightening *adj.* illuminating, revealing, instructive, helpful, edifying, informative, clarifying, educative, informing, eye-opening.
ant. obfuscatory, confusing, beclouding, muddying, unenlightening.

enlightenment *n.* learning, insight, comprehension, understanding, edification, revelation, *satori*.
ant. ignorance, error, confusion, bewilderment, delusion, obscurantism.

enlist *v.* enroll, engage, secure, obtain, procure, induce, recruit, register.

enliven *v.* animate, stimulate, spark, invigorate, vitalize, rouse, brighten, perk, excite, whet, exhilarate, inspirit, pep up.
ant. repress, dampen, dull, chill, depress, dispirit.

en masse TOGETHER.

enmesh *v.* entangle, ensnare, trap, ensnarl, involve, implicate, catch.

enmity *n.* hostility, hatred, animosity, antagonism, rancor, malice, animus, ill will, antipathy, strife, bad blood.
ant. friendship, amicability, harmony, good will, amity, affection.

ennoble *v.* improve, uplift, dignify, elevate, exalt, glorify, enhance, edify.
ant. degrade, cheapen, downgrade, debase.

ennui *n.* boredom, apathy, tedium, weariness, listlessness, lassitude, languor, doldrums, monotony, dreariness, malaise.

enormity n. **1** wickedness, baseness, depravity, sinfulness, vileness, heinousness, turpitude, evil. **2** *instance of depravity:* crime, atrocity, outrage, offense, sin, obscenity, iniquity, villainy. **3** enormousness, hugeness, vastness, largeness, immensity, amplitude.

ant. 3 smallness, insignificance, triviality, slightness.

enormous *adj.* huge, gigantic, immense, vast, monstrous, tremendous, colossal, astronomic, mountainous, titanic, elephantine, gargantuan, prodigious, stupendous.

ant. diminutive, small, petite, tiny, undersized, puny, minuscule.

enough *adj.* sufficient, ample, adequate, plenty, satisfactory.

ant. deficient, short, scanty.

enquire v. INQUIRE.

enquiry n. INQUIRY.

enrage v. anger, infuriate, aggravate, incense, madden, provoke, inflame, exasperate, make one's blood boil.

enraged *adj.* FURIOUS.

enrich v. enhance, improve, upgrade, cultivate, better, develop, endow, refine, ameliorate, step up.

ant. downgrade, degenerate, impoverish, cheapen.

enroll v. register, enlist, join, sign up, enter, matriculate, inscribe, record, list.

enrollment n. ROSTER.

ensconce v. settle, secure, nestle, snug, shelter, harbor, protect, cover, conceal, hide, blanket, screen, establish.

ensemble n. **1** totality, entirety, group, aggregate, assemblage, collection, whole, set, system. **2** suit, outfit, costume, wardrobe, toilet. **3** troupe, group, company, repertory, cast, chorus, stock company.

enshrined *adj.* cherished, hallowed, treasured, immortalized, revered, apotheosized, glorified, sanctified, venerated, worshiped, exalted.

enshroud v. COVER.

ensign n. banner, flag, pennant, standard, streamer.

enslave v. enthrall, bind, subjugate, subdue, yoke, overpower, dominate, control, subject, master.

ensnare v. entrap, snare, trick, catch, hook, bait, lure, decoy, seduce, entice, inveigle, enmesh.

ensue v. FOLLOW.

ensuing *adj.* following, subsequent, eventual, resultant, consequent, succeeding, later, next, sequent.

ant. antecedent, preceding, prior, foregoing, preliminary, previous.

ensure v. assure, insure, confirm, certify, establish, check, guarantee, secure, back, safeguard, warrant.

entail v. imply, involve, include, lead to, cause, result in, contain, encompass, comprise, embrace, necessitate, require.

entangle v. ensnare, embroil, enmesh, ensnarl, enlace, interlace, complicate, hamper, twist, stymie, snarl, web, perplex, embarrass, implicate, compromise, embroil, bewilder, mix up.

entente n. UNDERSTANDING.

enter v. **1** go in, come in, penetrate, pierce, invade, break in, board, trespass, intrude, insert, place, set, install, introduce, inject, insinuate. **2** join, enlist, enroll, sign up, affiliate. **3** begin, embark, commence, start, take up, launch, set out. **4** record, inscribe, register, note, log, list, post.

enterprise n. **1** undertaking, task, project, venture, job, endeavor, attempt, gamble, campaign, program. **2** boldness, initiative, ambition, drive, determination, push, ingenuity.

enterprising *adj.* bold, inventive, venturesome, ambitious, resourceful, aggressive, energetic, daring, intrepid, forceful, up-and-coming, adventurous, innovative.

ant. timid, meek, cautious, apathetic, lazy, indolent.

entertain v. **1** amuse, divert, engage, interest, engross, beguile. **2** receive, welcome, fete, wine, dine, regale. **3** contemplate, harbor, consider, cherish, hold, nurture, imagine, support, foster.

entertaining *adj.* amusing, diverting, funny, witty, sportive, humorous, interesting, engrossing.
ant. dull, tedious, dry, flat, uninteresting.

entertainment *n.* amusement, diversion, pleasure, fun, enjoyment, sport, show, pastime, performance, recreation, divertissement.

enthrall *v.* charm, fascinate, captivate, beguile, spellbind, rivet, seduce, bewitch, ravish, entrance, enrapture, hypnotize, transfix, enslave, overcome, overpower.

enthusiasm *n.* zeal, eagerness, ardor, zest, devotion, ebullience, fervor, passion, avidness, avidity, relish, warmth, heat.
ant. indifference, half-heartedness, apathy, coolness, listlessness.

enthusiast *n.* fan, aficionado, devotee, supporter, buff, booster, faddist, fanatic, follower, disciple, amateur, freak (*Slang*), nut (*Slang*).

enthusiastic *adj.* ardent, zealous, eager, whole-hearted, earnest, avid, fervent, hearty, impassioned.
ant. indifferent, lukewarm, half-hearted, apathetic, cool.

entice *v.* lure, tempt, attract, seduce, decoy, bait, lead on, inveigle, draw on, allure.

entire *adj.* complete, whole, total, full, livelong, unabridged, perfect, all-inclusive, plenary, integral, aggregate, intact, of a piece, undivided, unbroken, unitary, single.
ant. partial, incomplete, fragmentary, divided.

entirely *adj.* WHOLLY.

entirety *n.* UNITY.

entitle *v.* **1** authorize, qualify, empower, enable, permit, accredit, warrant, sanction, license, enfranchise, charter. **2** designate, name, call, title, style, dub, term, label, tag, christen.

entity *n.* thing, object, individual, person, organism, being, substance, re-

ality, existence, subsistence, presence, occurrence.

entomb *v.* bury, inter, inhume, cover, box in, incarcerate, immure, hide, enclose.
ant. exhume, uncover, dig up, unearth.

entombment *n.* BURIAL.

entourage *n.* associates, companions, attendants, retinue, cortege, escort, following, bodyguard, suite, train.

entr'acte *n.* INTERLUDE.

entrails *n.* viscera, guts, bowels, intestines, insides, innards.

entrance[1] *n.* **1** hallway, foyer, antechamber, vestibule, passageway, threshold, portal, gate, doorway, ingress, corridor, approach, access. **2** admission, admittance, entry, entrée, access, ingress, reception, acceptance.

entrance[2] *v.* **1** delight, charm, enrapture, fascinate, enchant, allure, enthrall, transport, spellbind. **2** hypnotize, bewitch, magnetize, mesmerize, hex.

entrancing *adj.* CHARMING.

entrant *n.* CONTESTANT.

entrap *v.* capture, catch, snare, bag, hook, nail, net, enmesh, trick, deceive, ensnare, entangle, entice, implicate, decoy, inveigle, involve, rope in.

entreat *v.* beg, plead, implore, beseech, pray, petition, urge, supplicate, request, press, adjure.

entreaty *n.* plea, supplication, request, prayer, cry, petition, suit, appeal, adjuration, invocation.

entrée *n.* ENTRY.

entrenched *adj.* established, fixed, rooted, stuck, ingrained, implanted, embedded, settled, ensconced, deep-seated, deep-rooted, profound.

entrust *v.* commit, commend, consign, charge, delegate, depute, vest, confide, invest, trust.

entry *n.* entrance, arrival, ingress, entrée, access, ingoing, penetration, intrusion, incursion, influx.

entwine *v.* TWIST.

enumerate *v.* list, tally, cite, detail, itemize, specify, catalog, inventory, count, numerate, tabulate.

enumeration *n.* LIST.

enunciate *v.* pronounce, articulate, utter, voice, vocalize, express, inflect, sound.

envelop *v.* engulf, enclose, wrap, surround, enfold, enwrap, encompass, encase, encircle, gird, embrace.

envelope *n.* wrapper, cover, jacket, cast, sheath, case, shell, hull, coating, skin, blanket, integument.

envenom *v.* POISON.

envious *adj.* jealous, grudging, covetous, greedy, jaundiced, green, resentful, petty, spiteful.
ant. generous, kind, open, giving, charitable.

environ *v.* SURROUND.

environment *n.* habitat, surroundings, ecosystem, medium, biosphere, milieu, atmosphere, climate, ambiance, scenery, background.

environs *n.* outskirts, suburbs, vicinity, neighborhood, outpost, surroundings, exurb.

envisage *v.* visualize, picture, imagine, conceive, conceptualize.

envision *v.* contemplate, see, foresee, anticipate, predict, view, regard, envisage.

envoy *n.* emissary, delegate, agent, messenger, ambassador, representative, legate, courier, minister, nuncio, *chargé d'affaires,* attaché.

envy *n.* jealousy, resentment, covetousness, greed, cupidity, spite, rivalry.
—*v.* begrudge, resent, grudge, be jealous of, want, crave, covet.

enwrap *v.* ENVELOP.

ephemeral *adj.* short-lived, transitory, brief, transient, passing, temporal, temporary, momentary, fleeting, perishable, evanescent, unstable.
ant. permanent, enduring, lasting, durable, stable, perpetual, abiding, constant.

epic *adj.* noble, grand, legendary, heroic, dramatic, exalted, sublime, lyric, Homeric, mythic.

epicene *adj.* ANDROGYNOUS.

epicure *n.* gourmet, epicurian, *bon vivant,* gastronomer, gourmand, hedonist, sensualist, sybarite, glutton, voluptuary.

epidemic *adj.* widespread, prevalent, far-reaching, pandemic, rife, rampant, general, extensive, wide-ranging, pervasive, sweeping.
ant. limited, contained, isolated.

epidermis *n.* SKIN.

epigram *n.* aphorism, adage, saying, *bon mot,* proverb, maxim, witticism, dictum, apothegm, slogan.

epigrammatic *adj.* pithy, witty, terse, pointed, biting, laconic, succinct, trenchant, aphoristic, apothegmatic.

epilogue *n.* SUPPLEMENT.

epiphany *n.* INSIGHT.

episode *n.* incident, occurrence, happening, event, circumstance, affair, scene, matter, business, adventure, experience, digression, interval, situation.

episodic *adj.* sporadic, intermittent, rambling, disjointed, digressive, aimless, disconnected, fitful, parenthetical, interpolative, disorganized, anecdotal.

epistle *n.* letter, missive, message, correspondence, communication, encyclical, circular.

epithet *n.* name, title, label, tag, designation, appellation, nickname, sobriquet, ascription.

epitome *n.* embodiment, essence, model, example, archetype, paradigm, prototype, substance, gist, abstract, abridgment, summary, condensation, synopsis, digest, précis, compendium.

epitomize *v.* typify, embody, represent, exemplify, encapsulate, condense, boil down.

epoch *n.* era, age, time, period, eon, generation, interval.

equable *adj.* serene, steady, tranquil, composed, equanimous, imperturbable, unruffled, even-tempered, unflappable.
ant. excitable, temperamental, quick-tempered, agitated, unstable.

equal *adj.* **1** identical, same, similar, alike, even, equivalent, uniform, parallel, tantamount, comparable, balanced, level, egalitarian, equalitarian. **2** fair, impartial, just, evenhanded, unbiased. —*v.* equalize, balance, even, level, rival, match, compare, parallel, amount to. —*n.* peer, rival, fellow, compeer, match, coequal.

   ant. *adj.* **1** disparate, unlike, uneven, lopsided. **2** biased, unfair, partial, prejudiced.

equalitarian *adj.* EQUAL.

equality *n.* parity, sameness, similarity, identity, equation, equivalence, likeness, uniformity, egalitarianism.

   ant. inequality, disparity, discrepancy.

equalize *v.* standardize, homogenize, regularize, smooth, balance, level, even.

equanimity *n.* serenity, calmness, repose, poise, self-possession, tranquility, composure, aplomb, imperturbability, self-control, coolness, placidity, *sang-froid*.

equate *v.* identify, liken, compare, match.

equation *n.* EQUALITY.

equilibrium *n.* **1** balance, stability, equipoise, steadiness, evenness, counterpoise, symmetry. **2** serenity, equanimity, steadiness, composure, poise, levelheadedness, self-control, stability.

equip *v.* furnish, supply, provide, attire, array, implement, outfit, arm, gird, rig, appoint, stock, endow, accouter.

equipage *n.* EQUIPMENT.

equipment *n.* supplies, gear, apparatus, furnishings, paraphernalia, rig, equipage, accouterment, materiel.

equipoise *n.* EQUILIBRIUM.

equitable *adj.* fair, just, evenhanded, impartial, objective, disinterested, unbiased, equal, proper, due, honorable, rightful.

   ant. biased, partial, prejudiced, unjust, uneven.

equity *n.* fairness, impartiality, justness, uprightness, justice, evenhandedness, fairmindedness, equitableness, fair shake (*Slang*).

equivalence *n.* EQUALITY.

equivalent *adj.* equal, alike, analogous, reciprocal, tantamount, same, similar, comparable, commensurate, interchangeable, homologous, isomorphic.

equivocal *adj.* ambiguous, indeterminate, vague, oblique, uncertain, doubtful, hazy, enigmatic, oracular, amphibolic, obscure.

   ant. definite, clear, precise, certain, specific, unequivocal, explicit, clearcut.

equivocate *v.* evade, quibble, hedge, fudge, temporize, tergiversate, dodge, dissemble, waffle, shuffle, sidestep, pussyfoot, straddle, back off, hem and haw.

era *n.* age, epoch, time, period, generation, cycle.

eradicate *v.* uproot, remove, extirpate, extract, destroy, demolish, abolish, erase, eliminate, wipe out, exterminate, kill, annihilate.

erase *v.* remove, eradicate, obliterate, efface, cancel, delete, strike out, expunge, wipe out, scratch.

erect *v.* **1** construct, build, raise, assemble, set up, mount, rear, fabricate, manufacture. **2** establish, formulate, construct, create, organize, found, devise, institute, frame.

erection *n.* construction, building, fabrication, raising, assembly, manufacture, formation.

ergo *adv.* THEREFORE.

erode *v.* eat, consume, corrode, wear, gnaw, abrade, grind.

erogenous *adj.* EROTIC.

erosion *n.* WEAR.

erotic *adj.* **1** amatory, erogenous, aphrodisiac, carnal, fleshly, prurient, sensual, sexy, raunchy (*Slang*). **2** passionate, amorous, voluptuous, lustful, libidinous, lewd, lecherous, lascivious, wanton, concupiscent, horny (*Slang*), hot (*Slang*).

err *v.* misjudge, miscalculate, blunder, slip, misconstrue, lapse, sin, trespass, offend, stray, transgress, misbehave, go wrong, bungle.

errand *n.* mission, venture, assignment, task, pursuit, undertaking.

errant *adj.* wayward, astray, deviate, devious, straying, aberrant, digressive.

erratic *adj.* eccentric, odd, peculiar, queer, capricious, deviant, abnormal, unpredictable, whimsical, changeable, straying, variable, aberrant, planetary, vacillating, volatile.
ant. normal, predictable, steady, regular, orderly.

erratum *n.* ERROR.

erroneous *adj.* wrong, false, incorrect, mistaken, untrue, inaccurate, faulty, fallacious, unfounded, invalid, unsound, inexact, off base, all wet (*Slang*).
ant. correct, proper, right, true, factual, valid, sound, accurate.

error *n.* **1** wrongness, wrongheadedness, fallaciousness, erroneousness, unsoundness. **2** mistake, inaccuracy, delusion, blunder, fallacy, untruth, oversight, erratum, miscalculation, misunderstanding, solecism, boo-boo (*Slang*). **3** fault, sin, transgression, wrongdoing, misdeed, vice, shortcoming, offense, misstep, delinquency, defect.

ersatz *adj., n.* SUBSTITUTE.

erstwhile *adj.* FORMER.

eruct *v.* BELCH.

erudite *adj.* learned, scholarly, knowledgeable, well-read, educated, lettered, literate, bookish, intellectual, pedantic, polymath, encyclopedic.
ant. illiterate, unlettered, ignorant, semiliterate.

erudition *n.* knowledge, learning, scholarship, literacy, proficiency, expertise, culture.

erupt *v.* burst, explode, gush, spout, spew, eject, discharge, hurl, rupture.

eruption *n.* outbreak, outburst, explosion, blowup, flare-up, sally, surge, rush, emanation.

escalate *v.* increase, intensify, expand, widen, magnify, heighten, amplify, step up, build up, aggravate, worsen, sharpen, deepen, enlarge.
ant. wind down, de-escalate, diminish, lessen, wane, abate, phase down.

escapade *n.* adventure, prank, caper, lark, antic, fling, spree.

escape *v.* **1** flee, run, fly, decamp, clear out, make off, abscond, skip. **2** elude, avoid, evade, dodge, shun, avert, skirt, circumvent. **3** leak, seep, ooze, issue, emanate, stream, emerge, flow, exude. —*n.* flight, getaway, break, exodus, deliverance, rescue, evasion, avoidance.

escapist *n.* dreamer, daydreamer, visionary, romantic, fantasist, utopian, Walter Mitty.

eschew *v.* shun, avoid, forswear, forgo, renounce, abstain, abandon, refrain from, swear off, give up, steer clear of, reject, spurn, abjure.

escort *v.* accompany, conduct, attend, usher, guide, lead, flank, support, chaperon. —*n.* companion, attendant, squire, partner, date, chaperon, bodyguard, guide, protector, retinue, entourage, cortege, convoy.

esculent *adj.* EDIBLE.

esoteric *adj.* abstruse, profound, deep, arcane, recondite, obscure, hidden, mysterious, enigmatic, cryptic, cabalistic, occult, difficult.
ant. intelligible, literal, accessible, clear, understandable, exoteric.

especial *adj.* exceptional, outstanding, special, particular, noteworthy, specific, specified, individual, uncommon, unique, extraordinary, unusual.
ant. general, ordinary, common, usual, commonplace.

especially *adv.* particularly, notably, principally, chiefly, specifically, expressly, precisely.

espial *n.* DISCOVERY.

esplanade *n.* AVENUE.

espouse *v.* adopt, embrace, support, maintain, take up, champion, defend, advocate, promulgate, favor, go in for, boost.

ant. reject, shun, repudiate, disown, spurn.

esprit *n.* SPIRIT.

esprit de corps solidarity, fellowship, fraternity, community, togetherness, morale, comradeship, camaraderie, brotherhood, sisterhood.

espy *v.* see, sight, observe, notice, discover, view, perceive, glimpse, spy, discern, descry, behold, make out, spot, witness, catch sight of.

essay *v.* try, attempt, endeavor, strive, undertake, venture, aim. —*n.* **1** composition, article, editorial, paper, monograph, theme, tract, treatise, discourse, dissertation. **2** endeavor, effort, attempt, trial, venture, purpose, undertaking, struggle, experiment, try, enterprise.

essence *n.* **1** nature, quintessence, quiddity, gist, substance, kernel, pith, core, heart, characteristic, marrow, lifeblood, soul, crux. **2** elixir, extract, distillation, concentrate.

essential *adj.* substantial, basic, fundamental, intrinsic, cardinal, primary, elementary, necessary, vital, indispensable, requisite, crucial. —*n.* necessity, basic, rudiment, element, fundamental, nitty-gritty (*Slang*).

ant. *adj.* incidental, accidental, peripheral, secondary, accessory, marginal.

establish *v.* **1** settle, fix, secure, entrench, ground, root, emplant, ensconce, consolidate, install, found, set up, institute, organize, create, place, enact, ordain, ratify, decree. **2** prove, substantiate, confirm, demonstrate, verify, authenticate.

establishment *n.* foundation, institution, enterprise, concern, association, business, firm, company, corporation, organization.

estate *n.* **1** property, possessions, wealth, fortune, belongings, goods, assets, effects, land, holdings, real estate, manor, plantation. **2** condition, state, status, situation, circumstance, lot, place, predicament.

esteem *n.* regard, respect, admiration, repute, honor, homage, approval, deference. —*v.* **1** value, prize, treasure, admire, praise, commend, respect, venerate, revere, appreciate. **2** deem, consider, regard, judge, think, hold, believe.

ant. *n.* scorn, disdain, contempt, disrespect, derision, ridicule. *v.* **1** scorn, deride, disdain, mock, insult, belittle, put down (*Slang*), dishonor.

estimable *adj.* reputable, honorable, worthy, laudable, exemplary, praiseworthy, admirable, commendable, venerable, august.

ant. contemptible, dishonorable, ridiculous, discredited, disgraced.

estimate *v.* calculate, guess, gauge, judge, evaluate, reckon, assess, figure, compute, consider, size up, weigh, ascertain. —*n.* guess, calculation, judgment, assessment, estimation, opinion, evaluation, valuation, appraisal, guesstimate (*Slang*).

estimation *n.* ESTIMATE.

estranged *adj.* alienated, disaffected, dissociated, disunited, at odds, on the outs, separated, irreconcilable, parted, removed, split, weaned.

etch *v.* engrave, stamp, impress, imprint, inscribe, carve, ingrain.

eternal *adj.* **1** *having no end:* everlasting, endless, perpetual, unending, undying, immortal, permanent, enduring, imperishable, incessant, unceasing, interminable, ceaseless, persistent, continuous, perennial, constant. **2** *independent of time:* timeless, ageless, unchangeable, immutable, indestructible, incorruptible.

ant. 1, 2 temporary, transitory, perishable, mortal, ephemeral, evanescent, transient, fleeting, short-lived, momentary, limited.

ethereal *adj.* light, airy, fine, subtle, exquisite, refined, rare, delicate, intangible, insubstantial, tenuous, rarefied, attenuated, spiritual.

ant. gross, crude, coarse, dense, thick, heavy, crass.

ethical *adj.* **1** moral, normative, prescriptive, deontological, moralistic. **2**

just, righteous, virtuous, moral, correct, proper, honest, good, upright, honorable, principled, decent, conscientious, scrupulous.

ant. 2 improper, immoral, dishonest, unethical, corrupt, unscrupulous, shady, crooked.

etiology *n.* cause, origin, attribution, derivation, responsibility, blame, source.

etiquette *n.* manners, customs, usage, decorum, protocol, formalities, convention, civility, courtesy, propriety, politeness, amenities, rules.

eulogize *v.* praise, laud, extol, glorify, applaud, celebrate, commend, compliment, honor, pay tribute.

eulogy *n.* praise, tribute, glorification, encomium, panegyric, homage, paean, accolade, testimonial.

euphonic *adj.* EUPHONIOUS.

euphonious *adj.* mellifluous, melodious, dulcet, mellow, harmonious, musical, consonant, euphonic, sweet, pleasant, agreeable, silvery.

ant. harsh, grating, hoarse, rasping, jarring, jangling, raucous.

evacuate *v.* **1** abandon, withdraw, desert, vacate, quit, leave, depart, retreat, pull out, forsake, decamp, clear out. **2** excrete, discharge, eject, empty, void, eliminate, defecate.

evacuation *n.* WITHDRAWAL.

evade *v.* escape, elude, avoid, dodge, shun, foil, neglect, shirk, duck, ditch, circumvent, sidestep, get around.

evaluate *v.* appraise, estimate, judge, assess, rate, weigh, calculate, reckon, gauge, size up.

evaluation *n.* appraisal, estimation, judgment, rating, assessment, opinion.

evanesce *v.* VANISH.

evanescent *adj.* ephemeral, passing, fleeting, short-lived, brief, fugitive, transient, momentary, swift, volatile.

ant. permanent, stable, lasting, enduring, durable.

evangelist *n.* MISSIONARY.

evaporate *v.* vanish, disappear, fade,

dissipate, volatilize, evanesce, dissolve, melt.

evasion *n.* subterfuge, avoidance, equivocation, dissemblance, deceit, concealment, cover-up, dodging, hedging, ducking.

evasive *adj.* equivocal, indirect, hedging, elusive, shifty, cagey, dissembling, oblique, unresponsive, fudging, wily, deceptive, tricky, misleading, casuistic.

ant. direct, candid, straightforward, forthright.

eve *n.* EVENING.

even *adj.* **1** flat, smooth, level, regular, plane, flush, straight, horizontal. **2** steady, constant, uniform, unvarying, equable, easy, stable, placid, calm, unruffled, serene, tranquil. **3** equal, fair, parallel, on a par, just, square, similar, comparable, commensurate, equitable, balanced, matching. —*v.* equalize, adjust, balance, match, square, accommodate, rectify, stabilize, level.

ant. *adj.* **1** rough, jagged, lumpy, uneven, askew. **2** irregular, variable, fluctuating, jumpy, unstable, excitable. **3** disparate, unequal, unfair, biased, favored, privileged.

evenhanded *adj.* FAIR.

evening *n.* **1** dusk, twilight, nightfall, eve, sundown, sunset, eventide, soirée. **2** decline, decay, wane, age, twilight, autumn, last legs, swan song.

evenly *adv.* FAIRLY.

evenness *n.* **1** smoothness, flatness, levelness, straightness. **2** steadiness, constancy, stability, placidity, equanimity, tranquillity, poise, serenity. **3** parity, equality, similarity, fairness, equitability, impartiality, balance.

ant. 1 roughness, bumpiness, unevenness. **2** volatility, jumpiness, moodiness, nervousness. **3** inequality, unsuitability, incongruity, bias, partiality.

event *n.* occurrence, happening, episode, incident, fact, circumstance, phenomenon, affair, matter, business, adventure, experience, milestone.

eventful *adj.* memorable, fateful, busy, lively, adventurous, active.
    ant. uneventful, empty, insignificant, trivial.

eventual *adj.* ultimate, final, inevitable, ensuing, subsequent, resultant, consequent, succeeding, future, later.

eventuality *n.* possibility, contingency, probability, chance, likelihood.

eventually *adv.* ULTIMATELY.

eventuate *v.* RESULT.

ever *adv.* ALWAYS.

everlasting *adj.* eternal, endless, perpetual, enduring, immortal, unending, imperishable, permanent, timeless, infinite, sempiternal.
    ant. temporary, limited, transitory, mortal, ephemeral, passing, shortlived.

evermore *adv.* ALWAYS.

everyday *adj.* **1** daily, day after day, quotidian. **2** common, usual, regular, ordinary, routine, habitual, mundane, commonplace, workaday, run-of-the-mill, frequent, prevalent.
    ant. 2 rare, unusual, extraordinary, infrequent, special, exceptional.

evict *v.* expel, dispossess, oust, remove, put out.

evidence *n.* proof, grounds, indication, data, facts, information, confirmation, substantiation, corroboration, documentation, testimony, exhibit.

evident *adj.* obvious, manifest, clear, apparent, plain, palpable, patent, tangible, demonstrable, unmistakable, certain, undeniable, indubitable, incontrovertible.
    ant. obscure, uncertain, doubtful, questionable, unsure.

evidently *adv.* apparently, seemingly, probably, ostensibly, obviously, clearly, plainly, unquestionably.

evil *adj.* **1** wicked, sinful, depraved, vile, villainous, black-hearted, vicious, bad, malevolent, evil-minded, maleficent, immoral, base, nefarious, unscrupulous, corrupt, venal, foul. **2** injurious, harmful, hurtful, perni-

cious, deleterious, unlucky, disastrous, detrimental, ruinous, calamitous, baneful, noxious, dire, insidious. **—n. 1** sinfulness, depravity, wickedness, crime, vice, iniquity, turpitude, baseness, degeneracy, villainy. **2** harm, injury, misfortune, adversity, catastrophe, ill, misery, affliction, disaster, mischief, calamity, woe.
    ant. *adj.* **1** good, just, virtuous, decent, noble, upright, moral, righteous. **2** beneficial, fortunate, lucky. *n.* **1** virtue, goodness, righteousness, rectitude, justness, saintliness.

evil-minded *adj.* EVIL.

evince *v.* display, show, manifest, exhibit, reveal, demonstrate, suggest, signify, express, present, indicate.

evoke *v.* summon, elicit, arouse, awaken, provoke, educe, call forth, induce, excite, draw, conjure up.

evolution *n.* development, progression, unfolding, change, metamorphosis, progress, growth, elaboration.

evolve *v.* develop, unfold, ripen, mature, grow, advance, progress, work out, unravel, become.

exacerbate *v.* aggravate, intensify, worsen, irritate, deepen, magnify, heighten, exaggerate, embitter, sour.
    ant. soothe, comfort, relieve, ease, alleviate, mitigate, soften, lessen, mollify, assuage.

exact *adj.* **1** definite, precise, explicit, express, unequivocal, specific, strict, careful, detailed, determinate, distinct. **2** accurate, correct, perfect, faultless, right, faithful, literal, true. **—v.** demand, insist, require, call for, compel, extort, impose, squeeze, extract.
    ant. *adj.* **1, 2** inexact, approximate, indeterminate, hazy, vague, fuzzy, ambiguous.

exacting *adj.* demanding, strict, meticulous, fastidious, finicky, particular, punctilious, rigorous, sever, stringent, unsparing, stern, difficult.
    ant. lenient, easygoing, lax, loose, flexible, relaxed.

exactness *n.* accuracy, precision, correctness, perfection, fidelity, faultlessness, exactitude.

exaggerate *v.* overstate, overrate, inflate, puff, overestimate, color, embroider, embellish, lay it on, oversell, boast, stretch, magnify, expand, heighten.

ant. minimize, belittle, underestimate, understate, underrate, depreciate.

exaggeration *n.* hyperbole, extravagance, caricature, puffery, tall tale, overstatement, embellishment, overkill.

ant. understatement, depreciation.

exalt *v.* GLORIFY.

exalted *adj.* extolled, esteemed, revered, august, noted, illustrious, glorified, venerated, praised, honored, ennobled, dignified.

ant. denigrated, ridiculed, belittled, downgraded, debased, humiliated, humbled, put down (*Slang*).

exam *n.* EXAMINATION.

examination *n.* inspection, scrutiny, observation, study, checkup, analysis, probe, test, quiz, exam, inquiry, inquest, investigation, interrogation, trial, questioning.

examine *v.* **1** inspect, scrutinize, investigate, probe, explore, study, analyze, test, quiz, question. **2** interrogate, cross-examine, try, hear, query, question, grill, pump.

example *n.* **1** specimen, sample, model, type, prototype, representation, illustration, instance, archetype, mockup, exemplar, paragon, exemplification. **2** warning, lesson, caution, precedent, test case.

exasperate *v.* irritate, annoy, infuriate, irk, vex, anger, enrage, exacerbate, needle, incense, rankle.

exasperating *adj.* ANNOYING.

excavate *v.* hollow, scoop, dig, unearth, mine, quarry, burrow, gouge.

excavation *n.* DITCH.

exceed *v.* surpass, outdo, outdistance, top, better, overshoot, excel, transcend, outstrip, beat, overdo, overstep, pass.

exceeding *adj.* EXTRAORDINARY.

exceedingly *adv.* extremely, exceptionally, too, very, inordinately, unusually, excessively, enormously, vastly.

excel *v.* outdo, surpass, outshine, outclass, outstrip, outdistance, top, eclipse, best, predominate, take precedence.

excellence *n.* superiority, distinction, eminence, fineness, supremacy, preeminence, superlativeness, virtuosity, genius.

ant. mediocrity, inferiority, inadequacy, deficiency, imperfection.

excellent *adj.* superior, exceptional, remarkable, great, splendid, nonpareil, unsurpassed, superb, outstanding, magnificent, surpassing, superlative, capital, choice, fine, unexcelled, bonny, first-class, first-rate, A-one, A-OK, top-notch, top-drawer, wonderful, tops (*Slang*), corking (*Slang*), super (*Slang*), nifty (*Slang*), swell (*Slang*), bang-up (*Slang*), topping (*Brit.*).

ant. mediocre, average, so-so, inferior, inadequate, deficient, secondrate, rotten, imperfect, defective, worthless.

except *v.* omit, exclude, leave out, reject, bar, eliminate, overlook, excuse, neglect, ignore, disregard, dismiss, elide.

exception *n.* **1** anomaly, irregularity, deviation, aberration, peculiarity, departure, oddity, eccentric, maverick, nonconformist, black sheep. **2** objection, complaint, quibble, disagreement, offense, demurral, dissent, challenge, criticism, caveat.

exceptional *adj.* outstanding, remarkable, extraordinary, unusual, uncommon, rare, unique, singular, special, unparalleled, phenomenal, noteworthy, atypical, wonderful.

ant. common, ordinary, usual, normal, customary, everyday, unexceptional, typical.

excerpt *n.* passage, extract, quotation, citation, selection, fragment, clipping.

excess *n.* **1** overabundance, surplus, superfluity, glut, oversupply, superabundance, plethora, overage, redundancy, profusion, surfeit, overload, overdose. **2** overindulgence, intemperance, extravagance, immoderation, profligacy, exorbitance, dissipation, dissoluteness.
ant. 1 shortage, lack, need, dearth, shortfall, deficiency, want. **2** moderation, temperance, self-control, frugality, abstinence, abstemiousness, austerity, asceticism.

excessive *adj.* immoderate, extreme, inordinate, overdone, overmuch, too much, exorbitant, outrageous, unreasonable, undue, redundant, cloying.
ant. moderate, reasonable, conservative, scanty, meager, spare.

exchange *n.* **1** barter, trade, swapping, traffic, interchange, give-and-take, reciprocity, banter, intercourse, repartee. **2** substitution, replacement, quid pro quo, alternate, surrogate.
—*v.* trade, swap, barter, convert, change, reciprocate, retaliate, requite, replace, substitute, alternate.

excitable *adj.* temperamental, highstrung, quick-tempered, emotional, hotheaded, hasty, irritable, volatile, moody, jumpy, irascible, nervous, edgy, passionate.
ant. calm, even, tranquil, placid, phlegmatic, cool, serene, self-controlled, equable, sedate.

excitation *n.* EXCITEMENT.

excite *v.* stimulate, arouse, animate, elate, evoke, stir, awaken, kindle, provoke, incite, foment, instigate, fire, agitate, galvanize, whet, precipitate, cause.

excitement *n.* **1** stimulation, agitation, arousal, excitation, electricity, provocation, ferment, flap (*Slang*), hoopla (*Slang*), frenzy, fever, fervor, heat. **2** kick, thrill, adventure, sensation.

exciting *adj.* stirring, rousing, thrilling, breathtaking, hair-raising, dramatic, electrifying, sensational, stimulating, titillating, provocative.
ant. dull, quiet, stodgy, flat, lifeless, tepid.

exclaim *v.* cry, shout, utter, blurt, clamor, ejaculate, proclaim.

exclamation *n.* outcry, clamor, expletive, utterance, ejaculation, interjection.

exclude *v.* **1** shut out, bar, debar, keep out. **2** leave out, omit, ignore, count out, except, pass over.
ant. 1 invite, ask in. **2** consider, evaluate, include, dwell on.

exclusive *adj.* **1** restrictive, restricted, select, private, discriminative, cliquish, clannish, personal, individual, unique, sole. **2** expensive, high-class, fancy, chic, fashionable, luxurious, elegant, posh (*Slang*). **3** complete, undivided, total, absolute, entire.
ant. 1 public, open, general, shared, common, collective, communal. **2** moderate, inexpensive, unpretentious, modest. **3** partial, half-hearted, divided.

excoriate *v.* **1** scratch, abrade, scrape, flay, chafe, skin, scarify. **2** denounce, assail, castigate, upbraid, berate, censure, condemn, reproach, criticize, vilify, revile, attack, chew out (*Slang*), scold.

excrement *n.* refuse, waste, feces, dung, stool, excreta, ordure, droppings, turd, crap.

excrescence *n.* growth, swelling, protuberance, tumor.

excreta *n.* EXCREMENT.

excrete *v.* evacuate, eliminate, void, discharge, defecate, expel, eject, exude.

excruciating *adj.* agonizing, acute, painful, searing, tormenting, punishing, grueling, racking, severe, torturous, unbearable, poignant, piercing, burning.

exculpate *v.* exonerate, clear, acquit, vindicate, absolve, excuse, pardon.
ant. incriminate, indict, charge, accuse, blame, convict.

excursion *n.* **1** outing, tour, cruise, trip, jaunt, junket, expedition, voyage. **2** digression, deviation, shift, sidetracking, departure, diversion, episode, tangent.

excusable *adj.* defensible, extenuating, justified, understandable, pardonable, forgivable, venial. **ant.** inexcusable, unforgivable, unpardonable, blameworthy, indefensible.

excuse *v.* **1** pardon, forgive, overlook, exonerate, absolve, condone, acquit, reprieve, amnesty, minimize, disregard, make allowances, tolerate. **2** release, dismiss, free, exempt, relieve, discharge, let off. —*n.* reason, explanation, alibi, defense, plea, pretext, rationalization, exemption, release.

execrable *adj.* abominable, accursed, hateful, appalling, abhorrent, despicable, damnable, odious, vile, detestable, loathsome, horrible.

execrate *v.* curse, condemn, revile, damn, excoriate, imprecate, anathematize, vilify, vituperate.

execration *n.* ABOMINATION.

execute *v.* **1** carry out, perform, effect, accomplish, do, achieve, exercise, complete, fulfill, discharge, consummate, administer, enforce, prosecute, finalize. **2** put to death, kill, dispatch.

execution *n.* **1** implementation, achievement, accomplishment, discharge, consummation, effectuation, performance, completion. **2** capital punishment, death penalty. **3** manner, style, expression, skill, touch, flair, delivery, rendition.

executive *adj.* managerial, directing, controlling, governing, supervisory, administrative, official. —*n.* official, director, administrator, officer, leadership, administration, management, hierarchy, higher-ups.

exegesis *n.* analysis, interpretation, exposition, explanation, commentary, elucidation, annotation.

exemplar *n.* model, pattern, paragon, ideal, nonpareil, example, standard, precedent, original, criterion, prototype.

exemplary *adj.* **1** commendable, admirable, estimable, nonpareil, superior, laudable, praiseworthy, worthy, ideal. **2** illustrative, representative, typical, characteristic, prototypical. **ant. 1** reprehensible, regrettable, wretched, worthless.

exemplify *v.* epitomize, illustrate, typify, embody, stand for, personify, symbolize, represent, depict, characterize, encapsulate, summarize.

exempt *adj.* free, excused, spared, clear, released, relieved, excepted, absolved, special, immune, pardoned, privileged, favored. **ant.** subject, accountable, responsible, answerable, liable, bound.

exercise *v.* **1** train, drill, work out, practice, condition, shape up, discipline, rehearse. **2** employ, use, wield, utilize, apply, exploit, enjoy, avail oneself of, take advantage. **3** perform, execute, apply, pursue, discharge, carry out, prosecute. —*n.* **1** execution, application, implementation, fulfillment, action, accomplishment. **2** workout, training, practice, discipline, drill, calisthenics, regimen, rehearsal. **3** problem, lesson, study, drill, task, homework, assignment.

exercised *adj.* harassed, agitated, distressed, upset, excited, concerned, perturbed, vexed, troubled, annoyed, beset, put upon. **ant.** calm, cool, composed, indifferent, unconcerned, unperturbed, unruffled.

exert *v.* apply, put forth, wield, use, employ, exercise, expend.

exertion *n.* work, effort, toil, labor, strain, exercise, struggle, pains, application, sweat.

exhaust *v.* **1** wear out, tire, fatigue, weaken, sap, enervate, enfeeble, weary, debilitate, devitalize, poop (*Slang*). **2** deplete, consume, use up, drain, empty, dissipate, expend, run out of, spend.

exhausted *adj.* **1** used up, spent, con-

sumed, drained, dissipated, emptied, depleted, gone. **2** fatigued, weary, worn out, tired, played out, jaded, weak, spent, done in, bushed, prostrate, tuckered out, pooped (*Slang*).
ant. 2 lively, refreshed, energetic, enlivened, invigorated, animated.

exhausting *adj.* tiring, wearying, fatiguing, arduous, grueling, taxing, debilitating, enervating, hard, strenuous.

exhaustion *n.* fatigue, weariness, tiredness, weakness, prostration, debility, collapse.

exhaustive *adj.* thorough, complete, full, total, comprehensive, all-inclusive, sweeping, intensive, deep, profound, thoroughgoing, radical, searching, in-depth.
ant. cursory, perfunctory, partial, sketchy, inadequate, incomplete, superficial.

exhibit *v.* display, present, expose, show, reveal, evince, manifest, evidence, demonstrate, express, indicate. —*n.* showing, exhibition, display, exposition, spectacle, retrospective.

exhibition *n.* showing, presentation, exposition, fair, display, demonstration, spectacle, exhibit.

exhilarate *v.* enliven, cheer, stimulate, elate, exalt, animate, invigorate, gladden, inspirit, perk up, quicken, hearten, energize.
ant. dampen, depress, sour, dispirit, discourage, deject, dishearten.

exhort *v.* urge, persuade, encourage, recommend, plead, spur, incite, prompt, entreat, press, goad, prod, admonish, caution, advise, enjoin.

exhortation *n.* advice, persuasion, counsel, entreaty, insistence, encouragement, plea, injunction, sermon, caution, warning, admonition.

exhume *v.* disinter, unearth, dig up, disentomb.

exigency *n.* **1** urgency, emergency, pressure, stress, necessity, imperativeness, crisis, fix, pinch, difficulty, strait, extremity, predicament. **2** requirement, need, demand, necessity.

exigent *adj.* critical, urgent, pressing, necessary, crucial, imperative, demanding, exacting, insistent, importunate, strict, stringent, tough.

exiguous *adj.* SCANTY.

exile *n.* **1** banishment, expatriation, expulsion, deportation, ostracism, extradition. **2** expatriate, deportee, displaced person, DP, émigré, refugee. —*v.* expel, oust, banish, deport, expatriate.

exist *v.* **1** be, stand, subsist, live, endure, stay, persist, prevail, abide, last, remain, breathe, survive. **2** occur, happen, take place, obtain, hold, arise, materialize.

existence *n.* being, subsistence, reality, actuality, living, breathing, persistence, presence, occurrence, situation, condition, state, life.

existent *adj.* LIVING.

exit *n.* **1** egress, outlet, way out, doorway, gate, avenue, vent. **2** departure, farewell, adieu, good-bye, emergence, leave-taking, parting, exodus, withdrawal, retirement, retreat, evacuation.

exodus *n.* EXIT.

exonerate *v.* acquit, exculpate, clear, vindicate, absolve, justify, pardon, excuse, exempt, let off, release, reprieve, amnesty.
ant. incriminate, charge, accuse, indict, convict, condemn, sentence, damn, censure.

exorbitant *adj.* excessive, extravagant, inordinate, unreasonable, outrageous, extreme, undue, inflated, egregious, unconscionable, enormous, overmuch.
ant. reasonable, moderate, modest, conservative, fair.

exotic *adj.* **1** foreign, alien, unfamiliar, strange, outside, external. **2** fascinating, intriguing, colorful, marvelous, quaint, different, peculiar, curious, strange, unusual.
ant. 1 native, indigenous, domestic, familiar. **2** ordinary, uninteresting, common, garden.

expand *v.* **1** enlarge, inflate, increase,

dilate, swell, blow up, distend, puff up, bloat, amplify, escalate. **2** extend, unfold, open, spread, stretch, unfurl, outstretch, unravel, grow, wax. **3** *of ideas:* develop, expound, elaborate, amplify, elucidate, evolve, expatiate, digress, draw out, protract, embellish, ramble.
ant. 1, 2 contract, diminish, deflate, shrink, shrivel, wither, wane, condense.

expanse *n.* stretch, area, space, tract, surface, plain, void, reach, immensity, vastness, extent.

expansion *n.* increase, enlargement, extension, dilation, growth, magnification, augmentation, amplification, swelling, spread.
ant. contraction, reduction, decrease, diminution, shrinkage, compression, condensation.

expansive *adj.* **1** broad, wide, vast, voluminous, extensive, spacious, far-reaching, widespread, comprehensive, inclusive. **2** outgoing, amiable, open, genial, affable, friendly, sociable, effusive, approachable, demonstrative, extroverted, talkative, garrulous.
ant. 1 limited, restricted, circumscribed, narrow, confined. **2** reserved, taciturn, inhibited, repressed, introverted.

expatiate *v.* elaborate, develop, enlarge, expand, explicate, descant, dwell on, ramble, drag out.

expatriate *n.* EXILE.

expect *v.* **1** anticipate, envisage, await, intend, hope, contemplate, foresee, predict, count on, figure on, look forward to. **2** require, want, wish, demand, call for, intend, insist. **3** presume, suppose, assume, surmise, guess, reckon, trust, think, gather.

expectancy *n.* EXPECTATION.

expectant *adj.* anticipating, awaiting, hopeful, contemplating, watchful, anxious, looking forward, on the lookout, eager, impatient.

expectation *n.* hope, expectancy, prospect, chance, probability, presumption, likelihood, promise.

expecting *adj.* PREGNANT.

expectorate *v.* SPIT.

expediency *n.* usefulness, suitability, fitness, aptness, effectiveness, advisability, pragmatism, utilitarianism, opportunism, manipulation, contrivance, Machiavellianism.
ant. inutility, impracticability, unworkableness, idealism.

expedient *adj.* suitable, advantageous, useful, prudent, politic, advisable, judicious, opportune, utilitarian, pragmatic, practical, profitable. —*n.* means, resort, device, measure, strategy, stratagem, method, tactic, contrivance, vehicle, instrument, resource.
ant. *adj.* impractical, unsuitable, inadvisable, useless, counterproductive.

expedite *v.* facilitate, speed, accelerate, hasten, dispatch, precipitate, rush, hurry.
ant. slow, hinder, delay, slacken, retard.

expedition *n.* journey, trip, excursion, mission, voyage, quest, junket, tour, march, tramp, trek, safari, campaign.

expeditious *adj.* quick, speedy, prompt, efficient, swift, fast, rapid, brisk, hasty, alacritous.
ant. slow, dawdling, sluggish, dilatory, dragging, procrastinating.

expel *v.* remove, dispel, banish, exile, eject, evict, oust, eliminate, discharge, throw out, send packing, drum out, cashier.

expend *v.* spend, disburse, pay out, give, shell out, fork out, use up, exhaust, consume, dissipate.

expendable *adj.* inessential, dispensable, superfluous, unnecessary, unneeded, extraneous, replaceable, marginal.
ant. indispensable, necessary, essential, nonexpendable, crucial, required, irreplaceable.

expenditure *n.* EXPENSE.

expense *n.* **1** cost, price, expenditure, outlay, charge, payment, disbursement, upkeep. **2** sacrifice, loss, cost, price, toll, forfeiture, penalty, deprivation.

expensive *adj.* costly, dear, precious, high-priced, steep, exorbitant, extravagant, prohibitive, stiff, beyond one's means.

ant. cheap, moderate, inexpensive, affordable.

experience *n.* **1** involvement, exposure, subjection, suffering, enjoyment, knowledge, understanding, wisdom, background, worldliness, skill, know-how, education, breeding, training, practice, apprenticeship. **2** adventure, encounter, ordeal, vicissitude, incident, event, occurrence, happening, situation, episode. —*v.* undergo, know, understand, feel, realize, discern, have, apprehend, perceive, suffer, endure, encounter, go through.

experienced *adj.* seasoned, mature, practiced, finished, accomplished, expert, knowing, weathered, hardened, salted, sophisticated, wise, worldly-wise, veteran, battle-scarred, toughened.

ant. green, immature, innocent, naive, fresh, untried.

experiential *adj.* EMPIRICAL.

experiment *n.* test, investigation, assessment, tryout, trial, check, proof, verification, assay, examination. —*v.* try, test, verify, assay, prove, examine.

experimental *adj.* empirical, tested, tried, verified, scientific, proven, confirmed, provisional, tentative, developmental.

experimentation *n.* research, testing, experiment, verification, investigation, trial and error, exploration, examination.

expert *n.* specialist, master, authority, professional, connoisseur, critic, old hand, past master, virtuoso. —*adj.* skillful, trained, dexterous, adept, handy, experienced, practiced, adroit, proficient, qualified, professional.

ant. *n.* apprentice, novice, beginner, layman, amateur, incompetent. *adj.* inexperienced, lay, inept, clumsy, incompetent, amateurish.

expertise *n.* skill, training, know-how, mastery, knowledge, authority, command, experience, proficiency, facility, background.

expiate *v.* atone, redeem, redress, compensate, rectify, make amends, do penance, make good, make reparation.

expiration *n.* termination, cessation, closing, ending, finish, windup, conclusion, completion, death.

ant. beginning, start, commencement, initiation, inauguration.

expire *v.* **1** die, pass away, decease, perish, kick off (*Slang*), kick the bucket (*Slang*), succumb, terminate, lapse, finish, close, end. **2** exhale, expel, breathe out, respire, blow, puff.

explain *v.* **1** clarify, explicate, illuminate, elucidate, expound, instruct, teach, demonstrate, enlighten, interpret, spell out, unravel, construe. **2** justify, excuse, account for, rationalize.

explanation *n.* **1** reason, account, explication, commentary, clarification, elucidation, interpretation, diagnosis, analysis, exegesis. **2** meaning, significance, sense, definition, description, connotation.

explanatory *adj.* interpretive, expository, illustrative, descriptive, explicative, illuminating, instructive, clarifying, didactic.

explicate *v.* EXPLAIN.

explicit *adj.* exact, categorical, distinct, definite, express, clear, precise, candid, frank, blatant, stated, straightforward, open, outspoken, blunt, patent.

ant. vague, indistinct, hazy, confusing, doubtful, equivocal, ambiguous.

explicitness *n.* CLARITY.

explode *v.* **1** detonate, blow up, erupt, discharge, fulminate, burst. **2** refute, puncture, disprove, debunk, belie, discredit, repudiate. **3** inflate, swell, expand, puff, boom, mushroom.

exploit *n.* deed, act, feat, stunt, action, performance, achievement, accomplishment, adventure, *tour de force.* —*v.* utilize, use, take advantage, manipulate, impose upon, capitalize on, profit by, milk, misuse.

exploitation *n.* utilization, manipulation, use, employment, benefit, advantage, profit.

exploratory *adj.* investigative, searching, probing, prying, analytic, fact-finding.

explore *v.* **1** travel, tour, survey, scout, reconnoiter. **2** examine, investigate, scrutinize, probe, delve, pry, search, look into, comb, research.

explosion *n.* detonation, blast, blowup, eruption, fulmination, bang, boom, report, outburst, outbreak, flareup, spurt, upheaval, convulsion, furor, paroxysm, tantrum.

explosive *adj.* **1** volcanic, eruptive, fulminatory, fiery, rabid. **2** charged, tense, violent, vehement, convulsive, paroxysmal, inflammatory.
ant. 1, 2 inert, stable, calm, peaceful, tranquil.

exponent *n.* spokesman, spokeswoman, interpreter, explicator, expounder, advocate, supporter, proponent, booster, example, representative, illustration, model, exemplar.

expose *v.* bare, display, reveal, uncover, disclose, show, exhibit, divulge, air, unmask, unearth.
ant. conceal, hide, cover up, veil, cloak, mask.

exposition *n.* commentary, explanation, exegesis, explication, elucidation, critique, interpretation, analysis, survey, overview.

exposure *n.* revelation, disclosure, exposé, discovery, baring, exhibition.

expound *v.* state, express, present, set forth, detail, formulate, elucidate, describe.

express *v.* utter, tell, assert, verbalize, articulate, put across, declare, communicate, enunciate, present, reveal, disclose, show, indicate. —*adj.* **1** speedy, rapid, nonstop, swift, fast, high-speed, expeditious. **2** EXPLICIT.
ant. *adj.* **1** slow, crawling, creeping, sluggish.

expression *n.* **1** communication, representation, manifestation, description, depiction, conveyance. **2** effectiveness, style, delivery, execution, eloquence, fluency, facility. **3** saying, phrase, utterance, term, idiom, locution, figure of speech.

expressive *adj.* meaningful, significant, indicative, suggestive, pregnant, telling, eloquent, pointed, poignant, moving, thoughtful.
ant. nondescript, meaningless, empty, unthinking.

expressly *adv.* exactly, precisely, definitely, unmistakably, strictly, absolutely, distinctly, clearly.
ant. uncertainly, vaguely, equivocally, ambiguously, tentatively.

expulsion *n.* ejection, ouster, eviction, removal, riddance, banishment, exile, dismissal, discharge, relegation.

expunge *v.* obliterate, erase, eradicate, remove, efface, blot out, delete, destroy, cancel, extirpate, elide, sponge, censor, clip, blip.

expurgate *v.* censor, bowdlerize, abridge, excise, cleanse, purge, purify, emasculate, blue-pencil, edit, sanitize, blip.

exquisite *adj.* delicate, fine, dainty, refined, sensitive, elegant, charming, precious, aesthetic, discriminating, consummate, perfect.
ant. gross, coarse, clumsy, inferior, rough, crass, vulgar, uncouth.

extant *adj.* remaining, existing, surviving, present, subsisting, continuing, current, visible.
ant. extinct, defunct, lost, vanished, destroyed.

extemporaneous *adj.* spontaneous, impromptu, improvised, unpremeditated, extemporary, extempore, offhand, informal, makeshift, off the cuff, unrehearsed, unprepared.

ant. premeditated, prepared, planned, contrived, memorized, rehearsed, formal, set.

extemporary *adj.* EXTEMPORANEOUS.

extempore *adj.* EXTEMPORANEOUS.

extemporize *v.* improvise, ad-lib, make up, devise, play it by ear.

extend *v.* **1** *of length:* stretch, straighten, unfurl, unroll, uncurl, lengthen, elongate. **2** *of time:* prolong, continue, protract, lengthen, postpone, delay, draw out, stay. **3** *of range or scope:* expand, enlarge, broaden, widen, diffuse, generalize, spread, outspread, augment, amplify. **4** offer, put forth, give, impart, bestow, tender, submit, proffer, present.

ant. **1** shorten, compress, contract, curl, constrict, roll, fold. **2** cut short, curtail, terminate, abort. **3** narrow, restrict, limit, curtail, reduce, telescope.

extension *n.* **1** expansion, stretching, lengthening, elongation, prolongation, continuance, increase, augmentation, enlargement, spread. **2** addition, attachment, adjunct, addendum, supplement, extra, increment, annex, wing, branch, continuation, postponement, deferment.

extensive *adj.* **1** ample, spacious, roomy, commodious, expansive, capacious, wide, broad, vast, large, huge. **2** widespread, considerable, prevalent, comprehensive, wholesale, sweeping, far-reaching, long-range, large-scale, general, pervasive. **ant.** **1** cramped, tiny, narrow, compact, small, compressed. **2** limited, contained, selected, exclusive, restricted, confined, isolated.

extent *n.* reach, size, measure, span, distance, dimension, magnitude, degree, intensity, scope, range, compass, area, volume, amplitude.

extenuating *adj.* excusable, defensible, mitigating, justifying, qualifying, palliating, softening, exonerating, exculpating.

exterior *adj.* EXTERNAL.

exterminate *v.* annihilate, demolish, destroy, root out, eradicate, remove, abolish, wipe out, kill, eliminate, extirpate, slaughter, massacre, waste (*Slang*).

external *adj.* **1** exterior, outer, outside, outlying, peripheral, distal. **2** objective, impersonal, real, ontological, extrinsic, foreign, extraneous. **3** superficial, shallow, meretricious, outward. —*n.* exterior, outside, surface, covering, face, crust, skin, shell, coating, veneer, integument, envelope, cover, wrapping.

ant. *adj.* **1** interior, internal, inner, inward, proximal. **2** subjective, personal, inherent, innate, intrinsic, essential, fundamental. **3** profound, solid, sincere, heartfelt.

externalize *v.* EMBODY.

externals *n.* effects, images, appearance, aspect, superficialities, look, semblance, veneer.

extinct *adj.* inactive, extinguished, defunct, dead, deceased, nonexistent, nonextant, vanished, gone. **ant.** living, alive, active, flourishing, thriving, extant.

extinction *n.* annihilation, extermination, death, obliteration, eclipse, destruction, oblivion, dissolution, extirpation.

extinguish *v.* quench, douse, put out, snuff out, suppress, crush, stifle, put down, kill, abolish, exterminate, eliminate, destroy, wipe out, annihilate, extirpate.

extirpate *v.* ERADICATE.

extol *v.* praise, laud, exalt, celebrate, acclaim, eulogize, glorify, magnify, panegyrize, elevate. **ant.** humble, belittle, disparage, discredit, denounce.

extort *v.* blackmail, extract, wring, wrest, exact, bully, coerce, bleed, squeeze, shake down (*Slang*), rip off (*Slang*).

extra *adj.* additional, more, supplementary, spare, extraneous, surplus, reserve, further, excess, superfluous, supererogatory, supernumerary. —*n.* addition, supplement, extension, accessory, adjunct, appendage, affix, codicil, appendix, bonus, plus, supererogation.

extract *v.* **1** withdraw, remove, extirpate, uproot, pull out, excise, pry, pluck, extort, elicit, squeeze, force. **2** derive, obtain, gather, reap, collect, glean. —*n.* **1** essence, concentrate, elixir, juice, distillation, spirit, infusion. **2** excerpt, passage, selection, quotation, clipping, citation, fragment.

extraction *n.* ANCESTRY.

extraneous *adj.* incidental, irrelevant, peripheral, extrinsic, immaterial, inessential, external, adventitious, marginal, extra, accidental, superfluous, beside the point.

  ant. inherent, essential, central, germane, apt, apropos, pertinent, relevant.

extraordinary *adj.* unusual, amazing, marvelous, uncommon, remarkable, exceptional, incredible, exceeding, phenomenal, odd, rare, fantastic, unprecedented, unheard-of.

  ant. ordinary, commonplace, customary, expected, normal, everyday, unexceptional.

extravagance *n.* **1** wastefulness, lavishness, prodigality, profligacy, thriftlessness, profuseness, squandering. **2** outlandishness, outrageousness, exaggeration, preposterousness, wildness, folly, excess, exorbitance, intemperance.

  ant. 1 thrift, parsimony, frugality.

extravagant *adj.* **1** spendthrift, profligate, lavish, wasteful, improvident, profuse. **2** immoderate, excessive, exorbitant, intemperate, fantastic, wild, fanciful, outlandish, unrestrained, ornate, far-out (*Slang*).

  ant. 1 thrifty, parsimonious, tight, stingy, miserly. **2** conservative, restrained, modest, moderate, sober, sensible.

extreme *adj.* **1** utmost, outermost, farthest, ultimate, supreme, final, greatest, most, radical, ultra, excessive, rabid, fanatical, revolutionary. **2** abnormal, bizarre, freakish, *outré*, unprecedented, exaggerated, drastic, dire, severe, intense, harsh. —*n.* limit, extremity, height, pinnacle, depth, apex, maximum, acme, ultimate.

extremely *adv.* exceedingly, markedly, very, utterly, intensely, quite, mighty, terribly, awfully.

extremist *n.* radical, fanatic, revolutionary, zealot, die-hard.

extremity *n.* **1** limit, edge, termination, end, brink, extreme, tip, precipice, border, periphery. **2** desperation, adversity, wretchedness, desolation, despair, distress, need, trouble, destitution, hardship, misery.

extricate *v.* release, free, rescue, disentangle, disengage, liberate, deliver, disembarrass, emancipate, disencumber.

  ant. implicate, embroil, entangle, involve.

extrinsic *adj.* EXTRANEOUS.

exuberance *n.* **1** enthusiasm, vitality, buoyance, *élan*, zestfulness, liveliness, jauntiness, exhilaration. **2** abundance, copiousness, plenitude, overflow, profusion, outpouring, lavishness, richness.

  ant. 1 dreariness, despondency, grimness, solemnity, dejection, depression, glumness. **2** shortage, lack, need, insufficiency, meagerness.

exuberant *adj.* **1** high-spirited, enthusiastic, exhilarated, buoyant, elated, light-hearted, cheerful, zestful. **2** plentiful, abundant, bounteous, lavish, copious, abounding, overflowing, rich.

  ant. 1 heavy-hearted, glum, grim, solemn, sober, downcast, dispirited. **2** scarce, meager, short, skimpy, limited.

exude *v.* **1** ooze, trickle, seep, escape, leak, emit, effuse, excrete, secrete, perspire, sweat. **2** manifest, exhibit, display, radiate, emanate.

exult *v.* rejoice, glory, revel, cheer, jubilate, celebrate, gloat, crow, boast.

exultant *adj.* jubilant, gleeful, triumphant, elated, overjoyed, rejoicing, delighted, joyous.

    ant. disappointed, dejected, defeated, crushed, subdued, downcast, glum.

exultation *n.* rejoicing, triumph, elation, glee, jubilation, delight, celebration, gloating.

    ant. disappointment, dejection, depression.

eye *v.* observe, scrutinize, study, watch, regard, peruse, perceive, stare at, gaze at, survey, scan, look at, take in, view.

eyeball *v. Slang* STARE.

eyeful *n. Slang* sight, spectacle, eye-opener, show, dazzler, stunner (*Slang*), knockout (*Slang*), beauty.

eyeless *adj.* BLIND.

eye-opener *n.* EYEFUL.

eyesight *n.* SIGHT.

eyewash *n. Slang* nonsense, hogwash, balderdash, buncombe, rubbish, humbug, bunk (*Slang*), baloney (*Slang*), malarky (*Slang*), bull (*Slang*), hooey (*Slang*).

F

fable *n.* myth, legend, tale, story, parable, allegory, romance, invention, fiction, fantasy, yarn.

fabled *adj.* famous, legendary, historic, storied, famed.

fabric *n.* **1** cloth, textile, material, stuff, knit, weft, dry goods, yard goods. **2** structure, texture, construction, manufacture, constitution, organization, configuration, substance, make-up.

fabricate *v.* **1** make, assemble, manufacture, construct, create, produce, build, devise, compose, fashion. **2** concoct, invent, feign, forge, contrive, make up.

fabricated *adj.* FAKE.

fabrication *n.* lie, deceit, falsehood, fib, deception, untruth, fiction, forgery, invention, concoction, prevarication.

    ant. truth, fact, reality, verity, actuality.

fabulous *adj.* **1** mythical, legendary, fictitious, fantastic, unreal, imaginary, apocryphal. **2** unbelievable, incredible, untrue, absurd, amazing.

    ant. 2 factual, true, real, proven, credible, actual, normal.

facade *n.* mask, deception, front, veneer, show, semblance, pose, affectation, guise.

face *n.* **1** countenance, visage, physiognomy, features, puss (*Slang*), mug (*Slang*), kisser (*Slang*). **2** front, surface, right side, obverse, facet. **3** appearance, guise, show, front, look, expression, semblance, display, bravado. —*v.* **1** realize, acknowledge, confront, brave, meet, admit. **2** line, cover, dress, smooth, decorate, appliqué.

facet *n.* aspect, side, component, phase, angle, plane, slant, view, perspective.

facetious *adj.* humorous, jocular, clever, droll, funny, pungent, waggish, comical, witty, jesting, playful, flippant.

    ant. serious, sober, weighty, grave, solemn.

face to face confronting, opposing, head to head, nose to nose, eyeball to eyeball (*Slang*).

face value VALUE.

facile *adj.* **1** easy, simple, uncomplicated. **2** dexterous, quick, ready, skillful, clever, glib, fluent, adroit, proficient.

    ant. 1 difficult, complex, complicated, hard, laborious, arduous. **2** awkward, clumsy, ponderous, plodding, painstaking.

facilitate v. simplify, expedite, smooth, accelerate, lighten, promote.

facilities n. means, conveniences, aid, resources, ways and means.

facility n. **1** dexterity, skill, proficiency, ease, readiness, adroitness. **2** office, bureau, accommodation.

facing adj. OPPOSITE.

facsimile n. duplicate, reproduction, replica, copy, likeness.

fact n. actuality, reality, truth, datum, statistic, verity, certainty, occurrence, particular, specific, given.

faction n. party, clique, sect, cabal, division, splinter group.

factious adj. PARTISAN.

factitious adj. artificial, false, spurious, made-up, synthetic, sham, unnatural, mannered, affected.

ant. genuine, natural, real, artless, simple.

factor n. element, cause, part, constituent, influence, component, instrument.

factory n. plant, installation, manufactory, shop, works, mill.

factual adj. true, literal, real, proven, actual, certain, sure, exact, accurate, correct, genuine, authentic.

ant. untrue, fictitious, fictional, imaginary, fanciful, whimsical, speculative.

faculty n. **1** sense, endowment, power, skill, gift, talent, knack, ability, aptitude, capacity. **2** staff, department, professoriat, teachers.

fad n. craze, rage, fancy, fashion, vogue, caprice, mania.

faddish adj. modish, ephemeral, passing, transitory, temporary, fleeting, in.

ant. permanent, lasting, enduring, perennial, classic, traditional.

fade v. dim, pale, wane, wither, age, dwindle, abate, decline, blur, vanish, disappear, dissolve.

fagged adj. tired, exhausted, weary, overworked, fatigued, jaded, worn out, beat, pooped (Slang).

fail v. **1** miss, abort, miscarry, collapse, misfire, fold, crash, desert, forsake, lose, flop, flunk, bomb (Slang). **2** weaken, droop, sicken, decline, sink. **3** neglect, omit, forgo, avoid, evade.

ant. **1** succeed, accomplish, win, achieve, triumph. **2** thrive, flourish, prosper. **3** fulfill, perform, discharge, execute.

failing n. foible, fault, peccadillo, shortcoming, imperfection, defect, weakness, frailty.

ant. strength, steadiness, firmness, stability, integrity.

failure n. **1** miscarriage, lapse, decline, disappointment, collapse, fiasco, debacle, bankruptcy, insolvency, ruin, downfall, defeat. **2** loser, bankrupt, dud, washout (Slang), bomb (Slang).

ant. **1** success, victory, triumph, conquest, achievement, prosperity, fortune, luck, hit. **2** winner, victor, success, achiever.

faint v. pass out, black out, collapse, swoon, languish. —adj. **1** timid, weak, feeble, irresolute, cowardly, frightened, ineffectual, pusillanimous. **2** indistinct, dim, slight, inconspicuous, soft, tenuous, low, vague, pianissimo. —n. blackout, syncope, swoon, collapse.

ant. adj. **1** courageous, firm, resolute, brave, bold, stout, intrepid. **2** strong, clear, bright, sharp, distinct, definite, unequivocal, resonant, resounding.

faint-hearted adj. TIMID.

fair adj. **1** clear, open, attractive, beautiful, sunny, spotless, unblemished, distinct, clean, pleasant, handsome, comely, lovely. **2** just, upright, honest, impartial, evenhanded, disinterested, equitable, reasonable, unbiased. **3** passable, adequate, middling, decent, mediocre, average, satisfactory, so-so. —n. exhibit, show, mart, exhibition, exposition, pageant, bazaar.

ant. *adj.* **1** cloudy, stormy, inclement, dirty, ugly, nasty, ill-favored, foul. **2** partial, prejudiced, biased, bigoted.

fair-and-square *adj.* HONEST.

fair-haired *adj.* FAVORITE.

fairly *adv.* **1** justly, equitably, impartially, evenly, equally, squarely. **2** moderately, tolerably, rather, somewhat, passably.

fair-minded *adj.* just, equitable, open-minded, unbiased, reasonable, impartial, irreproachable, honest, scrupulous, unprejudiced, evenhanded, disinterested.

ant. biased, narrow-minded, close-minded, bigoted, prejudiced, unjust, partial, partisan, intolerant, mean-spirited.

fairness *n.* justice, impartiality, equity, honesty, evenhandedness, fair shake (*Slang*).

ant. partiality, favoritism, inequity, unfairness, bias, prejudice, one-sidedness.

fair shake *Slang* FAIRNESS.

fair-spoken *adj.* POLITE.

fair-weather *adj.* UNTRUSTWORTHY.

fairy *n.* elf, spirit, sprite, pixy, gnome, leprechaun, brownie, goblin, hobgoblin, hob.

faith *n.* belief, credence, confidence, trust, religion, creed, credo, troth, allegiance, loyalty, constancy, fidelity, faithfulness, dependence, reliance.

ant. skepticism, doubt, disbelief, incredulity, mistrust, atheism.

faithful *adj.* **1** trustworthy, true, loyal, constant, staunch, steadfast, devoted, true-blue. **2** exact, accurate, true, close, conscientious, precise, careful.

ant. **1** inconstant, treacherous, disloyal, faithless, deceitful, untrustworthy, unfaithful, dishonest, false. **2** inaccurate, imprecise, careless, erroneous, loose, inexact.

faithless *adj.* disloyal, untrue, treacherous, deceptive, unreliable, deceitful, false, perfidious, recreant, unfaithful, untrustworthy, dishonest, two-faced, irresponsible.

ant. true, loyal, faithful, unwavering, staunch, steadfast, constant, devoted.

faithlessness *n.* TREACHERY.

fake *n.* fraud, counterfeit, sham, imitation, impostor, deception, fabrication, falsification, forgery, humbug, hoax, phony (*Slang*), put-on (*Slang*). —*adj.* false, imitation, spurious, sham, fraudulent, forged, fabricated, counterfeit, make-believe, phony (*Slang*). —*v.* feign, make believe, counterfeit, sham, fabricate, falsify, forge, doctor, simulate, pretend, dissemble, dissimulate, affect, put on (*Slang*).

ant. *adj.* authentic, real, true, genuine, right, pure, honest, unadulterated.

falderal *n.* nonsense, foolery, balderdash, gibberish, jargon, humbug, piffle, rubbish, blather.

fall *v.* **1** drop, collapse, droop, sag, sink, buckle, topple, tumble, plummet, plunge, descend, decline, crash. **2** lessen, diminish, descend, dwindle, decrease, abate, subside, depreciate, weaken. **3** surrender, succumb, capitulate, topple. —*n.* descent, drop, plunge, tumble, decline, decrease, diminution, subsidence, lessening, spill, collapse, downfall, ruin, overthrow, failure, defeat, capitulation.

ant. *v.* **1** rise, climb, soar, ascend, surge, take off, mount. **2** grow, increase, expand, extend, enlarge, swell, appreciate, multiply. **3** resist, withstand, rebuff, repel, hold out. *n.* rise, ascent, climb, increase, heightening, advance, expansion, augmentation.

fallacious *adj.* false, untrue, wrong, deceptive, erroneous, illusory, misleading, delusive.

ant. true, accurate, exact, factual, real.

fallacy *n.* error, mistake, delusion, illusion, sophistry, sophism, deception, misconception.

fall back recede, retreat, concede, withdraw, recoil, retire.

ant. advance, progress, gain, improve, proceed, prosper.

fall guy *Slang* DUPE.

falling-out *n.* QUARREL.

fallout *n.* byproduct, spinoff.

fall out QUARREL.

fallow *adj.* unused, idle, dormant, inactive, quiescent, unproductive, inert.
ant. active, productive, rich, fertile, prolific, fruitful, creative.

fall short lack, want, fail, disappoint, miss, lose.
ant. succeed, come through, win, suffice, serve, satisfy.

fall through fail, collapse, fizzle, misfire, abort, evaporate, peter out.
ant. work out, materialize, succeed, bear fruit.

false *adj.* **1** untrue, inaccurate, unreal, misleading, wrong, lying, dishonest, deceitful, deceptive, mendacious, hypocritical, faithless, treacherous, unfaithful. **2** artificial, synthetic, spurious, imitation, ersatz, fake, sham, bogus, pseudo, make-believe.
ant. **1** true, loyal, faithful, honest, constant, steady, staunch, direct, straightforward. **2** genuine, authentic, real, original, pure, veritable, correct.

falsehood *n.* lie, untruth, deception, prevarication, equivocation, fabrication, fiction, evasion, perjury, fib, whopper (*Slang*).
ant. truth, fact, verity, reality, certainty.

false step BLUNDER.

falsification *n.* LIE.

falsify *v.* misrepresent, disguise, misstate, adulterate, fake, mislead, doctor, gloss.

falsity *n.* untruth, unreality, illusion, lie, dishonesty, fraud, fraudulence, deceit.
ant. truth, authenticity, reality, certainty, verity, honesty, candor.

falter *v.* hesitate, waver, stumble, totter, shake, reel, tremble, stagger, dodder, stammer, stutter.

faltering *adj.* halting, hesitant, uncertain, tentative, stumbling, wavering.

ant. sure, firm, agile, sure-footed, adroit, graceful, facile, fluent.

fame *n.* reputation, renown, celebrity, repute, notice, distinction, eminence, prestige, prominence, kudos, publicity, famousness, notability, esteem, mark, notoriety.
ant. obscurity, anonymity, retirement, seclusion.

famed *adj.* renowed, well-known, celebrated, noted, eminent, illustrious.

familiar *adj.* **1** acquainted, versed, informed, conversant, cognizant, apprised, aware. **2** intimate, close, friendly, near, amicable, cordial. **3** bold, disrespectful, rude, presuming, forward, impudent, intrusive. **4** common, frequent, well-known, everyday, ordinary, mundane, routine, customary, accustomed.
ant. **1** ignorant, uninformed, unaware. **2** distant, formal, remote, faraway. **3** shy, retiring, discreet, respectful, cautious, circumspect. **4** extraordinary, remarkable, unusual, rare, prodigious, marvelous, uncommon, phenomenal, unheard-of.

familiarity *n.* knowledge, acquaintance, awareness, cognizance, comprehension, grasp, experience, understanding, know-how.

family *n.* **1** clan, house, lineage, brood, household, menage, kin, kindred, relatives, relations, offspring, issue, progeny. **2** class, group, kind, genus, genre, order, system, network.

famish *v.* STARVE.

famous *adj.* well-known, renowned, celebrated, illustrious, noted, eminent, distinguished, prominent, esteemed, publicized, lionized, notorious.
ant. obscure, unknown, humble, hidden, retiring, undistinguished.

famousness *n.* FAME.

fan *n.* devotee, admirer, aficionado, follower, rooter, fancier, enthusiast, fanatic, buff, freak (*Slang*). —*v.* STIR.

fanatic *n.* enthusiast, monomaniac, zealot, extremist, visionary, bigot, hothead, nut (*Slang*).

fanatical *adj.* zealous, overenthusiastic, extreme, radical, monomaniacal, rabid, irrational.

ant. temperate, reasonable, prudent, detached.

fancier *n.* expert, aficionado, devotee, follower, connoisseur, votary, breeder.

fanciful *adj.* imaginary, illusory, fictional, unreal, whimsical, fantastic, romantic, flighty, capricious, visionary, ideal, chimerical.

ant. prosaic, everyday, ordinary, humdrum, realistic, mundane, down-to-earth.

fancy *n.* **1** imagination, notion, whim, whimsy, caprice, idea, conceit, conception, image, vision, reverie, illusion, delusion, chimera. **2** liking, fondness, craving, desire, taste, inclination, want. —*adj.* elaborate, ornamental, decorative, ornate, elegant, fine, extravagant, fussy, purple. —*v.* suppose, imagine, guess, reckon, speculate, conjecture, believe, surmise, assume.

ant. *adj.* plain, unadorned, simple, natural, chaste, austere, utilitarian.

fanfare *n.* publicity, demonstration, fuss, to-do, propaganda, puffery, buildup, ballyhoo.

fantasize *v.* daydream, imagine, invent, envision, speculate.

fantastic *adj.* odd, grotesque, eerie, bizarre, strange, weird, unearthly, wild, capricious, peculiar, outlandish, uncanny, marvelous, wonderful, awesome, eldritch.

ant. ordinary, everyday, mundane, prosaic, humdrum, staid, sober.

fantasy *n.* fancy, imagination, image, dream, daydream, reverie, phantasy, notion, whim, whimsy, caprice, vision, invention, fabrication, figment.

far *adj.* distant, remote, faraway, removed, separated, estranged, alienated.

ant. near, close, neighboring, adjacent, contiguous, familiar.

faraway *adj.* **1** DISTANT. **2** ABSENT-MINDED.

farce *n.* COMEDY.

farcical *adj.* absurd, comical, laughable, ludicrous, ridiculous, droll, funny.

ant. serious, grave, solemn, earnest, sober, tragic.

fare *v.* get on, make out, do, manage, get along, succeed, prosper, thrive. —*n.* food, nourishment, victuals, provisions, provender, viands, edibles, comestibles, board, table, commons, regimen, diet, cheer.

farewell *n.* good-by, adieu, leave-taking, valedictory, au revoir, godspeed, send-off.

far-fetched *adj.* improbable, unlikely, unnatural, implausible, illogical, dubious, doubtful, strained, forced, abstruse, recherché, outlandish, cockamamie (*Slang*).

ant. plausible, credible, reasonable, logical, believable, rational.

far-flung *adj.* WIDESPREAD.

farm *v.* cultivate, till, plow, hoe, plant, sow, raise, grow, reap, harvest.

farmer *n.* cultivator, grower, raiser, tiller, husbandman, agriculturist.

farming *n.* agriculture, husbandry, cultivation, growing, raising, tillage, culture, agronomy, agribusiness.

farness *n.* DISTANCE.

far-off *adj.* distant, remote, faraway, removed.

far-out *adj.* *Slang* unconventional, avant-garde, advanced, wild, outlandish, bizarre, weird, strange, odd, outré, way-out (*Slang*).

ant. traditional, conventional, ordinary, standard, conservative, square (*Slang*), straight (*Slang*).

farrago *n.* MEDLEY.

far-reaching *adj.* wide, extensive, broad, sweeping, significant, far-flung, reverberating, momentous, critical, fateful.

farseeing *adj.* WISE.

farsighted *adj.* wise, prudent, provident, farseeing, watchful, judicious, prescient, sage, shrewd, thoughtful.

ant. heedless, rash, thoughtless, headstrong, improvident, careless.

fascinate *v.* attract, captivate, enthrall, charm, engross, bewitch, enchant, transfix, seduce, enrapture.

fascinating *adj.* enthralling, captivating, spellbinding, bewitching, charming, engrossing, enchanting, absorbing, engaging, alluring, riveting, entrancing, attractive, seductive.

ant. dull, vapid, lackluster, uninteresting, insipid, prosaic.

fascination *n.* attraction, charm, spell, absorption, enchantment, lure, pull, magic, glamor, seduction, bewitchment, captivation.

fashion *n.* style, mode, manner, method, way, practice, custom, usage, convention, vogue, couture, craze, rage. —*v.* shape, form, make, manufacture, fabricate, model, create, design, mold, sculpt.

fashionable *adj.* stylish, modish, elegant, customary, conventional, voguish, smart, à la mode, tony.

ant. outdated, unfashionable, démodé, outmoded, old-fashioned.

fast *adj.* **1** firm, secure, tight, steady, close, fixed, permanent, immovable, constant, steadfast, staunch, loyal, unwavering, tenacious, stationary. **2** rapid, quick, swift, speedy, deft, fleet, hasty, precipitate, expeditious, instant, accelerated, presto, lickety-split (*Slang*). **3** dissipated, loose, wanton, reckless, extravagant, profligate, prodigal, rakish, giddy, intemperate, lascivious, licentious. —*adv.* **1** firmly, securely, soundly, thoroughly, tightly, closely, immovably. **2** quickly, swiftly, rapidly, hastily, speedily, apace, instantly, presto. **ant.** *adj.* **1** insecure, unsteady, wavering, shaky, loose, tenuous, uncertain, inconstant. **2** slow, tardy, sluggish, inert, torpid, inactive, plodding, crawling, deliberate. **3** prim, staid, sober, respectable, decent, decorous, prudish, square (*Slang*). *adv.* **1** loosely, insecurely, slackly. **2** slow, slowly, leisurely, moderately.

fasten *v.* attach, secure, connect, tie, bind, fix, affix, make fast, join, unite.

fastidious *adj.* discriminating, particular, punctilious, delicate, precise, finicky, meticulous, finical, fussy, choosy, picky, squeamish, precious.

fasting *n.* ABSTINENCE.

fat *adj.* **1** corpulent, obese, plump, stout, stocky, heavy, overweight, chubby, rotund, roly-poly, fleshy, portly, paunchy, pudgy, tubby, pursy. **2** oily, greasy, sebaceous, adipose, unctuous, oleaginous. **3** rich, prosperous, thriving, comfortable, rewarding, remunerative, lucrative, profitable, flourishing, fruitful, luxuriant, cushy (*Slang*).

ant. **1** lean, thin, slender, skinny, slim, wiry, bony, slight. **3** meager, scanty, poor, barren, unproductive.

fatal *adj.* deadly, destructive, mortal, ruinous, lethal, calamitous, pernicious, malignant, cataclysmic.

fatality *n.* death, mortality, casualty.

fate *n.* destiny, fortune, lot, providence, kismet, outcome, issue, result, upshot.

fateful *adj.* critical, momentous, crucial, decisive, ominous, portentous, far-reaching, prophetic.

fathead *n. Slang* ASS.

father *n.* founder, originator, maker, author, inventor, benefactor. —*v.* **1** beget, sire, engender, procreate. **2** found, create, make, originate, establish, institute, organize.

fatherland *n.* country, homeland, birthplace, old country.

fathom *v.* **1** sound, plumb, cast. **2** understand, comprehend, penetrate, probe, figure out, investigate, divine, interpret, bottom, get to the bottom of.

fatigue *n.* exhaustion, weariness, tiredness, lassitude, enervation, boredom, languor, malaise, ennui. —*v.* tire, exhaust, weary, bore, enervate, jade, fag, poop (*Slang*).

fatness *n.* corpulence, obesity, plumpness, stoutness, overweight, stockiness, fleshiness, portliness, chubbiness, paunchiness.

fatty *adj.* **1** adipose. **2** greasy, oily, suety, sebaceous, unctuous.

ant. 1 lean.

fatuous *adj.* stupid, foolish, silly, dull, asinine, obtuse, inane, vacuous, witless, vapid.

ant. shrewd, perceptive, clearsighted, astute, discerning.

fault *n.* **1** defect, imperfection, misdeed, peccadillo, flaw, blemish, shortcoming, weakness, foible, error, snag, glitch (*Slang*), frailty, infirmity. **2** responsibility, blame, guilt, culpability, error, lapse. —*v.* blame, accuse, criticize, reprove, impeach, impugn, take to task, censure.

faultfinding *adj.* captious, critical, carping, disapproving, censorious, caviling, hypercritical, nitpicking.

ant. tolerant, lenient, indulgent, forbearing, easygoing, generous.

faultless *adj.* perfect, flawless, ideal, blameless, spotless, immaculate, impeccable, nonpareil, exemplary.

ant. flawed, marred, defective, imperfect.

faulty *adj.* defective, imperfect, unsound, impaired, wrong, incorrect, unsatisfactory, corrupt, blameworthy, culpable, erroneous, false, untrue.

ant. perfect, faultless, flawless, blameless.

faux pas impropriety, gaucherie, blunder, misstep, indiscretion, error, lapse, mistake, gaffe, goof (*Slang*).

favor *n.* **1** benefit, benefaction, boon, kindness, dispensation, indulgence, accommodation. **2** approval, good will, patronage, esteem, grace, support, favoritism, bias, partiality. —*v.* approve, commend, encourage, support, countenance, indulge, advocate, aid, assist, foster, spare, spoil.

favorable *adj.* **1** beneficial, advantageous, convenient, helpful. **2** promising, auspicious, propitious, fortunate, opportune, lucky.

ant. 1 inconvenient, unsatisfactory,

disadvantageous, adverse, contrary, discouraging. **2** inauspicious, threatening, foreboding, unlucky, ominous, ill-starred.

favored *adj.* PRIVILEGED.

favorite *adj.* preferred, choice, dearest, popular, pet, fair-haired. —*n.* pet, darling, idol, fair-haired boy, choice, preference, predilection.

favoritism *n.* partiality, bias, preference, onesidedness, partisanship.

fawn *v.* cringe, toady, flatter, grovel, truckle, bootlick.

fawning *adj.* obsequious, slavish, servile, sycophantic, truckling, bootlicking, flattering, cringing.

faze *v.* worry, disturb, disconcert, upset, intimidate, discourage, daunt.

fealty *n.* FIDELITY.

fear *n.* **1** dread, apprehension, anxiety, uneasiness, alarm, fright, terror, horror, awe, panic, trepidation, timidity, concern, misgiving, dismay. **2** bogy, bugbear, nightmare, specter. —*v.* dread, distrust, apprehend.

fearful *adj.* afraid, frightened, scared, anxious, timid, timorous, apprehensive, nervous, worried, panicky, faint-hearted, cowardly.

ant. courageous, bold, valiant, intrepid, fearless, brave.

fearless *adj.* brave, bold, courageous, valiant, valorous, gallant, intrepid, dauntless, daring, unafraid, unfearing, undaunted, mettlesome, game, confident, stout-hearted, heroic, indomitable.

ant. timid, cowardly, faint-hearted, afraid, fearful.

fearlessness *n.* BRAVERY.

fearsome *adj.* formidable, alarming, frightening, awesome, dismaying, menacing, threatening, daunting.

feasible *adj.* possible, practicable, workable, attainable, suitable, expedient, practical, viable, operable, reasonable.

ant. unworkable, impractical, impossible.

feast *n.* banquet, treat, repast, spread, blowout (*Slang*).

feat *n.* achievement, deed, exploit, accomplishment, act, stunt, trick.

feature *n.* highlight, characteristic, earmark, attribute, lineament, hallmark, imprint, cachet, idiosyncrasy. —*v.* emphasize, highlight, stress, headline, star, play up.

featured *adj.* emphasized, highlighted, stressed, starred, leading.

feces *n.* excrement, dung, excreta, stool, waste, manure, ordure, muck, droppings.

feckless *adj.* USELESS.

fecund *adj.* fertile, fruitful, prolific, teeming, rich, productive, creative, inventive.
  ant. barren, sterile, dry, arid, bare, unproductive, jejune.

federate *v.* AMALGAMATE.

fee *n.* payment, charge, bill, tip, gratuity, remuneration, reward, recompense, stipend, honorarium.

feeble *adj.* **1** weak, infirm, ailing, frail, sickly, debilitated, nerveless, fragile, puny, decrepit, invalid, valetudinarian. **2** ineffective, powerless, weak, lame, ineffectual, inadequate, flimsy, spiritless, paltry.
  ant. 1 strong, vigorous, healthy, hale, robust, fit, hardy. **2** forceful, cogent, powerful, firm, decisive, sound, convincing, effective.

feeble-minded *adj.* retarded, backward, dull, handicapped, stupid, moronic, imbecilic, idiotic, senile, half-witted, doltish, foolish, brainless, crazy, insane, dimwitted (*Slang*), daft.
  ant. intelligent, quick-witted, sane, normal, alert, sound.

feed *v.* nourish, nurture, sustain, strengthen, foster, support, maintain, serve, cater, regale, fuel, feast, dine, provision. —*n.* fodder, ensilage, silage, provender, forage, provision, pasture, pasturage.
  ant. *v.* starve, famish, exhaust, weaken, deprive, undernourish, emaciate.

feel *v.* **1** sense, perceive, experience, sustain, suffer, detect, discriminate, react, discern, notice, apprehend. **2** touch, handle, palpate, finger,

thumb, grope, stroke, rub, paw, maul. —*n.* aptitude, flair, talent, gift, cleverness, faculty, knack, forte, proclivity, genius, ability.

feeler *n.* antenna, tentacle, palp, palpus, whisker, proboscis, finger.

feeling *n.* **1** sensation, sense, emotion, reaction, response, impression, sentiment, sentience, awareness. **2** opinion, conviction, view, point of view, judgment, conclusion, estimate, evaluation, viewpoint, attitude, belief, intuition, credo, stand, stance, position, assumption, presumption, inference.

feelings *n.* emotions, sensitivities, passions, sensibilities, susceptibilities, ego, pride.

feign *v.* simulate, dissemble, pretend, dissimulate, sham, counterfeit, affect, assume, pose, imitate, misrepresent, play at, act, fake.

feint *n.* ruse, pretense, trick, wile, swindle, sham, pretext, artifice, stratagem, expedient, blind, gambit, dodge, plot, trap, maneuver.

felicitous *adj.* appropriate, apt, relevant, germane, timely, opportune, pertinent, to the point, apropos, seasonable, suitable, well-timed, right on (*Slang*).
  ant. inappropriate, untimely, unwelcome, irrelevant, unsuitable, out of place, clumsy, inept.

fell[1] *v.* level, cut down, hew, floor, ground, prostrate, raze, flatten, knock down.
  ant. raise, grow, put up, nourish, support, prop.

fell[2] *adj.* FIERCE.

fellow *n.* **1** man, boy, person, individual, human being, creature, mortal, someone, somebody, character, figure, guy, chap, jack, bloke (*Brit. Slang*). **2** equal, mate, companion, peer, partner, co-worker, colleague, associate, brother, twin, double, alter ego, counterpart, duplicate, equivalent, parallel.

fellowship *n.* **1** companionship, friendship, camaraderie, comradeship, brotherliness, amity, intimacy, closeness, familiarity, friendliness, companionability, congeniality. **2** club, society, fraternity, association, guild, membership, union, league, alliance, federation, confederation, sodality, sisterhood, sorority.

felon *n.* criminal, lawbreaker, wrongdoer, culprit, miscreant, malefactor, offender, delinquent, convict, gangster.

felonious *adj.* malicious, villainous, wicked, base, vicious, heinous, infamous, iniquitous, vile, corrupt, pernicious, cruel, noxious, criminal.

fence *n.* barrier, enclosure, wall, boundary, paling, stockade, palisade, hedge, ha-ha, rail, railing, bulkhead. —*v.* **1** separate, surround, encircle, girdle, enclose, confine, restrict, exclude. **2** parry, equivocate, quibble, hedge, dodge, shift, evade, elude, cavil, fudge, avoid, deflect, block, stonewall (*Slang*).

fend for provide, manage, cope, survive, shift, contend with, get along, make out, take care.

fend off repulse, ward off, parry, resist, beat off, elude, evade, circumvent, escape, keep off, drive back, repel, oppose, rebuff, reject.

ant. succumb, capitulate, give in, submit, yield, collapse, knuckle under.

feral *adj.* WILD.

ferment *v.* agitate, stir up, provoke, foment, incite, trouble, shake, disturb, disquiet, perturb, rouse, roil, excite, seethe, boil, fester. —*n.* excitement, agitation, stir, disturbance, fomentation, tumult, turbulence, commotion, confusion, uproar, fever, disquiet, unrest, disorder.

ant. *v.* calm, soothe, relax, still, quiet, compose, allay. *n.* calm, order, peace, quiet, serenity, apathy, inertia.

ferocious *adj.* savage, bloodthirsty, cruel, fierce, rapacious, bestial, brutal, predatory, ravenous, inhuman,

barbarous, murderous, fiendish, untamed, feral.

ant. tame, docile, mild, unaggressive, civilized, humane, gentle.

ferocity *n.* CRUELTY.

ferret out discover, reveal, disclose, find, dig up, search out, track down, trace, hunt, disinter, unearth, root out, pry into, worm out, fish out, smell out.

ant. bury, hide, conceal, inter, cover, cache.

fertile *adj.* **1** fecund, procreative, generative, yielding, rich, productive, fruitful, copious, plenteous, plentiful, teeming, abundant. **2** creative, inventive, productive, prolific, formative, fruitful, teeming, exuberant, resourceful, ingenious, rich, seminal.

ant. 1 sterile, barren, dry, arid, bare, fallow, unyielding. **2** unproductive, impoverished, inactive, feeble, poor.

fervent *adj.* ardent, zealous, impassioned, fervid, passionate, vehement, fiery, intense, keen, perfervid, fierce, heated, burning, glowing, throbbing, impatient, violent.

ant. cool, apathetic, phlegmatic, impassive, dispassionate, chilly, detached, unmoved.

fervid *adj.* FERVENT.

fervor *n.* ardor, zeal, passion, intensity, enthusiasm, gusto, zest, drive, fire, eagerness, vehemence, excitement, animation, verve.

ant. apathy, boredom, detachment, coolness, dispassion, ennui.

fester *v.* **1** suppurate, ulcerate, run. **2** irritate, annoy, rankle, gall, chafe, fret, roil, rile, plague, torment, vex, nettle. —*n.* ulcer, sore, pustule, abscess, boil, carbuncle, inflammation, infection, pimple, discharge.

festival *n.* celebration, carnival, jubilee, fete, feast, holiday, carousal, merrymaking, fiesta, festivities, gala.

festive *adj.* gay, joyful, convivial, joyous, merry, mirthful, gala, sportive, holiday, jovial, jolly, celebrative, jubilant, playful, convivial, lighthearted.

ant. doleful, gloomy, sad, dreary, dismal, depressing, joyless, somber.

festivity *n.* festival, gaiety, merrymaking, party, carousal, revelry, rejoicing, joyousness, jollity, merriment, mirth, glee, sport, conviviality, do, bash (*Slang*).

festoon *v.* garland, bedeck, deck, wreathe, trim, ornament, adorn, decorate, beribbon.

fetch *v.* bring, get, carry, tote, go for, retrieve, transport, obtain, bear, procure, convey, deliver, secure.

fetching *adj.* attractive, fascinating, captivating, taking, appetizing, intriguing, charming, entrancing, engaging, interesting, disarming, winsome, exciting, provocative, alluring, enticing, inviting, smashing (*Brit.*).
ant. unattractive, displeasing, offputting, repulsive, nauseating, disgusting, distasteful.

fete *n.* FESTIVAL.

fetid *adj.* foul, rank, malodorous, stinking, noisome, gamy, mephitic, rotten, rotting, putrid, putrescent, reeking, stenchy, funky, frowsty (*Brit.*).
ant. fragrant, fresh, aromatic, perfumed, scented, sweet-smelling.

fetter *n.* restraint, curb, rein, chain, shackle, manacle, bridle, bind, tie, bond, trammel, yoke, leash, gyve, hindrance, pinion, gag, brake, straitjacket. —*v.* restrain, curb, leash, chain, bridle, bind, tie, hinder, shackle, manacle, straitjacket, muzzle, gag, tether, confine.
ant. *v.* release, set free, liberate, unbind, loose, unfetter.

fettle *n.* state, condition, shape, form, circumstance, order, plight, footing, standing, mood, disposition, spirits.

feud *n.* quarrel, strife, conflict, hostility, contention, vendetta, enmity, dissension, controversy, dispute, fracas, breach, schism, animosity, clash, ill will. —*v.* quarrel, contend, fight, war, contest, clash, combat, wrestle, duel, dispute, rival, bicker, squabble.
ant. *n.* agreement, peace, harmony,

concord, détente, amity, understanding, friendship. *v.* agree, get on, concur, cooperate, collaborate.

fever *n.* excitement, enthusiasm, passion, ardor, fervor, zeal, agitation, ferment, frenzy, craze, obsession, distraction, ecstasy, heat, fire, hysteria, delirium.
ant. calm, serenity, detachment, dispassion, composure, tranquillity, cool (*Slang*).

feverish *adj.* **1** flushed, fevered, hot, febrile, hectic, delirious, pyretic, parched, inflamed. **2** excited, eager, impatient, frenzied, overwrought, agitated, hectic, frenetic, frantic, impassioned, violent, giddy, uncontrolled, driven.
ant. **2** calm, cool, serene, self-controlled, composed, phlegmatic, orderly.

few *adj.* limited, sparse, scant, scanty, scarce, infrequent, rare, meager, thin, paltry, skimpy, lacking, insufficient.
ant. many, numerous, ample, sufficient, common, frequent, generous.

fey *adj.* ECCENTRIC.

fiasco *n.* failure, disaster, mess, botch, ruin, rout, defeat, miscarriage, dud, fizzle, flop, bomb (*Slang*), washout (*Slang*), bummer (*Slang*).
ant. success, triumph, victory, achievement, hit, coup, smash.

fiat *n.* COMMAND.

fib *n.* lie, falsehood, untruth, fabrication, invention, fiction, fish story, myth, prevarication, falsification, half-truth, canard, deception, deceit. —*v.* lie, fabricate, falsify, invent, prevaricate, fictionalize, pretend, misrepresent, misstate, distort, embroider, exaggerate.
ant. *n.* truth, fact, accuracy, actuality, veracity, authenticity. *v.* level, own up, come clean (*Slang*).

fiber *n.* **1** thread, filament, strand, tendril, hair, web, line, ribbon, string. **2** character, quality, texture, essence, makeup, nature, kind, sort, substance, constitution, temperament, disposition, stamp, stripe, spirit.

fickle *adj.* changeable, inconstant, erratic, irresolute, mercurial, capricious, unreliable, undependable, unpredictable, volatile, inconsistent, indecisive, vacillating, whimsical, flighty.

ant. constant, reliable, dependable, faithful, consistent, settled, definite, unwavering.

fiction *n.* story, tale, yarn, improvisation, brainchild, invention, fantasy, fancy, misrepresentation, falsehood, lie, fib, fabrication, concoction, coinage, creation.

ant. fact, truth, reality, accuracy, verity.

fictional *adj.* IMAGINARY.

fictitious *adj.* imaginary, untrue, false, counterfeit, unreal, invented, improvised, created, feigned, imagined, fanciful, mythical, legendary, fantastic, fabricated.

ant. true, real, genuine, factual, actual, proven, verifiable.

fictive *adj.* IMAGINARY.

fiddle *v.* tinker, toy, putter, potter, dabble, mess, fool with, dawdle, fritter, idle, fuss, diddle, dilly-dally, trifle.

fidelity *n.* faithfulness, loyalty, constancy, allegiance, honesty, integrity, exactness, accuracy, reliability, trustworthiness, dependability, devotion, fealty.

ant. disloyalty, treachery, faithlessness, unfaithfulness, infidelity, unreliability, apostasy.

fidget *v.* squirm, fuss, twitch, fret, chafe, wriggle, fiddle, jitter, jiggle, bustle.

field *n.* **1** area, region, pasture, arena, lea, meadow, grassland, plot, green, battleground, theater, scene, turf, domain, sphere, realm. **2** profession, department, specialty, vocation, calling, discipline, line, trade, job, occupation, pursuit, metier, business, activity.

fiend *n.* **1** devil, demon, hellhound, archfiend, Satan, Mephistopheles, Beelzebub, Evil One, dybbuk, incubus, succubus, Lucifer. **2** monster, ogre, beast, brute, barbarian, swine, savage, villain, scoundrel, cutthroat, sadist, ghoul.

ant. 1 angel, seraph, cherub, archangel, saint.

fiendish *adj.* diabolical, villainous, evil, monstrous, satanic, savage, bestial, brutal, barbarous, sadistic, cruel, infernal, demonic, inhuman, horrible, Mephistophelian.

ant. angelic, cherubic, saintly, spiritual, pure, good, humane.

fierce *adj.* violent, savage, ferocious, furious, cruel, fell, vehement, passionate, extreme, wild, ravenous, murderous, merciless, fiery, impassioned.

ant. gentle, tame, moderate, meek, mild, placid, calm, kind.

fiery *adj.* blazing, burning, glowing, flaming, fierce, passionate, spirited, ardent, smoldering, fevered, impassioned, red-hot, wrathful, choleric, hotheaded.

ant. cool, quenched, dampened, phlegmatic, dispassionate, calm, apathetic, low-key.

fight *v.* **1** battle, combat, war, assault, contest, skirmish, brawl, wrestle, box, spar, scuffle, duel, feud, quarrel, clash, bombard. **2** oppose, contend, struggle, resist, repulse, contest, strive, dispute, argue, wrangle, bicker, protest, defy. —*n.* **1** battle, conflict, combat, encounter, contest, engagement, fracas, skirmish, quarrel, brawl, match, duel, scrimmage, dogfight, set-to, altercation, row. **2** struggle, attempt, contention, effort, campaign, contest, competition, striving, strife.

fighter *n.* contender, battler, combatant, warrior, disputant, soldier, contestant, assailant, opponent, arguer, adversary, dissenter, brawler, wrangler, bruiser, pugilist, boxer, scrapper, campaigner.

figment *n.* fiction, creation, improvisation, invention, fabrication, fancy, fable, concoction, production, product, yarn, story, prevarication, fib, untruth.

ant. truth, fact, reality, actuality, verity, certainty, certitude.

figuration *n.* CONFIGURATION.

figurative *adj.* metaphorical, allegorical, symbolic, poetic, figured, imagistic, imaginative, graphic, vivid, pictorial, allusive, indirect, elliptical, fanciful.

ant. literal, straightforward, prosaic, factual, direct, unembellished.

figure *n.* **1** shape, outline, form, contour, configuration, structure, silhouette, format. **2** body, physique, build, shape, embodiment, corpus, representation, likeness, image. **3** illustration, diagram, drawing, pattern, design, delineation, sketch, picture, depiction, tracing. **4** number, numeral, digit, integer, ordinal, cipher, quantity. —*v.* **1** compute, tally, reckon, estimate, calculate, score, count, enumerate, measure, assess, evaluate. **2** think, believe, predict, opine, assume, guess, conjecture, conclude, reckon, presume, suppose, feel, infer, deduce, hold, maintain.

figurehead *n.* front, dummy, straw man, man of straw, blind, puppet, instrument, dupe, tool, nonentity, ornament, adornment, token, emblem, nobody, cipher, window-dressing.

ant. power, force, leader, commander, authority, policymaker, decision-maker, strongman.

figure on EXPECT.

figure out 1 reckon, ascertain, discover, determine, detect, contrive, devise, imagine. **2** solve, fathom, understand, comprehend, resolve, decipher, unravel, explain, clear up.

filament *n.* thread, fiber, hair, web, strand, tendril, wire, string, twist, coil, cilia, line.

filch *v.* steal, rob, lift, purloin, snatch, embezzle, cheat, rook, bilk, thieve, pinch (*Slang*), swipe (*Slang*), heist (*Slang*).

file *n.* record, dossier, folder, sheaf, data, information, source, portfolio. —*v.* **1** sort, organize, classify, alphabetize, record, catalog, list, calendar, register, store, preserve, chronicle. **2** apply, request, petition, claim, solicit, seek, canvas, enroll.

fill *v.* occupy, suffuse, pervade, put in, saturate, soak, steep, replenish, load, pack, cram, inflate, distend, overspread, stock, puff up, complete, stretch, crowd, congest.

ant. empty, drain, exhaust, deplete, use up, remove, void.

fill-in *n.* substitute, replacement, pinch hitter, alternate, understudy, proxy, deputy, stand-in, surrogate, standby, extra.

fill in complete, fill up, replenish, refill, shoal, shore up.

ant. dig out, scoop, excavate, hollow, burrow.

fillip *n.* impetus, provocation, stimulus, spice, lure, invitation, enticement, spur, magnet, drawing-card, come-on (*Slang*), bait.

fill out 1 fatten, enlarge, distend, round out, inflate, batten, swell, bloat, puff up, expand, wax, tumefy, balloon. **2** fill in, complete, finish, make out, write in.

ant. 1 reduce, slenderize, taper, wane, narrow, deflate.

film *n.* **1** coating, layer, membrane, skin, integument, veil, scale, lamina, sheet, scum. **2** haze, mist, blur, shadow, cloud, fog, gauze, cloudiness, opacity, mistiness, fogginess, indistinctness. **3** movie, movies, cinema, motion picture, motion pictures, moving picture, moving pictures, screen, flick (*Slang*), flicks (*Slang*), —*v.* photograph, shoot.

filmy *adj.* **1** misty, hazy, veiled, coated, membranous, blurred, blurry, shadowy, cloudy, opaque, murky, foggy, indistinct, milky, opalescent, unclear. **2** gauzy, cobwebby, sheer, transparent, diaphanous, chiffon, delicate, thin, fragile.

ant. 1 distinct, clear, lustrous, sharp, bright.

filter *n.* strainer, sieve, screen, clarifier, colander. —*v.* strain, sift, filtrate, purify, clarify, refine, percolate, seep, ooze, drain, pass through, winnow, drip.

filth *n.* **1** dirt, ordure, dung, excrement, feces, garbage, pollution, foulness, filthiness, putrefaction, putrescence, sewage, muck, mud, slime. **2** grossness, indecency, lewdness, nastiness, rottenness, vileness, defilement, obscenity, smut, pornography.

ant. 2 purity, virtue, cleanliness, high-mindedness, spirituality, innocence.

filthy *adj.* **1** dirty, polluted, putrified, putrid, excremental, fecal, foul, squalid, sordid, stained, unclean, piggish, unwashed, muddy, slimy, besmirched. **2** gross, indecent, lewd, nasty, swinish, shameless, foulmouthed, corrupt, foul, obscene, smutty, pornographic.

ant. 1 cleansed, clean, washed, purified, sanitary, hygienic, washed. **2** decent, virtuous, high-minded, uncorrupted, pure.

finagle *v.* arrange, maneuver, wangle, manage, con, bamboozle, trick, gyp, deceive, cheat, do, dupe, hook, hoax, take in, bilk, swindle, defraud, rook, hoodwink, rip off (*Slang*).

final *adj.* last, ultimate, finishing, end, concluding, conclusive, terminal, terminating, extreme, decisive, definitive, irrevocable, closing, latest.

ant. first, original, beginning, opening, earliest, introductory, prime, primal.

finale termination, end, finis, expiration, consummation, culmination, wind-up, dead end, curtains (*Slang*).

ant. origin, opening, beginning.

finality *n.* conclusiveness, definitiveness, decisiveness, completeness, resolution.

ant. inconclusiveness, incompleteness, indecision.

finalize *v.* wind up, conclude, complete, terminate, consummate, culminate, finish, end, mop up, wrap up.

finally *adv.* ULTIMATELY.

finance *n.* banking, economics, purse strings, budget. —*v.* subsidize, underwrite, contribute, fund, subscribe, pay for, endow, aid, assist, pension, pledge.

finances funds, resources, treasure, money, capital.

financial *adj.* monetary, fiscal, pecuniary, bursal, budgetary.

financier *n.* banker, capitalist, investor, backer, broker, tycoon, baron, angel, underwriter.

find *v.* discover, come on, experience, meet with, observe, notice, ascertain, perceive, discern, remark, detect, meet, recover, locate, espy, come up with.

ant. lose, misplace, overlook, miss, mislay, neglect.

finding *n.* result, conclusion, deduction, inference, observation, discovery, decision, judgment, verdict, solution, disclosure, exposure, resolution, answer, outcome.

find out learn, discover, detect, uncover, hear, trace, perceive, unravel, verify, realize, observe, note.

fine[1] *adj.* **1** excellent, admirable, superior, choice, rare, quality, topdrawer, select, outstanding, first-rate, exemplary, top-notch, distinguished, first-class, exceptional, A-one. **2** agreeable, pleasant, enjoyable, sunny, cloudless, clear, bright, pure, unmarred, lovely, delightful. **3** delicate, airy, gossamer, light, cobwebby, diaphanous, sheer, tiny, minute, finegrained, flimsy, sifted, ground, powdery, pulverized, refined. **4** slim, sharp, thin, narrow, attenuated, slender, keen. **5** cultivated, refined, polished, acute, elegant, delicate, finished, brilliant, fastidious, sensitive, dainty, discriminating. **6** subtle, intricate, exacting, precise, hairsplitting, nice.

ant. 1 mediocre, inferior, middling, common, so-so, second-rate. **2** disagreeable, cloudy, unpleasant, marred, flawed, impure. **3** coarse, crude, thick, heavy, gross, large. **4** blunt, dull, dulled. **5** uncouth, rough, unrefined, rude, crude, insensitive. **6** gross, coarse, heavy-handed.

fine[2] *n.* forfeit, penalty, punishment, forfeiture, damages, settlement, amercement.

fine-spun *adj.* SUBTLE.

finesse *n.* skill, adroitness, tact, subtlety, savoir faire, delicacy, discretion, polish, refinement, sophistication, know-how, artfulness, diplomacy, cleverness, savvy (*Slang*).
ant. ineptitude, clumsiness, crudeness, tactlessness, heavy-handedness, stupidity, maladroitness.

finger *v.* **1** touch, handle, toy with, feel, thumb, stroke, manipulate, caress, palpate, paw, maul. **2** *Slang* point out, designate, indicate, identify, sell out (*Slang*), double-cross (*Slang*), betray, deliver, turn in.

finical *adj.* FINICKY.

finicking *adj.* FINICKY.

finicky *adj.* fussy, fastidious, squeamish, prim, prissy, precious, overneat, overprecise, niggling, meticulous, exacting, finical, finicking, punctilious, picky, nit-picking, hair-splitting.
ant. careless, offhand, slapdash, uncritical, sloppy, untidy.

finis *n.* END.

finish *v.* **1** complete, conclude, end, terminate, close, cease, stop, achieve, discharge, discontinue, desist, culminate, break, expire, drop, wind up, finalize. **2** use up, exhaust, deplete, dispose of, consume, empty, drain, polish off. —*n.* **1** conclusion, end, termination, completion, close, cessation, windup, culmination, crown, stop, finale, expiration, denouement, limit, boundary, death, expiration, curtains (*Slang*). **2** polish, elegance, cultivation, refinement, perfection, completeness, poise, suavity, urbanity, savoir faire, breeding, gentility, courtliness.
ant. *v.* **1** begin, start, commence, embark on, set out, open, launch. *n.* **1** beginning, start, commencement,

opening, prologue, birth. **2** crudity, vulgarity, coarseness, roughness, awkwardness, ingenuousness, naiveté.

finished *adj.* **1** polished, elegant, refined, well-bred, cultivated, civilized, urbane, suave, expert, accomplished, perfected, gifted, exquisite. **2** ruined, undone, bankrupt, depleted, destroyed, overthrown, wrecked, failed, annihilated, pauperized, destitute, wiped out, devastated, defeated.
ant. **1** crude, coarse, rough, boorish, ill-mannered, plebian, amateurish, tactless. **2** up-and-coming, successful, making out, well-off, flush, in the chips (*Slang*).

finite *adj.* limited, bounded, temporal, numbered, measured, measurable, confined, circumscribed, fixed, partial, terminable, temporary, fleeting, transitory, ephemeral.
ant. infinite, eternal, perpetual, everlasting, unbounded, endless, immeasurable.

fink *n.* *Slang* louse (*Slang*), rat (*Slang*), rat fink (*Slang*), wretch, dog, snake, cur, caitiff, scab, lowlife, scum, skunk, toad, bastard.

fink out *Slang* BACK OUT.

fire *n.* **1** flame, light, heat, combustion, conflagration, holocaust, bonfire, wildfire, blaze, fuel, flare, spark, glow, incandescence, effulgence, sparkle, torch, brand. **2** ardor, passion, zeal, fever, fervor, spirit, fireworks, pyrotechnics, virtuosity, éclat, glory, dazzle. **3** ordeal, trial, torment, anguish, suffering, tragedy, calamity, agony, scourge, purgatory, hell. —*v.* **1** ignite, light, kindle, burn, set aflame, set ablaze. **2** excite, inflame, impassion, heat, incite, inspire, stimulate, rouse, arouse, fan, electrify, galvanize, foment, spur, whet. **3** shoot, discharge, detonate, bombard, shell, snipe, strafe, torpedo, hurl, rake, pepper, fling, sling, pelt, strike, blitz.
ant. *n.* **2** boredom, dullness, apathy,

nonchalance, torpor, cool (*Slang*).
v. **1** extinguish, bank, put out,
quench, smother, blow out. **2** dampen, cool, quell, calm, soothe, dispirit,
lull, discourage.

firebrand *n.* agitator, troublemaker, instigator, incendiary, rabble-rouser,
agent provocateur, hothead, mutineer, insurgent, rebel, revolutionary.

firebug *n.* pyromaniac, arsonist.

fireplace *n.* hearth, fireside, grate, hob,
ingle (*Brit.*).

firm[1] *adj.* **1** solid, compact, compressed, rigid, stiff, unyielding,
dense, concentrated, substantial,
stocky, stuffed, stout. **2** stable, unfluctuating, fixed, stationary, secure,
settled, established, confirmed, rooted, anchored, riveted, moored, fast.
3 enduring, steadfast, constant, true,
strong, determined, unwavering, resolved, resolute, decided, decisive,
unflinching, unfaltering, obdurate,
immovable, unyielding, tough, hardnosed (*Slang*).
ant. 2 unstable, fluctuating, shaky,
adrift, mercurial. **3** undecided, irresolute, uncertain, weak, wavering, faltering.

firm[2] *n.* company, business, organization, enterprise, partnership, house,
establishment, concern, corporation,
conglomerate.

firmament *n.* sky, heaven, heavens,
blue, welkin, vault.

first *adj.* **1** original, earliest, preceding,
foregoing, previous, prior, eldest,
premier, prime, primary, primal, primeval, primordial. **2** closest, nearest,
proximal, proximate. **3** highest, chief,
principal, outstanding, main, preeminent, cardinal, leading, key, ruling,
greatest, foremost. **4** primary, basic,
rudimentary, fundamental.
ant. 1 last, end, final, concluding,
terminating, closing. **2** farthest, last,
remotest, outside, extreme. **3** undistinguished, least, lowest, smallest. **4**
advanced, unessential.

first-class *adj.* SUPERIOR.

first-rate *adj.* finest, best, choice, prime,

select, elite, superior, outstanding,
excellent, distinguished, incomparable, exclusive, hand-picked, A-one,
nonpareil, exemplary, tip-top, topdrawer, topflight, top-notch, tops
(*Slang*).
ant. mediocre, average, ordinary, undistinguished, run-of-the-mill, so-so,
tolerable.

fisherman *n.* angler, fisher, piscator.

fish for angle, look for, seek, solicit, ask
for, hope for, bid for, wheedle, cajole, coax.

fish story FIB.

fishy *adj.* shady, dubious, questionable,
improbable, unlikely, suspicious,
slippery, unsound, unreasonable, unbelievable, doubtful, implausible,
queer, odd.
ant. likely, plausible, cogent, convincing, believable, sound, reasonable.

fissure *n.* cleft, crevice, cleavage, opening, split, crack, break, cranny, rift,
slit, chink, chasm, cut, crevasse,
fracture, fault, flaw.

fit[1] *adj.* **1** suitable, proper, fitting, pertinent, germane, apt, apposite, relevant, timely, seasonable, meet, felicitous, becoming, well-chosen. **2**
trained, prepared, ready, primed,
healthy, strong, capable, hardy, rugged, muscular, sound. —*v.* **1** suit,
conform, correspond, befit, accord,
coincide, match, answer. **2** outfit,
furnish, clothe, appoint, supply, provide, accouter.
ant. *adj.* **1** improper, unsuitable, inappropriate, unfit, out of place, illadvised. **2** weak, unsound, puny,
flabby, feeble, flaccid.

fit[2] *n.* spasm, convulsion, paroxysm,
seizure, attack, spell, outburst, spurt,
fury, frenzy, explosion, tantrum,
snit, conniption.

fitful *adj.* spasmodic, intermittent, irregular, uneasy, uneven, discontinuous, sporadic, fluctuating, broken,
disordered, aberrant, erratic, variable, flickering.

ant. regular, even, steady, smooth, flowing, continuous, unbroken.

fitting *adj.* fit, suitable, proper, becoming, befitting, meet, correct, right, applicable, appropriate, seemly, apropos, *comme il faut*, decent, acceptable. —*n.* fixture, part, piece, unit, component, mechanism, attachment, adjunct, accessory.

ant. *adj.* improper, wrong, tasteless, incorrect, unsuitable, unacceptable.

fittings *n.* furnishings, furniture, decor, equipment, appurtenances, accessories, conveniences, apparatus, gear, outfit, paraphernalia, things, trappings, fixtures, installation.

fix *v.* **1** attach, secure, focus, position, fasten, connect, bind, tie, rivet, nail, affix, join, pin, immobilize, impale, cement. **2** decide, determine, nail down, settle, agree on, resolve, establish, arrange, stipulate, choose, name, specify, designate. **3** repair, mend, heal, tend to, adjust, patch, rearrange, renovate, renew, improve on, refurbish, tidy, readjust, rebuild, recondition, overhaul. —*n.* jam, spot, bind, dilemma, trouble, quandary, predicament, impasse, mess, corner.

ant. *v.* **1** loosen, undo, unfasten, remove, disconnect. **3** break, tear, split, mutilate, damage.

fixation *n.* obsession, compulsion, neurosis, infatuation, monomania, fetishism, *idée fixe*, complex, preoccupation, passion.

fixed *adj.* **1** STABLE. **2** RESOLUTE.

fixture *n.* installation, attachment, equipment, appendage, appurtenance, contrivance, facility, gimmick.

fizzle *v.* peter out, fail, miscarry, misfire, fall flat, fall through, crash, collapse, come to nothing, draw a blank, poop out (*Slang*), lay an egg (*Slang*), bomb (*Slang*), fold (*Slang*). —*n.* dud, flop, frost, failure, miscarriage, fiasco, botch, bomb (*Slang*), bust (*Slang*), lemon (*Slang*), washout (*Slang*).

ant. *v.* make it, hit the jackpot, suc-

ceed, come through, click (*Slang*). *n.* hit, smash, success, triumph, winner, achievement.

flabbergast *v.* CONFOUND.

flabbergasted *adj.* amazed, astonished, astounded, confounded, overcome, dumbfounded, staggered, breathless, stunned, shocked, stupefied, speechless, knocked for a loop (*Slang*), thrown (*Slang*).

ant. unimpressed, apathetic, cool, unmoved, impassive.

flabby *adj.* soft, flaccid, feeble, limp, weak, infirm, baggy, droopy, sagging, unfit, slack, lax, ineffective, insipid, sickly.

ant. firm, fit, muscular, strong, solid, robust.

flaccid *adj.* FLABBY.

flag[1] *n.* banner, standard, ensign, pennant, streamer, colors, gonfalon, oriflamme, bunting, guidon, banderol. —*v.* signal, wave, salute, dip, semaphore.

flag[2] *v.* WEAKEN.

flagellate *v.* WHIP.

flagellation *n.* flogging, whipping, lashing, scourging, thrashing, birching, caning, switching, drubbing, strapping, hiding, flailing, paddling, corporal punishment.

flagging *adj.* weakening, failing, drooping, sagging, declining, languishing, sinking, ebbing, fading, tiring, wearying, deteriorating, waning, wasting.

ant. improving, strengthening, waxing, rising, unflagging, increasing.

flagitious *adj.* WICKED.

flagrant *adj.* glaring, brazen, undisguised, scandalous, notorious, outrageous, infamous, out-and-out, audacious, shocking, barefaced, indecent, disgraceful, shameless, blatant.

ant. hidden, clandestine, surreptitious, sneaky, undercover, concealed.

flail *v.* BEAT.

flair *n.* talent, aptitude, feel, feeling, sensibility, taste, discernment, touch, style, chic, dash, elegance, genius, gift, knack, panache.

flak *n.* criticism, fault-finding, disparagement, condemnation, hostility, sarcasm, carping, disapproval.

ant. kudos, applause, approval, salvo, salute, praise, respect.

flake *n.* fleck, scale, disk, paten, lamina, sheet, leaf, foil, wafer, slice, shaving, layer, film, lamella, plate, scurf, squama. —*v.* peel, scale, laminate, layer, chip, desquamate, strip, skin, shave, shed, moult.

flake out *Slang* RETIRE.

flamboyant *adj.* ornate, vivid, flashy, showy, bright, loud, garish, jazzy, ostentatious, florid, overdone, wild, exaggerated, theatrical, attention-getting, campy.

ant. muted, drab, plain, dull, quiet, colorless, inconspicuous.

flame *n.* fire, blaze, flare, light, flash, spark, incandescence, corruscation, glow, gleam, flicker. —*v.* **1** blaze, burn, flash, glare, flare, gleam, sparkle, spark, corruscate, shimmer, glow, glisten, glint, redden. **2** rant, roar, fume, flare up, explode, burn, glare, rage, erupt.

ant. *v.* **2** calm down, simmer down, cool off, abate.

flammable *adj.* combustible, inflammable.

ant. fireproof, flameproof, fire-resistant, fire-retarded, fire-resistive, fire-retardant.

flank *v.* ABUT.

flap *n.* **1** tab, lap, lappet, overlap, lapel, wing, attachment, extension. **2** *Slang* dither, fluster, panic, ferment, sweat, fever, jitters, shakes, tizzy (*Slang*). **3** *Slang* crisis, emergency, furore, uproar, commotion, hubbub, brouhaha, hullabaloo. —*v.* slap, beat, flail, flutter, oscillate, wave, flick, swing, swish, whoosh, whisk, smack, swat, paddle, whack, thwack.

flare *v.* **1** blaze, burn, ignite, flash, flame, glare, sparkle, gleam, glow. **2** erupt, break out, blow up, explode, burn, fulminate, rage, glare, fume, thunder. **3** widen, open, spread, dilate, expand, enlarge, broaden, distend, amplify, stretch. —*n.* blaze, flash, flame, glare, sparkle, gleam, glow.

ant. *v.* **2** calm down, cool off, simmer down, relax, subside, abate, diminish, wane. **3** contract, narrow, close, shrink, condense.

flare-up *n.* outburst, eruption, explosion, storm, blast, scene, fury, furor, blaze, tantrum, fit, paroxysm.

flash *v.* **1** flare, flame, spark, sparkle, gleam, glitter, glisten, glimmer, shimmer, shine, scintillate, glint, corruscate, twinkle, dazzle. **2** streak, race, run, dash, rush, sweep, speed, fly, dart. **3** wire, telegraph, signal, cable, radio, broadcast, announce, report. **4** show, display, reveal, disclose, expose, uncover, exhibit, flaunt, flourish. —*n.* **1** gleam, glint, point, sparkle, streak, scintilla, spark, twinkle, burst. **2** eruption, outburst, explosion, outbreak. **3** instant, moment, second, twinkling, breath, blink, trice, wink, jiffy.

flashy *adj.* showy, gaudy, garish, cheap, tawdry, pretentious, gimcrack, flamboyant, vulgar, meretricious, tasteless, loud, tinsel, jazzy (*Slang*).

ant. somber, muted, inconspicuous, toned-down, sober, tasteful, decorous.

flask *n.* vial, phial, bottle, vessel, cruet, ampule, retort, jug, decanter, canteen, flagon, crock.

flat *adj.* **1** level, horizontal, even, unbroken, oblate, unwrinkled, smooth, uniform, flush, plane, regular. **2** positive, absolute, unequivocal, unqualified, peremptory, direct, plain, downright, unmistakable, decisive, categorical, explicit, unreserved. **3** stale, tasteless, insipid, dead, vapid, weak, watery, indifferent, dull.

ant. **1** round, rounded, rough, curved, arched, uneven, bumpy, ridged. **2** indecisive, qualified, unclear, questionable, vague, puzzling, ambiguous. **3** bubbly, effervescent, sparkling, frothy, fizzing, vital, animated, stimulating, interesting.

flat-footed *adj.* RESOLUTE.

flatness *n.* **1** levelness, horizontality, evenness, smoothness, regularity, uniformity. **2** staleness, insipidity, vapidity, tastelessness, weakness, indifference, dullness.
ant. 1 bumpiness, unevenness, roughness, irregularity. **2** effervescence, fizz, sparkle, bubbles, freshness, life, liveliness, vitality, animation, interest.

flatter *v.* compliment, praise, overpraise, adulate, puff, extol, eulogize, blandish, cajole, salve, soft-soap, jolly, bootlick, fawn, toady, court, cotton up to, beguile, please, gratify, butter up, sweet-talk.
ant. deride, insult, belittle, criticize, deprecate, put down (*Slang*).

flatterer *n.* sycophant, adulator, eulogist, panegyrist, booster, fawner, bootlicker, flunkey, toady, blandisher, yes-man, apple polisher (*Slang*).
ant. faultfinder, knocker, critic, belittler, detractor.

flattering *adj.* **1** complimentary, commendatory, laudatory, eulogistic, praising, honoring, honeyed, unctuous, congratulatory, sycophantic, panegyric. **2** becoming, attractive, decorative, ornamental, beautifying, enhancing.
ant. 1 uncomplimentary, critical, derogatory, derisive, disparaging, unflattering. **2** unbecoming, unsuitable, plain, unattractive, unflattering.

flattery *n.* adulation, acclaim, compliments, plaudits, applause, eulogy, praise, sycophancy, obsequiousness, fawning, cajolery, blandishment, blarney, sweet talk, honey, soft soap, buildup, snow job (*Slang*), taffy.
ant. criticism, derogation, deprecation, belittling, carping, put-down (*Slang*).

flatulent *adj.* pretentious, pompous, bombastic, turgid, inflated, swollen, long-winded, wordy, prolix, garrulous.
ant. simple, concise, terse, pithy, succinct.

flaunt *v.* display, show off, disport, swagger, strut, boast, vaunt, air, brandish, flourish, blazon, parade.
ant. conceal, cloak, cover, disguise, minimize.

flavor *n.* **1** taste, savor, tang, flavoring, seasoning, spice, extract, spirit, tincture, lacing. **2** aspect, type, characteristic, essence, nature, trait, feature, earmark, brand, cast, stamp, quality, property, attribute, smack. —*v.* season, spice, salt, distinguish, characterize, imbue, infuse, instill, impregnate, aromatize, leaven, tinge, color, tincture.

flaw *n.* defect, blemish, fault, disfigurement, imperfection, spot, deformity, taint, stain, blot, blotch, smudge, tear, scar, crack, break, fissure.

flawless *adj.* PERFECT.

flay *v.* castigate, excoriate, scalp, skin, attack, assail, slash, scathe, roast, scorch, blister, rip into, tear into, damn, savage, inveigh, revile, abuse, vilify, curse, execrate, cut up.

fleck *n.* SPECK.

fledgling *n.* novice, tyro, new hand, novitiate, beginner, entrant, neophyte, greenhorn, tenderfoot, freshman, gosling, infant, newcomer, rookie (*Slang*).
ant. veteran, professional, old hand, old-timer, master, dean, authority, past master, pro.

flee *v.* escape, vanish, decamp, depart, take off, scud, disappear, dodge, run away, fly, make off, bolt, avoid, shun, evade, split (*Slang*).
ant. remain, confront, stay, tarry, stand ground.

fleece *v.* cheat, defraud, rob, bleed, pluck, rook, bilk, skin, diddle, swindle, mulct, pilfer, filch, dupe, gull, hoodwink, take (*Slang*).

fleer *v.* SNEER.

fleet[1] *adj.* fast, swift, rapid, speedy, quick, hurried, mercurial, nimble, spry, agile.
ant. sluggish, slow, plodding, lingering, unhurried, indolent, lagging.

fleet[2] *n.* flotilla, navy, armada, squadron, tonnage, vessels, shipping, ships, transport, sea power, argosy, convoy, line.

fleeting *adj.* brief, transitory, transient, evanescent, ephemeral, short-lived, impermanent, flitting, temporary, temporal, momentary, vanishing.
ant. abiding, permanent, enduring, ageless, lasting, remaining, eternal.

flesh *n.* **1** meat, tissue, muscle, fat, weight, brawn, heft, food. **2** body, corpus, soma, substance, corporeality, fleshliness, mortality, carnality, matter, materiality.
ant. 2 spirit, psyche, soul, anima, spirituality, immateriality, shadow, soulfulness.

flesh out AUGMENT.

fleshy *adj.* **1** plump, fat, stout, obese, overweight, corpulent, beefy, chubby, portly, well-padded, thickset, rotund, heavy, hefty, heavy-set, stocky. **2** pithy, firm, succulent, meaty, pulpy, plump, juicy.
ant. 1 bony, skinny, thin, lean, spare, scrawny, underweight. **2** dry, wrinkled, mealy, shriveled, withered, desiccated.

flex *v.* bend, tilt, crook, angle, curve, arch, bow.
ant. straighten, relax, unbend.

flexibility *n.* RESILIENCE.

flexible *adj.* **1** pliable, pliant, plastic, rubbery, elastic, lithe, supple, willowy, malleable, ductile, stretchy, extensible, tensile. **2** versatile, adaptable, pliant, compliant, tractable, adjustable, affable, manageable, docile, responsive, giving, relaxed, soft, lenient, indulgent.
ant. 1 rigid, stiff, brittle, hard, inflexible, adamantine, breakable. **2** stubborn, obdurate, set, fixed, unyielding, resolute, intransigent.

flick[1] *v.* flip, strike, tap, peck, dab, rap, hit, touch, remove, dart, move, start, leap, spurt, flit, dash, skim. —*n.* stroke, pat, rap, jab, blow, peck, dab, touch, slap.

flick[2] *n. Slang* FILM.

flicker *v.* glimmer, shimmer, glisten, gleam, flash, blink, scintillate. —*n.* glimmer, shimmer, gleam, flash, ember, flame, ray, scintilla.

flighty *adj.* capricious, unstable, frivolous, silly, scatterbrained, giddy, thoughtless, irresponsible, unreliable, dizzy, heedless, fickle, impulsive, impetuous, foolish.
ant. settled, sober, stable, thoughtful, responsible, dependable, cautious.

flimsy *adj.* **1** weak, breakable, unsubstantial, sleazy, shoddy, thin, frail, fragile, delicate, rickety, unsteady, ramshackle, jerrybuilt, tumbledown, unreliable, perishable. **2** inadequate, ineffective, trivial, feeble, unsatisfactory, foolish, unconvincing, poor, implausible, inept, inane, meaningless.
ant. 1 substantial, strong, solid, serviceable, well-made, well-built, durable. **2** convincing, cogent, effective, plausible, sensible, acceptable.

flinch *v.* shrink, wince, withdraw, draw back, shy, retreat, cringe, cower, quiver, quail, recoil, blench, dodge, duck.
ant. confront, face, breast, meet, accept, endure, stand fast.

fling *v.* hurl, throw, toss, cast, project, pitch, put, flip, sling, dash, send, launch, chuck, pelt. —*n.* **1** throw, toss, pitch, dash, heave, lob, shot, discharge, serve. **2** hazard, attempt, venture, try, gamble, flier, risk, trial, effort, essay, undertaking, crack, stab, go.

flinty *adj.* obdurate, hard, stony, steely, adamant, unyielding, inflexible, rigid, coldhearted, unsympathetic, unfeeling, hardhearted, cold, unmerciful, heartless.
ant. compassionate, sympathetic, humane, generous, flexible, accommodating.

flip *v.* jerk, flick, toss, twirl, throw, spin, fling, pitch, flounce, cast. —*n.* jerk, toss, twirl, spin, flick, pitch, throw, yank, twitch, start, jiggle.

flip out *Slang* freak out (*Slang*), lose

one's cool (*Slang*), go ape (*Slang*), flip one's lid (*Slang*).

ant. calm down, cool it (*Slang*), keep one's cool (*Slang*).

flip over *Slang* rave, get excited, go wild, go crazy, enthuse, carry on, lose control.

ant. disregard, ignore, neglect, disdain, criticize.

flippant *adj.* impertinent, impudent, disrespectful, flip, saucy, sassy, unconcerned, frivolous, insolent, cheeky, brazen, rude, fresh (*Slang*).

ant. serious, mannerly, polite, respectful, courteous, thoughtful.

flirt *v.* trifle, toy, tease, coquet, dally, philander, lead on, entice, tantalize, pique, beguile. —*n.* coquette, trifler, tease, philanderer, playboy, vamp (*Slang*).

flirtation *n.* coquetry, dalliance, coyness, teasing, enticement, allurement, trifling, toying.

flirtatious *adj.* coquettish, coy, enticing, alluring, dallying, wanton, provocative, come-hither (*Slang*), on the make (*Slang*).

flit *v.* whisk, dart, flutter, flitter, skim, wing, fly, float, speed, race, scurry, scamper, hasten, hurry, career, pass, elapse, go by.

flitter *v.* FLUTTER.

float *v.* skim, drift, waft, swim, glide, soar, sail, hover, levitate, hang, poise.

ant. sink, submerge, hit bottom, drown, go under.

floater *n.* drifter, vagrant, vagabond, itinerant, gypsy, wanderer, hobo, tramp, migrant, nomad, ne'er-do-well, rover, good-for-nothing, loafer, beachcomber.

flock *n.* **1** group, company, gathering, herd, pack, bevy, drove, roundup, fold, brood, flight, swarm, band, colony, cluster, gaggle. **2** congregation, parish, community, assembly, assemblage, crowd, band, troop, horde, body, host, multitude, convention, gang, group.

flog *v.* whip, beat, scourge, thrash, horsewhip, lash, flagellate, cane, birch, switch, paddle, swinge, welt, strike, trounce, thwack, whack. **2** spur, goad, prod, sweat, overwork, push, burden, tax, oppress, drive, overexert, strain, punish.

flood *n.* overflow, inundation, deluge, downpour, river, stream, spate, outpouring, torrent, swell, rush, cascade, sea, surge. —*v.* deluge, inundate, overflow, overwhelm, drown, submerge, drench, engulf, swamp, bury, glut, cloy, saturate, oversupply.

flood tide CLIMAX.

floor *n.* story, level, tier, stage, flight. —*v.* confound, baffle, puzzle, nonplus, stagger, stump, throw, disconcert, bewilder, confuse, discomfit, befuddle, perplex, bamboozle.

flop *v.* **1** thud, thump, bump, plod, clomp, clump, plump, plunk, plonk. **2** foil, close, fold (*Slang*), bomb (*Slang*), lay an egg (*Slang*), go under. —*n.* dud, fizzle, failure, fiasco, debacle, disaster, turkey (*Slang*), bomb (*Slang*), washout (*Slang*), bust (*Slang*).

ant. *v.* flourish, succeed, thrive, make it (*Slang*), hit the jackpot. *n.* hit, smash, sensation (*Slang*), success, triumph.

floppy *adj.* droopy, sagging, limp, boneless, soft, baggy, pendulous, flapping, wilting, listless, dangling, loose-jointed.

ant. stiff, firm, rigid, upright, unbending, erect.

florid *adj.* ornate, flowery, overdecorated, gaudy, embellished, overelaborate, rococo, high-flown, fussy, fancy, euphuistic, overwritten, circumlocutory.

ant. simple, plain, straightforward, unadorned, understated, spare, functional.

flotilla *n.* FLEET.²

flotsam *n.* wreckage, rubbish, debris, trash, sweepings, odds and ends, leavings, garbage, refuse, scraps, castoffs, jetsam, junk, crap (*Slang*).

flounder *v.* struggle, stumble, wallow,

fumble, grope, limp, hobble, blunder, stammer, waver, hesitate, falter, shamble, shuffle, totter.

flourish v. **1** fatten, bear fruit, flower, bloom, grow, burgeon, thrive, succeed, wax, prosper, triumph, get ahead, peak, rise, arrive, batten. **2** wave, brandish, swing, shake, flutter, wag, wield, flaunt, display, exhibit. —n. decoration, ornament, embellishment, display, parade, fanfare, curl, curlicue, plume, panache, show, adornment, blazon.

ant. v. **1** wither, weaken, fail, dry up, shrivel, decline, wane.

flout v. deride, mock, jeer, scoff, gibe, taunt, sneer at, ridicule, scorn, defy, spurn, sass, chaff, guy.

ant. respect, conform, obey, defer to, abide by.

flow v. stream, run, issue, emanate, pour, gush forth, surge, spring, originate, sweep, roll, ripple, cascade, course. —n. stream, river, gush, course, current, sweep, emanation, flux, fluxion, spate, flood, cascade, outpouring, fountain, wave, rush.

flower v. bloom, blossom, burgeon, sprout, peak, effloresce, develop, grow, mature, unfold, ripen, evolve, maturate, arrive. —n. bloom, blossom, inflorescence, floret, floweret, bud, posy.

fluctuate v. waver, vary, oscillate, vacillate, undulate, alternate, flicker, flutter, sway, veer, alter, wobble, teeter, totter, falter.

ant. stabilize, settle, freeze, solidify, firm up (*Slang*).

fluent adj. smooth, flowing, effortless, facile, graceful, uninterrupted, articulate, expert, practiced, ready, unconstrained, effusive, easy, glib.

ant. halting, constrained, tongue-tied, hesitant, uneven, limping.

fluff n. **1** nap, down, lint, pile, feather, shag, hair, fleece, fuzz, dust, flocking, kapok, eiderdown. **2** error, mistake, blunder, slip, misreading, boo-boo (*Slang*), boner (*Slang*), howler, gaffe, faux-pas.

fluffy adj. downy, feather, airy, light, shaggy, foamy, fleecy, fuzzy, woolly, hairy, soft, silky, gossamer, filmy, gauzy.

ant. stiff, heavy, substantial, flat, hard-surfaced, enameled, lacquered.

fluid adj. **1** liquid, flowing, running, liquefied, melted, watery, streaming, pouring, gushing, moist, wet. **2** unfixed, fluctuating, varying, variable, unsettled, changeable, alterable, in flux, versatile, adaptable, flexible, elastic. **3** smooth, even, fluent, unbroken, graceful, easy, unconstrained, elegant, eloquent, facile.

ant. **1** solid, congealed, frozen, dammed up, solidified, dry. **2** invariable, fixed, set, settled, unalterable, rigid, inflexible. **3** stumbling, hesitant, halting, faltering, constrained, inhibited.

fluke n. windfall, godsend, luck, boon, blessing, break, serendipity, hap, happenstance, accident, chance, stroke of fate, quirk of fate, contingency, fortuity, mishap, mischance, misadventure.

flummery n. HUMBUG.

flunky n. lackey, servant, assistant, bootlicker, toady, valet, page, sycophant, yes-man, hanger-on, tool, jackal, drudge, minion, vassal, slave, go-fer (*Slang*).

flurry v. FLUSTER.

flush v. **1** blush, redden, glow, crimson, burn, color, suffuse, flame. **2** wash, swab, flood, douche, syringe, spray, rinse, cleanse, irrigate, hose down, drain. —n. blush, redness, reddening, fever, pink, red, rosiness, floridness, ruddiness, flame, glow, excitement, elation, high spirits, flurry, emotion. —adj. abundant, copious, full, rich, overflowing, lavish, wealthy, affluent, plentiful, abounding, in the chips (*Slang*), in the money (*Slang*). —adv. directly, squarely, exactly, straight, precisely, spang, unswervingly, on target.

ant. v. **1** blanch, whiten, pale, fade. n. pallor, whiteness, paleness, grayness, dullness, low spirits, funk, depression. *adj.* meager, sparse, low, scarce, indigent, needy, impoverished. *adv.* blindly, wildly, carelessly, wide of the mark.

fluster *v.* flurry, bewilder, confuse, addle, upset, perturb, agitate, rattle, disconcert, discombobulate, ruffle, disquiet, muddle, faze, unhinge, unsettle, unstring. —*n.* stir, commotion, to-do, bustle, flutter, agitation, excitement, fuss, disturbance, ado, confusion, hubbub.
ant. *v.* calm, quiet, reassure, soothe, smooth. *n.* peace, order, serenity, quiet, calm, stillness.

flutter *v.* flap, wave, flit, flitter, fritter, tremble, shake, quiver, vibrate, flicker, beat, palpitate, oscillate, agitate, throb, swish, toss, bat.

flux *n.* flow, change, stream, current, motion, passage, tide, variety, fluctuation, instability, unrest, shift, inconstancy, transition.
ant. stasis, rest, balance, equilibrium, standstill, inactivity, freeze.

fly *v.* **1** wing, soar, take flight, ascend, rise, skim, sail, mount, take off, zoom, shoot, rush. **2** escape, flee, shun, avoid, decamp, disappear, skip, depart, get away, split (*Slang*).
ant. 1 land, light, come down, alight, settle, arrive, reach.

flyspeck *n.* SPECK.

foam *n.* froth, effervescence, bubbles, spume, head, fizz, suds, lather, scum, spray, scud, spindrift, spritz. —*v.* froth, bubble, effervesce, fizz, spume, lather.

foamy *adj.* bubbly, frothy, sudsy, effervescent, fizzy, soapy, lathery, spumy, spumescent, sparkling, ebullient, light, aerated, airy, lively.
ant. flat, dull, still, glassy, smooth.

fob off FOIST.

focal point FOCUS.

focus *n.* center, hub, heart, eye, point, bull's eye, axis, focal point, core, nerve, limelight, nucleus, target, spotlight, magnet, cynosure. —*v.* concentrate, pinpoint, center on,

converge, scrutinize, examine, study, zoom in on, highlight, underline, emphasize, zero in on.
ant. *n.* margin, outside, outskirts, edge, fringe, sidelight.

foe *n.* enemy, adversary, antagonist, rival, opponent, competitor, contender, contestant, combatant, disputant.
ant. ally, friend, comrade, associate, brother, sister, confederate.

fog *n.* **1** mist, steam, haze, vapor, smog, murkiness, overcast, veil, cloud, brume, cloudiness, soup (*Slang*). **2** bewilderment, confusion, daze, muddle, perplexity, stupor, uncertainty, mystification, disorientation, trance, stupefaction, befuddlement.

foggish *adj.* OLD-FASHIONED.

foggy *adj.* **1** hazy, misty, steamy, murky, overcast, cloudy, blurred, indistinct, filmy, veiled, unclear, brumous, nebulous, vague, inexact, soupy. **2** bewildered, confused, dazed, perplexed, muddled, uncertain, mystified, disoriented, unhinged, befuddled, spacey (*Slang*).
ant. 1 clear, sunny, cloudless, bright, sharp, distinct, precise. **2** clearheaded, alert, lucid, self-possessed, on the qui vive, together (*Slang*).

foible *n.* weakness, frailty, flaw, fault, crack, defect, failing, shortcoming, deficiency, quirk, eccentricity, kink, vulnerability.
ant. strength, strong point, forte, asset.

foil[1] *v.* frustrate, thwart, circumvent, counter, check, discomfit, disconcert, balk, hinder, nullify, outwit, confound, cripple, hamstring.
ant. abet, support, further, promote, advance, cooperate, collaborate.

foil[2] *n.* contrast, antithesis, background, backdrop, counterpart, complement, setoff.

foist *v.* insinuate, sneak in, tuck in, palm off, slip in, fob off, pass off, put over, misrepresent, falsify.

fold[1] *v.* **1** crease, pleat, close, collapse, enclose, wrap up, double, surround, bend, shut, lap, overlap, dog-ear, hem, crumple, crinkle, corrugate. **2** *Slang* FLOP. —*n.* crease, wrinkle, pleat, dog-ear, crimp, lap, flap, overlap, furrow, corrugation, pucker.

ant. *v.* **1** smooth, even, flatten, open, separate, iron, unfold.

fold² *n.* **1** pen, cote, enclosure, corral, yard, pale, close, barnyard, stockade, pound, compound, sty. **2** flock, congregation, parishioners, worshipers, group, tribe, sect, herd, community, coreligionists, believers, gathering, meeting, party members, followers, adherents, loyalists.

ant. 2 dissenters, individualists, rebels, black sheep, outsiders, dissidents, independents, loners.

folder *n.* **1** file, portfolio, dossier, envelope, container. **2** leaflet, brochure, pamphlet, flier, handbill, throwaway, booklet.

foliage *n.* leaves, verdure, leafage, greenery.

folk *n.* people, tribe, nation, race, population, caste. —*adj.* indigenous, popular, local, native, primitive, aboriginal, autochthonous, local, vernacular, regional, parochial, unschooled, unsophisticated, unpolished, amateur.

ant. *adj.* cultivated, polished, professional, sophisticated, high, highbrow, elegant.

folksy *adj.* homey, informal, unpretentious, warm, neighborly, hospitable, unassuming, simplehearted, everyday, natural, unpolished, friendly, spontaneous.

ant. formal, distant, mannered, cool, stilted, artificial, starchy.

follow *v.* **1** result, ensue, come after, eventuate, proceed, succeed, supplant, happen, emanate, arise, issue. **2** trail, dog, track, pursue, hunt, hound, tail, shadow, chase, stalk. **3** imitate, conform to, model after, heed, obey, comply with, be guided by, regard, pattern, echo, duplicate, mimic. **4** comprehend, understand, get, see, appreciate, catch on,

fathom, perceive, gather, deduce, infer.

ant. 1 antedate, precede, come before, forerun. **4** misunderstand, misconstrue, misinterpret, misjudge.

follower *n.* disciple, adherent, devotee, believer, admirer, partisan, fan, convert, proselyte, enthusiast.

ant. dissenter, detractor, critic, renegade, apostate.

following *n.* entourage, followers, retinue, clientele, clients, customers, fans, boosters, attendants, circle, coterie, suite, cortege, bodyguard.

follow through complete, conclude, consummate, finish, see through, round out, finalize, end, polish off, clinch, wrap up, mop up.

follow-up *n.* reinforcement, supplement, addition, strengthening, follow-through, continuation, furtherance, boost, support, advancement, augmentation, replenishment, buttress, extension.

folly *n.* **1** foolishness, silliness, mindlessness, madness, irrationality, brainlessness, senselessness, idiocy, inanity, lunacy, imprudence, asininity, goofiness (*Slang*), dopiness (*Slang*). **2** mistake, blunder, misstep, indiscretion, false move, goof (*Slang*), boo-boo (*Slang*), faux pas.

ant. 1 wisdom, sanity, prudence, good sense, mindfulness, astuteness, penetration.

foment *v.* incite, stir up, agitate, roil, provoke, disturb, instigate, foster, kindle, enflame, excite, arouse, fire, exhort, quicken, embolden.

ant. inhibit, hinder, arrest, obstruct, discourage.

fond *adj.* affectionate, devoted, partial, warm, liking, loving, tender, attached, close, friendly.

ant. distant, averse, hostile, cool, uninterested.

fondle *v.* caress, pet, stroke, cuddle, nuzzle, spoon, neck (*Slang*), smooch (*Slang*), make out (*Slang*).

font *n.* origin, source, fountainhead, root, germ, seed, spring, womb, cradle, wellspring, genesis, basis, nucleus.

food *n.* **1** fare, nutriment, aliment, victuals, foodstuff, eats, diet, viands, comestibles, provender, provisions, pabulum, flesh, chow (*Slang*), grub (*Slang*). **2** sustenance, nourishment, support, maintenance.

foodstuff *n.* FOOD.

fool *n.* idiot, moron, simpleton, dope (*Slang*), half-wit, loon, loony, nincompoop, blockhead, dolt, pinhead, dunce, buffoon, jester, jokester, clown, chucklehead, ninny, dunderhead, tomfool, zany, dupe, butt, sap (*Slang*), saphead (*Slang*), meatball (*Slang*). —*v.* deceive, trick, dupe, take in, kid, bamboozle, cheat, hoodwink, gull, hoax, diddle, bluff, mislead, hook, con (*Slang*), sell (*Slang*).

fool around fritter, dabble, putter, mess, dawdle, diddle, idle, loiter, hang around, poke, loll, lounge, loaf.
ant. get going (*Slang*), get on the ball (*Slang*), get it together (*Slang*), get cracking (*Slang*), shape up.

foolhardy *adj.* reckless, rash, daring, venturesome, hot-headed, heedless, precipitate, imprudent, daredevil, impetuous, unthinking, injudicious, devil-may-care.
ant. cautious, careful, prudent, timid, wary, circumspect.

foolish *adj.* unwise, ill-advised, stupid, thoughtless, injudicious, imprudent, preposterous, absurd, tomfool, inane, harebrained, asinine, silly, empty-headed, extravagant, inappropriate, improper, senseless.
ant. wise, sensible, prudent, well-advised, reasonable, intelligent.

fool with meddle, mess, toy, play, poke, tamper, handle, romp, frolic, cavort.
ant. let alone, let be, stay out of, lay off (*Slang*).

foot *n.* bottom, base, pedestal, extremity, basis, lowest part, end, foundation, heel, sole, underneath, floor, nadir.

ant. head, top, summit, acme, peak, crown.

footdragging *n.* delay, lagging, dawdling, dilatoriness, reluctance, unwillingness, disinclination, averseness, repugnance, balkiness, mulishness, noncooperation, refractoriness, recalcitrance.
ant. alacrity, promptness, eagerness, enthusiasm, cooperation, ardor, zeal.

foothold *n.* **1** grip, toehold, hold, footing, standing, base, foundation, support. **2** bridgehead, beachhead, vantage, vantage point, vantage ground.

footing *n.* **1** surface, foundation, support, standing, purchase, grip, hold, foothold. **2** basis, ground, groundwork, foundation, position. **3** terms, relationship, relations, standing.

footloose *adj.* unattached, fancy-free, uncommitted, unsettled, on the move, free, independent, unbound, uncurbed, detached, drifting, carefree.
ant. settled, involved, committed, engaged, tied down, rooted.

footprint *n.* footmark, footstep, trace, track, spoor, impression, mark.

footstep *n.* **1** pace, stride, walk, footfall, tread, step, stepping, gait. **2** FOOTPRINT.

fop *n.* dandy, beau, dude, buck, peacock, coxcomb, popinjay, swell, fashion plate, blade, Beau Brummell, gallant, clotheshorse, tailor's dummy, toff (*Brit.*).
ant. bumpkin, peasant, rustic, boor, mess, slob.

foppish *adj.* overdressed, overcourteous, overfastidious, pretentious, finicky, precious, dandyish, affected, swish (*Brit.*).
ant. casual, informal, folksy, sporty, messy.

forage *v.* SEARCH.

foray *v.* raid, reconnoiter, explore, invade, descend on, sneak up on, board, move in on, venture, assault. —*n.* raid, exploration, reconnaissance, invasion, incursion, inroad, venture, assault, attack, siege, storm, march.

forbear *v.* abstain, refrain, desist, pause, hang back, leave off, stay, discontinue, renounce, withhold, restrain, eschew, tolerate, endure, abide, bear with.

ant. rush into, pursue, insist on, persist.

forbearance *n.* patience, restraint, understanding, sympathy, tolerance, acceptance, self-control, meekness, indulgence, mildness, mercy, temperance, humanity, gentleness, clemency.

ant. impatience, vindictiveness, intolerance, rancor, vengefulness, ruthlessness.

forbearing *adj.* patient, abstinent, renouncing, restrained, tolerant, accepting, understanding, sympathetic, long-suffering, uncomplaining, self-controlled, restrained, philosophical, unruffled.

ant. impatient, intolerant, cranky, critical, self-indulgent, unsympathetic, resentful.

forbid *v.* prohibit, ban, enjoin, interdict, veto, proscribe, debar, exclude, bar, disallow, taboo, shut, stop, suppress, outlaw.

ant. allow, permit, let, sanction, authorize, approve, assent.

forbidding *adj.* frightening, repulsive, scary, repellent, alarming, disagreeable, menacing, horrifying, hideous, grisly, sinister, threatening, grim, stony, icy.

ant. pleasant, agreeable, friendly, encouraging, warm, inviting, cordial.

force *n.* **1** power, energy, vigor, might, strength, dint, compulsion, coercion, impact, weight, duress, influence, pull, push, drive, clout (*Slang*). **2** efficacy, validity, effectiveness, potency, cogency, effect. **3** army, troops, legion, host, battalion, body, corps, squad, squadron, division, posse, gang, vigilantes. —*v.* compel, impel, coerce, push, drive, pull, influence, enforce, necessitate, oblige,

constrain, effect, overpower, propel, press, urge, exact, extort.

ant. *n.* **1, 2** weakness, impotence, feebleness, infirmity, debility, invalidity, ineffectiveness.

forced *adj.* strained, affected, unnatural, labored, feigned, artificial, grudging, constrained, contrived, factitious, stiff, mannered, insincere, simulated.

ant. spontaneous, natural, effortless, easy, sincere, genuine, unforced.

forceful *adj.* powerful, strong, vigorous, impressive, efficient, mighty, dynamic, potent, energetic, emphatic, intense, vehement, robust.

ant. weak, powerless, insipid, impotent, ineffectual, lackadaisical, namby-pamby.

forcible *adj.* compelling, compulsory, coercive, drastic, violent, aggressive, strong, warlike, armed, combative, mighty, forceful.

ant. peaceable, amicable, reasonable, noncoercive, pacifist, nonaggressive.

fore *adj.* first, foremost, leading, frontal, headmost, front, forward, anterior, chief, head, advance, forehand, prime, primary.

ant. last, posterior, rear, aft, tail, back, hindmost.

forebear *n.* ANCESTOR.

forebode *v.* PORTEND.

foreboding *n.* premonition, presentiment, omen, portent, apprehension, dread, forewarning, presage, sign, indication, foreshadowing, misgiving, intuition, prescience.

forecast *v.* foretell, predict, augur, prognosticate, presage, prophesy, foresee, anticipate, envisage, prearrange, predetermine, contrive, devise, scheme, plan, plot, conspire. —*n.* prediction, prophecy, prognostication, foresight, foreknowledge, prescience, prevision, anticipation, conjecture, prognosis, precognition, extra-sensory perception, ESP.

forefather *n.* ancestor, forbear, forerunner, begetter, procreator, progenitor, primogenitor, originator, ancient, predecessor, precursor, author, patriarch.

forefront *n.* front, lead, first place, fore, foreground, vanguard, avant garde, spearhead, prow, helm.
ant. last, rear guard, background, tail, end, tail end.

foregoing *adj.* previous, preceding, antecedent, former, prior, antedating, earlier, precursory, late, recent, prefatory, introductory, old.
ant. later, latter, following, coming, future, new, concluding, final.

foregone *adj.* determined, previous, premeditated, calculated, intended, fixed, set, bygone, inexorable, predestined, inevitable, fated, foreordained.
ant. undecided, open, undetermined, uncertain, chancy.

foreground *n.* forefront, lead, fore, front, front and center, vanguard, spotlight, limelight, prominence.
ant. background, shadow, shade, back, rear.

forehanded *adj.* THRIFTY.

foreign *adj.* **1** alien, exotic, outlandish, unfamiliar, strange, unknown, imported, distant, exterior. **2** aberrant, abnormal, uncharacteristic, unnatural, unrelated, unexpected, unbefitting, odd, unusual, irregular, unaccountable.
ant. **1** native, indigenous, aboriginal, homegrown, known, familiar. **2** typical, characteristic, usual, natural, expected.

foreigner *n.* ALIEN.

foreknowledge *n.* FORESIGHT.

foremost *adj.* first, leading, prime, primary, initial, inaugural, forward, front, uppermost, head, chief, supreme, capital, starring, preeminent.
ant. rearmost, last, bottom, hindmost, least.

forensic *adj.* arguable, argumentative, polemical, controversial, debatable, disputable, rhetorical, equivocal, moot, unsettled, dialectic.
ant. settled, decided, closed, unequivocal, undebatable.

foreordain *v.* PREDETERMINE.

forerunner *n.* precursor, herald, harbinger, announcer, outrider, usher, proclaimer, messenger, scout, informant, reporter, trumpeter, envoy, omen, portent, prognostic, token, sign, augury.

foresee *v.* anticipate, presage, augur, divine, forebode, foretell, prophesy, predict, prognosticate, forecast, expect, envision, envisage, surmise.

foreshadow *v.* prefigure, signal, signify, bode, forebode, foretoken, foreshow, presage, betoken, portend, augur.

foreshow *v.* FORESHADOW.

foresight *n.* prophecy, clairvoyance, forethought, precognition, foreknowledge, prevision, prediction, prescience, preconception, presentiment, premonition, prudence, precaution, good sense, care, planning.
ant. afterthought, hindsight, retrospect.

forest *n.* woods, woodland, grove, timberland, timber, copse, coppice, thicket, bosk, brush, brake, bracken, wilderness, wild.

forestall *v.* ward off, frustrate, avert, preclude, prevent, hinder, hamper, deter, fend off, head off, repel, guard against, debar, thwart, counteract, circumvent.
ant. encourage, abet, incite, impel, provoke, rouse, induce, initiate.

foretaste *n.* sample, preview, whiff, scent, introduction, sip, prelude, preliminary, example, demonstration.

foretell *v.* prophesy, predict, forecast, prognosticate, divine, foresee, soothsay, foretoken, augur, bode, foreshadow, herald, signify, presage, forewarn.

forethought *n.* PRUDENCE.

foretoken *v.* FORESHADOW.

forever *adv.* always, ever, endlessly, incessantly, unceasingly, perpetually, everlastingly, eternally, unremittingly, continually, constantly, ceaselessly, interminably, infinitely.

foreword *n.* preface, introduction, preamble, proem, prologue, prelude, exordium, preliminary, prolegomenon. **ant.** epilogue, appendix, postscript, afterthought, coda.

forfeit *v.* lose, pay, be liable, give up, sacrifice, surrender, yield, waive, forgo, renounce, resign. —*n.* penalty, fine, cost, loss, payment, pledge, assessment, amercement, damages.

forgather *v.* MEET.

forge[1] *v.* **1** mold, cast, hammer out, shape, fashion, create, model, contrive, devise, invent, coin, produce, fabricate, originate, chisel. **2** counterfeit, falsify.

forge[2] *v.* plod, slog, push, progress, drive on, press forward, advance, spurt, gain.
ant. lag, drop back, fall behind, retrogress, recede, regress, retreat.

forgery *n.* FAKE.

forgetful *adj.* **1** absent-minded, oblivious, amnesiac, unmindful, out of it (*Slang*). **2** neglectful, careless, negligent, unmindful, oblivious, heedless, mindless.

forgive *v.* excuse, pardon, exonerate, exculpate, absolve, acquit, clear, remit, release, reprieve.
ant. accuse, impeach, condemn, charge, blame, convict.

forgiveness *n.* pardon, exoneration, absolution, dispensation, acquittal, reprieve, amnesty, mercy, forbearance, grace, exculpation, deliverance, indulgence, clemency, compassion, charity.
ant. vindictiveness, vengefulness, implacability, rancor, resentment, hardheartedness.

forgiving *adj.* MERCIFUL.

forgo *v.* give up, do without, relinquish, renounce, forfeit, surrender, waive, eschew, abandon, abjure, forswear, dispense with.
ant. retain, keep, cling to, enjoy, revel in, safeguard.

fork *v.* branch, divide, bifurcate, split, divurge, ramify, bend, part, deviate.

forlorn *adj.* abandoned, deserted, miserable, pitiable, pitiful, desolate,

bereft, forsaken, dejected, woeful, woebegone, wretched, doleful, dismal, hopeless.
ant. cheerful, happy, optimistic, befriended, cherished.

form *n.* **1** shape, contour, figure, outline, silhouette, build, construction, structure, condition, appearance, configuration, pattern, set, format, arrangement, image, semblance. **2** species, type, variety, genus, kind, sort, class, category, classification, order. **3** formula, method, system, style, manner, procedure, mode, way, technique. **4** behavior, conduct, convention, usage, ritual, manners, custom, ceremony, decorum, deportment, etiquette, punctilio. **5** document, application, questionnaire. —*v.* **1** shape, mold, fashion, sketch, contour, carve, outline, sculpt, cast, delineate, manufacture. **2** devise, conceive, envision, imagine, create, concoct. **3** organize, coalesce, frame, produce, combine, erect, build. **4** grow into, develop, become, appear, crystallize, acquire, beget, engender, eventuate. **5** make up, make, comprise, constitute, compose.

formal *adj.* **1** official, regulated, methodical, correct, ceremonial, conventional, orthodox, authoritative, systematic, fixed, prescribed, conformist, *pro forma*. **2** rigid, aloof, stiff, punctilious, standoffish, off-putting, unbending, distant, reserved, starched, unsociable, high-hat, highfalutin.
ant. **1** unconventional, irregular, unusual, bohemian, nonconformist, unorthodox, oddball (*Slang*). **2** warm, friendly, casual, folksy, informal, spontaneous, natural.

formality *n.* **1** conventionality, orthodoxy, conformism, ritualism, methodology, propriety, ceremoniousness, orderliness, formalism, red tape, regularity. **2** etiquette, form, custom, usage, manners, decorum, ritual, rite, ceremony, tradition, politesse, observance.

ant. 1 unorthodoxy, nonconformism, bohemianism, spontaneity, irregularity, eccentricity, improvisation. **2** aberration, faux pas, gaffe, rudeness, boner (*Slang*), blooper (*Slang*).

format *n.* plan, arrangement, blueprint, ground plan, outline, drawing, sketch, projection, scheme, method, system, schedule, syllabus, prospectus, proposal, layout, formula, diagram, mockup.

formation *n.* development, evolution, evolvement, organization, construction, structure, delineation, creation, production, genesis, makeup, nature, constitution, arrangement, synthesis, lineament, contour.

former *adj.* preceding, prior, previous, aforementioned, earlier, antecedent, aforesaid, late, quondam, precursory, one-time, erstwhile, ci-devant.
ant. latter, later, following, subsequent, consequent, ensuing.

formidable *adj.* **1** awesome, impressive, forbidding, portentous, intimidating, dreadful, dire, fearful, redoubtable, terrible, awful, appalling, threatening. **2** difficult, arduous, toilsome, burdensome, wearisome, strenuous, challenging, overpowering, herculean, monumental, colossal, staggering.
ant. 1 ordinary, insignificant, weak, unimpressive, powerless. **2** simple, easy, manageable, unchallenging, light, minuscule.

formless *adj.* shapeless, amorphous, chaotic, unformed, asymmetrical, irregular, free, unshapely, crude, rough, rough-hewn, untidy, sloppy.

formula *n.* **1** banality, commonplace, shibboleth, cliché, platitude, truism, slogan, byword. **2** format, blueprint, system, construct, convention, code, recipe, prescription, method, plan, schedule, layout, arrangement, outline, guide, procedure.
ant. 1 invention, coinage, improvisation, fancy, new slant, impromptu.

formulate *v.* define, specify, stipulate, outline, designate, particularize, detail, delimit, analyze, itemize, systematize, indicate, list, synthesize.

fornication *n.* copulation, sexual intercourse, sex, cohabitation, adultery, intimacy, congress, liaison, seduction, carnal knowledge.

forsake *v.* renounce, abandon, give up, forswear, abjure, quit, jettison, repudiate, forgo, discard, disavow, apostatize, reject, neglect, forfeit.
ant. cling to, remain, continue, care for, adhere.

fort *n.* fortress, fortification, bastion, castle, citadel, stronghold, bulwark, stockade, garrison, keep, redan, redoubt.

forte *n.* specialty, strong point, talent, strength, gift, aptitude, capability, ability, accomplishment, asset, skill, proficiency, endowment, shtick (*Slang*), number (*Slang*).
ant. deficiency, weakness, ineptitude, foible.

forthcoming *adj.* **1** available, ready, accessible, handy, obtainable, convenient, on hand, on tap. **2** in the works, prospective, impending, upcoming, coming, approaching, in the offing, in view.
ant. 1 doubtful, unavailable, inconvenient, impossible, inaccessible.

forthright *adj.* straightforward, direct, frank, candid, blunt, open, honest, plain-spoken, outspoken, sincere, unreserved, explicit, undisguised, plain.
ant. devious, guarded, indirect, veiled, equivocal, circuitous, misleading.

forthwith *adv.* immediately, at once, instantly, quickly, promptly, speedily, directly, presently, in a jiffy, right away, straightaway, pronto (*Slang*).
ant. later, any time, whenever, slowly, afterward, another time, ultimately.

fortification *n.* fort, defense, fortress, bastion, citadel, emplacement, stronghold, stockade, garrison, redan, redoubt, rampart, entrenchment, wall, parapet.

fortified *adj.* ARMED.

fortify v. **1** arm, man, defend, blockade, barricade, wall, entrench, guard, militarize. **2** strengthen, reinforce, stiffen, brace, encourage, inspirit, buttress, harden, embolden, hearten, toughen, reassure, invigorate, heighten, boost.
ant. 2 undermine, demoralize, sap, weaken, discourage, disable, demolish.

fortitude n. courage, grit, pluck, stoutheartedness, heroism, hardihood, bravery, intrepidity, valor, endurance, strength, mettle, spirit, spunk.
ant. cowardice, timidity, faintheartedness, funk, panic, weakness, cold feet.

fortuitous adj. accidental, unexpected, unanticipated, incidental, haphazard, casual, adventitious, chance, random, unintended, unintentional, unforeseen.
ant. scheduled, planned, ordained, expected, foreseen, anticipated.

fortunate adj. lucky, favored, blessed, flourishing, happy, thriving, well-off, felicitous, blissful.
ant. ill-fated, unlucky, unfortunate, hapless, miserable, wretched, cursed.

fortune n. fate, chance, lot, luck, destiny, share, star, hap, circumstance, karma, future, kismet, portion, prospect, providence.

fortuneteller n. prophet, seer, clairvoyant, soothsayer, sibyl, oracle, medium, crystal-gazer, forecaster, predictor, prophesier, prognosticator, magician.

forum n. assembly, meeting, congregation, audience, gathering, panel, platform, arena, hustings, symposium, seminar, hearing.

forward adj. bold, brash, presumptuous, eager, pert, ready, flippant, brazen, impudent, saucy, sassy, self-assertive, pushy, fresh (*Slang*).
ant. retiring, timid, shy, deferential, loath, unwilling, bashful.

fosse n. DITCH.

foster v. **1** rear, raise, bring up, mother, tend, nourish, care for, take care of, nurture. **2** advance, promote, further, abet, forward, help, maintain, nurse, encourage, cultivate, feed, harbor.
ant. 2 neglect, discourage, starve, hamper, disregard, abandon, frustrate.

foul adj. **1** disgusting, offensive, nauseating, putrid, spoiled, rotten, putrescent, filthy, rank, mephitic, noisome, tainted, dirty, polluted, repulsive. **2** smutty, lewd, obscene, coarse, vulgar, filthy, dirty, low, nasty, offensive, indecent, blasphemous, scurrilous, risqué. —n. collision, irregularity, entanglement, jam, hindrance, obstacle, misplay, infraction. —v. **1** befoul, dirty, soil, defile, taint, pollute, corrupt, disease, infect, blemish, stain, smirch, sully, contaminate, smear. **2** entangle, snarl, catch, jam, collide, encumber, impede, twist, disorder, kink.
ant. adj. **1** spotless, attractive, pure, fresh, clean, untainted, appetizing. **2** proper, decent, inoffensive, respectable, polite, euphemistic, respectful. n. order, regularity, fair play. v. **1** clean, wash, purify, decontaminate, freshen. **2** untangle, straighten, smooth.

foul play treachery, evil intent, perfidy, crime, murder, assassination, barbarity, savagery, inhumanity, liquidation, homicide, assault, villainy, skulduggery, criminality, outrage, dirty work.

foul up *Slang* BUNGLE.

found v. establish, set up, originate, create, institute, inaugurate, launch, produce, engineer, start, construct, erect, build.

foundation n. basis, grounds, root, substructure, base, substratus, footing, rudiments, support, bed, bottom, bedrock, underpinning, framework, skeleton, armature.

founder v. collapse, cave in, fail, fall, sink, break down, run aground, hit bottom, go under, topple, perish, crash, disintegrate, come apart, go to pieces, miscarry.

ant. stand firm, hold, endure, survive, last, weather.

fountain *n.* **1** fount, jet, spray, spring, font, stream, spout, geyser, gush, outflow. **2** origin, source, root, cradle, wellspring, fountainhead, genesis, beginning, cause, author, womb, birthplace.

four-letter word obscenity, indecency, impropriety, indelicacy, profanity, vulgarity, taboo word, vulgarism, expletive.

fox *n.* schemer, plotter, dodger, intriguer, smooth talker, sly-boots, swindler, dissembler, maneuverer, opportunist, strategist, Machiavelli, con man (*Slang*), shyster, wheeler-dealer (*Slang*).

ant. innocent, babe, ingenue, naif, gull, dupe, easy mark, sap (*Slang*), pigeon (*Slang*).

foxy *adj.* sly, crafty, devious, scheming, underhand, slick, tricky, cunning, wily, shifty, insidious, untrustworthy, artful, subtle.

ant. gullible, naive, ingenuous, credulous, aboveboard, trustworthy, honest.

foyer *n.* lobby, entrance, hall, reception room, waiting room, anteroom, vestibule, antechamber, corridor, passageway, green room.

fracas *n.* brawl, scrimmage, scuffle, uproar, hubbub, fistfight, set-to, row, donnybrook, free-for-all, melee, fray, rhubarb (*Slang*).

fraction *n.* part, portion, fragment, section, division, bit, chip, piece, particle, scrap, morsel, swatch, sample, shaving, shard, crumb, bite.

ant. whole, entirety, all, totality, everything, aggregate, sum.

fractious *adj.* rebellious, unruly, cross, petulant, cranky, intractable, irritable, captious, perverse, churlish, grumpy, contrary, recalcitrant, perverse, froward.

ant. docile, pleasant, obliging, obedient, agreeable, amiable, willing.

fracture *n.* crack, break, cleft, breach, cleavage, split, fissure, hiatus, cranny, opening, gap. —*v.* break, crack, split, fragment, chip, shatter, splinter.

fragile *adj.* breakable, delicate, brittle, frail, frangible, weak, feeble, infirm, friable, flimsy, thin, decrepit, worn out.

ant. strong, sturdy, durable, unbreakable, flexible, firm, robust.

fragment *n.* portion, fraction, part, piece, shard, splinter, segment, chip, snip, sample, division, installment.

ant. whole, entirety, totality, all, everything, ensemble, total.

fragmentary *adj.* incomplete, unfinished, broken, partial, fractional, segmented, separated, disconnected, disjointed, rough, uneven, impaired, choppy.

ant. unified, unbroken, connected, smooth, intact, whole, entire.

fragrance *n.* perfume, aroma, scent, odor, smell, bouquet, redolence, freshness, sweetness.

ant. stench, stink, fetor, reek, malodorousness, foulness, miasma.

frail *adj.* fragile, delicate, weak, breakable, wispy, thin, feeble, infirm, slender, unsupported, slight, brittle, tottery, doddering, puny, rickety, vulnerable.

ant. strong, robust, resistant, stout, fit, vigorous, sturdy.

frailty *n.* WEAKNESS.

frame *v.* draw up, formulate, articulate, utter, think out, conceive, devise, concoct, imagine, embody, incorporate, fashion, construct, shape, contrive. —*n.* **1** framework, armature, skeleton, scaffolding, arrangement, constituents, constitution, scheme, schema, plan. **2** physique, anatomy, body build, morphology, figure, structure, form, soma, anatomy, shape, chassis (*Slang*).

frame of mind mood, disposition, attitude, humor, temper, feeling, construct, mental state, slant, posture, viewpoint, sentiment, inclination, outlook, leaning, bent.

framework *n.* structure, arrangement, plan, armature, construct, construction, frame of reference, ideology, blueprint, mockup, scheme, schema, skeleton, ground plan, scaffold.

frangible *adj.* FRAGILE.

frank *adj.* honest, candid, open, straightforward, evident, unconcealed, undisguised, unambiguous, unequivocal, blunt, direct, patent, forthright, aboveboard, plainspoken, free-spoken, open-faced.

ant. guarded, devious, ambiguous, constrained, hypocritical, sly, veiled, covert.

frantic *adj.* agitated, overexcited, frenzied, unhinged, frenetic, panicky, crazed, distraught, overwrought, maddened, deranged, raving, beside oneself.

ant. cool, composed, self-possessed, self-controlled, dispassionate, stoic, calm.

fraternal *adj.* brotherly, comradely, familial, kindred, consanguineous, affiliated, allied, congenial.

fraternity *n.* brotherhood, brotherliness, comradeship, consanguinity, congeniality, kinship, fellowship, fellow-feeling, matiness (*Brit.*).

fraternize *v.* socialize, consort, associate, band together, cooperate, harmonize, unite, hobnob, mingle, amalgamate, coalesce, unionize, affiliate, pal around (*Slang*).

ant. avoid, stand aloof, withdraw, snub, high-hat, keep one's distance.

fraud *n.* **1** deception, trickery, guile, fakery, counterfeit, deceit, duplicity, imposture, chicanery, swindle, sham, hoax, fake, sell (*Slang*), hype (*Slang*). **2** faker, swindler, liar, impostor, counterfeiter, cheat, double-dealer, crook, law-breaker, shady character, charlatan, rogue, scoundrel.

ant. 1 honesty, integrity, decency,

uprightness, authenticity, trustworthiness, reliability.

fraudulent *adj.* deceptive, dishonest, sham, fake, counterfeit, duplicitous, illegal, lying, shady, treacherous, underhand, crooked, bogus, spurious.

ant. honest, upright, legal, reliable, truthful, trustworthy, law-abiding.

fraught *adj.* laden, weighted, heavy with, involving, full, abounding, pregnant, freighted, charged, loaded, burdened, replete.

fray[1] *n.* fracas, brawl, fight, set-to, battle, row, quarrel, commotion, rumpus, disturbance, melee, scuffle, skirmish, war, rumble (*Slang*).

ant. agreement, concord, peace, truce, quiet, tranquillity.

fray[2] *v.* ravel, wear out, wear thin, rip, tatter, frazzle, shred, abrade, disintegrate, come apart.

frazzled *adj.* worn out, fatigued, beat, worried, anxious, edgy, enervated, exhausted, weary, vexed, fagged out, pooped (*Slang*).

ant. relaxed, rested, energetic, fit, lively, peppy.

freak *n.* **1** abnormality, aberration, monster, monstrosity, grotesque, mutation, irregularity, abortion, deviation, sport, teratism, anomaly. **2** *Slang* NUT. —*adj.* atypical, exceptional, strange, unusual, weird, unexpected, unforeseen, uncommon, peculiar, unaccountable, extraordinary, queer, odd.

ant. *adj.* normal, ordinary, typical, usual, common, everyday, run of the mill.

freakish *adj.* monstrous, grotesque, aberrant, malformed, abnormal, anomalous, bizarre, strange, unnatural, teratoid, outré, outlandish, misshapen.

free *adj.* **1** independent, liberated, unconfined, unconstrained, unfettered, at liberty, autonomous, self-governing, emancipated, uncurbed, footloose, unrestricted, unattached. **2** at no cost, gratis, for nothing, complimentary, giveaway, gratuitous, with-

out charge, on the house. **3** unoccupied, available, open, idle, vacant, void, devoid, rid, unfilled, unobstructed, unused, unemployed. **4** forthright, frank, candid, easygoing, relaxed, forward, impertinent, free-and-easy, unreserved, brash, impudent. —*v.* liberate, release, rid, deliver, exempt, emancipate, clear, extricate, unburden, ransom, acquit, disengage, loose, untie, unfetter, unleash, unloose, unshackle.
ant. *adj.* **1** confined, imprisoned, dependent, enslaved, burdened, fettered, curbed. **3** occupied, taken, busy, employed, in use, unavailable. **4** guarded, reserved, constrained, tense, hesitant. *v.* curb, restrain, constrain, burden, tie, enmesh.
freedom *n.* **1** liberty, autonomy, independence, liberation, self-rule, emancipation, scope, range, elbowroom, margin, flexibility, option, privilege, right, prerogative. **2** exemption, immunity, release, unconstraint, exception, discharge, impunity, irresponsibility, reprieve, acquittal, absolution.
ant. 1 dictatorship, authoritarianism, slavery, enslavement, bondage, dependence. **2** onus, burden, responsibility, constraint, arrest, pressure.
free-spoken *adj.* FRANK.
freethinker *n.* agnostic, atheist, nonreligionist, skeptic, humanist, materialist, nonbeliever, rationalist, nihilist, doubter, dissenter, secularist.
ant. believer, sectarian, denominationalist, churchgoer, pietist, religionist.
free-will *adj.* VOLUNTARY.
freezing *adj.* FRIGID.
freight *n.* load, shipment, cargo, charge, consignment, express, goods, merchandise, mail, poundage, tonnage. —*v.* load, burden, weigh down, pile on, weight, encumber, saddle, clog, fill, oppress, tax, hamper.
ant. *v.* lighten, alleviate, ease, remove, unload, disencumber, lift.
frenetic *adj.* distraught, distracted, ma-

niacal, raving, wild, frantic, frenzied, crazed, unbalanced, overexcited, overwrought, hyperactive, manic, hyped up (*Slang*), hyper (*Slang*).
ant. calm, composed, serene, phlegmatic, lethargic, tranquil, self-possessed.
frenzy *n.* agitation, excitement, mania, transport, delirium, passion, fury, rage, derangement, lunacy, madness.
ant. normality, stability, balance, self-possession, sanity.
frequency *n.* constancy, commonness, repetition, periodicity, regularity, recurrence, reiteration, steadiness, prevalence.
ant. rarity, oddity, singularity, infrequency, irregularity.
frequent *adj.* common, usual, habitual, regular, persistent, everyday, recurrent, continual, ordinary, repeated, familiar, customary, incessant, constant. —*v.* revisit, haunt, dwell, sojourn, stay, inhabit, occupy, hang out at (*Slang*), hang around in (*Slang*).
ant. *adj.* rare, sporadic, unusual, uncommon, infrequent, extraordinary.
fresh[1] *adj.* **1** new, recent, novel, modern, up-to-date, vital, vivid, striking, bright, unspoiled, wholesome, glowing, flourishing, verdant, green. **2** further, additional, added, more, renewed, replenished, refreshed, extra, supplementary, appended, attached, another, auxiliary. **3** refreshing, healthy, invigorating, rosy, blooming, flourishing, fair, bright, undimmed, unfading.
ant. 1 trite, used, dated, outmoded, second-hand, imitative, unoriginal. **3** worn, tired, faded, sickly, wan, polluted.
fresh[2] *adj. Slang* nervy (*Slang*), snotty (*Slang*), smart-alecky, snippy, sassy, flippant, discourteous, disrespectful, brazen, cheeky, presumptuous, forward, rude, impolite, thoughtless.
ant. polite, deferential, courteous, respectful, mannerly, obliging.
freshman *n.* beginner, novice, tyro,

newcomer, recruit, apprentice, neophyte, tenderfoot, learner, greenhorn, novitiate, amateur, rookie (*Slang*).

ant. veteran, master, old hand, senior, expert, pro (*Slang*), authority.

fret *v.* irritate, worry, annoy, bother, upset, disquiet, tease, pester, agitate, pick on, frazzle, vex, irk, rile, nettle, harass, torment.

ant. please, gratify, delight, soothe, calm, lull.

fretful *adj.* cranky, peevish, irritable, touchy, sulky, crotchety, cantankerous, complaining, querulous, faultfinding, crabby, ill-tempered, cross, impatient.

ant. agreeable, pleasant, relaxed, cheerful, good-natured, easygoing.

friable *adj.* crumbly, breakable, brittle, fragile, powdery, chalky, pulverable, frangible, delicate, mealy.

ant. solid, firm, unbreakable, flexible, compact, substantial, rugged.

friction *n.* **1** abrasion, attrition, erosion, rubbing, chafing, grating, grinding, filing, scraping, scouring, rasping. **2** antagonism, discord, conflict, disagreement, dissension, clash, contention, quarrel, disharmony, strife, dissidence, incompatibility, cross-purposes, animosity, hostility.

ant. 2 harmony, agreement, compatibility, congeniality, concurrence, cooperation.

friend *n.* intimate, comrade, pal, crony, familiar, confidant, companion, chum, acquaintance, well-wisher, *amigo*, buddy, pardner, sidekick (*Slang*).

ant. enemy, rival, adversary, foe, opponent.

friendless *adj.* alone, apart, isolated, solitary, lonesome, reclusive, withdrawn, sequestered, forlorn, forsaken, ostracized, abandoned, desolate, deserted, unpopular.

ant. accepted, included, befriended, cherished, cared for, popular.

friendly *adj.* sociable, amiable, amicable, chummy, congenial, clubby, convivial, comradely, familiar, folksy, informal, close, neighborly, helpful, cooperative.

ant. cool, formal, distant, standoffish, aloof, unfriendly, reserved, hostile.

friendship *n.* amity, congeniality, closeness, nearness, familiarity, chumminess, neighborliness, sociability, friendliness, comradeship, camaraderie, companionship, fellowship, affection, regard, consideration, loyalty.

ant. coolness, indifference, detachment, disloyalty, antagonism, hostility, enmity.

fright *n.* fear, panic, alarm, scare, terror, dread, horror, shock, apprehension, funk, trepidation, the shakes, the shivers, cold sweat, cold feet, the jitters, the willies (*Slang*), the creeps (*Slang*).

ant. reassurance, composure, courage, fearlessness, calm.

frighten *v.* scare, alarm, terrify, shock, horrify, affright, intimidate, terrorize, daunt, awe, faze, petrify, dismay, unnerve, appall.

ant. reassure, hearten, encourage, inspirit, embolden, nerve.

frightening *adj.* terrifying, alarming, scary, fearful, awesome, intimidating, horrifying, threatening, unnerving, bloodcurdling, hair-raising, appalling, menacing.

ant. reassuring, encouraging, calming, heartening, emboldening, soothing, cheering.

frightful *adj.* dreadful, awful, horrible, horrendous, gruesome, grisly, ghastly, shocking, terrible, hideous, repulsive, horrid, disgusting, grim.

ant. pleasant, attractive, inviting, fetching, lovely, charming.

frigid *adj.* **1** freezing, icy, cold, gelid, frosty, frozen, wintry, bitter, arctic, glacial, chilled, chilly. **2** coldhearted, stiff, formal, cool, distant, remote, unbending, chilly, austere, forbidding, reserved, unyielding. **3**

inhibited, repressed, unsexual, over-controlled, unresponsive.

ant. 1 melting, thawing, temperate, moderate, warm, lukewarm. **2** informal, folksy, cordial, friendly, outgoing, convivial, sociable. **3** responsive, ardent, passionate, uninhibited.

frill *n.* ruffle, ruff, ruche, ruching, furbelow, edging, flounce.

frills *n.* ostentation, showiness, superfluity, fanciness, fussiness, falderal, frippery, excess, caparison, froufrou, affectation.

ant. simplicity, severity, practicality, necessity, essentiality.

frilly *adj.* ruffly, ruffled, flouncy, ruched, gathered, fancy, fussy, dainty, curly, ornate, frothy, showy, foppish, overdressed, overornamented, gussied up (*Slang*).

ant. plain, unadorned, severe, tailored, simple, understated, basic.

fringe *n.* **1** border, trimming, ruff, edging, fimbriation, frizz. **2** margin, edge, border, boundary, brink, rim, selvage, ledge, frontier, outskirts, outpost, curb, hem, limit, periphery, perimeter.

ant. 2 center, core, inside, heart, middle, hub.

frippery *n.* showiness, foppery, ostentation, gaudiness, frills, frilliness, froufrou, preciosity, fussiness, affectation, flossiness, tawdriness, flashiness, vulgarity, pretentiousness.

ant. simplicity, precision, good taste, refinement, restraint, necessity.

frisk *v.* **1** frolic, gambol, caper, leap, skip, romp, spring, cavort, prance, bounce, play, dance, sport, jump, trip. **2** *Slang* search, rummage through, hunt for, ransack.

frisky *adj.* lively, playful, frolicsome, bouncy, animated, nimble, vivacious, spry, jaunty, merry, rollicking, prankish, spirited, sprightly, kittenish, coltish.

ant. indolent, dull, moping, morose, lumpy, heavy, cloddish.

fritter away waste, squander, dissipate,

exhaust, use up, deplete, misspend, run through.

ant. economize, conserve, budget, skimp, stint, scrimp, save.

frivolity *n.* LEVITY.

frivolous *adj.* petty, trivial, unimportant, trifling, superficial, silly, nonsensical, irreverent, giddy, flighty, light-headed, light-minded, lightsome, scatterbrained, flippant, carefree, foolish, slap-dash.

ant. weighty, serious, substantial, significant, consequential, earnest, sensible.

frock *n.* dress, gown, robe, outfit, costume, creation, garment, clothing, get-up, number (*Slang*), rags (*Slang*), glad rags (*Slang*).

frolic *n.* romp, revel, caper, party, dance, ball, picnic, outing, gala, fete, gathering, spree, jamboree, bash (*Slang*). —*v.* cavort, frisk, romp, carouse, caper, skip, play, sport, prance, dance, leap, spring, make merry, jollify, have a ball (*Slang*).

frolicsome *adj.* playful, lighthearted, merry, frisky, blithe, carefree, gleeful, rollicking, sportive, larky, vivacious, prankish, fun-loving, coltish, kittenish.

ant. gloomy, sullen, dour, careworn, plodding, cloddish, lumpy.

front *n.* **1** surface, face, facade, forehead, brow, entrance, facing, exterior, outside, frontage, forefront, features, visage, covering, externality. **2** unity, coalition, solidarity, union, cooperation, amalgamation, merger, alliance, affiliation, league, syndicate, federation, collaboration. **3** deportment, manner, bearing, demeanor, semblance, superficiality, persona, show, display, mien, air, guise, face, exterior, flash, trappings, mask.

ant. 1 back, rear, underside, inside, interior, lining, background. **2** antagonism, disunion, friction, separateness, estrangement, dissension. **3** essence, nature, feelings, reality, substance.

frontage *n.* FRONT.

frontier *n.* **1** boundary, border, limit, edge, confines, outskirts, march, hinterland, outpost, dividing line, backwoods. **2** *terra incognita,* unknown, outer limits, new terrain, unbroken ground, threshold, outpost, virgin territory.

frontiersman *n.* PIONEER.

frosty *adj.* **1** icy, rimy, freezing, hoary, nippy, icicled, frigid, gelid, ice-capped, frost-nipped, wintry. **2** cold-hearted, aloof, distant, icy, forbidding, unfriendly, chilly, formal, haughty, unapproachable, disdainful, imperious.

ant. 1 temperate, warm, pleasant, melting, balmy, comfortable. **2** friendly, warm-hearted, informal, amiable, folksy, sympathetic, encouraging.

froth *n.* **1** bubbles, foam, spume, spray, effervescence, scud, spindrift, fizz, lather, head, suds, spritz. **2** frivolity, triviality, frill, foolishness, frippery, frou-frou, nonsense, bagatelle, trivia, absurdity.

ant. 2 essential, necessity, fundamental, weight, substance, seriousness.

frothy *adj.* frivolous, trivial, foolish, nonsensical, unnecessary, trifling, slight, flimsy, petty, superficial, shallow, surface.

ant. weighty, substantial, necessary, essential, fundamental, serious, important.

froward *adj.* CONTRARY.

frown *v.* scowl, wrinkle, glower, disapprove, fret, discountenance, disfavor, discourage, restrict, censor, look askance, take a dim view.

ant. smile, approve, favor, like, encourage, countenance, tolerate.

frowzy *adj.* messy, slovenly, unkempt, sloppy, dirty, disheveled, smelly, slatternly, blowzy, bedraggled, frumpy, untidy, disarranged.

ant. well-groomed, neat, clean, tidy, meticulous, *soigné.*

frozen *adj.* FRIGID.

frugal *adj.* economical, saving, sparing, cautious, prudent, penny-pinching, canny, thrifty, parsimonious, stingy, tight, scrimping, close-fisted.

ant. extravagant, profligate, prodigal, spendthrift, liberal, generous, open-handed.

fruit *n.* yield, crop, harvest, produce, production, return, reward, consequence, issue, outcome, result, profit, benefit, advantage.

fruitful *adj.* fertile, productive, profitable, rewarding, advantageous, successful, gratifying, worthwhile, valuable, satisfying.

ant. vain, useless, futile, fruitless, unproductive, unrewarding.

fruition *n.* fulfillment, result, attainment, accomplishment, yield, achievement, success, gratification, satisfaction, realization, consummation, culmination, happy ending.

ant. frustration, disappointment, failure, misfortune, incompletion, miscarriage, nothing.

fruitless *adj.* useless, vain, unproductive, purposeless, futile, unprofitable, unfruitful, abortive, idle, worthless, unsuccessful, unavailing, unrewarding, inadequate.

ant. successful, profitable, productive, rewarding, effective, valuable, gratifying.

frumpy *adj.* dowdy, shabby, dingy, dreary, drab, slovenly, unattractive, colorless, unfashionable, frowzy, unsightly, tacky.

ant. stylish, elegant, well-dressed, chic, smart, tasteful, *soigné.*

frustrate *v.* foil, thwart, circumvent, checkmate, short-circuit, defeat, nullify, abort, cross, check, contravene, block, counteract, impede, hamper, stymie, interrupt, forestall, spoil.

ant. encourage, foster, abet, promote, support, nourish, aid.

frustration *n.* defeat, miscarriage, circumvention, contravention, abortion, block, impediment, bar, check, interruption, interference, obstruction, hindrance, curb, bafflement.

ant. fulfillment, success, fruition,

achievement, encouragement, attainment.

fuddy-duddy *n.* old fogy, back number, nit-picker, fuss-budget, fusspot, stuffed shirt, crank, dodo, fossil, perfectionist, fault-finder, sourpuss (*Slang*), conservative, traditionalist.
ant. pacesetter, iconoclast, radical, swinger (*Slang*).

fudge *n.* nonsense, foolishness, hogwash, humbug, twaddle, gibberish, rubbish, drivel, babbling, prattle, rot, piffle, bilge (*Slang*), bull (*Slang*), crap (*Slang*). —*v.* hedge, dodge, quibble, weasel, stall, straddle, equivocate, hem and haw.

fuel *n.* **1** combustible, inflammable. **2** nourishment, food, wherewithal, sustenance, provisions, rations, supplies, subsidy, provocation, incitement, stimulus, motive, energy, encouragement, inspiration. —*v.* fire, light, kindle, ignite, stoke, feed, nourish, sustain, inflame, energize, activate, fan, incite, stimulate.
ant. *n.* **2** damper, wet blanket, barrier, hindrance, deterrent, starvation. *v.* dampen, bank, starve, discourage, cool, quench, extinguish.

fugitive *adj.* fleeting, transitory, transient, ephemeral, shifting, errant, short-lived, evanescent, uncertain, unfixed, unsettled, passing, brief, momentary. —*n.* runaway, deserter, renegade, refugee, outlaw, outcast, wanderer, absconder, pariah.
ant. *adj.* permanent, abiding, long-lasting, constant, enduring, settled, fixed.

fulcrum *n.* support, rest, prop, foundation, base, basis, mainstay, pillar, underpinning, buttress, crutch, staff, brace, platform, backbone, spine.

fulfill *v.* consummate, finish, satisfy, effect, effectuate, achieve, accomplish, attain, complete, bring about, carry out, execute, realize, close.
ant. leave off, withdraw, abandon, fail, give up.

fulfillment *n.* consummation, achievement, satisfaction, end, realization,

completion, execution, culmination, pinnacle, attainment, summit, observance, acquittal, delivery.
ant. frustration, disappointment, failure, lack, deficiency, abandonment, imperfection.

fulgent *adj.* RADIANT.

full *adj.* **1** satisfied, replete, filled, sated, satiated, brimming, gorged, glutted, saturated, loaded, crammed, bursting. **2** whole, complete, entire, intact, well-supplied, unabridged, detailed, uncut, solid, undivided, exhaustive, undiminished, perfect. **3** crowded, dense, abounding, teeming, rife, plentiful, abundant, overloaded, overflowing, plenary, jammed, packed, maximum, utmost, optimum, greatest, highest.
ant. **1** hungry, underfed, undernourished, unsatisfied, empty, famished, unsated. **2** partial, incomplete, abridged, cut, fragmentary, divided, imperfect. **3** scant, skimpy, sparse, minimum, least, lightest.

full-blooded *adj.* THOROUGHBRED.

full-fledged *adj.* professional, qualified, trained, full-blown, schooled, experienced, able, proficient, expert, adept, versed, knowing, skilled, masterly, authoritative, top-flight, senior.
ant. green, inexperienced, untrained, unschooled, untried, uninitiated, half-baked.

full-grown *adj.* adult, mature, ripe, grown-up, full-blown, full-fledged, complete, developed.
ant. immature, adolescent, unripe, undeveloped, young, green.

fullness *n.* **1** satiety, glut, satiation, satisfaction, fill, repletion, saturation, surfeit, enough, sufficiency, abundance, engorgement, plethora, overload. **2** wholeness, totality, entirety, completeness, all, voluminousness, details, particulars, plenitude, indivisibility, aggregate, sum, everything.
ant. **1** hunger, insufficiency, emptiness, lack, need, want, privation. **2** incompleteness, sketchiness, abridg-

ment, sparseness, paucity, scarcity, lack.

full-scale *adj.* all-out, maximum, thoroughgoing, major, exhaustive, intensive, comprehensive, complete, sweeping, unrestricted, lavish, wholehearted, unlimited, total, outright, full-dress.
ant. partial, halfhearted, minor, perfunctory, indifferent, incomplete.

fulminate *v.* denounce, execrate, vituperate, curse, damn, berate, anathematize, revile, scathe, impugn, vilify, stigmatize, castigate, imprecate.

fulsome *adj.* excessive, extravagant, nauseating, sickening, overstated, immoderate, gross, inordinate, exaggerated, sycophantic, idolatrous, specious, blatant, saccharine.
ant. tempered, subtle, measured, suitable, due, considered, well-balanced.

fumble *v.* grope, bumble, flounder, stumble, muff, bungle, blunder, botch, mishandle, boggle, mess, spoil, miscalculate.

fume *n.* smoke, exhalation, reek, smog, miasma, fetor, exhaust, stench, haze, effluvium, malodorousness. —*v.* smolder, simmer, boil, seethe, rant, rage, bluster, storm, explode, chafe, mutter, flare up, carry on (*Slang*), burn up (*Slang*), blow one's stack (*Slang*).
ant. *v.* subside, cool off, simmer down, let up, calm down, lay off (*Slang*).

fumigate *v.* exterminate, disinfect, decontaminate, smoke out, gas, sterilize, cleanse, purify, sanitize, vaporize, steam.

fun *n.* diversion, amusement, enjoyment, mirth, merriment, jollity, comedy, play, game, sport, laughter, humor, gaiety, joke, wit, romp, gas (*Slang*). —*adj.* amusing, entertaining, diverting, lively, funny, comical, witty, enjoyable, convivial, vivacious, enlivening.
ant. *n.* boredom, dullness, ennui, tedium, monotony. *adj.* boring, dull, uninteresting, uncongenial, tiresome.

function *n.* **1** role, use, activity, place, duty, pursuit, job, position, capacity, sphere, realm, province, station, assignment. **2** party, social, get-together, do, occasion, reception, gathering, ceremony, gala, fete, bash (*Slang*).

functional *adj.* practical, suitable, operative, useful, serviceable, efficient, adapted, fitted, workable, utilitarian, convenient, pragmatic.
ant. impractical, overcomplicated, unsuitable, unworkable, inefficient.

functionary *n.* bureaucrat, official, activist, leader, office-holder, politico, politician, manager, specialist, power, commissioner, commissar, *apparatchik*, brass (*Slang*), wheel (*Slang*), big shot (*Slang*).

fund *n.* **1** money, stock, capital, cash, subsidy, bank account, savings, endowment, investment, nest egg. **2** reservoir, reserve, store, lode, supply, source, stock, hoard, treasure, backlog, cache, accumulation, mine, well. —*v.* capitalize, subsidize, endow, invest, support, contribute, provide, finance, pension, bequeath, back, promote, stake.

fundamental *adj.* basic, essential, indispensable, primary, chief, foremost, major, underlying, key, cardinal, vital, necessary, requisite, principal. —*n.* foundation, basis, first principle, rudiment, *sine qua non*, cornerstone, base, essence, source, creed, ethos, core, abc's.
ant. *adj.* superficial, subsidiary, secondary, minor, auxiliary, unnecessary. *n.* afterthought, supplement, superstructure, trimming, adjunct, extra.

funds *n.* money, assets, capital, revenue, income, riches, cash, wealth, means, wherewithal, finances, bankroll, wad, loot (*Slang*), moola (*Slang*), bread (*Slang*), lettuce (*Slang*), dough (*Slang*).

funereal *adj.* mournful, somber, doleful, sepulchral, elegiac, melancholy, lugubrious, grave, solemn, sorrowful, depressing, dark, heavy-hearted. **ant.** joyful, happy, lighthearted, bright, festive, smiling, jubilant.

funk *n.* **1** panic, cold sweat, flutter, trepidation, fright, fear, timidity, faint-heartedness, cowardice, anxiety. **2** depression, doldrums, dumps, distress, misery, despair.

ant. 2 elation, joy, rapture, bliss, ecstacy.

funky *adj.* **1** smelly, stinking, malodorous, fetid, reeking, rank, foul, noisome, noxious, miasmic, offensive. **2** *Slang* earthy, sensual, sexual, sexy, blue, soulful, low-down, (*Slang*), dirty (*Slang*).

funnel *v.* siphon, channel, sift, pass through, filter, pipe, convey, conduct, sieve, burrow.

funny *adj.* **1** comical, laughable, ludicrous, amusing, droll, clownish, humorous, slapstick, farcical, entertaining, facetious, absurd, witty, ridiculous. **2** peculiar, odd, unusual, puzzling, strange, freak, weird, mysterious, baffling, bizarre, outlandish, perplexing, uncommon, offbeat (*Slang*).

ant. 1 boring, depressing, sober, sad, melancholy, tearful, funereal. **2** normal, ordinary, usual, understandable, everyday, accustomed.

furbelow *n.* ORNAMENT.

furbish *v.* RENOVATE.

furious *adj.* **1** angry, infuriated, raging, mad, irate, enraged, incensed, wrathful, boiling, fuming, rabid, raving, inflamed, exasperated, on the warpath, up in arms. **2** turbulent, wild, violent, fierce, savage, vehement, stormy, intense, rampant, ferocious, mighty, clamorous, unrestrained, unleashed.

ant. 1 pleased, gratified, affable, unruffled, self-controlled. **2** tame, bland, weak, moderate, mild, calm.

furlough *n.* VACATION.

furnish *v.* equip, outfit, supply, provide, stock, rig, arm, give, grant, appoint, accouter, cater, administer, bestow, distribute.

furnishings *n.* fittings, trappings, rig, outfit, gear, apparel, decor, furniture, equipment, appointments, accouterments, necessaries, appurtenances.

furniture *n.* household goods, appointments, effects, furnishings, property, possessions, movables, chattels.

furor *n.* excitement, enthusiasm, craze, mania, to-do, commotion, fervor, fever, ardor, rapture, transport, passion, rage, tumult, uproar, hullabaloo, brouhaha, hoopla (*Slang*), flap (*Slang*).

ant. apathy, indifference, nonchalance, dispassion, impassivity, torpor, cool (*Slang*).

furrow *n.* groove, wrinkle, crease, line, dent, channel, trench, rut, hollow, concavity, rabbet, corrugation, indentation, seam.

ant. rise, mound, hill, bump, protuberance.

furry *adj.* soft, downy, hairy, woolly, fluffy, fleecy, flocked, bushy, shaggy, fuzzy, pilose.

further *adv.* additionally, besides, also, moreover, furthermore, together with, in addition, too, to boot, over and above, as well as, along with, yet.

furthermore *adv.* FURTHER.

furtive *adj.* secret, stealthy, sly, covert, sneaky, surreptitious, clandestine, underhand, concealed, conspiratorial, skulking, secretive, slinking.

ant. overt, open, direct, straightforward, manifest, public.

fury *n.* **1** rage, anger, fit, tantrum, wrath, explosion, outburst, furor, ire, passion, paroxysm, madness, snit. **2** ferocity, vehemence, frenzy, disturbance, storm, rampage, violence, severity, intensity, savagery, brutality, riot, uproar.

ant. 1 calm, self-control, self-possession, dispassion, detachment, cool (*Slang*). **2** mildness, tranquillity, serenity, peace, quiet, tameness.

fuse v. weld, melt, join, solder, merge, consolidate, blend, alloy, agglutinate, adhere, commingle, intermingle, amalgamate, coalesce, combine.
ant. separate, disjoin, divide, come apart, split, segment, crack.

fusion n. blend, coalescence, coalition, merger, union, alliance, mixture, intermingling, amalgamation, synthesis, unification, confederation, league, combination, incorporation.
ant. split, separation, division, disjunction, factionalism, sectarianism, separatism.

fuss n. **1** ado, to-do, bustle, stir, agitation, excitement, flutter, bother, flurry, display, stew, twitter, commotion, disturbance. **2** objection, protest, quarrel, disagreement, wrangle, contention, squabble, dispute, tiff, complaint, argument, challenge. —v. fret, fidget, whimper, complain, chafe, whine, snivel, pule, wail, mewl, bawl, cry.

fussbudget n. worrywart, fusspot (*Slang*), nit-picker, fault-finder, fuddy-duddy, crank, malcontent, complainer, worrier, perfectionist, crank.

fussy adj. **1** fastidious, dainty, nice, particular, finicky, picky, choosy. **2** fidgety, fretful, nervous, anxious, edgy, agitated, cranky, irritable, impatient, upset, restless, antsy (*Slang*).
ant. **1** imprecise, vague, inexact, careless, sloppy. **2** calm, collected, serene, tranquil, relaxed.

fustian n. bombast, purple prose, grandiloquence, rhetoric, pomposity, verbiage, wordiness, rigmarole, rant, hot air (*Slang*), wind.
ant. simplicity, succinctness, terseness, crispness, brevity.

fusty adj. **1** musty, moldy, rank, funky, stuffy, stale, airless, foul, malodorous, close, frowsty (*Brit.*). **2** fogeyish, old-fashioned, outdated, passé, obsolete, antiquated, motheaten, doddering, superannuated, outmoded, antediluvian, archaic, anachronistic, square (*Slang*).
ant. **1** fresh, sweet-smelling, clean, pure, fragrant. **2** modern, current, fashionable, up-to-date, new, in (*Slang*), with it (*Slang*).

futile adj. useless, vain, unproductive, wasted, unavailing, fruitless, bootless, sterile, ineffectual, worthless, unsuccessful, abortive.
ant. rewarding, successful, fruitful, productive, worthwhile, gratifying.

future n. tomorrow, time to come, by-and-by, offing, futurity, hereafter, outlook, forecast, destiny, fate, unknown, posterity, coming events, *mañana*. —adj. coming, eventual, prospective, impending, next, subsequent, succeeding, later, unborn, approaching, destined, fated.
ant. n. past, yesterday, years ago, days gone by, heretofore, long ago. adj. past, bygone, remembered, previous, prior, former, old.

fuzz[1] n. down, hair, frizz, nap, flocking, fur, fluff, lint, fibers, wool, pile, thistledown, swansdown, eiderdown, bloom.

fuzz[2] n. *Slang* POLICE.

fuzzy adj. **1** downy, hairy, frizzy, woolly, flocked, napped, fibrous, fluffy, velvety, linty. **2** vague, blurred, unfocused, indistinct, unclear, misty, smudged, beclouded, bleary, hazy, indefinite, ambiguous.
ant. **2** distinct, sharp, clear, well-defined, explicit, pointed, focused.

G

gab *n.* talk, conversation, chatter, chit-chat, rap (*Slang*), palaver, twaddle, tête-à-tête, tittle-tattle. —*v.* talk, gossip, chatter, chit-chat, rap (*Slang*), jabber, prate, prattle, tittle-tattle, jaw (*Slang*).

gabble *v.* babble, chatter, blabber, blab, blather, jabber, prate, prattle, gaggle, gibber, sputter, splutter. —*n.* babble, chatter, blabber, blab, blather, jabber, prattle, gibberish.

gabby *adj.* talkative, loquacious, garrulous, wordy, chatty, prolix, voluble, verbose, windy, long-winded, clamorous, talky, glib.
ant. taciturn, terse, reticent, quiet, reserved, laconic.

gad *v.* roam, wander, ramble, rove, stroll, gallivant, meander, traipse, tramp, stray, saunter, cruise.

gadabout *n.* wanderer, rambler, gallivanter, gypsy, meanderer.

gadfly *n.* PEST.

gadget *n.* device, contrivance, contraption, gimmick, jigger, doodad, doohickey, thing, thingamajig.

gaff *n.* GUFF.

gaffe *n.* mistake, blunder, gaucherie, faux pas, boo-boo (*Slang*), boner (*Slang*), goof (*Slang*), blooper (*Slang*), howler, error, contretemps, no-no.

gag *n.* joke, quip, jest, spoof, crack, wisecrack, witticism, pleasantry. —*v.* **1** suppress, silence, muzzle, muffle, squelch, stifle, censor, quell, contain, curb, inhibit, check, obstruct, throttle, choke. **2** throw up, retch, heave, puke, disgorge, spew, upchuck (*Slang*).

gage *n., v.* GAUGE.

gaggle *v.* GABBLE. —*n.* GROUP.

gaiety *n.* merriment, merrymaking, cheerfulness, joy, *joie de vivre,* frolicsomeness, festivity, conviviality, glee, jollity, joviality, mirth, buoyancy, vivacity, hilarity.
ant. sadness, misery, depression, melancholy, dejection.

gain *v.* **1** earn, win, accomplish, achieve, get, obtain, acquire, procure, secure, attain, realize, reach, reap, profit, cash in on, harvest. **2** reach, attain, acquire, augment, clear, net, realize. **3** improve, better, progress, advance, develop, grow, forward, approach, near, further, thrive, flourish, prosper, succeed, bloom, blossom. —*n.* **1** profits, assets, earnings, benefits, yields, proceeds, returns, winnings, dividends, receipts, pay. **2** improvement, advantage, betterment, advancement, amelioration, furtherance, enrichment, promotion, growth, development, enhancement.
ant. *v.* **1** lose, fail, forfeit, deplete, waste, squander. **3** deteriorate, degenerate, recede, decline, wane, ebb. *n.* **1** losses, deficits, debts, shortages, defaults, arrears, obligations. **2** deterioration, degeneration, retrogression, disintegration, decline, decadence, impoverishment.

gainful *adj.* profitable, lucrative, remunerative, beneficial, rewarding, productive, paying, payable.
ant. unprofitable, profitless, unremunerative, unproductive, unrewarding.

gainsay *n.* **1** deny, contradict, refute, dispute, impugn, controvert, contravene, disprove. **2** oppose, refuse, reject, disavow, repudiate, dissent, disagree, disbelieve, differ.
ant. **1** affirm, maintain, aver, as-

severate, contend. **2** support, uphold, agree with, defend, back up.

gait *n.* walk, bearing, stride, step, tread, pace, carriage.

gala *n.* celebration, party, festival, festivity, feast, fete, fiesta, holiday, jamboree, banquet, ball, shindig (*Slang*). —*adj.* festive, festal, merry, gay, jolly, joyous.

gale *n.* outburst, burst, surge, outbreak, eruption, explosion, ejaculation, rush, flare-up flush.

gall[1] *n.* **1** bitterness, rancor, enmity, hatred, acrimony, hostility, antipathy, animosity, animus, venom, virulence, malevolence, detestation, abhorrence. **2** impudence, effrontery, rudeness, cheek, boldness, discourtesy, insolence, impertinence, chutzpah, nerve (*Slang*).

gall[2] *n.* **1** wound, sore, abrasion, cut, laceration, scratch, bruise, contusion, gash, nick, scrape, excoriation, lesion, scuff, irritant, scar. **2** irritation, annoyance, vexation, harassment, maltreatment, irritant, provocation, nuisance, aggravation, molestation, bother, botheration. —*v.* **1** chafe, injure, wound, excoriate, abrade, scarify, bruise, contuse, skin, nick, scratch, irritate, scuff, cut. **2** annoy, vex, irritate, harass, aggravate, irk, provoke, peeve, rile, molest, bother, maltreat.

gallant *adj.* **1** brave, daring, chivalrous, heroic, courageous, fearless, valiant, bold, spirited, high-spirited, valorous, intrepid, dauntless, undaunted, gutsy (*Slang*), game. **2** courteous, polite, mannerly, civil, gracious, chivalrous, courtly, cordial, noble, urbane, debonair. —*n.* **1** hero, daredevil, blade, stalwart, paladin. **2** ladies' man, suitor, lover, paramour, philanderer, flirt, flirter, wooer, wolf, ogler, lady-killer, masher (*Slang*). **3** fop, dandy, dude, swell, beau, Beau Brummell, blood, coxcomb.

ant. *adj.* **1** fearful, craven, pusillanimous, timid, timorous. **2** discourteous, impolite, ill-mannered, in-

solent, boorish, crude. *n.* **1** coward, craven, poltroon, dastard, milksop.

gallantry *n.* **1** courage, heroism, bravery, chivalry, valor, prowess, intrepidity, daring, fortitude, boldness, mettle, dauntlessness, fearlessness, stalwartness, stoutheartedness, manliness. **2** flirtatiousness, coquetry, courtesy, attentiveness, courtliness, chivalrousness, graciousness, politeness, gentleness.

ant. *n.* **1** cowardice, timidity, pusillanimity, poltroonery, dastardliness, unmanliness, cravenness. **2** boorishness, loutishness, discourtesy, rudeness, oafishness, cloddishness.

gallery *n.* passage, passageway, corridor, arcade, aisle, hall, hallway, balcony, loggia, veranda, piazza, porch, portico, cloister, ambulatory.

gallimaufry *n.* MEDLEY.

galling *adj.* chafing, irritating, vexatious, vexing, annoying, troublesome, aggravating, exasperating, distressing, distressful, grating, irksome, nettlesome.

ant. pleasant, pleasing, pleasurable, delightful, agreeable, soothing, enjoyable.

gallivant *v.* wander, stray, roam, ramble, rove, range, prowl, gad, traipse, stroll, meander, saunter, tramp, cruise.

gallivanter *n.* GADABOUT.

gallop *v.* **1** run, trot, canter, lope, rack, amble, pace, prance. **2** run, hurry, hasten, fly, race, scat, scud, hie, scoot, scamper, scurry, skedaddle, hotfoot, dash, rush.

galore *adj.* abundant, abounding, copious, plentiful, teeming, swarming, replete, profuse, lush, luxuriant, rich, overflowing.

ant. scarce, scant, scanty, sparse, meager.

galvanic *adj.* electrifying, stimulating, exciting, provocative, incisive, arousing, animating, quickening, vivifying, enlivening, stirring.

galvanize *v.* stimulate, electrify, excite, arouse, rouse, startle, provoke, quicken, pique, incite, vitalize, rally, stir, awaken, awake, wake, fire, foment.

gambit *n.* plan, stratagem, strategy, tactic, scheme, move, maneuver, design, plot, project, device, machination, artifice, trick, game plan.

gamble *v.* **1** bet, wager, risk, speculate, invest, stake, hazard, prospect, punt (*Brit.*). **2** lose, plunge, squander, waste, dissipate, fritter, blow. —*n.* bet, wager, stake, risk, plunge, hazard, flier, venture, pot, ante, investment.

gambol *v.* frolic, skip, leap, frisk, hop, caper, spring, romp, dance, bound, disport, prance, cavort, bounce, rollick. —*n.* frolic, skip, leap, frisk, rollick, hop, caper, spring, romp, dance, bound, cavort, bounce, prance.

game[1] *n.* **1** contest, competition, rivalry, engagement, match, tournament, tourney, event, meeting, race, conflict. **2** amusement, fun, sport, play, diversion, recreation, entertainment, pastime, jest, joke. **3** strategy, scheme, plan, game plan, stratagem, artifice, plot, tactic, gambit. —*adj.* plucky, spirited, intrepid, bold, brave, gamy, resolute, dauntless, gallant, fearless, unflinching, daring, cocky, gutsy (*Slang*).
ant. *adj.* timid, fainthearted, weak, shy, craven, cautious.

game[2] *adj.* LAME.

gamely *adv.* pluckily, courageously, fearlessly, intrepidly, valiantly, doggedly, unflinchingly, resolutely, bravely, boldly, gallantly, dauntlessly, daringly, heroically.
ant. cowardly, basely, dastardly, meanly, fearfully, timidly, cravenly.

gameness *n.* BRAVERY.

gamesome *adj.* PLAYFUL.

gamin *n.* **1** urchin, street urchin, ragamuffin, stray, vagabond, street Arab, guttersnipe, mudlark (*Brit.*), outcast, runaway, orphan. **2** lass, sprite, nymph, nymphet, fairy, sylph, maiden, damsel, flower child.

gammon *n.* HUMBUG.

gamut *n.* range, scope, compass, reach, sweep, ken, extent, area, field, scale, purview, horizon, orbit.

gamy *adj.* **1** plucky, brave, audacious, courageous, spirited, game, resolute, mettlesome, staunch, unflinching, unshrinking, spunky, determined, gutsy (*Slang*). **2** risqué, scandalous, spicy, off-color, suggestive, indecorous, indelicate, lewd, smutty, dirty, erotic, obscene, indecent, ribald, pornographic, porno, porn.
ant. **1** pluckless, apathetic, gritless, chicken-hearted, fainthearted. **2** proper, decorous, decent, seemly, fitting, conventional, moral, pure.

gander *n.* look, glance, glimpse, peep, peek, wink, blink, flash, *coup d'oeil.*

gang *n.* **1** group, crew, squad, team, outfit, shift, relay, company, body, force, troop, party, detachment, contingent. **2** group, club, ring, band, circle, coterie, league, alliance, order, lodge, clique, mob, knot, pack, batch, rabble.

gangling *adj.* tall, gangly, lank, lanky, spindly, rangy, rawboned, lean, spare, angular, gaunt, scrawny, skinny, slender, slim, thin.
ant. burly, husky, brawny, muscular, fleshy, sinewy, stout, fat.

gangster *n.* criminal, mobster, racketeer, gunman, thug, robber, crook, thief, hood (*Slang*), hoodlum, goon (*Slang*), tough, ruffian, bandit, mafioso.

gangway *n.* PASSAGE.

gaol *n. Brit.* JAIL.

gap *n.* **1** opening, break, parting, aperture, breach, rift, chasm, space, interval, cleft, crevice, fissure, split, chink, separation. **2** interruption, break, pause, interval, interim, hiatus, discontinuity, opening, lacuna, caesura, interference, hitch, stoppage, outage.

gape *v.* stare, gaze, peer, gaup, gawp, goggle, ogle, rubberneck (*Slang*), glare, gawk.

garb *n.* clothes, clothing, garment, apparel, dress, attire, outfit, costume, habit, get-up, uniform, vestment, livery, array. —*v.* clothe, dress, attire, outfit, robe, array, apparel, don, deck, gown.

garbage *n.* refuse, trash, rubbish, debris, waste, dirt, litter, scrap, dreck, swill, scum, discards, leavings, sweepings.

garble *v.* confuse, mix up, falsify, misrepresent, distort, pervert, interpolate, misread, misquote, misconstrue, misstate, misrender, doctor, twist. **ant.** clarify, resolve, clear up, explain, straighten out.

garden *adj.* ordinary, garden-variety, commonplace, routine, usual, customary, conventional, regular, average, familiar, wonted, workaday, unexceptional, everyday. **ant.** uncommon, unusual, irregular, exceptional, unique, rare, singular, extraordinary.

gargantuan *adj.* huge, big, large, gigantic, giant, colossal, vast, immense, enormous, mammoth, herculean, prodigious, monumental, elephantine, titanic. **ant.** tiny, small, little, miniature, puny, minuscule, diminutive, microscopic.

garish *adj.* glaring, showy, gaudy, flashy, ornate, tawdry, cheap, ostentatious, vulgar, meretricious, loud, conspicuous, obvious, blatant, tasteless, coarse. **ant.** elegant, refined, subtle, tasteful, fine.

garland *n.* wreath, chaplet, festoon, coronal, coronet, crown, diadem, bay, laurel, laureate, fillet, lei, headband.

garment *n.* clothes, clothing, garb, gear, apparel, attire, dress, outfit, costume, vestment, wraps, togs, toggery, vesture, raiment, habiliments, rags, glad rags (*Slang*).

garner *v.* store, gather, collect, accumulate, assemble, amass, aggregate, hoard, marshal, muster, lay in, lay up, mass, round up, squirrel away.

ant. spread, disperse, strew, broadcast, distribute, scatter.

garnish *v.* decorate, embellish, adorn, ornament, grace, enhance, beautify, trim, deck, bedeck, array, spruce, bedizen. —*n.* garnishment, garniture, decoration, embellishment, adornment, ornament, ornamentation, enhancement, bedizenment.

garnishment *n.* GARNISH.

garniture *n.* GARNISH.

garrison *n.* **1** troop, detachment, unit, militia, picket, guard, squad, watch, sentry. **2** fortification, fort, fortress, presidio, stronghold, hold, citadel, fastness, redoubt, bastion, bivouac, station, post, base, camp, encampment. —*v.* station, man, position, bivouac, camp, entrench, mount a guard, arm.

garrote *v.* strangle, strangulate, throttle, hang, choke, stifle, scrag, suffocate, smother, asphyxiate.

garrulity *n.* loquacity, talkativeness, garrulousness, loquaciousness, effusiveness, wordiness, volubility, verbosity, logorrhea, long-windedness, longiloquence. **ant.** taciturnity, reticence, reserve, laconism, terseness.

garrulous *adj.* talkative, loquacious, verbose, effusive, long-winded, windy, gabby, chatty, prolix, voluble, talky, glib, clamorous. **ant.** taciturn, terse, silent, quiet, laconic, reticent, reserved.

gas *n.* **1** air, vapor, ether, fume, steam, mist, fog, smoke, ozone, miasma. **2** bombast, braggadocio, grandiloquence, boastfulness, rant, gassiness, exaggeration, hot air (*Slang*), claptrap, fustian. **3** *Slang* merrymaker, gasser (*Slang*), cutup, good-time Charlie, card, wag, skylarker, playboy, fun lover, fun thing, partygoer, reveler, carouser.

gasconade *n.* BOAST.

gash *v.* cut, slice, slash, slit, lance, pierce, incise, wound, lacerate, rend, hew, penetrate. —*n.* cut, incision, slit, slash, rent, scission, wound, bruise, laceration, opening.

gasp v. gulp, pant, puff, blow, huff, heave, sigh. —n. gulp, pant, puff, blow, huff, heave, sigh.

gassy adj. **1** gaseous, vaporous, vapory, vaporish, ethereal, etheric, miasmal, miasmic, fumy, fuliginous. **2** flatulent, bloated, dyspeptic, windy. **3** pompous, vain, vainglorious, proud, conceited, boastful, snobbish, bombastic, pretentious, self-important, egotistic, flatulent.

gate n. door, doorway, gateway, opening, entry, entrance, entranceway, ingress, egress, exit, portal, passage, passageway, threshold, access, turnstile.

gatekeeper n. PORTER.

gateway n. GATE.

gather v. **1** collect, assemble, congregate, mass, amass, garner, store, hoard, accumulate, aggregate, marshal, muster, round up. **2** pick, harvest, pluck, reap, glean, cull, crop, garner. **3** conclude, infer, understand, deduce, assume, judge, derive, reckon, surmise, deem, reason.
ant. 1 separate, disperse, distribute, spread, scatter, strew.

gathering n. assembly, meeting, assemblage, crowd, multitude, throng, convocation, convention, congregation, conclave, concourse, affair, company, muster, collection.

gauche adj. boorish, awkward, wooden, gawky, clumsy, bungling, blundering, maladroit, ill-bred, ill-mannered, oafish, tactless, uncouth.
ant. suave, smooth, graceful, gracious, mannerly, deft, urbane.

gaucherie n. **1** mistake, gaffe, blunder, faux pas, boo-boo (*Slang*), boner (*Slang*), goof (*Slang*), blooper (*Slang*), howler, contretemps, nono, error. **2** clumsiness, tactlessness, oafishness, awkwardness, gracelessness, ponderousness, roughness, woodenness, gawkiness.
ant. 2 tactfulness, smoothness, grace-

fulness, graciousness, urbanity, suavity.

gaudy adj. garish, flashy, cheap, loud, unsubtle, blatant, showy, glaring, meretricious, tawdry, ostentatious, conspicuous, vulgar, coarse.
ant. elegant, tasteful, refined, fine, subtle, quiet.

gauge n. standard, criterion, measure, yardstick, touchstone, test, model, pattern, example, examplar, sample, basis, guide, rule, type. —v. estimate, judge, appraise, evaluate, compute, measure, figure, assess, count, calculate, rate, adjudge.

gaunt adj. **1** emaciated, thin, bony, meager, lank, haggard, lean, rawboned, spare, skinny, slim, scrawny, spindly, slender, cadaverous. **2** grim, desolate, bleak, forbidding, bare, barren, forlorn, wretched, forsaken, dismal, harsh, wild, uninhabited, laid waste.
ant. 1 obese, fat, stout, fleshy, plump, corpulent, portly, gross. **2** fertile, lush, luxuriant, lavish, rich, abundant, populous.

gauntlet n. CHALLENGE.

gauze n. MIST.

gauzy adj. thin, slight, unsubstantial, delicate, filmy, misty, transparent, see-through, translucent, sheer, silken, diaphanous, gossamer, hazy.
ant. thick, tight, substantial, dense, heavy, opaque.

gawk v. GAPE. —n. dolt, ignoramus, lout, clod, oaf, moron, imbecile, idiot, boob, simpleton, fool, boor, dunce, halfwit, nitwit.

gawky adj. awkward, clumsy, gauche, dull, ungainly, uncouth, foolish, boorish, unpolished, oafish, wooden, simple-minded, maladroit.
ant. polished, suave, deft, intelligent, quick-witted, discerning.

gay adj. **1** joyous, joyful, merry, high-spirited, gleeful, jovial, jolly, happy, convivial, sunny, cheerful, hearty, buoyant, delighted, jubilant. **2** brilliant, showy, bright, fine, vivid, splendid, sparkling, shiny, fresh, intense, gorgeous, polychromatic, glittering, grand, lustrous.

ant. 1 unhappy, miserable, sad, wretched, doleful, melancholic, gloomy. **2** plain, dull, flat, dismal, somber, lackluster, colorless, dim.

gayety *n.* GAIETY.

gaze *v.* stare, scrutinize, gape, look, watch, regard, pore over, peer, glare, ogle, scan, rubberneck (*Slang*), survey, observe, study, examine. —*n.* stare, gape, look.

gazette *n.* newspaper, journal, periodical, paper, organ, publication, tabloid.

gear *n.* **1** equipment, tools, rigging, material, paraphernalia, trappings, belongings, apparatus, accouterment, accessories, effects, tackle, supplies. **2** clothes, clothing, garments, apparel, dress, attire, outfits. —*v.* clothe, harness, dress, outfit, rig, deck, fit, equip.

gelatinous *adj.* jellylike, viscous, viscid, glutinous, sticky, gluey, gummy, ropy, thick.

geld *v.* castrate, spay, sterilize, alter, desex, desexualize, emasculate.

gelid *adj.* cold, icy, ice-cold, frozen, frigid, arctic, glacial, frosty, chilly.

ant. hot, torrid, scorching, parching, fiery, warm.

gelt *n. Slang* MONEY.

gem *n.* **1** jewel, stone, precious stone, semiprecious stone, bijou, ice (*Slang*), rock (*Slang*), brilliant, solitaire. **2** masterpiece, masterwork, marvel, jewel, treasure, *rara avis*, nonpareil, nonesuch, prize.

gemütlichkeit *n.* GENIALITY.

genealogy *n.* descent, pedigree, lineage, line, derivation, extraction, ancestry, parentage, family tree, tree, stock.

general *adj.* **1** universal, catholic, ecumenical, all-inclusive, comprehensive, worldwide, broad, categorical, prevalent, unspecialized, common, popular, impartial, inclusive, generic. **2** unrestricted, unspecific, nonspecific, miscellaneous, vague, lax, indefinite, ill-defined, inexact, impre-

cise. **3** usual, customary, regular, ordinary, popular, accepted, widespread, prevailing, prevalent, normal, current, rife, conventional.

ant. 1 local, exclusive, iimited, restricted, individual. **2** restricted, specific, exact, definite, precise, explicit, categorical. **3** uncommon, unusual, extraordinary, unparalleled, exceptional, rare.

generality *n.* **1** majority, bulk, mass, preponderance, most, lion's share. **2** generalness, universality, catholicity, all-inclusiveness, comprehensiveness, ecumenicity.

generally *adv.* ordinarily, customarily, habitually, usually, normally, frequently, mainly, typically, principally, chiefly.

ant. infrequently, rarely, occasionally, seldom, unusually, now and then.

generalship *n.* LEADERSHIP.

generate *v.* **1** produce, create, construct, manufacture, form, fabricate, originate, frame, contrive, invent, compose, fashion, develop, forge, devise, effect. **2** procreate, propagate, reproduce, beget, get, create, breed, father, sire, mother, engender, bear, produce, yield, spawn.

generation *n.* **1** procreation, propagation, reproduction, fertilization, fructification, fecundation, impregnation, breeding, begetting, proliferation. **2** creation, production, formation, evolution, origination, development, genesis.

generative *adj.* procreative, procreant, propagative, reproductive, fertile, fecund, fructuous, prolific, productive, fruitful, life-giving.

generator *n.* CREATOR.

generic *adj.* general, universal, inclusive, comprehensive, collective, whole, wide, indefinite.

ant. particular, specific, special, distinctive, restricted, explicit.

generosity *n.* **1** liberality, munificence, charitableness, bounteousness, bountifulness, nobleness, disinterestedness, kindliness, open-handedness, large-heartedness. **2** gift, present, donation, grant, good deed, benefaction, largess, gratuity, alms.

ant. 1 smallness, meanness, meagerness, niggardliness, greediness.

generous *adj.* **1** munificent, magnanimous, bountiful, bounteous, beneficent, benevolent, liberal, open-handed, lavish, prodigal, abundant, plentiful, plenteous, copious, overflowing. **2** noble, high-minded, unselfish, honorable, humane, magnanimous, lofty, large-hearted.

ant. 1 tightfisted, stingy, mean, scarce, scanty, barren, meager. **2** ignoble, mean, small-minded, petty, narrow-minded.

genesis *n.* creation, origin, beginning, birth, source, provenance, root, rise, inception, commencement, fountain, spring, evolution.

ant. end, conclusion, termination, finish, finis.

genetic *adj.* causal, evolutionary, historical, basic, primary, underlying.

genial *adj.* **1** cordial, pleasant, affable, friendly, cheerful, blithe, sunny, lighthearted, warm, good-natured, well-disposed, sympathetic. **2** comfortable, enlivening, lively, warm, mild, pleasing, congenial, favorable, agreeable, desirable, promising.

ant. 1 uncongenial, churlish, ill-disposed, grouchy, surly, testy, morose. **2** uncomfortable, unpleasant, disagreeable, severe, harsh.

geniality *n.* kindliness, cheerfulness, cordiality, happiness, optimism, heartiness, lightheartedness, affability, sociability, *gemütlichkeit,* amiability, warmth, congeniality, friendliness.

ant. cheerlessness, unhappiness, disagreeableness, coldness, severity.

genius *n.* **1** brilliance, prowess, intelligence, intuition, cognition, subtlety, originality, judgment, invention, sagacity, wisdom, discernment, ingenuity. **2** gift, talent, flair, faculty, endowment, aptitude, quality,

knack, bent, aptness, penchant, proclivity, propensity, predilection. **3** prodigy, child prodigy, wizard, mental giant, mastermind, whiz (*Slang*).

ant. 3 idiot, imbecile, moron, fool, dullard.

genocide *n.* MASSACRE.

genre *n.* kind, sort, class, classification, style, type, set, category, group, nature, character, genus, species, variety.

genteel *adj.* **1** refined, elegant, well-bred, highbred, cultured, cultivated, courtly, polished, polite, courteous, ladylike, gentlemanly. **2** pretentious, ostentatious, affected, mannered, pompous, unnatural, highfalutin, high-hat, hoity-toity, showy.

ant. 1 common, inelegant, unrefined, impolite, discourteous, boorish, churlish. **2** unaffected, natural, simple, sincere.

gentility *n.* **1** refinement, breeding, cultivation, culture, civility, elegance, polish, grace, politeness, courtesy, courtliness, gentlemanliness, propriety, decorum. **2** aristocracy, nobility, gentry, second estate, gentlefolk, elite, society, blue bloods, upper class, county (*Brit.*).

ant. 1 coarseness, vulgarity, discourtesy, impropriety, barbarity.

gentle *adj.* **1** serene, peaceful, clement, kind, tender, humane, lenient, merciful, meek, mild, kindly. **2** soft, smooth, moderate, temperate, tempered, light, mild, gradual, balmy. **3** tame, docile, manageable, tractable, trained, peaceable, quiet, tempered, compliant, accommodating. **4** upperclass, wellborn, well-bred, high-class, highbred, noble, elegant, refined, polite, cultivated, cultured, polished, courteous. —*v.* sooth, calm, quiet, soften, allay, console, mitigate, lighten, comfort.

ant. *adj.* **1** cruel, harsh, heartless, truculent, merciless. **2** harsh, rough, immoderate, extreme, sudden, abrupt. **3** intractable, wild, noisy, active, headstrong, willful. **4** unrefined, impolite, unpolished, discourteous, low-class, low-bred. —*v.* agitate, provoke, stimulate, disturb, arouse, burden.

gentlefolk *n.* GENTRY.

gentlemanly *adj.* gentlemanlike, noble, well-bred, genteel, elegant, gallant, cultivated, aristocratic, refined, polished, courteous.

gentry *n.* **1** gentility, aristocracy, nobility, gentlefolk, elite, society, blue bloods, upper classes, county (*Brit.*). **2** folk, folks, people, mankind, society.

genuine *adj.* **1** real, authentic, legitimate, veritable, proven, tested, unadulterated, unalloyed, actual, factual, pukka. **2** frank, sincere, true, honest, candid, ingenuous, straightforward, aboveboard, plain, open, guileless.
ant. **1** spurious, bogus, sham, counterfeit, fake, fallacious. **2** affected, hypocritical, insincere, sly, cunning, disingenuous.

genus *n.* kind, class, classification, sort, set, group, order, type, category, genre.

germ *n.* **1** microbe, microorganism, bacterium, bug, virus, pathogen, infection. **2** source, rudiment, root, seed, origin, nucleus, beginning, embryo, womb, principle, spring, fountainhead.

germane *adj.* relevant, pertinent, apropos, apt, appropriate, to the point, applicable, pat, suited, apposite, fit, material.
ant. inept, foreign, beside the point, extraneous, incidental, irrelevant.

germicide *n.* antiseptic, bactericide, disinfectant, prophylactic, antibiotic.

germinal *adj.* SEMINAL.

germinate *v.* sprout, bud, develop, grow, push up, shoot, vegetate, burgeon, pullulate.

gestation *n.* pregnancy, gravidity, incubation, hatching, engendering, maturation, propagation.

gesticulate *v.* GESTURE.

gesture *n.* sign, signal, movement, gesticulation, indication, motion, by-play, dumb show, body English, mimicry. —*v.* gesticulate, signal, mime, pantomime, motion.

get *v.* **1** obtain, receive, acquire, earn, reap, fetch, gain, procure, win, achieve. **2** persuade, cause, induce, prevail on, influence, dispose. **3** comprehend, see, understand, follow, take in, perceive, fathom, apprehend, grasp, sense, learn, dig (*Slang*). **4** become, grow, wax, turn.

get ahead succeed, prosper, flourish, thrive, do well, make good, advance, progress, prevail, make it (*Slang*).

get along **1** leave, go, go away, get away, move off, pull out, quit, buzz off (*Slang*), bug out (*Slang*), bug off (*Slang*). **2** succeed, manage, contrive, make out, shape up, prosper, shift, fare, progress, develop, make headway, turn out.

get at **1** reach, arrive at, gain access to, come upon, hit upon, get hold of. **2** intend, mean, imply, hint, intimate, lead up to.

getaway *n.* escape, start, dash, departure, exit, exodus, break, breakout, flight, disappearance.

get away escape, depart, start, break loose, leave, disengage, go free, go, withdraw, elude.

get off **1** dismount, descend from, alight from, disembark, deplane, step off. **2** depart, leave, set out, go, start, move off, sally forth, shove off.

get on make out, get along, progress, develop, advance, mature, flourish, succeed, manage, fare.

get out clear out, leave, decamp, break loose, extricate oneself, depart, escape, get clear.

get over recover, come round, revive, rally, pull through, survive, recuperate, convalesce, get better, mend, heal.

get through **1** complete, finish, conclude, accomplish, cover, wind up, carry out, dispose of, terminate, close. **2** endure, survive, live through, outlast, bear, tolerate, last, pass, withstand.

get to start, begin, take up, settle down to, broach, address oneself, apply oneself, plunge into, turn to, go ahead.

get together 1 collect, amass, accumulate, heap up, marshal, muster, assemble. **2** meet, congregate, assemble, associate, unite, integrate. **3** agree, come to terms, compromise, strike a bargain, negotiate, meet halfway.

get-up *n.* ensemble, outfit, appearance, aspect, guise, facade, composition, organization, accouterments, equipage, trappings, fashion, mode, costume.

get up 1 arise, rise, wake, awaken, bestir oneself, turn out, stand up, ascend, mount, spring up, rear, uprear. **2** prepare, arrange, improvise, organize, devise, assemble, scrape up, concoct, make ready, put together, compose, fashion.

gew-gaw *n., adj.* GIMCRACK.

ghastly *adj.* haggard, terrifying, deathlike, shocking, cadaverous, spectral, livid, repellent, fearful, terrible, grim, grisly, appalling.

ghost *n.* **1** spirit, apparition, wraith, phantom, shade, shadow, shape, spook, specter, manes, eidolon, phantasm. **2** trace, breath, iota, hint, shadow, suggestion, image, mirage.

ghostly *adj.* spectral, wraithlike, phantom, shadowy, incorporeal, illusory, phantasmal, phantasmic, eerie, uncanny.

ghoulish *adj.* macabre, sinister, scary, hair-raising, weird, gruesome, gothic, horrifying, eerie, fiendish, zombielike, monstrous, necrophilic, Grand Guignol.

giant *n.* colossus, leviathan, titan, whale, mammoth, mountain, monster, ogre, superman, behemoth, Goliath. —*adj.* gigantic, colossal, immense, huge, outsize, vast, enormous, mammoth, elephantine, prodigious, monstrous, mountainous, gargantuan, Brobdingnagian.

ant. *n.* dwarf, midget, pygmy, runt,

smidgeon, shrimp. *adj.* diminutive, picayune, toy, tiny, elfin, microscopic, Lilliputian.

gibber *v.* BABBLE. —*n.* GIBBERISH.

gibberish *n.* babble, gabble, double talk, gibber, gobbledygook, jabber, jargon, lingo, patter, twaddle, prattle, nonsense.

gibe *v.* mock, sneer, scoff, deride, taunt, ridicule, flout, jeer, twit, chaff, tease, fleer, rally, quip, scorn. —*n.* sneer, quip, taunt, jeer, crack, dig, twit, fleer, mock, scoff, flout, putdown (*Slang*).

giddy *adj.* **1** dizzy, reeling, lightheaded, faint, vertiginous. **2** flighty, silly, frivolous, daft, fluttery, foolish, volatile, unstable, impulsive, thoughtless, unbalanced.

ant. 2 reliable, serious, sober, steady, constant, prudent.

gift *n.* **1** present, gratuity, donation, handout, contribution, grant, offering, boon, favor, bonus, largesse. **2** talent, aptitude, knack, faculty, flair, endowment, bent, capacity, genius, ability.

gifted *adj.* talented, clever, endowed, well-endowed, capable, able, masterly, skilled, adept, superior, accomplished.

gigantic *adj.* colossal, huge, tremendous, enormous, immense, mammoth, gargantuan, vast, stupendous, prodigious, elephantine, Brobdingnagian.

ant. dwarfish, miniature, small, tiny, infinitesimal, microscopic, Lilliputian.

giggle *v.* titter, snigger, snicker, chuckle, chortle, twitter, cackle, crow, snort. —*n.* titter, snigger, twitter, snicker, chuckle, chortle, cackle, crow, snort.

gild *v.* gloss over, embellish, touch up, retouch, cover up, brighten, camouflage, color, embroider.

gimcrack *n.* trinket, bauble, gew-gaw, trifle, bagatelle, bijou, knickknack, thingamabob, kickshaw, toy, nothing. —*adj.* cheap, tawdry, showy, trashy, catchpenny, vulgar, meretricious, gaudy, garish, loud, flashy, paltry.

ant. *adj.* choice, tasteful, elegant, refined, extraordinary, superior, low-keyed.

gimmick *n.* scheme, stunt, twist, gadget, contrivance, wrinkle, gizmo, catch, device, artifice, trick, dodge, angle, ruse, stratagem, widgit (*Slang*), kicker (*Slang*).

gimpy *adj.* lame, crippled, limping, hobbling, halt, disabled, game.

gingerly *adv.* cautiously, carefully, warily, charily, circumspectly, guardedly, delicately, timidly, suspiciously, hesitantly, leerily.

ant. rashly, recklessly, headlong, precipitately, carelessly, confidently.

gird *v.* 1 circumscribe, encircle, circle, surround, girt, hem in, ring. 2 belt, bind, truss, strap, girdle, cinch, clinch, loop, band, wreathe.

girdle *n.* zone, belt, ring, compass, boundary, girth, band, loop, sash, collar, circumference, cinch, surcingle. —*v.* encircle, encompass, enclose, shut in, circle, surround, circumscribe, embrace, orbit, environ, bind.

girt *v.* GIRD.

girth *n.* GIRDLE.

gist *n.* substance, point, heart, core, essence, sense, crux, tenor, burden, spirit, drift, import, meaning.

give *v.* 1 donate, bestow, hand out, contribute, present, distribute, confer. 2 impart, express, deliver, supply, set forth, pronounce, publish, issue, show, produce, render, offer. 3 concede, yield, grant, allow, relinquish, render, accord, cede, part with. —*n.* RESILIENCE.

give-and-take *n.* compromise, reciprocation, evenhandedness, tit for tat, reciprocity, interchange, retaliation, counterbalancing, quid pro quo, exchange, trade-off.

give away 1 hand out, bestow, donate, part with, dispose of, dispense, spare. 2 divulge, reveal, disclose, uncover,

tattle, inform on, leak, betray, blab, blurt, squeal (*Slang*).

give back return, restore, replace, refund, rebate, repay, render, restitute, remit, remand, relinquish.

give in yield, collapse, submit, give up, quit, surrender, knuckle under, recant, renounce, cede, capitulate, comply, concede.

ant. persevere, resist, endure, stand firm, stick it out, insist.

given *n.* PREMISE.

give off emit, exude, produce, release, give forth, exhale, vent, smell of, expel, eject, discharge.

give out 1 emit, send forth, exhale, release, generate. 2 bestow, distribute, deal, pay out, disseminate, scatter, strew. 3 make known, publish, announce, proclaim, report, advertise.

give rise to cause, result in, occasion, bring about, lead to, bring on, entail, inaugurate, institute, effect, usher in, produce, foreordain.

give up surrender, cede, hand over, relinquish, abandon, waive, yield, quit, resign, desist, stop, cease.

ant. retain, persist, hoard, keep, hold fast, insist.

glabrous *adj.* BALD.

glacial *adj.* 1 cold, frigid, icy, freezing, frozen, wintry, gelid, congealed. 2 hostile, unfriendly, inimical, cutting, haughty, chilling, icy.

ant. 1 warm, torrid, hot, steaming, summery. 2 cheery, cordial, heartwarming, friendly, hearty.

glad *adj.* 1 happy, joyful, gay, merry, cheery, smiling, jocund, blithe, jolly, jovial. 2 gratifying, delightful, felicitous, pleasing, pleasant, cheering, heartwarming. 3 willing, amenable, delighted, pleased, inclined, eager, disposed, gratified.

ant. 1 tearful, sad, gloomy, dour, morose. 2 sorrowful, heartrending, distressing. 3 recalcitrant, resistant, loath, averse.

gladden *v.* elate, cheer, make happy,

please, gratify, hearten, encourage, exhilarate, delight, inspirit, rejoice.

ant. discourage, grieve, sadden, oppress, cast down, disappoint.

gladiator *n.* fighter, contestant, champion, battler, contender, competitor, militant, combatant.

gladsome *adj.* joyous, happy, merry, gay, satisfying, cheerful, jocund, blithe, jaunty, lighthearted.

ant. leaden, melancholy, heavy, cheerless, morose, sad, gloomy.

glamorous *adj.* fascinating, enchanting, alluring, dazzling, charismatic, magnetic, captivating, romantic, charming, interesting, resplendent.

glamour *n.* allure, charm, fascination, attraction, magnetism, magic, spell, witchery, aura, charisma, presence.

glance *v.* 1 ricochet, graze, carom, sideswipe, rebound, skim, flip, brush. 2 glimpse, peep, peek, look, peer. 3 flash, glint, glisten, shine, gleam, glitter, scintillate, coruscate. —*n.* 1 glimpse, look, peep, peek, squint. 2 *momentary gleam:* flash, sparkle, beam, glint, gleam, glitter, scintillation.

glare *v.* 1 dazzle, blaze, shine, flash, flare, sparkle, glitter, coruscate, glister, blind. 2 scowl, stare, glower, frown, gaze, lower, fixate, fix. —*n.* 1 *dazzling light:* blaze, dazzle, effulgence, incandescence, resplendence, brilliancy. 2 scowl, frown, stare, squint, gaze. 3 tinsel, gaudiness, dazzle, flashiness, tawdriness, spangle.

glaring *adj.* 1 scowling, frowning, staring, lowering, glowering, beetle-browed. 2 dazzling, brilliant, fulgent, beaming, glowing, blinding, vivid, blazing. 3 flagrant, arrant, conspicuous, outstanding, egregious, notable, obvious, blatant.

ant. 3 imperceptible, insignificant, restrained, trifling, negligible, low-keyed.

glary *adj.* dazzling, brilliant, glaring, gaudy, tawdry, blazing, glittering, flashy, garish, sparkling, blinding.

ant. dull, subdued, dark, dim, shadowy, obscure.

glassy *adj.* expressionless, glazed, fixed, dull, vacant, blank, uncomprehending, vapid, inexpressive, lifeless, stupid.

ant. meaningful, eloquent, significant, sparkling, bright, expressive.

glaze *v.* polish, lacquer, shine, varnish, luster, buff, gloss, furbish, burnish, shellac, coat. —*n.* polish, varnish, luster, burnish, glazing, icing, enamel, coat, finish, patina, veneer.

gleam *n.* flash, glint, glimmer, glow, ray, beam, sparkle, shine, glitter, flicker, spark, streak. —*v.* glimmer, glow, shine, flash, glint, ray, beam, sparkle, glitter, flicker, spark, streak.

glean *v.* 1 learn, piece together, root out, pick up, cull, hear, accumulate. 2 pluck, gather, harvest, reap, pick, crop, scavenge.

glee *n.* joy, gaiety, merriment, exultation, liveliness, hilarity, mirth, jollity, joviality, verve, exultation, elation, exhilaration.

ant. melancholy, sadness, sorrow, misery, dejection, depression.

gleeful *adj.* joyous, mirthful, exultant, delighted, blissful, jovial, joyful, jolly, merry, glad, festive, gay, exhilarated, hilarious, elated.

ant. wretched, sad, gloomy, miserable, melancholy, dejected.

glib *adj.* 1 fluent, voluble, loquacious, talkative, eloquent, gabby. 2 facile, plausible, smooth-tongued, artful, superficial, adroit, smooth, oily, slippery, ingratiating, fast-talking.

ant. 1 taciturn, reticent, quiet, silent. 2 considered, sincere, artless, guileless.

glide *v.* slip, slither, slide, stream, glissade, skate, float, skim, flow, plane, skid. —*n.* slide, slip, glissade, slipping, sliding.

glimmer *v.* flicker, sparkle, flash, twinkle, gleam, glow, shimmer, blink, glitter, scintillate. —*n.* flicker, gleam, shimmer, spark, flash, beam, ray, glimpse, glance, hint, trace, speck.

glimpse *n.* **1** *momentary view:* glance, peek, peep, squint, look, glint, flash. **2** inkling, glimmer, intimation, side-light, hint, notion, suggestion, idea. —*v.* catch sight of, espy, spy, spot, see, glance, squint, glint.

glint *v.* flash, coruscate, flicker, sparkle, glitter, glisten, beam, twinkle, glister, shine. —*n.* flash, beam, gleam, sparkle, glimmer, glitter, twinkle, flicker, glisten, shimmer.

glisten *v.* shine, shimmer, gleam, sparkle, twinkle, glow, glint, flash, glitter, beam, glister. —*n.* glint, flash, flicker, glimmer, twinkle, beam, gleam, sparkle, shine.

glister *v.* GLISTEN. —*n.* GLITTER.

glitch *n. Slang* mishap, malfunction, snag, hitch, blip, irregularity, discontinuity, jolt, pip, jounce.

glitter *v.* sparkle, gleam, scintillate, glint, flash, shine, twinkle, glisten, coruscate, flare, glow. —*n.* sparkle, brilliancy, flashing, coruscation, scintillation, twinkling, radiance, luster, refulgence, shine, glister, splendor, tinsel.

gloaming *n.* twilight, dusk, half-light, sundown, eventide, nightfall, gloom.

gloat *v.* exult, triumph, vaunt, crow, jubilate, rejoice, revel, bask, wallow, luxuriate.

global *adj.* **1** worldwide, universal, international, world, mundane, planetary, pandemic, general. **2** spherical, globate, globular, orbicular, circular, round.

globe *n.* **1** sphere, orb, ball, globule, bubble, bulb. **2** earth, planet, world, biosphere.

globe-trotter *n.* TOURIST.

globose *adj.* GLOBULAR.

globular *adj.* **1** spherical, rotund, globose, globate, orbicular, round, spheroid, globe-shaped. **2** GLOBAL.

gloom *n.* **1** depression, melancholy, dejection, despair, despondency, sorrow, dolor, woe, pessimism, misery, sadness, grief. **2** murk, darkness,

shade, obscurity, dimness, shadow, duskiness, twilight.

ant. 1 joy, glee, happiness, delight, frivolity, mirth. **2** brightness, effulgence, luminescence, glow.

gloomy *adj.* **1** moody, melancholy, morose, sad, dispirited, depressed, downcast, despondent, dumpy, sorrowful, glum, saturnine, atrabilious. **2** depressing, dreary, desolate, oppressive, dismal, uncomfortable, cheerless, comfortless, joyless. **3** dark, obscure, somber, clouded, dismal, shaded, inky, murky, overcast, crepuscular.

ant. 1 happy, joyful, elated, cheerful, gleeful, gay. **2** pleasing, enjoyable, delectable, gratifying, delightful. **3** sunny, bright, light, radiant, cloudless.

glorify *v.* **1** worship, honor, revere, exalt, consecrate, sanctify, reverence, venerate, idolize, apotheosize, beatify, enshrine, transfigure. **2** praise, extol, feature, eulogize, boost, puff, magnify, spotlight, celebrate, lionize, overrate.

ant. 1 mock, despise, revile, blaspheme. **2** degrade, abase.

glorious *adj.* splendid, magnificent, delightful, sublime, wonderful, heavenly, resplendent, brilliant, preeminent, admirable, noble.

glory *n.* **1** renown, distinction, honor, celebrity, prestige, fame, eminence, note, notability, repute. **2** adoration, worship, praise, hosanna, blessing, benediction, thanksgiving, Gloria. **3** radiance, splendor, magnificence, brilliance, effulgence, resplendence, grandeur, glitter, luster, illumination. —*v.* take pride, exult, rejoice, delight, revel, bask, triumph, vaunt, jubilate, luxuriate.

ant. *n.* **1** infamy, dishonor, disgrace, humiliation, shame, abasement. **3** gloom, darkness, obscurity, opacity, shade, dimness.

gloss[1] *n.* **1** shine, sheen, luster, glaze, brightness, polish, shimmer, glow. **2** semblance, pretense, facade, front, pretension, appearance, show, sham, pretext, mien. —*v.* shine, polish, furbish, burnish, varnish.

gloss[2] *n.* explanation, annotation, interpretation, scholium, footnote, note, comment, commentary, appendix, addendum, glossary.

glossary *n.* wordbook, lexicon, gloss, vocabulary, thesaurus, dictionary, key.

gloss over whitewash, disguise, color, falsify, explain away, extenuate, palliate, veil, cover up, sleek.

glossy *adj.* **1** lustrous, shiny, shining, polished, glazed, glassy, satiny, burnished, silky, smooth. **2** specious, spurious, tinsel, sham, meretricious, slick, plausible, illusory, artificial.
ant. 1 dull, matte, dim, tarnished, grainy. **2** plain, unvarnished, forthright, bald, genuine.

glow *v.* **1** gleam, radiate, shine, shimmer, glisten, incandesce, glitter, coruscate. **2** color, redden, blush, flush, tingle, twinkle, brighten, flare up. **3** burn, blaze, flame, kindle, redden. —*n.* **1** brightness, shine, shimmer, ruddiness, reddening, luminosity, incandescence. **2** fervor, enthusiasm, ardor, vehemence, gusto, impetuosity. **3** warmth, flush, blush, fever, bloom.

glower *v.* frown, scowl, glare, lower, stare. —*n.* scowl, glare, frown, lower, stare.
ant. *v.* smile, beam, grin.

glue *v.* paste, affix, stick, gum, cement, fix, plaster.

gluey *adj.* ADHESIVE.

glum *adj.* moody, sullen, morose, sulky, gloomy, ill-humored, low, doleful, crusty, sour, surly.
ant. cheerful, blithe, sunny, happy, carefree, gleeful.

glut *v.* **1** satiate, surfeit, gorge, stuff, cram, bolt, fill, gulp, wolf. **2** oversupply, flood, overload, dump, unload, surcharge. —*n.* plethora, excess, superabundance, surfeit, surplus, flood, deluge, congestion, repletion, saturation, redundance, superfluity.

ant. *n.* scarcity, dearth, lack, deficiency, want, paucity.

glutinous *adj.* gummy, sticky, tacky, viscid, viscous, gluey, adhesive, clinging, cohesive, tenacious, glairy.
ant. thin, serous, watery, fluid, dilute, tenuous.

glutton *n.* gourmand, pig, gorger, crammer, stuffer, cormorant, hog, gobbler, sensualist.

gluttonous *adj.* voracious, insatiable, greedy, ravenous, piggish, omnivorous, swinish, edacious, hoggish, rapacious.
ant. abstemious, temperate, moderate, abstinent, picky, anoretic.

gluttony *n.* voracity, voraciousness, overeating, insatiability, ravenousness, edacity, greed, rapaciousness, intemperance, crapulence, wolfishness, hoggishness, polyphagia.

gnarl *v.* twist, distort, contort, knot, deform, coil, bend, wring, screw, crook.

gnarled *adj.* **1** knotty, knurled, knobby, gnarly, cross-grained, knotted, nodular, snaggy. **2** weatherbeaten, twisted, crooked, wrinkled, leathery, distorted, deformed, rough, contorted. **3** querulous, hard-bitten, captious, crabbed, peevish, cantankerous, crabby, waspish, eccentric.

gnash *v.* GRIND.

gnaw *v.* **1** nibble, chew, bite, munch, gnash, masticate, champ, crunch. **2** erode, eat away, corrode, consume, wear. **3** rankle, worry, chafe, fester, fret, distress, obsess, torment.

gnome *n.* FAIRY.

gnomic *adj.* SENTENTIOUS.

gnostic *adj.* INTELLECTUAL.

go *v.* **1** proceed, move, progress, advance, pass along, hie, wend. **2** leave, depart, withdraw, betake oneself, go away, retire, quit. **3** pass away, vanish, cease, die, disappear, evaporate, fade, dissolve, elapse. **4** function, work, operate, run, perform, act, be in motion. **5** reach, extend, lie, connect, lead, stretch, span. —*n.* **1** energy, vigor, verve, vim, spirit, initiative, stamina, force, pep (*Slang*). **2**

attempt, stab, try, effort, turn, whirl, bid, endeavor, venture. —*adj.* operative, all right, OK, approved, in order, in readiness, functioning, clear.

goad *n.* spur, prod, incentive, inducement, motive, impulse, spring, motivation, urge, pressure. —*v.* prod, urge, poke, spur, incite, arouse, instigate, stimulate, impel, prick, badger, stir up.

go-ahead *n.* PERMISSION.

goal *n.* aim, end, purpose, design, object, intent, target, ambition, objective, intention, destination.

go along 1 accompany, attend, join, escort, wait on, convoy. **2** agree, assent, acquiesce, concur, consent, follow, cooperate.

goat *n.* SCAPEGOAT.

gob *n.* chunk, lump, gobbet, mass, piece, hunk, wad, clod, blob, glob, plug.

gobble *v.* **1** *swallow greedily:* bolt, gulp, raven, devour, cram, wolf. **2** *Slang* grab, snatch, snap up, pounce on, hog (*Slang*).

gobbledygook *n.* cant, jargon, balderdash, claptrap, gibberish, double talk, rigmarole, nonsense, bosh, buncombe, officialese, bunk (*Slang*).

go-between *n.* intermediary, mediator, broker, middleman, agent, negotiator, medium, arbiter, fixer, pander, bagman (*Slang*).

go by 1 pass, go beyond, overshoot, outstrip, exceed, beat, leave behind, eclipse. **2** conform to, be guided by, adapt to, accord with, follow, adopt, heed, observe, judge from.

god *n.* goddess, divinity, godhead, deity, idol, spirit, numen, demigod, demigoddess, daemon, genius, hero, heroine.

God-fearing *adj.* PIOUS.

godless *adj.* **1** atheistic, irreligious, heathen, freethinking, agnostic. **2** sinful, wicked, impious, ungodly, blasphemous, profane, unholy.

ant. 2 just, virtuous, God-fearing, pious, devout, pure.

godlike *adj.* divine, superhuman, heavenly, celestial, supernal, supernatural.

godly *adj.* pious, religious, devout, God-fearing, reverent, holy, righteous, saintly, reverential, pietistic, moral, good.

ant. sacrilegious, worldly, blasphemous, wicked, sinful, profane.

godsend *n.* blessing, boon, windfall, manna, miracle, mercy, find, prize.

go-getter *n.* hustler, live wire, doer, operator (*Slang*), activist, dynamo, eager beaver (*Slang*).

go in for engage in, take up, specialize in, practice, undertake, devote oneself to, pursue, adopt, enjoy, embrace, espouse.

going *n.* departure, withdrawal, disappearance, removal, retreat, retirement, leaving, moving, starting, exit. —*adj.* **1** continuing, ongoing, thriving, functioning, current. **2** extant, alive, existing, living, available, obtainable, accessible.

goings on behavior, conduct, actions, events, occurrences, happenings, activity, busyness, bustling, stir, commotion, trafficking, monkeyshines (*Slang*).

gold *n.* wealth, treasure, money, property, fortune, riches, lucre, capital, funds, substance.

goldbrick *v. Slang* SHIRK.

golden *adj.* precious, splendid, superb, extraordinary, exceptional, great, memorable, remarkable, glorious, admirable, outstanding.

gone *adj.* **1** ruined, done for, hopeless, lost, defeated, dead. **2** faint, weak, fatigued, exhausted, ailing, sick. **3** *Slang* first-rate, capital, excellent, splendid, superior, out of sight (*Slang*). **4** involved, absorbed, advanced, entangled, embroiled.

goo *n.* **1** mire, muck, sludge, mud, slime, ooze, slush, gunk, gumbo, guck (*Slang*), gook (*Slang*). **2** sentimentality, bathos, mawkishness, mush, emotionalism, mushiness, gush, schmaltz (*Slang*).

good *adj.* **1** satisfactory, serviceable, adequate, functional, competent, reliable, efficient, useful, favorable. **2** pleasing, admirable, striking, attractive, agreeable, excellent, first-rate, choice, select. **3** virtuous, kind, benevolent, righteous, honorable, moral, well-mannered, well-behaved. **4** orthodox, conforming, typical, true, dependable, reliable, suitable, exemplary, proper. **5** considerable, ample, tidy, sizable, full, substantial, large. —*n.* benefit, advantage, profit, well-being, behalf, welfare, prosperity, gain, enjoyment.
ant. 1 unsatisfactory, inadequate, incompetent, unreliable, inefficient. **2** displeasing, disagreeable, unattractive, mediocre, ordinary. **3** unkind, dishonorable, immoral, boorish, rude. **4** unconventional, atypical, unreliable, unsuitable, improper. **5** small, skimpy, insufficient, unsubstantial, scant. *n.* disadvantage, damage, drawback, loss, harm.

good-by *n.* farewell, adieu, leavetaking, parting, departure, Godspeed, leave, valediction, dismissal, send-off.

good-for-nothing *adj.* useless, worthless, ne'er-do-well, feckless, irresponsible, shiftless, paltry, valueless, idle, no-account.
ant. worthy, deserving, estimable, worthwhile, industrious, exemplary.

good-hearted *adj.* well-meaning, amiable, complaisant, kindly, benevolent, helpful, sympathetic, generous, considerate, liberal, good-natured, kind.
ant. ill-disposed, spiteful, malicious, selfish, mean, malevolent.

good-humored *adj.* GOOD-NATURED.

good-looking *adj.* attractive, handsome, beautiful, comely, becoming, fair, lovely, personable, well-favored, goodly, clean-cut, pretty.
ant. homely, ugly, plain, ill-favored, drab, repellent.

goodly *adj.* **1** comely, attractive, handsome, personable, pleasing, fair, good-looking, well-favored, graceful. **2** large, sizable, considerable, ample, substantial, tidy.
ant. 1 unattractive, homely, illfavored, unpleasant, disagreeable. **2** small, skimpy, insufficient, unsubstantial, scant.

good-natured *adj.* pleasant, amiable, kindly, complaisant, affable, agreeable, congenial, obliging, indulgent, tolerant, easygoing, good-humored, good-tempered.
ant. ill-tempered, morose, irritable, crotchety, surly, cantankerous.

goodness *n.* **1** virtue, honesty, rectitude, integrity, probity, righteousness, morality. **2** excellence, merit, value, superiority, worth, worthiness, quality. **3** kindness, good will, kindliness, benevolence, charity, generosity, humaneness.
ant. 1 wickedness, dishonesty, roguery, corruption, vice, evil. **2** mediocrity, imperfection, inferiority, badness, shoddiness. **3** malevolence, cruelty, malice, spite, brutality.

goods *n.* merchandise, property, material, possessions, wares, commodities, effects, stuff, furnishings, belongings, stock, inventory.

good-tempered *adj.* GOOD-NATURED.

good will 1 benevolence, friendliness, concern, kindness, favor, support. **2** willingness, consent, eagerness, readiness, zeal, acquiescence, ardor, alacrity, enthusiasm, heartiness.
ant. 1 animus, ill will, antipathy, animosity, bad blood, disfavor. **2** resentment, reluctance, hesitancy, indignation, demur, protest.

gooey *adj.* **1** sticky, smeary, thick, viscous, viscid, adhesive, adherent, glutinous. **2** sentimental, mawkish, maudlin, mushy, cloying, bathetic, emotional, saccharine.

goof *Slang n.* **1** fool, dolt, clown, ninny, numskull, nincompoop, blockhead, ignoramus, dunce, simpleton, screwball (*Slang*). **2** blunder, botch, bungle, muff, fumble, mess, slip, mistake, gaffe, faux pas. —*v.* blunder, botch, bungle, fumble, err, spoil, muff, stumble, flounder, trip.

gook *n.* GOO.

gooky *adj. Slang* sticky, messy, gooey, smeary, distasteful, unsavory, offensive, repugnant, repulsive, icky (*Slang*).

goon *n. Slang* **1** roughneck, thug, hoodlum, gangster, hooligan, ruffian, tough, bruiser, rowdy, hood (*Slang*). **2** fool, dunce, dolt, ass, addlepate, simpleton, imbecile, moron, bonehead, blockhead.

goose *n.* simpleton, ninny, scatterbrain, silly, ignoramus, nincompoop, booby, idiot, dunce, blockhead, dolt, numskull.

gore *v.* pierce, impale, horn, transfix, tusk, spear, stab, penetrate, spit, puncture, gouge.

gorge *n.* **1** ravine, canyon, defile, cleft, gully, fissure, crevasse, crack, chasm, pass. **2** throat, gullet, esophagus, maw. **3** anger, disgust, revulsion, repugnance, nausea. —*v.* stuff, satiate, gormandize, surfeit, glut, sate, overeat, gulp, pall, cloy.

gorgeous *adj.* **1** resplendent, magnificent, superb, glorious, sumptuous, splendid, sublime, beautiful, rich. **2** pretty, delightful, amusing, fine, lovely, swell (*Slang*). **ant. 1** poor, mean, humble, shabby, dim, ugly. **2** unattractive, homely, uninspiring, dull, awful.

gormandize *v.* overeat, stuff, surfeit, gobble, gorge, devour, raven, cram, bolt, gulp. **ant.** nibble, pick at, peck at, diet.

gory *adj.* bloody, bloodstained, sanguinary, ensanguined.

gossip *n.* **1** *idle talk:* hearsay, rumor, chitchat, tittle-tattle, scandal, prattle, small talk, report. **2** gossiper, scandalmonger, talebearer, prattler, quidnunc, tattler, babbler, magpie, newsmonger, chatterbox, busybody, yenta. —*v.* prattle, babble, tittle-tattle, chatter, chat, tattle, gabble.

gothic *adj.* **1** barbaric, uncouth, outlandish, uncivilized, barbarous, rude, inchoate. **2** weird, macabre, creepy, grotesque, freakish, bizarre.

go through 1 ransack, examine, investigate, look into, search, sift, analyze, review. **2** experience, undergo, meet with, stand, live through, bear with, endure. **3** use up, exhaust, consume, squander, waste, spend, expend. **ant. 3** save, preserve, conserve, keep, hoard.

gouge *n.* **1** groove, cut, channel, hollow, furrow, trench, notch, cavity, hole. **2** extortion, overcharge, stealing, cheating, swindle, rip-off (*Slang*). —*v.* **1** chisel, incise, hollow out, groove, furrow, corrugate, scoop, excavate, gash, dig out. **2** cheat, profiteer, chisel, bleed, overcharge, rip off (*Slang*).

go under be overwhelmed, fail, founder, succumb, sink, go down, collapse, lose out, fall, crash. **ant.** conquer, triumph, succeed, thrive, prosper.

go up increase, rise, ascend, climb, mount, expand, swell, inflate, mushroom, escalate. **ant.** decrease, decline, descend, lessen, lower.

gourmet *n.* connoisseur, epicurean, gastronome, gastronomer, bon vivant, gourmand, epicure.

govern *v.* **1** control, reign, hold sway, rule, command, manage, direct. **2** influence, incline, determine, decide, sway, establish, fix, dispose, overrule. **3** curb, discipline, tame, restrain, guide, check, correct, subdue.

government *n.* management, administration, control, dominion, rule, direction, domination, governance, sway, command, order, polity. **ant.** anarchy, chaos, mutiny, lawlessness, nihilism, insurrection.

governor *n.* director, supervisor, manager, overseer, controller, administrator, chief, head, leader, boss.

gown *n.* frock, garment, raiment, robe, dress, apparel, garb, costume, attire.

—*v.* costume, robe, bedeck, dress, array, attire, deck out.

ant. *v.* strip, disrobe, undress, divest.

grab *v.* **1** seize, snatch, capture, pluck, swoop, grasp. **2** confiscate, extort, commandeer, expropriate, plunder, appropriate. **3** *Slang* impress, strike, affect, rouse, involve, interest. —*n.* snatch, swoop, grasp, lunge, pass, seizure, clutch.

ant. *v.* **1** release, let go, loose, set loose, free. **2** surrender, cede, give up, yield, deliver.

grab bag miscellany, jumble, medley, assortment, gallimaufry, congeries, mélange, collection, aggregation, mass, heap.

grabby *adj.* grasping, acquisitive, pushy, greedy, avaricious, avid, aggressive, competitive, selfish, covetous.

ant. altruistic, benevolent, generous, unselfish, open-handed.

grace *n.* attractiveness, charm, elegance, accomplishment, breeding, urbanity, refinement, decorum, savoir faire, manners. —*v.* **1** adorn, enhance, embellish, beautify, decorate, ornament, trim. **2** dignify, honor, distinguish, ennoble, glorify, exalt, luster.

ant. *n.* ugliness, loutishness, crudity, awkwardness, boorishness, coarseness.

graceful *adj.* comely, shapely, attractive, pleasing, accomplished, elegant, charming, refined, beautiful, tasteful, well-bred, mannerly.

ant. awkward, clumsy, ungainly, uncouth, maladroit, rude.

graceless *adj.* **1** unregenerate, immoral, shameless, sinful, cursed, evil, impenitent, incorrigible, depraved, corrupt. **2** clumsy, awkward, gauche, ungainly, inelegant, unpolished, gawky, loutish, uncouth, ill-mannered, rough, boorish, ungraceful.

ant. **1** blessed, shriven, pure, virtuous. **2** graceful, cultivated, refined, elegant, well-bred, comely.

gracious *adj.* **1** kind, courteous, affable, compassionate, lenient, polite, cordial, amiable, benevolent, considerate, sympathetic. **2** gratifying, easeful, pampered, epicurean, easy, pleasurable, comfortable, discriminating, tasteful, spacious.

ant. **1** harsh, rough, ill-mannered, boorish, uncivil. **2** frugal, austere, cramped, parsimonious, straitened, uncomfortable.

gradation *n.* **1** progression, sequence, ordering, graduation, calibration, ranking, organization, grading, series, seriation, array. **2** step, degree, notch, echelon, rank, level, grade, tier, order, position, place.

grade *n.* **1** step, degree, increment, mark, level, rank, stage, gradation. **2** slope, incline, ramp, bank, slant, declivity, gradient, rise. —*v.* **1** rank, range, sort, seriate, classify, evaluate, class, gauge. **2** flatten, roll, level, smooth.

gradient *n.* slope, incline, slant, grade, rise, ramp, cant, tilt, inclination, steepness.

gradual *adj.* measured, stepwise, piecemeal, progressive, incremental, step-by-step, tapering, continual, continuous, moderate, imperceptible.

ant. sudden, precipitate, hasty, abrupt, intermittent, periodical.

graduate *v.* **1** calibrate, mark off, measure, standardize, grade. **2** sort, rank, range, arrange, classify, group, rate, stagger, space out.

graduation *n.* **1** calibration, grading, shading, gradation, ranking. **2** commencement, passing, promotion, certification, advancement, initiation, baptism.

graft[1] *n.* scion, transplant, implantation, slip, implant, insert, inset.

graft[2] *n.* spoils, booty, plunder, bribe, jobbery, loot, blackmail, extortion, pork (*Slang*), swag (*Slang*), payoff (*Slang*), payola (*Slang*).

grain *n.* **1** seed, kernel, cereal, corn, caryopsis. **2** pellet, particle, bit, speck, mite, fragment, morsel, dot, minim. **3** texture, **pattern**, surface, nap.

grainy *adj.* granular, particulate, crumbly, gritty, sandy, mealy, granulated, crystallized, grained, arenaceous.

ant. smooth, unctuous, creamy, satiny.

grand *adj.* **1** imposing, impressive, magnificent, great, mighty, sublime. **2** principal, main, chief, leading, highest, preeminent. **3** haughty, pretentious, ostentatious, pompous, arrogant, showy. **4** formal, dignified, eloquent, lofty, elevated, exalted. **5** first-rate, good, excellent, enjoyable, admirable.

ant. 1 ignoble, insignificant, lowly. **2** secondary, minor, lesser. **3** humble, modest, unassuming. **4** debased, commonplace, clownish. **5** mediocre, rotten, poor.

grandeur *n.* magnificence, sublimity, resplendence, pomp, majesty, exaltation, glory, nobility, splendor, distinction.

ant. squalor, abasement, ignominy, mortification, degradation, infamy.

grandiloquent *adj.* pompous, bombastic, high-flown, magniloquent, pretentious, florid, fustian, grandiose, rhetorical, stilted.

ant. matter-of-fact, prosaic, modest, plain-spoken, simple, down-to-earth.

grandiose *adj.* **1** impressive, imposing, majestic, magnificent, monumental, gigantic, stately, ambitious. **2** pompous, bombastic, pretentious, extravagant, flamboyant, high-flown, highfalutin.

ant. 1 paltry, trivial, picayune, insignificant, slight, piddling. **2** modest, down-to-earth, realistic, humble, lowly.

grandstand *v.* show off, swagger, clown, act up, strut, stunt, swank (*Slang*).

grant *v.* **1** give, award, present, accord, confer, bestow, donate, impart. **2** concede, allow, admit, yield, ac-

knowledge, accede, agree, consent. **3** transfer, dower, bequeath, convey, assign, leave, consign. —*n.* gift, award, allowance, bestowal, bequest, stipend, endowment, subvention.

ant. *v.* **1** refuse, withhold, deny. **2** deny, reject, dispute.

granular *adj.* grainy, particulate, gritty, pebbled, granulated, crumbly, rough, mealy, sandy, gravelly, arenose.

ant. smooth, creamy, silky, homogenized.

granulate *v.* grind, crumble, comminute, crystallize, pulverize, crack, crush, pound, triturate.

granule *n.* particle, speck, seed, pellet, crumb, corpuscle, atom, bit, dot, mote.

graphic *adj.* **1** vivid, effective, striking, clear, lifelike, telling, lucid, expressive, emphatic, picturesque. **2** pictorial, representational, visual, diagrammatic, symbolic, illustrative, tabular, delineated, pictured, explicit, mapped, plotted.

grapple *v.* **1** grasp, seize, grip, catch, make fast, clutch, clasp, fasten. **2** wrestle, attack, contend, cope, deal with, confront, struggle, encounter, contest, battle.

grasp *v.* **1** grip, clasp, hold, keep, clutch, retain. **2** snatch, seize, nab, capture, grab, pounce on. **3** understand, see, perceive, comprehend, encompass, envisage, imagine, sense. —*n.* **1** reach, grip, possession, hold, compass, tenure, holding. **2** understanding, scope, comprehension, ken, perception, insight.

ant. *v.* **1** lose, loose, free, drop, unhand, let go.

grasping *adj.* greedy, avaricious, covetous, miserly, selfish, acquisitive, mercenary, usurious, venal, predatory, rapacious.

ant. generous, open-handed, liberal, unselfish, magnanimous, charitable.

grass roots 1 citizenry, body politic, electorate, taxpayers, community, neighborhood, the country, hoi polloi, boondocks, sticks. **2** source, foundation, origin, root, basis, fountainhead.

grate *v.* **1** mince, shred, abrade, comminute, pulverize. **2** rasp, grit, grind, squeak, scrape. **3** annoy, fret, irk, exasperate, jar, irritate.

ant. 3 please, delight, soothe, stroke, calm, appease.

grateful *adj.* **1** thankful, beholden, indebted, appreciative, under obligation, obliged. **2** pleasing, gratifying, welcome, delightful, soothing, genial, pleasurable, agreeable, satisfying.

ant. 1 thankless, careless, thoughtless, unmindful, heedless, forgetful. **2** impolite, rude, irksome, irritating, upsetting.

gratification *n.* **1** satisfaction, enjoyment, contentment, pleasure, delight, happiness, fulfillment. **2** comfort, reward, recompense, solace, favor, indulgence, payment.

gratify *v.* **1** please, delight, charm, amuse, content, gladden, cheer, stimulate, enchant. **2** cater to, humor, pamper, indulge, give in to, coddle, spoil, favor, comply.

gratifying *adj.* pleasing, pleasant, delightful, acceptable, rewarding, satisfying, agreeable, welcome, soothing, cheering, grateful.

ant. irksome, harsh, vexatious, uncomfortable, unpleasant, disappointing.

grating *adj.* **1** harsh, rasping, strident, discordant, creaky, piercing. **2** annoying, irritating, jarring, offensive, abrasive, disagreeable, exasperating.

ant. 1 sweet, dulcet, pleasant, harmonious, musical. **2** lulling, soothing, pleasant, gratifying.

gratis *adj.* free, complimentary, unrequited, gratuitous.

gratitude *n.* thankfulness, appreciation, gratefulness, thanks, acknowledgment, recognition, obligation, thanksgiving.

gratuitous *adj.* **1** gratis, free, compli-

mentary, voluntary, donated, courtesy, unrequited, unrecompensed. **2** uncalled-for, unnecessary, unwarranted, superfluous, supererogatory, wanton, impertinent.

ant. 2 necessary, warranted, needed, demanded, essential.

gratuity *n.* gift, donation, tip, honorarium, bonus, lagniappe, perquisite, subvention, subsidy, handout, present, pourboire.

grave[1] *adj.* **1** momentous, important, critical, severe, exigent, urgent, crucial, vital, imperative. **2** dignified, sedate, solemn, sober, thoughtful, earnest, staid, sage. **3** somber, muted, subdued, plain, dull, quiet, leaden, heavy.

ant. 1 trivial, inconsequential, trifling, petty. **2** flippant, thoughtless, frivolous, heedless. **3** bright, cheerful, vivid, blithe.

grave[2] *n.* tomb, sepulcher, mausoleum, crypt, vault, catacomb, charnel, charnel house, barrow, tumulus, mound.

graven image IDOL.

graveyard *n.* CEMETERY.

gravitate *v.* be attracted, converge, tend toward, move toward, incline, approach, home in on, zero in on, descend, sink, fall.

ant. retreat, recede, diverge, separate.

gravitation *n.* attraction, pull, force, tendency, convergence, movement, bent, proclivity, inclination.

ant. divergence, repulsion, deviation, disinclination.

gravity *n.* **1** gravitation, attraction, heft, pull, pressure, heaviness, weight, mass. **2** seriousness, significance, magnitude, moment, import, consequence, importance, peril, danger. **3** dignity, reserve, sedateness, composure, calm, sobriety, solemnity, stolidity.

ant. 2 insignificance, triviality, smallness. **3** informality, casualness, spontaneity, frivolity.

gray *adj.* **1** salt-and-pepper, grizzled, hoary, ashen, silvery, dun. **2** aged, old, ancient, venerable, elderly. **3** cheerless, dismal, drab, overcast, dull, dim.
ant. 2 young, youthful, immature, green. **3** bright, sunny, clear, fair, cheery.

graze *v.* **1** skim, brush, touch, glance, swipe, kiss. **2** scrape, scratch, abrade, bruise, wing, scarify, skin.

grease *n.* fat, lubricant, petrolatum, lard, suet, tallow, oleate. —*v. Slang* bribe, suborn, corrupt, buy, fix.

greasy *adj.* **1** oily, waxy, buttery, fatty, smeary, messy, oleaginous. **2** unctuous, smooth, bland, slick, slippery.

great *adj.* **1** large, immense, huge, extensive, big, vast, broad, long, lengthy, prolonged, protracted, abundant, numerous, countless. **2** remarkable, eminent, important, outstanding, excellent, superior. **3** chief, main, principal, leading, major, superior. **4** adept, skilled, proficient, expert, crack, able, apt, good. **5** excellent, first-rate, fine, good, OK, terrific, tremendous, swell (*Slang*). —*adv.* well, successfully, excellently, favorably, happily, satisfactorily.
ant. *adj.* **1** small, tiny, little, narrow, short, few. **2** unimportant, unremarkable, unimpressive, inferior, mediocre. **3** minor, lesser, inferior, secondary. **4** poor, clumsy, maladroit, unskilled. **5** bad, awful, dreadful. *adv.* poorly, indifferently, so-so.

great-hearted *adj.* **1** courageous, lionhearted, intrepid, heroic, dauntless, chivalrous, brave, valorous. **2** magnanimous, noble, high-minded, generous, forgiving, charitable, liberal.
ant. 1 craven, fainthearted, pusillanimous, cowardly. **2** small, niggardly, mean, selfish, base, petty.

greed *n.* avarice, covetousness, craving, avidity, greediness, voraciousness, voracity, rapacity, desire, rapaciousness, insatiability, yearning, selfishness, cupidity.

ant. generosity, liberality, charity, munificence, bounty.

greedy *adj.* **1** covetous, avaricious, acquisitive, grasping, mercenary, avid, miserly. **2** gluttonous, swinish, ravenous, voracious, wolfish, hoggish, piggish, piggy, lickerish.
ant. 1 generous, unselfish, liberal, charitable, munificent. **2** abstemious, frugal, abstinent, temperate, moderate.

green *adj.* **1** youthful, fresh, alive, budding, live, verdant, burgeoning, blooming. **2** callow, unseasoned, unskilled, inexperienced, raw, halfbaked, unsophisticated, naive, unripe, immature. **3** pale, wan, ill, unhealthy, chlorotic. —*n.* lawn, sward, common, grass, herbage, foliage, greenery, verdure, vegetation.
ant. *adj.* **1** faded, jaded, sere, withered, declining, drooping. **2** ripe, ready, fit, mature, experienced, knowing. **3** rosy, flush, in the pink, robust, healthy.

greenhorn *n.* novice, tenderfoot, newcomer, neophyte, tyro, freshman, beginner, apprentice, amateur, ignoramus, know-nothing, babe.
ant. adept, past master, sophisticate, know-it-all, wiseacre.

green light approval, authorization, goahead, clearance, rubber stamp, endorsement, sanction, permission, confirmation, ratification, blessing, imprimatur.
ant. thumbs down, injunction, veto, taboo, blockage, denial.

greet *v.* **1** admit, receive, initiate, introduce, accost, meet. **2** welcome, hail, compliment, salute, bow to, nod, address. **3** *come into view:* meet, affect, strike, impinge upon, reach.

greeting *n.* **1** salutation, ovation, reception, obeisance, bow, salute, address, accosting. **2** welcome, ave, hail, greetings, congratulations, felicitations, compliments.

gregarious *adj.* social, sociable, companionable, convivial, genial, affable, accessible, friendly, outgoing, clubby, approachable, hail-fellow.

ant. solitary, reclusive, retiring, self-sufficient, private, reserved, aloof, standoffish.

grief *n.* **1** sorrow, anguish, distress, remorse, sadness, woe, heartbreak, agony. **2** disaster, affliction, tribulation, trouble, grievance, hardship, bereavement, loss.

ant. 1 joy, elation, contentment, felicity, bliss, happiness.

grief-stricken *adj.* inconsolable, heartsick, desolate, despairing, forlorn, wretched, ravaged, devastated, afflicted, agonized, broken-hearted, heartbroken.

ant. happy, joyous, elated, blissful, content.

grievance *n.* **1** injury, affliction, outrage, hardship, injustice, wrong, iniquity, unfairness, disservice. **2** suffering, annoyance, distress, worry, vexation.

grieve *v.* **1** sadden, dishearten, depress, crush, afflict, discourage, disappoint, burden, wound, hurt. **2** mourn, languish, sorrow, lament, pine, regret, rue, bemoan.

ant. 1 cheer, gladden, heal, soothe, buoy up. **2** rejoice, celebrate, delight, exult, revel.

grievous *adj.* **1** sad, unhappy, sorrowful, distressing, oppressive, heavy, lamentable, burdensome, painful, deplorable, baleful. **2** heinous, calamitous, severe, atrocious, dreadful, intolerable, gross, grave, flagrant, flagitous, baneful.

ant. 1 pleasurable, advantageous, delightful, agreeable, comforting. **2** harmless, trivial, minor, slight.

grill *v.* **1** broil, cook, roast, griddle, fry. **2** cross-examine, interrogate, catechize, question, interview, investigate, quiz, pump.

grim *adj.* **1** stern, forbidding, fierce, ferocious, heartless, savage. **2** unyielding, resolute, unflinching, firm, dogged, inflexible, implacable. **3** repellent, unpleasant, ghastly, sinister, grisly, gruesome.

ant. 1 amiable, inviting, congenial, pleasant, smiling. **2** submissive, soft, weak, malleable. **3** reassuring, attractive, benign.

grimace *n.* face, expression, moue, mow, mop, mug, pout, smirk, sneer, scowl, rictus. —*v.* make a face, mow, mop, mug, pout, smirk, sneer, scowl.

grime *n.* dirt, soot, filth, smudge, soil, smut, smear, dust, foulness.

grimy *adj.* dirty, grubby, soiled, gray, messy, begrimed, unclean, squalid, defiled, foul.

ant. clean, scrubbed, spotless, immaculate, bright.

grin *v.* smile, smirk, simper, beam. —*n.* smile, smirk, simper, beam, rictus.

grind *v.* **1** sharpen, whet, polish, smooth, scour, sand, abrade. **2** crush, pulverize, mill, powder, triturate, pound. **3** gnash, grit, crunch, rasp, rub. **4** oppress, harass, persecute, worry, torment. —*n.* tedium, toil, drudgery, sweat, treadmill, routine, slavery.

grinding *adj.* GRUELING.

grip *n.* **1** hold, seizure, grasp, clasp, clutch. **2** perception, understanding, ken, mastery, comprehension. **3** control, power, domination, influence, tyranny. **4** valise, suitcase, bandbox, traveling bag, gripsack. —*v.* **1** hold, keep, grab, grasp, clasp, clutch. **2** seize, capture, compel, transfix, mesmerize, fascinate.

ant. *v.* **2** release, let go, drop, let drop, let fall.

gripe *v.* **1** cramp, pinch, tweak, twinge, pain, twitch, seize. **2** *Slang* bother, vex, fret, annoy. **3** complain, grumble, whine, grouse, grouch, protest. —*n.* *Slang* complaint, protest, grievance, lament, grouchiness, complaining, faultfinding, grumbling.

gripes *n.* colic, cramps, bellyache, spasm, twinge.

grisly *adj.* terrifying, horrible, frightful,

hideous, sinister, appalling, gruesome, ghastly, forbidding, dreadful, grim.

ant. reassuring, genial, calming, agreeable, pleasant, soothing.

grit *n.* **1** sand, abrasive, dirt, gravel. **2** pluck, courage, stamina, backbone, tenacity, spunk, mettle, fortitude. —*v.* grind, gnash, grate, crunch, scrape, rub, rasp.

ant. *n.* **2** timidity, funk, cold feet, faintheartedness, fearfulness.

gritty *adj.* **1** sandy, granular, grainy, abrasive, grating, raspy, rough. **2** plucky, courageous, spirited, steadfast, persevering, resolute, self-reliant.

ant. 1 smooth, creamy, satiny. **2** cowardly, timid, weak.

grizzled *adj.* gray, salt-and-pepper, grayish, graying, white-tipped, hoary, silvery, gray-haired, leaden-hued.

groan *v.* moan, whimper, lament, murmur, keen, bemoan, complain, wail, bleat, bellow. —*n.* moan, cry, sob, whine, murmur, whimper, lament, wail, bellow, roar, bleat.

groggy *adj.* dazed, confused, unsteady, reeling, staggering, dizzy, swaying, stunned, shaky, punch-drunk, punchy.

groom *n.* bridegroom, husband, benedict, spouse, consort. —*v.* **1** care for, tend, curry, brush, rub down. **2** equip, dress, turn out, get up, spruce, tidy. **3** train, prepare, develop, drill, initiate, indoctrinate.

groove *n.* **1** furrow, channel, wrinkle, trench, hollow, flute, corrugation, chamfer, score. **2** routine, rut, wont, way, usage, custom, practice, procedure. —*v.* **1** furrow, score, hollow, channel, chamfer, rabbet, corrugate. **2** *Slang* dig (*Slang*), like, appreciate, love, enjoy, delight in, be satisfied, revel in, relish.

groovy *adj. Slang* wonderful, great, gorgeous, perfect, marvelous, delightful, satisfying, excellent.

grope *v.* fumble, feel, finger, handle, falter, hesitate, cast about, flounder.

gross *adj.* **1** glaring, flagrant, egregious, unsubtle, deplorable, grievous, heinous, shocking, dreadful. **2** coarse, uncouth, lumbering, hulking, massive, lumpish, bulky. **3** unseemly, indelicate, smutty, improper, vulgar, obscene. **4** unfeeling, obtuse, callous, insensitive, dull, hard.

ant. 1 venial, minor, trivial. **2** dainty, small, refined, graceful, elegant. **3** decent, decorous, clean, fit. **4** thin-skinned, sympathetic, responsive, alert.

grotesque *adj.* bizarre, incongruous, baroque, misshapen, contorted, gothic, eccentric, odd, absurd, outlandish, fanciful, fantastic, freakish, extravagant, strange.

ant. ordinary, normal, usual, familiar, everyday, routine.

grouch *v.* grumble, complain, growl, crab, sulk, mope, snap, grouse, whine, murmur, mutter. —*n.* **1** curmudgeon, malcontent, complainer, crosspatch, bear, grumbler, crab, faultfinder, crank. **2** complaint, grudge, grievance, lament, protest, objection, plaint, threnody, squawk (*Slang*).

grouchy *adj.* sulky, ill-tempered, peevish, cantankerous, surly, petulant, irritable, cross, testy, querulous, discontented, fretful, grumbling.

ant. good-humored, contented, agreeable, cheerful, easygoing, pleasant.

ground *n.* **1** soil, earth, dirt, loam, dust. **2** lot, yard, estate, turf, acres, property. **3** area, field, territory, sphere, region, tract, arena. —*v.* **1** found, establish, install, base, rest, anchor, plant, settle. **2** train, coach, tutor, initiate, indoctrinate, educate, instruct.

groundless *adj.* unwarranted, uncalled-for, unjustified, unfounded, needless, idle, unsubstantial, ungrounded, illusory, unreal.

ant. real, warranted, justified, substantial.

grounds *n.* basis, foundation, excuse, reason, considerations, premises, purpose, cause, arguments, motives, circumstances.

groundwork *n.* **1** foundation, basis, underpinning, footing, support, cornerstone, keystone. **2** preparation, spadework, preliminaries, arrangements, provisions.

group *n.* **1** gathering, cluster, assemblage, aggregation, bunch, crowd, throng, gang, gaggle, knot. **2** category, set, stratum, class, division, level, section, branch. —*v.* classify, sort, rank, marshal, cluster, arrange, bracket, grade, segregate, align. **2** mingle, congregate, associate, gather, collect, consort, hobnob, fraternize.

grouse *v.* grumble, complain, gripe, repine, fret, deplore, murmur, mutter, scold, growl. —*n.* complaint, gripe, plaint, lament, grievance, discontent, squawk (*Slang*).

grove *n.* wood, copse, coppice, thicket, spinney (*Brit.*), shrubbery, bosk, woodlot, plantation, covert, orchard.

grovel *v.* **1** crawl, creep, scrabble, cringe, slouch, stoop, cower, scramble. **2** toady, demean oneself, truckle, sponge, fawn, kowtow, crawl, blandish, wheedle.

grow *v.* **1** increase, expand, swell, enlarge, extend, lengthen. **2** sprout, shoot up, vegetate, germinate, spring up, burgeon, put forth. **3** flourish, thrive, prosper, improve, advance, progress, boom. **4** develop, become, turn into, wax, turn, get to be. **5** cultivate, produce, raise, propagate, breed.

ant. **1** decrease, shrink, reduce, lessen, shorten. **3** fail, fall short, fall through, worsen, collapse.

growl *n.* snarl, gnarl, grumble, rumble, roar, murmur, clamor, bellow —*v.* snarl, rumble, gnar, gnarl, grumble, snap, murmur, roar, bellow.

grown *adj.* MATURE.

grown-up *adj.* adult, full-grown, mature, senior, of age, big, ripe.

ant. childish, little, junior, budding, callow, juvenile.

growth *n.* **1** development, unfolding, burgeoning, evolution, expansion, growing, addition. **2** increase, advance, ascent, surge, rise, gain, bulge. **3** produce, harvest, height, flower, product, prime.

ant. **1** deterioration, degeneration, regression, retrogression, decay. **2** decrease, diminution, descent, lessening, contraction.

grub *v.* **1** dig, uproot, eradicate, weed out, pull up, extract, clear, deracinate. **2** drudge, toil, slave, moil, plod, grind, sweat. **3** rummage, ferret out, unearth, uncover, search, research. **4** *Slang* beg for, cadge, sponge, panhandle, petition, solicit, importune, mooch (*Slang*), scrounge (*Slang*). —*n.* **1** larva, worm, maggot, caterpillar. **2** drudge, fag, grind, hack, slave. **3** *Slang* food, victuals, bread, meat, fare, rations, eats.

grubby *adj.* dirty, messy, slovenly, frowzy, blowzy, unkempt, grimy, sloppy, seedy, untidy, negligent.

ant. neat, well-groomed, spruce, spick-and-span, clean, tidy.

grudge *v.* begrudge, resent, withhold, dole out, hold back, stint, pinch. —*n.* resentment, ill will, rancor, malice, malevolence, pique, spite, malignity, malignancy.

ant. *n.* benevolence, good will, generosity, friendliness, charity, liberality.

grueling *adj.* exhausting, taxing, arduous, punishing, crushing, excruciating, trying, backbreaking, grinding, severe.

ant. easy, effortless, simple, light, manageable.

gruesome *adj.* grisly, frightful, loathsome, hideous, awful, horrible, ghastly, repulsive, shocking, revolting, grim.

ant. delightful, soothing, charming, lovely, captivating, agreeable.

gruff *adj.* **1** abrupt, brusque, churlish, rude, rough, surly, crabbed, ill-humored, bluff. **2** hoarse, raucous, harsh, cracked, strident, guttural, croaking.

ant. **1** easy, pleasant, genial, friendly, civil. **2** clear, resonant, ringing, pleasant, dulcet.

grumble *v.* **1** complain, repine, gripe, whine, murmur, deplore, grouch, grouse. **2** mutter, growl, thunder, rumble, roll, roar. —*n.* **1** complaint, gripe, lament, grievance, fault-finding, discontent, repining. **2** rumble, thunder, growl, muttering, drumming, roll.

grumpy *adj.* grouchy, ill-tempered, fractious, cranky, surly, crabbed, crusty, pettish, cross-grained, peevish, disgruntled, cantankerous, irritable, out of sorts, moody.

ant. cheery, amiable, buoyant, sunny, winsome, pleasant.

guarantee *n.* **1** warranty, covenant, insurance, assurance, undertaking, endorsement. **2** bond, token, pledge, gage, earnest, security, hostage, collateral. —*v.* **1** certify, vouch for, undertake, contract, warrant, endorse, pledge, mortgage. **2** affirm, avow, promise, engage, assert, assure, maintain, swear, vow.

guarantor *n.* sponsor, voucher, underwriter, warrantor, bondsman, bailsman, signatory, seconder, surety.

guaranty *n.* **1** pledge, warranty, promise, covenant, surety, engagement, contract, insurance. **2** token, bond, pledge, gage, earnest, deposit, pawn, stake, collateral, security. —*v.* guarantee, certify, underwrite, insure, undertake, vouch for, warrant, promise.

guard *v.* watch over, watch, protect, safeguard, oversee, attend, shield, secure, preserve, defend, patrol, shelter. —*n.* **1** sentry, watchman, guardian, patrol, sentinel, watchdog, warder. **2** care, attention, vigilance, wariness, caution, supervision. **3** bul-

wark, protection, defense, safeguard, shield, screen, panoply.

guarded *adj.* cautious, restrained, reticent, circumspect, wary, careful, prudent, chary, hedged, unrevealing, ambiguous, attentive.

ant. careless, audacious, daring, outspoken, frank, reckless.

guardian *n.* custodian, protector, warden, patron, keeper, trustee, curator, caretaker, watchdog, defender, champion.

guess *v.* **1** estimate, conjecture, infer, surmise, theorize, hypothesize. **2** think, deem, believe, suppose, imagine, dare say. —*n.* estimate, conjecture, notion, assumption, suspicion, supposition, hypothesis, shot, presumption, theory, guesstimate (*Slang*).

guesstimate *n. Slang* GUESS.

guest *n.* **1** visitor, caller, company. **2** transient, habitue, resident, customer, client, patient.

guff *n. Slang* nonsense, bosh, poppycock, drivel, rubbish, bilge (*Slang*), humbug, gaff, impudence, boldness, sass, cheek, sauce, lip (*Slang*).

guffaw *n.* belly laugh, horselaugh, bray, roar, scream, howl, boff, boffo, boffola, shriek, yelp, yak (*Slang*). —*v.* heehaw, roar, howl, scream, bray, shriek, yelp, cachinnate.

guidance *n.* **1** leadership, direction, management, government, supervision, piloting, navigation, conduct, control, escort. **2** advice, counseling, counsel, caution, warning, recommendation, endorsement, urging, suggestion, lead.

guide *v.* **1** lead, direct, escort, conduct, accompany, attend, convoy. **2** steer, regulate, control, pilot, maneuver, train, handle, signal, wave. **3** manage, oversee, discipline, govern, manipulate, superintend, educate, sway. —*n.* **1** pilot, conductor, director, cicerone, leader, bellwether, model, counselor, mentor, teacher. **2** directory, manual, clue, key, sign, beacon, polestar, signal, signpost.

guideline *n.* specification, description, directive, stipulation, indication, outline, benchmark, parameter, criterion, restriction, rule, policy, lead.

guild *n.* society, association, alliance, league, company, fraternity, brotherhood, union, corporation, trade union, labor union, order.

guile *n.* cunning, trickery, craft, artfulness, chicanery, slyness, duplicity, deceit, fraudulence, artifice, fraud, treachery, deception, subtility, sophistry.
ant. ingenuousness, frankness, innocence, candor, sincerity, naivete.

guileful *adj.* sly, cunning, deceitful, wily, foxy, double-dealing, artful, crafty, treacherous, shifty, designing, tricky, fraudulent, devious, false.
ant. ingenuous, frank, innocent, candid, sincere, naive.

guileless *adj.* artless, ingenuous, simple, innocent, candid, natural, naive, open, honest, sincere, truthful, unsophisticated, aboveboard, pure, straightforward.
ant. guileful, sly, cunning, deceitful, crafty.

guilt *n.* **1** blameworthiness, culpability, reprehensibility, criminality, guiltiness, censurability. **2** shame, blame, wrong, evil, offensiveness, wickedness.
ant. **1** innocence, purity, honesty, faultlessness, sinlessness.

guiltless *adj.* innocent, irreproachable, sinless, blameless, pure, spotless, honest, unsullied, untarnished, immaculate, innocuous, sinless.
ant. guilty, culpable, blameworthy, erring, wrong, wicked, at fault, to blame.

guilty *adj.* **1** culpable, blameworthy, responsible, erring, convicted, redhanded, condemned, blamable. **2** ashamed, penitent, sheepish, repentant, remorseful, shamefaced, contrite, rueful.

ant. **1** innocent, pure, honest, faultless, sinless.

guise *n.* **1** appearance, aspect, shape, mode, mien, garb, habit, costume, fashion, form, manner. **2** pretense, disguise, show, masquerade, facade, semblance, seeming, mask.

gulf *n.* **1** abyss, chasm, pit, canyon, rift, cleft. **2** gap, barrier, space, distance, disparity, divergence.

gull *v.* trick, deceive, cheat, hoax, dupe, cozen, hoodwink, defraud, mislead, impose on. —*n.* dupe, cat's-paw, sucker, butt, mark, stooge, victim, fall guy (*Slang*).

gullet *n.* throat, maw, esophagus, gorge, craw, neck, fauces.

gullible *adj.* credulous, unsuspecting, trustful, naive, simple, innocent, confiding, trusting, green, believing, unskeptical, unsuspicious.
ant. suspicious, wary, skeptical, doubting, shrewd, sophisticated.

gully *n.* channel, watercourse, course, ravine, gutter, notch, washout, wadi, ditch, gorge, gulch, valley.

gulp *v.* **1** bolt, gobble, wolf, lap up, guzzle, consume, swallow, dispatch. **2** gasp, pant, sigh, swallow. —*n.* swallow, swig, draft, sip, bolt, mouthful, swallowing.

gum *n.* glue, resin, paste, adhesive, mucilage, exudate, ooze, gunk, goo, gook.

gummy *adj.* sticky, tacky, viscid, gluey, adhesive, viscous, thick, gooey, tenacious.
ant. watery, runny, thin, dry, powdery.

gumption *n.* initiative, enterprise, spirit, resourcefulness, shrewdness, sagacity, acumen, judgment, discernment, cleverness, ingenuity.
ant. ineptitude, dullness, vacuity, sloth, lassitude, indifference.

gumshoe *n. Slang* DETECTIVE.

gum up *Slang* bungle, ruin, botch, mismanage, obstruct, disable, inactivate, muff, spoil, mar, clog, stop up, jam, queer (*Slang*).

gung-ho *adj. Slang* enthusiastic, eager,

zealous, ardent, perfervid, vehement, impassioned, fanatical, extreme, spirited, earnest, strenuous.

ant. listless, indifferent, apathetic, lukewarm, languid.

gunman *n*. desperado, assassin, trigger-man, killer, mobster, gangster.

gurgle *v*. purl, babble, burble, sputter, bubble, ripple, guggle, murmur, boil, trill. —*n*. gargle, burble, babble, murmur, guggle, purl, trill, sputter.

guru *n*. teacher, mentor, pundit, preceptor, expert, guide, leader, authority, master.

gush *v*. **1** spout, spurt, squirt, pour forth, stream, jet, eject, burst, flow out. **2** sentimentalize, slobber, maunder, blather, emotionalize, emote, overstate. —*n*. **1** spurt, freshet, spout, jet, torrent, discharge, outflow, efflux, effusion, burst. **2** effusiveness, pathos, sentimentality, mawkishness, emotionalism, maudlinism.

ant. *n*. **2** reserve, cool, reticence, aloofness, restraint.

gushy *adj*. effusive, sentimental, mawkish, bathetic, maudlin, slushy, demonstrative, emotional.

ant. reserved, cool, reticent, aloof, restrained, quiet.

gust *n*. **1** squall, flurry, draft, puff, blast, rush, burst. **2** fit, paroxysm, frenzy, outburst, surge, access, fever.

gusto *n*. enjoyment, enthusiasm, zest, relish, appetite, appreciation, taste, palate, pleasure, vigor, fervor, exhilaration, delight.

ant. distaste, nausea, revulsion, loathing, reluctance.

gusty *adj*. variable, fitful, shifting, wayward, unsteady, squally, breezy, blustery, blowy, drafty, puffy, windy.

gut *v*. **1** eviscerate, disembowel. **2** raze, lay waste, destroy, despoil, ravage, pillage, ransack, rifle, strip, loot. —*adj*. *Slang* **1** basic, fundamental, central, vital, material, essential, preeminent, paramount, important, prime. **2** visceral, deep, deepest, deep-seated, heartfelt, ingrained, innate, instinctive, intuitive, spontaneous.

gutless *adj*. *Slang* cowardly, shiftless, submissive, weak, irresolute, abject, timid, faint-hearted, fearful, languid, chicken (*Slang*).

ant. aggressive, courageous, plucky, daring, dauntless, gutsy (*Slang*).

guts *n*. *Slang* stamina, backbone, mettle, courage, pluck, grit, fortitude, endurance, nerve, daring, intrepidity.

gutsy *adj*. *Slang* courageous, dauntless, audacious, spunky, venturesome, self-reliant, spirited, plucky, mettlesome, hardy, game, nervy, gutty (*Slang*), gritty.

ant. cowardly, timid, craven, spineless, cowed, faint-hearted.

gutter *n*. channel, trough, trench, drain, ditch, duct, conduit, groove, sluice, race.

guttersnipe *n*. riffraff, pariah, vagrant, panhandler, derelict, bum, outcast, gamin, urchin, rascal.

guttural *adj*. hoarse, harsh, rasping, gruff, cracked, croaking, rough, deep, throaty, thick, gargling.

ant. clear, high, dulcet, ringing, musical, pleasant.

gutty *adj*. *Slang* GUTSY.

guy *n*. fellow, man, person, individual, brother, gentleman, character, chap, lad, boy, cat (*Slang*), bozo (*Slang*) gink (*Slang*), bloke (*Brit. Slang*).

guzzle *v*. tipple, swill, imbibe, swizzle, tope, lap up, gulp, quaff, fuddle, nip.

gymnast *n*. athlete, acrobat.

gymnastic *adj*. athletic, calisthenic, acrobatic, agonistic.

gymnastics *n*. athletics, acrobatics, calisthenics, exercise, workout, conditioning.

gyp *v*. cheat, swindle, cozen, diddle, bamboozle, victimize, take advantage of, gull, hoodwink. —*n*. **1** swindle, imposture, plant, trick, shell game, hoax, fraud, confidence game, con game (*Slang*). **2** swindler, cheat, cozener, sharper, diddler, trickster, charlatan, crook, confidence man, con man (*Slang*).

gypsy *n.* nomad, wanderer, vagabond, rambler, vagrant, stray, migrant, gadabout, beachcomber, hobo, tinker (*Brit.*).

gyrate *v.* rotate, revolve, twirl, spin,

gyre, wheel, coil, whirl, circle, circulate, swirl. —*adj.* convoluted, curled, helical, corkscrew, spiral, twisted, winding, sinuous.

gyration *n.* spinning, whirling, turning, pirouette, convolution, rotation, spin, whirl, eddy, turn, roll.

H

habiliments *n.* CLOTHING.

habit *n.* routine, custom, practice, wont, usage, rule, habitude, fashion, manner, style, observance, way.

habitant *n.* INHABITANT.

habitation *n.* domicile, residence, home, dwelling, abode, lodgings, quarters, shelter, roof, hearth, accommodations, digs, pad (*Slang*).

habitual *adj.* customary, usual, inveterate, wonted, chronic, constant, regular, routine, persistent, established, fixed.

ant. occasional, rare, irregular, sporadic.

habituated *adj.* accustomed, acclimated, familiarized, used, adapted, conditioned, comfortable, at home, seasoned, hardened, disciplined, trained, inured, settled, addicted, adjusted.

habitude *n.* HABIT.

hack *v.* chop, cleave, hew, chip, slash, cut up, pick, mangle, mutilate, slice, sever.

hack it *Slang* COPE.

hackneyed *adj.* commonplace, trite, banal, stale, timeworn, shopworn, stock, stereotyped, warmed-over, run-of-the-mill, pedestrian, cliché, clichéd, platitudinous, motheaten, threadbare, bromidic.

ant. creative, original, fresh, inventive, novel.

haft *n.* HANDLE.

hag *n.* crone, beldam, granny, harridan, shrew, virago, vixen, ogress,

harpy, witch, termagant, gorgon, battle-ax.

haggard *adj.* weary, worn, exhausted, careworn, spent, tired out, rundown, debilitated, seedy, emaciated, wan, wasted, gaunt.

haggle *v.* ARGUE.

hail *v.* greet, salute, welcome, applaud, acclaim, cheer, honor, call, signal, summon, address, accost.

ant. shun, ignore, avoid, neglect, disregard, pass over.

hair-do *n.* haircut, hairstyle, hairset, coiffure, coif, headdress.

hairdresser *n.* hair stylist, beautician, *coiffeur,* haircutter, barber.

hairless *adj.* bald, baldheaded, baldpated, shorn, smooth, clean-shaven, beardless, depilitated, glabrous.

ant. hairy, shaggy, hirsute, bearded, unshaven.

hair-raising *adj.* frightful, bloodcurdling, spine-tingling, horrifying, terrifying, scary, petrifying, shocking, creepy, exciting, thrilling, breathtaking, alarming, startling.

hair-splitting *adj.* FINICKY.

hairy *adj.* 1 hirsute, shaggy, pilose, bushy, unshaven, bearded, bewhiskered. 2 *Slang* DIFFICULT.

ant. hairless, bald, shorn, smooth, clean-shaven.

halcyon *adj.* PEACEFUL.

hale[1] *adj.* healthy, sound, robust, fit, strong, wholesome, well, bouncy, hearty, vigorous, active, peppy, chipper, spry.

ant. sickly, weak, ailing, feeble, infirm.

hale² *v.* HAUL.

half-baked *adj.* premature, sophomoric, crude, slipshod, makeshift, naive, immature, shallow, superficial, ill-conceived, illogical, ignorant, untried.

half-hearted *adj.* apathetic, indifferent, lukewarm, passive, perfunctory, cool, lackadaisical, blasé, inert, lethargic, ambivalent.
ant. enthusiastic, eager, ambitious, determined, resolute.

half-truth *n.* FIB.

half-wit *n.* dolt, fool, nitwit, jackass, dunce, blockhead, dunderhead, moron, idiot, simpleton, dullard, imbecile, dimwit, numskull, nincompoop, ninny, donkey.

half-witted *adj.* SIMPLE-MINDED.

hall *n.* corridor, hallway, passageway, vestibule, foyer, entrance, antechamber, lobby, arcade, gallery.

hallmark *n.* SIGN.

hallow *v.* CONSECRATE.

hallowed *adj.* sacred, holy, sanctified, blessed, consecrated, sacrosanct, dedicated, beatified, venerable, saintly, divine, religious.

hallucination *n.* illusion, fantasy, image, vision, voices, apparition, mirage, appearance, figment, phantasmagoria, dream, delusion, daydream.

halt *n.* stop, cessation, standstill, pause, break, interruption, stoppage, arrest, breakdown, lapse, delay, recess, intermission, deadlock, suspension, impasse. —*v.* stop, cease, end, discontinue, quit, stall, hold, rest, check, interrupt, restrain, block, impede, obstruct, suspend, postpone.

halting *adj.* awkward, imperfect, limping, hobbling, stuttering, stammering, hesitant, faltering, stumbling, vacillating, perplexed, doubtful, wavering.
ant. confident, decisive, self-assured, fluent, graceful, smooth, facile.

hamlet *n.* VILLAGE.

hammer *v.* bang, beat, pound, whack, strike, tap, thump, knock, cudgel, ram, drive, drum, batter.

hamper *v.* impede, prevent, restrain, thwart, balk, inhibit, interfere, hinder, frustrate, hamstring, handicap, obstruct, curb, prevent, retard, cramp, undermine.
ant. assist, help, promote, encourage, support, facilitate, expedite.

hamstring *v.* CRIPPLE.

hamstrung *adj.* helpless, disabled, crippled, incapacitated, paralyzed, *hors de combat*, disarmed, hogtied, at a loss.

hand *n.* **1** role, part, responsibility, share, complicity. **2** worker, assistant, aide, employee, handyman, hired man, laborer, associate.

handicap *n.* disadvantage, drawback, disability, impediment, shortcoming, defect, encumbrance, penalty, burden, obstacle, stumblingblock. —*v.* impede, hinder, restrain, curb, check, bar, disable, inhibit, shackle, circumscribe, limit, frustrate, hamper, encumber.

handiwork *n.* CRAFT.

handkerchief *n.* kerchief, bandanna, babushka, scarf, neckerchief.

handle *v.* **1** touch, manipulate, hold, grasp, feel, finger, grip, clutch, fondle, wield. **2** control, direct, take care of, oversee, treat, deal with, steer, manage, run, supervise, administer, regulate. —*n.* grip, haft, halve, hilt, handgrip.

hand out distribute, disburse, mete, deal, dispense, apportion, parcel, circulate, disseminate.

hand over surrender, release, yield, turn over, deliver, give, present, donate, fork over (*Slang*).

handsome *adj.* **1** attractive, good-looking, comely, beautiful, becoming, graceful, elegant, stately, majestic, resplendent, gorgeous, pleasing, fair, well-proportioned, personable. **2** generous, liberal, abundant, magnanimous, ample, large, plentiful, gracious, bountiful, tidy, noble.

ant. 1 homely, ugly, repulsive, ungainly, plain, unsightly. **2** skimpy, meager, small, insignificant, paltry, scanty, inadequate.

handy *adj.* **1** convenient, accessible, useful, helpful, nearby, available, close, on hand. **2** skilled, adroit, adept, dexterous, proficient, apt, versatile, deft, inventive, ingenious.
ant. 1 inconvenient, useless, worthless, inaccessible. **2** inept, clumsy, awkward, ineffectual, bungling.

hang *v.* **1** dangle, suspend, hover, sag, droop, loll, lop, depend, project, drape, swing, fall, sling. **2** execute, lynch, string up, gibbet.

hang around loiter, dally, tarry, linger, frequent, haunt, hover, stay, cling to, tag along.

hangdog *adj.* ABJECT.

hanger-on *n.* PARASITE.

hang in *Slang* persevere, continue, persist, hold fast, endure, resist, stand pat, remain.
ant. yield, give in, give up, surrender, quit, concede, abandon.

hangout *n. Slang* RESORT.

hang-up *n. Slang* difficulty, inhibition, block, snag, obstacle, complication, hindrance.

hanker *v.* yearn, wish, desire, long, crave, covet, hunger, thirst, pine, itch, ache, lust.

hanky-panky *n. Slang* mischief, trickery, deception, shenanigans, deviltry, hoax, knavery, chicanery.

haphazard *adj.* random, aimless, accidental, arbitrary, purposeless, fortuitous, casual, incidental, chancy, indiscriminate, hit-or-miss.
ant. planned, controlled, deliberate, intentional, determined, designed.

hapless *adj.* unfortunate, ill-fated, ill-starred, luckless, jinxed, miserable, cursed, wretched.
ant. lucky, happy, charmed, blessed, fortunate.

happen *v.* occur, arise, befall, betide, take place, come to pass, ensue, turn up, crop up, eventuate, transpire, appear, come true, materialize.

happening *n.* event, occurrence, incident, episode, transaction, scene, proceeding, affair, occasion, circumstance, experience, adventure, phenomenon.

happy *adj.* **1** glad, pleased, joyous, delighted, elated, ecstatic, jubilant, exhilarated, exultant, joyful, merry, mirthful, cheerful, blissful, content, satisfied. **2** opportune, felicitous, auspicious, favorable, lucky, fortunate, propitious.
ant. 1 sad, miserable, depressed, gloomy, glum, wretched, downcast, dejected. **2** unfortunate, unlucky, inauspicious.

happy-go-lucky *adj.* carefree, irresponsible, easy-going, casual, improvident, shiftless, insouciant, devil-may-care, nonchalant, careless.
ant. responsible, prudent, concerned, sober.

harangue *n.* tirade, diatribe, oration, declamation, exhortation, lecture, sermon, screed. —*v.* declaim, spout, rant, exhort, preach, sermonize, orate, perorate.

harass *v.* annoy, bother, plague, disturb, vex, worry, harry, torment, bedevil, pester, badger, browbeat, bully, beleaguer, intimidate, threaten, persecute.

harassment *n.* ANNOYANCE.

harbinger *n.* forerunner, precursor, herald, omen, sign, messenger. —*v.* herald, presage, proclaim, announce, portend.

harbor *v.* **1** shelter, protect, hide, keep, shield, house, lodge. **2** entertain, cherish, foster, nurture, indulge, treasure, embrace, have, nurse, contemplate, consider, imagine.

hard *adj.* **1** solid, rigid, firm, impenetrable, stiff, compact, strong, set, petrified, ossified, sclerous. **2** difficult, arduous, formidable, complex, complicated, intricate, thorny, laborious, rigorous, tough, uphill, puzzling, Herculean. **3** harsh, severe, stern, ruthless, onerous, oppressive, unsparing, relentless, implacable, inexorable, immovable. **4** *of truth or facts:* bare, cold, plain, concrete, specific, verified, definite, actual, salient, unvarnished, undeniable, explicit, straightforward.

ant. 1 soft, pliable, plastic, flexible, fragile, malleable, elastic, resilient. **2** easy, simple, effortless, facile. **3** relaxed, benign, lenient, indulgent, comfortable, lax. **4** vague, intangible, impalpable, obscure, elusive, fuzzy.

hard-and-fast *adj.* BINDING.

hard-bitten *adj.* TOUGH.

hard-boiled *adj.* TOUGH.

hard-core *adj* **1** diehard, rigid, obstinate, extreme, steadfast, staunch, dedicated, radical, fundamental. **2** explicit, express, straightforward, frank.

harden *v.* **1** solidify, fortify, reinforce, brace, thicken, strengthen, stiffen, petrify, ossify, indurate, temper. **2** inure, toughen, discipline, season, desensitize, steel, embitter, brutalize. **ant. 1** soften, weaken, melt. **2** pamper, spoil, mollycoddle.

hard-fisted *adj.* MISERLY.

hard-headed *adj.* shrewd, practical, pragmatic, tough, tough-minded, sensible, realistic, hard-boiled, cool-headed, matter-of-fact, level-headed, no-nonsense, down-to-earth, hard-nosed (*Slang*). **ant.** impractical, idealistic, visionary, fanciful.

hard-hearted *adj.* callous, heartless, cruel, mean, pitiless, indifferent, stony, inhuman, merciless, ruthless, coldblooded. **ant.** compassionate, sympathetic, kind, sensitive, soft-hearted, merciful, tender, charitable.

hard-hitting *adj.* AGGRESSIVE.

hardihood *n.* COURAGE.

hardly *adv.* scarcely, barely, not quite, only just, no more than.

hardness *n.* **1** firmness, solidity, inflexibility, rigidity, density, compactness, impenetrability, stiffness. **2** severity, harshness, rigor, cal-

lousness, strictness, stringency, cruelty, coldness, insensitivity. **ant. 1** softness, pliancy, looseness, laxness, flaccidity. **2** gentleness, mildness, comfort, mercy, indulgence, tenderness, compassion, leniency, flexibility.

hard-nosed *adj. Slang* rigid, unyielding, fixed, stubborn, tough, obstinate, dogged, intractable, hard-bitten. **ant.** flexible, open-minded, receptive, accommodating, obliging.

hardship *n.* adversity, misfortune, privation, burden, difficulty, trouble, affliction, tribulation, trial.

hard up broke, bankrupt, penniless, straitened, impoverished, down-and-out, hard-pressed. **ant.** solvent, flush, affluent, prosperous.

hard-working *adj.* industrious, diligent, assiduous, busy, sedulous, laborious, indefatigable. **ant.** lazy, indolent, slothful, idle, easygoing.

hardy *adj.* **1** audacious, bold, rash, foolhardy, intrepid, cheeky, presumptuous, impudent, brazen, reckless. **2** durable, rugged, sturdy, tough, robust, strong, stalwart. **ant. 1** timid, fearful, shy, meek, cautious, prudent. **2** fragile, weak, frail, delicate.

harebrained *adj.* FOOLISH.

hark *v.* LISTEN.

harken *v.* LISTEN.

harlequin *n.* BUFFOON.

harlot *n.* whore, prostitute, trollop, tart, strumpet, tramp, slut, doxy, bawd, jade, wanton.

harm *n.* injury, damage, abuse, hurt, impairment, mischief, detriment, disservice. —*v.* injure, damage, hurt, impair, wrong, sabotage, ruin, mar, spoil, wound. **ant.** *n.* benefit, welfare, good, betterment, advantage, improvement. *v.* help, benefit, favor, repair, heal, cure.

harmful *adj.* injurious, detrimental, dangerous, hurtful, baneful, ruinous, deleterious, damaging, pernicious, prejudicial, disadvantageous, counterproductive.

ant. beneficial, advantageous, helpful, favorable.

harmless *adj.* innocuous, safe, benign, innocent, well-meaning, inoffensive, bland, scatheless.

ant. harmful, dangerous, injurious, malevolent.

harmonious *adj.* cordial, congenial, amicable, compatible, concordant, *en rapport*, conforming, consistent, coherent.

ant. discordant, conflicting, clashing, dissident, incongruous.

harmonize *v.* conform, blend, adapt, reconcile, conciliate, agree, attune, correspond, accommodate.

ant. clash, contradict, disagree, differ.

harmony *n.* accord, agreement, conformity, concordance, concurrence, consonance, consistency, sympathy, unanimity, congruity, rapprochement.

ant. conflict, discord, dissension, dissonance.

harness *v.* exploit, employ, control, utilize, mobilize, apply, operate, manage, channel.

harridan *n.* HAG.

harried *adj.* harassed, worried, anxious, upset, put-upon, agitated, beset, bothered, plagued, distressed, tormented, nervous, distraught.

harrow *v.* DISTRESS.

harrowing *adj.* traumatic, wrenching, searing, distressing, upsetting, tormenting, painful.

harsh *adj.* **1** grating, rasping, jarring, hoarse, discordant, grinding, squawky, strident, gruff, raucous, guttural. **2** severe, uncompromising, tough, strict, stringent, stern, rigorous, relentless, hard, brutal, punitive, Draconian.

ant. **1** smooth, pleasant, melodious, soothing. **2** lenient, indulgent, merciful, gentle, forgiving, permissive.

harshly *adv.* strictly, severely, strin-

gently, roughly, unsparingly, sternly, cruelly, relentlessly.

ant. mildly, gently, kindly, leniently, mercifully.

harum-scarum *adj.* RECKLESS.

harvest *n.* result, reward, fruit, consequence, product, aftermath, yield, profit, dividend, proceeds.

hash *n.* jumble, mess, confusion, chaos, mishmash, muddle, hodgepodge, mixture, conglomeration, potpourri.

hassle *Slang n.* quarrel, fight, squabble, run-in, set-to, scrap, row, argument, dispute, disagreement. —*v.* harass, harry, annoy, vex, argue, pick on, bother, irritate, bug (*Slang*).

haste *n.* speed, dispatch, rapidity, quickness, swiftness, celerity, posthaste, velocity.

ant. delay, slowness, sluggishness, slackness.

hasten *v.* hurry, speed, rush, scurry, quicken, hie, race, expedite, accelerate, step on it.

ant. delay, retard, slow, drag one's feet, slacken, brake.

hasty *adj.* speedy, swift, rapid, precipitate, rash, reckless, impetuous, sudden, impulsive, thoughtless.

ant. slow, deliberate, leisurely.

hatch *v.* concoct, devise, contrive, plot, scheme, draw up, design, draft, sketch.

hatchet job *Slang* CRITICISM.

hate *v.* detest, abhor, loathe, abominate, despise, execrate. —*n.* HATRED.

ant. *v.* like, admire, love, adore.

hateful *adj.* odious, loathsome, abominable, repugnant, obnoxious, detestable, heinous, abhorrent, execrable, revolting, disgusting.

ant. agreeable, likable, pleasant, attractive, decent.

hatred *n.* animosity, hate, revulsion, detestation, hostility, antagonism, enmity, rancor, animus, malice, venom, spite, asperity, aversion, abhorrence, antipathy, malevolence.

ant. friendliness, amiability, good will, love, affection, fondness.

haughtiness *n.* arrogance, conde-

scension, pride, conceit, vanity, hauteur, airs, disdain, insolence, imperiousness, superciliousness.
ant. humility, modesty, diffidence, deference, servility.

haughty *adj.* arrogant, patronizing, supercilious, conceited, vain, stuck-up, disdainful, uppish, pompous, imperious, condescending, snobbish, highfalutin, high and mighty, toplofty, upstage.
ant. humble, self-effacing, modest, unassuming, meek, servile.

haul *v.* drag, pull, tug, draw, hale, lug, tow, cart, carry, truck, transport.

haunt *v.* frequent, hang around, occupy, obsess, vex, preoccupy, prey, torment, plague, recur. —*n.* hideaway, stamping ground, hangout (*Slang*), turf (*Slang*).

haunted *adj.* obsessed, worried, preoccupied, plagued, tormented, uneasy, troubled.

haunting *adj.* unforgettable, indelible, persistent, disturbing, upsetting, distressing, disquieting.

have *v.* **1** possess, own, hold, acquire, get, include, contain, comprise, display, manifest. **2** undergo, suffer, experience, feel, enjoy, endure, sustain.

haven *n.* asylum, refuge, shelter, retreat, sanctuary, harbor, sanctum, cover, hideaway, haunt.

havoc *n.* destruction, ruin, devastation, upheaval, catastrophe, disaster, disruption, disorder, confusion, uproar, chaos, mayhem.

hawker *n.* peddler, huckster, vendor, crier.

hayseed *n. Slang* yokel, hick, rustic, bumpkin, rube (*Slang*), clodhopper, peasant, lout, provincial.
ant. dude, city slicker, sophisticate.

haywire *adj. Slang* confused, crazy, mixed up, wild, berserk, chaotic, tangled, out of order, out of commission, inoperative.

hazard *n.* danger, peril, jeopardy, menace, threat, risk, contingency, uncertainty, chance, accident. —*v.* risk, venture, attempt, gamble, dare,

chance, speculate, stake, wager, essay.

hazardous *adj.* dangerous, risky, perilous, chancy, precarious, insecure, threatening, uncertain, iffy.
ant. safe, reliable, secure, protected, safeguarded.

hazy *adj.* **1** cloudy, misty, smoky, foggy, murky, filmy, dim, translucent, shadowy, gauzy, blurred, turbid, crepuscular. **2** confused, vague, nebulous, obscure, muddled, obfuscated, uncertain, opaque, ambiguous.
ant. 1 clear, cloudless, transparent, distinct. **2** clear, plain, lucid, precise, exact, explicit, obvious.

head *n.* **1** top, crown, summit, acme, forefront, vanguard, beginning, origin, source. **2** leader, chief, ruler, commander, superior, boss, director, captain, chairman, ringleader. **3** *Slang* ADDICT. —*v.* lead, preside, command, direct, oversee, chair, control, rule, govern, supervise, run.

headache *n.* TROUBLE.

heading *n.* title, caption, name, rubric, topic, subject.

headlong *adv.* impetuously, precipitately, rashly, recklessly, hastily, impulsively, pell-mell, helter-skelter.
ant. cautiously, carefully, prudently, hesitantly.

head off FORESTALL.

head start ADVANTAGE.

headstrong *adj.* stubborn, obstinate, willful, intractable, obdurate, dogged, pigheaded, balky, perverse, refractory.
ant. obedient, docile, meek, obliging, submissive, compliant.

heads-up *adj. Slang* SMART.

headway *n.* progress, advance, improvement, furtherance, gain, accomplishment.

heal *v.* cure, remedy, ameliorate, mend, repair, restore, recuperate, treat.

healer *n.* physician, doctor, therapist, mender, medicine man, witch doctor, faith healer.

health *n.* **1** soundness, wholesomeness, well-being, vigor, robustness, fitness, strength, vitality. **2** condition, state, tone, shape, form.

ant. **1** illness, sickness, disease, infirmity, weakness.

healthful *adj.* wholesome, beneficial, salubrious, healthy, nutritious, invigorating, hygienic.

ant. unhealthy, harmful, detrimental, noxious, deleterious, pernicious, baneful, debilitating.

healthy *adj.* well, sound, hale, strong, robust, vigorous, hardy, sturdy, fit, able-bodied.

ant. sick, ill, diseased, weak, infirm, feeble, ailing.

heap *n.* pile, stack, mound, mass, collection, accumulation, agglomeration. —*v.* pile, gather, accumulate, stack, amass.

hear *v.* listen, hearken, heed, attend.

hearer *n.* listener, auditor, eavesdropper.

hearing *n.* **1** interview, examination, audition, tryout, audience, conference. **2** trial, investigation, inquest, inquiry, inquisition.

hearken *v.* LISTEN.

hearsay *n.* rumor, report, gossip, grapevine, say-so, talk, tales, canard.

heart *n.* **1** emotion, love, affection, compassion, tenderness, desire. **2** courage, fortitude, valor, spirit, nerve, mettle, resoluteness, pluck, stamina, grit, guts (*Slang*). **3** core, center, nucleus, pith, kernel, essence, gist, meat, substance, nub, crux.

heartache *n.* grief, sorrow, anguish, despair, pain, heartbreak, heartsickness, distress, suffering.

heartbreak *n.* GRIEF.

heartbreaking *adj.* pitiful, moving, touching, heart-rending, grievous, sorrowful, poignant, affecting.

heartbroken *adj.* grieved, forlorn, sorrowful, despondent, crushed, desolate, dejected, heartsick, disheartened, dispirited, downcast, crestfallen, disappointed.

hearten *v.* encourage, reassure, embolden, cheer, inspire, assure, strengthen, buck up.

ant. discourage, dishearten, daunt, dispirit, dampen.

heartfelt *adj.* sincere, genuine, profound, deep, devout, honest, earnest, fervent, ardent.

ant. insincere, feigned, artificial, superficial, shallow.

heartily *adv.* sincerely, cordially, enthusiastically, earnestly, warmly, genuinely, wholeheartedly, fervently, keenly, profusely.

ant. indifferently, half-heartedly, apathetically, coolly.

heartless *adj.* pitiless, hard-hearted, insensitive, cold, callous, cruel, mean, indifferent, uncaring, unfeeling, merciless.

ant. compassionate, kind, warm-hearted, tender, merciful, sympathetic, gracious.

heart-to-heart *adj.* frank, intimate, sincere, open, candid, straightforward, plain-spoken.

hearty *adj.* **1** genial, cordial, warm, friendly, effusive, enthusiastic. **2** vigorous, robust, healthy, strong, hardy, powerful, staunch, thorough, downright, utter.

ant. **1** cool, lukewarm, reserved, aloof, constrained. **2** weak, feeble, frail, mild.

heat *n.* **1** warmth, hotness, temperature, fever, fieriness, torridness, sultriness. **2** passion, excitement, intensity, frenzy, fury, fervor, zeal, ardor, temper.

ant. **1** cold, coolness, chill, frost, frigidity. **2** calm, tranquillity, control, restraint, composure, serenity.

heated *adj.* vehement, emotional, frenzied, passionate, angry, intense, violent, stormy, tempestuous, fierce.

ant. calm, cool, reasoned, deliberate, controlled.

heathen *n.* pagan, idolater, infidel, nonbeliever, idol-worshiper, polytheist, antichrist, atheist, agnostic.

heave *v.* **1** hoist, lift, raise, hurl, fling, heft, throw, cast, sling. **2** vomit, retch, throw up, regurgitate, chuck, puke, keck. —*n*. lift, hoist, pitch, sling.

heaven *n*. bliss, paradise, blessedness, rapture, ecstasy, joy, transport, nirvana.

ant. hell, purgatory, torment, agony, suffering.

heavenly *adj*. delightful, lovely, beautiful, glorious, blissful, sublime, divine, empyreal, exquisite.

heaviness *n*. **1** weightiness, gravity, ponderousness, massiveness, bulkiness, thickness, density. **2** oppressiveness, arduousness, onerousness.

ant. **1** lightness, weightlessness, airiness. **2** ease, agreeableness, pleasantness, tolerability.

heavy *adj*. **1** weighty, massive, bulky, dense, leaden, thick, laden, substantial. **2** oppressive, burdensome, intolerable, cumbersome, onerous, arduous, grueling, grinding, hard, taxing, exhausting. **3** grave, serious, ponderous, solemn, weighty, dreary, somber, dull, stodgy, tedious, graceless.

ant. **1** light, weightless, thin, ethereal, feathery, scanty. **3** trivial, frivolous, inconsequential, petty, light-hearted, delicate, dainty.

heavy-handed *adj*. clumsy, awkward, bungling, inconsiderate, insensitive, thoughtless, tactless, domineering, overbearing.

ant. adroit, tactful, diplomatic, delicate, sensitive.

heavy-hearted *adj*. sad, despondent, heartsick, depressed, melancholy, disheartened, discouraged, gloomy, dispirited.

ant. cheerful, lighthearted, gay, blithe, carefree, buoyant.

heckle *v*. taunt, provoke, bait, jeer, needle, harass, annoy, bother, snipe at, pick on, mock, gibe, hector.

hectic *adj*. chaotic, turbulent, tumultuous, flustering, flurrying, uproarious, frantic, frenzied, frenetic, feverish.

ant. calm, serene, tranquil, orderly, peaceful.

hector *v*. annoy, badger, bully, tease, harass, heckle, harry, bother, pester.

hedge *n*. barrier, fence, boundary, border, enclosure. —*v*. temporize, equivocate, dodge, evade, tergiversate, parry, shift, avoid, sidestep, pussyfoot, fudge, waffle.

hedonistic *adj*. self-indulgent, pleasure-seeking, epicurean, sybaritic, luxurious, voluptuous.

ant. ascetic, austere, abstinent, self-denying, self-abnegating.

heed *v*. listen, pay attention, regard, reck, obey, consider, advert, mind. —*n*. consideration, notice, attention, vigilance, care, caution.

heedful *adj*. attentive, careful, mindful, wary, cautious, considerate, thoughtful, aware.

ant. heedless, careless, reckless, inattentive, indifferent.

heedless *adj*. careless, reckless, foolhardy, uncaring, negligent, thoughtless, rash, headstrong.

ant. circumspect, considerate, careful, prudent.

heel *n*. *Slang* cad, bounder, scoundrel, rat, chiseler, louse, rogue, swine, blackguard, stinker, rotter (*Slang*), bastard.

heft *n*. heaviness, weight, weightiness, poundage, avoirdupois, mass, massiveness, bulkiness.

ant. lightness, buoyancy, airiness.

hefty *adj*. heavy, weighty, robust, brawny, husky, burly, strapping, stout, massive, powerful, sturdy, sinewy, muscular, strong, substantial.

ant. puny, flimsy, scanty, insignificant, feeble, weakly, fragile.

height *n*. **1** altitude, elevation, stature, tallness, loftiness, eminence, prominence. **2** acme, peak, depth, ultimate, apex, summit, crest, crown, capstone, climax, zenith, apogee, pinnacle.

heighten *v*. intensify, enhance, augment, sharpen, amplify, aggravate, strengthen, increase, reinforce, maximize, enlarge, advance, magnify, exaggerate, develop.

ant. abate, soften, mitigate, tone down, weaken.

heinous *adj.* atrocious, outrageous, unspeakable, shocking, revolting, abominable, ghastly, grisly, vicious, hideous, monstrous, odious, devilish, hateful, repugnant.

heist *Slang v.* steal, appropriate, seize, hijack, lift, take, grab, rip off (*Slang*), cop (*Slang*). —*n.* theft, robbery, holdup, stickup (*Slang*), rip-off. (*Slang*).

hell *n.* inferno, the pit, pandemonium, nether regions, lower world, the abyss, Hades, Gehenna, Tophet, perdition, limbo.
ant. paradise, Eden, heaven, bliss, felicity, beatitude, nirvana.

hellion *n.* madcap, firebrand, mischiefmaker, troublemaker, hothead, jackanapes, spitfire, fiend, demon, rascal, nuisance, rogue, devil, fire-eater, terror.

hellish *adj.* horrible, atrocious, brutal, savage, fiendish, infernal, damnable, diabolical, grim, barbarous, pitiless, merciless.
ant. heavenly, angelic, blissful, propitious, delightful.

helmet *n.* headpiece, hard hat, casque, dome, bubble, headgear, helm, basinet.

help *v.* **1** assist, aid, succor, second, sustain, abet, benefit, support, cooperate, befriend, stand behind, serve, further, contribute, pitch in. **2** ameliorate, ease, prevent, mitigate, allay, relieve, alleviate, mend, cure, remedy, control, restore.
ant. 1 hinder, stultify, block, oppose, harm. **2** worsen, aggravate, irritate.

helper *n.* assistant, aide, subordinate, servant, apprentice, underling, factotum, support, second, helpmate, helpmeet, prop, hand, partner, deputy, right hand, mainstay.

helpful *adj.* beneficial, advantageous, fortunate, favorable, useful, serviceable, supportive, cooperative, constructive, profitable, auspicious, practical, expedient, productive.

ant. useless, harmful, destructive, pointless, worthless, unresponsive, malign.

helpfulness *n.* cooperation, assistance, serviceability, usefulness, participation, collaboration, kindness, supportiveness, neighborliness, willingness, practicality, availability, readiness.
ant. opposition, hostility, recalcitrance, antagonism.

helpless *adj.* feeble, defenseless, powerless, paralyzed, weak, ineffectual, impotent, disabled, vulnerable, abandoned, bereft, rudderless, crippled, incapable, incompetent, destitute, entangled, trapped, disarmed, high and dry.
ant. strong, powerful, fortified, potent, invincible, resourceful.

helplessness *n.* weakness, feebleness, invalidism, disability, impotence, paralysis, incapacity, inadequacy, defenselessness, vulnerability, powerlessness, ineptitude, awkwardness, clumsiness, incompetence, incapacity, shiftless, fecklessness.
ant. strength, power, potency, effectiveness, might.

helpmate *n.* HELPER.

helter-skelter *adj.* DISORDERLY.

hem *n.* edge, border, bottom, flounce, fringe, periphery, rim, margin, pale, brim, boundary, brink, lip, verge, frame, hedge, fence, demarcation. —*v.* edge, border, frame, fringe, outline, demarcate, finish, trim, smoothe.

hem in shut in, enclose, restrict, limit, surround, box, constrain, confine.

hep *adj. Slang* HIP.

herald *n.* forerunner, harbinger, precursor, press agent, advance man, ambassador, envoy, crier, augury, portent. —*v.* usher in, announce, proclaim, prophesy, prefigure, reveal, forecast, foreshadow, advertise, promise, presage.

herculean *adj.* heroic, prodigious, titanic, mighty, formidable, laborious, stupendous, demanding, arduous, backbreaking, overwhelming.

herd *n.* **1** drove, pack, swarm, flock, group, gathering, troop. **2** throng, mob, rabble, horde, crowd, mass, multitude, congregation.

heresy *n.* APOSTASY.

heretic *n.* nonconformist, dissenter, dissident, skeptic, revisionist, deviationist, freethinker, apostate, unbeliever, defector, iconoclast, agnostic.

heretical *adj.* unorthodox, heterodox, schismatic, nonconformist, dissident, deviant, revisionist, unsound, idolatrous, freethinking.
   ant. orthodox, approved, devout, fundamentalist, pious, conventional.

heritage *n.* patrimony, birthright, portion, estate, endowment, legacy, inheritance, heritance, heirloom.

hermaphroditic *adj.* ANDROGYNOUS.

hermit *n.* recluse, eremite, solitary, anchorite, troglodyte.

hero *n.* champion, protagonist, principal, star, lead, cynosure, winner, exemplar, standard-bearer, adventurer.

heroic *adj.* fearless, daring, brave, stalwart, bold, resolute, herculean, great-hearted, magnanimous, dauntless, intrepid, doughty, courageous, valiant, gallant, noble.
   ant. pusillanimous, fearful, craven, faint-hearted, dastardly.

heroism *n.* valor, bravery, daring, prowess, courage, gallantry, boldness, fearlessness, chivalry, magnanimity, nobility, exaltation, intrepidity.
   ant. cowardice, weakness, baseness, cravenness, faint-heartedness.

hero-worship *n.* ADMIRATION.

hesitant *adj.* faltering, indecisive, irresolute, undecided, unsure, doubtful, wavering, halting, half-hearted, backward, tentative, diffident, reluctant, averse, loath, shilly-shally.
   ant. confident, assured, forward, firm, determined, positive.

hesitate *v.* pause, delay, hang back, lag, tarry, mark time, vacillate, waver, falter, scruple, balk, boggle.

hesitation *n.* delay, demurral, vacillation, reluctance, circumspection, scruple, doubt, misgiving, qualm, indecision, unwillingness, uncertainty.
   ant. haste, precipitancy, suddenness, abruptness, hastiness, hotheadedness.

heterodoxy *n.* DISSENT.

heterogeneous *adj.* varied, dissimilar, mixed, diverse, miscellaneous, assorted, unlike, motley, variegated, spotty, jumbled, complex.
   ant. homogeneous, homogenized, uniform, regular, matched, consonant.

hew *v.* chop, cut, axe, hack, sever, split, cleave, slash, lop, sunder, trim, carve, whittle, chisel.

hex *v.* jinx, bewitch, bedevil, curse, voodoo, haunt, possess. —*n.* spell, curse, hoodoo, evil eye, voodoo, enchantment, whammy (*Slang*), jinx, charm.

hiatus *n.* gap, break, interruption, omission, rift, discontinuity, lacuna, lapse, blank, void, vacuum.

hibernate *v.* retreat, retire, rusticate, lie dormant, estivate, vegetate, stagnate, lie low, hole up.

hick *n.* provincial, rustic, countryman, farmer, yokel, swain, naif, country cousin, clodhopper, hayseed (*Slang*), rube (*Slang*).

hidden *adj.* concealed, covert, cryptic, secret, dark, unseen, veiled, suppressed, latent, clandestine, arcane, occult.
   ant. exposed, overt, open, obvious, revealed, aboveboard.

hide[1] *v.* conceal, cover, secrete, screen, bury, cover up, cloak, mask, disguise, camouflage, veil, suppress.
   ant. display, reveal, expose, show, uncover.

hide[2] *n.* skin, pelt, fur, fell, epidermis, integument, husk, rind, coat, jacket, fleece, rawhide, leather.

hideaway *n.* RETREAT.

hidebound *adj.* NARROW-MINDED.

hideous *adj.* repulsive, shocking, revolting, dreadful, ghastly, repugnant, loathsome, appalling, grim, horrible, frightful, gruesome, monstrous, odious.

ant. attractive, charming, soothing, inviting, delightful, pleasant.

hideout *n.* RETREAT.

hiding *n.* flogging, beating, spanking, thrashing, trouncing, whipping, caning, drubbing, paddling, scourging.

hie *v.* HASTEN.

higgledy-piggledy *adj.* DISORDERLY.

high *adj.* **1** lofty, elevated, superior, tall, towering, alpine, soaring, prominent. **2** important, intense, forceful, advanced, exalted, strong, maximal, immoderate, climactic, great. **3** dear, expensive, costly, exorbitant, inflated, extravagant, excessive, immoderate, extortionate. **4** intoxicated, inebriated, drunk, besotted, manic, euphoric, delirious, stoned (*Slang*), muddled, turned on (*Slang*). —*n.* **1** maximum, peak, culmination, climax, zenith, acme, top, summit, crown. **2** euphoria, intoxication, trip, (*Slang*), delirium, transport, ecstasy, elation, drunkenness.

ant. *adj.* **1** low, little, short, insignificant, squat, truncated. **2** secondary, humble, weak, minimal, faint, insignificant. **3** modest, cheap, nominal, cut-rate, low-priced. **4** sober, low, detoxified, down, depressed. —*n.* **1** low, depression, trough, nadir.

high and dry HELPLESS.

high and mighty HAUGHTY.

highborn *adj.* noble, aristocratic, patrician, thoroughbred, pedigreed, blue-blooded, genteel, exalted.

ant. humble, common, plebeian, lowborn, proletarian.

highbrow *n.* intellectual, thinker, scholar, sage, savant, aesthete, classicist, mastermind, egghead (*Slang*), brain. —*adj.* intellectual, erudite, brainy, cultivated, scholarly, bookish, cultured, knowledgeable.

ant. *n.* ignoramus, lowbrow, Philistine, bourgeois, know-nothing. —*adj.* lowbrow, ignorant.

high-class *adj.* superior, first-rate, choice, distinguished, select, ranking, elite, excellent, notable, noble.

ant. commonplace, mediocre, humble, base, ordinary, vulgar.

highfalutin *adj.* POMPOUS.

high-flown *adj.* pretentious, inflated, grandiose, stilted, bombastic, affected, flowery, ostentatious, extravagant, grandiloquent, turgid, overblown.

ant. sober, commonplace, everyday, simple, plain, down-to-earth.

high-grade *adj.* SUPERIOR.

highhanded *adj.* overbearing, overweening, autocratic, authoritarian, domineering, despotic, peremptory, bossy, imperious, dictatorial, arrogant, arbitrary.

highhandedness *n.* presumptuousness, arrogation, lordliness, arrogance, autocracy, self-will, presumption, arbitrariness, dogmatism, despotism, tyranny, audacity.

high-hat *adj.* SNOBBISH.

highlight *n.* feature, crux, essence, key, mainstay, core, attraction, essential, detail, element, sine qua non. —*v.* emphasize, stress, underline, accentuate, flag, feature, mark, spotlight, point up.

ant. *v.* play down, gloss over, tone down, obfuscate, obscure, ignore.

highly *adv.* **1** very, very much, greatly, extremely, decidedly, eminently, profoundly, vastly, extraordinarily, intensely, deeply. **2** favorably, well, warmly, advantageously, enthusiastically, approvingly, sanguinely.

ant. **1** little, slightly, minimally, barely, scarcely, hardly. **2** critically, disparagingly, coldly, indifferently, reservedly.

high-minded *adj.* idealistic, lofty, magnanimous, reputable, incorruptible, noble, virtuous, estimable, elevated, principled, conscientious, honorable, chivalrous.

ant. mean, underhand, petty, venal, self-serving.

high-pressure *adj.* aggressive, enterprising, importunate, forceful, compelling, intensive, high-powered, dynamic, vigorous, coercive, hard-sell.

ant. relaxed, easygoing, languid, lackadaisical, apathetic, low-key, soft-sell.

high-sounding *adj.* grandiloquent, overblown, bombastic, pompous, strained, flamboyant, high-flown, extravagant, affected, stilted.

ant. sober, temperate, subdued, modest, plain, simple.

high-spirited *adj.* vivacious, dashing, animated, fun-loving, mettlesome, enthusiastic, fiery, sanguine, energetic, avid, bold, gallant, spunky, feisty, skittish.

ant. lethargic, sedate, listless, apathetic, gloomy, dull.

high-strung *adj.* temperamental, nervous, tense, irritable, excitable, taut, edgy, sensitive, susceptible, impatient, lively, skittish.

ant. phlegmatic, placid, impassive, stolid, even-tempered, relaxed.

high-toned *adj.* **1** fashionable, chic, smart, elegant, pompous, pretentious, high-flown, ostentatious, swank. **2** noble, lofty, dignified, elevated, honorable, stately, principled, meritorious.

highway *n.* road, thoroughfare, parkway, highroad, turnpike, artery, speedway, expressway, causeway, thruway, way, course, route.

hijack *v.* commandeer, steal, heist (*Slang*), seize, take over, expropriate, skyjack, coerce, dragoon, grab, pirate.

hijacker *n.* robber, bandit, brigand, gunman, thug, skyjacker, highwayman, thief, desperado.

hike *v.* walk, march, tramp, trudge, trek, journey, parade. —*n* journey, march, trek, walk, distance.

hilarious *adj.* laughable, sidesplitting, gleeful, jolly, merry, jovial, mirthful, funny, gay, rollicking, uproarious, boisterous.

ant. woebegone, lugubrious, miserable, sad, melancholy, dispirited.

hilarity *n.* glee, mirth, levity, merriment, gaiety, laughter, joviality, exhilaration, frivolity, amusement, jollity, cachinnation.

ant. gloom, sobriety, dejection, sorrow, depression.

hill *n.* elevation, rise, mound, heap, pile, hummock, hillock, hump, mount, knoll, prominence.

ant. hollow, valley, depression, hole, dell.

hillock *n.* HILL.

hilt *n.* HANDLE.

hind *adj.* rear, posterior, back, aft, rearward, backward, after, stern, dorsal, tail, trailing, lagging.

ant. fore, front, leading, anterior, ventral.

hinder[1] *v.* impede, stop, stay, halt, deter, check, delay, thwart, encumber, hamper, foil, frustrate, bar, block.

ant. facilitate, succor, help, abet, forward, enable.

hinder[2] *adj.* REAR.

hindmost *adj.* last, final, terminal, ultimate, back, rear, rearmost, concluding, trailing.

ant. front, foremost, leading, initial, primary.

hindrance *n.* obstruction, handicap, encumbrance, impediment, let, constraint, interference, drawback, blockage, curb, inhibition, difficulty, bar, restriction.

hinge *v.* depend, rest, hang, relate, turn, revolve, result, ensue, follow.

hint *n.* **1** tip, intimation, clue, lead, inkling, suggestion, innuendo, allusion, pointer, sign. **2** trace, tinge, touch, whiff, breath, pinch, suspicion, *soupçon*. —*v.* allude, intimate, suggest, imply, prompt, insinuate, cue, tip, let fall, remind.

hip *adj. Slang* aware, informed, privy to, in the know, hep (*Slang*), knowing, onto, wise, percipient, shrewd, alive to, cognizant, astute.

ant. naive, ignorant, innocent, ingenuous, uninformed.

hippodrome *n.* STADIUM.

hire *v.* employ, engage, retain, take on,

rent, lease, bespeak, charter, appoint, place.

hiss *v.* hoot, boo, whistle, shout down, clamor, jeer, mock, deride, scorn. **ant.** cheer, applaud, hurrah.

historic *adj.* notable, momentous, memorable, outstanding, celebrated, significant, renowned, red-letter, ground-breaking, unforgettable, remarkable. **ant.** insignificant, trivial, inconsequential, negligible, humdrum.

historical *adj.* recorded, documented, chronicled, attested, factual, verifiable, authentic, true, authoritative, well-founded, unchallengeable, veritable. **ant.** fictitious, legendary, conjectural, mythical, fabulous, imaginary.

history *n.* record, chronicle, annals, statement, story, account, recital, recapitulation, past, background.

histrionic *adj.* theatrical, dramatic, stagy, melodramatic, affected, bombastic, fustian, thespian, exhibitionist, hammy (*Slang*).

histrionics *n.* performance, staginess, dramatics, theatricality, rodomontade, rant, scene, tirade, tantrum, fuss, outburst.

hit *v.* strike, impinge, smack, smite, slap, tap, rap, knock, punch, slam, slug, club, bop (*Slang*), collide, touch. —*n.* **1** stroke, blow, shot, cuff, clout, slap, rap, knock. **2** success, triumph, conquest, winner, knockout (*Slang*). **ant.** *n.* **2** miss, failure, flop, bust (*Slang*), bomb (*Slang*).

hitch *n.* snag, catch, difficulty, drawback, obstacle, impediment, stumbling block, handicap, problem, bug, glitch (*Slang*). —*v.* fasten, join, tie, harness, bind, leash, attach, tether, yoke, grapple. **ant.** *v.* loose, free, release, let go, detach, untie.

hit man *Slang* ASSASSIN.

hit-or-miss *adj.* HAPHAZARD.

hoar *adj.* HOARY.

hoard *n.* stockpile, fund, aggregation, accumulation, heap, collection, mass, cache, supply, store. —*v.* accumulate, collect, amass, save, store, pile up, lay away, put by, cache, squirrel away. **ant.** *v.* disperse, squander, spend, scatter, use up, waste.

hoarder *n.* collector, miser, niggard, saver, scrimp, skinflint, tightwad (*Slang*). **ant.** spendthrift, wastrel, prodigal, profligate.

hoarse *adj.* harsh, rough, husky, throaty, rasping, raucous, croaky, gravelly, grating, cracked, croupy. **ant.** dulcet, melodious, bell-like, smooth, clear, piping.

hoary *adj.* old, ancient, grizzled, gray-haired, venerable, antiquated, aged, wintry, grizzly, hoar, gray, white-haired.

hoax *v.* trick, dupe, deceive, swindle, take in, gull, hoodwink, fool, cozen, con (*Slang*), put on (*Slang*). —*n.* trick, imposture, prank, fraud, deception, sham, subterfuge, counterfeit, dodge, spoof, flimflam, feint, quiz, humbug, racket, put-on (*Slang*).

hoaxer *n.* trickster, joker, spoofer, faker, practical joker, humbug, prankster, cheat, swindler, sharper, shyster.

hob *n.* FAIRY.

hobbled *adj.* limping, crippled, lame, disabled, fettered, constrained, hampered, trammeled, stumbling, shackled.

hobby *n.* pastime, avocation, diversion, sideline, toy.

hobgoblin *n.* FAIRY.

hobo *n.* tramp, vagrant, wanderer, drifter, vagabond, bum, floater, nomad, derelict, stray, beggar, loafer.

hock *v.* PAWN.

hocus-pocus *n.* trick, deception, sleight-of-hand, subterfuge, artifice, dodge, sham, flimflam, hanky-panky, abracadabra, mumbo-jumbo.

hodge-podge *n.* medley, jumble,

melange, hash, conglomeration, olio, patchwork, miscellany, muddle, gallimaufry, crazy quilt.

hog *n.* swine, pig, porker. —*v. Slang* gobble (*Slang*), take over, grab, annex, appropriate, commandeer, monopolize, corner, arrogate, usurp.

hoggish *adj.* greedy, selfish, gluttonous, dirty, filthy, swinish, gross, offensive, coarse, porcine, squalid, piggish, brutish.
ant. abstemious, self-denying, fastidious, refined, unselfish, generous.

hogwash *n.* nonsense, rubbish, foolishness, balderdash, gabble, piffle, trash, drivel, verbiage, tripe, twaddle, bilge (*Slang*).

hoi polloi masses, populace, commonalty, crowd, rank and file, grass roots, citizenry, people, rabble, riffraff, multitude, herd, mob.
ant. elite, aristocracy, leadership, establishment, upper crust.

hoist *v.* raise, elevate, jack, lift, erect, heave, furl, run up.

hoke up *v. Slang* fake, simulate, counterfeit, overact, put on, ham, pretend, exaggerate, dramatize, embroider.

hokum *n.* nonsense, claptrap, bunkum, poppycock, flummery, blather, guff (*Slang*), bunk (*Slang*), blah (*Slang*).

hold *v.* **1** grasp, embrace, clutch, grip, hug, steady, support, fondle. **2** consider, believe, regard, maintain, deem, view, assume, presume. **3** retain, keep, have, take, possess, own, secure, withhold, occupy. **4** persist, continue, last, endure, wear, hold out. —*n.* influence, authority, sway, weight, control, power, vantage, footing, rights, pull (*Slang*), clout (*Slang*).
ant. *v.* **1, 3** release, drop, reject, relinquish, yield, give up.

holder *n.* owner, possessor, proprietor, bearer, purchaser, keeper, custodian, occupant.

hold forth harangue, preach, declaim,

speechify, orate, sermonize, descant, discourse, speak, address.

holdings *n.* assets, property, resources, possessions, wealth, investments, estate, effects, belongings, goods.

hold on persist, persevere, dig in, endure, go on, keep up, continue, sustain, hold fast, carry on.
ant. give in, give up, let go, submit, relinquish, knuckle under.

hold out stand fast, endure, persist, persevere, continue, withstand, last, hang in, dig in, stick, carry on.
ant. give up, give in, lose heart, despair, cease.

hold-up *n.* **1** stoppage, delay, obstruction, impasse, deadlock, logjam, tie-up, bottleneck, blockage, snag. **2** robbery, theft, banditry, extortion, thievery, mugging, seizure, heist (*Slang*), shakedown (*Slang*), stickup (*Slang*).

hold up *v.* **1** support, prop, shore up, buttress, sustain, brace, jack up, bear. **2** last, endure, wear, stick, hold, survive, persist, continue, bear up. **3** delay, stop, impede, block, interrupt, prevent, obstruct. **4** rob, stick up (*Slang*), mug.

hole *n.* **1** aperture, opening, pore, hollow, crater, gap, perforation, cavity, cave, leak, space, puncture, slot, break, tear. **2** fault, defect, flaw, fallacy, error, loophole, omission, out. **3** dilemma, predicament, quandary, fix, imbroglio, pickle, scrape, quagmire, jam.

hole up *v.* hibernate, wait out, retreat, go to ground, hide out, shelter, lie low, retire, take refuge, take cover.

holiday *n.* festival, festivity, fete, fiesta, celebration, weekend, vacation, break, recess, sabbatical, leave, anniversary, respite, day off. —*v.* weekend, vacation, relax, knock off, take it easy.

holiness *n.* godhead, sanctity, godliness, divinity, spirituality, goodness, saintliness, piety, grace, sacredness, purity, transcendence, consecration.

holler *v.* shout, yell, bellow, cry, bawl,

bray, whoop, hail, clamor, protest. —*n.* shout, yell, roar, bellow, clamor, fuss, noise.

hollow *adj.* **1** void, empty, vacant, sunken, excavated, reamed, concave. **2** vain, vacuous, specious, insincere, vacant, empty, meaningless. —*n.* depression, cavity, dent, fissure, dimple, basin, hole, crater, excavation, indentation.
ant. *adj.* **1** solid, full, substantial. **2** pithy, cogent, significant. —*n.* bump, protuberance, knob, swelling, hillock, pimple.

hollowness *n.* emptiness, inanity, vacancy, vacuity, vanity, vapidity.

holocaust *n.* disaster, inferno, conflagration, fire storm, carnage, massacre, shambles, hecatomb, annihilation, devastation, genocide.

holy *adj.* consecrated, hallowed, saintly, sacrosanct, numinous, godly, pure, angelic, righteous, pious.
ant. profane, secular, worldly, mundane, cursed, diabolical.

homage *n.* deference, obeisance, honor, respect, adoration, tribute, veneration, reverence, submission, devotion.

home *n.* **1** residence, dwelling, abode, house, place, domicile, habitation, hearth, roof. **2** *place of origin or development:* cradle, center, territory, habitat, headquarters, fountainhead, haunt, stamping ground.

homeless *adj.* vagrant, vagabond, rootless, displaced, dispossessed, evicted, outcast, drifting, nomadic, forsaken, floating.
ant. domiciled, sheltered, settled.

homelike *adj.* comfortable, pleasant, cozy, domestic, intimate, familiar, congenial, cheerful, snug, warm, simple, plain.
ant. repellent, cold, forbidding, pretentious, strange, exotic.

homely *adj.* **1** unpretentious, simple, artless, natural, everyday, homespun, homelike, homey, unassuming, modest. **2** ugly, plain, ill-favored, drab, unattractive, graceless.

ant. **1** ostentatious, affected, vain, meretricious, sophisticated. **2** pretty, comely, personable, handsome, good-looking.

homespun *adj.* plain, simple, unpretentious, unaffected, artless, homely, crude, natural, rustic, native, homemade, folksy.
ant. polished, refined, artificial, exotic, sophisticated, arty.

homey *adj.* cozy, familiar, intimate, informal, comfortable, cheerful, domestic, inviting, simple, homelike, warm, wholesome.
ant. cheerless, forbidding, strange, cold, alien, unpleasant.

homicide *n.* murder, manslaughter, assassination, killing, bloodshed, slaughter.

homily *n.* SERMON.

homogeneous *adj.* consistent, uniform, unvarying, homogenized, alike, same, similar, homologous, identical, consonant, standardized, monolithic.
ant. mixed, heterogeneous, varied, variegated, miscellaneous, pluralistic.

homologous *adj.* ANALOGOUS.

hone *v.* sharpen, strop, whet, grind, file.

honest *adj.* **1** truthful, honorable, sincere, forthright, candid, upright, trustworthy, reliable, true, frank, veracious, scrupulous, guileless, square-shooting. **2** equitable, just, fair, bona fide, fair-and-square, impartial, unbiased, disinterested.
ant. **1** deceitful, treacherous, lying, false, scheming, disingenuous. **2** rigged, spurious, counterfeit, fixed, bogus, phony (*Slang*).

honesty *n.* integrity, rectitude, sincerity, probity, veracity, honor, uprightness, candor, frankness, truthfulness, faithfulness, openness.
ant. deceit, pretense, falsity, fraudulence, cheating, chicanery.

honey *n.* beauty, whopper, wonder, paragon, masterpiece, nonpareil, winner, jewel, delight, hit, prize, knockout (*Slang*).

honeyed *adj.* flattering, ingratiating, seductive, agreeable, soothing, cloying, smooth-tongued, unctuous, saccharine, cajoling, dulcet, alluring, oily.

honor *n.* 1 respect, regard, renown, esteem, prestige, glory, dignity, homage, deference, repute, fame, reverence, consideration. 2 integrity, rectitude, probity, honesty, principle, justice, uprightness, equity, fairness, nobleness. —*v.* 1 revere, esteem, regard, respect, venerate, adore, worship, hallow, value, glorify. 2 praise, commend, dignify, commemorate, laud, celebrate, decorate, fete, lionize, compliment, cite, recognize.

ant. *n.* 1 opprobrium, disgrace, humiliation, shame, odium, abasement. 2 perfidy, duplicity, venality, baseness, infamy, treachery. —*v.* 1 despise, scorn, disdain, abominate. 2 censure, castigate, humiliate.

honorable *adj.* ethical, virtuous, conscientious, scrupulous, just, estimable, trustworthy, upstanding, principled, creditable, candid.

ant. contemptible, disreputable, corrupt, perfidious, false, tricky.

honorary *adj.* nominal, titular, complimentary, voluntary, unpaid.

hooch *n. Slang* LIQUOR.

hood[1] *n.* cowl, bonnet, scarf, capote, parka, calash, kerchief, babushka.

hood[2] *n. Slang* HOODLUM.

hoodlum *n.* ruffian, rowdy, thug, criminal, cutthroat, tough, bruiser, hooligan, mobster, gangster, punk (*Slang*), hood (*Slang*).

hoodwink *v.* deceive, dupe, mislead, gull, cheat, cozen, hoax, inveigle, delude, decoy, defraud, entice, seduce.

hooey *n. Slang* NONSENSE.

hoof it WALK.

hook *n.* grapple, crook, crimp, barb, gaff, crotchet, clasp, claw, talon. —*v.* catch, hitch, gaff, seize, grapple, clasp, entrap, capture, snare, crimp.

hooked *adj. Slang* 1 addicted, habituated, caught, trapped. 2 fascinated,

taken with, devoted, enamored, ensnared, turned on (*Slang*).

hooker *n. Slang* 1 DRINK. 2 PROSTITUTE.

hooligan *n.* hoodlum, rowdy, tough, ruffian, roughneck (*Slang*), bully, bruiser, blackguard, terror, thug, ne'er-do-well.

hoop *n.* band, ring, loop, strap, circle, circlet, wheel, girdle.

hoopla *n. Slang* EXCITEMENT.

hoosegow *n. Slang* JAIL.

hoot *v.* jeer, deride, fleer, mock, clamor, boo, bray, bellow, hiss, scoff, shout. —*n.* howl, roar, bray, catcall, caterwauling, gibe, tumult, raspberry (*Slang*), Bronx cheer (*Slang*).

hop *v.* jump, bound, bounce, skip, leap, spring, caper, prance, bob, trip. —*n.* jump, bound, leap, spring, step.

hope *v.* trust, anticipate, await, aspire, contemplate, count on, rely, look forward, expect, believe, flatter one's self. —*n.* confidence, reliance, trust, faith, expectation, desire, prospect, expectancy, assumption, ambition.

ant. *v.* despair, give up, fear, doubt. —*n.* hopelessness, despair, despondency, pessimism, fear.

hopeful *adj.* promising, encouraging, favorable, auspicious, heartening, cheering, reassuring, optimistic, confident, sanguine, rosy, bright.

ant. hopeless, pessimistic, dim, cloudy, unfavorable.

hopefulness *n.* optimism, confidence, expectancy, buoyancy, cheerfulness, enthusiasm, anticipation, encouragement, promise.

ant. pessimism, despair, discouragement.

hopeless *adj.* despairing, despondent, desperate, foreboding, abject, disconsolate, incurable, useless, impossible, ill-omened, ominous, irrevocable.

ant. hopeful, favorable, promising, reassuring, rosy.

hopelessness *n.* despair, desperation, depression, dejection, despondency, melancholy, defeatism, pessimism, incurability, impossibility, futility, pointlessness, finality, incorrigibility. **ant.** optimism, buoyancy, cheerfulness, promise.

horde *n.* multitude, pack, swarm, throng, crush, press, crowd, mob, gang, legion, host, bevy, troop.

horizon *n.* purview, range, scope, vista, compass, limits, grasp, reach, sights, realm, domain, perspective, vision, prospect, outlook.

horizontal *adj.* level, even, flush, plane, flat, prostrate, recumbent.

horn *n.* excrescence, outgrowth, cornu, spur, spike, tusk, antler.

horn in *Slang* barge in, butt in, crash, trespass, interlope, intrude, interrupt, encroach, infringe, insinuate oneself, gate-crash (*Slang*).

horny *adj. Slang* LUSTFUL.

horrendous *adj.* frightful, dreadful, terrible, horrible, horrid, abhorrent, appalling, hideous, ghastly, shocking, awful. **ant.** fascinating, enchanting, wonderful, idyllic, marvelous.

horrible *adj.* horrifying, frightful, ghastly, hideous, horrid, grim, grisly, shocking, outrageous, execrable. **ant.** delightful, agreeable, fascinating, attractive, enchanting, delectable.

horrid *adj.* horrible, repugnant, dreadful, ghastly, frightful, obnoxious, hateful, shocking, appalling, abominable, grim, grisly, outrageous, nasty, vile.

horrify *v.* shock, appall, harrow, terrify, disgust, revolt, intimidate, dismay, daunt, repel, petrify, alarm, nauseate. **ant.** delight, soothe, calm, hearten, cheer, entrance.

horror *n.* terror, fear, alarm, dread, dismay, panic, disgust, antipathy, repugnance, aversion, loathing, abhorrence, consternation.

horse *n.* steed, equine, nag, pony, dobbin.

horse around *v.* clown, cut up, roughhouse, fool, act up, misbehave, cavort, frisk, romp, roister.

horseman *n.* equestrian, rider, jockey, caballero, cavalier, roughrider, cowboy, cowpuncher, centaur.

horseplay *n.* clowning, foolery, roughhousing, buffoonery, antics, pranks, harlequinade, romping, cutting up, tomfoolery.

horse sense COMMON SENSE.

horsewoman *n.* equestrienne, cowgirl.

hospitable *adj.* **1** neighborly, welcoming, convivial, cordial, companionable, sociable, genial, gregarious, gracious, amicable. **2** open-minded, receptive, accommodating, tolerant. **ant.** **1** antisocial, aloof, haughty, reserved, forbidding, unsociable. **2** resistant, inflexible, adamant, narrow-minded.

hospital *n.* infirmary, sanatorium, sanitarium, polyclinic, clinic, asylum, lazaretto.

hospitality *n.* conviviality, welcome, cordiality, friendliness, sociability, neighborliness, receptiveness, hospitableness, heartiness, cheer, warmth, largess.

host *n.* multitude, throng, legion, crowd, army, swarm, bevy, assemblage, flood, galaxy, myriad, drove. **ant.** handful, remnant, few, sprinkling.

hostage *n.* pledge, prisoner, pawn, guaranty, gage.

hostile *adj.* unfriendly, antagonistic, inimical, spiteful, ill-disposed, malevolent, rancorous, malign, virulent, aggressive, adverse, bellicose, opposing, warlike, opposed. **ant.** friendly, amiable, benevolent, peaceable, pacific, irenic.

hostilities *n.* WAR.

hostility *n.* animosity, enmity, ill will, dislike, antagonism, defiance, spite, malevolence, hatred, opposition, malice, animus, detestation, abhorrence, contempt. **ant.** friendliness, good will, affability, cordiality, benevolence, warmth.

hot *adj.* **1** burning, calorific, torrid,

fiery, blazing, sultry, thermal, boiling, heated, roasting, scorching, redhot, white-hot. **2** peppery, piquant, sharp, pungent, spicy, zesty, acrid, biting, keen, racy. **3** passionate, intense, violent, zealous, vehement, ardent, fervent, excited, raging, fervid. **4** controversial, sensitive, burning, contentious, debatable, sticky, live.

ant. 1 cold, frigid, freezing, icy, raw. **2** bland, insipid, mild, flat. **3** calm, collected, apathetic, cool. **4** moot.

hot air *Slang* blather, bombast, drivel, falderal, gabble, balderdash, bunkum, fustian, grandiloquence, hyperbole, gobbledygook, rhetoric, chatter, jabber, nonsense, rigmarole, bull (*Slang*).

hotbed *n.* den, nest, hatchery, sink, cradle, seedbed, source, well, nursery, fountain, incubator.

hot-blooded *adj.* excitable, passionate, fiery, impetuous, ardent, wild, impulsive, precipitate, rash, brash, fervent, intense.

ant. impassive, stolid, phlegmatic, apathetic, staid, cold.

hotel *n.* inn, hostelry, lodge, lodging house, caravansary, hostel, public house, motel, flophouse.

hotheaded *adj.* quick-tempered, fiery, impetuous, volatile, rash, hasty, precipitate, excitable, peppery, combustible, dashing, high-strung.

ant. equable, cool, deliberate, disciplined, steady, impassive, unflappable.

hound *v.* nag, bait, annoy, pester, harass, badger, dog, bedevil, harry, plague, torment, tease, wear down, molest, snipe at, rag (*Slang*).

hourly *adv.* constantly, frequently, periodically, regularly, steadily, continually, unfailingly, perpetually, ceaselessly, incessantly.

ant. seldom, occasionally, sporadically.

house *n.* **1** residence, dwelling, home, abode, shelter, domicile, habitation, household. **2** organization, establishment, business, company, firm, concern, shop, corporation. **3** lineage, line, family, tribe, race, dynasty, descent, family tree.

housebreaker *n.* burglar, robber, thief, intruder, prowler, yegg (*Slang*), secondstory man, cracksman.

household *n.* family, menage, house, home.

householder *n.* occupant, homeowner, tenant, resident.

housing *n.* **1** shelter, lodgings, habitation, lodgment, dwelling, quarters, domicile. **2** casing, case, niche, recess, enclosure, bracket, console, cabinet.

hovel *n.* hut, cabin, shack, sty, hole, den, shed, lean-to, shanty, cot, dump (*Slang*).

hover *v.* poise, hang, float, drift, stand by, impend, linger, brood, waver, vacillate, hang around.

howl *v.* wail, bay, bellow, ululate, yell, scream, yowl, whine, moan, clamor, shriek, roar.

howler *n.* BLUNDER.

hub *n.* center, pivot, axis, core, focal point, focus, nub, basis, nucleus, kernel, heart, keystone, crux.

hubbub *n.* tumult, uproar, noise, turmoil, confusion, commotion, racket, din, pandemonium, clamor, bedlam, hurly-burly, to-do, bustle, chaos.

ant. quiet, tranquillity, stillness, quiescence, peacefulness, silence.

hubris *n.* PRIDE.

huckster *n.* salesman, peddler, hawker, barker, adman, promoter, pitchman, publicist, coster (*Brit.*), bagman (*Brit.*).

huddle *v.* crowd, mass, bunch, herd, flock, gather, cram, pack, shove, snuggle, hug. —*n.* jumble, crowd, clump, clot, mass, bunch, ball, knot, muddle, hodge-podge, medley, mixup, conglomeration, scrum.

hue[1] *n.* color, shade, tint, tone, cast, tinge, complexion, coloration.

hue[2] *n.* shouting, tumult, outcry, clamor, bellowing, din, baying, hullabaloo, brouhaha, whooping, cry, fanfare, ado, bother.

huff *n.* ANGER.

huffy *adj.* **1** touchy, sensitive, thin-skinned, testy, hypersensitive, vulnerable, susceptible, irascible, choleric, cranky, querulous. **2** indignant, angry, irritated, offended, cross, wrathful, irate, peevish, distressed.
ant. 1 thick-skinned, tough, impassive, stolid, impervious, placid.

hug *v.* clasp, embrace, cuddle, hold, nestle, cradle, press, squeeze, enfold, clutch, grip, envelop, hold fast, clinch (*Slang*). —*n.* embrace, caress, clasp, squeeze.

huge *adj.* immense, tremendous, enormous, gigantic, vast, colossal, mammoth, elephantine, titanic, monstrous, great, stupendous, Brobdingnagian, extensive.
ant. tiny, minute, microscopic, minuscule, small, Lilliputian.

hugger-mugger *n.* CONFUSION.

hulking *adj.* bulky, unwieldy, ponderous, cumbersome, massive, hulky, clumsy, awkward, overgrown, ungainly, lumpish, lumbering, oafish.
ant. compact, diminutive.

hullabaloo *n.* uproar, tumult, clamor, hubbub, din, racket, commotion, pandemonium, bedlam, furor, to-do, brouhaha, blare, noise.
ant. peace, quiet, silence, calm.

hum *v.* buzz, whir, thrum, whizz, murmur, drone, trill, purr, croon, warble, intone, bombinate, vibrate.

human *adj.* mortal, manlike, fleshly, anthropic, anthropoid, hominid. —*n.* person, individual, human being, soul, mortal, body, man, tellurian, hominid.

humane *adj.* compassionate, tender, forbearing, kind, charitable, merciful, sympathetic, benevolent, clement, lenient, benignant, understanding.
ant. cruel, harsh, implacable, brutal, pitiless, savage, barbaric.

humanist *n.* classicist, scholar, savant, man of letters, pundit, sage.

humanitarian *n.* philanthropist, altruist, Good Samaritan, benefactor, do-gooder.
ant. misanthrope, cynic.

humanitarianism *n.* philanthropy, humanism, benevolence, beneficence, charity, good will, generosity, welfarism, Benthamism.

humanity *n.* **1** mankind, humankind, human race, Homo sapiens, man, mortality, world, flesh. **2** compassion, fellow feeling, charity, brotherhood, humaneness, fellowship, kindness, consideration, magnanimity, mercy, ruth.

humble *adj.* meek, modest, self-effacing, lowly, low-born, unpretentious, unpretending, obscure, insignificant, respectful, shy, biddable, simple, docile. —*v.* humiliate, abase, mortify, lower, demean, debase, shame, crush, abash, degrade, put down (*Slang*).
ant. *adj.* arrogant, illustrious, haughty, pretentious, proud, assertive. *v.* honor, exalt, elevate, raise, extol, glorify.

humbly *adv.* meekly, deferentially, modestly, submissively, subserviently, obsequiously, respectfully, diffidently, docilely, unassumingly.
ant. proudly, arrogantly, insolently, haughtily, pretentiously, grandly.

humbug *n.* nonsense, drivel, rubbish, flummery, bosh, gammon, piffle, poppycock, falderal, balderdash, bunkum, bunk (*Slang*), gobbledygook, double talk, absurdity, inanity.

humdrum *adj.* tedious, commonplace, unvarying, dull, pedestrian, prosy, tiresome, routine, mundane, ordinary, monotonous, insipid, dreary, uneventful, boring, wearisome, everyday.
ant. stimulating, interesting, exciting, piquant, striking, arresting.

humid *adj.* damp, moist, muggy, steamy, dank, dewy, misty, vaporous, oozy, watery, wet.
ant. dry, arid, parched, desiccated.

humiliate *v.* mortify, humble, belittle, abash, shame, degrade, chagrin, em-

barrass, discomfit, dishonor, disgrace, snub, put down (*Slang*).
ant. elevate, dignify, honor, exalt, puff up.
humiliation *n.* mortification, abasement, shame, chagrin, ignominy, disgrace, degradation, dishonor, embarrassment, humbling, denigration, put-down (*Slang*).
ant. honor, elevation, exaltation, glorification.
humility *n.* modesty, meekness, docility, humbleness, lowliness, self-abasement, submissiveness, unpretentiousness, shyness, sheepishness, subservience, diffidence, submission.
ant. pride, arrogance, self-assertion, self-importance, pretentiousness, hauteur.
humor *n.* **1** disposition, mood, bent, temperament, set, character, frame, temper, tendency, bias. **2** wit, comedy, comicality. —*v.* accommodate, indulge, pamper, spoil, gratify, mollify, cosset, go along with, coddle, baby.
ant. *v.* cross, contradict, confront.
humorist *n.* wag, wit, joker, comedian, comedienne, comic, farceur, jester, funnyman, prankster, clown, zany, wisecracker (*Slang*), merry-andrew.
humorous *adj.* comical, funny, witty, farcical, droll, amusing, laughable, facetious, jocose, waggish, whimsical, sportive, jocular, comic, risible.
ant. serious, sober, grave, stern, doleful, sad.
hump *n.* protuberance, knob, bump, swelling, mound, bulge, knoll, barrow, hillock, rise, lump.
hunch *n.* premonition, presentiment, intuition, feeling, suspicion, foreboding, intimation, impression, apprehension, sensation. —*v.* arch, hump, bend, huddle, stoop, crouch, bow, curve, squat.
hunger *n.* **1** starvation, famine, voraciousness, famishment, esurience, appetite. **2** desire, yearning, longing, lust, yen, itch, wish, mania, craving, stomach, need, demand. —*v.* crave,

starve, long, yearn, desire, hanker, pine, thirst, itch.
hungry *adj.* **1** *lacking food:* starving, famished, empty, malnourished, voracious, edacious, ravenous, starved, undernourished, hollow. **2** eager, covetous, desirous, avid, greedy, keen, craving, yearning, athirst, needful, insatiable, insatiate.
ant. **1** replete, sated, gorged, surfeited, satiated, anoretic. **2** indifferent, listless, satisfied, averse.
hung up *Slang* **1** delayed, detained, stuck, stalled, checked, impeded, slowed, arrested, held up, stayed, inhibited, handicapped. **2** obsessed, preoccupied, haunted, engrossed, entangled, exercised, fascinated, addicted, devoted, uptight (*Slang*).
ant. 1 expedited, unimpeded. **2** loose.
hunk *n.* chunk, piece, mass, wad, lump, gob, glob, gobbet, bolus, slab, slice, clod.
hunky-dory *adj.* OK, satisfactory, first-rate, fine, topping (*Brit.*), capital, excellent, admirable, splendid, good, pleasing, gratifying, go.
hunt *v.* pursue, seek, chase, search for, look for, reconnoiter, search, stalk, trail, track, shadow. —*n.* search, pursuit, quest, chase, inquiry, investigation, hunting, inquisition.
hunter *n.* sportsman, huntsman, Nimrod, pursuer, stalker.
hurdle *n.* obstacle, difficulty, barrier, fence, impediment, stumblingblock, roadblock, obstruction, hazard, barricade, hindrance, check, snag, wall. —*v.* vault, leap over, clear, surmount, scale, top, cap, leapfrog, jump, overcome, rise above.
hurl *v.* fling, propel, pitch, heave, launch, project, sling, catapult, let fly, toss, cast, throw.
hurly-burly *n.* HUBBUB.
hurried *adj.* hasty, rushed, slap-dash, speedy, swift, quick, headlong, impulsive, cursory, slipshod, superficial, careless, precipitate.
ant. slow, deliberate, dilatory, prolonged, careful, thorough.

hurry v. hasten, accelerate, speed up, quicken, spur, expedite, rush, fly, hustle, scamper, press, drive, urge, step on it. —n. haste, dispatch, precipitateness, speed, dash, rush, expedition, scampering, celerity, alacrity, darting, scurry.
ant. v. delay, slow, detain, impede, retard, check. n. dawdling, delay, slowness, sloth, indolence, sluggishness.
hurt v. 1 injure, harm, damage, wound, impair, mar, cripple, mutilate, torture, pain, ache. 2 offend, insult, wrong, abuse, ill-treat, vex, spite, spoil, distress, plague, victimize. —n. 1 wound, sore, bruise, blow, damage, harm, pain, pang, ache. 2 insult, affront, affliction, irritation, embarrassment, vexation, mortification, sorrow, humiliation.
hurtful adj. damaging, harmful, injurious, noxious, maleficent, baneful, unhealthy, prejudicial, detrimental, deleterious, baleful, mischievous, wounding, pernicious.
ant. beneficial, advantageous, good, helpful, salutary, remedial.
hurtle v. rush, charge, plunge, crash, dash, hurl, collide, lunge, roar, clatter, smash, fling, bump, clash.
husband n. married man, spouse, mate, man. —v. conserve, economize, store, save up, spare, reserve, safeguard, save, hold back, treasure, hoard.
ant. v. waste, squander, lavish, disperse, scatter, dissipate.
hush v. silence, quiet, soothe, mute, muffle, shush, soft-pedal, soften, deaden, allay, subdue, throttle, suppress, calm, mollify. —n. stillness, silence, quiet, quietness, lull, quietude, tranquillity, peacefulness.
husk n. hull, shell, shuck, pod, skin, rind, peel, crust, bark, covering, coating. —v. shell, shuck, strip, peel, decorticate.
husky[1] adj. hoarse, throaty, guttural, rough, harsh, rasping, cracked, raucous, gruff, strident, scraping.

ant. clear, musical, dulcet, soothing, sweet, melodious.
husky[2] adj. strong, muscular, burly, robust, brawny, powerful, beefy, hefty, strapping, stocky, hulking, thickset.
ant. puny, feeble, flabby, slight, weak, frail.
hussy n. baggage, hoyden, minx, wench, jade, wanton, tart.
hustle v. 1 jostle, push, shove, elbow, joggle, buffet, knock, poke, shoulder. 2 goad, spur, incite, urge on, hurry, drive, prod, hasten, accelerate. 3 (Slang) sell or obtain in an aggressive, underhanded manner: traffic, huckster, horse-trade, arrange, fix, swap, push (Slang), wheel and deal (Slang), solicit. —n. activity, bustle, movement, stir, excitement, fuss, flurry, ferment, agitation.
hut n. shack, shanty, cabin, shed, shelter, lean-to, cottage, cot, hovel, dump (Slang).
hutch n. 1 chest, box, locker, coffer, caddie, bin, crate, trunk, cupboard, strongbox. 2 shelter for animals: pen, coop, sty, cote, shed, kennel.
hybrid n. cross, crossbreed, mongrel, composite, mixture, mule, half-breed, half-caste, half-blood, mestizo, métis, mutt (Slang).
hygiene n. sanitation, cleanliness, prophylaxis, salubrity, hygienics, health.
hygienic adj. sanitary, clean, wholesome, salubrious, prophylactic, aseptic, sterile, healthful, germfree, preventive.
ant. polluted, unhealthy, contaminated, infected.
hymn n. anthem, paean, psalm, canticle, chant, chorale, plainsong.
hype Slang v. DECEIVE. —n. FRAUD.
hyperbole n. exaggeration, overstatement, embellishment, puffery, ballyhoo, magnification, amplification, enlargement, fish story.
hypercritical adj. captious, fussy, censorious, faultfinding, carping, finicky, persnickety, exacting, niggling, querulous, disparaging, hairsplitting, finical, nagging.

ant. easygoing, lenient, lax, appreciative, tolerant, indulgent.

hypnotic *adj.* **1** sleep-inducing, soporific, soothing, sedative, somniferous, anodyne, opiate, anesthetic, narcotic. **2** spellbinding, entrancing, mesmerizing, arresting, fascinating, gripping, enchanting, charming, irresistible, engaging.

hypnotize *v.* fascinate, entrance, spellbind, mesmerize, charm, dazzle, transfix, enchant, bewitch, enthrall, overpower, dominate.

hypocrisy *n.* pretense, dissembling, affectation, sham, duplicity, fakery, dissimulation, sanctimony, imposture, counterfeit, feigning, insincerity, disingenuousness, pharisaism. **ant.** sincerity, integrity, candor, forthrightness, honesty, directness.

hypocrite *n.* deceiver, dissembler, pretender, cheat, pharisee, charlatan, impostor, fraud, fake, Pecksniff, Janus.

hypocritical *adj.* insincere, duplicitous, false, deceptive, two-faced, dishonest, dissembling, fraudulent, affected, double-dealing, deceitful, double-faced, Janus-faced, phony (*Slang*), counterfeit, pharasaic. **ant.** genuine, heartfelt, honest, true, faithful.

hypothesis *n.* assumption, proposition, conjecture, presumption, speculation, explanation, theorem, theory, thesis, proposal, supposition, postulate, system, scheme, premise.

hypothetical *adj.* conjectural, assumed, speculative, presumptive, supposed, conditional, theoretical, postulated, theorized, imagined, suppositional, contingent. **ant.** factual, literal, indisputable, confirmed, demonstrable, veritable.

hysteria *n.* frenzy, agitation, delirium, madness, unreason, panic, conniptions.

I

ice *v. Slang* CLINCH.
ice-cold *adj.* ICY.
icky *adj. Slang* repulsive, disgusting, offensive, nasty, sticky, tacky, foul, sickening, distasteful, disagreeable, loathsome.
iconoclast *n.* skeptic, cynic, nihilist, dissenter, nonconformist.
icy *adj.* **1** freezing, frigid, frosty, ice-cold, chilled, glacial, slippery, glassy, cold, numbing, raw, biting, stinging. **2** unfriendly, forbidding, cool, chilly, glacial, coldhearted, unemotional, distant, aloof. **ant. 1** hot, torrid, warming, sizzling, blistering. **2** cordial, warm, emotional, passionate, genial.
idea *n.* thought, conception, impression, concept, notion, opinion, belief, conclusion.
ideal *adj.* **1** imaginary, conceptual, theoretical, abstract, intellectual, fanciful, illusory, unreal, impractical, unattainable, visionary, utopian. **2** perfect, pure, absolute, complete, flawless, faultless, consummate, supreme, excellent, exemplary, model. —*n.* standard, epitome, paragon, nonpareil, exemplar, model, example, pattern. **ant. adj. 1** actual, real, factual, literal, ordinary, commonplace, mundane. **2** imperfect, flawed, limited.
idealism *n.* perfectionism, devotion, dedication, selflessness, utopianism, quixotism, romanticism.

ant. cynicism, selfishness, realism, materialism.

idealist *n.* perfectionist, romantic, dreamer, visionary, utopian.
   ant. materialist, realist, cynic, skeptic.

idealistic *adj.* **1** principled, noble, honorable, right-minded, righteous, upright. **2** unrealistic, unpractical, romatic, visionary, naive, ingenuous, untried.
   ant. **1** mean, unprincipled, low, amoral. **2** practical, down-to-earth, battle-scarred, experienced, cynical.

idealize *v.* exalt, romanticize, deify, ennoble, apotheosize, glorify, magnify, rhapsodize, utopianize.
   ant. disparage, depreciate, degrade, debase, belittle, run down, defame, malign, vilify.

idée fixe OBSESSION.

identical *adj.* alike, same, one, very, selfsame, uniform, indistinguishable, tantamount, equal, equivalent, corresponding, synonymous, twin, duplicate, interchangeable, substitute.
   ant. different, separate, distinct, unlike, opposite, dissimilar, other, diverse, divergent.

identify *v.* recognize, single out, distinguish, determine, place, make out, know, name, specify, verify.

identity *n.* individuality, self, person, oneself, selfness, personality, singularity, uniqueness.

idiocy *n.* foolishness, folly, senselessness, fatuity, absurdity, silliness, craziness, madness, lunacy, stupidity, insanity, imbecility.
   ant. sense, soundness, common sense, intelligence, wisdom, sagacity, acumen.

idiom *n.* **1** expression, phrase, locution, colloquialism. **2** dialect, parlance, jargon, cant, patois, lingo, talk.

idiosyncrasy *n.* peculiarity, quirk, bent, trick, habit, eccentricity, mannerism, trait, mark, characteristic, trademark, shtick (*Slang*).

idiot *n.* fool, simpleton, blockhead, dunce, dummy, nitwit, dimwit

(*Slang*), nincompoop, halfwit, moron, natural, cretin, boob (*Slang*).

idiotic *adj.* senseless, stupid, foolish, fatuous, irrational, asinine, addled, obtuse, feebleminded, imbecilic.
   ant. bright, clever, smart, shrewd, intelligent.

idle *adj.* **1** unused, unoccupied, empty, vacant, inactive, jobless, unemployed, wasted, uncultivated, barren, fallow. **2** lazy, indolent, laggard, slothful, sluggish, shiftless, listless, dawdling, vegetative, vegetable. **3** useless, worthless, insignificant, irrelevant, trivial, unprofitable, fruitless, futile, ineffectual, vain. —*v.* dally, laze, loaf, lounge, loiter, loll, fritter away, while away.
   ant. *adj.* **1** employed, active, productive, operative, occupied. **2** energetic, busy, diligent, hard-working, indefatigable. **3** important, significant, effective, helpful, germane, relevant.

idol *n.* **1** image, statue, icon, effigy, simulacrum, graven image, symbol, fetish. **2** beloved, favorite, god, hero, darling, pet.

idolatrous *adj.* WORSHIPFUL.

idolize *v.* adore, worship, venerate, deify, revere, glorify, honor, admire, love, canonize, apotheosize.

idyllic *adj.* ROMANTIC.

iffy *adj.* uncertain, doubtful, chancy, risky, questionable, problematic, conditional, provisory, contingent.
   ant. certain, sure, settled, foregone, doubtless.

ignite *v.* **1** fire, light, kindle, burn, explode, blow up. **2** excite, stir up, agitate, brew, inflame, inspire.

ignoble *adj.* unworthy, degraded, contemptible, despicable, base, low, mean, inferior, vulgar.
   ant. noble, praiseworthy, admirable, excellent.

ignominious *adj.* dishonorable, disreputable, disgraceful, despicable, degrading, humiliating, shameful.

ant. worthy, creditable, reputable, honorable.

ignominy *n.* DISGRACE.

ignoramus *n.* simpleton, numskull, dunce, illiterate, fool, dolt, dullard, novice, greenhorn.

ignorance *n.* stupidity, dumbness, dullness, denseness, blindness, shallowness, uncomprehension, unenlightenment, benightedness, unawareness, nescience, unfamiliarity, inexperience, innocence.
ant. knowledge, understanding, comprehension, perspicacity, insight, enlightenment.

ignorant *adj.* **1** *lacking knowledge:* uninformed, unversed, stupid, uneducated, unschooled, illiterate, uncomprehending, untutored, unlettered, uncultivated. **2** *lacking awareness:* unaware, dense, obtuse, insensitive, unenlightened, uninitiated, unacquainted, unfamiliar, unknowing, unwitting, unconversant, inexperienced.
ant. **1** informed, intelligent, smart, learned, educated, knowledgeable, enlightened. **2** aware, understanding, knowing, sensitive, experienced.

ignore *v.* disregard, overlook, slight, neglect, pass over, skip, disdain, scorn, cut, snub, ostracize.
ant. acknowledge, recognize, heed, pay attention to.

ilk *n.* KIND².

ill *adj.* **1** sick, unwell, indisposed, ailing, diseased, afflicted, sickly, unhealthy, impaired, invalid, weak. **2** evil, bad, wicked, wrong, iniquitous, harmful, naughty, adverse, unkind, unfavorable, unfriendly, hostile. —*n.* harm, evil, wickedness, depravity, calamity, misfortune, mischief, misery, trouble, affliction, injury, hurt, pain.
ant. *adj.* **1** well, healthy, fine, sound, robust, hale. **2** good, favorable.

ill-advised *adj.* UNWISE.

ill-bred *adj.* RUDE.

ill-considered *adj.* UNWISE.

ill-disposed *adj.* UNFRIENDLY.

illegal *adj.* unlawful, illicit, wrong, criminal, felonious, lawless, illegitimate, unauthorized, prohibited, outlawed, banned, unlicensed, unconstitutional.
ant. legal, licit, lawful, authorized, permitted, sanctioned.

illegality *n.* unlawfulness, illicitness, illegitimacy, criminality, misconduct, malfeasance, wrong, crime, offense, violation.
ant. legality, lawfulness, legitimacy, rightfulness.

illegible *adj.* indecipherable, unreadable, scribbled, cramped, crabbed, unclear, obscure, unintelligible.
ant. legible, clear, plain, readable.

illegitimate *adj.* **1** bastard, unfathered, misbegotten, natural, baseborn. **2** illogical, unsound, spurious, invalid, unreasonable, irregular, improper, unprecedented. **3** unlawful, illicit, unauthorized, lawless.
ant. **2** logical, sound, cogent, valid. **3** lawful, legal.

ill-fated *adj.* UNFORTUNATE.

ill-favored *adj.* UGLY.

ill-founded *adj.* UNFOUNDED.

ill-humored *adj.* ILL-TEMPERED.

illiberal *adj.* NARROW-MINDED.

illicit *adj.* UNLAWFUL.

illimitable *adj.* BOUNDLESS.

ill-mannered *adj.* rude, discourteous, impolite, uncivil, ill-behaved, ill-bred, boorish, insolent, surly, uncouth, crude, unrefined.
ant. courteous, thoughtful, refined, cultivated, polished, suave.

ill-natured *adj.* unpleasant, unkind, unfriendly, malicious, contentious, irascible, spiteful, petulant, cranky, cross, sulky, morose, sullen, sour, dour.
ant. good-natured, kindly, pleasant, genial, amiable, friendly, cheerful, sanguine.

illness *n.* sickness, ailment, disease, malady, indisposition, disorder, complaint, affliction, infirmity.

illogical *adj.* fallacious, untenable, inconsistent, invalid, inconclusive, incorrect, false, senseless, far-fetched, unsound, specious, unreasonable, preposterous, absurd.

ant. logical, valid, correct, sound, reasonable, coherent.

ill-starred *adj.* UNFORTUNATE.

ill-tempered *adj.* cross, angry, ill-natured, ill-humored, irritable, cantankerous, irascible, acrimonious, quarrelsome, testy, sulky, morose, sullen, grouchy.

ant. good-natured, cheerful, pleasant, mild-mannered, genial, benign, sanguine.

ill-timed *adj.* INAPPROPRIATE.

ill-treat *v.* MALTREAT.

ill-treatment *n.* ABUSE.

illuminate *v.* **1** light up, illumine, spotlight, emblaze, brighten, irradiate. **2** elucidate, enlighten, clarify, reveal, explain, illustrate, demonstrate, instruct, edify.

ant. **1** darken, black out. **2** obscure, obfuscate, befog.

illuminating *adj.* revealing, enlightening, clarifying, instructive, illustrative, informative, edifying.

ant. obscuring, confusing, obfuscating, puzzling.

illumination *n.* **1** light, luminescence, florescence, incandescence, radiance, emanation, effulgence, flame, flash, flare, glow, gleam. **2** elucidation, enlightenment, knowledge, explanation, instruction, wisdom, discovery, insight, revelation.

illumine *v.* LIGHTEN.

ill-use *n.* mistreatment, maltreatment, misuse, abuse, ill-usage, mishandling, wrong, oppression, persecution, intimidation, torment, hurt, harm.

illusion *n.* **1** fantasy, imagination, fancy, image, appearance, impression, daydream, vision, apparition, phantasm, phantom, hallucination, will-o'-the-wisp, mirage, chimera. **2** misconception, misbelief, mistake, falsehood, falsity, error, fallacy, deception, delusion.

illusory *adj.* misleading, deceptive, mistaken, false, spurious, sham, delusive, apparent, seeming, ostensible, dreamlike.

ant. real, factual, practical, true, solid, reliable, down-to-earth, genuine, authentic.

illustrate *v.* **1** picture, depict, delineate, portray, represent, draw, adorn. **2** explain, elucidate, demonstrate, clarify, illuminate, make plain, typify, exemplify, embody.

illustration *n.* **1** picture, depiction, image, representation, reproduction, design, drawing. **2** example, case, instance, specimen, clarification, explication, illumination, explanation, comparison, analogy.

illustrious *adj.* famous, famed, renowned, celebrated, acclaimed, eminent, distinguished, remarkable, exalted, noble, splendid, glorious, brilliant.

ant. obscure, lowly, humble, meek, unassuming, mean, ignoble, infamous, notorious.

ill will antipathy, dislike, spite, grudge, bitterness, animosity, malice, hatred, hate, enmity, hostility, antagonism, animus.

ant. good will, friendliness, charity, amiability, congeniality, favor, cordiality.

image *n.* **1** representation, figure, form, picture, effigy, portrait, statue, idol, icon, reflection, appearance. **2** likeness, resemblance, semblance, similitude, counterpart, facsimile, copy, duplication. **3** idea, conception, impression, view, notion, ideal.

imaginary *adj.* unreal, nonexistent, hypothetical, assumed, conceived, fancied, fanciful, invented, fictitious, fictional, fictive, fabulous, ideal, shadowy, visionary, illusory, false, deceptive.

ant. real, actual, factual, true, genuine, known, proven, substantial, tangible.

imagination *n.* creativity, inspiration, originality, invention, inventiveness, ingenuity, enterprise, fertility, conception, thought, fancy, fancifulness, fantasy, vision.

imaginative *adj.* inventive, creative, original, fertile, enterprising, productive, fanciful, extravagant, fantastic, dreamy, visionary.
ant. prosaic, practical, pragmatic, realistic, uninspired, uninventive, imitative.

imagine *v.* conceive, picture, envision, visualize, invent, create, fancy, fabricate, devise, apprehend, realize, think, believe, surmise, assume, suppose, conjecture, hypothesize.

imbecile *n.* fool, simpleton, idiot, moron, cretin, half-wit, blockhead, dotard.

imbecility *n.* stupidity, idiocy, dullness, cretinism, feeble-mindedness, foolishness, irrationality, fatuity, silliness, incompetency.
ant. intelligence, soundness, reasonableness, understanding, comprehension, judgment, wisdom, sagacity, perspicacity.

imbibe *v.* drink, swallow, consume, partake, ingest, sip, lap, gulp, guzzle, quaff, swill, souse (*Slang*), tipple, swig, booze.

imbiber *n.* drinker, guzzler, quaffer, tippler, tosspot, toper, boozer, sponge, sot, souse (*Slang*), drunkard, inebriate.
ant. nondrinker, teetotaler, abstainer.

imbue *v.* **1** wet, saturate, infuse, steep, bathe, impregnate, permeate, pervade. **2** instill, ingrain, color, suffuse, animate, inspire, inculcate, indoctrinate, train, teach, brainwash, propagandize.

imitate *v.* copy, reproduce, simulate, repeat, reflect, parallel, duplicate, emulate, follow, echo, mirror, impersonate, mimic, ape, parrot.

imitation *n.* copy, duplicate, facsimile, likeness, resemblance, simulation, reproduction, replica, parody, deception, fraud, forgery, counterfeit. —*adj.* copied, simulated, reproduced, artificial, pseudo, feigned,

fake, false, counterfeit, spurious, ersatz, phony (*Slang*).
ant. *n.* original, prototype, model, the real McCoy. *adj.* authentic, original, pure, genuine, real, true, valid, unadulterated.

imitative *adj.* copied, simulated, reproduced, pseudo, counterfeit, bogus, quasi, derivative, secondhand, mimetic, mock, apish, parrotlike.

immaculate *adj.* **1** clean, spotless, unsullied, stainless, unsoiled, unblemished, untarnished, snowy, spick-and-span. **2** pure, irreproachable, faultless, flawless, unblemished, unsullied, perfect, impeccable, undefiled, sinless, guiltless, virtuous, innocent, virgin, chaste.
ant. **1** dirty, unclean, spotted, soiled, stained, tarnished. **2** impure, imperfect, tainted, corrupt, defiled, defamed, vile, sinful, guilty.

immanent *adj.* INHERENT.

immaterial *adj.* UNIMPORTANT.

immature *adj.* **1** unripe, inexperienced, unfledged, green, tender, raw, callow, young, precocious, juvenile, adolescent, childish, puerile, sophomoric, half-baked. **2** primitive, incomplete, unready, crude, inchoate, incipient, unformed, imperfect, undeveloped.
ant. **1** ripe, mature, adult, grown, mellow, aged. **2** developed, mature, complete, well-rounded, advanced, sophisticated.

immeasurable *adj.* BOUNDLESS.

immediate *adj.* **1** direct, primary, closest, next, nearest, contiguous, adjacent. **2** current, present, instant, instantaneous, prompt, speedy, sudden, swift, timely, punctual.
ant. **1** indirect, separated, removed, distant.

immediately *adv.* instantly, at once, right away, straightway, forthwith, now, promptly, presently, instantaneously, suddenly, speedily, closely, directly, *tout de suite*.
ant. shortly, soon, by and by, after a while, anon, later.

immense *adj.* huge, vast, great, enormous, tremendous, massive, mighty, gigantic, prodigious, colossal, mammoth, extensive, boundless, measureless, infinite.
ant. small, little, tiny, minute, puny.

immensity *n.* vastness, hugeness, greatness, largeness, stupendousness, boundlessness, infinity, infinitude.

imminent *adj.* immediate, coming, impending, approaching, near, at hand, looming, threatening.
ant. delayed, distant, far-off, remote.

immobile *adj.* STABLE.

immobilize *v.* FIX.

immoderate *adj.* extreme, excessive, inordinate, intemperate, extravagant, exorbitant, unreasonable, unbridled, unrestrained.
ant. moderate, restrained, mild, temperate, reasonable, judicious.

immodest *adj.* indelicate, indecorous, coarse, brazen, gross, indecent, shameless, bold, impudent, unreserved, forward, boasting, proud, vain.
ant. decent, decorous, modest, sober, restrained, genteel, unpretentious, humble, bashful.

immolate *v.* SACRIFICE.

immolation *n.* sacrifice, offering, oblation, killing, butchering, slaughter, holocaust, hecatomb, suttee.

immoral *adj.* wrong, bad, unprincipled, unethical, unscrupulous, corrupt, wicked, vicious, evil, sinful, impure, lewd, licentious, loose, depraved, self-indulgent, abandoned, dissipated, dissolute.
ant. moral, good, right, ethical, decent, honest, high-minded, noble, pure, virtuous.

immorality *n.* wrong, dishonesty, corruption, villainy, vice, sin, wickedness, impurity, venality, criminality, depravity, degeneracy, lewdness, profligacy, debauchery.
ant. purity, goodness, honesty, lawfulness, restraint, virtue.

immortal *adj.* deathless, eternal, undying, imperishable, endless, indestruct-

ible, immutable, ageless, timeless, infinite, lasting, enduring, abiding, unending, perpetual, ceaseless, everlasting. —*n.* god, goddess, deity, demigod, divinity.
ant. *adj.* mortal, perishable, ephemeral, transitory, temporary, fleeting, passing, forgettable.

immortality *n.* 1 deathlessness, imperishability, indestructability, incorruptibility, eternity, infinity, perpetuity. 2 celebrity, fame, glory, enshrinement, canonization, commemoration, memory.

immune *adj.* exempt, unsusceptible, invulnerable, free, protected, clear, safe, privileged.
ant. liable, susceptible, vulnerable, exposed.

immunity *n.* exemption, insusceptibility, clearance, protection, release, freedom, impunity, license, charter, prerogative, right, liberty, privilege.
ant. liability, susceptibility, vulnerability, exposure, openness, proneness, inclination, responsibility.

immure *v.* IMPRISON.

immutable *adj.* UNALTERABLE.

imp *n.* devil, demon, hobgoblin, elf, gnome, pixie, sprite, troublemaker, rogue, rascal, urchin, brat, minx, scamp, tyke.

impact *n.* 1 contact, blow, touch, impression, stroke, collision, percussion, crash, shock, clash, smash. 2 influence, effect, brunt, force, power, pressure.

impair *v.* injure, damage, harm, hurt, hinder, obstruct, vitiate, worsen, spoil, mar, cripple, ruin, destroy.

impale *v.* spear, spike, pierce, gore, stab, perforate, puncture, lance, stick, gouge, run through, transfix.

impart *v.* communicate, tell, relate, inform, convey, report, transmit, make known, disclose, divulge, confide, reveal.

impartial *adj.* unbiased, disinterested, nonpartisan, just, fair, equitable, unprejudiced, evenhanded, neutral, detached, objective.

ant. biased, partisan, partial, unjust, discriminatory, subjective.

impartiality *n.* fairness, justice, justness, equity, equality, evenhandedness, disinterestedness, nonpartisanship, neutrality, detachment, objectivity.

ant. bias, prejudice, partisanship, unfairness, favoritism, subjectivity.

impasse *n.* dead end, blind alley, cul-de-sac, stop, barrier, deadlock, stalemate, bottleneck, block, morass, snag, obstacle, quandary, predicament.

impassioned *adj.* fervent, ardent, animated, passionate, intense, vehement, stirring, exciting, vivacious, enthusiastic, zealous, raving, burning, fiery.

ant. reserved, cool, calm, placid, composed, quiet, tranquil, restrained.

impassive *adj.* unmoved, phlegmatic, stoical, stolid, insensible, imperturbable, unexcitable, reserved, self-contained.

ant. responsive, theatrical, dramatic, expressive, emotional, demonstrative.

impatience *n.* restiveness, agitation, irritability, anxiety, impetuosity, uneasiness, haste, precipitation, eagerness, restlessness, longing, expectancy, suspense.

ant. patience, calm, composure, control, forbearance, tolerance.

impatient *adj.* restless, restive, nervous, agitated, fidgety, fussy, chafing, peevish, irritable, impulsive, vehement, brusque, abrupt, rash, reckless, impetuous, hasty, hurried, precipitate, eager.

ant. patient, restful, quiet, calm, cool, composed, easygoing, imperturbable, tolerant.

impeccable *adj.* flawless, faultless, immaculate, spotless, stainless, unblemished, irreproachable, perfect, precise, pure, refined, polished, excellent.

ant. flawed, imperfect, defective, impaired, compromised, blameworthy.

impecunious *adj.* POOR.

impede *v.* hinder, hold back, obstruct, thwart, hamper, check, block, clog, cramp, balk, encumber, restrict, retard, slow, delay, frustrate, inhibit.

ant. aid, help, assist, facilitate, abet, support, encourage, expedite, promote, further.

impediment *n.* barrier, encumbrance, hindrance, bar, obstacle, obstruction, interference, blockage, delay, restriction, drawback, snag, difficulty.

ant. aid, help, assistance, support, benefit, advantage, relief, encouragement.

impel *v.* push, drive, press, prod, force, move, goad, spur, actuate, animate, stimulate, induce, incite, prompt, compel, urge, persuade, motivate.

ant. restrain, check, repulse, balk, rebuff, discourage.

impend *v.* THREATEN.

impending *adj.* imminent, coming, approaching, near, forthcoming, looming, brewing, destined, menacing, threatening.

impenetrable *adj.* incomprehensible, unfathomable, puzzling, baffling, insoluble, inexplicable, inscrutable, impervious, hidden, mysterious, enigmatic.

ant. comprehensible, understandable, clear, transparent, accessible.

impenitent *adj.* unrepentant, remorseless, uncontrite, unashamed, unapologetic, incorrigible, hardened, obdurate, defiant.

ant. penitent, contrite, shameful, apologetic, remorseful, regretful, humbled.

imperative *adj.* obligatory, binding, compulsory, mandatory, required, demanded, unavoidable, requisite, necessary, insistent, pressing, exigent, critical, urgent, decisive.

ant. inessential, unnecessary, optional, discretionary, voluntary.

imperfect *adj.* defective, impaired, flawed, faulty, deficient, marred, incomplete, unfinished, undeveloped, rudimentary, crude, unsound, limited, inferior.

ant. perfect, flawless, thorough, absolute, ideal.

imperfection *n.* deficiency, inadequacy, defectiveness, incompleteness, weakness, failing, defect, fault, flaw, lack, blemish, peccadillo.

ant. perfection, faultlessness, consummation, completeness, excellence, advantage.

imperil *v.* endanger, jeopardize, peril, hazard, risk, expose.

ant. protect, guard, safeguard, preserve, care for, secure.

imperious *adj.* domineering, commanding, overbearing, magisterial, lordly, autocratic, arbitrary, supercilious, peremptory, haughty, arrogant, despotic, dictatorial, tyrannical, bossy.

ant. humble, pliant, submissive, subservient, servile, obsequious, abject.

impermanent *adj.* temporary, transient, passing, fleeting, fugitive, ephemeral, transitory, elusive, provisional.

ant. permanent, lasting, stable, enduring, solid.

impersonal *adj.* **1** detached, disinterested, impartial, dispassionate, neutral, objective. **2** unsympathetic, cold, remote, formal, bureaucratic.

ant. 1 subjective, partisan, committed, personal, intimate, emotional. **2** friendly, warm, open, outgoing, accessible, sympathetic.

impersonate *v.* imitate, represent, act, enact, play, mimic, ape, mock.

impertinence *n.* INSOLENCE.

impertinent *adj.* impudent, rude, disrespectful, surly, insolent, pert, saucy, cheeky, brazen, presumptuous, audacious, nervy (*Slang*).

ant. civil, respectful, courteous, obliging, conciliating, complaisant.

imperturbable *adj.* unexcitable, unruffled, unflappable, unemotional, calm, nerveless, dispassionate.

ant. excitable, agitated, frantic, panicky, upset.

impervious *adj.* IMPENETRABLE.

impetuous *adj.* hasty, precipitate, headlong, rash, brash, impulsive, spontaneous, energetic, violent, fierce, vehement, headstrong, uncontrollable, impatient.

ant. prudent, cautious, careful, steady, composed, patient, hesitant, considered, calculated.

impetus *n.* stimulus, momentum, impulse, spur, motive, urge, incentive, push.

impinge *v.* strike, collide, touch, hit, jolt, push, thrust, intrude, infringe, encroach, trespass.

impious *adj.* irreverent, irreligious, ungodly, blasphemous, sacrilegious, iconoclastic, disrespectful, profane.

ant. pious, devout, reverent, respectful.

impish *adj.* mischievous, playful, elfin, puckish, prankish, rascally, naughty, annoying, vexatious, troublesome.

implacable *adj.* unappeasable, insatiable, relentless, inexorable, inflexible, unbending, uncompromising, irreconcilable, unrelenting, unforgiving, merciless.

ant. flexible, yielding, compromising, tolerant, lenient, merciful.

implausible *adj.* unbelievable, improbable, unreasonable, unlikely, doubtful, questionable, suspect, inconceivable, incredible, preposterous, absurd.

ant. believable, credible, plausible, reasonable, likely.

implement *n.* utensil, tool, instrument, apparatus, appliance, gadget, device, contrivance. —*v.* supplement, enforce, enable, expedite, effect, perform, execute, carry out, bring about, realize, achieve, accomplish, fulfill.

ant. *v.* hinder, hamper, impede, delay, weaken.

implementation *n.* execution, effectuation, performance, discharge, accomplishment, commission, attainment, achievement.

implicate *v.* involve, connect, associate, concern, entangle, impute, imply, incriminate, accuse, inculpate, blame, charge.

implication *n.* intimation, indication, import, purport, suggestion, connotation, overtone, hint, drift, tenor, innuendo, insinuation, assumption, presumption, supposition.

implicit *adj.* **1** unspoken, unexpressed, tacit, presupposed, denoted, signified, contained, latent, ingrained, immanent, intrinsic, inherent, potential. **2** absolute, unreserved, unconditional, unhesitating, undoubting, unequivocal, unqualified, firm, fixed, steadfast.
ant. 1 explicit, stated, expressed, specific, patent, obvious. **2** qualified, conditional.

implied *adj.* understood, indicated, tacit, implicit, suggested, presumed, intimated, indirect, insinuated, between the lines.

implore *v.* entreat, beseech, plead, beg, solicit, importune, crave, urge, pray for, supplicate.

imply *v.* suggest, intimate, hint, insinuate, indicate, connote, allude, import, signify, mean, denote, infer.

impolite *adj.* discourteous, rude, illbred, uncivil, unmannerly, ungracious, unrefined, unpolished.
ant. polite, courteous, well-bred, mannerly.

impolitic *adj.* TACTLESS.

importance *n.* significance, weight, moment, import, concern, consequence, seriousness, stress, emphasis.

important *adj.* substantial, considerable, weighty, serious, major, powerful, imposing, notable, valuable, prominent, influential, significant, meaningful, decisive, critical.
ant. unimportant, insignificant, slight, minor, weak, trivial, petty.

importunate *adj.* insistent, demanding, persistent, eager, officious, exigent, pressing, urgent, troublesome.

impose *v.* **1** place, put, lay, set, assign, appoint, prescribe, exact, demand, force, saddle, encumber, burden, inflict. **2** intrude, presume, encroach,

trouble, bother, take advantage, thrust, foist, butt in (*Slang*), domineer, bully.

imposing *adj.* grand, impressive, massive, striking, towering, lofty, monumental, magnificent, eminent, exalted, commanding, stately, majestic.
ant. insignificant, ordinary, petty, poor, mean.

impossible *adj.* inconceivable, unthinkable, unreasonable, unimaginable, incredible, unreal.
ant. conceivable, reasonable, likely, plausible.

impostor *n.* pretender, impersonator, deceiver, bluff, hypocrite, trickster, charlatan, fraud, cheat, counterfeit, phony (*Slang*).

impotent *adj.* powerless, weak, feeble, frail, enervated, exhausted, incapacitated, ineffectual, defenseless, incapable, unproductive.

impound *v.* IMPRISON.

impoverished *adj.* poor, indigent, destitute, poverty-stricken, bankrupt, broke.
ant. prosperous, well-off, rich, monied, affluent.

impracticable *adj.* IMPRACTICAL.

impractical *adj.* unrealistic, unfeasible, unworkable, impracticable, inexpedient, unviable, inoperable, theoretical, speculative, imaginative, abstract, far-fetched, ideal, quixotic, romantic, starry-eyed, romantic.
ant. realistic, practical, sensible, pragmatic, viable, prosaic, down-to-earth.

imprecation *n.* curse, malediction, anathema, execration, profanity, denunciation, vilification.

impregnable *adj.* unyielding, unassailable, tenable, secure, fast, redoubtable, invulnerable, invincible, unconquerable.
ant. vulnerable, pregnable, exposed, open.

impregnate *v.* fertilize, inseminate, fecundate, fructify, engender, beget, get with child.

impress *v.* **1** imprint, mark, indent,

stamp, press, print, seal, sign, engrave, shape, mold. **2** affect, touch, strike, reach, interest, influence, sway, move, stir, excite.

impression *n.* **1** mark, imprint, stamp, print, seal, brand, figure, trace, indentation, mold. **2** effect, influence, impact, sensation, emotion, idea, view, conception, opinion, sense, notion, hunch, fancy, supposition, remembrance, recollection.

impressionable *adj.* sensitive, responsive, receptive, emotional, susceptible, vulnerable, inexperienced, immature, ingenuous, naive.
ant. insensitive, hardened, jaded, blasé.

impressionistic *adj.* subjective, evocative, subtle, suggestive, vague, imprecise, sketchy, hazy, delicate, moody.
ant. objective, factual, realistic, precise, specific, detailed.

impressive *adj.* effective, convincing, serious, remarkable, admirable, grand, magnificent, splendid, wondrous, inspiring, profound, solemn, grave, awesome, overpowering, forcible, striking.
ant. unimpressive, unimportant, commonplace, plain, ordinary, slight, shallow, petty, trivial.

imprimatur *n.* APPROVAL.

imprint *v.* mark, stamp, press, impress, seal, sign, engrave, reproduce. —*n.* **1** *physical mark:* mark, stamp, seal, sign, indentation, character, figure. **2** *impression on the mind:* impression, effect, indication, impact, influence.

imprison *v.* jail, incarcerate, immure, impound, commit, lock up, trammel, confine, constrain, restrain, retain, detain, hold, keep, inclose.
ant. liberate, free, release, emancipate, discharge.

improbable *adj.* unlikely, rare, implausible, uncommon, doubtful, questionable, chancy, risky.
ant. likely, plausible, reasonable, common, apparent, evident.

impromptu *adj.* improvised, extemporaneous, extemporary, ad-lib, make-

shift, unrehearsed, offhand, unpremeditated, spontaneous, off the cuff.
ant. rehearsed, prepared, planned, considered, deliberate.

improper *adj.* unsuitable, inappropriate, unfit, inapt, unbecoming, unseemly, questionable, suggestive, offensive, indecorous, indelicate, indecent, off-color, lewd.
ant. suitable, proper, apt, right, fitting, correct, becoming, seemly, conventional, decent.

impropriety *n.* slip, mistake, blunder, gaucherie, ineptitude, oversight, inadvertence, gaffe, faux pas.

improve *v.* better, ameliorate, benefit, help, enhance, advance, promote, polish, purify, refine, reform, revise, amend, correct, right, rectify.
ant. impair, worsen, obstruct, vitiate, weaken, damage, debase.

improvement *n.* betterment, enrichment, amelioration, enhancement, advancement, promotion, reform, correction, amendment, reconstruction.
ant. decline, debasement, ruination, degeneration.

improvise *v.* extemporize, ad-lib, contrive, devise, wing it (*Slang*), concoct, hatch, make do, dream up, invent, originate.

imprudent *adj.* UNWISE.

impudence *n.* INSOLENCE.

impudent *adj.* insolent, rude, impertinent, forward, saucy, bold, brazen, presumptuous, cheeky, insulting, disrespectful.
ant. respectful, courteous, well-behaved, modest, timid, retiring, self-effacing.

impugn *v.* challenge, attack, oppose, assail, deny, negate, rebut, contradict, dispute, call in question, question.
ant. support, defend, advocate, authenticate.

impulse *n.* urge, stimulus, spur, itch, drive, instinct, desire, motive, inclination, penchant, propensity, need.

impulsive *adj.* rash, impetuous, excitable, emotional, spontaneous, unpremeditated, thoughtless, imprudent, incautious, hasty, sudden, abrupt, precipitate.

ant. cautious, considered, prudent, deliberate, premeditated.

impure *adj.* **1** dirty, unclean, foul, filthy, contaminated, polluted. **2** unchaste, immodest, loose, immoral, coarse, gross, unclean, smutty, indecent, lewd, obscene.

ant. 1 clean, spotless, immaculate. **2** chaste, pure, moral, decent, wholesome.

impurity *n.* pollutant, contaminant, adulteration.

imputation *n.* INSINUATION.

impute *v.* attribute, ascribe, assign, credit, refer, arrogate, allege, imply, insinuate, slur, reproach, blame, brand, charge, denounce.

in *adj.* CURRENT.

inability *n.* incapability, incapacity, weakness, impotence, powerlessness, incompetence, ineptitude, unskillfulness, clumsiness.

ant. ability, capacity, talent, potential, competence, power.

inaccuracy *n.* error, fault, mistake, slip, incorrectness, miscalculation, misinterpretation, typo.

inaccurate *adj.* unexact, imprecise, incorrect, faulty, erroneous, wrong, careless, loose, sloppy.

ant. accurate, precise, exact, correct.

inaction *n.* immobility, rest, standstill, inertia, suspension, stagnation, idleness, desuetude.

ant. activity, mobility, motion, fluidity, movement.

inactive *adj.* immobile, inert, motionless, stationary, inoperative, stagnant, quiescent, idle, dormant, torpid, passive, dilatory.

ant. energetic, active, busy, dynamic,

inadequate *adj.* insufficient, deficient, wanting, lacking, incomplete, incommensurate, unequal, unqualified, incompetent, unfit, unsatisfactory, imperfect, perfunctory, meager, scant, slight.

ant. ample, sufficient, competent, capable, fit, satisfactory.

inadvertent *adj.* unintentional, accidental, unintended, fortuitous, chance, thoughtless, inattentive, negligent, unmindful, unobservant, inconsiderate, careless.

ant. intentional, deliberate, purposeful, planned, calculated, careful.

inane *adj.* foolish, senseless, pointless, insignificant, trivial, fatuous, silly, ridiculous, absurd, empty, vapid, insipid, banal, bland, jejune.

ant. meaningful, significant, serious, profound, weighty.

inanity *n.* foolishness, silliness, absurdity, frivolity, folly, fatuity, imbecility.

inapplicable *adj.* irrelevant, unsuitable, unfitting, inapposite, impertinent, inconsistent, incompatible.

ant. appropriate, suitable, pertinent, relevant.

inapposite *adj.* IRRELEVANT.

inappreciable *adj.* NEGLIGIBLE.

inappropriate *adj.* unsuitable, inapt, unfit, incongruous, malapropos, discordant, improper, ill-timed, unseemly, tasteless.

ant. suitable, apt, appropriate, becoming, proper.

inapt *adj.* **1** INAPPROPRIATE. **2** INEPT.

inarticulate *adj.* incoherent, unintelligible, tongue-tied, garbled, indistinct, nonverbal.

ant. well-spoken, clear, articulate, distinct, intelligible, verbal, glib.

inattentive *adj.* unmindful, unobservant, unaware, absent-minded, distracted, dreamy, negligent, remiss, heedless, careless, inconsiderate, tactless.

ant. observant, aware, considerate, courteous.

inaugurate *v.* **1** install, induct, invest, instate, commission. **2** commence, begin, start, institute, initiate, originate, launch, activate, open, premiere.

inauguration *n.* **1** installation, induction, investiture, initiation, swearing-in. **2** commencement, beginning, opening, debut, inception, institution, premiere.

inauspicious *adj.* UNLUCKY.

inborn *adj.* congenital, inbred, innate, instinctive, native, natural, indigenous, inherited, ingrained, inherent, intrinsic.
ant. acquired, nurtured, foreign, extrinsic.

incalculable *adj.* immeasurable, countless, innumerable, infinite, numberless, inestimable, untold, unknown, enormous, limitless, immense.

incapable *adj.* unable, unfit, handicapped, inadequate, ineffective, inept, incompetent, powerless, unqualified.
ant. capable, competent, efficient, qualified, fit.

incapacitated *adj.* disabled, handicapped, crippled, lame, maimed, debilitated, exhausted, weakened, deprived, helpless, powerless, incapable, unfit.

incarcerate *v.* jail, imprison, immure, impound, lock up, commit, confine, restrain, retain, detain, hold, keep.

incarnate *v.* TYPIFY.

incautious *adj.* rash, headstrong, brash, reckless, careless, thoughtless, unwary, imprudent, injudicious, indiscreet, impolitic.
ant. cautious, wary, careful, considered, deliberate, prudent, discreet.

incendiary *adj.* provocative, inflammatory, rousing, rabble-rousing, factious, subversive, instigative, seditious.

incensed *adj.* enraged, angry, maddened, furious, inflamed, excited, provoked, exasperated, irritated, vexed, ireful, annoyed.

incentive *n.* motivation, motive, stimulus, spur, goad, provocation, instigation, incitement, mainspring, ground, cause, encouragement, enticement, inducement, reason, consideration.

inception *n.* start, beginning, commencement, initiation, outset, opening, origin, debut, inauguration.
ant. end, finish, close, conclusion, termination, denouement.

incertitude *n.* AMBIVALENCE.

incessant *adj.* ceaseless, constant, continuous, persistent, unending, perpetual, interminable, uninterrupted, unremitting, unrelenting, relentless.
ant. intermittent, occasional, periodic, recurrent, sporadic.

inchoate *adj.* INCIPIENT.

incident *n.* event, occurrence, episode, act, affair, happening, circumstance, adventure, experience. —*adj.* contingent, belonging, connected, linked, related, associated, dependent, accessory, subordinate, liable, likely.

incidental *adj.* **1** dependent, contingent, subject to, concomitant, associated, relating, liable, possible, occasional, eventual. **2** accidental, chance, fortuitous, casual, circumstantial, irregular, parenthetical, unimportant, nonessential, secondary, minor, subordinate.

incidentally *adv.* by the way, in passing, parenthetically, apropos, by chance, accidentally, fortuitously.

incipient *adj.* beginning, commencing, initial, elementary, rudimentary, inchoate, nascent, budding, embryonic.

incision *n.* cut, gash, slash, slit, penetration, section, operation.

incisive *adj.* acute, penetrating, piercing, sharp, keen, clear-cut, trenchant, biting, severe, distinct, direct, decisive, vigorous, bold.
ant. dull, dense, superficial, vague, bland.

incite *v.* instigate, stimulate, prompt, induce, encourage, urge, exhort, work up, prod, spur, goad, egg on, stir up, provoke, foment, arouse, inflame.
ant. restrain, dampen, deter, dishearten, dissuade.

inciter *n.* agitator, instigator, provoker, fomenter, incendiary, firebrand, provocateur, rabble-rouser.

incivility *n.* disrespect, impudence, discourtesy, impoliteness, unmannerliness, rudeness, coarseness, boorishness, uncouthness.

inclement *adj.* rough, harsh, raw, bitter, severe, rigorous, stormy, tempestuous, violent, nasty.
ant. mild, pleasant, temperate.

inclination *n.* tendency, disposition, penchant, bent, set, propensity, proclivity, predilection, stomach, partiality, preference, liking, taste, desire, fancy.

incline *v.* slant, slope, decline, descend, lean, skew, cant, bank, tilt, veer, bend, tip, diverge, deviate.

inclined *adj.* likely, apt, disposed, liable, prone, minded, willing, predisposed, partial, favorable.

include *v.* contain, comprise, involve, have, hold, embrace, encompass, comprehend, subsume, cover, admit, take in, embody, incorporate.
ant. exclude, preclude, eliminate, omit, debar.

incognito *adj.* ANONYMOUS.

incoherent *adj.* unintelligible, unclear, illogical, confused, muddled, rambling, wild, irrational, disjointed, disconnected, inconsistent, inarticulate.
ant. plain, clear, coherent, orderly, articulate.

incommode *v.* DISTURB.

incomparable *adj.* MATCHLESS.

incompatible *adj.* irreconcilable, unadapted, unsuitable, incongruent, discrepant, inharmonious, discordant, incongruous, unsympathetic, contradictory, opposed, antagonistic.
ant. compatible, appropriate, harmonious, congenial, alike, sympathetic.

incompetence *n.* inability, ineptitude, inefficiency, incapacity, inadequacy, insufficiency, unskillfulness.
ant. competence, proficiency, ability, skill.

incompetent *adj.* incapable, unfit, inadequate, ineffectual, unskilled, unqualified, inept, unhandy, maladroit, bungling.

ant. competent, skillful, expert, proficient, deft.

incomplete *adj.* unfinished, undone, half-finished, undeveloped, partial, wanting, fragmentary, defective, deficient, imperfect, sketchy, unpolished.
ant. whole, complete, finished, integral, unified.

incomprehensible *adj.* unintelligible, unfathomable, unimaginable, inconceivable, indecipherable, illegible, inscrutable, obscure, enigmatic, mysterious.
ant. understandable, clear, apparent, evident, obvious, manifest.

inconceivable *adj.* unthinkable, unimaginable, unbelievable, unlikely, improbable, unheard-of, incredible, strange, extraordinary, staggering, fantastic.
ant. believable, likely, credible, reasonable, plausible.

inconclusive *adj.* indecisive, indefinite, ambiguous, vague, undemonstrated, unconvincing, unpersuasive, unsettled, unverified, open.

incongruent *adj.* INCONGRUOUS.

incongruity *n.* DISPARITY.

incongruous *adj.* discordant, incongruent, inharmonious, clashing, ill-sorted, ill-suited, disparate, mismatched, unsuitable, unfit, unbecoming, inappropriate, discrepant, absurd, grotesque.
ant. appropriate, becoming, consistent, harmonious.

inconsequential *adj.* insignificant, unimportant, unessential, immaterial, worthless, negligible, irrelevant, trivial, petty, slight, flimsy.
ant. important, weighty, significant, far-reaching.

inconsiderable *adj.* TRIVIAL.

inconsiderate *adj.* thoughtless, selfish, negligent, careless, tactless, uncharitable, self-centered, rude, uncivil.
ant. considerate, thoughtful, attentive, concerned.

inconsistency *n.* contradiction, disagreement, discrepancy, incongruity, incompatibility, illogic, variance, vacillation, instability.

inconsistent *adj.* **1** incompatible, incongruent, discrepant, incoherent, unbalanced, self-contradictory, contrary, opposed. **2** erratic, changeable, volatile, vacillating, inconstant, capricious, fickle, fanciful.
ant. 1 coherent, orderly, uniform, homogeneous. **2** uniform, steady, reliable, stable, unchanging.

inconsonant *adj.* INHARMONIOUS.

inconspicuous *adj.* unremarkable, unobtrusive, unostentatious, retiring, unassuming, indistinct, dim, faint, undiscernible, unobserved.
ant. clear, obvious, visible, marked, noticeable.

inconstant *adj.* changeable, variable, vacillating, erratic, unstable, unreliable, perfidious, capricious, fickle, giddy.
ant. constant, steadfast, reliable, steady.

incontestable *adj.* UNDENIABLE.

incontrovertible *adj.* UNDENIABLE.

inconvenience *n.* awkwardness, annoyance, nuisance, disturbance, disruption, trouble, fuss, trial, bother, unwieldiness, encumbrance. —*v.* trouble, upset, disturb, discommode, bother, annoy, put out.

inconvenient *adj.* bothersome, annoying, troublesome, inadvisable, untimely, inopportune, awkward, unmanageable, cumbersome, unwieldy.
ant. convenient, handy, helpful.

incorporate *v.* include, take in, involve, cover, embody, incarnate, combine, unite, consolidate, subsume, compound, blend, mix, merge.

incorporeal *adj.* SPIRITUAL.

incorrect *adj.* **1** inaccurate, inexact, imprecise, faulty, erroneous, untrue, false, wrong. **2** unsuitable, unfit, inappropriate, unbecoming, unseemly, improper, ill-chosen.
ant. 1 accurate, exact, faultless, right, true. **2** proper, decorous, conventional, fastidious.

incorrigible *adj.* helpless, hopeless,

hardened, chronic, inveterate, shameless, incurable, irremediable, irreparable.

incorruptible *adj.* trustworthy, honest, conscientious, upright, blameless, impeccable, irreproachable, unimpeachable, righteous.
ant. corrupt, dishonest, venal.

increase *v.* grow, enlarge, add to, develop, expand, extend, dilate, distend, inflate, swell, multiply, proliferate, burgeon, intensify, augment, amplify, raise, magnify, escalate, prolong. —*n.* **1** growth, development, enlargement, augmentation, expansion, extension, addition. **2** rise, increment, accretion, accrual, margin, interval, spread, gain, profit, benefit.
ant. *v.* diminish, lessen, decrease, shrink, dwindle, reduce, cut, condense, abridge. *n.* **1** decrease, contraction, diminution, reduction. **2** decline, decrease, reduction, loss, drop.

incredible *adj.* unbelievable, inconceivable, implausible, improbable, doubtful, questionable, nonsensical, absurd, far-fetched, extraordinary, marvelous.

incredulous *adj.* disbelieving, skeptical, doubtful, dubious, distrustful, suspicious.
ant. gullible, unsuspecting, naive, ingenuous.

increment *n.* increase, addition, supplement, accumulation, accretion, growth, enlargement, gain, profit, benefit.

incriminate *v.* ACCUSE.

inculcate *v.* instill, infuse, imbue, implant, impart, instruct, teach, indoctrinate, enlighten, inspire, catechize.

incumbent *adj.* obligatory, binding, imperative, necessary, unavoidable, exigent, pressing, persistent. —*n.* officeholder, occupant, holdover.

incur *v.* contract, acquire, catch, bring upon oneself, expose oneself, subject oneself, provoke, arouse.

incursion *n.* infiltration, inroad, foray,

raid, sortie, invasion, assault, attack, infringement, trespass, violation.

indebted *adj.* obligated, beholden, obliged, bound, liable, accountable, responsible.

indebtedness *n.* obligation, liability, responsibility, gratitude.

indecency *n.* impropriety, indecorum, rudeness, discourtesy, incivility, offensiveness, bawdiness, lewdness, unwholesomeness, immorality.

indecent *adj.* improper, indecorous, indelicate, unbecoming, unseemly, offensive, immodest, obscene, licentious, lewd, coarse, dirty, filthy, distasteful, improper, immoral. **ant.** decorous, proper, befitting, appropriate, delicate, modest, respectable.

indecisive *adj.* **1** inconclusive, unconfirmed, questionable, doubtful, uneventful, unimportant. **2** hesitant, irresolute, vacillating, undecided, wishy-washy, weak, spineless. **ant.** **1** conclusive, clear-cut, definitive, final. **2** positive, determined, unhesitant, summary.

indeed *adv.* truly, really, veritably, actually, genuinely, undeniably, admittedly, certainly, positively, absolutely.

indefatigable *adj.* tireless, energetic, untiring, unflagging, unfaltering, hardworking, vigorous, diligent, dogged, persevering, unyielding. **ant.** sluggish, laggard, lackadaisical, reluctant.

indefensible *adj.* inexcusable, unjustifiable, unsupportable, unwarrantable, unforgivable, unpardonable, faulty, wrong. **ant.** justifiable, defensible, sound, reasonable, legitimate.

indefinable *adj.* indescribable, unspecific, vague, dim, obscure, subtle, ambiguous, equivocal, confusing. **ant.** clear, explainable, straightforward.

indefinite *adj.* imprecise, inexact, indistinct, loose, lax, uncertain, vague,
inexplicit, ambiguous, equivocal, confused. **ant.** precise, exact, specific, clear, certain.

indelible *adj.* ineradicable, fixed, fast, deep-dyed, ingrained, permanent, enduring, unforgettable, memorable. **ant.** eradicable, erasable, washable, removable, temporary, short-lived.

indelicate *adj.* improper, indecorous, unrefined, tactless, offensive, immodest, indecent, coarse, crude, broad, suggestive, off-color, risqué, lewd. **ant.** fastidious, sensitive, scrupulous, refined.

indent *v.* dent, press, impress, imprint, score, mark, hollow, pit, notch, nick, serrate, scallop, pink.

independence *n.* freedom, liberty, self-determination, emancipation, autonomy, sovereignty, self-government. **ant.** subjugation, subservience, subordination, subjection, bondage, control.

independent *adj.* self-governing, sovereign, autonomous, free, separate, distinct, unallied, nonaligned, unattached, self-reliant, self-sufficient, self-supporting, inner-directed, alone, individualistic, nonpartisan, impartial, unconstrained. —*n.* individualist, free lance, nonpartisan, loner, maverick. **ant.** *adj.* subject, subordinate, subservient, dependent, controlled, restrained, allied, subsidiary, dependent, submissive.

in-depth *adj.* thorough, intensive, penetrating, exhaustive, extensive, comprehensive, profound. **ant.** panoramic, bird's-eye, superficial, cursory.

indeterminate *adj.* indefinite, unfixed, undefined, unclear, imprecise, vague, uncertain, obscure, questionable. **ant.** fixed, determined, precise, clear, known.

index *n.* **1** pointer, guide, indicator, indicant, director, mark, sign, tracer. **2** manifestation, indication, guide, token, mark, clue, sign.

indicate v. signify, mean, point out, demonstrate, suggest, imply, infer, denote, refer, allude, prefigure, foreshadow, show, tell, evince, disclose, designate, specify, state, express, reveal, illustrate.

indication n. evidence, example, testimony, demonstration, expression, manifestation, suggestion, symptom, intimation, implication, token, hint, omen, illustration, reference.

indicator n. guide, pointer, index, sign, mark, earmark, gesture, signpost, guidepost, landmark, beacon, signal, alarm, gauge, meter.

indict v. ACCUSE.

indictment n. accusation, charge, allegation, implication, imputation, incrimination, arraignment, presentment, true bill, impeachment.

indifference n. apathy, unconcern, insensibility, disinterest, coolness, negligence, nonchalance, insouciance.
ant. concern, commitment, enthusiasm.

indifferent adj. 1 apathetic, unconcerned, unmoved, cool, lukewarm, uncaring, nonchalant, incurious, neutral, uninterested, disinterested, impartial, unbiased. 2 ordinary, moderate, mediocre, undistinguished, insignificant, unimportant, trivial, commonplace, so-so.
ant. 1 concerned, avid, enthusiastic, partisan. 2 distinctive, meaningful, outstanding, exceptional.

indigenous adj. native, aboriginal, endemic, autochthonous, natural, home-grown, domestic, innate, inborn, congenital, ingrained, inherent.
ant. naturalized, introduced, imported, exotic, foreign, alien.

indigent adj. needy, poor, reduced, pinched, poverty-stricken, penniless, impoverished, insolvent.
ant. well-off, affluent, prosperous, rich.

indignant adj. irate, incensed, wrathful, angry, provoked, exasperated.
ant. calm, tranquil, composed.

indignation n. ire, rage, wrath, fury, anger, scorn, resentment, huff, petulance, consternation.

indignity n. affront, insult, slight, slur, humiliation, disrespect, dishonor, ignominy, contempt, scorn, outrage.

indirect adj. 1 roundabout, circuitous, winding, zigzag, sidelong, oblique, devious, tortuous, meandering, rambling, circumlocutory. 2 secondary, incidental, subordinate, collateral, contingent, circumstantial, inferential, unintended, accidental, eventual, distant, remote.
ant. 1 straight, direct, undeviating, clear-cut, uninterrupted, straightforward. 2 explicit, express, direct, intended, predictable, immediate.

indirection n. circuitousness, circuity, meandering, roundaboutness, curving, twisting, deviation, divergence, wandering, rambling, zigzagging.

indiscreet adj. tactless, undiplomatic, impolitic, inconsiderate, imprudent, injudicious, incautious, hasty, reckless, rash, foolish, thoughtless.
ant. tactful, sensitive, politic, calculating, cautious.

indiscretion n. impropriety, misstep, faux pas, slip, lapse, misdeed, mistake, folly, blunder, gaffe, gaucherie.

indiscriminate adj. 1 uncritical, undiscriminating, casual, promiscuous, careless, sweeping, wholesale. 2 random, mixed, miscellaneous, motley, diversified, heterogeneous, confused.
ant. 1 selective, discriminating, strict, exclusive. 2 homogeneous, uniform, orderly.

indispensable adj. necessary, needed, requisite, exigent, critical, obligatory, imperative, essential, fundamental, basic, key, vital.
ant. unnecessary, nonessential, superfluous, dispensable, disposable.

indisposed adj. ailing, unwell, sickly, ill, sick, queasy, out of sorts, invalid, confined, bedridden.
ant. healthy, well, hardy, fit, fine, sound.

indisposition n. illness, sickness, ailment, infirmity, invalidism, confinement.

indisputable *adj.* incontestable, undeniable, irrefutable, unassailable, indubitable, definite, assured, certain, obvious, apparent, evident.

ant. questionable, doubtful, indefinite, uncertain, vague.

indissoluble *adj.* BINDING.

indistinct *adj.* **1** imperceptible, dim, faint, unclear, blurred, hazy, shadowy, cloudy, nebulous. **2** ill-defined, obscure, abstruse, vague, uncertain, confused.

ant. 1, 2 clear, distinct, defined, evident.

individual *adj.* **1** unique, single, one, sole, lone, solitary, distinct. **2** distinctive, characteristic, peculiar, particular, specific, special, exclusive, original, singular, personal, idiosyncratic, striking, exceptional, marked. —*n.* person, being, human, mortal, soul, creature, personage, somebody, personality, character.

ant. *adj.* **2** generic, common, ordinary, typical, unexceptional, stereotyped.

individualism *n.* self-direction, self-reliance, inner-direction, independence, self-interest, egocentricity.

ant. conformity, conventionalism, traditionalism, accommodation.

individualist *n.* nonconformist, independent, loner, egoist, original, eccentric, maverick.

individuality *n.* distinctiveness, uniqueness, peculiarity, personality, character, specialness, singularity, cachet, idiosyncrasy, originality.

individualize *v.* DISTINGUISH.

indoctrinate *v.* instruct, teach, tutor, inculcate, brief, imbue, instill, initiate, convert, proselytize, propagandize, brainwash.

indolent *adj.* inactive, inert, sluggish, torpid, listless, easygoing, slothful, idle, lazy.

ant. lively, energetic, bustling, busy, industrious.

indomitable *adj.* invincible, unconquerable, unyielding, resolute, firm, persistent, courageous.

ant. yielding, vulnerable, weak, irresolute.

indorse *v.* ENDORSE.

indubitable *adj.* CERTAIN.

indubitably *adv.* indisputably, undeniably, unquestionably, manifestly, surely, certainly.

induce *v.* persuade, prompt, influence, instigate, impel, move, urge, incite, spur, cause, produce, effect, result in, trigger.

inducement *n.* incentive, incitement, goal, attraction, enticement, allurement, temptation, motive, stimulus, cause, spur.

induct *v.* install, swear in, confirm, inaugurate, initiate.

indulge *v.* gratify, satisfy, placate, concede, yield to, favor, humor, pamper, coddle, spoil, baby, give in to.

ant. deny, forbid, thwart, frustrate, discipline.

indulgence *n.* **1** gratification, humoring, pampering, lenience, favor, liberality, kindness, tenderness. **2** privilege, favor, allowance.

indulgent *adj.* permissive, pampering, lenient, tolerant, kind, mild, gentle, tender.

ant. disciplined, strict, stern, forbidding.

indurate *v.* HARDEN.

industrious *adj.* diligent, assiduous, hard-working, sedulous, purposeful, zealous, energetic, busy, occupied, productive, indefatigable.

ant. lazy, indolent, idle, shiftless, slothful, lackadaisical.

industry *n.* diligence, application, assiduity, industriousness, exertion, perseverance, sedulousness, enterprise, activity, work.

ant. laziness, inactivity, idleness, indolence, sloth, inertia, inertness.

indwell *v.* INHABIT.

inebriated *adj.* intoxicated, drunk, drunken, besotted, tipsy, befuddled, boozy, high, potted (*Slang*), loaded (*Slang*).

ant. sober.

ineffective *adj.* ineffectual, unproductive, useless, vain, futile, fruitless, unfruitful, inconsequent, inconsequential, impotent, weak, unavailing, inadequate, inefficient.

ant. effective, productive, fruitful, potent, efficient, competent, satisfactory.

ineffectual *adj.* INEFFICIENT.

inefficient *adj.* incompetent, deficient, ineffective, inadequate, ineffectual, inoperative, inept, slipshod, bumbling, unskilled, unskillful.

ant. efficient, effective, competent, able, capable, skilled, skillful.

inelastic *adj.* INFLEXIBLE.

inelegant *adj.* unrefined, unpolished, graceless, ungraceful, tasteless, unvarnished, unadorned, indelicate, plain, crude, coarse, vulgar, blunt, boorish, unmannerly, uncultivated.

ant. elegant, refined, polished, graceful, fastidious.

ineligible *adj.* UNSUITABLE.

inept *adj.* unfit, unfitted, unsuitable, inappropriate, inapt, improper, malapropos, incompetent, unqualified, bungling, awkward, clumsy, graceless, maladroit, untalented, unskilled, unskillful.

ant. suitable, fit, proper, apt, competent, able, adroit, graceful.

inequitable *adj.* unjust, unfair, uneven, biased, one-sided, partial, partisan, prejudiced, discriminatory, bigoted, wrong.

ant. just, fair, impartial, even-handed, unbiased.

inequity *n.* injustice, unfairness, one-sidedness, favoritism, bias, partiality, prejudice, discrimination, partisanship, wrongfulness, bigotry.

ant. equity, justice, fairness, impartiality, fair play, even-handedness.

inert *adj.* motionless, unmoving, immobile, quiescent, inactive, stationary, lifeless, devitalized, sluggish, torpid, unresponsive.

ant. moving, mobile, motile, active, responsive, vital, energetic.

inertia *n.* inactivity, immobility, torpor, torpidity, unresponsiveness, lifelessness, passivity, quiescence, sluggishness, inertness.

ant. motion, motility, mobility, activity, change, liveliness.

inescapable *adj.* inevitable, unavoidable, inexorable, unpreventable, ineluctable, fated, destined, predestined, uncontrollable, certain, sure.

ant. avoidable, preventable, uncertain, doubtful, unsure.

inessential *adj.* unnecessary, superfluous, surplus, needless, extra, spare, excessive, dispensable, unessential, unrequired, uncalled-for, redundant, supernumerary, supererogatory, *de trop.* —*n.* superfluity, extra, excess, luxury, extravagance, frill, ornament, supererogation, unessential.

ant. *adj.* essential, necessary, needful, indispensable, requisite, vital, basic. *n.* necessity, need, requirement, requisite, must.

inevitable *adj.* unavoidable, destined, fated, predestined, inescapable, inexorable, determined, predetermined, sure, certain, established, ordained, fixed, unchangeable, unalterable, immutable.

ant. avoidable, escapable, uncertain, unsure, variable, changeable.

inexact *adj.* indefinite, vague, imprecise, incorrect, untrue, false, wrong, approximate, ill-defined, unclear, slipshod, ambiguous, questionable, uncertain, careless, unspecific, indeterminate, deceptive.

ant. exact, precise, accurate, definite, specific, correct, meticulous.

inexcusable *adj.* unforgivable, unpardonable, unjustifiable, indefensible, unwarrantable, unacceptable, outrageous.

ant. pardonable, justifiable, excusable, forgivable, unobjectionable, acceptable, understandable.

inexhaustible *adj.* **1** unlimited, boundless, endless, unbounded, infinite, illimitable, interminable, immeasurable, measureless. **2** tireless, untiring, indefatigable, unwearied, unwearying, dogged, unremitting, unflagging, undaunted, persevering.

ant. 1 limited, exhaustible, limitable, measurable, finite, measured. **2** flagging, tiring, wearied, daunted, enervated.

inexorable *adj.* UNYIELDING.

inexpedient *adj.* IMPRACTICAL.

inexpensive *adj.* reasonable, cheap, economical, *bon marché.*

ant. expensive, dear, costly, high-priced, exorbitant.

inexperienced *adj.* callow, immature, green, new, unpracticed, untried, unskilled, unseasoned, uninitiated, unfamiliar, raw, unknowing, unschooled, ignorant, unsophisticated, inexpert, unqualified, untrained.

ant. experienced, practiced, trained, able, versed, knowing, knowledgeable.

inexpert *adj.* AMATEURISH.

inexplicable *adj.* unexplainable, indefinable, unaccountable, indescribable, mysterious, enigmatic, obscure, unfathomable, baffling, puzzling, inscrutable, esoteric, occult, numinous.

ant. explainable, explicable, definable, understandable, clear, clear-cut, obvious.

infallible *adj.* **1** *incapable of error:* unerring, all-wise, all-knowing, omniscient, perfect, incontestable, irrefutable, unimpeachable, irreproachable, superhuman. **2** *not apt to fail:* unfailing, reliable, dependable, certain, sure, tried, tested, positive, trustworthy, assured.

ant. 1 fallible, errant, errable, mortal, human. **2** unreliable, undependable, uncertain, dubious, doubtful, unsure, untried.

infamous *adj.* notorious, scandalous, outrageous, disreputable, dishonorable, disgraceful, ignoble, execrable, ignominious, perfidious, villainous.

ant. esteemed, honorable, noble, vir-

tuous, honored, uncorrupted, reputable.

infamy *n.* dishonor, disrepute, disgrace, discredit, shame, scandal, opprobrium, shamefulness, wickedness, corruption, villainy, evil, abomination.

ant. honor, virtue, purity, nobility, high-mindedness, integrity, probity.

infancy *n.* commencement, beginning, beginnings, cradle, origin, inception, incipience, start, bud.

ant. conclusion, termination, finish, end, close, expiration, death.

infant *n.* BABY.

infantile *adj.* childish, babyish, immature, undeveloped, dependent, unreasoning, unreasonable.

ant. mature, developed, adult.

infatuated *adj.* beguiled, captivated, enchanted, fascinated, charmed, bewitched, enraptured, enthralled, enamored, possessed, spellbound, impassioned, intrigued.

infect *v.* **1** *communicate disease:* contaminate, disease, afflict, disorder, sicken, indispose, prostrate, lay low. **2** *influence harmfully:* taint, corrupt, debauch, deprave, defile, pollute, poison, pervert, warp, impair, damage, spoil, blight, smirch, besmirch, ruin.

infection *n.* **1** illness, disease, disorder, sickness, indisposition, contagion, contagiousness, contamination, pollution, poison, poisoning, epidemic, malaise. **2** *communication by example:* contagion, stimulation, provocation, inspiration, excitation, incitement, infusion, instigation.

infectious *adj.* contagious, catching, communicable, infective, transmittable, transmissible, transferable.

infective *adj.* INFECTIOUS.

infelicitous *adj.* UNFORTUNATE.

infer *v.* deduce, conclude, reason, gather, glean, presume, construe, suppose, estimate, reckon, surmise, interpret.

inference *n.* deduction, conclusion, intuition, presumption, assumption, construction, supposition, surmise, reading, corollary.

inferior *adj.* second-rate, poor, so-so, lower, mediocre, deficient, paltry, imperfect, indifferent, insignificant, inadequate, unsatisfactory, low-grade, wanting, subnormal.

ant. superior, first-class, outstanding, better.

inferiority *n.* mediocrity, deficiency, shortcoming, imperfection, insignificance, inadequacy, subnormality, subordination, subservience, poverty, worthlessness, baseness.

ant. superiority, ascendancy, dominance, eminence, excellence, advantage, edge.

infernal *adj.* hellish, diabolic, diabolical, devilish, satanic, fiendish, Mephistophelean, evil, dark, Stygian, accursed, wicked, damned.

ant. heavenly, celestial, angelic, seraphic, godlike, glorious.

inferno *n.* HELL.

infertile *adj.* sterile, barren, unproductive, nonproductive, unfruitful, impotent, arid, fallow, bare, desolate.

ant. fertile, productive, fruitful, fecund, generative.

infest *v.* overrun, beset, swarm, pervade, invade, fill, ravage, plague, bespread, overspread.

infidel *n.* unbeliever, nonbeliever, heathen, pagan, skeptic, atheist, agnostic, heretic, freethinker, materialist, nihilist, dissenter, noncomformist.

ant. believer, religionist, conformist, pietist, churchgoer.

infidelity *n.* disloyalty, unfaithfulness, faithlessness, treachery, perfidy, perfidiousness, betrayal, apostasy, treason, adultery, unbelief, disbelief, irreligion, ungodliness, impiety.

ant. fidelity, faith, faithfulness, loyalty, fealty, allegiance, steadfastness.

infiltrate *v.* permeate, pervade, penetrate, interpenetrate, percolate, imbue, saturate, infuse, suffuse, transfuse, steep, osmose.

infinite *adj.* endless, unending, immeasurable, limitless, unlimited, un-

bounded, boundless, countless, numberless, innumerable, incalculable, interminable, all-embracing, absolute, unconfined.

ant. finite, limited, restricted, measurable, circumscribed.

infinitesimal *adj.* minute, tiny, microscopic, imperceptible, inappreciable, diminutive, inconsiderable, insignificant, impalpable, undiscernible, wee.

ant. huge, vast, enormous, colossal, massive, tremendous, mountainous, gargantuan.

infinity *n.* endlessness, vastness, eternity, infinitude, myriad, illimitability, boundlessness, immeasurability, inexhaustibility, incalculability, innumerability.

ant. finitude, limit, bounds, end.

infirm *adj.* weak, feeble, frail, sickly, ailing, enfeebled, weakened, decrepit, unsound, debilitated, anile, shaky, irresolute, faltering, unstable, valetudinarian.

ant. robust, strong, vigorous, sturdy, forceful, healthy, hearty, sound.

infirmity *n.* weakness, disability, debility, feebleness, decrepitude, ailment, malady, disease, illness, sickness, invalidism, indisposition, decline.

ant. strength, soundness, vigor, health, well-being, stamina, vitality.

inflame *v.* kindle, ignite, fire, impassion, excite, arouse, fan, electrify, galvanize, intensify, aggravate, provoke, foment.

ant. soothe, calm, pacify, assuage, appease, lull, quell, quench, cool.

inflammable *adj.* FLAMMABLE.

inflate *v.* expand, distend, bloat, puff up, swell, fatten, stretch, aerate, enlarge, increase, magnify, grow, rise, exaggerate, escalate.

ant. deflate, shrink, compress, collapse, contract, diminish, lessen.

inflexibility *n.* OBSTINACY.

inflexible *adj.* **1** unyielding, firm, stubborn, steadfast, unalterable, determined, obstinate, rigid, inelastic, obdurate, mulish, pigheaded, intractable, resolute, adamant, unrelenting, unbending. **2** *incapable of being bent:* rigid, stiff, adamantine, steely.

ant. 1, 2 flexible, elastic, resilient, pliant, pliable, variable, plastic, supple.

inflict *v.* impose, exact, effectuate, administer, palm off, foist, put upon.

influence *n.* power, weight, importance, domination, dominance, control, supremacy, mastery, pressure, prestige, magnetism, appeal, charisma, pull, clout (*Slang*). —*v.* induce, incline, bend, sway, impel, compel, control, move, motivate, affect, prompt, dominate, manipulate, persuade, convince.

influential *adj.* powerful, weighty, consequential, potent, effective, forceful, persuasive, cogent, compelling, authoritative, important, commanding, charismatic.

infold *v.* EMBRACE.

inform *v.* **1** advise, apprise, acquaint, notify, enlighten, educate, tell, teach, instruct, explain. **2** accuse, denounce, charge, incriminate, disclose, divulge, impugn, inculpate, betray, tattle.

informal *adj.* unofficial, unceremonious, irregular, unconventional, casual, relaxed, easy, familiar, offhand, simple, free, unconstrained, unstudied, spontaneous.

ant. formal, ceremonious, conventional, constrained, stiff.

informality *n.* laxity, familiarity, casualness, ease, naturalness, offhandedness, simplicity, spontaneity, unconstraint, unconventionality, unceremoniousness.

ant. formality, stiffness, ritualism, constraint, conventionality, ceremoniousness.

informant *n.* respondent, informer, appriser, adviser, enlightener, herald, spokesman, spokeswoman, press agent, flack (*Slang*).

information *n.* knowledge, news, facts, data, intelligence, tidings, report, reportage, communication, communiqué, bulletin, message, proclama-

tion, announcement, word, notice, notification.

informative *adj.* enlightening, instructive, educational, edifying, revealing, informational, communicative, advisory, revelatory, revealing, heuristic.

informer *n.* accuser, denouncer, betrayer, informant, complainant, tattler, stool pigeon (*Slang*).

infraction *n.* breach, violation, infringement, transgression, encroachment, trespass, contravention, illegality, lawbreaking, dereliction, delinquency, unlawfulness.

infrequent *adj.* rare, uncommon, unusual, scarce, scant, sparse, odd, sporadic, spasmodic, fitful, irregular, occasional.

ant. frequent, often, common, usual, regular, plentiful, customary, habitual.

infrequently *adv.* seldom, rarely, uncommonly, fitfully, spasmodically, scarcely, hardly ever, occasionally, once in a while.

ant. frequently, often, commonly, regularly, constantly, perpetually, incessantly.

infringe *v.* violate, break, contravene, breach, transgress, disobey, encroach, impinge, trespass, intrude.

infuriate *v.* enrage, exasperate, incense, anger, madden, inflame, provoke, vex, rile, irritate, outrage, gall, inflame.

ant. appease, pacify, mollify, calm, soothe, propitiate, placate.

infuse *v.* instill, inculcate, imbue, inspire, inspirit, implant, impart, introduce, permeate, infiltrate, suffuse, pervade.

ingenious *adj.* clever, skillful, adroit, resourceful, creative, inventive, dextrous, deft, expert, handy, able, original, imaginative.

ant. unimaginative, pedestrian, imitative, unskilled, maladroit, inept, clumsy.

ingenuity *n.* cleverness, resourcefulness, originality, inventiveness, invention, creativity, talent, skill, skill-fulness, adroitness, aptitude, facility, flair, competence, expertness, expertise.

ant. ineptness, clumsiness, ineptitude, incompetence.

ingenuous *adj.* artless, unsophisticated, innocent, frank, honest, open, guileless, unaffected, natural, candid, direct, straightforward, simplehearted, trusting, genuine.

ant. disingenuous, insincere, sophisticated, wily, subtle, devious, crafty, worldly-wise, jaded.

ingest *v.* swallow, eat, imbibe, absorb, consume, gulp.

ant. vomit, spew, throw up, disgorge, regurgitate, expel.

inglorious *adj.* DISGRACEFUL.

ingrained *adj.* inherent, innate, inborn, inbred, intrinsic, rooted, deep, fixed, ineradicable, unalterable, unchangeable, thoroughgoing, deep-seated, organic.

ant. superficial, surface, external, acquired, superimposed, learned, alien.

ingratiate *v.* court, flatter, cajole, attract, captivate, blandish, disarm, fawn on, curry favor.

ingratitude *n.* ungratefulness, thanklessness, unthankfulness.

ant. gratitude, thanks, appreciation, thankfulness, acknowledgment, thanksgiving.

ingredient *n.* component, element, constituent, aspect, part, factor, item, module, section, piece.

ingulf *v.* ENGULF.

inhabit *v.* occupy, live, dwell, indwell, reside, populate, domicile, tenant, lodge, settle.

inhabitant *n.* **1** *of a house:* resident, dweller, occupant, occupier, resider, residentiary, tenant, lessee, addressee, renter, boarder, roomer, lodger. **2** *of a place:* native, citizen, indigene, dweller, habitant, settler, denizen, aborigine.

inhalation *n.* breath, breathing, inspiration, indraught, gasp, inhaling, sniff, sniffle, snuff, snuffle.

ant. exhalation, expiration, puff, blow, snort.

inhale *v.* breathe, inspire, inbreathe, gasp, sniff, sniffle, snuff, snuffle.

ant. exhale, expire, breathe out, blow, snort.

inharmonious *adj.* discordant, unharmonious, inconsonant, unmusical, unmelodious, jangly, jarring, incompatible, uncongenial, conflicting, dissident, clashing, grating, disagreeable.

ant. harmonious, concordant, melodious, harmonic, compatible.

inhere *v.* exist, reside, indwell, abide, belong, constitute, pertain, appertain.

inherent *adj.* innate, characteristic, natural, essential, intrinsic, immanent, basic, instinctive, instinctual, inborn, inbred, ingrained, congenital, inseparable, inalienable, ineradicable.

ant. extrinsic, superficial, imposed, superimposed, extraneous, supplementary, alien.

inheritance *n.* legacy, heritage, heritance, patrimony, bequeathal, devise, endowment, bestowal.

inhibit *v.* RESTRAIN.

inhibited *adj.* restrained, repressed, reticent, suppressed, withdrawn, constrained, guarded, checked, impeded, subdued, controlled, leashed, constricted.

ant. uninhibited, free, outgoing, spontaneous, unrestrained.

inhibition *n.* restraint, constraint, reserve, reticence, repression, suppression, restriction, control, check, clamp, curb, rein, block, hindrance, hang-up (*Slang*).

ant. laxity, freedom, spontaneity, unconstraint, liberty, ease.

inhuman *adj.* bestial, brutal, savage, cruel, bloodthirsty, ruthless, fiendish, diabolical, merciless, heartless, pitiless, vicious, barbarous, remorseless, inhumane.

ant. compassionate, brotherly, warmhearted, charitable, humane, tenderhearted, understanding.

inhumane *adj.* INHUMAN.

inhumanity *n.* cruelty, brutality, savagery, ferocity, bloodthirstiness, ruthlessness, fiendishness, malevolence, coldheartedness, brutishness, viciousness, bestiality, barbarity.
ant. humanity, humaneness.

inimical *adj.* **1** unfriendly, hostile, hateful, antagonistic, embattled, irreconcilable, disaffected, belligerent, antipathetic, rancorous, ill-willed, ill-disposed, acrimonious. **2** adverse, hurtful, harmful, damaging, destructive, contrary, counter, deleterious, injurious, pernicious, undermining, unfavorable, unpropitious.
ant. **1** friendly, amicable, well-disposed, amiable, kindly, congenial. **2** beneficial, favorable, salutary, helpful, useful, good.

inimitable *adj.* matchless, peerless, unrivaled, unequaled, unique, supreme, preeminent, unparalleled, incomparable, unsurpassed, unsurpassable, unexcelled, transcendent, nonpareil.

iniquity *n.* sinfulness, wickedness, sin, evil, evildoing, wrong, wrongdoing, vice, viciousness, transgression, infamy, crime, criminality, misdeed, lawlessness.
ant. rectitude, uprightness, virtue, probity, integrity, lawfulness.

initial *adj.* first, original, beginning, opening, primary, prime, germinal, inaugural, primal, incipient, introductory.
ant. last, final, closing, concluding, terminal, endmost, ultimate.

initiate *v.* **1** begin, originate, start, commence, introduce, establish, launch, pioneer, inaugurate, found, invent, create. **2** instruct, induct, indoctrinate, train, tutor, inculcate, prepare, qualify, brief, coach, clue in.
—*n.* beginner, novice, novitiate, entrant, neophyte, freshman, newcomer, recruit, tyro, apprentice, learner, probationer, proselyte.

initiation *n.* beginning, opening, commencement, inception, outset, start, incipience, inauguration, installation, entrance, debut, investiture, establishment, induction, briefing.

initiative *n.* enterprise, leadership, energy, independence, aggressiveness, drive, push, venturesomeness, vigor, ambition, ambitiousness.

initiatory *adj.* INTRODUCTORY.

inject *v.* **1** inoculate, instill, infuse, infix, imbue, intromit. **2** insert, introduce, interject.

injudicious *adj.* UNWISE.

injunction *n.* command, admonition, precept, mandate, bidding, requirement, direction, behest, regulation, ordinance, ruling, fiat, decree.

injure *v.* damage, hurt, harm, impair, wound, mar, deface, maim, bruise, mangle, deform, mutilate, lacerate, abuse, misuse, violate, debase.

injurious *adj.* harmful, hurtful, damaging, detrimental, pernicious, abusive, disadvantageous, adverse, deleterious, ruinous, offensive.
ant. beneficial, advantageous, salutary, healing, constructive, salubrious.

injury *n.* **1** *to the body:* wound, hurt, lesion, abrasion, gash, bruise, mutilation, disfigurement, damage, harm. **2** injustice, wrong, harm, damage, outrage, evil, ill, bane, abuse, misuse, indignity, grievance.
ant. **2** benefit, help, boon, blessing, favor.

injustice *n.* inequity, unfairness, partiality, one-sidedness, prejudice, bias, favoritism, partisanship, injury, wrong, grievance, offense, malpractice.
ant. justice, equity, right, fairness, rectitude, evenhandedness, impartiality.

inkling *n.* hint, intimation, indication, whisper, glimmer, glimpse, suggestion, clue, scent, suspicion, notion, touch, trace.

inky *adj.* BLACK.

inmate *n.* resident, occupant, dweller, occupier, denizen, inhabitant, indweller, habitant.

inmost *adj.* INTIMATE.

inn *n.* hotel, hostel, hostelry, guesthouse, lodge, caravansary, restaurant, tavern, bar, roadhouse, pub, public house, hospice, *auberge, bistro.*

innate *adj* inborn, congenital, inbred, natural, inherent, indigenous, constitutional, native, inherited, essential, intrinsic, ingrained.
ant. acquired, learned, superimposed, unnatural, extrinsic, alien, foreign.

inner *adj.* 1 interior, internal, inside, inward, proximal. 2 private, intimate, secret, hidden, concealed, shrouded, covert, unexposed, unrevealed, repressed.
ant. 1 outer, exterior, external, outlying, outward, outside, distal. 2 exposed, revealed, visible, overt, unconcealed, surface, obvious.

innocence *n.* blamelessness, innocuousness, harmlessness, guilelessness, artlessness, naiveté, simplicity, ingenuousness, purity, sinlessness, impeccability, unworldliness, inexperience, unimpeachability.
ant. guilt, reprehensibility, turpitude, sophisticated, artless, unworldly, inpeachability.

innocent *adj.* harmless, blameless, innocuous, unoffending, sinless, pure, spotless, impeccable, guiltless, uncorrupted, unsullied, naive, unsophisticated, artless, unworldly, ingenuous.
ant. guilty, sinful, culpable, reprehensible, corrupt, impure, wily.

innocuous *adj.* harmless, inoffensive, safe, mild, moderate, unstimulating, dull, uninspiring, banal, bland.
ant. noxious, harmful, injurious, unwholesome, deleterious, bad, damaging, dangerous, pernicious.

innovation *n.* novelty, change, variation, precedent, shift, modernism, invention.

innuendo *n.* insinuation, inference, implication, intimation, overtone, allu-sion, aspersion, imputation, indication, suggestion, hint.

innumerable *adj.* countless, numberless, incalculable, untold, infinite, myriad, unnumbered, unlimited, illimitable.
ant. calculable, finite, computable, measurable, limited.

inoculation *n.* injection, immunization, vaccination, infusion, shot.

inoffensive *adj.* harmless, innocuous, unoffending, unobjectionable, peaceable, innocent, quiet, safe, humble, gentle, mild, unobtrusive, retiring, bland.
ant. offensive, harmful, objectionable, irritating, provocative, abrasive, irksome.

inoperable *adj.* IMPRACTICAL.

inoperative *adj.* INEFFICIENT.

inopportune *adj.* untimely, inappropriate, inconvenient, unseasonable, mistimed, malapropos, untoward, unfavorable, unfortunate, unpropitious, inauspicious, undesirable, unsuitable, unsuited.
ant. timely, appropriate, convenient, opportune, suitable, favorable.

inordinate *adj.* excessive, exorbitant, extravagant, unreasonable, undue, unnecessary, immoderate, intemperate, prodigal, lavish, profuse, overflowing, overabundant, overweening, unrestrained, fulsome, egregious.
ant. moderate, reasonable, due, measured, meager, scanty, sparse.

inquiet *adj.* RESTLESS.

inquire *v.* 1 ask, query, question, interrogate, interview, quiz, cross-examine, catechize. 2 look into, probe, investigate, examine, explore, scan, scrutinize, search, research, study, inspect, pursue, pry.

inquiry *n.* 1 query, question, questioning, interrogation, interview, questionnaire, quiz, cross-examination, catechism, interrogatory, inquisition. 2 investigation, probe, examination, exploration, scanning, scrutiny, search, quest, study, inspection, analysis, survey.

inquisition *n.* INVESTIGATION.

inquisitive *adj.* curious, inquiring, prying, searching, quizzical, overcurious, nosy, snoopy.

ant. incurious, indifferent, uninterested, unquestioning.

inroad *n.* encroachment, incursion, invasion, assault, onslaught, infringement, attack, infiltration, trespass, injury, damage, impairment, dent, impression.

insane *adj.* **1** foolish, impractical, extravagant, scatterbrained, fanatic, senseless, fatuous, imbecilic, idiotic, moronic, simple-minded, bizarre, absurd, queer, odd, frenzied, frenetic, lunatic, unsound, loco (*Slang*). **2** *mentally ill:* deranged, demented, disoriented, distraught, psychotic, *non compos mentis.*

ant. 1, 2 sensible, practical, sound, normal, rational, lucid, sane, logical, reasonable, reasoned.

insanitary *adj.* UNSANITARY.

insanity *n.* **1** folly, foolishness, extravagance, giddiness, fanaticism, senselessness, fatuity, imbecility, idiocy, absurdity, eccentricity, madness, frenzy, lunacy, lightheadedness. **2** *mental illness:* derangement, dementia, psychosis, psychopathy.

ant. 1, 2 sanity, soundness, wisdom, sense, reason, reasonableness, normality, lucidity, rationality.

insatiable *adj.* ravenous, insatiate, unappeasable, voracious, unquenchable, bottomless, gluttonous, quenchless, unlimited, endless, infinite.

ant. satiable, appeasable, quenchable, limited, finite.

inscribe *v.* write, engrave, etch, impress, imprint, incise, carve, chisel, letter, mark, pen.

inscription *n.* engraving, impression, imprint, incision, carving, lettering, mark, marking, hallmark, dedication, motto, legend.

inscrutable *adj.* mysterious, enigmatic,

impenetrable, incomprehensible, inexplicable, unfathomable, unknowable, baffling, hidden, occult, shrouded, esoteric, sphinxlike.

ant. knowable, penetrable, comprehensible, transparent, obvious, patent, clear.

insecure *adj.* **1** unsafe, unstable, rickety, uncertain, perilous, dangerous, hazardous, risky, precarious, weak, shaky, wobbly, unsteady, tottering. **2** dubious, undecided, puzzled, adrift, threatened, vulnerable, exposed, diffident, anxious, uncertain.

ant. 1 safe, secure, stable, steady, sure, firm, reliable, substantial. **2** confident, secure, assured, poised, certain, decisive.

insecurity *n.* uncertainty, doubt, doubtfulness, instability, fallibility, unreliability, danger, risk, jeopardy, precariousness, vulnerability, hesitation, dubiety.

ant. safety, certainty, firmness, dependability, reliability, steadiness.

insensible *adj.* UNCONSCIOUS.

insensitive *adj.* unfeeling, insensible, impassive, indifferent, obtuse, blunted, dull, callous, crass, tactless, unresponsive, thick-skinned, numb, numbed, phlegmatic, apathetic, bovine.

ant. sensitive, sentient, responsive, susceptible, thin-skinned, emotional, touchy, volatile.

insert *v.* interpose, introduce, interpolate, inject, interject, imbed, intercalate, inset, impregnate, imbue, intromit, interlard, intersperse, pierce, implant, put in.

ant. remove, take out, withdraw, delete, excise, erase.

insertion *n.* inset, interpolation, infix, addition, supplement.

ant. extraction, withdrawal, erasure, excision, deletion, removal.

insider *n.* member, colleague, fellow, associate, cardholder, confederate, collaborator, teammate, comrade.

ant. outsider, alien, nonmember,

newcomer, stranger, interloper, intruder.

insidious *adj.* treacherous, duplicitous, conniving, sly, crafty, wily, cunning, tricky, deceptive, underhand, underhanded, Machiavellian, stealthy.
ant. frank, straightforward, overt, sincere, ingenuous, open.

insight *n.* perception, understanding, penetration, discernment, intuition, intuitiveness, perspicacity, epiphany, perspicuity, sagacity, grasp, *aperçu*, awareness.

insignia *n.* badge, emblem, mark, sign, label, regalia, decoration.

insignificant *adj.* meaningless, inconsequential, inessential, unimportant, petty, paltry, trifling, trivial, marginal, picayune, immaterial, incidental, slight, measly, worthless, piddling.
ant. significant, meaningful, important, vital, weighty, consequential, momentous.

insincere *adj.* hypocritical, false, dishonest, deceitful, disingenuous, dissembling, fraudulent, untruthful, perfidious, hollow, mealy-mouthed, two-faced, double-dealing.
ant. sincere, earnest, honest, truthful, direct, straightforward, plain-spoken, genuine.

insincerity *n.* HYPOCRISY.

insinuate *v.* hint, suggest, imply, intimate, indicate, whisper, convey, mean, signify, asperse.

insinuation *n.* innuendo, implication, suggestion, allusion, intimation, aspersion, imputation, hint, slur.

insipid *adj.* **1** tasteless, vapid, flat, savorless, bland. **2** unexciting, dull, tame, prosaic, uninteresting, pointless, jejune, weak, feeble, lukewarm, indifferent, vapid, vacant, namby-pamby, wishy-washy.
ant. 1 tasty, flavorful, savory, appetizing, delicious, sapid, toothsome. **2** exciting, interesting, stimulating, provocative, lively, engaging, appealing, vivid.

insist *v.* maintain, urge, demand, assert, contend, require, importune, enjoin, stress, emphasize, repeat, iterate, reiterate, claim, press, persist, stress.

insistence *n.* demand, assertion, contention, emphasis, stress, repetition, urging, reiteration, persistence, perseverance, single-mindedness, tenacity, doggedness, steadfastness, intransigence.

insistent *adj.* emphatic, urgent, pressing, persistent, importunate, pertinacious, assertive, necessary, needful, compelling, tenacious, dogged.

insolence *n.* impertinence, disrespect, rudeness, contempt, arrogance, haughtiness, presumption, surliness, presumptuousness, impudence, discourtesy, cheek, effrontery, temerity, gall, nerve (*Slang*).
ant. respect, courtesy, deference, mannerliness, civility, tact, esteem.

insolent *adj.* impertinent, discourteous, disrespectful, rude, insulting, arrogant, presumptuous, surly, disdainful, contemptuous, cheeky, brazen, nervy (*Slang*).
ant. deferential, courteous, respectful, civil, obedient, polite.

insoluble *adj.* inexplicable, unsolvable, insolvable, incomprehensible, unknowable, mysterious, baffling, undefinable, inscrutable, obscure, impenetrable, perplexing.
ant. solvable, soluble, understandable, explicable, comprehensible, penetrable.

insolvable *adj.* INSOLUBLE.

insolvency *n.* POVERTY.

insolvent *adj.* bankrupt, ruined, penniless, impecunious, straitened, indebted, overextended.
ant. solvent, sound, moneyed, solid, profit-making.

insouciant *adj.* carefree, lighthearted, unconcerned, unburdened, nonchalant, devil-may-care, heedless, happy-go-lucky, easygoing, gay, untroubled, unworried, free and easy, jaunty, *sans souci*.
ant. worried, anxious, burdened,

careworn, heavy-hearted, woebegone, troubled.

inspect *v.* examine, investigate, scan, scrutinize, check, eye, regard, pore over, explore, search, survey, contemplate, peruse, study, look over.

inspection *n.* examination, investigation, scanning, scrutiny, check, regard, contemplation, perusal, study, search, consideration, review.

inspiration *n.* stimulus, stimulation, influence, motive, motivation, incentive, afflatus, impulse, propulsion, provocation, demon, brainstorm.

inspire *v.* stimulate, motivate, prompt, stir, affect, propel, urge, spur, encourage, hearten, embolden, inspirit, animate, arouse, quicken, elevate.
ant. dispirit, discourage, dishearten, daunt, deter, deflate.

inspiring *adj.* inspirational, encouraging, stimulating, uplifting, enlightening, stirring, moving, motivating, elevating, heartening, eloquent, lofty, rousing, affecting.
ant. dispiriting, depressing, discouraging, disheartening, dull, boring, uninspired, uninspiring.

instability *n.* insecurity, unsteadiness, decrepitude, precariousness, infirmity, shakiness, unreliability, uncertainty, undependability, imbalance, variability, inconstance, disequilibrium.
ant. steadiness, equilibrium, firmness, balance, reliability, stability, equipoise.

instable *adj.* UNSTABLE.

install *v.* establish, place, position, locate, seat, induct, inaugurate, station, set up, initiate, ordain, admit, invest, put.

installment *n.* portion, section, serial, part, segment, subdivision, component, fragment, piece, chapter, fascicle, unit.

instance *n.* example, case, illustration, specimen, sample, prototype, specific, point, exemplification.

instant *adj.* immediate, direct, urgent, pressing, quick, instantaneous, un-

delayed, rapid, swift, hasty, compelling, crucial, critical, vital. —*n.* moment, second, flash, trice, twinkling, blink.

instantly *adv.* immediately, at once, urgently, swiftly, rapidly, instantaneously, hastily, directly, now, right away, instanter.

instigate *v.* incite, foment, provoke, urge, rouse, agitate, spur, prevail, press, exhort, stir up, stimulate, egg on, abet, suborn, whip up, prompt.
ant. quash, quell, check, repress, restrain, suppress, dampen, deter.

instigator *n.* agitator, rabble-rouser, inciter, formenter, troublemaker, spur, goad, whip, suborner, demagogue, incendiary, mischief-maker, *agent provocateur*.

instill *v.* infuse, impart, indoctrinate, impregnate, implant, plant, inseminate, teach, inculcate, instruct, propagandize, impress, imbue, brainwash.

instinct *n.* impulse, tendency, aptitude, proclivity, bent, leaning, prompting, inclination, flair, faculty, capacity, gift, talent, propensity, penchant.

instinctive *adj.* innate, inborn, inbred, inherent, instinctual, natural, automatic, spontaneous, involuntary, reflex, constitutional, characteristic, ingrained, intuitive, unpremeditated.
ant. learned, acquired, willed, premeditated, calculated, considered, mindful.

institute *v.* establish, inaugurate, introduce, originate, initiate, found, set up, erect, install, begin, commence, start, enact, effectuate. —*n.* organization, society, establishment, body, association, academy, school, league, fellowship, union.

institution *n.* **1** establishment, foundation, enactment, organization, corporation, society, league, fellowship, union, academy, school, hall. **2** custom, usage, practice, principle, law, convention, rite, ritual, code, regulation, canon.

institutional *adj.* established, settled,

conventional, societal, organized, bureaucratic, customary, usual, accepted, prevalent, formal.

instruct *v.* teach, inform, impart, explain, enlighten, educate, guide, direct, tutor, school, coach, indoctrinate, train, catechize, notify, apprise.

instruction *n.* teaching, information, education, indoctrination, training, schooling, counsel, guidance, bidding, prescription, enlightenment, coaching, edification, direction, order.

instructive *adj.* enlightening, informative, informing, educational, explanatory, guiding, edifying, pedagogical, preceptive, illuminating, revealing, heuristic, hortatory.

instructor *n.* teacher, educator, tutor, trainer, counsel, guide, adviser, pedagogue, master, preceptor, schoolmaster, lecturer, exponent, mentor.

instrument *n.* **1** implement, tool, means, device, wherewithal, machine, machinery, mechanism, equipment, gear, appliance, contrivance, invention. **2** agent, medium, agency, vehicle, hireling, puppet, tool, go-between, intermediary, expediter, lackey, servant, flunkey, pawn, cat's-paw.

instrumental *adj.* useful, helpful, serviceable, functional, contributory, conducive, effective, effectual, accessory, applicable, contingent, implemental, mediative, utilitarian.

instrumentality *n.* AGENCY.

insubordinate *adj.* DISOBEDIENT.

insubordination *n.* disobedience, revolt, rebellion, defiance, mutiny, insurgence, insurgency, sedition, unruliness, insolence, impudence, brass, intractability, contumacy. **ant.** obedience, compliance, submission, acquiescence, submissiveness, subservience, deference.

insubstantial *adj.* flimsy, frail, fragile, delicate, airy, gossamer, light, slight, incorporeal, ethereal, impalpable, weightless, disembodied, intangible, unsubstantial.

ant. substantial, real, strong, solid, firm, considerable, weighty.

insufferable *adj.* intolerable, unendurable, insupportable, unbearable, agonizing, outrageous, appalling, harrowing, tormenting, excruciating, killing, deadly. **ant.** bearable, tolerable, supportable, endurable.

insufficient *adj.* inadequate, deficient, incommensurate, scanty, meager, sparse, lacking, wanting, slim, skimpy, incomplete, stinted, sketchy. **ant.** sufficient, enough, adequate, ample, full, plentiful.

insular *adj.* isolated, insulated, parochial, provincial, lonely, circumscribed, limited, restricted, confined, cloistered, narrow, narrow-minded, hidebound, petty, intolerant. **ant.** worldly, urbane, tolerant, experienced, open-minded, broad-minded.

insulate *v.* isolate, separate, detach, set apart, segregate, quarantine, seclude, sequester, sequestrate, cut off, disengage, dissociate.

insult *v.* offend, affront, hurt, abuse, outrage, scorn, attack, misprise, undervalue, scorn, deride, rebuff, cut, ridicule, sneer, spurn, dishonor. —*n.* offense, affront, injury, attack, snub, cut, slight, indignity, derision, disdain, insolence, abuse. **ant.** *v.* compliment, praise, commend, honor, celebrate, applaud, respect. *n.* compliment, praise, commendation, honor, applause, homage.

insulting *adj.* offensive, cutting, abusive, hurtful, scornful, disrespectful, contemptuous, slighting, disparaging, nasty, insolent, scurrilous, disdainful, derisive, humiliating. **ant.** complimentary, flattering, laudatory, respectful, deferential.

insuperable *adj.* insurmountable, unconquerable, invincible, indomitable, unbeatable, unattainable, unachievable, impregnable, unassailable, impossible.

ant. surmountable, conquerable, accessible, attainable, doable, possible, reachable.

insupportable *adj.* INTOLERABLE.

insurance *n.* pledge, guarantee, assurance, warranty, indemnity, indemnification, premium, policy, contract, covenant, security.

insure *v.* ENSURE.

insurgent *adj.* REBELLIOUS.

insurrection *n.* uprising, revolt, rebellion, insurgence, mutiny, riot, insubordination, outbreak, strike, *putsch,* coup, *coup d'état,* turbulence, defiance, unruliness.

intact *adj.* whole, complete, unimpaired, undamaged, untouched, unaltered, unbroken, unharmed, unhurt, healthy, perfect, unflawed, undiminished, unspoiled.
ant. damaged, altered, broken, marred, flawed, diminished.

intangible *adj.* impalpable, imperceptible, immaterial, insubstantial, elusive, invisible, evanescent, shadowy, indefinite, incorporeal, illusory, imaginary, phantom, dreamlike, chimerical.
ant. tangible, substantial, material, visible, real, palpable.

integral *adj.* **1** whole, entire, complete, undivided, indivisible, total, aggregate, unified, integrated, one, unitary, composite. **2** component, constituent, elementary, essential.
ant. 1 discrete, separate, divided.

integrate *v.* **1** unify, combine, amalgamate, fuse, consolidate, coalesce, commingle, confederate, coordinate. **2** desegregate.
ant. 1 separate, disunite, disunify, divide, disintegrate, fragment, break up. **2** segregate.

integrity *n.* **1** honesty, rectitude, probity, uprightness, virtue, honor, principle, morality, trustworthiness, character, fair-mindedness, scrupulousness, incorruptibility. **2** wholeness, soundness, completeness, intactness, totality, unity.
ant. 1 dishonor, faithlessness, dis-

honesty, immorality, vice, viciousness. **2** division, fragmentation, segregation.

intellect *n.* mind, intelligence, understanding, reason, brain, brains, braininess, comprehension, mentality, acumen, intellectuality, rationality.

intellectual *adj.* cerebral, intelligent, rational, gnostic, brainy, mental, knowledgeable, informed, thoughtful, learned, bookish, scholarly, literate, unemotional, pensive. —*n.* thinker, savant, pundit, scholar, academician, bluestocking, highbrow, *bas bleu,* egghead (*Slang*).

intelligence *n.* **1** mind, brains, braininess, intellect, reason, rationality, intellectuality, perception, penetration, keenness, wit, wisdom, shrewdness, comprehension, understanding, acumen. **2** information, news, notice, instruction, data, facts, findings, tidings, knowledge, message, disclosure, account, report, revelation.

intelligent *adj.* bright, clever, discerning, astute, keen, sharp-witted, perspicacious, alert, quick, discriminating, knowing, knowledgeable, informed, smart, brainy, educated, enlightened.
ant. stupid, dull, dull-witted, obtuse, ignorant, uninformed.

intelligible *adj.* comprehensible, understandable, clear, obvious, distinct, lucid, coherent, clear-cut, unambiguous, decipherable, unmistakable, definite, well-defined.
ant. unintelligible, incomprehensible, unclear, confused, garbled, muddy, puzzling.

intemperate *adj.* **1** immoderate, excessive, unrestrained, inordinate, extravagant, extreme, unbridled, prodigal, uncontrolled, undisciplined, undue, unwarranted, exaggerated. **2** stormy, inclement, raging, tempestuous, severe, violent, turbulent, windswept, blustery, squally.
ant. 1 temperate, moderate, restrained, just, self-controlled, self-

disciplined. **2** calm, clement, mild, temperate, balmy, pleasant.

intend *v.* mean, plan, design, determine, resolve, aim, wish, hope, destine, contemplate, expect, incline, propose, figure, reckon.

intended *adj.* intentional, meant, planned, premeditated, designed, projected, purposeful, deliberate, studied, calculated, willful, ordained, providential.
ant. accidental, unintentional, unpremeditated, spontaneous, lucky.

intense *adj.* deep, extreme, concentrated, fervent, fervid, strenuous, passionate, poignant, energetic, vehement, vigorous, strong, arduous, acute, profound, ardent.
ant. weak, feeble, shallow, superficial, lax, relaxed, diluted.

intensify *v.* deepen, heighten, strengthen, increase, escalate, step up, concentrate, quicken, accelerate, aggravate, sharpen, whet, exacerbate, exaggerate, reinforce, emphasize.
ant. weaken, diminish, dilute, minimize, decrease, lessen, dull.

intensity *n.* depth, concentration, strength, extremity, passion, severity, profundity, energy, ardor, vigor, power, zeal, fervor, vehemence, purpose.
ant. weakness, shallowness, superficiality, laxity, coolness.

intensive *adj.* thorough, thoroughgoing, emphatic, strengthened, heightened, increased, accelerated, sweeping, exhaustive, all-embracing, inclusive, full, stepped-up.
ant. weakened, waning, superficial, careless, apathetic, hit-or-miss, feeble.

intent *adj.* concentrated, fixed, directed, earnest, channeled, determined, purposeful, assiduous, industrious, steadfast, attentive, engrossed, absorbed, rapt, regardful. —*n.* intention, meaning, purpose, aim, end, design, goal, inclination, leaning.

ant. *adj.* distracted, wandering, errant, purposeless, careless.

intention *n.* purpose, plan, design, meaning, determination, end, objective, goal, wish, resolve, resolution, point, ambition, project, idea, object, aim, target, reason, point.

intentional *adj.* deliberate, planned, intended, purposeful, willed, meant, considered, aimed, directed, premeditated, witting, calculated.
ant. unintentional, unintended, accidental, unpremeditated, fortuitous, haphazard.

inter *v.* bury, entomb, inhume, inurn.
ant. exhume, disinter, dig up.

intercede *v.* ARBITRATE.

intercept *v.* stop, arrest, check, seize, catch, impound, confiscate, commandeer, interfere, obstruct, debar, stay, restrain, hinder, detain.

intercourse *n.* **1** interchange, exchange, communication, discourse, conversation, intercommunication, correspondence, dealings, flow, current, reciprocity, colloquy, conference. **2** coitus, copulation, congress, cohabitation, fornication, carnal knowledge.

interdict *v.* PROHIBIT.

interest *n.* **1** attraction, curiosity, importance, consequence, magnetism, drawing power, charisma, regard, attention, notice, concern, care, inquisitiveness, significance, meaning, weight, moment. **2** profit, gain, boon, advantage, advancement, behalf, enrichment, self-regard. —*v.* attract, arouse, awaken, wake, absorb, hold, occupy, move, reach, impress, rouse, stir, entertain, delight, please.
ant. *n.* **1** boredom, apathy, coolness, disregard, insignificance, dispassion. *v.* bore, weary, tire, irk, burden, repel.

interested *adj.* attracted, engaged, absorbed, engrossed, involved, attentive, rapt, drawn, concerned, curious, inquisitive, diverted, beguiled.
ant. bored, wearied, uninterested,

unconcerned, detached, inattentive, *dégagé.*

interesting *adj.* absorbing, attractive, appealing, engaging, magnetic, provocative, exciting, entertaining, amusing, diverting, pleasing.

ant. uninteresting, boring, dull, tiring, tiresome, tedious, stale.

interfere *v.* intervene, meddle, oppose, clash, conflict, counter, intrude, interrupt, hinder, handicap, obstruct, interpose, restrain, intercede, butt in.

interference *n.* intervention, intrusion, interruption, hindrance, conflict, collision, opposition, handicap, obstruction, interposition, restraint, contravention, impediment, meddling, meddlesomeness.

interim *n.* interval, meantime, meanwhile, interlude, intermission, recess, pause, rest, respite, break, entr'acte. —*adj.* temporary, provisional, provisory, stopgap, makeshift, passing, transitional, transitory.

interior *adj.* internal, inside, inner, inward, proximal, enclosed, encapsulated, inland, remote. —*n.* inland, center, core, hinterland, upcountry, backwoods, bush.

ant. *adj.* external, exterior, outer, outside, distal, outward, exposed, surface.

interject *v.* INTERRUPT.

interjection *n.* interruption, interposition, interpolation, digression, intrusion, insertion, parenthesis, aside, apostrophe.

interloper *n.* intruder, trespasser, interposer, interferer, meddler, obtruder, invader, poacher, stranger, outsider.

interlude *n.* intermission, interval, recess, pause, respite, break, interim, interruption, entr'acte, interregnum, transition, bridge.

intermeddle *v.* MEDDLE.

intermediary *n.* mediator, go-between, middleman, representative, agent, emissary, medium, means, agency, negotiator, arbitrator, peacemaker, link, connection, broker, messenger, factor.

intermediate *adj.* intervening, intermediary, interposed, interpolated, medium, middle, halfway, median, medial, mean, transitional.

interment *n.* burial, burying, entombment, inhumation, funeral.

ant. exhumation, disinterment.

interminable *adj.* unending, endless, illimitable, unlimited, limitless, incessant, ceaseless, unceasing, boundless, unbounded, infinite, everlasting, eternal, perpetual, continuous.

ant. finite, limited, restricted, temporary, occasional.

intermingle *v.* mingle, mix, blend, combine, commingle, compound, fuse, interweave, amalgamate, intermix, merge, interfuse, incorporate, intertwine.

intermittent *adj.* discontinuous, interrupted, irregular, occasional, sporadic, alternating, fitful, spasmodic, periodic.

ant. continuous, incessant, perpetual, continual, constant.

intermix *v.* INTERMINGLE.

internal *adj.* inner, interior, inmost, innermost, inside, hidden, buried, secret, undisclosed, subjective, personal, private.

ant. exterior, outer, outside, outermost, revealed, unconcealed, exposed.

interpenetrate *v.* PERMEATE.

interpose *v.* **1** INSERT. **2** INTERRUPT.

interpret *v.* define, clarify, explain, elucidate, construe, expound, explicate, unravel, decode, decipher, solve, reveal, rephrase, reword, restate, describe, annotate, gloss, footnote.

interpretation *n.* explanation, explication, definition, clarification, construction, solution, paraphrase, restatement, exposition, exegesis, description, understanding, reading, version.

interpreter *n.* translator, definer, explicator, expounder, exponent, demonstrator, expositor, guide, conductor, commentator, annotator, spokesman, scholiast, mouthpiece.

interpretive *adj.* explanatory, exegetic, explicative, explicatory, expository, expositive, clarifying, elucidative, illuminative, enlightening, illustrative, exemplifying, annotative, scholiastic.

interrogate *v.* QUESTION.

interrogation *n.* questioning, investigation, examination, cross-examination, inquiry, inquisition, probe, grilling, catechism.

interrupt *v.* disturb, interfere, break, stop, punctuate, interject, interpose, divide, hinder, intercept, obstruct, check, disconnect, sever, cut, suspend, discontinue, delay.

interruption *n.* disturbance, interference, stoppage, disruption, hindrance, suspension, discontinuance, discontinuity, delay, break, pause, intermission, interval, recess, halt, rest.

intersect *v.* cross, divide, transverse, interrupt, crosscut, crisscross, bisect, cut across.

intersperse *v.* sprinkle, strew, scatter, interlard, interpose, pepper, broadcast, disseminate, interpolate, bestrew.

interstice *n.* APERTURE.

interval *n.* pause, rest, recess, break, intermission, gap, hiatus, distance, stretch, gulf, interim, meantime, meanwhile, respite, interlude, entr'acte, spell, lapse, discontinuity.

intervene *v.* interfere, mediate, interpose, intercede, arbitrate, negotiate, befall, betide, occur, supervene, ensue, arrive, arise, intrude.

intervention *n.* interference, interruption, intrusion, obtrusion, mediation, arbitration, agency, intercession, instrumentality, ministry, negotiation, interposition, encroachment, infringement.

interview *n.* meeting, parley, colloquy, consultation, conference, discussion, audience, conversation, reception, discourse, dialogue, assembly, *tête-à-tête*.

interweave *v.* INTERMINGLE.

inthrall *v.* ENTHRALL.

intimacy *n.* familiarity, closeness, companionship, fraternity, fellowship, friendship, brotherhood, amity, comradeship, camaraderie, chumminess. **ant.** alienation, aloofness, separation, apartheid.

intimate[1] *adj.* **1** *of friendship:* close, near, dear, familiar, confidential, personal, inseparable, chummy, fast, thick. **2** *of knowledge:* thorough, sound, special, deep, inmost, detailed, profound, solid. **3** sexual, carnal, physical, adulterous, fornicative. —*n.* familiar, friend, confidant, companion, comrade, mate, pal, buddy, chum.
ant. *adj.* **1** distant, formal, impersonal, remote, aloof. **2** superficial, slight, shallow, meager. *n.* stranger, outsider, alien.

intimate[2] *v.* insinuate, imply, hint, suggest, indicate, whisper, mean, signify, allude.

intimation *n.* insinuation, innuendo, implication, suggestion, allusion, indication, supposition, hint, whisper, cue, clue, glimmer, inkling.

intimidate *v.* frighten, menace, scare, dismay, affright, alarm, awe, daunt, cow, bully, abash, threaten, browbeat, unnerve, subdue.

intitle *v.* ENTITLE.

intolerable *adj.* insufferable, unendurable, insupportable, unbearable, excruciating, agonizing, harrowing, torturous, tormenting, maddening, racking, execrable, dreadful, loathsome.
ant. tolerable, bearable, endurable.

intolerance *n.* bigotry, narrow-mindedness, prejudice, rigidity, self-righteousness, illiberality, dogmatism, fanaticism, zealotry, one-sidedness, provincialism, parochialism.
ant. tolerance, open-mindedness, broadmindedness, understanding.

intolerant *adj.* bigoted, narrow-minded, prejudiced, rigid, fanatical, dogmatic, parochial, sectarian, one-sided, unreasonable, unyielding, inflexible, self-righteous.

ant. broadminded, understanding, unprejudiced.

intone *v.* chant, hum, croon, intonate.

intoxicated *adj.* inebriated, drunk, drunken, befuddled, besotted, tipsy, boozy, high, stoned (*Slang*), loaded (*Slang*), smashed (*Slang*), zonked (*Slang*).

ant. unintoxicated, sober, on the wagon.

intractability *n.* OBSTINACY.

intractable *adj.* obstinate, stubborn, refractory, unmanageable, uncontrollable, ungovernable, recalcitrant, rebellious, contrary, perverse, fractious, headstrong, ornery, willful, obdurate, unyielding.

ant. docile, compliant, willing, tractable, manageable, accommodating, complaisant.

intransigent *adj.* uncompromising, resolute, steadfast, unshakable, unyielding, inflexible, rigid, obdurate, adamant, diehard, fixed, principled, hard-nosed (*Slang*).

ant. compromising, flexible, irresolute, reconcilable, opportunistic, vacillating.

intrepid *adj.* fearless, courageous, brave, heroic, valorous, bold, valiant, daring, unflinching, stalwart, audacious, unafraid, game.

ant. cowardly, fearful, timid, craven, cautious, faint-hearted.

intricacy *n.* complexity, complication, entanglement, convolution, maze, labyrinth, mystery, involvement, tangle, knot, skein, network, intrigue.

ant. simplicity, bareness.

intricate *adj.* complex, complicated, overcomplicated, convoluted, labyrinthine, tangled, knotty, involved, mysterious, impenetrable, perplexing, obscure, puzzling.

ant. simple, plain, unadorned, uncomplicated, clear, easy.

intrigue *n.* 1 plot, scheme, ruse, stratagem, conspiracy, cabal, machination, maneuver, secret, connivance, collusion, trick, dodge, duplicity, chicanery, double-dealing. 2 love affair, liaison, flirtation, amour, intimacy. —*v.* plot, scheme, conspire, maneuver, connive, trick, hatch, brew, contrive, machinate.

intriguing *adj.* ENGROSSING.

intrinsic *adj.* inherent, essential, inner, internal, inborn, innate, inbred, ingrained, natural, native, fundamental, basic, inherited.

ant. extrinsic, outer, outward, external, acquired, superficial.

introduce *v.* 1 acquaint, present, familiarize. 2 begin, start, initiate, commence, inaugurate, originate, pioneer, embark, launch, lead, found. 3 insert, inject, infuse, implant, interject, put in.

introduction *n.* 1 beginning, commencement, initiation, start, innovation, launching, founding, pioneering. 2 insertion, injection, infusion. 3 preface, foreword, prelude, preamble, prologue, preliminary, prolegomenon, overture.

introductory *adj.* preliminary, prefatory, beginning, initial, initiatory, preparatory, inaugural, first.

ant. concluding, terminating, terminal, final, last.

introspective *adj.* pensive, brooding, reflective, subjective, meditative, contemplative, introverted, inner-directed.

intrude *v.* invade, interfere, interrupt, obtrude, interlope, encroach, meddle, infringe, intervene, trespass, overstep, impose, butt in.

intrusion *n.* interference, invasion, encroachment, obtrusion, infringement, trespass, intervention, imposition, aggression, inroad, incursion, meddling, officiousness, impertinence.

intrusive *adj.* interfering, obtrusive, meddlesome, aggressive, officious, importunate, impertinent, uncalled-for, unwelcome, unwanted, ill-timed, unbidden.

intrust *v.* ENTRUST.

intuition *n.* hunch, feeling, surmise, sixth sense, instinct, sense, insight.

intuitive *adj.* INSTINCTIVE.

inundate *v.* flood, deluge, overflow, engulf, overwhelm, drench.

inure *v.* habituate, harden, toughen, accustom, train, strengthen, discipline, desensitize.

invade *v.* **1** encroach, attack, trespass, raid, march on, assail, assault, strike. **2** spread, penetrate, enter, infect, infest, disease.

invalid[1] *n.* patient, shut-in, convalescent, valetudinarian.

invalid[2] *adj.* inoperative, null and void, weak, unbinding, unenforceable, ineffective, useless, pointless, impotent, vain, futile, illogical, unscientific.
ant. valid, forceful, cogent, viable, operative, enforceable, solid.

invalidate *v.* annul, cancel, nullify, undo, abrogate, overthrow, repeal, refute, rescind, override, overrule, countermand, quash, disable, disprove.
ant. validate, authorize, sanction, legalize, ratify, legitimize, empower.

invaluable *adj.* inestimable, priceless, precious, matchless, peerless, unparalleled, nonpareil, rare, indispensable, irreplaceable.

invariable *adj.* unchanging, unvarying, uniform, constant, unchangeable, immutable, unalterable, regular, stable, dependable, undeviating, homogeneous, consistent.
ant. variable, varied, changing, changeable, differing, irregular.

invasion *n.* incursion, raid, aggression, attack, encroachment, infringement, foray, intrusion, trespass, assault, inroad, offensive, sortie, hostility, onslaught.

invective *n.* abuse, denunciation, vituperation, censure, contumely, diatribe, sarcasm, satire, reproach, scurrility, opprobrium, contempt, disparagement, tongue-lashing.

inveigh *v.* denounce, censure, abuse, vilify, reproach, disparage, condemn, fulminate, objurgate, impugn, recriminate, castigate, execrate, upbraid, berate, vituperate.

inveigle *v.* entice, seduce, trick, beguile, decoy, entangle, ensnare, enmesh, tempt, delude, victimize, cozen, catch, mislead, bamboozle.

invent *v.* **1** create, devise, contrive, originate, fashion, concoct, improvise, conceive, hatch, fabricate. **2** lie, falsify, prevaricate, equivocate, fake, counterfeit, fib, misrepresent, simulate, misstate.

invention *n.* **1** creativity, creativeness, inventiveness, originality, genius, artfulness, ingenuity, ingeniousness, imagination, resourcefulness, freshness, newness, novelty. **2** creation, contrivance, design, device, concoction, improvisation, coinage, fancy. **3** falsehood, prevarication, lie, fib, fabrication, story, falsification, distortion, fiction.
ant. **1** imitativeness, unoriginality, dullness, staleness. **3** truth, fact, reality.

inventive *adj.* creative, ingenious, original, imaginative, improvisational, fertile, fecund, productive, gifted, fanciful.
ant. imitative, unimaginative, trite, pedestrian.

inventor *n.* originator, creator, pioneer, improviser, deviser, designer, father.

inverse *adj.* OPPOSITE.

invest *v.* empower, authorize, entitle, permit, endow, deputize, license, enfranchise, enable, delegate, charge, entrust, assign, ordain, sanction.

investigate *v.* inquire, search, examine, look into, study, scrutinize, probe, inspect, explore, analyze, reconnoiter, research, survey, track, trace.

investigation *n.* inquiry, search, research, examination, study, scrutiny, probe, inspection, analysis, survey, quest, reconnaissance, inquest, inquisition, review.

inveterate *adj.* habitual, chronic, established, confirmed, deep-rooted, deep-seated, long-standing, inbred, fixed, time-honored, ineradicable, age-old, customary, ingrained.

invidious *adj.* envious, begrudging, grudging, resentful, spiteful, malicious, malevolent, rancorous, offensive, unkind, hostile, hateful, baleful. **ant.** pleasant, gratifying, pleasing, kind, benevolent, generous.

invigorate *v.* ANIMATE.

invigorating *adj.* stimulating, bracing, energizing, animating, strengthening, fortifying, enlivening, vitalizing, restorative, wholesome, refreshing, quickening. **ant.** weakening, enervating, debilitating, devitalizing, enfeebling, incapacitating.

invincible *adj.* unconquerable, indomitable, insuperable, all-powerful, omnipotent, impregnable, titanic, unyielding, invulnerable, unassailable, unbeatable. **ant.** vulnerable, fallible, weak, unprotected, defenseless, powerless.

inviolate *adj.* unbroken, intact, unviolated, pure, virgin, whole, entire, unprofaned, unaltered, undisturbed, sacred, sacrosanct, consecrated, holy. **ant.** violated, broken, profaned, abused, desecrated.

invisible *adj.* unseeable, concealed, hidden, unseen, undiscernible, imperceptible, screened, veiled, covert, mysterious, unrevealed, undisclosed, microscopic, infinitesimal. **ant.** visible, patent, discernible, distinct, perceptible, obvious.

invitation *n.* bidding, summons, request, proposal, bid, inducement, encouragement, attraction, temptation, solicitation, provocation, allurement, spur, stimulus.

invite *v.* ask, call for, ask for, solicit, beckon, request, summon, seek, encourage.

inviting *adj.* attractive, charming, tempting, engaging, pleasing, winning, charismatic, magnetic, captivating, disarming, fetching, winsome, delightful, intriguing, alluring, seductive, appealing. **ant.** repellent, uninviting, unattractive, unappealing, off-putting.

invoke *v.* call, address, summon, supplicate, entreat, petition, implore, beseech, importune, evoke, appeal, plead.

involuntary *adj.* unintentional, unintended, instinctive, automatic, spontaneous, reflex, unwilled, unwilling, uncontrolled, disinclined, reluctant, coerced, forced. **ant.** voluntary, willing, intentional, volitional, unconstrained, optional.

involve *v.* affect, entail, include, implicate, contain, comprise, embrace, count in, connect, engage, consist of, incorporate.

involved *adj.* **1** engaged, committed, dedicated, occupied, concerned, engrossed, interested, absorbed, *engagé.* **2** implicated, ensnared, entangled, enmeshed, caught, trapped, embroiled, inveigled. **3** complicated, complex, tangled, intricate, elaborate, knotty, labyrinthine, convoluted. **ant.** **1** disengaged, disinterested, uninterested, unconnected, detached. **2** dissociated, divorced, free, liberated. **3** simple, simplified, uncomplicated, elementary, straightforward.

iota *n.* jot, particle, shred, speck, whit, scrap, bit, scintilla, grain, shadow, crumb, drop, trifle, hair, whiff, atom.

irascibility *n.* ASPERITY.

irascible *adj.* irritable, touchy, ill-humored, bad-tempered, excitable, testy, grumpy, choleric, impatient, cantankerous, quarrelsome, grouchy, peevish, quick-tempered. **ant.** even-tempered, imperturbable, calm, serene, placid, stolid.

irate *adj.* angry, angered, enraged, furious, incensed, infuriated, raging, provoked, wrathful, fuming, rabid, galled, riled, vexed.

ire *n.* anger, fury, rage, wrath, dudgeon, ill-temper, irritation, bile, rancor, spleen, vexation, choler.

irk *v.* annoy, irritate, anger, weary, upset, vex, rile, bother, perturb, trouble, nettle, fret, harass, displease, plague, peeve.
ant. please, satisfy, soothe, salve, calm, placate.

irksome *adj.* annoying, irritating, vexing, wearisome, troublesome, bothersome, unpleasant, displeasing, upsetting, unwelcome, trying, tiresome, exasperating.
ant. pleasing, pleasant, enjoyable, gratifying, agreeable, welcome.

iron *adj.* firm, hard, obdurate, unyielding, strong, inflexible, adamant, stony, grim, tough, rigid.
ant. soft, weak, malleable, flexible, yielding.

ironclad *adj.* UNALTERABLE.

iron out smooth, resolve, eliminate, simplify, erase, eradicate, clear up, expedite.

irrational *adj.* unreasonable, unreasoning, illogical, unthinking, unintelligent, unsound, mindless, emotional, mystical, unscientific, nonsensical, demented, brainless, foolish, absurd.
ant. rational, reasonable, sensible, intelligent, circumspect, sane, lucid.

irreconcilable *adj.* ESTRANGED.

irrecoverable *adj.* LOST.

irrefragable *adj.* UNDENIABLE.

irrefutable *adj.* UNDENIABLE.

irregular *adj.* **1** abnormal, erratic, uncontrolled, unregulated, unreliable, unconventional, exceptional, anomalous, disorderly, variable, improper, unusual, aberrant, fitful. **2** uneven, asymmetrical, rough, serrated, jagged, rugged, flawed, faulty, crooked.
ant. 1 regular, reliable, conventional, usual, proper, regulated, normal. **2** even, symmetrical, smooth, regular, balanced, classic.

irrelevancy *n.* non sequitur, inappropriateness, impertinence, unsuitability, disconnection, inappositeness.
ant. suitability, relevance, aptness, pertinence, appropriateness, point.

irrelevant *adj.* unrelated, inappropriate, inapplicable, immaterial, unsuitable, impertinent, extraneous, inapposite, unfitting, inconsequent, illogical, beside the point, incidental, off target, malapropos.
ant. relevant, pertinent, germane, apt, appropriate, to the point, fitting, apropos.

irreligious *adj.* impious, ungodly, irreverent, profane, unholy, blasphemous, atheistic, sacrilegious, freethinking, unbelieving.
ant. religious, pious, godly, worshipful, devout, pietistic.

irremovable *adj.* PERMANENT.

irreparable *adj.* PERMANENT.

irreproachable *adj.* BLAMELESS.

irresistible *adj.* overpowering, formidable, overwhelming, invincible, seductive, enchanting, masterful, potent, compelling, inexorable, indisputable, unquestionable.
ant. resistible, resistant, questionable, weak, powerless.

irresolute *adj.* wavering, undecided, unsure, uncertain, vacillating, hesitant, faltering, halting, indecisive, fluctuating, weak, pliable, feeble.
ant. resolute, determined, resolved, steadfast, firm, unhesitating, fixed.

irresponsible *adj.* unreliable, careless, undependable, untrustworthy, unpredictable, fickle, capricious, heedless, immature, scatterbrained, devil-may-care, frivolous, unsettled, harum-scarum.
ant. responsible, dependable, trustworthy, reliable, adult, sober.

irreverent *adj.* disrespectful, impertinent, rude, derisive, contemptuous, irreligious, iconoclastic, impious, mocking, sneering, unrespectful.
ant. reverent, worshipful, religious, respectful, deferential, awed.

irrevocable *adj.* UNALTERABLE.

irritability *n.* ASPERITY.

irritable *adj.* impatient, mean, ill-tempered, short-tempered, irascible, bad-tempered, touchy, fretful, excitable, high-strung, cantankerous, contentious, quarrelsome, fractious, grouchy, grumpy, waspish.
ant. calm, composed, even-tempered, good-natured, imperturbable, agreeable, unexcitable.

irritant *adj.* irritating, provoking, disturbing, nettlesome, exacerbating, irksome, chafing, vexing, vexatious, offensive, troubling, inflammatory, disquieting, unsettling. —*n.* irritation, annoyance, disturbance, exacerbation, thorn, nettle, sting, nuisance, vexation, provocation, spur, goad.
ant. *adj.* calming, soothing, quieting, relaxing, sedative, pleasing. *n.* tranquilizer, sedative, palliative, balm, salve, emollient.

irritate *v.* **1** exasperate, annoy, anger, irk, provoke, agitate, nettle, vex, offend, gall, disquiet, trouble, unsettle, pester, rub the wrong way. **2** inflame, chafe, exacerbate, acerbate, aggravate, sensitive, worsen, intensify, fester.
ant. 1 mollify, calm, comfort, soothe, please. **2** palliate, improve, relieve, ease, alleviate.

irritating *adj.* annoying, provoking, bothersome, troublesome, vexing, vexatious, disturbing, worrisome, offensive, chafing, displeasing, unpleasant, disagreeable, grating, disquieting, nagging, unsettling.
ant. soothing, calming, pleasant, comforting, agreeable, mollifying, assuaging.

irritation *n.* **1** annoyance, exasperation, anger, ire, provocation, disturbance, trouble, inflammation, exacerbation, disquietude, discomposure, tension, resentment, displeasure, impatience. **2** pest, tease, nuisance, heckler, thorn, wasp, irritant, goad, spur, bother, torment, trial, bore, sore, infection, inflammation.

ant. 1 calm, composure, serenity, pleasure, ease, quietude, tranquillity. **2** balm, salve, emollient, sedative, tranquilizer, relaxant.

irruption *n.* RAID.

island *n.* enclave, isle, islet, enclosure, escape, refuge, shelter, retreat, sanctuary, ivory tower.

islet *n.* ISLAND.

isolate *v.* **1** separate, set apart, detach, dissociate, segregate, insulate, sequester, seclude, circumscribe, banish, exile, excommunicate. **2** quarantine.

isolation *n.* **1** separation, separateness, solitude, aloneness, dissociation, detachment, segregation, banishment, seclusion, insulation, sequestration, apartheid, circumscription, exile, excommunication. **2** quarantine, confinement, restraint, *cordon sanitaire*.

issuance *n.* APPEARANCE.

issue *v.* give out, deal out, put out, distribute, emit, put forth, appear, emerge, come forth, come out, originate, emanate, discharge, arise. —*n.* **1** topic, subject, argument, matter, point, question, problem, desideratum, controversy, contention. **2** result, outcome, upshot, consequence, event, conclusion, effect, denouement, aftermath, eventually, termination. **3** offspring, progeny, children, family, descendants, young, posterity, line.

italicize *v.* EMPHASIZE.

itch *n.* **1** pruritis, scabies. **2** craving, longing, yen, yearning, want, desire, restlessness, hankering, appetite, lust, itchiness, hunger, thirst.

itchy *adj.* restless, edgy, itching, prurient, desirous, impatient, eager, unsatisfied, craving, thirsty, hungry, lustful, unsatisfied.

item *n.* article, entry, detail, particular, unit, element, feature, paragraph, piece, example, sample.

itemize *v.* specify, list, detail, enumerate, particularize, inventory, recount, recapitulate, take stock, instance, substantiate, spell out.

iterate *v.* REITERATE.

itinerant *adj.* wandering, nomadic, peripatetic, wayfaring, traveling, on the move, roving, roaming, migratory, vagrant, vagabond, unsettled.

ant. settled, established, fixed, rooted, stable, resident.

itinerary *n.* route, plan, course, path, road, way, trip, journey, tour.

J

jab *v.* poke, prod, punch, bump, bunt, tap, strike, push, hit, stab, thrust, lunge, feint. —*n.* poke, prod, punch, bump, blow, thrust, dig.

jabber *v.* chatter, gabble, prattle, prate, gab, mumble, palaver, gossip, waffle (*Brit.*), yap (*Slang*). —*n.* chatter, gabble, babble, prattle, palaver, gibberish, twaddle, blather, drivel, nonsense, yap (*Slang*).

jack *n.* **1** man, male, fellow, guy, chap, boy. **2** laborer, worker, toiler, hand. **3** sailor, seaman, seafarer, mariner, sea dog, salt, tar, gob (*Slang*).

jackal *n.* flunky, drudge, drone, legman, hack, puppet, tool, instrument, servant, slave, menial, vassal, minion.

jackanapes *n.* upstart, smart aleck, whippersnapper, bounder, pretender, parvenu, coxcomb, fop, dandy.

jackass *n.* fool, oaf, blockhead, nincompoop, idiot, imbecile, moron, dunce, simpleton, ignoramus, numskull, bungler.

jacket *n.* cover, case, casing, enclosure, wrapper, wrapping, envelope, folder, coat, skin, sheath.

jack-of-all-trades *n.* handyman, factotum, man Friday, hack, generalist, amateur.

ant. specialist, expert, adept, master, pro.

jack up *v.* **1** raise, lift, elevate, erect, hoist, heave, rear. **2** increase, advance, boost, raise, elevate, extend, up, put up, hike.

ant. 1 lower, drop, let down, take down, depress. **2** decrease, lower, reduce, cut.

jade *n.* wench, hussy, hag, flirt, wanton, shrew, trollop, slut, drab, harlot, whore.

jaded *adj.* worn-out, exhausted, fatigued, tired, weary, surfeited, satiated, sated, fagged, blasé, indifferent, bored, hardened, inured.

ant. fresh, alive, enthusiastic, spirited, interested, involved.

jag[1] *n.* notch, point, snag, barb, tooth, protuberance, denticulation.

jag[2] *n. Slang* spree, fit, bout, binge (*Slang*), spell, orgy, period, stretch, interim.

jagged *adj.* notched, saw-tooth, barbed, serrated, toothed, dentiform, denticulated, ragged, divided, uneven.

ant. smooth, straight, level, even.

jail *n.* prison, penitentiary, gaol, stockade, reformatory, borstal, house of correction, house of detention, workhouse, brig, keep, lockup, pen (*Slang*), coop (*Slang*), clink (*Slang*), jug (*Slang*), calaboose (*Slang*), cooler (*Slang*), stir (*Slang*), hoosegow (*Slang*). —*v.* imprison, incarcerate, immure, impound, lock up, intern, detain, confine, commit.

ant. *v.* release, let go, pardon, parole, spring (*Slang*).

jailbird *n.* prisoner, convict, inmate, con (*Slang*), ex-convict, parolee, criminal.

jailer *n.* warden, gaoler, warder, keeper, captor, guard, correction officer, turnkey, screw (*Slang*).

jam *v.* **1** wedge, squeeze, press, sandwich, cram, stuff, pack, ram, push, pack, force. **2** crowd, throng, mob, swarm, congest, blockade, block, crush, fill, pack. **3** crush, bend, dent, distort, bruise. **4** clog, obstruct, interfere with, interrupt, stall, stick, break, stop. —*n.* **1** crowd, horde, throng, mob, swarm, host, mass, pack, conglomeration, congestion, press, tie-up, bottleneck. **2** fix, bind, scrape, hole, hot water, pickle, plight, quandary, dilemma, predicament, embarrassment, trouble, difficulty. —*adv.* completely, entirely, wholly, altogether, fully, thoroughly, absolutely, overwhelmingly.

jamboree *n.* frolic, spree, fete, festival, celebration, carousal, festivity.

jangle *v.* **1** clang, clash, clatter, clank, rattle, vibrate. **2** quarrel, bicker, squabble, spat, altercate, wrangle, argue, dispute. —*n.* **1** clanging, clangor, clashing, clank, rattle, din, discord, dissonance. **2** quarrel, squabble, bickering, wrangle, tiff, imbroglio, feud, argument, altercation, discord.

janitor *n.* caretaker, superintendent, custodian, porter, doorkeeper, gatekeeper, concierge.

jape *v.* joke, jest, banter, twit, tease, lampoon, deride, ridicule. —*n.* joke, jest, gibe, banter, lampoon, ridicule, raillery, trick, caper, prank, horseplay.

jar[1] *n.* vessel, container, receptacle, crock, bottle, pot, jug, urn, vase, beaker.

jar[2] *v.* **1** vibrate, shake, rattle, jiggle, jog, jolt, jounce, rock, quake. **2** clang, jangle, clash, rattle, grate, grind. **3** annoy, irritate, grate on, disturb, rankle, offend, shock, outrage. —*n.* **1** jolt, jouncing, agitation, shock. **2** clang, jangle, clash, dissonance, cacophony. **3** strife, conflict, dissension,

discord, clash, quarrel, squabble, spat, tiff.

jargon *n.* **1** gibberish, gabble, babble, twaddle, rigmarole, mumbo jumbo, drivel, rubbish, bunk, gobbledygook, nonsense, double talk, doublespeak. **2** cant, parlance, idiom, argot, patois, shop talk, lingo (*Slang*).

jaundiced *adj.* **1** distorted, warped, twisted, biased, partial, intolerant, prejudiced, envious, jealous, bitter, embittered, hostile, resentful, spiteful. **2** yellow, sallow.

ant. 1 fair, impartial, tolerant, unprejudiced, generous, unselfish, magnanimous.

jaunt *n.* excursion, outing, tour, trip, ramble, tramp, stroll.

jaunty *adj.* sprightly, breezy, buoyant, lively, vivacious, frisky, blithe, winsome, airy, showy, dapper, debonair.

jaw *v. Slang* **1** chatter, jabber, babble, blab, gab, gossip, talk. **2** scold, berate, abuse, revile, vituperate.

jawbone *v. Slang* ENJOIN.

jazz *n. Slang* bunk, hokum, claptrap, poppycock, rubbish, drivel, nonsense.

jazz up *v. Slang* enliven, animate, pep up (*Slang*), intensify, enhance, heighten, improve.

jazzy *adj. Slang* **1** showy, flashy, splashy, garish, loud, exaggerated. **2** lively, swinging, syncopated, energetic, vivacious, spirited.

ant. 1 restrained, tasteful, elegant, understated.

jealous *adj.* **1** envious, covetous, jaundiced, mistrustful, suspicious, grudging, resentful, intolerant, hostile. **2** vigilant, watchful, alert, wary, protective, solicitous, anxious, zealous.

ant. 1 trusting, open, tolerant, generous. **2** relaxed, easygoing, careless.

jealousy *n.* envy, distrust, suspicion, misgiving, resentment, intolerance, covetousness, mistrust.

ant. trust, openness, tolerance, generosity.

jeer *v.* hoot, gibe, banter, taunt, mock, sneer, scoff, rail, deride, ridicule.

—*n.* gibe, taunt, banter, jest, sneer, scoff, ridicule.

jejune *adj.* **1** inadequate, lacking, deficient, wanting, insubstantial. **2** vapid, insipid, inane, wishy-washy, dull, prosaic, banal, flat. **3** unsophisticated, immature, puerile, juvenile, infantile, childish.
ant. 1 nourishing, invigorating, salubrious. **2** vital, exciting, inspired. **3** sophisticated, mature, knowing.

jell *v.* form, take form, shape up, crystallize, finalize, organize, congeal, harden, set, solidify.

jellyfish *n.* pushover (*Slang*), waverer, vacillator, softy (*Slang*), milksop, namby-pamby, trimmer, weakling, coward.
ant. stalwart, mule, bullhead, intransigent.

jeopardize *v.* imperil, endanger, expose, hazard, risk, chance, venture.

jeopardy *n.* peril, danger, precariousness, exposure, insecurity, risk, venture, hazard.
ant. security, safety, certainty.

jeremiad *n.* lamentation, lament, complaint, plaint, wail, cry.

jerk *v.* twitch, yank, jiggle, tweak, shake, snap, pluck, jolt, flip. —*n.* **1** twitch, yank, jiggle, snap, pull, spasm, convulsion. **2** *Slang* fool, simpleton, scatterbrain, goof (*Slang*), schlep (*Slang*), idiot, square (*Slang*), goon (*Slang*).

jerkwater *adj.* one-horse, hick (*Slang*), country, backwoods, remote, provincial, small, insignificant, unimportant.

jerky *adj.* **1** jolting, joggling, jouncy, shaky, twitchy, fidgety, jumpy. **2** foolish, idiotic, simple, stupid, asinine, crazy, silly, square (*Slang*).

jerrybuilt *adj.* shoddy, flimsy, gimcrack, unsubstantial, inferior, rickety, defective, faulty, shaky, weak.
ant. sturdy, solid, sound, well-built, well-constructed.

jest *n.* **1** joke, witticism, quip, mot, bon mot, pun, one-liner, gibe, sally, banter, raillery, prank. **2** fun, frivol-ity, pleasantry, humor, high spirits, sport. —*v.* joke, banter, tease, trifle, spoof, josh (*Slang*), gibe, jeer, deride, scoff.

jester *n.* joker, wag, wit, quipster, humorist, prankster, zany, comic, clown, fool.

jet[1] *adj.* black, ebony, sable, inky, coal-black, pitch-black, raven-black.

jet[2] *n.* **1** spurt, squirt, gush, shoot, spout, spray, stream, rush, flow. **2** nozzle, spout, hose, sprayer, sprinkler, atomizer. —*v.* spurt, squirt, shoot, gush, spray, spout, spew, emit, surge, well, pour, discharge.

jettison *v.* **1** eject, expel, discharge, throw, drop, dump, heave, evacuate, void. **2** discard, abandon, cast off, dispose, reject, remove, eliminate, dismiss.

jetty *n.* breakwater, sea wall, mole, wharf, pier, dock, quay.

jewel *n.* **1** gem, stone, brilliant, ornament, bauble, rock (*Slang*), ice (*Slang*). **2** rarity, paragon, worthy, pride, treasure, gem, pearl, wonder, charm, treat, prize, find.

jewelry *n.* gems, jewels, treasure, finery, trinkets.

Jezebel *n.* harlot, wanton, hussy, jade, adulteress, vixen, witch, hellcat, ogress, fury, she-monster, harridan, virago, bitch (*Slang*).

jib *v.* balk, recoil, shy, dodge, swerve, retreat, shrink, refuse.

jibe[1] *v.* accord, conform, fit, coincide, tally, square, agree, comport, correspond, complement, harmonize.
ant. contradict, conflict, differ, disagree.

jibe[2] *n., v.* GIBE.

jiffy *n.* instant, moment, second, minute, flash, trice, twinkling.

jig *v.* skip, gambol, caper, prance, frisk, romp, leap, bob, twitch, joggle, jiggle, wiggle.

jiggle *v.* jerk, jig, twitch, waggle, wiggle, wriggle, shimmy, shake, agitate, bob, hitch, flick. —*n.* twitch, jerk, wiggle, jig, wriggle, bob, shake.

jilt *v.* cast off, abandon, spurn, get rid

of, throw over, jettison, reject, discard, forsake, desert, quit, leave.

jingle v. tinkle, clink, ring, chink, tingle, chime, jangle. — n. tinkle, clink, ring, chink, jangle, rattle, tintinnabulation.

jingo n. chauvinist, flag-waver, ultranationalist, superpatriot, militarist, warmonger, hawk.

ant. internationalist, pacifist, peacemaker, peacemonger, dove.

jinx n. curse, evil eye, hex, hoodoo, whammy, bête noire, nemesis.

jitter v. fidget, tremble, flutter, quiver, shake, shiver.

jitters n. fidgets, shakes, willies (*Slang*), shivers, nervousness, tenseness, anxiety.

jittery adj. fidgety, skittery, shaky, jumpy, shaking, trembling, quivering, agitated, nervous, anxious.

ant. calm, cool, tranquil, composed, serene.

jive *Slang* n. bull (*Slang*), jazz (*Slang*), double talk, nonsense, claptrap. —v. mislead, confuse, fluster, rattle, muddle, befuddle, bewilder.

job n. 1 task, work, chore, stint, duty, assignment, mission, charge, errand, effort, activity, pursuit, venture, affair, business, undertaking, enterprise. 2 employment, position, situation, post, work, place, occupation, function, office, berth, career, vocation, trade, craft. 3 piece, lot, product, output, portion, share, batch, allotment, consignment.

jobless adj. unemployed, out of work, idle, unoccupied, inactive.

ant. employed, working, busy, occupied, active.

jockey v. 1 scheme, plot, maneuver, finagle, circumvent, insinuate, ingratiate, intrigue, engineer, navigate. 2 cheat, trick, manipulate, mislead, deceive, dupe, hoodwink.

jocose adj. JOCULAR.

jocular adj. jesting, joking, funny, playful, waggish, comical, teasing, witty, jocose, whimsical, droll, humorous, facetious, arch.

ant. unfunny, serious, earnest, humorless, sober, solemn, sedate, staid.

jocund adj. cheerful, merry, jovial, jolly, mirthful, frolicsome, gay, pleasant, blithe, elated, lively, debonair.

ant. sad, cheerless, sober, grave, serious.

jog v. 1 shake, jar, jostle, nudge, prod, press, push, poke, goad, jab, dig, bump, shove. 2 nudge, arouse, stimulate, prompt, remind, suggest, notify, warn. 3 poke, plod, trudge, lumber, shuffle, tramp, shamble, traipse. —n. push, nudge, prod, poke, goad, jab, dig.

joggle v. shake, jolt, jog, jostle, jerk, jiggle, wiggle, waggle, flip, flick. —n. shake, jolt, jog, jostle, jerk, wiggle, twitch, tremble, quaver.

john n. *Slang* TOILET.

joie de vivre zest, gusto, relish, elation, joy, enthusiasm, gaiety, cheerfulness, pleasure, enjoyment.

ant. lifelessness, apathy, weariness, ennui, indifference, jadedness.

join v. 1 connect, link, fasten, tie, attach, couple, yoke, unite, knit, cement, splice. 2 merge, combine, connect, meet, associate, consolidate, amalgamate, coalesce. 3 unite with, affiliate with, associate with, take part, participate, enroll, enlist, sign up, meet.

ant. 1 separate, split, sever, detach, break. 2 diverge, divide, deviate, branch. 3 leave, quit, disassociate, oppose, contest.

joint n. connection, link, union, junction, juncture, coupling, node, nexus, splice, seam, hinge, mortise, articulation. —adj. combined, united, shared, common, consolidated, mutual, allied, concerted, cooperative, collective, corporate. —v. 1 fasten, couple, link, connect, attach, join, affix, secure. 2 dismember, carve, dissect, disjoint, cut up, segment, section, divide, separate, sever, sunder.

ant. *v.* **1** separate, disconnect, sever, part, divide.

jointly *adv.* unitedly, together, conjointly, in conjunction, mutually, collectively.

joke *n.* **1** jest, witticism, story, yarn, repartee, crack, bon mot, quip, gag, prank, trick, jape, game, lark, fun, play. **2** laughingstock, butt, target, sport, laugh, farce, gag, folly, absurdity. —*v.* jest, banter, gibe, crack, josh, tease, chaff, mock, taunt.

joker *n.* **1** jokester, comic, jester, wit, punster, wisecracker, wag, humorist, comedian, prankster, trickster. **2** trap, snare, trick, subterfuge, plot, duplicity, ruse, cheat, swindle.

jollify *v.* FROLIC.

jolly *adj.* merry, jovial, cheerful, spirited, sprightly, light-hearted, fun-loving, playful, sportive, carefree. —*v.* flatter, soft-soap, cajole, wheedle, coax, encourage.

ant. *adj.* mirthless, sober, dour, morose.

jolt *v.* **1** strike, shake, stun, jar, jerk, bounce, shock, convulse. **2** surprise, startle, start, stagger, stun, upset, disturb, discompose. —*n.* **1** shake, bump, jerk, jar, jounce, jog, lurch, quiver, concussion. **2** surprise, shock, start, blow, thunderbolt, bombshell.

josh *v.* tease, poke fun at, kid (*Slang*), rib (*Slang*), sport with, guy, ridicule. —*n.* joke, jest, banter, pleasantry, sport, badinage, persiflage.

jostle *v.* push, bump, shove, joggle, shake, hustle, crowd, elbow, shoulder, joust, clash, collide, scuffle, scramble. —*n.* jolt, jar, bump, bounce, wobble, shake, tremor, collision.

jot *v.* write, note, record, register, take down, list, tally, scribble, indicate. —*n.* bit, iota, whit, particle, snippet, scrap, speck, mite, smidgen, trifle, scintilla.

jotting *n.* NOTE.

jounce *v.* bounce, jolt, jar, shake, jerk, bump, jostle, jiggle, joggle, stir, buffet. —*n.* bump, jolt, bounce, lurch, jerk, jostle, shake, quake, vibration, shock, concussion.

journal *n.* **1** diary, daybook, notebook, memoir, log, record, register, minutes, chronicle, calendar. **2** publication, periodical, serial, newspaper, paper, daily, gazette, review, magazine, bulletin, organ.

journalism *n.* news-gathering, news medium, press, fourth estate, communications, reporting, reportage.

journalist *n.* newsman, newswoman, reporter, correspondent, editor, columnist, stringer, leg man.

journey *n.* trip, tour, itinerary, passage, voyage, expedition, trek, excursion, jaunt, junket, pilgrimage, odyssey, quest. —*v.* travel, tour, voyage, range, roam, rove, traverse, trek, go, proceed, fare.

joust *n.* tilt, tourney, tournament, match, contest, fight, skirmish, competition, engagement, encounter. —*v.* tilt, jostle, duel, fight, skirmish, clash, strive, contest.

jovial *adj.* merry, mirthful, cheerful, gay, jolly, jocund, animated, zestful, sprightly, buoyant, convivial, cordial.

ant. cheerless, somber, sober, pensive.

joy *n.* **1** happiness, delight, gladness, pleasure, gaiety, elation, bliss, ecstasy, rapture. **2** treat, delight, pleasure, charm, jewel, gem, treasure, wonder.

ant. **1** sorrow, gloom, distress, despair. **2** trouble, worry, disappointment, affliction.

joyful *adj.* elated, gay, happy, delighted, lighthearted, buoyant, blissful, exuberant, glad, exultant, ecstatic, cheerful, joyous, merry, blithe, cheery, jovial, mirthful.

ant. sad, unhappy, melancholy, depressed.

joyless *adj.* cheerless, sad, unhappy, gloomy, dreary, downcast, melancholy, dejected, dismal, miserable.

ant. gay, happy, cheerful, mirthful, merry.

joyous *adj.* festive, merry, mirthful, cheerful, gleeful, gay, happy, heart-warming, exhilarating.

ant. depressing, grim, somber, heart-breaking, despairing.

jubilant *adj.* rejoicing, overjoyed, ecstatic, enraptured, elated, rollicking, exultant, triumphant.

ant. disappointed, dejected, downcast, forlorn.

jubilation *n.* exultation, elation, rejoicing, celebration, triumph.

ant. disappointment, dejection, melancholy, depression, the blues.

jubilee *n.* festivity, celebration, festival, fete, gala, commemoration, holiday, frolic, revelry.

Judas *n.* betrayer, deceiver, dissembler, snake, informer, turncoat, renegade, traitor, quisling.

judge *n.* **1** justice, jurist, magistrate, surrogate. **2** arbitrator, moderator, umpire, referee, czar, judicator, adjudicator, **3** arbiter, custodian, authority, expert, critic interpreter, connoisseur, epicure. —*v.* **1** try, sit, adjudge, adjudicate, determine, decide, rule, decree, pronounce, settle, sentence, find, award, assign, condemn, doom. **2** select, choose, find, decide, determine, settle, conclude, ascertain, resolve, arbitrate, umpire. **3** appraise, evaluate, appreciate, rate, assess, rank, value, gauge, weigh, size up, examine, review, criticize, interpret. **4** estimate, guess, reckon, calculate, deduce, infer, gather, suppose, surmise, presume. **5** consider, think, regard, believe, conclude, reckon, esteem, deem, opine.

judgment *n.* **1** determination, consideration, decision, arbitration, adjudication, conclusion. **2** ruling, decision, determination, finding, resolution, arbitration, opinion, pronouncement, decree, order, result, verdict, sentence, censure, condemnation, award. **3** opinion, notion, thought, determination, finding, eval-

uation, estimate, appraisal, diagnosis, assessment, appreciation, report, review, critique, criticism, censure. **4** wisdom, understanding, sagacity, prudence, intelligence, common sense, astuteness, acumen, perspicacity, discernment, discretion, discrimination.

ant. **4** imprudence, injudiciousness, indiscrimination, foolishness, obtuseness.

judicial *adj.* **1** legal, juridical, forensic, juristic, judiciary, judicatory. **2** discriminating, discerning, critical, acute, careful, exact, judicious.

ant. **2** hasty, imprecise, uncritical, cursory.

judicious *adj.* prudent, wise, enlightened, sensible, sound, sane, just, politic, discerning, circumspect, cautious.

ant. unreasonable, foolish, silly, fatuous, imprudent, unwise.

juggle *v.* manipulate, tamper with, alter, tinker with, maneuver, influence, modify.

juice *n.* **1** fluid, liquid, sap, serum, lymph, nectar, broth, extract, distillation. **2** essence, spirit, lifeblood, sap, kernel, pith, marrow, flame, force, vitality, energy.

juicy *adj.* **1** moist, wet, liquid, fluid, watery, sappy, succulent, pulpy, lush, luscious. **2** interesting, lively, colorful, irresistible, entrancing, zestful, tangy, piquant, spicy, racy, provocative, suggestive, sensational. **3** profitable, lucrative, money-making, rich, remunerative, productive.

jumble *n.* mixture, medley, hodgepodge, hash, scramble, conglomeration, muddle, mess, tangle, patchwork, snarl, disorder, confusion, farrago, gallimaufry.

jumbled *adj.* mixed, mingled, blended, miscellaneous, heterogeneous, indiscriminate, scrambled, muddled, scattered, confused, chaotic.

ant. ordered, organized, homogeneous, comparable, consistent.

jumbo *adj.* oversized, immense, huge,

giant, gigantic, mammoth, elephantine.

jump *v.* **1** spring, bound, leap, vault, hurdle, pounce, hop, skip, jerk, trip, prance. **2** miss, evade, pass over, leave out, skip, omit, avoid, neglect, shun. **3** increase, rise, gain, mount, surge. **4** assault, attack, charge, fall on, set on, surprise, catch offguard, mug (*Slang*). —*n.* **1** leap, bound, spring, hop, skip, vault, pounce. **2** increase, rise, advance, boost, upsurge, hike. **3** twitch, wrench, swerve, jerk, jolt, move, start, shock.
ant. *v.* **3** reduce, lower, cut back, mark down. *n.* **2** reduction, decrease, lowering, mark-down, cutback.

jumpy *adj.* **1** jerky, twitchy, skittish, springy, elastic, changeable, fluctuating, vacillating. **2** fidgety, jittery, fussy, fretful, agitated, restless, nervous, apprehensive, irritable.
ant. **2** calm, composed, unruffled, imperturbable.

junction *n.* joining, linking, coupling, union, fusion, merger, connection, attachment, meeting, confluence, crossing, crossroads, interchange, intersection.

juncture *n.* **1** union, joining, junction, connection, concurrence, confluence, convergence. **2** joint, connection, link, bond, seam, weld, knot, nexus, suture. **3** crisis, point, pass, pinch, strait, crux, emergency, exigency, quandary, predicament.

jungle *n.* forest, wilds, woods, thicket, bush, undergrowth.

junior *adj.* **1** subordinate, secondary, lesser, lower, minor, younger, inferior, second-string, subaltern. **2** youthful, immature, early, adolescent, juvenile.
ant. **1** senior, superior, primary, master. **2** adult, mature, older, later, advanced.

junk *n.* rubbish, trash, refuse, garbage, debris, scrap, waste, castoffs, leavings, schlock (*Slang*). —*v.* scrap, trash, dispose of, cast off, demolish, discard, dump, jettison.

junket *n.* TRIP.

junkie *n.* ADDICT.

junky *adj.* shoddy, tawdry, gaudy, cheap, tacky, ratty, rundown, ramshackle, tattered, dilapidated, schlocky (*Slang*).
ant. tasteful, refined, elegant, neat, well-maintained.

junta *n.* CLIQUE.

juridical *adj.* JUDICIAL.

jurisdiction *n.* **1** authorization, judicature, magistracy, commission, sanction, license, charter, warrant, authority, power, command, sovereignty, control, influence, direction. **2** sphere, range, compass, circuit, orbit, reach, bounds, zone, area, domain, district, province, dominion.

jurist *n.* **1** legalist, jurisprudent, jurisconsult, lawyer, attorney, counsel. **2** judge, justice, magistrate, surrogate.

juristic *adj.* JUDICIAL.

just *adj.* **1** virtuous, upright, honest, right, good, decent, honorable, straightforward, conscientious, blameless. **2** fair, impartial, reasonable, equitable, fair-minded, evenhanded, unbiased, scrupulous. **3** deserved, merited, worthy, proper, suitable, due, fit, fitting, apt, appropriate, reasonable, condign. **4** correct, accurate, exact, precise, true, sound, fit, appropriate, valid, legitimate, lawful, legal. —*adv.* **1** precisely, exactly, perfectly, positively, completely, fully. **2** only, merely, simply, but. **3** very, positively, quite, absolutely, simply.
ant. *adj.* **1** bad, iniquitous, base, dishonest. **2** unfair, partial, biased, warped. **3** undeserved, unearned, unwarrantable, improper, inappropriate. **4** false, wrong, illegitimate.

just about almost, nearly, well-nigh, not quite, all but, about, around, approximately, close to.

justice *n.* **1** integrity, honesty, honor, uprightness, virtue, merit, probity. **2** evenhandedness, impartiality, fairness, equity, justness, fair play. **3**

validity, correctness, rightfulness, lawfulness, legality, legitimacy, justness, truth, right, reasonableness.

ant. 1 injustice, wrong, dishonor, perifidy, dishonesty, impropriety. **2** unfairness, partiality, favoritism, bias. **3** invalidity, illegality, illegitimacy.

justifiable *adj* defensible, tenable, vindicable, warrantable, valid, legitimate, right, fit, proper, well-founded, plausible, sensible.

ant. indefensible, unwarranted, implausible, unsound.

justification *n.* **1** explanation, rationalization, defense, apology, excuse, vindication, extenuation, exoneration. **2** basis, grounds, reason, warrant, argument, defense, excuse, alibi.

justify *v.* **1** vindicate, legitimize, corroborate, confirm, verify, authorize, warrant, approve, sustain, uphold, support, establish. **2** clear, excuse, absolve, acquit, exculpate, exonerate.

jut *v.* project, protrude, extend, stand out, stick out, overhang, impend, beetle. —*n.* projection, protrusion, overhang, extension.

juvenile *adj.* young, youthful, junior, pubescent, adolescent, immature, undeveloped, childlike, childish, puerile, infantile, callow, unsophisticated. —*n.* youth, youngster, child, minor, boy, girl, teen-ager, kid, stripling.

ant. *adj.* mature, adult, grown-up, developed, advanced.

K

Kafkaesque *adj.* BIZARRE.

kaiser *n.* EMPEROR.

kaleidoscopic *adj.* variegated, everchanging, changeable, variable, mobile, fluid, unstable, fluctuating, many-sided, checkered, motley.

ant. stable, fixed, steady, uniform.

kaput *adj. Slang* DONE FOR.

keel over capsize, overturn, roll over, turn over, heel over, tip over, upset, founder.

keen *adj.* **1** sharp, cutting, knifelike, razor-sharp, edged, honed, fine, thin. **2** incisive, cutting, biting, penetrating, sharp, pointed, piercing, trenchant, caustic. **3** astute, discerning, clever, shrewd, brilliant, quick, sensitive, perceptive, acute, sharp. **4** intense, lively, animated, energetic, high-spirited, avid, ardent, enthusiastic, eager.

ant. 1 dull, blunt, flat, unedged. **2** pointless, unsophisticated, vulgar, gross. **3** obtuse, dense, stupid, dull,

blunt. **4** impassive, listless, bored, indifferent, nonchalant, apathetic, reluctant.

keep *v.* **1** hold, retain, have, possess, control. **2** maintain, manage, conduct, run, operate, deal in, trade in, stock. **3** observe, celebrate, commemorate, honor, perform, fulfill, hold, adhere to. **4** continue, sustain, maintain, stay, support, secure, preserve, protect. **5** detain, retain, reserve, restrain, confine, hold back, delay, hinder, retard. **6** remain, hold, hold to, hold fast, maintain, retain. —*n.* livelihood, support, means, maintenance, subsistence, sustenance, nourishment.

ant. 1 let go, hand over, release, drop. **3** forget, neglect, break, dishonor. **4** stop, interrupt, break, disturb. **5** release, let go, free, liberate, prompt.

keep back 1 restrain, hold back, check, curb, control, constrain, limit, restrict, prohibit. **2** withhold, reserve, hold aside, retain, preserve, suppress, hide.

ant. 1 release, let go, liberate, free. **2** release, give out, circulate, publish, announce.

keeper *n.* caretaker, overseer, guardian, guard, warden, curator, preserver.

keeping *n.* **1** custody, charge, care, maintenance, support, protection, possession, keep, trust, ward. **2** accord, line, accordance, conformity, compliance, agreement, harmony.

keep on continue, remain, prolong, endure, persist, persevere.

ant. stop, quit, give up, abandon.

keepsake *n.* souvenir, memento, remembrance, reminder, relic, token, emblem, symbol, memorial.

keep up match, maintain, keep pace, balance, emulate, rival, compete, contend.

ant. lag, trail, fall behind, abandon.

keg *n.* barrel, container, tank, drum, cask, tub, tun, butt, firkin.

ken *n.* **1** sight, vision, view, scope, range, field, compass. **2** knowledge, awareness, cognizance, acquaintance, perception, domain, mastery, grasp.

kerchief *n.* scarf, square, headpiece, babushka, neckcloth, neckpiece, neckware, handkerchief.

kernel *n.* **1** seed, grain, germ, nucleus, core, berry, pit, pip, stone, pith, marrow. **2** essence, gist, nub, core, heart, pith, germ, center, nucleus, quintessence.

kettle *n.* pot, teakettle, teapot, pan, vessel, caldron, boiler, vat, tureen.

key *n.* solution, answer, resolution, explanation, explication, elucidation, indicator, guide, pointer, sign, lead, clue, evidence. —*adj.* decisive, crucial, indispensable, salient, chief, vital, necessary, essential, fundamental, basic, material.

ant. *adj.* insignificant, immaterial, minor, secondary, peripheral.

keyed up TENSE.

keynote *n.* theme, essence, gist, nub, kernel, core, distinction, model, pattern, gravamen.

keystone *n.* basis, fundament, ground, principle, core, crux, cornerstone, mainspring.

kibitzer *n.* ONLOOKER.

kick *v.* **1** boot, punt, drop-kick. **2** object, protest, complain, gripe, grumble, remonstrate. **3** *Slang* quit, drop, give up, stop, abandon. —*n.* **1** blow, boot, punt, stroke, bang, bump. **2** zest, punch, pep, snap, dash, relish, tang, pungency, verve, vigor. **3** *Slang* thrill, bang (*Slang*), boot (*Slang*), stimulation, excitement, pleasure, enjoyment, gratification.

kick around 1 abuse, misuse, ill-treat, harass, persecute, oppress. **2** drift, knock around, loaf, bum (*Slang*), wander, roam, rove. **3** discuss, talk over, debate, argue, rap (*Slang*).

kickback *n.* **1** recoil, rebound, repercussion, ricochet, backfire, backlash, boomerang, bounce, spring. **2** graft, bribe, payoff, refund, ante, payment.

kicker *n.* SURPRISE.

kick in 1 pay, contribute, donate, give, subscribe, chip in, cough up (*Slang*). **2** *Slang* die, kick the bucket (*Slang*), croak (*Slang*), perish, expire, decease, succumb, pass away.

kickoff *n.* start, beginning, outset, send-off, opening, commencement.

ant. windup, finale, conclusion, finish, end.

kicky *adj. Slang* EXCITING.

kid *n.* CHILD. —*v.* tease, josh, toy, make sport of, jest, ridicule, deceive, delude, fool, hoodwink, bluff, trick, bilk, put on (*Slang*).

kidnap *v.* shanghai, impress, abduct, seize, hijack, skyjack.

kill *v.* **1** slay, execute, dispatch, put to death, do in, do away with, murder, assassinate, liquidate, annihilate, slaughter, massacre, butcher, rub out (*Slang*), zap (*Slang*). **2** end, halt, stop, arrest, defeat, destroy, extinguish, quench, stifle, smother. **3** counteract, offset, spoil, contravene, cancel, cross out, cut out, delete, scratch, excise, expunge, extirpate, censor. **4** overwhelm, stagger, amaze, astonish, astound, bewilder, bedazzle, dumbfound. —*n.* **1** prey, game, quarry, chase, carcass, meat, victim. **2** deathblow, *coup de grâce*, end, death, dispatch.

ant. *v.* **2** sustain, preserve, stimulate, encourage, create.

killer *n.* murderer, slayer, assassin, slaughterer, butcher, executioner, triggerman (*Slang*), cutthroat, hit man (*Slang*).

killing *n.* **1** murder, homicide, manslaughter, slaying, bloodshed, extermination, annihilation, slaughter, butchery, carnage, holocaust. **2** profit, windfall, coup, cleanup, success. —*adj.* **1** deadly, lethal, destructive, malign, virulent, pestilent, fatal, mortal. **2** exhausting, tiring, fatiguing, wearisome, demanding, difficult, painful. **3** irresistible, fascinating, captivating, arresting, engaging, alluring, attractive, entrancing.

killjoy *n.* spoilsport, wet blanket, dampener, sourpuss, dog in the manger, party-pooper (*Slang*).

kin *n.* **1** blood, descent, stock, flesh, family, kinfolk, kindred, kinship, extraction, relationship, consanguinity. **2** relatives, relations, family, kinfolk, kinsfolk, kindred, kith, folks, people. —*adj.* familial, akin, kindred, related, allied, cognate, germane, consanguine.

kind[1] *adj.* helpful, charitable, generous, good, friendly, accommodating, good-hearted, considerate, hospitable, benevolent, beneficent, gentle, mild, benign, tender, humane, gracious, loving, compassionate, indulgent, lenient, sympathetic, good-natured, Pickwickian.

ant. unsociable, inconsiderate, ill-disposed, ruthless, stern, harsh, unbending, forbidding, heartless, contrary, quarrelsome, disagreeable, spiteful.

kind[2] *n.* **1** variety, type, sort, breed, strain, class, stripe, stamp, form, make, brand, style, ilk, description. **2** essence, nature, character, disposition, style, manner, color, stripe, habit, persuasion.

kind-hearted *adj.* tender-hearted, gracious, humane, sympathetic, helpful, generous, considerate, indulgent.

ant. heartless, insensible, unsparing, cold, cruel.

kindle *v.* **1** ignite, fire, light, set on fire, burn, fuel. **2** excite, stimulate, animate, provoke, whet, rouse, incite, goad, arouse, inflame, stir up, foment. **3** warm, quicken, glow, fire, stir, thrill, brighten, illuminate.

ant. **2** discourage, dampen, stifle, extinguish.

kindly *adj.* **1** sympathetic, generous, genial, friendly, gentle, mild, benign, humane, considerate. **2** beneficial, benevolent, agreeable, pleasant, favorable, helpful, valuable. —*adv.* agreeably, pleasantly, good-naturedly, cordially, politely, thoughtfully.

ant. *adj.* **1** unsympathetic, inconsiderate, cold, cruel, hostile, inhumane. **2** unhelpful, unfavorable, disagreeable, unpleasant, adverse. —*adv.* disagreeably, unpleasantly, ungraciously, thoughtlessly, rudely.

kindness *n.* **1** goodness, good will, benevolence, graciousness, beneficence, tolerance, tenderness, mildness, grace, loving-kindness, sympathy, amiability, compassion. **2** good deed, benefaction, favor, treat, generosity, service, bounty, support, philanthropy, charity.

ant. **1** unkindness, meanness, cruelty, coldness, inhumanity.

kindred *adj.* **1** familial, akin, related, germane, cognate, fraternal, consanguine. **2** like, congenial, similar, resembling, akin, related, allied, affiliated, corresponding, analogous. —*n.* **1** blood, flesh, descent, stock, lineage, strain, kinship, relationship, consanguinity. **2** relatives, relations, family, kin, kinfolk, kith, folks, people. **3** affinity, relationship, similarity, correspondence, resemblance, conformity.

ant. *adj.* **2** unlike, uncongenial, unrelated, dissimilar, different.

kinetic *adj.* dynamic, animated, energetic, vigorous, forceful, active, mobile, motive, motile.

ant. static, motionless, fixed, immobile, inactive.

kinfolk *n.* KIN.

king *n.* leader, master, lord, power, boss, czar, autocrat, tycoon, baron. —*adj.* large, great, big, major, oversize, gross.

kingdom *n.* sphere, area, field, province, domain, realm, empire.

kingly *adj.* majestic, magnificent, splendid, glorious, august, noble, stately, regal, royal, princely, imperial, sovereign, autocratic.

kink *n.* **1** bend, twist, crimp, crinkle, coil, tangle, entanglement. **2** curl, knot, curlicue, frizz, ringlet, twirl, loop. **3** quirk, whim, crotchet, wrinkle, foible, notion, peculiarity, eccentricity, idiosyncrasy, fetish. **4** imperfection, defect, snarl, flaw, complication, difficulty, hindrance, obstruction, glitch (*Slang*). **5** crick, twinge, pinch, stitch, cramp, charley horse, pang.

kinky *adj.* **1** curly, knotted, frizzled, wiry, twisted, matted. **2** *Slang* odd, queer, bizarre, weird, peculiar, eccentric, esoteric, perverse, idiosyncratic, quirky.

ant. **2** conventional, stereotyped, hackneyed, conservative, square (*Slang*).

kinsfolk *n.* KIN.

kinship *n.* **1** family, blood, flesh, stock, lineage, kindred, relationship, consanguinity. **2** affinity, connection, relationship, affiliation, association.

kinsman *n.* RELATIVE.

kismet *n.* fate, destiny, Providence, fortune, lot, portion, end, doom.

kiss *n.* touch, caress, brush, graze, glance, shave, contact. —*v.* **1** touch, caress, brush, glance, graze, scrape,

skim, pat. **2** osculate, buss, smooch (*Slang*).

kit *n.* outfit, gear, tackle, rig, set, supplies, tools, utensils, equipment, implements.

kittenish *adj.* playful, coquettish, flirtatious, coy, teasing.

klutz *n. Slang* OAF.

knack *n.* talent, skill, bent, gift, genius, cleverness, facility, aptitude, adroitness, flair.

knave *n.* rogue, scoundrel, cheat, swindler, charlatan, shyster, villain.

knavery *adj.* roguery, cunning, chicanery, craftiness, trickery, dishonesty, deceit, deception, corruption, villainy.

ant. decency, honor, trustworthiness, uprightness, principle.

knavish *adj.* roguish, crafty, cunning, conniving, tricky, fraudulent, unprincipled, dishonorable.

ant. decent, honorable, upright, trustworthy.

knead *v.* **1** mix, work, stir, form, press, compound. **2** massage, rub, stroke, rub down, manipulate.

knickknack *n.* trinket, trifle, bauble, gimcrack, gewgaw, knack, bric-a-brac, bagatelle, bibelot, nicknack.

knife *v.* **1** stab, stick, cut, pierce, hack, slash, wound. **2** undermine, undercut, double-cross, frustrate, thwart, betray, stab in the back.

knightly *adj.* chivalrous, gallant, gracious, urbane, gentlemanly, courtly, noble, valiant, courageous, heroic.

ant. common, vulgar, rude, ignoble, base.

knit *v.* fasten, join, link, connect, attach, affix, unite, bind, secure, intertwine, interlace, weave.

ant. separate, part, split, divide.

knob *n.* protuberance, protrusion, bump, lump, knurl, swelling, bulb, button, nub, stud, hump, boss, prominence, process.

knobby *adj.* bumpy, knotty, lumpy, gnarled, warty, bulbous, embossed.

knock *v.* **1** bang, strike, hit, smack, punch, slap, thump, rap, hammer, clobber, smash. **2** drive, impel, hit, slam, belt, crack, pound, tap, bat, swat, wallop. **3** bump, collide, clash, buffet, jolt, jar, jostle, meet, encounter. **4** rap, pound, beat, strike, thump, tap, hammer, rattle. **5** *Slang* belittle, slam, disparage, deprecate, criticize, condemn, censure, carp, cavil. —*n.* **1** blow, crack, punch, smack, whack, thump, clout, bang, hit, rap, clap, stroke, pounding, banging. **2** criticism, slam, rap (*Slang*), faultfinding, blame, censure, rebuke. **3** upset, reversal, setback, mishap, rebuff, rejection.

ant. *v.* **5** praise, approve, extol, acclaim, laud. *n.* **2** praise, approval, acclaim, commendation, compliment. **3** boost, assist, assistance, lift, backing.

knockabout *adj.* **1** rambunctious, boisterous, roisterous, rowdy, unruly, wild, rough-and-tumble. **2** rugged, hardy, sturdy, rough-and-ready, casual, informal.

knock around 1 rough up, abuse, mistreat, manhandle, buffet, strike, hit. **2** gad, wander, roam, rove, ramble, kick about.

knockdown *adj.* powerful, potent, mighty, forceful, formidable, overpowering, overwhelming.

ant. weak, feeble, impotent, delicate.

knockout *adj.* stunning, crushing, stupefying, overwhelming, overpowering. —*n. Slang* dazzler, stunner, beauty, charmer, winner.

ant. *n.* dog (*Slang*), lemon (*Slang*), flop, disaster, bomb (*Slang*).

knoll *n.* mound, hillock, hill, hump, hummock, dune, down, butte, barrow, elevation, eminence.

knot *n.* **1** tie, bow, hitch, loop, rosette, braid, plait. **2** tangle, snarl, entanglement, bend, kink, cluster, mat, bunch, mass. **3** gnarl, knurl, burl, tuber, excrescence, bulb, lump, tumescence, swelling, node, joint, protuberance, knob, bulge, projection. **4** bond, union, tie, juncture, junction, connection, link, hitch, ligature. **5**

group, bunch, cluster, swarm, gathering, crowd, band, crew, gang, circle, clique. **6** problem, bind, difficulty, complication, entanglement, puzzle, complexity. —*v.* **1** tie, loop, hitch, ligate. **2** secure, fasten, attach, connect, affix, bind, lash. **3** unite, bond, join, link, yoke, couple.

ant. *v.* **1** untie, undo, unloosen, unbind, unhitch. **2** disconnect, unfasten, detach, disengage. **3** separate, split, sever, divide.

knotty *adj.* **1** bumpy, knotted, gnarled, lumpy, knurly, clotted, rough, rugged. **2** intricate, complex, thorny, spiny, involved, difficult, hard, troublesome.

ant. **1** smooth, flat, level, plane. **2** simple, clear, obvious, manifest.

know *v.* **1** understand, comprehend, realize, apprehend, appreciate, perceive, discern, see, recognize, experience, undergo. **2** distinguish, differentiate, discriminate, identify, discern, perceive.

know-how *n.* expertise, savvy (*Slang*), aptitude, ability, skill, talent, bent, knack, art, competence, proficiency.

ant. inexperience, backwardness, incompetence, ignorance.

knowing *adj.* **1** perceptive, astute, discerning, sagacious, perspicacious, acute, keen, experienced. **2** sophisticated, worldly-wise, canny, clever, sharp, shrewd, cunning, meaningful.

ant. **1** obtuse, undiscerning, shortsighted, insensitive. **2** uninitiated, naive, artless, simple, ingenuous.

knowledge *n.* **1** learning, education, erudition, scholarship, experience, familiarity, information, facts, data, acquirements, accomplishments. **2** ability, capacity, know-how, judgment, wisdom, understanding, insight, enlightenment. **3** awareness, consciousness, comprehension, apprehension, perception, discernment, intelligence, cognizance.

ant. **1** ignorance, benightedness, darkness, obscurity. **2** incapacity, unenlightenment, foolishness, folly.

3 unawareness, ignorance, incomprehension.

knowledgeable *adj.* well-informed, conversant, familiar, experienced, learned, erudite, intelligent, wise, aware, understanding, appreciative. **ant.** uninformed, unversed, unaware, ignorant.

know-nothing *n.* ignoramus, lout, oaf, lowbrow, illiterate, vulgarian, philistine, dunce, moron.

knuckle under yield, submit, succumb, surrender, capitulate, give in, defer to, accede, acquiesce. **ant.** resist, oppose, defy, flout, brave.

knurl *n.* protuberance, gnarl, burl, node, knot, lump, bulb, bulge, projection, ridge.

kook *n. Slang* weirdo (*Slang*), oddball (*Slang*), freak (*Slang*), character, eccentric, crackpot, crazy (*Slang*).

kooky *adj. Slang* unpredictable, wild, capricious, whimsical, individualistic, original, eccentric, odd, peculiar, weird, freakish. **ant.** staid, conservative, moderate, sensible, predictable.

kosher *adj. Slang* proper, fit, all right, okay, acceptable, allowed, permitted, legitimate, genuine. **ant.** illicit, improper, outré.

kowtow *v.* **1** kneel, stoop, bend, bow, genuflect. **2** toady, fawn upon, truckle, bow and scrape, cringe, court, flatter, pander to, butter up, softsoap.

kudos *n.* glory, fame, honor, repute, credit, praise, acclaim, applause, cheers, ovation. **ant.** dishonor, censure, brickbat, defamation.

L

lab *n.* LABORATORY.

label *n.* **1** tag, ticket, sticker, docket, slip, stamp, seal. **2** characterization, description, sketch, stereotype, definition, specification, classification, summation, epitome. —*v.* classify, designate, characterize, class, name, describe, call, tag, define, identify, brand, ticket, stereotype.

labile *adj.* CHANGEABLE.

labor *n.* work, toil, drudgery, effort, travail, pains, exertion, grind, sweat, industry, diligence, task. —*v.* work, toil, drudge, plod, slave, strain, strive, travail, sweat, struggle. **ant.** *n.* idleness, inaction, ease, inactivity, sloth, indolence. *v.* idle, loaf, laze, shirk, rest.

laboratory *n.* workshop, lab, workroom, atelier.

labored *adj.* strained, painstaking, laborious, forced, elaborate, overwrought, studied, overdone, stiff, awkward, ponderous. **ant.** effortless, facile, easy, offhand, simple, relaxed.

laborer *n.* worker, blue-collar worker, toiler, prole, proletarian, wage earner, workman, hand, drudge, coolie, helper, peon, day laborer.

laborious *adj.* toilsome, arduous, burdensome, difficult, onerous, labored, strenuous, hard, wearisome, tiresome, irksome, herculean. **ant.** easy, light, simple, paltry, facile, dainty.

labyrinth *n.* maze, intricacy, tangle, coil, entanglement, puzzle, perplexity, confusion, convolution, meander, mare's nest.

lace *n.* openwork, mesh, lacework, network, fancywork, braid, embroidery, edging, filigree. —*v.* fasten, do up, tie, bind, string, wind, lash, hitch, tether, knot.

lace into attack, scold, castigate, storm at, call down, reprimand, thrash, lash, light into (*Slang*), chastise, berate, dress down, trounce.

lacerated *adj.* **1** *of flesh:* mangled, torn, broken, cut, wounded, raw, punctured, bleeding. **2** *of feelings:* injured, hurt, tormented, agonized, distressed, pained, bruised, harrowed.

laceration *n.* lesion, bruise, wound, tear, gash, mutilation, injury, mangling, tearing, clawing, rawness.

lacework *n.* LACE.

lachrymose *adj.* TEARFUL.

lacing *n.* thrashing, hiding, beating, trouncing, switching, caning, whipping, lambasting, flogging, flagellation, punishment.

lack *v.* miss, be without, need, want, require. —*n.* **1** deficiency, shortcoming, want, absence, gap, shortness, insufficiency, failure. **2** essential, necessity, desideratum, requirement, need, requisite.
ant. *n.* **1** surplus, extra, plethora, amplitude.

lackadaisical *adj.* listless, languishing, apathetic, languid, indolent, lethargic, unconcerned, indifferent, weak, inert, otiose.
ant. lively, enthusiastic, keen, zestful, spirited, energetic.

lackey *n.* flunky, toady, sycophant, hanger-on, bootlicker, yesman, stooge, flatterer, tool, gofer (*Slang*), slave.

lackluster *adj.* dim, dull, drab, lusterless, pallid, leaden, dun, flat, lifeless, dead, somber.
ant. radiant, vivid, lively, bright, shiny, splendid.

laconic *adj.* terse, concise, succinct, pithy, short, compendious, compact, brief, curt, sententious, concentrated, summary.
ant. loquacious, verbose, prolix, long-winded, voluble, talkative.

lacuna *n.* gap, break, blank, void, space, hiatus, omission, interval, vacancy, hole.

lad *n.* boy, youth, youngster, juvenile, youngling, stripling, chap, fellow, schoolboy, kid, guy.

ladder *n.* steppingstone, bridge, toehold, boost, leg up, head start, hand, stake.

lade *v.* BURDEN.

laden *adj.* burdened, fraught, charged, weighted, encumbered, trammeled, weighed down, oppressed, loaded, taxed, hampered.
ant. free, clear, unencumbered, exempt, unburdened, empty.

lading *n.* LOAD.

lady *n.* gentlewoman, matron, mistress, grande dame, dame, noblewoman, peeress.

lady-killer *n.* ladies' man, philanderer, womanizer, Lothario, Don Juan, libertine, roué, rake, heartbreaker, masher, lecher, seducer, profligate, wolf (*Slang*).

ladylike *adj.* refined, genteel, polite, elegant, well-bred, well-mannered, proper, modest, well-behaved, courtly, cultured.
ant. rude, coarse, crass, tomboyish, shameless, forward.

lag *v.* fall behind, dawdle, drag, linger, hang back, retard, loiter, stall, tarry, falter, delay, shuffle, idle, hesitate. —*n.* lingering, dawdling, delay, hesitation, retardation, interval, intermission, interim, pause, interlude.
ant. *v.* hasten, sprint, bound, dash, speed, hurry.

laggard *n.* loiterer, lingerer, dawdler, slowpoke, snail, dallier, saunterer, idler, drag (*Slang*), stick-in-the-mud, also-ran.

laggardly *adv.* slowly, tardily, dilatorily, backwardly, belatedly, slackly, pokily, hesitantly, sluggishly, languidly.
ant. smartly, quickly, readily, briskly, speedily, willingly.

lagniappe *n.* GRATUITY.

laid up sick, incapacitated, injured, bedridden, disabled, abed, bedfast, ill, housebound, immobilized.

lair *n.* den, burrow, covert, nest, couch, earth, mew, form, hole, cover, haunt, retreat.

laird *n.* LORD.

lake *n.* pond, pool, tarn, mere, basin, reservoir, catchment, loch.

lam *v. Slang* BEAT.

lamb *n. gentle or innocent person:* innocent, babe, angel, cherub, pet, dear, dove, honey, child, pussycat.
ant. fox, shark, crank, spitfire, tartar, bear.

lambaste *v. Slang* 1 scold, castigate, censure, berate, upbraid, light into (*Slang*), dress down, lash, rebuke, rail at, reprimand. 2 BEAT.
ant. 1 laud, approve, extol, praise, honor, glorify.

lambent *adj.* 1 dancing, flickering, undulating, gliding, wavering, touching, brushing. 2 radiant, luminous, shimmering, glowing, lustrous, glistening, refulgent.

lame *adj.* 1 crippled, disabled, limping, halt, handicapped, game, deformed, gimpy. 2 poor, sorry, halting, weak, inadequate, faltering, unconvincing, imperfect, ineffective.
ant. 1 agile, nimble, active, functioning, good. 2 sound, plausible, convincing, satisfactory, persuasive.

lamentable *adj.* unfortunate, regrettable, grievous, woeful, disheartening, discouraging, wretched, miserable, unsatisfactory, unhappy.
ant. fortunate, encouraging, joyful, cheerful, satisfactory, happy.

lamentation *n.* moaning, wailing, keening, plaint, wail, moan, dirge, murmuring, howling, ululation.
ant. rejoicing, exultation, jubilation, cheering, applause, elation.

lamp *n.* light, torch, bulb, lantern, beacon.

lampoon *n.* satire, travesty, broadside, skit, squib, pasquinade, tirade, attack, burlesque, parody. —*v.* satirize, burlesque, ridicule, travesty,

parody, squib, attack, abuse, disparage.
ant. *v.* extol, applaud, celebrate, acclaim, compliment, praise.

lance *n.* shaft, spear, pike, harpoon, javelin, assegai, dart, pole, stick, weapon.

land *n.* 1 earth, ground, soil, turf, crust, continent, territory, field, acreage. 2 country, nation, homeland, state, realm, domain, sphere, province, fatherland, motherland, home. —*v.* 1 alight, debark, disembark, descend, set down, deplane, put in, anchor, unship, unload. 2 obtain, win, gain, get, secure, catch, hook, grasp, snatch.
ant. *v.* 1 take off, embark, set off, emplane, board.

landholder *n.* LANDLORD.

landing *n.* debarkation, docking, disembarkation, arrival, mooring, berthing, beaching, unloading, deplaning.
ant. embarkation, casting off, boarding, sailing, setting sail.

landlord *n.* proprietor, owner, lessor, freeholder, landlady, landowner, holder, landholder.

landmark *n.* milestone, watershed, turning point, cornerstone, keystone, highlight, feature, monument, benchmark, signpost, occasion.

landscape *n.* vista, view, scene, aspect, outlook, prospect, panorama, scenery, surroundings, environs, countryside, environment.

landslide *n.* avalanche, rockfall, landslip, glissade.

lane *n.* alley, passage, aisle, byway, road, thoroughfare, bypass, passageway, way, path, track, trail, avenue.

language *n.* 1 verbalization, tongue, voice, utterance, parlance, speech, writing. 2 communication, signification, demonstration, symbolism, interchange, expression, signaling. 3 jargon, vernacular, lingo, cant, dialect, argot, lingua franca.

languid *adj.* drooping, listless, lackadaisical, apathetic, languorous, weak, weary, fatigued, sluggish, indifferent.

ant. active, energetic, vigorous, animated, eager, lively.

languish v. **1** flag, droop, fail, tire, fade, decline, wither, sicken. **2** suffer, despond, brood, grieve, sorrow, pine. **3** long, yearn, sigh, pine, thirst, hunger, hanker.

ant. 1 rally, recover, perk up, revive, refresh. **2** flourish, bloom, luxuriate, thrive, prosper.

languishing adj. weakening, flagging, pining, drooping, sagging, sickening, sinking, withering, wilting, declining, tiring, wasting away.

ant. thriving, flourishing, waxing, blooming, vigorous.

languor n. lassitude, depression, dullness, torpor, listlessness, inertia, apathy, ennui, sluggishness, indolence, weariness, torpidity, weakness.

ant. verve, enthusiasm, elan, liveliness, vigor, vitality.

lank adj. LANKY.

lanky adj. scrawny, lean, skinny, gangling, rangy, weedy, gawky, rawboned, gaunt, lank, spare, emaciated, bony.

ant. chubby, plump, rotund, well-rounded, pudgy, roly-poly.

lantern n. light, lamp, torch, taper, hurricane lamp, flashlight.

lap v. OVERLAP.

lapse v. **1** slip, fall, sink, subside, pass into, merge, fade, regress. **2** elapse, expire, terminate, run out, cease, stop, fail. —n. **1** elapse, respite, interval, interim, pause, passage, lull, intermission. **2** slip, error, blunder, mistake, inadvertence, dereliction, neglect.

larcenist n. THIEF.

larcenous adj. thieving, light-fingered, rapacious, fraudulent, peculating, pilfering, kleptomaniac, predatory, dishonest.

ant. honest, upright, trustworthy, aboveboard, incorruptible.

larceny n. theft, stealing, embezzlement, appropriation, peculation,

cheating, fraud, swindling, fleecing, pilferage, burglary, robbery.

large adj. **1** big, great, ample, substantial, sizable, largish, large-scale, bulky, immense, vast, huge, gargantuan. **2** comprehensive, grandiose, spacious, extensive, capacious, generous, liberal.

ant. 1 small, minute, tiny, diminutive, baby. **2** narrow, mean, pinched, restricted, limited.

largely adv. generally, mostly, extensively, chiefly, by and large, as a rule, mainly, usually, principally, primarily.

ant. rarely, exceptionally, hardly, scarcely, seldom.

large-scale adj. LARGE.

largesse n. GIFT.

largish adj. LARGE.

lark n. escapade, caper, prank, frolic, gambol, skylark, romp, trick, spree, jape, revel, fling.

larrikin n. ROWDY.

larrup v. BEAT.

lascivious adj. lustful, lewd, wanton, prurient, lecherous, licentious, lickerish, raunchy (Slang), horny (Slang), randy, goatish, satyric, nymphomaniac.

ant. chaste, celibate, prudish, continent, abstinent, virginal.

lash n. **1** whip, thong, scourge, strap, knout, rawhide, flail, whiplash, cat, cat-o'-nine-tails. **2** stroke, blow, whip, prick, swipe, goad, spur, fillip. —v. **1** urge, drive, goad, impel, rouse, thrash, stir up. **2** thrash, flail, beat, dash, snap, wave, whip. **3** attack, censure, criticize, berate, upbraid, castigate, lecture, sting, rebuke.

lashing n. **1** fastening, tie, lacing, binding, bonds, strapping, wrapping. **2** scolding, trouncing, calling down, berating, castigation, rebuke, admonition. **3** BEATING.

lash out 1 strike out, attack, lay about, flail, go berserk, hit out, lay into. **2** explode, burst out, protest, attack, denounce, fulminate.

lass *n.* girl, miss, schoolgirl, lassie, colleen, damsel, maid, maiden.

lassie *n.* LASS.

lassitude *n.* weariness, enervation, fatigue, languor, listlessness, inertia, torpor, lethargy, fatigue, exhaustion, debility, apathy, sluggishness, malaise.
ant. vigor, vivacity, enthusiasm, animation, vitality, élan.

lasso *n.* rope, riata, lariat, slip noose, noose, snare.

last[1] *adj.* **1** final, terminal, closing, concluding, eventual, ultimate. **2** latest, newest, current, immediate, up-to-the-minute. **3** farthest, remotest, extreme, rearmost, final, ultimate.
ant. **1** first, prime, initial, introductory. **2** earliest, original, oldest, primal. **3** nearest, imminent, first, paramount.

last[2] *v.* endure, persevere, hold out, survive, carry on, stand up, persist, subsist, hold on, continue, abide, remain.
ant. expire, give up, fail, give out, cease, die.

lasting *adj.* continuing, durable, permanent, enduring, perdurable, protracted, chronic, abiding, stable, perennial, unremitting, unceasing, fixed.
ant. temporary, perishable, fleeting, ephemeral, short-lived, transitory.

lastly *adv.* ULTIMATELY.

last word **1** ultimatum, final say, summation, finis. **2** perfection, *crème de la crème,* best, ultimate, crown, capstone, *ne plus ultra.* **3** vogue, *dernier cri,* rage, latest, fashion, newest.

latch *v.* fasten, catch, bolt, secure, snap, bar, hook, shut, close.
ant. unlatch, unfasten, open, unhook.

late *adj.* **1** tardy, behindhand, slow, backward, laggard, overdue, delayed. **2** recent, advanced, modern, developed, mature, novel, new. **3** deceased, defunct, departed, dead.
ant. **1** prompt, early, timely, punctual, expeditious. **2** primal, em-

bryonic, inchoate, early, old. **3** living, extant, existing, alive, surviving.

lately *adv.* recently, of late, just now, latterly, yesterday.
ant. formerly, once, long ago.

latency *n.* ABEYANCE.

latent *adj.* dormant, hidden, quiescent, potential, abeyant, suspended, inactive, lurking, smoldering, unrealized, rudimentary, undeveloped, passive.
ant. patent, evident, manifest, active, kinetic, apparent.

lateral *adj.* side, sideways, sideward, sidelong, glancing, tangential, oblique, marginal, skirting, flanking, abreast.

later on subsequently, afterwards, thereupon, thereafter, then, later.
ant. earlier on, previously, beforehand, prior to, earlier, before.

latitude *n.* **1** freedom, liberty, opportunity, license, indulgence, elbowroom, leeway, play. **2** scope, range, reach, amplitude, field, sweep, extent.

latitudinarian *adj.* PERMISSIVE.

latrine *n.* TOILET.

latter-day *adj.* modern, contemporary, current, recent, up-to-date, present, advanced, novel, new, late, newfangled.
ant. time-worn, old-fashioned, antiquated, obsolete, venerable, traditional.

lattice *n.* openwork, framework, trellis, grid, grating, grille, grate, screen, reticulum, network, fretwork, fret, frame.

laud *v.* praise, extol, acclaim, glorify, celebrate, honor, commend, applaud, magnify, esteem, compliment, approve.
ant. censure, denigrate, disparage, minimize, belittle, decry.

laudable *adj.* praiseworthy, admirable, commendable, estimable, exemplary, creditable, meritorious, model, deserving, worthy, excellent.
ant. blameworthy, censurable, culpable, reprehensible, chargeable.

laudation *n.* PRAISE.

laudatory *adj.* praising, eulogizing,

complimentary, flattering, favorable, approbatory, approving, commendatory, eulogistic, adulatory, panegyrical.

ant. denigratory, condemnatory, belittling, abusive, scornful.

laugh *v.* snicker, chuckle, giggle, cackle, chortle, titter, snigger, heehaw, guffaw, cachinnate, roar. —*n.* laughter, chuckle, smile, grin, snigger, giggle, guffaw, chortle, hee-haw, snicker, roar.

ant. *v.* cry, wail, weep, moan, howl, mourn. *n.* groan, wail, cry, howl, weeping.

laughable *adj.* ridiculous, droll, ludicrous, comic, comical, risible, funny, amusing, farcical, humorous, whimsical, hilarious, sidesplitting.

ant. pitiable, sad, serious, melancholy, solemn, mournful.

laugh at belittle, ridicule, scoff, jeer, taunt, jibe, fleer, deride, sneer, disparage, flout.

laugh off minimize, pooh-pooh, scout, shrug off, flout, deride, belittle, scoff, scorn, brush off, turn aside, ridicule, disdain.

ant. heed, appreciate, note, take to heart, listen to.

laughter *n.* merriment, hilarity, ridicule, mockery, derision, glee, mirth, hooting, howling, tittering, sniggering, snickering, mocking.

ant. wailing, lamentation, keening, murmuring, groaning, susurration.

launch *v.* **1** propel, send off, set afloat, eject, push, discharge, set going. **2** initiate, inaugurate, install, institute, start, begin, broach.

launch out START.

laureate *adj.* EMINENT.

laurels *n.* honor, kudos, glory, reward, award, fame, renown, distinction, recognition, credit, applause, commendation.

lavatory *n.* washroom, rest room, bathroom, powder room, toilet, privy, water closet, w.c., can (*Slang*), outhouse, men's room, ladies' room, loo (*Brit.*), latrine, john (*Slang*).

lave *v.* WASH.

lavish *adj.* **1** profuse, abundant, bountiful, copious, generous, luxuriant, prodigal, lush, myriad, extravagant. **2** exaggerated, unrestrained, exuberant, immoderate, intemperate, bombastic, measureless, fulsome, sweeping. —*v.* squander, waste, dissipate, deluge, shower, spill, spend, pour out, disperse, deplete.

ant. *adj.* **1** sparing, meager, skimpy, exiguous, scant. **2** restrained, qualified, faint, moderate, cool. *v.* stint, restrain, skimp, limit, confine.

law *n.* rule, order, code, principle, statute, decree, edict, ordinance, mandate, commandment, regulation, command, formula.

law-abiding *adj.* governable, obedient, dutiful, compliant, submissive, controllable, responsible, loyal, orderly, legitimate, lawful.

ant. lawless, delinquent, mutinous, anarchic, disobedient, noncompliant.

law-breaker *n.* violator, offender, miscreant, transgressor, outlaw, delinquent, criminal, crook, felon, perpetrator, culprit, scofflaw.

lawful *adj.* legitimate, licit, authorized, permitted, constitutional, warranted, legal, legalized, allowable, just, rightful, permissible.

ant. unlawful, prohibited, illicit, illegal, unconstitutional, unauthorized.

lawgiver *n.* LEGISLATOR.

lawless *adj.* illegal, delinquent, illegitimate, felonious, resistant, mutinous, defiant, disobedient, insurgent, anarchic, nihilistic, criminal, sinful.

ant. law-abiding, compliant, legitimate, lawful, controllable, obedient.

lawmaking *n.* LEGISLATION.

lawn *n.* grass, sward, greensward, grounds, yard, meadow, lea, park, turf, glade.

lawsuit *n.* action, suit, cause, case, proceedings, litigation, contest, dispute, argument, trial, prosecution.

lawyer *n.* attorney, counsel, advocate, solicitor, jurist, barrister, attorney at law, counselor, legist, prosecutor, pettifogger, mouthpiece (*Slang*).

lax *adj*. **1** yielding, slack, soft, flabby, loose, flaccid, flexible, pliable, plastic, ductile, relaxed. **2** lenient, permissive, negligent, slack, remiss, derelict, loose, unprincipled, careless.

ant. 1 rigid, taut, firm, tense, hard. **2** strict, unyielding, rigorous, stringent, severe.

laxative *n*. cathartic, aperient, physic, carminative, purge, purgative, purgation, salts.

lay¹ *v*. **1** put, place, set, deposit, settle, locate, repose, station. **2** attribute, ascribe, assign, impute, allege, assert. **3** impose, apply, assess, burden, saddle, charge, encumber. —*n*. arrangement, conformation, configuration, orientation, alignment, position, attitude, disposition, form.

lay² *adj*. nonprofessional, unprofessional, amateur, secular, laic, profane, popular, inexpert, inexperienced.

ant. professional, initiate, expert, informed, clerical.

lay³ *n*. ballad, song, poem, ditty, verse, air, melody, rhyme, refrain, folk song.

layabout *n*. idler, good-for-nothing, sluggard, drone, do-nothing, lounger, beachcomber, dawdler, laggard, parasite, vagrant, bum.

lay aside LAY AWAY.

lay away store up, save, hoard, stockpile, accumulate, stow, stash, put aside, lay aside, amass, collect, shelve, preserve, squirrel, secrete.

ant. squander, disperse, scatter, spend, use, dispense.

lay before put forward, present, submit, proffer, tender, offer, advance, introduce, volunteer, propose.

layer *n*. thickness, stratum, fold, lamina, seam, tier, course, bed, ply, lap, lay.

lay into attack, fall upon, assail, set upon, tackle, assault, bear down on, abuse, castigate, lash, berate, censure, lambaste (*Slang*).

layman *n*. outsider, nonprofessional, amateur, lay person, laic.

ant. expert, initiate, professional, insider, specialist.

layoff *n*. dismissal, disemployment, discharge, firing, ouster, shutdown, closing, idling, termination, retirement.

lay off 1 dismiss, discharge, oust, drop, fire, turn out, bounce, cashier. **2** discontinue, recess, take a breather, rest, quit, vacation, flake out (*Slang*).

ant. 1 take on, hire, employ, sign on, engage. **2** keep on, persist, stick to, continue, persevere.

lay on BEAT.

lay siege to BESIEGE.

lazaretto *n*. HOSPITAL.

lazy *adj*. indolent, slothful, sluggish, inactive, idle, shiftless, slow, laggard, languorous, apathetic, torpid, slack, remiss, inert.

ant. industrious, active, energetic, bustling, diligent, indefatigable.

lazybones *n*. LOAFER.

leach *v*. percolate, extract, lixiviate, elute, wash out, dissolve, remove, run off, demineralize, seep.

lead *v*. **1** guide, escort, direct, conduct, accompany, pilot, usher. **2** supervise, manage, direct, govern, boss, command, induce, influence. **3** precede, head, open, start, excel, outstrip, surpass. —*n*. **1** leadership, predominance, priority, primacy, initiative, vanguard, direction, supremacy. **2** advantage, head start, jump, edge, precedence, margin. **3** clue, hint, tip, pointer, suggestion, indication, cue, trace.

ant. *n*. **1** followership, subordination, service. **2** disadvantage, impediment, handicap, burden, encumbrance. **3** misdirection, diversion, red herring, distraction.

leaden *adj*. **1** heavy, oppressive, wearisome, crushing, burdensome, onerous. **2** dull, sluggish, languid, dreary, listless, somber, inanimate.

ant. 1 buoyant, airy, weightless,

light, lightsome. **2** bright, animated, sprightly, vivacious, buoyant.

leader *n.* chief, commander, director, head, superior, chieftain, captain, foreman, boss, conductor, guide, supervisor, torchbearer, bellwether, honcho (*Slang*), *Führer*.
ant. follower, disciple, myrmidon, subordinate, acolyte, adherent.

leadership *n.* hegemony, charisma, dominance, predominance, forcefulness, primacy, superiority, supremacy, domination, generalship, magnetism, influence, strength.
ant. followership, subordination, obedience, subservience, dependence, meekness.

leading *adj.* **1** foremost, first, principal, dominant, front, outstanding, main, chief, greatest, primary. **2** suggestive, provocative, manipulative, prejudicial, insidious, artful, tricky.

lead-off *n.* BEGINNING.

lead off start, begin, open, set out, wade in, set in motion, break the ice, embark, launch, commence, institute, inaugurate.

lead on entice, tempt, lure, seduce, decoy, entrap, inveigle, bewitch, induce to, contribute to, entail, pre-

lead to result in, cause, bring about, give rise to, induce, generate, conduce to, contribute to, entail, precede, herald.

league *n.* alliance, association, union, coalition, compact, confederation, company, society, combine, entente, cartel, band, pool, partnership, federation.

leak *n.* **1** opening, fissure, break, hole, chink, crack, puncture, perforation, crevice. **2** breech, lapse, defect, weakness, imperfection, disclosure, exposure, deficiency, flaw. —*v.* ooze, seep, percolate, escape, trickle, spill, drip, dribble, exude, discharge.

lean[1] *v.* **1** slope, slant, cant, incline, tilt, tip, bow. **2** rely, depend, count on, bank on, prop, rest on, recline against. **3** tend, favor, incline, verge, trend, gravitate. —*n.* LEANING.

lean[2] *adj.* **1** thin, spare, gaunt, skinny, lank, lanky, scrawny, rawboned. **2** sparse, unproductive, meager, scanty, exiguous, deficient, inadequate, poor, barren.
ant. **1** fleshy, chubby, fat, plump, well-rounded. **2** rich, bountiful, prosperous, productive, abundant.

leaning *n.* inclination, tendency, disposition, propensity, proclivity, penchant, bias, bent, flair, proneness, set, aptitude, lean.

leap *v.* jump, spring, start, bound, vault, skip, hop, bounce, caper, gambol, frolic. —*n.* bound, vault, jump, spring, hop, skip, bounce, start, caper, frisk, antic.

learn *v.* **1** acquire, master, memorize, study, pore over, imbibe, read. **2** ascertain, determine, discover, find out, detect, hear, divine.

learned *adj.* erudite, polymath, scholarly, profound, intellectual, educated, well-read, lettered, informed, omniscient, philosophic, knowledgeable, deep, abstruse.
ant. unlettered, illiterate, ignorant, nonintellectual, lowbrow, shallow.

learning *n.* education, schooling, study, knowledge, skill, lore, culture, wisdom, erudition, scholarship, inquiry, research, exploration, information, enlightenment.
ant. ignorance, illiteracy, obscurantism, nescience, know-nothingism, anti-intellectualism.

lease *v.* let, rent, lend, hire, engage, charter, secure, employ, sublease, demise.

leash *n.* lead, line, thong, rope, tether, string, rein, restraint. —*v.* restrain, tether, tie, hold, rein, curb, check, hold back, bind, snub.

least *adj.* smallest, slightest, minutest, fewest, tiniest, lowest, shortest, poorest, minimal, minimum, minim, minority.
ant. most, greatest, biggest, best, largest.

leave[1] *v.* go, depart, quit, move on, begone, exit, set forth, retire, resign, relinquish, withdraw, vamoose (*Slang*).

ant. arrive, come, enter, approach, attain, take.

leave² *n.* **1** permission, license, authorization, liberty, sanction, consent, allowance, tolerance, sufferance. **2** furlough, vacation, departure, recess, holiday, absence.

ant. 1 prohibition, taboo, veto, restriction, injunction, proscription.

leave off CEASE.

leave out omit, exclude, except, neglect, forget, overlook, ignore, disregard, slight, shun, rebuff.

ant. include, remember, take in, cover, cherish.

leave-taking *n.* FAREWELL.

leavings *n.* **1** scraps, scrap, leftovers, remnant, residue, excess, orts, rest, remainder. **2** refuse, offal, garbage, waste, dregs, rubbish, sweepings, junk, lees.

lecher *n.* debauchee, rake, libertine, sensualist, womanizer, Don Juan, roué, profligate, goat, fornicator, satyr.

ant. celibate, ascetic, puritan, monk, family man.

lecherous *adj.* lewd, lustful, licentious, debauched, concupiscent, salacious, lascivious, sensual, prurient, profligate, carnal, goatish, horny (*Slang*).

ant. chaste, celibate, pure, abstinent, monkish, virginal.

lechery *n.* sensuality, venery, lasciviousness, carnality, debauchery, concupiscence, salaciousness, lewdness, prurience, lust, satyriasis, nymphomania.

ant. chastity, abstinence, virginity, frigidity, celibacy, purity.

lecture *n.* **1** talk, discourse, address, oration, speech, harangue, sermon, preachment, discussion, class. **2** reprimand, talking-to, dressing-down, reproof, censure, scolding, castigation. —*v.* **1** teach, preach, discourse, hold forth, declaim, recite, talk, harangue. **2** rebuke, reprove, admon-

ish, scold, reprimand, remonstrate, berate, chide.

ledge *n.* shelf, projection, ridge, shoulder, abutment, border, molding, cornice, eaves, sill, mantle, course, strip.

lee *n.* shelter, protection, cover, refuge, asylum, shield, sanctuary, screen, guard, safety, safekeeping, haven, shade, shadow.

leech *n.* bloodsucker, hanger-on, parasite, toady, barnacle, sponger, sycophant, lickspittle, flatterer, deadbeat (*Slang*).

leer *n.* ogle, smirk, wink, squint, grimace, fleer, gloat, eye. —*v.* fleer, smirk, gloat, goggle, stare, ogle, wink, grimace, eye, coquet.

leery *adj.* suspicious, wary, cautious, distrustful, dubious, skeptical, doubtful, unsure, chary, uncertain, skittish, shy.

ant. trustful, credulous, secure, confident, gullible, assured.

lees *n.* SEDIMENT.

leeway *n.* margin, scope, latitude, elbowroom, reserve, allowance, range, slack, play, room, leverage, headroom, clearance.

left-handed *adj.* insincere, malicious, indirect, backhanded, enigmatic, ambiguous, contradictory, dubious, sardonic, doubtful, awkward.

ant. sincere, straightforward, candid, open, direct, guileless.

leftist *adj.* LEFT-WING.

leftover *n.* remainder, scrap, residue, remnant, leaving, ort, paring, surplus, spare, extra, balance.

left-wing *adj.* radical, liberal, socialistic, communistic, pink, red, revolutionary, extremist, leftist, Whig.

ant. right-wing, conservative, Tory, reactionary, rightist.

legacy *n.* **1** bequest, estate, inheritance, devise, heirloom. **2** birthright, heritage, endowment, throwback, reversion, patrimony, inheritance.

legal *adj.* lawful, legitimate, licit, permissible, rightful, litigious, legalistic, juridical, juristic, judiciary, legislative, statutory, de jure.

ant. unlawful, illicit, illegal, extralegal, extrajudicial, invalid.

legalistic *adj.* litigious, contentious, disputatious, polemical, hair-splitting, controvertible, disputable, actionable, theoretical, literal, strict.

legalize *v.* sanction, authorize, validate, approve, legitimate, legitimize, warrant, prescribe, ordain, legislate, enact.

ant. outlaw, proscribe, interdict, disallow, repudiate, deny.

legate *n.* ENVOY.

legation *n.* mission, deputation, delegation, consulate, foreign office, chancery, chancellery, embassy, ministry, representation.

legend *n.* **1** myth, saga, fable, fiction, tradition, story, old wives' tale. **2** prodigy, phenomenon, wonder, miracle, spectacle, marvel, celebrity, hero, heroine, luminary. **3** inscription, motto, device, imprint, lettering, figure.

legendary *adj.* traditional, mythical, storied, fictitious, epic, mythic, fabulous, apocryphal, fanciful, imaginary, word-of-mouth, tralatitious.

ant. historical, factual, documented, actual, real, true.

legerdemain *n.* DECEPTION.

legible *adj.* readable, decipherable, plain, clear, easy-to-read, distinct, clear-cut, comprehensible, understandable, fair.

ant. illegible, unclear, unreadable, undecipherable, scrawly.

legion *n.* multitude, horde, myriad, host, crowd, throng, mass, spate, crush, mob, army, congregation.

legislate *v.* enact, ordain, establish, set up, act, constitute, pass, codify, put through, draft, institute.

legislation *n.* **1** lawmaking, enactment, codification, government, establishment, regulation. **2** ruling, measure, statute, charter, act, law, enactment, constitution.

legislative *adj.* statutory, constitutional, judicial, lawmaking, jurisdictive,

legal, juridical, authorized, prescribed, admissible.

legislator *n.* lawmaker, politician, statesman, lawgiver, parliamentarian, congressman, assemblyman, senator.

legislature *n.* parliament, congress, assembly, diet, senate, house.

legit *n. Slang* LEGITIMATE.

legitimate *adj.* **1** lawful, licit, legal, permitted, rightful, permissible, constitutional, warranted. **2** genuine, valid, authoritative, authentic, real, reliable, OK, legit (*Slang*). —*v.* LEGITIMIZE.

ant. **1** illegitimate, prohibited, unlawful, illegal. **2** spurious, false, fake, meretricious, unauthorized, counterfeit.

legitimize *v.* justify, condone, legitimate, legalize, decriminalize, sanction, authorize, endorse, approve, support, validate, vindicate.

ant. inculpate, proscribe, incriminate, denounce, repudiate, outlaw.

leisure *n.* ease, freedom, rest, recess, vacation, holiday, liberty, pause, interlude, retirement, unemployment.

ant. work, labor, employment, toil, drudgery, exertion.

leisurely *adj.* deliberate, slow, unhurried, measured, gradual, easy, gentle, inactive, lazy, lethargic, indolent, quiescent, torpid.

ant. hurried, precipitate, hasty, rushed, swift, breakneck.

lemon *n. Slang* disappointment, failure, reject, botch, flop, dud, fiasco, miss, bungle, miscarriage, wreck, bomb (*Slang*), loser, bust (*Slang*).

ant. success, hit, smash, achievement, winner, honey.

lend *v.* **1** loan, lease, advance, let, entrust, accommodate with, commit. **2** impart, give, bestow, afford, confer, furnish, grant, invest.

length *n.* **1** *of linear extent:* extension, distance, extent, reach, linearity, compass, magnitude. **2** *of time:* duration, continuance, term, period, space, span, stretch, extent. **3** segment, portion, piece, unit, section, span, measure.

lengthen v. elongate, expand, extend, stretch, prolong, protract, spin out, continue, increase, draw out.

ant. shorten, curtail, abridge, decrease, abbreviate, cut.

lengthy adj. overlong, interminable, long-drawn, protracted, extensive, sustained, elongated, endless, prolix, long-winded, far-reaching, outstretched, long.

ant. short, concise, brief, cursory, contracted, fleeting.

leniency n. mercifulness, indulgence, softness, blandness, mildness, gentleness, compassion, patience, pity, mercy, charity, humanity, benevolence, laxity, lenity.

ant. harshness, roughness, mercilessness, sternness, severity, implacability.

lenient adj. merciful, mild, indulgent, tolerant, bland, soft, gentle, softhearted, forbearing, kind, permissive, compassionate, tender, patient.

ant. hard, harsh, stern, unrelenting, strict, severe.

lenitive adj. SOOTHING.

lenity n. LENIENCY.

leprechaun n. elf, fairy, sprite, fay, brownie, gnome, pixy, imp, hobgoblin, goblin, banshee.

lesion n injury, hurt, sore, trauma, wound, bruise, blemish, harm, abnormality, excrescence, impairment, disorder, disfigurement.

less adj. **1** smaller, fewer, lesser, negative, minus, shorter, slighter, reduced, stinted. **2** inferior, minor, secondary, subordinate, mere, lesser, lower, nether, unimportant.

ant. 1 more, bigger, plus, extra, larger. **2** superior, preferable, major, better, important.

lessen v. decrease, shrink, diminish, abate, decline, dwindle, reduce, attenuate, contract, wane, subside, erode, wind down, de-escalate, phase out.

ant. increase, enlarge, grow, wax, augment, multiply.

lessening n. abatement, shrinkage, diminution, decrease, let-up, decline, reduction, waning, dwindling, mitigation, minimization, moderation, de-escalation.

ant. increase, reinforcement, enhancement, growth, intensification, increment.

lesson n. assignment, division, section, exercise, recitation, lecture, reading, portion, session, class, stint, task.

let[1] v. **1** allow, permit, suffer, warrant, authorize, tolerate, concede, admit, leave, grant. **2** rent, assign, lease, hire, lend, charter, sublet, farm.

ant. 1 disallow, prevent, hinder, impede, forbid, prohibit.

let[2] n. HINDRANCE.

letdown n. disappointment, disillusionment, anticlimax, frustration, discomfiture, humiliation, mortification, disgruntlement, adversity, blow, chagrin, balk.

ant. fulfillment, satisfaction, culmination, contentment, gratification.

let down disappoint, disillusion, fail, frustrate, fall short, sell out, foil, depress, disconcert, balk, betray.

ant. fulfill, come through, deliver, help, succor, satisfy.

lethal adj. fatal, deadly, mortal, noxious, baneful, malignant, virulent, killing, internecine, pernicious, dangerous, destructive, devastating.

ant. harmless, benign, nonlethal, innocuous, safe, protective.

lethargic adj. drowsy, apathetic, languid, lazy, sleepy, sluggish, torpid, comatose, listless, soporific, somnolent, slothful, slow, costive.

ant. energetic, animated, lively, active, strenuous, vital.

lethargy n. stupor, drowsiness, sleepiness, apathy, inactivity, sluggishness, laziness, indifference, lassitude, languor, torpor, listlessness, coma, malaise.

ant. animation, enthusiasm, verve, vitality, liveliness, gusto.

lethe *n.* OBLIVION.

let in ADMIT.

let off 1 emit, discharge, release, expel, leak, exude, excrete. **2** excuse, dismiss, exempt, absolve, exonerate, spare, adjourn, relieve.
ant. 1 build up, accumulate, increase, hold, confine. **2** hold, retain, blame, keep, constrain.

let on pretend, profess, feign, simulate, dissemble, dissimulate, affect, assume, counterfeit, sham, insinuate, intimate.

letter *n.* **1** symbol, character, sign, figure. **2** missive, note, dispatch, epistle, memo, communiqué, notice, bulletin, message, billet, comunication.

lettered *adj.* LITERATE.

letter-perfect *adj.* PERFECT.

letters *n.* literature, belles-lettres, humanities, scholarship, learning, liberal arts, books, writing, classics, erudition, culture.

lettuce *n. Slang* MONEY.

let-up *n.* stopping, cessation, pause, lull, surcease, slackening, relief, interlude, recess, slowdown, interval, respite, remission, vacation.
ant. intensification, acceleration, speedup, increase, worsening, crackdown.

let up slacken, subside, abate, ebb, decrease, diminish, wane, ease, moderate, relax, ameliorate, let down, soften, weaken, ease up.
ant. augment, intensify, increase, rise, revive, accelerate.

levee *n.* embankment, dike, dam, bank, escarpment, ridge, terrace, mole, breakwater, wall.

level *adj.* **1** flat, even, horizontal, plane, smooth, uniform, flush. **2** commensurate, equivalent, comparable, proportionate, balanced, aligned. **3** equal, co-equal, mated, matched, like, similar, congenial. **4** calm, sensible, well-balanced, equable, steady, stable, self-possessed, even. —*n.* 1

plane, flat, horizontal, plain. **2** height, altitude, elevation, stratum, stage. **3** rank, position, standing, status, percentile. —*v.* raze, knock down, demolish, destroy, collapse, disassemble.
ant. *adj.* **1** sloping, uneven, vertical, rough, aslant, perpendicular. **2** unequal, uneven, unbalanced, disproportionate. **3** unequal, mismatched, alien, inimical. **4** excitable, temperamental, erratic, freakish, fitful. *v.* build, erect, establish, construct.

level-headed *adj.* sensible, composed, judicious, prudent, sapient, sage, sane, wise, deliberate, circumspect, dependable, steady, sound, practical.
ant. fatuous, thoughtless, flighty, foolish, absurd, impulsive.

lever *n.* **1** crowbar, crow, pry, jimmy, handspike. **2** trigger, fuse, switch, button, wedge, push button, tool, instrument.

leverage *n.* pull, influence, weight, clout (*Slang*), power, priority, rank, ascendancy, control, seniority, precedence.

leviathan *n.* colossus, monster, mammoth, giant, whale, jumbo, behemoth, mountain, hulk, prodigy, Titan.
ant. mite, mote, gnat, atom, speck, grain.

levitate *v.* RISE.

levity *n.* lightness, humor, frivolity, flippancy, volatility, whimsy, triviality, silliness, horseplay, giddiness, trifling, hilarity, merriment, fun.
ant. gravity, sobriety, heaviness, solemnity, sternness, seriousness.

levy *v.* impose, assess, demand, collect, charge, tithe, tax, wrest, seize, require, draft. —*n.* **1** imposition, assessment, collection, gathering, exaction, extortion, muster. **2** tax, dues, toll, tithe, tribute, revenue, assessment, contribution.

lewd *adj.* **1** lustful, lascivious, licentious, lubricious, adulterous, lickerish, goatish. **2** obscene, bawdy, ribald, smutty, salacious, dirty, filthy, pornographic, Rabelaisian, raunchy (*Slang*).

ant. 1 chaste, continent, celibate, virginal, abstinent. **2** decent, priggish, moral, modest, prudish, pure.

lexicon *n*. dictionary, wordbook, vocabulary, glossary, thesaurus, code book, gloss, index.

liability *n*. **1** accountability, answerability, indebtedness, obligation, culpability, responsibility, vulnerability. **2** drawback, obstacle, disadvantage, handicap, hindrance, impediment, cross, minus, encumbrance, drag.

ant. 1 exemption, impunity, freedom, exoneration, privilege. **2** advantage, edge, plus, support, assistance, help.

liable *adj*. **1** responsible, answerable, accountable, chargeable, obligated, obliged, amenable, exposed. **2** likely, apt, probable, prone, open, subject, susceptible.

ant. 1 unaccountable, excusable, clear, exempt, protected. **2** unlikely, improbable, inapt, secure, exempt.

liaison *n*. **1** bond, alliance, union, interrelationship, association, connection, coupling, link. **2** amour, affair, romance, intrigue, flirtation, conquest, adventure, dalliance.

libation *n*. DRINK.

libel *n*. slander, calumny, denigration, smear, slur, defamation, obloquy, vilification, aspersion, innuendo, attack, scandal. —*v*. defame, disparage, slander, traduce, denigrate, vilify, malign, abuse, revile, scandalize, smear.

libelous *adj*. defamatory, slanderous, scurrilous, derogatory, injurious, abusive, denigrating, malicious, vilifying, maligning, traducing, reviling, offensive.

liberal *adj*. **1** generous, bounteous, abundant, lavish, munificent, ample, open-handed, full. **2** progressive, latitudinarian, advanced, libertarian, radical, reformist, left-wing. **3** broadminded, tolerant, enlightened, charitable, lenient, indulgent, dispas-

sionate. **4** *not literal or exact:* general, loose, broad, free, figurative, metaphoric, oblique, elliptical, inexact, lax, careless.

ant. 1 stingy, penurious, miserly, niggardly, sparse. **2** conservative, reactionary, die-hard, regressive, rightwing. **3** bigoted, prejudiced, biased, partial, narrow-minded. **4** strict, literal, rigorous, narrow, exact, precise.

liberality *n*. **1** generosity, bounty, largess, munificence, open-handedness, beneficence, charity, philanthropy. **2** broad-mindedness, tolerance, catholicity, universality, magnanimity, liberalism.

ant. 1 stinginess, avarice, parsimony, closeness, meanness. **2** prejudice, bigotry, intolerance, dogmatism, narrowness.

liberalize *v*. broaden, ease, expand, soften, relax, moderate, modify, stretch, extend, loosen, mitigate, ameliorate, temper.

ant. limit, constrict, narrow, toughen, tighten, restrict.

liberate *v*. free, emancipate, deliver, rescue, release, manumit, disengage, discharge, redeem, unshackle, extricate, let out, let loose.

ant. capture, enslave, immure, subjugate, overpower, imprison.

liberation *n*. freedom, liberty, deliverance, redemption, emancipation, manumission, disengagement, release, salvation, rescue, enfranchisement, extrication.

ant. subjugation, captivity, servitude, enslavement, domination, enthrallment.

libertine *n*. debauchee, sensualist, voluptuary, profligate, rake, roué, womanizer, sybarite, satyr, goat, rip. —*adj*. DISSOLUTE.

ant. *n*. ascetic, puritan, prude, celibate, abstainer, family man.

liberty *n*. **1** freedom, independence, emancipation, liberation, dismissal, release. **2** permission, leave, right, privilege, franchise, license. **3** familiarity, impertinence, audacity, effrontery, impudence, boldness.

ant. 1 imprisonment, bondage, captivity, oppression. **2** proscription, veto, denial, taboo, ban. **3** propriety, circumspection, discretion, hesitation, timidity.

libidinous *adj.* LUSTFUL.

libido *n.* LUST.

license *n.* **1** franchise, permit, authority, permission, right, charter, privilege, leave, sufferance. **2** disorder, unruliness, licentiousness, lawlessness, anarchy, excess, laxity, impropriety. —*v.* authorize, permit, allow, sanction, endorse, warrant, approve, commission.

ant. *n.* **1** prohibition, proscription, ban, veto, denial, curb. **2** moderation, order, restraint, sobriety, propriety. *v.* prohibit, ban, oppose, forbid, check.

licentious *adj.* wanton, lewd, libidinous, dissolute, lubricious, promiscuous, libertine, dissipated, debauched, concupiscent, unrestrained, lascivious, ruttish.

ant. ascetic, restrained, puritanical, strait-laced, moderate, prudish.

licit *adj.* LAWFUL.

lick *v.* **1** lap, lave, ripple, brush, touch, tongue, flick, trickle, wash. **2** thrash, beat, defeat, trounce, drub, best, punish, overcome. —*n.* little, speck, bit, touch, dab, snip, hint, stroke, brush, rub.

lickerish *adj.* LUSTFUL.

lickety-split *adv. Slang* FAST.

lickspittle *n.* TOADY.

lid *n.* cover, top, stopper, cap, cork, plug, stopple, throttle.

lie[1] *v.* rest, recline, sprawl, repose, loll, lounge, couch, extend, lean, be, sit.

lie[2] *n.* falsehood, fabrication, falsification, fib, untruth, story, deceit, prevarication, mendacity, perjury, misrepresentation, equivocation. —*v.* equivocate, prevaricate, perjure, misstate, palter, fib, invent, misrepresent, mislead, falsify, deceive.

ant. *n.* truth, verity, fact, gospel, veracity, sooth.

liege *n.* LORD.

lie low *Slang* hide, hole up, take cover, skulk, go underground, hide away, hide out, disappear, rusticate, vegetate, hibernate.

lieu *n.* place, stead.

lieutenant *n.* aide, assistant, deputy, right hand, agent, second, representative, adjutant, steward, factotum, man Friday, henchman.

life *n.* **1** animation, sentience, being, vitality, existence, subsistence, lifetime. **2** spirit, heart, kernel, breath, soul, essence, center. **3** duration, term, span, existence, career, lifetime.

ant. 1 death, extinction, mortality, cessation, nonbeing, oblivion.

lifeblood *n.* ESSENCE.

lifeless *adj.* **1** dead, inanimate, deceased, defunct, inorganic, nonliving, inert, departed, extinct. **2** dull, listless, torpid, sluggish, spiritless, passive, inert, spent, lackluster.

ant. 1 live, breathing, animate, alive, living. **2** animated, lively, spirited, active, energetic.

lifelike *adj.* realistic, natural, graphic, photographic, faithful, exact, authentic, real, undistorted, representational, representative.

ant. unnatural, mechanical, wooden, unrealistic, fake.

lift *v.* **1** raise, hoist, elevate, boost, uplift, hold up, heft, rear, heave, heighten. **2** steal, pilfer, plagiarize, pirate, appropriate, crib, thieve, snatch, pocket, take. —*n.* glow, exaltation, rapture, bliss, euphoria, transport, inspiration, elation, high (*Slang*).

ant. *v.* **1** lower, drop, sink, plunge, depress. *n.* depression, dumps, gloom, blues, melancholy, low.

ligate *v.* TIE.

light[1] *n.* radiance, gleam, illumination, luminosity, shining, brightness, luminescence, incandescence, effulgence, brilliance, day, dawn. —*adj.* bright, sunny, illuminated, lighted, shining, gleaming, lustrous, vivid, visible. —*v.* **1** kindle, ignite, set afire, burn. **2** illuminate, switch on, turn on. **3** beam, brighten, animate, irradiate, lighten.

ant. *n.* darkness, gloom, blackness, dark, night. *adj.* dark, shaded, obscure, overcast, shadowy. *v.* **1, 2** douse, quench, extinguish, put out, turn off. **3** darken, deaden, becloud.

light[2] *adj.* **1** *of weight:* slight, sparse, little, underweight, scant. **2** *of force or strength:* weak, moderate, mild, soft, puny, slight, modest. **3** easy, effortless, simple, undemanding, unexacting, facile. **4** gay, cheerful, unimportant, inconsequential, carefree, airy, blithe.

ant. **1** ponderous, heavy, hefty, weighty. **2** strong, dense. **3** onerous, burdensome, difficult, arduous, taxing, hard, wearisome. **4** important, serious, grave, sad, sober.

lighten[1] *v.* illuminate, brighten, enlighten, light up, clarify, clear up, irradiate, illumine, gleam, shine, elucidate.

ant. darken, obscure, dim, overshadow, obfuscate, shade.

lighten[2] *v.* **1** reduce, diminish, disencumber, unburden, unload, lessen, alleviate, take from. **2** encourage, relieve, cheer, enliven, gladden, ameliorate, ease.

ant. **1** load, burden, weight, encumber, increase. **2** worsen, discourage, deteriorate, sadden, depress.

light-footed *adj.* NIMBLE.

light-headed *adj.* **1** dizzy, delirious, giddy, disoriented, confused, distracted, incoherent, rambling, unbalanced, spinning, reeling, hazy, foggy. **2** FRIVOLOUS.

ant. **1** self-possessed, clear-headed, composed, lucid, steady, sober.

lighthearted *adj.* carefree, gay, untroubled, joyous, cheerful, easygoing, sprightly, happy, merry, cheery, blithe, joyful, glad, lightsome, careless, insouciant.

ant. grave, sober, despondent, sad, anxious, worried.

lighting *n.* illumination, radiance, incandescence, luminescence, candlepower.

ant. obfuscation, shadow, darkness, darkening.

light-minded *adj.* FRIVOLOUS.

lightness[1] *n.* **1** brightness, pellucidity, illumination, glow, glistening, shining, shimmer, gleaming. **2** paleness, pallor, dimness, colorlessness, bloodlessness, blondness, translucence.

ant. **1** darkness, gloom, shadow, obscurity, shadiness. **2** color, brightness, intensity, darkness.

lightness[2] *n.* **1** buoyancy, weightlessness, volatility, imponderability, levity, airiness. **2** cheerfulness, heedlessness, frivolity, levity, insouciance, flippancy. **3** nimbleness, grace, facility, agility, ease, finesse.

ant. **1** weight, ponderousness, heaviness, weightiness, ponderability. **2** seriousness, gravity, solemnity, sobriety, grimness. **3** clumsiness, awkwardness, laboriousness, heaviness, leadenness.

lightning *adj.* fast, swift, rapid, sudden, speedy, instant, flashing, instantaneous, explosive, electric, darting.

ant. slow, gradual, gentle, deliberate, hesitant, sluggish.

light out DEPART.

lightsome *adj.* **1** LIGHTHEARTED. **2** NIMBLE. **3** FRIVOLOUS.

light upon happen on, stumble on, come across, encounter, discover, chance on, find, meet, find out, hit on.

like[1] *v.* **1** enjoy, relish, savor, appreciate, delight in, fancy. **2** care for, dote on, be fond of, cherish, love, esteem. **3** prefer, choose, wish, elect, want, desire.

like[2] *adj.* similar, identical, equal, equivalent, akin, parallel, allied, analogous, homologous, comparable, same. —*n.* equivalent, counterpart, equal, analogue, peer, mate, match, sort, stamp.

ant. *adj.* different, diverse, other, opposite, unlike, else. *n.* opposite, antithesis, reverse, contrary, contrast, contradiction.

likelihood *n.* **1** probability, possibility, chance, contingency, potentiality, prospect, liability. **2** CREDIBILITY.

likely *adj.* probable, reasonable, plausible, liable, credible, reliable, acceptable, expected, anticipated.

    ant. implausible, incredible, farfetched, unreasonable, preposterous.

liken *v.* compare, match, relate, juxtapose, link, equate.

likeness *n.* **1** resemblance, similarity, analogy, form, guise, appearance, disguise, semblance. **2** picture, copy, representation, portrait, image, reproduction, effigy, model, replica, spitting image, depiction.

likes *n.* preferences, inclinations, wishes, desires, wants, tastes, needs.

    ant. aversions, pet peeves, dislikes.

likewise *adv.* also, moreover, similarly, too, in addition, as well, further, besides, additionally.

liking *n.* fondness, taste, preference, partiality, inclination, disposition, desire, tendency, propensity, bent, appetite, craving.

    ant. antipathy, dislike, aversion, distaste, loathing, hatred, revulsion.

Lilliputian *adj.* SMALL.

lilt *n.* swing, sway, pulsation, beat, wave.

lily-livered *adj.* COWARDLY.

lily-white *adj.* PURE.

limb *n.* appendage, member, part, extension, leg, arm, wing, bough.

limber *adj.* flexible, lithe, agile, supple, loose-jointed, elastic, pliant, nimble, pliable, malleable.

    ant. stiff, inflexible, unbending, awkward, clumsy, rigid.

limbo *n.* oblivion, purgatory, exile, banishment, neglect.

limelight *n.* prominence, fame, notoriety, spotlight, celebrity, notice, publicity.

limerick *n.* jingle, rhyme, doggerel.

limit *n.* **1** boundary, terminus, end,

border, bourn, periphery, confines, margin, circumference, perimeter, fringe, enclosure. **2** end, length, reach, bound, restraint, restriction, check. —*v.* restrict, bound, demarcate, circumscribe, check, restrain, bar, specify, proscribe, ration.

limitation *n.* restriction, condition, impediment, hindrance, handicap, obstruction, block, check, qualification, disadvantage, proscription, hitch, catch.

limited *adj.* restricted, controlled, restrained, checked, confined, special, circumscribed, fixed, defined, particular, conditional, diminished, reduced.

    ant. free, total, complete, unrestrained, general, liberal, unconditional, absolute.

limitless *adj.* infinite, boundless, unbounded, unending, endless, unlimited, eternal, immeasurable, countless.

    ant. limited, finite, measurable, confined, controlled, definite, fixed.

limn *v.* **1** draw, paint, sketch, copy, delineate, depict, portray, illustrate. **2** describe, narrate, represent, depict, portray, relate.

limp[1] *v.* halt, hobble, jerk, hitch, falter.

limp[2] *adj.* flaccid, weak, soft, floppy, slack, flabby, lax, ductile, yielding, pendent, droopy.

    ant. firm, tough, rigid, hard, stiff, unyielding.

limpid *adj.* **1** clear, transparent, pure, crystalline, pellucid. **2** intelligible, lucid, plain, clear, logical, straightforward, comprehensible, understandable, direct, clear-cut, unequivocal.

    ant. **1** muddy, turbid, opaque, foul, polluted. **2** confused, obscure, unclear, muddled, fuzzy, abstruse.

line *n.* **1** string, cord, rope, strand, thong, filament. **2** mark, stroke, stripe, band, groove, notch, dash, furrow, wrinkle, scratch, slash, slit. **3** row, rank, queue, series, column, file, train, procession, alignment, array, arrangement. **4** course, route, method, procedure, plan, concept, way, vocation, business, calling, scope, range. **5** series, sequence, progression, set, succession, lineage, descent, ancestry, descendants. **6** pitch, spiel (*Slang*), song and dance (*Slang*), ballyhoo, hype (*Slang*).

lineage *n*. descent, ancestry, family, derivation, parentage, line, stock, extraction, heredity, genealogy, blood, breed.

lineament *n*. FEATURE.

lineup *n*. ARRAY.

line up organize, assemble, set up, arrange, provide, marshal, coordinate, consolidate.

linger *v*. delay, dawdle, idle, tarry, wait, loiter, procrastinate.
ant. hurry, hasten, rush, scurry, dash, speed.

lingo *n*. language, tongue, dialect, jargon, idiom, vernacular, patois, talk, speech.

linguist *n*. **1** polyglot. **2** philologist, semanticist, phonetician, phonologist, morphologist, glossologist.

lining *n*. coating, facing, filling, stuffing, interlining, interfacing, reinforcement.

link *n*. connection, tie, bond, attachment, association, liaison, relationship, part, constituent, component, element, member. —*v*. attach, join, couple, fuse, combine, connect, unite, associate, merge, fasten, splice, consolidate, concatenate.
ant. *v*. divide, disconnect, untie, uncouple, sever, part, separate, detach, disengage, split, divorce.

linkage *n*. connection, union, relationship, alliance, bond, association, attachment, conjunction, linkup, league, liaison.
ant. separation, disjunction, cleavage, breach, rupture, break, disruption, division, disconnection, gap.

linkup *n*. LINKAGE.

lint *n*. down, fuzz, fluff.

lion *n*. **1** hero, prodigy, wonder, strong-man, superman, brave, warrior, champion, gladiator. **2** DIGNITARY.
ant. **1** weakling, coward, craven, milquetoast, mouse, sissy.

lionhearted *adj*. BRAVE.

lionize *v*. acclaim, celebrate, honor, praise, admire, glorify, flatter, revere, adore, worship.
ant. belittle, depreciate, underestimate, underrate, ignore, neglect.

lip *n*. **1** edge, rim, margin, brim, brink, curb, threshold, verge. **2** *Slang* sass, backtalk, impudence, rudeness, cheek, gall (*Slang*), chutzpah (*Slang*).

liquefy *v*. melt, dissolve, thaw, liquesce, run, deliquesce.
ant. solidify, harden, freeze, congeal, petrify, consolidate.

liquid *adj*. **1** fluid, wet, moist, damp, melted, molten, liquefied, aqueous. **2** flowing, smooth, graceful, mellifluous, dulcet, soft, sweet. —*n*. fluid, solution, juice, sap, liquor, secretion, nectar.
ant. *adj*. **1** hard, solid, condensed, dry, compact, cohesive, crystallized, frozen. **2** harsh, rough, ragged, jarring, staccato.

liquidate *v*. settle, pay, discharge, dispose, cancel, defray, wipe out, pay off.

liquor *n*. alcohol, spirits, drink, intoxicant, grog, booze, firewater, sauce (*Slang*), schnapps, hooch (*Slang*).

lissom *adj*. flexible, lithe, nimble, agile, sprightly, pliant, supple, quick, lively, active.
ant. clumsy, gawky, awkward, cloddish, sluggish, stiff, ponderous.

list[1] *n*. roll, catalog, series, inventory, schedule, enumeration, listing, slate, register, docket, directory, file, enumeration, index, record. —*v*. enumerate, set down, record, arrange, codify, rank, register, enroll, chronicle.

list[2] *v*. lean, tilt, incline, bend, slant, slope, careen, heel.

listen *v*. hear, pay attention, hearken,

listing 394 **live**

attend, heed, hark, give ear, eavesdrop.

ant. ignore, neglect, shun, disregard.

listing *n*. LIST[1].

listless *adj.* languid, lackadaisical, indifferent, spiritless, apathetic, torpid, lethargic, enervated, inattentive, lazy, indolent, sluggish, lymphatic, inactive, dull, drowsy.

ant. vigorous, energetic, spirited, active, lively, animated, vivacious, mettlesome.

litany *n*. list, repetition, catalog, refrain, enumeration, account, tale.

literal *adj.* **1** exact, precise, verbatim, faithful, textual, strict, undeviating. **2** matter-of-fact, prosaic, unimaginative, prosy, blunt, colorless, dull, mechanical, exact, factual, realistic, unexaggerated, authentic, veritable, bona fide.

ant. 1 metaphorical, symbolic, paraphrased, adapted, figurative, allegorical. **2** poetic, fanciful, imaginative, romantic, fantastic, creative, visionary, whimsical.

literally *adv.* verbatim, exactly, word for word, literatim, rigorously, precisely, actually, indeed, utterly.

ant. figuratively, metaphorically, more or less, vaguely.

literary *adj.* bookish, well-read, learned, lettered, scholarly, bibliophilistic.

literate *adj.* educated, schooled, lettered, cultured, informed, versed, cultivated, knowledgeable.

ant. illiterate, uninformed, ignorant, untaught, unschooled.

literatim *adv.* LITERALLY.

literature *n*. writings, books, letters, belles-lettres, publications.

lithe *adj.* limber, supple, pliant, pliable, bendable, flexible, agile, nimble, lissom, graceful, lithesome.

ant. stiff, clumsy, awkward, rigid, heavy, graceless.

lithesome *adj.* LITHE.

litigious *adj.* contentious, quarrelsome, argumentative, legalistic, disputatious.

ant. pacific, calm, placid, easygoing, peaceful, accommodating.

litter *n*. **1** couch, sedan chair, palanquin. **2** refuse, trash, junk, garbage, waste, mess, rubbish, disorder, debris, detritus, jumble. —*v*. strew, scatter, disorder, clutter, dishevel, mess up.

ant. *v*. clean, tidy, spruce up, police.

littérateur *n*. WRITER.

little *adj.* **1** small, diminutive, tiny, minute, slight, reduced, petite, wee, dinky, miniature, minuscule, mini. **2** young, immature, undeveloped, callow, babyish. **3** mean, petty, narrow-minded, small-minded, bigoted, selfish, illiberal, cheap, niggardly, close, pusillanimous, ungenerous, uncharitable. **4** weak, slight, scant, deficient, ineffective, ineffectual, feeble, faint, impotent, insufficient, meager, puny, paltry.

ant. 1 large, big, great, sizable, huge, giant, gross, hulking. **2** old, mature, grown, adult. **3** generous, liberal, magnanimous, noble, broad-minded. **4** mighty, considerable, powerful, strong, effective.

little by little gradually, progressively, step by step, slowly, successively, by degrees, imperceptibly.

ant. suddenly, abruptly, hastily, instantaneously, unexpectedly, all at once.

littoral *n*. SHORE.

liturgy *n*. rite, worship, service, ritual, ceremony, sacrament.

livable *adj.* habitable, agreeable, comfortable, fit, satisfactory, convenient, decent, pleasant, sociable, amicable, harmonious.

ant. uninhabitable, disagreeable, unfit, unpleasant.

live[1] *v*. **1** exist, be, subsist, breathe, continue, endure, persist, last, remain, survive, prevail. **2** reside, dwell, abide, lodge, stay, inhabit, settle, occupy.

ant. 1 die, pass away, disappear, perish, expire, decease, decline, fade, vanish.

live² *adj.* **1** alive, living, quick, existent, animate, extant, vital, breathing. **2** lively, vital, energetic, interesting, compelling, vivid, active, alert, wide-awake, eager, ardent, spirited, dynamic, intense, vigorous.
ant. 1 dead, inert, nonexistent, extinct, deceased, late, lifeless, inanimate, defunct. **2** dull, sluggish, dispirited, tedious, boring, vapid, inactive, torpid, blah (*Slang*).

livelihood *n.* living, subsistence, occupation, job, work, trade, business, calling, vocation, profession, employment, career.

livelong *adj.* ENTIRE.

lively *adj.* **1** energetic, active, vivacious, bouncy, alive, spirited, ardent, buoyant, brisk, animated, vivid, intense, enthusiastic, peppy, perky, keen. **2** joyful, gay, merry, ebullient, confident, joyous, upbeat.
ant. 1 inert, sluggish, dull, lazy, impassive, slothful, torpid, indolent. **2** unhappy, dismal, mournful, doleful, depressing, gloomy.

liverish *adj.* PEEVISH.

livery *n.* uniform, suit, costume, vestments, dress, raiment.

livid *adj.* **1** bruised, discolored, black-and-blue, purple. **2** pallid, ashen, pale, wan, grayish, leaden. **3** angry, furious, wrathful, raging, mad, infuriated, irate, inflamed, choleric, wroth, indignant, beside oneself.
ant. 2 healthy, ruddy, blooming, rosy-cheeked. **3** peaceful, calm, unruffled, serene, mild, tranquil, composed.

living *adj.* **1** alive, live, animate, existent, extant, quick. **2** continuing, persisting, current, active, operative, ongoing, in use. —*n.* LIVELIHOOD.
ant. 1 dead, defunct, deceased, gone, inanimate, nonexistent, kaput (*Slang*). **2** extinct, dead, disused, obsolete, discarded, discontinued.

load *n.* **1** cargo, freight, goods, lading, shipment. **2** burden, care, trouble, oppression, worry, encumbrance, impediment, strain, stress, tribula-

tion. —*v.* **1** fill, lade, stack, pack, stuff, weight, heap. **2** burden, oppress, encumber, weigh down, overwhelm, overcharge, crush, afflict, hinder, hamper, strain.
ant. v. 1 unpack, unship, unload, discharge, offload, dump. **2** relieve, disburden, free, deliver, liberate, emancipate.

loaded *adj. Slang* WEALTHY.

loafer *n.* idler, loiterer, drone, bum, wastrel, lazybones, sluggard, laggard, sponger, deadbeat (*Slang*), ne'er-do-well, shirker, goldbrick (*Slang*).
ant. go-getter, hustler, dynamo, live wire, ball of fire.

loan *n.* advance, credit, allowance, mortgage.

loath *adj.* unwilling, averse, disinclined, reluctant, indisposed, loth, against, counter, hostile, opposed.
ant. willing, eager, anxious, avid, fain, desirous.

loathe *v.* abhor, detest, hate, despise, scorn, disdain, abominate, shun.
ant. love, adore, worship, admire, relish.

loathing *n.* disgust, aversion, abhorrence, dislike, detestation, contempt, enmity, scorn, repugnance, horror, revulsion, antipathy, odium.
ant. love, admiration, desire, adoration, longing, yearning, ardor, fondness, partiality.

loathly *adj.* LOATHSOME.

loathsome *adj.* repulsive, disgusting, horrible, loathly, abominable, unbearable, revolting, evil, rank, reprehensible, vile, nauseating, nasty, contemptible, hateful, odious.
ant. charming, delightful, beautiful, lovely, attractive, sweet, winning.

lob *v.* throw, pitch, loft, heave, hurl, upthrow, sky (*Brit.*), pop up.

lobby *n.* **1** vestibule, foyer, hall, antechamber, lounge, entrance hall, gallery, court, porch, waiting room. **2** pressure group, coterie, influence peddlers. —*v.* influence, promote, solicit, pressure, pull strings.

lobe *n.* projection, protuberance, pendant, convexity, knob, bulge, division, lobule.

lobule *n.* LOBE.

local *adj.* **1** regional, limited, circumscribed, confined, spatial, near, close, adjacent, adjoining, nearby. **2** parochial, insular, provincial, small-town. **ant.** **1** general, broad, universal, worldwide, cosmic, endless, unlimited, infinite. **2** cosmopolitan, urbane, sophisticated, worldly.

locale *n.* LOCALITY.

locality *n.* place, position, locale, region, neighborhood, vicinity, territory, district, zone, area, spot, site, situation.

localize *v.* limit, locate, assign, pinpoint, spot, situate, restrict, circumscribe, confine, contain, concentrate, quarantine, restrain, narrow. **ant.** broaden, enlarge, widen, amplify, expand, dilate, universalize.

locate *v.* **1** find, discover, detect, discern, fix upon, pinpoint, track down, unearth, come across. **2** settle, establish, move in, squat, camp, take root. **ant.** **2** leave, move out, decamp, depart, go away.

located *adj.* situated, placed, found, based, stationed, sited, positioned, quartered, living, residing.

location *n.* place, position, site, locale, spot, district, area, neighborhood, station.

lock[1] *n.* **1** fastening, bolt, padlock, hook, catch, clamp, clasp, latch, bar, deadbolt. **2** junction, hold, interlocking, fastening, securing, grasp, clutch, clinch, embrace. —*v.* **1** secure, fasten, bolt, clamp, latch. **2** join, link, interweave, entwine. **ant.** *v.* **1** undo, unfasten, unlock, loosen, release, open, disengage, disconnect.

lock[2] *n.* tress, tuft, ringlet, curl, hank, skein, coil.

locker *n.* chest, cabinet, closet, compartment, wardrobe, armoire.

locket *n.* pendant, case, charm, lavaliere.

lock, stock, and barrel totally, thoroughly, completely, absolutely, uncompromisingly. **ant.** partially, half-heartedly, moderately.

lockup *n.* JAIL.

lock up **1** close, shut, secure, fasten, stabilize, settle, fix. **2** confine, jail, imprison, restrain, incarcerate, detain. **ant.** **1** open, unlock, unfasten. **2** release, liberate, discharge, set free, let out, spring (*Slang*).

loco *adj. Slang* INSANE.

locomotion *n.* movement, progress, advance, travel, headway, motion, step, gait. **ant.** stillness, rest, immobility, inactivity, inertia, stasis.

locomotive *adj.* moving, ambulatory, motile, mobile, traveling, progressing. **ant.** stationary, static, immobile, motionless, fixed.

locus *n.* place, site, point, locality, spot, location.

locution *n.* **1** accent, manner, phrasing, discourse, pronunciation, inflection, intonation, cadence. **2** expression, idiom, phrase, wording, term, verbalism.

lodestar *n.* guide, ideal, standard, beacon, model, criterion, pattern, archetype.

lodge *v.* **1** house, shelter, harbor, protect, quarter, accommodate, put up. **2** place, proffer, file, confer, invest, repose, present, bestow, vouchsafe. —*n.* hut, cottage, cabin, gatehouse.

lodger *n.* boarder, roomer, tenant, renter.

lodging *n.* home, abode, lodgment, quarters, residence, dwelling, pied-à-terre, diggings, digs, pad (*Slang*).

lodgment *n.* LODGING.

loft *n.* attic, garret, mansard, gallery, balcony, clerestory. —*v.* upthrow, heave, lob, pop up, sky (*Brit.*). **ant.** *n.* cellar, basement, vault, crypt.

lofty *adj.* **1** tall, high, soaring, towering, elevated, raised. **2** exalted, noble, dignified, stately, sublime, grand, superior, elevated, majestic. **3** haughty, arrogant, proud, disdainful, insolent, scornful, lordly, patronizing, self-important.

ant. 1 low, deep, depressed, sunken, short, stunted, squat, dwarfish. **2** base, mean, petty, banal, everyday, mundane, common, shabby. **3** humble, meek, modest, unassuming, lowly, submissive.

log *n.* **1** trunk, beam, chunk, block, stump, timber. **2** record, account, journal, logbook, daybook, diary, schedule, listing. —*v.* record, tally, chart, enter, note, tabulate, score, report, mark down, list.

loge *n.* box, stall, balcony, parterre, parquet.

logic *n.* **1** reason, reasoning, argument, induction, deduction, inference, analysis, dialectics, clarity, accuracy, precision. **2** connection, relationship, association, link, chain, inevitability.

logical *adj.* clear, rational, coherent, valid, sound, cogent, relevant, pertinent, consistent, analytical, sensible.

ant. confused, chaotic, illogical, irrational, specious, inconsistent, untenable.

logorrhea *n.* GARRULITY.

logy *adj.* dull, lethargic, sleepy, drowsy, weary, tired, torpid, inert, inactive, stupefied, sluggish, enervated, comatose.

ant. energetic, active, brisk, spirited, vigorous, lively, animated.

loiter *v.* linger, loaf, dawdle, laze, delay, tarry, procrastinate, lag, idle, potter, shuffle, ramble, stroll.

ant. hurry, bustle, hasten, hustle, rush, speed, dash, scurry.

loiterer *n.* vagrant, bum, idler, dawdler, loafer, layabout (*Brit.*), ne'er-do-well.

ant. hustler, demon, go-getter.

loll *v.* recline, lean, lounge, relax, slump, flop, sprawl, repose, loaf, languish, droop, sag.

lone *adj.* solitary, isolated, single, unac-

companied, sole, individual, separate, detached, only, exclusive, one.

lonely *adj.* **1** deserted, solitary, unfrequented, desolate, remote, secluded, withdrawn, private, deserted, out-of-the-way, uninhabited, unpopulated. **2** lonesome, friendless, desolate, forsaken, forlorn, estranged, outcast, destitute.

ant. 1 busy, crowded, bustling, thronged, frequented, populous, congested. **2** gregarious, popular, sociable.

loner *n.* solitary, recluse, hermit, misanthrope, eccentric, maverick, outsider.

ant. mixer, joiner, fraternizer.

lonesome *adj.* LONELY.

long[1] *adj.* **1** *of space:* extended, extensive, stretched, expanded, lengthy, considerable, great. **2** *of time:* prolonged, protracted, drawn-out, sustained, continuing. **3** copious, multitudinous, numerous, profuse, full, abundant, plentiful. **4** slow, tedious, tiresome, dragging, interminable, boring, monotonous, endless, wearisome, long-winded.

ant. 1 short, contracted, reduced, compact, curtailed. **2** brief, short, fleeting, quick, sudden, transitory. **3** scant, skimpy, small, meager, lean. **4** terse, concise, brief, economical, pointed, pithy.

long[2] *v.* yearn, covet, crave, desire, hanker, pine, wish, hunger, want, lust.

longheaded *adj.* SHREWD.

longiloquence *n.* GARRULITY.

longing *n.* craving, yearning, wish, desire, hunger, eagerness, hankering, aspiration. —*adj.* desirous, eager, yearning, craving, pining, wishful, hungry, ardent, anxious, impatient, fervent, avid.

ant. *n.* distaste, aversion, reluctance, antipathy, coldness. —*adj.* cool, disinclined, reluctant, averse, loath.

long-range *adj.* lengthy, long, longish, continuous, long-lasting, long-term, protracted, prolonged, extensive, extended.

ant. short-range, brief, temporary, transient, experimental.

long-standing *adj.* long-lasting, long-lived, long-established, lasting, long, perennial, perpetual, continual, permanent, immemorial, infinite, ancient.

ant. short-lived, temporary, short, passing, transient, transitory.

long-winded *adj.* verbose, wordy, prolix, garrulous, voluble, windy, gabby, overlong, prolonged, talky, talkative, copious, diffuse, tedious, long, lengthy, rambling, fustian, boring, meandering.

ant. short, brief, terse, taciturn, concise.

long-windedness *n.* GARRULITY.

look *v.* **1** see, gaze, regard, sight, view, eye, stare, glance, watch, squint, discern, espy. **2** search, seek, examine, research, inquire, survey, scrutinize, contemplate, study, ogle, leer, peep, gape, stare, spy. **3** *appear to be:* seem, appear, present, show, evidence, exhibit, manifest. —*n.* aspect, expression, demeanor, appearance, mien, manner, air, complexion, face, countenance, bearing, behavior, carriage, cast, guise, expression, effect, semblance.

look after watch over, care for, mind, tend to, protect, guard, attend to, nurse, keep an eye on, supervise, oversee.

ant. neglect, ignore, slight, forget, disregard.

look-alike *n.* double, duplicate, twin, equivalent, counterpart, parallel, replica, facsimile, copy, reproduction.

look down on despise, scorn, misprize, disdain, spurn, contemn, snub, sneer, detest, disregard, undervalue, hold in contempt, high-hat.

ant. admire, look up to, respect, esteem, regard.

looker-on *n.* ONLOOKER.

look forward to anticipate, look toward, expect, count upon, long for,

await, wait for, hope for, look for, rely on.

ant. despair of, lose hope, despond, lose heart, give up.

looking-glass *n.* MIRROR.

look into examine, investigate, inquire, scrutinize, study, inspect, check out, look over, probe, explore, delve, pursue, plumb, dig into, poke into, sound, fathom.

look like resemble, take after, appear like, favor, duplicate, match, simulate, imitate, parallel, copy, echo, counterfeit, smack of, mimic.

look-out *n.* **1** watchfulness, vigilance, attention, readiness, alertness, circumspection, wakefulness, guardedness, prudence, heed, surveillance, awareness, cognizance, mindfulness, precaution, diligence. **2** post, overlook, citadel, tower. **3** sentry, sentinel, monitor, watchman, guard, watcher, watchdog, observer, warner, spy, signalman, patrol, spotter, vedette, surveillant.

ant. 1 inattentiveness, oblivion, laxness, absent-mindedness, carelessness, neglect, indifference.

look over LOOK INTO.

look up to ADMIRE.

loom *v.* take shape, bulk, hulk, form, appear, arise, ascend, emerge, hover, impend, mount, show, wax, figure, portend, bode, threaten.

ant. disappear, evaporate, dissolve, sink, settle, wane, recede.

loon *n.* FOOL.

loony *Slang adj.* foolish, erratic, nutty (*Slang*), imbecilic, moronic, irrational, asinine, ludicrous, preposterous, nonsensical, silly, daft, zany, lunatic, demented, mad, crazy, insane. —*n.* FOOL.

ant. *adj.* wise, prudent, rational, sensible, clever, reasonable.

loop *n.* circle, spiral, whorl, twirl, knot, ring, ringlet, eye, eyelet, circuit, fastener, noose, grommet, catch. —*v.* encircle, connect, double, join, knot, bend, twist, turn, furl, hoop, wind, round, curve, whirl, curl, spiral, twirl, coil, braid.

looped *adj. Slang* DRUNK.

loose *adj.* **1** unattached, unsecured, untied, unfastened, free, unbound, unfettered, unrestrained, unconfined, unyoked, untethered, unshackled, released. **2** slack, lax, careless, uncaring, negligent, neglectful, heedless, remiss, permissive, indulgent, imprudent, thoughtless, indifferent, unmindful, forgetful, rash. **3** friable, grainy, granular, crumbly, powdery, gritty, pulverized, sandy, lumpy, thin, unpacked. **4** free, at liberty, liberated, unconfined, independent, at large, scot-free, relaxed, limber, unencumbered, easy, unrestricted, unrestrained, unimpeded. **5** lewd, unchaste, licentious, immoral, vulgar, wanton, libertine, dissolute, impure, ribald, debauched, profligate, fallen, sinful. **6** imprecise, inexact, general, vague, indefinite, ill-defined, indeterminate, indistinct, diffuse, rambling. —*v.* LOOSEN.

ant. **1** bound, fettered, tied, restrained, trussed. **2** careful, vigilant, wary, alert, chary, circumspect, judicious. **3** tight, packed, hard, compact, firm, solid, compressed. **4** confined, shut-in, restrained, detained, incarcerated, imprisoned. **5** moral, chaste, pure, clean, virtuous, wholesome. **6** precise, exact, specific, detailed, comprehensive, complete.

loose-jointed *adj.* LIMBER.

loosen *v.* **1** untie, undo, unclasp, unshackle, unfasten, unfetter, unyoke, untether, unlock, unbind, unloose, loose. **2** release, free, set free, let go, liberate, unloose, unchain, unbridle, unshackle, untie, deliver, unbind, extricate. **3** relax, reduce, dissolve, dilute, soften, diffuse, break up, melt, thaw, liquefy, macerate, crumble. **4** relax, slacken, ease, let up, mitigate, soften, reduce, diminish, ameliorate, lessen, weaken, moderate, alleviate, decrease.

ant. **1** tie, bind, clasp, shackle, fasten,

yoke, fetter. **2** imprison, incarcerate, enchain, bridle, capture. **3** harden, stiffen, tighten, compress, condense, thicken. **4** tighten, strengthen, increase, reinforce.

loot *v.* plunder, rob, despoil, devastate, lay waste, ransack, pillage, rape, fleece, ravage, rifle, raid, filch. —*n.* plunder, pillage, booty, prize, goods, spoils, take, haul, pilferage.

lop *v.* cut, sever, hack, chop, detach, amputate, dock, crop, trim, truncate, prune, slice off, mow, mutilate, clip.

lope *v.* bound, gallop, canter, coast, sweep, skim, course, saunter, amble, cruise, roll along, meander, skip along, jog.

lop-sided *adj.* uneven, askew, asymmetric, unbalanced, overbalanced, tilting, topheavy, inclined, leaning, oblique, one-sided, disproportionate, unequal, irregular, tipped, tilted, slanted, listing.

ant. even, balanced, equal, proportioned, symmetric, straight.

loquacious *adj.* talkative, chatty, verbose, garrulous, vociferous, voluble, prolix, wordy, long-winded, windy, gabby, profuse, copious, babbling, gushy, diffusive.

ant. taciturn, reticent, terse, silent, quiet, reserved.

loquacity *n.* GARRULITY.

lord *n.* ruler, monarch, crown, sovereign, overlord, leader, noble, liege, potentate, paramount, master, superior, headman, governor, peer, laird, suzerain, emperor, czar, autocrat, seignior.

ant. vassal, subject, commoner, liegeman, underling, minion.

lord it boss around, domineer, tyrannize, oppress, put on airs, act big, overawe, coerce, dictate, control, intimidate, browbeat, swagger, vaunt.

lordly *adj.* **1** lofty, noble, grand, magnificent, majestic, regal, royal, kingly, princely, aristocratic, dignified, proud. **2** haughty, insolent, arrogant, lofty, domineering, imperious, disdainful, overbearing, supercilious, despotic, dictatorial, tyrannical.

ant. 1 servile, menial, submissive, obsequious, cringing. **2** humble, obedient, lowly, meek, modest, unpretentious, unassuming.

lore *n.* wisdom, folk wisdom, folktales, tales, sayings, stories, legends, folkways, beliefs, teachings, traditions, customs.

lose *v.* **1** mislay, misplace, miss, misdirect, let slip, go astray, vanish, lose track of, wander off. **2** fail, default, fall short, miss, forfeit, flunk, flub, succumb, fall, miscarry, abort, collapse, submit, yield, capitulate, surrender, come a cropper. **3** outdistance, leave behind, outrun, escape, elude, evade, slip away, dodge, outdo, outstrip, outshine, eclipse, surpass, outpace.

ant. 1 find, locate, retrieve, recover, regain, get back. **2** succeed, triumph, win, vanquish, achieve, forge ahead, surmount.

loser *n.* FAILURE.

loss *n.* **1** deficit, debit, debt, minus, shrinkage, deficiency, depletion. **2** privation, deprivation, harm, damage, ruin, trouble, disadvantage, injury, defeat, destruction, detriment, forfeiture, impairment, misfortune, bereavement.

ant. 1 excess, plus, surplus, overage, profit. **2** gain, profit, return, improvement, acquisition.

lost *adj.* **1** mislaid, misplaced, missing, missed, wayward, gone, misdirected, astray. **2** wasted, exhausted, depleted, dissipated, abandoned, depraved, dissolute, corrupt, profligate, licentious, gone to pot, helpless, on the ropes, down and out. **3** squandered, wasted, misspent, dissipated, misused, frittered away. **4** rapt, absorbed, abstracted, engrossed, preoccupied, entranced, spellbound, bewildered, confused, perplexed, stymied, dazed, puzzled, befogged, befuddled, mystified. **5** passé, past, forgotten, bygone, gone by, lapsed,

irrecoverable, unrecollected, unremembered, out-of-date, disappeared, antiquated, obsolete, extinct, dead, outmoded.

ant. 1 found, located, retrieved, recovered, regained. **2** wholesome, moral, uncorrupted, healthy, pure. **3** laid away, hoarded, amassed, treasured up, saved. **5** present, contemporary, current, up-to-date, modern, au courant.

lot *n.* **1** portion, share, allotment, apportionment, measure, allowance, quota, ration, piece, part, percentage. **2** chance, fate, accident, kismet, fortune, plight, destiny, heritage, estate, condition, predicament. **3** group, bunch, collection, company, package, set, clique, coterie, host, cluster, body. **4** acreage, parcel, plot, tract, field, patch, property, division.

loth *adj.* LOATH.

Lothario *n.* seducer, rake, philanderer, libertine, roué, debauchee, debaucher, lecher, sensualist, profligate, wolf (*Slang*), lover, Don Juan, Casanova, Romeo, skirt chaser, ladies' man, lady-killer.

lotion *n.* cosmetic, conditioner, cream, preparation, base, wash, unguent, salve, balm, ointment, liniment, freshener.

lots *n.* many, plenty, good deal, great deal, scads, slew, heaps, piles, numbers, scores, droves, stacks.

lottery *n.* drawing, draw, chance, raffle, gamble, wager, bet, venture, stake.

loud *adj.* **1** noisy, clamorous, resounding, tumultuous, deafening, booming, earsplitting, ear-piercing, loudmouthed, stentorian, boisterous, riotous, vociferous, hurly-burly, uproarious, rip-roaring, rowdy. **2** gaudy, flashy, showy, garish, splashy, obtrusive, vulgar, obvious, blatant, flaunting, loudmouthed, rude, crude, cheap, coarse.

ant. 1 quiet, soft, silent, peaceful. **2** tasteful, sedate, artistic, elegant.

loudmouthed *adj.* LOUD.

lounge *v.* **1** stretch out, recline, loll,

laze, relax, lie around, repose, languish, take it easy, slouch, slump, flop. **2** loaf, dally, dillydally, idle away, waste time, trifle away, fritter away, laze, dawdle, loiter, vegetate, stagnate, mark time. —*n*. lobby, waiting room, reception room, vestibule, anteroom.

louse *n. Slang* scoundrel, rat (*Slang*), heel (*Slang*), stinker, cad, bounder (*Brit*.), villain, knave, rascal, rogue, cuss, cur, viper, swine, skunk, dog.

louse up mismanage, foul up, botch, snarl, bungle, muff, blunder, spoil, ruin, bollix (*Slang*), screw up (*Slang*), mess up, trip up, muddle, butcher.
ant. straighten out, put in order, rectify, adjust, correct, untangle.

lousy *adj. Slang* **1** dirty, filthy, disgusting, revolting, foul, squalid, grimy, repulsive, putrid, rotten. **2** contemptible, mean, hateful, execrable, horrible, outrageous, abominable, atrocious, awful, dreadful. **3** inferior, poor, second-rate, paltry, shabby, puny, low-grade, deficient, worthless, uninspiring, schlocky (*Slang*).
ant. 1 clean, pure, pristine, immaculate. **3** superior, first-rate, top-notch, worthy, admirable, quality.

lout *n*. boor, oaf, churl, clown, ape, bumpkin, lummox, rustic, clodhopper, yokel, boob (*Slang*), dunce.

loutish *adj.* boorish, oafish, churlish, clownish, awkward, uncouth, gross, rough, ungainly, vulgar, rude, gawky, gauche, unpolished.
ant. gentlemanly, genteel, gracious, well-mannered, suave, smooth.

lovable *adj.* amiable, winning, winsome, sweet, charming, endearing, engaging, taking, attractive, lovely, fetching, delightful, adorable, likable, cuddly, captivating.
ant. hateful, odious, detestable.

love *n*. **1** fondness, liking, attachment, affection, friendliness, amity, inclination, cordiality, geniality, regard, devotion, warmth, adoration, ten-

derness, endearment. **2** passion, desire, amour, infatuation, craving, longing, yearning, coveting, ardor, rapture, crush, flame. —*v*. **1** like, adore, adulate, worship, cherish, yearn for, hold dear, pine for. **2** enjoy, like, delight in, savor, fancy, admire. **3** caress, fondle, embrace, kiss, cuddle, hug, pamper.
ant. *n*. **1** hatred, dislike, loathing, enmity, bitterness, antipathy, distaste, aversion, disgust, repugnance. *v*. **1** detest, abhor, abominate, hate, loathe, scorn.

loveless *adj.* **1** unloved, disliked, hated, unpopular, forsaken, lovelorn, cut off, unlamented, friendless, spurned, deserted, rejected. **2** unloving, cold, indifferent, unresponsive, heartless, hard, unfeeling, lukewarm, icy, cold-hearted.
ant. 1 loved, beloved, well-liked, popular. **2** loving, warm, amiable, affectionate, ardent.

lovelorn *adj.* LOVESICK.

lovely *adj.* **1** beautiful, attractive, handsome, comely, charming, exquisite, winning, winsome, nice, gracious, grand, swell. **2** enjoyable, delightful, gratifying, satisfying, enchanting, fascinating, inviting, captivating, pleasing, pleasant, felicitous, sweet, agreeable.
ant. 1 ugly, hideous, homely, uncomely, plain. **2** unpleasant, revolting, repugnant, offensive, unsavory.

lover *n*. **1** sweetheart, beau, admirer, boy friend, girl friend, fiancé, fiancée, suitor, flame, mistress, wooer, courter, spooner, paramour, wolf (*Slang*), Don Juan, Lothario, Casanova, Romeo, ladies' man, swain, lady-killer, philanderer, trifler, vamp (*Slang*), coquette, flirt. **2** devotee, aficionado, follower, fan, enthusiast, admirer, supporter.

lovesick *adj.* pining, lovelorn, yearning, languishing, longing, desiring.

loving *adj.* adoring, affectionate, passionate, hot-blooded, warm-hearted, demonstrative, tender, yearning, devoted, fond, doting, adulatory, amatory, amorous, erotic, romantic, worshipful, reverential, enamored, smitten, infatuated, uxorious.

ant. unloving, cold, frigid, indifferent, detached.

loving-kindness *n.* KINDNESS.

low *adj.* **1** slight, limited, modest, paltry, niggardly, pitiful, sorry, slender, slim, unimportant, superficial, insignificant, trivial, nugatory. **2** substandard, low-grade, inferior, poor, mediocre, puny, wretched, deficient, faulty, unsatisfactory, shabby, worthless. **3** depressed, melancholy, dejected, sad, miserable, unhappy, dispirited, downcast, morose, blue, morbid, gloomy, despondent. **4** humble, lowly, meek, obscure, low-born, poor, plain, plebeian, coarse, vulgar, base, rude, crude, rough, common, simple, inglorious, unpretentious. **5** scant, depleted, exhausted, meager, sparse, insufficient, thin, lean, used up, dried up, spent, short, expended, drained, consumed.

ant. 1 considerable, significant, substantial, abundant, sizable, ample. **2** superior, first-class, first-rate, highgrade, excellent. **3** happy, elated, cheerful, optimistic. **4** exalted, high, estimable, aristocratic. **5** abundant, overflowing, plentiful, excessive.

low-born *adj.* HUMBLE.

low-bred *adj.* VULGAR.

low-down[1] *n. Slang* TRUTH.

low-down[2] *adj.* MEAN.

lower[1] *adj.* **1** inferior, lesser, smaller, subordinate, secondary, junior, minor, second-class, low-level, subsidiary, ancillary, subservient, tributary, marginal, expendable. —*v.* **1** let down, drop, depress, take down, bring down, sink, dip, submerge, plunge, level. **2** reduce, decrease, sink, fall, diminish, lessen, slacken, weaken, ease, shorten, contract, dwindle, pare, minimize, subtract, moderate, prune, temper. **3** humble, degrade, abase, humiliate, disgrace,

dishonor, demote, debase, weaken, undermine.

ant. *adj.* superior, preferred, ranking. *v.* **1** raise, lift, elevate. **2** increase, add, enlarge, extend. **3** honor, glorify, revere, esteem, respect.

lower[2] *v., n.* SCOWL.

lowering *adj.* **1** overcast, threatening, cloudy, dark, ominous, forbidding, black, murky, gloomy, heavy, gray. **2** frowning, sullen, scowling, gloomy, minatory, somber, dismal, menacing, funereal.

ant. 1 sunny, cloudless, bright, fine. **2** smiling, beaming, happy, cheerful.

lower world HELL.

low-key *adj.* understated, low-pressure, calm, subdued, muted, muffled, restrained, moderate, controlled, lowpitched, soft, gentle.

ant. overstated, intensive, high-pressure, forceful.

lowly *adj.* inferior, subordinate, subject, secondary, unassuming, simple, plebeian, meek, modest, humble, plain, common, commonplace, average, ordinary.

ant. superior, exalted, unexcelled, elevated.

low-minded *adj.* VULGAR.

low-spirited *adj.* DEPRESSED.

loyal *adj.* faithful, true, devoted, constant, steadfast, reliable, staunch, trustworthy, unswerving, unwavering, scrupulous, dependable, dutiful, firm, reputable, punctilious, conscientious, resolute.

ant. faithless, disloyal, treacherous, perfidious, traitorous, false.

loyalty *n.* allegiance, fidelity, faithfulness, devotion, constancy, fealty, faith, reliability, dependability, obedience, firmness, steadfastness, singlemindedness.

ant. treachery, perfidy, faithlessness, disloyalty.

lubber *n.* lout, boor, churl, rustic, yokel, hick, slob (*Slang*), hayseed (*Slang*), bumpkin, peasant, lummox, bungler, clodhopper.

lucent *adj.* **1** luminous, bright, brilliant, radiant, resplendent, lucid, beaming, glowing, vivid, gleaming, illuminated, glistening, sparkling, lustrous, blazing. **2** translucent, clear, pellucid, limpid, crystalline, semitransparent, diaphanous.

ant. 1 dull, dark, dim, murky, cloudy. **2** opaque, dense, solid.

lucid *adj.* **1** clear, understandable, comprehensible, transparent, pellucid, intelligible, plain, unmistakable, obvious, manifest, distinct, evident, clear-cut, luculent. **2** rational, sound, reasonable, clear-headed, sensible, sane, sober, competent.

ant. 1 confusing, unclear, dark, unintelligible, fuzzy, enigmatic, vague. **2** deranged, irrational, muddled, incompetent, fuzzy-minded, confused.

Lucifer *n.* DEVIL.

luck *n.* **1** chance, fortune, lot, accident, happenstance, providence, fate, kismet, karma, destiny, hazard, wheel of fortune, fortuity. **2** good fortune, success, advantage, windfall, prosperity, fluke, Midas touch, godsend, break, manna, serendipity.

ant. 2 misfortune, adversity, mishap.

luckless *adj.* unlucky, unfortunate, jinxed, cursed, accursed, ill-fated, ill-starred, star-crossed, hapless.

ant. lucky, fortunate, blessed.

lucky *adj.* **1** fortunate, blessed, fortuitous, happy, favored, successful, providential. **2** auspicious, propitious, favorable.

ant. 1 unfortunate, unlucky, luckless, ill-starred, ill-fated.

lucrative *adj.* profitable, remunerative, fruitful, gainful, money-making, beneficial, productive, rich, fat.

ant. unprofitable, unproductive, marginal.

lucre *n.* money, riches, wealth, gain, pelf, mammon, gelt (*Slang*).

lucubration *n.* STUDY.

ludicrous *adj.* laughable, absurd, ridiculous, preposterous, farcical, amusing, comical, silly, funny, droll,

senseless, crazy, outlandish, zany, screwy (*Slang*).

ant. serious, solemn, sensible.

lug[1] *n. Slang* lout, blockhead, ass, dolt, dunce, fool, oaf, boor, gawk, ape, clod, bumpkin, loon, klutz (*Slang*), numskull, bonehead (*Slang*), fathead (*Slang*).

lug[2] *v.* drag, tug, tow, pull, tote, heave, draw, haul, bear, carry, schlep (*Slang*).

luggage *n.* baggage, bags, suitcases, pack, things, gear, effects, accouterments, equipment, paraphernalia.

lugubrious *adj.* sad, mournful, dismal, doleful, sorrowful, melancholy, gloomy, depressing, miserable, crestfallen, woeful, depressed, downcast, rueful, woebegone.

ant. cheerful, happy, content, joyous.

lukewarm *adj.* **1** tepid, mild, warm. **2** half-hearted, indifferent, neutral, uninterested, cool, aloof, detached, unconcerned, apathetic, phlegmatic, languid, dispassionate, uncaring.

ant. 2 avid, concerned, involved, eager, curious.

lull *v.* calm, allay, alleviate, mitigate, quiet, placate, soothe, tranquilize, pacify, mollify, appease. —*n.* pause, suspension, breather, interval, let-up calm, interlude, respite, hush, slack, break, intermission, caesura, *entr'acte*.

ant. *v.* provoke, incite, stir up, agitate.

lulu *n. Slang* dandy, jim-dandy, honey, pip (*Slang*), whiz (*Slang*), dilly (*Slang*), nifty (*Slang*), corker (*Slang*), crackerjack (*Slang*), humdinger (*Slang*), peach (*Slang*).

lumber *v.* plod, trudge, stamp, shamble, drag, stumble, shuffle, barge, jog, clump, fumble, hobble, waddle, flounder.

luminary *n.* notable, celebrity, personage, immortal, laureate, star, hero, lion, somebody, VIP, dignitary, worthy, big name, name, leading light, brass (*Slang*).

ant. nonentity, nobody.

luminous *adj.* **1** shining, brilliant, lustrous, bright, lucid, lucent, radiant, resplendent, lit, alight, lighted, refulgent, illuminated, aglow, glowing, lambent, luminescent, incandescent. **2** comprehensible, clear, understandable, intelligible, perspicuous, plain, lucid, rational, transparent, evident.

ant. 1 dark, black, subdued, dull. **2** confused, cloudy, obscure, vague, abstruse, opaque.

lummox *n.* lout, oaf, clod, clown, lubber, yokel, bumpkin, boor, klutz (*Slang*), gawk, blunderbuss, lug (*Slang*), ape, zombie.

lump *n.* **1** hunk, chunk, gob, pile, clod, clot, wad, heap, clump, batch. **2** protuberance, swelling, distention, tumescence, mass, bulge, puff, bump, excrescence, nodule, tumor. —*v.* **1** group, collect, assemble, amass, join, gather, heap, cluster, rake up, round up. **2** *treat as one:* combine, associate, pool, merge, blend, consolidate, amalgamate, link, fuse, unite.

ant. *v.* **1** scatter, disperse, spread around. **2** separate, part, split, break up.

lumpish *adj.* STUPID.

lumpy *adj.* cloddy, clotted, lumpish, caked, granular, grainy, coagulated, curdled, clabbered, thick, chunky, knobby, knotty.

ant. smooth.

lunacy *n.* **1** insanity, madness, irrationality, craziness, derangement, mania, idiocy, dementia, psychosis. **2** foolishness, senselessness, folly, foolhardiness, absurdity, irrationality, asininity, idiocy, imbecility, nonsense.

ant. 1 sanity, rationality, lucidity. **2** common sense, soundness, sensibleness, reasonableness.

lunatic *adj.* **1** insane, mad, crazy, demented, deranged, unbalanced, psychopathic, unhinged, daft, psychotic,

raving, touched, loco (*Slang*), off one's rocker (*Slang*), nuts (*Slang*). **2** irrational, foolish, foolhardy, unsound, rash, moonstruck, crackbrained, nutty (*Slang*), batty (*Slang*), cuckoo (*Slang*), crackpot (*Slang*), screwy (*Slang*). —*n.* madman, crackbrain, psychopath, maniac, nut (*Slang*), psycho (*Slang*).

ant. *adj.* **1** sane, lucid, rational, normal. **2** rational, sober, sound, sensible.

lunch *n.* luncheon, bite, brunch, snack, tiffin (*Brit.*), repast, collation.

luncheon *n.* LUNCH.

lunge *n.* **1** thrust, pass, jab, attack, charge, stab, push. **2** plunge, dash, lurch, pitch, dive. —*v.* thrust, pass, jab, attack, charge, stab, plunge, dash, lurch, pitch, dive.

lurch *v.* pitch, toss, careen, teeter, cant, sway, swing, reel, tilt, roll, stagger, stumble, swag, sag, flounder.

lure *n.* enticement, attraction, allurement, bait, inducement, magnet, decoy, trap, snare, temptation, tease, come-on (*Slang*), pitfall, hook, siren song, drawing card. —*v.* entice, attract, allure, draw, inveigle, invite, tempt, solicit, seduce, bewitch, charm, cajole, bait, beckon.

ant. *v.* repel, dissuade, repulse, drive away, discourage.

lurid *adj.* violent, terrible, sensational, gruesome, ghastly, shocking, startling, awful, grisly, Grand-Guignol.

luscious *adj.* delicious, juicy, delectable, palatable, savory, tasty, succulent, sweet, ambrosial, pleasing, gustatory, appetizing, mouth-watering.

ant. unsavory, unpalatable, disgusting, nauseating, sickening, insipid.

lush[1] *adj.* **1** juicy, tender, succulent, fresh, ripe. **2** luxuriant, rich, abundant, profuse, prolific, teeming, dense. **3** elaborate, extravagant, overdone, plush, ornate, posh.

ant. sparse, barren, arid, meager.

lush[2] *n. Slang* DRUNKARD.

lust *n.* **1** desire, craving, passion, appetite, eagerness, cupidity, longing, thirst. **2** lechery, concupiscence, carnality, libido, salaciousness, licentiousness, lubricity, license, lasciviousness, libertinism, wantonness, pruriency, lewdness, goatishness, satyrism, venery. —*v.* desire, hunger for, crave, need, want, demand, thirst, long for, covet, yearn for.

ant. *n.* **2** purity, chastity, virtue, continence.

luster *n.* **1** sheen, gloss, glitter, glisten, radiance, brightness, illumination, incandescence, luminosity, dazzle, glow, glint. **2** excellence, brilliance, distinction, splendor, glory, merit, repute, honor, renown, eminence, celebrity, dash, flair, panache, élan, éclat.

ant. 1 dullness, dimness, drabness, lusterlessness.

lustful *adj.* passionate, desirous, amorous, erotic, loving, sexy, sex-starved, lascivious, concupiscent, wanton, lickerish, salacious, goatish, libidinous, sensual, randy, raunchy, carnal, lubricious, satyric, horny (*Slang*).

lustrous *adj.* bright, burnished, luminous, effulgent, glossy, radiant, illuminated, dazzling, glowing, incandescent, glistening.

ant. dull, dim, drab, dark.

lusty *adj.* vigorous, hearty, robust, strong, healthy, sturdy, stout, rough, rugged, hale, sound, virile, hefty.

ant. weak, faint, frail, unhealthy, puny.

luxuriance *n.* richness, ornateness, extravagance, floridness, gaudiness, flashiness, flamboyance, abundance, copiousness, exuberance, fertility, lushness, fruitfulness, bounty.

ant. barrenness, aridity, dryness, sparseness, exiguity.

luxuriant *adj.* **1** teeming, abundant, exuberant, flourishing, wild, rank,

overgrown, overrun, copious, profuse, rich, fertile, lush, replete, dense, prolific, fruitful, lavish, bountiful. **2** extravagant, ornate, gaudy, florid, adorned, flowery, ornamented, fancy, showy, flashy, bedecked, flamboyant.

ant. 1 meager, barren, infertile, fallow, arid. **2** somber, plain, unadorned.

luxurious *adj.* **1** epicurean, voluptuous, self-indulgent, sybaritic. **2** splendid, sumptuous, ornate, rich, opulent, well-appointed, magnificent, plush, posh, ritzy (*Slang*), tony.

ant. 1 austere, spartan, spare. **2** poor, squalid, shabby, decrepit.

luxury *n.* **1** high living, wealth, ease, richness, well-being, comfort, bed of roses, life of Riley, elegance, clover, velvet, sybaritism, self-indulgence, prodigality, self-gratification. **2** treat, rarity, delicacy, bauble, frill, choice bit, trinket, trifle, ornament, adornment, trappings, finery.

lying *n.* untruthfulness, deceit, deception, fabrication, prevarication, mendacity, guile, fraud, fibbing, hypocrisy, dissimulation, falseness, falsification, storytelling, duplicity, dishonesty, calumny, perjury, dissembling. —*adj.* mendacious, false, untrue, deceptive, perfidious, deceitful, dissembling, dishonest, insincere, uncandid, evasive, fabricating, crooked, treacherous, two-faced, hypocritical, faithless.

ant. *n.* truth-telling, honesty, straightforwardness, openness. *adj.* truthful, sincere, frank, honest, guileless, scrupulous.

lymphatic *adj.* LISTLESS.

lyric *adj.* musical, melodious, melodic, tuneful, singing, euphonious, mellifluous.

ant. cacophonous, harsh, grating, tuneless.

M

ma *n.* MOTHER.

macabre *adj.* gruesome, grisly, grim, deathlike, deathly, cadaverous, ghastly, eerie, ghostly, unearthly, weird, dreadful, horrible, horrific.

mace *n.* CLUB.

Machiavellian *adj.* unscrupulous, unprincipled, expedient, opportunistic, conniving, calculating, scheming, crafty, cunning, insidious, cynical, hypocritical, double-dealing, two-faced, deceitful.
ant. idealistic, visionary, principled, honorable, conscientious.

machinate *v.* SCHEME.

machination *n.* scheming, plotting, intriguing, conspiring, contriving, manipulating, engineering, finagling, wirepulling, wheeling and dealing (*Slang*).

machine *n.* **1** mechanism, machinery, engine, motor, appliance, apparatus, instrument, movement, device, contrivance, contraption, gadget. **2** automaton, robot, puppet, creature, instrument, yes-man, tool, pawn, drudge, menial, slave. **3** organization, administration, institution, establishment, bureaucracy, apparat, instrument, power brokers, clubhouse, backroom, gang, crowd, bunch, faction, camp, city hall.

machinery *n.* means, procedure, system, process, ways and means, wherewithal, resources, devices, setup, agency, instrumentality, mechanism, *modus operandi*.

macrocosm *n.* UNIVERSE.

macula *n.* SPOT.

mad *adj.* **1** insane, crazy, lunatic, deranged, demented, unbalanced, cracked, daft, possessed, psychotic, berserk, delirious, ravening, rabid,

raging, madding, nutty (*Slang*), screwy (*Slang*), loony (*Slang*). **2** overwhelmed, overwrought, frantic, frenzied, consumed, distraught, hysterical, raging, infuriated, indignant, angry, furious, fuming, irate, sore. **3** foolish, silly, inane, wacky (*Slang*), goofy (*Slang*), asinine, witless, wild, reckless, foolhardy, harebrained.
ant. 1 rational, lucid, sound, responsible. **2** composed, self-possessed, level-headed, sober. **3** sensible, reasonable, credible, thoughtful.

madcap *adj.* WILD.

madden *v.* anger, infuriate, enrage, exasperate, gall, provoke, outrage, aggravate, upset, distract, vex.
ant. placate, calm, soothe, mollify, appease.

maddening *adj.* infuriating, enraging, exasperating, galling, outrageous, aggravating, inflammatory, provoking, provocative, vexatious, irritating.

madding *adj.* MAD.

made-up *adj.* fictitious, make-believe, fictional, mythical, fabricated, concocted, plotted, contrived, invented, artificial, cooked-up, trumped-up, specious.
ant. true, realistic, authentic, actual, veritable.

madhouse *n.* bedlam, pandemonium, confusion, chaos, commotion, turmoil, rumpus, hubbub, racket, Babel, muddle, mix-up.

madman *n.* lunatic, maniac, psychotic, psychopath, nut (*Slang*), loon.

maelstrom *n.* **1** whirlpool, vortex, eddy, whirl, surge, twirl, torrent, rapids, shoot, white water, riptide, Charybdis. **2** passion, emotion, agitation, ferment, turmoil, turbulence, perturbation, fluster, unrest.

maestro *n.* MASTER.

magazine *n.* periodical, serial, journal.

magic *n.* **1** sorcery, witchcraft, wizardry, wonderworking, enchantment, conjuration, divination, necromancy, theurgy, shamanism, mumbo jumbo, voodooism, black art, witchery, black magic, demonism, diabolism, exorcism. **2** sleight-of-hand, illusionism, prestidigitation, legerdemain, hocus pocus, trickery, juggling, thaumaturgy. **3** glamour, allure, fascination, spell, bewitchery, enchantment, attraction, charm, appeal, charisma, magnetism.

magical *adj.* fascinating, enchanting, entrancing, bewitching, spellbinding, irresistible, charismatic, glamorous, magnetic, mesmerizing, hypnotic.

magician *n.* **1** wizard, sorcerer, necromancer, diviner, conjuror, Merlin, magus, theurgist, thaumaturge, shaman, warlock, diabolist, exorcist, illusionist, prestidigitator, legerdemainist, sleight-of-hand artist, trickster, juggler. **2** genius, marvel, wonder, miracle man, wonder-worker, wizard, spellbinder, charmer.

magisterial *adj.* commanding, authoritative, masterful, assertive, majestic, august, lordly, imperious, overbearing, high-handed, haughty, arbitrary, arrogant, domineering, peremptory.
ant. modest, meek, humble, diffident, timorous.

magnanimity *n.* greatness, nobility, high-mindedness, large-mindedness, loftiness, bigheartedness, bigness, charity, liberality, selflessness, generosity.
ant. pettiness, meanness, small-heartedness.

magnanimous *adj.* noble, high-minded, large-minded, big, big-hearted, handsome, princely, chivalrous, unselfish, self-sacrificing, selfless, liberal, generous.
ant. petty, mean, selfish, base, grudging.

magnate *n.* leader, chief, power, giant, bigwig, empire builder, VIP, king, prince, duke, lord, seigneur, grandee, captain, baron, czar, tycoon, mogul, nabob.

magnet *n.* lure, spell, inducement, enticement, temptation, cynosure, charmer, enticer, tempter, temptress, sorcerer, sorceress, siren, seducer, bait, decoy.

magnetic *adj.* fascinating, captivating, alluring, entrancing, enthralling, enticing, tantalizing, ravishing, seductive, charismatic, intriguing, provocative, persuasive, dynamic, hypnotic, mesmerizing, galvanic.
ant. repellent, repulsive, offensive, forbidding.

magnetism *n.* attraction, fascination, appeal, allure, spell, magic, power, pull, charisma, glamour, romance.

magnetize *v.* CHARM.

magnificence *n.* splendor, grandeur, impressiveness, nobility, majesty, stateliness, glory, brilliancy, polish, elegance, style, luxury, sumptuousness, pomp.

magnificent *adj.* **1** grand, splendid, impressive, imposing, glorious, superb, sublime, exalted, transcendent, majestic, noble, august, stately, grandiose. **2** lavish, sumptuous, elaborate, spectacular, luxurious, gorgeous, plush (*Slang*), brilliant, radiant, glossy, gaudy, ostentatious. **3** EXCELLENT.
ant. 1, 2 unostentatious, unassuming, unpretentious, humble, modest, ordinary.

magnifico *n.* PERSONAGE.

magnify *v.* **1** enlarge, increase, amplify, augment, extend, raise, boost, spread, dilate. **2** intensify, strengthen, reinforce, concentrate, heighten, deepen, enhance, overdo, overstate, exaggerate, overrate, embroider, stretch, strain, aggravate, worsen, exacerbate.
ant. 1 reduce, diminish, decrease, lessen, scale down, compress. **2** minimize, belittle, diminish, disparage, underrate.

magnitude *n.* **1** size, bulk, mass, bigness, largeness, enormousness, vastness, volume, capacity, immensity, amplitude, space, extent, expanse, measure, proportions, might, strength, intensity. **2** importance, significance, consequence, weight, weightiness, eminence, prominence, enormity, distinction, greatness, nobility, fame.

magpie *n.* GOSSIP.

maid *n.* MAIDEN.

maiden *n.* girl, maid, miss, damsel, lass, coed, gal, chick (*Slang*). —*adj.* first, initial, original, untried, initiatory, inaugural, virgin, introductory, beginning, primary, leading, prime.

mail[1] *v.* post, send, dispatch, address, consign, direct, airmail, ship, freight, express, export, transmit, expedite, forward.

mail[2] *n.* armor, coat of mail, panoply, harness.

maim *v.* mutilate, mangle, wound, injure, hurt, tear, rend, lacerate, dismember, cripple, lame, disable, hamstring, incapacitate.

main *n.* conduit, conductor, cable, line, wire, pipe, tube, channel, duct, drain, sewer. —*adj.* principal, chief, major, leading, premier, prime, primary, head, first, foremost, dominant, paramount, cardinal, capital, topflight, ranking, featured, star.

mainly *adv.* MOSTLY.

mainstay *n.* backbone, bulwark, support, buttress, staff, pillar, anchor, reinforcement, backing, refuge, hope, confidence, encouragement.

maintain *v.* **1** continue, carry on, keep going, keep up, protract, prolong, perpetuate, extend, preserve. **2** repair, service, overhaul, restore, remedy, fix, mend, condition, reclaim, conserve, preserve, save, secure, keep. **3** support, sustain, provide for, keep, pay for, finance, uphold, supply, nourish. **4** claim, declare, state, profess, contend, say, hold, aver, avow, assert, affirm, allege, stress, insist, emphasize.

ant. 1 cease, discontinue, refrain, terminate, quit. **2** ruin, wreck, demolish, spoil, ravage. **3** neglect, slight, skimp, shirk, abandon. **4** deny, repudiate, dispute, refute, disavow.

maintenance *n.* **1** repair, good repair, service, upkeep, condition, custodianship, conservation. **2** support, upkeep, backing, payment, subsistence, provisions, keep, custody, sustenance, supplies, necessaries.

majestic *adj.* stately, dignified, exalted, noble, regal, princely, imperial, splendid, grand, grandiose, impressive, imposing, monumental, sublime, solemn.

majesty *n.* stateliness, grandeur, magnificence, splendor, glory, nobility, distinction, dignity, eminence, portliness, grandiosity, regalness, pomp.

major *adj.* **1** larger, greater, bigger, better, higher, superior, uppermost, considerable, important. **2** principal, leading, main, senior, eminent, superior, predominant, primary, foremost, supreme, sovereign, unrivaled, peerless, unequaled. **3** serious, grave, important, significant, crucial, critical, pressing, urgent, weighty, formidable, vital, life-and-death, severe, dire, acute, radical.

ant. 1 smaller, lesser, lower, inferior. **2, 3** minor, secondary, subordinate, insignificant, inconsequential.

majority *n.* **1** preponderance, bulk, mass, best part, body, gross, lion's share, predominance. **2** maturity, adulthood, seniority, manhood, womanhood.

ant. 1 minority, few, little. **2** minority, juniority, nonage, immaturity.

make *v.* **1** build, construct, fabricate, manufacture, produce, assemble, put together, fashion, form, shape, create, forge, frame, erect, put up. **2** cause, bring about, effect, produce, occasion, effectuate, breed, generate, do, manage, work out, bring to pass, achieve, accomplish, realize. **3** conceive, make up, concoct, contrive, devise, fabricate, invent, draft, formulate, create, hatch, compose, project. **4** earn, acquire, get, gain, accumulate, obtain, procure, come by, reap. **5** compel, force, induce, impel, oblige, necessitate, require, demand, constrain, drive, enforce. —*n.* **1** structure, composition, form, shape, construction, arrangement, build, frame, architecture, makeup, cut, stamp, texture, fabric. **2** brand, trademark, model, variety, type, kind, style, name, designation. **ant.** *v.* **1** destroy, wreck, dismantle, disassemble.

make-believe *adj.* pretended, unreal, imagined, artificial, synthetic, stagy, theatrical, simulated, dummy, false, sham, counterfeit, fake, phony (*Slang*). **ant.** real, authentic, solid, actual, tangible.

make do settle for, get by, eke out, manage, improvise, scrape along, get along with, make out, contrive, muddle through, keep afloat, suffice, serve.

make good SUCCEED.

make off with steal, take, filch, pilfer, purloin, appropriate, cop (*Slang*), lift, pinch (*Slang*), snitch (*Slang*), swipe (*Slang*).

make out 1 see, behold, sight, observe, glimpse, spy, descry, spot, notice, detect, perceive, view, discern, discover, distinguish, recognize. **2** comprehend, understand, apprehend, realize, perceive, sense, know, conceive, fathom, see through, penetrate, identify, place, distinguish, recognize. **3** succeed, manage, work out, bring off, get on, put over, prevail. **ant. 3** fail, founder, miss, disappoint, slip up.

maker *n.* builder, manufacturer, producer, fabricator, industrialist, inventor, originator, founder, creator, pioneer, author.

makeshift *adj.* temporary, substitute, provisional, alternate, ersatz, slapdash.

ant. permanent, durable, lasting, solid, sound.

makeup *n.* **1** composition, constitution, construction, organization, arrangement, formation, format, assembly, structure, components, make, build, fabric. **2** cosmetics.

make up 1 compose, devise, invent, create, concoct, contrive, originate, generate, compound, mix, fabricate, cook up, hatch, improvise, coin. **2** comprise, consist of, constitute, be. **3** reconcile, settle, arrange, adjust, compose, accommodate, harmonize, fix, mend, patch up, come to terms, shake hands, make peace. **4** compensate, recompense, indemnify, redress, make amends, offset, counteract, requite, balance, propitiate, atone for.

making *n.* manufacturing, production, construction, formation, fabrication, composition, building, execution, erection, creation, preparation, forming.

makings *n.* ingredients, substance, potential, potentiality, possibilities, nucleus, soul, heart.

maladjusted *adj.* disaffected, alienated, estranged, malcontent, dissident, out-of-step, ill-adjusted, neurotic, unfit, hung up (*Slang*), abnormal. **ant.** well-adjusted, normal, stable, well-balanced.

maladroit *adj.* CLUMSY.

malady *n.* disease, sickness, illness, ailment, disorder, infection, unhealthiness, indisposition, complaint, affliction, infirmity, disability, affection.

malaise *n.* **1** uneasiness, disquiet, nervousness, alienation, anxiety, apprehension, restlessness, discontent, angst, dissatisfaction, disaffection, misgiving, qualm. **2** weakness, lassitude, languor, frailty, debility, enervation, exhaustion, fatigue. **ant. 1** contentment, serenity, complacency, well-being, restfulness. **2** vigor, vim, heartiness, hardiness.

malapropos *adj.* INAPPROPRIATE.

malarky *n. Slang* nonsense, stuff, rubbish, humbug, baloney (*Slang*), bunk (*Slang*), bunkum, hooey (*Slang*), hokum (*Slang*), tripe, hot air (*Slang*).

malcontent *adj.* discontented, dissident, dissatisfied, displeased, disgruntled, querulous, ill-humored, irascible, out of humor, quarrelsome. —*n.* troublemaker, agitator, fomenter, rebel, die-hard, extremist, mischief-maker.
ant. *adj.* complacent, easygoing, conciliatory, untroubled.

malediction *n.* curse, anathema, imprecation, execration, damnation, vilification, aspersion, calumny, opprobrium, diatribe, abuse, invective.

malefactor *n.* criminal, lawbreaker, perpetrator, offender, felon, gangster, hoodlum, thug, delinquent, culprit, wrongdoer, malfeasant, troublemaker, scoundrel, villain, evildoer, transgressor, sinner.

maleficent *adj.* EVIL.

malevolent *adj.* spiteful, vicious, malicious, antagonistic, hostile, ill-natured, pernicious, invidious, malign, hateful, bitter, mean, malignant, evil, baleful.
ant. benevolent, kind, amicable, cordial, friendly, compassionate.

malfeasance *n.* MALPRACTICE.

malformed *adj.* DEFORMED.

malfunction *n.* breakdown, failure, fault, flaw, snag, glitch (*Slang*), impairment.

malice *n.* spite, ill will, maliciousness, bitterness, rancor, malevolence, hate, hatred, aversion, malignity, antipathy, animosity, hostility, antagonism.
ant. amity, benevolence, kindness, affection.

malicious *adj.* spiteful, vicious, harmful, hateful, treacherous, viperous, hostile, malignant, wanton, merciless, ruthless, pernicious, vindictive, diabolical, baleful, evil.

malign *v.* slander, vilify, defame, revile, abuse, disparage, calumniate, denigrate, traduce, blacken, slur, de-

preciate, discredit, smear. —*adj.* MALEVOLENT.

malignancy *n.* **1** rancor, virulence, malice, spite, ill will, bile, distemper, gall, venom, truculence. **2** cancer, carcinoma, tumor, growth.

malignant *adj.* **1** spiteful, vile, ill-intentioned, baleful, evil, malicious, harmful, hurtful, detrimental, vicious, wicked, malign, dire. **2** cancerous, metastatic, tumorous, malign, virulent.
ant. **1** beneficial, favorable, pleasing, efficacious, salubrious. **2** benign, harmless, dormant, inactive.

malignity *n.* MALICE.

malingerer *n.* shirker, idler, do-nothing, quitter, slacker, goldbrick (*Slang*), welsher (*Slang*), faker, loafer.

malleable *adj.* docile, impressionable, compliant, susceptible, trainable, teachable, formable, pliant, pliable, moldable, flexible, responsive, receptive, ready, willing.
ant. rigid, intractable, refractory, unmanageable, unyielding.

malodorous *adj.* foul, smelly, stinking, noxious, reeking, noisome, rank, high, strong, obnoxious, fetid, vile, putrid, rancid, rotten, putrescent, offensive.

malpractice *n.* wrong, error, offense, dereliction, wrongdoing, misconduct, malfeasance, abuse, misdeed, transgression, ill-treatment, misuse, mismanagement, misbehavior.

maltreat *v.* MISTREAT.

mamma *n.* MOTHER.

mammon *n.* riches, wealth, profit, gain, gold, lucre, materialism, worldliness.

mammoth *adj.* colossal, gigantic, huge, immense, massive, enormous, titanic, gargantuan, prodigious, stupendous, elephantine, ponderous, monstrous.
ant. dainty, petite, tiny, pygmy, puny, elfin.

mammy *n.* MOTHER.

man *n.* **1** human being, human, person, individual, being, mortal, soul, creature, hominid, *Homo sapiens*. **2** male, youth, fellow, gentleman, chap, guy, employee, hired hand, assistant, member, menial, servant, manservant, attendant, boy, lad, valet, retainer. **3** MANKIND.

manacle *n.* handcuff, cuff, iron, shackle, fetter, bond, chain, trammel.

manage *v.* **1** direct, conduct, supervise, administer, carry on, control, operate, work, run, head, lead, drive, guide, steer, pilot, mastermind, preside over, regulate. **2** manipulate, handle, use, control, maneuver, engineer, wangle, make use of, utilize, wield, apply, work, employ.

manageable *adj.* governable, tractable, yielding, submissive, docile, acquiescent, compliant, untroublesome, obedient, pliant, pliable, tame, wieldy, handy, convenient.

ant. uncontrollable, contrary, refractory, unwieldy, inconvenient.

management *n.* **1** operation, direction, control, regulation, supervision, jurisdiction, handling, running. **2** authorities, government, leadership, administration, direction, directorate, board, regime, ins, the Establishment.

manager *n.* director, head, leader, supervisor, chief, administrator, overseer, superintendent, foreman, boss, conductor, governor, chairman, honcho (*Slang*).

mandarin *n.* pundit, sage, master, guru, authority, oracle, Brahmin, savant, scholar, Nestor, intellectual, highbrow, egghead (*Slang*).

mandate *n.* command, order, injunction, directive, instructions, commandment, writ, direction, bidding, behest, summons, dictate, charge, commission, warrant, license, authorization.

mandatory *adj.* obligatory, required, necessary, imperative, compulsory, peremptory, binding, commanding, incumbent on, exigent.

ant. voluntary, optional, discretionary, self-willed, free, volitional.

maneuver *n.* **1** war game, exercise, practice, training, action, operation, movement, mission, campaign. **2** move, action, execution, turn, passage, performance, feat, stunt. **3** scheme, plot, stratagem, strategy, tactic, ploy, gambit, game, device, dodge, shift, feint, machination, manipulation, connivance, intrigue, ruse, subterfuge, trick. —*v.* **1** manage, conduct, plan, run, lead, handle, steer, pilot, navigate, exercise, carry out. **2** manipulate, scheme, connive, jockey, engineer, plot, angle, wangle, intrigue, trick, outsmart, outwit, finesse, evade, circumvent, machinate.

manful *adj.* MANLY.

mangle *v.* mutilate, disfigure, wreck, break, smash, splinter, shatter, crush, flatten, press, lacerate, maim, demolish, ruin, mar, spoil.

mangy *adj.* shabby, threadbare, shoddy, frayed, ragged, frazzled, seedy, trashy, sordid, cheap, mean, squalid.

manhandle *v.* abuse, mistreat, rough up, knock about, maltreat, ill-treat, maul, batter, ill-use.

mania *n.* craze, madness, rage, passion, obsession, compulsion, preoccupation, fascination, fixation, enthusiasm, infatuation, thing.

maniac *n.* madman, lunatic, psychotic, nut (*Slang*), screwball (*Slang*), crackbrain.

manic *adj.* excited, agitated, high, hyped up (*Slang*), elated, frenzied, hysterical, worked up, hyperactive, up.

ant. depressed, sluggish, down, low.

manifest *adj.* obvious, evident, clear, plain, patent, palpable, unmistakable, unquestionable, incontrovertible, self-evident, undeniable, indisputable. —*v.* reveal, show, display, exhibit, demonstrate, evidence, evince, express, present, indicate.

ant. *adj.* questionable, dubious, ambiguous, vague, uncertain, indefinite. *v.* conceal, hide, secrete, disguise, dissemble.

manifestation *n.* example, instance, indication, illustration, representation, evidence, sign, mark, clue, proof, grounds.

manifesto *n.* declaration, proclamation, pronouncement, statement, announcement, affirmation, edict, pronunciamiento, credo.

manifold *adj.* 1 numerous, multiple, innumerable, abundant, prolific, countless, many, copious, plenteous, profuse, bountiful, teeming, swarming, divers, various, myriad, multitudinous, considerable. 2 complex, diversified, varied, many-sided, assorted, variegated, omniform, polymorphous, multifarious, multiform, multifold.
ant. 1 few, scanty, limited, meager, scarce. 2 simple, elementary, fundamental, uncomplicated, plain, rudimentary.

manikin *n.* DWARF.

manipulate *v.* 1 handle, operate, use, make use of, wield, utilize, employ, work, run, apply. 2 influence, control, maneuver, engineer, jockey, machinate, steer, wangle, trick.

mankind *n.* humanity, human species, human race, humankind, *Homo sapiens,* man, people, mortals.

manly *adj.* courageous, valiant, hardy, stouthearted, brave, bold, stalwart, determined, intrepid, resolute, strong-willed, gallant, chivalrous, masculine, gritty, virile, manful.
ant. timid, pusillanimous, cowardly, meek.

man-made *adj.* ARTIFICIAL.

manner *n.* 1 way, practice, mode, method, procedure, routine, habit, custom, usage, wont, fashion. 2 demeanor, bearing, aspect, air, mien, tone, tenor, cast, turn, conduct, behavior, comportment. 3 style, mode, fashion, sort, type, kind, variety, vein, aspect, character, nature, form, method, school, genre, usage, idiom, persuasion, species, breed, stamp, brand.

mannered *adj.* affected, stilted, artificial, unnatural, formal, precious, overrefined, brittle, studied, pretentious, stagy, theatrical.
ant. natural, unaffected, down-to-earth, artless, spontaneous, naive, unsophisticated.

mannerism *n.* 1 idiosyncrasy, peculiarity, trait, characteristic, quirk, habit, mark, cast. 2 affectation, affectedness, theatricality, artificiality, preciosity.

mannerly *adj.* polite, civil, courteous, well-behaved, well-bred, genteel, courtly, gentlemanly, gallant, urbane, suave.
ant. rude, discourteous, unpolished, gauche.

manners *n.* politeness, civility, etiquette, decorum, breeding, gentility, refinement, propriety, formalities, amenities, ceremony, protocol.
ant. impoliteness, discourteousness, ill-breeding, coarseness.

mannikin *n.* DWARF.

mansion *n.* estate, palace, castle, villa, chateau, manor house, manse, lodge, palazzo.

manslaughter *n.* KILLING.

mantle *n.* 1 cloak, cape, wrap, poncho, serape, shawl, garment, coat, overgarment, tunic, smock, frock, robe. 2 cover, covering, coat, coating, envelope, blanket, vestment, curtain, canopy, shield, veil, concealment, pall. —*v.* conceal, disguise, obscure, veil, mask, curtain, screen, shroud, shield, veneer, cover, wrap, envelop, put on, blanket, overspread, superimpose.
ant. *v.* uncover, divest, disclose, reveal, manifest, bare, expose.

manual *adj.* physical, blue-collar, arduous, laborious, menial. —*n.* handbook, guidebook, guide, directory, primer.
ant. *adj.* sedentary, white-collar, office.

manufactory *n.* FACTORY.

manufacture *v.* 1 make, produce, fabricate, construct, mass-produce, build, put together, assemble, form, fashion, frame. 2 devise, concoct, invent, fabricate, cook up, hatch, trump up, fake, sham, falsify.

manufacturer *n.* producer, maker, builder, industrialist.

manumit *v.* EMANCIPATE.

manure *n.* dung, droppings, excrement, waste, feces, excreta, ordure, fertilizer, compost.

many *adj.* numerous, uncounted, countless, divers, manifold, multitudinous, considerable, myriad, abundant. —*n.* 1 numbers, quantities, multitude, myriad, abundance, mass, array, host, swarm, flock, legion, scores. 2 masses, multitude, majority, crowd, herd, horde, mob, rabble, hoi polloi.
ant. *adj.* few, several. *n.* 2 elite, select, pick, cream, aristocracy.

map *n.* itinerary, plan, chart, projection, blueprint, sketch, outline, design, profile, scheme, plot.

map out plan, arrange, outline, project, chart, plot, lay out, blueprint, diagram, devise, design, delineate, organize, program, orchestrate, stage-manage.

mar *v.* 1 harm, injure, hurt, impair, spoil, damage, upset, disrupt, ruin, wreck, botch. 2 disfigure, deface, blemish, mark, stain, spot, mutilate, maim, scar.

maraud *v.* raid, assault, attack, invade, prey on, depredate, plunder, pillage, ravage, ransack, despoil, loot, sack.

marauder *n.* plunderer, pillager, looter, sacker, spoiler, depredator, pirate, corsair, freebooter.

march[1] *n.* 1 walk, pace, tramp, hike, movement, passage, procession, promenade, parade. 2 progress, advance, progression, course, passage, movement. —*v.* 1 walk, step, tread, tramp, trudge, strut, hike, promenade, parade, file. 2 progress, advance, move forward, go, proceed, continue, travel, make headway, forge ahead.

march[2] *n.* FRONTIER.

mare's nest *n.* 1 delusion, deception, fake, fraud, hoax, bubble, chimera, myth, fairytale, moonshine, will-o'-the-wisp, fool's paradise, fool's gold. 2 disorder, chaos, muddle, confusion, mix-up, mess, hassle, foul-up (*Slang*), can of worms, Pandora's box.

margin *n.* 1 edge, border, verge, side, boundary, rim, fringe, hem, skirt, ledge, flange. 2 extra, more, spare, surplus, allowance, supplement, bonus, premium, contingency. 3 leeway, elbow room, latitude, range, scope, space, room, play, wide berth.

marginal *adj.* unimportant, insignificant, slight, minor, trivial, indifferent, secondary, borderline, negligible, expendable, replaceable.
ant. primary, crucial, principal, capital, compelling, sovereign.

marine *adj.* 1 oceanic, salt-water, pelagic, oceanographic, aquatic. 2 MARITIME.

mariner *n.* sailor, seaman, seafarer, navyman, salt, gob (*Slang*), tar, sea dog, Jack, mate, deck hand, navigator, helmsman, skipper, boatman, yachtsman.

marionette *n.* PUPPET.

marital *adj.* matrimonial, conjugal, connubial, nuptial, wedded, married, wifely, husbandly, spousal.

maritime *adj.* 1 coastal, littoral, seaside, shore, marine, riparian. 2 nautical, seagoing, marine, ocean-going, oceanic, naval, seafaring.

mark *n.* 1 impression, impress, sign, stroke, line, score, streak, marking, blaze, scratch, incision, cut, notch, nick, bruise. 2 signpost, guide, beacon, touchstone, pointer, marker. 3 characteristic, feature, sign, symptom, peculiarity, earmark, trait, cachet, attribute, quality, property. 4 target, goal, aim, end, objective, destination, standard, stage, degree, bound, limit, extent. —*v.* 1 identify, distinguish, indicate, label, earmark, check, stamp, demarcate, imprint, impress, brand, blaze, score, notch. 2 typify, characterize, embody, personify, exemplify, illustrate, represent, symbolize. **3** notice, note, observe, attend to, heed, pay attention to, remark, look, see to. **4** reveal, manifest, indicate, evidence, evince, show, signify, point to, denote. **5** grade, rank, rate, evaluate, assess, gauge, appraise, class.

marked *adj.* prominent, eminent, notable, noticeable, remarkable, striking, special, signal, noteworthy, distinguished, memorable.

ant. undistinguished, ordinary, commonplace, mediocre, middling, second-rate, insignificant.

market *n.* **1** market place, square, plaza, bazaar, mart, emporium, piazza, agora. **2** trade, commerce, business, dealings, traffic, truck, exchange, intercourse, transactions, demand. **3** buyers, customers, consumers, shoppers, clientele, patronage, public, constituency, audience.

marketable *adj.* COMMERCIAL.

marking *n.* coloring, mark, patch, brand, score, blaze, spot, blot, stain, speck.

mark time postpone, procrastinate, delay, put off, stand still, pause, defer, hold back.

ant. move out, push on, advance, progress.

maroon *v.* abandon, desert, cast away, leave behind, quit, forsake, jettison.

marriage *n.* **1** matrimony, wedlock, match, union, wedding, nuptials, nuptial rites, spousal. **2** linking, combination, coupling, union, junction, tie-in, liaison.

marriageable *adj.* nubile, unmarried, mature, marriable, single, unwed, eligible.

married *adj.* conjugal, connubial, nuptial, matrimonial, hymeneal, marital, wedded, united, hitched (*Slang*), mated, yoked.

ant. single, unmarried.

marrow *n.* core, essence, kernel, gist, nub, pith, nucleus, center, substance, matter, essential, heart, soul, spirit.

ant. exterior, surface, veneer.

marry *v.* wed, espouse.

marsh *n.* swamp, marshland, estuary, bog, moor, everglade, fen, bottoms, mud, mire, sump, slough, morass, quagmire, quicksand.

marshal *n.* deputy, adjutant, chief of staff, officer, coordinator. —*v.* organize, arrange, collect, order, compose, systematize, coordinate, group, line up, dispose, distribute, fix, array, rally.

marshy *adj.* swampy, boggy, oozy, spongy, squashy, squishy, miry, soggy, muddy.

mart *n.* MARKET.

martial *adj.* military, soldierly, militant, combative, Spartan, warlike, belligerent, bellicose.

martinet *n.* disciplinarian, taskmaster, slave-driver, stickler, authoritarian, drillmaster, dictator, despot, tyrant, Simon Legree.

martyr *v.* persecute, torment, hound, harass, plague, molest, beset, afflict, aggravate, harrow, torture, punish, rack.

marvel *v.* wonder, gape, stare. —*n.* wonder, phenomenon, astonishment, sensation, spectacle, curiosity, rarity, prodigy, miracle, sign, mystery, whiz (*Slang*).

marvelous *adj.* **1** remarkable, exceptional, amazing, wonderful, striking, singular, extraordinary, astonishing, surprising, stupendous, prodigious, phenomenal. **2** supernatural, preternatural, unearthly, fantastic, incredible, abnormal, fabulous, spiritual, psychic, transcendental, miraculous, wonder-working, inexplicable, mysterious.

ant. **1** commonplace, ordinary, familiar, prosaic, banal. **2** natural, rational, literal, normal, matter-of-fact.

mascot *n.* charm, totem, pet, fetish, talisman, amulet.

mash *n.* pulp, mush, paste, squash, sauce, hash, dough, stew, mishmash, mess, potpourri, farrago. —*v.* crush, squash, pulp, macerate, smash, crunch, pulverize, grind, thrash, mill, grate, pound, beat, stamp.

mask *n.* **1** disguise, false front, image, face, facade, window dressing, camouflage, guise, cloak, veil. **2** shield, screen, face mask, face guard, cover, covering, mantle. **3** subterfuge, pretext, pretense, dissimulation, false front, falsification, sham, masquerade, mummery. **4** MASQUERADE. —*v.* **1** cover, protect, shield, put over, spread over, screen, blanket, cloak, mantle, envelop, sheathe. **2** hide, conceal, disguise, cloak, veil, screen, obscure, camouflage, cover up, falsify, misrepresent.

ant. *v.* **1, 2** disclose, uncover, reveal, expose, bare, divest, unmask.

masque *n.* MASQUERADE.

masquerade *n.* **1** masked ball, costume party, ball, masque, mask, *bal masqué*. **2** disguise, mummery, deceit, hypocrisy, false front, dissimulation, affectation, show, pòmp, bluster, deception, imposture. —*v.* pose, pretend, dissemble, dissimulate, disguise, pass for, impersonate, simulate, counterfeit, fool, bluff, impersonate, mislead, delude.

ant. *n.* **2** sincerity, authenticity, naturalness, artlessness, unsophistication.

mass *n.* **1** assemblage, aggregate, accumulation, collection, concretion, pile, quantity, batch, bunch, pack, group, heap, load. **2** lump, hunk, piece, chunk, block, wad, cake, substance, solid. **3** majority, bulk, preponderance, most, best part, generality, plurality. **4** size, extent, bulk, volume, heft, quantity, amount, measure, dimensions. —*v.* AMASS.

ant. 2 minority, less, smaller, handful.

massacre *n.* slaughter, bloodbath, carnage, butchery, bloodletting, mass murder, decimation, liquidation, purge, genocide, pogrom. —*v.* slaughter, butcher, decimate, exterminate, murder, kill, liquidate, purge, annihilate, wipe out.

massage *n.* rubdown, kneading, manipulation, chiropractic. —*v.* rub down, manipulate, knead, flex, stretch.

masses *n.* people, populace, multitude, commonalty, folk, common folk, lower classes, proletariat, crowd, rabble, mob, hoi polloi, plebeians.

ant. elite, aristocracy, upper class.

massive *adj.* **1** bulky, hulking, hefty, ponderous, husky, ample, broad, large, bullish, sizable, massy. **2** substantial, large, far-ranging, extensive, major, imposing, sweeping, great, impressive.

ant. 1 diminutive, slight, fine-boned, delicate, elfin. **2** restricted, parochial, local, modest, minor.

massy *adj.* MASSIVE.

master *n.* **1** controller, manager, governor, boss, head, skipper, chief, headman, sahib, leader, principal, superior, author, administrator, possessor, owner, employer. **2** expert, mastermind, authority, professional, genius, artist, artisan, maestro, impresario, craftsman, virtuoso, technician. **3** original, prototype, basis, key, source, wellspring. —*adj.* **1** chief, head, principal, leading, main, first, central, primary, foremost, supreme, paramount, dominant, commanding, controlling. **2** expert, authoritative, professional, experienced, accomplished, proficient, practiced, skilled.

ant. *n.* **1** subordinate, follower, underling, assistant. **2** amateur, beginner, tyro, greenhorn, bungler. **3** copy, facsimile, reproduction, replica. —*adj.* **1** subordinate, auxiliary, assistant. **2** amateurish, unskilled, incompetent, unfit, inept.

masterful *adj.* accomplished, skillful, commanding, craftsmanlike, virtuoso, able, cunning, sharp, canny, sensible, wise, authoritative, masterly.

ant. inept, amateurish, incompetent, unskillful, unable.

masterly *adj.* MASTERFUL.

mastermind *n.* genius, wonder, wizard, prodigy, master, pundit, sage, guru, intellect, mentor, authority, whiz (*Slang*). —*v.* manage, direct, supervise, lead, govern, conduct, engineer, quarterback, administer, officiate.

master of ceremonies toastmaster, M.C., emcee, chairman, announcer.

masterpiece *n.* masterwork, classic, *chef d'oeuvre*, old master, brainchild, prizewinner, *ne plus ultra*.

mastery *n.* **1** power, control, rule, command, influence, prestige, prowess, proficiency, dominion, sway, jurisdiction, sovereignty. **2** victory, triumph, success, conquest, superiority, ascendancy, domination.

masticate *v.* CHEW.

masturbation *n.* onanism, self-abuse.

mat *n.* pad, rug, carpet, pallet, cover, shield, mattress, bedding.

match *n.* **1** equal, peer, equivalent, like, fellow, mate, double, counterpart, complement, competition, rival, par. **2** pair, couple, duet, combination, combo, team, club, group. **3** contest, competition, engagement, game, meet, encounter, bout, tourney, event, set-to, rivalry, conflict, fight. —*v.* **1** resemble, approximate, parallel, agree with, correspond with, coincide, measure up to, keep pace with. **2** pair, couple, mate, team, group, yoke, equate, correlate, collate, screen, balance, align, equalize. **3** contest, equal, rival, test, engage, duel, emulate.

matchless *adj.* incomparable, unrivaled, excellent, unparalleled, unexcelled, unequaled, peerless, unsurpassed, unbeatable, supreme, superlative, nonpareil, first-rate, tops (*Slang*).
ant. pedestrian, undistinguished, lackluster, second-rate.

mate *n.* **1** associate, comrade, fellow, companion, partner, colleague, confederate, pal, chum, buddy, crony, sidekick (*Slang*). **2** spouse, partner, match, companion, consort, wife, bride, husband, groom.

material *n.* **1** substance, matter, constituents, elements, stuff, body, texture.

2 data, facts, source material, evidence, circumstances, background. **3** cloth, fabric, textile, dry goods, goods, drapery, yard goods. —*adj.* **1** physical, tangible, organic, concrete, palpable, corporeal, fleshly, bodily, sensible, substantial, real. **2** significant, important, crucial, relevant, substantive, signal, striking, salient.
ant. *adj.* **1** ideal, spiritual, incorporeal, otherworldly, theoretical, unreal. **2** inconsequential, immaterial, irrelevant, trivial, slight.

materialize *v.* appear, emerge, turn up, take shape, come to pass, finalize, form, embody, reify, objectify, incarnate, personify.
ant. vanish, dissipate, disappear, evaporate.

materia medica MEDICINE.

materiel *n.* supplies, provisions, materials, equipment, gear, furnishings, fixtures, fittings, appurtenances, paraphernalia, impedimenta.

mathematical *adj.* exact, precise, disciplined, clear-cut, strict, definite, positive, absolute, unerring, rigid, rigorous, meticulous, scientific.

matrimony *n.* MARRIAGE.

matrix *n.* mold, form, cast, template, die, punch, stamp, mint, negative, stencil, cutout.

matte *adj.* DULL.

matted *adj.* tangled, gnarled, knotted, snarled, massed, clustered, twisted, tousled, disheveled, rumpled, uncombed, shaggy.

matter *n.* **1** substance, material, stuff, elements, tissue, constituents, gist. **2** importance, significance, consequence, import, concern, note, interest, moment, weight, gravity, urgency. **3** content, text, thesis, theme, substance, proposition, work, composition. **4** issue, affair, business, concern, subject, topic, transaction, proceeding, question, problem. —*v.* concern, signify, count, import, carry weight, affect, influence.

matter-of-fact *adj.* straightforward, down-to-earth, natural, unaffected, factual, sensible, practical, unemotional, unsentimental, unromantic, prosaic, commonplace, mundane, ordinary.

ant. impractical, theoretical, unrealistic, speculative, blue-sky.

maturate v. MATURE.

mature adj. **1** full-grown, grown-up, adult, full-fledged, grown, ripe, mellow, big, of age. **2** *of character or ability:* developed, experienced, wise, seasoned, practiced, fulfilled, capable, enriched. **3** *highly developed:* advanced, complete, detailed, elaborate, sophisticated, complex, complicated. —v. **1** age, grow, develop, maturate, ripen, progress, advance, mellow, season, come of age, flower, blossom. **2** complete, finish, conclude, end, round off, top off, perfect.

ant. adj. **1** immature, unripe, raw, green, tender, young, unfledged. **2** undeveloped, inexperienced, callow. **3** embryonic, unsophisticated, incomplete, inchoate.

maturity n. **1** competence, capability, readiness, development, sophistication, experience, wisdom. **2** ripeness, full bloom, maturation, aging, seasoning, development, adulthood, majority.

ant. 1 inexperience, incompleteness, crudeness, imperfection, ineptness.

maudlin adj. sentimental, mawkish, emotional, bathetic, mushy, schmaltzy (*Slang*), teary, weepy, nostalgic.

maul v. beat, batter, pound, buffet, bruise, pummel, scuff, knock about, rough up, mistreat, ill-treat, manhandle, abuse.

mausoleum n. TOMB.

maverick n. independent, nonconformist, oddball (*Slang*), nonpartisan, neutral, mugwump, outsider, dissenter, original, eccentric, loner, apostate.

mawkish adj. **1** sentimental, maudlin, emotional, nostalgic, schmaltzy (*Slang*). **2** disgusting, offensive, repulsive, foul, vile, obnoxious, sickening, nauseous, nauseating.

maxim n. saying, adage, saw, byword, truism, platitude, proverb, motto, axiom, aphorism, moral, apothegm, epigram, dictum, precept, belief, tenet, dogma.

maximal adj. MAXIMUM.

maximize v. enhance, exalt, magnify, heighten, raise, boost, reinforce, augment, intensify, increase, extend, enlarge.

ant. minimize, belittle, depreciate, disparage, undervalue.

maximum n. most, optimum, utmost, lead, primacy, priority, supremacy, preeminence, leadership, climax, apex, zenith, acme, limit, extremity. —adj. maximal, greatest, largest, most, utmost, biggest, highest, dominant, top, supreme, optimum, superlative, preeminent, predominant.

ant. n. least, minimum, fragment, fraction, iota. adj. minimal, smallest, least, slightest, shortest.

maybe adv. perhaps, possibly, conceivably, imaginably, feasibly, perchance, mayhap.

ant. certainly, surely, doubtless, undoubtedly.

mayhap adv. MAYBE.

mayhem n. violence, brutality, savagery, bestiality, barbarity, viciousness, ruthlessness, chaos, disorder.

maze n. **1** labyrinth, meander, tangle, snarl, complex, knot, jungle, wild. **2** perplexity, bewilderment, confusion, fluster, muddle, uncertainty, quandary, stew, daze, haze, fog.

meadow n. pasture, field, mead, grassland, lea, park, parkland, range, prairie, pampas, green, yard, plot.

meager adj. scant, scanty, inadequate, deficient, sparse, paltry, skimpy, scattered, exiguous, little, slight, token.

ant. plentiful, generous, abundant, profuse, copious, inexhaustible.

meal n. dinner, repast, refreshments, spread, mess, table, board, eats, feed, feast, snack, supper, nosh.

mealy-mouthed *adj.* INSINCERE.

mean[1] *v.* **1** intend, plan, have in mind, purpose, propose, design, hope, expect, anticipate, aim, desire, wish, look forward. **2** denote, signify, stand for, refer to, indicate, purport, import, express, convey, betoken, suggest, imply, connote. **3** portend, foreshadow, herald, promise, adumbrate, augur, forebode, prefigure, foretell, suggest, imply, threaten, menace.

mean[2] *adj.* **1** low-grade, inferior, second-rate, poor, paltry, base, inadequate, coarse, sorry, sad, pitiful. **2** humble, modest, lowly, lowborn, poor, plebeian, common, ordinary, plain, undistinguished, proletarian. **3** worthless, valueless, unimportant, insignificant, unprofitable, fruitless, trivial, petty, picayune. **4** shabby, tawdry, sloppy, shoddy, scruffy, squalid, slovenly, slipshod, unkempt, disheveled, unruly. **5** unkind, ignoble, narrow-minded, petty, small, base, low, low-down, intolerant, parochial, contemptible, despicable, selfish, ungenerous, grudging, tight, niggardly, close-fisted, stingy, miserly, cheap, penny-pinching.
ant. 1 first-rate, superior, prime, excellent, select, choice. **2** highborn, patrician, aristocratic, noble, thoroughbred, genteel. **3** important, crucial, momentous, marked, critical. **4** stylish, elegant, exquisite, tasteful, delicate. **5** generous, unselfish, obliging, considerate, altruistic.

mean[3] *n.* average, medium, golden mean, middle, measure, balance, moderation, normal, rule. —*adj.* medium, average, middle, medial, mid, intermediate, intermediary, normal, standard, midmost, equidistant, central.

meander *v.* twist, turn, wind, twine, snake, worm, corkscrew, wander, ramble, rove, divagate, convolute, convolve, go astray.

meaning *n.* **1** intention, aim, intent, design, import, point, plan, purport,

object. **2** denotation, sense, significance, idea, implication, connotation, effect, force, drift, tenor, gist, definiens.

meaningful *adj.* significant, important, crucial, profound, deep, pointed, expressive, vivid, eloquent, pregnant, telling, cogent.
ant. meaningless, absurd, inane, empty, senseless.

meaningless *adj.* senseless, nonsensical, aimless, purposeless, hollow, insignificant, absurd, foolish, vacant, vapid, empty.
ant. significant, meaningful, rich, profound, important.

means *n.* **1** way, method, system, procedure, process, *modus operandi,* wherewithal, resources, measures, steps, expedient, medium, form, mode, manner, fashion, style. **2** wealth, money, assets, funds, capital, finances, resources, property, tangibles.

meantime *adv.* MEANWHILE.

meanwhile *adv.* meantime, in the interim, simultaneously, concurrently.

measly *adj. Slang* skimpy, paltry, meager, pitiful, pathetic, scanty, wretched, puny, petty.
ant. substantial, considerable, abundant, generous.

measurable *adj.* quantitative, limited, restricted, unexceptional, circumscribed, restrained, unexcessive, temperate, moderate, reasonable.
ant. incalculable, immense, vast, infinite, inexhaustible, extraordinary.

measure *n.* **1** dimensions, extent, proportions, size, range, reach, portion, largeness, capacity, volume, spread, amplitude. **2** moderation, restraint, constraint, control, bounds, limitation, boundaries, borders, limits, extent. **3** action, course, step, proceeding, operation, shift, means, expedient, device. —*v.* **1** calculate, compute, figure, ascertain, gauge, cipher, tally, survey, enumerate, count, calibrate, graduate, size, rank, mark off, set apart. **2** compare, judge, weigh, adjudge, assess, consider, check, appraise, size up, balance, set over against, juxtapose, match, liken, oppose, contrast.

ant. *n.* **2** immoderation, intemperance, extravagance, unrestraint, excess, prodigality.

measured *adj.* **1** slow, sedate, gradual, deliberate, considered, balanced, weighed, studied, calculated, grave, solemn, sober, stately. **2** restrained, limited, due, controlled, tempered, moderate, proper, frugal, sparing.

ant. **1** hasty, hurried, precipitate, thoughtless, peremptory, abrupt, brisk. **2** excessive, exorbitant, unreasonable, immoderate, outrageous.

measureless *adj.* unlimited, incalculable, immeasurable, endless, boundless, immense, infinite, eternal, everlasting.

ant. finite, limited, restricted, moderate.

measurement *n.* calculation, computation, quantification, mensuration, measure, gauging, enumeration, rating, determination, assessment, evaluation.

measure up equal, match, compare, correspond, come up, amount, fulfill, parallel, tie, rival, vie with.

ant. fall short, fail, come a cropper.

meat *n.* **1** flesh, game, viands. **2** food, victuals, edibles, provender, comestibles, fare, eats, chow (*Slang*), grub (*Slang*), feed, meal. **3** essence, gist, kernel, pith, nub, heart, marrow, stuff, sum and substance, core, nucleus.

meatball *n. Slang* FOOL.

meaty *adj.* stimulating, suggestive, pointed, pregnant, profound, deep, pithy, eloquent, meaningful, significant, substantial.

ant. trivial, inconsequential, shallow, flimsy, picayune, frivolous.

mecca *n.* goal, destination, aim, target, end, shrine, sanctuary.

mechanical *adj.* **1** routine, habitual, automatic, automated, programmatic, machinelike, reflex, involuntary, au-

tonomic, cybernetic. **2** lifeless, lackluster, expressionless, blank, phlegmatic, emotionless, dull, insensible, leaden, matter-of-fact. **3** handy, skilled, proficient, expert, competent, workmanlike, adept, adroit, dexterous.

ant. **1** spontaneous, instinctive, natural, extemporaneous, unpremeditated. **2** exuberant, emotional, expressive, dramatic, vivid, graphic. **3** bungling, clumsy, inept, maladroit, awkward, all thumbs, left-handed.

mechanism *n.* **1** mechanics, workings, operation, functioning, action. **2** process, procedure, method, system, means, medium, agency, instrumentality, program, way, technique, execution, technic. **3** MACHINE.

medal *n.* medallion, award, decoration, insignia, ribbon, riband, laurel, citation, prize, honor, reward, wreath, blue ribbon, star.

medallion *n.* MEDAL.

meddle *v.* interfere, intervene, intrude, butt in, tamper, mix in, obtrude, intermeddle, interject, put in, kibitz, horn in (*Slang*).

ant. hold aloof, refrain, keep out, shun, abstain, avoid.

meddler *n.* busybody, snoop, pest, kibitzer, interferer, quidnunc, troublemaker, talebearer, gossip, prier, buttinsky (*Slang*), yenta (*Slang*).

meddlesome *adj.* intrusive, officious, obtrusive, pushing, forward, impertinent, audacious, bothersome, kibitzing, meddling, interfering, prying, pushy.

ant. aloof, reserved, restrained, indifferent, reticent, offish.

medial *adj.* ORDINARY.

mediate *v.* settle, reconcile, intercede, intervene, referee, pacify, moderate, negotiate, arbitrate, propitiate, interpose, interfere, step in, compromise.

mediation *n.* intercession, interposition, intervention, peacemaking, pacification, conciliation, arbitration, negotiation, appeasement, reconciliation, parley, instrumentality.

medical *adj*. **1** clinical, iatric, therapeutic, diagnostic, professional. **2** medicinal, restorative, medicative, sanative, remedial, therapeutic, healing, curative.

medicament *n*. MEDICINE.

medication *n*. MEDICINE.

medicine *n*. **1** medication, medicament, remedy, nostrum, drug, physic, specific, dose, materia medica. **2** healing, therapeutics, treatment, hygiene.

mediocre *adj*. middling, ordinary, commonplace, so-so, second-rate, indifferent, unimpressive, passable, pedestrian, average, medium, fair, inferior. **ant.** impressive, outstanding, exceptional, singular, superior.

meditate *v*. consider, think, contemplate, muse, ponder, ruminate, cogitate, reason, brood, reflect, concentrate, deliberate, study, puzzle, mull.

meditation *n*. contemplation, thought, cogitation, reflection, pensiveness, abstraction, rumination, thoughtfulness, study, musing, pondering, reverie, consideration, speculation.

medium *n*. **1** mean, middle, average, rule, median, compromise, moderation. **2** environment, element, ambience, surroundings, circumstances, milieu, condition. **3** means, agency, instrument, channel, mechanism, wherewithal, intermediary. **4** clairvoyant, spiritualist, necromancer, oracle, crystal gazer, soothsayer, seer. —*adj*. intermediate, middling, middle, average, moderate, run-of-the-mill, so-so, ordinary, commonplace, normal, mediocre. **ant.** *n*. **1** extreme, excess, aberration, departure, deviation. *adj*. extraordinary, unusual, different, odd, extreme, exceptional.

medley *n*. jumble, miscellany, confusion, mélange, hodgepodge, mixture, mishmash, olio, potpourri, gallimaufry, pastiche, hash, salmagundi, farrago.

meed *n*. REWARD.

meek *adj*. gentle, submissive, compliant, tractable, docile, patient, long-suffering, amenable, agreeable, unassertive, obedient, timid, weak-kneed, mild, pusillanimous, passive, cowardly. **ant.** aggressive, self-assertive, rebellious, refractory, pushing, unruly, disobedient.

meet[1] *v*. **1** encounter, run into, face, come across, happen on, find, chance on, bump into. **2** make acquaintance, get to know, shake hands. **3** converge, join, cross, intersect, touch, unite, forgather, collide. **4** satisfy, fulfill, conform, comply, perform, carry out, answer. **ant. 1** evade, miss, dodge, avoid, shun. **3** diverge, separate, deviate, branch off, part. **4** disappoint, fall short, refuse, fail, miss.

meet[2] *adj*. suitable, appropriate, fit, proper, becoming, seemly, fitting, apt, opportune, felicitous, agreeable, apposite, happy. **ant.** inappropriate, unmeet, improper, unseemly, gauche, awkward.

meeting *n*. **1** encounter, junction, confluence, concourse, convergence, agreement, union, connection, collision. **2** congregation, assembly, gathering, conference, convention, congress, college, council, powwow, get-together, confabulation, rap session (*Slang*). **ant. 1** parting, separation, divergence, dispersal, split, gap.

megrims *n*. MELANCHOLY.

melancholia *n*. MELANCHOLY.

melancholy *adj*. **1** gloomy, sad, glum, low-spirited, despondent, unhappy, downcast, dejected, depressed, mirthless, miserable, melancholic, blue. **2** discouraging disheartening, depressing, dismal, saddening, dire, tragic, woeful, sad. —*n*. depression, dejection, gloom, despondency, blues, dumps, unhappiness, woe, dolor, sorrow, sadness, melancholia, megrims. **ant.** *adj*. **1** happy, glad, joyful, gay, lively, manic. **2** encouraging, promising, cheering, fortunate, happy. *n.* happiness, vivacity, euphoria, gaiety, exhilaration.

mélange *n.* medley, mixture, miscellany, hodgepodge, jumble, mishmash, confusion, hash, olio, potpourri, gallimaufry, pastiche.

ant. system, homogeneity, structure, array, arrangement, order.

meld *v.* merge, blend, combine, fuse, coalesce, amalgamate, unite, mingle, mix, commingle.

ant. separate, divide, dissociate, disunite, split, rive.

melee *n.* brawl, free-for-all, fracas, broil, dogfight, Donnybrook, pandemonium, battle royal, fisticuffs, row, riot, fight, fistfight.

meliorate *v.* IMPROVE.

mellifluent *adj.* SMOOTH.

mellifluous *adj.* SMOOTH.

mellow *adj.* **1** mild, matured, ripened, aged, smooth, velvety. **2** rich, full, dulcet, mellifluous, pear-shaped, pure. **3** understanding, seasoned, gentle, mature, wise, compassionate.

ant. **1** harsh, raw, crude, biting, green. **2** strident, reedy, squeaky, thin, shrill, harsh. **3** authoritarian, narrow, childish, intolerant, crabbed.

melodic *adj.* MELODIOUS.

melodious *adj.* tuneful, lilting, carolling, musical, melodic, lyric, singing, dulcet, euphonious, mellifluous, warbling, ringing.

ant. harsh, cacophonous, scrannel, grating, noisy, unmelodious.

melodrama *n.* **1** thriller, cliffhanger, soap opera, penny dreadful (*Brit.*), tear-jerker (*Slang*). **2** scene, histrionics, dramatics, melodramatics, carrying-on, production (*Slang*), emoting, ranting, hysteria.

melodramatic *adj.* sensational, stagy, histrionic, overwrought, theatrical, frenzied, exciting, thrilling, spectacular, flamboyant, camp, campy.

ant. understated, sober, humdrum, prosaic, commonplace, matter-of-fact.

melodramatics *n.* MELODRAMA.

melody *n.* tunefulness, euphony, mellifluousness, music, harmoniousness, concord, tune, strain, air, trilling.

ant. noise, discord, cacophony, jangle, clangor, dissonance.

melt *v.* **1** fuse, dissolve, liquefy, thaw, deliquesce, disintegrate. **2** disappear, dissipate, fade, disperse, vanish, evaporate, erode. **3** relent, mollify, soften, pacify, disarm, appease, warm.

ant. **1** freeze, harden, solidify, jell, set. **2** gather, grow, appear, come together, snowball. **3** toughen, steel, stiffen, embitter, harden.

member *n.* **1** enrollee, fellow, associate, initiate, registrant, constituent, unit. **2** limb, organ, appendage, part, segment, division, section. **3** element, component, part, ingredient, factor, piece, division, constituent.

ant. **3** whole, aggregate, entirety, body, composite.

membership *n.* rank and file, body, roster, members, associates, community, constituency, company, population, personnel, society.

membrane *n.* sheet, film, tissue, web, layer, envelope, sheath, covering, coat, flap, coating, lining, pellicle, skin, integument, leaf.

memento *n.* souvenir, keepsake, remembrance, token, memorial, reminder, relic, gift, trophy, record, sign, memory.

memo *n.* MEMORANDUM.

memoir *n.* REPORT.

memoirs *n.* autobiography, journal, memories, recollections, reminiscences, confessions, adventures, experiences, diary, life, story, reflections, holograph.

memorable *adj.* noteworthy, historic, momentous, significant, important, red-letter, notable, signal, crucial, impressive, unforgettable, extraordinary, great.

ant. commonplace, unimportant, trivial, humdrum, routine, insignificant.

memorandum *n.* note, record, memo,

reminder, *aide-memoire,* minute, brief, notation, summary, recapitulation, recap, communication, jotting, scribble.

memorial *adj.* commemorative, retrospective, celebrative, remindful, honoring, reminiscent, perpetuating, ritual, celebrating, immortalizing, eulogizing, hallowed, solemn, preserving.

memorialize *v.* COMMEMORATE.

memory *n.* **1** remembrance, recollection, reminiscence, recall, recreation, recognition, mnemonics. **2** commemoration, remembrance, celebration, memorial, honor, tribute, testimonial, immortalization.
ant. 1 oblivion, forgetfulness, block, Lethe, blank, amnesia.

menace *v.* threaten, imperil, portend, impend, forebode, lower, overhang, presage, augur, intimidate. —*n.* peril, danger, threat, warning, endangerment, intimidation, threatening, troublemaker, risk, plague.

menacing *adj.* threatening, dire, dangerous, fearful, dreadful, ominous, portentous, impending, appalling, intimidating, frightful, fateful, awful, terrible.
ant. pacific, harmless, reassuring, comforting, heartening, soothing.

mend *v.* **1** repair, patch, fix, recondition, overhaul, restore. **2** reform, improve, rectify, correct, ameliorate, amend. **3** heal, recuperate, cure, restore, moderate, abate.
ant. 1 tear, break, damage, mar, wear. **2** deteriorate, worsen, aggravate, decline, err. **3** sicken, regress, relapse, languish, worsen.

mendacious *adj.* deceitful, lying, dishonest, untruthful, false, fraudulent, deceptive, story-telling, dissembling, guileful, tricky, double-dealing.
ant. veracious, honest, truthful, true, sincere, creditable.

mendicant *n.* BEGGAR.

menial *adj.* **1** humble, lowly, routine, tedious, unskilled, humdrum, low, degrading. **2** servile, base, subservient, fawning, slavish, obsequious,

ingratiating, meek. —*n.* servant, domestic, underling, factotum, retainer, laborer, lackey, slavey, drudge, attendant.
ant. *adj.* **1** prestigious, honorable, dignified, skilled, responsible. **2** domineering, overbearing, arrogant, proud, assertive.

menopause *n.* change of life, climacteric.

mental *adj.* **1** cerebral, intellectual, meditative, thoughtful, conscious, reflective, rational, thinking, reasoning. **2** psychiatric, disoriented, irrational, disturbed, psychotic, mad, insane.
ant. 1 reflex, unthinking, unconscious, automatic, brainless. **2** sane, rational, reasonable, lucid, normal.

mentality *n.* outlook, attitude, set, bias, cast, disposition, makeup, constitution, psychology, consciousness, temperament, personality, character, point of view.

mention *v.* speak of, allude, name, instance, specify, refer to, observe, say, remark, enumerate. —*n.* **1** reference, naming, allusion, comment, word, observation, remark, utterance, inkling. **2** citation, selection, nomination, designation, recognition, singling out.

mentor *n.* teacher, guide, counselor, guru, big brother, advisor, protector, sponsor, coach, tutor, master, swami, pundit.

mephitic *adj.* FOUL.

mercantile *adj.* commercial, trade, trading, business, merchant, merchandising.

mercenary *adj.* **1** greedy, venal, avaricious, materialistic, self-seeking, corrupt, acquisitive, bribable, purchasable, sordid. **2** hired, paid, purchased. —*n.* soldier of fortune, adventurer, hireling, Hessian, free lance.
ant. *adj.* **1** idealistic, generous, high-minded, public-spirited, incorruptible. **2** voluntary, volunteer.

merchandise *n.* goods, wares, commodities, stock, products, articles, staples, produce. —*v.* trade, deal, market, distribute, traffic, sell, promote, push, handle.

merchant *n.* tradesman, tradeswoman, storekeeper, trader, dealer, salesman, saleswoman, shopkeeper, businessman, businesswoman, entrepreneur, retailer, vendor, hawker, bourgeois, capitalist.

merchantable *adj.* commercial.

merciful *adj.* compassionate, humane, lenient, clement, soft-hearted, gentle, tender, mild, forgiving, gracious, kind, sympathetic.
ant. merciless, pitiless, implacable, cruel, relentless, callous.

merciless *adj.* pitiless, implacable, relentless, heartless, cruel, ruthless, inhumane, unrelenting, unmerciful, remorseless, ferocious, callous, fell, fierce.
ant. merciful, compassionate, humane, clement, lenient, forgiving.

mercurial *adj.* **1** volatile, changeable, capricious, fickle, inconstant, unstable, flighty. **2** lively, quick, ingenious, nimble, vivacious, sprightly, eloquent, lighthearted.
ant. 1 constant, steadfast, stable, unvarying, predictable. **2** saturnine, gloomy, clumsy, stodgy.

mercy *n.* **1** compassion, benevolence, kindness, forbearance, pity, charity, grace, clemency, lenity, forgiveness. **2** godsend, blessing, boon, benison, windfall, grace.
ant. 1 sternness, vindictiveness, harshness, retaliation, cruelty. **2** scourge, calamity, plague, malediction, curse.

mere[1] *adj.* only, nothing but, utter, simple, sheer, unadorned, bare, pure, stark.

mere[2] *n.* POOL.[1]

meretricious *adj.* tawdry, specious, garish, flashy, gaudy, tinsel, pinchbeck, sham, spurious, paste, false, bogus, plastic (*Slang*).
ant. classic, genuine, tasteful, quiet, unobtrusive, authentic.

merge *v.* blend, coalesce, fuse, amal-

gamate, integrate, mingle, weld, mix, combine, unite, unify, desegregate.
ant. separate, disunite, segregate, diverge, part.

merger *n.* consolidation, amalgamation, combine, cartel, conglomerate, union, confederation, alliance, incorporation, syndicate, trust, pool.

meridian *n.* zenith, culmination, peak, acme, climax, high noon, flood tide, flowering, golden age, summit, pinnacle, crest, apex.
ant. nadir, ebb tide, decline, low, depths, minimum.

merit *n.* **1** worthiness, desert, meed, due, title, right, claim. **2** worth, virtue, value, integrity, excellence, quality, good.
ant. 2 unworthiness, dishonor, demerit, corruption, shame.

meritorious *adj.* praiseworthy, deserving, estimable, laudable, admirable, first-rate, excellent, exemplary, commendable, creditable, good.
ant. unworthy, undeserving, blameworthy, disreputable, deplorable, reprehensible, flagrant.

Merlin *n.* MAGICIAN.

merriment *n.* gaiety, mirth, hilarity, glee, fun, jocularity, levity, jollity, cheer, joy, sport, joviality, laughter, frolic, merrymaking.
ant. melancholy, gloom, woe, sadness, sorrow, despondency.

merry *adj.* mirthful, cheery, blithe, gay, jovial, joyful, high-spirited, jolly, gleeful, fun-loving, frolicsome, jocund, vivacious, lighthearted, happy.
ant. sober, downcast, sad, staid, pensive, melancholy.

merry-andrew *n.* CLOWN.

merry-go-round *n.* carousel, whirligig, roundabout (*Brit.*).

merrymaking *n.* MERRIMENT.

mesh *n.* **1** space, interstice, grid, aperture, opening, hole. **2** network, plexus, reticulation, web, screen, sieve, netting, openwork. —*v.* engage, fit together, connect, catch, interlock, align, meet, dovetail, occlude.

mesmerize *v.* fascinate, enthrall, hypnotize, transfix, dominate, spellbind, bewitch, captivate, entrance, transport, charm.

mess *n.* **1** confusion, disorder, muss, dishevelment, untidiness, litter, tangle, dirtiness, conglomeration, jumble. **2** dilemma, quandary, predicament, plight, trouble, muddle, pickle, fix, kettle of fish. **3** serving, plateful, batch, meal, dish. —*v.* MESS UP.
ant. *n.* **1** tidiness, orderliness, symmetry, order, neatness, cleanliness.

message *n.* **1** signal, indication, sign, portent, omen, information, communication. **2** notice, memorandum, notification, communication, letter, bulletin, missive. **3** moral, principle, point, theme, meaning, gist, conclusion.

mess around dabble, putter, dawdle, fiddle, fritter, tinker, trifle, busy oneself, while away, beguile, fuss.
ant. buckle down, concentrate, slave, settle down, apply oneself, work.

messenger *n.* courier, emissary, envoy, runner, scout, liaison, delegate, nuncio, intermediary, agent, delivery boy, bellhop, page, bellman, Mercury.

Messiah *n.* liberator, standard-bearer, emancipator, savior, redeemer, leader, bellwether, prophet, guru, oracle.

mess up **1** befoul, mess, muss, dirty, disarrange, tangle, smear, smirch, damage, litter, pollute. **2** bungle, botch, muddle, foul up (*Slang*), screw up (*Slang*), fail, flunk, louse up (*Slang*).
ant. **1** clean up, tidy, mend, fix, organize, sort out. **2** come through, measure up, succeed.

messy *adj.* mussy, untidy, rumpled, disarranged, unkempt, disheveled, tousled, tangled, confused, muddled.
ant. tidy, trim, orderly, neat, shipshape.

metallic *adj.* *of sounds:* hard, harsh, grating, clashing, raucous, strident, jarring, clanging, clangorous, piercing, brassy, brazen.
ant. dulcet, euphonious, harmonious, bell-like, silvery, soft.

metamorphosis *n.* transformation, transfiguration, transmutation, conversion, transmogrification, mutation, alteration, permutation, change, rebirth, transubstantiation.

metaphor *n.* figure of speech, allusion, allegory, comparison, trope, simile, metonymy.

metaphysical *adj.* abstract, abstruse, recondite, transcendental, inscrutable, theoretical, conjectural, hypothetical, philosophical, profound, immaterial, arcane, esoteric.
ant. concrete, simple, plain, perceptible, material, real.

meteoric *adj.* flashing, swift, sudden, brilliant, spectacular, remarkable, ephemeral, evanescent, brief, cometic.
ant. obscure, slow, pedestrian, plodding, steady, long-drawn.

mete out apportion, measure out, allot, dispense, dole, parcel out, assign, distribute, deal, allocate.

meter¹ *n.* gauge, scale, measure, rule.

meter² *n.* measure, cadence, beat, rhythm, stress.

method *n.* **1** procedure, technique, way, mode, *modus operandi*, fashion, manner, system, process, style. **2** regularity, order, arrangement, organization, structure, design, plan, system, causality.
ant. **2** randomness, chance, disorganization, chaos.

methodical *adj.* orderly, systematic, routine, businesslike, efficient, regular, undeviating, cut-and-dried, thorough, well-defined, disciplined, matter-of-fact, organized.
ant. haphazard, random, casual, hit-or-miss, aimless, inefficient.

methodize *v.* SYSTEMATIZE.

meticulous *adj.* finical, painstaking, punctilious, exacting, careful, fastidious, finicky, precise, perfectionist, fussy, scrupulous, nice.

ant. careless, slovenly, slap-dash, perfunctory, negligent, sloppy.

métier *n.* PROFESSION.

metropolis *n.* capital, city, megalopolis, hub, center, seat.

metropolitan *adj.* urban, municipal, megalopolitan, citified, urbanized.
ant. rural, suburban, rustic, countrified, bucolic.

mettle *n.* **1** caliber, nature, kind, temper, character, disposition, kidney. **2** courage, spirit, fortitude, bravery, resolution, valor, fearlessness, pluck, heart, guts (*Slang*).
ant. 2 timidity, apathy, irresolution, weakness, backwardness, velleity.

mettlesome *adj.* courageous, spirited, ardent, fiery, spunky, dashing, bold, lively, animated, energetic, plucky, brisk, sprightly, feisty.
ant. listless, backward, irresolute, shrinking, lackadaisical, timorous.

mewl *v.* CRY.

miasma *n.* effluvium, mephitis, stench, reek, pollution, smog, fog, contagion, vapor, mist, cloud, smoke, steam.

microbe *n.* MICROORGANISM.

microcosm *n.* miniature, model, microcopy, miniaturization, Lilliput, reflection, echo, epitome, image, copy.
ant. macrocosm, magnification, blowup.

microorganism *n.* microbe, animalcule, germ, amoeba.

microscopic *adj.* minuscule, minute, infinitesimal, imperceptible, diminutive, tiny, wee, minimal.
ant. macroscopic.

micturate *v.* URINATE.

mid *adj.* MIDWAY.

middle *adj.* **1** central, midway, medial, mid, equidistant, median. **2** intermediate, betwixt and between, halfway, intervening, transitional, inside, inner. —*n.* **1** center, midway, midpoint, inside, focus, mean. **2** waist, midriff, midsection, torso, trunk.
ant. *adj.* **1, 2** peripheral, terminal, outer, end, outside, extreme. *n.* **1**

end, terminus, periphery, extreme, outside. **2** extremity, appendage.

middleman *n.* intermediary, go-between, broker, agent, factor, medium, liaison.

middle-of-the-road *adj.* moderate, compromising, fence-straddling, uncommitted, nonpartisan, impartial, neutral, centrist, neutralistic, noncommittal.
ant. extremist, radical.

middling *adj.* **1** medium, mid, secondrate, moderate, so-so, average, mediocre, OK. **2** *of health:* bearable, tolerable, fairish, indifferent, passable, so-so.
ant. 1, 2 first-rate, fine, good, excellent, splendid, glowing.

midge *n.* MIDGET.

midget *n.* **1** dwarf, Lilliputian, midge, gnome, pygmy, peewee, runt, shrimp. **2** miniature, mite, toy, peewee, pygmy, runt.
ant. 1, 2 giant, colossus, titan, mammoth, whale, monster.

midst *n.* middle, interior, center, thick, hub, bosom, heart, core, eye, nucleus.
ant. periphery, outskirts, edge, outside, beyond.

midway *adj.* mid, central, middle, mean, medial, intermediate, halfway, midmost, focal, inside, equidistant, intervening.
ant. end, outer, peripheral, terminal, extreme.

mien *n.* bearing, demeanor, expression, deportment, manner, carriage, air, look, style, attitude, guise, presence.

miff *v.* irritate, offend, vex, affront, provoke, irk, nettle, exasperate, rile, chagrin, annoy, rub the wrong way.
ant. pacify, mollify, placate, flatter, please, soft-soap.

might *n.* strength, power, potency, force, vigor, greatness, prowess, puissance, intensity, energy, sinew.
ant. puniness, weakness, frailty, infirmity, deficiency.

mighty *adj.* **1** powerful, strong, omnipotent, puissant, stalwart, potent, sturdy, stout. **2** gigantic, huge, prodigious, tremendous, vast, stupendous, extraordinary, great.

ant. 1 weak, puny, infirm, powerless, feeble. **2** small, insignificant, trivial, paltry, slight.

migrant *n.* nomad, transient, emigrant, vagrant, itinerant, drifter, gypsy, hobo, Okie, tinker (*Brit.*). —*adj.* MIGRATORY.

migrate *v.* move, journey, travel, wander, emigrate, pass, trek, rove, relocate, immigrate, resettle.

ant. settle, bide, sojourn, alight, remain.

migration *n.* emigration, nomadism, vagabondage, relocation, resettlement, travel, trek, journey, pilgrimage, voyage, passage, expedition.

migratory *adj.* roving, nomadic, wandering, unsettled, wayfaring, migrant, itinerant, transient, ranging, mobile, vagabond, vagrant.

ant. resident, settled, rooted, immobile, stationary.

mild *adj.* **1** gentle, kind, benign, easygoing, considerate, amiable, meek. **2** temperate, balmy, clement, bland, moderate, tame, smooth.

ant. 1 curt, rough, unpleasant, irascible, nasty. **2** strong, harsh, stormy, fierce, sharp.

mileage *n. length of service:* usefulness, advantage, service, benefit, return, good, help, yield, harvest, profit, gain, sustenance.

milieu *n.* surroundings, environment, setting, ambience, element, background, scene, locale, circumstances, condition, position, circle, ecosystem.

militant *adj.* fighting, combatant, aggressive, bellicose, assertive, self-assertive, activist, active, combative, pushing, warring, contentious. —*n.* belligerent, activist, firebrand, agitator, combatant, fighter, scrapper, battler.

ant. *adj.* passive, nonmilitant, peaceful, quiescent, withdrawn, inactive.

n. peacemaker, quietist, pacifist, nonactivist, dove.

militarism *n.* hawkishness, jingoism, chauvinism, bellicosity, saber-rattling, flag-waving, warmongering, preparedness, belligerence, aggressiveness.

ant. pacifism, dovishness, nonaggression, neutrality, neutralism.

military *adj.* martial, soldierly, bellicose, warlike, armed, militant, fighting, belligerent, combative, militaristic. —*n.* army, troops, soldiery, force, militia, Pentagon.

ant. *adj.* peaceable, pacific, irenic, peaceful, unmilitary.

militate *v.* influence, affect, carry weight, weigh, resist, obstruct, contravene, interfere, oppose, conflict.

milk *v.* **1** extract, tap, pump, drain, siphon, squeeze, press, draw off. **2** exploit, take advantage, squeeze, pressure, blackmail, use, manipulate.

milk-and-water *adj.* WEAK.

milksop *n.* mollycoddle, sissy, milquetoast, sheep, namby-pamby, coward, weakling, dastard, poltroon, pansy.

ant. he-man, macho, superman, brute, cave man, Neanderthal.

milky *adj.* **1** whitish, opaque, cloudy, filmy, chalky, turbid, hazy, pearly, lacteal, lactic, pellucid. **2** TIMID.

ant. 1 clear, watery, transparent, colorless.

mill *n.* factory, manufactory, shop, plant, works, foundry.

millenium *n.* utopia, golden age, nirvana, peace, bliss, heaven, Eden, New Jerusalem, Shangri-la, promised land, cloud nine (*Slang*).

millstone *n.* burden, drag, encumbrance, load, weight, hindrance, impediment, clog, cumber, incubus, affliction, cross.

milquetoast *n.* MILKSOP.

mime *n.* pantomime, mummery, dumb show, mimicry, gesture, body English, role playing. —*v.* pantomime, mum, gesticulate, mimic, act out, role-play.

mimic *v.* imitate, copy, ape, take off, caricature, simulate, counterfeit, echo, mock, repeat, parody, mime, burlesque, reproduce. —*n.* copycat, imitator, mimicker, echo, parrot, mime, ape, mocker.

mimicry *n.* imitation, parody, burlesque, takeoff, mockery, mimicking, aping, caricature, travesty, paraphrase.

minatory *adj.* THREATENING.

mind *n.* **1** intelligence, brain, intellect, mentality, wits, head. **2** opinion, view, thinking, conception, viewpoint, point of view, judgment. **3** desire, inclination, wish, intention, purpose. **4** sanity, reason, senses, wits, faculties, rationality. —*v.* **1** attend to, notice, mark, remark, observe. **2** obey, heed, comply, follow, defer to. **3** tend, attend, look after, watch over, take care of, guard, protect, nurse, baby-sit.
ant. *v.* **1** ignore, overlook, skip, dismiss. **2** disobey, defy, resist, rebel. **3** neglect, lose sight of, abandon, desert.

mindful *adj.* heedful, heeding, cognizant, alert, aware, attentive, careful, solicitous, watchful, conscious, informed, sensible, conversant, alive.
ant. heedless, oblivious, unaware, forgetful, unmindful, mindless.

mindless *adj.* **1** unintelligent, stupid, simple, foolish, witless, idiotic, moronic, imbecile. **2** careless, heedless, inattentive, unmindful, oblivious, absent-minded.
ant. **1** intelligent, acute, smart, clever, brainy. **2** mindful, careful, attentive, alert, watchful.

mine *n.* **1** quarry, excavation, pit, deposit, lode, seam, crater. **2** source, store, mother lode, fountain, well, spring, wellspring, treasure-trove. —*v.* **1** delve, excavate, dig, quarry, shovel, work, extract, tunnel. **2** probe, investigate, look into, sound out, quiz, pump, delve, tap, pipe, siphon, elicit, get to the bottom of.

mingle *v.* **1** mix, blend, unite, combine, coalesce, merge, compound, commingle. **2** hobnob, fraternize, associate, socialize, consort, mix, participate.
ant. **1** separate, divide, dissociate, segregate, detach. **2** hold aloof, withdraw, break, retire, keep one's distance.

mini *adj.* MINIATURE.

miniature *adj.* small-scale, diminutive, tiny, minute, small, little, dwarf, baby, minuscule, microscopic, wee, petite, mini.
ant. full-scale, large, vast, enormous, huge, elephantine.

minimal *adj.* MINIMUM.

minimize *v.* **1** reduce, shrink, attenuate, miniaturize, curtail, lessen, diminish, abbreviate. **2** belittle, play down, detract, decry, gloss over, disparage, depreciate, derogate.
ant. **1** increase, enlarge, maximize, magnify, expand. **2** maximize, stress, exaggerate, emphasize, blow up.

minimum *n.* least, lowest, smallest, slightest, bottom, trough, nadir, low. —*adj.* minimal, lowest, smallest, slightest, bottom, least.
ant. *n.* maximum, most, greatest, peak, high. *adj.* maximal, greatest, peak, most, maximum.

minion *n.* underling, henchman, myrmidon, dependent, hanger-on, flunky, attendant, favorite, parasite, yesman, apple polisher (*Slang*).

minister *n.* **1** clergyman, priest, parson, preacher, cleric, religious, divine, pastor, churchman, ecclesiastic, man of the cloth. **2** administrator, ambassador, executive, envoy, consul, delegate, official. **3** agent, subordinate, aide, steward, assistant, servant, underling, factotum. —*v.* serve, succor, relieve, aid, support, sustain, attend, assist, uphold, wait on, nourish, nurse.
ant. *n.* **1** layman, laic, secular. *v.* neglect, abandon, forsake, ignore.

ministration *n.* help, aid, assistance, succor, relief, service, accommodation, subvention, support, favor, advocacy, patronage, aegis, championship.

ministry *n.* service, instrumentality, intervention, aid, agency, mediation, intercession, subvention, ministration, interposition, assistance, operation.

minor *adj.* **1** less, lesser, smaller, fewer, junior, lower. **2** secondary, inferior, subordinate, subsidiary, inconsiderable, unimportant, petty, trivial, slight. —*n.* child, adolescent, teen-ager, junior, infant.
ant. *adj.* **1** bigger, more, greater, larger, senior. **2** principal, major, considerable, outstanding, signal. *n.* adult, grown-up.

minority *n.* infancy, childhood, nonage, juvenility, salad days, immaturity, youth.
ant. adulthood, maturity, majority, seniority.

mint *n.* heap, lots, abundance, quantities, million, scores, loads, scads, pile. —*v.* **1** coin, stamp, strike, cast, punch, issue, monetize. **2** invent, fabricate, devise, forge, coin, fashion, produce. —*adj.* unused, fresh, brand-new, firsthand, unmarred, original, virgin, new.
ant. *n.* few, little, drop, scrap, bit, pinch. *adj.* used, secondhand, worn, marred.

minus *prep.* without, sans, less. —*adj.* negative, inferior, second-rate, poor, weak, bad. —*n.* defect, drawback, disadvantage, deficiency, failure, want, lack, demerit, weakness, blemish.
ant. *prep.* plus, with, as well as. *adj.* positive, plus, superior, first-rate, strong, good. *n.* plus, advantage, bonus, gain, success.

minuscule *adj.* MINUTE.²

minute¹ *n.* moment, instant, flash, breath, wink, twinkling, shake, trice, second, jiffy.

minute² *adj.* **1** minuscule, infinitesimal, imperceptible, diminutive, miniature, wee. **2** unimportant, trifling, inconsiderable, insignificant, inconse-

quential, minor. **3** precise, particular, correct, circumstantial, punctilious, nice, detailed, exacting.
ant. **1** large, great, enormous, big, huge. **2** significant, major, momentous, important, weighty. **3** general, loose, careless, casual, imprecise.

minutes *n.* proceedings, record, journal, report, transactions, summary, memorandum, log, digest, notes, diary, abstracts.

minutiae *n.* trivia, trifles, niceties, particulars, details, subtleties, elaborations, pedantries.

minx *n.* hussy, hoyden, saucebox, wench, tomboy, jade, baggage, nymphet, witch, teenybopper (*Slang*).

miracle *n.* marvel, wonder, sensation, curiosity, oddity, rarity, portent, sign, prodigy.

miraculous *adj.* wonderful, strange, marvelous, extraordinary, incredible, remarkable, wondrous, supernatural, preternatural, unnatural, inscrutable, superhuman.
ant. usual, natural, commonplace, ordinary, everyday, prosaic.

mirage *n.* delusion, chimera, will-o'-the-wisp, ignis fatuus, illusion, dream, castle in the air, hallucination, wild-goose chase, fantasy.

mire *n.* slush, mud, ooze, muck, gumbo, bog, slime, fen, marsh, swamp. —*v.* bog down, sink, wallow, welter, flounder, slump.

mirror *n.* **1** looking-glass, glass, reflector. **2** reflection, image, copy, exemplar, standard, model, prototype. —*v.* reflect, echo, represent, imitate, repeat, copy, show, manifest, simulate, display.

mirth *n.* gaiety, merriment, jollity, levity, laughter, hilarity, glee, delight, enthusiasm, festivity, jocularity, playfulness, happiness.
ant. sadness, heaviness, depression, sorrow, melancholy, despondency.

mirthful *adj.* merry, gay, jolly, gleeful, blithe, vivacious, festive, genial, frolicsome, jocular, hilarious.

ant. sad, dreary, gloomy, morose, sorrowful, tearful.

miry *adj.* MUDDY.

misadventure *n.* misfortune, mishap, mischance, slip, accident, contretemps, infelicity, adversity, affliction, reverse, setback, catastrophe, hardship, calamity, disaster.
ant. luck, windfall, fortune, godsend, blessing, boon.

misanthrope *n.* curmudgeon, grouch, cynic, pessimist, crab, crank, scrooge.
ant. philanthropist, humanitarian, altruist, benefactor, Good Samaritan.

misappropriate *v.* misapply, filch, defraud, peculate, embezzle, defalcate, steal, swindle, rifle, purloin, cheat, plunder, rob.

misbegotten *adj.* illegitimate, illicit, bastard, unlawful, spurious, abortive, deformed, ill-conceived.
ant. legitimate, well-favored, licit, lawful.

misbehavior *n.* impropriety, misconduct, immorality, misdoing, misdeed, lapse, delinquency, fault, indiscretion, trespass, offense, naughtiness, rudeness, impertinence.

miscalculate *v.* mistake, err, misjudge, miscompute, misinterpret, miscount, blunder, miss, confuse, misconceive, misconstrue, misgauge.

miscarriage *n.* **1** abortion, stillbirth, prematurity. **2** failure, fiasco, slip-up, defeat, frustration, miss, error, collapse, accident.
ant. 2 success, accomplishment, fruition, triumph, achievement, implementation.

miscarry *v.* fail, fizzle, fall through, flounder, go wrong, go amiss, fall short, abort, falter, collapse.
ant. succeed, flourish, progress, prosper, triumph, make good.

miscellaneous *adj.* varied, mixed, heterogeneous, various, sundry, divers, manifold, diversified, indiscriminate, motley, mingled, promiscuous.
ant. uniform, homogeneous, unalloyed, specific, unmixed, like.

miscellany *n.* collection, medley, potpourri, mixture, blend, mélange, omnium-gatherum, compilation, anthology, gallimaufry, pastiche, jumble, olio, salmagundi.

mischance *n.* MISHAP.

mischief *n.* **1** trick, prank, naughtiness, devilment, shenanigans, jape, roguishness, foolery, playfulness, horseplay, hijinks. **2** damage, harm, trouble, detriment, hurt, evil, injury, disaster.
ant. 2 advantage, help, good, benefit, improvement, favor.

mischievous *adj.* **1** annoying, troublesome, rascally, impish, teasing, naughty, sly, playful. **2** injurious, harmful, malicious, noxious, vicious, pernicious, damaging.
ant. 1 well-behaved, orderly, obedient, manageable, quiet. **2** benign, propitious, favorable, benevolent, salutary.

misconceive *v.* MISUNDERSTAND.

misconduct *n.* misprision, malfeasance, transgression, dereliction, delinquency, negligence, wrongdoing, impropriety, misbehavior, misdeed, malversation, peccadillo.
ant. propriety, uprightness, morality, lawfulness, integrity, decency.

misconstrue *v.* MISUNDERSTAND.

miscreant *n.* evildoer, villain, scoundrel, rascal, knave, wretch, rogue, reprobate, sinner, criminal, malefactor. —*adj.* villainous, evil, wicked, vicious, iniquitous, corrupt, infamous, nefarious, depraved, degenerate.
ant. *adj.* virtuous, ethical, moral, good, righteous, noble.

miscue *n.* mistake, slip, slip-up, error, lapse, fumble, blunder, muff, bungle, fault, bobble, fluff, trip.
ant. success, bull's-eye, hit, score, slam.

misdeed *n.* offense, sin, transgression, violation, trespass, misdemeanor, fault, misconduct, misbehavior, injury, wrong, scandal.

misdemeanor *n.* offense, infringement,

trespass, fault, lapse, misbehavior, transgression, misdeed, misconduct, wrong, injury, violation.

misdo v. BUNGLE.

misemploy v. MISUSE.

miser n. skinflint, penny pincher, hoarder, niggard, cheapskate (*Slang*), scrooge, usurer, skimper, piker, tightwad (*Slang*).

ant. prodigal, wastrel, spendthrift, spender, waster, philanthropist.

miserable adj. **1** wretched, poor, piteous, pathetic, unfortunate, dismal, unhappy, accursed, lamentable. **2** distressing, inconvenient, oppressive, uncomfortable, unfortunate, regrettable, severe, grievous, bothersome. **3** inferior, worthless, shoddy, second-rate, trashy, unsatisfactory, flimsy. **4** shameful, detestable, disgraceful, pitiable, sorry, menial, abject, forlorn.

ant. 1 prosperous, affluent, happy, blessed, fortunate, contented. **2** light, minor, inconsequential, insignificant, bearable. **3** first-rate, superior, satisfactory, good, valuable. **4** respectable, enviable, dignified, great.

miserly adj. grasping, stingy, mean, covetous, parsimonious, tight, tight-fisted, hard-fisted, cheap, close, close-fisted, niggardly, ungenerous, selfish, avaricious, sordid, penurious, penny-pinching.

ant. generous, open, bountiful, munificent, unselfish, liberal.

misery n. **1** suffering, distress, anguish, agony, grief, woe, sorrow. **2** hardship, affliction, misfortune, adversity, complaint, calamity, trouble, disaster.

ant. 1 happiness, joy, felicity, cheerfulness, well-being. **2** blessing, benison, boon, benefit, welfare.

misfire v. fail, miscarry, break down, hang fire, fall through, collapse, peter out, go wrong, abort, fizzle, miss, go astray.

ant. succeed, prosper, carry through, triumph, make good, advance.

misfit n. nonconformist, eccentric,

crank, individualist, loner, malcontent, sorehead, deviate, fanatic, fifth wheel, freak (*Slang*), crackpot (*Slang*), oddball (*Slang*).

ant. conformist, joiner, member, insider.

misfortune n. **1** adversity, sorrow, misery, trouble, evil, ruination, bad luck, mischief. **2** calamity, injury, harm, mishap, blow, hurt, accident, reverse, setback.

ant. 1 happiness, fortune, prosperity, good, luck. **2** fluke, godsend, windfall, advantage, blessing.

misgiving n. doubt, premonition, apprehension, anxiety, suspicion, mistrust, reservation, qualm, scruple, distrust, hesitation, disquiet, foreboding.

ant. confidence, reliance, faith, trust, certitude, assurance.

misguided adj. mistaken, ill-advised, unwise, unwarranted, injudicious, imprudent, indiscreet, foolish, uncalled-for, unsound, misdirected, misled, erroneous.

ant. judicious, wise, prudent, sound, well-advised, sagacious.

mishandle v. mismanage, botch, bungle, fumble, blunder, stumble, spoil, mar, upset, mess up, misconduct, foul up (*Slang*).

ant. master, succeed, make good, redeem, accomplish, benefit.

mishap n. mischance, misadventure, reverse, adversity, affliction, misfortune, contretemps, slip, woe, harm, grief.

ant. luck, fortune, felicity, success, prosperity, happiness.

mishmash n. hodge-podge, jumble, mélange, hash, medley, conglomeration, olio, muddle, patchwork, crazy quilt, gallimaufry.

misinform v. misrepresent, mislead, misguide, misdirect, misstate, deceive, lie, lead on, lead astray, delude, bamboozle, humbug, put on (*Slang*).

misinterpret v. MISUNDERSTAND.

misjudge v. err, miscalculate, mistake,

misapprehend, misunderstand, prejudge, misconceive, blunder, misconstrue, misinterpret.

mislay v. misplace, lose, forget, miss, displace.

ant. find, locate, retain, place, keep.

mislead v. misguide, misdirect, misinform, deceive, delude, beguile, decoy, lure, gull, inveigle, misconduct.

ant. edify, enlighten, direct, advise, undeceive.

misleading adj. deceptive, delusive, ambiguous, seductive, beguiling, specious, fallacious, disingenuous, sophistical, demagogic.

ant. enlightening, candid, aboveboard, guileless, informative, honest.

mislike v. DISLIKE.

mismanage v. mishandle, botch, bungle, fumble, mess up, spoil, upset, misrule, misconduct, blunder, stumble, mar, foul up (*Slang*).

ant. master, preserve, benefit, accomplish, succeed, make good.

mismatch n. discrepancy, disparity, irregularity, anomaly, dissonance, clash, incongruity, misfit, discord, unconformity, misalliance, mismating.

ant. agreement, harmony, fit, match, mate, conformity.

misnomer n. malapropism, solecism, inexactitude, slip, mistake, misusage, barbarism.

misplace v. MISLAY.

misplay v. err, slip up, stumble, blunder, fumble, slip, fluff, trip. —n. mistake, error, slip, lapse, miscue, blunder, slip-up, fumble, misstep, misdeal.

misprint n. typo, erratum, corrigendum.

misprision n. MISCONDUCT.

misprize v. DESPISE.

misread v. MISUNDERSTAND.

misrepresent v. falsify, belie, garble, distort, slant, twist, color, misstate, caricature, disguise, mislead.

misrepresentation n. falsification, distortion, caricature, exaggeration, misdirection, dissembling, perversion, contortion, garble, misstatement, simulation.

ant. truth, exactitude, accuracy, verisimilitude, veracity, verity.

misrule n. misgovernment, mismanagement, maladministration, disorder, anarchy, lawlessness, turmoil, chaos, laxity, malfeasance.

ant. order, concord, control, law, tranquillity, discipline.

miss[1] n. girl, young lady, lass, maiden, maid, schoolgirl, mademoiselle, teenager, youngster, spinster, Ms.

miss[2] v. **1** fail, lose, muff, overlook, omit, fall short, miscarry. **2** avoid, skip, neglect, pass by, escape, leave out, overlook. **3** lack, require, need, desire, want, long, yearn.

ant. **1** succeed, understand, get, see, catch. **2** include, undergo, utilize, attend, avail. **3** have, possess, own, enjoy, use.

misshapen adj. deformed, shapeless, distorted, ill-made, malformed, misproportioned, awry, warped, contorted, ungainly, twisted, gnarled, askew, ill-formed, grotesque.

ant. shapely, graceful, symmetrical, trim, well-turned, well-balanced.

missile n. projectile, bolt, shaft, lance, dart, boomerang, grenade, ball, bullet, weapon.

missing adj. absent, lost, gone, away, out, invisible, wanting, lacking, mislaid, misplaced, forgotten, astray, omitted.

ant. present, at hand, existing, near, nearby, here.

mission n. **1** task force, delegation, deputation, commission, legation, embassy. **2** task, goal, business, objective, aim, assignment, service, calling, vocation.

missionary n. missioner, evangelist, proselytizer, propagandist, popularizer, advance man, publicist.

missive n. letter, dispatch, epistle, message, communication, note, report, memorandum, circular, bulletin, memo.

misspent *adj.* debauched, dissolute, wasted, frittered, dissipated, squandered, unprofitable, intemperate, depraved, wild, prodigal.

ant. temperate, sober, dutiful, exemplary, estimable, profitable.

misstatement *n.* falsification, inexactitude, misrepresentation, dissembling, blunder, howler, spoonerism, distortion, mistake, untruth, garble.

ant. exactitude, truth, verity, gospel.

misstep *n.* ERROR.

mist *n.* haze, fog, dew, film, blur, cloud, vapor, smog, drizzle, steam, moisture, smoke, gauze.

mistake *n.* error, blunder, lapse, misunderstanding, misconception, omission, inaccuracy, oversight, slip-up, botch, aberration, failure, flaw, miscue, muff, boo-boo (*Slang*), clinker (*Slang*). —*v.* err, misinterpret, misjudge, confuse, misapprehend, confound, misconceive, misunderstand.

mistaken *adj.* **1** incorrect, false, wrong, erroneous, untrue, inexact, inaccurate, fallacious, specious. **2** misguided, misled, misinformed, deceived, deluded, foolish, confused, wrong.

ant. 1 true, correct, exact, right, accurate. **2** enlightened, informed, just, reasonable, right.

mister *n.* fellow, lad, buddy, young man, jack, mac, brother, pal, man, master, gentleman, esquire, sir.

mistreat *v.* abuse, maltreat, misuse, illuse, wrong, injure, harm, mishandle, oppress, outrage, pervert.

ant. cherish, protect, treasure, care for, shield, guard.

mistreatment *n.* abuse, misuse, misusage, ill-treatment, maltreatment, illuse, oppression, harassment, unkindness, injury, cruelty, persecution, harm, wrong, mishandling.

ant. kindness, ministration, succor, indulgence, benevolence, protection.

mistress *n.* **1** head, chief, supervisor, boss, principal, matron, housewife. **2** paramour, sweetheart, inamorata, concubine, doxy, lover, flame

(*Slang*). **3** expert, specialist, authority, connoisseur, adept, virtuoso, maven.

mistrust *n.* suspicion, distrust, doubt, uncertainty, skepticism, apprehension, misgiving, dubiety, fear, presentiment. —*v.* doubt, suspect, distrust, apprehend, beware, question, demur, scruple, disbelieve.

ant. *n.* confidence, reliance, certainty, faith, trust. *v.* rely, accept, believe, trust, swallow.

mistrustful *adj.* suspicious, wary, doubtful, dubious, skeptical, leery, cautious, hesitant, uncertain, apprehensive, anxious, fearful.

ant. trustful, confident, assured, secure, certain, fearless.

misty *adj.* murky, hazy, foggy, opaque, indistinct, fuzzy, smoky, vaporous, steamy, clouded, dewy, filmy.

ant. clear, unclouded, transparent, limpid, distinct, bright.

misunderstand *v.* mistake, misread, misinterpret, misconstrue, misconceive, misapprehend, misreckon, misjudge, confuse, confound.

ant. understand, comprehend, see, fathom, master, perceive.

misunderstanding *n.* **1** mistake, misinterpretation, misapprehension, miscalculation, blunder, error, misconception, misreading. **2** quarrel, disagreement, breach, dissension, discord, difference, rupture, conflict.

ant. 1 comprehension, understanding, enlightenment, perception, recognition. **2** agreement, accord, harmony, amity, concord.

misunderstood *adj.* unappreciated, underestimated, slighted, undervalued, disregarded, unrecognized, misjudged, scorned, misprized, unacknowledged, despised, rejected.

ant. esteemed, valued, admired, recognized, honored, cherished.

misusage *n.* **1** MISUSE. **2** MISTREATMENT.

misuse *n.* **1** misapplication, misemployment, misusage, desecration, perversion, impropriety, profanation, abuse, prostitution, exploitation, debasement. **2** MISTREATMENT. —*v.* **1** misapply, misemploy, prostitute, pervert, corrupt, debase, profane, desecrate. **2** MISTREAT.

mite *n.* grain, particle, atom, bit, mote, smidgen, dab, sliver, trifle, pinpoint, modicum, iota, corpuscle.

ant. mountain, load, abundance, lot, mass, giant.

mitigate *v.* moderate, alleviate, ameliorate, extenuate, assuage, relieve, soften, temper, allay, soothe, placate, mollify, ease, lighten.

ant. intensify, aggravate, worsen, magnify, increase, harden, exacerbate.

mix *v.* **1** unite, compound, blend, shake, amalgamate, stir, knead, combine, join, admix, synthesize, commingle, integrate. **2** participate, socialize, associate, fraternize, take part, mingle, get along. —*n.* combination, mixture, medley, composite, blend, variety, diversity, mélange.

ant. *v.* **1** separate, isolate, divide, segregate, analyze. **2** withdraw, retire, retreat, hibernate.

mixed-up *adj.* confused, bewildered, perplexed, deranged, disturbed, distraught, addled, wrong-headed, irrational, puzzled, muddled.

ant. lucid, clear-headed, composed, self-possessed, level-headed, sensible.

mixture *n.* blend, combination, assortment, jumble, miscellany, compound, association, amalgamation, admixture, composite, hodge-podge, mélange, conglomeration, medley, variety.

mix-up *n.* confusion, muddle, disorder, mess, clutter, complication, misunderstanding, quandary, tangle, maze, entanglement.

ant. order, enlightenment, clarification, simplification, explanation, solution.

moan *n.* groan, lament, murmur, sough, wail, lamentation, sob. —*v.* **1** groan, bemoan, keen, lament, bewail,

mourn, complain, grieve, deplore. **2** *of nonhuman sounds, as the wind:* sough, sigh, murmur, wail, sob, groan, squeak.

moat *n.* ditch, trench, fosse, trough, dike, entrenchment, gutter.

mob *n.* **1** crowd, masses, rabble, populace, multitude, riffraff, hoi polloi, throng, crush, horde, gathering. **2** *Slang* gang, underworld, band, conspiracy, syndicate, family. —*v.* crowd around, hem in, rough up, jostle, surround, overcome, inundate.

mobile *adj.* **1** movable, locomotive, portable, ambulatory, motile. **2** changeable, vivacious, expressive, sensitive, spirited, mercurial, volatile. **3** *of a social system:* progressive, shifting, dynamic, free, open, pluralistic.

ant. 1 immobile, stationary, immovable, sessile. **2** torpid, stiff, expressionless, dull. **3** hidebound, rigid, hierarchical, stratified, closed, monolithic.

mobilize *v.* assemble, organize, call up, muster, marshal, activate, summon, ready, prepare, catalyze, animate.

ant. disband, relax, demobilize, dissipate, dismiss, disperse.

mobster *n. Slang* GANGSTER.

mock *v.* **1** scorn, ridicule, scoff, deride, burlesque, flout, mimic, jeer, ape, sneer at. **2** deceive, delude, disappoint, dupe, mislead, fool. **3** defy, challenge, taunt, disparage, goad, dare, stultify. —*adj.* imitation, sham, counterfeit, fake, spurious, pretended, feigned, artificial, make-believe, ersatz, phony (*Slang*).

ant. *v.* **1** honor, esteem, praise, acclaim. **2** reward, satisfy, gratify, make good. **3** encourage, rally, urge on, hearten. *adj.* genuine, authentic, real, true, natural.

mockery *n.* **1** derision, contempt, ridicule, scorn, sarcasm, burlesque, jeering, contumely, mimicry. **2** laughingstock, butt, target, mock, dupe, gull, fool, clown, buffoon. **3** travesty, pretense, imitation, counterfeit, sham, pretext, satire.

ant. 1 respect, deference, homage, courtesy, regard. **3** paragon, exemplar, ideal, model, standard.

mocking *adj.* derisive, scornful, disrespectful, rude, taunting, sardonic, contemptuous, insulting, scoffing, ironic, sarcastic, insincere, pert.

ant. respectful, courteous, civil, sincere, polite, sympathetic.

mockup *n.* MODEL.

mode *n.* **1** manner, way, method, system, fashion, form, style, rule, procedure, *modus operandi.* **2** vogue, style, fad, fashion, craze, rage.

model *n.* **1** miniature, facsimile, mockup, representation, duplicate, copy, figure, imitation. **2** ideal, exemplar, paradigm, mold, archetype, prototype, paragon, pattern. **3** sitter, poser, mannequin, lay figure, dummy, puppet, clotheshorse (*Slang*). **4** analogue, description, representation, construct, analogy. —*v.* **1** copy, reproduce, imitate, take after, pattern after. **2** make, fashion, shape, form, mold. **3** wear, don, parade, display, show, demonstrate, pose, sit. —*adj.* exemplary, ideal, typical, admirable, standard, archetypal, paradigmatic.

moderate *adj.* **1** limited, ordinary, typical, measured, unexceptional, customary, balanced, reasonable. **2** centrist, conventional, middle-of-the-road, popular. **3** temperate, mild, gentle, calm, balmy, quiet. **4** average, mediocre, indifferent, pedestrian, commonplace, humdrum, unexceptional, so-so, fair. —*n.* middle-of-the-roader, centrist. —*v.* **1** abate, lessen, ease, diminish, subside, modify, decrease, quiet, temper, limit. **2** preside, mediate, chair, arbitrate, keep order, regulate, control.

ant. *adj.* **1** extreme, excessive, undue, drastic, far-out (*Slang*). **2** partisan, radical, revolutionary, fanatical, excessive. **3** inclement, harsh, violent, stormy, rough. **4** exceptional, extraordinary, outstanding, remarka-

ble. *n.* revolutionary, radical, fanatic, partisan, extremist. *v.* **1** intensify, magnify, exacerbate, aggravate, increase.

moderation *n.* temperance, moderateness, self-control, discipline, golden mean, restraint, self-restraint, forbearance, frugality, sobriety, continence, abstemiousness.

ant. excess, license, immoderation, overindulgence, debauchery, licentiousness.

moderator *n.* chairman, chairperson, chairwoman, mediator, referee, presiding officer, master of ceremonies, emcee, president, leader, umpire, arbitrator, ombudsman.

modern *adj.* **1** contemporary, present-day, current, recent, late, present, neoteric. **2** up-to-date, modernistic, fashionable, modish, novel, original, ultramodern, fresh, new, with-it (*Slang*). —*n.* contemporary, modernist.

ant. *adj.* **1** ancient, former, olden, historical, archaic. **2** antique, old-fashioned, passé, antiquated, old. *n.* ancient, predecessor, forebear, old fogy.

modernity *n.* **1** modernism, up-to-dateness, contemporaneity, recency, newness, futurism. **2** novelty, *dernier cri,* latest, last word, vogue, innovation.

ant. 1 antiquity, obsolescence, venerability, fustiness, staleness. **2** fossil, relic, antique, throwback, antiquity.

modernize *v.* renew, rejuvenate, update, regenerate, refurbish, renovate, refresh, revamp, streamline, recondition.

ant. age, date, antiquate, outdate, antique.

modest *adj.* **1** reserved, proper, humble, demure, chaste, shy, simple, sober. **2** moderate, limited, middling, unpretentious, inexpensive, medium, smallish.

ant. 1 bold, flamboyant, self-important, vain, proud, shameless. **2** excessive, grand, unlimited, imposing, pretentious.

modesty *n.* **1** humility, unpretentiousness, meekness, simplicity, constraint, shyness, reserve, diffidence. **2** propriety, decorum, pudency, decency, purity, virtue, continence, chastity.

ant. 1 vanity, pride, self-assertion, pretentiousness, ambition. **2** impropriety, immodesty, shamelessness, lewdness, wantonness.

modicum *n.* bit, little, minimum, smidgen, particle, grain, morsel, trifle, sliver, grain, iota, fragment, drop.

ant. lot, much, plenty, abundance, surfeit, masses.

modification *n.* alteration, change, qualification, refinement, variation, transformation, conversion, adjustment, mutation, shift, moderation, permutation.

modify *v.* alter, vary, change, moderate, modulate, temper, reduce, lessen, slacken, transform, transfigure, transmute, convert, adjust, reshape, adapt.

modish *adj.* stylish, fashionable, chic, smart, high-style, voguish, current, now, in (*Slang*), trendy (*Slang*).

ant. dated, passé, dowdy, old-fashioned, out (*Slang*).

modulate *v.* regulate, adjust, attune, modify, temper, equalize, true, align, focus, fix, balance, arrange, coordinate, correct.

modulation *n.* adjustment, regulation, modification, alignment, balance, equalization, coordination, correction, alteration, softening, slackening, decrease, lessening.

module *n.* unit, component, constituent, gauge, standard, measure, integer, part, model, norm, division, dimension.

modus operandi operating procedure, operation, technique, method, system, means, treatment, practice, way, process, workings, technology, praxis.

mogul *n.* magnate, potentate, power, personage, somebody, bigwig, V.I.P., figure, heavyweight, tycoon, notable, big wheel (*Slang*), big shot (*Slang*).

ant. nobody, cipher, nullity, nothing, lightweight, cog, underling.

moil *v.* TOIL.

moist *adj.* damp, wet, watery, humid, dank, dewy, misty, muggy, vaporous, clammy, dripping, humidified.

ant. dry, unmoistened, parched, dehumidified, arid.

moisten *v.* dampen, wet, moisturize, humidify, spray, bedew, sponge.

ant. dry, parch, dehumidify.

moisture *n.* damp, dampness, dew, wet, wetness, humidity, evaporation, sweat, perspiration, vapor, mist, dankness, drizzle, droplets.

ant. dryness, aridity, dehumidification, desiccation.

moisturize *v.* MOISTEN.

mold *n.* **1** form, matrix, frame, contour, shape, stamp, last, die, punch, seal, outline, pattern, cast, format. **2** character, stripe, type, category, kind, peculiarity, individuality, singularity, idiosyncrasy, bent, temperament, nature, complexion. —*v.* **1** cast, form, shape, fashion, devise, model, sculpt, figure, contour, construct. **2** influence, indoctrinate, affect, modify, transform, control, guide, determine.

molder *v.* decay, rot, dry out, desiccate, decompose, disintegrate, crumble, wither, dehydrate.

ant. freshen, bloom, quicken, renew, revive.

moldy *adj.* musty, stale, dank, timeworn, shabby, dusty, moldering, old, rusty, crumbling, disintegrating, deteriorating, frowsty (*Brit.*).

ant. fresh, new, bright, sparkling, flourishing.

mole *n.* nevus, birthmark, beauty mark, spot, blemish, macula, freckle.

molest *v.* **1** annoy, bother, disturb, pester, plague, vex, trouble, inconvenience, harass, heckle, hector, kibitz, bully. **2** accost, abuse, make advances, affront, insult, attack, maltreat, misuse, make a pass at (*Slang*).

mollify *v.* **1** appease, pacify, conciliate, soothe, calm, compose, tranquilize, propitiate, quiet, placate, humor, console. **2** lessen, lower, temper, allay, abate, ease, mitigate, palliate, soften, dull, blunt, still, subdue, check, tone down.

ant. 1 anger, enrage, ruffle, provoke, exasperate, infuriate. **2** heighten, intensify, aggravate, sharpen, worsen, stimulate.

mollycoddle *n.* milksop, mamma's boy, sissy, baby, weakling, milquetoast, coward, crybaby, cream puff (*Slang*), pansy (*Slang*), nance (*Slang*). —*v.* overprotect, cosset, coddle, pamper, baby, overindulge, spoil, cater to, give in to.

molt *v.* shed, slough off, cast off, exuviate, throw off, doff.

molten *adj.* melted, liquefied, smelted, fusible, red-hot.

ant. solid, annealed, hard, cold.

mom *n.* MOTHER.

moment *n.* **1** instant, second, trice, twinkling, flash, jiffy, wink, breath. **2** point, juncture, hour, stage, date, present, here and now, the times, the time being, nonce. **3** significance, importance, weight, consequence, seriousness, gravity, influence, value, merit, concern, import, magnitude, substance, note.

ant. 3 insignificance, triviality, unimportance.

momentarily *adv.* SHORTLY.

momentary *adj.* brief, short, fleeting, transitory, quick, hasty, ephemeral, instantaneous, abrupt, transient, temporary, flashing, short-lived.

ant. prolonged, long, lasting, lengthy, extended.

momentous *adj.* important, weighty, serious, consequential, grave, significant, decisive, substantial, noteworthy, far-reaching, memorable, outstanding, eventful, signal.

ant. trivial, insignificant, inconsequential, petty, ordinary, frivolous.

momentum *n.* motion, movement, impetus, impulse, activity, drive, thrust, action, propulsion, energy, go, vigor, dash.

ant. inertia, immobility, passivity, inactivity, rest.

monarch *n.* **1** sovereign, king, queen, ruler, H.R.H., royal highness, emperor, empress, crowned head, majesty. **2** chief, champion, ace, lord, master, star, winner, head, leader, top dog (*Slang*).

monastic *adj.* ascetic, abstinent, reclusive, withdrawn, cloistered, solitary, hermitic, self-denying, self-disciplined, dedicated, austere, unworldly, antisocial, celibate.

ant. worldly, sybaritic, pleasure-loving, self-indulgent, abandoned, convivial.

monetary *adj.* fiscal, financial, pecuniary, budgetary, sumptuary, numismatic.

money *n.* **1** currency, cash, coin, specie, exchange medium, negotiable instrument, legal tender, paper money, bills. **2** profit, gain, assets, wealth, means, funds, wherewithal, riches, affluence, pelf, substance, capital, scratch (*Slang*), dough (*Slang*), bread (*Slang*), lettuce (*Slang*), gelt (*Slang*), wampum.

ant. 2 poverty, need, penury, indigence.

moneyed *adj.* wealthy, rich, prosperous, affluent, well-off, well-to-do, solvent, flush, well-heeled (*Slang*), loaded (*Slang*).

ant. poor, bankrupt, insolvent, indigent, broke.

money-making *adj.* profitable, gainful, paying, productive, lucrative, rewarding, successful, worthwhile, remunerative, going.

ant. unprofitable, losing, wasteful, unrewarding, bankrupt.

monger *n.* dealer, trader, merchant, retailer, seller, handler, storekeeper, peddler, hawker, huckster, vendor, tradesman, shopkeeper.

mongrel *n.* **1** hybrid, mixed breed,

crossbreed, half-breed, half-blood, mutt, cur. **2** incongruity, impurity, intermixture, miscegenation, mismatch, hodge-podge, hash. —*adj.* hybrid, crossbred, impure, mongrelized, bastardized, mixed, miscellaneous, interbred, heterogeneous, unpedigreed.

ant. *adj.* pure, unmixed, homogeneous, pedigreed.

moniker *n. Slang* NAME.

monition *n.* WARNING.

monitor *n.* adviser, guide, overseer, authority, mentor, watchdog, director, guiding light, beacon. —*v.* check, watch over, keep an eye on, oversee, spy, keep tabs on, survey, keep track of, eavesdrop, bug.

monkey business *Slang* horseplay, hijinks, high jinks, tomfoolery, boisterousness, clowning, mischief, capers, buffoonery, skylarking, roguery, shenanigans, monkeyshines (*Slang*).

ant. sobriety, dignity, seriousness, sedateness.

monkeyshines *n. Slang* MONKEY BUSINESS.

monkey with trifle, meddle, tamper, fool, fiddle, tinker, interfere, examine, explore, handle, poke into, mess with (*Slang*).

monograph *n.* treatise, tome, paper, publication, article, report, dissertation, thesis, study, investigation, disquisition, biography, exposition.

monolith *n.* slab, block, monument, plinth, obelisk, stone, dolmen.

monolithic *adj.* **1** massive, monumental, solid, imposing, substantial, colossal, impressive, permanent, enduring. **2** indivisible, unitary, one, undivided, intact, whole, homogeneous, like, unchanging, undeviating, uniform, monistic.

ant. **1** puny, unimpressive, ephemeral. **2** various, several, multiform, multifaceted, individualized, pluralistic.

monologue *n.* soliloquy, one-man show, apostrophe, discourse, lecture, disquisition, talk, sermon, oration, address, speech, tirade, diatribe, routine, number.

ant. dialogue, conversation, give-and-take, colloquy.

monomania *n.* fanaticism, single-mindedness, obsession, obsessiveness, zealotry, passion, craze, compulsiveness, compulsion, extremism, irrationality, madness, *idée fixe*.

monopolistic *adj.* exclusive, privileged, uncompetitive, restrictive, private.

ant. competitive, laissez-faire, public.

monopolize *v.* control, corner, take over, dominate, appropriate, regulate, direct, manage, cartelize, hog (*Slang*).

ant. democratize, share, compete.

monotonous *adj.* tiresome, repetitious, unvaried, unending, dull, dreary, wearisome, boring, droning, toneless, uninteresting, flat, tedious, humdrum, colorless, blah (*Slang*).

ant. varied, interesting, absorbing, diversified, engrossing, colorful, exciting.

monotony *n.* tedium, uniformity, dullness, repetition, dreariness, boredom, ennui, sameness, rote, rut, routine, humdrum.

ant. variety, change, excitement, interest, stimulation, surprise.

monster *n.* **1** monstrosity, freak, aberration, abnormality, abortion, oddity, curiosity, phenomenon, sport, wonder. **2** ogre, ghoul, troll, devil, fiend, terror, sadist, vampire, incubus, succubus, dragon, chimera, gorgon, nightmare. **3** giant, colossus, mammoth, leviathan, Titan, mastodon, gargantua, goliath, behemoth, Brobdingnagian. —*adj.* enormous, gigantic, colossal, huge, monstrous, giant, great, mammoth, gargantuan, jumbo, immense, tremendous, titanic, stupendous, mountainous.

ant. *n.* **3** runt, pygmy, dwarf, midget, peewee. *adj.* tiny, undersized, wee, pygmy.

monstrosity *n.* MONSTER.

monstrous *adj.* **1** grotesque, unnatural,

freakish, aberrant, abnormal, weird, bizarre, peculiar, outré, odd, off, outlandish, wild. **2** enormous, huge, colossal, great, monster, giant, mammoth, gargantuan, jumbo, immense, titanic, stupendous, mountainous. **3** hideous, atrocious, hateful, intolerable, ghoulish, fiendish, satanic, sadistic, heinous, gruesome, macabre, horrible, horrifying, revolting, grisly, ghastly. **4** absurd, incredible, unbelievable, outrageous, ludicrous, ridiculous, extravagant, flagrant, preposterous, exaggerated, shocking, amazing, astonishing, blatant, egregious.
ant. 1 typical, natural, regular, normal, usual. **2** undersized, tiny, midget, dwarf, peewee. **3** charming, fetching, pleasant, agreeable. **4** reasonable, believable, sensible, convincing.

monument *n.* **1** memorial, statue, monolith, obelisk, plinth, pillar, slab, cairn, tablet, shrine, dolmen, pyramid. **2** masterpiece, masterwork, magnum opus, *chef d'oeuvre*, epic, landmark, legacy, heritage, accomplishment, contribution. **3** tomb, tombstone, cenotaph, mausoleum, gravestone, headstone, sepulchre, vault.

monumental *adj.* huge, impressive, outstanding, significant, enduring, memorable, enormous, massive, colossal, lofty, towering, gigantic, exalted, mighty.
ant. insignificant, trivial, negligible, small.

mooch *v. Slang* BEG.

moocher *n. Slang* BEGGAR.

mood *n.* disposition, humor, frame of mind, state, inclination, condition, temper, vein, streak, mind, spirit, tenor, temperament.

moody *adj.* temperamental, unstable, melancholy, sullen, mopish, petulant, cranky, touchy, mercurial, volatile, morose, broody, capricious, changeable, unpredictable, erratic.
ant. stable, balanced, phlegmatic, calm, stoic.

moon *v.* MOPE.

moonshine *n.* NONSENSE.

moonstruck *adj.* **1** LUNATIC. **2** ROMANTIC.

moony *adj.* ABSENT-MINDED.

moor[1] *v.* anchor, fix, secure, tie, chain, fasten, tether, settle, bind, lash, rope, make fast.
ant. loose, unchain, untie, unfasten, set sail.

moor[2] *n.* heath, waste, wasteland, downs, plain, desert, tundra, marsh, prairie, pampas, steppe, veldt, savanna, mesa, plateau.

moorings *n.* harbor, anchor, anchorage, dock, marina, slip, haven, port, seaport, roads, berth, basin, wharf, pier, landing, quay.

moot *adj.* **1** debatable, arguable, unresolved, unsettled, undetermined, undecided, disputable, questionable, controversial, controvertible, contestable, problematical, open. **2** academic, hypothetical, philosophical, unreal, metaphysical, conjectural, theoretical, suppositional. —*v., n.* DEBATE.
ant. *adj.* **1** settled, resolved, determined, decided, incontrovertible, indisputable. **2** practical, real, pragmatic, common-sense.

mop *v.* swab, sponge, wipe, clean, rub, wash, brush.

mope *v.* brood, sulk, fret, moon, whine, grieve, agonize, repine, despond, gloom, languish, worry, pout, grumble, grouse.

mopey *adj.* listless, dejected, mopish, depressed, blue, downcast, gloomy, downhearted, despondent, crestfallen, dispirited, glum, morose, down.
ant. lighthearted, cheerful, energetic, up.

moppet *n.* CHILD.

moral *adj.* **1** ethical, principled, dutiful, upright, just, conscientious, honorable, incorruptible, scrupulous, righteous, honest, high-minded. **2** good, virtuous, chaste, pure, puritanical, innocent, respectable, virginal, decorous, prissy, prudish. —*n.* lesson, truism, maxim, adage, proverb, byword, meaning, significance, motto, precept, dictum, teaching, homily.

ant. *adj.* **1** opportunistic, unprincipled, unethical, unscrupulous, dishonorable, base. **2** immoral, loose, promiscuous, wild, wanton, abandoned, debauched.

morale *n.* spirit, heart, mood, disposition, state of mind, frame of mind, temper, will, confidence, resolve, hope.

morality *n.* virtue, goodness, righteousness, uprightness, high-mindedness, conscientiousness, incorruptibility, probity, rectitude, integrity, worthiness.

ant. evil, immorality, opportunism, depravity, profligacy, vice.

moralize *v.* sermonize, preach, lecture, speechify, exhort, expound, advocate, teach, enlighten, admonish, uplift, evangelize.

morals *n.* morality, conduct, behavior, life style, ethics, scruples, standards, principles, discretion, conventionality, guidelines, restraints, constraints.

morass *n.* **1** marsh, fen, bog, swamp, quagmire, slough, mire, wetlands, quicksand. **2** muddle, mess, mixup, dilemma, booby trap, jam, hole, predicament, squeeze, bind, fix, spot, mare's nest, hornet's nest, can of worms.

moratorium *n.* suspension, discontinuance, discontinuation, reprieve, respite, halt, stay, postponement, cessation, abeyance, standstill, letup.

morbid *adj.* **1** diseased, pathological, infected, infectious, affected, contaminated, malignant, decaying, festering, purulent, degenerative. **2** gruesome, grisly, macabre, unwholesome, sick, abnormal, neurotic, depressed, melancholy, black, suicidal.

ant. **1** sound, healthy, normal, robust, flourishing. **2** cheerful, sunny,

sanguine, buoyant, hopeful, wholesome.

mordant *adj.* biting, cutting, sarcastic, stinging, acid, acerbic, waspish, caustic, pungent, incisive, acrimonious, scornful, venomous.

ant. bland, charitable, soothing, innocuous.

more *adj.* greater, additional, extra, other, second, supplementary, auxiliary, fresh, new, replenished, added, augmented. —*n.* increase, addition, plus, extra, refill, supplement, replenishment, increment, dividend, bonus, extension, surplus, excess, gain.

ant. *adj.* less, lower, reduced, diminished, lessened. *n.* decrease, reduction, diminution, loss.

more or less MOSTLY.

mores *n.* customs, traditions, conventions, observances, code, standards, usages, rituals, practices, uses, rules, forms, ethos.

moribund *adj.* dying, failing, obsolescent, expiring, devitalized.

ant. vital, strong, healthy, potent, viable.

morning *n.* dawn, sunrise, sunup, forenoon, a.m.

ant. sunset, twilight, evening, p.m., afternoon.

moron *n.* retardate, defective, subnormal, simpleton, ninny, dunce, dummy, dullard, dolt, blockhead, imbecile, dimwit (*Slang*).

moronic *adj.* ASININE.

morose *adj.* gloomy, glum, melancholy, downcast, sad, crestfallen, blue, sullen, mopey, surly, cranky, pessimistic, unhappy, dispirited, depressed, down.

ant. cheerful, happy, optimistic, convivial, light-hearted.

morsel *n.* **1** *of food:* bite, taste, tidbit, dollop, scrap, drop, mouthful, bit, piece, swallow, chyme. **2** *of anything:* fraction, segment, scrap, drop, tidbit, bit, piece, shaving, paring, sliver, snip, speck, whit, shred, particle, chip, flake, snippet, sample, iota.

mortal *adj.* **1** human, earthly, corporeal, temporal, ephemeral, perishable, impermanent, transitory, fleeting, short-lived, vulnerable. **2** fatal, lethal, life-and-death, critical. **3** unrelenting, deadly, out-and-out, unremitting, murderous, implacable, inexorable, relentless, bitter, bloodthirsty, irreconcilable, remorseless, savage. —*n.* HUMAN.
ant. *adj.* **1** immortal, eternal, undying, incorporeal, imperishable, permanent, lasting.

mortality *n.* death, destruction, fatality, holocaust, carnage, ruin, havoc, undoing, waste, bloodshed, doom, slaughter, extermination.

mortgage *v.* pledge, promise, pawn, post, put up, stake, encumber.

mortician *n.* undertaker, funeral director, embalmer.

mortification *n.* humiliation, shame, chagrin, embarrassment, abashment, abasement, discomfiture, discomposure, self-reproach.
ant. self-esteem, self-satisfaction, pride, self-regard.

mortified *adj.* ASHAMED.

mortify *v.* humiliate, shame, abash, chagrin, dismay, embarrass, discomfit, humble, disgrace, deflate, lower, crush, chasten, put down (*Slang*).
ant. uplift, extol, exalt, praise.

mortuary *n.* funeral home, funeral parlor, morgue, crematory, crematorium, charnel house.

mosey *v. Slang* SAUNTER.

most *adj.* maximum, maximal, optimum, optimal, top, superlative, utmost, supreme, unsurpassed, chief, foremost, peerless, incomparable, unequaled, nonpareil.
ant. least, lowest, bottom, poorest.

mostly *adv.* principally, for the most part, chiefly, especially, primarily, predominantly, particularly, mainly, above all, generally, as a rule, more or less.

mote *n.* speck, particle, flake, fragment, grain, bit, crumb, spot, pinch, whit, atom.

moth-eaten *adj.* **1** worn-out, dilapidated, threadbare, old, ragged, tattered, unwearable, seedy, musty, moldy. **2** outworn, outmoded, outdated, old-fashioned, obsolete, stale, antiquated, superannuated, unfashionable, antediluvian, tired.
ant. **1** fresh, new, intact. **2** current, up-to-date, contemporary, now, trendy (*Slang*).

mother *n.* **1** mom, mama, mamma, ma, mommy, mummy, mammy, matriarch, matron, progenitrix, mater (*Brit.*), maw (*Slang*), old lady (*Slang*). **2** source, origin, originator, pioneer, creator, begetter, producer, fountainhead, womb, seed, wellspring, genesis, cradle. —*v.* nurture, nurse, cherish, care for, nourish, love, sustain, foster, protect, guard, baby, spoil, overprotect. —*adj.* native, natural, parental, original, natal, indigenous.

motherhood *n.* maternity.

motherly *adj.* maternal, protective, parental.

motif *n.* theme, subject, topic, keynote, thread, reprise, refrain.

motion *n.* **1** movement, displacement, change, move, transition, drift, shift, passage, gesture, action, stir, transit, dislocation, removal, transfer. **2** recommendation, proposition, proposal, suggestion, measure, plan, question. —*v.* gesture, move, gesticulate, indicate, point, beckon, signal, wave.
ant. *n.* **1** repose, rest, stasis, immobility, inertia.

motionless *adj.* inert, immobile, immobilized, still, calm, quiet, undisturbed, frozen, rigid, stiff, fixed, at rest, static, stationary, paralyzed, unresponsive.
ant. mobile, moving, changing, shifting, unsettled.

motion picture MOVIE.

motivate *v.* induce, activate, propel, stir, move, instigate, stimulate, arouse, impel, provoke, inspirit, hearten, influence, prompt, persuade, goad.

ant. discourage, deter, dissuade, dishearten.

motivation *n.* MOTIVE.

motive *n.* reason, cause, inducement, motivation, provocation, stimulus, spur, rationale, grounds, purpose, incentive, aim.

motley *adj.* assorted, varied, various, miscellaneous, mixed, divers, diverse, multifarious, manifold, variegated, differing, multiple, heterogeneous, diversified, jumbled.

ant. uniform, homogeneous, similar, like.

motor *n.* machine, engine, dynamo, generator, mechanism, appliance, transformer. —*adj.* **1** mobile, locomotive, driving, propellent, propulsive. **2** mechanical, motorized, mechanized, power-driven, vehicular. **3** neuromuscular, autonomic.

mottled *adj.* variegated, dappled, pied, piebald, spotted, shaded, streaked, marbled, checkered, brindled, blotched, blotchy, flecked, freckled, motley.

ant. solid, homogeneous, uniform.

motto *n.* slogan, cry, byword, watchword, maxim, proverb, rule, adage, precept, principle, formula, saw.

mound *n.* heap, pile, mass, accumulation, stack, rick, hill, hillock, knoll, rise, dune, ridge, hummock.

ant. pit, hole, burrow, hollow, dugout.

mount[1] *v.* **1** ascend, rise, climb, go up, scale, clamber, shinny. **2** increase, grow, soar, escalate, pile up, accrue, accumulate, heighten, enlarge, amplify, gain, swell, multiply. —*n.* MOUNTING.

ant. *v.* **1** descend, go down. **2** decrease, lessen, lower, fall, diminish, decline, plunge.

mount[2] *n.* MOUNTAIN.

mountain *n.* **1** mount, eminence, height, alp, elevation, highland, peak, tor, cliff, butte, range. **2** mass,

pile, abundance, accumulation, ocean, ton, slew, overflow, pile-up.

ant. 1 valley, hollow, dale, glen.

mountainous *adj.* alpine, hilly, elevated, craggy, rocky, steep, high.

ant. flat, low, level, unbroken.

mountebank *n.* charlatan, quack, fraud, cheat, rascal, swindler, humbug, faker, bluffer, liar, phony (*Slang*), con man (*Slang*), grifter (*Slang*).

mounting *n.* frame, mount, support, backing, setting, framework, background, set, base, pedestal, stand, mount, trestle, easel, surroundings, environment, *mise en scene,* frame of reference.

mourn *v.* grieve, sorrow, lament, weep, cry, keen, sob, wail, bewail, suffer, elegize.

mournful *adj.* lugubrious, rueful, disconsolate, grief-stricken, sorrowful, funereal, melancholy, woeful, somber, gloomy, inconsolable, heavyhearted, broken-hearted, grieving, woebegone.

ant. cheerful, joyous, lighthearted.

mourning *n.* grieving, lamenting, sorrowing, suffering, lamentation, bereavement, grief, dolor, sorrow, sadness, anguish, affliction.

ant. rejoicing, celebration, gaiety, merrymaking.

mouse *n.* shrinking violet, rabbit, sissy, coward, weakling, milksop, milquetoast.

mousy *adj.* timid, quiet, bashful, shy, self-effacing, reserved, withdrawn, inconspicuous, unobtrusive, unnoticed, dull, colorless, vapid.

ant. bold, brazen, self-assertive, noisy, jazzy.

mouth *n.* **1** maw, gullet, muzzle, lips, jaws, trap (*Slang*), kisser (*Slang*), yap (*Slang*). **2** opening, entrance, access, ingress, orifice, hole, aperture, inlet, top, vent, spout, gateway, entry, avenue, approach, adit. —*v.* declaim, speechify, orate, echo, repeat, spout, harangue, mince, rant, imitate, duplicate, mimic, reiterate.

mouthpiece *n. Slang* LAWYER.

mouthy *adj.* TALKATIVE.

movable *adj.* portable, transferable, transportable, mobile, ambulatory, conveyable, changeable, unattached, detached.
ant. fixed, immobile, stationary, immovable.

move *v.* **1** go, shift, depart, leave, set out, stir, migrate, veer, budge, travel, hie, walk. **2** progress, advance, proceed, act, commence, start, get going, inaugurate, initiate, go forward, press on, further, promote, develop. **3** propose, present, offer, submit, recommend, urge, advocate, propound, put forth. **4** arouse, influence, agitate, instigate, provoke, stir, incite, embolden, impassion, inspirit, affect, encourage, excite, rouse, activate. —*n.* **1** maneuver, strategy, tactic, ploy, stratagem, machination, scheme, plan, plot, subterfuge, dodge, coup, tour de force. **2** MOVEMENT.
ant. *v.* **1** stay, remain, rest. **2** stall, stop, idle, stagnate. **4** dull, blunt, discourage.

movement *n.* **1** move, motion, stir, shift, departure, transfer, change, displacement, progress, advance, advancement, action, operation, procedure. **2** gesture, nod, shake, twist, turn, step, rotation, gyration, spin, act, exercise, pantomime, dance. **3** trend, inclination, drift, tendency, leaning, proclivity, propensity, swing, drive, push, crusade, campaign.
ant. **1** inertia, rest, stagnation, decline.

movie *n.* motion picture, film, moving picture, photoplay, picture show, show, picture, screening, run, showing, flick (*Slang*).

movies *n.* the cinema, films, the screen, motion pictures, moving pictures, filmmaking, cinematography, Hollywood, flicks (*Slang*).

moving *adj.* touching, affecting, stirring, poignant, heart-rending.

ant. flat, sterile, unaffecting, perfunctory.

moving picture MOVIE.

mow *v.* cut, scythe, trim, hack, clip, shorten, lop, crop, shear.

mow down slaughter, annihilate, demolish, destroy, exterminate, liquidate, machine-gun, wipe out, slay, shoot, butcher, massacre, decimate, waste (*Slang*), rub out (*Slang*).

much *adj.* great, considerable, appreciable, high, deep, abundant, ample, plentiful, sufficient, sizable, substantial, extensive, broad, far-reaching, thorough.
ant. little, small, inadequate, insufficient, sparse.

muck *n.* **1** mud, slime, ooze, mire, slop, filth, dirt, dung, compost, sludge, sewage. **2** mudslinging, smear, slander, vilification, defamation, muckraking, character assassination, name-calling, libel, scandal, dirt, filth.

mucky *adj.* MUDDY.

mud *n.* **1** mire, muck, ooze, slime, dirt. **2** mudslinging, smear, slander, vilification, defamation, muckraking, character assassination, name-calling, libel, scandal, dirt.

muddle *v.* **1** jumble, mess up, muss, ruffle, scramble, disorder, disarrange, tangle, entangle, upset, disorganize, pi. **2** bewilder, confuse, addle, bemuse, disorient, mix up, fuddle, befuddle, perplex, puzzle, rattle, unsettle, unhinge. **3** muddy, roil, stir up, disturb. **4** bungle, botch, mismanage, spoil, muff, make a mess of, fumble, flounder, bumble, foul up (*Slang*), louse up (*Slang*). —*n.* **1** jumble, mess, confusion, tangle, snarl, disorder, chaos, complication, predicament, quandary, mix-up, foul-up (*Slang*), snafu (*Slang*). **2** befuddlement, bewilderment, perplexity, disorientation, fog, fix, bind, uncertainty, discomposure, discomfiture.
ant. *v.* **1** neaten, straighten out, arrange, organize. **2** clarify, solve, re-

solve, elucidate, simplify. **3** clarify, clear, sift. **4** carry off, carry through, cope, succeed. *n.* **1** order, neatness, organization, arrangement. **2** clarity, clear-headedness, perspicacity, keenness.

muddy *adj.* **1** bemired, bespattered, boggy, mucky, muddied, messy, dirty, swampy, marshy, slushy, miry, sodden. **2** confused, unclear, disordered, bewildered, vague, fuzzy, muddled, muddle-headed, perplexed, baffled, disorderly. —*v.* confuse, muddle, mess up, disorder, mix up, becloud, bedim, befuddle, ruffle, disorient, obscure.

ant. *adj.* **2** clear, lucid, organized, orderly, understandable. *v.* clear up, clarify, elucidate.

mudslinging *n.* ASPERSION.

muff *v.* blunder, bungle, botch, fumble, boggle, flounder, fail, miss, lose out, mismanage, miscalculate, foul up (*Slang*).

ant. carry off, bring off, succeed, come through.

muffle *v.* **1** wrap, swathe, envelop, cover, drape, conceal, shroud, veil, hide, disguise, mask, enfold, swaddle. **2** hush, tone down, quiet, deaden, suppress, stifle, silence, gag, mute, dampen, cushion, soft-pedal, drown out.

ant. **1** unwrap, uncover, reveal, lay bare. **2** heighten, brighten, accent, soup up (*Slang*).

muffler *n.* scarf, shawl, tippet, boa, stole, stock, comforter.

mug *n.* **1** stein, tankard, toby, cup, goblet, stoup, flagon. **2** *Slang* FACE. —*v.* **1** assault, set upon, attack, strong-arm, beset, rob, hold up. **2** *Slang* make faces, grimace, mime, overact, show off, clown around, sport, horse around, ham (*Slang*), ham it up (*Slang*).

mugging *n.* assault, attack, robbery, beating, battery, hold-up, stick-up (*Slang*).

muggy *adj.* humid, damp, sticky, sultry, stuffy, clammy, oppressive, close, steamy.

ant. fresh, breezy, airy, dry, pleasant.

mulct *v.* **1** fine, amerce, assess, penalize, punish. **2** defraud, cheat, exploit, milk, rook, dupe, swindle, fleece, bilk, skin, take (*Slang*), rip off (*Slang*).

mulish *adj.* stubborn, recalcitrant, obstinate, refractory, perverse, unreasonable, balky, ungovernable, willful, pig-headed, rigid, inflexible, ornery, unaccommodating, unyielding, uncooperative.

ant. accommodating, reasonable, obedient, yielding, complaisant, flexible.

mull over ponder, cogitate, think about, consider, examine, reflect, study, chew, ruminate, meditate, deliberate, weigh, pore over.

multifarious *adj.* diversified, heterogeneous, manifold, variegated, varied, protean, motley, miscellaneous, mixed, multiple, multiplex, diverse, multiform.

ant. uniform, homogeneous, solid, pure, unmixed.

multifold *adj.* MANIFOLD.

multiform *adj.* MULTIFARIOUS.

multiple *adj.* many, manifold, multiplex, plural, divers, sundry, numerous, multitudinous, several, assorted, variable, varied.

ant. single, sole, only, singular.

multiplex *adj.* MULTIPLE.

multiply *v.* increase, propagate, grow, augment, extend, spread, proliferate, amplify, swell, burgeon, expand, mushroom, soar.

ant. decrease, diminish, lessen, dwindle, drop.

multitude *n.* crowd, mass, horde, throng, mob, assemblage, press, crush, flock, sea, army, legion, troop.

multitudinous *adj.* NUMEROUS.

mum *adj.* silent, mute, dumb, quiet, still, uncommunicative, tight-lipped, tongue-tied, secretive, closemouthed, taciturn.

ant. talkative, voluble, effusive, informative.

mumble *v.* mutter, murmur, hem and haw, grunt, stammer, grumble, hesitate, drone, rumble, falter, whisper, swallow one's words. —*n.* mutter, murmur, grunt, grumble, stammer, drone, rumble.

ant. *v.* speak up, articulate, communicate. *n.* clarity, eloquence, articulation.

mumbo jumbo gobbledygook, doublespeak, abracadabra, rigmarole, obscurantism, hocus pocus, nonsense, humbug, flummery, sophistry, cant, gibberish, double talk, obfuscation.

ant. sense, meaning, directness, straightforwardness.

munch *v.* chew, crunch, chomp, champ, gnaw, grind, masticate, ruminate, bite.

mundane *adj.* **1** ordinary, practical, everyday, usual, regular, humdrum, day-to-day, common, commonplace, habitual, routine, pedestrian, accustomed. **2** earthly, worldly, temporal, mortal, terrestrial, secular, human.

ant. **1** extraordinary, unusual, rare, special. **2** immortal, spiritual, divine, eternal.

munificent *adj.* generous, bountiful, liberal, open-handed, lavish, prodigal, princely, extravagant, philanthropic, unstinting, magnanimous.

ant. stingy, mean, grudging, tightfisted.

munitions *n.* materiel, arms, armaments, ammunition, ordnance, guns, weapons, ammo (*Slang*).

murder *v.* kill, slay, assassinate, slaughter, massacre, execute, butcher, mow down, do in, finish off, annihilate, wipe out, rub out (*Slang*), erase (*Slang*).

murderous *adj.* **1** homicidal, slaughterous, deadly, internecine, fatal, lethal, poisonous, mortal, deathly. **2** ferocious, violent, frenzied, bloodthirsty, sanguinary, raging, wild, maniacal, menacing, venomous, savage, barbarous, brutal.

murky *adj.* **1** obscure, arcane, ambiguous, esoteric, perplexing, unclear, nebulous, mystifying, obfuscated, impenetrable, veiled, inscrutable, unplumbed. **2** misty, hazy, foggy, cloudy, overcast, dim, gray, sunless, cheerless, dismal, dreary, lowering.

ant. **1** obvious, plain, explicit, distinct, straightforward. **2** sunny, bright, clear, brilliant, radiant, cloudless.

murmur *n.* drone, buzz, susurrus, susurration, rustle, purr, sigh, sough, swish, purl. —*v.* hum, drone, buzz, bombinate, rustle, whisper, purr, swish, purl, sigh, sough.

muscle *n.* **1** strength, brawn, prowess, robustness, power, heft, muscularity, endurance, fitness, vigor, stamina, sturdiness, might, vim. **2** force, power, effectiveness, potency, forcefulness, authority, weight, influence, impact, clout (*Slang*). —*v.* elbow, shove, push, butt, batter, shoulder, poke, jostle, ram, trample, crowd, squeeze, ride roughshod.

ant. *n.* **1** flabbiness, frailty, debility, decrepitude, flaccidity, flab. **2** ineffectuality, powerlessness, helplessness, impotence.

muscular *adj.* powerful, strong, brawny, fit, well-developed, robust, sturdy, sinewy, athletic, burly, strapping, husky, limber, vigorous.

ant. flabby, weak, flaccid, frail, soft.

muse *v.* ponder, meditate, reflect, deliberate, cogitate, dream, daydream, ruminate, puzzle over, review, imagine, mull over, contemplate, speculate, consider.

museum *n.* institute, gallery, repository, exhibition hall, exposition hall, treasure house, collection.

mush *n.* **1** mash, pap, pulp, paste, squash, semifluid, semisolid, semiliquid. **2** sentimentality, sentimentalism, mawkishness, bathos, melodramatics, gush, slush, goo, schmaltz (*Slang*), corn (*Slang*).

mushroom *v.* spread, grow, take over, multiply, shoot up, crop up, spring up, proliferate, abound, flourish, burgeon, pullulate.

mushy *adj.* SENTIMENTAL.

music *n.* harmony, melody, tunefulness, lyricism, melodiousness, strain, air, lilt, refrain, cadence, euphony.
ant. noise, cacophony, discordance, dissonance.

musical *adj.* harmonious, melodious, tuneful, lyrical, lilting, cadenced, euphonious, mellifluent.
ant. discordant, cacophonous, dissonant, shrill, noisy.

musing *adj.* THOUGHTFUL.

muss *v.* mess, rumple, disorder, crease, disarrange, dishevel, disturb, tousle, crumple, jumble, bedraggle. —*n.* MESS.
ant. *v.* neaten, straighten, tidy, arrange, smooth.

mussy *adj.* messy, disarranged, rumpled, disordered, disheveled, disturbed, tousled, crumpled, creased, jumbled, bedraggled, lumpy, uneven.
ant. neat, tidy, arranged, even, starched.

must *n.* essential, requirement, indispensable, basic, emergency, fundamental, requisite, obligation, necessity, duty, necessary, responsibility, commitment, urgency, ultimatum. —*adj.* essential, required, indispensable, basic, exigent, necessary, fundamental, obligatory, requisite, imperative, mandatory, compulsory, important, compelling.

muster *v.* **1** assemble, summon, mobilize, call, gather, line up, convene, marshal, convocate, round up, rally. **2** brace, arm, nerve, steel, dredge up, summon up, invoke, brave, face. —*n.* turnout, assemblage, gathering, lineup, roundup, rally, congregation, convocation, parade, review, roll call, body, mobilization.
ant. *v.* **1** disperse, scatter, fall out, withdraw.

musty *adj.* **1** moldy, stale, rotting, rotten, decayed, decaying, mildewed, rancid, tainted, putrescent, airless,

dank, foul, funky. **2** trite, dull, motheaten, lifeless, obsolete, hackneyed, worn-out, threadbare, vapid, dry, colorless.
ant. **1** fresh, pure, sweet, refreshing. **2** lively, new, original, exciting, now.

mutable *adj.* **1** variable, changeable, flexible, alterable, adjustable, adaptable, versatile, kaleidoscopic, mercurial, volatile, metamorphic, transformable, pliable. **2** fickle, unstable, inconstant, unreliable, erratic, unpredictable, irresponsible, undependable, wayward, capricious, flighty, inconsistent, fitful, unsteady.
ant. **1** rigid, inflexible, immutable, unalterable. **2** dependable, reliable, predictable, steadfast, firm, stable.

mute *adj.* silent, dumb, wordless, soundless, mum, speechless, voiceless, tongue-tied, aphasic, aphonic, uncommunicative, pantomimic. —*v.* muffle, damp, dampen, soften, lower, deaden, dull, moderate, hush, drown, tone down, soft-pedal.
ant. *adj.* voiced, sounded, spoken, talkative, audible. *v.* amplify, heighten, brighten, raise, intensify.

mutilate *v.* **1** maim, amputate, castrate, mangle, dismember, disfigure, cripple, lame, deform. **2** spoil, botch, damage, impair, destroy, devitalize, demolish, truncate, hack up, butcher, wreck, make mincemeat of.

mutineer *v.* MUTINY.

mutinous *adj.* seditious, revolutionary, insurrectionary, insurgent, insubordinate, rebellious, unruly, defiant, intractable, ungovernable, turbulent, riotous.
ant. obedient, compliant, submissive, acquiescent.

mutiny *n.* rebellion, revolt, uprising, insurrection, insurgency, insubordination, upheaval, takeover, strike, coup. —*v.* mutineer, revolt, rebel, riot, strike, sabotage, disobey.

mutt *n.* mongrel, cur.
ant. purebreed.

mutter *v.* **1** mumble, growl, sputter, grunt, whisper, murmur, rumble. **2**

complain, grumble, grouse, grouch, disapprove, gripe, carp, deplore, resent, criticize.

mutual *adj.* reciprocal, reciprocated, shared, common, similar, joint, interchangeable, interdependent, communal, interrelated, equivalent, cooperative.

ant. exclusive, sole, singular, unique.

muzzle *v.* suppress, restrain, stifle, gag, squelch, curb, throttle, silence, censor, strangle, crush, hogtie, hamstring.

ant. free, liberate, loose, disencumber.

myopia *n.* shortsightedness, nearsightedness, obtuseness, stupidity, blindness, incomprehension, insensibility, fatuity, foolishness, folly, inanity.

ant. insight, intelligence, awareness, acuteness.

myriad *n.* multitude, infinity, infinitude, army, sea, swarm, host, profusion.

mysterious *adj.* inexplicable, puzzling, baffling, inscrutable, unexplained, unfathomable, weird, uncanny, arcane, enigmatic, perplexing, occult, mystical, hidden.

ant. obvious, clear, reasonable, patent.

mystery *n.* **1** puzzle, enigma, riddle, perplexity, quandary, unknown, question mark. **2** secrecy, obscurity, opacity, concealment, unfathomability, impenetrability, inscrutability, inexplicableness.

ant. 1 solution, answer, open book.

mystic *adj.* **1** occult, arcane, esoteric, ritualistic, cabalistic, mystical, antirational, magic, magical, oracular,

shamanistic. **2** mysterious, mystifying, eerie, spooky, weird, unfathomable, inscrutable, unknowable, impenetrable, veiled, shrouded, sphinxlike.

ant. 1 rational, logical, scientific, rationalist, pragmatic. **2** obvious, clear, overt, manifest, straightforward.

mystical *adj.* inexplicable, intuitive, nonrational, irrational, spiritual, numinous, instinctive, unjustifiable, inspirational, transcendental, metaphysical, inscrutable, inner.

ant. reasonable, logical, demonstrable.

mystify *v.* confuse, perplex, mislead, bewilder, deceive, confound, misrepresent, hoodwink, stump, nonplus, buffalo (*Slang*), flummox (*Slang*).

ant. clarify, enlighten, illuminate, explain.

mystifying *adj.* recondite, obscure, mysterious, arcane, enigmatic, ambiguous, abstruse, unclear, baffling, difficult, complex.

ant. obvious, direct, clear, simple, unambiguous.

mystique *n.* charisma, aura, quality, spirit, ambiance, appeal, magic, glamour, glory, cult, awe, veneration, cultishness.

myth *n.* **1** legend, story, allegory, folk tale, fable. **2** untruth, fiction, error, nonsense, foolishness, pretense, fallacy, misconception, inaccuracy, absurdity, superstition.

mythical *adj.* imaginary, fictitious, imagined, unreal, fantastic, untrue, chimerical, illusory, fanciful, nonexistent, invented.

ant. real, factual, actual, true, palpable.

N

nab *v.* arrest, apprehend, pinch (*Slang*), catch, capture, collar, seize, snatch, trap, grab, snag, snare.

ant. set free, let go, release, loose, liberate.

nabob *n.* millionaire, multimillionaire,

billionaire, Croesus, moneybags (*Slang*), *nouveau riche,* coupon clipper, nawab.

nadir *n.* base, foundation, bedrock, floor, bottom, foot, minimum, root, zero, nothing.

ant. zenith, acme, apex, pinnacle, summit.

nag[1] *v.* torment, harass, pester, harry, berate, hector, badger, heckle, importune, irritate, annoy, vex, henpeck, carp, harp. —*n.* scold, pest, *kvetch,* nuisance, complainer, hector, shrew, virago, hag, termagant, vixen, battleax (*Slang*).

nag[2] *n.* *old horse:* hack, jade, tit, plug, dobbin.

nagging *adj.* persistent, tenacious, continual, continuous, constant, steady, stubborn, repeated.

ant. sporadic, occasional, infrequent, rare, uncommon.

naif *adj.* NAIVE.

nail *n.* fingernail, claw, talon, hoof, unguis.

naive *adj.* unsophisticated, simple, ingenuous, natural, unaffected, unsuspecting, artless, guileless, innocent, candid, frank, open, plain, fresh, amateurish, naif.

ant. sophisticated, disingenuous, artful, calculating, worldly-wise.

naiveté *n.* simplicity, ingenuousness, naturalness, artlessness, unaffectedness, candor, sincerity, frankness, openness, innocence, greenness, inexperience, childishness, naivety.

ant. sophistication, artfulness, experience, urbanity, savoir faire.

naivety *n.* NAIVETÉ.

naked *adj.* 1 bare, nude, unclothed, undressed, uncovered, stripped, unclad, in the altogether, in the raw. 2 defenseless, unprotected, exposed, unguarded, unarmed, vulnerable, pregnable, powerless, helpless, unsafe, precarious.

ant. 1 clothed, dressed, clad, covered. 2 protected, guarded, shielded, impregnable.

namby-pamby *adj.* wishy-washy,

vapid, insipid, dull, insubstantial, mawkish, jejune, sentimental, mediocre, simpering, weak, thin, mushy.

name *n.* 1 appellation, title, tag, label, designation, cognomen, nickname, moniker (*Slang*), sobriquet, epithet. 2 reputation, repute, character, credit, fame, worth, note, esteem, distinction, renown, eminence, honor, praise. —*v.* 1 call, dub, label, denominate, title, entitle, characterize, cite, term, style, christen, baptize, nickname. 2 cite, specify, indicate, nominate, mention, designate, identify, set, label, characterize, commission, delegate, ordain, authorize.

nap[1] *n.* sleep, doze, snooze, siesta, wink, forty winks, drowse, nod, catnap. —*v.* sleep, doze, snooze, drowse, nod, drop off, catnap, catch forty winks.

nap[2] *n.* pile, shag, fuzz, fluff, hair, bristle, down.

nappy *adj.* shaggy, velvety, downy, hairy, woolly, fleecy, rough, velutinous.

narcissist *n.* EGOTIST.

narcotic *adj.* soporific, hypnotic, sleep-inducing, somniferous, sedative, opiate, somnolent.

narrate *v.* tell, describe, relate, recount, detail, report, recite, chronicle, repeat, recapitulate, retell, portray, set forth.

narration *n.* 1 writing, storytelling, chronicling, emceeing, recounting, recital, description. 2 NARRATIVE.

narrative *n.* story, account, recital, history, chronicle, tale, description, anecdote, report, yarn, saga, narration.

narrator *n.* author, writer, storyteller, tale-teller, storywriter, raconteur, relater, emcee, anecdotist, chronicler, annalist, romancer, fabulist.

narrow *adj.* 1 slender, slim, thin, tight, tapered, threadlike, fine, spare, slight. 2 limited, close, circumscribed, contracted, confined, confining, pent, shrunken, cramped, incapacious, restricted, pinched. 3

bigoted, illiberal, narrow-minded, small-minded, small, biased, partial, prejudiced, intolerant, petty.

ant. 1 wide, fat, thick, broad. **2** capacious, roomy, ample, spacious. **3** liberal, broad-minded, open-minded, tolerant.

narrow-minded *adj.* prejudiced, bigoted, biased, intolerant, illiberal, small, small-minded, short-sighted, partial, partisan, petty, sectarian, provincial, hidebound, opinionated, arbitrary, little.

ant. liberal, broad-minded, tolerant, unprejudiced.

nascent *adj.* beginning, commencing, forming, prime, primal, primitive, aboriginal, introductory, incipient, emerging, dawning, rudimentary, elementary, embryonic, developing, inchoate.

ant. dying, passing, ceasing, waning, terminating, ending.

nasty *adj.* **1** filthy, disgusting, dirty, foul, unclean, loathsome, impure, defiled, polluted, nauseous, slimy, soiled. **2** immoral, indecent, sordid, obscene, smutty, indelicate, gross, profligate, ribald, lewd, licentious, pornographic, immodest. **3** ill-natured, mean, bad-tempered, vicious, spiteful, ugly, disagreeable, unpleasant, hateful, snotty (*Slang*).

ant. 1 clean, pure, unsoiled, spotless. **2** moral, pure, virtuous, decent. **3** pleasant, good-natured, good-tempered, amiable.

nation *n.* **1** country, state, realm, community, commonwealth, commonweal, land, domain, dominion, city-state, polis, polity. **2** race, tribe, ethnic group, people, stock, population.

nation-wide *adj.* country-wide, national, coast-to-coast.

native *adj.* **1** indigenous, autochthonous, endemic, original, native-born, aboriginal, natural, domestic, local. **2** NATURAL. —*n.* citizen, countryman, inhabitant, dweller, aborigine, autochthon.

ant. *adj.* **1** imported, alien, foreign. *n.* foreigner, alien, immigrant.

native-born *adj.* NATIVE.

nativity *n.* BIRTH.

natty *adj.* smart, spruce, tidy, trim, sharp, chic, well-dressed, well-turned-out, well-tailored, dapper, foppish.

natural *adj.* **1** inborn, native, inherent, inbred, intrinsic, incarnate, ingrained, congenital, born, hereditary, instinctive, normal, implanted, genetic. **2** instinctive, intuitive, automatic, unaffected, artless, unstudied, impulsive, ingenuous, straightforward, blunt, frank, direct, candid, matter-of-fact. —*n.* IDIOT.

ant. *adj.* **1** extraneous, incidental, extrinsic. **2** studied, guarded, purposeful, disingenuous, subtle.

naturally *adv.* simply, normally, informally, intuitively, spontaneously, unaffectedly, unassumedly, genuinely, unpretentiously, honestly, sincerely, frankly, candidly.

ant. strangely, affectedly, studiedly, pretentiously, disingenuously.

nature *n.* **1** essence, character, qualities, attributes, features, traits, properties, identity, constitution. **2** kind, sort, character, type, species, genus, quality, stamp, cast, stripe, color, kidney, style, brand, designation, mold. **3** disposition, character, temperament, temper, spirit, frame of mind, personality, makeup, traits, humor.

naught *n.* nothing, zero, cipher, nil, null, nought, goose egg (*Slang*), zilch (*Slang*).

naughty *adj.* disobedient, wayward, contrary, perverse, disrespectful, mischievous, bad, wanton, wicked, recalcitrant, stubborn, unmanageable, obstinate, perverse.

ant. obedient, good, dutiful, governable, compliant.

nausea *n.* queasiness, motion sickness, car sickness, seasickness, sickness, throwing up, vomiting, retching, heaving, emesis, upset stomach, squeamishness, biliousness.

nauseate *v.* sicken, revolt, disgust, turn one's stomach, repel, offend, repulse.

nauseated *adj.* queasy, sick, sickened, ill, unwell, disgusted, repelled, squeamish, qualmish, qualmy, nauseous.

nauseating *adj.* NAUSEOUS.

nauseous *adj.* **1** nauseating, emetic, disgusting, revolting, offensive, repulsive, sickening, loathsome, nasty, repellent, abhorrent. **2** NAUSEATED.

nautical *adj.* marine, maritime, naval.

naval *adj.* NAUTICAL.

navigate *v.* steer, manage, guide, control, direct, conduct, pilot, convey.

navy *n.* fleet, flotilla, task force, armada.

nawab *n.* NABOB.

near *adj.* **1** close, nigh, nearby, at hand, adjacent, touching, contiguous, proximal, proximate, bordering, adjoining, abutting. **2** related, connected, familiar, intimate, attached, allied, close, devoted, friendly. —*v.* approach, move toward, draw near to, advance on, make for, close in on, steer for, head for.

nearby *adj.* near, at hand, close by, adjacent, next, immediate, nigh, handy, convenient.

nearly *adv.* almost, well-nigh, just about, approximately, all but, for the most part, close to, roughly.

nearness *n.* proximity, closeness, vicinity, contiguity, propinquity, approximation, neighborhood.

nearsighted *adj.* myopic, shortsighted.

neat *adj.* **1** orderly, ordered, clean, immaculate, tidy, spruce, trim, smart, nice, methodical, correct, uniform, shipshape, spick-and-span. **2** clever, adroit, sharp, deft, effective, ingenious, apt, handy, dexterous, skillful, competent, capable. *ant.* **1** slovenly, sloppy, unkempt, disorderly. **2** awkward, clumsy, inept, unskillful, ineffectual.

nebulous *adj.* indistinct, hazy, vague, unclear, confused, indefinite, cloudy, ambiguous, obscure, dark, murky, indeterminate, dim, mixed-up. *ant.* distinct, clear, discernible, obvious, definite.

necessaries *n.* essentials, needs, requirements, necessities, basics, fundamentals, exigencies.

necessary *adj.* **1** unavoidable, inevitable, inexorable, necessitous, ineluctable, inescapable, unpreventable, irresistible, fated, certain. **2** essential, required, indispensable, needed, needful, requisite, *de rigueur,* obligatory, vital, compulsory, imperative, exigent, central, basic, principal. *ant.* **2** unnecessary, dispensable, unessential, unrequired, peripheral.

necessitous *adj.* needy, destitute, poverty-stricken, poor, impecunious, out of pocket, insolvent, bankrupt, impoverished, penurious, indigent, broke, hard up, strapped. *ant.* rich, well-off, in the chips, well-to-do, wealthy.

necessity *n.* **1** requirement, demand, requisite, essential, necessary, want, *sine qua non,* prerequisite, requirement, exigency. **2** needfulness, indispensability, need, essentiality, requirement, demand, want, exigency, lack, deficiency. *ant.* **2** dispensability, superfluity, redundancy, abundance, plenitude.

neck of the woods NEIGHBORHOOD.

need *v.* require, want, lack, call for, necessitate, crave, demand, covet, hunger for. —*n.* lack, want, necessity, demand, needfulness, exigency, urgency, emergency, shortcoming, deficiency, requirement.

needful *adj.* needed, necessary, required, indispensable, essential, irreplaceable, vital, requisite, prerequisite, demanded. *ant.* unnecessary, dispensable, unessential, nonessential, superfluous.

needle *v.* heckle, goad, provoke, prod, tease, bait, badger, harass, hector, taunt, jeer, challenge.

needless *adj.* useless, unneeded, unnecessary, superfluous, redundant, excessive, useless, unessential, nonessential, purposeless, repetitious.

ant. useful, needed, necessary, essential, required.

needy *adj.* poor, destitute, impoverished, indigent, poverty-stricken, necessitous, in want, beggarly, penniless, insolvent, moneyless, bankrupt, broke, strapped.

ant. rich, prosperous, in the chips, wealthy, well-off.

ne'er-do-well *n.* good-for-nothing, wastrel, black sheep, loser, idler, loafer, bum.

nefarious *adj.* heinous, wicked, atrocious, flagrant, infamous, villainous, iniquitous, abominable, detestable, horrible, flagitious, base, vile, dreadful, horrendous, sinister, vicious.

ant. virtuous, good, noble, honest, exalted.

negate *v.* nullify, abrogate, void, cancel, revoke, neutralize, disallow.

negation *n.* nullity, nonentity, nonexistence, nothingness, vacuity, blank, void, obscurity.

negative *adj.* contradictory, contrary, converse, opposite, reverse, contrasting, inverse, conflicting, opposed, clashing, inimical, antagonistic, inconsistent. —*n.* **1** no, not, nix (*Slang*), nay, by no means. **2** opposite, contra, converse, reverse, antithesis, other side of the coin, *vis-à-vis*, the contrary, counter. —*v.* DENY.

ant. *adj.* positive, affirmative, similar, in agreement. *n.* **1** yes, affirmative, check. **2** same, positive.

neglect *v.* ignore, disregard, slight, overlook, omit, forget, let ride, leave alone, blink at, wink at, pass over, pass up, pass by, take no notice of, let slip, let go, skimp, shirk, gloss over. —*n.* oversight, forgetfulness, neglectfulness, inattention, inaction, procrastination, disregard, omission, indolence, laxity, laxness, slackness, evasion, negligence, dereliction, remissness, carelessness, heedlessness, indifference.

ant. *v.* regard, attend, mind, notice, care for. *n.* regard, attention, care, notice, mindfulness.

neglectful *adj.* remiss, disregardful, careless, negligent, inattentive, heedless, thoughtless, indifferent, uncaring, slack, sloppy, lax, uncaring, indolent, evasive.

ant. regardful, attentive, thoughtful, careful, mindful.

negligence *n.* neglect, disregard, omission, inattention, indifference, heedlessness, remissness, carelessness, inattentiveness.

ant. thoughtfulness, alertness, carefulness, regard, attention.

negligent *adj.* neglectful, careless, inattentive, thoughtless, remiss, unmindful, heedless, slack, lax, unwatchful, indifferent, inconsiderate.

ant. regardful, attentive, careful, considerate, thoughtful.

negligible *adj.* inconsiderable, minor, minute, inappreciable, nominal, meager, modest, slight, small, unimportant, petty, trifling, piddling.

ant. large, considerable, appreciable, goodly, sizable.

negotiate *v.* **1** bargain, arrange, settle, mediate, intercede, intervene, interpose, arbitrate, parley, confer, dicker, umpire, haggle, compromise, meet halfway. **2** surmount, cross, pass through, hurdle, overleap, clear, engineer.

neigh *v.* whinny, nicker.

neighborhood *n.* vicinity, precincts, environs, environment, region, surroundings, locale, locality, place, area, section, community, neck of the woods.

nemesis *n.* retribution, retaliation, vengeance, revenge, punishment, justice, an eye for an eye, deserts.

neophyte *n.* beginner, novice, novitiate, amateur, tyro, trainee, greenhorn, rookie, tenderfoot, recruit, apprentice, pupil, student.

ant. old hand, expert, authority,

adept, past master, crackerjack (*Slang*).

nepotism *n.* favoritism, partisanship, patronage, bias, partiality, prejudice, discrimination.

ant. fairness, equity, equality, impartiality, justice.

nerve *n.* **1** *Slang* effrontery, boldness, brazenness, impudence, temerity, gall, cheek, crust, insolence, brass. **2** fearlessness, courage, bravery, firmness, fortitude, resolution, resoluteness, endurance, pluck, boldness, daring, grit.

ant. 1 shyness, modesty, reserve, bashfulness. **2** cowardice, timidity, faintheartedness, fearfulness.

nerveless *adj.* **1** FEEBLE. **2** IMPERTURBABLE.

nerve-racking *adj.* irritating, exasperating, trying, jarring, grating, nettlesome, vexing, annoying, rankling, galling, maddening, harassing.

nervous *adj.* excitable, high-strung, tense, uneasy, edgy, restless, neurotic, strained, jumpy, skittish, disquieted, anxious, fidgety, jittery.

ant. relaxed, calm, serene, cool, in control.

nervy *adj. Slang* brazen, impudent, bold, brash, cheeky, brassy, insulting, saucy, cocky, fresh, presumptuous.

ant. unassuming, polite, gracious, modest, shy.

nescience *n.* IGNORANCE.

nest *n.* retreat, hideaway, den, haunt, resort, hangout, stamping ground, snuggery (*Brit.*), refuge, sanctuary, purlieu, hermitage, cloister.

nestle *v.* snuggle, cuddle, nuzzle, settle, settle down, snug.

net[1] *n.* netting, mesh, network, meshwork, seine, toils, trawl, trammel. —*v.* snare, ensnare, enmesh, trap, entrap, catch, capture, take captive, take, seize, bag, grab, snag, entangle.

net[2] *n.* yield, proceeds, gains, profit, earnings, winnings, returns. —*v.* profit, realize, clear, return, gain, pocket, earn, pay, reap, clean up, make, win.

nether *adj.* lowest, lower, under, bottom, inferior, bottommost, underlying, basal, nethermost.

netting *n.* NET.[1]

nettle *v.* annoy, irritate, bother, vex, beset, harass, exasperate, irk, harry, chafe, prickle, sting, bait, get one's goat, grate, gall, burn up.

nettlesome *adj.* VEXATIOUS.

network *n.* complex, maze, interlacing, labyrinth, plexus, filigree, grid, gridiron, web, mesh, crisscross, reticulum, reticulation.

neuter *adj.* sexless, asexual, neutral.

neutral *adj.* **1** uninvolved, impartial, unbiased, evenhanded, unaligned, nonaligned, uncommitted, unprejudiced, nonpartisan, disinterested, aloof, detached, remote. **2** indifferent, intermediate, middling, indefinite, uncertain, indeterminate, undefined, indistinct, indecisive, unformed.

ant. 1 partisan, biased, prejudiced, aligned, committed. **2** definite, distinct, determined, well-defined, decisive.

neutralize *v.* counterbalance, balance, offset, set off, counteract, counterpoise, nullify, cancel, negate, dilute, compensate for.

nevertheless *conj., adv.* nonetheless, however, yet, in spite of, on the other hand, anyway, anyhow, notwithstanding, just the same, still, in any event, after all, regardless.

new *adj.* **1** up-to-date, up-to-the-minute, fashionable, recent, modern, modernistic, latest, current, novel, fresh, green, maiden, virgin, spanking, new-fangled, brand-new. **2** renewed, recurring, renascent, reborn, recreated, modernized, refreshed, reconstructed, refurbished, rebuilt, remodeled, revived, restored. **3** unfamiliar, unknown, unheard-of, unprecedented, uncharted, unexplored, remote, unexampled, untried, recent.

4 more, additional, added, further, fresh, extra, supplementary, spare.
ant. 1 old, stale, used, old-fashioned, dated, obsolete. **3** tried-and-true, familiar, well-charted.

newborn *n.* infant, baby, suckling, nursling, weanling, cub, whelp, neonate.

new-fangled *adj.* NEW.

news *n.* information, intelligence, report, tidings, data, dispatch, message, copy, story, article, announcement, bulletin, flash, release, communiqué, account.

next *adv.* subsequently, consequently, thereafter, whereupon, whereafter, from that time, after that time, at a later time, since, later, following, ensuing, successively, closely, from that moment.

nexus *n.* link, tie, bond, bind, connection, interconnection, association, yoke, knot, relationship, kinship, liaison.

nib *n.* **1** tip, point, peak. **2** beak, neb, bill, pecker, rostrum.

nibble *v.* nip, bite, chew, crunch, munch, peck.

nice *adj.* **1** pleasant, pleasing, agreeable, delightful, enjoyable, satisfying, desirable. **2** good, kindly, friendly, warm, amiable, pleasant, winning, gracious, cordial, genial, charming. **3** precise, exact, accurate, skilled, fastidious, exacting, critical, scrupulous, strict, rigorous, demanding, discerning, discriminating, subtle, fine, refined, delicate. **4** refined, elegant, proper, exquisite, fastidious, correct, formal, cultured, cultivated, polished.
ant. 1 disagreeable, unpleasant, undesirable. **2** unkind, cold, distant. **3** uncritical, inaccurate, unrefined. **4** gauche, boorish, rough.

nicety *n.* exactness, accuracy, subtlety, particularity, discrimination, precision, correctness, meticulousness, rigor, fastidiousness.
ant. sloppiness, inaccuracy, imprecision, carelessness.

niche *n.* **1** recess, hollow, nook, opening, hole, cavity, cranny, corner. **2** position, place, slot, cubbyhole, pigeonhole.

nick *n.* notch, cut, dent, indentation, scratch, scoring, score, gash, mark, marking, mar, jag, incision, scar. —*v.* notch, cut, dent, indent, injure, scar, scarify, damage, mark, mar, gash, scratch.

nicker *v.* NEIGH.

nicknack *n.* KNICKKNACK.

nickname *n.* sobriquet, cognomen, agnomen, appellation, handle, epithet, diminutive, designation.

nictitate *v.* BLINK.

nifty *adj.* *Slang* EXCELLENT.

niggard *n.* MISER.

niggardly *adj.* **1** stingy, parsimonious, miserly, penurious, tightfisted, closefisted, mean, small, cheap, mercenary, avaricious, niggard, stinting, ungenerous, frugal, grudging. **2** scanty, measly, niggard, spare, paltry, insufficient, inadequate, pitiful, small, miserable, lean, beggarly.
ant. 1 generous, unstinting, charitable, openhanded, munificent. **2** abundant, profuse, overflowing, plentiful, plenteous.

niggling *adj.* finicky, fussy, fastidious, pettifogging, quibbling, caviling, picayune, trifling, small, petty, piddling, nit-picking, finicking.

nigh *adj.* NEAR.

night *n.* nighttime, nightfall, evening, eventide, dark, darkness, sundown, bedtime.
ant. day, daytime, daylight, daybreak, dawn.

nightfall *n.* NIGHT.

nightmare *n.* ordeal, tribulation, trouble, calamity, tragedy, trial, horror, torment, purgatory, hell.

nighttime *n.* NIGHT.

nil *n.* nothing, null, zero, naught, cipher, negation, nullity, zip (*Slang*), goose egg (*Slang*), zilch (*Slang*).

nimble *adj.* spry, lively, agile, sprightly, lithe, brisk, quick, light, light-footed,

lissome, limber, lithesome, lightsome, spirited, fleet, fast, swift.
ant. clumsy, plodding, slow, heavy, fumbling.

nincompoop *n.* numskull, blockhead, muddlehead, imbecile, simpleton, dolt, nitwit, moron, fool, ninny, jackass, idiot, dunce, boob (*Slang*), fathead (*Slang*), jerk (*Slang*), noodle (*Slang*).

ninny *n.* NINCOMPOOP.

nip[1] *v.* **1** bite, pinch, compress, squeeze, press, clamp, tweak, grip. **2** cut, check, truncate, shorten, clip, lop, curtail, discourage, destroy, prevent, thwart, frustrate.
ant. 2 encourage, feed, foster, further, promote, advance.

nip[2] *n.* sip, drop, swallow, taste, swig, dram, mouthful, sample, soupçon.

nipping *adj.* NIPPY.

nipple *n.* teat, tit, udder, pap, papilla, breast, dug.

nippy *adj.* chilly, biting, cool, cold, frosty, chilling, sharp, cutting, wintry, crisp, raw, snappy, bitter, piercing, penetrating, nipping.
ant. balmy, pleasant, warm, mild, temperate.

nirvana *n.* tranquillity, serenity, peace, joy, heaven, bliss, paradise, happiness, ecstasy, oblivion.
ant. torment, conflict, anguish, suffering.

nite *n.* NIGHT.

nit-picker *n.* perfectionist, precisionist, purist, pettifogger, pedant, quibbler, caviler, hair-splitter, fussbudget, fusspot (*Slang*).

nit-picking *adj.* finicky, fussy, captious, hypercritical, overprecise, overscrupulous, demanding, pedantic, pettifogging, hair-splitting, quibbling.
ant. easygoing, uncritical, undemanding, careless, slipshod.

nitty-gritty *n. Slang* fundamentals, basics, essentials, essence, core, hard core, heart of the matter, brass tacks, bedrock, bottom line (*Slang*).
ant. superficialities, unessentials, surface, irrelevancies.

nitwit *n.* fool, clown, muddlehead, simpleton, nincompoop, halfwit, numskull, jackass, dummy, moron, clod, imbecile, idiot, dolt, dunce, jerk (*Slang*).

nix *Slang v.* veto, forbid, prohibit, taboo, deny, ban, cancel, interdict, negate, reject. —*n.* NO.
ant. *v.* agree to, sanction, permit, allow, go along with.

no *n.* negation, denial, refusal, noncompliance, veto, thumbs down, nix (*Slang*).
ant. yes, affirmation, agreement, assent, compliance.

nobility *n.* **1** grandeur, majesty, loftiness, preeminence, rank, exaltation, eminence, prestige, prominence, stateliness, magnificence, peerage, high birth, high station. **2** moral fiber, morality, heroism, honor, rectitude, uprightness, incorruptibility, principle, virtue, integrity, chivalry, high-mindedness, character.
ant. 1 lowliness, obscurity, simplicity, insignificance. **2** baseness, immorality, cowardice, untrustworthiness.

noble *adj.* **1** high-born, aristocratic, high-ranking, feudal, princely, lordly, titled, landed, ducal, blue-blooded, upper-class, patrician. **2** high-minded, virtuous, heroic, magnanimous, unselfish, chivalrous, altruistic, lofty, generous, honorable, elevated, admirable, exemplary, exalted. **3** imposing, grand, impressive, magnificent, memorable, majestic, stately, regal, strong, dignified, august, splendid, imperious, commanding, powerful.
ant. 1 low-born, lowly, lower-class. **2** ignoble, base, mean, cowardly, self-serving. **3** weak, unimpressive, common, unprepossessing, undignified.

nobody *n.* nothing, zero, cipher, nullity, nonentity, cog, underling, mediocrity, menial, flunky, lightweight, small fry, has-been.
ant. somebody, VIP, personage, star, champion.

noddy *n.* DUNCE.

node *n.* knot, knob, swelling, lump, bump, protuberance, growth, bulge, tumescence, gnarl, nodule, cyst, wen.

nodule *n.* NODE.

noise *n.* clamor, disturbance, disquiet, din, sound, outcry, racket, riot, clatter, uproar, hubbub, commotion, hullabaloo, to-do.
ant. quiet, serenity, silence, peacefulness, stillness.

noise about bruit about, publicize, make public, make known, advertise, promulgate, circulate, spread the word, rumor, gossip, air.
ant. keep secret, keep quiet, hide, conceal, cover.

noiseless *adj.* quiet, hushed, still, silent, soundless, muted, muffled, mute, inaudible, peaceful, tomblike, deathlike.
ant. noisy, bustling, loud, audible, lively.

noisome *adj.* **1** reeking, stinking, rank, odorous, smelly, fetid, foul, rancid, putrid, malodorous, mephitic, rotten, gamy, nauseating, funky. **2** injurious, noxious, harmful, destructive, hurtful, detrimental, deleterious, unhealthy, sickening, unwholesome, pernicious, poisonous, baneful, toxic.
ant. 2 beneficial, wholesome, healthful, curative.

noisy *adj.* loud, clamorous, lively, bustling, humming, buzzing, riotous, disturbing, hectic, uproarious, animated, resounding, rackety, deafening, ear-splitting.
ant. quiet, still, hushed, peaceful, dead, noiseless.

nomad *n.* wanderer, rover, pilgrim, migrant, vagabond, drifter, vagrant, itinerant, gypsy, tramp, hobo, beachcomber, bedouin, bird of passage, bum.

nomadic *adj.* wandering, roving, unsettled, migrant, migratory, vagabond, drifting, itinerant, vagrant, footloose, peripatetic.
ant. settled, rooted, established, installed, tethered, resident.

nom de plume PSEUDONYM.

nominal *adj.* **1** so-called, purported, ostensible, in name only, supposed, alleged, soi-disant, self-styled, surface, would-be, professed, manqué. **2** trivial, slight, picayune, inconsiderable, small, moderate, low, inconsequential, petty, minute, niggling, trifling, insignificant.
ant. 1 real, actual, factual, genuine, true. **2** large, great, high, considerable, exorbitant.

nominate *v.* name, designate, propose, put up, present, offer, appoint, assign, slate, commission, depute, delegate, deputize, choose, propose, select, empower.

nominee *n.* candidate, office-seeker, contestant, entrant, aspirant, competitor, vote-seeker, party favorite, dark horse.

nonchalance *n.* unconcern, indifference, sang-froid, equanimity, composure, detachment, self-possession, insouciance, dispassion, objectivity, casualness, calm, imperturbability, cool (*Slang*).
ant. concern, involvement, regard, anxiety, passion.

nonchalant *adj.* casual, indifferent, blasé, unconcerned, dispassionate, detached, cool, uninterested, lackadaisical, devil-may-care, insouciant, easygoing, apathetic, uninvolved, insensitive.
ant. impassioned, disturbed, concerned, involved, anxious.

noncommittal *adj.* uncommitted, undecided, neutral, uncommunicative, taciturn, detached, tepid, equivocal, nonpartisan, ambiguous, unclear, cautious, guarded, wary, indecisive.
ant. definite, decisive, outspoken, involved, partisan.

non compos mentis INSANE.

nonconformist *n.* rebel, heretic, dissenter, protester, original, reformer, bohemian, individualist, radical, iconoclast, renegade, schismatic, dissident, eccentric, oddball (*Slang*), kook (*Slang*), crazy (*Slang*).

ant. conformist, believer, follower, sheep, philistine.

nondescript *adj.* unclassifiable, indistinct, indefinite, indescribable, amorphous, indeterminate, characterless, colorless, ordinary, commonplace, uninteresting, vague, blah (*Slang*).
ant. distinct, distinctive, distinguishable, definite.

nondrinker *n.* teetotaler, abstainer, dry, prohibitionist, nephalist.

nonentity *n.* nobody, nullity, cipher, nothing, zero, underling, cog, lightweight, mediocrity, menial, unknown, has-been, unperson.
ant. somebody, name, personage, VIP, star, headliner.

nonessential *adj.* extraneous, extrinsic, external, unnecessary, unrequired, auxiliary, ancillary, marginal, tangential, supplementary, extra, surplus, excessive, superfluous, expendable, *de trop*.
ant. essential, intrinsic, indispensable, necessary, basic, crucial.

nonesuch *n.* NONPAREIL.

nonobjective *adj.* NONREPRESENTATIONAL.

nonpareil *adj.* unequaled, unmatched, unique, nonesuch, nonsuch, one-of-a-kind, supreme, unsurpassed, unrivaled, choice, elite, prize, blue-ribbon, exceptional, preeminent, paramount, extraordinary, super (*Slang*). —*n.* wonder, phenomenon, miracle, marvel, one in a million, paragon, gem, prize, diamond, nonesuch, nonsuch, oner, humdinger (*Slang*), knockout (*Slang*), superman, record-breaker.
ant. *adj.* commonplace, everyday, ordinary, average, mediocre, standard, usual.

nonpartisan *adj.* neutral, detached, uncommitted, independent, impartial, disinterested, objective, unbiased, uninvolved, noncommittal, dispassionate, nonparticipating, aloof, unprejudiced.
ant. biased, partial, prejudiced, partisan, involved.

nonplus *v.* baffle, perplex, bewilder, confuse, muddle, confound, rattle, bemuse, disorient, daze, puzzle, stump, mystify, distract, dumbfound.

nonplussed *adj.* DAZED.

nonproductive *adj.* UNPRODUCTIVE.

nonpublic *adj.* private, restricted, exclusive, cliquish, selective.
ant. public, free, unrestricted, community.

nonrepresentational *adj.* nonobjective, abstract, nonfigurative, expressionist, abstract expressionist.
ant. representational, pictorial, figurative, realistic.

nonresistant *adj.* OBEDIENT.

nonsense *n.* **1** silliness, foolishness, asininity, fatuity, poppycock, rubbish, bosh, balderdash, rot, claptrap, piffle, drivel, twaddle, moonshine, babble, punk (*Slang*), bunk (*Slang*), baloney (*Slang*), boloney (*Slang*), hot air (*Slang*), eyewash (*Slang*), hooey (*Slang*), waffle (*Brit.*). **2** trash, garbage, frippery, junk, gimcrackery, trivia, trivialities, bagatelles, gewgaws, furbelows, trifles, tinsel.
ant. **1** sense, logic, cogency. **2** substance, essentials, basics, necessities.

nonsensical *adj.* INCREDIBLE.

nonsuch *n.* NONPAREIL.

nonviable *adj.* impracticable, unworkable, impossible, useless, unfeasible, hopeless, inutile, valueless, inoperative, ineffective, unachievable, futile, nonfunctioning.
ant. viable, workable, practicable, effectual, useful.

nonviolent *adj.* nonaggressive, peaceful, peaceable, pacific, pacifist, pacifistic, unwarlike, passive, nonbelligerent, reasonable, rational, sober, judicious, cool, coolheaded.
ant. aggressive, hostile, violent, warlike, irrational.

nonworking *adj.* unemployed, out of work, idle, jobless, laid-off, inactive, retired, at liberty, on the dole (*Brit.*).
ant. employed, salaried, working.

noodle *n. Slang* NINCOMPOOP.

nook *n.* recess, niche, hideaway, shelter, den, hole, alcove, cubbyhole, refuge, retreat, inglenook, snuggery (*Brit.*).

noose *n.* loop, bight, halter, lasso, lariat, riata, snare, hangman's knot.

norm *n.* standard, model, average, representative, type, pattern, rule, gauge, yardstick, measuring rod, barometer, touchstone, criterion, guideline, guidepost, prototype.

normal *adj.* **1** regular, standard, usual, model, representative, typical, habitual, orthodox, conventional, general, expected, traditional, accustomed. **2** average, mean, median, medium.
ant. 1 unusual, irregular, extraordinary, atypical, bizarre, freakish.

nosedive *n., v.* PLUNGE.

nosh *n.* SNACK.

nostrum *n.* cure-all, panacea.

nosy *adj.* inquisitive, prying, snooping, intrusive, curious, overcurious, snoopy, all ears, meddlesome, eavesdropping.

notable *adj.* noteworthy, distinguished, prominent, important, remarkable, noted, famous, famed, renowned, storied, momentous, consequential, outstanding, significant, distingué, exceptional, remarkable. —*n.* dignitary, personage, luminary, worthy, name, personality, VIP, somebody, celebrity, headliner, mogul, leader, bigwig.
ant. *adj.* undistinguished, unimportant, inconsequential, ordinary, anonymous, unknown. *n.* nobody, underling, second-rater, also-ran, man on the street.

notably *adv.* ESPECIALLY.

notation *n.* NOTE.

notch *n.* **1** nick, cut, dent, mark, marking, cleft, score, serration, incision, crimp, gash. **2** gap, gully, gulch, pass, divide, gorge, defile, passage, chasm, canyon, ravine, crevasse.

note *n.* **1** reminder, notation, memo, memorandum, jotting, entry, record, annotation, comment, gloss, footnote, commentary. **2** minutes, record, chronicle, summary, summation, diary, log, daybook. **3** NOTICE. —*v.* **1** set down, put down, write down, jot down, record, enter, annotate, gloss, footnote, inscribe, chronicle, log, scribble, register, scrawl. **2** mention, emphasize, underline, italicize, remark on, point to, look into, call attention to, highlight, spotlight, allude to, stress. **3** NOTICE.

noted *adj.* NOTABLE.

noteworthy *adj.* significant, important, consequential, unusual, remarkable, singular, celebrated, noted, notable, exceptional, outstanding, prominent, extraordinary.
ant. insignificant, unimportant, unexceptional, inconsequential.

nothing *n.* **1** nothingness, nonexistence, nonbeing, nil, void, nirvana, oblivion, *nada*. **2** nobody, zero, cipher, nonentity, mediocrity, cog, nullity, bagatelle, nonsense, bubble, bauble, gewgaw, trifle, *petit rien*. **3** zero, naught, cipher, aught, none, goose egg (*Slang*), zip (*Slang*), zilch (*Slang*).
ant. 1 being, existence. **2** somebody, something. **3** infinity.

nothingness *n.* NOTHING.

notice *v.* **1** note, heed, pay attention, be aware of, see, perceive, sense, observe, glance at, recognize, make out, discern, espy, discover. **2** mention, comment on, remark on, call attention to, refer to, allude to, point to, speak of, touch on, report on, describe. —*n.* **1** observation, heed, attention, glance, eye, awareness, perception, recognition, discernment, espial, discovery, note, cognizance, look, survey, once-over (*Slang*). **2** announcement, notification, statement, proclamation, declaration, pronouncement, warning, admonishment, caution, forewarning, caveat.
ant. *v.* **1** miss, overlook, be unaware of. **2** ignore, neglect, gloss over. *n.* **1**

inattention, unawareness, insensibility.

notification *n.* NOTICE.

notify *v.* inform, advise, tell, acquaint, apprise, let know, serve notice, send word, enlighten, instruct, tip off.

notion *n.* **1** thought, idea, opinion, intimation, impression, conception, feeling, belief, view, conclusion. **2** intention, inclination, desire, impulse, whim, fancy, bent, wish, hankering, penchant, disposition, predisposition, yen.

notoriety *n.* infamy, disrepute, ill repute, dishonor, disgrace, shame, degradation, scandal, discredit, flagrancy, ignominy, bad odor.
ant. decency, goodness, honor, virtue, nobility.

notorious *adj.* scandalous, infamous, disreputable, shameless, ignominious, dishonored, discredited, outrageous, flagrant, recognized, outstanding, glaring, well-known, blatant.
ant. reputable, decent, virtuous, concealed, hidden, covert.

notwithstanding *adv.* ANYHOW.

nought *n.* NAUGHT.

nourish *v.* **1** feed, sustain, provide for, nurture, nurse, strengthen, suckle, breast-feed. **2** support, maintain, foster, cultivate, further, abet, promote, encourage, boost.
ant. **1** starve, deprive. **2** discourage, undermine, retard.

nourishing *adj.* NUTRITIOUS.

nourishment *n.* food, nutriment, sustenance, feed, subsistence, provender, provisions, victuals, viands, bread, meat, pabulum, eats.

novel *adj.* new, unfamiliar, striking, original, innovative, unusual, fresh, unexpected, unconventional, unique, odd, different, unorthodox, offbeat (*Slang*).
ant. imitative, trite, timeworn, typical, tired.

novelty *n.* innovation, change, surprise, departure, variation, wrinkle.

novice *n.* beginner, tyro, trainee, apprentice, learner, neophyte, novitiate, freshman, newcomer, student, amateur, new hand, probationer, colt, rookie (*Slang*).
ant. veteran, old hand, master, expert, authority.

novitiate *n.* NOVICE.

noxious *adj.* injurious, harmful, hurtful, destructive, poisonous, unwholesome, unhealthy, pernicious, lethal, deadly, virulent, dangerous, ruinous, bad.

nuance *n.* shade, degree, shadow, variation, distinction, modulation, nicety, touch, trace, refinement.

nub *n.* **1** protuberance, node, knob, nubbin, knot, bump, bulge, swelling, growth, protrusion. **2** essence, pith, heart, core, nucleus, kernel, crux, gist, point, meaning, nitty-gritty (*Slang*).
ant. **1** hollow, dent, hole, concavity, dimple.

nucleus *n.* kernel, seed, center, pith, core, heart, nub.

nude *adj.* naked, bare, unclothed, uncovered, bared, undressed, unclad, denuded, stripped, bare-skinned, disrobed, *au naturel*, in the raw, in the buff.
ant. dressed, covered, clad, clothed, robed.

nudge *v.* shove, elbow, poke, push, jostle, prod, jog, touch, jolt, press. —*n.* shove, push, poke, elbowing, pressure, prod, jog, touch, jolt.

nugget *n.* lump, ball, clump, chunk, hunk, piece, pellet.

nuisance *n.* bother, vexation, annoyance, irritation, inconvenience, pest, pain, burden, affliction, thorn, misfortune, blight, aggravation.
ant. pleasure, delight, joy, balm.

null *adj.* ineffectual, powerless, inoperative, void, nugatory, nonexistent, invalid, immaterial, inconsequential, ineffective, insignificant, valueless, unimportant.
ant. valid, effective, effectual, operative, valuable.

nullify *v.* cancel, veto, void, kill, invalidate, annul, negate, rescind, repeal, abrogate, destroy, override, overrule, scrap, undo, counteract, obliterate. **ant.** enforce, validate, uphold, enact, strengthen.

nullity *n.* nonexistence, invalidity, impotence, ineffectuality, inoperativeness, insignificance, nothingness, negation, oblivion. **ant.** existence, viability, effectiveness, power.

numb *adj.* insensitive, frozen, paralyzed, immobilized, numbed, anesthetized, insensible, unfeeling, benumbed, unresponsive, deadened, narcotized, stupefied, comatose. **ant.** sensitive, responsive, reactive, alert, alive.

number *n.* **1** digit, integer, unit, figure, numeral. **2** amount, quantity, aggregate, sum, volume, total, multitude, mass, preponderance. —*v.* **1** count, figure, enumerate, total, compute, quantify, reckon, tally, tell, calculate, cast up. **2** include, comprise, contain, encompass, consist of, amount to, constitute.

numberless *adj.* countless, innumerable, incalculable, multitudinous, endless, infinite, myriad, illimitable, boundless, measureless, unbounded, unending, unnumbered. **ant.** numbered, limited, finite, restricted.

number-one *adj.* CHIEF.

numeral *n.* number, symbol, character, letter, integer, digit, cipher, figure.

numerate *v.* ENUMERATE.

numerous *adj.* many, abundant, countless, innumerable, myriad, profuse, plentiful, copious, multitudinous. **ant.** scant, sparse, few, meager, limited, scarce.

numskull *n.* NINCOMPOOP.

nuncio *n.* MESSENGER.

nuptials *n.* wedding, marriage, matrimony, espousals.

nurse *v.* **1** take care of, minister to, look after, watch over, attend, tend, care for, help, wait on, cater to, aid, succor. **2** suckle, feed, breast-feed,

wet-nurse. **3** promote, develop, nurture, foster, support, protect, cultivate, keep alive, further, help, aid, advance.

nurture *v.* **1** feed, nourish, sustain, strengthen, nurse, mother. **2** bring up, raise, educate, rear, school, teach, train, cultivate, civilize, acculturate, develop, prepare, foster, discipline. —*n.* upbringing, raising, rearing, child rearing, child raising, parenthood, development, indoctrination, training, acculturation, preparation, cultivation, education, fostering.

nut *n. Slang* **1** lunatic, madman, maniac, psychopath, eccentric, crackpot, character, oddball (*Slang*), screwball (*Slang*), kook (*Slang*). **2** enthusiast, devotee, fanatic, fan, zealot, expert, monomaniac, demon, bug (*Slang*), buff, freak (*Slang*), maven, aficionado, groupie (*Slang*).

nutrient *adj.* nutritional, nourishing, nutritious, nutritive, wholesome, healthful, alimentary. —*n.* NUTRIMENT.

nutriment *n.* food, nourishment, sustenance, aliment, provisions, provender, nutrient, victuals, eats, meat, bread, pabulum.

nutritious *adj.* nourishing, nutrient, nutritional, nutritive, wholesome, healthful, beneficial, body-building, sustaining.

nuts *Slang adj.* crazy, demented, deranged, insane, irrational, lunatic, unbalanced, cracked, daft, *non compos mentis*, loony (*Slang*), cuckoo (*Slang*), batty (*Slang*), nutty (*Slang*). **ant.** sane, rational, lucid, normal, sensible.

nuts about *Slang* **1** infatuated with, enthralled by, in love with, mad for, bewitched by, enamored of, smitten by, wild about, crazy about. **2** enthusiastic about, engrossed by, wrapped up in, keen on, hipped on (*Slang*), turned on by (*Slang*).

ant. 1, 2 uninterested in, bored by, cool to.

nutty *Slang adj.* NUTS.

nuzzle *v.* SNUGGLE.

nymph *n.* beauty, belle, goddess, charmer, Venus, dream girl, sylph, cover girl, dazzler, enchantress, doll (*Slang*), looker (*Slang*), eyeful (*Slang*), knockout (*Slang*).

O

oaf *n.* booby, dunce, simpleton, clod, ignoramus, imbecile, dullard, ninny, lout, boor, fool, nincompoop, boob (*Slang*), klutz (*Slang*), meatball (*Slang*).
ant. sophisticate, intellect, brain, sage, smart aleck, wiseacre.

oasis *n.* refuge, island, retreat, sanctuary, shelter, resort, haven, harbor, sanctum, ivory tower.
ant. crossroads, mainstream, thick, midst, hurly-burly, jungle.

oath *n.* **1** word, promise, pledge, vow, deposition, affidavit, affirmation, declaration. **2** blasphemy, profanity, curse, imprecation, swearword, expletive, malediction.
ant. 2 benediction, piety, blessing, piousness, sanction.

obduracy *n.* OBSTINACY.

obdurate *adj.* hard, unyielding, stubborn, relentless, pitiless, merciless, unbending, adamant, inflexible, inexorable, callous, tenacious, obstinate, dogged, hard-nosed (*Slang*).
ant. flexible, tractable, soft-hearted, amenable, compliant, malleable.

obedience *n.* submissiveness, compliance, subservience, willingness, meekness, docility, biddability, submission, respectfulness, conformability, dutifulness, respect.
ant. disobedience, defiance, obstinacy, recalcitrance, stubbornness, insurgency.

obedient *adj.* docile, compliant, submissive, nonresistant, subservient, dutiful, deferential, tractable, amenable, respectful, yielding, acquiescent, conformable, law-abiding.
ant. disobedient, contumacious, rebellious, insubordinate, obstinate, recalcitrant.

obeisance *n.* deference, respect, reverence, homage, veneration, subjection, submission, honor, esteem, courtesy, allegiance, fealty.
ant. disrespect, insolence, impertinence, impiety, discourtesy, slight.

obese *adj.* fat, corpulent, overweight, heavy, fleshy, portly, stout, porky, gross, rotund, plump.
ant. thin, underweight, emaciated, skinny, gaunt, lean.

obey *v.* heed, submit, accede, execute, conform, mind, comply, concur, carry out, answer, respond, assent, serve.
ant. disobey, defy, ignore, rebel, disregard, transgress.

obfuscate *v.* obscure, muddle, confuse, bewilder, befog, complicate, blur, becloud, stupefy, confound, fluster.
ant. clarify, enlighten, simplify, disentangle, clear up, untangle.

obiter dictum REMARK.

object[1] *v.* **1** dissent, disapprove, oppose, remonstrate, complain, kick, expostulate, protest. **2** *offer contrary arguments:* counter, argue, charge, instance, allege, appeal, evidence, observe.
ant. 1 approve, applaud, agree, support, invite. **2** advocate, justify, second, espouse, reinforce, favor.

object[2] *n.* **1** entity, substance, body,

thing, something, subject, mark, target, butt, article. **2** aim, goal, purpose, objective, end, aspiration, intention, target, design, scheme.

ant. 1 nothingness, void, space, illusion, vacuum, shadow.

objection *n.* exception, rebuttal, contradiction, challenge, expostulation, dispute, complaint, protest, demurrer, imputation, stricture.

ant. concession, agreement, acceptance, affirmation, endorsement, accord.

objectionable *adj.* offensive, displeasing, repugnant, unseemly, unacceptable, deplorable, disagreeable, unwholesome, undesirable, intolerable, insufferable, unsavory, noxious, regrettable.

ant. unexceptionable, pleasing, acceptable, desirable, agreeable, welcome.

objective *adj.* **1** material, physical, real, factual, external, actual, outward. **2** detached, unbiased, disinterested, unprejudiced, impersonal, fair, equitable, impartial, judicial. —*n.* object, aim, purpose, intention, destination, termination, target, goal, end.

ant. *adj.* **1** mental, internal, sensory, intellectual, subjective. **2** biased, personal, prejudiced, intolerant, subjective. *n.* cause, origin, inception, premise, preliminary.

objurgate *v.* REBUKE.

obligated *adj.* beholden, bound, indebted, committed, constrained, obliged, compelled, required, forced, impelled.

ant. unconstrained, uncommitted, clear, exempt, quit, free.

obligation *n.* **1** indebtedness, engagement, requirement, accountability, responsibility, liability, duty, compulsion, constraint. **2** debt, pledge, burden, bond, stipulation, responsibility, agreement, contract, covenant, promise.

obligatory *adj.* imperative, compulsory, mandatory, requisite, binding, required, enforced, coercive, peremptory, imperious, essential, necessary.

ant. optional, discretionary, voluntary, elective, conditional.

oblige *v.* accommodate, favor, serve, convenience, gratify, please, benefit, obligate, aid, provide, assist, furnish.

ant. disoblige, inconvenience, put out, discommode, displease, hinder.

obliging *adj.* kind, accommodating, agreeable, good-natured, complaisant, amiable, considerate, indulgent, gracious, thoughtful, hospitable, cheerful.

ant. inconsiderate, disobliging, sullen, ill-disposed, churlish, hostile.

oblique *adj.* **1** slanting, crosswise, inclined, aslant, diagonal, tilted, transverse, cater-corner, sidelong. **2** indirect, allusive, devious, sly, furtive, covert, underhand, crooked.

ant. 2 candid, foursquare, open, straightforward, direct.

obliterate *v.* **1** destroy, eradicate, exterminate, raze, extirpate, ruin, deracinate, crush, extinguish, pulverize, stamp out. **2** erase, blot, delete, cancel, efface, remove, rub out.

ant. 1 create, make, build, construct. **2** restore, repair, preserve, stet, reinstate.

oblivion *n.* extinction, eclipse, invisibility, obscurity, neglect, obliteration, blackout, nullity, void, unconsciousness, disregard, Lethe, nirvana.

ant. recognition, prominence, eminence, fame, notoriety, remembrance.

oblivious *adj.* unaware, distracted, forgetful, unmindful, heedless, insensible, unconscious, careless, neglectful, inattentive, undiscerning, disregardful.

ant. mindful, aware, alert, watchful, heedful, careful.

oblong *adj.* elongated, rectangular, elongate, elliptical.

obloquy *n.* **1** censure, denunciation, reprobation, vilification, defamation, calumny, opprobrium, rebuke, abuse, dressing-down. **2** ignominy,

disgrace, shame, odium, disfavor, contempt, humiliation, degradation.
ant. 1 praise, eulogy, panegyric, adoration, adulation. **2** honor, regard, favor, esteem, respect.

obnoxious *adj.* offensive, disgusting, repulsive, odious, repugnant, abhorrent, hateful, revolting, repellent, invidious, reprehensible, pernicious, abominable, distasteful.
ant. gratifying, agreeable, congenial, pleasant, grateful, welcome.

obscene *adj.* **1** offensive, filthy, scatological, disgusting, foul, smutty, indecent, gross, improper. **2** licentious, lewd, lubricious, pornographic, lascivious, libidinous, goatish.
ant. 1 inoffensive, decent, proper, refined, respectable. **2** innocent, chaste, virginal, modest, moral.

obscenity *n.* offensiveness, indecency, licentiousness, pornography, indelicacy, smuttiness, ribaldry, grossness, filth, lewdness, immodesty, coarseness, vulgarity, repulsiveness, unchastity.
ant. decency, propriety, decorum, delicacy, innocence, chastity.

obscure *adj.* **1** dim, dark, dusky, gloomy, overcast, murky, unlit, shadowy, cloudy. **2** vague, abstruse, ambiguous, recondite, cryptic, equivocal, occult, enigmatic. **3** undefined, concealed, remote, distant, out-of-the-way, unnoticed, hidden, secluded, apart. —*v.* **1** conceal, screen, hide, cover, shield, disguise. **2** muddle, becloud, befog, confuse, obfuscate, confound.
ant. *adj.* **1** bright, sunny, resplendent, lighted, ablaze. **2** distinct, obvious, clear, plain, evident. **3** manifest, noted, celebrated, distinguished, famous, conspicuous. *v.* **1** reveal, show, demonstrate, exhibit, expose. **2** clarify, explain, simplify, elucidate, resolve.

obsequious *adj.* fawning, servile, subservient, sycophantic, ingratiating, slavish, bootlicking, toadying, truckling, deferential, menial.

ant. swaggering, arrogant, imperious, contumelious, overbearing.

observance *n.* **1** celebration, observation, performance, fulfillment, discharge, compliance, attention, honoring, heed. **2** custom, usage, form, rite, practice, habit, ceremony.
ant. 1 nonobservance, disregard, default, breach, omission, evasion.

observant *adj.* attentive, alert, watchful, sharp, perceptive, keen, quick, wide-awake, heedful, mindful, aware, heads-up (*Slang*).
ant. heedless, careless, indifferent, nodding, dreamy, preoccupied.

observation *n.* **1** perception, examination, cognizance, consideration, study, observance, experience, attention, knowledge, notice. **2** remark, statement, comment, utterance, assertion, declaration, opinion, announcement.
ant. 1 inattention, absent-mindedness, detachment, abstraction, apathy, woolgathering.

observe *v.* **1** see, notice, watch, study, survey, scrutinize, examine, perceive, look, view, espy, attend to, discern. **2** conform to, abide by, submit to, heed, obey, follow, acknowledge, respect, keep. **3** celebrate, solemnize, commemorate, remember, consecrate, sanctify, honor, keep. **4** say, mention, comment, opine, state, declare, exclaim, remark.
ant. 1 neglect, ignore, overlook, disregard. **2** disobey, flout, ignore, transgress, disregard. **3** desecrate, violate, dishonor, forget, ignore.

observer *n.* spectator, onlooker, bystander, watcher, examiner, overseer, inspector, viewer, witness, scrutineer, student, watch, lookout, eyewitness.

obsess *v.* preoccupy, harass, haunt, engross, plague, enthrall, craze, distress, torment, pursue, harry.
ant. shake off, disburden, purge, liberate, rid, exorcise.

obsession *n.* fixation, preoccupation, delusion, mania, hang-up (*Slang*), infatuation, compulsion, *idée fixe,* conviction, enthusiasm, craze, passion, fetish, fantasy, quirk.

obsessive *adj.* compulsive, besetting, gripping, intrusive, compelling, haunting, irresistible, immoderate, worrisome, preoccupying, excessive, fanatical, irrational.

obsolescent *adj.* OBSOLETE.

obsolete *adj.* outmoded, archaic, out-of-date, passé, old-fashioned, antiquated, dated, obsolescent, disused, outworn, outdated, ancient, effete, extinct, old, old hat, out.
ant. current, up-to-date, modern, present-day, prevalent, new, *à la mode.*

obstacle *n.* hindrance, obstruction, stumblingblock, impediment, barrier, hurdle, block, snag, roadblock, difficulty, catch, restriction, check, interference, let.
ant. aid, support, assistance, crutch.

obstinacy *n.* stubbornness, doggedness, obduracy, determination, single-mindedness, pertinacity, persistence, tenacity, resoluteness, resolution, refractoriness, intractability, inflexibility, incorrigibility, pig-headedness, orneriness, wrong-headedness, mulishness.
ant. docility, tractability, pliancy, compliance, submissiveness, flexibility.

obstinate *adj.* **1** stubborn, pig-headed, dogged, froward, headstrong, mulish, wrong-headed, obdurate, unyielding, determined, single-minded, resolute, unshakable, pertinacious, tenacious, refractory, ornery. **2** *of a disease:* persistent, uncontrollable, intractable, stubborn, tenacious, refractory, chronic.
ant. **1** pliant, compliant, flexible, pliable, submissive. **2** remediable, curable, eradicable, tractable, amenable.

obstreperous *adj.* **1** clamorous, boisterous, loud, vociferous, noisy, roistering, tumultuous, uproarious. **2** refractory, difficult, unmanageable, troublesome, obstinate, contrary,

perverse, uncontrollable, unruly, problem.
ant. **1** quiet, peaceful, calm, silent, harmonious. **2** obedient, docile, submissive, disciplined, compliant.

obstruct *v.* **1** choke, clog, stop, impede, retard, check, bar, barricade, hinder. **2** hide, screen, shield, obscure, cut off, curtain, block, prevent, bar.
ant. **1** further, abet, assist, aid, encourage, favor. **2** reveal, expose, open up, unveil, show.

obstruction *n.* hindrance, obstacle, barrier, hurdle, impediment, encumbrance, difficulty, bottleneck, barricade, block, bar, check, stopper.
ant. aid, furtherance, encouragement, assistance, sustenance.

obtain *v.* **1** acquire, get, gain, procure, attain, secure, earn, win, gather. **2** exist, persist, prevail, subsist, hold, abound, stand, continue.
ant. **1** lose, forfeit, forgo, give up, spend, dispense.

obtrude *v.* **1** encroach, insinuate, butt in (*Slang*), barge in, intrude, trespass, infringe, interject, foist. **2** extrude, push out, stick out, eject, protrude, advance, expel.
ant. **1** draw back, withdraw, retreat, retire, vacate. **2** contain, confine, enclose, retain, embrace.

obtrusive *adj.* **1** conspicuous, prominent, salient, blatant, glaring, garish, protruding, striking. **2** pushing, officious, bold, forward, impertinent, meddlesome, interfering, importunate.
ant. **1** unobtrusive, inconspicuous, imperceptible, covert, concealed. **2** reserved, diffident, retiring, modest, decorous.

obtuse *adj.* **1** blunt, rounded, dull. **2** insensitive, imperceptive, dull, sluggish, stupid, phlegmatic, unintelligent, slow, stolid, dense, lumpish, vapid, vacant, costive.
ant. **1** acute, sharp. **2** alert, sharp, quick, sensitive, clever, keen.

obverse *n.* FACE.

obviate *v.* preclude, ward off, turn

aside, prevent, circumvent, avert, forestall, remove, avoid, evade, anticipate.

ant. necessitate, entail, enforce, constrain, permit, bring on.

obvious *adj.* evident, perceptible, manifest, distinct, unmistakable, patent, plain, apparent, clear, self-evident, palpable, visible.

ant. indistinct, obscure, abstruse, ambiguous, vague, hidden.

occasion *n.* **1** event, occurrence, happening, juncture, time, turn, opportunity, incident. **2** celebration, gala, pageant, festivity, fete, festival, carnival, holiday. —*v.* cause, bring about, entail, effect, produce, create, give rise to, originate.

ant. *v.* terminate, end, halt, stop, cease, quit.

occasional *adj.* intermittent, infrequent, irregular, sporadic, accidental, casual, uncertain, unreliable, capricious, spasmodic, incidental, uncommon, rare.

ant. regular, frequent, sure, certain, systematic, planned.

occasionally *adv.* sometimes, now and then, intermittently, sporadically, seldom, fitfully, at times, casually, irregularly, periodically, once in a while.

ant. constantly, frequently, often, continuously, continually, regularly.

occlude *v.* shut up, block off, obstruct, throttle, choke, trammel, stanch, clog, plug, retard, close.

ant. unplug, open, clear, ream, unclog.

occult *adj.* mysterious, supernatural, mystical, cabalistic, esoteric, secret, abstruse, recondite, unrevealed, veiled, hidden, unknown, invisible.

ant. open, intelligible, natural, manifest, plain, self-evident.

occupancy *n.* possession, engagement, inhabitation, use, tenure, occupation, enjoyment, acquisition, retention, lodgment, holding, tenancy, control, sojourn.

ant. vacancy, relinquishment, evacuation, desertion, eviction, release.

occupant *n.* resident, tenant, inhabitant, householder, inmate, addressee, occupier, dweller, owner, lessee.

occupation *n.* business, calling, trade, pursuit, vocation, avocation, profession, craft, employment, work, job, métier.

occupy *v.* **1** seize, invade, conquer, garrison, possess, capture. **2** *of space or time:* take up, employ, fill, utilize, use, inhabit. **3** *of an office or position:* fill, hold, conduct, carry out, maintain, run.

ant. **1** evacuate, withdraw, retreat, vacate, abandon. **3** depart, quit, resign, give up, vacate.

occur *v.* happen, come about, arise, take place, befall, appear, transpire, develop, eventuate.

occurrence *n.* happening, event, accident, proceeding, experience, incident, episode, circumstance, transaction, adventure, affair, occasion.

ocean *n.* **1** sea, main, deep, brine, tide. **2** infinity, immensity, flood, abundance, profusion, multitude, sea, quantities, lots.

ant. **2** drop, trickle, sprinkling, modicum, minim, particle.

odd *adj.* **1** occasional, casual, sporadic, incidental, chance, fragmentary, intermittent. **2** peculiar, eccentric, weird, singular, extraordinary, uncanny, eldritch, bizarre, fantastic, strange.

ant. **1** regular, systematic, continual, predictable, habitual, fixed. **2** common, unexceptional, everyday, ordinary, usual, commonplace.

oddball *n. Slang* eccentric, nonconformist, character, original, case, individualist, crank, loner, specimen, deviate, crackpot (*Slang*), freak (*Slang*).

ant. conformist, bourgeois, everyman, square (*Slang*).

oddity *n.* singularity, peculiarity, curiosity, anomaly, prodigy, rarity, incongruity, wonder, freak, natural, caution.

ant. commonplace, banality, mediocrity, stereotype, triteness.

oddment *n.* scrap, remnant, leaving, snippet, fragment, shred, crumb, gobbet, sliver, chip, paring, ort, discard.

oddments *n.* ODDS AND ENDS.

odds *n.* chance, likelihood, probability, advantage, lead, edge, difference, disparity, superiority, supremacy, balance.

odds and ends fragments, scraps, oddments, miscellany, remnants, leavings, shavings, leftovers, particles, sweepings, refuse, chips, rummage.

ode *n.* poem, lyric, verse, song, rhyme.

odious *adj.* hateful, repugnant, disgusting, abhorrent, abominable, detestable, loathsome, repulsive, nasty, nauseous, revolting, repellent, offensive.

ant. delightful, agreeable, attractive, pleasing, entrancing, charming.

odium *n.* offensiveness, opprobrium, repugnance, disgust, abhorrence, obloquy, detestation, antipathy, enmity, hatred, hatefulness, repulsiveness, dishonor.

odor *n.* **1** smell, aroma, scent, redolence, fragrance, perfume, bouquet, stench, stink. **2** air, aura, flavor, atmosphere, quality, character, semblance, appearance.

odoriferous *adj.* ODOROUS.

odorous *adj.* fragrant, odoriferous, scented, redolent, aromatic, perfumed, sweet-smelling, heady, spicy, ambrosial.

ant. malodorous, smelly, noisome, fetid, rancid, noxious.

odyssey *n.* pilgrimage, peregrination, quest, expedition, crusade, voyage, travels, wandering, journey, journeying, sojourn.

off *adj.* **1** remote, far, distant, faraway, afar, outlying, further. **2** wrong, inaccurate, subpar, subnormal, incorrect, poor, inferior. **3** null, inoperative, cancelled, nonexistent, unavailing, disconnected, inefficacious.

4 odd, eccentric, bizarre, unusual, singular, peculiar, strange.

ant. **1** near, close, adjacent, beside, nearby. **2** standard, normal, good, right, correct. **3** on, engaged, operative, effective, working. **4** ordinary, normal, everyday, habitual, usual.

offal *n.* rubbish, refuse, garbage, trash, leavings, waste, slag, junk, ordure, scum, dregs, grounds, scurf.

offbeat *adj. Slang* unconventional, unusual, uncommon, eccentric, novel, odd, strange, outré, singular, peculiar, bizarre, unorthodox, bohemian, kinky (*Slang*), far-out (*Slang*), way-out (*Slang*).

ant. conventional, traditional, stereotyped, ordinary, orthodox, wonted.

off-color *adj.* indecent, offensive, indelicate, risqué, tasteless, vulgar, suggestive, coarse, smutty, obscene, improper, unseemly, spicy.

ant. seemly, respectable, bowdlerized, decent, proper.

offend *v.* displease, anger, outrage, affront, provoke, vex, annoy, irritate, disoblige, nettle, gall, upset, antagonize, insult, mortify.

ant. please, soothe, delight, mollify, placate, compliment.

offender *n.* perpetrator, transgressor, law-breaker, malefactor, sinner, wrongdoer, delinquent, culprit, miscreant, trespasser, violator, outlaw, scofflaw.

offense *n.* **1** fault, sin, outrage, injury, hurt, crime, vice, scandal. **2** assault, attack, siege, onslaught, aggression, sortie, battery, charge.

ant. **1** innocence, honor, virtue, good, benefit. **2** defense, protection, retreat, submission, resistance.

offensive *adj.* **1** disagreeable, displeasing, repugnant, disgusting, vexatious, irritating, outrageous, obnoxious, abusive, nauseous. **2** aggressive, belligerent, warlike, hostile, quarrelsome, pugnacious, assailant, attacking, invading.

ant. **1** agreeable, soothing, amiable, delightful, pleasing. **2** defensive, conciliatory, retiring, peaceable, placative, meek.

offer *v.* **1** present, proffer, put forward, tender, exend, give, donate. **2** bid, submit, suggest, advance, propound, propose. —*n.* **1** attempt, try, move, essay, endeavor, venture. **2** bid, proposal, proposition, overture, invitation, suggestion.

ant. *v.* **1, 2** refuse, take back, deny, withold, withdraw, disclaim. *n.* **2** refusal, denial, disclaimer, withdrawal, rejection, repudiation.

offering *n.* submission, contribution, presentation, bid, gift, grant, donation, present, sacrifice, oblation, award, proposal.

offhand *adj.* extemporaneous, unstudied, extempore, unrehearsed, unpremeditated, impromptu, casual, hasty, haphazard, spontaneous, approximate, impetuous, impulsive.

ant. studied, informed, considered, deliberate, premeditated, rehearsed.

office *n.* **1** duty, trust, function, role, province, task, charge. **2** position, appointment, incumbency, post, commission, billet. **3** ceremony, rite, observance, sacrament, solemnity, service.

officer *n.* official, dignitary, executive, functionary, bureaucrat, officeholder, appointee, commissioner, minister, director, agent.

official *adj.* **1** administrative, ministerial, bureaucratic, legislative, executive, departmental. **2** authoritative, formal, studied, ceremonious, veritable, authentic, indisputable, undeniable, real. —*n.* bureaucrat, officeholder, dignitary, officer, executive, functionary, commissioner, apparatchik, minister, director, appointee, agent.

ant. *adj.* **2** unofficial, doubtful, unreliable, dubious, informal, casual.

officiate *v.* preside, administer, serve, direct, lead, function, regulate, manage, superintend, head, handle, act, oversee, chair, emcee.

officious *adj.* meddlesome, interfering,

inquisitive, impertinent, intrusive, busy, prying, nosy, snooping, forward, overbold, obtrusive.

ant. reticent, reserved, indifferent, aloof, retiring, withdrawn.

offish *adj.* ALOOF.

offset *n.* counterbalance, compensation, counterpoise, balance, equivalent, reparation, antidote, recompense. —*v.* compensate, counterbalance, equalize, countervail, balance, neutralize, redeem, counterweight.

offshoot *n.* APPENDAGE.

offspring *n.* progeny, descendant, offshoot, issue, scion, children, young, spawn, seed, posterity, generation, succession, litter.

ant. ancestor, forebear, progenitor, begetter, parent, forerunner.

oft *adv.* OFTEN.

often *adv.* repeatedly, frequently, oftentimes, oft, habitually, commonly, recurrently, customarily, usually, generally, much.

ant. seldom, infrequently, scarcely, occasionally, rarely.

oftentimes *adv.* OFTEN.

ogle *v.* stare, goggle, eye, leer, gaze, coquet. —*n.* eyeful, leer, fleer, stare, gaze.

ogre *n.* monster, bogeyman, bugbear, fiend, brute, devil, beast, demon, incubus, harpy, ghoul.

oily *adj.* **1** greasy, fatty, oleaginous, lubricative, fat, sebaceous, lipoid, slick. **2** unctuous, ingratiating, glib, lubricious, smooth, slick, suave, plausible, devious, subservient.

ointment *n.* salve, balm, unguent, emollient, lenitive, lotion, nard, spikenard, pomade, pomatum.

OK *adj.* correct, approved, all right, satisfactory, acceptable, adequate, agreeable, good, accurate. —*n.* endorsement, approval, rubber stamp, consent, approbation, agreement, support, permission, commendation, encouragement.

ant. *adj.* unsatisfactory, faulty, incorrect, wrong, unacceptable, poor. *n.*

veto, disapproval, prohibition, condemnation, thumbs down.

old *adj.* **1** aged, mature, experienced, elderly, sedate, advanced, skilled. **2** remote, immemorial, ancient, antique, primeval, olden, dateless, primitive, antediluvian. **3** previous, former, once, past, erstwhile, olden, pre-existing, preceding, one-time, bygone. **4** shabby, worn-out, trite, stale, gray, dilapidated, senile, decayed, deteriorated.

ant. 1 immature, inexperienced, young, fresh, juvenile. **2** new, up-to-date, recent, current, modern. **3** future, coming, recent, late, succeeding. **4** unused, vigorous, fresh, new, blooming.

olden *adj.* OLD.

old-fashioned *adj.* dated, obsolete, antiquated, passé, unfashionable, démodé, outdated, out-of-date, fusty, archaic, unmodish, antique, ancient, old, fogyish, nostalgic.

ant. up-to-date, new-fangled, modern, modish, new, chic, *à la mode.*

old hat *Slang* OUT-OF-DATE.

old-line *adj.* traditional, conservative, established, ingrained, conventional, fundamentalist, reactionary, fixed, rigid, hardshell, die-hard, right-wing.

ant. latter-day, liberal, up-to-date, modern, progressive.

oleaginous *adj.* OILY.

olfaction *n.* SMELL.

oligarch *n.* RULER.

olio *n.* medley, jumble, mélange, miscellany, potpourri, gallimaufry, muddle, hash, conglomeration, variety, mixture, farrago, patchwork.

Olympian *adj.* lofty, majestic, towering, sublime, grand, grandiose, exalted, imperious, superior, haughty, overbearing, supercilious, high-and-mighty.

ant. lowly, meek, humble, submissive, inferior, ignoble.

omen *n.* portent, sign, augury, harbinger, warning, indication, auspice, stormy petrel, precursor, foreboding. —*v.* indicate, presage, augur, portend, foreshadow, bode, foretell, threaten.

ominous *adj.* sinister, threatening, foreboding, portentous, fateful, minatory, inauspicious, menacing, unpropitious, premonitory, monitory, suggestive, presaging, prophetic.

ant. auspicious, propitious, favorable, felicitous, encouraging, happy.

omission *n.* **1** neglect, oversight, disregard, negligence, default, absence, exception, delinquency, exclusion, failure. **2** blank, hiatus, gap, break, lapse, lacuna, hole, lack.

ant. 1 inclusion, admission, enclosure, attention, fulfillment, success.

omit *v.* leave out, neglect, ignore, overlook, slight, disregard, forget, bypass, skip, miss, except, exclude, let go, elide.

ant. include, enter, accept, add, insert, introduce.

omnipotence *n.* power, invincibility, might, puissance, predominance, prepotency, sovereignty, supremacy, dominion, mastery, primacy.

ant. weakness, vulnerability, inferiority, helplessness, impotence, powerlessness.

omnipotent *adj.* mighty, almighty, powerful, authoritative, puissant, all-powerful, irresistible, supreme, preeminent, prepotent, invincible, dominant, masterful.

ant. impotent, weak, unavailing, powerless, feeble, effete.

omnipresent *adj.* ubiquitous, infinite, universal, pervasive, widespread, prevalent, pervading.

onanism *n.* MASTURBATION.

oncoming *adj.* approaching, impending, looming, imminent, immediate, developing, advancing, arriving, nearing, onrushing, growing, successive.

ant. retreating, receding, retiring, remote, distant, subsiding.

one *adj.* united, whole, undivided, entire, integral, single, individual, complete, coordinated, integrated, intact, unitary, total.

ant. multiple, manifold, plural, many, split, divided.

one-horse *adj.* UNIMPORTANT.

oneness *n.* **1** singleness, sameness, identity, unity, solidarity, integrity, wholeness, unification, individuality. **2** agreement, concord, harmony, accord, amity, unity, coherence, union. **ant. 1** plurality, division, multiplicity, difference, variation. **2** discord, disagreement, dissension, dissidence, strife.

onerous *adj.* arduous, burdensome, exacting, oppressive, heavy, weighty, difficult, hard, formidable, toilsome, taxing, distressing, cumbersome, demanding, overpowering, overwhelming. **ant.** insignificant, trifling, easy, light, facile, agreeable.

one-sided *adj.* **1** partial, unfair, biased, unjust, prejudiced, warped, partisan. **2** unequal, unbalanced, uneven, lopsided, mismatched, runaway. **ant. 1** even-handed, just, equitable, fair, conscientious. **2** balanced, even, close, tight.

one-time *adj.* FORMER.

one-track *adj.* single-minded, limited, undiversified, restricted, circumscribed, undeviating, narrow, cramped, inhibited, compulsive, unimaginative, persistent. **ant.** diversified, far-ranging, liberal, exploratory, adventurous, various.

ongoing *adj.* continuing, progressing, functioning, proceeding, forward-moving, advancing, operating, progressive, prosperous, growing, developing, successful, workable, viable, unfolding, evolving. **ant.** regressive, declining, deteriorating, flagging, concluding, terminating, abortive.

onlooker *n.* spectator, bystander, observer, witness, looker-on, viewer, beholder, watcher, eyewitness, attendant, kibitzer.

only *adv.* solely, merely, exclusively, uniquely, singly, alone, just, but, no more than. —*adj.* alone, sole, single, solitary, unique, exclusive, distinct, lone.

onrush *n.* onset, flux, torrent, flood, assault, attack, storm, deluge, access, outburst. **ant.** let-up, lull, remission, recession, subsidence, cessation.

onset *n.* OUTSET.

onslaught *n.* attack, incursion, assault, raid, foray, aggression, invasion, offensive, charge, onset, offense, encounter, push, putsch, coup. **ant.** retreat, rout, flight, stampede, recession.

onus *n.* **1** burden, obligation, duty, responsibility, load, cross, burden of proof. **2** blame, responsibility, stigma, liability, debt, dishonor, imputation, shame. **ant. 1** relief, release, exemption, liberation, easement. **2** pardon, exoneration, forgiveness, justification, remission.

onward *adv.* forward, ahead, on, forth, along, in advance, beyond, frontward, headward. **ant.** backward, rearward, behind, astern, aft.

oodles *n.* MANY.

ooze[1] *v.* leak, seep, percolate, filter, exude, leach, transpire, strain, emit, discharge, dribble, drain, escape.

ooze[2] *n.* MUD.

opacity *n.* impermeability, density, imperviousness, obscurity, opaqueness, cloudiness, dullness, thickness, darkness, shadiness. **ant.** translucence, transparency, permeability, clearness, limpidity, glassiness.

opaque *adj.* **1** impervious, murky, obfuscated, dense, turbid, clouded, obscure. **2** stupid, dense, obtuse, thick, thickheaded, ignorant, unenlightened, unintelligent, crass, insensitive, cloddish, dull. **ant. 1** transparent, clear, lucid, limpid, bright. **2** enlightened, intelligent, quick, lucid, clear-headed.

open *adj.* **1** unobstructed, unlocked, unsealed, agape, accessible, ajar, unbarred, unclosed. **2** public, accessible, available, vacant, unoccupied, unrestricted, free. **3** unconcealed, overt, clear, apparent, exposed, uncovered, manifest. **4** unbiased, receptive, disinterested, fair, fair-minded, nonpartisan, unprejudiced, hospitable, amenable, generous. **5** frank, ingenuous, candid, artless, guileless, blunt, straight, plain, honest. —*v.* **1** unlock, unbar, undo, unclose, uncork, unstop. **2** rupture, perforate, puncture, pierce, prick, come apart, separate. **3** unfold, expand, unfurl, unroll, dilate, enlarge, spread out. **4** begin, start, commence, initiate, broach, launch, usher in, inaugurate. **ant.** *adj.* **1** barred, shut, blocked, stopped, closed. **2** occupied, restricted, taken, closed, limited. **3** hidden, secret, buried, concealed, latent. **4** intolerant, prejudiced, narrow, warped, closed. **5** artful, sly, wily, reticent, secretive. *v.* **1** lock, close, bar, shut, stop up. **2** join, close, seal, plug, unite. **3** fold, wrap, surround, shut, close. **4** conclude, end, finish, terminate, close.

open-and-shut *adj.* simple, obvious, clear, unmistakable, unquestionable, plain, transparent, manifest, incontrovertible, distinct, easy, determinable, bald, apparent, patent, unarguable.
ant. intricate, complicated, puzzling, indeterminate, difficult, knotty.

open-eyed *adj.* WATCHFUL.

open-faced *adj.* FRANK.

open-handed *adj.* generous, munificent, bountiful, charitable, lavish, ungrudging, unstinting, prodigal, liberal, magnanimous, extravagant, altruistic, princely, handsome.
ant. closefisted, stingy, miserly, grudging, grasping, avaricious.

open-hearted *adj.* candid, unreserved, sincere, ingenuous, guileless, frank, artless, generous, straightforward, direct, naive, unsophisticated, open, honest.

ant. disingenuous, sly, devious, artful, insincere, sophisticated.

opening *n.* **1** hole, gap, aperture, passage, breach, orifice, fissure, interspace, loophole, chasm, cleft, gulf, chink, lacuna. **2** beginning, prelude, commencement, start, dawn, opportunity, occasion, chance, vacancy.
ant. 1 closure, stoppage, plug, obstruction, seal. **2** ending, finish, termination, conclusion, close.

open-minded *adj.* receptive, unbiased, broad-minded, amenable, tolerant, unprejudiced, impartial, undogmatic, reasonable, tractable.
ant. narrow-minded, dogmatic, prejudiced, intolerant, opinionated, bigoted.

open-mouthed *adj.* NOISY.

operable *adj.* FEASIBLE.

operate *v.* **1** function, work, run, go, behave, effect, cause. **2** conduct, manage, carry on, manipulate, transact, superintend, guide, run.
ant. 1 fail, stop, stall, falter, break down.

operation *n.* **1** working, performance, procedure, process, effecting, proceeding, manipulation, activation, functioning, running, performing. **2** transaction, act, affair, process, course, action, business. **3** campaign, exercise, maneuver, offensive, assault.

operational *adj.* functional, ready, set, usable, activated, active, operative, effective, working, workable, viable, conditioned, repaired.
ant. inoperative, ineffective, unusable, nonfunctional, abortive, broken.

operative *adj.* **1** effective, in effect, applicable. **2** working, functional, operational, usable, running, acting, readied, set, activated.
ant. 1 ineffective, inapplicable. **2** inoperative, powerless, nonfunctioning, unusable.

operator *n.* **1** operative, worker, technician, mechanic, handler, workman, conductor, pilot. **2** *Slang* shyster, fraud, adventurer, finagler, shark, manipulator, wheeler-dealer (*Slang*), swindler.

opiate *n.* soporific, sedative, hypnotic, narcotic, tranquilizer, calmative, somnifacient, anodyne, nepenthe, downer (*Slang*).

ant. stimulant, excitant, bracer, upper (*Slang*), pep pill (*Slang*).

opine *v.* think, state, conjecture, suggest, say, volunteer, offer, hold, consider, deem, reckon, guess, allow.

opinion *n.* conclusion, judgment, estimate, evaluation, assessment, view, idea, notion, belief, conviction, persuasion, impression, conception, feeling, sentiment.

opinionated *adj.* obstinate, pig-headed, obdurate, unyielding, pertinacious, biased, bigoted, opinionative, inflexible, overbearing, headstrong, stubborn, impervious, self-important.

ant. open-minded, compliant, yielding, flexible, receptive, tractable.

opinionative *adj.* OPINIONATED.

opponent *n.* antagonist, adversary, foe, competitor, contestant, challenger, resister, contender, rival, assailant, disputant, enemy.

ant. ally, associate, partner, colleague, helper, friend.

opportune *adj.* timely, auspicious, convenient, favorable, fortunate, well-chosen, seasonable, pat, fit, felicitous, suitable, lucky, appropriate, propitious, right.

ant. inopportune, untimely, unseasonable, inconvenient, inappropriate, unfortunate.

opportunism *n.* pragmatism, expediency, realism, realpolitik, Machiavellianism, timeserving, utilitarianism, unscrupulousness.

ant. idealism, probity, altruism, high-mindedness, principle, conscientiousness.

opportunist *n.* ADVENTURER.

opportunity *n.* occasion, chance, juncture, time, moment, possibility, scope, advantage, opening, situation, means, contingency, turn.

oppose *v.* **1** resist, combat, withstand, antagonize, contravene, thwart, obstruct, prevent, contradict. **2** contrast, counterbalance, offset, compare, equate, parallel, match, confront.

ant. **1** concur, support, aid, help, cooperate. **2** merge, combine, blend, mingle, fuse.

opposed *adj.* CONTRARY.

opposing *adj.* CONTRADICTORY.

opposite *adj.* facing, opposed, fronting, contrary, contradictory, antithetical, inverse, unlike. —*n.* reverse, contrary, antithesis, antipode, contradiction, counterpart, complement, reversal.

ant. *adj.* identical, same, similar, consistent, like. *n.* similarity, agreement, image, identity, duplicate.

opposition *n.* **1** antagonism, hostility, animosity, aversion, resistance, conflict, repulsion. **2** antithesis, contradiction, inconsistency, contrariety, contrast, dualism, symmetry, paradox. **3** obstruction, check, impediment, obstacle, hindrance, bar, restraint, restriction.

ant. **1** cooperation, collaboration, synergism, attraction, combination. **2** correspondence, agreement, reciprocity, concurrence, consistency. **3** assistance, aid, furtherance, help, hand.

oppress *v.* subjugate, abuse, crush, tyrannize, subdue, overpower, persecute, harass, afflict, burden, weigh down, overwhelm, suppress, enslave, trample, squelch.

ant. liberate, emancipate, free, unburden, deliver, disencumber.

oppressed *adj.* downtrodden, disadvantaged, underprivileged, dispossessed, deprived, handicapped, abused, humble, prostrate, abject.

ant. exalted, privileged, powerful, advantaged, elite, favored.

oppression *n.* tyranny, injustice, persecution, subjugation, autocracy, despotism, bullying, maltreatment, brutality, harshness, abuse, coercion.

ant. justice, benevolence, clemency,

deliverance, compassion, humaneness.

oppressive *adj*. **1** burdensome, tyrannical, exacting, severe, heavy, overpowering, overwhelming. **2** depressing, worrisome, discouraging, gloomy, uncomfortable, close, dismal, painful.
ant. 1 negligible, lenient, gentle, easy, soft. **2** cheering, heartening, encouraging, propitious, restorative.

oppressor *n*. tyrant, taskmaster, despot, autocrat, bully, dictator, martinet, tormentor, scourge, slave-driver, browbeater.

opprobrious *adj*. **1** abusive, scurrilous, insolent, insulting, vituperative, reproachful, offensive, contemptuous. **2** shameful, disgraceful, hateful, disreputable, infamous, despicable, dishonorable.
ant. 1 complimentary, flattering, gratifying, pleasant, praising. **2** honorable, reputable, commendable, estimable, distinguished.

opprobrium *n*. infamy, disgrace, dishonor, disrepute, contempt, reproach, shame, humiliation, stigma, ignominy, discredit.
ant. respect, esteem, honor, regard, deference, repute.

opt *v*. choose, elect, decide on, select, pick, single out, settle on, fix on, prefer.
ant. reject, dismiss, decide against, rule out, turn down, exclude.

optimal *adj*. OPTIMUM.

optimistic *adj*. cheerful, hopeful, confident, enthusiastic, sanguine, roseate, blithe, buoyant, upbeat, sunny, forward-looking, inspiriting, rousing.
ant. pessimistic, gloomy, despairing, hopeless, dejected, mournful.

optimum *adj*. best, optimal, superlative, unequaled, excellent, peerless, most, greatest, highest, choicest, utmost, unmatched, select.
ant. lowest, poorest, minimal, least, worst, inferior.

option *n*. **1** franchise, decision, discretion, self-determination, volition, suffrage, voice, election, choice. **2** alternative, choice, selection, possibility, preference, desire, liking, predilection.

optional *adj*. elective, discretionary, facultative, conditional, voluntary, selective, indeterminate, open, open-ended, permissible, allowable.
ant. compulsory, obligatory, mandatory, imperative, required, requisite.

opulence *n*. wealth, affluence, luxury, riches, fortune, prosperity, comfort, treasure, money, resources, capital.
ant. poverty, squalor, penury, need, degradation, beggary.

opulent *adj*. wealthy, rich, affluent, well-off, moneyed, well-to-do, prosperous, comfortable, well-fixed, well-heeled (*Slang*).
ant. destitute, indigent, needy, poor, down-and-out, impecunious.

opus *n*. composition, work, creation, piece, brainchild, invention, *oeuvre*, production, effort, product.

oracle *n*. seer, sage, authority, pundit, savant, mastermind, prophet, soothsayer, forecaster, high priest, wizard, guru, sibyl, clairvoyant.

oracular *adj*. prophetic, predictive, prescient, prognostic, authoritative, magisterial, wise, knowing, sage.

oral *adj*. spoken, verbal, verbalized, voiced, viva-voce.

orate *v*. speechify, lecture, declaim, perorate, preach, sermonize, discourse, hold the floor.

oration *n*. address, speech, discourse, declamation, salutatory, disquisition, sermon, recital, talk, lecture, peroration.

orator *n*. speaker, discourser, lecturer, rhetorician, talker, sermonizer, preacher.

oratorical *adj*. rhetorical, eloquent, elocutionary, declamatory, sermonizing, grandiloquent, silver-tongued, orotund, bombastic, magniloquent.
ant. chatty, intimate, informal, conversational.

oratory *n*. public speaking, speechmaking, rhetoric, declamation, elocution, eloquence, speechifying, sermonizing, grandiloquence, bombast, preaching.

orb *n.* sphere, globe, ball, globule, moon, spheroid.

orbicular *adj.* ROUND.

orbit *n.* **1** path, road, way, route, pathway, passage, circuit, course, cycle, trajectory. **2** domain, realm, scope, sphere, field, province, reach, grasp, locus, power, compass, territory, sway, bounds.

orchestrate *v.* stage-manage, synchronize, put together, coordinate, combine, organize, direct, carry out, arrange, put into shape.

ordain *v.* **1** order, decree, establish, dictate, command, rule, prescribe, pronounce, enact, legislate, constitute, institute. **2** predestine, destine, fate, predetermine, foredoom, foreordain, predestinate, preordain.

ordeal *n.* tribulation, trial, torment, nightmare, torture, anguish, vexation, agony, misery, pain, horror, curse, trouble, affliction, hell.
ant. joy, delight, pleasure, breeze.

order *n.* **1** method, system, organization, formation, formulation, arrangement, procedure, convention, usage, custom, distribution, sequence, classification, neatness, tidiness, orderliness, propriety. **2** condition, shape, state, form, fettle, repair, commission. **3** command, decree, rule, regulation, ordinance, dictate, injunction, instruction, behest, charge, fiat, ultimatum, mandate, say-so. —*v.* **1** command, direct, bid, rule, dictate, prescribe, enjoin, decree, charge, mandate, compel, require, ordain, instruct, summon. **2** systematize, arrange, methodize, classify, regulate, coordinate, codify, catalogue, grade, class, categorize, rank, tabulate.
ant. *n.* **1** disorder, mess, jumble, hodge-podge, chaos, anarchy. *v.* **2** disorder, scramble, disarrange, jumble, mix up, mess up.

orderliness *n.* ORDER.

orderly *adj.* **1** neat, systematic, organized, systematized, methodical, methodized, regular, regulated, regularized, classified, shipshape, tidy. **2** disciplined, law-abiding, well-behaved, peaceful, quiet, proper, civil, tractable.
ant. **1** scrambled, messy, disorderly, chaotic, higgledy-piggledy. **2** unruly, undisciplined, lawless, mutinous.

ordinance *n.* decree, rule, ruling, statute, law, regulation, edict, act.

ordinarily *adv.* usually, commonly, mostly, generally, habitually, as a rule, by and large, regularly, conventionally, customarily, normally, routinely.
ant. rarely, infrequently, seldom, uncommonly.

ordinary *adj.* **1** common, usual, everyday, regular, habitual, accustomed, conventional, expected, customary, prevailing, familiar, normal, medial, stock, established, standard. **2** mediocre, commonplace, humdrum, undistinguished, run-of-the-mill, tolerable, passable, so-so, insipid, tame, unimpressive, uninspired, banal, uninteresting.
ant. **1** unusual, odd, rare, irregular, freak, uncommon. **2** outstanding, impressive, extraordinary, significant, noteworthy.

ordnance *n.* armaments, arms, munitions, artillery, weapons, guns.

ordure *n.* excrement, feces, dung, manure, excreta, droppings, stool, guano, coprolite, sewage, filth, *merde.*

organ *n.* voice, publication, periodical, vehicle, instrument, mouthpiece, medium, sheet, journal, channel.

organic *adj.* **1** living, live, animate, biological. **2** somatic, structural, bodily, corporeal, organized, inherent, physical, systemic, constitutional, innate, morphological, intrinsic.
ant. **1** inorganic, inanimate, mineral.

organism *n.* body, creature, animal, plant, microorganism, cell, bacterium.

organization *n.* **1** method, order, system, procedure, regularity, methodization, methodology, arrangement, formulation, systematization, coordination, classification, tabulation, structure, plan. **2** federation, association, alliance, affiliation, company, corporation, guild, club, league, school, society, institute, party, corps.
ant. 1 disorder, disorganization, chaos, confusion.

organize *v.* systematize, order, methodize, regularize, classify, sort, group, coordinate, tabulate, catalogue, structure, codify, categorize.
ant. scramble, jumble, confuse, mix up, disarrange, disorganize.

orgiastic *adj.* wanton, abandoned, libertine, debauched, bacchanalian, drunken, undisciplined, riotous, licentious, hedonistic, sybaritic, saturnalian, Dionysian, wild.
ant. temperate, moderate, disciplined, monastic, ascetic.

orgy *n.* **1** revelry, debauch, debauchery, saturnalia, carousal, wassail, bacchanal, bacchanalia, drunk. **2** overindulgence, excess, feast, riot, fit, bout, spree, kick (*Slang*), jag (*Slang*), binge (*Slang*).

orient *v.* adjust, adapt, align, accustom, acculturate, reconcile, acclimate, acclimatize, fit, conform, accommodate, orientate.

orientate *v.* ORIENT.

orientation *n.* bearings, position, point of view, attitude, stance, adjustment, adaptation, acclimation, accommodation, acculturation, familiarization, indoctrination.

orifice *n.* opening, aperture, hole, mouth, perforation, vent, pore, cavity, crack, split, gap, slot, puncture, lacuna, fistula.

origin *n.* **1** source, commencement, beginning, birth, genesis, seed, womb, cradle, germ, fountain, spring, root, dawn, inauguration, inception, origination. **2** parentage, ancestry, lineage, extraction, descent, line, pedi-

gree, antecedents, derivation, genealogy, heredity.
ant. 1 end, finish, conclusion, death, grave.

original *adj.* **1** first, primary, primal, earliest, aboriginal, elementary, fundamental, introductory, underlying, basic, primeval. **2** inventive, generative, seminal, creative, imaginative, causal, germinative, dormative. **3** new, fresh, clever, unconventional, unexpected, unusual, different, unorthodox, atypical, singular, unique, unprecedented. —*n.* **1** archetype, prototype, pattern, model, master, paradigm, example, precedent, pioneer, exemplar, norm, standard. **2** eccentric, character, individual, anomaly, genius, prodigy, iconoclast, nonconformist, odd duck, oddball (*Slang*), weirdo (*Slang*), kook (*Slang*).
ant. *adj.* **1** last, final, ultimate, end, concluding. **2** unproductive, imitative, unimaginative, sterile, barren. **3** stale, trite, typical, hackneyed. *n.* **1** copy, imitation, duplicate, reproduction, replica. **2** conformist, traditionalist, Babbitt.

originality *n.* creativity, inventiveness, imagination, cleverness, unconventionality, unorthodoxy, genius, uniqueness, iconoclasm, newness, freshness, singularity, novelty, nonconformity, boldness.
ant. imitativeness, staleness, traditionalism, conformity, orthodoxy.

originate *v.* **1** create, initiate, invent, make, devise, concoct, pioneer, inaugurate, introduce, conceive, coin, compose, start, engender, give birth to. **2** be born, come from, arise, emanate, derive, stem, be rooted in, be shaped by, spring from.

origination *n.* ORIGIN.

originator *n.* CREATOR.

orison *n.* PRAYER.

ornament *n.* adornment, decoration, embellishment, trimming, enrichment, garnish, accessory, ornamentation, elaboration, furbelow. —*v.*

adorn, embellish, decorate, enrich, beautify, trim, garnish, enrich, elaborate, dress up, brighten, festoon.

ornamental *adj.* decorative, enhancing, beautifying, enriching, pretty, picturesque.

ornamentation *n.* adornment, embellishment, decoration, decor, trim, garnish, accessories, glitter, embroidery, elaborateness, elaboration.

ornate *adj.* elaborate, sumptuous, baroque, rococo, florid, flowery, fussy, showy, flashy, pretentious, overdone. **ant.** simple, plain, severe.

ornery *adj.* mean, low, disagreeable, unpleasant, mulish, stubborn, unruly, surly, cranky, churlish, refractory, uncooperative, perverse, cussed. **ant.** pleasant, agreeable, cooperative, reasonable, civil.

orotund *adj.* resonant, reverberating, resounding, sonorous, oratorical, pompous, bombastic, florid, declamatory, inflated, pretentious.

orthodox *adj.* **1** unquestioning, dogmatic, rigid, conformist, strict, hidebound, narrow, devout. **2** accepted, approved, customary, conventional, conservative, established, official, traditional, standard, proper, prevailing, usual, normal. **ant. 1** heretical, heterodox, radical, schismatic. **2** unusual, innovative, unconventional, untried, individualistic.

orthodoxy *n.* devoutness, faith, piety, observance, belief, devotion, reverence, credo, conformity, conformism, conservatism, tradition, traditionalism, rigidity, inflexibility. **ant.** heterodoxy, heresy, impiety, nonconformism, innovation, flexibility.

oscillate *v.* **1** swing, librate, vibrate, pulsate, pulse, alternate, wave, **2** vacillate, fluctuate, waver, vary, change, shilly-shally, hesitate, hem and haw. **ant. 2** decide, resolve, settle, choose.

osculate *v.* KISS.

ostensible *adj.* seeming, apparent, professed, declared, evident, probable, likely, plausible, manifest, surface, implied, presumable, avowed, visible, ostensive.

ostensive *adj.* OSTENSIBLE.

ostentation *n.* pretentiousness, display, show, showiness, flourish, frills, affectation, airs, flashiness, flaunting, gaudiness, flamboyance. **ant.** unpretentiousness, humility, reserve, modesty, simplicity, inconspicuousness.

ostentatious *adj.* pretentious, showy, flashy, affected, boastful, conspicuous, flamboyant, immodest, garish, grandiose, pompous. **ant.** simple, modest, plain, unpretentious, inconspicuous.

ostracism *n.* exclusion, disapproval, boycott, avoidance, rejection, excommunication, exile, isolation, expulsion, ouster, blacklisting, blackballing, cold shoulder. **ant.** acceptance, inclusion, approval, welcome, embrace, invitation.

ostracize *v.* exclude, avoid, shun, reject, banish, oust, expel, blacklist, blackball, excommunicate, isolate, boycott, cold-shoulder. **ant.** include, accept, approve, invite, mingle with.

other *adj.* **1** different, distinct, separate, dissimilar, unlike, disparate, unrelated. **2** additional, added, further, second, another, alternate, alternative, extra, spare, auxiliary, supplementary, more, remaining. **ant. 1** like, alike, similar, same. **2** fewer, less.

otiose *adj.* **1** lazy, indolent, languid, inactive, resting, slothful, sluggish, dormant, idle, somnolent. **2** useless, futile, vain, unproductive, unavailing, ineffective, worthless, superfluous, powerless, bootless, unrewarding. **ant. 1** active, energetic, busy, dynamic. **2** useful, effective, worthwhile, rewarding.

ottoman *n.* hassock, pouf, footstool,

seat, sofa, divan, couch, taboret, cushion.

oust v. eject, throw out, expel, turn out, cast out, evict, banish, dispossess, dismiss, unseat, kick out, remove, depose, overthrow, dethrone, fire, boot out (*Slang*), bounce (*Slang*).
ant. install, admit, seat, induct, receive, invite.

ouster n. dispossession, ejection, dismissal, expulsion, discharge, firing, overthrow, eviction, banishment, removal, bounce (*Slang*), boot (*Slang*).
ant. installation, invitation, admission, reception, induction.

out adj. **1** OUTSIDE. **2** extinguished, exhausted, smothered, doused, finished, ended, done, over, concluded, at an end, elapsed, expired, past. —n. excuse, dodge, escape, explanation, alibi, defense, justification, reason, loophole, solution, answer.
ant. adj. **2** on, ongoing, current, live, continuing.

out-and-out adj. thoroughgoing, unmitigated, consummate, blatant, utter, complete, total, unmistakable, outright, unqualified, flagrant, downright.

outbreak n. **1** eruption, epidemic, outburst, explosion, invasion. **2** mutiny, insurrection, upheaval, uprising, revolt, insurgence, revolution, disturbance, riot, uproar, violence.

outburst n. explosion, eruption, outpouring, rush, discharge, burst, blast, thunder, fulmination, paroxysm, outbreak.

outcast n. exile, displaced person, D.P., pariah, persona non grata, fugitive, vagabond, derelict, outlaw, untouchable, leper.

outclass v. surpass, outdo, exceed, outstrip, outdistance, outshine, cap, top, beat, eclipse, overshadow, dominate, lead, tower over, transcend.

outcome n. result, consequence, effect, aftermath, end, upshot, issue, sequel, payoff, outgrowth, aftereffect, repercussion, denouement, harvest.

outcry n. clamor, tumult, uproar, noise, scream, yell, hue and cry, protest, demonstration, outburst, agitation, hullaballoo, racket, howl.

outdated adj. OUT-OF-DATE.

outdistance v. **1** outrun, outstrip, outreach, go beyond, overtake, leave behind. **2** outdo, surpass, exceed, eclipse, top, cap, prevail, dominate, transcend, overshadow, outshine, master.

outdo v. surpass, exceed, excel, top, cap, eclipse, outshine, outdistance, outclass, lead, master, transcend, beat.

outdoor adj. out-of-door, outside, open-air, fresh-air, alfresco, exterior.
ant. indoor, interior, inside, enclosed.

outer adj. exterior, external, farther, outside, extramural, outward, distal, peripheral, remote, outlying, outermost.
ant. inner, nearer, closer, proximal, inside.

outface v. DEFY.

outfit n. **1** equipment, gear, rig, ensemble, clothes, trousseau, apparel, costume, clothing, getup, furnishings, supplies, provisions, accouterments, paraphernalia, necessaries, necessities. **2** group, troop, gang, troupe, company, detachment, detail, band, force, squad, corps, team, crew, muster. —v. equip, provision, rig, fit out, deck, supply, furnish, dress, costume, appoint, gear, garb, accouter.

outflank v. OUTWIT.

outflow n. stream, gush, jet, flow, outpouring, effusion, spring, river, spurt, emanation, effluence, effluent, issue, emergence, outgo.
ant. inflow, inrush, input, income.

outfox v. OUTWIT.

outgo v. outstrip, outdistance, go beyond, exceed, surpass, outdo, overtake, shoot ahead, leave behind, pass. —n. expense, outlay, expenditure, price, cost, disbursement, payment.
ant. n. income, earnings, profit.

outgoing *adj.* **1** departing, retiring, withdrawing, superseded, replaced, late. **2** extroverted, friendly, sociable, convivial, cordial, approachable, warm, demonstrative, unreserved, informal, amiable.

ant. 1 incoming, new. **2** introverted, withdrawn, reticent, reserved, repressed, taciturn.

outgrowth *n.* offshoot, byproduct, excrescence, upshot, outcome, result, effect, derivative, development, product, yield, fruit, aftereffect, emergence, outcropping.

outguess *v.* OUTWIT.

outhouse *n.* privy, backhouse, latrine, toilet, outbuilding.

outing *n.* excursion, junket, jaunt, trip, holiday, expedition, ramble, tour, turn, airing.

outlander *n.* ALIEN.

outlandish *adj.* bizarre, freaky, freakish, weird, barbaric, strange, grotesque, eccentric, peculiar, queer, ridiculous, outré, mad, nutty (*Slang*), kooky (*Slang*).

ant. ordinary, familiar, usual, inconspicuous, commonplace.

outlast *v.* outlive, survive, outwear, endure, outstay.

outlaw *n.* criminal, fugitive, lawbreaker, desperado, pariah, hooligan, bandit, gunman, thug, gangster. —*v.* prohibit, ban, bar, debar, forbid, suppress, boycott, circumscribe, constrain, quash, proscribe, taboo.

ant. *v.* sanction, permit, legalize.

outlay *n.* expenditure, expense, cost, charge, disbursement, fee, outgo, payment, price.

outlet *n.* **1** vent, passage, spout, nozzle, valve, mouth, hole, spigot, duct, pore, opening, orifice, exit. **2** avenue, way, path, channel, means.

outline *n.* **1** sketch, diagram, line drawing, delineation, lineament, border, shape, contour, boundary, edge, silhouette, profile, periphery. **2** synopsis, resumé, blueprint, plan, map, draft, graph, scenario, précis, prospectus, summary, brief, digest, rough. —*v.* **1** sketch, draw, delineate, trace, diagram, silhouette, limn. **2** summarize, digest, abridge, rough out, recapitulate, sum up, abstract, compress.

outlive *v.* outlast, survive, endure, live through, overcome, recover from, recuperate from.

outlook *n.* **1** view, scene, scenery, panorama, vista, aspect, spectacle, landscape. **2** expectation, anticipation, prospect, future, course, forecast, probability, likelihood, hope, speculation, promise, tendency. **3** point of view, attitude, viewpoint, slant, frame of mind, perspective, standpoint, position, stance, construct, angle.

outlying *adj.* peripheral, out-of-the-way, suburban, exurban, rural, remote, outer, backwoods, far-off, provincial, exterior.

outmoded *adj.* OUT-OF-DATE.

out-of-bounds *adj.* UNCALLED-FOR.

out-of-date *adj.* outdated, outmoded, outworn, old-fashioned, obsolete, moth-eaten, superseded, antiquated, extinct, dead, passé, unfashionable, irrelevant, tired, stale.

ant. up-to-date, current, fashionable, new, in.

out-of-door *adj.* OUTDOOR.

out of it *Slang* ABSTRACTED.

out-of-the-way *adj.* remote, secluded, distant, far-off, isolated, lonely, unfrequented, forlorn, godforsaken, backwoods, outlying, unspoiled, unpopulated, inaccessible.

ant. nearby, close, adjacent, thriving, active.

outpouring *n.* effusion, outflow, spate, stream, gush, jet, flow, river, spring, spurt, effluence, effluent, outgo, rain, downfall, torrent.

output *n.* production, productivity, achievement, accomplishment, manufacture, yield, run, product, produce, crop, harvest, end product.

outrage *n.* **1** atrocity, barbarism, brutality, transgression, havoc, excess, enormity, cruelty, savagery, fiendishness, inhumanity. **2** insult, slander, libel, insolence, contempt, contumely, offense, affront, gall, effrontery, scurrility, slap, blow, provocation, humiliation. **3** fury, rage, anger, resentment, wrath, indignation, self-righteousness, acrimony, asperity, passion, vexation, rankling. —*v.* **1** violate, abuse, ill-use, wrong, maltreat, brutalize, insult, injure, harm, assault, persecute, humiliate, ravage. **2** infuriate, enrage, anger, vex, shock, scandalize, incense, provoke, madden, gall, affront, offend. **3** RAPE.

outrageous *adj.* **1** atrocious, monstrous, fiendish, diabolical, contemptible, vicious, inhuman, inhumane, barbarous, despicable, brutal, savage, cruel. **2** indecent, immoral, scandalous, shocking, improper, flagrant, excessive, notorious, wanton, wicked, immoderate, intolerable, unrestrained.

outré *adj.* bizarre, odd, freakish, extravagant, outlandish, eccentric, freaky, curious, exaggerated, unconventional, shocking, conspicuous, deviant, kooky (*Slang*), kinky (*Slang*).
ant. usual, everyday, inconspicuous, conventional, ordinary.

outright *adj.* downright, out-and-out, forthright, unreserved, unrestrained, complete, utter, unmitigated, all-out, thorough, thoroughgoing, direct, blunt, total, consummate.
ant. partial, conditional, indirect, ambiguous, covert.

outset *n.* start, beginning, opening, commencement, inception, onset, inauguration, origin, initiation, first, overture, birth, dawn.
ant. end, conclusion, finish, consummation, finale.

outshine *v.* SURPASS.

outside *n.* exterior, face, facade, front, appearance, surface, look, externals, aspect. —*adj.* **1** outer, out, exterior, external, surface, visible, apparent. **2** foreign, alien, outlying, exotic, unfamiliar. **3** extreme, overgenerous,

maximal, maximum, full, ample, high, inordinate, excessive. **4** slight, inconsequential, small, marginal, unlikely, improbable, remote.
ant. *n.* inside, interior, center. *adj.* **1** interior, inside, internal, hidden, unrevealed. **2** familiar, home, local, neighborhood. **3** minimal, cautious, careful, low. **4** probable, certain, sure, likely.

outsider *n.* alien, stranger, foreigner, outlander, noncitizen, nonmember, nonparticipant, bystander, observer, interloper, intruder, newcomer.
ant. insider, member, participant, comrade, colleague.

outskirts *n.* suburbs, suburbia, exurbia, purlieu, periphery, faubourg, banlieue, border, limits, environs.

outsmart *v.* OUTWIT.

outspoken *adj.* frank, forthright, direct, blunt, unreserved, straightforward, candid, honest, opinionated, articulate.
ant. reticent, taciturn, reserved, timid, uncommunicative, tongue-tied, silent.

outspread *v.* EXTEND.

outstanding *adj.* **1** preeminent, noted, noteworthy, famous, well-known, prominent, conspicuous, noticeable, striking, obtrusive, visible, glaring, important, eye-catching. **2** unresolved, unsettled, continuing, remaining, unconcluded, surviving, pending, existing, unfinished.
ant. 1 inconspicuous, ordinary, dull. **2** resolved, settled, concluded, finished.

outstretch *v.* EXPAND.

outstrip *v.* **1** OUTDISTANCE. **2** EXCEL.

outward *adj.* **1** exterior, outer, external, outside, visible, evident, observable, apparent. **2** superficial, surface, extrinsic, adventitious, incidental, extraneous.
ant. 1 inner, inward, inside, interior. **2** inherent, innate, essential, intrinsic.

outwear *v.* OUTLAST.

outweigh *v.* overshadow, overweigh

override, predominate, preponderate, supersede, invalidate, counteract, cancel, nullify, dwarf.

outwit v. outsmart, outguess, outfox, outclass, outshine, outflank, get around, fool, dupe, trick, take in, best, worst, foil, trap, snare, psych out (*Slang*).

outworn adj. OUT-OF-DATE.

oval adj. ovoid, ovate, ovoidal, egg-shaped, elliptical, ellipsoid, ovular, oviform.

ovate adj. OVAL.

ovation n. acclamation, applause, tribute, fanfare, salvo, salute, bravos, cheers, homage, adulation, clapping. **ant.** booing, hissing, heckling, razzing (*Slang*), Bronx cheer (*Slang*).

over adv. above, overhead, aloft, high, on high. —adj. finished, done, completed, ended, concluded, past, gone, elapsed, expired, dead, terminated, closed, *fini*, *finito*. **ant.** adv. below, low, earthward. adj. ongoing, in progress, current, unfinished.

overabundance n. REDUNDANCY.

overact v. OVERDO.

overage n. SURPLUS.

overall adj. all-inclusive, comprehensive, exhaustive, all-embracing, unlimited, sweeping, extensive, widespread, thoroughgoing, far-reaching, total, entire. **ant.** partial, fragmentary, incomplete, sketchy.

overbear v. DOMINATE.

overbearing adj. 1 arrogant, dictatorial, bossy, officious, self-important, pompous, imperious, lordly, supercilious, highhanded, haughty, overweening, patronizing, self-assertive. 2 overriding, compelling, dominant, supreme, utmost, cardinal, paramount, imperative, pressing, major. **ant.** 1 deferential, humble, modest, timid, self-effacing. 2 inconsequential, minor, lesser, unimportant.

overblown adj. exaggerated, inflated, pretentious, excessive, puffed up, disproportionate, immoderate, undue, preposterous, flamboyant, fatuous, florid, flowery, overdone. **ant.** moderate, modest, unpretentious, simple.

overcast adj. cloudy, clouded, beclouded, gloomy, dark, murky, sunless, gray, threatening, heavy, lowering, smoggy, foggy, dim. **ant.** clear, bright, sunny, brilliant, cheerful.

overcome v. defeat, conquer, overrun, surmount, triumph, prevail, win, best, subdue, overpower, subjugate, override, master, weather, survive.

overconfident adj. arrogant, brash, rash, presumptuous, egotistical, foolhardy, reckless, heedless, headstrong, overweening, conceited, boastful. **ant.** timid, timorous, insecure, unsure, self-doubting.

overdo v. 1 overreach, overtax, exhaust, overwork, overburden, strain, overexert, tire, drudge, drive oneself. 2 exaggerate, overplay, overact, overstate, blow up, lay it on (*Slang*), ham (*Slang*), hoke up (*Slang*). **ant.** 2 understate, underplay, minimize.

overflow v. flood, deluge, run over, spill over, slop over, inundate, swamp, pour in, rush in, gush, surge. —n. REDUNDANCY.

overhang v. 1 project over, jut over, hang over, protrude. 2 impend, loom, forbode, threaten, darken, cast a shadow, cast a pall, hover, foreshadow, menace, portend. —n. projection, eave, jut, brow, ledge, shelf, ridge, salient, extension, gallery, balcony.

overhaul v. inspect, repair, examine, renovate, check, test, fix, restore, go over, recondition, service. —n. checkup, going-over, examination, repair, reconditioning, renovation, servicing.

overjoyed adj. ecstatic, enraptured, rapturous, delighted, enchanted, transported, elated, carried away, blissful, thrilled, delirious, euphoric.

ant. miserable, heartbroken, woebegone, disappointed.

overlap v. overlay, overlie, overhang, pleat, lap, lap over, fold back on, extend over, superimpose, overspread, imbricate.

overlay v. OVERLAP.

overlie v. OVERLAP.

overlook v. **1** miss, neglect, forget, scant, skip, slight, omit, overpass, disregard, ignore. **2** disregard, ignore, excuse, forgive, condone, pardon, wink at. **3** supervise, oversee, direct, survey, watch, keep an eye on, manage, inspect, scrutinize, superintend.

overlord n. LORD.

overly adv. too, unduly, excessively, exceedingly, inordinately, immoderately, unnecessarily, unfairly, disproportionately, needlessly, overmuch, acutely, unreasonably.

ant. inadequately, insufficiently, sparingly.

overmatch v. SURPASS.

overmuch adv. OVERLY.

overpass v. **1** SURPASS. **2** OVERLOOK.

overplay v. OVERDO.

overpower v. subdue, overcome, conquer, master, crush, overwhelm, subjugate, overthrow, overturn, vanquish, outdo, beat, triumph over, enslave, immobilize, paralyze.

overpowering adj. OVERWHELMING.

overrated adj. overesteemed, overassessed, overpopular, oversold, overpraised, overpublicized, overvalued, overestimated, overprized, misrepresented, exaggerated, disappointing.

ant. underrated, underestimated, neglected, belittled, ignored.

override v. **1** vanquish, conquer, dominate, overbear, quell, overcome, overwhelm, subdue, ride roughshod over, prevail over. **2** disregard, overrule, neglect, flout, nullify, cancel, annul, counteract, countermand, supersede, set aside.

overriding adj. compelling, primary, principal, chief, transcendent, over-

powering, overwhelming, paramount, supreme, dominant, predominant, obligatory.

ant. negligible, minor, insignificant, trivial.

overrule v. nullify, cancel, invalidate, override, repeal, countermand, annul, set aside, revoke, abrogate, rescind, vacate.

overrun v. infest, plague, invade, swarm over, encroach upon, overspread, inundate, deluge, beset, permeate, pervade.

oversee v. direct, supervise, survey, watch, see to, overlook, superintend, boss, eye, keep an eye on, scrutinize, watch over, administer, regulate, conduct.

overseer n. director, superintendent, supervisor, foreman, boss, administrator, chief, head, captain, manager, governor, taskmaster, slave-driver.

oversell v. EXAGGERATE.

overshadow v. eclipse, dominate, domineer, control, prevail over, lead, outshine, outrank, outdo, outclass, override, surpass.

overshoot v. EXCEED.

oversight n. neglect, negligence, neglectfulness, absent-mindedness, omission, blunder, inattention, disregard, inadvertence, heedlessness, carelessness.

overstate v. EXAGGERATE.

overstep v. exceed, overdo, trespass, impinge, encroach, infringe, transgress, violate, intrude, usurp, misbehave, go too far.

ant. confine, limit, restrain.

oversupply n. EXCESS.

overt adj. manifest, apparent, obvious, clear, patent, straightforward, unconcealed, outright, visible, plain, public, undisguised, direct.

ant. covert, concealed, hidden, underhand.

overtake v. catch up with, reach, gain on, arrive at, go by, pass, outstrip, outrun, go beyond, outdo, outdistance, leave behind.

overthrow v. **1** upset, knock down,

throw over, displace, overturn, topple, capsize, upend, tumble. **2** defeat, depose, oust, vanquish, overcome, master, take over, unseat, overpower. —*n.* upset, displacement, overturn, triumph, victory, mastery, coup, dethronement, revolution.

overtop *v.* SURPASS.

overture *n.* proposal, approach, offer, suggestion, presentation, proposition, advance, suggestion, opening, invitation, bid, recommendation.

overturn *v.* **1** capsize, upset, throw over, displace, knock over, knock down, upend. **2** defeat, overthrow, ruin, master, overpower, overwhelm, vanquish, best, overcome, turn out, depose, unseat, oust.

overview *n.* survey, review, study, investigation, scrutiny, inspection, observation, examination.

overweening *adj.* presumptuous, arrogant, overbearing, haughty, patronizing, pompous, overconfident, egotistical, imperious, domineering, supercilious, proud, highhanded. **ant.** modest, self-effacing, deferential, timid.

overweigh *v.* OUTWEIGH.

overweight *n.* obesity, corpulence, stoutness, chubbiness, pudginess, paunchiness, fleshiness, plumpness, heaviness. —*adj.* obese, corpulent, stout, chubby, pudgy, paunchy, fleshy, plump, heavy, chunky, overstuffed, well-padded, fat. **ant.** *n.* underweight, emaciation, undernourishment. *adj.* undernourished, emaciated, skinny, scrawny.

overwhelm *v.* **1** overflow, flood, inundate, cover, bury, submerge, drown, deluge, overrun, swamp, swallow up, immerse, engulf, whelm. **2** overcome, defeat, crush, overpower, override, destroy, conquer, shatter, beat, wipe out, paralyze, immobilize.

overwhelming *adj.* crushing, devastating, stunning, overpowering, severe, immobilizing, paralyzing, shattering, ruinous, stupefying.

overwork *v.* **1** drive, weary, wear out, overexert, overtax, exploit, overburden, tire, oppress, fatigue, strain, slave-drive. **2** belabor, overdo, overuse, repeat.

overwrought *adj.* agitated, worked up, wrought up, stirred up, hysterical, uncontrolled, unstrung, unhinged, overexcited, frantic, distracted, distraught, seething, beside oneself. **ant.** calm, controlled, dispassionate, cool, self-contained.

ovoid *adj.* OVAL.

ovular *adj.* OVAL.

ovule *n.* EGG.

ovum *n.* EGG.

owing *adj.* due, outstanding, unpaid, payable, unsettled, owed, overdue, debited. **ant.** paid, settled, collected.

owlish *adj.* serious, solemn, wise, judicious, unblinking, knowing, appraising, perceptive, penetrating.

own *v.* **1** possess, have, hold, have title to, retain, maintain, keep. **2** acknowledge, admit, concede, allow, grant, yield, profess, confess.

owner *n.* possessor, partner, proprietor, landlord, proprietary, proprietress, landowner, landholder, copartner.

ownership *n.* possession, title, entitlement, holding, tenure, proprietorship, partnership, copartnership.

own up to confess, admit, acknowledge, disclose, lay bare, come clean, reveal, make a clean breast of, tell the truth, plead guilty, spill (*Slang*). **ant.** conceal, hide, lie, play dumb (*Slang*).

P

pabulum *n.* FOOD.

pace *n.* **1** step, footstep, stride, tread, length, unit. **2** *manner of movement:* gait, stride, walk, step, tread, canter, trot, gallop, prance, jaunt, saunter, amble, stalk. **3** rate, speed, velocity, movement, motion, progress, career, clip, stride. —*v.* walk, step, tread, traverse, step off, mark out, count off, measure, calculate, span, track.

pacific *adj.* **1** calm, peaceful, tranquil, serene, quiet, placid, peaceable, smooth, halcyon, untroubled, harmonious. **2** PEACEABLE.
ant. **1** troubled, agitated, turbulent, tumultuous, restless, ruffled, overwrought.

pacification *n.* PEACE.

pacifist *adj.* PEACEABLE.

pacifistic *adj.* PEACEABLE.

pacify *v.* appease, allay, mollify, placate, propitiate, calm, relax, tranquilize, soothe, soften, tame, chasten.
ant. agitate, arouse, perturb, discompose, unsettle, alarm, ruffle.

pack *n.* **1** bundle, packet, package, bale, truss, trunk, load, weight, burden, fardel. **2** set, bunch, group, batch, sum, portion, block, mass, suite, string, collection, aggregate. **3** band, gang, bunch, group, body, crew, party, outfit, company, crowd, boodle, caboodle, troop, herd, flock, school, covey, swarm, drove. —*v.* fill, load, stuff, stow, cram, compress, crowd, jam, gorge, wad, pad, stack, heap, bag, charge.

package *n.* **1** parcel, packet, pack, bundle, box, bale, case, container. **2** combination, combo, compound, union, fusion, alliance, composite, blend, amalgam.

packed *adj.* full, filled, stuffed, replete, chock-full, chock-a-block, brimful, crowded, jammed, overloaded, overflowing, teeming, congested.
ant. empty, depleted, vacant, wanting, lacking.

packet *n.* PARCEL.

pact *n.* agreement, treaty, compact, contract, covenant, convention, alliance, concordat, protocol, charter, understanding, stipulation.

pad[1] *n.* **1** cushion, mat, pillow, bolster, buffer, mattress, wadding, padding, stuffing. **2** tablet, notebook, ledger, album. **3** *Slang* ABODE. —*v.* **1** stuff, fill, pack, cram, wad, protect, line, face, inlay. **2** protract, spin out, elaborate, dwell on, lengthen, embellish, expand, extend.

pad[2] *v.* walk, tramp, hike, march, trek, stroll, traipse, tiptoe, pussyfoot, creep, sneak, steal.

padding *n.* **1** PAD. **2** REDUNDANCY.

paddle *n.* oar, blade, scull, sweep, board, pole, stick, rod, ruler, switch, cane. —*v.* **1** row, oar, propel, punt, pull, scull. **2** beat, batter, wallop, thrash, whale, lambaste, flog, cane, drub, spank, punish.

paddock *v.* CORRAL.

paean *n.* HYMN.

pagan *n.* heathen, idolater, infidel, unbeliever, atheist, skeptic.

page[1] *n.* attendant, messenger, errand boy, office boy, girl Friday, bellboy, bellhop, usher. —*v.* SUMMON.

page[2] *n.* **1** leaf, sheet, side, paper, folio. **2** phase, stage, period, time, point, occasion, incident, chapter, episode.

pageant *n.* drama, spectacle, exhibition, exhibit, display, play, show, presentation, extravaganza, charade, tableau, parade, procession.

pageantry *n.* **1** spectacle, extravaganza, display, ritual, drama, show, exhibition, parade, theatrics, theatricalism, flourish, splendor, grandeur. **2** ostentation, showiness, pomp, exhibitionism, staginess, gaudiness, flashiness, glitter, pretension.
ant. **2** drabness, lackluster, dullness, grayness, dreariness.

pail *n.* bucket, scuttle, hod, can, dipper, bail, container, receptacle, vessel.

pain *n.* **1** ache, soreness, hurt, irritation, twinge, pang, discomfort, tenderness, hurting, sensitivity, suffering, distress, misery, agony. **2** anxiety, grief, anguish, woe, heartache, misery, distress, affliction, wretchedness, agony, torment, pang. **3** *Slang* nuisance, bother, annoyance, irritation, headache, vexation, pest, bore, drag (*Slang*), pill (*Slang*). —*v.* hurt, ache, wound, irritate, afflict, ail, chafe, inflame, aggravate, trouble, torment, bother, grieve, distress, offend, disquiet.

painful *adj.* **1** distressing, irritating, grievous, hurtful, hurting, inflamed, sensitive, sore, raw, smarting, tender, acute, sharp, stabbing, throbbing. **2** difficult, hard, troublesome, arduous, tough, strenuous, onerous, bothersome, irksome.
ant. **1** pleasing, agreeable, welcome, delightful, enjoyable. **2** effortless, easy, facile, slight.

pain-killer *n.* analgesic, anodyne, anesthetic, palliative, pacifier, tranquilizer, sedative, calmative.

painstaking *adj.* meticulous, exacting, finicky, fussy, careful, demanding, assiduous, diligent, punctilious, particular, vigilant, thoroughgoing, precise, scrupulous, conscientious.
ant. sloppy, slipshod, clumsy, negligent, careless, thoughtless.

paint *n.* pigment, color, coloring, tincture, oil, stain, dye, tint, hue, shade. —*v.* **1** cover, coat, brush on, daub, color, smear. **2** describe, recount, tell, relate, picture, portray, delineate, represent.

painter *n.* artist, dauber, old master, colorist, illustrator.

pair *n.* couple, two, mates, twosome, doubles, duplicates, twins, counterparts, brace, dyad, set, unit, team. —*v.* couple, mate, match, team, yoke, bracket, league, affiliate, ally, merge, unite, combine, marry, wed.

pal *n.* FRIEND.

palace *n.* mansion, edifice, castle, manor house, villa, chateau, homestead, residence, home, abode.

paladin *n.* champion, defender, crusader, advocate, protector, apologist, knight-errant, hero, brave, gallant, Galahad.

palatable *adj.* **1** tasteful, tasty, delicious, flavorful, toothsome, appetizing, mouth-watering, savory, piquant, delectable, luscious, ambrosial. **2** acceptable, satisfactory, agreeable, eligible, admissible, all right, fair, tolerable.
ant. **1** distasteful, unsavory, nauseating, bitter. **2** unsatisfactory, abhorrent, repugnant, objectionable, inadmissible.

palate *n.* TASTE.

palatial *adj.* magnificent, splendid, grand, glorious, superb, imposing, sumptuous, luxurious, majestic, princely, stately, grandiose.
ant. unpretentious, humble, mean, ramshackle.

palaver *n.* discussion, conference, talk, parley, consultation, conclave, council, powwow, confab, talkfest, rap session (*Slang*). —*v.* chatter, gabble, chat, gab, prattle, babble, jabber, jaw (*Slang*), gossip, talk.

pale[1] *n.* **1** picket, stake, stick, stalk, shaft, palisade, cane, peg, pile. **2** territory, terrain, area, zone, region, field, circuit, enclosure, confines, limits, boundary, bounds, border, edge, frontier.

pale[2] *adj.* whitish, pallid, wan, ashen, pasty, ashy, sallow, colorless, faded, washed-out, bloodless, waxen, waxy, anemic, white, bleached, blanched, light.

ant. florid, flushed, ruddy, rosy, sanguine, blooming.

palisade *n.* **1** FENCE. **2** CLIFF.

pall[1] *n.* **1** shroud, mantle, cover, canopy, veil, vestment, shield, blanket, cloth, fabric. **2** cloud, haze, shadow, darkness, eclipse, shade, curtain, obscurity, veil, gloom, blanket, wet blanket.

pall[2] *v.* fade, decline, weaken, dim, flag, bore, cloy, satiate, dull, blunt, dismay, appall, displease, disaffect.
ant. stimulate, incite, invigorate, inflame, animate, arouse.

palladium *n.* SAFEGUARD.

palliate *v.* **1** excuse, extenuate, mitigate, minimize, soften, apologize for, gloss over, varnish. **2** ease, relieve, alleviate, assuage, allay, sooth, soften, lessen, moderate, diminish, temper, relax.
ant. 1, 2 aggravate, inflame, exaggerate, magnify, intensify.

palliative *adj.* curative, healing, helpful, corrective, remedial, therapeutic, calmative, easing, soothing, softening.
ant. aggravating, inflaming, irritating, provoking.

pallid *adj.* pale, wan, sallow, ashen, pasty, white, anemic, colorless, haggard, drawn.
ant. florid, ruddy, flushed, rubicund, glowing, hale, flush.

pallor *n.* paleness, wanness, sallowness, pastiness, ashenness, bloodlessness, anemia.

palmy *adj.* PROSPEROUS.

palpable *adj.* **1** tangible, solid, concrete, material, physical, corporeal, substantial, touchable, tactile. **2** perceptible, observable, perceivable, discernible, noticeable, apparent, visible, sensible, distinct. **3** obvious, manifest, evident, apparent, ostensible, self-evident, conspicuous, plain, clear, explicit.
ant. 1 spiritual, ethereal, spectral, disembodied. **2** invisible, imperceptible, indistinct, unseen. **3** ambig-

uous, obscure, vague, inconclusive, indefinite, questionable.

palpate *v.* PRESS.

palpitate *v.* quiver, throb, tremble, pulsate, pulse, flutter, beat, pant, vibrate, pitter-patter, quaver, shiver, thrill.

palsy *n.* paralysis, trembling, quiver, shakes.

palter *v.* TRIFLE.

paltry *adj.* petty, trivial, meager, trifling, mere, worthless, niggardly, mean, poor, sorry, sad, scant, scanty, slight, pitiful, miserable, wretched, exiguous.
ant. major, considerable, significant, superior, outstanding, weighty, striking.

pamper *v.* coddle, spoil, indulge, cater to, gratify, humor, mollycoddle.

pamphlet *n.* brochure, folder, leaflet, circular, manual, text, primer, booklet, book, tract.

pan *n.* pot, utensil, vessel, container, holder, saucepan, skillet. —*v.* criticize, castigate, assail, attack, animadvert, knock (*Slang*), slam, rap (*Slang*), flay, roast.

panacea *n.* CURE-ALL.

panache *n.* verve, dash, zest, gusto, spirit, liveliness, animation, passion, *brio*, splash, flourish, jauntiness, smartness, chic, style, flair, *éclat*.

pandemic *adj.* EPIDEMIC.

pandemonium *n.* uproar, commotion, chaos, disorder, tumult, disturbance, rumpus, fracas, hubbub, bedlam, riot, racket, clamor.

pander *n.* procurer, pimp, go-between, runner, procuress, bawd, madam.

panegyric *n.* EULOGY.

panel *n.* committee, conference, group, board, assembly, commission, forum, round table, tribunal, chamber, court, inquest, jury, venire.

pang *n.* ache, pain, stab, twinge, throe, stitch, wrench, crick, shock, agony, anguish, discomfort, affliction, irritation, torment.

panhandle *v.* BEG.

panic *n.* alarm, terror, fright, fear,

scare, distress, dread. —*v.* terrify, frighten, scare, startle, shake, shock, appall, unnerve, alarm, terrorize.

panicky *adj.* panic-stricken, alarmed, unnerved, stunned, shocked, terrified, frightened, fearful, dismayed, aghast, stupefied, immobilized, speechless.

ant. composed, imperturbable, unruffled, cool, steady.

panic-stricken *adj.* PANICKY.

panoply *n.* regalia, trappings, array, turnout, get-up, insignia, raiments, pageantry, pomp, spectacle.

panorama *n.* overview, perspective, bird's-eye view, prospect, vista.

pan out eventuate, culminate, turn out, end up, come out, work out, fare, result, develop, conclude, wind up.

pant *v.* 1 gasp, puff, wheeze, sigh, blow, breathe, respire. 2 pulsate, palpitate, pulse, throb, tremble, quiver, quaver, flutter, shake, beat, drum.

pant for yearn for, desire, want, ache for, seek, need, covet, hope for.

ant. spurn, reject, discard.

pantomime *n.* mime, charade, dumb show, tableau, pageant, play, spectacle.

pants *n.* trousers, breeches, slacks, pantaloons, culottes, dungarees, bell-bottoms, trunks, pedal-pushers, knickers, jodhpurs.

pantywaist *n. Slang* SISSY.

paper *n.* 1 document, manuscript, original, record, instrument, registry, notation, memorandum. 2 composition, work, writing, manuscript, essay, assignment, treatment, examination, report, theme, dissertation, thesis, study, analysis, treatise, article, monograph.

papers *n.* documents, records, archive, registry, file, dossier, identification, registration.

papilla *n.* NIPPLE.

papoose *n.* BABY.

par *n.* standard, rule, guideline, guidepost, guide, rule of thumb, precedent, convention, grade, mark, measure, caliber, scale, stage.

parable *n.* fable, allegory, tale, folktale, lesson, moral, story, legend, myth.

parabola *n.* ARC.

parade *n.* 1 procession, cavalcade, review, train, column, march, promenade, walk, stroll, saunter. 2 ostentation, show, display, pageantry, pomp, spectacle. —*v.* 1 march, file, defile, pace, step, walk, tread, promenade, stroll, saunter, amble. 2 flaunt, flourish, display, exhibit, brandish, show off, emblazon, swagger, prance, strut, grandstand.

paradigm *n.* pattern, original, mold, matrix, form, lead, precedent, prototype, example, exemplar, archetype.

paradise *n.* heaven, hereafter, Promised Land, Valhalla, Nirvana, utopia, millennium, bliss, glory, felicity, beatitude, harmony, elation, euphoria.

ant. hell, misery, wretchedness, desolation, despair, suffering.

paradox *n.* contradiction, inconsistency, incompatibility, self-contradiction, disparity, discord, dilemma, quandary, perplexity, mystery, enigma, puzzle, conundrum, riddle, problem, question.

paragon *n.* ideal, model, epitome, apotheosis, exemplar, symbol, example, standard, pattern, criterion, representative, illustration, lesson.

parallel *adj.* equal, coordinate, complementary, corresponding, comparable, matching, similar, like, duplicate, twin, analogous. —*n.* 1 counterpart, like, complement, correspondent, duplicate, twin, double, equal, equivalent, match, mate. 2 comparison, analogy, likeness, similarity, resemblance, correspondence. —*v.* correspond, approximate, approach, complement, equal, match, measure up to, balance.

paralysis *n.* 1 palsy, paresis, immobility, immobilization, numbness, paraplegia, quadriplegia. 2 impotence, inaction, powerlessness, unresponsiveness, immobility, inertia, apathy, listlessness, lethargy.

ant. 2 vigor, power, energy, dynamism, potency.

paralytic *adj.* **1** immobilized, palsied, paretic, powerless, immobile, nonambulatory. **2** impotent, inactive, stunned, benumbed, stupefied, flabbergasted.

ant. 2 vigorous, decisive, clearheaded, responsive.

paralyze *v.* stun, benumb, stupefy, immobilize, incapacitate, cripple, hamstring, throttle, strangle, muzzle, handcuff, disarm, disable, debilitate.

parameter *n.* GUIDELINE.

paramount *adj.* foremost, principal, chief, main, leading, highest, greatest, dominant, preeminent, overruling, superior, supreme, uppermost, ranking, crowning, cardinal, primary.

ant. least, minimum, slightest, minor, immaterial.

paramour *n.* lover, mistress, kept woman, sugar daddy (*Slang*), gigolo, concubine, courtesan, hetaera, inamorata, inamorato.

paranoiac *adj.* PARANOID.

paranoid *adj.* suspicious, distrustful, paranoiac, fearful, wary, apprehensive, uptight (*Slang*).

parapet *n.* barrier, breastwork, rampart, barricade, battlement, bulwark, palisade, stockade, earthwork, bulkhead, bank, embankment, buffer, wall, fence, bar, gate.

paraphernalia *n.* belongings, things, furnishings, possessions, trappings, gear, accouterments, accessories, appurtenances, fixtures, equipment, outfit, apparatus, equipage, impedimenta, materiel.

paraphrase *n.* rewording, précis, summary, synopsis, resumé, version, restatement, rendering, interpretation, transcription, sketch, outline, gloss, brief, digest, condensation, abridgment. —*v.* reword, rephrase, restate, render, summarize, outline, sketch, brief, epitomize, abridge, encapsulate, transcribe, translate, interpret.

paraplegia *n.* PARALYSIS.

parasite *n.* freeloader, scrounger (*Slang*), sponger, hanger-on, drone, dependent, leech, bloodsucker, cadger, deadbeat (*Slang*), moocher (*Slang*).

parasitic *adj.* freeloading, sponging, scrounging, leechlike, dependent, bloodsucking, cadging, mooching (*Slang*).

parcel *n.* **1** package, bundle, packet, pack, box, carton, bale, fardel. **2** group, assortment, collection, bunch, pack, band, company, mass, gathering, gang, throng, horde, multitude.

parcel out distribute, dispense, deal out, portion out, dole out, mete out, apportion, allocate, assign, allot, divide, ration, budget.

parched *adj.* dry, desiccated, dehydrated, withered, scorched, baked, burnt, blistered, sere, singed, shriveled, waterless, arid.

pardner *n.* FRIEND.

pardon *v.* forgive, excuse, condone, absolve, release, discharge, remit, reprieve, acquit, exonerate, exculpate, amnesty. —*n.* forgiveness, excuse, release, dismissal, waiving, remission, acquittal, exemption, exoneration, exculpation, indemnity, absolution, amnesty.

ant. *v.* accuse, blame, indict, charge, incriminate, condemn, inculpate.

pare *v.* trim, cut away, prune, clip, crop, strip, dock, lop, peel, eliminate, retrench.

parent *n.* **1** progenitor, procreator, mother, father, sire, ancestor, forefather, begetter, generator, originator, author, agent. **2** source, wellspring, origin, beginning, egg, seed, nucleus, embryo, root, head, rise, fountainhead, derivation, principle, occasion, ground, basis, cause.

parenthesis *n.* ASIDE.

par excellence SUPREME.

pariah *n.* outcast, leper, undesirable, untouchable, outlaw, Ishmael, derelict, castaway, vagabond, fugitive, exile, expatriate, maverick.

parish *n.* congregation, church, flock, fold, assembly, society, celebrants, communicants, churchgoers, brethren, community, diocese, see.

parity *n.* equivalence, equality, equilibrium, par, likeness, sameness, parallelism, correspondence, comparison, resemblance, approximation, symmetry, analogy.
ant. inequality, disparity, difference, diversity, disproportion, variableness, dissimilitude.

park *n.* **1** green, common, playground, square, plaza, enclosure, grounds, field, lawn, meadow, quadrangle, quad. **2** reservation, reserve, preserve, sanctuary, chase (*Brit.*), range, parkland, woodland, woods, forest, grove, grassland.

parkland *n.* PARK.

parlance *n.* speech, language, lingo, jargon, argot, cant, phraseology, talk, tongue, idiom.

parlay *v.* increase, enlarge, extend, augment, build up, pyramid, trade on, capitalize on, take advantage of, exploit, use, manage, manipulate.

parley *n.* conference, discussion, council, meeting, conclave, colloquy, assembly, consultation, deliberation, palaver, confabulation, confab, powwow.

parliament *n.* legislature, assembly, council, congress, convocation, meeting, body.

parliamentary *adj.* legislative, lawmaking, deliberative, governmental, congressional.

parlor *n.* living room, sitting room, front room, drawing room, visiting room, reception room, salon, foyer.

parlous *adj.* PERILOUS.

parochial *adj.* limited, restricted, narrow, provincial, insular, unenlightened, sheltered, shortsighted, myopic, nearsighted, unsophisticated.
ant. cosmopolitan, broad-minded, sophisticated, broad, catholic, farsighted, farseeing.

parody *n.* **1** imitation, burlesque, travesty, take-off, caricature, send-up

(*Brit. Slang*). **2** *poor imitation:* mockery, farce, joke, laugh, travesty, caricature, absurdity. —*v.* travesty, burlesque, take off, send up (*Brit. Slang*), mock, caricature, satirize, poke fun at.

parole *n.* PROMISE.

paroxysm *n.* **1** seizure, attack, fit, convulsion, grip, spasm, stroke, cramp, apoplexy, throe, crackup, breakdown. **2** outburst, rage, frenzy, furor, fury, tantrum, fit, flare-up, explosion, eruption.

parrot *v.* ape, copycat, copy, mimic, imitate, repeat, echo, mirror, reflect, simulate, borrow.

parry *v.* avoid, evade, dodge, sidestep, duck, hedge, pussyfoot, hold off, keep off, hold at bay, rebuff, repulse, repel, ward off, fend off, stave off. —*n.* evasion, hedge, dodge, diversion, deflection, pussyfooting, sidestepping, quibbling, circumvention, shift, subterfuge, escape.
ant. *v.* confront, challenge, encounter, brave, meet, defy.

parsimonious *adj.* stingy, miserly, niggardly, closefisted, pennypinching, tight, mean, cheap, penurious, scrimping, sparing, frugal, thrifty.
ant. extravagant, lavish, spendthrift, prodigal, wasteful, squandering.

parsimony *n.* stinginess, miserliness, tightness, cheapness, pennypinching, niggardliness, penury, thriftiness, frugality, meanness, pettiness.

parson *n.* MINISTER.

part *n.* **1** portion, piece, segment, section, fragment, subdivision, fraction, share, particle, detail, element, component, ingredient, constituent, module, member, offshoot, organ, limb. **2** side, interest, cause, party, faction, division, sect, group, circle, team, set, clique, coterie. —*v.* **1** divide, split, separate, break up, partition, sever, dissever, dismantle, disassemble, disunite, detach, divorce, cleave, sunder. **2** depart, go away, leave, part company, take leave, split up, separate, break up. —*adj.* PARTIAL.

ant. *n.* **1** whole, total, sum, all, mass, aggregate. *v.* **1** join, connect, merge, meld, fasten, link, marry, unite, fuse. **2** meet, arrive, return, reunite, make up.

partake in participate, take part in, enter into, join in, have a hand in, contribute to, share in, enjoy, engage in.

partake of 1 consume, eat, feed on, feast on, stuff oneself, put away, dispatch, dispose of, enjoy, relish, appreciate. **2** exhibit, reveal, manifest, show, demonstrate, evince, disclose, compare with, approximate, look like, resemble.

partial *adj.* **1** incomplete, fragmentary, fractional, part, halfway, unfinished, deficient, inadequate, undeveloped, immature. **2** biased, prejudiced, partisan, predisposed, one-sided, factional, sectarian, interested, involved.

ant. 1 complete, thorough, total, entire, exhaustive, all-inclusive, definitive. **2** neutral, detached, objective, disinterested, impartial, unbiased, equitable, fair.

partiality *n.* bias, partisanship, onesidedness, prejudice, unfairness, preference, favoritism, predisposition, factionalism, sectionalism, clannishness, nepotism.

ant. fairness, impartiality, evenhandedness, neutrality, fair play, equity, disinterestedness.

partially *adv.* PARTLY.

partial to fond of, taken with, keen on, devoted to, enamored of, stuck on, sweet on.

participant *n.* participator, actor, contributor, activist, party, accessory, member, joiner, partner.

participate *v.* take part, engage, enter into, have a hand, join, share, contribute, perform, partake.

participation *n.* involvement, contribution, collusion, entanglement.

particle *n.* bit, piece, scrap, speck, trace, mite, iota, jot, morsel, item, fragment, segment, fraction, section, portion, subdivision, modicum, minimum.

particular *adj.* **1** definite, specific, exact, precise, distinct, express, certain, exclusive, singular, sole, unique, distinctive, individual, peculiar, special, characteristic, typical. **2** unusual, extraordinary, especial, uncommon, unheard-of, marked, pronounced. **3** detailed, precise, minute, selective, fussy, exacting, finicky, fastidious, meticulous, punctilious, discriminating, painstaking, critical, scrupulous, conscientious. —*n.* detail, fact, specific, instance, item, point, case, technicality, nicety, matter, article, thing, particularity, feature, mark, trait.

ant. *adj.* **1** ordinary, common, widespread, general, familiar, shared, prevailing, abundant. **2** usual, frequent, customary, habitual, prevalent, normal. **3** slipshod, careless, sloppy, casual, negligent.

particularity *n.* **1** PARTICULAR. **2** PECULIARITY. **3** PRECISION.

particularize *v.* SPECIFY.

particularly *adv.* especially, expressly, specifically, decidedly, pointedly, singularly, emphatically, notably, unusually, extremely, strikingly, extraordinarily.

parting *n.* departure, leaving, going, leave-taking, good-by, farewell, adieu, send-off, exit, withdrawal, passing.

ant. arrival, coming, return, meeting, welcome, reception.

partisan *n.* **1** supporter, backer, follower, promoter, champion, advocate, attendant, regular, party-liner, stalwart, devotee, votary. **2** guerrilla, maquis, irregular, saboteur. —*adj.* factional, prejudiced, biased, one-sided, factious, partial, sectarian, interested, committed, undetached, opinionated.

ant. *n.* **1** apostate, renegade, maverick, independent. *adj.* neutral, impartial, unbiased, equitable, independent, objective, uncommitted.

partition *n.* **1** division, separation, severance, split, demarcation, segregation, cleavage. **2** wall, divider, room divider, barrier, panel, separation, curtain, screen, fence, hedge, rampart. —*v.* divide, separate, set apart, subdivide, split, segment, section, wall off, fence off, screen.
ant. *v.* join, unite, merge, connect, link, consolidate.

partly *adv.* somewhat, partially, slightly, relatively, comparatively, incompletely, partway, halfway, qualifiedly.

partner *n.* associate, colleague, copartner, collaborator, ally, confederate, confrere, companion, fellow, mate, compatriot, pardner.

parturition *n.* BIRTH.

part with give up, relinquish, yield, surrender, render up, cede, give away, abandon, renounce, sacrifice, drop, waive, dispose of.

party *n.* **1** organization, affiliation, machine, faction, camp, wing, group, band, body, division, interest, side, association, assembly, bureaucracy, apparat. **2** person, individual, being, human, personage, participant, contributor, collaborator, participator, sharer, accessory, copartner. **3** festivity, celebration, revelry, fete, gala, merrymaking, jamboree, soirée, blowout (*Slang*), dance, ball, hop, occasion, gathering, shindig (*Slang*).

parvenu *n.* UPSTART.

pass *v.* **1** go ahead, go, move, get ahead of, leave behind, overtake, distance, outdistance, outdo, surpass, exceed, proceed, progress, travel. **2** traverse, extend, cross, cover, travel over, ford, bypass, penetrate, permeate. **3** disregard, overlook, ignore, neglect, omit, slight, skip, miss. **4** qualify, satisfy, complete, pass muster, accomplish, get by, finish, achieve, graduate. **5** *of time:* spend, fill, while away, occupy, consume, expend, employ, put in, lead, devote. **6** approve, endorse, validate, sanction, authorize, confirm, certify, enact, put

through, ratify, legislate. **7** end, finish, close, cease, expire, disappear, vanish, wane, elapse, dissolve, melt, ebb, dwindle, fade, evaporate, sink. —*n.* **1** passage, movement, course, transit, advance, progress, progression. **2** way, route, trail, channel, corridor, passage, course, lane, artery, narrows, strait, ravine, defile, col, gorge, notch, gap, break, breach, opening, access. **3** permit, permission, passport, authorization, warrant, license, leave, sanction, consent, allowance, safe-conduct. **4** situation, condition, state, position, point, turning, turning point, turn, plight, lot, juncture, pinch, pickle, crisis, predicament, emergency, exigency. **5** thrust, lunge, feint, swing, jab, gesture, parry.
ant. *v.* **1** fall behind, lag, falter, delay, drag. **3** notice, regard, heed, observe, perceive, attend, study. **4** fail, flunk, miss, succumb, lose. **6** disapprove, disallow, reject, refuse, veto. **7** endure, continue, last, stay, persist.

passable *adj.* acceptable, tolerable, adequate, satisfactory, all right, respectable, presentable, admissible, decent, fair, moderate, mediocre, so-so, OK, pedestrian.
ant. exceptional, extraordinary, superlative, singular, superior, incomparable.

passage *n.* **1** corridor, hall, hallway, way, passageway, gangway, gallery, loggia, arcade, alley, avenue, artery, channel, conduit, breezeway, aisle, lobby, vestibule. **2** passing, course, moving, progress, movement, march, advance, motion, transit, transition, change, conversion, flow, current. **3** excerpt, section, portion, part, selection, fragment, extract, quotation, phrase. **4** enactment, enaction, ratification, approval, passing, legislation. **5** PASSAGEWAY.

passageway *n.* corridor, avenue, channel, artery, way, path, conduit, alley, lane, passage, pass, gateway, threshold, access, inlet, opening, entrance, outlet, exit.

pass away DIE.

passé *adj.* unfashionable, out-of-date, dated, outmoded, old-fashioned, stale, fusty, musty, faded, obsolete, superannuated, past, dead, extinct, antiquated, archaic.

ant. stylish, chic, fashionable, with-it (*Slang*), trendy (*Slang*).

passenger *n.* commuter, fare, rider, straphanger, traveler, motorist.

passerby *n.* onlooker, bystander, looker-on, observer, viewer, witness, eyewitness, rubberneck (*Slang*).

passing *adj.* transitory, fleeting, short-lived, transient, temporary, fading, impermanent, momentary, ephemeral, vanishing, brief, short. —*n.* DEATH.

ant. permanent, enduring, imperishable, eternal.

passion *n.* **1** devotion, zeal, enthusiasm, fascination, infatuation, obsession, craze, mania, ardor, fervor, excitement, zest, gusto, agitation, stimulation. **2** love, desire, ardor, lust, fervor, infatuation, affection, emotion, adoration, feeling, appetite. **3** rage, anger, fury, frenzy, tantrum, vehemence, irritation, perturbation, flare-up, outburst.

passionate *adj.* **1** emotional, hotheaded, quick-tempered, fiery, excitable, fervent, impassioned, avid, eager, ardent, keen, zestful, enthusiastic. **2** inflamed, fevered, flushed, agitated, turbulent, perturbed, frenzied, vehement, fierce, furious, violent. **3** amorous, erotic, lustful, ardent, aroused, infatuated, desirous, wrought-up, inflamed, hot, hot-blooded.

ant. **1** phlegmatic, apathetic, unconcerned, unresponsive. **2** composed, serene, unruffled, imperturbable, placid, self-possessed. **3** cold, distant, chilly, cool, frigid.

passive *adj.* unassertive, unresponsive, listless, spiritless, apathetic, docile,

deferential, acquiescent, compliant, resigned, unresisting, submissive.

ant. aggressive, self-assertive, vigorous, obtrusive, enterprising, energetic, resolute.

pass out **1** distribute, hand out, circulate, disperse, scatter, sow, broadcast, propagate, issue, deal out. **2** faint, black out, keel over, swoon, drop.

past *adj.* **1** ancient, olden, bygone, old-time, one-time, former, early, antique, archaic, extinct, time-honored, venerable, immemorial. **2** recent, previous, preceding, former, late, foregoing, erstwhile, quondam. —*n.* history, antiquity, yesteryear, heretofore.

paste *n.* adhesive, mucilage, glue, fixative, binder, cement, stickum. —*v.* stick, glue, bind, cement, fasten, weld.

pastime *n.* recreation, diversion, relaxation, divertissement, amusement, entertainment, enjoyment, pleasure, lark, frolic, romp, play, sport, fun, avocation, hobby.

past master EXPERT.

pastor *n.* MINISTER.

pastoral *adj.* rustic, bucolic, Arcadian, natural, simple, rural, country.

pasty *adj.* PALE².

pat¹ *v.* slap, tap, rap, dab, flip, flick, touch, caress, pet, fondle. —*n.* clap, slap, rap, hit, dab, flip, stroke, caress.

pat² *adj.* **1** suitable, fitting, appropriate, apt, apposite, apropos, neat, felicitous, happy. **2** facile, glib, thoughtless, smooth, simplistic, conventional, familiar, commonplace, banal.

ant. **1** unsuitable, inappropriate, unbecoming, inapt, irrelevant, incompatible. **2** thoughtful, attentive, conscientious, reflective, complicated, serious.

patch *n.* **1** cover, layer, panel, sheet, leaf, coat, overlay, plate, slab, ply. **2** ground, land, tract, field, lot, plot, parcel, clearing, space, area. **3** scrap, shred, tatter, snatch, bit, stitch, rag, morsel, blotch, spot. —*v.* mend, repair, fix, overhaul, vamp, condition, recondition, ready, sew up.

patchwork *n.* JUMBLE.

patchy *adj.* SPOTTY.

patent *adj.* self-evident, manifest, apparent, evident, obvious, plain, clear, transparent, explicit, unmistakable, undeniable, incontrovertible.

   ant. obscure, vague, indefinite, cryptic, equivocal, perplexing, unfathomable, recondite.

path *n.* **1** walk, way, lane, trail, road, track, pathway, byway, bypath, beat, round, course, route. **2** *way of life or course of action:* course, route, road, itinerary, trail, track, wake, trace, line, plan, design, mode, style, form, manner, means.

pathetic *adj.* pitiful, sad, woeful, piteous, pitiable, sorry, lamentable, deplorable, moving, touching, affecting.

pathway *n.* PATH.

patience *n.* **1** endurance, perseverance, persistence, fortitude, stick-to-itiveness, doggedness, tenacity, application, concentration, diligence, resignation, stoicism. **2** tolerance, forbearance, indulgence, leniency, sufferance, sympathy, regard, understanding, responsiveness, bigness, generosity.

   ant. **1** restlessness, restiveness, impatience, nervousness, hastiness, impetuosity. **2** intolerance, peremptoriness, strictness, aloofness.

patient *adj.* **1** persistent, persevering, enduring, diligent, steadfast, dogged, tenacious, assiduous, unfaltering, indefatigable, resigned, stoic. **2** tolerant, indulgent, forbearing, lenient, understanding, permissive, sympathetic, compassionate, big-hearted, generous.

   ant. **1** restless, fidgety, impatient, hurried, hasty, impetuous. **2** intolerant, peremptory, strict, inflexible.

patina *n.* COATING.

patois *n.* JARGON.

patriarch *n.* elder, father, forefather, forebear, ancestor, founder, paterfamilias, grandfather, graybeard, sire, progenitor, procreator, sage, master, guru.

patrician *n.* aristocrat, nobleman, noblewoman, noble, peer, gentleman, gentlewoman, blue blood, grandee, lady, lord, thoroughbred, Brahmin. —*adj.* aristocratic, noble, wellborn, well-bred, highborn, high, exalted, thoroughbred, blue-blooded, silk-stocking, genteel.

   ant. *adj.* lower-class, proletarian, vulgar, humble, common, lowborn, plebeian, uncultivated.

patriot *n.* loyalist, nationalist, flag-waver, chauvinist, jingo.

   ant. traitor, subversive.

patriotism *n.* loyalty, loyalism, nationalism, flag-waving, chauvinism, jingoism.

   ant. treason, subversion.

patrol *n., v.* GUARD.

patron *n.* **1** benefactor, sponsor, patroness, champion, advocate, supporter, backer, promoter, exponent, protagonist, financer, angel, booster. **2** client, customer, frequenter, regular, shopper, buyer, purchaser, prospect, visitor.

patronage *n.* **1** support, backing, sponsorship, promotion, advancement, encouragement, auspices, assistance, aid, abetment, care, championship, tutelage. **2** condescension, presumptuousness, hauteur, imperiousness, noblesse oblige, superciliousness, self-complacency, haughtiness, snobbery, cockiness, insolence, arrogance.

patronize *v.* **1** condescend, presume, deign, stoop, descend, humiliate, put down (*Slang*). **2** trade with, deal with, do business, frequent, shop.

patronizing *adj.* condescending, presumptuous, arrogant, supercilious, haughty, lofty, top-lofty, high-handed, imperious, inconsiderate, humiliating, insolent.

   ant. respectful, tactful, humble, discreet.

patter[1] *v.* pelt, tap, pat, pitter-patter, rat-a-tat, tattoo, drum, rap, pulsate, palpitate, throb, pummel, thump, buffet, batter, beat, pound.

patter[2] *n.* chat, chatter, spiel (*Slang*), pitch, monologue, palaver, chitchat, discourse, talk, causerie.

pattern *n.* **1** model, guide, standard, criterion, precedent, example, paradigm, prototype, archetype, paragon, ideal, exemplar, original, mold, matrix, cast, stamp, stereotype. **2** design, arrangement, markings, figure, motif, theme, scheme, form, composition, representation, image, sketch, outline, drawing. —*v.* copy, imitate, reproduce, repeat, simulate, reflect, mirror, echo, ape, parrot, mimic, emulate, follow, model after, take after.

paucity *n.* **1** scarcity, sparsity, scarceness, scantiness, dearth, shortage, want, lack, deficiency, inadequacy, poverty, uncommonness, rarity. **2** smallness, slightness, spareness, puniness, meagerness, leanness, pittance.

ant. 1 excess, surplus, redundance, overflow, glut, plethora, abundance. **2** greatness, vastness, largeness, magnitude, enormousness, immensity.

paunch *n.* abdomen, stomach, belly, pot, potbelly, tummy, corporation, breadbasket (*Slang*), bay window (*Slang*).

pauper *n.* indigent, down-and-out, beggar, hobo, debtor, bankrupt, insolvent.

pauperism *n.* POVERTY.

pauperize *v.* RUIN.

pause *v.* rest, recess, suspend, delay, interrupt, take a break, take a breather, discontinue, let up, break, stay, knock off, quit, cease, stop, halt. —*n.* rest, break, recess, respite, time-out, breather, let-up, standstill, lull, lapse, halt, stay, suspension, interruption, interlude, interval, interim, intermission, caesura, entr'acte.

ant. *v.* continue, persist, carry on, persevere, maintain.

pave *v.* surface, cover, top, lay over, spread over, cement, blacktop, asphalt, macadamize.

pavement *n.* sidewalk, paving, walkway, footway.

pavilion *n.* hall, structure, edifice, shelter, annex, outbuilding, kiosk, rotunda, pergola, arbor, bower, summerhouse, tent, canopy, canvas, awning.

paw *n.* foot, forepaw, forefoot, hand, claw, pad, hoof. —*v.* **1** scrape, scratch, rub, scuff, chafe, scrub, scour, brush. **2** handle, maul, manhandle, buffet, pound, manipulate, touch, pat, stroke, rub, fondle, caress, pet, mash (*Slang*).

pawn[1] *n.* puppet, toy, plaything, cat's-paw, creature, agent, medium, organ, slave, robot, instrument, tool, vehicle, stooge, dupe, patsy, fall guy (*Slang*).

pawn[2] *v.* pledge, secure, post, stake, deposit, hock, put, place, offer, hazard, chance, risk, venture, gamble, mortgage.

pay *v.* **1** spend, expend, disburse, render, tender, compensate, reimburse, defray, recompense, remunerate, finance, back, support, bankroll, stake, capitalize, subsidize, reward, treat, foot the bill. **2** profit, benefit, reward, compensate, return, yield, bring in, reimburse, recoup, capitalize, cash in on. **3** requite, return, answer, repay, reciprocate, retort, retaliate, atone, make amends. —*n.* wages, salary, income, payment, earnings, fee, allowance, stipend, returns, honorarium, compensation, recompense, remuneration, emolument, take (*Slang*), takings, gain, reward, reckoning, bonus, commission, bounty, dividend.

pay back reimburse, repay, pay up, settle with, square accounts, ante up (*Slang*), discharge, return, refund.

payment *n.* **1** requital, reparation, amends, redress, indemnity, restitu-

unexcelled, superlative, nonpareil, outstanding, superior, super (*Slang*). **ant.** inferior, second-rate, pedestrian, commonplace, ordinary.

peeve *v.* irritate, annoy, irk, bother, disturb, upset, pique, gall, gripe, chafe, miff, nettle, exasperate, vex.

peevish *adj.* irritable, testy, grouchy, touchy, crabby, cross, ill-humored, fretful, petulant, querulous, liverish, atrabilious, moody, curmudgeonly, ill-tempered, bad-tempered, sullen, surly. **ant.** good-natured, amiable, jovial, affable, good-humored, genial, complaisant.

peewee *adj.* TINY.

peg *n.* **1** projection, protuberance, pin, point, stick, rod, knob, boss, button, stud, spur, hook, shaft, pile, stake, picket. **2** excuse, pretext, alibi, guise, pretense, out, handle, justification, apology, reason. **3** rank, grade, degree, level, step, position, stage, notch, mark, round, rung, measure, extent, standing, station, status. —*v.* pin, tack, nail, skewer, wedge, jam, clasp, join, connect, fasten, secure, affix.

pejorative *adj.* disparaging, derogatory, depreciatory, deprecatory, negative, unpleasant. **ant.** approving, commendatory, favorable, benign, positive.

pelf *n.* WEALTH.

pellet *n.* ball, sphere, spherule, globule, globelet, drop, droplet, bulb, bead, shot, marble, pea, pearl, pebble, blob.

pell-mell *adv.* helter-skelter, posthaste, hastily, precipitately, slapdash, rashly, feverishly, swiftly, quickly. —*n.* helter-skelter, hubbub, topsy-turvy, bustle, flurry, fuss, jumble, commotion, rumpus, scramble, tumult, disorder, confusion. **ant.** *adv.* calmly, serenely, placidly, orderly, methodically.

pellucid *adj.* LUCID.

pelt[1] *n.* hide, fur, coat, skin, pile.

pelt[2] *v.* **1** strike, beat, batter, buffet, pummel, baste, hammer, thrash, thump, pound, knock, attack, assail, lambaste. **2** rush, speed, hasten, hurry, race, scurry, bound, tear, scamper, barrel (*Slang*), flit, whiz, whisk, zip, dash, whistle, dart.

pen[1] *v.* WRITE.

pen[2] *n. Slang* PRISON.

penalize *v.* punish, discipline, correct, pass judgment, set to rights, sentence, chastise.

penalty *n.* **1** punishment, penalization, discipline, correction, chastening, chastisement, castigation, scourge, infliction, payment. **2** consequence, result, outcome, upshot, outgrowth, harvest, fruit, issue.

penance *n.* repentance, remorse, atonement, expiation, redemption, mortification, redress, amends, restitution, contrition, compunction.

penchant *n.* inclination, tendency, habit, turn, bent, leaning, bias, proneness, readiness, aptitude, propensity, proclivity, predisposition, partiality, predilection.

pendant *adj.* PENDENT.

pendent *adj.* hanging, drooping, dangling, hung, suspended, pendulous, pendant, pendulant, pensile, swinging.

pending *adj.* unfinished, unsettled, undetermined, unresolved, undecided, in suspense, up in the air, forthcoming, upcoming, in the offing, looming, impending, imminent, threatening.

pendulous *adj.* PENDENT.

penetrable *adj.* ABSORBENT.

penetrate *v.* **1** pierce, perforate, puncture, break through, broach, tap, prick, punch, stick, stab, impale, run through. **2** permeate, pervade, infuse, invade, suffuse, transfuse, diffuse, infiltrate, impregnate, spread, fill, occupy, leaven, tinge.

penetrating *adj.* **1** intrusive, penetrative, piercing, incisive, acid, acerbic, cutting, sharp, severe, biting, stinging, bitter, spicy, strong, pungent, heady, harsh, shrill, shattering, clangorous, deafening, screeching, ear-splitting. **2** discerning, insightful, perceptive, perspicacious, astute, sagacious, searching, profound, acute, incisive, keen, shrewd, thoughtful, profound, deep, in-depth.

ant. 1 bland, dull, soft, muted, subdued, blunt, muffled. **2** shallow, superficial, obtuse, thoughtless, dense.

penetration *n.* ACUMEN.

penetrative *adj.* PENETRATING.

penitence *n.* repentance, remorse, contrition, self-reproach, self-condemnation, atonement, expiation, mortification, reparation.

penitent *adj.* repentant, contrite, remorseful, penitential, conscience-stricken, abject, apologetic, sorry, humble.

ant. impenitent, hardened, callous, shameless, incorrigible, unregenerate.

penitential *adj.* PENITENT.

penitentiary *n.* PRISON.

penman *n.* WRITER.

penmanship *n.* handwriting, writing, longhand, hand, script, manuscript, calligraphy, chirography, graphology.

pen name PSEUDONYM.

pennant *n.* pennon, banner, banneret, flag, streamer, standard, ensign, colors, bunting.

penniless *adj.* indigent, destitute, impoverished, poverty-stricken, bankrupt, beggared, broke, down-and-out, strapped, poor, needy, in want.

ant. rich, affluent, prosperous, wealthy, well-off.

pennon *n.* PENNANT.

penny-wise *adj.* TIGHT-FISTED.

pensile *adj.* PENDENT.

pension *n.* annuity, social security, benefits, allowance.

pensive *adj.* **1** reflective, meditative, thoughtful, contemplative, ruminative, absorbed, dreamy, rapt, engrossed, preoccupied, serious, sober, musing. **2** wistful, nostalgic, downcast, melancholy, troubled.

ant. 1 unreflective, thoughtless, un-

thinking, flighty, heedless. **2** cheerful, frolicsome, lighthearted, carefree.

pent-up *adj. of emotions:* repressed, suppressed, muffled, inhibited, restrained, checked, stifled, subdued, smothered, confined, reserved, reticent.

ant. expressed, uninhibited, displayed, unchecked.

penurious *adj.* frugal, sparing, thrifty, prudent, provident, economic, parsimonious, penny-pinching, tight-fisted, mean, petty, cheap, grudging, stingy, miserly, ungenerous.

ant. extravagant, spendthrift, prodigal, lavish, thriftless, generous.

penury *n.* POVERTY.

people *n.* **1** population, inhabitants, citizens, nationals, natives, dwellers, compatriots, countrymen, community, society, commonwealth. **2** folk, stock, race, culture, ethnic group, breed, lineage, nationality, house, family, clan, tribe. **3** human beings, persons, individuals, humans, mankind, man, humanity, folks, populace, public, grass roots, community, society, commonality, masses, multitude, constituency, electorate, citizens. —*v.* populate, inhabit, settle, colonize, locate, relocate, establish, found.

pep *n. Slang* vim, verve, energy, kick, zip, dash, drive, punch, sprightliness, push, starch, ginger, vigor, force, vivacity, spryness, juice (*Slang*), pizzazz (*Slang*).

pepper *v.* spatter, shower, riddle, pelt, sprinkle, speck, dot, bespot, bombard, barrage.

peppery *adj.* quick-tempered, hot-tempered, short-tempered, fiery, hot, hotheaded, passionate, impetuous, hasty, volatile, unpredictable, contentious, argumentative, quarrelsome, feisty.

ant. unperturbed, cool-headed, placid, serene, restrained, apathetic.

peppy *adj.* LIVELY.

pep up invigorate, energize, animate, enliven, liven, prime, quicken, stimulate, exhilarate, inspire, jazz up (*Slang*), juice up (*Slang*).

peradventure *adv.* PERHAPS.

perambulate *v.* STROLL.

perceive *v.* **1** see, sight, discern, behold, view, observe, regard, watch, look at, spy, glimpse, descry, espy, apprehend, spot, discover, notice, distinguish, recognize, make out. **2** understand, comprehend, know, apprehend, realize, conceive, learn, grasp, absorb, assimilate, digest, fathom, appreciate, discern, recognize.

percentage *n.* proportion, ratio, fraction, percent, portion, measure, rate, quota, share, part, piece, cut, interest, dividend, allotment, commission, allowance, divvy (*Slang*).

perceptible *adj.* noticeable, visible, discernible, ascertainable, observable, appreciable, recognizable, evident, patent, plain, clear, definite, distinct, obvious, unmistakable, conspicuous. **ant.** imperceptible, inconspicuous, insignificant, inconsequential, intangible, scant.

perception *n.* **1** vision, sight, seeing, eyesight, discernment, perspicacity, acumen, sensation, impression, consciousness, awareness. **2** cognition, comprehension, appreciation, knowledge, grasp, consciousness, awareness, realization, discernment, understanding, judgment, sense, wisdom. **3** insight, intuition, astuteness, acumen, sensitivity. **ant.** **1** blindness, sightlessness. **2** incomprehension, unawareness, ignorance. **3** dullness, obtuseness, insensitivity.

perceptive *adj.* insightful, discerning, perspicacious, percipient, astute, intuitive, sensitive, judicious, sagacious, canny, hip (*Slang*), knowing, shrewd, sharp, clever, alert. **ant.** dull, insensitive, dense, undiscerning, obtuse.

perceptiveness *n.* ACUMEN.

perch *n.* roost, vantage, elevation, height, rise, altitude, eminence, aerie. —*v.* roost, settle, sit on, squat,

rest, settle down, get down, alight, land.

perchance *adv.* PERHAPS.

percipient *adj.* PERCEPTIVE.

percolate *v.* filter, filtrate, seep, ooze, leach, seethe, steep, ripple, gurgle, perk, distill, strain, sift, separate, screen, sieve, clarify, refine, sublimate.

percussion *n.* impact, shock, concussion, clash, collision, brunt, blow, hit, knock, bump, smash, butt, thrust.

perdition *n.* **1** Hell, Hades, underworld, inferno, abyss, pit, pandemonium. **2** ruin, destruction, devastation, havoc, loss, ravage, wrack and ruin, damnation, punishment.

peregrinate *v.* TRAVEL.

peregrinations *n.* travels, journeys, trips, journeying, meandering, wanderings, comings-and-goings, passage, tours, voyages, roaming, odysseys, globetrotting.

peremptory *adj.* **1** final, conclusive, decisive, binding, irrevocable, absolute, categorical, unequivocal, indisputable, commanding, imperative, authoritative. **2** obstinate, arbitrary, overbearing, dogmatic, opinionated, arrogant, dictatorial, imperious, domineering, highhanded, autocratic, absolute. **ant.** **1** inconclusive, indecisive, disputable, untenable, unproved, flimsy, fallacious. **2** pliant, conformable, cooperative, accommodating, flexible.

perennial *adj.* enduring, durable, lasting, persistent, perpetual, evergreen, constant, continuous, ongoing, permanent, lifelong, recurrent, unceasing, never-ending, unbroken.

perfect *adj.* **1** absolute, complete, comprehensive, full, total, utter, sheer, pure, ideal, consummate, faultless, flawless, unblemished, superb, outright, unqualified, categorical, exhaustive, downright. **2** accomplished, practiced, able, capable, qualified, skilled, well-equipped, well-endowed, gifted, talented, effi-

cient. **3** accurate, correct, exact, right, precise, letter-perfect, unerring, rigorous, meticulous, strict. —*v.* **1** finish, end, complete, conclude, terminate, carry out, get done, round out, top off, consummate, accomplish, perform, produce, execute, achieve, attain, fulfill. **2** develop, train, cultivate, polish, improve, better, advance, promote, mature, refine.
ant. *adj.* **1** flawed, faulty, defective, deficient, limited, partial. **2** inadequate, incapable, ineffectual, inept, unqualified. **3** inaccurate, inexact, unreliable, unsound, fallacious.

perfection *n.* flawlessness, faultlessness, ideal, fulfillment, exactness, exactitude, correctness, precision.

perfectionist *n.* stickler, precisionist, pedant, purist, quibbler, fuddy-duddy, fuss-budget.

perfervid *adj.* FERVENT.

perfidious *adj.* treacherous, false, false-hearted, unfaithful, disloyal, double-dealing, shifty, tricky, hypocritical, two-faced, Janus-faced, unreliable, traitorous, treasonous, apostate.
ant. loyal, trustworthy, devoted, dependable, steadfast, reliable, upright.

perfidy *n.* treachery, betrayal, treason, disloyalty, infidelity, faithlessness, falsity, duplicity, hypocrisy, double-dealing, deceitfulness, inconstancy, apostasy, double-cross (*Slang*), sell-out.

perforate *v.* pierce, puncture, penetrate, prick, punch, stab, stick, broach, tap, hole, bore, drill, auger, impale.

perforation *n.* HOLE.

perform *v.* **1** do, carry out, bring about, work out, execute, dispatch, enact, produce, effect, achieve, complete, finish, conclude, perfect, work, go, run, serve, function. **2** fulfill, discharge, live up to, satisfy, comply with, observe, keep, heed, attain, realize. **3** act, play, enact, play-act, role-play, represent, characterize,

portray, depict, render, exhibit, stage, appear, put on, execute.

performance *n.* **1** operation, practice, action, conduct, working, functioning, running, handling, management, production, exercise. **2** deed, accomplishment, action, achievement, attainment, feat, effort, enterprise, exploit, adventure, maneuver, doing, proceeding. **3** show, production, play, presentation, representation, entertainment, spectacle, exhibit, display, showing, engagement, stand, portrayal, characterization, part.

performer *n.* actor, actress, player, entertainer, star, lead, tragedian, tragedienne, comedian, comedienne, Thespian, trouper, mummer, mime, personality, ham (*Slang*).

perfume *n.* fragrance, scent, aroma, breath, whiff, bouquet, odor, smell, redolence, emanation, nosegay, incense, essence, aromatic, attar.

perfunctory *adj.* **1** routine, superficial, mechanical, habitual, repetitive, conventional, standard, unthinking, automatic, formal. **2** apathetic, spiritless, unconcerned, blasé, half-hearted, listless, cool, lukewarm, uninterested, disinterested, dispassionate, lackadaisical.
ant. **1** wholehearted, thoughtful, intense, earnest, careful. **2** absorbed, attentive, interested, alert, engrossed, dedicated.

perhaps *adv.* maybe, possibly, conceivably, perchance, mayhap.

peril *n.* danger, risk, hazard, jeopardy, insecurity, unsafeness, unsteadiness, unreliability, endangerment, imperilment. —*v.* IMPERIL.
ant. *n.* safety, security.

perilous *adj.* dangerous, hazardous, risky, insecure, unsound, unsafe, precarious, unreliable, shaky, uncertain, exposed, unprotected, vulnerable, endangered, parlous, chancy, tricky.
ant. safe, secure, guarded, guaranteed, reliable, trusty, solid, dependable, harmless.

perimeter *n.* PERIPHERY.

period *n.* **1** time, era, eon, age, interval, epoch, term, span, season, course, spell, duration, stage, cycle, date. **2** finis, stop, terminus, end, conclusion, termination, completion, expiration, finish, term, limit, closure, close, omega.

ant. 2 beginning, introduction, onset, start, initiation, alpha.

periodic *adj.* recurrent, intermittent, cyclic, alternate, recurring, rhythmic, circular, seasonal, epochal, repeated, pulsating, regular, routine.

ant. incessant, continued, irregular, chance, random, unceasing.

periodical *n.* publication, magazine, serial, review, journal, fascicle.

peripatetic *adj.* walking, itinerant, perambulatory, wandering, roving, rambling, tramping, pedestrian, ambling, ambulant, migrant.

ant. stationary, immobile, settled, rooted.

peripheral *adj.* **1** marginal, tangential, incidental, circumstantial, secondary, nonessential, borderline, outlying, surrounding. **2** distal, external, surface, outermost, exterior, outer.

ant. 1 basic, primary, central, essential, intrinsic, nuclear. **2** focal, proximal, central, underlying, inner.

periphery *n.* bounds, confines, compass, boundary, border, perimeter, circumference, limit, ambit, circuit, margin, surface.

ant. hub, core, middle, heart, center, inside.

periphrasis *n.* CIRCUMLOCUTION.

perish *v.* die, pass away, expire, pass on, wither, vanish, fade away, decay, molder, disappear, evaporate.

ant. survive, endure, persist, thrive, remain, abide.

perjure *v.* LIE.

perjury *n.* LIE.

perk *v.* PERCOLATE.

perk up rally, take heart, cheer up, recover, revive, mend, improve, look up, brighten, buck up, bear up, strengthen, recuperate.

ant. lose heart, flag, droop, languish, pine, tire.

perky *adj.* SPIRITED.

permanence *n.* durability, fixity, stability, perdurability, endurance, survival, perpetuity, permanency, immortality, continuance, fixedness, duration.

ant. evanescence, impermanence, transience, mortality, fleetingness, brevity.

permanency *n.* PERMANENCE.

permanent *adj.* durable, stable, fixed, lasting, irremovable, irreparable, immutable, perdurable, enduring, continuing, unchanging, perpetual, persistent, abiding, unchangeable, steadfast.

ant. ephemeral, temporary, unstable, impermanent, fleeting, transient.

permeable *adj.* ABSORBENT.

permeate *v.* pervade, diffuse, saturate, penetrate, infiltrate, impregnate, interpenetrate, sink in, ooze, seep, spread, drench, imbue, pass through, osmose, transfuse.

permissible *adj.* allowable, permitted, lawful, legal, legitimate, admissible, sufferable, tolerated, proper, fitting, free, unprohibited, authorized.

ant. forbidden, illegal, taboo, prohibited, unauthorized.

permission *n.* authorization, consent, sufferance, leave, warrant, liberty, freedom, franchise, license, enfranchisement, authority, dispensation, allowance, permit, go-ahead.

ant. prohibition, refusal, proscription, taboo, injunction, inhibition.

permissive *adj.* tolerant, lenient, indulgent, latitudinarian, acquiescent, easygoing, patient, lax, soft, yielding, compliant, forbearing, complaisant, agreeable.

ant. stern, strict, strait-laced, unyielding, harsh, Draconian.

permit *v.* allow, consent to, let, authorize, warrant, sanction, grant, tolerate, suffer, empower, charter, license, accord, agree to, endure. —*n.* PERMISSION.

ant. *v.* prohibit, forbid, prevent, refuse, enjoin, ban.

permutation *n.* ALTERATION.

permute *v.* ALTER.

pernicious *adj.* destructive, deadly, baneful, malignant, noxious, deleterious, harmful, hurtful, injurious, detrimental, damaging, ruinous, virulent, lethal, fatal.
ant. innocuous, beneficial, healthful, invigorating, tonic, salubrious.

pernickety *adj.* PERSNICKETY.

perorate *v.* HARANGUE.

perpetrate *v.* commit, do, perform, carry out, effect, execute, enact, practice, transact, bring about, inflict, actuate, act.

perpetrator *n.* offender, transgressor, malefactor, miscreant, delinquent, culprit, wrongdoer, trespasser, lawbreaker, violator, outlaw, scofflaw, suspect, prisoner.

perpetual *adj.* **1** eternal, everlasting, immortal, endless, permanent, sempiternal, enduring, infinite, unending. **2** incessant, continual, perennial, interminable, repetitious, ceaseless, uninterrupted, continuous, constant, unfailing.
ant. **1** temporary, finite, impermanent, transient, transitory. **2** interrupted, discontinuous, inconstant, unstable, momentary.

perpetuate *v.* continue, immortalize, preserve, eternize, eternalize, prolong, sustain, maintain, keep up, protract, extend.
ant. terminate, discontinue, finish off, end, cut off, kill.

perplex *v.* confuse, puzzle, baffle, nonplus, mix up, bewilder, confound, muddle, distract, dumbfound, disconcert, mystify, daze, dismay.
ant. explain, solve, enlighten, reassure, instruct, clarify.

perplexed *adj.* DAZED.

perplexing *adj.* CONFUSING.

perplexity *n.* bewilderment, confusion, dismay, distraction, bafflement, puzzlement, agitation, hesitation, uncertainty, embarrassment, disturb-

ance, astonishment, amazement, mystification, doubt.
ant. sureness, understanding, self-possession, coolness, facility, composure.

perquisite *n.* PRIVILEGE.

persecute *v.* harass, badger, oppress, torment, victimize, harry, afflict, punish, torture, beset, distress, worry, molest, annoy, vex.
ant. benefit, support, gratify, comfort, sustain, relieve.

persecution *n.* oppression, harassment, torment, abuse, molestation, annoyance, harrying, pursuit, tyranny, maltreatment, punishment, torture, outrage.
ant. benefaction, indulgence, protection, reward, succor.

perseverance *n.* steadfastness, tenacity, persistence, resolution, endurance, insistence, doggedness, stamina, diligence, zeal, stick-to-itiveness, determination, firmness, constancy, dedication, immovability, devotion.
ant. irresolution, vacillation, shilly-shally, hesitation.

persevere *v.* persist, endure, carry on, strive, hold out, continue, hang on, keep on, stand firm, last, hold on, pursue.
ant. vacillate, waver, shilly-shally, hesitate.

persevering *adj.* PERSISTENT.

persiflage *n.* BANTER.

persist *v.* **1** continue, persevere, insist, strive, plod, struggle, hold on, pursue. **2** endure, last, abide, continue, survive, prolong, linger, remain, stay.
ant. **1** vacillate, waver, falter, shillyshally. **2** vanish, perish, end, disappear, die.

persistence *n.* perseverance, determination, steadfastness, resolution, firmness, doggedness, obstinacy, tenacity, stamina, constancy, insistence, stick-to-itiveness, diligence, tirelessness, zeal, devotion.

persistent *adj.* **1** firm, persevering, resolute, dogged, tireless, steadfast, indefatigable, tenacious, insistent, importunate, demanding, pig-headed. **2** enduring, permanent, tenacious, durable, lasting, chronic, ineradicable, unceasing, immovable, fixed, unchangeable, changeless, unaltered.

ant. 1 irresolute, inconstant, vacillating, changeable. **2** short-lived, temporary, fleeting, impermanent, unstable.

persnickety *adj.* fastidious, fussy, over-precise, pernickety, prissy, prim, painstaking, old-maidish, nit-picking, exact, accurate, careful, nice, scrupulous, punctilious.

ant. careless, slap-dash, haphazard, hit-or-miss, sloppy, nonchalant.

person *n.* **1** human being, individual, human, one, somebody, someone, anyone. **2** body frame, soma, flesh, carcass, phenotype, presence. **3** self, personality, being, soul, life, spirit, ego, identity, self-image, psyche.

persona *n.* ROLE.

personable *adj.* attractive, good-looking, comely, handsome, pretty, lovely, fair, graceful, pleasing, winning, charming, seemly, fetching.

ant. homely, ugly, unattractive, ill-favored, plain, unlovely.

personage *n.* dignitary, notable, luminary, eminence, magnifico, nabob, bigwig, somebody, VIP, leader, pillar of society, personality, celebrity, big shot (*Slang*), panjandrum, chief.

ant. nobody, cipher, plebeian, pawn, lightweight (*Slang*).

personal *adj.* **1** private, individual, intimate, own, privy, particular, idiosyncratic, special, peculiar, exclusive. **2** bodily, physical, corporeal, carnal, corporal, sensual, material, external, exterior.

ant. 1 public, common, communal, general, social. **2** spiritual, inner, inward, disembodied, impalpable.

personality *n.* **1** character, nature, disposition, temperament, temper, individuality, complexion, stripe, genius, style. **2** charm, attractiveness, allure, fascination, magnetism, charisma,

animation, dynamism, friendliness. **3** celebrity, personage, notable, dignitary, luminary, worthy, star, superstar.

ant. 3 nobody, nonentity, has-been, cipher, nullity, drag (*Slang*).

personification *n.* EMBODIMENT.

personify *v.* typify, embody, represent, symbolize, exemplify, incorporate, substantiate, incarnate, externalize, impersonate, imitate, copy, materialize.

personnel *n.* persons, staff, force, crew, workers, retinue, helpers, employees, work force.

perspective *n.* **1** discrimination, proportion, judgment, relativity, background, configuration, context, frame of reference. **2** vista, prospect, view, outlook, horizon, aspect, distance.

perspicacious *adj.* discerning, keen, shrewd, sharp-witted, perspicuous, understanding, sagacious, astute, perceptive, acute, penetrating, lucid, sharp, clear-sighted.

ant. dull, stupid, slow, obtuse, dim-witted, simple.

perspicaciousness *n.* ACUMEN.

perspicacity *n.* ACUMEN.

perspicuity *n.* CLARITY.

perspicuous *adj.* **1** LUCID. **2** PERSPICACIOUS.

perspiration *n.* SWEAT.

perspire *v.* SWEAT.

persuade *v.* induce, convince, coax, prevail upon, influence, dispose, impel, lead, urge, win over, cajole, incite, entice, get.

ant. dissuade, discourage, deter, prevent, turn from, admonish.

persuasion *n.* **1** inducement, conversion, counseling, guidance, argumentation, influencing, suasion. **2** belief, assent, certainty, certitude, conviction, opinion, view. **3** cogency, potency, persuasiveness, influence, seductiveness, force, validity.

ant. 1 dissuasion, discouragement, expostulation, warning, remonstrance. **2** disbelief, skepticism, uncertainty, dissent, doubt. **3** speciousness, dubiety, ambiguity, delusiveness, fallaciousness.

persuasive *adj.* convincing, influential, assuring, cogent, compelling, moving, powerful, credible, logical, valid, sound, weighty, seductive, telling, eloquent, incontrovertible, undeniable. **ant.** unconvincing, dubious, lame, inconclusive, invalid, ambiguous.

pert *adj.* **1** impudent, forward, impertinent, saucy, disrespectful, flippant, bold, arch, cheeky, insolent, brash. **2** comely, lively, vivacious, nimble, sprightly, jaunty, brisk, dapper. **ant. 1** respectful, demure, reserved, shy, courteous, retiring. **2** dull, homely, sluggish, shabby, indolent, lethargic.

pertain *v.* refer, relate, appertain, apply, concern, affect, bear on, touch, regard, connect, tie in, adhere, answer, belong, involve.

pertinacious *adj.* dogged, stubborn, tenacious, unyielding, persistent, headstrong, willful, strong-willed, obstinate, mulish, inflexible, wayward, determined, persevering, firm, relentless. **ant.** compliant, flexible, pliable, submissive, relenting, pliant.

pertinacity *n.* OBSTINACY.

pertinence *n.* RELEVANCE.

pertinent *adj.* relevant, applicable, germane, material, apposite, apropos, significant, related, suited, apt, pat, appropriate, fitting. **ant.** irrelevant, extraneous, inappropriate, impertinent, foreign, inapplicable.

perturb *v.* disquiet, disturb, alarm, agitate, upset, annoy, fluster, distress, bother, discompose, flurry, trouble, worry, vex, disconcert, excite, harass, pique. **ant.** compose, soothe, quiet, calm, pacify, tranquilize.

perturbation *n.* ALARM.

perusal *n.* SCRUTINY.

peruse *v.* READ.

pervade *v.* permeate, penetrate, diffuse,

imbue, infuse, spread, fill, interfuse, pass through, infiltrate, impregnate, saturate, suffuse, soak, traverse, affect.

pervasive *adj.* widespread, commonplace, diffuse, general, rife, common, universal, omnipresent, wide-ranging, inescapable, ineluctable. **ant.** spotty, localized, occasional, uncommon, sparse, rare.

perverse *adj.* **1** abnormal, deviant, incorrect, improper, cranky, eccentric, topsy-turvy, backward, counter. **2** wicked, corrupt, immoral, perverted, bad, depraved, dissolute, debauched. **3** obstinate, unreasonable, wrong-headed, contrary, balky, mulish, refractory, froward, wayward, restive, contentious, pigheaded, ornery. **ant. 1** normal, right, regular, standard, correct, proper. **2** good, honorable, pure, chaste, moral, upright. **3** complaisant, amenable, yielding, agreeable, tractable, docile.

perversion *n.* deviation, abnormality, aberration, degeneration, corruption, depravity, immorality, vitiation, debauchment, debasement, prostitution, injury, impairment.

pervert *v.* **1** misconstrue, misinterpret, distort, falsify, garble, stretch, twist, scramble. **2** corrupt, debase, entice, vitiate, misdirect, lead astray, deprave, seduce, debauch. —*n.* deviate, delinquent, aberrant, deviant, debauchee. **ant. v. 1** amend, correct, rectify, remedy, clarify. **2** elevate, reclaim, uplift, convert, reform.

perverted *adj.* corrupt, abnormal, deviant, aberrant, depraved, distorted, misguided, sick, impaired, debased, injurious, debauched, vitiated, wicked, immoral. **ant.** normal, healthy, virtuous, straight, pure, good.

pervious *adj.* ABSORBENT.

pesky *adj.* annoying, troublesome, irksome, vexatious, galling, wearisome, exasperating, bothersome, pestiferous, plaguy, detestable, cursed, blessed, importunate.

ant. soothing, pleasant, delightful, agreeable, welcome, comforting.

pessimism *n.* GLOOM.

pessimistic *adj.* gloomy, cynical, hopeless, misanthropic, distrustful, despondent, despairing, dyspeptic, cloudy, dark, foreboding, depressed, glum, grim, dejected.

ant. optimistic, hopeful, sanguine, confident, bright, rosy.

pest *n.* nuisance, pain (*Slang*), pain in the neck (*Slang*), bother, irritation, worry, bore, thorn, thorn in one's side, trouble, bane, gadfly, critic, carper, faultfinder, annoyance, aggravation, headache.

pester *v.* harass, annoy, tease, bait, molest, disturb, vex, tantalize, plague, harry, worry, heckle, badger, torment, nettle, beset, taunt.

ant. please, pamper, pet, soothe, cosset, delight.

pestiferous *adj.* PESKY.

pestilence *n.* epidemic, plague, pandemic, scourge, pest, contagion, infestation, visitation, infection, virulence, malignancy.

pesty *adj.* ANNOYING.

pet[1] *adj.* cherished, favorite, darling, beloved, precious, dear. —*v.* stroke, caress, fondle, dandle, cuddle, baby.

ant. *adj.* detested, despised, scorned, disliked, unloved.

pet[2] *n.* PIQUE.

peter out run dry, expire, sink, fail, dwindle, give out, ebb, fade, dissolve, evaporate, wind down.

petite *adj.* diminutive, dainty, small, slight, little, tiny, wee, undersized.

ant. gross, large, ample, big.

petition *n.* request, supplication, suit, appeal, entreaty, plea, solicitation, prayer, invocation, application, round robin. —*v.* entreat, supplicate, pray, plead, sue, solicit, appeal, beg, ask, apply.

petrified *adj.* AGHAST.

petrify *v.* **1** harden, solidify, indurate, calcify, fossilize, mineralize, set. **2**

immobilize, paralyze, transfix, stupefy, dumbfound, spellbind, stun.

ant. 1 liquefy, soften, melt.

pettifogger *n.* NITPICKER.

pettish *adj.* PETULANT.

petty *adj.* **1** unimportant, paltry, small, contemptible, inconsequential, insignificant, trifling, trivial, small-time (*Slang*), negligible, bush-league (*Slang*), minor, subordinate. **2** small-minded, mean, spiteful, stingy, grudging, ungenerous, miserly, cheap, shabby, ornery.

ant. 1 important, consequential, worthy, leading, commanding, great. **2** broad-minded, generous, magnanimous, lofty, largehearted, noble.

petulance *n.* ANGER.

petulant *adj.* pettish, fretful, peevish, grumpy, cross, irascible, irritable, querulous, waspish, captious, complaining, whining, ill-humored, touchy.

ant. agreeable, even-tempered, debonair, cheerful, pleasant, sunny.

phalanx *n.* corps, troop, column, force, group, body, wedge, formation, cadre, army, mass.

phantasm *n.* PHANTOM.

phantasy *n.* FANTASY.

phantom *n.* **1** illusion, figment, dream, vision, shadow, will-o'-the-wisp, chimera, ignis fatuus, mirage. **2** apparition, specter, wraith, ghost, phantasm, spirit, revenant. **3** bugbear, spook, bugaboo, bogy, goblin, monster, ogre. —*adj.* illusory, unreal, imaginary, spectral, hallucinatory, dreamy, ghostly, chimerical, fanciful, spurious.

ant. *adj.* material, real, flesh-and-blood, realistic, down-to-earth, practical.

pharisaic *adj.* HYPOCRITICAL.

pharisaism *n.* HYPOCRISY.

pharisee *n.* HYPOCRITE.

pharmacist *n.* DRUGGIST.

phase *n.* stage, aspect, facet, guise, appearance, condition, status, level, chapter, grade, step, angle, side, state, attitude, position.

phaseout *n.* TERMINATION.

phase out taper off, wind up, wind down, close, run down, wrap up, ease off, retire, settle, end, diminish, deactivate, terminate.

ant. embark on, initiate, set in motion, start, tool up, get under way.

phenomenal *adj.* **1** material, physical, objective, sensible, substantial, real, corporeal, natural. **2** miraculous, marvelous, prodigious, preternatural, striking, remarkable, noteworthy, outstanding.

ant. 1 immaterial, subjective, incorporeal, transcendent, noumenal. **2** everyday, ordinary, familiar, natural, routine.

phenomenon *n.* prodigy, marvel, curiosity, spectacle, wonder, sight, rarity, sensation, miracle, portent, nonpareil.

philander *v.* DALLY.

philanderer *n.* flirt, gallant, lady-killer, ladies' man, trifler, lover, Don Juan, adulterer, rake, rakehell, libertine, lecher.

philanthropic *adj.* charitable, munificent, magnanimous, liberal, humanitarian, humane, beneficent, bounteous, public-spirited, altruistic, benevolent, compassionate, eleemosynary.

ant. misanthropic, hardhearted, miserly, egotistical, selfish, morose.

philanthropy *n.* charity, benefaction, magnanimity, benevolence, good will, public-spiritedness, humanitarianism, humanity, generosity, munificence, altruism, almsgiving, openhandedness.

ant. misanthropy, cynicism, ill will, malevolence, animosity, hostility.

philistine *n.* conformist, vulgarian, ignoramus, Babbitt, yahoo, peasant, bourgeois, boor, barbarian, upstart, parvenu.

ant. aesthete, connoisseur, dilettante, critic, cognoscente.

philosopher *n.* savant, scholar, metaphysician, thinker, theorist, rationalist, dialectician, logician, polymath, speculator, pundit, solon, guru.

philosophical *adj.* reasonable, calm, patient, thoughtful, unruffled, serene, imperturbable, resigned, impassive, composed, tranquil, reflective, stoical, cool, unmoved.

ant. impatient, rash, excitable, emotional, overwrought, passionate.

philosophy *n.* **1** knowledge, laws, thought, wisdom, learning, theory, principles, metaphysics, science. **2** ideology, ism, doctrine, system, rationale, life style, apologia, values, tenets, *Weltanschauung.*

philter *n.* POTION.

phlegmatic *adj.* indifferent, calm, dull, undemonstrative, apathetic, stolid, stoic, languid, listless, unemotional, unresponsive, halfhearted, impassive, sluggish, inert, frigid, tame.

ant. sanguine, excitable, eager, demonstrative, hotheaded, lively.

phobia *n.* fear, dislike, antipathy, aversion, apprehension, repugnance, distaste, abhorrence, dread, loathing, disgust, horror, hatred.

ant. attraction, addiction, taste, liking, enjoyment, love.

phoney *adj.* PHONY.

phony *Slang adj.* counterfeit, fake, spurious, false, fraudulent, specious, sham, bogus, artificial, hypocritical. —*n.* fake, fraud, humbug, counterfeit, facade, front, hoax, imitation, sham, hypocrite, pretense, imposture.

ant. *adj.* genuine, authentic, bona fide, veritable, true, sincere. *n.* the real McCoy.

photo *n.* PHOTOGRAPH.

photograph *n.* photo, picture, photoprint, print, snapshot, shot, exposure, take, still, glossy, halftone, blowup, enlargement, positive, negative, transparency, slide. —*v.* take, shoot, film, snap, expose, run, record.

photographic *adj.* vivid, detailed, lifelike, cinematic, visual, realistic, exact, pictorial, graphic, representative, convincing, natural, faithful, eidetic, filmic.

ant. impressionistic, hazy, inexact, unrealistic.

phrase *n.* expression, catchword, locution, word, idiom, tag, epithet, byword, saying, motto, saw. —*v.* word, couch, express, style, voice, put, pronounce, term, call, denominate, designate, describe, present, dub, name.

phraseology *n.* WORDING.

phrasing *n.* WORDING.

physic *n., v.* PURGE.

physical *adj.* **1** material, palpable, sensible, substantial, tangible, phenomenal, objective, corporeal, real, solid. **2** bodily, carnal, fleshly, somatic, mortal, vital, corporeal, corporal, incarnate, external.

ant. 1 impalpable, subjective, delusional, unreal, unnatural, apparent. **2** mental, psychic, disembodied, spiritual, internal.

physician *n.* doctor, medico, practitioner, healer, medic, medical examiner, M.D., doc (*Slang*).

physiognomy *n.* PHYSIQUE.

physique *n.* anatomy, body, structure, conformation, figure, build, shape, makeup, habit, configuration, organization, constitution, physiognomy, type.

piazza *n.* **1** PORCH. **2** SQUARE.

picaresque *adj.* ROGUISH.

picayune *adj.* **1** little, paltry, trivial, trifling, worthless, insignificant, slight, skimpy. **2** petty, small-minded, mean, shallow, narrow-minded, spiteful, niggling, nit-picking, argumentative.

ant. 1 large, important, significant, considerable, valued. **2** generous, great-hearted, broad-minded, liberal, magnanimous.

pick *v.* **1** select, cull, choose, single out, fix on, prefer, settle on. **2** detach, pluck, pull, take, gather, cut, get. **3** provoke, bring on, instigate, kindle, stir up, foment, incite, egg on. —*n.* **1** selection, choice, option, choosing,

decision, preference, fancy. **2** best, cream, choicest, prize, elite, gem, paragon.

ant. *v.* **1** pass over, leave out, ignore, reject, refuse. **3** allay, calm, cool, pacify, cancel. *n.* **2** worst, refuse, reject, lees, jetsam, cull.

picket *n.* **1** stake, paling, pale, peg, post, rail, palisade, stanchion, tether. **2** guard, sentinel, watch, detail, patrol, warder, spotter, lookout, scout, sentry.

pickings *n.* **1** leavings, gleanings, scraps, leftovers, culls, rejects, scrapings, residue. **2** spoils, loot, booty, plunder, payoff, rewards, return, yield, gravy (*Slang*).

pickle *n.* fix, stew, dilemma, plight, quandary, predicament, crisis, scrape, mess, corner, jam, spot (*Slang*), hot water (*Slang*).

pick-me-up *n.* STIMULUS.

pick on tease, annoy, harass, pester, needle, worry, nag, torment, heckle, goad, rile, badger, hector, bait, bug (*Slang*).

ant. indulge, cater to, please, encourage, cosset, praise.

pickup *n.* **1** acceleration, speedup, revving, quickening. **2** improvement, gain, advance, revival, recovery, comeback, rally, strengthening, intensification, enhancement.

ant. 1 deceleration, slowdown, moderation. **2** waning, downturn, decline, reversal, decrease, slump.

pick up 1 raise, take up, grasp, lift, hoist, take hold, seize, grab. **2** tidy, straighten, arrange, neaten, smarten, dispose, spruce, clear, clean, redd.

ant. 1 drop, let fall, loose, throw away, discard, toss away. **2** litter, strew, clutter, mess up, disorder.

Pickwickian *adj.* KIND[1].

picky *adj.* choosy, fussy, finicky, fastidious, particular, discriminating, squeamish, difficult, overcritical, meticulous, faultfinding, nice, captious, demanding, exacting.

ant. undemanding, easygoing, uncritical, promiscuous, undiscriminating, unselective.

pictorial *adj.* graphic, illustrated, illustrative, picturesque, representational, vivid, scenic, cinematic, picturable, attractive, imaginative, photogenic.

picture *n.* **1** *visual:* image, semblance, delineation, illustration, likeness, portrait, representation, depiction, painting, sketch, drawing, tracing. **2** *verbal:* description, representation, depiction, delineation, scene, sketch, portrayal. —*v.* draw, sketch, outline, represent, limn, delineate, illustrate, depict, describe.

picturesque *adj.* **1** pictorial, photogenic, cinematic, filmic. **2** quaint, charming, old-fashioned, singular, peculiar, interesting, whimsical, fanciful, odd.

ant. 2 commonplace, dull, banal, uninteresting, ordinary.

piddle *v.* TRIFLE.

piebald *adj.* MOTTLED.

piece *n.* **1** portion, element, member, part, chunk, fragment, section, segment, unit, module, division, bit, scrap, amount. **2** *object used in games:* counter, disk, chip, token, checker, figure, tile.

ant. 1 entirety, set, whole, total, assemblage, sum.

piecemeal *adj.* gradual, step-by-step, incremental, stepwise, erratic, fragmentary, spotty, partial, interrupted, intermittent, disparate, patchy.

pied *adj.* MOTTLED.

pier *n.* **1** upright, buttress, pillar, support, column, post, shoulder, brace. **2** jetty, wharf, dock, breakwater, sea wall, quay, landing, mole.

pierce *v.* penetrate, perforate, run through, puncture, impale, transfix, prick, stab, stick, probe, enter, pink, gore, bore, drill.

piercing *adj.* **1** SHRILL. **2** ACUTE.

pietism *n.* PIETY.

piety *n.* **1** sanctity, pietism, godliness, devoutness, piousness, holiness, grace, devotion, reverence, religion. **2** devotion, dutifulness, respect, rev-

erence, patriotism, loyalty, fidelity, allegiance, fealty, obedience.

ant. 1 ungodliness, irreverence, impiety, apostasy, blasphemy. **2** faithlessness, infidelity, impiety, irreverence, disrespect.

piffle *n.* NONSENSE.

pig *n.* **1** swine, porker, piglet, hog, sow, shoat, boar. **2** glutton, guzzler, beast, animal, hog, swine, cormorant, slob (*Slang*).

pigeon *n. Slang* DUPE.

piggish *adj.* GREEDY.

piggy *adj.* GREEDY.

pig-headed *adj.* OBSTINATE.

pig-headedness *n.* OBSTINACY.

pigmy *n., adj.* PYGMY.

piker *n. Slang* MISER.

pilaster *n.* COLUMN.

pile[1] *n.* heap, mass, hoard, lot, stack, accumulation, quantity, load, collection, assemblage, store. —*v.* load, heap, stack, amass, assemble, accumulate, collect, hoard.

ant. *v.* disperse, spread out, unload, scatter, distribute, strew.

pile[2] *n.* pier, post, column, stake, support, foundation, piling.

piles *n.* hemorrhoids.

pile-up *n.* ACCUMULATION.

pile up accumulate, amass, agglomerate, assemble, heap up, bring together, hoard, collect, gather, aggregate, scrape together.

ant. scatter, disperse, waste, spend, dissipate, level.

pilfer *v.* steal, filch, purloin, lift, crib, thieve, take, finger, rifle, sneak, palm, appropriate, pick, snatch.

pilferage *n.* **1** ROBBERY. **2** LOOT.

pilgrim *n.* wanderer, wayfarer, itinerant, palmer, crusader, hadji, devotee, sojourner, nomad, journeyer, traveler.

pilgrimage *n.* journey, expedition, voyage, travel, passage, excursion, tour, mission, sojourn, hadj, visit, trip.

pill *n.* **1** pellet, tablet, capsule, lozenge, medicine, medication, remedy, dose. **2** pest, nuisance, headache, bore, drip (*Slang*), pain (*Slang*), jerk (*Slang*), schlep (*Slang*).

pillage *n.* robbery, looting, plundering, devastation, destruction, spoliation, rapine, vandalism, depredation, sack. —*v.* loot, plunder, despoil, desecrate, rape, sack, ravage, rifle, strip, rob, spoil.

pillager *n.* BRIGAND.

pillar *n.* **1** column, shaft, post, pier, colonnade, stanchion, pilaster, monument, tower, obelisk, needle. **2** leader, worthy, support, upholder, prop, supporter, maintainer.

pillar of society PERSONAGE.

pillory *v.* RIDICULE.

pillow *n.* cushion, pad, support, headrest, bolster.

pilose *adj.* HAIRY.

pilot *n.* helmsman, steersman, navigator, leader, commander, guide, captain, conductor, director, operator. —*v.* steer, guide, conduct, direct, operate, lead, engineer, navigate, shepherd.

pimp *n.* pander, procurer, bawd, whoremonger, go-between, white slaver.

pimple *n.* pustule, papule, ruck, blotch, eruption, lesion, sore, bleb, blister, fester, vesicle, pock, verruca, wart, wheal, carbuncle.

pin *n.* **1** skewer, fastener, peg, bar, bolt, fastening, support. **2** brooch, ornament, medal, clasp, badge, clip, decoration, button. —*v.* **1** fasten, affix, join, attach, staple, secure, rivet, clamp, bolt, nail. **2** immobilize, hold down, restrain, hold fast, fix, pinion, press down.

pinch *v.* **1** squeeze, compress, tweak, cramp, crush, bind, nip, contract, gripe, crimp. **2** *Slang* arrest, nab, collar, apprehend, capture, grab, restrain, catch. —*n.* emergency, crisis, predicament, plight, difficulty, exigency, strait, strain, vicissitude, stress.

pinch-hit *v.* RELIEVE.

pine *v.* weaken, languish, droop, dwin-dle, wither, flag, peak, waste, diminish, decline, sicken, sink, decay.

ant. flourish, burgeon, wax, bloom, prosper, batten.

pine for crave, long for, hanker for, lust after, thirst for, yearn, sigh for, hunger for, covet.

ant. spurn, reject, disdain, put off.

pinhead *n. Slang* FOOL.

pinion *v.* shackle, restrain, bind, manacle, fetter, handcuff, straitjacket, leash, strap, trammel, hamstring, hobble, chain, tether, fasten.

ant. loosen, free, liberate, release, unloose, unshackle.

pink *v.* prick, stab, pierce, penetrate, puncture, perforate, run through, wound, cut, transfix, impale, nick.

pinnacle *n.* acme, peak, apex, summit, top, zenith, meridian, cap, crown, crest, climax, culmination, eminence, tower, maximum.

ant. nadir, depths, bottom, base, foot, minimum.

pinpoint *v.* localize, zero in on, define, spot, identify, home in on, locate, fix on, triangulate.

pioneer *n.* forerunner, innovator, harbinger, frontiersman, originator, inventor, developer, avant-gardist, ancestor, midwife, first. —*v.* explore, originate, launch, initiate, develop, introduce, invent, inaugurate, lead, establish, found, discover, create.

ant. *n.* follower, disciple, imitator, successor, descendant. *v.* copy, follow, imitate, trail, succeed.

pious *adj.* **1** devout, godly, reverent, consecrated, righteous, God-fearing, saintly, holy, religious, devotional, sacred. **2** pietistic, holier-than-thou, insincere, hypocritical, unctuous, sanctimonious, Pecksniffian.

ant. **1** impious, sacrilegious, profane, sinful, blasphemous, unholy.

piousness *n.* PIETY.

pip[1] *n.* **1** *Slang* prodigy, honey, gem, wonder, marvel, nonpareil, dandy, paragon, masterpiece, model, exemplar, dream, winner, humdinger (*Slang*). **2** PIT[2].

ant. 1 botch, reject, second-rater, bummer (*Slang*), lemon (*Slang*), loser.

pip² *v.* PEEP.

pipe *n.* **1** hookah, calumet, narghile, meerschaum, briar, corncob pipe. **2** duct, conduit, pipeline, conveyor, tube, hose, main, conductor, line. —*v.* **1** toot, play, trill, shrill, tootle, tweet, chirp, sing, sound, whistle. **2** convey, conduct, siphon, channel, transport, transmit, guide.

pipe dream DAYDREAM.

piquancy *n.* SPICE.

piquant *adj.* **1** pungent, tart, sapid, tasty, zesty, savory, appetizing, flavorsome, sharp, tangy, spicy. **2** racy, interesting, titillating, spirited, lively, intriguing, provocative, stimulating, winsome, sparkling.

ant. 1 bland, flat, insipid, tasteless, unappetizing. **2** stodgy, tedious, dull, uninteresting, unattractive.

pique *n.* irritation, resentment, pet, spite, snit, grudge, umbrage, vexation, displeasure, anger. —*v.* **1** irritate, nettle, offend, chafe, vex, wound, provoke, affront, sting, incense. **2** stimulate, whet, spur, excite, goad, arouse, incite, instigate, urge, provoke, stir up, turn on (*Slang*).

ant. *n.* delight, pleasure, felicity, happiness, comfort. *v.* **1** please, delight, mollify, compliment, soothe. **2** bore, quiet, calm, turn off (*Slang*).

piracy *n.* plagiarism, theft, infringement, cribbing, lifting, borrowing, copying, stealing, appropriation.

pirate *n.* freebooter, buccaneer, corsair, plunderer, filibuster, picaroon, marauder, privateer, sea rover. —*v.* plagiarize, steal, crib, borrow, lift, copy, appropriate.

pistol *n.* handgun, small arm, revolver, gun, automatic.

pit¹ *n.* cavity, hole, excavation, mine, abyss, chasm, crater, burrow, hollow, shaft, well.

ant. hill, rise, elevation, mound, heap, mountain.

pit² *n.* stone, kernel, seed, core, nut, pip.

pitch *v.* **1** erect, set up, establish, locate, settle, plant, fix, place. **2** throw, toss, cast, fling, hurl, heave, put, send, launch. **3** lurch, plunge, dive, stagger, topple, drop, fall, wobble. —*n.* slant, elevation, declivity, inclination, slope, dip, grade, angle, steepness, obliquity.

ant. *v.* **1** dismantle, pull down, strike, remove, take apart.

pitch-black *adj.* BLACK.

pitch-dark *adj.* DARK.

pitcher *n.* ewer, jug, flask, jar, beaker, pot, vase, cruse, cruet, vessel, amphora, urn, toby, bottle.

pitch in 1 buckle down, plunge into, start, set about, tackle, undertake, begin, go ahead, set out, get busy, get cracking (*Slang*). **2** participate, join in, lend a hand, cooperate, help, contribute, take part in, partake, assist.

pitchman *n.* SALESPERSON.

pitchwoman *n.* SALESPERSON.

pitchy *adj.* DARK.

piteous *adj.* distressing, poignant, heart-rending, affecting, touching, moving, pitiful, pitiable, pathetic, wretched, miserable, heartbreaking, woeful, sad, deplorable.

ant. pleasant, joyful, heart-warming, delightful, fine, happy.

pitfall *n.* trap, ambush, snare, danger, quagmire, deadfall, booby trap, land mine, gin, toils, springe, quicksand, stumblingblock, hurdle.

pith *n.* substance, essence, soul, heart, quintessence, core, kernel, marrow, gist, point, root, rudiment, nucleus, medulla.

ant. integument, layer, skin, surface, cortex.

pithy *adj.* concentrated, concise, succinct, terse, effective, forceful, forcible, convincing, cogent, well-taken, compendious, laconic, summary, powerful.

ant. redundant, maundering, weak, digressive, ineffective, diluted.

pitiable *adj.* PITIFUL.

pitiful *adj.* **1** lamentable, pathetic, deplorable, pitiable, miserable, touching, piteous, heartbreaking, distressing, wretched, moving, affecting. **2** paltry, insignificant, contemptible, despicable, inadequate, worthless, sorry, abject, mean, base.
ant. 1 enviable, fortunate, happy, prosperous, flourishing. **2** ample, respectable, powerful, superior, honored, adequate.

pitiless *adj.* merciless, unmerciful, ruthless, cruel, hardhearted, obdurate, relentless, coldblooded, inexorable, implacable, unfeeling, mean, harsh, barbarous, inhuman.
ant. compassionate, softhearted, merciful, clement, kind, sympathetic.

pittance *n.* dole, mite, trifle, driblet, modicum, ration, insufficiency, allotment, alms, allowance, charity.
ant. bounty, excess, abundance, largess, sufficiency, bonus.

pitted *adj.* marked, scarred, rough, indented, honeycombed, dented, dimpled, gouged, pockmarked, blemished.
ant. smooth, unmarked, flat, plane, regular.

pity *n.* sympathy, compassion, commiseration, mercy, empathy, ruth, fellow feeling, condolence, charity, humanity, tenderness, kindness. —*v.* sympathize, commiserate, have mercy, relent, compassionate, condole, be sorry for, solace, feel for, grieve for, forbear, weep for.
ant. *n.* mercilessness, ruthlessness, harshness, apathy, rancor, pitilessness.

pivot *n.* turning point, fulcrum, swivel, kingbolt, axis, hinge, kingpin, center, axle, focus, joint. —*v.* turn, hinge, revolve, depend, hang, swing, oscillate, wheel, whirl, swivel, spiral.

pixilated *adj.* **1** CRAZY. **2** DROLL.

pixy *n.* fairy, elf, brownie, sprite, fay, hobgoblin, imp, leprechaun, kobold, puck, peri.

pizzazz *n. Slang* SPICE.

placable *adj.* TRACTABLE.

placard *n.* notice, sign, poster, bill, advertisement, flier, bulletin, broadside, handbill, circular.

placate *v.* appease, propitiate, humor, pacify, conciliate, mollify, reconcile, soothe, satisfy, calm, assuage, quiet, tranquilize.
ant. exacerbate, irritate, anger, displease, dissatisfy, rouse.

place *n.* **1** locus, location, spot, point, space, plot, locality, area, region, section. **2** quarters, site, abode, room, chamber, home, residence, dwelling. **3** square, mall, piazza, plaza, alley, court, courtyard, lane, crescent. **4** position, station, rank, appointment, function, office, employment, degree. —*v.* **1** situate, pose, put, lay, seat, fix, set, deposit. **2** rank, range, group, array, order, arrange, allocate, organize, catalog. **3** appoint, install, establish, assign, nominate, induct, commission, settle.

placement *n.* positioning, location, establishment, installation, arrangement, disposal, distribution, organization, ordering, disposition, emplacement, seating

placid *adj.* quiet, calm, serene, composed, pacific, peaceful, unruffled, self-possessed, tranquil, undisturbed, unmoved, collected, equable, gentle, even.
ant. agitated, aroused, choleric, stormy, turbulent, seething.

placidity *n.* QUIETNESS.

plagiarism *n.* piracy, cribbing, plagiary, infringement, theft, stealing, copying, lifting, borrowing, exploitation.

plagiarize *v.* pirate, copy, crib, lift, steal, borrow, infringe, thieve, exploit.

plagiary *n.* PLAGIARISM.

plague *n.* **1** pestilence, epidemic, pandemic, scourge, visitation, outbreak, pest, influx. **2** nuisance, pest, bother, affliction, bane, curse, scourge, annoyance, blight. —*v.* harass, distress, torment, harry, worry, disturb, annoy, burden, tantalize, pester, tease.

ant. *n.* **2** blessing, pleasure, aid, angel, godsend. *v.* comfort, placate, soothe, please, relieve.

plaguy *adj.* TROUBLESOME.

plain *adj.* **1** easy, simple, slight, effortless, trifling, uncomplicated, light. **2** clear, understandable, obvious, unmistakable, transparent, patent, apparent, visible, lucid. **3** common, simple, humble, modest, unaffected, artless, down-to-earth, unsophisticated, solid, unassuming. **4** unadorned, restrained, severe, stark, frugal, lean, undisguised, unornamented. **5** homely, ill-favored, unattractive, ill-looking, ugly, unprepossessing, gawky.

ant. 1 complicated, hard, difficult, laborious, cumbersome, exacting. **2** clouded, murky, unclear, indistinct, hidden. **3** affected, extraordinary, uncommon, artful, sophisticated. **4** adorned, ornate, fancy, rich, luxurious. **5** pretty, comely, attractive, good-looking, well-favored, beautiful.

plainly *adv.* clearly, obviously, distinctly, frankly, bluntly, point-blank, candidly, honestly, sincerely, evidently, unmistakably, patently, openly, simply.

ant. abstrusely, furtively, darkly, secretly, covertly.

plain-spoken *adj.* FRANK.

plaint *n.* COMPLAINT.

plait *v.* BRAID.

plan *n.* program, design, scheme, blueprint, system, chart, scenario, script, arrangement, proposal, method, way, process, procedure, conception, orchestration. —*v.* **1** contrive, devise, design, outline, plot, organize, scheme, invent, sketch, arrange, itemize, concoct, orchestrate, stage-manage. **2** intend, propose, contemplate, purpose, aim, envision, envisage, project, consider, foresee.

plane *n.* **1** plateau, table, flat, horizontal, plain, horizon, smooth. **2** rank, stratum, sphere, tier, grade, level, stage, step, condition, status, notch,

rung. —*adj.* level, even, smooth, flat, horizontal, tabular, plain, flush, unwrinkled.

ant. uneven, rough, pitted, jagged, wrinkled, perpendicular.

planetary *adj.* ERRATIC.

plank *n.* **1** board, slab, beam, timber, two-by-four. **2** PLATFORM.

planner *n.* ARCHITECT.

plant *n.* **1** herb, vegetable, greenery, foliage, holophyte, organism. **2** factory, facility, workshop, foundry, shop, works, mill. —*v.* **1** seed, sow, scatter, implant, set. **2** place, install, implant, lodge, set down, put, establish, embed, fix, instill.

plaque *n.* tablet, disk, slab, plate, medallion, inscription, intaglio, cameo, badge.

plash *n.*, *v.* SPLASH.

plastered *adj. Slang* DRUNK.

plastic *adj.* **1** pliable, malleable, sculptural, soft, formable, tractable, yielding, impressionable, pliant, ductile. **2** *Slang* sham, meretricious, counterfeit, substitute, factitious, spurious, synthetic, artificial, specious, bogus, factoidal.

ant. 1 rigid, stiff, stubborn, unresponsive, unyielding, hard. **2** genuine, natural, bona fide, valid, legitimate.

plat[1] *n.*, *v.* PLOT.

plat[2] *v.* BRAID.

plate *n.* dish, vessel, platter, saucer, porringer, dinnerware, china. —*v.* metallize, electroplate, coat, laminate, galvanize, anodize, foil.

plateau *n.* tableland, table, plain, highland, mesa, upland, savanna, down, prairie, steppe, platform, level.

platform *n.* **1** dais, rostrum, stage, pulpit, soapbox, stump, scaffold, skid, stand, boards. **2** program, plank, plan, principle, policy, tenet, objective, belief, line, party line, stance, position.

platitude *n.* bromide, truism, commonplace, cliché, banality, inanity, chestnut, saw.

platitudinous *adj.* BANAL.

platter *n.* tray, trencher, plank, plate, dish, charger, salver.

plaudits *n.* praise, applause, kudos, congratulations, cheers, hurrahs, approval, commendation, approbation, honor, compliments.
ant. censure, boos, disapproval, catcalls, reprimand, rebuke.

plausibility *n.* CREDIBILITY.

plausible *adj.* believable, specious, credible, likely, convincing, reasonable, respectable, misleading, deceptive, sophistical, devious, colorable.
ant. implausible, unlikely, incredible, unconvincing, unbelievable, absurd.

play *v.* **1** amuse oneself, entertain, enjoy oneself, revel, frolic, sport. **2** compete, contend, participate, join in, take part, game. **3** flash, flicker, coruscate, glitter, flutter, frisk, dance, skip. **4** perform, imitate, enact, act, mimic, make believe, impersonate, represent. **5** bet, wager, gamble, stake, risk, speculate, chance, hazard, put. —*n.* **1** diversion, entertainment, recreation, sport, amusement, pleasure, game, merrymaking. **2** move, turn, inning, go, spell. **3** operation, action, activity, behavior, deportment, transaction, employment, function. **4** joking, humor, fun, foolery, trifling, prank, jest. **5** drama, spectacle, show, entertainment, theatricals, performance. **6** lambency, animation, flickering, fluttering, movement, rippling, variegation, hovering, action.

play down minimize, gloss over, make light of, decry, deprecate, depreciate, disparage, detract, hush up, poohpooh, belittle, derogate, whitewash, ridicule, slur.
ant. stress, emphasize, play up, underline, call attention to, praise.

player *n.* **1** participant, contestant, athlete, opponent, competitor, entrant. **2** thespian, performer, trouper, mummer, actor, actress. **3** musician, performer, artist, instrumentalist, virtuoso.

playfellow *n.* PLAYMATE.

playful *adj.* **1** frolicsome, lively, frisky, rollicking, kittenish, sportive, gamesome, jaunty, sprightly. **2** humorous, joking, arch, coy, jocular, jolly, merry, amusing, droll, mirthful.
ant. 1, 2 staid, sedate, sober, grave, solemn, earnest.

playmate *n.* playfellow, companion, comrade, friend, cohort, buddy, pal, chum.

play on exploit, take advantage of, capitalize on, profit by, utilize, turn to account, presume on, count on, impose on, use.

plaything *n.* toy, bauble, amusement, trifle, trinket, knickknack, gew-gaw, bagatelle, pastime, game.

playtime *n.* leisure, recess, intermission, liberty, breather, vacation, holiday, break, interlude, pause, time, freedom.

play up emphasize, stress, call attention to, praise, extol, show off, accentuate, promote, highlight, feature, point up, underline.
ant. play down, minimize, decry, make light of, deprecate, gloss over.

play up to fawn, flatter, toady, curry favor, court, soft-soap, pander, humor, blandish, woo, dance attendance, truckle.
ant. disdain, patronize, condescend to, spurn, cold-shoulder.

plaza *n.* square, marketplace, mall, rialto, place, piazza, shopping center, common, park, court, exchange.

plea *n.* **1** prayer, appeal, entreaty, request, petition, suit, intercession. **2** excuse, pretext, justification, apology, alibi, claim, vindication, apologia.

plead *v.* implore, entreat, sue, appeal, solicit, importune, pray, beg, beseech, supplicate, request, press, crave, ask.

pleasant *adj.* pleasing, agreeable, gratifying, enjoyable, satisfying, pleasurable, congenial, refreshing, welcome, amiable, cheerful, affable, engaging, diverting, delectable.
ant. unpleasant, distasteful, distress-

ing, annoying, forbidding, provoking.

pleasantry *n.* joke, quip, banter, sally, whimsy, witticism, waggery, badinage, mot, funny, squib, quirk, wisecrack (*Slang*).

please *v.* **1** gratify, pleasure, satisfy, delight, amuse, entertain, gladden, elate, cheer, charm, rejoice, captivate, flatter, warm, humor, divert, attract, indulge. **2** wish, desire, will, choose, like, prefer, elect, want, opt.
ant. 1 displease, offend, vex, injure, distress, trouble.

pleasing *adj.* PLEASANT.

pleasurable *adj.* PLEASANT.

pleasure *n.* **1** enjoyment, diversion, amusement, play, entertainment, gratification, cheer, comfort, elation, relish, gusto, gladness, satisfaction, dissipation, treat, beer and skittles, cakes and ale. **2** choice, desire, bent, preference, wish, will, inclination, mind, selection, desideratum.
ant. 1 unhappiness, pain, discomfort, deprivation.

plebeian *n.* commoner, man in the street, John Doe, everyman, proletarian, peasant. —*adj.* vulgar, crude, low, lowborn, coarse, mean, base, common, undistinguished, obscure, humble, ignoble, popular.
ant. *n.* aristocrat, blue blood, elitist, notable, noble. *adj.* highborn, aristocratic, lordly, refined, noble, elite.

pledge *v.* **1** pawn, stake, mortgage, hazard, venture, bet, gamble, risk. **2** promise, guarantee, vow, engage, contract, affirm, bind. —*n.* **1** guaranty, promise, assurance, covenant, vow, word, oath, undertaking, avowal. **2** pawn, gage, token, collateral, surety, bail, stake, deposit, earnest, bond.

plenary *adj.* full, whole, total, entire, complete, general, open, unrestricted, unlimited.
ant. partial, limited, short, shy, restricted.

plenitude *n.* FULLNESS.

plenteous *adj.* PLENTIFUL.

plentiful *adj.* abundant, abounding, ample, bounteous, copious, lavish, plenteous, replete, rife, teeming, profuse, overflowing, bountiful, generous, plenty.
ant. scarce, scanty, sparse, insufficient, inadequate, skimpy, exiguous, meager.

plenty *n.* **1** abundance, copiousness, profusion, plenitude, bounteousness, ampleness, repletion, muchness, fullness. **2** load, loads, lot, lots, scads, stack, slew, pile, oodles, acres, enough, sufficiency, abundance. —*adj.* PLENTIFUL.
ant. 1 scarcity, shortage, paucity, lack, dearth, need, want. **2** bit, scrap, drop, smidgen.

pleonasm *n.* REDUNDANCY.

plethora *n.* excess, superabundance, surplus, surfeit, glut, overabundance, superfluity, redundancy, overload, overage, overflow.
ant. shortage, deficiency, lack, scarcity, scantiness.

plexus *n.* NETWORK.

pliability *n.* RESILIENCE.

pliable *adj.* **1** flexible, limber, lithe, lithesome, pliant, supple, plastic, ductile. **2** docile, tractable, adaptable, compliant, pliant, flexible, manageable, malleable, submissive, unresisting, impressionable, yielding, obedient.
ant. 1 rigid, stiff, hard, firm. **2** stubborn, unbending, refractory, fixed, obdurate, unyielding, intractable, resolute, firm.

pliancy *n.* RESILIENCE.

pliant *adj.* PLIABLE.

plight[1] *n.* predicament, difficulty, dilemma, quandary, straits, pinch, fix, scrape, trouble, jam, mess, pickle.

plight[2] *n.* pledge, promise, vow, oath, word, guarantee, assurance, parole, commitment, avouchment. —*v.* pledge, swear, promise, vow, vouch, guarantee, warrant, betroth, affiance, engage, contract.

plod *v.* **1** trudge, slog, tramp, lumber, trek, pace, drag, march, stomp, stamp, tread, clump. **2** grind, drudge, toil, labor, sweat, moil, grub, plow, plug.

plodder *n.* DRUDGE.

plodding *adj.* PEDESTRIAN.

plop *v.* drop, flop, plump, plunk down. —*n.* thump, thud, plump.

plot *n.* **1** tract, lot, parcel, area, patch, plat, field, acre, land, estate. **2** conspiracy, scheme, plan, intrigue, design, machination, collusion, racket, blueprint. **3** narrative, theme, story, thread, scenario, action, outline, summary, précis. —*v.* **1** map, chart, plat, draft, draw, outline, diagram, sketch. **2** conspire, intrigue, scheme, machinate, plan, hatch, cabal, concoct, engineer, maneuver, connive.

plotter *n.* TRAITOR.

plow *v.* till, cultivate, prepare, furrow, harrow, hoe, dig, work, farm, groove, gouge, score.

ploy *n.* stratagem, maneuver, ruse, trick, device, pretext, artifice, dodge, bluff, game, tactic, subterfuge.

pluck *v.* **1** pick, pull, yank, extract, tug, jerk, snatch, grab, tear. **2** plunk, strum, thrum, play, finger, pick. —*n.* **1** nerve, guts, boldness, courage, bravery, mettle, backbone, grit, confidence, assurance, spirit, fortitude, stamina, doggedness. **2** twitch, yank, pull, tug, jerk.

ant. *n.* **1** trepidation, cowardice, faint-heartedness, reluctance, vacillation, nervousness.

plucky *adj.* courageous, brave, fearless, bold, undaunted, valiant, spirited, game, hardy, daring, resolute, spunky, unflinching, intrepid.

ant. fearful, timid, cowardly, afraid, scared, hesitant, wavering, reluctant.

plug *n.* **1** stopper, cork, stopple, bung, lid, cap, wad, closure. **2** *Slang* boost, promotion, promo (*Slang*), advertisement, publicity, blurb, buildup, puff. —*v.* **1** close, shut, seal, occlude, stop, stopper, stopple, block, cork, cap. **2** *Slang* boost, promote, advertise, publicize, puff, ballyhoo, push, praise, advocate. **3** persevere, persist,

grind, plod, toil, drudge, peg away, carry on, stick it out.

ant. *v.* **1** open, unplug, unstop, uncork. **2** belittle, disparage, criticize, pan, knock (*Slang*), run down. **3** quit, discontinue, give up.

plum *n.* prize, find, bonus, treasure, gem, pearl, cream, nugget, pick, choice.

plumb *adj.* **1** vertical, perpendicular, upright, straight, sheer, erect, right-angled. **2** sheer, complete, absolute, downright, total, full, unqualified, unreserved. —*v.* probe, fathom, penetrate, delve, explore, investigate, solve, unravel, explain, figure out, comprehend.

ant. *adj.* **1** oblique, crooked, slanting, leaning, awry.

plume *v.* PREEN.

plummet *v.* plunge, drop, fall, dive, descend, nosedive, tumble, plunk.

ant. rise, lift, ascend, soar.

plump¹ *adj.* swollen, bloated, full, puffy, distended, chubby, pudgy, podgy, rotund, round, portly, stout, buxom, fleshy, corpulent, well-fed.

ant. bony, thin, angular, lean, skinny, slender, emaciated.

plump² *v.* fall, drop, sink, slip, slide, thud, slump, plunk, cast, hurl, dump, plop, flop.

plump for support, choose, back, side with, come out for, endorse, favor, champion, advocate.

ant. oppose, reject, fight, take issue with.

plunder *v.* sack, pillage, loot, depredate, despoil, ravage, strip, ransack, rifle, maraud, steal, rob. —*n.* **1** booty, loot, spoil, swag (*Slang*), prey, prize, pillage. **2** rapine, pillage, depredation, sack, spoiling, looting, robbery.

plunderer *n.* BRIGAND.

plunge *v.* **1** dip, immerse, sink, submerge, douse, dunk, cast, thrust. **2** dive, jump, fall, plummet, nosedive, splash, duck, plop, descend, swoop, pitch, tumble, toboggan. **3** lunge, lurch, hurtle, dash, rush, lash, pitch, spurt, start, spring, career. —*n*. dive, descent, fall, drop, submersion, immersion, sinking, nosedive, swoop.

ant. *v.* **2** rise, lift, ascend, soar. *n*. rise, elevation, ascent.

plunk *v.* **1** plump, crash, thud, plop, drop, fall, keel over, tumble, plummet, slump. **2** PLUCK.

plural *adj*. multiple, many, several, numerous, manifold, multiplex, multitudinous, divers.

ant. single, singular, unique, sole, solitary, lone.

plurality *n.* **1** numerousness, multiplicity, diversity, variety. **2** majority, preponderance, bulk, mass, multitude, excess, most.

ant. 1 singleness, uniqueness, individuality. **2** minority, handful, fraction, few.

plus *adj*. extra, added, more, additional, supplemental, supplementary. —*n*. **1** addition, addendum, extra, supplement, gain, extension, attachment, increment. **2** desideratum, asset, prize, bonus, treasure, good, benefit, advantage, premium.

ant. *n.* **2** liability, disadvantage, minus, drawback.

plush *adj*. *Slang* luxurious, sumptuous, elegant, opulent, fancy, posh (*Slang*), palatial, de luxe, extravagant, classy (*Slang*).

ant. austere, spare, stark, poor, simple, bare, Spartan.

plutocrat *n.* capitalist, tycoon, magnate, industrialist, monopolist, millionaire, moneybags (*Slang*), nabob, bigwig, fat cat (*Slang*), big shot (*Slang*), big wheel (*Slang*).

ply[1] *v.* bend, flex, mold, shape, form, warp, fold, press. —*n*. layer, sheet, fold, thickness, web, slice, stratum, leaf, lamina, plate.

ply[2] *v.* **1** practice, follow, pursue, undertake, engage in, devote oneself to, exercise, carry on. **2** importune, press, beset, bombard, assail, urge, coax, entreat, implore, harass.

poach *v.* trespass, raid, invade, intrude,

encroach, impinge, steal, plunder, rob, rustle, appropriate.

pock *n.* PIMPLE.

pocket *n.* **1** pouch, bag, sack, fob. **2** opening, hollow, cavity, hole, ditch, pit, socket, crater, receptacle, container. —*v*. filch, pilfer, appropriate, embezzle, purloin, steal, take, lift, swipe (*Slang*), help oneself.

pocketbook *n.* purse, handbag, case, bag, moneybag.

podgy *adj*. PUDGY.

podium *n.* dais, platform, rostrum, stage, pulpit, soapbox.

poem *n.* verse, rhyme, lyric, ode, sonnet, ballad, idyll, epic, elegy, jingle.

poesy *n.* POETRY.

poet *n.* versifier, bard, lyricist, troubadour, laureate, sonneteer, rhymer, rhymster, poetaster.

poetaster *n.* POET.

poetic *adj*. **1** bardic, lyric, metrical, rhyming. **2** creative, imaginative, esthetic, inspired, romantic, fanciful, dreaming, visionary.

ant. 2 prosaic, unimaginative, practical, matter-of-fact, stolid, literal.

poetry *n.* verse, poems, meter, rhyme, song, poesy, poetics, versification, numbers, stanzas, balladry.

pogrom *n.* MASSACRE.

poignant *adj*. **1** heartbreaking, moving, touching, pathetic, agonizing, excruciating, piercing, sharp, acute, tormenting, bitter, painful. **2** keen, cutting, barbed, sharp, acid, biting, caustic, vitriolic, trenchant, mordant, stinging.

point *n.* **1** tip, apex, vertex, nib, cusp, peak, spike, prong, tine, extremity. **2** feature, characteristic, attribute, peculiarity, trait, mark, aspect, property, quality. **3** thrust, theme, topic, motif, focus, idea, essence, substance, gist, crux, heart, core, nucleus, issue. **4** place, position, location, spot, site, stage, juncture, time, instant, moment. **5** detail, item, step, particular, instance, section, piece, article, part. **6** purpose, object, end, design, aim, use, goal, reason, value, objective. —*v.* aim, direct, train, level, beam, face, turn, fix, focus.

pointblank *adj.* DIRECT.

pointed *adj.* apt. pertinent, acute, incisive, accurate, penetrating, sharp, aimed, telling, appropriate, fitting, to the point.

ant. vague, aimless, pointless, inappropriate, irrelevant.

pointless *adj.* meaningless, nonsensical, vague, inane, insipid, stupid, absurd, ridiculous, vapid, aimless, inappropriate, irrelevant, senseless.

ant. significant, telling, pertinent, apt, fitting, appropriate, meaningful, to the point.

point of view 1 orientation, position, angle, frame of reference, perspective, standpoint, outlook. 2 attitude, opinion, viewpoint, view, judgment, posture, bias, sentiment, feeling, belief, conviction.

point out show, note, indicate, reveal, refer, allude, mention, specify, emphasize, remind, underscore.

poise *v.* hold, support, position, suspend, float, balance, hover, hang. —*n.* 1 balance, equilibrium, stability, equipoise, steadiness, counterpoise. 2 composure, aplomb, equanimity, self-assurance, self-control, self-possession, coolness, calmness, presence, presence of mind, dignity, serenity, cool (*Slang*), stability, self-confidence, savoir faire.

ant. *n.* 1 imbalance, instability, shakiness. 2 excitability, nervousness, edginess, awkwardness, clumsiness.

poison *n.* 1 toxin, venom, bane. 2 bane, virus, blight, curse, cancer, malignancy, rot, plague, infection, miasma. —*v.* infect, contaminate, envenom, corrupt, debauch, pollute, taint, defile, ruin, deprave, corrode, undermine, subvert, pervert, vitiate.

ant. *n.* 1 antitoxin, antidote, remedy, cure. 2 benefit, blessing, panacea, help, uplift, edification, redemption. *v.* neutralize, counteract, redeem, purify, edify, improve, uplift, benefit.

poisonous *adj.* toxic, lethal, fatal, deadly, venomous, baneful, noxious, pernicious, virulent.

ant. healthy, beneficial, wholesome, harmless, innocuous, salubrious.

poke *v.* 1 push, prod, shove, jab, elbow, hit, punch, press, jostle, bump, dig, thrust. 2 intrude, meddle, interfere, tamper, nose, butt in (*Slang*), horn in (*Slang*), obtrude, kibitz, pry, snoop, peek. 3 dawdle, putter, delay, idle, dillydally, lag, crawl, tarry, drag, linger, loiter.

ant. 3 hasten, dash, scurry, scoot, speed, bustle.

poky *adj.* 1 SPIRITLESS. 2 SHABBY.

pol *n. Slang* POLITICIAN.

polar *adj.* opposite, antithetical, antipodal, contrary, contradictory, reverse, opposed, counter, conflicting, antagonistic.

ant. similar, alike, same, identical, of a kind.

polarity *n.* opposition, duality, dichotomy, division, split, schism.

polarization *n.* SPLIT.

polarize *v.* SPLIT.

pole[1] *n.* antipode, extremity, terminus, hub, pivot, swivel.

pole[2] *n.* rod, shaft, bar, stick, staff, post, mast, stilt, axle, beam, stem, perch.

polemic *n.* ARGUMENT.

polemical *adj.* disputatious, controversial, contentious, argumentative, quarrelsome, critical, carping, propagandistic.

ant. conciliatory, harmonious, agreeable, flexible, amenable, diplomatic, accommodating.

polemics *n.* controversy, disputation, argument, argumentation, debate, wrangling, dispute, contention, logomachy.

police *n.* authorities, cops, troopers, guard, patrol, force, constabulary, *gendarmerie*, fuzz (*Slang*), the law. —*v.* 1 protect, regulate, control, supervise, oversee, safeguard, guard, patrol. 2 clean up, straighten, tidy, clear up, spruce up, keep up, neaten.

ant. *v.* **2** neglect, mess, dilapidate, disarray.

policy *n.* procedure, program, practice, platform, system, method, approach, line, principle, code, guideline, custom, rule, protocol.

polish *n.* **1** gloss, shine, sheen, smoothness, glossiness, luster, brightness, glaze, varnish. **2** refinement, style, elegance, finesse, grace, cultivation, urbanity, class (*Slang*), accomplishment, finish, culture, savoir faire, presence, suaveness. —*v.* **1** shine, burnish, buff, smoothe, glaze, wax, varnish, furbish, rub. **2** refine, perfect, cultivate, civilize, improve, uplift.

ant. *n.* **1** dullness, flatness, roughness, rawness, dimness. **2** crudeness, boorishness, vulgarity, coarseness, grossness, awkwardness, crassness. *v.* **1** dull, dim, mat, roughen. **2** vulgarize, cheapen, brutalize, debase, coarsen.

polished *adj.* REFINED.

polite *adj.* courteous, civil, well-mannered, courtly, gracious, considerate, cultivated, genteel, polished, proper, nice, refined, elegant, well-bred, civilized.

ant. rude, discourteous, impolite, impudent, insolent, crude, uncouth, crass, boorish, barbarous.

politeness *n.* civility, courtesy, manners, decorum, propriety, *politesse*, graciousness, gallantry, courtliness, chivalry, breeding.

ant. discourtesy, rudeness, insolence, unseemliness, indelicacy, vulgarity.

politic *adj.* prudent, judicious, tactful, shrewd, wise, sagacious, artful, wary, expedient, discreet, diplomatic, sensible.

ant. careless, blundering, imprudent, rash, tactless, rude.

political *adj.* governmental, civic, civil, administrative, public, elective, partisan.

politician *n.* politico, pol (*Slang*), candidate, office-holder, office-seeker, front-runner, dark horse, statesman, stateswoman.

politico *n.* POLITICIAN.

polity *n.* GOVERNMENT.

poll *n.* **1** head, crown, cranium, skull, pate, noggin, noodle (*Slang*), bean (*Slang*), dome (*Slang*). **2** survey, census, sampling, canvass. —*v.* survey, canvass, question, inquire, interview, interrogate.

pollutant *n.* contaminant, impurity, effluvium, adulterant, filth, dirt, scum, slime.

pollute *v.* **1** foul, contaminate, befoul, soil, infect, poison, tarnish, dirty, adulterate. **2** desecrate, defile, profane, debase, corrupt, debauch, sully, besmirch, violate, dishonor, pervert.

ant. 1 purify, cleanse, clean, sanitize. **2** redeem, respect, honor, revere, elevate, ennoble.

poltroon *n.* COWARD.

polymath *n.* SCHOLAR.

polymorphous *adj.* PROTEAN.

pommel *v.* beat, punch, pound, hit, strike, hammer, pummel, cuff, box, belt, club, whack, wallop, batter, maul, knock.

pomp *n.* flourish, grandeur, magnificence, splendor, pageantry, ceremony, spectacle, showiness, ostentation, grandiosity, pomposity, vainglory, pretension.

ant. modesty, simplicity, austerity, plainness, spareness, lowliness, humbleness.

pomposity *n.* POMP.

pompous *adj.* **1** grandiose, overbearing, arrogant, magisterial, haughty, grandiloquent, top-lofty, imposing, self-important, high-sounding, overweening, patronizing, supercilious, high-handed, highfalutin. **2** STATELY.

ant. 1 unassuming, modest, meek, humble, timid, retiring, self-effacing, diffident.

pond *n.* POOL.[1]

ponder *v.* deliberate, examine, consider, contemplate, study, think, meditate, muse, reflect, brood, dwell, cogitate, ruminate, speculate, mull, pore over.

ponderous *adj.* **1** heavy, bulky, weighty, massive, cumbrous, cumbersome, hefty, unwieldy. **2** dull, lumbering, heavy, tedious, pedantic, labored, stuffy, long-winded, bombastic, fustian, prolix, verbose, dry, turgid.
ant. 1 light, flimsy, airy, fragile, delicate. **2** breezy, light, entertaining, witty, subtle.

poniard *n.* DAGGER.

pontifical *adj.* pompous, dogmatic, preachy, positive, opinionated, peremptory, assertive, smug, patronizing, condescending, sanctimonious.
ant. hesitant, uncertain, unassuming, humble, diffident, modest, shy.

pontificate *v.* SERMONIZE.

pooh-pooh *v.* dismiss, belittle, scorn, disparage, slight, disregard, disdain, reject, ridicule, deride, sneer, scoff, sniff, spurn, brush aside.
ant. respect, admire, consider, heed, ponder.

pool[1] *n.* puddle, pond, plash, spring, water hole, swimming hole, lake, lagoon, tarn, mere, reservoir.

pool[2] *n.* coalition, partnership, collaboration, cooperative, union, alliance, merger, collective, team. —*v.* ally, coordinate, join, combine, merge, amalgamate, unite, consolidate, associate, band together.

pooped *adj. Slang* TIRED.

poor *adj.* **1** needy, indigent, impoverished, poverty-stricken, destitute, insolvent, bankrupt, penniless, hard up, pauperized, impecunious, beggarly, broke, down-and-out, stony (*Slang*), necessitous, straitened, pinched, mendicant. **2** deficient, inferior, shabby, shoddy, sorry, substandard, worthless, lacking, inadequate, faulty, unsatisfactory. **3** pitiable, wretched, miserable, unlucky, unfortunate, hapless, sad, dismal, abject, unhappy, ill-fated.
ant. 1 affluent, wealthy, rich, prosperous, well-heeled (*Slang*), flush, solvent, well-to-do, well-off, moneyed. **2** excellent, superior, adequate,

sufficient, ample, good, worthy. **3** enviable, lucky, fortunate, happy.

pop[1] *v.* **1** bang, burst, bust, clap, crack, explode, detonate, fulminate, snap. **2** dart, leap, jump, rush, dash, run, tear, spring, flash, break. **3** thrust, plunge, stick, poke, throw, toss. **4** protrude, bulge, jut, project, protuberate, stick out, extrude, swell. —*n.* bang, report, detonation, discharge, blast, explosion, clap.

pop[2] *adj.* POPULAR.

poppycock *n.* NONSENSE.

populace *n.* public, people, multitude, masses, citizenry, commonalty, commons, mob, crowd, herd, rabble, folk, hoi polloi.

popular *adj.* **1** public, general, extensive, widespread, conventional, prevailing, universal, standard, current, rampant, prevalent. **2** well-liked, sought-after, lionized, honored, illustrious, renowned, esteemed, respected, admired, favored, approved, welcomed, well-received, famous, in. **3** pop, middlebrow, lowbrow, philistine, vulgar, folk, mass, plebeian, common, masscult.
ant. 1 exclusive, private, restricted, selective. **2** disliked, outcast, friendless, ostracized, rejected, despised. **3** highbrow, arty, intellectual, cultured.

popularity *n.* acclaim, approval, acceptance, favor, support, regard, fame, repute, esteem, celebrity, renown, admiration.
ant. unpopularity, disrepute, disfavor, dislike, disregard.

populate *v.* PEOPLE.

populated *adj.* inhabited, peopled, settled, occupied, colonized.
ant. deserted, vacant, evacuated, empty, depopulated.

population *n.* inhabitants, residents, people, folk, citizenry, populace, denizens, community, society.

populous *adj.* crowded, teeming, overpopulated, full, dense, swarming, packed, jammed, concentrated.

ant. sparse, scattered, vacant, underpopulated.

porch *n.* stoop, veranda, piazza, portico, sun parlor, deck, terrace, balcony.

pore *n.* hole, opening, orifice, aperture, stoma.

pore over scrutinize, examine, study, peruse, comb, inspect, check, ponder, contemplate, consider. **ant.** skim, skip over, glance at, scan.

porky *adj.* OBESE.

pornographic *adj.* obscene, lewd, lascivious, salacious, licentious, erotic, smutty, bawdy, indecent, immodest, prurient, suggestive, risqué, blue, porn (*Slang*), porno (*Slang*).

porous *adj.* ABSORBENT.

port *n.* harbor, haven, shelter, dock, berth, seaport, wharf, pier, quay, landing, mooring, anchorage.

portable *adj.* movable, transferable, transportable, conveyable, compact, lightweight, pocket. **ant.** stationary, fixed, anchored, immovable, standing.

portal *n.* gateway, entrance, entry, approach, door, doorway, passageway.

portend *v.* augur, presage, bode, forebode, forewarn, warn, foreshadow, predict, prefigure, signify, herald, indicate, harbinger, betoken.

portent *n.* OMEN.

portentous *adj.* ominous, foreboding, premonitory, threatening, impending, menacing, alarming, disquieting, sinister, fateful, prophetic. **ant.** encouraging, auspicious, propitious, cheering, comforting.

porter[1] *n.* bearer, carrier, redcap, attendant, steward.

porter[2] *n.* doorkeeper, doorman, concierge, gatekeeper, watchman, guard, sentry.

portico *n.* PORCH.

portion *n.* **1** piece, section, fragment, part, segment, slice, scrap, morsel, division, fraction, percentage. **2** allotment, share, ration, quota, cut, allowance, dose, measure, dividend. **3**

fate, lot, destiny, fortune, luck, kismet, end, future, doom.

portliness *n.* **1** CORPULENCE. **2** MAJESTY.

portly *adj.* **1** stout, pudgy, plump, rotund, round, chubby, corpulent, fleshy, heavy, fat, obese, porcine. **2** stately, imposing, majestic, dignified, august, magisterial, impressive, lordly, lofty, noble, venerable. **ant. 1** thin, lean, bony, slender, angular, skinny.

portrait *n.* **1** likeness, representation, sketch, image, painting, drawing, picture, photograph, snapshot, profile, head. **2** portrayal, account, description, depiction, profile, sketch, vignette.

portray *v.* **1** delineate, represent, draw, sketch, limn, illustrate, photograph, depict, caricature. **2** picture, depict, show, describe, characterize, profile, delineate.

portrayal *n.* REPRESENTATION.

pose *n.* **1** posture, stance, attitude, position, aspect, bearing, mien, carriage. **2** affectation, posturing, pretense, attitudinizing, mannerism, facade, front, mask, act, show, role, masquerade, air. —*v.* **1** sit, stand, model, posture. **2** pretend, posture, attitudinize, profess, simulate, feign, affect, dissemble, act, sham.

poser[1] *n.* POSEUR.

poser[2] *n.* PROBLEM.

poseur *n.* poser, hypocrite, faker, imposter, humbug, phony (*Slang*), pretender, masquerader, sham, fraud, charlatan.

posh *adj. Slang* luxurious, plush, fancy, elegant, sumptuous, palatial, de luxe, swanky. **ant.** austere, bare, simple, humble, spare.

posit *v.* POSTULATE.

position *n.* **1** stance, posture, pose, aspect, bearing, carriage, manner, mien, arrangement, placement. **2** location, place, site, spot, bearings, locale, station, locus, whereabouts, point, area. **3** status, rank, prestige, standing, reputation, station, footing, place, level, caste, class. **4** post, job, employment, occupation, situation, role, duty, capacity, office, assignment, appointment. **5** opinion, attitude, stand, policy, point of view, belief, bias, conviction, outlook, viewpoint, orientation. —*v.* set, place, fix, establish, install, insert, arrange, put, poise, situate.

positive *adj.* **1** actual, existing, real, genuine, certain, sure, assured, undeniable, incontestable, decisive, conclusive, well-founded, sound, incontrovertible, conclusive, unquestionable. **2** absolute, emphatic, explicit, express, categorical, flat, unequivocal, unqualified, definite, distinct, precise. **3** confident, assured, self-possessed, sure, cocksure, decided, resolute, opinionated, assertive, dogmatic, arrogant, peremptory, obstinate, stubborn. **4** constructive, helpful, useful, practical, beneficial, effective, productive, effectual.

ant. 1 uncertain, doubtful, dubious, questionable, iffy, unsound, fallacious, disputable, debatable. **2** tentative, qualified, hedging, equivocal, vague. **3** unsure, uncertain, hesitant, diffident, timid. **4** negative, destructive, malicious, hostile.

positively *adv.* absolutely, certainly, surely, undeniably, indubitably, assuredly, categorically, without doubt, definitely, expressly.

ant. possibly, perhaps, maybe.

possess *v.* own, have, hold, enjoy, acquire, keep, retain, inherit, receive, maintain, grasp, cling.

possessed *adj.* bedeviled, bewitched, hexed, haunted, cursed, seized, obsessed, frenzied, crazed, maddened, raving.

possession *n.* ownership, title, custody, proprietorship, retention, monopoly, hold, grip, occupancy, control, grasp.

possessions *n.* BELONGINGS.

possessive *adj.* acquisitive, covetous, selfish, greedy, grasping, dominating,

controlling, overprotective, clinging, tenacious.

possibility *n.* **1** likelihood, feasibility, potentiality, chance, plausibility, attainability, achievability. **2** eventuality, prospect, event, contingency, expectation, chance.

possible *adj.* potential, feasible, realizable, conceivable, imaginable, thinkable, attainable, achievable, practicable, doable, contingent.

ant. impossible, inconceivable, unthinkable, absurd, out of the question, unfeasible.

post¹ *n.* stake, pole, stud, standard, stilt, upright, pile, pillar, column, pilaster. —*v.* affix, fasten, place, set, attach, display, exhibit, announce, broadcast, publicize, proclaim, advertise, circulate, promulgate, disseminate.

post² *n.* **1** station, beat, position, lookout. **2** base, camp, fort, encampment, garrison, headquarters. **3** POSITION.

post³ *v.* **1** mail, send, dispatch, ship, transmit. **2** inform, notify, fill in on, report to, apprise, brief, advise, enlighten. **3** hasten, speed, rush, scurry, race, dash, hurry, whiz, scamper, run, fly, zip, hurtle, hie, scuttle.

ant. 3 slacken, slow down, crawl, drag, lag.

poster *n.* bill, notice, placard, sign, advertisement, broadside, circular, announcement.

posterior *adj.* rear, hind, back, hindmost, behind, after, subsequent, succeeding, following, later, ensuing, latter.

ant. anterior, antecedent, prior, ahead, previous, fore.

posterity *n.* descendents, progeny, offspring, children, issue, heirs, scions, spawn.

ant. ancestors, forebears, progenitors, forefathers.

posthaste *n.* HASTE. —*adv.* QUICKLY.

postpone *v.* defer, delay, put off, shelve, stay, suspend.

postponement *n.* deferral, delay, stay,

suspension, adjournment, recess, respite, break, abeyance, moratorium.

postscript *n*. SUPPLEMENT.

postulate *n*. premise, assumption, supposition, presupposition, axiom, given, hypothesis, theorem, thesis, truism, proposition. —*v*. **1** claim, insist, stipulate, demand, contend, lay down, determine, specify, require. **2** posit, assume, surmise, hypothesize, suppose, presuppose, submit, advance, theorize.

posture *n*. **1** bearing, attitude, stance, position, pose, aspect, demeanor, carriage, mien. **2** situation, state, circumstance, condition, status, shape, position. **3** attitude, mood, disposition, frame of mind, inclination, outlook, feeling, point of view, temperament, temper. —*v*. POSE.

pot *n*. **1** saucepan, boiler, kettle, cauldron, pan, skillet, casserole. **2** mug, cup, stein, tankard.

potation *n*. DRINK.

potbelly *n*. PAUNCH.

potency *n*. POWER.

potent *adj*. **1** powerful, effective, strong, stiff, high-powered, efficacious. **2** convincing, persuasive, cogent, compelling, forceful, powerful, trenchant, telling, impressive, unassailable, weighty, serious. **3** authoritative, influential, dominant, ruling, prevailing, commanding, ascendant, puissant, mighty.

ant. **1** weak, mild, feeble, ineffectual, ineffective. **2** shaky, dubious, weak, unconvincing, inconsequential, flimsy, lame. **3** impotent, helpless, powerless, ineffective.

potentate *n*. sovereign, ruler, governor, power, monarch, king, czar, chieftain, satrap, mogul, prince, lord, despot.

potential *adj*. possible, realizable, latent, dormant, inherent, future, implicit, embryonic, budding, promising. —*n*. APTITUDE.

ant. *adj*. actual, existent, realized.

pother *v*., *n*. BOTHER.

potion *n*. brew, philter, draft, cup, dose, mixture, concoction, dram, elixir, tonic.

potpourri *n*. MEDLEY.

potted *adj*. *Slang* DRUNK.

potter *v*. PUTTER.

potty *adj*. CRAZY.

pouch *n*. bag, sack, pocket, container, poke, purse.

pounce *v*. swoop, jump, leap, spring, attack, assault, dive, fall, drop, surprise, strike. —*n*. jump, leap, attack, assault, spring, strike, pass.

pound[1] *n*. pen, fold, enclosure, shelter, coop, sty, kennel, corral, paddock.

pound[2] *v*. strike, beat, pommel, batter, thrash, buffet, hammer, clobber (*Slang*), trounce, bruise, maul, wallop, smash, lambaste (*Slang*).

pour *v*. **1** spill, decant, splash, sprinkle, trickle, shower, drop, sluice, cascade. **2** emit, gush, effuse, spout, spew, flow, ooze, exude, give vent to, chatter, babble, prattle, gab, ramble. **3** swarm, teem, throng, stream, crowd, mob, stampede, overrun.

pourboire *n*. TIP[2].

pout *v*. sulk, fret, scowl, frown, glower, grouch, grouse, grumble, mope. —*n*. sullenness, peevishness, ill-humor, sulkiness, grouchiness, petulance, moodiness, surliness, crossness, grumpiness, crankiness.

ant. *v*. smile, beam, laugh. *n*. cheerfulness, good humor, pleasantness, sunniness.

poverty *n*. **1** penury, pauperism, indigence, pennilessness, need, want, insolvency, privation, destitution, impecuniousness, mendicancy, beggary. **2** lack, dearth, shortage, insufficiency, paucity, scantiness, scarcity, deficiency, skimpiness. **3** meagerness, inadequacy, exiguity, scantiness, paucity, aridity, sterility, barrenness, dullness, monotony, jejuneness.

ant. **1** wealth, affluence, prosperity, luxury, opulence. **2** abundance, plenitude, bounty, adequacy, sufficiency, ampleness, copiousness. **3** richness, fertility, imaginativeness, creativity.

poverty-stricken *adj*. POOR.

powder *n.* dust, grain, grit, sand, flour, meal, efflorescence. —*v.* dust, sprinkle, spray, strew, spread, scatter, dredge.

power *n.* **1** potency, strength, effectiveness, force, capacity, efficacy, potential, capability, faculty, ability, energy, vigor, muscle, intensity. **2** authority, control, domination, sway, mastery, supremacy, puissance, command, sovereignty, prerogative, hegemony, warrant, authorization, *carte blanche.* —*v.* force, shove, push, plow, muscle, thrust, bulldoze (*Slang*), plunge, press.

ant. *n.* **1** weakness, feebleness, ineffectiveness, debility, incompetence, infirmity. **2** helplessness, powerlessness, impotence.

powerful *adj.* **1** mighty, strong, forceful, energetic, vigorous, intense, overwhelming, potent. **2** puissant, controlling, dominant, supreme, ruling, commanding, ascendant, authoritative, predominant. **3** cogent, potent, convincing, irresistible, forceful, valid, effective, conclusive, compelling, impressive, persuasive.

ant. **1** weak, feeble, fragile, debilitated, frail. **2** powerless, impotent, helpless, subjugated, subdued, dominated. **3** unconvincing, flimsy, trivial, invalid, inconsequential, shaky.

powerhouse *n. Slang* TITAN.

powerless *adj.* **1** helpless, weak, impotent, feeble, unable, incapable, disabled, incapacitated, paralyzed, immobilized, crippled, debilitated. **2** helpless, defenseless, unlicensed, unauthorized, prostrate, disfranchised, ineffective, dependent, subject.

ant. **1** able, strong, powerful, potent, vigorous. **2** autonomous, independent, empowered, authorized.

powwow *n.* MEETING.

practicable *adj.* PRACTICAL.

practical *adj.* **1** utilitarian, pragmatic, realistic, down-to-earth, businesslike, matter-of-fact, factual, hard-headed, efficient, applied, empirical, experi-

ential. **2** useful, feasible, practicable, possible, workable, achievable, attainable, doable, viable, operable, expedient, functional, performable.

ant. **1** theoretical, hypothetical, conjectural, speculative, idealistic, romantic, visionary. **2** useless, impractical, impossible, unworkable, unfeasible.

practically *adv.* **1** VIRTUALLY. **2** ALMOST.

practice *v.* **1** exercise, employ, act, perform, do, discharge, observe. **2** ply, follow, pursue, carry on, undertake, engage in, specialize. **3** train, drill, rehearse, exercise, prepare, discipline, study, perfect, sharpen, work out, polish. —*n.* **1** habit, wont, routine, custom, observance, usage, procedure, policy, praxis, method, way, course, fashion, *modus operandi.* **2** execution, performance, application, discharge, accomplishment, commission, realization, activity. **3** career, profession, trade, pursuit, study, business, vocation, discipline. **4** exercise, rehearsal, training, preparation, workout, discipline.

practiced *adj.* experienced, trained, proficient, able, expert, skilled, qualified, accomplished, versed, seasoned, veteran, salted.

ant. unskilled, inexperienced, raw, untutored, green, neophytic.

practitioner *n.* worker, performer, specialist, expert, professional, technician, craftsman, artisan.

pragmatic *adj.* **1** practical, useful, expedient, efficacious, workable, functional, efficient, applicable. **2** businesslike, utilitarian, matter-of-fact, realistic, materialistic, hard-headed, busy, down-to-earth, practical.

ant. **1** impractical, unworkable, unrealistic, theoretical, speculative, abstract. **2** dreamy, romantic, idealistic, sentimental, thoughtful.

prairie *n.* meadow, plain, range, grassland, pasture, lea, moor, savanna, veld, steppe, tundra, heath.

praise *v.* applaud, commend, laud, eu-

logize, honor, acclaim, compliment,
flatter, boost, extol, magnify, glorify,
exalt, venerate, adore. —*n.* compliment, commendation, acclaim, applause, plaudit, eulogy, laudation,
tribute, approbation, celebration,
flattery, kudos, puffery, soft soap,
panegyric, encomium.

ant. *v.* disparage, belittle, condemn,
censure, criticize, disapprove, denounce. *n.* condemnation, denunciation, censure, disapproval, rebuke.

praiseworthy *adj.* commendable, laudable, admirable, fine, meritorious,
worthy, honorable, exemplary.

ant. disgraceful, contemptible, dishonorable, base, ignoble, detestable,
despicable.

prance *v.* **1** swagger, strut, stalk, stride,
swank (*Slang*), show off. **2** gambol,
caper, cavort, romp, frolic, skip,
dance, frisk, bounce, trip.

prank *n.* joke, trick, antic, escapade,
gambol, lark, caper, practical joke,
shenanigan, mischief.

prankish *adj.* FROLICSOME.

prate *v., n.* PRATTLE.

prattle *v.* prate, chatter, babble, blab,
jabber, jaw (*Slang*), blather, gab,
twaddle, yak, drivel, twaddle, palaver. —*n.* prate, babble, gab, twaddle, blab, blather, yak, chit-chat, hot
air (*Slang*).

pray *v.* invoke, plead, implore, beg, entreat, supplicate, petition, importune, beseech, sue, adjure, ask, request.

prayer *n.* worship, veneration, adoration, orison, devotion, invocation,
plea, entreaty, petition, supplication,
suit, request.

preach *v.* **1** lecture, sermonize, preachify, evangelize, orate, homilize, hold
forth, moralize. **2** urge, exhort, harangue, advise, admonish, counsel,
caution, declaim.

preacher *n.* parson, minister, pastor,
clergyman, chaplain, homilist, sermonizer, pulpiteer, evangelist, reviv-
alist, apostle.

preachify *v.* PREACH.

preachment *n.* LECTURE.

preachy *adj.* pietistic, sanctimonious,
pontifical, self-righteous, holier-than-
thou, moralizing, canting, pharisaic.

preamble *n.* PROLOGUE.

prearrange *v.* ARRANGE.

precarious *adj.* **1** uncertain, doubtful,
questionable, dubious, shaky, iffy,
unreliable, unpredictable, slippery,
tricky. **2** hazardous, dangerous, insecure, risky, perilous, unstable, critical, parlous, treacherous, unsafe.

ant. **1** certain, sure, predictable, assured, firm, reliable. **2** safe, secure,
stable.

precaution *n.* preparation, foresight,
wariness, prudence, providence,
care, caution, provision, anticipation, prevention, safeguard, obviation.

precautionary *adj.* PREVENTIVE.

precede *v.* forerun, forego, antedate,
preface, lead, introduce, head, spearhead, herald, usher, pave the way,
anticipate, preexist.

ant. succeed, follow, postdate, result,
ensue.

precedence *n.* **1** priority, antecedence,
precession, previousness, anteriority.
2 priority, superiority, supremacy,
preference, advantage, rank, seniority, primacy, preeminence, importance, dominance.

precedent *adj.* PRECEDING. —*n.* ORIGI-
NAL.

preceding *adj.* prior, foregoing, precedent, antecedent, precursory, preliminary, anterior, previous, earlier, former.

ant. succeeding, following, subsequent, later, resultant, ensuing, latter.

precept *n.* maxim, rule, principle, commandment, teaching, dictate, canon,
axiom, law, prescript, motto.

preceptor *n.* TEACHER.

precinct *n.* district, zone, neighborhood, quarter, bailiwick, parish,
ward, confines, enclosure, vicinity,
environs, section, ambit, barrio.

preciosity *n.* AFFECTATION.

precious *adj.* **1** costly, priceless, valuable, expensive, dear, invaluable, inestimable, rare, fine, exquisite. **2** beloved, dear, cherished, darling, prized, treasured, adored, esteemed, loved. **3** overnice, fastidious, particular, overrefined, hair-splitting, fussy, finical, meticulous, exacting, finicky. **ant. 1** cheap, worthless, trashy, shoddy, common, tawdry. **2** disliked, rejected, spurned, despised, scorned. **3** careless, sloppy, slipshod, perfunctory.

precipice *n.* brink, edge, rim, height, cliff, bluff, escarpment, steep, palisade.

precipitant *adj.* PRECIPITATE.

precipitate *adj.* **1** headlong, precipitant, rushing, plunging, rapid, swift, abrupt, breakneck, sudden, instantaneous, immediate. **2** hasty, rash, impetuous, impulsive, reckless, brash, heedless, wild, unpremeditated, spontaneous. —*v.* expedite, hasten, speed, quicken, accelerate, hurry, dispatch, advance, facilitate, spur, press. **ant.** *adj.* **1** gradual, slow, easy, gentle, leisurely, prolonged, progressive, step-by-step. **2** deliberate, premeditated, planned, considered, cautious, careful. *v.* retard, delay, slacken, inhibit, slow, drag, hinder.

precipitous *adj.* steep, sheer, sharp, abrupt, perpendicular, vertical, bluff, high. **ant.** gradual, gentle, sloping, rolling, low, graded.

précis *n.* SUMMARY.

precise *adj.* **1** exact, accurate, correct, definite, specific, explicit, distinct, neat, express, unequivocal, strict, pinpoint, nice, clear-cut, literal. **2** punctilious, scrupulous, rigid, meticulous, exacting, uncompromising, strict, conforming, fastidious, particular, finicky, fussy, hypercritical, prim, prissy. **ant. 1** vague, hazy, indeterminate, approximate, ambiguous, equivocal.

2 flexible, easygoing, relaxed, casual, informal.

precision *n.* accuracy, preciseness, exactness, correctness, rigor, fidelity, nicety, definiteness, particularity, rightness, perfection, clarity, definition. **ant.** vagueness, inaccuracy, indeterminacy, ambiguity, approximation.

preclude *v.* prevent, hinder, forestall, inhibit, anticipate, obviate, check, foil, thwart, head off, nip in the bud, debar, intercept, avert, deter. **ant.** help, encourage, facilitate, expedite, permit, allow.

preclusive *adj.* PREVENTIVE.

precocious *adj.* forward, advanced, premature, early, bright. **ant.** backward, immature, undeveloped, dull.

precognition *n.* FORESIGHT.

preconception *n.* FORESIGHT.

precondition *n.* REQUIREMENT.

precursor *n.* forerunner, predecessor, herald, harbinger, vanguard, pioneer, initiator, originator, leader. **ant.** follower, successor, heir, disciple, imitator.

precursory *adj.* ANTECEDENT.

predacious *adj.* PREDATORY.

predate *v.* ANTEDATE.

predatory *adj.* **1** raptorial, predacious, rapacious, carnivorous, hunting, ravening. **2** rapacious, marauding, plunderous, ravaging, pillaging, despoiling, piratical, thieving, larcenous.

predecessor *n.* **1** forerunner, antecedent, precursor. **2** ancestor, forebear, forefather, progenitor, parent, father, mother, elder. **ant. 1** successor, inheritor, heir. **2** descendant, offspring, scion, child, heir.

predestine *v.* PREDETERMINE.

predetermine *v.* foreordain, preordain, predestine, preestablish, doom, determine, prearrange, plan, fate.

predicament *n.* dilemma, fix, plight, strait, quandary, difficulty, corner, pinch, mess, jam, pickle, scrape, pretty pass, complication, trouble, spot, hole.

predicate *v.* declare, affirm, assert, aver, maintain, say, insist, state, allege, contend.

predicate on base, found, ground, establish, postulate, build, maintain, sustain.

predict *v.* **1** foretell, foresee, prognosticate, prophesy, forecast, foreknow, divine, presage, vaticinate. **2** estimate, judge, anticipate, expect, envision, guess, calculate, reckon, figure, gauge, ascertain, bet.

prediction *n.* forecast, prognosis, prognostication, prophecy, divination, expectation, anticipation, foretelling, warning, promise, threat, portent, omen, augury.

predilection *n.* liking, fondness, preference, appetite, taste, affinity, partiality, inclination, proclivity, desire, penchant, propensity, attraction, stomach.

ant. aversion, revulsion, dislike, antipathy, distaste.

predispose *v.* DISPOSE.

predominance *n.* ASCENDANCY.

predominant *adj.* superior, paramount, primary, dominant, controlling, ruling, regnant, supreme, ascendant, major, prevailing, preponderant, overriding, overruling, principal, prime.

ant. subordinate, lesser, inferior, minor, secondary, subservient, subsidiary.

predominantly *adv.* MOSTLY.

predominate *v.* PREVAIL.

preeminent *adj.* EMINENT.

preempt *v.* APPROPRIATE.

preen *v.* adorn, bedeck, primp, prink, plume, doll up (*Slang*), spruce up, dress up.

preface *n.* foreword, introduction, prologue, proem, prelude, preamble, preliminary, prolegomenon, exordium. —*v.* introduce, begin, commence, initiate, start, lead into, launch, open.

ant. *n.* epilogue, supplement, appen-

dix, postscript. *v.* end, close, summarize, conclude, sum up, wind up.

prefatory *adj.* INTRODUCTORY.

prefer *v.* **1** favor, choose, select, elect, pick, fancy, single out, opt for. **2** advance, promote, elevate, raise, upgrade, aggrandize, graduate.

ant. **1** reject, exclude, pass over. **2** demote, lower, downgrade, suppress, hold back.

preferable *adj.* better, worthier, superior, favored, choicer, desirable, attractive, advantageous.

ant. worse, inferior, poorer.

preference *n.* **1** partiality, favoritism, bias, prejudice, precedence, predisposition, predilection, inclination, partisanship. **2** choice, selection, pick, option, alternative, priority, pleasure, vote.

ant. **1** fairness, justness, detachment, disinterest, impartiality, evenhandedness.

preferential *adj.* favored, special, privileged, better, superior, partial, partisan, one-sided, select, choice.

prefigure *v.* foreshadow, foreshow, foretoken, bode, adumbrate, signify, portend, augur, indicate, betoken, herald, presage.

pregnable *adj.* VULNERABLE.

pregnant *adj.* **1** with child, expecting, gravid, heavy, big, *enceinte*, gestating, carrying, in the family way. **2** significant, meaningful, weighty, suggestive, pointed, telling, fraught, indicative, important, consequential, momentous. **3** fruitful, fertile, creative, prolific, rich, imaginative, fecund, productive.

ant. **2** insignificant, meaningless, empty, trivial, senseless. **3** dull, barren, sterile, arid.

prehistoric *adj.* PRIMORDIAL.

prejudice *n.* **1** bias, preconception, prejudgment, prepossession, blind spot, *parti pris*, partiality, predisposition, partisanship, unfairness, narrowmindedness, subjectivity. **2** bigotry, intolerance, racism, sexism, chauvinism, ethnocentrism, xenophobia, discrimination. —*v.* influence, bias, sway, predispose, slant, distort, warp, color, prepossess, indoctrinate, brainwash, poison, turn against, undermine, damage.

ant. *n.* **1** objectivity, fairness, open-mindedness, detachment. **2** brotherhood, sisterhood, tolerance, liberality, charity.

prejudicial *adj.* detrimental, injurious, harmful, hurtful, damaging, undermining, hostile, antagonistic, deleterious, inimical.

ant. favorable, beneficial, helpful, advantageous, friendly.

preliminary *adj.* introductory, prefatory, preparatory, opening, beginning, commencing, incipient, inchoate, exordial, initiatory, antecedent, prior.

ant. final, ending, concluding.

prelude *n.* introduction, overture, preface, opening, beginning, commencement, preamble, preliminary, curtain raiser.

ant. finale, conclusion, ending, finis.

premature *adj.* early, untimely, hasty, unseasonable, previous, ill-timed, precipitate, sudden, abortive, unripe, unready, unprepared.

ant. overdue, belated, overripe, late.

premeditated *adj.* planned, deliberate, intentional, prearranged, plotted, schemed, contrived, calculated, conscious, willful, purposeful, aforethought.

ant. impulsive, spontaneous, instinctive, unconscious, accidental, unpremeditated, unplanned.

premier *adj.* **1** principal, chief, main, primary, major, leading, first, head, top, prime, foremost, senior. **2** first, earliest, original, primal, maiden, initial, inaugural, premiere, introductory. —*n.* prime minister, chancellor.

ant. *adj.* **1** subordinate, assistant, ancillary, auxiliary, minor, supporting. **2** subsequent, later, following, last.

premiere *n.* opening, debut, bow, first night. —*adj.* PREMIER.

premise *n.* supposition, assumption, postulate, given, hypothesis, proposition, theorem, lemma, argument, thesis, assertion, presupposition.

premium *n.* reward, bonus, prize, bounty, gift, remuneration, payment, recompense, guerdon, gratuity.

premonition *n.* omen, portent, warning, forewarning, foreshadowing, presage, presentiment, apprehension, foreboding, misgiving, hunch, augury, inkling, intimation, intuition.

preoccupied *n.* engrossed, engaged, absorbed, abstracted, lost, rapt, occupied, involved, obsessed, haunted.

preoccupy *v.* ENGAGE.

preordain *v.* PREDETERMINE.

preparation *n.* **1** arrangement, groundwork, development, formation, training, grooming, apprenticeship, education, provision, preparedness, readiness, alertness. **2** concoction, compound, composition, mixture, confection.

preparatory *adj.* PRELIMINARY.

prepare *v.* **1** arrange, anticipate, form, forearm, adapt, fit, prime, coach, train, qualify, groom, ready, shape up, tune up. **2** outfit, provide, fit out, equip, array, rig out, furnish, appoint, accouter.

preparedness *n.* READINESS.

preponderance *n.* predominance, primacy, extensiveness, prevalence, influence, supremacy, superiority, lead, majority, bulk, control, importance, weight, power.

ant. unimportance, inferiority, smallness, minority.

preponderant *adj.* PREDOMINANT.

preponderate *v.* PREVAIL.

prepossessing *adj.* ATTRACTIVE.

preposterous *adj.* ridiculous, absurd, foolish, impossible, unthinkable, idiotic, irrational, silly, ludicrous, insane, senseless, nonsensical, fantastic.

ant. reasonable, sensible, realistic, plausible.

prerequisite *adj.* REQUIRED. —*n.* REQUIREMENT.

prerogative *n.* PRIVILEGE.

presage *n.* omen, portent, warning, auspice, sign, augury, threat, presentiment, premonition, foreboding, apprehension. —*v.* portend, bode, augur, signify, herald, foreshadow, presignify, betoken, prefigure.

prescience *n.* FORESIGHT.

prescient *adj.* CLAIRVOYANT.

prescribe *v.* command, designate, enjoin, ordain, order, dictate, direct, assign, require, decree, institute, establish.

prescript *n.* PRESCRIPTION.

prescription *n.* **1** direction, designation, ordering, injunction, dictation, requiring. **2** instruction, imperative, mandate, order, prescript, requirement, dictum, direction, recipe, formula, precept, directive, commandment.

presence *n.* **1** attendance, occurrence, existence, being, visibility, appearance, company, manifestation, nearness, propinquity, proximity, neighborhood, vicinity. **2** bearing, manner, air, aura, appearance, aspect, mien, carriage, demeanor, look, profile, image, comportment.

presence of mind SELF-CONTROL.

present[1] *adj.* **1** attending, occurring, existing, found, nearby, at hand, available, visible, manifest, ubiquitous, omnipresent. **2** current, recent, contemporary, present-day, latter-day, modern, up-to-date, topical, latest.
ant. **1** absent, away, off, remote, distant. **2** past, bygone, ancient, former, future, coming.

present[2] *v.* **1** introduce, acquaint with. **2** display, show, introduce, exhibit, air, expose, demonstrate, put on, stage. **3** raise, suggest, introduce, offer, submit, proffer, propose, invite, produce. **4** donate, give, award, grant, bestow, confer, accord, render.

presentable *adj.* acceptable, bestowable, suitable, appropriate, decent, respectable, passable, proper, tasteful,
fit, satisfactory, neat, agreeable, personable.
ant. unacceptable, objectionable, inappropriate, shabby, shoddy, unsuitable, unworthy.

presentation *n.* **1** donation, bestowal, award, conferment, grant, contribution, endowment. **2** introduction, ceremony, courtesy, debut. **3** showing, airing, exhibition, staging, performance, production, exposure, viewing, offering, submission, proposal, forwarding.

present-day *adj.* PRESENT.

presentiment *n.* foreboding, presage, apprehension, premonition, forethought, foretaste, anticipation, expectation, hunch.

presently *adv.* SHORTLY.

preserve *v.* **1** guard, safeguard, defend, save, protect, secure, shield, shelter. **2** maintain, conserve, keep, sustain, perpetuate, continue, uphold, support, care for. —*n.* retreat, refuge, asylum, haven, shelter, sanctuary, reserve, reservation.
ant. *v.* **2** destroy, damage, ruin, break, neglect, dilapidate, scrap, discard.

preside *v.* chair, moderate, head, lead, direct, supervise, oversee, manage, administer, officiate.

presignify *v.* PRESAGE.

press *v.* **1** push, poke, palpate, depress, compress, bear, shove, mash, crush, weigh down, compact. **2** squeeze, extract, express, wring, pat, smooth, iron, flatten, level, crowd, cram, jam, pack, compact, condense. **3** hug, embrace, cuddle, nestle, nuzzle, snuggle, clasp, grip, grasp, huddle. **4** force, impel, drive, propel, compel, thrust, push, move. **5** importune, urge, plead, entreat, solicit, exhort, demand, insist, persuade, prevail, prompt, egg on, oblige, hasten, prod. —*n.* **1** crowd, throng, mob, host, herd, flock, crush, swarm, pack, jam, legion, multitude. **2** pressure, stress, strain, demands, compulsion, rat race (*Slang*).

pressing *adj.* urgent, exigent, imperative, important, vital, necessary, serious, critical, crucial, demanding, insistent, crying.

ant. frivolous, trivial, inconsequential, unimportant, unnecessary.

pressure *n.* **1** pressing, crushing, pushing, squeezing, compression, pinching, weighing down. **2** compulsion, coercion, constraint, obligation, demand, push, strain, duress, harassment, necessity. —*v.* compel, coerce, constrain, persuade, force, bear down upon, twist one's arm, high-pressure, drive, coax, influence.

prestidigitation *n.* SLEIGHT OF HAND.

prestige *n.* status, authority, influence, weight, importance, distinction, prominence, repute, renown, eminence, preeminence, esteem, regard, respect.

ant. insignificance, obscurity, lowliness, disgrace, disrepute, ignominy.

prestigious *adj.* esteemed, renowned, respected, prominent, eminent, distinguished, illustrious, reputable, high-class, superior, notable, outstanding, exalted, celebrated, important.

ant. discredited, inconsequential, unknown, disreputable, petty, inferior, ignominious.

presto *adv., adj.* FAST.

presume *v.* **1** assume, arrogate, appropriate, usurp, dare, venture, make bold, take the liberty, impose, abuse, exploit, take advantage. **2** suppose, assume, posit, postulate, hypothesize, predicate, presuppose, consider, surmise, infer, gather, guess.

presumption *n.* **1** arrogance, audacity, forwardness, impertinence, insolence, brass, effrontery, gall, contumely, nerve, cheek, impudence, familiarity, chutzpah, hubris. **2** assumption, supposition, presupposition, postulate, premise, inference, belief, opinion, theory. **3** probability, likelihood, chance, plausibility, grounds, evidence, reason.

ant. **1** modesty, humility, politeness, courtesy, civility, respect.

presumptive *adj.* PROBABLE.

presumptuous *adj.* forward, audacious, bold, brazen, assuming, insolent, haughty, arrogant, impertinent, contumelious, brash, conceited, flippant, familiar, smart-alecky.

ant. meek, timid, humble, modest, civil, polite, courteous, unassuming, respectful.

presuppose *v.* ASSUME.

pretend *v.* **1** feign, fake, simulate, affect, imitate, impersonate, sham, counterfeit, dissemble, dissimulate. **2** claim, profess, purport, allege, contend, assert, lie, prevaricate. **3** make believe, act, play, imagine, suppose.

pretended *adj.* SHAM.

pretense *n.* **1** make-believe, sham, acting, feigning, imitation, mimicry, role-playing. **2** ruse, pretext, stratagem, wile, artifice, excuse, dodge, bluff, feint, trick, tactic. **3** mask, show, facade, veneer, affectation, appearance, pose, posturing, dissimulation, charade, cloak, disguise, veil, coloration, cover.

ant. **3** truth, candor, openness, honesty, artlessness, naturalness, frankness.

pretension *n.* **1** claim, presumption, allegation, profession, assertion, arrogation. **2** affectation, display, show, airs, snobbery, ostentation, hypocrisy, pomposity, pretentiousness.

ant. **1** renunciation, repudiation, rejection, abdication, forswearing. **2** simplicity, sincerity, plainness, modesty, naturalness.

pretentious *adj.* **1** affected, self-important, pompous, conceited, high-flown, grandiloquent, inflated, mannered, precious, lofty, highfalutin, boastful. **2** showy, ostentatious, grandiose, conspicuous, flamboyant, overblown, extravagant, ornate, fancy, gaudy, elaborate.

ant. **1** humble, unassuming, natural, modest. **2** simple, modest, plain, ascetic, austere, spare.

preternatural *adj.* SUPERNATURAL.

pretext *n.* excuse, device, ruse, subterfuge, guise, justification, alibi, cover-up, bluff, stall, evasion, red herring, pretense, ploy.

prettify *v.* adorn, gild, decorate, beautify, primp, furbelow, embellish, bedizen, bedeck, fix up.
ant. mar, blemish, spoil, deface, uglify.

pretty *adj.* dainty, delicate, fair, personable, attractive, comely, bonny, handsome, good-looking, seemly, graceful. —*adv.* moderately, fairly, reasonably, tolerably, somewhat, passably.
ant. *adj.* homely, plain, ugly, gross, unattractive, unsightly, ungainly.

prevail *v.* conquer, overcome, triumph, withstand, win, succeed, override, overrule, predominate, preponderate, reign, obtain, endure, abide, stand.
ant. lose, fail, fall, surrender, knuckle under, collapse.

prevailing *adj.* current, common, dominant, operative, popular, fashionable, present, in force, in effect, predominant, preponderant, influential, controlling, powerful, effective, effectual.
ant. outmoded, passé, ineffectual, ineffective.

prevalent *adj.* widespread, commonplace, pervasive, extensive, sweeping, rife, rampant, epidemic, popular, prevailing, frequent, universal, general.
ant. limited, rare, uncommon, infrequent, isolated, restricted.

prevaricate *v.* LIE.

prevarication *n.* LIE.

prevent *v.* **1** avert, forestall, preclude, deter, avoid, obviate, inhibit, stave off, head off, nip in the bud. **2** hinder, thwart, foil, obstruct, block, arrest, cramp, impede, stop, balk, frustrate, inhibit, bar, prohibit.
ant. **1** cause, instigate, provoke, effectuate, engender. **2** abet, help, encourage, further, allow, expedite.

prevention *n.* precaution, safeguard, preclusion, inhibition, deterrence, avoidance, anticipation, obviation, prophylaxis.

preventive *adj.* deterrent, preclusive, inhibitory, precautionary, protective, prophylactic, counteractive.

previous *adj.* **1** earlier, anterior, antecedent, former, erstwhile, preceding, prior, foregoing, aforesaid, aforementioned, first. **2** premature, precipitate, untimely, inopportune, unseasonable.
ant. **1** later, following, posterior, subsequent, ensuing, succeeding, sequent. **2** timely, opportune.

prevision *n.* FORESIGHT.

prey *n.* **1** catch, quarry, kill, chase, game, victim, mark, target, dupe, fall guy. **2** booty, loot, pillage, plunder, spoils, prize, swag (*Slang*).

prey on exploit, cheat, defraud, swindle, rob, rip off (*Slang*), fleece, bleed, manipulate, blackmail, victimize.

price *n.* **1** cost, outlay, expense, amount, charge, value, worth, assessment, expenditure, fee, tab, payment. **2** sacrifice, toll, cost, penalty, consequence, dues, wages.

priceless *adj.* **1** invaluable, precious, inestimable, costly, dear, valuable, expensive. **2** amusing, funny, riotous, hilarious, fantastic, absurd, wonderful, extraordinary, fabulous, splendid, rich, witty, droll.
ant. **1** cheap, ordinary, worthless, common. **2** dull, vapid, banal, tedious, trite, hackneyed, stock, insipid.

prick *v.* **1** pierce, puncture, prickle, stab, jab, poke, stick, perforate, lance, impale, spear. **2** grieve, distress, hurt, dismay, upset, touch, wound, move, cut, sting. **3** goad, prod, spur, press, urge, impel, needle, drive. **4** sting, bite, tingle, smart, itch, pinch, chafe, nip. —*n.* **1** puncture, perforation, cut, gash, wound, nick. **2** sting, prickle, smarting, tingle, burning, itch. **3** pang, twinge, feeling, spasm, wrench, gnawing, scruple, spur, compunction.

prickle *n.*, *v.* PRICK.

prickly *adj.* stinging, sharp, tingling, tickly, itchy, crawling, creeping.

pride *n.* **1** arrogance, conceit, vanity, egotism, self-importance, haughtiness, hauteur, presumption, hubris, vainglory, airs, loftiness, self-satisfaction, disdain, snobbery. **2** self-esteem, self-respect, dignity, self-worth, *amour-propre*. **3** elite, best, cream, glory, aristocracy, treasure, pride and joy, pick, flower.
ant. **1** modesty, humility, unpretentiousness, demureness, meekness. **2** self-loathing, abjectness, servility, obsequiousness, sycophancy.

prideful *n.* PROUD.

priest *n.* minister, ecclesiastic, cleric, clergyman, pastor, divine, chaplain, parson, rabbi, lama, father, father confessor, guru.

priestly *adj.* sacerdotal, hieratic, pastoral, ecclesiastical, ministerial, clerical.
ant. lay, secular.

prig *n.* stuffed shirt, prude, bluenose, pedant, stiff (*Slang*), precisionist, authoritarian, schoolmarm, old maid, fuddy-duddy.

priggish *adj.* stuffy, self-righteous, prudish, pedantic, prim, strait-laced, pompous, self-satisfied, narrow-minded, stiff, formal, starchy.
ant. casual, liberal, relaxed, informal.

prim *adj.* proper, strait-laced, prissy, fussy, formal, stiff, rigid, starchy, unbending, prudish, puritanical.
ant. libertine, relaxed, easy-going, loose, casual, flexible, informal.

primacy *n.* supremacy, leadership, command, ascendancy, dominance, superiority, championship, preeminence.
ant. inferiority, subordination, mediocrity.

primal *adj.* PRIMARY.

primarily *adv.* MOSTLY.

primary *adj.* **1** first, original, earliest, oldest, initial, primal, prime, primordial, germinal, primitive, embryonic, elementary, rudimentary. **2** first, top, chief, prime, primal, leading, head, highest, ruling, senior, premier, principal, main, dominant. **3** basic, elemental, fundamental, ultimate, underlying, primitive, radical, basal, essential.
ant. **1** last, later, subsequent, resultant, following. **2** secondary, subordinate, assistant, junior, lower. **3** derivative, secondary, composite, compounded.

prime *adj.* **1** first-rate, first-class, top, excellent, A-one, top-notch, top-drawer, superior, optimal, prize, select. **2** PRIMARY. —*n.* **1** heyday, golden age, flower, bloom, summer. **2** best, top, optimum, choice, pick, prize, plum, elite.
ant. *adj.* **1** second-rate, average, mediocre, inferior, run-of-the-mill, lesser. *n.* **1** dotage, decline, wane, decay, decrepitude, autumn, evening.

primeval *adj.* PRIMORDIAL.

primitive *adj.* **1** early, original, primordial, primeval, antediluvian, pristine, embryonic, incipient, budding, inchoate, rudimentary, aboriginal, atavistic, uncivilized, savage. **2** simple, plain, crude, rough, rustic, homespun, undeveloped, unsophisticated.
ant. **1** developed, civilized, cultivated, evolved. **2** ornate, polished, elaborate, fancy, sophisticated.

primogenitor *n.* ANCESTOR.

primordial *adj.* primitive, primeval, original, early, ancient, prehistoric, pristine, ancestral, antediluvian.
ant. modern, recent, current, developed, mature.

primp *v.* preen, prink, dress up, doll up (*Slang*), titivate, smarten, fuss, groom, adorn.

princely *adj.* **1** noble, regal, distinguished, stately, lordly, grand, august, majestic, lofty, magnificent, splendid. **2** generous, liberal, kind, benevolent, magnanimous, gracious, munificent, sumptuous, open-handed, bountiful.

ant. 1 lowly, base, ignoble, vulgar, common. **2** miserly, niggardly, stingy, mean, petty, small-minded.

principal *adj.* main, central, foremost, paramount, prime, cardinal, major, essential, key, chief, capital, primary, leading, dominant. —*n.* **1** protagonist, party, participant, actor. **2** headmaster, headmistress, director, dean, master, rector. **3** star, lead, headliner.

ant. *adj.* minor, secondary, peripheral, lesser, incidental, accessory.

principally *adj.* MOSTLY.

principle *n.* **1** rule, law, truth, verity, regulation, axiom, canon, proposition, creed, guide, morality, integrity, high-mindedness, standards, ethics. **2** essence, workings, explanation, character, rationale, theory, nature, mode, key, quality. **3** cause, origin, basis, source, groundwork, fundamentals, rudiments, ABC's.

principled *adj.* ethical, moral, high-minded, just, right-minded, righteous, upright, honorable, conscientious, trustworthy, reputable, scrupulous, incorruptible, rigorous, judgmental.

ant. unscrupulous, unprincipled, corrupt, treacherous, opportunistic, amoral.

prink *v.* PRIMP.

print *n.* imprint, impression, mark, seal, stamp, brand, impress. —*v.* mark, stamp, impress, imprint, offset, engrave.

prior *adj.* previous, preceding, anterior, earlier, former, antecedent, aforementioned, foregoing, precursive, preexistent, erstwhile, quondam.

ant. subsequent, following, later, latter, posterior.

priority *n.* **1** precedence, antecedence, previousness, preexistence, anteriority. **2** privilege, preference, advantage, preeminence, ascendancy, seniority, supremacy, prerogative, leverage, pull, clout (*Slang*).

ant. 1 subsequence, posteriority, futurity.

prison *n.* **1** jail, penitentiary, jailhouse, reformatory, lockup, brig, pen (*Slang*), clink (*Slang*), jug (*Slang*), cooler (*Slang*), pokey (*Slang*), gaol (*Brit.*). **2** cage, cell, pen, coop, tomb, vault, cloister, dungeon, enclosure, pound.

prisoner *n.* **1** convict, jailbird, inmate, accused, lawbreaker, felon, criminal, con (*Slang*). **2** captive, hostage, slave, internee, victim, pawn, serf, peon, vassal.

prissy *adj.* fussy, prim, prudish, smug, self-righteous, precise, overprecise, punctilious, particular, priggish, puritanical, squeamish, overcautious, finical, precious.

ant. casual, relaxed, unihibited, natural, free-wheeling, reckless.

pristine *adj.* **1** primeval, primitive, aboriginal, primal, rudimentary, inchoate, prehistoric, initial, earliest, original. **2** pure, uncontaminated, undefiled, untouched, unmarred, unsullied, unspoiled, virgin, virginal, immaculate, impeccable.

ant. 2 contaminated, spotted, tainted, spoiled, overused.

privacy *n.* seclusion, sequestration, retirement, isolation, aloofness, unsociability, retreat, self-sufficiency, withdrawal, segregation, purdah.

private *adj.* **1** secluded, sequestered, cloistered, closeted, retired, isolated, alone, aloof, withdrawn, hermitic, monastic. **2** confidential, secret, hidden, covert, unrevealed, clandestine, furtive, undisclosed, unpublished, undercover, off-the-record, classified, top-secret, hush-hush (*Slang*). **3** personal, individual, particular, intimate, peculiar, subjective, singular, own, self-contained, unique. **4** restricted, nonpublic, exclusive, special, nonofficial, autonomous, independent.

ant. 1 available, accessible, sociable. **2** overt, revealed, publicized, straightforward, open. **3** general, popular, communal, inclusive, shared. **4** public, official, community, governmental, unrestricted, municipal.

privation *n.* **1** deprivation, lack, need, want, insufficiency, inadequacy, paucity, deficiency, scarcity, shortage, shortfall, deficit, exiguity. **2** poverty, penury, hardship, want, indigence, pauperism, destitution, misery, distress.

ant. 1 excess, overflow, oversupply, sufficiency. **2** riches, wealth, affluence, comfort, ease, plenty, fulfillment, privilege.

privilege *n.* **1** perquisite, prerogative, priority, advantage, exemption, authority, franchise, sanction, benefit, immunity, leverage, influence, pull (*Slang*), clout (*Slang*). **2** entitlement, right, authorization, benefit, liberty, freedom, sanction, birthright, claim, due.

privileged *adj.* **1** advantaged, favored, ascendant, powerful, established, entrenched, ruling, preeminent, unaccountable, elite, dominant, prevailing, on top. **2** *of information:* special, exceptional, preferential, extraordinary, inside.

ant. 1 underprivileged, disadvantaged, powerless, exploited, downtrodden, deprived.

privy *n.* outhouse, toilet, w.c., latrine, backhouse, john (*Slang*), can (*Slang*).

privy to in on, on to, aware of, apprised of, cognizant of, wise to, informed, clued in, in the know (*Slang*), hip (*Slang*).

ant. in the dark, ignorant, unaware.

prize *n.* **1** reward, award, honor, accolade, trophy, distinction, recognition, payment, loot, winnings, windfall, haul, take, purse. **2** ambition, desideratum, aim, end, goal, hope, attainment, conquest, gain, desire. —*v.* VALUE. —*adj.* prize-winning, outstanding, first-rate, top-notch, blue-ribbon, acclaimed, champion, note-

worthy, valuable, esteemed, valued, cherished, invaluable, inestimable.

ant. *adj.* ordinary, mediocre, worthless, pedestrian, third-rate.

probability *n.* likelihood, presumption, prospect, possibility, expectation, gamble, risk, odds, chance, contingency.

probable *adj.* likely, expected, anticipated, presumed, presumptive, seeming, presumable, reasonable, conceivable, plausible, verisimilar.

ant. unlikely, improbable, inconceivable, implausible, unexpected, rare.

probation *n.* TEST.

probe *v.* investigate, look into, research, examine, question, grill, study, interrogate, cross-examine, ferret out, peer into, delve into, scrutinize. —*n.* investigation, scrutiny, research, examination, cross-examination, study, grilling, inspection, analysis, search, detection.

probity *n.* integrity, virtue, honesty, high-mindedness, righteousness, morality, character, uprightness, dependability, trustworthiness, honor, principle, incorruptibility, scrupulousness, conscience.

ant. perfidy, duplicity, corruption, unscrupulousness, dishonesty, crookedness.

problem *n.* **1** puzzle, riddle, question, conundrum, poser. **2** dilemma, enigma, labyrinth, maze, question mark, unknown, complexity, mystery, paradox, quandary, predicament, perplexity, impasse, hornet's nest, can of worms. —*adj.* difficult, refractory, obstreperous, stubborn, unmanageable, perverse, disconcerting, baffling, intractable.

ant. *n.* **1** solution, answer. **2** open book, easy sailing. *adj.* simple, normal, predictable, manageable.

problematic *adj.* uncertain, questionable, doubtful, contingent, chancy, unsettled, undetermined, unsure, debatable, moot, dubious, risky, tricky.

ant. definite, certain, settled, sure, decided, undoubted.

procedure *n.* **1** course, way, manner, conduct, action, process, modus operandi, method, measure, plan, policy, strategy, scheme. **2** protocol, form, routine, methodology, punctilio, regulations, conventions, proceedings, proprieties, etiquette, standards, ins and outs, red tape.

proceed *v.* go on, go forward, go ahead, continue, move on, advance, progress, extend, move along, flow, forge ahead, make headway, get on with, pursue, set in motion, initiate. **ant.** stall, stop, regress, back up, back out.

proceeding *n.* act, action, transaction, process, procedure, plan, method, system, event, situation, incident, occurrence, undertaking, venture, deed.

proceedings *n.* records, minutes, transactions, doings, goings-on, activities, agenda, archives, annals, reports, business.

proceeds *n.* income, return, profit, gain, take, return, remuneration, assets, receipts, yield, revenue, net, gross, gate.

process *n.* **1** method, technique, procedure, formula, chemistry, modus operandi, routine, way, workings, functioning, practice, praxis, manner, mode, system. **2** progress, proceeding, development, continuation, continuity, movement, action, unfolding, growth, expansion, evolution, formation. —*v.* treat, prepare, ready, adapt, handle, engineer, regulate, deal with. **ant.** *n.* **2** decline, decay, retrogression, stasis.

procession *n.* line, line of march, parade, cavalcade, march, progress, file, caravan, column, queue, cortege, pageant, review, retinue.

proclaim *v.* announce, declare, state, promulgate, inform, expound, publicize, advertise, blazon, herald, report, broadcast, communicate, profess, avow, expatiate, aver. **ant.** retract, recant, disavow.

proclamation *n.* announcement, declaration, statement, report, pronunciamento, manifesto, utterance, profession, information, notice, notification, decree, edict, pronouncement.

proclivity *n.* disposition, tendency, penchant, inclination, bias, leaning, idiosyncrasy, foible, weakness, taste, partiality, affinity, propensity, liking, predilection, bent, prejudice. **ant.** disinclination, dislike, aversion, distaste.

procrastinate *v.* put off, defer, postpone, delay, stall, shelve, hesitate, shilly-shally, suspend, temporize, prolong, dally, remand. **ant.** settle, dispose of, decide, rush into.

procreate *v.* beget, engender, father, mother, generate, multiply, reproduce, breed, propagate, proliferate, produce, bear, sire, fecundate, impregnate.

procreation *n.* PROPAGATION.

proctor *n.* agent, proxy, deputy, substitute, representative, steward, second, surrogate, delegate, aide, alternate, lieutenant, spokesman, spokeswoman.

procumbent *adj.* PRONE.

procure *v.* obtain, acquire, get, gain, attain, secure, come by, win, buy, purchase, appropriate, pick up, gather, receive, earn.

procurer *n.* pimp, procuress, pander, madam, bawd, go-between, brothelkeeper, ponce (*Brit. Slang*).

prod *v.* **1** poke, push, punch, nudge, lash, whip, spur, goad. **2** urge, arouse, motivate, impel, incite, nag, excite, animate, provoke, move, prompt, quicken, exhort, instigate, drive. —*n.* **1** goad, poker, spur, thorn, prick, stick. **2** incentive, motivation, prodding, encouragement, impulse, compulsion, impetus, catalyst, prompting, nagging, provocation, inspiration, urge, urging, push, shove, pressure, drive.

ant. *v.* **2** deter, discourage, dissuade, restrain, daunt, stop. *n.* **2** deterrent, warning, restraint.

prodigal *adj.* **1** extravagant, wasteful, spendthrift, improvident, profligate, excessive, wanton, reckless, squandering, overgenerous, free, openhanded, unselfish. **2** bountiful, abundant, lavish, lush, profuse, rich, teeming, rife, replete, luxuriant, luxurious, prodigious, copious, sumptuous. —*n.* spendthrift, wastrel, profligate, wanton.

ant. *adj.* **1** thrifty, cautious, economical, provident, stinting, selfish. **2** scarce, sparse, scant, limited, insufficient. *n.* miser, penny-pincher, skinflint, tightwad (*Slang*).

prodigious *adj.* huge, monumental, mammoth, enormous, gigantic, stupendous, colossal, immense, vast, immeasurable, oversized, giant, massive, tremendous, inordinate.

ant. puny, small, picayune, scant, insufficient.

prodigy *n.* MARVEL.

produce *v.* **1** yield, bear, bring forth, generate, beget, breed, hatch, procreate, supply, render, furnish, fructify, progenerate. **2** invent, create, devise, originate, concoct, form, fashion, coin, conceive, frame, shape, formulate, dream up, make, contrive. **3** provoke, engender, lead to, result in, cause, occasion, give rise to, promote, stir up, kindle, raise, begin, effect, effectuate. **4** manufacture, fabricate, make, turn out, build, construct, assemble, process, market, mass-produce.

producer *n.* manufacturer, fabricator, factory, plant, mill, shop, craftsman, artificer, maker, seller, industrialist, farmer, grower, processor.

ant. consumer, user, buyer, customer.

product *n.* end result, commodity, merchandise, artifact, output, produc-

tion, creation, invention, concoction, produce, yield.

production *n.* manufacture, output, fabrication, mass production, creation.

ant. consumption, use.

productive *adj.* **1** fertile, prolific, creative, inventive, imaginative, generative, seminal, original, ingenious, resourceful, copious, rich, fecund. **2** fruitful, useful, valuable, gratifying, advantageous, profitable, worthwhile, rewarding, beneficial.

ant. 1 barren, sterile, poor, impoverished, exhausted. **2** futile, useless, unproductive, fruitless, ineffective, worthless.

proem *n.* PREFACE.

prof *n.* PROFESSOR.

profanation *n.* SACRILEGE.

profane *v.* desecrate, degrade, debase, abuse, misuse, blaspheme, violate, contaminate, pervert, prostitute, sin, transgress. —*adj.* **1** irreverent, sacrilegious, blasphemous, disrespectful, impious, iconoclastic, irreligious, wicked, sinful, obscene, vicious, evil. **2** secular, worldly, earthly, mundane, temporal, lay.

ant. *v.* exalt, honor, worship, glorify, respect. *adj.* **1** God-fearing, religious, pious, devout, virtuous, reverent, good. **2** godly, sacred, spiritual, ecclesiastical.

profanity *n.* **1** irreverence, blasphemy, impiety, obscenity, cursing, swearing, cussing. **2** swearword, oath, cussword, four-letter word, unprintable.

ant. 1 reverence, respect, propriety, virtue, decency.

profess *v.* **1** avow, affirm, announce, proclaim, contend, confirm, state, depose, maintain, certify, warrant, hold, claim. **2** dissemble, pretend, purport, feign, sham, counterfeit, allege, simulate, affect.

profession *n.* **1** calling, occupation, specialty, vocation, discipline, field, career, métier, job, work, area, line, business, employment, activity. **2** announcement, avowal, declaration, statement, proclamation, contention, claim, deposition, testimony, allegation, pronouncement, pledge, manifesto, word, credo, dictum.

professional *n., adj.* EXPERT.

professor *n.* academician, teacher, instructor, tutor, educator, savant, don, prof.

professorial *adj.* ACADEMIC.

proffer *v.* offer, tender, volunteer, present, give, donate, supply, submit, hand, deliver, bestow, bid.
ant. withhold, keep, retain, reserve.

proficiency *n.* competence, ability, skill, expertise, expertness, aptitude, facility, talent, knack, cleverness, faculty, capability, mastery, know-how, fluency, familiarity, knowledge, background.
ant. incompetence, ineptitude, inadequacy, bungling.

proficient *adj.* competent, skillful, expert, talented, able, dextrous, well-trained, capable, apt, adroit, adept, skilled, learned, qualified, gifted.
ant. bungling, incompetent, inefficient, clumsy, green.

profile *n.* **1** side view, outline, contour, likeness, silhouette, face, portrait, drawing, picture. **2** biography, sketch, vignette, characterization, résumé, rundown, *curriculum vitae*, vita.

profit *n.* benefit, advantage, gain, good, return, proceeds, avail, use, value, harvest, yield, reward, advancement, boon. —*v.* benefit, gain, avail, advance, reap, serve, contribute, help, improve, reward, promote, aid.
ant. *n.* loss, detriment, disadvantage, drawback, harm. *v.* handicap, hinder, retard, harm.

profitable *adj.* advantageous, lucrative, gainful, beneficial, worthwhile, useful, availing, rewarding, remunerative, valuable, desirable, expedient, productive, fruitful, money-making.
ant. vain, useless, unrewarding, un-

profitable, harmful, damaging, losing.

profligacy *n.* **1** dissipation, debauchery, wantonness, abandon, dissoluteness, immorality, viciousness, depravity, promiscuity, licentiousness, debasement, sinfulness, corruption, degeneracy, delinquency. **2** wastefulness, extravagance, prodigality, recklessness, improvidence, lavishness, sumptuousness, excess.
ant. **1** decency, virtue, propriety, self-discipline. **2** thrift, economy, stinginess, providence, moderation.

profligate *adj.* **1** immoral, dissipated, debauched, wanton, wild, abandoned, vicious, depraved, licentious, debased, promiscuous, corrupt, degenerate, sinful, evil, delinquent. **2** wasteful, extravagant, prodigal, reckless, spendthrift, improvident, heedless, overgenerous, excessive, unthrifty, immoderate.
ant. **1** moral, upright, virtuous, decent, prim. **2** thrifty, provident, cautious, tight-fisted, stingy, miserly, penny-pinching.

profound *adj.* **1** insightful, penetrating, deep, wise, weighty, thoughtful, philosophical, scholarly, informed, incisive, sagacious, knowing, learned, erudite, serious, sage, abstruse, shrewd. **2** complete, thoroughgoing, total, exhaustive, far-reaching, far-ranging, all-inclusive, sweeping, full, entire, comprehensive, all-embracing, all-out, unrestricted.
ant. **1** thoughtless, frivolous, shallow, superficial, silly, meaningless. **2** fragmentary, partial, light, incomplete, inadequate.

profundity *n.* **1** WISDOM. **2** INTENSITY.

profuse *adj.* **1** generous, extravagant, lavish, prodigal, open-handed, munificent, spendthrift, sumptuous, unstinting, immoderate, excessive, fulsome. **2** teeming, abounding, luxuriant, plentiful, abundant, copious, plenteous, bounteous, limitless, unending, ample, overflowing, prolific, rich, rife.

ant. 1 stingy, miserly, mean, stinting, selfish. **2** thin, meager, sparse, inadequate, insufficient, scarce.

profusion *n.* abundance, excess, oversupply, copiousness, overflow, fullness, surplus, glut, plethora, lavishness, bounty, multiplicity, myriad, crowd.

ant. scarcity, paucity, sparseness, insufficiency, want, lack.

progenitor *n.* **1** ancestor, forefather, forebear, parent, sire, begetter, father, mother, dam, procreator, predecessor. **2** source, originator, fountainhead, wellspring, creator, inspiration, author, pioneer, founder, inventor, cause, forerunner, precursor. **ant. 1** descendants, offspring, issue, progeny, children. **2** follower, imitator, inheritor.

progeny *n.* offspring, descendants, issue, young, children, line, posterity, stock, family.

ant. ancestry, parentage, forebears, forefathers, progenitors.

prognosis *n.* PREDICTION.

prognosticate *v.* PREDICT.

prognostication *n.* PREDICTION.

program *n.* **1** list, listing, schedule, itemization, tabulation, regimen, itinerary, enumeration, docket, timetable, calendar, bulletin. **2** plan, course, routine, procedure, recipe, platform, plank, policies, manifesto, proceedings, scenario, evolution, scheme, plot, arrangement, prearrangement, organization. —*v.* **1** list, arrange, order, range, itemize, tabulate, organize, systematize. **2** schedule, book, engage, line up, prearrange, sign up.

progress *n.* **1** headway, advance, progression, movement, locomotion, acceleration, motion, time. **2** improvement, betterment, advancement, promotion, amelioration, achievement, gain, refinement, uplift, humanization, enterprise, dynamism. —*v.* **1** move forward, make headway, accelerate, advance, proceed, continue, forge ahead, overtake,

lead. **2** improve, ameliorate, develop, achieve, gain, blossom, grow, burgeon, flourish, perfect, fulfill.

ant. *n.* **1** retreat, standstill, retardation. **2** regression, retrogression, decadence, decay, loss, degradation, brutalization. *v.* **1** stall, stop, lose ground, retreat, back up. **2** decline, decay, fade, fail, degenerate.

progression *n.* **1** progress, headway, advance, furtherance, advancement, promotion, procession, improvement, betterment, development, gain. **2** series, sequence, succession, flow, continuity, train, cycle, chain, parade, cavalcade.

ant. 1 regression, retrogression, decline, lowering.

progressive *adj.* **1** advancing, continuing, ongoing, successive, increasing, intensifying, accelerating, escalating, developing, continuous, sequential, unbroken, dynamic, enterprising. **2** meliorative, improving, reformist, liberal, forward-looking. —*n.* reformer, liberal, left-winger, meliorist, activist.

ant. *adj.* **1** retrogressive, diminishing, declining. **2** reactionary, conservative, backward-looking, unchanging. *n.* reactionary, conservative, right-winger, stand-patter.

prohibit *v.* forbid, ban, interdict, outlaw, prevent, disallow, constrain, hinder, deny, bar, debar, impede, restrict, block, check, obstruct.

ant. legalize, allow, permit, decriminalize, encourage, approve.

prohibition *n.* **1** hindrance, constraint, prevention, restriction, block, check, rein, barrier, forbiddance, exclusion, negation. **2** ban, interdict, embargo, disallowance, veto, proscription, estoppel, injunction, taboo, debarment, stay, outlawing.

ant. 1, 2 freedom, license, allowance, permission, acceptance, legalization, encouragement.

project *n.* plan, undertaking, venture, enterprise, job, course, scheme, task, objective, assignment, pursuit, experiment. —*v.* **1** extend, overhang, jut, beetle, protrude, stick out, arch, vault. **2** propel, eject, shoot, expel, discharge, emit, deliver, throw, cast, ejaculate, hurl, launch, fire. **3** predetermine, extrapolate, estimate, plan, rough out, outline, approximate, gauge, compute, reckon, guess.

projectile *n.* missile, shot, pellet, bullet, shaft, arrow.

projection *n.* **1** overhang, eave, extension, jut, protrusion, brow, prominence, ledge, sill, swell, bump, knob, bulge, vault, arch. **2** prediction, extrapolation, estimate, estimation, predetermination, approximation, guess, prospectus, forecast, evaluation, assessment, computation, reckoning, guesstimate (*Slang*).

ant. *n.* **1** indentation, undercut, recess, hollow, niche, relief, intaglio.

proliferate *v.* multiply, abound, swarm, increase, teem, spawn, run riot, superabound, propagate, overproduce, overrun.

prolific *adj.* fecund, fruitful, abundant, luxuriant, bountiful, copious, proliferating, productive, procreative, progenitive, multiplying, fertile.

ant. barren, sterile, impotent, jejune, infertile.

prolix *adj.* WORDY.

prolixity *n.* REDUNDANCY.

prologue *n.* **1** preface, introduction, prelude, preamble, proem, opening, exordium. **2** beginning, opening, initiation, precursor, preparation, preliminary, warmup, foretaste, preview, premonition, basis, foundation, prefigurement, antecedent.

ant. **1** epilogue, postlude, coda, peroration. **2** sequel, aftermath, consequence, result, outgrowth.

prolong *v.* extend, lengthen, continue, prolongate, stretch, protract, draw out, drag out, attenuate, perpetuate, maintain, delay, temporize, filibuster.

ant. shorten, abbreviate, limit, curtail, cut short.

promenade *n.* walk, saunter, stroll, air-

ing, jaunt, meander, ramble, tramp, hike. —*v.* strut, parade, swagger, flounce.

prominence *n.* **1** eminence, note, fame, notability, conspicuousness, renown, leadership, popularity, distinction, loftiness, reputation, illustriousness, superiority, notoriety, salience. **2** promontory, peak, crest, height, protuberance, extension, elevation, jut, projection, crag, overhang, pinnacle, salience.

prominent *adj.* **1** jutting, projecting, protuberant, overhanging, beetling, protrusive. **2** conspicuous, notable, noticeable, visible, salient, striking, eye-catching, remarkable, obvious, marked, evident, pronounced, unmistakable, obtrusive, unavoidable. **3** eminent, outstanding, famous, well-known, distinguished, top, leading, renowned, celebrated, honored, important, illustrious, significant, noteworthy.

ant. **1** recessive, undercut, underslung, indented, concave. **2** inconspicuous, hidden, unobtrusive, imperceptible, unnoticeable. **3** unknown, insignificant, undistinguished, average, ordinary, mediocre.

promiscuity *n.* PROFLIGACY.

promiscuous *adj.* **1** mixed, jumbled, heterogeneous, haphazard, motley, miscellaneous, varied, variegated, illassorted, scrambled, chaotic, diverse, unselective, random, undifferentiated, hit-or-miss. **2** undiscriminating, indiscriminate, lax, loose, casual, wanton, dissolute, profligate.

ant. **1** homogeneous, selected, orderly. **2** discriminating, choosy, deliberate.

promise *n.* **1** pledge, vow, assurance, word, parole, oath, warrant, guarantee, covenant, contract, agreement, stipulation, compact, bond, commitment. **2** endowment, talent, gift, ability, aptitude, capacity, intelligence, flair. —*v.* **1** pledge, vow, swear, guarantee, assure, contract, stipulate, engage, vouch, plight, warrant. **2** indicate, augur, imply, bode, portend, foretoken, presage, betoken, point to, suggest.

promising *adj.* **1** hopeful, auspicious, favorable, likely, propitious, rosy, reassuring, encouraging, heartening, bright, optimistic. **2** gifted, talented, able, intelligent, enterprising, capable, favored, endowed, precocious.

ant. 1 threatening, bleak, hopeless, inauspicious. **2** untalented, ordinary, unpromising, unlikely.

promontory *n.* headland, highland, eminence, prominence, peak, height, ness, precipice, point, head, jut, projection.

promote *v.* **1** further, encourage, stimulate, influence, extend, heighten, intensify, exacerbate, cultivate, engender, help, support, abet, expedite, develop, foster, contribute to, boost, back. **2** upgrade, elevate, advance, move up, raise, reward. **3** advocate, advertise, support, sell, publicize, tout, push, popularize, praise, recommend, back, espouse, champion, endorse, ballyhoo, puff.

ant. 1 discourage, disable, immobilize, stifle, hinder, dishearten. **2** demote, downgrade, retard. **3** condemn, denounce, disapprove, criticize, quash.

promotion *n.* **1** advancement, upgrading, elevation, exaltation, glorification, raise, reward, honor. **2** furtherance, development, progress, encouragement, cultivation, stimulation, extension, augmentation, broadening, heightening. **3** advertising, publicity, advocacy, testimonial, praise, recommendation, backing, endorsement, championship, touting, boosting, popularization, promulgation, sell, salesmanship, hoopla (*Slang*), ballyhoo, puffery, hype (*Slang*).

ant. 1 demotion, downgrading, debasement, humiliation. **2** limitation, decline, diminution.

prompt *v.* **1** incite, instigate, inspire,

provoke, motivate, cause, induce, occasion, move, activate, encourage, hearten, inspirit. **2** cue, remind, suggest, help, hint, prod, jog, push, nudge. —*adj.* **1** quick, rapid, ready, swift, alert, speedy, efficient, attentive, wide-awake, responsive, eager, cooperative, energetic, on the ball (*Slang*). **2** punctual, on time, undelayed, early, punctilious.

ant. *v.* **1** discourage, deter, dissuade. *adj.* **1** laggard, unresponsive, slow, leisurely. **2** late, delayed, tardy, overdue, unpunctual.

promptly *adv.* QUICKLY.

promulgate *v.* announce, make known, publicize, spread, broadcast, proclaim, advertise, promote, noise abroad, noise about, circulate, disseminate, bruit, herald, propagandize.

prone *adj.* **1** flat, horizontal, procumbent, prostrate, recumbent, reclining, supine. **2** apt, likely, liable, disposed, inclined, partial, predisposed, subject.

ant. 1 erect, upright, vertical, standing. **2** disinclined, averse, reluctant.

prong *n.* tine, point, tip, fang, tooth, tusk, spike, barb, hook, nib, spur.

pronounce *v.* **1** proclaim, utter, assert, declare, decide, judge, deem, consider, hold, opine, maintain. **2** articulate, say, enunciate, express, speak, sound, accent, emphasize, stress, syllabify.

pronounced *adj.* marked, distinct, noticeable, evident, obvious, decided, conspicuous, prominent, major, unmistakable, positive, undisguised, strong, clear, unambiguous.

ant. inconspicuous, subtle, questionable, minor.

pronouncement *n.* declaration, announcement, pronunciamento, manifesto, ukase, dictum, decision, judgment, proclamation, edict, decree, dictate, mandate, notice.

pronto *adv. Slang* QUICKLY.

pronunciamento *n.* PRONOUNCEMENT.

pronunciation *n.* diction, speech, articulation, accent, enunciation, stress, emphasis, expression, intonation, register, orthoepy.

proof *n.* **1** verification, validation, authentication, establishment, documentation, attestation, corroboration, affirmation, confirmation. **2** trial, test, experiment, demonstration, assay, check, examination, research, analysis, investigation, inquiry, interrogation, probe. **3** evidence, argument, documents, testimony, facts, grounds, results, statistics, logic, support, vindication.

prop *v.* support, hold up, brace, buttress, shore, truss, stay, bolster, reinforce. —*n.* support, brace, buttress, shoring, truss, bolster, reinforcement, mainstay, stay, stanchion, shim, wedge.

propagandize *v.* INDOCTRINATE.

propagate *v.* **1** breed, generate, reproduce, multiply, increase, procreate, hatch, spawn, beget, proliferate. **2** disseminate, spread, promulgate, diffuse, publicize, propagandize, circulate, broadcast, scatter, publish, proclaim, repeat, radiate.

propagation *n.* **1** reproduction, increase, multiplication, proliferation, begetting, procreation, breeding, spawning, hatching. **2** dissemination, promulgation, diffusion, spread, distribution, publicity, broadcasting, reporting, promotion, circulation, communication, contagion.

propel *v.* push, drive, move, urge, impel, prompt, activate, motivate, launch, start, thrust, shove, send, poke, prod.

propensity *n.* tendency, disposition, leaning, predisposition, proclivity, bias, partiality, bent, penchant, prejudice, inclination, predilection, preference, taste, appetite, affinity, appetence.
ant. disinclination, aversion, reluctance, distaste.

proper *adj.* **1** *specially suited:* appropriate, suitable, suited, meet, fit, fitting, seemly, apt, well-chosen, be-

coming, right. **2** *conforming to a standard:* accurate, standard, correct, right, orthodox, standardized, conventional, accepted, fitting, seemly, preferred, traditional, normal, usual, indicated. **3** genteel, respectable, decorous, polite, mannerly, punctilious, prim, priggish, prudish, prissy, *comme il faut.*
ant. **1** unsuitable, incongruous, inappropriate, malapropos. **2** unorthodox, unusual, unconventional, odd, outré, incorrect. **3** impolite, objectionable, rude, brash, gross, vulgar.

property *n.* **1** possessions, belongings, acquisitions, effects, assets, estate, capital, chattels, wealth, goods, resources, means. **2** real estate, land, acreage, acres, holding, domain, parcel, title, realty, freehold (*Brit.*). **3** attribute, characteristic, quality, essential, trait, feature, peculiarity, aspect, mark, distinction, constituent, ingredient.

prophecy *n.* prediction, forecast, prognosis, augury, foretelling, portent, prognostication, divination, revelation, precognition, warning.

prophesy *v.* foretell, predict, forecast, divine, presage, prognosticate, soothsay, augur, bode, forewarn, foresee.

prophet *n.* prophetess, seer, seeress, predictor, diviner, forecaster, soothsayer, prognosticator, magician, Cassandra, oracle, prophesier, fortuneteller, sibyl, crystal-gazer.

prophetic *adj.* prescient, sibylline, prognostic, predictive, oracular, apocalyptic, foreshadowing, presaging, ominous, threatening, portentous.

prophylactic *adj.* PREVENTIVE.
prophylaxis *n.* PREVENTION.
propinquity *n.* NEARNESS.
propitiate *v.* appease, conciliate, placate, mollify, pacify, reconcile, soothe, beguile, disarm, humor, soften, satisfy, calm.
ant. anger, irritate, vex, provoke, inflame.

propitious *adj.* auspicious, promising,

hopeful, favorable, felicitous, lucky, fortunate, happy, rosy, providential, timely, reassuring, opportune, encouraging, advantageous.

ant. ominous, threatening, inauspicious, unfavorable.

proponent *n.* advocate, champion, supporter, exponent, defender, upholder, partisan, subscriber, patron, backer, friend, booster, spokesman, spokeswoman, sympathizer, fellow-traveler.

ant. opponent, critic, enemy, adversary, fault-finder.

proportion *n.* **1** balance, harmony, symmetry, correspondence, agreement, congruity, analogy. **2** allotment, quota, measure, percentage, ration, dividend, slice, cut, percent, fraction.

proportional *adj.* PROPORTIONATE.

proportionate *adj.* proportional, commensurate, commensurable, balanced, even, just, equitable, due, comparable, equivalent, uniform, like, similar.

ant. uneven, lopsided, disproportionate, off, incommensurate.

proportions *n.* size, dimensions, measurements, measure, amplitude, magnitude, expanse, scope, volume, capacity, range.

proposal *n.* offer, proposition, bid, overture, presentation, resolution, motion, suggestion, plan, program, request, theory, theorem, thesis, hypothesis, construct, trial balloon.

propose *v.* **1** offer, present, proffer, tender, intend, aim, move, suggest, purpose, request, propound, broach, contemplate, theorize, submit, resolve, bid. **2** nominate, name, indicate, specify, invite, designate, dub, authorize, choose, select.

proposition *n.* **1** scheme, proposal, plan, program, bill, bid, motion. **2** theory, thesis, offer, hypothesis, idea, notion, suggestion, postulate, resolution, axiom, construct.

propound *v.* propose, present, suggest, broach, introduce, theorize, submit,

ask, set forth, offer, pose, contend, postulate.

proprietor *n.* OWNER.

propriety *n.* decorum, politeness, politesse, respectability, decency, modesty, conventionality, manners, rectitude, uprightness, diplomacy, tact, punctilio, savoir faire.

ant. misconduct, misbehavior, rudeness, impropriety, *faux pas.*

propulsion *n.* momentum, drive, push, shove, projection, impulse, force, thrust, pressure, ram, impetus, motivation, catalysis.

prosaic *adj.* unimaginative, commonplace, dull, ordinary, humdrum, prosy, everyday, pedestrian, uninteresting, tame, tedious, trite, platitudinous, vapid.

ant. unusual, exciting, different, extraordinary, imaginative, provocative.

proscribe *v.* denounce, condemn, prohibit, interdict, outlaw, banish, ban, bar, exile, boycott, embargo, censure, exclude, forbid, excommunicate.

ant. approve, sanction, favor, advocate.

proscription *n.* PROHIBITION.

prosecute *v.* **1** persist, pursue, continue, wage, carry through, see through, follow through, stick with, persevere, attain, complete, finish, effect, effectuate. **2** engage in, practice, perform, handle, work at, administer, manage, transact. **3** sue, indict, try, arraign, charge, accuse, impeach, litigate, challenge, seek redress.

ant. **1** abandon, discontinue, leave off, withdraw.

proselyte *n.* CONVERT. —*v.* PROSELYTIZE.

proselytize *v.* convert, persuade, propagandize, brainwash, win over, proselyte, indoctrinate, inculcate, reorient.

prospect *n.* **1** expectation, probability, likelihood, chance, anticipation, promise, certainty, assurance, assumption, presumption. **2** view, panorama, outlook, scene, exposure, vista, aspect, perspective, angle, spectacle, scenery, landscape, setting.

prospective *adj.* anticipated, future, anticipatory, expected, presumed, coming, impending, approaching, forthcoming, destined, eventual, awaited, imminent.

prospects *n.* chances, opportunities, promise, odds, outlook, likelihood, possibilities, openings, future, expectations.

prospectus *n.* summary, outline, résumé, synopsis, blueprint, digest, draft, bulletin, recapitulation, abstract, précis, condensation, brief, syllabus, catalog.

prosper *v.* thrive, flourish, succeed, burgeon, bloom, gain, wax, fatten, advance, boom, get ahead, make it (*Slang*).
ant. fail, founder, decline, waste away.

prosperity *n.* wealth, success, good fortune, affluence, riches, ease, boom, plenty, well-being, luxury.
ant. depression, recession, hard times, failure, want, poverty.

prosperous *adj.* successful, wealthy, thriving, booming, flourishing, well-off, rich, prospering, affluent, moneyed, privileged, blooming, opulent, palmy.
ant. failing, declining, bankrupt, needy, indigent.

prostitute *n.* **1** whore, harlot, trollop, strumpet, call girl, slut, streetwalker, bawd, tart, hustler (*Slang*), hooker (*Slang*), quean, trull, hussy, camp follower, *poule.* **2** tool, pawn, cat's-paw, opportunist, hireling, gull, toad, instrument, mercenary. —*v.* **1** debase, besmirch, degrade, corrupt, pervert, contaminate, abuse, debauch, defile, disgrace, dishonor, taint, soil, sully, lower, humble, dirty, pollute. **2** whore, hustle (*Slang*), pimp, procure, pander.

prostrate *adj.* **1** prone, procumbent, flat, horizontal, reclining, supine. **2** depressed, down, low, exhausted, tired, overtired, weary, spent, fagged out, overpowered, fatigued, laid low, overcome, worn out. **3** defenseless, helpless, powerless, paralyzed, immobilized, crippled, incapacitated, disabled, vulnerable. —*v.* **1** bow, kneel, grovel, scrape, kowtow, genuflect, cringe, fawn, beg. **2** overcome, overpower, exhaust, weary, debilitate, cripple, weaken, fatigue, tire, depress, lay low, impair, sap, paralyze, immobilize, enervate.
ant. *adj.* **1** erect, standing. **2** energetic, peppy, energized, lively. *v.* **2** energize, strengthen, encourage, cure.

prostration *n.* exhaustion, debility, weakness, vulnerability, fatigue, impairment, weariness, illness, enervation, decrepitude, collapse, helplessness.
ant. strength, soundness, health, vigor, pep.

prosy *adj.* PROSAIC.

protagonist *n.* leader, hero, heroine, chief, head, doer, actor, champion, star, advocate, principal, pioneer, trailblazer, spokesman, spokeswoman, commander.

protean *adj.* changeable, versatile, polymorphous, polymorphic, multiform, metamorphic, kaleidoscopic, mercurial, variable, many-sided, volatile.
ant. unchangeable, invariable, constant, unvarying, uniform, fixed.

protect *v.* guard, shield, defend, screen, watch over, look after, champion, care for, safeguard, secure, shelter, fortify, bulwark, cover, harbor, chaperon.
ant. abandon, desert, forsake.

protection *n.* security, safeguard, defense, watch, shelter, safety, cover, shield, armor, preservation, conservation, care, custody, safekeeping, aegis.
ant. vulnerability, exposure, peril, destruction.

protective *adj.* guiding, tutelary, paternal, maternal, helpful, assisting, sheltering, insulating, tender, warm, loving.

protégé *n.* disciple, ward, student, pupil, follower, protégée.
ant. mentor, coach, manager, director.

pro tempore TEMPORARY.

protest *n.* objection, complaint, remonstrance, outcry, demonstration, expostulation, confrontation, protestation, revolt, mutiny, challenge, dissidence, agitation, uproar, strike. —*v.* object, remonstrate, demonstrate, expostulate, complain, disapprove, dissent, oppose, contend, strike, picket, mutiny.

protestation *n.* **1** disputation, controversy, dispute, opposition, demurral, objection, outcry, protest, remonstrance, complaint, dissent, polemics, argumentation. **2** PROTEST.
ant. 1 agreement, accord, settlement, capitulation.

protocol *n.* **1** draft, compact, charter, pledge, agreement, pact, covenant. **2** etiquette, propriety, decorum, politesse, manners, customs, good form, conventions, usages, amenities, formalities, civilities, courtesies, rites, correctness, savoir faire.

prototype *n.* model, original, archetype, first, standard, norm, pattern, exemplar, example, paradigm, precedent, ideal, sample, ancestor, absolute.
ant. copy, imitation, rerun, facsimile, reproduction.

protract *v.* prolong, extend, draw out, lengthen, delay, continue, perpetuate, drag out, attenuate, stretch out.
ant. shorten, abbreviate, condense, cut.

protracted *adj.* extended, overextended, prolonged, lengthy, drawnout, never-ending, unending, diffuse, rambling, long-winded, interminable, extensive.
ant. brief, short, limited, concise, abbreviated.

protrude *v.* push out, stick out, project,

shoot out, swell, beetle, jut, overhang, belly, bulge, obtrude.

protrusion *n.* PROJECTION.

protuberance *n.* swelling, bump, knob, node, nodule, prominence, projection, jut, bulge, belly, convexity, hill, lump, growth, ridge, process, excrescence, outgrowth.
ant. hollow, concavity, hole, dimple.

proud *adj.* **1** honored, gratified, pleased, delighted, prideful, appreciative, glad, satisfied, self-respecting. **2** arrogant, overbearing, immodest, high-handed, conceited, smug, egotistical, haughty, disdainful, condescending, patronizing, supercilious, top-lofty, overweening, uppity, high-and-mighty. **3** gratifying, rewarding, pleasing, satisfying, exalting, ennobling, enriching, memorable.
ant. 1 ashamed, sorry, regretful, humiliated, abashed. **2** modest, humble, deferential, self-effacing. **3** humiliating, painful, regrettable, humbling.

prove *v.* **1** demonstrate, confirm, substantiate, validate, verify, corroborate, authenticate, bear out, attest to, uphold, vindicate. **2** test, try, analyze, check, probe, assay, investigate, research.
ant. 1 refute, controvert, disprove, invalidate, contradict.

proven *adj.* tested, tried, confirmed, verified, proved, certified, checked, authentic, established, factual, correct, empirical, experiential.
ant. untried, unfounded, speculative, hypothetical, theoretical, conjectural, alleged.

provenance *n.* SOURCE.
provender *n.* PROVISIONS.
provenience *n.* SOURCE.

proverb *n.* adage, saying, apothegm, aphorism, byword, truism, dictum, maxim, axiom, saw, bromide, example, legend, commonplace, rule.

proverbial *adj.* typical, common, well-known, familiar, commonplace, legendary, recognized, stock, trite, time-honored, conventional, accepted, customary, traditional, established.

ant. new, fresh, original, unusual, unfamiliar.

provide *v.* **1** supply, furnish, procure, get, contribute, offer, cater, submit, stock, bestow. **2** produce, render, afford, yield, give, engender, bring, impart, lend, add.

provide for 1 prepare for, plan for, anticipate, forearm, insure, store. **2** look after, take care of, support, sustain, tend to, minister to, nurture, nourish, maintain, keep.

providence *n.* forethought, foresight, preparation, prearrangement, provision, anticipation, prudence, precaution, farsightedness, discretion.

ant. imprudence, carelessness, shortsightedness.

provident *adj.* **1** prudent, cautious, farsighted, precautionary, prepared, circumspect, heedful, forearmed, vigilant, shrewd. **2** thrifty, frugal, parsimonious, economical, sparing, saving, abstemious, self-denying.

ant. **1** reckless, heedless, shiftless, devil-may-care. **2** wasteful, spendthrift, prodigal, self-indulgent.

providential *adj.* heavenly, divine, inspired, felicitous, lucky, happy, opportune, timely, welcome, heaven-sent, miraculous, unexpected, glorious, wonderful, serendipitous.

ant. accursed, unlucky, dreadful, disastrous.

province *n.* **1** territory, region, borough, precinct, area, neighborhood, section, subdivision, jurisdiction, department, dominion, county, colony, community, dependency. **2** sphere, orbit, domain, responsibility, concern, compass, arena, ambit, extent, limits, scope, area, authority.

provinces *n.* hinterland, backwoods, boondocks, sticks, country, backwater, outback.

ant. metropolis, oligopolis.

provincial *adj.* **1** rustic, rural, outlying, bucolic, countrified, unspoiled, exur-

ban, out-of-the-way, agrarian, backwoods. **2** narrow, parochial, insular, naive, insulated, unworldly, unsophisticated, uninformed, backward, narrow-minded, hidebound, intolerant, small-town, square (*Slang*).

ant. **1** urban, metropolitan, central. **2** worldly, urbane, open-minded, broad-minded, tolerant, sophisticated, hip (*Slang*).

provision *n.* **1** prearrangement, arrangement, groundwork, spadework, preparation, readiness, precaution, procurement, accommodation. **2** proviso, requirement, stipulation, condition, if, qualification, reservation, prerequisite, restriction, exception, obligation, promise.

provisional *adj.* temporary, provisory, conditional, limited, *pro tem, ad hoc,* improvised, impermanent, makeshift, transitional, tentative, stopgap.

ant. permanent, perpetual, entrenched, well-established, unalterable.

provisions *n.* food, provender, victuals, supplies, purveyance, necessaries, essentials, staples, sustenance, nourishment, edibles, groceries, rations, foodstuffs.

proviso *n.* PROVISION.

provisory *adj.* PROVISIONAL.

provocateur *n.* AGITATOR.

provocation *n.* **1** instigation, incitement, excitation, challenge, motivation, irritation, vexation, exasperation, perturbation. **2** stimulus, impulse, taunt, dare, challenge, slur, slap, prick, outrage, grievance, affront, injury, insult, atrocity, cruelty, red flag, last straw.

provocative *adj.* stimulating, exciting, inspiring, disturbing, suggestive, moving, interesting, challenging, tantalizing, shocking, intriguing, irritating, annoying, outrageous.

ant. bland, dull, meaningless, boring, soothing.

provoke *v.* **1** irritate, vex, annoy, nettle, rile, anger, aggravate, perturb, exasperate, affront, pique, upset, offend, incense, enrage, infuriate. **2** cause, arouse, stir up, stimulate, incite, instigate, precipitate, result in, lead to, occasion, produce, generate, impel. **ant. 1** calm, mollify, propitiate, soothe, please. **2** deaden, put down, quell, stop.

provoking *adj.* VEXATIOUS.

prow *n.* nose, stem, bow, beak, front, fore, figurehead, bowsprit, boom. **ant.** tail, fin, aft, rear.

prowess *n.* strength, skill, expertise, expertness, ability, know-how, forte, capability, power, puissance, competence, mastery, achievement, preeminence, command, muscle. **ant.** weakness, inadequacy, feebleness, incompetence.

prowl *v.* stalk, hunt, sneak, steal, range, roam, slink, pursue, prey on, tiptoe, scavenge, plunder.

proximal *adj.* NEAR.

proximate *adj.* NEAR.

proximity *n.* closeness, nearness, propinquity, adjacency, contiguity, apposition, approximation, affinity, compatibility, kinship, similarity, correspondence. **ant.** distance, remoteness, difference, gap.

proxy *n.* deputy, agent, alternate, proctor, substitute, surrogate, representative, second, delegate, aide, lieutenant, steward, emissary.

prude *n.* prig, puritan, touch-me-not, old maid. **ant.** wanton, libertine, swinger (*Slang*).

prudence *n.* **1** caution, care, discretion, thought, judgment, mindfulness, heed, heedfulness, foresight, forethought, providence, judiciousness, circumspection, common sense, mother wit. **2** economy, thrift, frugality, thriftiness, self-discipline, self-denial, parsimony, provision, moderation, abstinence. **ant. 1** indiscretion, mindlessness, folly, profligacy. **2** wastefulness, prodigality, improvidence, openhandedness, self-indulgence.

prudent *adj.* **1** cautious, careful, discreet, politic, circumspect, judicious, mindful, sensible, chary, shrewd, vigilant, wary, calculating, levelheaded, cool. **2** frugal, thrifty, economical, parsimonious, abstinent, moderate, temperate, self-denying, sparing, provident, penurious, stingy. **ant. 1** careless, reckless, foolish, indiscreet, unwary. **2** prodigal, wasteful, spendthrift, liberal, openhanded, self-indulgent.

prudish *adj.* priggish, prissy, puritanical, touch-me-not, strait-laced, prim, standoffish, sanctimonious, old-maidish, Victorian, self-righteous, inhibited, repressed, over-modest, punctilious. **ant.** natural, free, uninhibited, fast, wanton, promiscuous.

prurient *adj.* lewd, salacious, lustful, concupiscent, sensual, smutty, indecent, obscene, lascivious, lecherous, unwholesome, pornographic, voyeuristic.

pry[1] *v.* peer, snoop, peep, peek, stare, gawk, ferret, nose, meddle, intrude, interfere, butt in.

pry[2] *v.* raise, lift, elevate, open, move, hoist, prize, force, jimmy, lever. —*n.* LEVER. **ant.** shut, close, seal, fasten, lock.

pseudo *adj.* FALSE.

pseudonym *n.* pen name, alias, *nom de plume*, professional name, assumed name, sobriquet, anonym.

psyche *n.* soul, spirit, self, I, mind, ego, superego, id, consciousness, personality, selfhood, self-awareness, life force.

psychic *adj.* clairvoyant, extrasensory, precognitive, prescient, telepathic, mediumistic, telekinetic, psychokinetic, parapsychological, delphic, oracular.

psychological *adj.* psychic, mental, subjective, cognitive, conscious, subconscious, unconscious, innermost, emotional.

psychopathic *adj.* PSYCHOTIC.

psychotic *adj.* mentally ill, emotionally disturbed, psychopathic, certifiable, *non compos mentis*, insane, deranged, demented, unbalanced.
ant. sane, *compos mentis*.

psych out *Slang* 1 DEMORALIZE. 2 OUTWIT. 3 UNDERSTAND.

pub *n. Brit.* TAVERN.

public *adj.* 1 general, social, societal, human, national, popular, widespread, universal, comprehensive, civic, communal, group, common. 2 free, unrestricted, open, community, neighborhood, municipal. 3 publicized, well-known, patent, obvious, ventilated, aired, open, divulged, avowed, acknowledged, exposed, unconcealed. —*n.* society, people, populace, country, electorate, population, citizenry, community, commonality, mankind, humanity, masses, rank and file, grass roots.
ant. *adj.* 1 individual, personal, private. 2 sectarian, parochial, private, restricted. 3 covert, secret, concealed, hidden, closet, covered-up.

publication *n.* 1 printing, airing, appearance, announcement, promulgation, dissemination, circulation, publicizing, publicity, broadcasting, reporting, presentation, issuance. 2 book, journal, newspaper, magazine, periodical, serial, fascicle, edition, issue.

public house *Brit.* TAVERN.

publicity *n.* information, news, promotion, propaganda, dissemination, promulgation, ballyhoo, public relations, press-agentry, buildup, puffery, hype (*Slang*).

publicize *v.* air, advertise, circulate, promote, disseminate, promulgate, spread, broadcast, ballyhoo, propagandize, noise about, bruit about, build up, spotlight, puff (*Slang*), plug (*Slang*).
ant. conceal, hide, cover up, hush up.

public-spirited *adj.* PHILANTHROPIC.

publish *v.* reveal, announce, print, air, broadcast, publicize, promote, disseminate, promulgate, spread, circulate.
ant. censor, cover up, conceal, hide, hush up.

puck *n.* SPRITE.

pucker *v.* wrinkle, pleat, gather, fold, purse, compress, contract, crinkle, furrow, crumple, corrugate. —*n.* crease, wrinkle, pleat, fold, furrow, crinkle, contraction, pinch, ridge, accordion pleat, shirring, gathering.
ant. *v.* smooth out, flatten, straighten, even, lie flat.

puckish *adj.* mischievous, playful, sportive, coy, waggish, droll, arch, impish, prankish, gamesome.
ant. solemn, earnest, serious, grave.

puddle *n.* pool, pond, mudhole, wallow.

pudgy *adj.* plump, roly-poly, chunky, fat, fleshy, flabby, overweight, podgy, squat, stocky, dumpy, chubby, paunchy, hefty, flaccid, tubby, pursy, rotund, zaftig (*Slang*).
ant. skinny, bony, lanky, gangling, underweight, raw-boned, angular.

puerile *adj.* childish, immature, silly, callow, sophomoric, juvenile, babyish, infantile, jejune, irresponsible, inane, thoughtless, mindless, simple-minded, injudicious, naive.
ant. mature, adult, sensible, responsible, thoughtful, experienced.

puff *n.* 1 gust, breath, blow, exhalation, waft, draft, whiff, emanation, cloud, plume, vapor. 2 smoke, draw, pull, drag (*Slang*). —*v.* 1 blow, gust, waft, emanate. 2 pant, huff, wheeze, gasp. 3 swell, dilate, distend, inflate, expand, balloon, bloat, belly, stretch, increase, enlarge, blow up.
ant. *v.* 3 deflate, decrease, flatten, puncture.

puffery *n.* PRAISE.

puffy *adj.* swollen, distended, bloated, bulgy, enlarged, inflated, billowy, tumid, tumescent, expanded, bulbous, edematous, puffed up.

pugilist *n.* FIGHTER.

pugnacious *adj.* quarrelsome, combative, contentious, bellicose, belligerent, aggressive, hostile, hot-tempered, hot-headed, disputatious, argumentative, fractious, choleric, scrappy, feisty.

ant. meek, friendly, conciliatory, peaceable, good-natured, forbearing.

puissant *adj.* POWERFUL.

puke *v., n.* VOMIT.

pukka *adj.* GENUINE.

pulchritude *n.* BEAUTY.

pule *v.* cry, whimper, whine, snivel, complain, mewl, wail, weep, fret, fuss, blubber.

pull *v.* **1** drag, tug, tow, haul, lug, jerk, twitch, yank, attract, lure, magnetize. **2** remove, take out, extract, draw out, yank, dislocate, pluck out, withdraw, snatch, uproot, wrest, root out, dig out, extirpate. —*n.* **1** tug, yank, tow, twitch, jerk, pluck, removal, dislocation, snatch, wrench, attraction, gravitation. **2** handle, bar, knob, crank, handlebar, grip, lug, trigger. **3** effort, exertion, haul, endeavor, struggle, grind, stretch, push, drudgery, industry, strain, travail, sweat. **4** influence, power, weight, leverage, drag (*Slang*), clout (*Slang*).

ant. *v.* **1** push, shove, thrust. **2** insert, introduce, put in.

pull apart fragment, destroy, tear, tear asunder, rend, dismember, disjoint, break, split, cleave, disunite, rive, separate, sever, detach, demolish, mangle, mutilate.

ant. mend, unite, attach, bond.

pullback *n.* PULLOUT.

pull for root for, back, boost, strive for, cheer on, support, stand behind, encourage.

ant. undermine, sabotage, discourage.

pullout *n.* withdrawal, retreat, pullback, removal, takeoff, departure, exit, relocation, exodus, flight, evacuation, recall.

pull through survive, recover, heal, outlive, come through, rally, revive, convalesce, come around, weather, endure, overcome, suffer, bear.

ant. succumb, go under, worsen, capitulate.

pulp *n.* mash, flesh, squash, pith, mush, pap, crush, paste, sponge, dough, batter, semiliquid, semisolid.

pulpit *n.* **1** stand, desk, platform, rostrum, lectern, stump, soapbox. **2** clergy, ministry, priesthood, preaching, sermonizing, proselytizing, clergymen, the cloth, the church, religion, ecclesiastics, pastorate.

pulpy *adj.* fleshy, mushy, squashy, spongy, doughy, pasty, pithy, semiliquid, semisolid, semifluid, mashed, macerated, viscous, gelatinous, thick, grumous.

pulsate *v.* throb, beat, pulse, vibrate, quiver, tick, pound, flutter, drum, palpitate, shake, quaver, tremble, reverberate, oscillate, thrum.

pulsation *n.* PULSE.

pulse *n.* **1** pulsation, throbbing, beat, beating, reverberation, pounding, drumming, thrumming, ticking, vibration. **2** mood, feeling, sense, reaction, temper, disposition, tenor, humor, drift, spirit, inclination, preference, will, frame of mind, disposition, opinion, wish. —*v.* PULSATE.

pulverize *v.* crush, grind, comminute, demolish, annihilate, atomize, pound, granulate, mince, shatter, destroy, break down, trample, exterminate, triturate, extirpate, vanquish, undo, suppress.

pummel *v.* POMMEL.

pump *v.* interrogate, question, query, cross-examine, interpellate, probe, pry, grill, worm out, pick the brains of (*Slang*).

punch *v.* **1** strike, hit, box, wallop, pommel, cuff, swing at, clip, clout, slam (*Slang*), whack, thwack, smash, smack, sock (*Slang*), swat. **2** prod, poke, push, goad, shove, jostle. —*n.* **1** wallop, clout, smash, smack, swing, swat, clip, chop, wham (*Slang*), sock (*Slang*), slam (*Slang*), whack, thwack. **2** nudge, shove, thrust, prod, poke, push, jostle. **3** vitality, force, impact, effectiveness, zip, energy, vim, verve, vigor, zing, snap, potency, wallop (*Slang*), kick (*Slang*), pizzazz (*Slang*).

punch-drunk *adj.* PUNCHY.

puncheon *n.* TIMBER.

punchinello *n.* BUFFOON.

punchy *adj.* **1** punch-drunk, dazed, confused, groggy, reeling, staggering, stupefied, bewildered, disoriented, befuddled, unsteady. **2** lively, snappy, zippy, energetic, vital, vigorous, forceful, aggressive, effective, dynamic, spirited, potent, strong, zestful.

ant. 1 alert, on one's toes, clearheaded, together (*Slang*). **2** tame, weak, sluggish, mild, ineffectual, lax, tepid.

punctilio *n.* nicety, fine point, formality, particular, rule, standard, convention, nuance, distinction, subtlety, ritual, observance.

punctilious *adj.* scrupulous, meticulous, exact, precise, conventional, proper, fussy, ceremonious, formal, ritualistic, rigorous, finicky, starchy, exacting, demanding, overnice.

ant. casual, careless, negligent, slipshod.

punctual *adj.* prompt, on time, precise, on the dot, dependable, reliable, punctilious, seasonable, regular, timely.

ant. late, tardy, behindhand, undependable, irregular.

punctuate *v.* emphasize, stress, underline, italicize, accent, underscore, point up, heighten, mark, harp on, dwell on, accentuate.

ant. understate, minimize, make light of, de-emphasize.

puncture *v.* **1** pierce, prick, perforate, knife, stab, open, lance, punch, bite, sting, bore, drill, spike, spear, penetrate. **2** deflate, disabuse, disenchant, discourage, dishearten, flatten, humble, disillusion, take down a peg. —*n.* hole, perforation, opening, leak, damage, pit, prick, cut, slit, break, nick, space.

pundit *n.* expert, sage, guru, thinker,

guide, mentor, savant, authority, philosopher, master, wizard, mastermind, oracle, prophet, forecaster.

ant. know-nothing, ignoramus, fool.

pungent *adj.* **1** aromatic, tangy, spicy, acrid, seasoned, peppery, sharp, piquant, appetizing. **2** poignant, piercing, penetrating, pointed, stimulating, moving, irritating, affecting, painful, distressing, provocative, stirring. **3** keen, cutting, caustic, telling, pointed, barbed, sharp, incisive, acidulous, biting, sarcastic, stinging, on the mark.

ant. 1 bland, odorless, tasteless, flavorless. **2** dull, pointless, uninteresting, soothing. **3** bland, vapid, empty.

punish *v.* **1** penalize, castigate, condemn, sentence, chasten, correct, discipline, confine, fine, revenge, retaliate. **2** injure, hurt, harm, abuse, maltreat, torture, misuse, violate, oppress, batter, brutalize, bruise, victimize, torment.

punishing *adj.* taxing, demanding, grueling, exhausting, oppressive, tormenting, arduous, trying, burdensome, onerous, painful, wearisome, wearing, enervating, fatiguing.

ant. light, relaxing, simple, invigorating.

punishment *n.* **1** penalty, retribution, pain, suffering, affliction, loss, chastening, tax, fine, penance, damages, humiliation, consequences, confinement, disgrace. **2** chastisement, castigation, imprisonment, penalization, condemnation, discipline, correction, infliction, chastening, retaliation, vengeance, sentencing. **3** injury, damage, impairment, abuse, hurt, harm, misuse, oppression, victimization, torture, pain, maltreatment, misfortune, beating, mutilation, ruin.

punk *n.* *Slang* **1** NONSENSE. **2** HOODLUM.

puny *adj.* small, slight, insignificant, picayune, inferior, tiny, feeble, petty, weak, substandard, undersized, trivial, trifling, piddling, niggling, anemic.

ant. large, sizable, considerable, important, weighty, significant.

pupil *n.* student, schoolboy, schoolgirl, schoolmate, learner, scholar, undergraduate, disciple, follower, matriculant, apprentice, charge, trainee. **ant.** teacher, instructor, tutor, master.

puppet *n.* dummy, marionette, figurehead, front, tool, mouthpiece, pawn, cat's-paw, instrument, slave, servant, agent, medium.

ant. manipulator, manager, boss, power, *éminence grise*.

purchase *v.* buy, pay for, invest in, acquire, obtain, get, gain, win, collect, procure, attain, come by, secure, ransom, redeem, sacrifice. —*n.* buy, investment, acquirement, acquisition, procurement, possession, property, asset, gain, advantage, foothold.

ant. *v.* sell, divest, offer, supply.

pure *adj.* **1** unadulterated, unpolluted, unmixed, unmodified, unalloyed, pristine, clear, clean, untainted, homogeneous, straight, flawless, unimpaired, spotless. **2** righteous, highminded, faultless, perfect, proper, wholesome, moral, sincere, honest, unimpeachable, upright, exemplary, irreproachable, impeccable. **3** chaste, innocent, simple, virtuous, virginal, unsullied, undefiled, lily-white, uncorrupted, unspoiled, unworldly, maidenly. **4** theoretical, speculative, abstract, hypothetical, metaphysical, ideal, visionary, fundamental, mathematical.

ant. 1 adulterated, impaired, mixed, muddy, spoiled. **2** questionable, faulty, base, low, corrupt. **3** debauched, wicked, corrupted, sinful. **4** applied, practical, functional.

pureness *n.* PURITY.

purgation *n.* CATHARSIS.

purge *v.* **1** eliminate, remove, get rid of, do away with, wipe out, kill, exterminate, eradicate, annihilate, liqui-

date, root out, suppress, crush, silence, banish, exile, extirpate. **2** physic, cleanse, catheterize. **3** PURIFY. —*n.* **1** witch hunt, reign of terror, extermination, annihilation, elimination, suppression, crushing, murder, slaughter, imprisonment, exile, banishment, liquidation, removal, expulsion. **2** physic, cathartic, laxative, purgative, enema, carminative, emetic, aperient.

purification *n.* CATHARSIS.

purify *v.* **1** clean, cleanse, improve, purge, strain, filter, sterilize, fumigate, aerate, sift, wash, sublimate, scour, scrub, boil, pasteurize. **2** exalt, ennoble, sublimate, uplift, hallow, better, edify, sanctify, absolve.

ant. 1 pollute, contaminate, soil. **2** debase, degrade, defile, debauch.

purism *n.* strictness, orthodoxy, rigor, precision, classicism, formalism, rigidity, inflexibility, purity, correctness, punctiliousness, exactitude. **ant.** compromise, eclecticism, adaptability, progressivism, mélange.

puritan *n.* PRUDE.

puritanical *adj.* strict, righteous, self-righteous, rigid, narrow, austere, forbidding, disapproving, sanctimonious, dogmatic, strait-laced, blue-nosed, witch-hunting, holier-than-thou.

ant. pleasure-loving, self-indulgent, sybaritic, lenient, permissive, broadminded.

purity *n.* pureness, cleanliness, wholesomeness, innocence, spotlessness, virtue, homogeneity, asepsis, blamelessness, incorruptibility, integrity, principle, idealism.

ant. contamination, impairment, admixture, impurity, baseness.

purl *v.* WHIRL.

purlieu *n.* OUTSKIRTS.

purloin *v.* steal, filch, pilfer, rob, thieve, lift, misappropriate, take, snatch, grab, heist (*Slang*), swipe (*Slang*), pinch (*Slang*), rip off (*Slang*).

purple *n.* EMINENCE. —*adj.* FANCY.

purport v. **1** signify, imply, mean, convey, express, say, indicate, denote, intimate, suggest, betoken, bespeak, point to, promise, signalize, foretoken. **2** pretend, profess, claim, allege, pose as, feign, represent, misrepresent. —n. MEANING.

purportedly adj. SUPPOSEDLY.

purpose n. **1** plan, design, aim, ambition, desire, wish, intention, desideratum, scheme, goal, target, objective, object, end, motive, rationale. **2** resolve, determination, drive, will, grit, spine, diligence, single-mindedness, firmness, tenacity, persistence, steadfastness, resolution, willpower, stick-to-itiveness. —v. intend, plan, hope, aim, want, resolve, mean, aspire, work, propose.
ant. n. **2** irresolution, purposelessness, weakness, uncertainty, vacillation.

purposeful adj. intentional, intended, ambitious, energetic, determined, goal-directed, designed, designing, single-minded, tenacious, aggressive. **ant.** random, unfocused, accidental, unambitious, unintentional, irresolute.

purposeless adj. aimless, pointless, drifting, haphazard, random, desultory, uncalculated, uncalculating, unmotivated, accidental, fortuitous, irresolute, indecisive, irrational, uncalled-for. **ant.** purposeful, resolute, planned, intentional.

purse n. **1** pouch, bag, handbag, pocketbook, sack, carryall, reticule, tote, wallet. **2** prize, money, cash, award, endowment, resources, means, wherewithal, treasury, subsidy, scholarship, stake, ante, proceeds, winnings, receipts, profit, take (Slang).

pursue v. **1** chase, follow, trail, tail, stalk, shadow, hunt, track, go after, dog, run after. **2** long for, yearn, aspire, crave, desire, hanker for, aim, work toward, purpose. **3** proceed, advance, progress, move forward, forge ahead, cultivate, maintain, perpetuate, bring about, forward. **4** work at, ply, practice, conduct, carry on, labor at, participate in, engage in, perform, operate. **5** harass, hound, harry, hunt down, besiege, beset, plague, threaten, badger, pester, exhaust, haunt, bug (Slang).

pursuit n. **1** chase, hunt, quest, aspiration, ambition, purpose, procedure, execution, undertaking, venture, performance, progress, advancement, perpetuation, achievement, **2** vocation, profession, calling, practice, career, occupation, preoccupation, hobby, business, job, employment, project, plan, scheme, specialty.

pursy adj. PUDGY.

purulent adj. PUSSY.

purvey v. furnish, provide, provision, cater, sell, offer, supply, trade in, equip, outfit, fit out, deal in, retail.

purveyance n. PROVISIONS.

purview n. **1** scope, extent, range, realm, dominion, domain, orbit, ken, reach, spectrum, area, empire, territory, field, arena. **2** overview, understanding, outlook, perspective, experience, standpoint, attitude, point of view, viewpoint, slant, angle.

pus n. suppuration, discharge, purulence, festering.

push v. **1** shove, elbow, jostle, propel, press, drive, nudge, force, thrust, heave, poke, ram, butt, prod, jam, squeeze. **2** promote, advocate, tout, publicize, recommend, boost, advertise, eulogize, extol, glorify, puff, plug (Slang). —n. **1** thrust, jolt, shove, pressure, propulsion, impulse, impulsion, nudge, prod, poke, punch, start, prompting. **2** energy, drive, ambition, determination, dynamism, snap, momentum, aggressiveness, purposefulness, vitality, vigor, get-up-and-go.

pushing adj. **1** enterprising, energetic, dynamic, aggressive, vigorous, ambitious, determined, driving, snappy, hard-hitting, purposeful, hardworking, industrious, on the go, on the make, persevering, diligent, spirited. **2** pushy, impertinent, self-assertive, opinionated, presumptuous, assertive, contentious, bossy, brash, bold, forward, bumptious, officious.

ant. 1 lazy, sluggish, inert, unambitious. **2** modest, deferential, self-effacing, humble, mousy.

pushover *n. Slang* **1** child's play, snap, breeze, setup, walkaway, walkover, cinch (*Slang*), duck soup (*Slang*), no sweat (*Slang*). **2** dupe, gull, foil, easy mark, pigeon, sitting duck, sap (*Slang*), sucker (*Slang*), poor fish (*Slang*), chump.

pushy *adj.* PUSHING.

pusillanimous *adj.* weak-willed, cowardly, craven, spineless, timorous, timid, lily-livered, ignoble, fearful, faint-hearted, apprehensive, afraid, yellow, spiritless, scared.

ant. courageous, bold, heroic, reckless, fearless.

puss *n. Slang* FACE.

pussy *adj. full of pus:* suppurating, abscessed, festering, purulent, infected, inflamed, diseased, pustulous, pustular, suppurative.

put *v.* **1** place, lay, set, situate, bring, establish, set up, bring about, deposit, plant, post, install, lodge, locate, station. **2** apply, impose, press, bring to bear, use, employ, resort to, superimpose, add, levy, affix, saddle with, inflict, administer.

ant. 1, 2 remove, take, dislodge.

putative *adj.* REPUTED.

put by SALT AWAY.

put-down *n. Slang* slur, sneer, insult, prick, cut, snub, dig, slap, rebuff, knock, taunt, barb, humiliation, disparagement, derogation, derision, sarcasm.

ant. build-up, boost, praise, flattery, plug (*Slang*).

put down 1 repress, crush, quell, quash, silence, subdue, break, destroy, overcome, overpower, overwhelm, demolish, shatter, wreck, stamp out, suppress. **2** degrade, demote, humble, humiliate, deflate,

shame, disgrace, discountenance, discomfit, reduce, derogate, disparage, chasten, sneer.

ant. 1 encourage, abet, create, build. **2** build up, inflate, compliment, flatter, upgrade.

put off 1 delay, postpone, shelve, table, defer, protract, pigeonhole, suspend, procrastinate, adjourn, dawdle, temporize, dally, remand, stall. **2** disconcert, discomfit, abash, discountenance, confuse, discompose, unsettle, nonplus, rattle, bemuse, disorient, muddle, bewilder, perplex, perturb, discombobulate.

ant. 1 dispose of, attend to, settle, act on, address. **2** charm, win over, disarm, attract.

put-on *n. Slang* HOAX.

put on 1 don, wear, clothe, cover, dress, attire, garb, accouter, array, add. **2** assume, pretend, simulate, counterfeit, play-act, sham, make believe, affect, fake, feign, imitate, role-play. **3** *Slang* fool, deceive, dupe, tease, hoax, gull, josh, spoof, joke, kid (*Slang*), take in (*Slang*).

ant. 1 take off, doff, undress, divest.

put out 1 extinguish, smother, quench, stifle, douse, snuff. **2** expel, eject, evict, throw out, dispossess, dislodge, oust, remove. **3** inconvenience, discommode, disconcert, discompose, discountenance, irritate, embarrass, bother, trouble, vex, displease, disgruntle, discomfit, provoke, upset, exasperate, irk, disquiet. **4** *Slang use extra effort:* sweat, strain, slave, strive, drive oneself, push oneself, go all-out, knock oneself out (*Slang*), pull out all the stops (*Slang*).

ant. 1 light, kindle, ignite, turn on. **2** install, lodge, seat. **4** goof off (*Slang*), take it easy, hold back.

putrefy *v.* decay, rot, fester, putresce, spoil, decompose, taint, pollute, gangrene, infect, molder, deteriorate.

putrid *adj.* rotting, rotten, rancid, putrescent, putrefactive, decaying, decayed, spoiled, moldering, moldy, rank, fetid, contaminated, decomposed, stinking, reeking.

ant. fresh, healthy, pure, wholesome.

putsch *n.* REBELLION.

putter *v.* tinker, potter, fool around, dawdle, waste time, fritter, fiddle around, piddle, poke, dillydally.

put up 1 erect, build, establish, construct, fabricate, raise. **2** accommodate, house, board, lodge, entertain, take in, shelter, quarter. **3** incite, egg on, instigate, goad, bring about, encourage, back, support, favor.

ant. 1 tear down, raze, level, demolish. **2** turn away, turn out, put out. **3** discourage, retard, resist, oppose.

put-upon *adj.* beset, harried, harassed, plagued, bedeviled, imposed on, put out, beleaguered, abused, victimized, exploited, vexed, burdened, saddled, besieged, bugged (*Slang*).

put up with tolerate, endure, abide, stand, stand for, submit to, bear, brook, suffer, stomach, swallow, take, withstand, permit, allow.

puzzle *v.* confuse, confound, perplex, mystify, baffle, bewilder, nonplus, bemuse, stump, stick, beat, elude, frustrate, bedevil. —*n.* enigma, problem, maze, puzzler, poser, stopper, mystery, riddle, paradox, quandary, labyrinth.

puzzlement *n.* mystification, obfuscation, bafflement, bewilderment, frustration, perplexity, disorientation, ambiguity, uncertainty, complexity, quandary, muddle, difficulty.

ant. clarification, solution, certainty, simplicity.

puzzling *adj.* CONFUSING.

pygmy *adj.* diminutive, dwarfish, dwarf, short, undersized, stunted, runty, tiny, wee, miniature, Lilliputian, pocket-sized, toy, small, midget, minuscule. —*n.* **1** nonentity, nobody, mediocrity, pipsqueak, cipher, lightweight, small fry, zero. **2** midget, dwarf, runt, shrimp, miniature, peewee, bantam, toy.

ant. *adj.* giant, oversize, huge, mammoth, enormous, gigantic. *n.* **1** somebody, personage, giant, heavyweight, big wheel (*Slang*). **2** giant, elephant, mountain, leviathan.

pyramid *v.* escalate, increase, rise, spiral, soar, climb, go up, accrue, pile up, accumulate, build up, amass, appreciate, gain, multiply.

ant. decrease, dwindle, diminish, fall, plunge, plummet.

Q

quack[1] *v.* gaggle, gabble, clack, cackle, cluck.

quack[2] *n.* charlatan, fraud, fake, humbug, impostor, bluffer, dissembler, pretender, cheat, mountebank, empiric, fourflusher (*Slang*), con man (*Slang*).

quackery *n.* deceit, charlatanism, fakery, dissimulation, duplicity, fraudulence, make-believe, pretense, affectation, counterfeiting, sham, show.

ant. probity, integrity, sincerity, veracity, candor, honesty.

quaff *v.* guzzle, toss off, gulp, swig, ingurgitate, swill, imbibe, drink, swallow, down, sip, lap up.

quaggy *adj.* BOGGY.

quagmire *n.* **1** bog, swamp, morass, marsh, fen, slough, ooze, quicksand. **2** predicament, plight, jam, quandary, dilemma, fix, impasse, entanglement, imbroglio, pass, hole.

quail *v.* cower, recoil, blench, flinch,

shrink, wince, quake, give way, falter, hesitate, tremble, shake, droop, faint.

ant. defy, brave, confront, face up to, resist, withstand.

quaint *adj.* charming, old-fashioned, fanciful, old-world, picturesque, archaic, antiquated, antique, whimsical, droll, unusual, dainty.

ant. modern, new-fangled, up-to-date, current, everyday, novel.

quake *v.* shudder, shake, shiver, quaver, tremble, quiver, throb, pulsate, rock, waver, stagger, wobble, vibrate, cower, quail.

quaky *adj.* TREMULOUS.

qualification *n.* **1** competence, capability, suitability, eligibility, aptitude, adaptation, fitness. **2** requisite, desideratum, property, skill, talent, gift, ability. **3** restriction, caveat, condition, limitation, proviso, stipulation, reservation, exception, modification.

qualified *adj.* **1** competent, eligible, capable, able, adept, fit, adequate, fitted, equipped, efficient. **2** restricted, modified, limited, conditional, contingent, delimited, conditioned, circumscribed, bounded, confined.

ant. **1** deficient, unfit, inept, unable, unqualified, impotent. **2** unconditional, categorical, unqualified, unlimited, absolute, complete.

qualify *v.* **1** prepare, fit, ready, capacitate, empower, condition, equip, adapt, train. **2** limit, restrict, lessen, soften, moderate, temper, mitigate, restrain, modify. **3** describe, characterize, name, call, designate, label, define, delineate, signify, dub, distinguish.

ant. **1** disable, unfit, disqualify, incapacitate, invalidate. **2** intensify, reinforce, magnify, enlarge, aggravate.

quality *n.* **1** attribute, nature, characteristic, property, essence, feature, character, trait, flavor, constitution, quintessence. **2** excellence, distinction, stature, preeminence, grandeur, importance, caliber, standing, dig-

nity, worth, value. —*adj.* good, excellent, first-rate, superior, select, fine, estimable, exclusive, classy (*Slang*).

ant. *n.* **2** mediocrity, inferiority, indifference, poverty, triviality. *adj.* poor, shoddy, inferior, low-grade, second-rate, schlocky (*Slang*).

qualm *n.* pang, twinge, scruple, compunction, uneasiness, regret, misgiving, fear, apprehension, demur, remorse, uncertainty.

ant. confidence, security, invulnerability, comfort, easiness, firmness.

quandary *n.* predicament, dilemma, plight, perplexity, bewilderment, entanglement, fix, jam, impasse, uncertainty, difficulty, doubt, crisis, quagmire, hornet's nest.

ant. certainty, relief, ease, assurance, child's play, plain sailing.

quantitative *adj.* MEASURABLE.

quantity *n.* amount, number, measure, magnitude, size, volume, greatness, extent, mass, bulk, total, aggregate, sum, lump sum, store, lot.

quarrel *n.* dispute, misunderstanding, contention, altercation, falling-out, run-in, brawl, bickering, controversy, disagreement, feud, set-to, squabble, fuss, fracas, fray, argument, spat, rhubarb (*Slang*). —*v.* **1** dispute, contend, fight, fall out, disagree, differ, squabble, bicker, argue, wrangle, clash, brawl, spar. **2** cavil, find fault, disapprove, object, complain, pick, decry, carp, nitpick.

ant. *n.* agreement, accord, amity, unity, concord, sympathy. *v.* **1** agree, cooperate, concur, resolve, patch up, make up. **2** approve, support, uphold, concur, go along, back.

quarrelsome *adj.* combative, disputatious, contentious, argumentative, irritable, truculent, irascible, choleric, pugnacious, belligerent, aggressive, bellicose, fractious, fiery, hot-tempered, cross.

ant. peaceable, easygoing, friendly,

imperturbable, agreeable, accommodating.

quarry *n.* game, prey, victim, quest, prize, aim, objective, goal.

quarter *n.* **1** source, place, origin, spring, well, fount, mainspring, stock, root. **2** mercy, clemency, compassion, forbearance, ruth, leniency, benevolence, pity. —*v.* lodge, station, billet, accommodate, put up, house, locate, post, board, reside, abide.

ant. *n.* **2** cruelty, ruthlessness, barbarity, ferocity, brutality, harshness.

quarters *n.* lodgings, residence, dwelling, chambers, rooms, accommodations, apartment, flat, berth, abode, habitation, billets, barracks, domicile, shelter, home, pad (*Slang*), *pied-à-terre*.

quash *v.* **1** annul, void, nullify, set aside, overthrow, cancel, invalidate, abolish. **2** put down, suppress, subdue, quell, extinguish, quench, crush, repress, root out, stamp out, destroy, extirpate.

ant. **1** authorize, validate, sanction, sustain, reinforce. **2** abet, incite, arouse, instigate, encourage.

quasi *adj.* pseudo, would-be, manqué, nominal, self-styled, so-called, partial, imitation, epigonic, synthetic, counterfeit, sham, mock, bogus.

ant. genuine, authentic, bona fide, real, certified, legitimate.

quaver *v.* tremble, shake, quiver, vibrate, falter, hesitate, quake, trill, shudder, waver, shiver, oscillate, thrill, twitter. —*n.* trembling, shaking, tremor, quiver, shiver, quake, catch, break, sob, trill, shudder.

quay *n.* wharf, dock, pier, landing, levee, jetty, mole, bank.

quean *n.* PROSTITUTE.

queasy *adj.* **1** nauseated, sick, nauseous, squeamish, qualmish, seasick. **2** uneasy, troubled, uncomfortable, restless, fidgety, queer, edgy, ill at ease.

ant. **2** comfortable, untroubled, relaxed, content, easy.

queen *n.* first lady, doyenne, prima donna, empress, diva, belle, star, goddess, flower.

queer *adj.* **1** unusual, strange, odd, peculiar, weird, curious, singular, droll, fantastic, grotesque, peculiar, eldritch. **2** mysterious, puzzling, suspicious, suspect, funny, disquieting, eerie, uncanny, anomalous, weird, ominous, rum (*Brit. Slang*). **3** eccentric, unbalanced, deranged, peculiar, odd, touched, crack-brained, pixilated, daft, off, unconventional, idiosyncratic, quirky, spacey (*Slang*). —*v.* jeopardize, spoil, mess up, botch, compromise, harm, imperil, endanger, hurt, ruin.

ant. *adj.* **1** ordinary, common, usual, familiar, commonplace. **2** patent, plain, evident, obvious. **3** normal, composed, sane, self-possessed, conventional. *v.* clinch, secure, strengthen, assure, support.

queerness *n.* oddness, oddity, strangeness, freakishness, eccentricity, peculiarity, singularity, curiosity, unusualness, outlandishness, fantasy, rarity, anomaly, aberration, weirdness, grotesqueness.

ant. familiarity, normality, conformity, standardization, commonness, regularity.

quell *v.* suppress, extinguish, crush, quash, repress, overcome, overpower, put out, quench, subdue, stifle, smother, curb, put down, restrain.

ant. incite, arouse, instigate, foment, encourage, foster.

quench *v.* **1** extinguish, put out, suppress, repress, cool, quell, crush, quash. **2** slake, satisfy, allay, sate, appease, satiate, abate, refresh, slacken.

ant. **1** light, kindle, set, start, begin. **2** aggravate, whet, worsen, increase.

quenchless *adj.* INSATIABLE.

querulous *adj.* fretful, faultfinding, complaining, carping, captious, disparaging, critical, censorious, petulant, peevish, plaintive, irritable, discontented, whining, testy.

ant. easygoing, carefree, contented, complacent, pleased, cheerful.

query *v.* investigate, look into, probe, inquire into, scrutinize, examine, explore, survey, ask about, interrogate, cross-examine, quiz, inspect. —*n.* QUESTION.

quest *n.* search, pursuit, pilgrimage, exploration, expedition, seeking, hunt, investigation, examination, inquiry, enterprise, journey, adventure.

question *n.* **1** query, inquiry, interrogatory, poser, problem, examination, investigation, interrogation. **2** issue, topic, subject, theme, argument, debate, problem, thesis. **3** doubt, uncertainty, misgiving, dispute, controversy, contention, confusion, qualm. —*v.* **1** interrogate, inquire, query, catechize, interview, pump, examine, ask, sound out, interpellate. **2** doubt, dispute, challenge, mistrust, impugn, object, disbelieve, discredit.

ant. *n.* **1** answer, reply, response, rejoinder, result. **3** assurance, confidence, conviction, certainty, resolution. *v.* **1** answer, inform, reply, state, say. **2** agree, attest, affirm, confirm, avow.

questionable *adj.* **1** debatable, controversial, hypothetical, ambiguous, doubtful, unproven, undecided, provisional, controvertible, arguable, tentative, unsure, moot, iffy. **2** suspect, fishy, dubious, equivocal, queer, disreputable, suspicious, shady, improper, unseemly.

ant. **1** indubitable, obvious, definite, proven, assured. **2** proper, legitimate, seemly, unimpeachable, conventional.

queue *n.* line, file, cordon, string, row, chain, train, sequence, series, tier.

quibble *n.* equivocation, cavil, quiddity, evasion, subterfuge, shift, hairsplitting, objection, dodge, prevarication, sophism. —*v.* equivocate, palter, cavil, prevaricate, split hairs, tergiversate, dodge, carp, evade, shuffle.

quick *adj.* **1** expeditious, brisk, prompt, speedy, fast, swift, rapid, fleet, nimble, hasty, precipitous, brief, stepped-up, hurried. **2** alert, sensitive, perceptive, responsive, receptive, keen, smart, prompt, ready, apt.

ant. **1** slow, gradual, unhurried, deliberate, sluggish. **2** dull, stupid, sluggish, backward, slow.

quicken *v.* **1** hasten, accelerate, speed up, hurry, expedite, dispatch, press on. **2** stimulate, resuscitate, enliven, revive, animate, vivify, excite, restore, arouse.

ant. **1** slow, hinder, delay, hamper, impede. **2** deaden, kill, block, suppress, discourage.

quickly *adv.* rapidly, soon, promptly, swiftly, speedily, fast, instantly, immediately, at once, presently, instanter, hastily, headlong, expeditiously, fleetly, pronto (*Slang*), posthaste.

ant. slowly, gradually, deliberately, tardily, later, afterwards.

quick-tempered *adj.* IRASCIBLE.

quick-witted *adj.* keen, alert, intelligent, penetrating, perceptive, ready, quick, smart, knowing, sharp, clever, brilliant, responsive, witty, incisive.

ant. dull, stupid, unintelligent, slow, plodding.

quiddity *n.* **1** ESSENCE. **2** QUIBBLE.

quidnunc *n.* GOSSIP.

quiescent *adj.* inactive, quiet, still, dormant, latent, tranquil, silent, resting, potential, abeyant, motionless, placid, calm, serene.

ant. active, astir, manifest, patent, dynamic, aroused.

quiet *adj.* **1** still, calm, motionless, immobile, tranquil, peaceful, restful, pacific, secluded, undisturbed, serene, placid. **2** silent, noiseless, soundless, mute, still, inaudible, dumb, hushed. **3** unobtrusive, conservative, subdued, sober, inconspicuous, low-key, restrained, repressed. —*n.* peace, calm, quietness, quietude, tranquillity, stillness, serenity, repose, calm, rest, silence. —*v.* shush, hush up, quieten (*Brit.*), lull, still, silence, muffle.

ant. *adj.* **1** restless, disturbed, rough, tumultuous, blustering. **2** noisy, loud, roaring, deafening, tumultuous. **3** gaudy, loud, florid, blatant, vivid. *n.* disturbance, perturbation, tumult, uproar, bluster. *v.* blare, roar, thunder, deafen, bang.

quietness *n.* **1** repose, quietude, stillness, tranquillity, calm, calmness, peace, seclusion, serenity, placidity, ease, quietism. **2** silence, stillness, hush, inaudibility, muteness, soundlessness, noiselessness.

ant. 1 disturbance, flurry, agitation, turbulence, fuss, ado. **2** clamor, hubbub, resonance, uproar, noisiness, tumult.

quietude *n.* QUIETNESS.

quintessence *n.* essence, heart, distillation, quiddity, extract, soul, core, marrow, pith, essential.

ant. adjunct, accidental, nonessential, contingency, excrescence, extra.

quip *n.* gibe, jest, witticism, joke, pleasantry, sally, squib, sarcasm, taunt, retort, jeer, wisecrack (*Slang*), comeback (*Slang*). —*v.* gibe, ridicule, taunt, jeer, jest, mock, deride, twit, joke, guy, wisecrack (*Slang*).

quirk *n.* idiosyncrasy, mannerism, peculiarity, quiddity, foible, eccentricity, crotchet, oddity, vagary, characteristic, habit, trait, quality, whimsy, caprice, hang-up (*Slang*), schtick (*Slang*).

quirky *adj.* peculiar, unpredictable, idiosyncratic, crotchety, eccentric, capricious, whimsical, odd, pixilated, droll, queer, weird, erratic, zany, kinky (*Slang*), spacey (*Slang*).

ant. normal, predictable, dependable, steady, usual, conventional.

quisling *n.* traitor, collaborationist, fifth columnist, subversive, renegade,

turncoat, betrayer, apostate, Judas, Benedict Arnold.

ant. loyalist, patriot, partisan.

quit *v.* **1** cease, desist, give up, renounce, relinquish, discontinue, drop, leave off, halt, abandon, conclude, stop. **2** leave, go away, depart, take off, go, withdraw, retire, decamp, remove, exit, forsake, drop out, abandon, split (*Slang*).

ant. 1 continue, persist, persevere, keep on, endure. **2** remain, stay, stand fast, tarry, abide.

quite *adv.* completely, fully, totally, thoroughly, very, considerably, positively, really, perfectly, precisely, nearly, wholly, entirely, mostly, rather.

ant. barely, hardly, scarcely, somewhat, slightly, merely.

quitter *n.* dropout, shirker, slacker, coward, defeatist, deserter, malingerer, loser, piker (*Slang*), welsher (*Slang*).

quiver *v.* vibrate, tremble, shake, flutter, quaver, quake, shiver, flicker, twitch, palpitate, shudder, oscillate.

quixotic *adj.* romantic, impractical, unrealistic, idealistic, visionary, lofty, fanciful, fantastic, chimerical, freakish, chivalrous, impracticable, Utopian, zany, fey, unworldly.

ant. realistic, practical, pragmatic, hardheaded, matter-of-fact, prosaic.

quiz *n.* **1** test, examination, questioning, inquiry, interrogation, catechism, investigation, inquisition, questionnaire, check, trial. **2** HOAX. —*v.* **1** examine, question, pump, query, interrogate, sound out, crossexamine, catechize, inquire, interpellate, check. **2** RIDICULE.

ant. *v.* **1** answer, reply, respond, state, say, inform.

quizzical *adj.* **1** mocking, teasing, bantering, arch, derisive, coy, elliptical, joking, impudent, insolent. **2** perplexed, puzzled, curious, inquiring, baffled, questioning, inquisitive, searching. **3** queer, odd, eccentric, erratic, quaint, funny, strange, off-beat (*Slang*).

ant. 1 serious, respectful, attentive, sober, obsequious. **2** uninterested, indifferent, incurious, unconcerned, unaware. **3** normal, standard, ordinary, usual, everyday.

quondam *adj.* FORMER.

quota *n.* part, share, portion, allotment, allowance, ration, proportion, percentage, apportionment, quantity, contingent.

quotation *n.* selection, quote, excerpt, passage, extract, repetition, citation, reference, clipping, cutting.

quote *v.* repeat, cite, name, instance, adduce, paraphrase, refer to, plagiarize, extract, take, excerpt, detail, attest, exemplify. —*n.* QUOTATION.

quotidian *adj.* DAILY.

R

rabble *n.* riffraff, mob, masses, canaille, herd, commonalty, hoi polloi, populace, crowd, lumpen proletariat, trash, dregs, scum.

Rabelaisian *adj.* BAWDY.

rabid *adj.* **1** fanatical, zealous, dedicated, gung-ho (*Slang*), bigoted, intolerant, hot-headed, hot-tempered, all-out, unreasonable, deranged. **2** furious, raging, mad, violent, frantic, frenzied, infuriated, amok.

ant. 1 moderate, reasonable, sound, sober, discerning, normal. **2** calm, sane, tame, reasonable, gentle, quiet.

race[1] *n.* people, stock, breed, tribe, type, class, kind, group, ethnic group, division, clan, parentage, ancestry, family, paternity, generation.

race[2] *n.* contest, competition, chase, dash, run, course, trial, career. —*v.* contest, contend, vie, compete, run, dash, course, hurry, hasten, speed, tear, scamper, career.

raciness *n.* SPICE.

rack *n.* frame, grating, framework, lattice, crate, scaffold, stand, skeleton, crib. —*v.* **1** fit in, rig, place, array, arrange, dispose, deploy, marshal, group, order. **2** torment, strain, harass, wring, torture, pain, afflict, punish, oppress, try.

ant. *v.* **1** dismantle, take apart, remove, jumble, knock down. **2** comfort, soothe, cheer, lull, support.

racket[1] *n.* paddle, bat, battledore.

racket[2] *n.* **1** clatter, noise, hubbub, clamor, din, tumult, commotion, disturbance, uproar, fracas. **2** graft, fraud, swindle, extortion, confidence game, scheme, game, rip-off (*Slang*), shakedown (*Slang*), con game (*Slang*).

ant. 1 silence, quiet, hush, peace, calm, tranquillity.

racketeer *n.* swindler, extortionist, outlaw, gangster, pirate, confidence man, bully, hooligan, shakedown artist (*Slang*), con man (*Slang*).

rackety *adj.* NOISY.

racking *adj.* ACUTE.

raconteur *n.* STORYTELLER.

racy *adj.* **1** spirited, vigorous, lively, animated, keen, interesting, entertaining, stimulating, foreceful. **2** spicy, piquant, risqué, immodest, suggestive, off-color, indelicate, ribald, indecent.

ant. 1 dispirited, languid, morose, dejected, dull. **2** bland, modest, decent, inoffensive, delicate.

raddle *v.* BRAID.

raddled *adj.* **1** DAZED. **2** DILAPIDATED.

radiant *adj.* **1** shining, refulgent, fulgent, luminous, glowing, bright, brilliant, lustrous, sparkling. **2** happy, ecstatic, pleased, beaming, glowing, delighted, joyful, elated, blithe, merry, overjoyed. **ant. 1** dull, dim, murky, dark, blurred. **2** sad, dull, gloomy, somber, downcast.

radiate *v.* **1** shine, gleam, beam, shed, emit, diffuse, scatter, illuminate, send out. **2** spread out, diverge, part, issue, proliferate, branch out, emanate, ramify, disperse, splay. **ant. 2** converge, coalesce, close in, unite, gather, absorb.

radical *adj.* **1** thoroughgoing, basic, extreme, fundamental, profound, deep-rooted, deep-seated, essential, complete, unqualified. **2** extremist, revolutionary, insurgent, intransigent, fanatical, leftist. —*n.* extremist, revolutionary, freethinker, iconoclast, fanatic, firebrand, leftist. **ant.** *adj.* **1** superficial, shallow, extraneous, incomplete, partial, cosmetic. **2** conservative, traditional, reactionary, legitimate, established. *n.* conservative, reactionary, standpatter, traditionalist, mossback.

radius *n.* sphere, scope, limit, range, orbit, compass, sweep, reach, span, field, area, extent, command.

raffish *adj.* TAWDRY.

raft[1] *n.* float, pontoon, boom, platform.

raft[2] *n.* pile, heap, conglomeration, jumble, multitude, stack, mass, slew, lot, assortment, hash, hodge-podge, mess. **ant.** trace, smidgen, trickle, bit, few, little.

rafter *n.* TIMBER.

rag *v. Slang* TEASE.

ragamuffin *n.* gamin, tatterdemalion, scarecrow, derelict, urchin, beggar, wretch, street Arab, waif.

ragbag *n.* miscellany, potpourri, medley, olio, mélange, gallimaufry, omnium-gatherum, mixture, hash, pastiche, salmagundi, jumble, compila-

tion, anthology, miscellany, hodge-podge.

rage *n.* **1** anger, wrath, fury, frenzy, ire, indignation, vehemence, furor, rampage. **2** craze, vogue, fad, fashion, mania, style, mode. —*v.* storm, bluster, fulminate, seethe, rave, fume, chafe, boil, madden, fret, bridle. **ant.** *n.* **1** equanimity, serenity, composure, restraint, peace, calm. *v.* lull, mollify, moderate, subdue, calm, soothe.

ragged *adj.* **1** frayed, shabby, raggedy, threadbare, seedy, mean, tattered, torn, shredded, rent, slovenly. **2** rough, shaggy, poor, crude, unfinished, uneven, harsh, rugged, jagged. **ant. 1** whole, new, unused, smooth, neat. **2** refined, finished, elegant, sleek, polished, smooth.

raggedy *adj.* RAGGED.

raid *n.* incursion, attack, assault, foray, invasion, inroad, irruption, seizure, operation, capture. —*v.* attack, assault, pillage, ravage, fall upon, invade, assail, set upon, forage, plunder, lay waste.

rail *n.* RAILING.

rail against castigate, abuse, scold, revile, censure, vituperate, upbraid, reproach, rebuke, chastise, harangue, lambaste (*Slang*), cry down, dress down. **ant.** acclaim, congratulate, approve, cry up, praise, compliment.

railing *n.* rail, barrier, fence, balustrade, guard, bar, banister, parapet, paling, boundary.

raillery *n.* jesting, teasing, sport, banter, riding, chaff, ridicule, sarcasm, persiflage, badinage, pleasantry, merriment, joking, satire, irony, ribbing (*Slang*). **ant.** seriousness, sobriety, sympathy, commiseration, forbearance.

railroad *v.* rush, push, force, press, shove, expedite, hurry, hasten.

raiment *n.* CLOTHING.

rain *n.* shower, sprinkle, drizzle, downpour, deluge, fall, scattering, dispersal, flow, flood. —*v.* fall, pour down, shower, drizzle, spatter, sprinkle, scatter, strew, deluge, overwhelm.

raise *v.* 1 lift, elevate, boost, heighten, loft, jack up, hoist, uplift, heave. 2 erect, rear, set up, fashion, frame, build, construct, establish, fabricate. 3 increase, advance, intensify, elevate, heighten, enhance, amplify, up, strengthen, animate. 4 breed, grow, cultivate, propagate, engender, bring about, produce, rear, cause. 5 arouse, suggest, spur, bring up, incite, evoke, excite, stir up, awaken, elicit. —*n.* increase, addition, gain, rise, elevation, supplement, advance, augmentation, improvement, growth, expansion.
ant. *v.* 1 lower, put down, drop, depress, debase. 2 fell, demolish, raze, overthrow, level. 3 weaken, lessen, abridge, curtail, reduce. 4 eradicate, kill, destroy, prevent, cut down. 5 discourage, pacify, lull, dispirit, depress. *n.* decrease, curtailment, lowering, lessening, decline.

rake[1] *v.* gather, scrape up, pull together, heap up, collect, amass, scratch.
ant. disperse, scatter, spread out, strew, blow away.

rake[2] *n.* libertine, roué, sensualist, lecher, profligate, rakehell, seducer, debauchee, Don Juan, Lothario.
ant. ascetic, puritan, celibate, family man, hermit, monk.

rakish[1] *adj.* dashing, jaunty, sprightly, smart, dapper, swanky, natty, chic, stylish, showy, sporty, voguish, saucy.
ant. dowdy, drab, frowzy, shabby, unkempt, old-fashioned.

rakish[2] *adj.* DISSOLUTE.

rally[1] *v.* 1 bring together, muster, assemble, convene, mobilize, convoke, summon, call. 2 revive, recover, perk up, improve, rebound, refresh, rejuvenate, recuperate. —*n.* 1 assembly, mass meeting, meet, convention, convocation, assemblage, gathering, protest, revival. 2 recovery, revival,

rebirth, rebound, improvement, renewal, renaissance.
ant. *v.* 1 disband, demobilize, disperse, 2 worsen, sink, weaken, regress, relapse. *n.* 2 relapse, decline, weakening, sinking, worsening.

rally[2] *v.* TEASE.

ram *v.* 1 strike, dash against, butt, run into, batter, pound, collide, crash into. 2 cram, force down, stuff, tamp, press, plug, choke.

ramble *v.* 1 roam, meander, wander, rove, stroll, stray, saunter, amble, peregrinate. 2 maunder, digress, drivel, blather, wander, babble. —*n.* rambling, stroll, roaming, wandering, amble, excursion, tour, roving, walk, peregrination, junket.

rambunctious *adj.* unruly, refractory, headstrong, obstreperous, unmanageable, stubborn, strong-minded, insubordinate, defiant, strong-willed, self-willed, intractable, aggressive, mulish, contrary, perverse.
ant. tractable, amenable, submissive, obedient, tame, quiet.

ramification *n.* offshoot, branch, result, consequence, outgrowth, aftermath, extension, excrescence, development, circumstance, subdivision, sequel, scion.

ramify *v.* DIVIDE.

ramp *n.* slope, incline, grade, rise, gradient, acclivity, ascent, access, plane, adit.

rampage *n.* outbreak, agitation, uproar, excitement, frenzy, ferment, tumult, ebullition, storm, rage, tempest. —*v.* storm, rage, go berserk, tear, rant, rave, bluster, run amok, run riot.
ant. *n.* serenity, peace, quiet, calm, stillness, repose.

rampant *adj.* 1 unrestrained, wild, excessive, unbridled, flagrant, egregious, excessive, boisterous, rampaging, ungovernable, menacing. 2 widespread, unchecked, epidemic, rife, prevalent, far-flung, universal, comprehensive.
ant. 1 mild, bland, calm, decorous,

dispassionate. **2** confined, moderate, local, limited, contained.

rampart *n.* embankment, bulwark, fortification, earthwork, guard, barrier, barricade, elevation, mound, wall, security, defense, palisade.

ramshackle *adj.* dilapidated, unsteady, shaky, battered, rickety, decrepit, tumble-down, unstable, flimsy, tottering, crumbling.

ant. solid, sound, strong, steady, substantial, rugged.

rancid *adj.* sour, spoiled, noisome, musty, fusty, malodorous, putrid, fetid, putrescent, stinking, rank, rotten, tainted.

ant. fresh, wholesome, sweet, fragrant, pure, savory.

rancor *n.* enmity, malice, spite, hatred, hostility, malevolence, ill will, animosity, bitterness, aversion, antipathy, grudge, venom.

ant. affection, good will, benevolence, regard, kindness, love.

random *adj.* chance, casual, haphazard, fortuitous, accidental, adventitious, contingent, incidental, unplanned, desultory, irregular, aimless, stray, vagrant.

ant. intentional, planned, designed, purposeful, particular, specific.

range *n.* extent, scope, reach, compass, limits, latitude, sweep, gamut, area, field, command. —*v.* **1** order, align, rank, arrange, array, dispose, class, classify, categorize, seriate. **2** move over, wander, roam, course, traverse, cover, pass over, cruise, survey, rove, migrate, extend.

ant. *v.* **1** jumble, disarrange, mix up, confound, randomize.

rangy *adj.* SLENDER.

rank¹ *n.* **1** line, row, series, tier, file, range, group. **2** level, standing, caste, echelon, position, degree, station, rung. **3** quality, standing, eminence, position, grade, distinction, status. —*v.* arrange, align, grade, line up, classify, sort, array, order, range, dispose, class.

ant. *v.* disorder, disarrange, mix up, upset, scatter, jumble.

rank² *adj.* **1** luxuriant, flourishing, dense, exuberant, abundant, vigorous, proliferating, burgeoning, blooming. **2** rancid, gamy, foul, fusty, noisome, rotten, fetid, sour. **3** utter, total, flagrant, gross, egregious, absolute, complete, glaring, bald, blatant.

ant. **1** sparse, scanty, scraggly, meager, sickly. **2** sweet, fresh, fragrant, pure, wholesome. **3** covert, half-hearted, indifferent, latent, poor.

rankle *v.* **1** irritate, embitter, chafe, gall, gripe, gnaw, eat away. **2** fester, suppurate, ulcerate.

ant. **1, 2** heal, cure, ease, improve, mend.

ransack *v.* search, scour, rifle, rummage, comb, search out, strip, sack, plunder, pillage, loot, despoil, ravish.

rant *v.* rave, spout, declaim, bellow, vociferate, gibber, babble, carry on, clamor, yell. —*n.* bombast, rodomontade, swagger, balderdash, fustian, exaggeration, bluster, declamation, fanfaronade, cant, rubbish, nonsense.

ant. *v.* murmur, whisper, breathe, mutter, mumble.

rap *v.* **1** hit, slap, strike, cuff, whack, tap, knock, clobber (*Slang*), punch, sock (*Slang*). **2** *Slang* criticize, roast, censure, castigate, lampoon, satirize, assail, attack, ridicule, pillory, blast, knock (*Slang*). **3** *Slang* talk, thrash out, discuss, converse, parley, palaver, commune, deliberate, chew the fat (*Slang*). —*n.* **1** blow, hit, cuff, tap, slap, whack, knock. **2** *Slang* blame, roasting, censure, criticism, attack, blast, knock (*Slang*). **3** *Slang* talk, parley, palaver, discussion, dialogue, colloquy, converse, communion, bull session (*Slang*).

ant. *v.* **2** approve, extol, praise, applaud, laud. *n.* **2** approval, applause, plaudit, praise, eulogy.

rapacious *adj.* greedy, grasping, ravening, voracious, wolfish, predatory, thievish, marauding, avaricious, covetous, extortionate, plundering, ravenous.

ant. charitable, liberal, hospitable, giving, generous, abstemious.

rape *v.* ravish, violate, seduce, molest, outrage, attack, debauch, maltreat, assault, force. —*n. any gross violation or abuse:* violation, abuse, despoliation, maltreatment, pillage, rapine, ravaging, plunder, depredation, assault, desecration.

ant. *n.* conservation, preservation, defense, safekeeping, protection, guard.

rapid *adj.* speedy, swift, fast, fleet, quick, hasty, instantaneous, agile, expeditious, light-footed, express, smart, mercurial.

ant. deliberate, leisurely, slow, laggard, sluggish.

rapine *n.* plunder, pillage, looting, spoiling, ravin, destruction, marauding, depredation, spoliation, rape, robbery, seizure.

rapport *n.* accord, harmony, sympathy, affinity, empathy, relation, fellowship, mutuality, compatibility, agreement, understanding.

ant. hostility, alienation, strangeness, disagreement, incompatibility, antagonism.

rapprochement *n.* RECONCILIATION.

rapscallion *n.* RASCAL.

rapt *adj.* enraptured, transported, engrossed, intent, preoccupied, absorbed, fascinated, spellbound, carried away, entranced, enchanted, ecstatic, delighted, inspired, charmed, turned-on (*Slang*).

ant. distracted, unimpressed, apathetic, indifferent, inattentive, listless.

raptorial *adj.* PREDATORY.

rapture *n.* joy, ecstasy, delight, felicity, transport, exultation, delectation, bliss, beatitude, enchantment, passion, rejoicing, ravishment.

ant. distress, misery, affliction, revulsion, discontent, disgust.

rapturous *adj.* ecstatic, joyful, delighted, exalted, enchanted, perfervid, enraptured, overjoyed, entranced, transported, radiant, blissful, impassioned, turned-on (*Slang*), high.

ant. distressed, afflicted, disappointed, discontented, unmoved, apathetic.

rare *adj.* **1** infrequent, unusual, uncommon, singular, extraordinary, sporadic, scarce, exceptional, sparse, unique. **2** choice, fine, excellent, meritorious, distinctive, admirable, first-rate, superb, inimitable, elegant, exquisite, incomparable.

ant. 1 common, frequent, current, ordinary, manifold, usual. **2** inferior, mediocre, worthless, commonplace, base, indifferent.

rarefy *v.* refine, purify, attenuate, clarify, clear, cleanse, sublimate, extract, purge, winnow, spin out.

ant. pollute, contaminate, coarsen, muddy, obfuscate.

rarely *adv.* seldom, infrequently, uncommonly, scarcely, occasionally, sparingly, hardly, barely, now and again, once in a while.

ant. often, frequently, usually, continually, time and again.

raring *adj.* EAGER.

rarity *n.* **1** uncommonness, scarcity, shortage, sparseness, singularity, unwontedness, infrequency, strangeness. **2** curio, find, marvel, prodigy, treasure, miracle, wonder, spectacle, treasure trove.

rascal *n.* scoundrel, rapscallion, scamp, tease, rogue, imp, knave, mischiefmaker, trickster, prankster, scapegrace, miscreant, villain, scalawag.

rash *adj.* reckless, precipitate, headstrong, adventurous, ill-advised, thoughtless, impulsive, headlong, hasty, ill-considered, audacious, foolhardy, heedless, careless, unwary, madcap.

ant. careful, calculating, circumspect, cautious, prudent, discreet.

rasp *v.* GRATE.

rasping *adj.* RASPY.

raspy *adj.* harsh, grating, strident, dissonant, rasping, hoarse, raucous, gruff, husky, discordant, noisy, clangorous, guttural, grinding, scraping.
ant. harmonious, dulcet, musical, soothing, sweet, pleasant.

rate¹ *n.* **1** price, value, cost, worth, valuation, tariff, impost, levy. **2** class, degree, rank, status, rating, position, standing, sphere, station. —*v.* estimate, appraise, rank, grade, consider, regard, reckon, assess, adjudge, evaluate, deem, class, hold, assay, place.

rate² *v.* SCOLD.

rather *adv.* **1** preferably, sooner, liefer, more, first, before. **2** somewhat, moderately, fairly, comparatively, pretty, tolerably, slightly, quite.
ant. 2 highly, very, hugely, extremely, inordinately, excessively.

ratification *n.* APPROVAL.

ratify *v.* sanction, confirm, approve, endorse, validate, attest, certify, corroborate, support, uphold, substantiate, establish, subscribe to, authorize.
ant. veto, oppose, disapprove, invalidate, disagree, repudiate.

rating *n.* evaluation, classification, grade, standing, assessment, status, rank, placing, position, level, designation, assignment, degree, sphere, consignment, disposition, rate.

ratio *n.* relation, proportion, rate, percentage, share, comparison, proportionality, quota, correspondence, degree.

ratiocinate *v.* REASON.

ratiocination *n.* REASONING.

ration *n.* portion, share, allowance, allotment, quota, measure, meed, pittance, dole, provision, part. —*v.* allot, dole, distribute, apportion, mete, deal, issue, give out, supply, parcel out.

rational *adj.* **1** cognitive, reasoning, intellectual, mental, deductive, logical, analytical, ratiocinative. **2** sane, reasonable, sound, lucid, sober, competent, clear-headed. **3** sensible, sagacious, wise, judicious, enlightened, realistic, knowing, intelligent, discreet.
ant. 1 intuitive, irrational, nonrational, visionary, unreasoning, emotional. **2** irrational, insane, incompetent, unreasonable, dazed. **3** injudicious, indiscreet, stupid, unwise, idiotic.

rationale *n.* basis, reason, reasoning, explanation, key, grounds, motivation, theory, principle, logic, cause, why.

rationalize *v.* explain away, justify, excuse, gloss over, extenuate, vindicate, account for, alibi, cover up, whitewash.
ant. own up, confess, make a clean breast of.

rations *n.* food, provender, provisions, comestibles, victuals, meat, sustenance, bread, groceries, commons, grub (*Slang*).

rat on *Slang* BETRAY.

ratter *n. Slang* TRAITOR.

rattle *v.* **1** clatter, racket, clack, clank, hammer, bang, clink, chatter. **2** gibber, chatter, prate, babble, prattle, jabber, gabble. **3** confuse, fluster, upset, embarrass, disconcert, bewilder, daze, muddle, put out, discountenance. —*n.* racket, clicking, clack, clatter, clinking, clangor, din, noise, hubbub.
ant. *v.* **3** compose, reassure, clear up, relieve, ease. *n.* quiet, hum, murmur, silence, stillness.

rattled *adj.* DAZED.

ratty *adj. Slang* RUN-DOWN.

raucous *adj.* **1** harsh, hoarse, discordant, cacophonous, strident, raspy, grating. **2** noisy, rowdy, boisterous, tumultuous, obstreperous, uproarious, disorderly, vociferous, clamorous, turbulent.
ant. 1 harmonious, dulcet, musical, sweet, pleasant. **2** quiet, calm, tranquil, peaceful, serene.

raunchy *adj. Slang* LEWD.

ravage *v.* lay waste, despoil, ruin, destroy, wreak havoc, pillage, plunder, ransack, desolate, exterminate, harry, raze, devastate, sack.

ant. organize, establish, build, repair, reinstate, construct.

rave *v.* **1** babble, rant, roar, gibber, rage, prattle, prate, fume. **2** extol, boost, rhapsodize, praise, gush, enthuse, eulogize, magnify. —*n.* tribute, boost, eulogy, encomium, acclaim, accolade, blurb, kudos, applause.

ant. *v.* **2** cry down, disparage, rap (*Slang*), censure, detract. *n.* criticism, denunciation, knock, rap (*Slang*), put-down (*Slang*).

ravel *v.* fray, unravel, undo, pull apart, separate, loosen, untwist, unwind, disentangle, divide.

ant. knit, wind, knot, stitch up, sew, mend.

raven *adj.* BLACK.

ravening *adj.* **1** RAPACIOUS. **2** MAD.

ravenous *adj.* **1** hungry, voracious, famished, starved, insatiable, gluttonous, devouring. **2** eager, greedy, grasping, rapacious, avid, predatory, exigent, exacting, covetous.

ant. **1** satisfied, replete, sated, full, satiated. **2** subdued, meek, undemanding, docile, content.

ravine *n.* gorge, gully, gulch, gap, flume, pass, canyon, valley, chasm, cleft.

raving *adj.* FURIOUS.

ravish *v.* RAPE.

ravishing *adj.* pleasing, attractive, delightful, fascinating, enchanting, seductive, striking, alluring, gorgeous, becoming, comely, captivating, outstanding.

ant. repulsive, revolting, loathsome, disgusting, ugly, nasty.

raw *adj.* **1** uncooked, fresh, unbaked, natural, rare, undone. **2** crude, unrefined, rough, unprocessed, untreated, unprepared, unpainted. **3** bleak, chilling, harsh, cold, piercing, wintry, chilly, bitter. **4** inexperienced, undisciplined, immature, unskilled, unseasoned, callow, green, untried, untrained, new. **5** vulgar,

off-color, risqué, crude, rude, indecent, improper, obscene, suggestive.

ant. **1** baked, cooked, heated, well-done. **2** refined, treated, processed, prepared, manufactured. **3** comfortable, warm, summery, halcyon, pleasant. **4** skilled, mature, seasoned, experienced, trained. **5** pure, chaste, decent, proper, polite.

raw-boned *adj.* GAUNT.

ray *n.* **1** *of light:* beam, flash, shaft, stream, streak, pencil, sliver, gleam, glimmer. **2** *slight amount or indication:* spark, scintilla, flicker, breath, glimmer, hint, trace, speck, bit, touch.

raze *v.* tear down, demolish, dismantle, topple, pull down, level, overthrow, flatten, overturn, knock down, destroy, ruin, scatter, smash.

ant. build, erect, raise, construct, set up, rear.

re *prep.* REGARDING.

reach *v.* **1** extend, stretch out, lengthen, unfold, sprawl, untwist, dilate. **2** present, deliver, hand over, pass, convey, render, consign, transmit, transfer. **3** touch, grasp, make contact, arrive at, come to, achieve, gain access, get to, gain. **4** amount to, total, come to, aggregate, add up to, rise to, attain, suffice. —*n.* **1** span, stretch, distance, spread, extent, scope, sweep, latitude, limit, amplitude, compass, purview, range, capacity, dominion, grasp, mastery. **2** vista, expanse, sweep, stretch, view, limit, distance.

ant. *v.* **1** retract, withdraw, flinch, draw back, recoil. **2** take, deprive, hold back, keep, retain. **3, 4** fall short, fail, give out, lose, disappoint.

react *v.* respond, answer, reciprocate, backfire, echo, requite, offset, rebound, recoil, repay, return, counterbalance.

reaction *n.* **1** response, reply, answer, interaction, reciprocation, repercussion, echo, consequence, result, effect. **2** counteraction, reversal, backlash, reversion, recoil, regression, retrogression, antagonism, resistance, rebound.

ant. 1, 2 action, instigation, stimulus, impetus, catalysis, initiation.

reactionary *n.* ultraconservative, right-winger, die-hard, Bourbon, standpatter, rightist, tory, conservative, mossback.

ant. liberal, radical, revolutionary, left-winger, reformer, leftist.

read *v.* understand, interpret, react to, construe, decipher, peruse, infer, deduce, see, comprehend, gather, discover.

readable *adj.* legible, decipherable, clear, plain, understandable, comprehensible, unmistakable, distinct, clear-cut, undisguised.

ant. illegible, unclear, undecipherable, unreadable, obliterated, defaced.

readiness *n.* **1** preparedness, vigilance, alertness, preparation, wariness, punctuality, promptness. **2** skill, dexterity, adroitness, facility, finesse, proficiency, ease, address.

reading *n.* **1** perusal, study, education, literacy, letters, knowledge, erudition, edification, scholarship. **2** interpretation, version, performance, conception, impression, rendering, rendition, treatment, idea.

ready *adj.* **1** *quick to act or understand:* prepared, prompt, alert, quick, on one's toes, facile, ripe, fitted, sharp. **2** *mentally prepared:* willing, inclined, disposed, prompt, alert, punctual, eager, keyed up, psyched up (*Slang*). **3** accessible, near, handy, convenient, available, at hand, possible. —*v.* prepare, complete, arrange, contrive, devise, provide for, develop, fit.

ant. *adj.* **1** unfit, unprepared, unready, off balance. **2** doubtful, disinclined, unwilling, indisposed. **3** inconvenient, awkward, hard, remote, difficult.

real *adj.* **1** actual, objective, material, existent, tangible, sensible, physical, solid. **2** genuine, true, authentic, demonstrable, veritable, verifiable,

bona fide, essential, literal, authorized. **3** unaffected, unpretentious, sincere, natural, genuine, unfeigned, faithful, simple, complete, intrinsic.

ant. 1 imaginary, nonexistent, fancied, unreal, ideal. **2** artificial, counterfeit, apparent, supposed, ostensible. **3** affected, pretentious, superficial, insincere, deceptive.

realistic *adj.* genuine, lifelike, authentic, natural, representational, objective, photographic, naturalistic, practical, unromantic, unadorned, down-to-earth.

ant. nonobjective, impressionistic, romantic, idealistic, fuzzy, nonrepresentational.

reality *n.* **1** genuineness, authenticity, validity, verisimilitude, materiality, realism, truth. **2** fact, verity, truth, entity, actuality, being, phenomenon.

ant. 1 fraudulence, misrepresentation, falseness, pretense, unreality. **2** chimera, dream, illusion, lie, myth.

realization *n.* **1** understanding, awareness, comprehension, recognition, knowledge, insight, appreciation, acquaintance. **2** obtaining, acquisition, gaining, earning, profit, attainment, achievement, receipt.

ant. 1 ignorance, unawareness, blindness, incomprehension, obliviousness. **2** shortfall, deficiency, loss, want, failure.

realize *v.* **1** understand, appreciate, grasp, apprehend, take in, comprehend, recognize, conceive. **2** reify, concretize, objectify, externalize, body, embody, substantiate. **3** gain, profit, obtain, reap, effect, earn, accomplish, produce.

ant. 1 misunderstand, miss, neglect. **2** internalize, imagine, dream, exorcise, dismiss. **3** lose, relinquish, give up.

really *adv.* truly, genuinely, unquestionably, veritably, very, undoubtedly, certainly, verily, indubitably, literally, quite, positively.

ant. doubtfully, questionably, possibly.

realm *n.* domain, sphere, field, territory, orbit, world, department, province, region, beat, ambit, extent.

reanimate *v.* REVIVE.

reap *v.* realize, obtain, gain, earn, acquire, win, harvest, get, procure, derive, produce, profit.
ant. lose, forfeit, waste, spend, dissipate, fall short.

rear[1] *adj.* hindmost, last, back, hind, hinder, rearward, aft, tail, stern, caudal, posterior, after, following.
ant. front, forward, leading, fore, advance, first, anterior.

rear[2] *v.* **1** raise, erect, elevate, lift, hoist, loft, boost. **2** bring up, nurture, foster, train, raise, care for, cherish, educate, nurse. **3** RAISE.
ant. **1** level, drop, lay down, let fall, lower.

reason *n.* **1** cause, motive, basis, ground, purpose, end, goal, object, view, design, target. **2** excuse, explanation, rationale, defense, justification, alibi, rationalization, interpretation, theory, apologia. **3** reasoning, ratiocination, cognition, thought, logic, judgment, ideation, conceptualization, argument, thinking. **4** sanity, rationality, sense, understanding, lucidity, intelligence, common sense, soundness. —*v.* **1** think, deliberate, ratiocinate, cogitate, speculate, analyze, deduce, infer, consider, conclude. **2** argue, debate, dispute, remonstrate, expostulate, convince, influence, contend.
ant. *n.* **4** nonsense, stupidity, dullness, insanity, madness. *v.* **2** agree, comply, encourage, abet, back up.

reasonable *adj.* **1** rational, credible, considered, plausible, logical, reasoned, sound, thoughtful, enlightened, sagacious. **2** moderate, fair, modest, just, tolerable, suitable, proper, acceptable, equitable, inexpensive, legitimate, OK.
ant. **1** illogical, insane, irrational, thoughtless, prejudiced. **2** extreme,

excessive, immoderate, unconscionable, outlandish.

reasoning *n.* logic, thought, thinking, reason, ratiocination, analysis, deduction, induction, deliberation, reflection, cogitation.

rebel *v.* resist, revolt, mutiny, defy, disobey, strike, break with, riot. —*n.* nonconformist, mutineer, dissenter, heretic, traitor, insurgent, agitator, insurrectionist, malcontent, apostate, schismatic. —*adj.* REBELLIOUS.
ant. *v.* obey, comply, conform, submit, adapt. *n.* conformist, loyalist, yes-man, myrmidon, slave.

rebellion *n.* resistance, revolt, defiance, insubordination, disobedience, mutiny, revolution, revolt, overthrow, putsch, coup, coup d'état, insurrection, sedition.
ant. obedience, submission, conciliation, peace, repression.

rebellious *adj.* insubordinate, disobedient, refractory, contumacious, mutinous, insurgent, intractable, uncontrollable, defiant, rebel, recalcitrant, unmanageable, difficult, contrary, stubborn, froward.
ant. subordinate, submissive, docile, obedient, tractable, manageable, agreeable.

rebirth *n.* RENASCENCE.

rebound *v.* recover, recoup, rally, perk up, bounce back, ricochet, spring back, return, improve. —*n.* recoil, recovery, comeback, bounce, kick, ricochet, reaction, return, echo.

rebuff *v.* reject, refuse, repel, resist, check, beat back, turn away, snub, oppose, slight, cut, high-hat. —*n.* repulse, denial, check, defeat, snub, slight, discouragement, resistance, opposition, put-down (*Slang*).
ant. *v.* accept, abet, encourage, support, welcome. *n.* boost, encouragement, support, welcome, help.

rebuke *v.* reprove, reprimand, objurgate, castigate, chide, censure, upbraid, berate, reproach, reprehend, admonish, scold, take to task, dress down. —*n.* disapproval, objurgation, reproof, reprimand, castigation, admonition, reproach, blame, censure, scolding, dressing-down.

ant. *v.* approve, applaud, extol, eulogize, praise. *n.* approval, praise, approbation, applause, eulogy.

rebut *v.* dispute, disprove, refute, contradict, confute, counter, retort, negate, negative, overturn, controvert, oppose, parry, deny.

ant. prove, substantiate, validate, establish, demonstrate, verify.

rebuttal *n.* refutation, contradiction, negation, confutation, invalidation, denial, disagreement, disproof, overthrow, retort, upset.

ant. verification, validation, proof, demonstration, establishment, substantiation, corroboration.

recalcitrant *adj.* obstinate, rebellious, refractory, stubborn, headstrong, intractable, defiant, unruly, ungovernable, willful, disobedient, unwilling, reluctant, loath.

ant. amenable, biddable, tractable, docile, obedient, willing.

recall *v.* 1 recollect, remember, recapture, summon up, evoke, commemorate, revive, review, retrace. 2 take back, revoke, countermand, retract, repeal, withdraw, abjure, repudiate, rescind. —*n.* remembrance, retention, recollection, memory, reminiscence, recreation, recapture.

ant. *v.* 1 forget, lose sight of. 2 reinforce, reiterate, invoke, ratify, enforce. *n.* amnesia, forgetfulness, oblivion, nirvana, Lethe.

recant *v.* withdraw, take back, renounce, revoke, abjure, repudiate, retract, forswear, disavow, deny, disclaim, rescind, recall, abrogate.

ant. confirm, acknowledge, admit, reaffirm, insist, repeat.

recap *v.* RECAPITULATE. —*n.* RECAPITULATION.

recapitulate *v.* restate, review, recap, sum up, summarize, run through, reiterate, rephrase, recount, repeat, outline, epitomize, encapsulate.

recapitulation *n.* summary, summa-

tion, recap, synopsis, abstract, compendium, précis, abridgment, digest, outline, résumé.

recapture *v.* RECALL.

recast *v.* reword, rephrase, refashion, paraphrase, restate, reconstruct, remodel, rearrange, transliterate, translate.

recede *v.* 1 move back, withdraw, retreat, retire, back out, ebb. 2 fade, shrink, diminish, disappear, wane, sink, evanesce.

ant. 1 proceed, advance, press on, progress, rise. 2 approach, bulk, loom, stand out.

receipt *n.* reception, receiving, taking, acceptance, acquisition, assumption, admittance, admission, possession, custody.

ant. removal, rejection, exclusion, expulsion, emission.

receive *v.* 1 take, acquire, possess, gain, pick up, accept, win, collect, have. 2 perceive, hear, learn, gather, gain, glean, believe, understand. 3 undergo, experience, meet with, encounter, suffer, sustain, endure, put up with, absorb, take. 4 admit, greet, welcome, entertain, show in, take in, usher in, shelter.

ant. 1 reject, refuse, lose, deliver, expend. 2 tell, broadcast, publish, spread, transmit. 3 avoid, escape, elude, evade, miss. 4 rebuff, reject, expel, refuse, repulse.

recent *adj.* modern, fresh, new, late, novel, young, contemporary, up-to-date, current, latter-day, now, present-day.

ant. old, ancient, former, early, old-time, once.

receptacle *n.* container, vessel, holder, depository, repository, reservoir, box, basket, vase, case, well, bin, hopper.

reception *n.* welcome, greeting, recognition, salutation, salute, acknowledgment, response, reaction, entertainment, acceptance.

receptive *adj.* open, responsive, hospitable, accessible, approachable, friendly, amenable, flexible, tolerant, favorable, inclined.

ant. hostile, unresponsive, inhospitable, antagonistic, closed, intolerant.

recess *n.* **1** depression, indentation, niche, cleft, alcove, chink, nook, crypt, crevice, slot. **2** intermission, cessation, interruption, pause, lull, respite, interlude, halt, break, entr'acte. —*v.* interrupt, break, suspend, intermit, discontinue, pause, rest, dismiss, postpone, put off.

ant. *v.* persist, continue, persevere, prolong, keep on, carry on.

recession *n.* WITHDRAWAL.

recessive *adj.* receding, backward, regressive, retrograde, retrogressive, diminishing, declining, ebbing, retiring, shrinking, latent, dormant.

ant. forward, progressive, ongoing, advancing, increasing, growing.

recherché *adj.* REFINED.

recidivism *n.* REGRESSION.

recipe *n.* prescription, instructions, formula, means, plan, program, scenario, procedure, scheme, system, strategy, design, method, modus operandi, standard operating procedure, SOP.

reciprocal *adj.* mutual, interchangeable, equivalent, complementary, correlative, corresponding, alternate, correspondent, common, countervailing.

reciprocate *v.* interchange, requite, retaliate, return, remunerate, pay back, trade, barter, swap, exchange, interact, settle with.

recital *n.* retelling, narration, recitation, recapitulation, repetition, relation, description, account, statement, narrative, story, history.

recitation *n.* **1** recital, repetition, declamation, reiteration, elocution, rehearsal, narration, instruction. **2** talk, speech, address, reading, lecture, piece, lesson, recitative.

recite *v.* **1** declaim, deliver, perform, repeat, speak, rehearse, recount. **2**

report, particularize, itemize, relate, enumerate, detail, impart, recount.

reck *v.* HEED.

reckless *adj.* rash, careless, irresponsible, venturesome, foolhardy, daring, fearless, daredevil, devil-may-care, thoughtless, heedless, precipitate, headlong, hasty, improvident, negligent, imprudent, harum-scarum, wild, ill-considered.

ant. careful, circumspect, prudent, cautious, wary, provident.

reckon *v.* **1** count, compute, calculate, figure, estimate, enumerate, number, cast up. **2** look upon, regard, esteem, consider, deem, judge, class, assess, rate. **3** rely, depend, count on, bank on, plan, trust, lean, expect, hope for, bargain for.

reckoning *n.* **1** retribution, requital, retaliation, settlement, atonement, judgment, recompense, satisfaction, reciprocation, tit for tat. **2** appraisal, estimate, calculation, evaluation, summation, account, opinion.

reclaim *v.* recycle, restore, regenerate, redeem, reform, rescue, retrieve, recover, regain, get back, reinstate.

ant. discard, waste, abandon, neglect, reject, lose.

recline *v.* lie down, lie back, loll, sprawl, lounge, stretch, rest, repose, couch, incline, lean.

ant. stand, rise, get up, arise, rear, tower.

recluse *n.* hermit, solitary, eremite, loner, troglodyte, anchorite, ascetic. —*adj.* RECLUSIVE.

ant. *n.* joiner, mixer, socializer, bon vivant, boon companion.

reclusive *adj.* secluded, withdrawn, solitary, recluse, retiring, isolated, ascetic, monastic, eremitic, cloistered.

ant. gregarious, sociable, worldly, convivial, companionable, accessible, clubbable.

recognition *n.* **1** recollection, remembrance, awareness, avowal, identification, memory, discovery. **2** attention, notice, appreciation, citation, acknowledgment.

recognize v. 1 identify, know, remember, recollect, recall, place. 2 realize, perceive, apprehend, see, admit, discern, observe. 3 acknowledge, approve, appreciate, salute, bow, accede, concede.

recoil v. shrink, spring back, rebound, ricochet, draw back, pull back, flinch, retreat, withdraw, retire, blench, quail, retract. —n. shrinking, rebound, reaction, revulsion, repercussion, kick, boomerang.

recollect v. recall, remember, reflect, reminisce, call to mind, remind, recreate, think.
ant. forget.

recollection n. memory, remembrance, reminiscence, impression, recall, reconstruction.
ant. oblivion, forgetfulness, forgetting, amnesia.

recommend v. 1 commend, praise, endorse, approve, sanction, acclaim, applaud, laud, promote. 2 advise, urge, counsel, advocate, suggest, prescribe, propose, advance, exhort, enjoin.
ant. 1 disparage, disapprove, denigrate, condemn, cry down. 2 warn, discourage, deter, remonstrate, caution.

recommendation n. commendation, praise, approbation, endorsement, backing, advocacy, approval, sanction, blessing, urging.
ant. disapproval, objection, censure, aspersion, criticism, animadversion.

recompense v. 1 pay, repay, reward, compensate, requite, remunerate, satisfy. 2 reimburse, make good, redress, make up for, make amends, repair, redeem, indemnify, pay for. —n. requital, compensation, repayment, reward, retribution, reckoning, remuneration, satisfaction, wages, return, assets, payment, stipend, take (Slang).

reconcile v. 1 appease, conciliate, pacify, reunite, placate, propitiate, disarm. 2 of a dispute: settle, adjust, compose, resolve, heal, make up. 3

of differences: harmonize, adjust, attune, conform, square, fit, regulate.
ant. 1 anger, disturb, arouse, antagonize. 2 incite, exacerbate, arouse, stir up. 3 differ, clash, conflict, collide.

reconciliation n. rapprochement, understanding, conciliation, détente, pacification, appeasement, reunion, accommodation, adjustment, agreement, settlement.
ant. antagonism, misunderstanding, hostility, anger, enmity.

recondite adj. abstruse, involved, profound, deep, complicated, complex, abstract, difficult, obscure, arcane, esoteric, mysterious.
ant. simple, obvious, plain, easy, well-known, superficial.

reconnaissance n. survey, exploration, examination, inspection, view, scrutiny, observation, reconnoitering, investigation, pass, scan, overview.

reconnoiter v. SURVEY.

reconsider v. reevaluate, rethink, review, reexamine, ponder, mull over, reassess, reflect, revise, amend, correct, think better of, change one's mind.

reconstruct v. REMODEL.

record n. 1 account, log, report, chronicle, reminder, memento, memorandum, journal, diary, recording, trace, evidence. 2 career, performance, track record, achievement, history, case history, background, experience, course, conduct, acquirements, life, vita, résumé. —v. chronicle, log, register, set down, enter, indicate, preserve, inscribe, note, enroll, list.
ant. v. expunge, erase, cancel, remove, obliterate, delete.

recount v. narrate, describe, tell, detail, recite, report, repeat, convey, communicate, divulge, make known, portray, delineate.

recoup v. RECOVER.

recourse n. resource, resort, refuge, haven, option, expedient, choice, means, remedy, way out, recipe, device.

recover v. 1 regain, recoup, retrieve,

reclaim, restore, repossess, win back, make up for, recapture, redeem. **2** get well, recuperate, rally, get better, heal, mend, survive, come around, pull through, get over, convalesce.

ant. 2 worsen, weaken, debilitate, fail, succumb.

recovery *n.* rehabilitation, restoration, rallying, restitution, reestablishment, recuperation, healing, reclamation, retrieval, redemption, improvement, revival, renascence, rejuvenation.

recreant *adj.* **1** FAITHLESS. **2** COWARDLY. —*n.* COWARD.

recreation *n.* **1** refreshment, relaxation, diversion, amusement, regeneration, revitalization, reinvigoration, revival, recuperation. **2** pastime, hobby, diversion, amusement, fun, sport, stimulation, breather, pleasure, delight, festivity, break.

ant. 2 drudgery, toil, labor, grind, travail.

recriminate *v.* ACCUSE.

recrimination *n.* accusation, countercharge, counterattack, retaliation, vindication, retort, sally, riposte, reproach, rejoinder, quarrel, dissension, strife, bickering, hostility.

recrudesce *v.* REVIVE.

recrudescence *n.* REVIVAL.

recruit *v.* muster, proselytize, enlist, impress, supply, replenish, round up, draft, mobilize, enroll, convince, win over. —*n.* trainee, apprentice, proselyte, convert, neophyte, novice, beginner, tyro, probationer, greenhorn, freshman, rookie (*Slang*).

ant. *n.* veteran, master, old hand.

rectify *v.* correct, amend, remedy, repair, set right, redress, reform, revise, emend, straighten out, fix up, regulate.

rectitude *n.* uprightness, righteousness, high-mindedness, principle, morality, honor, probity, integrity, decency, trustworthiness, incorruptibility, evenhandedness, impartiality, scrupulousness.

ant. turpitude, corruption, crookedness, iniquity, laxity, immorality.

recuperate *v.* **1** recover, get better, get well, convalesce, rally, mend, heal, survive, come around, pull through, strengthen, improve. **2** recoup, regain, restore, repossess, reclaim, retrieve, replace, redeem, recapture.

ant. 1 sicken, worsen, weaken, fail, succumb.

recurrent *adj.* recurring, repeated, repeating, periodic, regular, intermittent, cyclical, chronic, repetitious, frequent, repetitive, episodic, reappearing, unending.

ant. singular, unusual, rare, freak, isolated.

recycle *v.* RECLAIM.

redact *v.* EDIT.

red-blooded *adj.* VIGOROUS.

redden *v.* BLUSH.

redeem *v.* **1** regain, repossess, ransom, cash in, claim, reclaim, recover, trade in, retrieve, convert, reconvert, swap, exchange, trade. **2** fulfill, make good, discharge, satisfy, abide by, carry out, keep one's word, complete, come through.

ant. 2 renege, back out, rescind, retract, forsake.

redemption *n.* repossession, reclamation, recovery, retrieval, ransom, restoration, reestablishment, reparation, compensation, repurchase, release, discharge fulfillment, *quid pro quo,* payoff.

red-hot *adj.* HOT.

red-letter *adj.* MEMORABLE.

redolence *n.* AROMA.

redolent *adj.* fragrant, odorous, perfumed, sweet-smelling, aromatic.

redoubt *n.* fort, fortification, stronghold, buttress, defense, rampart, bulwark, bastion, fortress, citadel, stockade, battlement, parapet, barricade, shelter, trench.

redoubtable *adj.* formidable, awesome, fearsome, invulnerable, powerful, awe-inspiring, commanding, fearful, dread, overpowering, indomitable, invincible, impregnable, threatening, menacing.

ant. vulnerable, weak, puny, exposed, unprotected, unimpressive.

redound *v.* result in, lead to, eventuate, effect, effectuate, cause, yield, affect, influence, contribute.

redress *v.* set right, repair, compensate, avenge, revenge, retaliate, correct, make up for, rectify, square, recompense, amend, remedy, repay, requite, reward. —*n.* reparation, amends, restoration, correction, compensation, damages, satisfaction, rectification, remedy, recompense, retribution, requital, appeasement, propitiation.

reduce *v.* **1** diminish, lessen, decrease, lower, cut, subtract, abridge, shorten, deduct, curtail, wind down, phase out, truncate, compress, contract, constrict. **2** classify, systematize, order, organize, arrange, categorize, grade, label, methodize, codify, tabulate, itemize, list, computerize, index. **3** degrade, debase, devalue, demote, humble, humiliate, shame, detract, derogate, deflate, cheapen, depreciate, discredit, bring down, put down (*Slang*). **4** subdue, conquer, break, bankrupt, put down, subjugate, immobilize, paralyze, crush, enfeeble, weaken, debilitate, overcome, overpower.

ant. 1 lengthen, increase, extend, amplify. **3** enhance, upgrade, exalt, inflate, lift.

reduction *n.* decrease, curtailment, cut, diminution, lowering, lessening, phaseout, compression, constriction, dwindling, depletion, attenuation, deduction, shortening, abridgment, abatement.

ant. increase, addition, enlargement, extension, amplification, growth.

redundancy 1 superfluity, excess, superfluousness, excessiveness, overflow, overdose, surfeit, overabundance, plethora, oversupply, congestion, profusion, glut. **2** repetition, reiteration, wordiness, pleonasm, verbiage, prolixity, verbosity, tautol-

ogy, diffuseness, circumlocution, padding, hot air (*Slang*).

ant. 1 insufficiency, paucity, scarcity, shortage, sparseness, lack. **2** terseness, directness, pithiness, brevity, compactness.

redundant *adj.* **1** superfluous, unnecessary, expendable, extra, supererogatory, marginal, inessential, wasteful, useless, additional, dispensable. **2** repetitious, wordy, inflated, pleonastic, prolix, tautological, diffuse, circumlocutory, circumambient, reiterative, verbose, padded, loose, inflated, windy.

ant. 1 necessary, essential, central, indispensable, exigent. **2** concise, terse, brief, direct, to the point.

reduplicate *v.* COPY.

reef *n.* ridge, shelf, atoll, ledge, bar, sandbar, flat, shoal, shallow.

reel *v.* stagger, sway, lurch, totter, stumble, falter, flounder, shake.

reenforce *v.* REINFORCE.

refection *n.* REFRESHMENT.

refer *v.* **1** consign, send, pass on, turn to, confer, consult, ask, relegate, entrust, deliver, recommend, transfer, turn over to, research. **2** allude, assign, attribute, ascribe, impute, advert, credit, accredit, invest, lay to, trace to, attach to, associate with, connect with, charge with, arrogate.

referee *n.* mediator, arbitrator, umpire, adjudicator, peacemaker, arbiter, conciliator, decision-maker, judge, moderator, intermediary, go-between, negotiator, ombudsman.

reference *n.* **1** direction, relegation, consignment, referral, assignment, imputation, association. **2** allusion, suggestion, connotation, indication, note, notation, footnote, mention, citation, hint, innuendo, insinuation, intimation, quotation, extract. **3** source, data bank, authority, dictionary, compendium, encyclopedia. **4** regard, connection, relation, respect, conjunction, answer, relevance, bearing. **5** recommendation, testimonial, certification, attestation, affirmation, deposition, certificate, warrant, voucher, good word.

referral *n.* reference, direction, relegation, consignment, assignment, consultation, application, allusion, recommendation, buck-passing (*Slang*).

refine *v.* **1** purify, cleanse, clean, clarify, filter, distill, rarefy, sieve, strain, sift. **2** improve, polish, uplift, civilize, perfect, better, elaborate, develop, cultivate, reform, finish, advance, enhance, elevate, upgrade.

ant. 1 pollute, muddy, thicken, coarsen. **2** debase, vulgarize, downgrade, brutalize, degrade.

refined *adj.* **1** polished, elegant, recherché, civilized, urbane, cultivated, tasteful, finished, smooth, mannerly, well-bred, fine, aristocratic. **2** subtle, nuanced, precise, exact, fastidious, discriminating, punctilious, nice, discerning, sensitive, elegant, critical, finicky, precious, mannered, particular.

ant. 1 crude, rough, barbarous, vulgar, boorish, coarse, humble. **2** undiscerning, gross, obvious, blatant.

refinement *n.* fineness, elegance, polish, finish, finesse, delicacy, cultivation, sensitivity, subtlety, good taste, breeding, urbanity, civility, discernment, *politesse*.

ant. vulgarity, coarseness, boorishness, insensitivity, grossness, roughness.

reflect *v.* **1** mirror, echo, return, reverberate, revert, repeat, resound, rebound, careen. **2** manifest, show, indicate, display, signify, reveal, express, demonstrate, evince, imply, disclose, exhibit, denote, bespeak, register. **3** ponder, cogitate, think about, muse, deliberate, weigh, contemplate, mull over, cerebrate, study, consider, meditate, reason, wonder, speculate.

reflection *n.* **1** thought, meditation, deliberation, contemplation, study, examination, cogitation, consideration, speculation, reasoning, review, lucubration, inspection, scrutiny, going-

over. **2** aspersion, insult, imputation, innuendo, accusation, slander, defamation, disparagement, slur, blot, smear, knock, slap, rap (*Slang*).

reflective *adj.* thoughtful, pensive, meditative, deliberative, contemplative, speculative, intellectual, cerebral, cogitative, cognitive, philosophical, introspective, introverted, withdrawn.

ant. thoughtless, spontaneous, impulsive, rash.

reflex *n.* response, reaction, habit, impulse, second nature, wont, habituation, custom, rule.

reflux *n.* RETURN.

reform *v.* improve, better, regenerate, rehabilitate, repent, amend, meliorate, ameliorate, correct, mend, recant, purify, rectify, uplift, civilize. —*n.* correction, improvement, betterment, melioration, amelioration, rectification, uplift, progress, rehabilitation, gradualism, advancement, elevation, reformation.

ant. *v.* worsen, degenerate, deteriorate, backslide, regress. *n.* degeneration, deterioration, degradation, corruption, abuse, reaction, regression.

refractory *adj.* **1** stubborn, obstinate, mulish, uncooperative, perverse, unmanageable, willful, difficult, recalcitrant, opinionated, balky, bullheaded, disruptive, inflexible, obdurate, immovable, ornery. **2** *of a disease:* chronic, stubborn, incurable, resistant, unresponsive, persistent, protracted, prolonged.

ant. 1 agreeable, cooperative, flexible, willing, amenable. **2** curable, responsive, temporary, remediable.

refrain *v.* forbear, abstain, forgo, renounce, resist, avoid, quit, stop, withdraw, cease, desist, eschew, refuse, leave off, relinquish.

ant. continue, persist, indulge, yield.

refresh *v.* **1** freshen, renew, revitalize, invigorate, revive, clean, cleanse, air, brighten, cheer, exhilarate, lift, animate, reanimate, inspirit, energize. **2** remind, stimulate, jog, stir, arouse, activate, awaken, prompt, kindle, quicken, summon up, recall. **3** RE-PLENISH.

ant. 1 exhaust, deaden, weaken, depress, undermine. **2** dull, blunt, benumb, stultify.

refreshing *adj.* invigorating, exhilarating, bracing, fresh, novel, bright, new, original, pleasing, delightful, heartening, gratifying, exciting, stimulating.

ant. stultifying, boring, stale, dull, depressing.

refreshment *n.* **1** renewal, revitalization, freshening, nourishment, invigoration, refection, brightening, exhilaration, lift, cheer, animation, vitality, vigor, energy, stimulation, awakening, quickening. **2** repast, snack, bite, meal, refection, tidbit, morsel, pickup, tea (*Brit.*), elevenses (*Brit.*), nourishment, nosh.

ant. 1 deadening, stultification, fatigue, dullness, torpor, devitalization.

refuge *n.* **1** shelter, protection, security, safety, recourse, cover, assurance, delivery, rescue, preservation, defense, seclusion, privacy, resort. **2** asylum, sanctuary, haven, harbor, cloister, citadel, nest, preserve, hideout, lair, home, stronghold, hideaway, hole, burrow.

refulgent *adj.* RADIANT.

refund *v.* return, repay, pay back, give back, rebate, reimburse, recompense, remunerate, remit, adjust, make restitution, redress.

refurbish *v.* RENOVATE.

refusal *n.* rejection, nonacceptance, turndown, noncompliance, denial, dissent, no, veto, disapproval, nay, noncooperation, disavowal, repudiation, balkiness, unwillingness, objection, defiance.

ant. acceptance, agreement, compliance, cooperation, yes, approval, support.

refuse[1] *v.* decline, turn down, resist, balk, object, veto, demur, shrink from, stick at, stand firm, disavow, reject, spurn.

ant. accept, comply, agree, cooperate, conform, assent, concur, defer, acquiesce.

refuse[2] *n.* rubbish, waste, garbage, dross, swill, slops, dregs, litter, sweepings, trash, debris, junk, leavings, jetsam, dust (*Brit.*).

refute *v.* rebut, confute, negate, disprove, dispute, contend, controvert, deny, contradict, contravene, impugn, invalidate, answer, debate, gainsay.

ant. substantiate, corroborate, uphold, agree, consent, assent.

regal *adj.* ROYAL.

regale *v.* **1** delight, enchant, charm, amuse, comfort, entrance, transport, enrapture, gratify, divert, please, bewitch, enthrall, entertain. **2** wine and dine, feast, banquet.

ant. 1 bore, tire, irritate. **2** stint, economize.

regard *v.* **1** look at, observe, notice, gaze at, scan, stare at, mark, eye, remark, watch, peruse, scrutinize, note, ogle, inspect, size up. **2** consider, deem, look on, hold, think, suspect, conceive, fancy, conclude, view, suppose, imagine, presume, judge, opine. —*n.* **1** consideration, attention, contemplation, thought, judgment, opinion, meditation, study, reflection, diligence, assiduity, mindfulness, mind, heed, attentiveness. **2** respect, esteem, admiration, approval, favor, homage, honor, note, approbation, recognition, affection, warmth, appreciation, friendship, friendliness. **3** REFERENCE.

ant. *n.* **1** thoughtlessness, inattention, heedlessness, neglect. **2** scorn, contempt, disrespect, disapproval, coolness.

regardful *adj.* heedful, careful, watchful, vigilant, alert, circumspect, attentive, aware, observant, cautious, mindful, open-eyed, awake, wideawake, on the beam (*Slang*), headsup (*Slang*).

ant. unobservant, nodding, mindless, rash, careless.

regarding *prep.* in reference to, with regard to, considering, with respect to, in connection with, touching on, in the matter of, re, anent, as to, as for, apropos, concerning.

regardless *adj.* heedless, careless, negligent, remiss, thoughtless, inattentive, unobservant, unmindful, unaware, rash, reckless, mindless, imprudent, lax, sloppy.

ant. circumspect, cautious, attentive, alert, careful, thoughtful, reflective.

regards *n.* greetings, good wishes, respects, remembrances, salutations, devoirs, compliments.

regenerate *v.* **1** reform, rehabilitate, uplift, improve, better, remedy, change, save, redeem, reclaim, reconstruct, convert, civilize, edify, enlighten. **2** reestablish, recreate, rebuild, reproduce, remake, redo, rejuvenate, resurrect, refashion, reconstitute, reanimate, revitalize, overhaul. —*adj.* regenerated, reformed, rehabilitated, redeemed, converted, changed, reconstructed, edified, enlightened, uplifted, saved, cleansed, straight (*Slang*).

ant. *v.* **1** corrupt, debase, deprave, degenerate, lower, defile, **2** undo, finish off, crush, kill, demolish. *adj.* unredeemed, lost, degenerate, unregenerate, unreconstructed.

regime *n.* administration, government, rule, reign, dynasty, system, sovereignty, command, power, control, direction, leadership, jurisdiction, party, apparatus, *apparat.*

regiment *v.* systematize, methodize, regulate, order, standardize, control, dominate, subjugate, dehumanize, bureaucratize, mechanize, brutalize, propagandize, brainwash, depersonalize.

region *n.* **1** area, place, territory, expanse, space, section, district, locality, zone, tract, clearing, terrain, corridor, locale, vicinity, spot, setting, neighborhood, barrio. **2** realm, sphere, domain, world, province, scene, area, arena, activity, interest, field, bailiwick, turf (*Slang*), beat (*Slang*).

regional *adj.* sectional, district, community, neighborhood, parochial, provincial, limited.

register *n.* **1** record, registry, archive, annal, roll, roster, chronicle, schedule, list, daybook, guestbook, log, diary, calendar. **2** item, entry, fact, datum, inscription, notation, posting, registration, jotting, memo, memorandum. —*v.* **1** enroll, sign up, enter, inscribe, write, subscribe, post, chronicle. **2** express, indicate, signify, reflect, show, exhibit, denote, bespeak, betoken, display, reveal, manifest. **3** impress, affect, make an impression, get through, reach, come across, get to, penetrate, sink in, ring a bell, hit the mark.

registry *n.* REGISTER.

regnant *adj.* **1** PREDOMINANT. **2** WIDESPREAD.

regorge *v.* VOMIT.

regress *v.* recede, retrogress, go back, move back, ebb, revert, relapse, lose ground, retreat, wane, back up, backslide, withdraw, deteriorate, degenerate. —*n.* RETURN.

ant. progress, advance, go forward, develop, proceed, make headway.

regression *n.* retrogression, backsliding, relapse, reversion, retreat, recidivism, recoil, reaction, withdrawal, deterioration, decline.

ant. progress, progression, advancement, headway, improvement.

regressive *adj.* RETROGRADE.

regret *v.* rue, repent, deplore, repine, sorrow, mourn for, bemoan, brood. —*n.* remorse, contrition, sorrow, grief, self-reproach, guilt, humiliation, qualms, compunction, repentance, penitence, anguish, bitterness, misgivings, rue.

regretful *adj.* remorseful, contrite, sorry, rueful, apologetic, repentant, sorrowful, guilty, conscience-stricken, penitent, anguished, heavy-

hearted, woebegone, self-reproach-ful.
ant. pleased, self-satisfied, self-con-gratulatory, smug, complacent, de-fiant.

regrettable *adj.* unfortunate, unlucky, ill-fated, deplorable, lamentable, sorry, sad, grievous, ill-starred, un-happy, woeful, pitiful, grave, calami-tous, untoward, inauspicious, dismal. **ant.** lucky, fortunate, happy, propi-tious, felicitous.

regular *adj.* **1** standard, normal, uni-form, even, symmetrical. **2** methodi-cal, systematic, orderly, predictable, dependable, fixed, set, systematized, routinized, standardized, method-ized, regularized, regulated, un-changing, undeviating, stable, efficient, steady, exact, precise, un-varied, punctilious. **3** routine, cus-tomary, habitual, classic, orthodox, pat, proper, usual, accepted, accepta-ble, ordinary, everyday, established, correct, sanctioned, received (*Brit.*). **ant. 1** unregulated, uneven, abnor-mal, freakish. **2** variable, disorderly, unpredictable, sloppy, lax, free, flexi-ble. **3** unaccustomed, unusual, un-orthodox, unconventional, idiosyn-cratic.

regularize *v.* REGULATE.

regulate *v.* **1** systematize, methodize, organize, control, standardize, man-age, direct, determine, govern, super-vise, oversee, codify, police, pilot, administer. **2** adjust, balance, equili-brate, regularize, set right, reset, re-adjust, equalize, true, even, correct, rectify, moderate, reconcile, adapt.

regulation *n.* **1** organization, stan-dardization, order, classification, ad-justment, alignment, rectification, codification, regularity, balance, equilibrium, normalcy, supervision, discipline, administration, manage-ment. **2** rule, statute, law, system, procedure, routine, method, princi-ple, control, requirement, order, convention, red tape, must, norm.

ant. 1 disorganization, disorder, chaos, license, anarchy.

rehabilitate *v.* RESTORE.

rehearse *v.* practice, run through, coach, repeat, learn, prepare, ready, direct, train, study, polish, perfect, drill, go over and over.

reign *n.* sovereignty, regime, domina-tion, power, rule, sway, preemi-nence, dominion, ascendancy, en-thronement, dynasty, supremacy, might, government. —*v.* rule, pre-vail, govern, dominate, lead, predom-inate, command, master, head, control, administer, run, guide, pre-ponderate.

reimburse *v.* pay back, recompense, re-fund, remunerate, rebate, compen-sate, pay up, remit, make restitution.

rein *n.* restraint, check, control, deter-rent, restriction, constraint, curb, leash, barrier, bridle, brake, pres-sure, repression, limitation. —*v.* check, guide, halt, stop, slow down, control, restrict, curb, leash, limit, constrain, repress, inhibit, encumber. **ant.** *n.* spur, goad, encouragement. *v.* unleash, speed, free, spur on.

reinforce *v.* strengthen, buttress, brace, steel, revitalize, reenforce, invigor-ate, encourage, fortify, harden, in-tensify, refresh, sustain, support, augment, beef up (*Slang*). **ant.** undermine, weaken, debilitate, sap, water down.

reinstate *v.* RESTORE.

reinvigorate *v.* REJUVENATE.

reiterate *v.* repeat, iterate, do over, em-phasize, stress, din, drum, restate, rephrase, retell, hammer, recapit-ulate, rehash.

reiteration *n.* REPETITION.

reject *v.* **1** turn down, refuse, dismiss, spurn, scorn, jilt, snub, cold-shoulder, blackball, blacklist, veto, rule out, discount, disbelieve, dis-credit, disallow, decline, disdain, ig-nore, overrule. **2** expel, discard, throw away, cast off, throw out, spit out, vomit, throw up, eliminate, scrap, oust, jettison, get rid of, abandon, relegate, dump. —*n.* discard, waste, castoff, second, jetsam, outcast, damaged goods, pariah, refuse, junk, scrap, exile, deportee, Ishmael, loser (*Slang*), 4-F, untouchable.

ant. *v.* **1** accept, include, believe, embrace, endorse, grant, recognize. **2** hold, keep, retain, save.

rejoice *v.* exult, revel, delight, gladden, jubilate, celebrate, crow, glory, bask, exhilarate, elate, transport, brighten.

ant. mourn, lament, sadden, depress, regret, mope.

rejoin *v.* ANSWER.

rejoinder *n.* answer, response, retort, riposte, rebuttal, reply, refutation, counterclaim, countercharge, remonstrance, back talk, comeback (*Slang*).

rejuvenate *v.* revitalize, invigorate, reinvigorate, refresh, restore, renew, animate, energize, regenerate, rekindle, revivify, recondition, overhaul.

ant. age, debilitate, weaken, exhaust, enervate, deplete.

relapse *v.* **1** weaken, sicken, worsen, deteriorate, fade, fail, sink. **2** regress, retrogress, degenerate, deteriorate, backslide, revert, recidivate, fall from grace. —*n.* regression, retrogression, backsliding, deterioration, degeneration, weakening, worsening, recidivism, decline.

ant. *v.* **1** strengthen, improve, get over, get well. **2** advance, progress, reform, rehabilitate. *n.* progress, advancement, advance, improvement, betterment.

relate *v.* **1** narrate, tell, speak of, describe, report, communicate, recount, go over, detail, recite, inform, impart, convey, express, apprise. **2** connect, link, bring together, coordinate, join, conjoin, associate, compare, correlate, ally, tie, unite, mingle, attach, juxtapose.

ant. 2 separate, disconnect, isolate, set apart.

related *adj.* **1** connected, linked, associated, joined, correlated, comparable, cognate, agnate, affiliated, interdependent, correlative, congenial, similar, adjoining, contiguous, coupled. **2** kindred, akin, consanguineous, fraternal.

ant. 1 separate, different, independent, isolated, unconnected. **2** unrelated, alien, nonconsanguineous.

relater *n.* NARRATOR.

relation *n.* **1** relationship, connection, link, tie, tie-in, correlation, interrelation, interdependence, mutuality, similarity, coupling, comparison, association, rapport, liaison. **2** reference, allusion, regard, response. **3** narration, report, account, description, recital, telling, narrating, storytelling, communication, expression, recountal. **4** RELATIONSHIP. **5** RELATIVE.

ant. 1 independence, isolation, separateness.

relations *n.* relationship, contact, association, dealings, rapport, liaison, bonds, actions, policies, terms, treatment, procedure, understanding, intimacy, vibrations (*Slang*), vibes (*Slang*).

relationship *n.* **1** kinship, relation, consanguinity, bond, blood. **2** rapport, communication, give-and-take, exchange, accord, association, friendship, connection, interdependence, intimacy, communion, union, liaison, affair. **3** RELATION.

relative *adj.* **1** relevant, connected with, pertinent, relating to, regarding, respecting, applicable, apropos, germane. **2** comparative, contingent, dependent, variable, unfixed, flexible, interdependent, partial, relativistic, referential, reciprocal, limited. —*n.* relation, kinsman, kinswoman, kin, cousin.

ant. *adj.* **1** irrelevant, unrelated, inapplicable, separate, remote. **2** absolute, autonomous, invariable, unique, independent.

relax *v.* **1** loosen, ease, unbend, unwind, thaw, loosen up, free, let go, let it all hang out (*Slang*), let one's hair down. **2** waive, soften, modify, moderate, weaken, breach, except, abrogate. **3** abate, slacken, let up, calm down, taper off, slow down, subside, diminish, lower, reduce, ease off, cool (*Slang*). **4** rest, take one's ease, loll, lounge, loaf, laze, potter, fritter, slow down.

ant. 1 inhibit, tighten, bind, stiffen. **2** apply, enforce. **3** accelerate, heighten, intensify, step up, escalate. **4** toil, labor, sweat, apply oneself, put out (*Slang*).

relaxation *n.* **1** slackening, easing, loosening, forbearance, leniency, weakening, exception, modification, clemency, mercy, softening, decrease, abatement, reduction, let-up. **2** rest, repose, recreation, loafing, self-indulgence, unwinding, lounging, enjoyment, vacation, lull, recess, breather, time out, leisure.

ant. 1 intensification, increase, step-up, escalation, speedup.

release *v.* **1** free, liberate, emancipate, let go, parole, manumit, let out, let loose. **2** deliver, relieve, disengage, excuse, discharge, exempt, unbind, untie, unfetter, unshackle, extricate, loosen, undo. —*n.* freedom, liberation, emancipation deliverance, liberty, relief, disengagement, discharge, extrication, disentanglement, manumission, pardon, rescue, ransom, parole, amnesty.

ant. 1 imprison, jail, cage, hold, enslave. **2** bind, tie, chain, fetter. —*n.* imprisonment, entanglement, slavery, repression.

relegate *v.* consign, assign, refer, classify, entrust, transfer, delegate, remand, authorize, commission, convey, dispatch, separate, pass the buck (*Slang*).

relent *v.* soften, weaken, give in, relax, yield, bend, accede, succumb, acquiesce, melt, submit, forbear, forgive.

ant. hold out, stiffen, toughen, harden.

relentless *adj.* **1** unremitting, continuous, eternal, uninterrupted, persistent, stubborn, tenacious, dogged,

undeviating, determined, unrelieved, unfaltering, ceaseless, incessant, unabated. **2** pitiless, obdurate, stony, unfeeling, cold, cruel, ruthless, adamant, hard-hearted, remorseless, merciless, inhuman, inhumane, fierce, vindictive.

ant. 1 intermittent, occasional, brief. **2** merciful, compassionate, sympathetic, yielding.

relevance *n.* pertinence, applicability, aptness, relatedness, suitability, connection, relation, appropriateness, bearing, relationship, application, compatibility, reference, congruity.

ant. disparity, divergence, irrelevance, inappropriateness, inapplicability.

relevant *adj.* pertinent, apposite, apt, apropos, fitting, related, contingent, applicable, right, germane, suitable, connected, appropriate, to the point, on target.

ant. irrelevant, beside the point, inappropriate, unrelated.

reliable *adj.* dependable, trustworthy, loyal, constant, faithful, regular, stable, responsible, truthful, honest, conscientious, scrupulous, accurate, infallible, authentic, exact.

ant. capricious, questionable, irresponsible, erratic, inconstant.

reliant *adj.* dependent, conditioned, ancillary, accessory, sustained, supported, interconnected, subordinate, attendant, parasitic.

ant. autonomous, free, self-determined, independent.

relic *n.* **1** vestige, trace, remains, ruin, fossil, antiquity, antique. **2** archaism, tradition, rite, ritual, custom, leftover, carry-over, hangover, atavism, throwback, ghost, echo. **3** memento, keepsake, heirloom, reminder, remembrance, memory, token, evocation, souvenir, diary, memoir, reminiscence.

relief *n.* **1** respite, alleviation, mitigation, relaxation, breather, break, let-up, pause, assuagement, riddance, abatement, cessation, lessening, diminishment, diminution, freedom, liberation, release, emancipation. **2** cure, remedy, help, assistance, aid, comfort, anodyne, palliative, salve, balm, panacea, corrective, prescription, medicine, antidote.

ant. 1 exacerbation, intensification, worsening, heightening, relapse. **2** disease, discomfort, distress.

relieve *v.* **1** alleviate, mitigate, relax, assuage, abate, rid, dwindle, diminish, free, liberate, let up, lessen, slacken, emancipate, loosen, unbind. **2** aid, help, assist, solace, comfort, support, sustain, cure, strengthen, treat, medicate, soothe, refresh, improve, succor. **3** exempt, excuse, release, remit, reprieve, relegate, substitute, spell, replace, deliver, parole, spare, discharge, take over, pinch-hit.

ant. 1 intensify, heighten, bind, press. **2** hamper, irritate, abuse, undermine.

religion *n.* **1** faith, theology, persuasion, denomination, affiliation, church, sect, piety, holiness, dogma, doctrine, belief, creed, credo. **2** commitment, passion, love, enthusiasm, life, interest, thing (*Slang*).

religious *adj.* **1** devout, pious, spiritual, godly, holy, sanctified, reverent, pietistic, orthodox, saintly, sacred, God-fearing, churchgoing, sectarian. **2** conscientious, scrupulous, faithful, strict, meticulous, mindful, unswerving, unquestioning, zealous, loyal, blind, credulous, worshipful, fervent. **ant. 1** irreligious, disbelieving, agnostic, atheistic. **2** lax, casual, careless, unconcerned.

relinquish *v.* give up, abandon, abjure, cede, leave, renounce, disclaim, renege, disavow, submit, surrender, retire, abdicate, forswear, waive, drop. **ant.** keep, retain, claim, cling to, insist on, hold.

relinquishment *n.* ABNEGATION.

relish *n.* **1** appetite, appreciation, liking, zest, enthusiasm, enjoyment, pleasure, satisfaction, taste, gusto, gratification, delight, savor. **2** tang,

piquancy, flavor, pungency, spice, bite, liveliness, zip, punch, excitement, appeal, fascination, allure, thrill, kick (*Slang*), pizzazz (*Slang*). **3** hint, trace, suggestion, shadow, whiff, whisper, bit, evocation, sign, tinge, glimmer, scent, token, indication, *soupçon*. —*v.* like, enoy, appreciate, savor, delight in, luxuriate in, bask in, revel in, prefer, look forward to.

ant. *n.* **1** dislike, antipathy, distaste, displeasure. **2** vapidness, tastelessness, flatness, dullness, boredom, blandness. —*v.* dislike, shun, avoid, detest, abhor.

reluctant *adj.* disinclined, unwilling, loath, averse, hesitant, slow, unenthusiastic, balky, foot-dragging, laggard, recalcitrant, resentful, grudging, hesitant, squeamish.

ant. enthusiastic, eager, willing, cooperative, quick, ready.

rely *v.* trust, lean, depend, count, bank, reckon, believe, swear by, follow, build on, confide, credit, look to.

ant. distrust, suspect, disbelieve, question.

remain *v.* **1** stay behind, outstay, outlive, survive, outlast, linger, loiter, tarry, hang around, wait. **2** stay put, stay, continue, live, dwell, reside, rest, roost, lodge, persist, cling, go on, persevere, inhabit, settle. **3** prevail, endure, last, abide, drag on, wear, weather, hold up, hang on, hang in (*Slang*).

ant. 1 go, leave, go under, die. **2** move, change, transfer, gad about. **3** fade, fail, decline, give up.

remainder *n.* rest, balance, excess, overage, surplus, residue, remains, leftovers, superfluity, trace, dregs, scraps, vestige, ghost, relic.

remains *n.* **1** remnants, oddments, odds and ends, scraps, leavings, waste, dregs, residue, refuse, remainder, debris, ruins, relics, discards, junk. **2** corpse, body, cadaver, mummy, carcass.

remake v. REMODEL.

remark n. **1** comment, observation, saying, utterance, mention, assertion, expression, statement, pronouncement, articulation, avowal, dictum, obiter dictum. **2** notice, perception, awareness, note, attention, heed, reflection, thought, mindfulness, regard, look, acknowledgment, recognition, grasp, detection. —v. **1** say, comment, mention, state, express, pronounce, avow, observe, hold, declare, assert, aver, affirm, voice, utter, articulate, verbalize, communicate, asseverate. **2** notice, observe, see, note, take note of, take in, heed, regard, detect, attend, perceive, make out, mark, register, respond, find, feel, sense.

ant. n. **2** inattention, disregard, neglect v. **2** overlook, neglect, ignore, disregard.

remarkable adj. **1** noteworthy, striking, memorable, unforgettable, eminent, outstanding, distinguished, exceptional, special, glorious, renowned, illustrious, significant, red-letter, marvelous, stunning. **2** unexpected, extraordinary, unusual, miraculous, unforeseen, unique, singular, odd, freakish, bizarre, strange, surprising, astounding, amazing, incredible.

ant. **1, 2** ordinary, inconspicuous, usual, average, routine, unexceptional.

remedial adj. corrective, therapeutic, curative, correctional, reformative, medicinal, beneficial, restorative, prophylactic, healing, meliorative.

ant. harmful, damaging, pernicious, destructive.

remedy v. cure, heal, correct, repair, set right, rectify, reform, improve, better, restore, redress, right, relieve, help, alleviate, fix, adjust. —n. **1** medicine, treatment, cure, regimen, corrective, medication, medicament, therapy, restorative, relief, help, panacea, stimulant, dose, prescription, modality. **2** solution, help,

cure, correction, alleviation, betterment, resolution, satisfaction.

ant. v. impair, damage, harm, hurt, undermine, exacerbate.

remember v. **1** recall, summon up, recollect, retrieve, reminisce, look back, call up, dredge up, review, recover, retrace, bethink, think back, dig up, revive, relive, call to mind, bring to mind. **2** keep in mind, bear in mind, think upon, commemorate, memorialize. **3** reward, tip, bequeath, hand down, bestow, endow, will, devise.

ant. **2** forget, draw a blank (Slang), lose sight of.

remembrance n. **1** recall, recollection, review, retrieval, reminiscence, nostalgia, retrospect, retrospection, commemoration, memorization, memorialization. **2** gift, memento, keepsake, souvenir, relic, trophy, memorial. **3** MEMORY.

remind v. bring to mind, recall, cue, allude to, hint, suggest, prompt, prod, jog, refresh, review.

reminiscence n. recall, review, nostalgia, memoir, diary, autobiography, journal, chronicle, remembrance, recollection, reflection, retrospection.

remiss adj. negligent, careless, lax, inattentive, derelict, delinquent, slack, neglectful, sloppy, culpable, irresponsible, oblivious, slipshod, forgetful, unmindful, offhand, absentminded.

ant. careful, scrupulous, heedful, meticulous, dutiful, blameless.

remission n. **1** pardon, release, exemption, amnesty, reprieve, forgiveness, exoneration, clearance, remittal, discharge, indulgence, acquittal, absolution, excuse. **2** abatement, alleviation, amelioration, assuagement, abeyance, lapse, let-up, cessation, stop, breather, break, interruption, relief, relaxation, respite, decrease.

ant. **2** continuation, increase, prolongation, intensification, exacerbation.

remit v. **1** exempt, excuse, pardon, forgive, clear, condone, overlook, discharge, exonerate, discharge, acquit, free, reprieve, release. **2** restore, replace, return, give back, pay back, send back, settle, reimburse, compensate, rectify, indemnify. **3** postpone, delay, put off, set aside, pigeonhole, lay over, table, procrastinate. **4** diminish, abate, lessen, relax, decrease, reduce, moderate, soften, calm, alleviate, temper, slacken, extenuate, weaken, dwindle.

ant. 4 intensify, worsen, deteriorate, aggravate, increase.

remittal *n.* REMISSION.

remnant *n.* shred, scrap, fragment, leftover, vestige, shard, relic, carry-over, hangover, trace, remainder, residue, reminder, evocation, token, souvenir.

remodel *v.* reconstruct, reshape, rebuild, refashion, redo, reform, reestablish, convert, alter, change, refurbish, update, streamline, overhaul, make over, remake, revamp, renovate, tune up.

remonstrance *n.* PROTEST.

remonstrate *v.* protest, object, argue, demur, expostulate, oppose, complain, dispute, contend, dissent, differ, challenge, knock (*Slang*), beef (*Slang*).

ant. accept, agree, support, comply, assent.

remorse *n.* self-reproach, contrition, guilt, regret, penitence, sorrow, repentance, compunction, ruefulness, anguish.

remorseful *adj.* regretful, contrite, sorry, repentant, self-reproachful, penitent, conscience-stricken, rueful, guilt-ridden, anguished, tormented, heavy-hearted.

ant. self-satisfied, self-righteous, untroubled, smug.

remorseless *adj.* merciless, ruthless, pitiless, cruel, inhumane, hardhearted, unfeeling, coldblooded, heartless, bloodless, fiendish, savage, brutal, callous, unrelenting, unremorseful.

ant. compassionate, merciful, humane, sympathetic, kindhearted.

remote *adj.* **1** far-off, distant, outlying, backwoods, faraway, out-of-the-way, inaccessible, unreachable, godforsaken, isolated, sequestered, removed. **2** prehistoric, ancient, antediluvian, age-old, primitive, immemorial, forgotten, unremembered, buried. **3** unrelated, separate, foreign, irrelevant, unconnected, far-fetched, extraneous, off-target, immaterial, alien, disparate, incompatible, distant. **4** faint, subtle, vague, slight, small, meager, indistinct, improbable, unlikely, minimal, limited, imperceptible, slim, slender. **5** withdrawn, reserved, cold, aloof, unapproachable, starchy, reticent, introverted, unsociable, off-putting, frosty, forbidding, unfriendly, standoffish, formal, introspective.

ant. 1 nearby, close, neighboring, **2** current, recent, contemporary. **3** germane, apposite, relevant, related. **4** distinct, obvious, visible, marked, large. **5** friendly, warm, outgoing, affable.

removal *n.* **1** displacement, dislocation, withdrawal, pullout, transfer, dislodgment, uprooting, transplantation, relocation, transportation, cartage, erasure, obliteration, deletion. **2** dismissal, ousting, ouster, firing, ejection, discharge, eviction, dethronement, expulsion, banishment.

ant. 2 installation, hiring, enthronement, election.

remove *v.* **1** take away, move away, take off, depart, pull out, transfer, relocate, dislocate, reposition, withdraw, dislodge, uproot, divest, carry away. **2** get rid of, do away with, erase, elide, extirpate, obliterate, cancel, wipe out, clean, eliminate, eradicate, purge, undo, discard, delete, expunge. **3** dismiss, displace, eject, oust, depose, unseat, dethrone, banish, exile, expel, discharge, fire, lay off, kick out (*Slang*), bounce (*Slang*), sack (*Slang*), can (*Slang*).

4 take out, extract, pull out, yank, purify, sift, sieve, strain, disconnect, detach, separate, cut off, sever, trim, simplify.

ant. 1 put back, come back, resettle, replace. **2** restore, keep, retain, include, stet. **3** hire, install, seat. **4** put in, insert, attach, connect.

remunerate *v.* PAY.

remuneration *n.* payment, repayment, compensation, recompense, reimbursement, reward, tip, stipend, fee, honorarium, indemnification, remembrance, satisfaction, reparation, settlement.

renaissance *n.* RENASCENCE.

renascence *n.* rebirth, revival, renaissance, reestablishment, recrudescence, regeneration, reemergence, restoration, resurrection, revitalization, rejuvenation, reawakening, resurgence, reappearance.

rend *v.* **1** tear apart, split, part, break, fragment, pull, wrench, sunder, rive, shatter, sever, cleave, crack. **2** distress, move, wring, hurt, stab, anguish, disturb, upset, overwhelm, sadden.

ant. 1 put together, unite, cement, mend, join.

render *v.* **1** give, present, submit, provide, furnish, perform, do, supply, offer, turn over, accomplish, impart, lend, relinquish, deliver. **2** represent, depict, translate, play, portray, rephrase, transmute, reword, interpret, explicate, delineate, execute, define, express.

ant. 1 keep, withhold, retain.

rendezvous *n.* appointment, meeting, date, assignation, tryst, retreat, nest, haunt, hideaway, hideout, hangout (*Slang*), twosome, tête-à-tête.

rendition *n.* version, interpretation, performance, edition, reading, representation, depiction, portrayal, expression, delineation, impersonation, characterization, translation, rendering, execution.

renegade *n.* **1** traitor, apostate, turncoat, defector, secessionist, sep-

aratist, recusant, heretic, insurgent, betrayer, dissenter, Benedict Arnold, quisling. **2** rebel, nonconformist, independent, maverick, mugwump, oddball, dissident, hippie, outsider, malcontent, iconoclast, mutineer, deserter, outcast, expatriate, weirdo (*Slang*). —*adj.* traitorous, heretical, rebellious, insurgent, recusant, nonconformist, dissident, mutinous, maverick, apostate, disloyal, unfaithful, recreant, perfidious, treasonable.

ant. *adj.* loyal, faithful, steadfast, uncritical, obedient, unswerving.

renege *v.* back out, back down, double-cross (*Slang*), let down, default, repudiate, shirk, deceive, welsh (*Slang*).

ant. fulfill, satisfy, come through, make good.

renew *v.* **1** remake, remodel, revise, refashion, reshape, reform, recreate, regenerate, redo, renovate, reestablish, overhaul, refresh, refurbish, modernize. **2** resume, begin again, return, take up, recommence, resurrect.

renounce *v.* repudiate, disclaim, disavow, abjure, forswear, abnegate, disown, relinquish, give up, forgo, abandon, resign, hand over, reject.

ant. accept, claim, keep, cling to, insist on.

renovate *v.* refurbish, modernize, renew, redo, overhaul, revamp, remodel, refresh, rejuvenate, furbish, convert, repair, redecorate, redesign.

renown *n.* fame, repute, celebrity, note, acclaim, publicity, prominence, popularity, status, notoriety, eminence, prestige, elevation, illustriousness, notability, importance.

renowned *adj.* famous, celebrated, well-known, outstanding, prominent, conspicuous, noteworthy, eminent, notable, acknowledged, noted, remarkable, popular, acclaimed, leading, notorious.

ant. unknown, obscure, anonymous, unrecognized.

rent[1] *v.* lease, let, sublet, sublease.

rent[2] *n.* **1** hole, slit, tear, damage, rip, flaw, puncture, chink, tatter, cleft, leak, aperture, perforation, slot, lacuna. **2** schism, split, rift, breach, rupture, wrench, break, estrangement, disunion, cleavage, division.

renter *n.* tenant, lessee, leaser, subtenant, sublessee, leaseholder, occupant.

renunciation *n.* repudiation, disclaimer, disavowal, abjuration, forswearing, relinquishment, abandonment, resignation, abnegation, rejection, abdication, recantation, refusal, waiver, expulsion.
ant. acceptance, claim, adherence, avowal.

reopen *v.* RESUME.

repair *v.* **1** restore, fix, mend, recondition, overhaul, refresh, renovate, renew, refurbish, patch up, tune up, revamp, rehabilitate, freshen, readjust, rejuvenate. **2** compensate for, make up for, correct, remedy, redress, set right, square, rectify, requite, make good, repay, recompense, remunerate, pay back, relieve, alleviate, appease. —*n.* reparation, renovation, restoration, renewal, refurbishment, rehabilitation, compensation, correction, remedy, redress, repayment, recompense, relief, alleviation.

reparable *adj.* remediable, curable, salvageable, retrievable, mendable, rectifiable, correctable, corrigible.
ant. irreparable, beyond repair, incurable, irremediable, hopeless.

reparation *n.* atonement, expiation, amends, satisfaction, redress, recompense, propitiation, damages, compensation, requital, remuneration, apology.

repartee *n.* badinage, persiflage, banter, pleasantries, chit-chat.

repast *n.* meal, food, refreshment, snack, spread, feast, banquet, bite, tea (*Brit.*), victuals, eats, nosh.

repay *v.* **1** pay back, refund, rebate, reimburse, reward, indemnify, return, recompense, make good, square accounts, settle up. **2** get even, retaliate, compensate, redeem, avenge, get back at, requite, reciprocate, revenge, reward, strike back, vindicate.

repeal *v.* rescind, revoke, nullify, cancel, void, abrogate, retract, countermand, invalidate, override, set aside, annul, abolish, do away with, withdraw, delete. —*n.* revocation, nullification, rescission, cancellation, abrogation, rescindment, retraction, invalidation, annulment, abolition, recall, reversal, termination, withdrawal, deletion.

repeat *v.* **1** reiterate, iterate, say again, retell, redo, remake, reaffirm, reassert, emphasize, reexperience, reinform, harp on, recapitulate, restate. **2** reveal, divulge, give away, spill, talk, rat (*Slang*).

repel *v.* **1** reject, refuse, rebuff, turn down, turn away, repudiate, disown, renounce, disapprove, oppose, object to, spurn, scorn, disdain, decline. **2** disgust, repulse, nauseate, sicken, revolt, alienate, irritate, offend, turn off (*Slang*). **3** REPULSE.
ant. 1 accept, approve, encourage. **2** please, attract, gratify.

repellent *adj.* **1** repulsive, disgusting, nauseating, sickening, offensive, revolting, unsavory, off-putting, loathsome, odious, repugnant, obnoxious, insufferable, distasteful, unappetizing. **2** REPULSIVE.
ant. attractive, agreeable, pleasing, congenial, likable, charming.

repent *v.* regret, rue, bewail, bemoan, lament, deplore, repine.

repentance *n.* regret, remorse, contrition, penitence, sorrow, compunction, lamentation, grief, self-reproach, guilt, anguish, qualms, bitterness, misgivings.
ant. smugness, self-satisfaction, self-righteousness.

repercussions *n.* consequences, aftereffects, aftermath, results, upshot, fruit, developments, rewards, effects, reverberations, ripples, waves.

repetition *n.* **1** repetitiousness, iteration, reiteration, redoing, remaking, recapitulation, restatement, recurrence, reappearance, duplication, reversion, replication, rote, *déjà vu*. **2** copy, duplicate, replica, reproduction, facsimile, recording, refrain, encore, litany, echo, repeat, double, ditto, rehash.

ant. 1 newness, freshness, uniqueness, singularity, precedence.

repetitious *adj.* repetitive, boring, dull, tiresome, monotonous, unvaried, unchanging, repeated, habitual, redundant, pleonastic, tautological, humdrum, tedious, routinized, rehashed.

ant. fresh, new, interesting, varied, changing, excited, unexpected.

repetitive *adj.* REPETITIOUS.

rephrase *v.* RECAST.

repine *v.* mope, languish, fret, droop, brood, sulk, despond, despair, lament, bewail, bemoan, complain, grumble, beef (*Slang*), bitch (*Slang*).

replace *v.* supersede, supplant, substitute, take the place of, substitute for, displace, succeed, follow, understudy, represent, fill in for, relieve, alternate.

replacement *n.* substitute, alternate, understudy, surrogate, proxy, agent, pinch-hitter, bench-warmer, second, refill, replica, fill-in, equivalent, makeshift, ersatz.

replenish *v.* restore, refresh, refill, stock, restock, reload, reorder, store, provision, contribute, load up, fill up, replace, provide for.

ant. deplete, use up, consume, exhaust, empty.

replete *adj.* **1** full, filled, packed, loaded, jammed, overflowing, crammed. **2** satiated, gorged, full, sated, brimming, bursting, overfed, stuffed.

ant. 1 empty, vacant, unpopulated, unoccupied. **2** hungry, ravenous, unsated, starving.

replica *n.* duplicate, facsimile, copy, reproduction, photocopy, print, reprint, double, imitation, counterpart,

likeness, simulacrum, ditto, twin, transcript.

ant. original, master, archetype, pattern.

replicate *v.* COPY.

reply *v.* **1** answer, respond, retort, refute, rejoin, rebut, riposte. **2** react, reciprocate, retaliate, respond, requite, return, report, strike back. —*n.* answer, response, retort, riposte, rebuttal, refutation, confirmation, rejoinder, reaction, retaliation, reciprocation, comeback.

ant. *v.* **1** question, ask, inquire. *n.* stimulus, question, query.

report *v.* **1** relate, narrate, describe, detail, divulge, reveal, inform, tell, disclose, air, announce, publicize, publish, broadcast, bruit about, apprise. **2** repeat, relay, communicate, advise, retail, retell, restate, bring word, rehash, transmit, deliver. —*n.* **1** account, story, release, description, revelation, disclosure, announcement, statement, summary, dossier, communiqué, communication, bulletin, record, narration, memorandum, memoir. **2** rumor, gossip, hearsay, common knowledge, insinuation, chit-chat, *on-dit*, tidbit, scuttlebutt (*Slang*). **3** fame, character, reputation, repute, name, standing, prestige, regard, influence, rank, position, status, caliber, note. **4** explosion, detonation, shot, bang, crack, salvo, reverberation, discharge, volley, blast, boom, burst.

repose *n.* **1** rest, sleep, relaxation, calm, peacefulness, quiet, quietude, inertia, quiescence, dormancy, slumber, passivity, respite, stillness, inactivity. **2** composure, serenity, tranquillity, poise, peace of mind, placidity, dignity, self-possession, equanimity, stability, balance, self-assurance, sang-froid, cool (*Slang*).

ant. 1 excitement, activity, bustle, noise, disturbance. **2** anxiety, jitters, fidgets, nervousness.

repository *n.* **1** depository, closet, cupboard, bin, catch-all, warehouse, storehouse, armoire, drawer, container, receptacle, vault, cabinet. **2** museum, library, archives, treasury, treasure-house, store, mine, source, reserve, thesaurus.

reprehend v. CRITICIZE.

reprehensible *adj.* blameworthy, culpable, remiss, censurable, blamable, delinquent, criminal, immoral, unethical, objectionable, disreputable, wrong, wicked, damnable, heinous, derelict, sinful, miscreant, villainous. **ant.** irreproachable, blameless, innocent, guiltless, law-abiding, commendable.

represent v. **1** symbolize, express, exemplify, typify, depict, stand for, denote, mean, betoken, indicate, embody, signalize, illustrate, imply. **2** impersonate, enact, play, perform, portray, mime, mimic, pantomime, counterfeit. **3** show, present, depict, evoke, delineate, etch, limn, sketch, mirror, reflect, picture, conjure.

representation *n.* **1** indication, expression, exemplification, impersonation, performance, portrayal, delineation, characterization, spectacle, show, depiction, substitution, designation, replacement. **2** likeness, symbol, type, model, specimen, example, image, icon, token, picture, photograph, effigy. **3** argument, presentation, proof, thesis, demonstration, evidence, argumentation, polemics, demagogy, propaganda, position, proposition, doctrine, ism, line, pitch.

representative *adj.* **1** characteristic, typical, symbolic, illustrative, emblematic, descriptive, indicative, exemplary, archetypal, prototypal. **2** substitute, deputized, delegated, authorized, accredited, commissioned, proxy, alternate, surrogate, backup. —*n.* **1** type, symbol, example, model, specimen, instance, archetype, exemplar, paradigm, exemplification, embodiment, illustration, personification, incarnation, norm. **2** delegate, agent, deputy, envoy, proxy, emissary, legislator, law-maker, substitute, surrogate, backup, alternate, second, legate, ambassador, appointee, advocate, ombudsman.

ant. *adj.* **1** atypical, unusual, exceptional, odd, abnormal, aberrant, anomalous. *n.* **1** freak, anomaly, oddity, abnormality, exception, aberration.

repress v. **1** restrain, control, inhibit, stifle, block, hamper, hinder, leash, squelch, hold back, hold in, hamstring, swallow, suppress, check, sit on, curb. **2** put down, quell, quash, subdue, overpower, vanquish, censor, subjugate, overwhelm, defeat, dominate, master, undo, silence, stamp out, crush.

ant. 1 encourage, liberate, free, let loose, express. **2** allow, permit, sanction, authorize.

repression *n.* subjugation, domination, censorship, mastery, suppression, tyranny, regimentation, quashing, prohibition, subjection, defeat, coercion, control, domination, bondage, constraint, duress.

ant. liberation, freedom, emancipation.

reprieve v. remit, relieve, suspend, stay, abate, alleviate, relax, respite, exonerate, remand, slacken, pardon. —*n.* suspension, respite, abeyance, breather, breathing spell, alleviation, mitigation, truce, amnesty, cessation, remission, stay, pardon, relief.

reprimand v. reprove, censure, rebuke, reproach, chide, admonish, scold, chastise, upbraid, take to task, find fault with, reprehend, tell off, chew out (*Slang*). —*n.* reproof, rebuke, reproach, scolding, condemnation, censure, dressing-down, talking-to, tongue-lashing, admonishment, disapprobation, denunciation, upbraiding, castigation, tirade, chewing out (*Slang*), what for (*Slang*).

ant. *v.* approve, endorse, applaud, praise, compliment. *n.* approval, endorsement, praise, commendation.

reprisal *n.* counterattack, counterblow,

countermove, counteroffensive, retaliation, retribution, revenge, vengeance, repayment, requital, tit for tat, *lex talionis,* revanchism.

reproach *v.* blame, rebuke, charge, chide, take to task, criticize, reprimand, chastise, reprove, scold, disapprove of, call to account, accuse, chew out (*Slang*). —*n.* **1** reproof, charge, censure, criticism, disapproval, lecture, accusation, condemnation, scolding, dressing-down, disparagement, tirade, denunciation. **2** disgrace, discredit, shame, ignominy, dishonor, obloquy, opprobrium, disrepute, humiliation, scorn, degradation.

ant. *v.* approve, endorse, praise, commend. *n.* **1** approval, endorsement, praise, commendation. **2** esteem, glory, honor, renown.

reprobate *adj.* depraved, corrupt, profligate, debauched, abandoned, immoral, sinful, unprincipled, roguish, shameless, dissolute, degenerate, evil, wicked, irredeemable, damned. —*n.* profligate, degenerate, wastrel, rounder, debauchee, sinner, good-for-nothing, ne'er-do-well, roué, libertine, scoundrel, bum, rotter (*Brit.*). —*v.* CONDEMN.

ant. *adj.* moral, upright, virtuous, pure.

reproduce *v.* **1** copy, redo, remake, recreate, reflect, repeat, duplicate, reprint, trace, mirror, echo, match, transcribe, photocopy, recast. **2** breed, bear, procreate, multiply, clone, proliferate, generate, beget, propagate, hatch, spawn, fructify, populate.

reproduction *n.* **1** duplication, reduplication, transcription, printing, tracing, taping, photocopying, copying, imitation, forging, counterfeiting, engraving. **2** propagation, insemination, fertilization, cloning, spawning, hatching, laying, dropping, fission. **3** copy, facsimile, remake, print, lithograph, tracing, replica,

photocopy, recording, record, tape, transcript.

ant. 3 original, master, first.

reproductive *adj.* generative, sexual, progenitive, genitive, genital, procreative, germinative, propagative, life-giving.

ant. sterile, barren, jejune.

reproof *n.* censure, reproach, reprimand, rebuke, admonition, blame, scolding, chastisement, punishment, faultfinding, tongue-lashing, dressing-down, disapproval, denunciation, condemnation, scorn, disdain.

ant. approval, praise, commendation, endorsement.

reprove *v.* **1** censure, reproach, reprimand, rebuke, chastise, punish, scold, admonish, twit, correct, castigate, chasten, take to task, accuse, chew out (*Slang*). **2** disapprove of, condemn, sneer at, disdain, disparage, frown on, run down, belittle, discredit, object to, take a dim view of, knock (*Slang*), put down (*Slang*).

ant. 1, 2 praise, commend, endorse, approve.

repudiate *v.* **1** reject, disclaim, contravene, abjure, revoke, deny, gainsay, protest, override, repeal, disavow, discredit, disbelieve, contradict. **2** cast off, disown, discard, divorce, renounce, cut off, ignore, disregard, dismiss, exile, banish, relegate, dodge.

ant. 1 accept, agree, believe, concede. **2** embrace, adopt, welcome.

repugnance *n.* aversion, dislike, loathing, detestation, antipathy, distaste, displeasure, repulsion, revulsion, abhorrence, disgust, animosity, hostility, reluctance, unwillingness.

ant. enthusiasm, pleasure, sympathy, eagerness.

repugnant *adj.* REPULSIVE.

repulse *v.* **1** repel, drive back, push back, beat off, withstand, counteract, check, stop, halt, thwart, rout, frustrate, fight off. **2** rebuff, snub, cold-shoulder, put off, reject, disdain, ig-

nore, disregard, discountenance, discomfit. **3** REPEL.
ant. 1 yield, submit, capitulate. **2** accept, welcome, receive.

repulsive *adj.* **1** repugnant, repellent, disgusting, obnoxious, loathsome, nauseating, distasteful, abhorrent, hateful, detestable, aversive, disagreeable, revolting, hideous, offensive. **2** forbidding, off-putting, aloof, austere, snobbish, unfriendly, unsympathetic, distant, cold, icy, remote, unapproachable, unresponsive, repellent.
ant. 1 attractive, charming, pleasing, pleasant, likable, enchanting, disarming. **2** warm, friendly, gregarious, sociable, affable, approachable.

reputable *adj.* estimable, honorable, notable, honored, esteemed, respected, reliable, upright, respectable, scrupulous, trustworthy, well-regarded, honest, dependable, unimpeachable, trusted.
ant. disreputable, shady, corrupt, unreliable, questionable, notorious.

reputation *n.* name, repute, standing, regard, odor, esteem, estimation, reliability, honor, honesty, report, note, fame, prominence, stature.
ant. obscurity, anonymity, disrepute, disregard.

repute *n.* REPUTATION.

reputed *adj.* considered, supposed, accepted, estimated, seeming, accounted, regarded, judged, assumed, reported, putative, ostensible, apparent.

request *v.* ask for, petition, requisition, apply, appeal, solicit, seek, invoke, desire, pray, wish, importune, entreat, beseech, beg, plead. —*n.* desire, favor, want, need, answer, wish, requirement, requisition, petition, application, solicitation, appeal, importuning, plea, entreaty.

require *v.* **1** need, crave, hanker, yearn for, covet, miss, lack, hunger for, thirst for. **2** demand, insist on, want, call for, necessitate, impose.

required *adj.* requisite, necessary, indispensable, needful, prerequisite, called-for, demanded, mandatory, obligatory, compulsory, essential, vital, wanted, basic, fundamental, imperative.
ant. optional, elective, dispensable, unnecessary, marginal.

requirement *n.* requisite, prerequisite, requisition, request, need, want, necessity, essential, precondition, obligation, demand, command, order, must, constraint, dictate, rule, dictum, ukase.

requisite *adj.* REQUIRED. —*n.* REQUIREMENT.

requisition *n., v.* REQUEST.

requital *n.* RECOMPENSE.

requite *v.* repay, reward, fulfill, return, satisfy, recompense, compensate, reciprocate, respond, make good, remember, reimburse, pay back, retaliate, revenge, give tit for tat.

rescind *v.* cancel, void, repeal, annul, recall, retract, withdraw, invalidate, abrogate, countermand, abolish, revoke, nullify, override, vacate.
ant. uphold, validate, confirm, approve.

rescission *n.* REPEAL.

rescue *v.* save, free, liberate, deliver, redeem, recover, ransom, emancipate, preserve, salvage, reclaim, extricate, rehabilitate, help. —*n.* deliverance, release, redemption, liberation, recovery, ransom, emancipation, extrication, freedom, salvation, relief, narrow escape, close call, assistance.

research *n.* investigation, inquiry, study, probing, scrutiny, experimentation, fact-finding, analysis, theorizing, exploration, digging, delving. —*v.* investigate, inquire, study, probe, dig, experiment, analyze, pioneer, explore, scrutinize, delve, theorize, test.

resemblance *n.* similarity, likeness, correspondence, kinship, similitude, approximation, closeness, relationship, analogy, parallelism, affinity, sameness, congruence, connection, tie, comparability.

ant. difference, contrast, dissimilarity, disparity.

resemble *v.* look like, take after, approximate, duplicate, parallel, echo, mirror, match, correspond.

resentful *adj.* indignant, hurt, wounded, upset, angry, offended, piqued, bitter, rancorous, huffy, outraged, exasperated, provoked, sore.

ant. well-disposed, good-natured, forgiving, complacent.

resentment *n.* indignation, anger, ill will, pique, rancor, outrage, exasperation, bitterness, hostility, animosity, acrimony, vindictiveness, antagonism.

ant. good will, understanding, forgiveness, complacency.

reservation *n.* **1** doubt, skepticism, limitation, condition, qualification, objection, exception, restriction, caveat, but, stipulation, exemption, proviso, criticism. **2** enclave, preserve, settlement, retreat, colony, enclosure, confines, close, tract, territory, grounds, domain, habitation, home, turf (*Slang*).

reserve *v.* hold back, set aside, arrange for, delay, save, retain, keep, cache, store, earmark, hang on to, postpone, book, schedule, engage. —*n.* **1** stock, store, backlog, cache, hoard, nest egg, savings, capital, reservoir, supply, stockpile, accumulation, resources, wherewithal. **2** restraint, reluctance, constraint, reticence, coolness, shyness, distance, taciturnity, aloofness, diffidence, composure, inhibition, hesitancy, unwillingness, secretiveness, evasiveness.

ant. *n.* **2** straightforwardness, boldness, openness, spontaneity, friendliness, directness, warmth, insouciance.

reserved *adj.* restrained, undemonstrative, reticent, self-effacing, taciturn, cool, shy, diffident, distant, inhibited, formal, uncommunicative, retiring, bashful.

ant. outgoing, gregarious, sociable, warm, friendly, uninhibited.

reservoir *n.* reserve, store, stock, supply, fund, mine, repository, depository, hoard, accumulation, resource, source, wherewithal, backlog, sufficiency.

reside *v.* dwell, live, inhabit, stay, occupy, domicile, remain, lodge, settle, nestle, nest, keep house, encamp.

reside in inhere, exist, dwell, lie, belong, rest, be inherent, be vested.

residence *n.* home, habitation, dwelling, domicile, lodging, quarters, house, place, abode, living quarters, household, apartment, flat, pad (*Slang*), address, residency.

residency *n.* RESIDENCE.

resident *n.* dweller, inhabitant, occupant, tenant, lodger, addressee, housekeeper, denizen, sojourner, householder, settler, citizen. —*adj.* residing, living, settled, dwelling, inhabiting, occupying, lodged, lodging, installed, domiciled, established.

ant. *n.* traveler, wanderer, gypsy, vagrant, vagabond, stranger, alien. *adj.* foreign, alien.

residue *n.* remainder, remains, leavings, scraps, ashes, rest, balance, leftovers, remnants, residuum, dregs, odds and ends, refuse, trash.

resign *v.* **1** relinquish, give up, quit, abdicate, depart, leave, renounce, vacate, disclaim, hand over, withdraw, reject, desert, forsake, relegate, abandon. **2** submit, yield, reconcile oneself, surrender, brook, bear with, cope with, capitulate, acquiesce, bow to, give in, accede.

ant. **1** continue, pursue, go on, carry out, cling to. **2** fight against, battle, contest, resist, oppose.

resignation *n.* **1** withdrawal, retirement, leave-taking, notice, relinquishment, quitting, abdication, rejection, abandonment, departure, divorce, relegation, renunciation, divestment. **2** patience, submission,

submissiveness, sufferance, endurance, nonresistance, forbearance, surrender, capitulation, self-sacrifice, meekness, passivity, tolerance, acquiescence.
ant. 1 involvement, attachment, continuation. **2** resistance, opposition, impatience.

resigned *adj.* submissive, patient, enduring, forbearing, meek, tolerant, acquiescent, self-sacrificing, reconciled, uncomplaining, stoical, docile, subservient, put-upon, abject.
ant. resistant, rebellious, unwilling, defiant, belligerent, unyielding.

resilience *n.* **1** elasticity, stretch, bounce, resiliency, springiness, spring, tensility, ductility, give, flexibility, pliancy, pliability, adjustability. **2** flexibility, adaptability, pliancy, pliability, buoyancy, responsiveness, amenability, complaisance.
ant. 1 stiffness, rigidity, inflexibility, friability. **2** stolidity, unresponsiveness, rigidity, stubbornness.

resiliency *n.* RESILIENCE.

resilient *adj.* **1** elastic, flexible, springy, rubbery, stretch, tensile, rebounding, adjustable. **2** responsive, buoyant, sprightly, lively, perky, relaxed, free, adaptable, amenable, agreeable, complaisant.
ant. 1 rigid, inflexible, fixed, set. **2** stolid, unaccommodating, unresponsive, stultified.

resist *v.* fight, struggle against, foil, frustrate, thwart, withstand, battle, defy, repulse, flout, contest, obstruct, dispute, recoil.
ant. comply, give in, yield, surrender, capitulate.

resistance *n.* struggle, opposition, defiance, intransigence, repulsion, obstruction, frustration, protest, recalcitrance, rebellion, refusal, counteraction, insubordination, disobedience, refusal.
ant. compliance, cooperation, capitulation, surrender.

resolute *adj.* determined, purposeful, decisive, firm, steady, constant, fixed, unswerving, unyielding, flat-footed, resolved, convinced, strong-willed, decided, steadfast, persevering, persistent, adamant.
ant. weak, changeable, unsteady, faltering, purposeless, aimless.

resolution *n.* **1** resolve, determination, decision, dedication, ambition, perseverance, constancy, tenacity, devotion, persistence, patience, assiduity, conviction, heart, stick-to-itiveness, purposefulness. **2** plan, scheme, proposal, proposition, purpose, aim, end, ambition, target, intention, motion, undertaking, objective, goal, project, enterprise. **3** outcome, end, result, denouement, settlement, solution, upshot, conclusion, windup, termination, culmination, disposition, accommodation, conciliation, payoff, aftermath, fallout.
ant. 1 uncertainty, indecision, aimlessness, inconstancy, fickleness.

resolve *v.* **1** decide, determine, intend, aim, persevere, persist, plan, propose, set out, undertake, set about, will, take steps, venture, pursue, desire. **2** separate, split up, analyze, break up, take apart, reduce, convert, dissolve, transmute, catalyze, metabolize, transform. **3** solve, explain, answer, untangle, unravel, settle, straighten, interpret, unriddle, establish, reveal, fathom, penetrate, clear up, elucidate, crack. —*n.* **1** decision, plan, resolution, undertaking, purpose, objective, target, enterprise, choice, commitment, pledge, vow, course, conclusion. **2** RESOLUTION.
ant. *v.* **2** integrate, coalesce, combine, reconstitute. **3** complicate, tangle, confuse, obfuscate.

resort *v.* frequent, visit, repair to, revisit, haunt, attend, betake oneself, head for, habituate, hang out (*Slang*). —*n.* **1** hotel, inn, club, lodge, spa, watering place (*Brit.*), camp. **2** RECOURSE.

resort to have recourse, apply, refer, turn to, make use of, use, utilize, employ, apply.

resound *v.* **1** reverberate, resonate, echo, ring, vibrate, reecho. **2** clang, boom, chime, roar, rumble, roll, peal, thunder, bellow.

resourceful *adj.* ingenious, clever, capable, inventive, able, improvisational, talented, enterprising, aggressive, industrious, imaginative, creative, expert, skillful, cunning, competent, shrewd, practical, pragmatic.
ant. helpless, dependent, incompetent, unimaginative, orthodox.

resources *n.* **1** means, capabilities, strengths, essentials, wherewithal, materials, power, capacity, know-how, expertise, instrumentality, reserves. **2** wealth, capital, money, savings, funds, nest egg, assets, riches, cash, property, portfolio.

respect *v.* esteem, honor, revere, look up to, defer to, appreciate, prize, venerate, praise, value. —*n.* **1** esteem, regard, honor, reverence, appreciation, veneration, deference, consideration, obedience, compliance, acknowledgment, submission. **2** aspect, detail, facet, regard, sense, point of view, particular, feature, angle, condition.
ant. *v.* disrespect, dishonor, deride, scorn. *n.* **1** contempt, disdain, discourtesy, disobedience, disregard.

respectable *adj.* **1** admirable, worthy, estimable, honorable, praiseworthy, venerable, valuable, august, commendable, meritorious. **2** proper, acceptable, conventional, correct, decorous, orthodox, punctilious, genteel, reputable, polite, appropriate, seemly, suitable, conformist, *comme il faut.* **3** appreciable, considerable, sizable, fair, definite, distinct, apparent, noticeable, evident, goodly, substantial, reasonable.
ant. **1** contemptible, dishonorable, worthless, despicable, pitiable. **2** unconventional, raffish, unacceptable. **3** poor, small, insignificant, picayune.

respected *adj.* admired, honored, es-

teemed, revered, praised, venerated, deferred to, valued, appreciated, exalted, obeyed.
ant. scorned, despised, pitied, sneered at, mocked, disobeyed.

respectful *adj.* deferential, obedient, reverent, admiring, courteous, accommodating, self-effacing, compliant, regardful, humble, submissive, solicitous, attentive.
ant. rude, disobedient, contemptuous, rebellious, irreverent.

respire *v.* BREATHE.

respite *n.* **1** postponement, delay, suspension, adjournment, deferment, remission, tabling, shelving, stay, reprieve, moratorium. **2** rest, recess, interval, abeyance, relief, relaxation, pause, intermission, let-up, break, breathing spell, lull, interim, interlude, entr'acte, breather (*Slang*).

resplendent *adj.* splendid, gorgeous, dazzling, brilliant, effulgent, radiant, glorious, lustrous, blazing, shimmering, sparkling, scintillating, bright, showy, bejeweled.
ant. dull, drab, inconspicuous, plain, gray, mousy.

respond *v.* reply, answer, retort, rejoin, return, acknowledge, notice, recognize, react, act.
ant. ignore, disregard, overlook, neglect.

response *n.* reaction, reply, answer, retort, rejoinder, rebuttal, acknowledgment, riposte, reciprocation, retaliation.

responsibility *n.* accountability, liability, obligation, commitment, onus, burden, duty, trust, charge, assignment, chore, observance, debt, contract, guarantee.

responsible *adj.* **1** accountable, answerable, liable, reliable, dependable, stable, solid, trustworthy, creditable, dutiful, solvent, subject, bound, beholden, indebted. **2** sane, rational, ethical, moral, sound, adult, mature, right-minded, logical, *compos mentis,* lucid, sober, judicious.
ant. **1** unaccountable, untrustworthy,

undependable, irresponsible, bankrupt, fly-by-night, fickle. **2** insane, irrational, psychotic, *non compos mentis.*

responsive *adj.* **1** reactive, retaliative, reciprocal, retaliatory, retributive, counteractive. **2** sympathetic, understanding, receptive, sensitive, aware, alert, warm, friendly, affectionate, demonstrative, outgoing, openhearted, forthcoming, enthusiastic, perceptive, impressionable, susceptible.
ant. 1 inert, inactive, passive. **2** cold, unfriendly, insensitive, dense, thick-skinned, distant, aloof, unapproachable.

rest[1] *v.* **1** relax, sit, lie, idle, laze, doze, nap, sleep, be still, quiet down, retire. **2** depend, hinge, rely, turn, revolve, lean, result, follow, hang.
—*n.* **1** relaxation, idleness, indolence, somnolence, lassitude, inactivity, recuperation, refreshment, revitalization, leisure, sleep, repose, retirement, nap, doze, lull, siesta, snooze. **2** recess, pause, intermission, break, breather, cessation, interlude, time-out. **3** peace, calm, tranquillity, quiet, restfulness, surcease, serenity, quietude, placidity, stillness, composure, peacefulness, motionlessness, immobility.
ant. *v.* **1** work, toil, bustle, hustle. *n.* **1** work, activity, bustle, exertion, sweat, toil. **3** agitation, excitement, disturbance, noise, perturbation, turmoil.

rest[2] *n.* remains, remainder, leftovers, residue, remnants, leavings, ends, balance, excess, surplus, extras, discards, scraps, oddments, odds and ends.

restaurant *n.* eatery, chophouse, diner, hash house (*Slang*), beanery, café, cafeteria, luncheonette, bistro, dining room, brasserie.

restful *adj.* **1** relaxing, calming, tranquilizing, refreshing, revitalizing, recuperative, reposeful, leisurely, peaceful, lulling, soothing, comfort-

ing, unhurried, slow, undemanding, unpressured. **2** calm, quiet, peaceful, serene, indolent, placid, tranquil, unruffled, lazy, relaxed, undisturbed, composed.
ant. 1 exciting, stimulating, unnerving, disquieting. **2** agitated, disturbed, noisy, bustling, nervous, restless, antsy (*Slang*).

restitution *n.* restoration, repayment, reimbursement, recompense, compensation, satisfaction, return, rebate, refund, indemnification, amends, redress, recovery, retrieval, replevin.

restive *adj.* restless, fidgety, edgy, on edge, unruly, balky, bored, impatient, fretful, uneasy, disobedient, rebellious, fractious, intractable, resentful, agitated, antsy (*Slang*).
ant. quiet, relaxed, patient, unhurried, calm.

restless *adj.* **1** disturbed, agitated, fretful, interrupted, fitful, sleepless, uncomfortable, unrelaxed, turbulent, exhausting, unquiet, awake, tiring. **2** uneasy, impatient, restive, anxious, worried, fidgety, irritable, excited, excitable, twitchy. **3** driven, aggressive, ambitious, on the go, bustling, hurried, pushy, pushing, striving, on the make, compulsive, pressured.
ant. 1 peaceful, reposeful, refreshing, uninterrupted. **2** relaxed, serene, tranquil, calm. **3** passive, sluggish, lazy, unambitious, vegetative.

restoration *n.* **1** reestablishment, reinstatement, replacement, reinsertion, reinstallation, return, comeback, renascence, renaissance, rebirth, revival, reappearance. **2** renovation, repair, renewal, reconstruction, rehabilitation, refreshment, rejuvenation, revitalization, reanimation.
ant. 1 loss, disappearance, death. **2** decline, decay, dilapidation, debility.

restore *v.* **1** reestablish, reinstitute, resuscitate, revive, regenerate, recreate, reconstitute, bring back. **2** repair, renew, retouch, remodel, refashion, rebuild, revamp, refurbish, reclaim, freshen, fix, make over, redo, recondition, overhaul, patch up, retrieve, recover. **3** reinstate, put back, reinstall, reelect, replace, reset, reinsert. **4** rehabilitate, remedy, cure, refresh, relieve, rejuvenate, reanimate, heal, fortify, energize, strengthen, invigorate, ameliorate, revitalize.

ant. 1 do away with, wipe out, oppose, undermine. **3** throw out, oust, banish, exile.

restrain v. **1** hinder, repress, inhibit, constrain, hold back, hamper, control, check, bridle, tether, handicap, restrict, limit, leash, trammel. **2** arrest, hold, imprison, capture, lock up, impound, jail, straitjacket, handcuff, manacle, put away, confine, coop up, detain, shut in.

ant. 1 impel, encourage, urge on, speed, spur. **2** free, liberate, release, discharge, let go.

restraint n. **1** constraint, prevention, obstruction, restriction, limitation, circumscription, arrest, house arrest, confinement, detention, captivity, repression, blockage, curtailment, hindrance, imprisonment. **2** rein, check, brake, bridle, tether, leash, trammel, handcuff, straitjacket, curb, muzzle, gag, manacle, hobble, bar. **3** stricture, taboo, ban, interdiction, forbiddance, warning, injunction, interference, disapproval, censure, blockade, embargo, no-no (*Slang*). **4** self-control, self-discipline, moderation, temperance, reserve, judgment, sobriety, willpower, firmness, poise, self-possession, levelheadedness, calmness, reticence, dignity, cool (*Slang*).

ant. 1 freedom, liberty, acceleration, flow. **2** spur, goad, stimulus, impetus, propellant. **3** inducement, incitement, incentive. **4** abandon, profligacy, excess, self-indulgence.

restrict v. limit, confine, circumscribe, restrain, constrain, bind, constrict, cramp, narrow, hem in, straiten, regulate, qualify, handicap, immobilize.

ant. loose, loosen, free, open, widen, broaden, enlarge.

restricted adj. limited, confined, exclusive, private, restrictive, qualified, circumscribed, segregated, handicapped, demarcated, obstructed, controlled.

ant. public, open, free, accessible.

restriction n. restraint, limitation, control, handicap, obstruction, check, qualification, deterrent, curb, warning, boundary, ban, stricture, condition, stipulation, proviso, caveat.

ant. encouragement, spur, stimulus, goad, incitement, provocation.

restrictive adj. RESTRICTED.

result n. **1** outcome, effect, upshot, conclusion, aftereffect, denouement, outgrowth, aftermath, consequence, harvest, reward, end, fruit, product, sequent, spin-off, fallout. **2** remainder, balance, rest, net, surplus, overage, residue, product, answer. —v. **1** follow, ensue, happen, evolve, eventuate, emerge, turn out, work out, pan out, come about, emanate. **2** end, conclude, cause, make, effect, bring about, determine, contribute to, terminate, wind up, yield, come to.

ant. n. **1** cause, origin, seed, beginning.

resume v. reopen, reestablish, reinstitute, take up, continue, proceed, go on, recommence, reembark, revert.

ant. drop, discontinue, close, leave off.

résumé n. SUMMARY.

resumption n. reopening, renewal, reestablishment, recreation, continuation, recommencement, reembarking, fresh start.

resurgence n. resurrection, revival, renewal, renascence, renaissance, recrudescence, rebirth, return, reflow, reappearance, comeback, rally, resuscitation, reanimation, recovery, revitalization, rejuvenation.

ant. decline, decay, downfall, degeneration.

resurrection *n.* revival, renewal, rebirth, revitalization, reappearance, comeback, return, restoration, resurgence, reestablishment, renascence.

resuscitate *v.* revive, rescue, save, reanimate, resurrect, restore, bring to, bring around.

retain *v.* **1** keep, hold, hang on to, save, reserve, withhold, clutch, clench, grasp. **2** maintain, preserve, cling to, adhere to, nail down, detain, immobilize, fix, restrain, grip, buttress, contain, keep up, sustain, prolong, protract. **3** keep in mind, remember, memorize, bear in mind, treasure, recall, recollect, know, look back on, retrace. **4** hire, engage, employ, pay, consult, commission, book, reserve. **ant. 1** give, hand over, let go of. **2** abandon, leave, loosen, give up. **3** forget. **4** discharge, let go, lay off.

retainer *n.* servant, hireling, dependent, attendant, aide, assistant, valet, squire, flunkey, lackey, sycophant, equerry.

retaliate *v.* avenge, revenge, requite, repay, pay off, even the score, get back at, strike back, reciprocate, vindicate, reward. **ant.** forget, forgive, overlook, excuse, condone, bury the hatchet.

retard *v.* delay, impede, hold back, hold up, hinder, slow up, detain, decelerate, arrest, slow down, slacken, brake, defer, postpone, stall, handicap. **ant.** speed, rush, hasten, accelerate, move ahead.

retch *v.* VOMIT.

retention *n.* **1** possession, keeping, holding, safekeeping, reservation, acquisition, accumulation, amassment, hoarding, custody, tenacity, grip, hold. **2** memory, remembrance, recall, retentiveness, review, retrospection.

rethink *v.* RECONSIDER.

reticent *adj.* shy, diffident, withdrawn, retiring, reserved, low-key, uncommunicative, subdued, quiet, restrained, self-effacing, bashful, secretive, silent, taciturn, closemouthed, mum. **ant.** bold, outspoken, opinionated, talkative, aggressive, forward.

retinue *n.* **1** retainers, train, suite, following, followers, cortege, entourage, escort, convoy, equipage. **2** hangers-on, satellites, lackeys, sycophants, hirelings, admirers, claque, groupies (*Slang*), yes-men, henchmen.

retire *v.* **1** quit, resign, leave, withdraw, abdicate, pull out, depart, vacate. **2** go away, withdraw, absent oneself, leave, step out, exit, vanish. **3** *go to bed:* bed down, turn in, call it a day, hit the hay (*Slang*), hit the sack (*Slang*), sack out (*Slang*). **4** fall back, retreat, move back, recede, evacuate, lose ground, decamp, withdraw, pull out, regroup, flee. **ant. 1, 2** stay on, continue. **3** stay up. **4** advance, proceed, gain ground, stand fast.

retired *adj.* inactive, emeritus, pensioned, superannuated.

retirement *n.* **1** retreat, withdrawal, pullout, pullback, evacuation, flight, rout, regrouping. **2** inactivity, relaxation, disengagement, leisure, abdication, departure, seclusion, rest. **ant. 1** advance, gain.

retiring *adj.* shy, modest, reserved, self-effacing, timid, withdrawn, reticent, bashful, unassuming, diffident, quiet, distant, withdrawn, modest, mousy. **ant.** aggressive, assertive, bold, gregarious.

retort *v.* respond, answer, reply, return, rebut, retaliate, counterclaim, argue, contend, sass. —*n.* rejoinder, riposte, comeback, quip, sally, give-and-take, put-down (*Slang*).

retract *v.* **1** take back, disavow, disclaim, recant, renege, back down, give in, rescind, unsay, revoke, recall, countermand, repeal, repudiate, eat one's words. **2** pull back, withdraw, draw in, hide, cover, sheathe. **ant. 1** uphold, maintain, repeat. **2** expose, uncover, unsheathe.

retreat *v.* go back, withdraw, flee, depart, pullout, retire, ebb, back away, recoil, recede, reverse, move back, back up, vacate, abandon, regress, turn tail. —*n.* **1** withdrawal, pullout, pullback, backup, retirement, departure, abandonment, repositioning, evacuation, flight, escape, about-face, reversal, *volte-face*. **2** refuge, haven, sanctuary, asylum, recourse, resort, covert, cloister, den, lair, hideaway, shelter, cave, burrow, hideout.

ant. *v.* advance, proceed, move ahead, push on, stand fast. *n.* **1** advance, advancement, progress.

retrench *v.* economize, scrimp, scrape, cut back, cut costs, tighten one's belt, curtail, reduce, lessen, cut down.

ant. waste, overspend, squander, fritter away.

retribution *n.* punishment, retaliation, requital, justice, revenge, vengeance, reprisal, just deserts, vindication, penalty, price, reckoning, comeuppance, *lex talionis*.

retrieve *v.* **1** regain, get back, repossess, ransom, recover, redeem, reclaim, salvage, recoup. **2** remedy, make up for, rectify, correct, restore, repair, make good, satisfy, atone, put right, redress. **3** REMEMBER.

retrograde *adj.* **1** regressive, backward, recessive, retreating, retiring. **2** retrogressive, declining, deteriorating, worsening, reverting, relapsing, debilitating. —*v.* DEGENERATE.

ant. **1** progressive, proceeding, onward. **2** improving, evolving, progressive.

retrogress *v.* DEGENERATE.

return *v.* **1** come back, reappear, go back, turn back, retreat. **2** requite, retaliate, give back, repay, recompense, compensate, reciprocate. **3** revert, remember, review, recapture, recollect, reflect, echo, repeat. **4** answer, respond, reply, retort, acknowledge, rebut, rejoin. **5** put back, bring back, restore, replace, reset,

reposition, reinstate, reestablish, reinstall. **6** yield, produce, net, avail, bear fruit, render, furnish, result in. —*n.* **1** restoration, replacement, reflux, regress, reinstatement, retrieval, recapture. **2** reappearance, recurrence, echo, rerun, reverberation, nostalgia, rebound, revival, recrudescence, resurrection, renascence, renaissance, rebirth, repetition. **3** repayment, recompense, compensation, reciprocation, retaliation, requital, reward, stipend, allowance, allotment, remittance, reimbursement. **4** profit, revenue, yield, income, net, gain, assets, interest, proceeds, benefit, take (*Slang*). **5** response, answer, reply, retort, rejoinder, riposte, rebuttal, comeback.

ant. *v.* **1** leave, go, depart. **4** ask, question, claim, assert. **5** take away, remove, displace, borrow. *n.* **1, 2** loss, disappearance, decline, death. **4** outlay, expense, cost, investment, debit.

revamp *v.* RENOVATE.

reveal *v.* **1** disclose, divulge, make known, declare, tell, announce, communicate, publish, confess, notify, tattle, broadcast, inform, let out, leak, exhume. **2** expose, bare, uncover, display, show, exhibit, unmask, unearth, unveil, strip, divest, bring to light, manifest, evince.

ant. **2** cover, hide, conceal, disguise, bury, screen.

revel *v.* **1** delight, enjoy, bask, luxuriate, rejoice, relish, wallow, lap up, savor, love, thrive on, gloat, crow. **2** carouse, make merry, feast, celebrate, frolic, romp, skylark, have a ball (*Slang*), roister, party. —*n.* merrymaking, carousal, romp, party, fete, festivity, spree, gala, ball, celebration, saturnalia, wassail, orgy, carnival, festival, fiesta, jamboree, bash (*Slang*).

ant. *v.* **1** dislike, shrink from.

revelation *n.* disclosure, eye-opener, exposé, news, surprise, shock, exposure, shocker, bombshell.

revelry *n.* rejoicing, merrymaking, carousal, merriment, boisterousness, celebration, feasting, roistering, romping, skylarking, ball, gala, festival, carnival, jamboree, bash (*Slang*).

revenge *n.* vengeance, retaliation, vindication, requital, reprisal, retribution, repayment, compensation, satisfaction, vindictiveness, counterattack. —*v.* retaliate, avenge, repay, vindicate, hit back, exact, reward, punish, counterattack, reciprocate, get back at, get even, settle a score.

revengeful *adj.* vengeful, vindictive, resentful, spiteful, unforgiving, retaliatory, retributive, punitive, unmerciful, merciless, retaliative, remorseless, recriminatory, grudgeful, grudge-bearing, mean-spirited.
ant. forgiving, forbearing, understanding, charitable.

reverberate *v.* RESOUND.

reverberation *n.* **1** resounding, echoing, echo, resonance, reecho, reflection. **2** consequence, aftereffect, repercussion, aftermath, result, sequel.

revere *v.* venerate, respect, adore, worship, esteem, honor, idolize, deify, glorify, exalt, sanctify, beatify, look up to, kneel to, put on a pedestal.
ant. scorn, disdain, look down on, disparage.

reverence *n.* **1** esteem, worship, awe, veneration, adoration, honor, glorification, exaltation, regard, deference, admiration, homage, devotion, humility. **2** obeisance, bow, curtsy, genuflection, salute, salaam, devoirs, prostration, kneeling, prayer.
ant. 1 scorn, disdain, contempt, disrespect, arrogance, mockery.

reverend *adj.* venerable, venerated, estimable, holy, righteous, sacred, exalted, honorable, worthy, lofty, esteemed, valued, meritorious. —*n.* CLERGYMAN.
ant. unworthy, contemptible, base, infamous.

reverent *adj.* worshipful, respectful, reverential, adoring, awed, deferential, obeisant, pious, devout, humble, submissive, idolatrous.
ant. scornful, disdainful, impious, blasphemous, irreverent.

reverential *adj.* REVERENT.

reverie *n.* daydreaming, fantasizing, musing, daydream, fantasy, fancy, illusion, meditation, woolgathering.

reversal *n.* REVERSE.

reverse *adj.* backward, opposite, contrary, counter, inverse, converse, inverted, reversed, transposed. —*n.* **1** opposite, contrary, contradiction, inverse, converse, underside, counterpart, antithesis. **2** reversal, about-face, turnabout, backlash, rebound, boomerang, reversion, inversion, transposition. **3** misfortune, mishap, setback, upset, comedown, contretemps, reversal, downfall, overthrow, calamity, adversity, undoing, loss, disaster, accident, comeuppance. —*v.* **1** invert, transpose, turn about, evert, back up, exchange, swap, upend, overturn. **2** annul, repeal, retract, cancel, veto, countermand, overrule, abolish, set aside, undo, override, withdraw, vacate, rescind, nullify.

reversion *n.* return, regression, retrogression, reversal, relapse, atavism, throwback, backsliding, recidivism, nostalgia, revival, reflux.
ant. progression, advancement, pioneering.

revert *v.* go back, turn back, regress, retrogress, repeat, return, revive, reverse, relapse, backslide, recidivate, recall, remember, review, relive, rebound.
ant. progress, advance, move on, pioneer.

review *v.* **1** go over, repeat, recapitulate, interpret, study, prepare for. **2** recall, reflect, remember, retrace, look back on, retrospect, brood over, mull over, dredge up, ruminate, reminisce. **3** study, survey, evaluate, consider, examine, assess, reexamine, reconsider, reevaluate, criticize, weigh, ponder, analyze, scrutinize. —*n.* examination, study, survey, retrospective, analysis, scrutiny, going-over, evaluation, critique, commentary, exegesis, exposition.

revile *v.* vilify, calumniate, curse, defame, denigrate, libel, slander, smear, disparage, vituperate, malign, inveigh, desecrate, blaspheme, denounce.

   ant. praise, extol, eulogize, acclaim.

revise *v.* **1** edit, rewrite, redact, emend, correct, emendate, polish, blue-pencil. **2** change, alter, modify, redo, refashion, revamp, remodel, overhaul, vary, recast, remold, remake, transform, reconstruct, reform.

revision *n.* redaction, rewriting, updating, emendation, editing, blue-penciling.

revitalization *n.* REVIVAL.

revitalize *v.* REVIVE.

revival *n.* restoration, renewal, revitalization, recrudescence, revivification, renascence, renaissance, resuscitation, exhumation, nostalgia, resurgence, rediscovery.

revive *v.* reanimate, resuscitate, rescue, bring back, restore, reanimate, recrudesce, revitalize, revivify, resurrect, rally, refresh, renew, rejuvenate.

revivify *v.* REVIVE.

revocation *n.* REPEAL.

revoke *v.* annul, rescind, cancel, repeal, nullify, recall, override, abrogate, void, withdraw, abolish, vacate, retract, invalidate, recant, repudiate.

   ant. uphold, validate, enact, support, maintain.

revolt *n.* **1** uprising, rebellion, insurrection, mutiny, revolution, insurgence, upheaval, takeover, coup d'état, coup, putsch. **2** protest, resistance, balkiness, insubordination, disobedience, confrontation, defection, sedition, mutiny, subversion, defiance, opposition. —*v.* **1** rise, rise up, rebel, mutiny, take over, strike, defect, secede, riot. **2** disgust, repel, nauseate, sicken, turn one's stomach,

abhor, shrink from, loathe, horrify, scandalize, appall, offend, outrage.

   ant. *n.* **2** obedience, compliance, cooperation, capitulation. *v.* **1** obey, comply, cooperate. **2** attract, charm, lure, please.

revolting *adj.* abhorrent, disgusting, loathsome, nauseating, sickening, repulsive, appalling, offensive, outrageous, repugnant, obnoxious, horrible, nasty, foul.

   ant. pleasing, agreeable, attractive, charming.

revolution *n.* **1** rotation, spin, turn, gyration, revolving, circuit, whirl, twirl, pirouette, twist, winding, whirling, spinning. **2** round, cycle, lap, course, circuit, recurrence, repetition, circle, spin. **3** revolt, rebellion, coup d'état, coup, takeover, insurrection, insurgence, putsch.

revolutionary *adj.* insurgent, insurrectionary, mutinous, seditious, radical, subversive, extremist. —*n.* revolutionist, insurrectionist, subversive, insurgent, rebel, radical, extremist, mutineer, agitator, rabble-rouser, sansculotte.

revolutionize *v.* change, transform, transfigure, refashion, remold, transmute, transmogrify.

   ant. conserve, preserve, stabilize, maintain.

revolve *v.* spin, rotate, whirl, twirl, circle, gyrate, twist, wind, coil, spiral, pirouette, turn, eddy, wheel.

revulsion *n.* **1** recoil, withdrawal, change of heart, reversal, transformation, rebound, backlash, boomerang, *volte-face.* **2** disgust, loathing, nausea, aversion, distaste, repulsion, detestation, abhorrence, antipathy, queasiness, hatred, animosity, repugnance, contempt, disdain.

   ant. 2 sympathy, liking, affection.

rev up 1 ACCELERATE. **2** STIMULATE.

reward *n.* recompense, payment, repayment, compensation, wages, prize, accolade, meed, award, bonus, acknowledgment, gratuity, tip, deserts, requital, remembrance, retaliation. —*v.* recompense, compensate, award, acknowledge, tip, remember, recognize, honor, remunerate, retaliate, requite, pay back, give tit for tat.

rewarding *adj.* gratifying, satisfying, pleasing, welcome, delightful, enriching, productive, advantageous, beneficial, fruitful, elevating, profitable, valuable, favorable, happy, fulfilling.

ant. futile, empty, useless, wasted, unproductive, barren.

reword *v.* RECAST.

rewrite *v.* REVISE.

rhapsody *n.* paean, eulogy, effusion, extravaganza, rapture, idealization.

rhetoric *n.* **1** expressiveness, style, eloquence, articulateness, fluency. **2** bombast, fustian, grandiloquence, verbosity, wordiness, pomposity, prolixity, turgidity, pretentiousness, floridity, flamboyance, talk, bull (*Slang*), bunkum, bunk, hot air (*Slang*), jive (*Slang*).

rhetorical *adj.* **1** expressive, eloquent, fluent, articulate, well-spoken, oratorical. **2** bombastic, grandiloquent, pompous, exaggerated, pretentious, flowery, florid, flamboyant, purple, overdone, fustian, prolix, wordy.

ant. 1 tongue-tied, inarticulate, fumbling, ill-spoken.

rhizome *n.* ROOT.

rhubarb *n. Slang* QUARREL.

rhyme *n.* **1** poem, verse, song, lay, lyric, ballad, epic, ode, sonnet, rhapsody, dithyramb, ditty, doggerel, jingle, rime. **2** poetry, verse, song, poetics, versification, prosody, poesy, rime.

rhythm *n.* beat, pulse, cadence, throb, pulsation, lilt, swing, tempo, accent, stress, meter, measure, numbers, vibration, oscillation, alternation, repetition.

rib *v. Slang* TEASE.

ribald *adj.* improper, indecent, unseemly, off-color, bawdy, risqué, racy, spicy, smutty, dirty, earthy, raw, rude, coarse, vulgar, gross, lewd, obscene, salacious, pornographic.

rich *adj.* **1** wealthy, affluent, prosperous, moneyed, flush, well-heeled (*Slang*), well-to-do, well-off, comfortable. **2** abundant, plentiful, ample, profuse, abounding, copious, replete, generous, bountiful, productive, fruitful, fertile, fecund, prolific, fat, pregnant, prodigal. **3** luxuriant, extravagant, lavish, sumptuous, elaborate, ornate, exuberant, flowery, flamboyant, gorgeous, showy, splendid.

ant. 1 poor, destitute, penniless, indigent, pinched, strapped, impoverished. **2** scarce, lean, unplentiful, meager, scant. **3** unadorned, simple, natural, severe, drab, plain, undecorated.

riches *n.* **1** possessions, goods, money, property, funds, assets, fortune, treasure, substance, lucre, pelf, bounty, wealth. **2** abundance, richness, profusion, plenitude, copiousness, liberality, opulence, profuseness, prodigality, luxuriance, exuberance.

ant. 2 poverty, meagerness, inadequacy, want, lack, need.

rickety *adj.* shaky, wobbly, tottering, flimsy, decrepit, unsubstantial, jerry-built, unstable, unsteady, teetering, feeble, infirm.

ant. solid, sound, substantial, rugged, resistant, durable, sturdy.

ricochet *v.* rebound, bounce, glance off, spring back, fly back, recoil, deflect, deviate, backfire, boomerang.

rid *v.* eliminate, remove, dispel, expel, disperse, unload, reject, purge, exterminate, weed out, shake off, throw off, do away with, free of, dispose of.

riddle[1] *v.* **1** pierce, puncture, perforate, honeycomb, pepper, pelt, penetrate, punch, prick, tap, shoot, fire, snipe. **2** permeate, spread through, infiltrate, damage, injure, spoil, mar, corrupt, debase, impair, weaken.

riddle[2] *n.* **1** puzzle, conundrum, rebus, problem, poser, brain twister, knot, perplexity, charade. **2** enigma, mystery, Sphinx, secret, question, problem, labyrinth. —*v.* SOLVE.

ride *v.* **1** travel, move, go, progress, fare, traverse, drive, tour, journey, cruise, speed, drift, race. **2** tease, kid (*Slang*), rib (*Slang*), razz, jolly, haze, heckle, hector, pester, bait, roast, ridicule, deride, irritate, irk, nettle. —*n.* drive, spin, whirl, turn, trip, outing, tour, journey, excursion, jaunt, junket.

ride on DEPEND.

rider *n.* SUPPLEMENT.

ridge *n.* crest, spine, hill, hillock, mound, hump, saddle, rib, backbone, promontory, hogback, chine.

ridicule *n.* derision, mockery, banter, jeering, ribbing (*Slang*), twitting, gibing, raillery, scoffing, taunting, scorn, contempt. —*v.* deride, mock, ride, razz, make fun of, poke fun at, kid (*Slang*), rib (*Slang*), taunt, chaff, twit, roast, pillory, quiz.

ridiculous *adj.* ludicrous, laughable, absurd, nonsensical, senseless, foolish, asinine, crazy, preposterous, outrageous, derisive, outlandish, incredible, unbelievable.

ant. sensible, sound, serious, rational, credible, logical.

rife *adj.* prevalent, widespread, common, rampant, plentiful, abundant, innumerable, ample, teeming, abounding, swarming, epidemic, extensive.

ant. scarce, rare, scanty, unusual, uncommon.

riffraff *n.* RABBLE.

rifle *v.* search, ransack, rummage, scour, comb, rake, turn inside out, rob, steal, plunder, pillage, sack, burgle, burglarize.

rift *n.* **1** fissure, fault, fracture, flaw, rent, split, breach, opening, gap, crack, crevice, cleft, cranny, chink, chasm, gulf, abyss. **2** falling-out, quarrel, alienation, estrangement, division, separation, rupture, break, breakup, split, breach. —*v.* SPLIT.

rig[1] *v.* furnish, fit out, outfit, equip, fit,

provide, supply, appoint, dress, clothe, costume, suit, deck, array, turn out, habit, caparison, accouter. —*n.* equipment, fixtures, fittings, gear, equipage, outfit, apparatus, tackle, machinery, appointments, accouterments, paraphernalia.

rig[2] *v.* manipulate, fix, arrange, prearrange, manage, maneuver, control, influence, finagle, juggle, jockey.

right *adj.* **1** virtuous, moral, honest, righteous, honorable, ethical, noble, just, good, suitable, responsible, proper, fitting, correct, fair. **2** accurate, correct, exact, precise, definite, positive, true, valid, unerring, faultless, perfect. **3** sound, wholesome, unimpaired, normal, solid, rightminded, sane, reasonable, rational, healthy, hale, hearty. **4** right-wing, rightist, conservative, Tory, reactionary, unprogressive, orthodox, traditional, conventional, standpat, moss-backed, die-hard. —*adv.* **1** justly, morally, honorably, honestly, uprightly, ethically, rightfully, properly, correctly, conscientiously, responsibly. **2** accurately, correctly, precisely, exactly, unerringly, faultlessly, flawlessly, perfectly. **3** thoroughly, completely, altogether, entirely, wholly, perfectly, absolutely, positively, decidedly, exceedingly, quite, very, utterly. —*n.* **1** goodness, righteousness, justness, justice, fairness, propriety, probity, uprightness, integrity, honesty, rectitude, impartiality, truth. **2** prerogative, due, power, authority, control, command, say, say-so, demand, license, privilege, claim, title, interest, equity, estate, appanage, birthright. **3** rightism, right wing, conservatism, reactionaryism, Toryism, orthodoxy, hideboundness, standpattism. —*v.* **1** straighten, position, fix, square, true, restore, normalize, adjust, regulate, rectify. **2** organize, arrange, order, regulate, repair, fix, systematize, straighten up, tidy up. **3** correct, remedy, emend, revise, reform, redress, rectify, amend. **4** redress, requite, repay, retaliate for, avenge, punish.

ant. *adj.* **1** immoral, unjust, wrong, bad, unfair, improper. **2** incorrect, erroneous, false, inexact, imprecise. **3** unwholesome, unhealthy, sick, impaired, unbalanced. **4** left-wing, leftist, radical, revolutionary, liberal. *adv.* **1** unjustly, immorally, improperly, unethically, unfairly, irresponsibly. **2** inaccurately, inexactly, faultily, incorrectly, imperfectly. **3** incompletely, inadequately, partially, noway, nowise, not at all. *n.* **1** wrong, injustice, inequity, misdoing, impropriety, dishonesty, evil. **3** leftism, left wing, left, radicalism, liberalism. *v.* **1** upset, overturn, invert, upend, tip over, capsize. **2** disarrange, muddle, scatter, displace, confuse, shuffle, tangle.

righteous *adj.* just, virtuous, good, blameless, right, noble, elevated, magnanimous, unselfish, incorrupt, moral, pure, honest, upright.

ant. unjust, unfair, wrong, immoral, corrupt, evil, wicked.

rightful *adj.* **1** just, due, fair, sanctioned, authorized, valid, bona fide, authentic, genuine, legitimate, legal, licit. **2** suitable, proper, fit, correct, appropriate, becoming, fitting.

ant. **1** unjust, unfair, dishonest, unjustifiable, unwarranted, illegal. **2** inappropriate, improper, unsuitable, inapt, incongruous, alien.

rightism *n.* RIGHT.

rightist *adj.* RIGHT.

rightly *adv.* **1** correctly, accurately, exactly, precisely, unerringly, faultlessly, truthfully, faithfully, perfectly, expressly. **2** honorably, upstandingly, justly, honestly, uprightly, scrupulously, conscientiously, morally. **3** aptly, properly, correctly, fittingly, becomingly, appropriately, suitably.

ant. **1** erroneously, inaccurately, mistakenly, faultily, unreliably. **2** unjustly, immorally, dishonorably, iniquitously, wrongfully. **3** inappro-

priately, unsuitably, inaptly, unbecomingly, unfittingly.

right-minded *adj.* SOUND.

rightness *n.* **1** PRECISION. **2** INTEGRITY. **3** aptness, correctness, fitness, suitability, appropriateness, propriety.

right-thinking *adj.* SOUND.

right-wing *adj.* RIGHT.

right wing RIGHT.

rigid *adj.* **1** stiff, hard, firm, inflexible, unpliable, unmalleable, inelastic, ramrod, taut, tense, tight. **2** inflexible, undeviating, uncompromising, intransigent, adamant, ironbound, rigorous, strict, severe, stern, stringent.

ant. **1** pliable, limp, flexible, malleable, flaccid, supple. **2** relaxed, easygoing, nonchalant, conciliatory, forbearing.

rigmarole *n.* falderal, humbug, mumbo jumbo, poppycock, bunk (*Slang*), baloney (*Slang*), tommyrot, rubbish, blather, twaddle, bosh, blarney, nonsense.

rigor *n.* **1** strictness, severity, austerity, harshness, stringency, firmness, rigidity, inflexibility, stubbornness. **2** discomfort, hardship, adversity, privation, distress, ordeal, trial, tribulation, challenge, difficulty. **3** exactitude, precision, preciseness, accuracy, correctness, meticulousness, punctiliousness, fussiness, finicalness, nicety, thoroughness.

ant. **1** negligence, laxness, looseness, indolence, relaxation. **2** ease, comfort, blessings, creature comforts, luxury. **3** vagueness, imprecision, inaccuracy, carelessness, sloppiness, indifference.

rile *v.* **1** irk, irritate, vex, pique, miff, gall, gripe, chafe, nettle, hector, plague, pain, exasperate, roil, provoke, bother, aggravate. **2** ROIL.

rill *n.* STREAM.

rim *n.* edge, border, brim, margin, lip, fringe, brink, hem, side, verge, flange, perimeter, circumference.

rime *n.* RHYME.

rind *n.* skin, peel, crust, layer, cover,

coat, integument, bark, hide, cuticle, husk.

ring¹ *n.* **1** band, circle, loop, oval, orb, disk, belt, girdle, collar, cincture, hoop, halo. **2** circumference, perimeter, border, rim, band, circuit, cordon, loop. **3** gang, group, crew, band, club, outfit, pack, troupe, bunch, knot, cell, circle, clique, coterie, junta, cabal. —*v.* encircle, circle, surround, environ, encompass, girdle, loop, wreathe, belt, band.

ring² *v.* sound, resound, resonate, reverberate, peal, clang, toll, knell, clamor, gong, chime, echo. —*n.* **1** pealing, clanging, chiming, tolling, knelling, clangor, clang, din, tintinnabulation, reverberation, resounding, echo. **2** quality, nature, character, property, substance, tenor, tone, flavor, mark, stamp, hint, suggestion, implication, feeling.

ringer *n. Slang* TWIN.

ringleader *n.* chief, leader, instigator, inciter, provoker, agitator, fomenter, troublemaker.

rinse *v.* clean, cleanse, launder, wash, immerse, flush, soak, bathe. —*n.* wash, washing, laundering, rinsing, cleaning, cleansing, soak, bath.

rinsing *n.* RINSE.

riot *n.* **1** disorder, disturbance, row, rioting, panic, tumult, ruckus (*Slang*), hubbub, commotion, unruliness, fracas, brawl, broil, uprising, violence, tumult, insurgence, revolt. **2** outburst, flare-up, fit, uproar, storm, scene, roar, burst, outbreak, explosion, eruption, boisterousness. **3** laugh, scream, howl, giggle (*Brit.*), uproar, panic, hoot (*Brit. Slang*), romp, frolic, lark, sensation, wow (*Slang*). —*v.* **1** rampage, run amuck, rage, run riot, go berserk, rise up, rebel, revolt. **2** revel, romp, carouse, gambol, frolic, roister, caper, celebrate, make merry, cut loose, have a ball (*Slang*).

riotous *adj.* wild, tumultuous, rambunctious, turbulent, boisterous, roister-

ous, loud, noisy, rollicking, knockabout, rough-and-tumble, rowdy.

rip *v.* **1** tear, cut apart, split, separate, divide, part, rift, rend, rent, cleave, rive. **2** rush, race, dash, dart, scoot, scamper, scurry, scramble, tear, sprint, hustle, fly, zip, run, speed, hasten, hurry. —*n.* tear, split, slit, rift, slash, rending, rent, perforation, gap, gape.

ripe *adj.* **1** mature, full-grown, mellow, of age, full-blown, full-fledged, adult, old, grown-up, grown, big, developed, matured, seasoned. **2** prepared, ready, set, in condition, fit, disposed, inclined, primed, avid, keen.

ant. **1** raw, green, unripe, tender, young, premature. **2** unprepared, unready, unfit, disinclined, averse.

ripen *v.* mature, age, grow, develop, maturate, mellow, season, come of age, progress, advance, grow old.

rip into attack, assail, lash out at, pitch into, light into (*Slang*), go at, beset, assault, charge, strike at.

rip-off *n. Slang* gyp, swindle, racket, extortion, exploitation, dishonesty, thievery, illegality, fraud, robbery, larceny, theft, heist, shakedown (*Slang*).

rip off *Slang* cheat, defraud, swindle, rob, gouge, bilk, steal, steal from, thieve, take, swipe, burglarize, cop (*Slang*), pinch (*Slang*), lift, filch, pilfer.

ripost *n.* retort, rejoinder, reply, repartee, comeback, return, response, rebuttal, wisecrack, quip.

ripping *adj. Brit. Slang* SPLENDID.

ripple *v.* undulate, wave, riffle, flow, purl, trill, spurtle, gurgle, bubble, burble, dribble, trickle. —*n.* wavelet, wave, undulation, riffle, rimple, crinkle, wrinkle, crumple, rumple, corrugation, ridge.

rise *v.* **1** ascend, soar, climb, levitate, go up, mount, scale, spire, slant, rake, pitch. **2** progress, advance, improve, develop, get ahead, make good, make headway, prevail, arrive, triumph. **3** increase, intensify, reinforce, inflate, heighten, advance, grow, gain, mount, wax. **4** stand up, arise, get up, get to one's feet, spring up, uprise, raise, uprear. **5** REVOLT. **6** ARISE. —*n.* **1** ascent, rising, ascension, uprise, climb, upgrade, uphill, acclivity. **2** height, elevation, hill, mound, knoll, hillock, slope, rise, eminence. **3** advance, progress, furtherance, increase, growth, gain, boost, upturn, upswing, step-up, jump, inflation.

ant. *v.* **1** descend, drop, fall, plunge, go down. **2** decline, fail, fall, fade, diminish. **3** depreciate, decline, slump, tumble, drop. **4** sit down, repose, recline, lie down. *n.* **1** descent, plunge, falling, sinking, drop. **2** dip, valley, depression, hollow, pocket, concavity, trough. **3** decline, deterioration, decrease, failing, retrogression, waning, comedown, fall, slump, setback.

risible *adj.* HUMOROUS.

risk *n.* danger, peril, jeopardy, threat, unsafeness, precariousness, vulnerability, insecurity, shakiness, hazard, chance, contingency. —*v.* endanger, imperil, jeopardize, hazard, peril, venture, chance.

ant. *n.* safety, security, protection, safeness.

risky *adj.* dangerous, perilous, hazardous, unsafe, precarious, insecure, unprotected, unsound, venturesome, chancy, dicey, adventurous, venturous, uncertain, unsure.

ant. safe, guarded, secure, certain, sure.

risqué *adj.* off-color, spicy, racy, suggestive, indelicate, improper, daring, ribald, bawdy, dirty, vulgar, lewd.

rite *n.* **1** ceremony, observance, formality, ceremonial, celebration, ritual, function, exercise, service, liturgy, sacrament, sacrifice, initiation, mystery, solemnization. **2** RITUAL.

ritual *n.* **1** prescription, form, code, protocol, formality, ritualism, ceremonialism, formalism, ceremony,

show, solemnity. **2** ceremony, ceremonial, rite, procedure, practice, pattern, routine, convention, custom, tradition, habit.

ritualism *n.* RITUAL.

ritzy *adj. Slang* LUXURIOUS.

rival *n.* **1** competitor, contestant, contender, opponent, adversary, player, antagonist, challenger, emulator, assailant, enemy, combatant, foe. **2** equal, match, peer, fellow, equivalent, compeer. —*v.* emulate, vie with, compete with, race, keep pace with, contend with, engage, strive with, challenge, contest, reach, match, touch, measure up to. —*adj.* competing, competitive, contending, contesting, opposing, striving, emulous, vying, disputing.

ant. *n.* **1** collaborator, colleague, partner, associate, teammate, ally, helpmate. *adj.* cooperative, collaborating, affiliated, associated, allied.

rivalry *n.* competition, race, contest, struggle, striving, vying, emulation, match, duel, opposition, contention, engagement, antagonism.

ant. cooperation, collaboration, teamwork, alliance, partnership, coalition.

rive *v.* SPLIT.

river *n.* **1** stream, course, watercourse, current, rapids, headstream, tributary, branch, fork, brook, creek, rivulet, freshet, rill, kill. **2** abundance, profusion, mass, quantity, volume, plenitude, flow, flux, rush, surge, torrent, flood, deluge, ocean.

rivet *v.* **1** fasten, secure, attach, join, bind, couple, weld, bolt, pin, nail, tack, staple. **2** engross, engage, grip, hold, attract, arrest, fix, monopolize, absorb, immerse, preoccupy, fascinate, excite, enthrall.

rivulet *n.* STREAM.

road *n.* street, roadway, thoroughfare, avenue, boulevard, concourse, highway, expressway, thruway, turnpike, freeway, artery, route, itinerary, course, way, channel, track, trail, path, lane, byway.

roadblock *n.* OBSTACLE.

roadway *n.* ROAD.

roam *v.* wander, rove, range, ramble, saunter, meander, drift, jaunt, gad about, stroll, tramp, trek, hike, walk, travel.

roar *v.* **1** bellow, bawl, howl, yowl, holler, whoop, hoot, yell, scream, shout, call, cry, yelp. **2** boom, bang, thunder, rumble, roll, blare, blast, crash, clap, bang, crack, clamor. —*n.* **1** bellow, bawl, howl, yowl, holler, whoop, hoot, yell, shout, call, scream, cry, yelp. **2** boom, bang, thunder, rumble, roll, blare, blast, crash, clap, bang, crack, clamor, hubbub, uproar, tumult.

roast *v.* ridicule, deride, ride, kid (*Slang*), rib (*Slang*), tease, mock, travesty, burlesque, parody, twit, taunt, criticize, scorch, slam, pan.

rob *v.* **1** steal, burglarize, burgle, thieve, hold up, stick up (*Slang*), filch, pilfer, swipe (*Slang*), take, cop (*Slang*), pinch (*Slang*), rip off (*Slang*), plunder, pillage, ransack, loot. **2** deprive, take away from, strip, wrest, divest, usurp, annex, exact, do out of, cheat, defraud, swindle.

robbery *n.* stealing, thievery, burglary, holdup, stick-up (*Slang*), theft, steal, rip-off (*Slang*), job, caper, swiping, lifting, snatching, pilfering, pilferage, filching, looting.

robe *n.* gown, dressing gown, bathrobe, housecoat, caftan, cloak, mantle, cape, tunic, toga, muumuu, smock. —*v.* CLOTHE.

robot *n.* **1** automaton, android, computer. **2** puppet, pawn, tool, dummy, flunky, menial, drudge, workhorse, laborer, serf, slave, vassal.

robust *adj.* **1** strong, sound, rugged, hardy, sturdy, stout, stalwart, strapping, able-bodied, vigorous, lusty, hearty, healthy, hale. **2** boisterous, roisterous, blustering, tumultuous, rude, coarse, raw, earthy, funky (*Slang*).

ant. 1 feeble, delicate, fragile, frail, puny, debilitated. **2** restrained, inhibited, reserved, delicate, refined, effete.

rock[1] *n.* **1** stone, boulder, pebble, gravel, marble, granite, limestone. **2** support, defense, stronghold, pillar, tower, refuge, haven, shelter, asylum, sanctuary, Gibraltar.

rock[2] *v.* sway, roll, pitch, swing, lurch, shake, swagger, bob, wobble, waver, reel, stagger.

rocket *v.* SKYROCKET.

rocky[1] *adj.* **1** stony, rocklike, stonelike, flinty, gritty, gravelly, pebbly, jagged, craggy, bumpy, rough. **2** difficult, hard, tough, rugged, rigorous, thorny, uphill, laborious, Herculean, formidable, challenging.

ant. 2 easy, effortless, simple, slight, unchallenging.

rocky[2] *adj.* wobbly, shaky, tottery, trembly, quivering, quavering, unsteady, unstable, dizzy, groggy, faint, sickish, ill, seedy, under the weather, out of sorts.

ant. sound, strong, rugged, stout, firm, tough, durable, hardy, robust.

rod *n.* pole, stick, bar, shaft, stalk, spar, post, dowel, staff, scepter, baton, mace, wand.

rodomontade *n.* BLUSTER.

rogue *n.* scoundrel, good-for-nothing, ne'er-do-well, black sheep, knave, rotter (*Brit. Slang*), dastard, villain, mischief-maker, scamp, scapegrace, rascal, scalawag, wag, cutup, imp, elf.

roguish *adj.* **1** mischievous, prankish, mischief-loving, playful, waggish, puckish, impish, elfish, devilish, tricky. **2** unscrupulous, unprincipled, knavish, crafty, villainous, crooked, dishonest, corrupt, criminal, scheming, picaresque.

ant. 1 solemn, grave, staid, humorless, earnest. **2** honest, honorable, trustworthy, conscientious, law-abiding.

roil *v.* **1** muddy, stir up, churn, rile, muck, mire, agitate, disturb. **2** RILE.

roister *v.* swagger, bluster, swashbuckle, rollick, vaunt, flourish, bluff, sputter.

role *n.* character, part, portrayal, characterization, impersonation, persona, facade, face, image, function, position, capacity.

roll *v.* **1** rotate, revolve, turn, spiral, gyrate, spin, swirl, reel, twirl, swivel, pivot, swing, wheel. **2** rock, swing, pitch, sway, reel, waver, lurch, stagger, lumber, swagger. **3** progress, advance, proceed, go forward, cover ground, move on, propel, impel, push, trundle, bowl, troll. —*n.* **1** rotation, revolution, turn, spin, spinning, reeling, swiveling, pivoting, swinging, wheeling, whirl, cycle, gyration. **2** list, register, roster, muster, census, inventory, catalogue, file, index, enumeration, tally, tabulation. **3** sway, swing, pitch, reel, waver, lurch, stagger, swagger, saunter.

rollicking *adj.* frolicsome, spirited, lighthearted, animated, exuberant, vivacious, playful, gay, carefree, joyous.

roll up accumulate, amass, pile up, rake in, heap up, collect, gather.

roly-poly *adj.* PUDGY.

romance *n.* **1** adventure, daring, enterprise, fascination, mystery, lure, attraction, interest, charm, glamour, appeal, captivation, flair, color, picturesqueness, exoticism. **2** love affair, affair, liaison, entanglement, intrigue, flirtation, infatuation, *amour.*

romantic *adj.* **1** glamorous, colorful, exotic, captivating, fabulous, legendary, mythical, picturesque, idyllic, adventurous, venturous, audacious, daring, heroic. **2** loving, amorous, adoring, affectionate, devoted, tender, demonstrative, emotional, passionate, ardent, fervent, impassioned, lovelorn, sentimental. **3** visionary, utopian, quixotic, idealistic, moonstruck, starry-eyed, optimistic, dreamy, impractical, unrealistic, fanciful, fantastic. —*n.* idealist, dreamer, wishful thinker, visionary,

enthusiast, adventurer, knight-errant, hero, lover.

ant. *adj.* **1** familiar, homely, commonplace, timorous, faint-hearted. **2** cold, aloof, unemotional, unromantic, frigid. **3** practical, pragmatic, hardheaded, cynical, pessimistic.

romp *v.* **1** frolic, sport, play, gambol, frisk, caper, disport, cut up, rollick, horse around. **2** win, win hands down, succeed, make a killing, triumph, conquer, score. —*n.* **1** frolic, gambol, horseplay, caper, rollick, lark, fun, sport, play. **2** walkover, walkaway, pushover, snap, sweep, triumph, conquest, victory.

ant. *n.* **2** debacle, collapse, rout, defeat.

rood *n.* CROSS.

rook *v.* CHEAT.

rookie *n. Slang* RECRUIT.

room *n.* **1** chamber, cubicle, cell, cubbyhole, closet, den, apartment. **2** space, capacity, volume, accommodation, measure, clearing, leeway, margin, elbowroom, swing, play, scope, latitude. **3** opportunity, chance, occasion, scope, opening, place, season, time, moment.

roomy *adj.* spacious, commodious, large, sizable, vast, generous, ample, broad, wide, extensive, capacious, comfortable.

ant. crowded, tight, cramped, compact, small.

roost *n.* **1** perch, henhouse, hutch, pen, coop, cage, dovecote, aviary, rookery, aerie, nest. **2** home, hearth, fireside, berth, den, quarters, lodgings, residence, domicile, abode, pad (*Slang*). —*v.* settle, dwell, reside, park, take up quarters, drop anchor, perch, nest, berth, camp, bunk.

root[1] *n.* **1** shoot, rootlet, rootstock, taproot, tap, radical, radix, root hair, tuber, bulb, bulbil, corm, rhizome. **2** source, origin, beginning, fountainhead, derivation, mainspring, germ, seed, egg, nucleus, embryo, womb, matrix, essence, basis, principle, fundamental. —*v.* establish, fix, implant, ground, entrench, anchor, moor.

root[2] *v.* rummage, poke, burrow, pry, dig, delve, nose around, ferret, grub, search, explore, rout.

root for support, back, bolster, boost, promote, sponsor, encourage, cheer, acclaim, hail, applaud.

rootlet *n.* ROOT.

root out get rid of, dispose of, cut out, weed out, tear out, dig up, uproot, purge, pluck out, extirpate, extract, eradicate.

rootstock *n.* ROOT.

rope *n.* cord, cable, strand, line, hawser, wire, string, cordage, rope-work, rigging, tackle.

ropy *adj.* stringy, wiry, threadlike, fibrous, cartilaginous, viscous, viscoid, gelatinous, glutinous.

roseate *adj.* 1 RUDDY. 2 ROSY.

roster *n.* list, listing, register, roll, panel, slate, ticket, census, cadre, team, muster, enrollment.

rostrum *n.* PLATFORM.

rosy *adj.* 1 fresh, blooming, healthy, glowing, warm, rubicund, ruddy, flushed, blushing, florid. 2 favorable, promising, encouraging, reassuring, optimistic, auspicious, hopeful, confident, cheering, bright, sunny, roseate.
ant. 1 pallid, pale, wan, ashen, gray. 2 discouraging, disheartening, gloomy, unpromising, unfavorable.

rot *v.* 1 decompose, decay, spoil, putrefy, fester, mold, mildew, turn, go bad, disintegrate, crumble. 2 degenerate, decline, slip, lapse, backslide, regress, spoil, ruin, corrupt, degrade. —*n.* 1 decomposition, decay, rotting, spoliation, spoilage, putrefaction, foulness, corruption, pollution, defilement, blight, poison, affliction, disintegration, dissolution, destruction. 2 NONSENSE.

rotary *adj.* revolving, rotating, turning, rotational, rotatory, gyral, axial, rolling, swirling, whirling.

rotate *v.* 1 revolve, turn, go round, pivot, circle, swivel, spin, swirl,

swing, reel, wheel, gyrate, gyre, twist, screw, wind, crank. 2 alternate, intermit, cycle, recur.

rotation *n.* 1 revolution, turning, spinning, gyration, whirling, swirling, swiveling, pivoting, rolling, spin, turn, swirl. 2 alternation, succession, recurrence, sequence, periodicity, intermittence, rhythm, return.

rotatory *adj.* ROTARY.

rote *n.* routine, repetition, mechanization, perfunctoriness, system, order, conformity, convention, habitude, custom, habit, wont, practice, rut, groove.

rotten *adj.* 1 decayed, decomposed, spoiled, putrid, foul, tainted, rank, stale, rancid, sour, high, fetid, smelly, contaminated. 2 untrustworthy, unreliable, unscrupulous, dishonest, crooked, fraudulent, corrupt, base, weak, unsound, infirm, unstable, unsupported, insubstantial. **ant.** 1 fresh, unspoiled, green, sweet, refreshing, pure. 2 honest, scrupulous, reliable, solid, substantial, sound.

rotter *n. Brit. Slang* ROGUE.

rotund *adj.* 1 spherical, rounded, round, circular, globular, spheriform, ringlike, global, discoid, orbicular, annular. 2 plump, corpulent, stout, portly, chubby, pudgy, tubby, chunky, stocky, thickset, burly, fat, puffy, bloated. 3 full-toned, resonant, sonorous, round, rich, ringing, vibrant, orotund, mellifluous, grandiloquent.
ant. 2 thin, trim, slim, slender, lean, svelte. 3 pinched, squeaky, thin, shrill, piping, reedy.

roué *n.* RAKE.[2]

rough *adj.* 1 uneven, unsmooth, irregular, broken, bumpy, jagged, craggy, snaggy, choppy, gnarled, knotted, corrugated, scabrous, stubbled, granulated, rugged. 2 shaggy, stubby, bushy, bristly, fuzzy, nappy, coarse, matted, ragged, tousled, rumpled, uncombed, ruffled, disheveled, unkempt, disordered. 3 violent, fierce, furious, severe, intense, rigorous, harsh, tough, agitated, stormy, tempestuous, turbulent, choppy, raging, wild. **4** uncouth, boorish, rude, coarse, loutish, uncultivated, unpolished, unrefined, uncivil, ungentle, crude, crass, gross, rank, rugged, rowdy, boisterous, raw, blunt, earthy, ribald. **5** unpolished, unworked, unfashioned, unfinished, rough-hewn, homespun, formless, shapeless, amorphous, crude, patchy, sketchy, cursory, rudimentary, vague, approximate, hasty. **6** difficult, trying, hard, arduous, strenuous, laborious, rugged, austere, severe, unsparing, uncomfortable, inconvenient. —*n.* sketch, draft, outline, layout, skeleton.

ant. *adj.* **1** smooth, level, flat, plane, uniform. **2** satiny, glossy, slick, neat, trim. **3** calm, still, gentle, unruffled, serene, placid. **4** elegant, delicate, refined, polished, cultivated, tasteful, urbane. **5** flawless, well-made, crafted, masterful, finished. **6** easy, soft, light, undemanding, mild, lenient.

rough-and-tumble *adj.* DISORDERLY.

roughneck *n.* ROWDY.

rough up *v.* mistreat, manhandle, maltreat, ill-treat, batter, bruise, maul, buffet, knock about, abuse.

round *adj.* **1** spherical, circular, rounded, rotund, globular, cylindrical, ringlike, disklike, orblike, spheriform, global, discoid, orbicular, annular. **2** plump, rotund, chubby, tubby, pudgy, portly, stocky, corpulent. —*n.* **1** circle, ring, sphere, globe, orb, cylinder, loop, halo, aureole, disk, crown, annulus. **2** circuit, revolution, orbit, turn, cycle, loop, beat, route, course, trajectory, itinerary, tour, sequence, schedule, arrangement, routine, process, procedure, layout, order, system. **3** outburst, flare-up, burst, blast, rush, outbreak, eruption, salvo, volley, barrage, fusillade, spray. —*v.*

encircle, circle, go round, circuit, circumnavigate, compass, skirt, flank.

ant. *adj.* **2** slim, slender, thin, trim, lean.

roundabout *adj.* indirect, circuitous, winding, twisting, serpentine, sinuous, labyrinthine, tortuous, devious, oblique, ambiguous, backhanded, digressive, evasive.

ant. direct, straight, unswerving, straightforward, unambiguous.

roundaboutness *n.* INDIRECTION.

rounder *n.* REPROBATE.

roundly *adv.* **1** thoroughly, completely, entirely, wholly, fully, totally, utterly, altogether, absolutely, perfectly. **2** severely, rigorously, sharply, intensely, bluntly, fiercely, furiously, vehemently, bitterly, scathingly, violently, cruelly.

ant. 1 partially, partly, somewhat, incompletely, comparatively. **2** gently, mildly, softly, lightly, moderately.

roundness *n.* rotundity, sphericalness, sphericity, sphericality, cylindricality, cylindricalness, globularity, globularness.

roundup *n.* ASSEMBLY.

round up gather, collect, assemble, bunch, cluster, group, amass, accumulate, scare up, scrape up, glean, hunt down, pursue, corral, herd, drive, rally, muster, mobilize.

rouse *v.* **1** wake, wake up, awake, awaken, arouse, call, summon, get up, arise, stir. **2** excite, stir up, arouse, animate, stimulate, exhilarate, move, provoke, pique, incite, inflame, foment.

ant. 1 sedate, tranquilize, narcotize, sleep, rest. **2** calm, restrain, pacify, quell, curb.

rousing *adj.* **1** stimulating, exciting, moving, stirring, exhilarating, breathtaking, electric, galvanic, provocative, inciting, agitating, inflammatory. **2** lively, spirited, vigorous, vivacious, brisk, quick, sprightly, animated, active, bustling, dynamic, rushing.

ant. 1 drab, flat, monotonous, uninteresting, tiresome, boring. **2** slow, inactive, tired, dull, sluggish.

rout[1] *n.* retreat, flight, stampede, panic, withdrawal, evacuation, exodus, recession, repulse, reversal, rebuff, setback, collapse, defeat, debacle, downfall, ruin, shambles. —*v.* defeat, vanquish, conquer, overpower, overwhelm, clobber (*Slang*), subdue, subjugate, crush, humble, repulse, repel, rebuff.

rout[2] *n.* ROOT.[2]

route *n.* **1** itinerary, way, course, passage, circuit, beat, run, round, orbit, trajectory, artery, channel, detour, bypass. **2** road, street, roadway, thoroughfare, passage, passageway, artery, channel, corridor, track, trail, avenue, boulevard, highway, thruway, turnpike. **3** means, medium, agency, steps, instrumentality, way, system, *modus operandi*, method, procedure, practice, process, course. —*v.* channel, direct, send, point, aim, head, steer, drive, maneuver, pilot.

routine *n.* **1** procedure, program, method, system, practice, schedule, formula, recipe, rule, model, prescription, order, arrangement, sequence. **2** custom, habit, tradition, usage, wont, convention, formality, practice, grind. —*adj.* **1** customary, ordinary, habitual, usual, accustomed, accepted, regular, everyday, standard, familiar, conventional, normal. **2** uninspired, unimaginative, uninventive, unoriginal, dull, dry, sterile, perfunctory, mechanical, automatic, compulsive, unconscious. **ant.** *adj.* **1** extraordinary, exceptional, unusual, singular, abnormal, unfamiliar. **2** spontaneous, impulsive, extemporaneous, unpremeditated, inspired.

rove *v.* ramble, roam, wander, range, travel, drift, prowl, jaunt, stray, gad about, meander, straggle, stroll, traipse, gallivant, walk, tramp, hike.

row[1] *n.* series, sequence, succession, progression, course, run, arrange-

ment, pattern, line, rank, file, string, thread, queue, bank, tier.

row[2] *n.* quarrel, dispute, argument, squabble, set-to, wrangle, fight, scrap, tiff, spat, feud, fuss, disturbance, commotion, controversy, uproar, rumpus, ruckus (*Slang*), brawl, fracas, rumble (*Slang*). —*v.* quarrel, dispute, argue, squabble, wrangle, bicker, spat, scrap, fall out, fight, set to, broil, brawl, riot, feud, tiff.

rowdy *n.* troublemaker, roughneck (*Slang*), rough, tough, ruffian, brawler, hooligan, larrikin, scrapper, boor, lout, churl. —*adj.* unruly, disorderly, obstreperous, boisterous, rambunctious, wild, roughneck (*Slang*), rough, coarse, crude, boorish, loutish. **ant.** *adj.* orderly, well-behaved, disciplined, mannerly, decorous, peaceable.

royal *adj.* regal, royalist, monarchical, kingly, kinglike, queenly, queenlike, sovereign, imperial, princely, noble, aristocratic, majestic, stately, magisterial, purple.

royalty *n.* sovereignty, regnancy, regality, majesty, kingship, kinghood, queenhood, queenship, supremacy, dominion, prerogative, rule, sway, scepter, purple, right, power, potency, rank.

rub *v.* **1** spread, apply, press, massage, knead, stroke, scrub, scrape, brush, graze, skim, touch, feel, handle, scour, buff, polish, gloss, shine, burnish. **2** irritate, chafe, grate, rasp, abrade, burn, inflame, fret, fray, wear away, frazzle. —*n.* **1** contact, touch, friction, scraping, massage, kneading, stroking, fingering, scrubbing, scouring, polishing. **2** obstacle, hindrance, obstruction, barrier, snag, hitch, catch, drawback, difficulty, deterrent, frustration.

rubberneck *n.* TOURIST.

rubberstamp *v.* APPROVE.

rubber stamp OK.

rubbish *n.* **1** trash, refuse, waste,

debris, litter, rubble, scrap, junk, clutter, dust (*Brit.*), garbage, leavings, dregs. **2** nonsense, baloney (*Slang*), bosh, trumpery, bunk (*Slang*), hogwash, falderal, malarky (*Slang*), poppycock, tommyrot (*Slang*), foolishness, absurdity.

rubdown *n.* MASSAGE.

rub down MASSAGE.

rube *n. Slang* RUSTIC.

rubicund *adj.* RUDDY.

rub out *Slang* KILL.

rub the wrong way IRRITATE.

ruckus *n. Slang* COMMOTION.

ruddy *adj.* **1** reddish, red, rubicund, scarlet, crimson, incarnadine, roseate, ruby, rosy. **2** healthy, robust, hearty, blowzy, florid, flushed, blooming, rosy, blushing, sanguine.
ant. 2 pallid, ashen, sallow, sickly, wan.

rude *adj.* **1** impolite, uncivil, discourteous, disrespectful, unmannerly, ill-behaved, ill-bred, uncouth, impertinent, blunt, boorish, vulgar, crude, gross. **2** unfinished, raw, rough, crude, rough-hewn, coarse, natural, undeveloped, unrefined, uncultured, unskillful, untrained, unlearned, untaught, inexperienced. **3** robust, sturdy, stout, hearty, hardy, vigorous, strong, lusty. **4** barbarous, barbaric, barbarian, brutish, savage, untamed, wild, uncivilized, primitive, rough.
ant. 1 polite, courteous, well-mannered, tactful, civil, gracious. **2** polished, faultless, seasoned, experienced, artificial. **3** weak, infirm, faint, frail, invalid, anemic. **4** civilized, sophisticated, cultivated, genteel, restrained.

rudeness *n.* discourtesy, incivility, impudence, impertinence, insolence, audacity, brashness, crudeness, grossness, cheek, brass, gall, nerve.
ant. courtesy, civility, politeness, tact, savoir faire.

rudimentary *adj.* elementary, fundamental, essential, introductory, beginning, initial, primary, original,

basic, underlying, embryonic, germinal, early, undeveloped, imperfect.
ant. final, concluding, finished, developed, complete.

rudiments *n.* basics, fundamentals, ABC's, essentials, principles, axioms, theories, facts, core, basis.

rue *v.* regret, deplore, reproach oneself for, lament, bemoan, bewail, repine, repent, sorrow for.

rueful *adj.* regretful, sorry, repentant, penitent, contrite, self-reproachful, conscience-stricken, remorseful, pitying, sorrowful, grieved, woeful, mournful, dolorous, melancholy, lugubrious.
ant. remorseless, impenitent, negligent, gay, cheerful.

ruffian *n.* hoodlum, thug, hooligan, criminal, crook, hood (*Slang*), bully, tough, rough, brute, rowdy.

ruffle *n.* **1** frill, flounce, furbelow, trimming, edging, border, crimp, pleat, fold, tuck, gather, ornament, wrinkle. **2** disturbance, commotion, confusion, hassle (*Slang*), muddle, bother, mix-up, snafu (*Slang*), flurry, fluster, discomposure, discomfiture. —*v.* **1** unsettle, disturb, ripple, stir, churn, trouble, roughen, flurry, rumple, dishevel, tousle, disarrange, muddle, discompose, muss up, mix up. **2** irritate, disturb, vex, upset, annoy, chafe, gall, nettle, roil, rile, pique, peeve, gripe, provoke, exasperate, aggravate.

rug *n.* carpet, mat, pad, carpeting, floor covering, throw rug, scatter rug.

rugged *adj.* **1** uneven, rough, bumpy, unsmooth, unlevel, irregular, ridged, rippled, corrugated, crinkled, furrowed, jagged, craggy. **2** difficult, hard, strenuous, laborious, rigorous, stringent, rough, tough, severe, demanding, trying. **3** robust, hardy, sturdy, stout, vigorous, hearty, husky, brawny, able-bodied, stalwart. **4** ROUGH.
ant. 1 smooth, level, plane, straight, flat. **2** easy, undemanding, effortless,

simple, unexacting, soft. **3** frail, weak, delicate, feeble, infirm.

ruin *n.* **1** collapse, crash, fall, overthrow, downfall, decay, overturn, breakup, demolition, destruction, devastation, ravage, havoc, catastrophe. **2** undoing, downfall, ruination, curse, affliction, Waterloo, nemesis, bête noire. —*v.* **1** destroy, demolish, wreck, obliterate, devastate, dismantle, raze, level, crush, subdue, overwhelm, exterminate, annihilate, decimate, defeat. **2** disgrace, dishonor, humiliate, debase, crush, humble, shame, mortify, embarrass, bankrupt, break, impoverish, pauperize.

ruination *n.* **1** destruction, devastation, obliteration, dissolution, disruption, breakup, annihilation, ravage, havoc, catastrophe, cataclysm. **2** downfall, undoing, ruin, curse, affliction, nemesis, bête noire, Waterloo.

ruinous *adj.* disastrous, devastating, calamitous, catastrophic, cataclysmic, destructive, wasting, ravaging, pernicious, deleterious, detrimental, baneful, deadly, fatal.

rule *n.* **1** power, authority, control, dominion, command, sovereignty, supremacy, jurisdiction, leadership, management, direction, sway, reign, government. **2** procedure, method, course, action, pattern, habit, custom, practice, regimen, regime. **3** regulation, instruction, directive, ruling, direction, dictum, dictate, charge, injunction, code, precept, decree, edict, ordinance, mandate, maxim, tenet, dogma, law, statute, measure, proposition, enactment, canon. —*v.* **1** govern, command, dominate, control, supervise, direct, manage, head, lead, preside over, reign. **2** influence, affect, move, prompt, induce, persuade, dispose, sway, decide, determine.

rule out 1 eliminate, exclude, debar, reject, ban, leave out, dismiss, cut out, excise, strike out, expunge, extirpate, delete, obliterate. **2** preclude, prohibit, prevent, deter, avert, discourage, obstruct, hamper, hinder, obviate, ward off.

ruler *n.* sovereign, monarch, potentate, dynast, autocrat, despot, dictator, oligarch, satrap, tyrant, governor, commander, leader.

ruling *n.* RULE.

rum *adj. Brit. Slang* QUEER.

rumble *v.* boom, thunder, roll, roar, resound, reverberate, drum, crash, bang, clap, explode. —*n.* boom, thunder, roll, roar, reverberation, crash, bang, clap, drumming.

ruminant *adj.* THOUGHTFUL.

ruminate *v.* meditate, contemplate, ponder, brood, muse, reflect, mull over, consider, think about, speculate, weigh, deliberate.

rummage *v.* ransack, root, poke, pry, hunt out, probe, scour, comb, rifle, delve, burrow, explore, search, seek, look. —*n.* ODDS AND ENDS.

rummy *n. Slang* DRUNKARD.

rumor *n.* report, story, tale, talk, gossip, hearsay, bruit, innuendo, hint, insinuation, tattle, babble, buzz, whisper, scuttlebutt (*Slang*), dirt, canard. —*v.* report, gossip, talk of, whisper, noise abroad, bruit about, spread, broadcast, chatter, tattle, prate.

rump *n.* buttocks, posterior, hindquarters, haunches, behind, backside, butt, fundament, bottom, stern, rear (*Slang*), tail (*Slang*), seat.

rumple *v.* wrinkle, crease, fold, crinkle, crumple, ruffle, tousle, muss up, dishevel, rimple, ripple, furrow, corrugate. —*n.* wrinkle, crease, fold, crinkle, crumple, ruffle, furrow, crimp, pucker, corrugation.

rumpus *n.* COMMOTION.

run *v.* **1** race, speed, sprint, rush, dash, tear, dart, scurry, scamper, scoot, fly, spurt, zip, hotfoot it. **2** flee, retreat, take flight, bolt, skip, clear out, cut loose, make off, cut and run, decamp, abscond. **3** extend, reach, stretch, go, range, cover, proceed, continue, endure, last, persist, remain, stay, hold. **4** flow, stream, rush, surge, pour, gush, spill, flood, flush, course, drip, leak, bleed, sweat, perspire, weep. **5** function, perform, go, work, act, behave, operate, manipulate, manage, regulate, handle. **6** manage, direct, control, govern, conduct, regulate, carry on, supervise, oversee, administer, superintend, mastermind, lead. —*n.* **1** scurry, scamper, scuttle, scout, rush, dash, tear, race, sprint, jog, canter, trot, gallop. **2** flow, movement, flux, motion, sweep, surge, course, current, stream, rush, passage. **3** series, succession, sequence, progression, course, round, cycle, span, spell, period, season, bout, trend, tendency, bent, bias, drift, course, direction. **4** type, class, order, kind, sort, variety, set, character, group, ilk, species, stamp, brand.

run across RUN INTO.

runaway *n.* fugitive, escapee, refugee, deserter, turntail.

rundown *n.* summary, sketch, synopsis, résumé, outline, draft, précis, review, brief, digest, abridgment, condensation, abstract, capitulation, epitome.

run-down *adj.* **1** exhausted, tired, weary, fatigued, worn-out, faint, feeble, frail, seedy, sickly, ailing. **2** broken-down, dilapidated, ramshackle, rickety, crumbling, tumbledown, shabby, ratty, decayed, timeworn, deteriorated, battered, damaged, ruined.

ant. 1 robust, strong, vigorous, healthy, hale, ruddy. **2** solid, substantial, sturdy, well-constructed, durable, fresh, new.

run down 1 chase, pursue, track, track down, trail, seek, hunt, hound, run to earth, overtake. **2** disparage, belittle, depreciate, degrade, debase, discredit, defame, malign, slander, soil, knock (*Slang*).

run-in *n.* QUARREL.

run into meet, encounter, run across, come across, come upon, bump into, see, confront.

runnel *n.* STREAM.

run-of-the-mill *adj.* ORDINARY.

run out expire, give out, end, elapse, cease, stop, close, finish, conclude, run dry, vanish, disappear.

runt *n.* pygmy, dwarf, midget, shrimp, peewee, elf, gnome, manikin, Tom Thumb, Lilliputian.

rupture *n.* **1** break, fracture, breach, crack, split, rent, fissure, rift, fault, flaw, cleft, tear, cut, severance. **2** falling-out, breach, split, break, schism, rift, separation, divorce, alienation, estrangement, disaffection, quarrel, squabble, wrangle, scrap. —*v.* break, burst, split, crack, open, breach, cleave, divide, rift, rend.

rural *adj.* rustic, country, countrified, up-country, Arcadian, pastoral, bucolic, hick, unsophisticated, provincial, simple, uncomplicated.

ant. urban, citified, sophisticated, urbane.

ruse *n.* trick, stratagem, subterfuge, device, dodge, scheme, shift, gimmick, artifice, deception, deceit, chicanery, dishonesty, swindle, fraud, flim-flam.

rush *v.* **1** run, race, speed, scurry, scamper, scoot, scramble, sprint, tear, dash, bolt, fly, tear, bound, surge, hurry, hasten, hustle. **2** attack, chase, assault, assail, charge, sail into, go at, have at, pitch into, raid, storm, beset, beleaguer. —*n.* **1** movement, speed, velocity, drive, surge, acceleration, expedition, swiftness, rapidity, activity, haste, hurry, dash, scramble, bustle, hustle, flurry. **2** demand, pressure, press, run, drain, spurt, burst, explosion, outburst, eruption, torrent, exigency.

ant. *n.* **1** stoppage, cessation, halt, stay, rest, respite, lull.

rustic *adj.* **1** rural, countrified, country, agrarian, agricultural, pastoral, bucolic, Arcadian. **2** unrefined, uncultured, unpolished, uncouth, unsophisticated, artless, rude, awkward, boorish, cloddish, lumpish, hickish. —*n.* **1** farmer, countryman, agriculturist, cultivator, tiller, gardener, husbandman, yeoman (*Brit.*), sharecropper, tenant farmer. **2** hick, yokel, rube (*Slang*), hayseed (*Slang*), bumpkin, clodhopper, farmer, churl.

ant. *adj.* **2** sophisticated, worldly-wise, blasé, stylish, chic, elegant, citified.

rustle *v.* swish, whisk, whish, ruffle, shuffle, riffle, hustle, bustle.

rusty *adj.* stale, inept, slow, deficient, inadequate, impaired, unpolished,

inexpert, unpracticed, unskilled, unprepared.

ant. practiced, fluent, skilled, finished, polished.

rut *n.* groove, furrow, trench, trough, ditch, gutter, gouge, gash, cut, score, fluting, crack, channel, dike, canal, track, trail, road, pathway, passage.

ruth *n.* COMPASSION.

ruthless *adj.* merciless, pitiless, unmerciful, unpitying, heartless, relentless, unfeeling, hardened, callous, cold, cruel, brutal, savage, bestial.

ant. compassionate, pitying, sympathetic, tenderhearted, softhearted, indulgent, gentle.

S

sabbatical *n.* HOLIDAY.

saber *n.* SWORD.

sable *adj.* BLACK.

sabotage *v.* subvert, disable, incapacitate, undermine, sap, wreck, vandalize, damage, hamper, obstruct, hinder, scotch.

ant. strengthen, reinforce, enhance, assist, abet, cooperate.

sac *n.* pouch, pocket, cavity, cyst, bladder, bag, sack, pod, vesicle, bursa, capsule.

saccharine *adj.* sweet, syrupy, sugary, oversweet, cloying, honeyed, candied, mellific, sugared, mellifluous.

ant. sour, acerb, sharp, biting, vinegary, acid.

sacerdotal *adj.* priestly, clerical, churchly, pontifical, apostolic, ecclesiastical, ministerial, canonical, pastoral, monastic.

ant. lay, secular, laic, worldly, profane, mundane.

sack[1] *n.* bag, pouch, pocket, poke, purse, satchel, knapsack, pocket-

book, handbag, ditty-bag. —*v. Slang* fire, dismiss, discharge, let go, release, oust, cashier, drop, shelve, discard, turn out, bounce (*Slang*).

ant. *v.* hire, employ, engage, retain, take on, appoint.

sack[2] *v.* plunder, pillage, ravage, devastate, lay waste, despoil, loot, strip, spoil, desolate, destroy, demolish, ruin, reduce.

sacrament *n.* covenant, pledge, affirmation, vow, ceremonial, troth, plight, obligation, solemnity, ceremony, rite, ministration.

sacred *adj.* **1** consecrated, hallowed, religious, holy, divine, sanctified, venerable, dedicated, blessed, devoted. **2** solemn, inviolable, inviolate, incorruptible, protected, invulnerable, unassailable, immune, sacrosanct, defended.

ant. **1** profane, secular, impious, unsanctified, sinful. **2** violable, vulnerable, corruptible, assailable.

sacredness *n.* SANCTITY.

sacrifice *n.* **1** offering, oblation, immolation, lustration, slaughter, piaculum, hecatomb, corban, mactation. **2** victim, scapegoat, martyr, offering, incense, holocaust. **3** abnegation, self-sacrifice, self-denial, surrender, renunciation, capitulation, yielding, cession, abandonment, relinquishment. —*v.* give up, yield, surrender, forgo, forfeit, renounce, cede, abandon, waive, part with, immolate.

ant. *n.* **3** seizure, gain, usurpation, confiscation, appropriation. *v.* keep, guard, cleave to, clutch, grip, hold tight.

sacrilege *n.* violation, profanation, blasphemy, desecration, impiety, profanity, iniquity, irreverence, irreligion, mockery.

ant. consecration, sanctification, piety, reverence, devoutness, observance.

sacrilegious *adj.* blasphemous, godless, impious, unholy, irreligious, profane, ungodly, irreverent, sinful, desecrating, disrespectful, unregenerate, wicked.

ant. pious, godly, reverent, devout, religious, holy.

sacrosanct *adj.* sacred, inviolable, consecrated, hallowed, sanctified, inviolate, holy, divine, godly, heavenly, celestial, spiritual, religious.

ant. sacrilegious, ungodly, unsanctified, unholy, impious.

sad *adj.* **1** sorrowful, depressed, mournful, dejected, despondent, disconsolate, miserable, unhappy, melancholy, downcast, heavy-hearted, downhearted, gloomy, morose, disheartened, pessimistic, sullen, glum, down, blue, *triste.* **2** deplorable, grievous, lamentable, pitiful, disastrous, dire, sorry, worthless, distressing, wretched.

ant. **1** happy, glad, cheerful, sprightly, jolly. **2** fortunate, propitious, flourishing, promising, prosperous.

sadden *v.* grieve, sorrow, depress, deject, desolate, dishearten, crush, dis-

courage, dash, subdue, burden, languish, mourn, lament.

ant. gladden, delight, cheer, encourage, gratify, please.

saddle *v.* burden, load, weigh down, encumber, tax, shackle, overload, charge, assign, handicap, hamper, obstruct, overwhelm, trouble.

ant. relieve, disburden, lighten, free, alleviate, allay.

sadistic *adj.* CRUEL.

sadness *n.* SORROW.

safari *n.* EXPEDITION.

safe *adj.* **1** secure, impregnable, immune, protected, unendangered, rescued, guarded, snug. **2** unhurt, unscathed, intact, alive, unharmed, undamaged, whole, sound, saved. **3** reliable, certain, sure, dependable, secure, trustworthy, tried-and-true, conservative.

ant. **1** hazardous, exposed, dangerous, perilous. **2** damaged, hurt, injured, harmed, hit. **3** unreliable, insecure, uncertain, risky, chancy.

safe-conduct *n.* PASS.

safeguard *n.* precaution, defense, protection, security, shield, screen, armor, palladium, charm, amulet, guard. —*v.* defend, guard, shield, screen, secure, protect, preserve, conserve, armor, fortify.

ant. *n.* peril, danger, hazard, threat, plight. *v.* expose, danger, imperil, jeopardize, risk.

safekeeping *n.* protection, custody, guardianship, charge, care, preservation, conservation, surveillance, ward, auspices, tutelage.

ant. negligence, neglect, laxity, carelessness, indifference, slackness.

safety *n.* security, protection, safeness, preservation, safekeeping, shelter, asylum, refuge, surety, immunity, custody, sanctuary.

ant. danger, peril, risk, hazard, jeopardy.

sag *v.* droop, bow, slump, bend, give way, settle, decline, sink, curve, swag, bulge, dip, lean.

saga *n.* narrative, legend, chronicle,

story, tale, yarn, epic, myth, romance, gest, history.

sagacious *adj.* intelligent, acute, discerning, clear-sighted, keen, perspicacious, judicious, shrewd, practical, astute, sharp-witted, cunning, rational, sage, wise.

ant. unwise, irrational, fatuous, stupid, foolish, shortsighted.

sagacity *n.* ACUMEN.

sage *n.* philosopher, pundit, intellectual, savant, authority, scholar, solon, guru, oracle, Nestor, Solomon, highbrow, egghead (*Slang*). —*adj.* wise, prudent, profound, learned, sagacious, judicious, enlightened, sensible, sapient, sane.

ant. *n.* simpleton, ignoramus, dolt, fool, idiot. *adj.* foolish, imprudent, shallow, simple, silly.

sahib *n.* MASTER.

sail *v.* soar, glide, fly, float, scud, skim, cruise, drift, sweep, stream, coast, wing.

sail into ASSAIL.

sailor *n.* mariner, seaman, shipmate, seafarer, salt, tar, navigator, voyager, sea dog, gob (*Slang*), yachtsman.

saint *n.* paragon, angel, worthy, model, cherub, martyr. —*v.* VENERATE.

ant. sinner, rascal, scoundrel, wrongdoer, reprobate, scapegrace.

sainted *adj.* SAINTLY.

saintly *adj.* **1** godly, holy, blessed, sainted, beatific, pious, devout. **2** benevolent, charitable, kindly, righteous, virtuous, blameless, moral, upright.

ant. 1 ungodly, impious, wicked, sinful, diabolical. **2** flawed, frail, corruptible, malicious, immoral.

sake *n.* **1** purpose, motive, reason, objective, end, aim, cause, principle. **2** interest, regard, consideration, account, advantage, welfare, benefit, enhancement, good.

ant. 2 disadvantage, detriment, damage, harm, misfortune, peril.

salaam *n., v.* BOW.

salable *adj.* COMMERCIAL.

salacious *adj.* lascivious, lustful, lecherous, rakish, prurient, libidinous, concupiscent, pornographic, wanton, lewd, carnal, loose, incontinent, lickerish.

ant. strait-laced, prudish, modest, proper, chaste, puritanical.

salary *n.* payment, compensation, remuneration, earnings, emolument, stipend, pay, wages, income, fee, allowance, hire.

sale *n.* exchange, transfer, auction, transaction, trade, deal, disposal, selling, bargain, vending, marketing, barter.

salesgirl *n.* SALESPERSON.

saleslady *n.* SALESPERSON.

salesman *n.* SALESPERSON.

salesperson *n.* salesclerk, salesgirl, saleslady, salesman, saleswoman, clerk, merchandiser, drummer, huckster, pitchman, pitchwoman, peddler, vendor, shopkeeper, storekeeper.

saleswoman *n.* SALESPERSON.

salience *n.* PROMINENCE.

salient *adj.* **1** prominent, outstanding, conspicuous, noticeable, important, significant, striking, remarkable, impressive, signal. **2** projecting, jutting, protruding, prominent, bulging, protuberant, swelling.

ant. 1 insignificant, unimportant, trivial, minor, inconspicuous. **2** indented, recessed, sunken, depressed, dimpled.

saliva *n.* spit, spittle, drivel, slaver, slobber, drool, salivation, sputum, water, froth, foam.

sallow *adj.* jaundiced, yellowish, yellow, sickly, anemic, wan, muddy, ashen, livid, chlorotic, greensick.

ant. ruddy, florid, rosy, blooming, flushed.

sally *v.* rush out, debouch, erupt, issue, set out, attack, dash, spring. —*n.* **1** sortie, foray, excursion, expedition, debouchment, raid, attack, jaunt. **2** witticism, quip, joke, pleasantry, gibe, squib, quirk, fancy.

ant. *v.* retreat, subside, fall back, retire, give way.

salmagundi *n.* MEDLEY.

salon *n.* drawing room, living room, sitting room, lounge, parlor, reception room.

saloon *n.* bar, pub, barroom, lounge, taproom, tavern, bistro, cabaret, ginmill (*Slang*), public house (*Brit.*), grogshop (*Brit.*), beer parlor, beer hall, beer garden.

salt away store up, save, stockpile, hoard, squirrel away, put by, cache, stow away, accumulate, amass, conserve, preserve.

   ant. spend, scatter, fritter away, disperse, use, waste.

salted *adj.* EXPERIENCED.

salty *adj. of speech, etc.:* piquant, witty, pungent, sharp, acerb, earthy, peppery, colorful, humorous, racy, immodest, risqué, ribald, vulgar, coarse, gross, obscene.

   ant. inspired, boring, stale, refined, delicate, prudish.

salubrious *adj.* wholesome, healthful, salutary, therapeutic, beneficial, invigorating, bracing, tonic, protective, healthy.

   ant. debilitating, deleterious, harmful, enfeebling, pernicious, baneful.

salutary *adj.* 1 beneficial, helpful, advantageous, useful, productive, serviceable, profitable, practical, favorable, good, remedial, corrective. 2 SALUBRIOUS.

   ant. 1 harmful, detrimental, counterproductive, unpropitious, adverse, bad.

salutation *n.* greeting, salute, obeisance, reverence, recognition, homage, address, welcome, hail, bow, curtsy, kowtow, salaam.

salutatory *n.* ORATION.

salute *v.* 1 greet, welcome, hail, accost, address, recognize, nod to, call. 2 honor, celebrate, mark, praise, compliment, congratulate, recognize. —*n.* greeting, recognition, salutation, address, welcome, ovation, honor, commemoration, celebration, fanfare, obeisance, honoring.

salvage *v.* save, retrieve, salve, recover, restore, rescue, redeem, cull, rehabilitate, recycle.

   ant. waste, destroy, discard, scatter, expend.

salvation *n.* redemption, absolution, deliverance, sanctification, reformation, regeneration, conversion, rebirth.

   ant. damnation, excommunication, anathema, malediction, doom, judgment.

salve[1] *n.* emollient, ointment, unguent, cerate, balm, lotion, dressing, liniment.

salve[2] *v.* SALVAGE.

salver *n.* TRAY.

salvo *n.* discharge, burst, volley, fusillade, broadside, drumfire, cannonade, blast, shower, spray, hail, eruption, salute.

same *adj.* 1 identical, equal, alike, selfsame, equivalent, like, duplicate, twin, ditto, corresponding, interchangeable, very similar. 2 unchanged, immutable, consistent, constant, regular, unvarying, continuing.

   ant. 1 different, other, unlike, dissimilar, unequal, opposite. 2 changed, inconstant, varying, shifting, irregular.

sample *n.* 1 portion, piece, part, specimen, sip, taste, slip, chip, slice, representative, aliquot. 2 instance, example, illustration, case, specimen, exemplification, exemplar, case in point. —*v.* test, taste, try, experience, partake of, dip into, try out, assay, judge, analyze.

sanative *adj.* THERAPEUTIC.

sanatorium *n.* sanitarium, hospital, infirmary, asylum, home, retreat, spa, watering place, baths.

sanctify *v.* 1 consecrate, dedicate, set apart, beautify, hallow, devote, enshrine, anoint, bless. 2 purify, absolve, cleanse, redeem, atone for, shrive, expiate for.

   ant. 1 desecrate, profane, defile, pollute. 2 condemn, damn, execrate, excommunicate.

sanctimonious *adj.* hypocritical, pharisaical, pietistic, holier-than-thou, self-righteous, unctuous, affected, canting, preachy, bigoted, dissembling.

sanctimony *n.* hypocrisy, sanctimoniousness, pharisaism, pietism, Tartuffery, cant, preachiness, religiosity, self-righteousness, dissembling, pretense.

sanction *v.* approve, countenance, allow, endorse, confirm, ratify, support, certify, encourage, accredit, favor. —*n.* **1** confirmation, approval, ratification, commendation, acceptance, justification, approbation, permission, indulgence, encouragement. **2** decree, order, fiat, law, ruling, command, warrant. **ant.** *v.* interdict, disapprove, forbid, hinder, denounce, censure. *n.* **1** disapproval, objection, hindrance, restraint, exclusion.

sanctioned *adj.* ACCREDITED.

sanctity *n.* saintliness, purity, godliness, piety, spirituality, sacredness, holiness, grace, goodness, inviolability, virtue, righteousness, religiousness. **ant.** godlessness, irreverence, wickedness, sacrilege, impiety, worldliness.

sanctuary *n.* **1** sanctum, shrine, temple, altar, adytum, holy of holies, church. **2** refuge, asylum, haven, shelter, preserve, protection, cover, retreat.

sanctum *n.* SANCTUARY.

sandwich *v.* insert, enclose, layer, wedge in, interject, interpose, bracket, intercalate, interlard.

sandy *adj.* gritty, granular, grainy, arenaceous, powdery.

sane *adj.* sound, sensible, wise, rational, lucid, reasonable, sober, normal, healthy, sapient, sage, judicious, prudent. **ant.** deranged, demented, irrational, disturbed, insane, frenzied.

sang-froid *n.* COMPOSURE.

sanguinary *adj.* bloodthirsty, bloodstained, bloody, murderous, gory, savage, ruthless, merciless, pitiless, fell, cruel, truculent.

sanguine *adj.* hopeful, confident, enthusiastic, optimistic, buoyant, expectant, elated, animated, spirited, lively, cheerful. **ant.** hopeless, somber, gloomy, despondent, pessimistic, morose.

sanitarium *n.* SANATORIUM.

sanitary *adj.* hygienic, germfree, clean, sterile, unpolluted, uninfected, disinfected, aseptic, sterilized, salubrious, healthy, healthful. **ant.** unsanitary, unhealthy, septic, infected, dirty, filthy.

sanitize *v.* EXPURGATE.

sanity *n.* rationality, saneness, common sense, levelheadedness, sensibleness, mental health, lucidity, reason, coherence, horse sense, soundness, reasonableness, moderation. **ant.** insanity, derangement, folly, fanaticism, madness, dementia.

sansculotte *n.* REVOLUTIONARY.

sap[1] *n. Slang* FOOL.

sap[2] *v.* weaken, destroy, debilitate, disable, enervate, enfeeble, drain, impair, cripple, exhaust, impoverish, prostrate, undermine. **ant.** strengthen, build up, restore, regenerate, fortify, toughen.

saphead *n. Slang* FOOL.

sapient *adj.* WISE.

sapling *n.* YOUNGSTER.

saponaceous *adj.* SOAPY.

sappy *adj. Slang* SILLY.

sarcasm *n.* sneering, irony, scorn, derision, ridicule, contempt, disparagement, mockery, jeering, taunting, gibing, scoffing, bitterness, invective, aspersion, vitriol. **ant.** flattery, approval, soft soap, admiration, eulogy, commendation.

sarcastic *adj.* taunting, caustic, bitter, biting, mordant, cutting, cynical, derisive, scornful, sneering, sardonic, contemptuous, ironic, satiric. **ant.** complimentary, ingratiating, flattering, gracious, fawning.

sardonic *adj.* scornful, derisive, sneering, mocking, cynical, sarcastic, satiric, caustic, malignant, bitter, malicious, mordant.

sash *n.* band, scarf, stole, ribbon, cincture, belt, girth, waistband, tie, cummerbund, girdle, obi.

sashay *v.* strut, glide, swagger, flounce, bounce, prance, sidle, parade, promenade, step, move.

sass *n.* impudence, back talk, sauce, flippancy, cheek, brashness, disrespect, impertinence, pertness, boldness. —*v.* snap at, mock, heckle, sauce, talk back to, insult, sneer at, scoff at, twit, ridicule.

ant. *n.* respect, decorum, courtesy, modesty, reserve.

sassy *adj.* saucy, impudent, impertinent, flippant, pert, cheeky, brazen, bratty, forward, disrespectful.

ant. timid, mannerly, diffident, respectful, meek, sedate.

Satan the Devil, Beelzebub, Old Nick, Prince of Darkness, Belial, the Evil One, the Tempter, Lucifer, Apollyon, Mephistopheles.

satanic *adj.* evil, diabolical, infernal, hellish, fiendish, malicious, devilish, vicious, vile, wicked, malignant, corrupt, cruel.

ant. angelic, virtuous, righteous, benevolent, good, heavenly.

satchel *n.* bag, grip, case, valise, sack, reticule, gripsack, suitcase, briefcase, handbag.

sate *v.* SATIATE.

satellite *n.* **1** moon, sputnik, orbiter, space station, capsule. **2** attendant, minion, hanger-on, retainer, sycophant, dependent, disciple, follower, vassal.

satiate *v.* satisfy, gratify, sate, surfeit, pall, gorge, cloy, glut, suffice, fill, overfill, stuff, weary.

satire *n.* ridicule, sarcasm, irony, exposure, mockery, derision, wit, burlesque, lampooning, pasquinade, denunciation, humor.

satirical *adj.* sarcastic, mordant, mocking, caustic, biting, ironic, sardonic, malicious, derisive, taunting, cynical, scornful.

satirize *v.* lampoon, ridicule, take off, censure, mock, deride, burlesque, parody, travesty, ape, abuse, lash.

satisfaction *n.* **1** gratification, repletion, pleasure, enjoyment, contentment, satiety, felicity, delight, comfort. **2** fulfillment, expiation, atonement, reimbursement, restitution, compensation, vindication, reparation, settlement, payment.

ant. 1 displeasure, discomfort, discontent, resentment, want.

satisfactory *adj.* adequate, gratifying, pleasing, sufficient, acceptable, enough, competent, all right, OK, suitable, fitting, convincing, conclusive.

ant. unsatisfactory, substandard, inadequate, disappointing, insufficient, incompetent.

satisfy *v.* **1** fulfill, make good, discharge, supply, surfeit, repay, defray, recompense, appease. **2** please, gratify, content, delight, relieve, amuse, cheer, indulge. **3** convince, answer, allay, persuade, settle, assure, meet, quiet, dispel.

ant. 1 renege, deny, fail, deplete, drain. **2** displease, trouble, disturb, sadden, vex.

satisfying *adj.* pleasing, gratifying, agreeable, cheering, comforting, enjoyable, welcome, pleasant, satisfactory, grateful, refreshing, nice.

ant. disagreeable, irksome, unsatisfactory, painful, unpleasant, galling.

satrap *n.* RULER.

saturate *v.* soak, imbue, permeate, drench, suffuse, impregnate, pervade, infuse, wet, ret, fill.

ant. dry, drain, evaporate, dehydrate, ted.

saturnine *adj.* morose, gloomy, dour, sullen, sad, heavy, crabbed, glum, sardonic, somber, surly, leaden, dull, grave.

ant. cheerful, urbane, genial, pleasant, happy.

satyr *n.* profligate, lecher, libertine, voluptuary, sensualist, womanizer, roué, rake, goat, debauchee, Don Juan, seducer.

ant. celibate, ascetic, puritan, monk, monogamist, family man.

sauce *n.* 1 relish, condiment, dressing, topping, puree, gravy. 2 SASS.

saucy *adj.* disrespectful, impudent, sassy, impertinent, brazen, flippant, pert, forward, cheeky, rude, bratty, presumptuous, fresh (*Slang*).

ant. respectful, mannerly, well-bred, well-behaved, amiable, demure.

saunter *v.* stroll, promenade, ramble, roam, stray, wander, amble, traipse, meander, idle, dawdle, lounge, mosey (*Slang*). —*n.* stroll, turn, promenade, meander, walk, ramble, airing, amble.

savage *adj.* 1 feral, wild, untamed, untameable. 2 fierce, ferocious, fell, barbarous, merciless, brutal, cruel, inhuman. 3 uncivilized, primitive, uncultivated, rude, barbaric, barbarian, wild. —*n.* 1 primitive, aborigine, barbarian, autochthon, native, indigene. 2 monster, beast, butcher, cutthroat, brute, assassin, vandal, fiend, killer, murderer, yahoo. —*v.* beat, maul, manhandle, abuse, thrash, mangle, drub, brutalize, torture, lacerate, waste (*Slang*).

ant. *adj.* 1 domesticated, tame, trained, housebroken. 2 gentle, tender, mild, merciful, kind. 3 civilized, cultivated, cultured, advanced, developed.

savagery *n.* cruelty, bloodthirstiness, ferocity, fiendishness, sadism, mercilessness, brutality, inhumanity, barbarousness, barbarity, fierceness, atrocity.

ant. mildness, clemency, gentleness, kindness, humanity, mercy, lenity.

savant *n.* scholar, intellectual, sage, guru, pundit, authority, expert, philosopher, solon, oracle, Nestor.

ant. ignoramus, dolt, know-nothing, lowbrow, illiterate, simpleton.

save *v.* 1 rescue, preserve, redeem, salvage, deliver, safeguard, help, ransom, recover, keep. 2 hoard, put by,

store, set aside, accumulate, reserve, hold, amass, husband, lay up.

ant. 1 sacrifice, surrender, abandon, give up, lose, fail. 2 spend, squander, scatter, dissipate, disperse, waste.

savior *n.* rescuer, preserver, deliverer, benefactor, liberator, champion, defender, protector, redeemer, salvation, guardian.

ant. bane, curse, betrayer, nemesis, Judas, traitor.

savor *n.* 1 taste, smell, flavor, tang, scent, aroma, fragrance, odor. 2 aura, quality, air, suggestion, essence, redolence, indication, nature. —*v.* 1 taste, smell, smack, reek, betoken, indicate, suggest, resemble. 2 enjoy, relish, fancy, like, appreciate, delight in, value, cherish, admire.

savorless *adj.* INSIPID.

savory *adj.* 1 appetizing, tasty, flavorful, palatable, piquant, toothsome, flavorsome, delicious, good, spicy. 2 reputable, respectable, unimpeachable, righteous, moral, proper, decent, honorable, edifying.

ant. 1 unpalatable, distasteful, sickening, nauseating, acrid, bland. 2 unsavory, shady, questionable, shameful, scandalous, disreputable.

savvy *Slang* *v.* UNDERSTAND. —*n.* KNOW-HOW. —*adj.* SHREWD.

saw *n.* proverb, saying, maxim, adage, axiom, aphorism, dictum, apothegm, byword, platitude, truism, bromide.

saw-toothed *adj.* serrate, jagged, notched, dentate, crenulate, denticulate, chipped, scored, nicked.

say *v.* 1 speak, utter, articulate, pronounce, remark, tell, express, state, recite, declare. 2 allege, claim, hold, maintain, aver, assert, avow, advance, cite, imply.

ant. 2 deny, gainsay, dispute, oppose, contradict, contravene.

saying *n.* 1 utterance, speech, talk, statement, enunciation, voicing, expression, declaration, communication. 2 maxim, saw, proverb, aphorism, dictum, adage, motto, apothegm, byword.

scab *n.* crust, eschar, incrustation, scale, slough, scurf, proud flesh, granulation tissue.

scabrous *adj.* **1** rough, uneven, harsh, coarse, rugged, scurfy, squamous, scaly, flaky, scraggy, rugose. **2** suggestive, salacious, indecent, scandalous, risqué, unseemly, improper, coarse, offensive, grimy, squalid.
ant. 1 smooth, glabrous, velvety, soft, fine. **2** decent, proper, seemly, delicate, polite.

scads *n.* abundance, plenty, plethora, superabundance, profusion, much, lots, heaps, host, mass, ocean, flood, wealth.
ant. dearth, paucity, scarcity, smidgen, little, mite.

scaffold *n.* PLATFORM.

scalawag *n.* RASCAL.

scale¹ *n.* plate, flake, lamina, squama, chip, peel, layer, lamella, eschar, scurf, crust, scab.

scale² *n.* **1** calibration, graduation, gauge, measure, system, series, steps, degrees, rule. **2** hierarchy, gradation, progression, gamut, system, chart, ranking, ladder. —*v.* **1** climb, ascend, rise, mount, clamber, escalade, surmount, go up. **2** prorate, convert, regulate, adjust, transpose, size.
ant. *v.* **1** descend, dismount, fall, go down, get down.

scaly *adj.* flaky, squamous, scurfy, scalelike, scutellate, scabrous, foliated, spathic.
ant. smooth, glabrous, mirrorlike, even.

scamp *n.* RASCAL.

scamper *v.* scurry, scuttle, scud, rush, hasten, hurry, hie, scoot, sprint, bolt, skedaddle, vamoose (*Slang*), run, race, dart, trip, trot.
ant. lag, dawdle, creep, loiter, crawl, inch.

scan *v.* **1** peruse, scrutinize, examine, peer, observe, study, pore over, inspect, survey. **2** glance at, skim, browse, skip through, leaf through, thumb through.

scandal *n.* outrage, offense, abomina-tion, shame, transgression, infringement, sin, excess, vice, crime, enormity, shocker, dereliction, infraction.

scandalize *v.* OUTRAGE.

scandalous *adj.* disgraceful, disreputable, ignominious, odious, unseemly, shocking, scabrous, shameful, infamous, notorious, outrageous, dishonorable, slanderous, opprobrious.

scant *adj.* meager, exiguous, skimpy, scanty, sparse, insufficient, spare, thin, short, scarce. —*v.* restrict, limit, stint, grudge, light, skimp, withhold, cut short, skim, dole out.
ant. *adj.* plentiful, profuse, copious, abundant, ample. —*v.* overwhelm, glut, engulf, surfeit, cloy.

scanty *adj.* deficient, exiguous, meager, sparse, skimpy, poor, scant, inadequate, scarce, few, paltry, small, thin, restricted.
ant. ample, plentiful, copious, excessive, exuberant, gross.

scapegoat *n.* goat, whipping boy, fall guy (*Slang*), straw man.

scapegrace *n.* ROGUE.

scar *n.* **1** cicatrix, pockmark, pit. **2** mark, injury, stigma, disfigurement, trauma, reminder, memento, brand. —*v.* mark, brand, mar, hurt, traumatize, disfigure, blemish, injure, wound.

scarce *adj.* rare, unusual, uncommon, singular, exceptional, unique, out-of-the-way, spare, scanty, scant, sparse, insufficient, unplentiful, exiguous.
ant. plentiful, common, abundant, manifold, profuse.

scarcely *adv.* barely, just, only just, hardly, only, no more than, merely, at most.

scarcity *n.* scantiness, insufficiency, dearth, deficiency, paucity, poverty, shortage, want, lack, need, deficit, undersupply.
ant. wealth, excess, surfeit, glut, superabundance, plethora.

scare *v.* frighten, intimidate, daunt, alarm, terrorize, appall, cow, terrify, shock, dismay, affright, startle, surprise. —*n.* fright, start, alarm, shock, terror, dismay, panic, horror. —*adj.* alarming, sensational, lurid, startling, threatening, frightening, ominous, disturbing, hair-raising, terrifying.

ant. *v.* lull, soothe, pacify, calm, reassure, tranquilize.

scarf *n.* stole, neckpiece, muffler, band, bandanna, tie, cravat, shawl, babushka, mantilla, tippet, comforter.

scarify *v.* **1** SCRATCH. **2** CRITICIZE.

scarp *n.* SLOPE.

scary *adj.* alarming, frightening, eerie, weird, awesome, ominous, startling, threatening, fearful, terrifying, uncanny, awful, horrendous.

ant. reassuring, soothing, heartening, harmless, encouraging, comforting.

scat *v.* scoot, shoo, go away, leave, decamp, quit, get away, beat it (*Slang*), scram (*Slang*), get lost (*Slang*), vamoose (*Slang*), make tracks (*Slang*), bug off (*Slang*), begone, avaunt.

scathe *v.* CRITICIZE.

scatheless *adj.* HARMLESS.

scathing *adj.* blasting, withering, scorching, searing, merciless, caustic, cutting, fierce, trenchant, mordant, severe, ferocious, savage.

ant. mild, gentle, soothing, benign, bland, unctuous.

scatter *v.* **1** strew, disseminate, broadcast, throw about, sprinkle, spread, sow. **2** disperse, dissipate, dispel, rout, separate, break up, diffuse, disunite, disband.

ant. **1** assemble, collect, amass, gather, cluster. **2** rally, unite, converge, assemble, meet.

scatter-brained *adj.* heedless, flighty, giddy, thoughtless, frivolous, impulsive, erratic, unstable, volatile, capricious, harebrained, inattentive, rash.

ant. reliable, sober, careful, steadfast, trustworthy, attentive.

scenario *n.* **1** plot, script, screenplay, synopsis, story line, story, resumé,

outline. **2** outline, plan, orchestration, agenda, synopsis, program, design, master plan, scheme.

scene *n.* **1** landscape, view, prospect, picture, outlook, tableau, panorama, sight, spectacle. **2** setting, set, scenery, backdrop, cyclorama, background, locale, milieu, ambience, environment, arena. **3** outburst, tantrum, exhibition, display, explosion, spectacle, production, sight, storm.

scenic *adj.* picturesque, pictorial, artistic, paintable, panoramic, pleasing, charming.

scent *n.* odor, smell, perfume, essence, aroma, fragrance, bouquet, redolence, tang, incense, savor. —*v.* smell, detect, inhale, perceive, sniff, get wind of, sense.

scented *adj.* ODOROUS.

scepter *n.* STAFF.

sceptic *n.* SKEPTIC.

schedule *n.* agenda, timetable, outline, program, catalog, table, roll, inventory, list, plan, recipe. —*v.* plan, time, organize, slate, assign, appoint, list, enter, enroll.

schema *n.* SUMMARY.

scheme *n.* **1** plan, program, project, design, outline, system, framework, device. **2** plot, stratagem, strategy, intrigue, machination, conspiracy, cabal, contrivance. —*v.* plot, conspire, collude, concoct, hatch, contrive, intrigue, cook up, plan, machinate.

scheming *adj.* ARTFUL.

schism *n.* division, split, breach, rupture, rift, separation, faction, dissension, break, disruption, discord, disharmony.

ant. union, fusion, harmony, agreement, unification, compromise.

schlemiel *n.* DUPE.

schlep *Slang v.* drag, carry, lug, haul, tug, trail, bundle, plod, struggle, shuffle. —*n.* **1** trudge, trek, tramp, plod, haul, pilgrimage, journey, struggle. **2** JERK.

schlock *Slang n.* JUNK. —*adj.* JUNKY.

schlocky *Slang adj.* JUNKY.

schnapps *n.* LIQUOR.

scholar *n.* **1** savant, authority, specialist, academician, pundit, professor, polymath, intellectual, philosopher, sage. **2** student, pupil, learner, schoolboy, schoolgirl, neophyte, apprentice, disciple.

   ant. 1 illiterate, know-nothing, simpleton, ignoramus, blockhead. **2** teacher, tutor, mentor, instructor, pedagogue.

scholarly *adj.* learned, erudite, academic, lettered, educated, intellectual, profound, literate, literary, well-read, bookish, informed.

   ant. ignorant, uninformed, illiterate, uneducated.

scholarship *n.* learning, erudition, lore, knowledge, enlightenment, education, culture, wisdom, reading, accomplishment.

scholastic *adj.* educational, scholarly, instructional, pedagogic, learning, bookish, academic, professorial, pedantic, learned, lettered, literary, intellectual.

school *n.* **1** academy, institute, gymnasium, seminary, college, alma mater. **2** group, sect, faction, denomination, persuasion, faith, fellowship, clique, set. —*v.* instruct, educate, teach, train, indoctrinate, coach, prepare, discipline, drill, rule.

schoolbook *n.* TEXTBOOK.

schooling *n.* instruction, training, education, teaching, tuition, pedagogy, tutelage, preparation, grounding, indoctrination, guidance.

schoolmate *n.* PUPIL.

science *n.* knowledge, expertness, art, craft, skill, dexterity, cunning, expertise, efficiency, discipline.

scientific *adj.* systematic, empirical, phenomenal, demonstrable, objective, material, physical, verifiable, tangible, technical, technological.

   ant. transcendental, unscientific, spiritual, noumenal, intuitive, ineffable.

scintilla *n.* trace, iota, particle, atom, spark, speck, grain, jot, bit, modicum, hint, glimmer.

   ant. mountain, mass, heap, profusion, horde, oceans.

scintillate *v.* SPARK.

scintillating *adj.* brilliant, witty, dazzling, coruscating, sparkling, bright, clever, quick-witted, effervescent, irrepressible, keen, flashing.

   ant. obtuse, dense, dull, slow, stolid, dreary.

scion *n.* child, descendant, issue, progeny, offspring, get, heir, offshoot, seed, posterity.

sclerotic *adj.* DENSE.

scoff *v.* deride, mock, jeer, flout, fleer, belittle, pooh-pooh, scout, ridicule, scorn, sneer, taunt, rail, gibe, contemn.

   ant. praise, exalt, extol, commend, appreciate, value.

scold *v.* berate, find fault, rate, upbraid, rebuke, reproach, reprimand, reprove, chide, blame, censure, vituperate, rail, revile, castigate, call down, dress down, chew out (*Slang*).

scoop *n.* shovel, trowel, spoon, ladle, bucket, dipper, bail. —*v.* excavate, hollow out, shovel, gouge, ladle, lade, bail, dip out, dig out, burrow, mine.

scoot *v.* dart, skedaddle, scamper, scurry, dash, scuttle, bolt, scud, flee, skip, rush, hie, run, hasten, hurry.

   ant. dawdle, lounge, saunter, amble, idle, creep.

scope *n.* range, field, sphere, reach, breadth, amplitude, latitude, purview, orbit, compass, ambit, elbow room, play, freedom, space.

scorch *v.* **1** wither, sear, shrivel, parch, singe, char, dry out. **2** CRITICIZE.

score *n.* tally, count, record, reckoning, total. —*v.* **1** mark, nick, scratch, cut, crosshatch, notch. **2** delete, scratch, eliminate, cancel, rule out, cross out. **3** win, gain, tally, register, make, record, achieve, count. **4** grade, evaluate, mark, rate, rank, assay. **5**

scourge, criticize, berate, excoriate, denounce, censure, scold. **6** succeed, triumph, win, prevail, prosper, flourish.

ant. *v.* **6** fail, flop, founder, falter.

scores *n.* many, multitude, mass, numbers, lot, horde, swarm, host, army, crowd, throng, mob, myriad.

ant. few, little, some, couple, several.

scoria *n.* ASHES.

scorn *n.* contempt, disdain, scoffing, derision, haughtiness, disregard, opprobrium, distaste, mockery, despite, contumely. —*v.* despise, contemn, reject, spurn, look down on, slight, flout, rebuff, disdain, mock, detest, scout, gibe.

ant. *n.* esteem, affection, respect, approval, appreciation. *v.* respect, look up to, value, defer to, esteem, admire.

scornful *adj.* contemptuous, disdainful, haughty, arrogant, supercilious, patronizing, presumptuous, superior, insolent, contumelious, derisive, mocking, discourteous.

ant. respectful, approving, appreciative, admiring, deferential.

scotch *v.* quash, suppress, stamp out, crush, thwart, block, stop, put to rest, kill, cover up, hinder, confound.

ant. encourage, promote, spread, abet, nurse, feed.

scoundrel *n.* villain, blackguard, crook, swindler, trickster, sharper, scamp, knave, rascal, cheat, rogue, cad, bounder, reprobate, dog, miscreant.

scour[1] *v.* clean, scrape, cleanse, scrub, wash, rub, brush, burnish, buff, polish.

scour[2] *v.* ransack, comb, rake, delve, scrutinize, range, search, explore, rummage, burrow, probe, rifle.

scourge *n.* **1** whip, lash, strap, thong, cat-o'-nine-tails, discipline, cat, knout, flail. **2** punishment, affliction, bane, plague, disaster, calamity, curse, visitation, doom. —*v.* flog, chastise, whale, trounce, thrash, lash, flagellate, switch, discipline.

scout *n.* spy, advance man, explorer,

lookout, patrol, spotter, investigator, emissary, precursor, outrider. —*v.* spy, observe, survey, explore, search, reconnoiter, look over, examine, investigate, scrutinize, inquire, case (*Slang*).

scowl *n.* frown, lower, glower, moue, glare, grimace, stare, face, pout, dirty look. —*v.* frown, lower, glower, glare, sulk, pout, look daggers.

scrabble *v.* SCRATCH.

scrag *v.* GARROTE.

scraggly *adj.* irregular, uneven, jagged, ragged, unkempt, shaggy, tattered, rough, straggly, stringy, frayed, untrimmed.

ant. neat, even, smooth, trim, tidy, regular.

scraggy *adj.* SCRAWNY.

scram *v. Slang* go away, get away, decamp, scoot, leave, scamper, skedaddle, quit, depart, get lost (*Slang*), begone, beat it (*Slang*), bug off (*Slang*), make tracks (*Slang*).

scramble *v.* **1** clamber, crawl, scrabble, struggle, scuffle, strive, jostle, scrimmage. **2** mix, jumble, shuffle, muddle, disarrange, disorder, disorganize, confuse. —*n.* struggle, contest, race, free-for-all, encounter, scrabble, scuffle, tussle, skirmish.

ant. *v.* **2** align, organize, arrange, classify, sort, order.

scrap[1] *n.* bit, fragment, piece, morsel, portion, crumb, snippet, segment, part, particle, dab, shard, chip, bite. —*v.* discard, shed, junk, cast off, jettison, slough, reject, throw away, get rid of.

ant. *v.* reclaim, salvage, restore, rehabilitate, retrieve, maintain.

scrap[2] *n.* fight, quarrel, squabble, rumpus, fracas, brawl, dispute, tiff, row, ruction, free-for-all, melee, hassle (*Slang*), ruckus (*Slang*).

scrape *v.* **1** abrade, scuff, graze, rasp, rub, grind, bark, file. **2** amass, gather, assemble, heap up, get, acquire, glean. —*n.* **1** scratch, abrasion, scar, scuff, rub, squeak, shuffle.

2 dilemma, difficulty, predicament, quandary, perplexity, pickle, embarrassment, fix.

scrappy *adj.* combative, pugnacious, aggressive, competitive, gritty, tough, spunky, plucky, quarrelsome, bellicose, mettlesome, spirited, resolute, feisty.

ant. pusillanimous, timid, meek, mild, unaggressive, retiring.

scratch *v.* **1** scarify, scrape, abrade, scrabble, score, lacerate, file, grate, rasp, gash. **2** cancel, eliminate, cross out, rule out, erase, annul, withdraw, disqualify, exclude, delete. —*n.* **1** incision, mark, furrow, wound, laceration, scrape, striation, nick, cut, gash. **2** *Slang* MONEY.

scrawl *v.* scribble, scratch, scrabble, doodle, jot.

scrawny *adj.* lean, bony, scraggy, lanky, gaunt, raw-boned, skinny, spare, thin, lank, underweight, undernourished, angular.

ant. fleshy, plump, brawny, well-fed, muscular, stout.

scream *v.* yell, screech, shriek, screak, wail, yowl, shrill, cry, howl, whine, bellow, roar, ululate. —*n.* **1** cry, shriek, screech, screak, yell, howl, outcry, ululation. **2** card, character, sensation, riot, comedian, joker, wit, laugh, boff (*Slang*), boffola (*Slang*), wow (*Slang*).

screech *n.*, *v.* SHRIEK.

screed *n.* HARANGUE.

screen *n.* **1** sieve, mesh, grating, net, strainer, filter, lattice, netting, colander. **2** shield, barrier, partition, wall, hedge, cover, guard, fence, fender. —*v.* **1** shield, conceal, hide, shroud, protect, shelter, cover. **2** sift, sieve, winnow, filter, strain. **3** classify, sort, gauge, cull, evaluate, process, scan, size up.

screw *v.* **1** twist, turn, rack, wind, twirl, wrench, gyre. **2** *Slang* defraud, oppress, harm, cheat, betray, thwart, cross, shaft (*Slang*).

screwball *n. Slang* ECCENTRIC.

screwed-up *adj. Slang* **1** disorganized, disorderly, botched, bungled, awry, mismanaged, untidy, messy, chaotic. **2** unbalanced, deranged, demented, disturbed, disoriented, confused, neurotic, distressed, irrational, screwy (*Slang*).

ant. **1** organized, neat, orderly, well-run, tidy. **2** rational, self-possessed, well-balanced, clear-headed, calm, serene.

screw up *Slang* botch, mess up, bungle, snarl, mismanage, muddle, confuse, disorganize, derange, disorder, damage, tangle, spoil, break.

ant. repair, put to rights, adjust, regulate, fix, order.

screwy *adj. Slang* **1** SCREWED-UP. **2** ECCENTRIC.

scribble *v.* scrawl, scratch, doodle, scrabble, jot, pen. —*n.* scrawl, doodle, jotting, scratching.

scribe *n.* scrivener, clerk, copyist, amanuensis, stenographer, secretary, chirographer, calligrapher, copier, recorder, notary.

scrimp *v.* skimp, save, hoard, stint, grudge, hold back, economize, begrudge, withhold, scrape, retrench, dole out.

ant. waste, spend, squander, pour out, lavish.

scrimpy *adj.* SKIMPY.

scrip *n.* WRITING.

script *n.* handwriting, penmanship, cursive, calligraphy, chirography, writing, hand, longhand.

scrivener *n.* SCRIBE.

scrooge *n.* miser, misanthrope, skinflint, tightwad (*Slang*), curmudgeon, niggard, killjoy, cynic, grouch, sourpuss (*Slang*).

ant. philanthropist, altruist, benefactor, giver, Good Samaritan, dogooder.

scrounge *v. Slang* **1** pilfer, steal, purloin, snatch, filch, sneak, lift. **2** sponge, panhandle, freeload, borrow, impose on, beg, mooch (*Slang*).

scrub[1] *v.* rub, scour, cleanse, brush, swab, clean, wash.

scrub[2] *adj.* undersized, inferior, puny, insignificant, stunted, scruffy, runty, deficient, mean, shabby, scrubby.

ant. superior, well-developed, strong, choice, flourishing.

scrubby *adj.* STUNTED.

scruffy *adj.* shabby, seedy, ragged, threadbare, moth-eaten, scrubby, dilapidated, mangy, faded, worn, mean, poor, wretched, squalid.

ant. spruce, trim, smart, neat.

scrumptious *adj. Slang* elegant, stylish, splendid, delectable, exquisite, luscious, toothsome, excellent, delightful, ambrosial, great, fine.

ant. inferior, distasteful, second-rate, wretched, worthless, unpleasant.

scruple *n.* doubt, uncertainty, hesitation, reluctance, qualm, demur, compunction, second thought, misgiving, objection, delicacy, sensitivity, conscience, restraint, caution, caveat. —*v.* hesitate, waver, boggle, falter, hang back, vacillate, stick, balk, demur, protest, doubt.

scrupulous *adj.* cautious, conscientious, careful, punctilious, precise, principled, ethical, honest, meticulous, upright, exact, painstaking.

ant. unprincipled, dishonest, careless, remiss, negligent, underhanded.

scrutinize *v.* examine, observe, inspect, probe, scan, investigate, dissect, inquire into, sift, search, pore over, study, survey, watch.

ant. neglect, slight, skip, wink at, overlook, ignore.

scrutiny *n.* inspection, investigation, examination, perusal, surveillance, dissection, study, inquisition, inquiry, research, probing, survey, exploration, search, watching.

scuff *v.* **1** SHUFFLE. **2** SCRAPE.

scuffle *n.* fracas, brawl, rumpus, skirmish, tussle, squabble, scrap, melee, struggle, set-to, bout, fight, commotion. —*v.* SHUFFLE.

sculpt *v.* SCULPTURE.

sculpture *n.* **1** carving, modeling, shaping, fashioning, chiseling, molding. **2** figure, statuary, carving, statue, relief. —*v.* sculpt, carve, chisel, fashion, model, mold, shape, form, cut, engrave, cast, hew.

scum *n.* **1** crust, film, froth, flotsam, dross, slick, scoria, slag. **2** rabble, mob, riffraff, trash, herd, pariah, outcast.

ant. 2 elite, cream, aristocracy, upper class, peerage.

scurfy *adj.* SCALY.

scurrilous *adj.* offensive, indecent, insulting, scandalous, opprobrious, coarse, abusive, obscene, vulgar, vituperative, reproachful, gross, low, foul.

scurry *v.* scamper, scuttle, dart, dash, scoot, hurry, rush, bolt, sprint, race, hasten, scud, hie, run, skedaddle.

ant. lag, loiter, creep, dawdle, crawl, inch.

scurvy *adj.* low, contemptible, despicable, mean, shabby, base, vile, abject, pitiful, sorry, worthless, vulgar.

ant. honorable, dignified, admirable, noble, good, exalted.

scutellate *adj.* SCALY.

scuttle[1] *n.* hatch, hatchway, porthole, trapdoor, manhole, bulkhead, skylight, transom. —*v.* wreck, destroy, demolish, raze, blast, gut, smash, sabotage, subvert, blight, ruin, scratch, abort.

ant. *v.* preserve, restore, save, salvage, maintain.

scuttle[2] *v.* SCURRY.

scuttlebutt *n. Slang* rumor, gossip, tittle-tattle, hearsay, prattle, chit-chat, trivia, chatter, whispering, talk.

sea *n.* **1** ocean, water, deep, main, flood, brine. **2** plethora, mass, ocean, abundance, torrent, Niagara, quagmire, den, pit, slough.

sea dog SAILOR.

seafarer *n.* SAILOR.

seal *n.* **1** imprint, stamp, cachet, impression, impress, mark, brand, logo, trademark, label. **2** pledge, token, indication, confirmation, authentication, imprimatur, guarantee, ratification, endorsement, signature, certification, cachet. —*v.* **1** authenticate,

validate, certify, underwrite, sign, stamp, confirm, guarantee, settle, conclude, execute, come to terms, finalize, clinch, cinch (*Slang*). **2** fasten, close, secure, shut, stop, stopper, plug, waterproof, glue, paste, lock, bar, bolt.
   ant. *v.* **2** unfasten, leak, unplug, loosen.

seam *n.* junction, joining, line, ridge, gusset, tuck, groove, closure, joint, suture, scar, cicatrix, bond, connection, miter.
   ant. opening, gap, cut, space.

seaman *n.* SAILOR.

seamy *adj.* sordid, squalid, degraded, offensive, disagreeable, corrupt, unpleasant, rundown, ramshackle, shabby, dirty, unclean, foul, disreputable, unwholesome.
   ant. wholesome, clean, refreshing, decent, respectable, pleasant.

sear *v.* **1** wither, dry up, parch, dry out, fade, dehydrate, desiccate, blight, shrivel. **2** burn, scorch, cauterize, brand, singe, char, bake, blister, blast, roast. —*adj.* dried, withered, blasted, parched, blighted, burnt, desiccated, scorched, shriveled, faded.
   ant. *v.* **1** bloom, blossom, flourish. *adj.* fresh, succulent, blooming.

search *v.* **1** seek, hunt, explore, probe, investigate, research, inquire into, examine, scrutinize, delve, track, forage, ransack, rifle, rummage. **2** frisk (*Slang*), examine. —*n.* hunt, exploration, investigation, probe, quest, chase, inquiry, pursuit, study, scrutiny, research, reconnoitering, perusal, questioning, interrogation, going-over.

searching *adj.* penetrating, speculative, inquisitive, inquiring, inquisitorial, keen, sharp, probing, poignant, meaningful, quizzical, evaluating, piercing, curious.
   ant. casual, blank, enigmatic, bland, poker-faced.

season *n.* era, time, epoch, period, stage, tenure, spell, course, duration, term, while, interval, stretch, span. —*v.* **1** spice, salt, flavor, lace. **2** soften, temper, mitigate, moderate, tame, abate, allay, subdue, muffle, tone down, soft-pedal.
   ant. *v.* **2** harden, intensify, aggravate, sharpen.

seasonable *adj.* TIMELY.

seasoned *adj.* experienced, mature, veteran, knowing, expert, ripe, tough, weathered, battle-scarred, practiced, inured, hardened, toughened.
   ant. green, immature, untried, innocent, wide-eyed, starry-eyed.

seasoning *n.* spice, salt, relish, zest, condiment, herb, flavoring, essence, dressing, sauce, taste, gusto.

seat *n.* locus, location, site, center, headquarters, source, post, region, locale, habitat, area, venue, place, roost, perch, wellspring.

sebaceous *adj.* FATTY.

secede *v.* withdraw, leave, quit, retire, abandon, bolt, repudiate, renounce, differ, dissent, forsake, break with, disaffiliate, defect, split.

secession *n.* withdrawal, abandonment, repudiation, renunciation, disaffiliation, defection, apostasy, desertion, break, split, splinter, schism, breach.

seclude *v.* ISOLATE.

secluded *adj.* separated, withdrawn, isolated, cloistered, closeted, sequestered, reclusive, monastic, private, quarantined, segregated, shut in, cut off, confined, hidden.
   ant. public, accessible, participating, open.

seclusion *n.* solitude, retirement, privacy, isolation, sequestration, separation, quarantine, confinement, withdrawal, removal, remoteness, unavailability, concealment, exile.
   ant. accessibility, worldliness, participation, publicity.

second[1] *n.* instant, moment, minute, trice, twinkling, second, wink, flash, jiffy, tick, two shakes (*Slang*).

second[2] *v.* support, promote, abet, stimulate, encourage, assist, endorse, uphold, back, root for, aid, help, fur-

ther, stand behind, side with. —*adj.*
SECONDARY.
ant. *v.* oppose, hinder, undermine,
discourage.

secondary *adj.* subordinate, subsidiary,
second, lesser, minor, dependent,
auxiliary, accessory, complementary, supplementary, extra, additional, indirect, ancillary, inferior,
smaller, unimportant, contingent,
marginal.
ant. primary, major, first, prime,
leading, principal, main, crucial.

second-best *adj.* SECOND-CLASS.

second-class *adj.* inferior, inadequate,
second-rate, third-rate, second-best,
second-string, also-ran, mediocre,
outclassed, deficient, imperfect, so-
so, pedestrian, undistinguished.
ant. first-class, prime, A-one, excellent, prize, best.

secondhand *adj.* **1** used, worn, old,
hand-me-down, discarded, shop-
worn, shabby, deteriorated, frowzy,
seedy. **2** indirect, through the grapevine, rumored, reported.
ant. **1** fresh, new, untouched, un-
worn, pristine. **2** firsthand, direct.

second-rate *adj.* SECOND-CLASS.

second-string *adj.* SECOND-CLASS.

secrecy *n.* concealment, secretiveness,
privacy, surreptitiousness, stealth,
cover, covertness, furtiveness, silence, underhandedness, invisibility,
inconspicuousness, darkness, incognito, camouflage.
ant. publicity, overtness, straightforwardness, conspicuousness.

secret *adj.* **1** hidden, unseen, concealed,
private, confidential, unrevealed, unavowed, unacknowledged, quiet, silent, hush-hush, privileged, under
wraps, surreptitious, covert, undisclosed, disguised, clandestine,
sneaky, stealthy, furtive. **2** secluded,
withdrawn, sequestered, isolated,
cloistered, buried, invisible, unavailable, solitary, unfrequented, out-of-
the-way. —*n.* **1** confidence, intrigue,
conspiracy, cabal. **2** mystery,
enigma, code, puzzle, conundrum,

sphinx. **3** key, answer, basis, clue,
cause, foundation, explanation, essence, root, source.
ant. *adj.* **1** overt, publicized, avowed,
revealed, admitted, open. **2** public,
available, lively, frequented, accessible.

secretary *n.* amanuensis, stenographer,
scribe, aide, girl Friday, man Friday,
clerk.

secrete *v.* conceal, hide, cache, cover,
bury, mask, shroud, harbor, cloak,
withhold, disguise, stow, screen,
stash, store, horde, squirrel away.
ant. reveal, uncover, bare, take out.

secretion *n.* exudation, transmission,
discharge, flow, outflow, emission.
ant. absorption, intake, inflow.

secretive *adj.* taciturn, uncommunicative, furtive, closemouthed, cagy,
reticent, evasive, cryptic, wary,
laconic, secret, private, diffident, reserved, withdrawn.
ant. open, frank, trusting, talkative,
communicative, gossipy.

sect *n.* faction, denomination, splinter
group, clique, ism, cult, split, wing,
deviation, opposition, persuasion,
school, camp.

sectarian *adj.* partisan, parochial, prejudiced, cultist, cultish, fanatic, cliquish, exclusive, narrow-minded, hidebound, clannish, faithful, factional,
rigid, doctrinaire.
ant. nonsectarian, nonpartisan,
broad-minded.

section *n.* **1** part, division, fraction,
portion, piece, unit, subdivision, segment, measure, percent, share, fragment, component, constituent, module, element. **2** district, area, region,
neighborhood, community, department, borough, zone, sector, province, parish, precinct, ward, colony,
ghetto, enclave, barrio, turf (*Slang*).
ant. **1** whole, entirety, totality, all.

sector *n.* class, category, division, caste,
group, hierarchy, stratum, sphere,
bailiwick, grouping, circle, sect, clan,
clique, community.

secular *adj.* **1** worldly, temporal, mate-

rial, materialistic, terrestrial, earthly, mundane, profane, fleshly. **2** lay, civil, civic, laic, popular, public, political.
ant. 1 spiritual, godly, eternal, heavenly. **2** ecclesiastical, sacred, religious, holy.

secure *adj.* **1** safe, safeguarded, protected, immune, sheltered, cloistered, unexposed, shielded, invulnerable, guarded. **2** confident, certain, convinced, sure, bold, assured, positive, easy, relaxed, untroubled, carefree, fearless, courageous, self-reliant. **3** firm, fast, locked, unbreakable, invulnerable, impregnable, unassailable. **4** reliable, steady, dependable, stable, steadfast, established, definite, positive, sound, tried and true, solid. —*v.* **1** protect, safeguard, shelter, shield, guard, fortify, harbor, hide, conceal, cover, watch over, look after, conserve. **2** fasten, tighten, tie, seal, fix, set, immobilize, bind, lash, anchor, rivet. **3** insure, guarantee, indemnify, pledge, underwrite, warrant, vouch, assure, stand behind, stake. **4** obtain, get, come by, acquire, procure, achieve, attain, earn, reap, make, inherit, pick up.
ant. *adj.* **1** imperiled, endangered, unsafe, unguarded, unprotected, vulnerable, exposed. **2** hesitant, anxious, unconvinced, dubious, skeptical, unsure. **3** loose, unlocked, open. **4** unreliable, hit-or-miss, undependable, tenuous. *v.* **1** imperil, endanger, menace, expose. **2** loosen, untie, unlock, open. **4** lose, let slip, miss out.

security *n.* safety, protection, immunity, certainty, confidence, privilege, shelter, cover, insurance, invulnerability, impregnability, unassailability, independence, anchorage, peace of mind.
ant. exposure, vulnerability, hazard, anxiety, fearfulness, doubt.

sedate *adj.* calm, composed, staid, unruffled, serene, sober, demure,

unflappable, prim, undemonstrative, retiring, unresponsive, settled, cool.
ant. agitated, fidgety, excitable, demonstrative, giddy.

sedative *adj.* soothing, tranquilizing, calming, settling, soporific, sleep-inducing, narcotic, comforting, relaxing, sedating, opiate, narcotizing.
ant. stimulating, agitating, irritating.

sediment *n.* dregs, lees, grounds, silt, remains, precipitate, settlings, mud, sludge.

sedition *n.* mutiny, rebellion, revolt, disobedience, defiance, insurrection, uprising, lawlessness, subversion, treason, disloyalty, treachery.
ant. obedience, submission, loyalty.

seditious *adj.* rebellious, mutinous, revolutionary, subversive, defiant, disloyal, lawless, treasonable, insubordinate, insurrectionary, riotous, insurgent, underground.
ant. submissive, obedient, loyal, faithful.

seduce *v.* tempt, entice, mislead, attract, lure, pervert, corrupt, demoralize, debauch, ensnare, captivate, induce, lead astray.

seduction *n.* enticement, temptation, lure, snare, inducement, charm, blandishment, attraction, spell, magnet.

seductive *adj.* enticing, tempting, luring, alluring, charming, attractive, appealing, flirtatious, captivating, beguiling, enchanting, irresistible, siren.
ant. unattractive, uninteresting, off-putting, offensive.

sedulous *adj.* assiduous, diligent, industrious, persevering, hard-working, painstaking, patient, purposeful, plodding, ambitious, resolute, serious, dedicated.
ant. lazy, indolent, shiftless, careless, aimless.

see *v.* **1** look at, watch, regard, behold, view, eye, witness, sight, spot, gaze at, glimpse, attend, stare at, survey, scan. **2** perceive, comprehend, understand, register, catch on, know, remark, realize, appreciate, conceive, intuit, grasp, get. **3** ask about, inquire, ascertain, look into, find out, inspect, verify, discover, corroborate, learn, determine, investigate, research, detect, test, get to the bottom of. **4** encounter, meet, interview, receive, entertain, visit, run into, date, come across, happen upon, greet, speak to. **5** mull over, contemplate, think about, consider, weigh, ponder, deliberate, gauge, judge, cogitate.

seed *n.* **1** ovule, ovum, egg, egg cell, gamete, embryo, seedlet, seedling, spore. **2** source, origin, nucleus, root, spring, element, cradle, matrix, wellspring, basis, beginning, foundation, start, font. **3** sperm, semen, spermatozoon, spermatocyte. —*v.* sow.

seedbed *n.* HOTBED.

seedy *adj.* ragged, shabby, squalid, mangy, tacky, down-at-heel, dilapidated, run-down, threadbare, frayed, grubby, poor, disheveled, unkempt, messy. **ant.** crisp, fresh, dapper, elegant.

seek *v.* **1** search for, look for, strive for, aspire to, hope for, hope to, quest, go after, pursue, cast about, hunt, crave, yearn for, hunger for, want, desire. **2** request, inquire about, ask for, solicit, need, requisition.

seem *v.* appear, look, manifest.

seeming *adj.* ostensible, surface, superficial, calculated, feigned, contrived, assumed, designed, supposed, putative, skin-deep, deceptive, misleading, artful, fake, phony (*Slang*), counterfeit, spurious, bogus, hypocritical. **ant.** genuine, true, authentic, real.

seemly *adj.* **1** proper, appropriate, becoming, fitting, right, suitable, decorous, conventional, polite, decent, due, correct, well-bred, civil, diplomatic, felicitous. **2** attractive, becoming, comely, handsome, pleasing, good-looking, charming, fetching, winning, engaging, appealing, pleasant, personable, graceful, pretty.

ant. **1** rude, impolite, shocking, outrageous, uncivil. **2** unattractive, ugly, repulsive, unseemly.

seep *v.* ooze, soak through, leak, exude, drip, exudate, filter, dribble, percolate, permeate, osmose.

seer *n.* prophet, oracle, fortuneteller, sage, soothsayer, predictor, medium, clairvoyant, psychic, sybil, necromancer, augur, diviner, divinator, witch, wizard, stargazer, astrologist.

seesaw *n.* teeter-totter. —*v.* alternate, fluctuate, oscillate, teeter, shuttle, shift, hem and haw, hedge, waver, shilly-shally.

seethe *v.* **1** boil, foam, bubble, simmer, fizz, brew, steam. **2** rage, storm, smolder, bluster, carry on, fume, boil over, flare up, burn.

see through 1 get to the bottom of, penetrate, see the light, be on to, be wise to, detect. **2** aid, protect, support, succor, assist, look after, finance, help, stand by, stick with, back, second. **3** finish, complete, achieve, persevere, consummate, follow through, carry out, execute, accomplish, bring about, hang in (*Slang*). **ant.** **2** abandon, forsake, leave in the lurch, desert. **3** quit, give up.

segment *n.* section, portion, part, cutting, slice, piece, fragment, component, constituent, fraction, subdivision, sector, bit, clipping, snip, snippet. **ant.** whole, entirety, all, totality.

segmentation *n.* division, partition, fragmentation, subdivision, separation, slicing, cutting, slipping, cleavage, articulation, apportionment, allotment, scission, dissection, segregation. **ant.** amalgamation, unification, consolidation, wholeness, oneness, integration.

segregate *v.* isolate, separate, cut off, sequester, set apart, ostracize, discriminate, differentiate, exclude, seclude, quarantine, ghettoize. **ant.** integrate, desegregate, unify.

segregation *n.* discrimination, exclusion, separation, ostracism, differentiation, sequestration, apartheid, ghettoization.

ant. integration, desegregation, unification.

seignior *n.* LORD.

seize *v.* **1** take hold of, hold, grab, grasp, clutch, snatch, grip. **2** understand, perceive, see, get, comprehend, catch on, register, realize, grasp, apprehend. **3** confiscate, impound, appropriate, expropriate, preempt, possess, commandeer, hijack, skyjack. **4** capture, take, wrest, usurp, shanghai, impress, kidnap, nab, abduct, arrest, collar, pinch (*Slang*).

seizure *n.* **1** grip, grasp, hold, confiscation, appropriation, expropriation, usurpation, preemption, arrogation, dispossession, capture, kidnaping, impoundment, abduction, arrest. **2** attack, fit, convulsion, paroxysm, stroke, siege, spell, throe, incident, episode, visitation, pang.

ant. 1 relinquishment, release, relaxation.

seldom *adv.* rarely, infrequently, hardly ever, scarcely, uncommonly, sporadically, now and then, occasionally, sometimes.

ant. often, frequently, usually, regularly, always.

select *v.* choose, pick, prefer, cull, winnow, single out, elect, opt for, distinguish, abstract, sift, decide on, excerpt, favor. —*adj.* chosen, elite, choice, prime, preferred, handpicked, exclusive, blue-ribbon, outstanding, best, leading, distinguished.

ant. *v.* reject, turn down, ignore, pass over. *adj.* run-of-the-mill, ordinary, mediocre, random.

selection *n.* **1** discrimination, election, partiality, determination, distinction, selectivity, specification, judgment, designation, nomination, vote, winnowing, culling, picking. **2** preference, choice, favorite, winner, nominee, excerpt, option, pick, elect.

ant. 1 rejection, exclusion, impartiality, abstention.

selective *adj.* discriminating, choosy, particular, fussy, critical, exclusive, specific, hard-to-please, finicky, opinionated, exacting, fastidious, discerning, percipient.

ant. unselective, random, undemanding, inclusive.

self *n.* **1** ego, I, psyche, soul, selfhood, oneself, superego. **2** individuality, character, identity, nature, being, essence, autonomy, separateness, uniqueness, spirit, personality, singularity, soul, temperament, particularity.

self-abnegation *n.* self-sacrifice, self-denial, self-control, self-restraint, selflessness, unselfishness, martyrdom, self-discipline, self-effacement, altruism, generosity.

ant. self-interest, selfishness, self-indulgence, self-assertion.

self-abuse *n.* MASTURBATION.

self-assurance *n.* self-confidence, self-respect, self-esteem, poise, independence, boldness, equanimity, nerve, self-possession, presence, aplomb, imperturbability, composure, unflappability, cool (*Slang*).

ant. self-doubt, apprehensiveness, timidity, anxiety, nervousness.

self-assured *adj.* CONFIDENT.

self-centered *adj.* selfish, self-important, self-serving, egotistical, self-seeking, self-absorbed, conceited, narcissistic, immodest, smug, complacent, subjective.

ant. self-effacing, self-sacrificing, generous, charitable.

self-command *n.* SELF-CONTROL.

self-confidence *n.* CONFIDENCE.

self-confident *adj.* CONFIDENT.

self-conscious *adj.* ill at ease, nervous, anxious, abashed, insecure, uncomfortable, embarrassed, out of countenance, discountenanced, diffident, shy, uneasy, edgy, jittery, shamefaced, affected, nervous, uptight (*Slang*).

ant. spontaneous, relaxed, easygoing, self-confident.

self-contained *adj.* IMPASSIVE.

self-contradictory *adj.* INCONSISTENT.

self-control *n.* self-discipline, self-command, self-possession, self-restraint, self-mastery, self-government, willpower, independence, character, equilibrium, stability, temperance, moderation, balance, level-headedness, presence of mind, fortitude, stoicism.

ant. weakness, instability, excitability, hotheadedness.

self-denial *n.* self-restraint, self-sacrifice, self-abnegation, selflessness, unselfishness, self-discipline, asceticism, monasticism, stoicism, spartanism.

ant. self-indulgence, wantonness, profligacy, sybaritism.

self-denying *adj.* ASCETIC.

self-evident *adj.* self-explanatory, obvious, patent, evident, manifest, plain, apparent, axiomatic, glaring, undeniable, distinct, palpable, unavoidable, explicit, inescapable, unarguable, incontrovertible.

ant. questionable, doubtful, hypothetical, arguable, ambiguous.

self-explanatory *adj.* SELF-EVIDENT.

self-government *n.* SELF-CONTROL.

self-importance *n.* CONCEIT.

self-important *adj.* conceited, arrogant, overbearing, cocky, pompous, vain, egotistical, self-centered, haughty, boastful, smug, opinionated, supercilious, swaggering, overweening, swell-headed.

ant. self-effacing, humble, shy, deferential.

selfish *adj.* self-centered, egocentric, self-absorbed, self-interested, egotistical, egoistic, ungenerous, self-serving, self-seeking, greedy, grudging, grasping, uncharitable, acquisitive, stingy, mean, tight.

ant. generous, altruistic, selfless, charitable.

selfless *adj.* unselfish, altruistic, self-sacrificing, self-denying, self-abnegating, generous, giving, liberal,

thoughtful, considerate, charitable, unstinting.

ant. selfish, self-seeking, greedy, grasping, self-absorbed.

self-possession *n.* SELF-CONTROL.

self-reliant *adj.* independent, autonomous, self-possessed, self-governed, self-supporting, self-sufficient, self-controlled.

ant. dependent, reliant, contingent, parasitic.

self-restraint *n.* SELF-CONTROL.

self-righteous *adj.* smug, complacent, holier-than-thou, sanctimonious, pietistic, puritanical, intolerant, didactic, preachy, self-satisfied, pontificating, bombastic, high and mighty, pedantic.

ant. self-critical, modest, tolerant, understanding.

selfsame *n.* SAME.

self-satisfaction *n.* smugness, complacency, self-righteousness, conceit, egotism, narcissism, pride, vanity, self-esteem, self-respect.

ant. self-criticism, self-hatred, anxiety, guilt, humility, modesty.

self-seeking *adj.* self-serving, self-interested, self-concerned, selfish, calculating, grasping, greedy, pushing, pushy, self-indulgent, opportunistic, acquisitive, on the make.

ant. selfless, generous, altruistic, charitable.

self-sufficient *adj.* SELF-RELIANT.

self-supporting *adj.* SELF-RELIANT.

sell *v.* market, vend, retail, wholesale, deal in, trade in, advertise, merchandise, promote, peddle, hawk, handle, offer.

ant. buy, purchase, shop for.

seller *n.* vendor, retailer, wholesaler, tradesman, shopkeeper, dealer, storekeeper, merchant, marketeer, handler, promoter, peddler, jobber, middleman, salesperson.

ant. buyer, customer, shopper, purchaser.

sell out betray, play false, abandon, cheat, dupe, deceive, break faith, stab in the back, doublecross

(*Slang*), squeal (*Slang*), rat (*Slang*).
ant. stand by, support.
semblance *n.* look, appearance, aspect, resemblance, likeness, similarity, image, exterior, air, sameness, affinity, guise, mien, counterpart, duplicate, persona.
semicircle *n.* ARCH.[1]
seminal *adj.* productive, generative, developmental, germinal, creative, formative, fertile, fruitful, visionary, original, useful, yielding, basic, fundamental, pregnant, rich, pioneering. **ant.** sterile, useless, unproductive, hackneyed, worn-out.
sempiternal *adj.* EVERLASTING.
send *v.* **1** transmit, dispatch, forward, ship, mail, export, post, broadcast, radio, send off, dismiss, consign, relegate. **2** emit, discharge, project, throw off, give off, give forth, erupt, gush, shoot, deliver, pour forth, emanate, radiate.
ant. 1, 2 receive, get, take, admit.
send for summon, call, order, call for, ask for, command, invite, muster, direct, subpoena.
send packing DISMISS.
senior *adj.* elder, older, oldest, firstborn, father, sire. —*n.* **1** veteran, head, superior, master, founder, sire, chief, higher-up. **2** senior citizen, patriarch, elder, dean, doyen, doyenne, oldster.
ant. *adj.* junior, younger, son, youngest. *n.* **1** junior, son, apprentice, underling, subordinate, assistant, newcomer. **2** youngster, offspring, stripling, tadpole, child.
senior citizen SENIOR.
sensation *n.* **1** feeling, sense, reaction, response, impression, feel, aura, emotion, state of mind, air, mood. **2** perception, apperception, sensibility, sensitivity, awareness, consciousness, intuition, receptivity, responsiveness, sentience.
ant. 2 unconsciousness, insensibility, paralysis, anesthesia.
sensational *adj.* **1** sensory, receptive,

responsive, perceptive, affective, sentient, perceptual, apperceptive, percipient, feeling, reactive. **2** shocking, startling, lurid, melodramatic, electrifying, sensationalistic, dramatic, scandalous, staggering, hair-raising, eye-opening, mind-blowing (*Slang*).
ant. 1 unresponsive, inert, unfeeling, numb. **2** bland, routine, dull, humdrum.
sensationalistic *adj.* SENSATIONAL.
sense *n.* **1** faculty, feeling, sensation, reaction. **2** capacity, appreciation, capability, receptivity, responsiveness, talent, taste, knack, discernment, ability, gift, flair. **3** perception, awareness, impression, consciousness, apprehension, realization, presentiment, suspicion, supposition, prescience, intuition, precognition. **4** common sense, reason, logic, judgment, intelligence, mother wit, rationality, sanity, plausibility, coherence, clear-headedness, lucidity, consistency, intelligibility. **5** meaning, signification, import, definition, denotation, connotation, implication, nuance, gist, explanation, content, intention, drift, coloration, message, definiens. **6** consensus, opinion, weight, drift, will, tenor, majority, tendency, direction, course, sentiment, feeling. **7** SENSATION.
ant. 1 atrophy, anesthesia, paralysis, numbness.
senseless *adj.* **1** unconscious, comatose, insensible, stunned, blacked-out, anesthetized, insentient, dazed, insensate, unresponsive, numb, paralyzed, out. **2** foolish, inane, stupid, silly, nonsensical irrational, meaningless, purposeless, idiotic, brainless, empty-headed, scatterbrained, mad, crazy.
ant. 1 conscious, aware, responsive, sentient. **2** sensible, logical, rational, reasonable, meaningful.
sensibility *n.* **1** sensitiveness, sensitivity, responsiveness, susceptibility, reactivity, reflexivity, sentience, affect, hypersensitivity, allergy, irritability.

2 awareness, intuition, perceptiveness, acumen, insight, discrimination, taste, delicacy, sympathy, empathy, feeling, nuance, appreciation, receptivity, vibes (*Slang*).
ant. 1 unconsciousness, numbness, insensibility. **2** unawareness, blindness, toughness, denseness, obtuseness, insensitivity.

sensible *adj.* **1** astute, perceptive, knowing, wise, alert, intelligent, logical, shrewd, insightful, canny, sagacious, reasonable, rational, sane, sound, sharp, able, keen, sage. **2** sensitive, reactive, reflexive, responsive, conscious, sentient, sensitized, susceptible, affected, alive to, hypersensitive, tender. **3** perceptible, appreciable, conceivable, knowable, palpable, tangible, substantial, considerable, detectable, evident, apparent, manifest. **4** SENSITIVE.
ant. 1 obtuse, dense, thick, irrational, scatterbrained, impractical. **2** insensitive, unfeeling, numb, anesthetized, desensitized, deadened. **3** imperceptible, unappreciable, invisible, inconceivable.

sensitive *adj.* **1** receptive, responsive, reactive, conscious, delicate, sensible, intuitive, aware, perceptive, insightful, sympathetic, aesthetic, discriminating, cultivated, tuned-in (*Slang*). **2** hypersensitive, irritated, sore, tender, irritable, raw, aching. **3** touchy, thin-skinned, oversensitive, querulous, huffy, quick-tempered, temperamental, excitable, impatient, quarrelsome, testy, choleric, irascible, petulant. **4** *capable of indicating slight changes:* fine, delicate, responsive, subtle. **5** SENSORY.
ant. 1 unresponsive, unreceptive, unfeeling, blind. **2** healed, desensitized, callous, inured. **3** thick-skinned, obtuse, gross, insensitive. **4** crude, coarse.

sensory *adj.* sensitive, sensorial, perceptual, receptive, reactive, responsive, reflexive.

sensual *adj.* **1** fleshly, carnal, bodily,

self-indulgent, sybaritic, pleasure-loving, sexual, worldly, lusty, corporeal, physical, hedonistic. **2** lewd, lecherous, lascivious, salacious, sexy, concupiscent, prurient, wanton, lustful, voluptuous, gross, animalistic, brutish, licentious.
ant. 1 spiritual, soulful, intellectual, cerebral, spartan, ascetic.

sensuous *adj.* **1** sensory, sensual, receptive, responsive, perceptual. **2** epicurean, self-indulgent, sybaritic, pleasure-loving, hedonistic, voluptuous, dissolute.
ant. 2 ascetic, monastic, spartan, spiritual, otherworldly.

sentence *n.* opinion, judgment, decree, determination, verdict, ruling, finding, order, pronouncement, decision, adjudication, fiat, regulation, command, writ. —*v.* condemn, punish, penalize, ordain, convict, adjudge, fine, doom.

sententious *adj.* **1** terse, pithy, aphoristic, to the point, epigrammatic, gnomic, succinct, concise, compact, laconic, meaningful, trenchant, pointed, compressed. **2** moralistic, preachy, didactic, pedantic, judgmental, bombastic, self-righteous, pietistic, holier-than-thou, sanctimonious, homiletic.
ant. 1 long-winded, circumlocutory, wordy, verbose. **2** laissez-faire, live-and-let-live, tolerant.

sentient *adj.* responsive, sensitive, aware, feeling, susceptible, live, alive, conscious, sensible, discerning, reactive, perceptive.
ant. unresponsive, insensitive, insensible, comatose, unconscious.

sentiment *n.* **1** sensibility, feeling, tenderness, delicacy, emotion, point of view, attitude, bias, opinion, judgment, tenor, affect, response. **2** message, toast, greeting, verse, salute, respects, felicitations, congratulations. **3** SENTIMENTALITY.

sentimental *adj.* mawkish, maudlin, gushy, melodramatic, emotional, mushy, weepy, sloppy, syrupy, gooey, tear-jerking (*Slang*), soupy, spoony, nostalgic, bathetic, corny (*Slang*), schmaltzy (*Slang*), theatrical, stirring, tender, touching.

ant. matter-of-fact, practical, sensible, understated, realistic, hardheaded.

sentimentality *n.* mawkishness, sentiment, sloppiness, gush, melodramatics, mush, soupiness, nostalgia, bathos, inanity, goo, corn (*Slang*), schmaltz (*Slang*), hearts and flowers.

ant. matter-of-factness, understatement, hard-headedness, tough-mindedness.

sentinel *n.* SENTRY.

sentry *n.* guard, sentinel, watch, watchman, lookout, patrol, ranger, guardian, warden, warder, watchdog.

separable *adj.* divisible, detachable, discrete, separate, dissoluble, fissionable, severable, scissile, distinguishable.

ant. inseparable, indivisible, welded, inextricable.

separate *v.* **1** sever, cut, tear, sunder, break, disconnect, detach, part, disjoin, disunite, cleave, divorce, split, dissociate, unyoke, rive, fragment, rend, disengage. **2** divide, come between, demarcate, distinguish, partition, polarize, section, intervene, alienate, disunite, disjoin, sunder, part, set at odds, pit against, estrange, classify, sort out, allocate. **3** isolate, segregate, sift, filter, screen, eliminate, cull, select, set aside, pick out, exclude, abstract. —*adj.* distinct, individual, discrete, detached, unconnected, disunited, unjoined, divorced, isolated, severed, discontinuous, particular, single, unattached, disconnected, separated.

ant. *v.* **1** unite, unify, connect, put together, join. **3** blend, homogenize, mix. —*adj.* joint, joined, attached, connected, unified, united, continuous.

separation *n.* disconnection, severance, detachment, disengagement, divi-

sion, cleavage, rift, partition, break, alienation, exclusion, isolation, dissociation, segregation, apartheid, gap, space.

ant. connection, attachment, unification, unity, continuity, mixture, homogeneity, integration.

septic *adj.* putrid, putrescent, rotten, decayed, putrefactive, rotting, rancid, diseased, infected, putrifying, festering, contaminated, toxic, noxious, infectious.

ant. germ-free, pure, antiseptic, sterilized, germicidal.

sepulcher *n.* tomb, vault, grave, crypt, mausoleum, pit, catacomb.

sepulchral *adj.* dismal, funereal, ghostly, ghastly, morbid, ashen, melancholy, depressing, somber, cheerless, joyless, gloomy, dreary, lugubrious.

ant. lively, vivacious, bright, cheerful, inviting.

sequel *n.* continuation, consequence, development, result, outcome, outgrowth, upshot, epilogue, repercussion, aftermath, supplement, aftereffect, corollary, denouement, payoff.

sequence *n.* **1** succession, order, arrangement, serialization, timing, spacing, continuity, regularity, prolongation, procedure, progression, tabulation, organization, filing, listing. **2** series, chain, line, lineup, procession, cycle, round, routine, schedule, calendar, file, serial, run, scale, column.

ant. **1** discontinuity, disorder, irregularity, permutation.

sequent *n.* RESULT.

sequential *adj.* SERIAL.

sequester *v.* **1** separate, isolate, segregate, quarantine, sequestrate, remove, banish, exile, exclude, lock up, set apart, blacklist. **2** withdraw, retire, seclude, confine, hide, hibernate, estivate, go off, shelter, cloister, bury, retreat, avoid, rusticate.

ant. **1** include, accept, invite. **2** socialize, mingle, participate.

sequestrate *v.* SEQUESTER.

seraph *n.* ANGEL.

serene *adj.* **1** clear, bright, fair, balmy, pleasant, cloudless, unclouded, unruffled, untroubled, undimmed. **2** relaxed, tranquil, calm, peaceful, stable, composed, pacific, self-contained, imperturbable, poised, placid, sedate, cool, self-possessed, unflappable.

ant. 1 stormy, cloudy, turbulent, forbidding, threatening. **2** anxious, nervous, disturbed, hectic.

serf *n.* SLAVE.

serial *adj.* continuous, successive, consecutive, sequential, serialized, ordered, scheduled, progressive, tabulated, orderly, uninterrupted. —*n.* PERIODICAL.

ant. discontinuous, intermittent, disordered, irregular.

series *n.* succession, order, chain, cycle, circuit, course, progression, sequence, schedule, regimen, calendar, docket, ring, routine, scale, run, serialization, lineup, string, permutation.

serious *adj.* **1** grave, earnest, sincere, thoughtful, sober, pensive, staid, heavy, solemn, grim, somber. **2** difficult, complicated, complex, demanding, laborious, exacting, strenuous, burdensome, onerous, painful, exhausting, intricate, troublesome, knotty, involved. **3** important, far-reaching, profound, consequential, long-range, weighty, major, decisive, urgent, vital, momentous, basic, fundamental, considerable, influential, appreciable, radical. **4** severe, dangerous, critical, dire, fearful, acute, mortal, lethal, deadly, virulent, life-and-death, hazardous, perilous, alarming.

ant. 1 lighthearted, frivolous, puckish, humorous, irreverent. **2** easy, light, simple, undemanding. **3** inconsequential, trivial, superficial, short-range. **4** mild, bland, superficial.

sermon *n.* lecture, homily, preachment, exhortation, moralizing, preaching, homiletics, diatribe, declamation, admonition, discourse, lesson, disquisition, address, instruction.

sermonize *v.* preach, lecture, instruct, uplift, moralize, exhort, declaim, pontificate, admonish, warn, discourse, harangue, instruct, teach, edify, enlighten, speechify.

serpent *n.* SNAKE.

serpentine *adj.* **1** winding, zigzag, coiling, snaking, devious, circuitous, meandering, tortuous, snaky, slithery, sinuous, undulating, undulatory. **2** subtle, cunning, sneaky, devious, crooked, snaky, sly, shrewd, canny, underhand, insidious, conniving, perfidious, slippery, treacherous, untrustworthy, unscrupulous.

ant. 1 straight, unswerving. **2** straightforward, forthright, candid, direct, ingenuous.

serrate *adj.* SAW-TOOTHED.

servant *n.* domestic, housekeeper, retainer, maid, butler, valet, factotum, hired help, household help, *bonne*.

serve *v.* **1** wait on, work for, aid, help, attend, promote, minister to, accommodate, benefit, oblige, assist, enlist, enroll, fight for, support, boost. **2** obey, revere, honor, follow, reverence, respect, please, defer to. **3** suffice, do, satisfy, fulfill, avail, suit, answer, fill the bill, pass muster.

service *n.* **1** attention, accommodation, ministration, deference. **2** division, branch, arm, office, section, command, post, department, category, sector. **3** installation, maintenance, repair, upkeep, overhauling. **4** assistance, aid, benefit, use, utility, help, usefulness, good, avail, enjoyment. **5** ritual, ceremony, rite, liturgy, observance, celebration, formality, ceremonial, tradition, litany, sacrament. —*v.* maintain, repair, overhaul, check, recondition, tune up, keep up, fix, conserve, readjust, inspect, go over.

serviceable *adj.* practical, utilitarian, beneficial, useful, sturdy, helpful, everyday, workable, dependable, economical, rugged, effective, functional.

ant. useless, impractical, unavailing, flimsy, fragile.

servile *adj.* slavish, abject, menial, subservient, submissive, groveling, fawning, obsequious, humble, sycophantic, meek, pusillanimous, cowardly, craven, dependent.

ant. masterful, overbearing, powerful, proud, defiant.

servitude *n.* slavery, enslavement, bondage, subjugation, submissiveness, indenture, serfdom, vassalage, thrall, thralldom, dependence, oppression, durance, duress.

ant. freedom, liberty, independence, power, mastery, emancipation, manumission.

session *n.* meeting, assembly, sitting, conference, congress, council, consultation, discussion, séance, interview, seminar, get-together, rap (*Slang*), rap session (*Slang*), bull session, powwow.

set[1] *v.* **1** put, place, fix, position, locate, establish, situate, stick, glue, harden, cement, fasten, implant, lodge, embed. **2** appoint, assign, allocate, establish, schedule, calendar, time, arrange, inaugurate, institute, relegate, entrust, invest, prescribe, delegate. **3** wane, decline, recede, ebb, sink, diminish, fade, disappear, descend, fall, lower, subside, vanish, die. **4** solidify, congeal, firm, harden, thicken, gel, jellify, gelatinize, take shape, condense, coagulate, cake. —*adj.* **1** established, authorized, customary, conventional, pat, orthodox, prescribed, agreed on, appointed, scheduled, determined, usual, accepted, habitual, normal, standard. **2** formal, rehearsed, predetermined, deliberate, systematic, regulated, formulated, impersonal, unspontaneous, settled, formalized, traditional, hard and fast, standardized. **3** motionless, fixed, rigid, immobile, immobilized, hardened, cemented, immovable, locked, lodged, settled, un-

budging. **4** obstinate, inflexible, opinionated, adamant, stubborn, firm, unyielding, unbending, obdurate, bigoted, narrow, unchangeable, sclerotic, unalterable, unresponsive. —*n.* placement, setting, position, arrangement, tilt, hang, angle, bearing, carriage, posture, shape, fix, drape, fit.

ant. *v.* **1** remove, dislocate, loosen, dislodge, yank, uproot, extirpate. **3** wax, rise, appear, ascend. **4** melt, liquefy, flow. *adj.* **1** unusual, unconventional, unorthodox, heterodox, eccentric. **2** spontaneous, informal, improvised, original. **3** pliable, tensile, flexible. **4** tractable, responsive, broad-minded, open, flexible.

set[2] *n.* **1** class, group, clique, coterie, association, club, fraternity, faction, claque, caucus, sect, tribe, crowd, gang, bunch, ring. **2** category, series, sequence, program.

setback *n.* reversal, reverse, misfortune, disappointment, loss, mischance, relapse, misstep, adversity, rebuff, defeat, slump, regression, drawback.

ant. headway, progress, gain, advance, advantage.

set forth SET OUT.

setoff *n.* balance, offset, compensation, contrast, trade-off, accent, counter, counterweight, counterbalance, equivalency, equivalent, counterpart, complement, foil, *quid pro quo*.

set off SET OUT.

set out begin, start, set forth, set off, commence, undertake, launch, embark on, inaugurate, enter on, set up, venture, go, tackle, institute.

ant. conclude, finish, wind up, terminate.

setting *n.* **1** position, degree, angle, set, positioning, situation, placement, location, fix, tilt, posture. **2** frame, mounting, enclosure, border. **3** environment, surroundings, background, decor, scenery, *mise-en-scène*, period, habitat, scene, milieu, circumstances, locale, ambience, site, situation.

settle v. **1** put in order, straighten out, neaten, regulate, arrange, set to rights, stabilize, compose, assort, classify, order. **2** establish, fix, live, reside, inhabit, colonize, populate, abide, lodge, roost, install, allocate, situate, root, anchor, locate. **3** calm, quiet, sedate, tranquilize, pacify, mollify, soothe, relax, lull, allay, mitigate, relieve. **4** decide, determine, judge, resolve, find, mediate, reconcile, arbitrate, rectify, rule, adjudicate, conclude, umpire, referee, decree. **5** pay, repay, satisfy, recompense, compensate, dispose of, square accounts, adjust, liquidate, clear, close, terminate, compromise. **6** come to rest, light, sit, alight, land, descend, perch. **7** sink, subside, wane, ebb, drop, lower, abate, fall, dwindle.

ant. 1 disarrange, upset, scramble, mess up. **3** excite, agitate, irritate, roil, exacerbate. **7** wax, increase, heighten, rise.

settlement n. **1** arrangement, ordering, sequence, order, neatening, neatness, tidiness, placement, stabilization, composition, classification, assortment. **2** decision, determination, agreement, adjustment, conciliation, compromise, accommodation, disposition, conclusion, arbitration, quittance, payment, reconciliation, satisfaction, payment.

ant. 1 disorder, disarrangement, displacement, untidiness, mess.

settlings n. DREGS.

set-to n. QUARREL.

setup n. arrangement, plan, organization, scheme, system, structure, basis, coordination, circumstances, elements, constituents, framework, blueprint, layout, outline, apparatus, *apparat*.

set up 1 construct, build, erect, raise, rear, put up, fabricate, produce, assemble, put together, fashion, form, frame, structure, organize. **2** em-

power, authorize, install, seat, commission, license, enfranchise, accredit, appoint, assign, induct, invest, entitle, sanction. **3** found, establish, inaugurate, initiate, begin, open, launch, institute, originate, start, create, undertake, embark, commence.

ant. 1 tear down, raze, level, take down, dismantle. **2** divest, discredit, depose, oust. **3** discontinue, close, finish, terminate.

set upon attack, assail, besiege, beleaguer, beset, harass, strike, hit, assault, maul, charge, fall upon, ambush, molest, mug (*Slang*).

sever v. **1** separate, cut, rend, part, disjoin, break, detach, cleave, split, dissever, fragment, disconnect, section, splinter, segment. **2** discontinue, end, terminate, cease, dissolve, break off, suspend, abandon, drop, leave off, quit, break up.

ant. 1 connect, attach, join, unify. **2** continue, maintain, keep on.

several adj. **1** numerous, divers, some, sundry, various, certain, few. **2** separate, individual, particular, respective, single, private, own, distinct, distinctive, peculiar, independent, different, unique, personal, marked.

severe adj. **1** difficult, trying, painful, extreme, acute, burdensome, arduous, taxing, nerve-wracking, worrisome, demanding, grievous, vexatious, agonizing, sore, intense, profound, unendurable, unrelenting. **2** unsparing, merciless, harsh, rigid, strict, inhuman, drastic, inflexible, pitiless, remorseless, nasty, unfeeling, cold, brutal, Draconian. **3** serious, grave, staid, austere, unsmiling, puritanical, self-denying, formal, earnest, repressed, starchy, unbending, unyielding. **4** plain, unadorned, functional, unembellished, undecorated, tailored, classic, restrained, ascetic, bare, minimal, spare, austere.

ant. 1 pleasant, painless, mild, light. **2** gentle, compassionate, merciful, sympathetic, lenient. **3** frivolous, informal, affable, folksy. **4** ornate, rococo, baroque, fancy, embellished.

sex *adj.* SEXUAL.

sex appeal ALLURE.

sexless *adj.* neuter, asexual, nonsexual, epicene, androgynous, hermaphrodite, eunuchoid, parthenogenetic.
ant. sexed, sexual, sexy, masculine, feminine.

sexual *adj.* reproductive, procreative, genital, sex, sexed, progenitive, childbearing.
ant. sterile, barren, asexual, neuter, parthenogenetic.

sexy *adj.* **1** seductive, provocative, exhibitionistic, stimulating, tantalizing, titillating, irresistible, intriguing, suggestive, alluring, exciting, desirable, sensual, oversexed. **2** prurient, lewd, bawdy, pornographic, lurid, coarse, vulgar, indecent, salacious, risqué, ribald, smutty, obscene, off-color. **3** *Slang* sensational, spectacular, topical, effective, new, hot, rich, dramatic, stirring, exciting, popular, compelling.
ant. 3 tedious, washed-out, uninteresting, hackneyed, boring.

shabby *adj.* **1** threadbare, worn, ragged, seedy, poor, faded, mangy, frowzy, rundown, frayed, sorry, impoverished, ratty, down-at-heel, dowdy. **2** mean, paltry, poky, picayune, ungenerous, low, wretched, miserable, mean-spirited, scurvy, sneaky, unfair, ungentlemanly, dishonorable, ignoble.
ant. 1 spruce, dapper, debonair, new, spanking. **2** generous, admirable, spendthrift.

shack *n.* shanty, hut, cabin, hovel, cottage, shed, lean-to, dump (*Slang*).

shackle *n.* **1** fetter, handcuff, chain, manacle, hobble, gyve, iron, trammel, bilbo, clamp. **2** impediment, restraint, straitjacket, muzzle, encumbrance, millstone, handicap, dead weight, yoke, brake, bridle, injunction, taboo, deterrent. —*v.* restrain, confine, impede, straitjacket,

muzzle, hamstring, fetter, tether, rein, forbid, constrain, stifle, subjugate, repress, suppress, strangle, prevent, limit.
ant. *v.* free, liberate, allow, permit, encourage.

shade *v.* **1** screen, protect, shadow, veil, cover, hide, shutter, curtain, shield, shroud, eclipse, mask, shelter, cloak. **2** darken, bedim, becloud, befog, blur, blot out, gray, tone down, overshadow, mute, obscure, adumbrate. **3** blend, graduate, scale, gradate, mix, intensify, darken, lighten. —*n.* **1** gradation, differentiation, shading, variation, subtlety, tone, tinge, chiaroscuro, tint, nicety, degree. **2** screen, cover, shield, film, veil, visor, hood, blind, parasol, shutter, drape, curtain, jalousie. **3** SHADOW. **4** GHOST.
ant. *v.* **1** uncover, bare, reveal, expose. **2** brighten, lighten, illuminate.

shadow *n.* **1** shade, dimness, sunlessness, dark, darkness, murk, murkiness, obscurity, grayness, dusk, twilight, cloudiness, gloaming, crepuscule. **2** foreshadowing, symbol, omen, remnant, vestige, trace, shred, drop, bit, scintilla, suspicion, tinge, hint. **3** gloom, cloud, sadness, blot, blight, smear, stigma, tarnish, pall, gloominess, melancholy, depression, sorrow, desolation, the blues, wet blanket. **4** GHOST. —*v.* **1** follow, trail, spy on, track, trace, hound, dog, pursue, pry, watch, tag after, tail, keep tabs on. **2** SHADE.
ant. *n.* **1** sunlight, light, brightness, glare, dazzle, brilliance. **3** cheerfulness, joy, gaiety.

shadowy *adj.* **1** dark, shady, sunless, murky, unlit, gloomy, somber, sepulchral, umbrageous, shaded, gray, veiled, screened. **2** vague, dim, obscure, misty, cloudy, beclouded, befogged, indistinct, dusky, crepuscular, unclear, blurred, murky, soupy, turbid, opaque, fuzzy, filmy, nebulous. **3** unreal, ghostly, eerie, spectral, occult, chimerical, mysterious, intangible, impalpable, incorporeal, phantom, haunted, dreamlike, improbable, wispy.

ant. 1 bright, sunny, sunlit, brilliant, dazzling. **2** distinct, clear, sharp, definite. **3** real, palpable, tangible, corporeal, substantial.

shady *adj.* **1** suspicious, suspect, questionable, devious, illicit, disreputable, dishonest, ambiguous, unreliable, untrustworthy, fishy, dubious, slippery, crooked, unscrupulous. **2** SHADOWY.

ant. honest, upright, reputable, esteemed, reliable.

shaft *n.* **1** rod, arrow, spear, lance, handle, hilt, pole, mast, stack, staff, stave, dart, wand, baton. **2** barb, sting, blow, jibe, jeer, cut, affront, thrust, wound, attack, slap, dig, knock, put-down (*Slang*). **3** beam, ray, stream, streak, ribbon, arc, glint, radiance, glimmer. **4** passageway, conduit, tunnel, flue, vent, hole, chimney, excavation, adit, well, pit. —*v. Slang* malign, slander, smear, insult, abuse, offend, impugn, hurt, attack, wound, affront, revile, backbite, bad-mouth (*Slang*).

shaggy *adj.* woolly, long-haired, fuzzy, shock, hairy, bushy, nappy, downy, hirsute, unshorn.

ant. sleek, smooth, shorn.

shake *v.* **1** jiggle, joggle, wiggle, jounce, jog, bounce, bobble, waggle, shog. **2** vibrate, tremble, totter, quiver, shimmy, churn, convulse, dodder, wave, flap, palpitate, quaver, shiver, shudder, quake, oscillate, rock. **3** weaken, disturb, undermine, dissuade, unsettle, discourage, unnerve, dishearten, sap, drain, startle, ruffle, flurry, disquiet, perturb, confuse.

ant. 3 strengthen, encourage, fortify, nerve, steel.

shaky *adj.* **1** rickety, decrepit, jiggly, quivering, infirm, wavering, fluctuating, flimsy, unsteady, teetering, broken-down, insecure, tumbledown, ramshackle, jerry-built. **2** dubious, questionable, ungrounded, untena-

ble, half-baked, weak, unsupported, unsound, inconclusive, groundless, improbable, faulty, arguable, flawed, doubtful, speculative, uncertain. **3** undependable, unreliable, shady, inconstant, fickle, variable, unbalanced, unstable, shifty, slippery, untrustworthy, indecisive.

ant. 1 solid, firm, well-built, strong. **2** conclusive, valid, well-grounded, proven, tested. **3** balanced, steady, reliable, constant.

shallow *adj.* superficial, surface, skin-deep, trivial, frivolous, frothy, immature, sketchy, insignificant, cursory, empty-headed, unthinking, puerile, silly, meaningless.

ant. profound, serious, meaningful, in-depth, deep, thoroughgoing.

sham *adj.* false, pretended, counterfeit, mock, fraudulent, fake, spurious, artificial, simulated, specious, trumped-up, insincere, affected, synthetic, pseudo, phony (*Slang*). —*n.* **1** hoax, deception, imitation, counterfeit, fake, fraud, forgery, mockery, trickery, swindle, fabrication, lie, put-on (*Slang*), spoof. **2** artificiality, pretension, pretentiousness, insincerity, airs, affectation, meretriciousness, affectedness, speciousness, dissimulation, showiness, tinsel, flash, vulgarity, tawdriness, trumpery. —*v.* COUNTERFEIT.

ant. *adj.* authentic, real, true, honest, legitimate. *n.* **2** authenticity, genuineness, honesty, sincerity.

shamble *v.* SHUFFLE.

shambles *n.* **1** chaos, upheaval, madhouse, mess, havoc, uproar, confusion, cataclysm, devastation, destruction, holocaust, ruin, wreck, jumble. **2** SLAUGHTERHOUSE.

shame *n.* **1** remorse, regret, guilt, embarrassment, sorrow, self-reproach, repentance, contrition, shamefacedness, grief, pain, chagrin, dismay, perturbation, sadness, agony. **2** humiliation, disgrace, abasement, dishonor, degradation, ignominy, disrepute, infamy, odium, ill-repute, contempt, opprobrium. —*v.* **1** embarrass, discomfit, reproach, chagrin, humiliate, mortify, humble, abash, upset, bother, agitate. **2** disgrace, dishonor, degrade, derogate, smear, sully, vilify, calumniate, besmirch, defile, brand, stigmatize, expose, reduce.

ant. *n.* **1** pride, self-satisfaction, self-righteousness. **2** honor, glory, exaltation. *v.* **2** honor, exalt, praise, glorify.

shamefaced *adj.* ASHAMED.

shameful *adj.* disgraceful, scandalous, disreputable, dishonorable, ignoble, ignominious, base, despicable, contemptible, deplorable, vile, odious, infamous, detestable, opprobrious.

ant. honorable, respectable, reputable, estimable.

shameless *adj.* impudent, brazen, immodest, wanton, indecent, bold, barefaced, immoral, unabashed, unblushing, tough, fresh, audacious, pert, saucy, cheeky, brassy, insolent, unseemly, lewd.

ant. proper, prissy, moralistic, prim, priggish.

shanghai *v.* KIDNAP.

shanty *n.* SHACK.

shape *n.* **1** form, contour, figure, configuration, aspect, appearance, guise, silhouette, outline, lineaments, likeness, semblance, build, measurements, physique. **2** pattern, mold, diagram, sketch, blueprint, cast, die, punch, stamp, format, model, layout, matrix. **3** condition, state, circumstances, form, fitness, trim, fettle, health. **4** GHOST. —*v.* **1** mold, fashion, ply, manipulate, form, devise, prepare, contour, delineate, outline, pattern, cast, model, sculpt, whittle. **2** adjust, modify, adapt, fit, alter, trim, streamline, reshape, reform, remodel, accommodate, frame, transfigure, reconstruct. **3** guide, define, pattern, characterize, condition, steer, chart, govern, determine, delineate, fix.

shapeless *adj.* amorphous, formless,

lumpy, dumpy, unformed, amoeboid, irregular, unstructured, vague, inchoate.

ant. contoured, delineated, formed, formal, distinct.

shapely *adj.* well-formed, well-proportioned, graceful, symmetrical, well-made, comely, well-turned, curvaceous, sightly, good-looking, Junoesque.

ant. misshapen, ill-shaped, ugly, unbecoming, ill-proportioned.

share *n.* portion, allotment, due, lot, quota, percent, part, fraction, helping, serving, allowance, dividend, segment, dole, cut (*Slang*), divvy (*Slang*). —*v.* **1** apportion, allot, divide, dole, portion, measure, mete, partition, deal, allocate, parcel. **2** participate in, partake of, enjoy, use, have in common.

shark *n.* SWINDLER.

sharp *adj.* **1** honed, pointed, edged, keen-edged, cutting, piercing, razorlike, razor-edged. **2** clear, distinct, unmistakable, well-defined, unequivocal, unambiguous, blatant, striking, emphatic. **3** quick, perceptive, insightful, acute, keen, canny, sharp-witted, discerning, penetrating, shrewd, alert, attentive, vigilant, brainy, aware, quick-witted, astute, wide-awake, smart. **4** harsh, cutting, hurtful, acerbic, barbed, stinging, strong, edged, acrimonious, catty, shrewish, heated, fiery, biting, mordant, sarcastic, trenchant, nasty, incisive, smarting. **5** tart, sour, acid, vinegary, lemony, pungent, nippy, astringent, piquant, spicy, tangy. **6** *Slang* stylish, dapper, chic, debonair, well-dressed, well-groomed, slick, spruce, showy, flashy, fancy, elegant. —*n.* SWINDLER.

ant. **1** blunt, dull, obtuse. **2** vague, ambiguous, indistinct, fuzzy, blurred. **3** dense, thick, slow-witted, foolish, gullible. **4** placatory, bland, inoffensive, conciliatory. **5** bland, tasteless. **6** shabby, dowdy, sloppy.

sharpen v. hone, edge, whet, strop, grind, file, taper, acuminate.
ant. dull, blunt.

sharper n. SWINDLER.

sharp-witted adj. INTELLIGENT.

shatter v. **1** break, burst, fragment, explode, shiver, implode, fracture, smash, blow up, pop, splinter, crack, crumble, crash. **2** destroy, ruin, damage, demolish, undermine, undo, wreck, devastate, blast, topple, crush, break down, spoil, end.
ant. 2 build, strengthen, fortify.

shattering adj. OVERWHELMING.

shave v. **1** crop, trim, shear, razor, mow, clip, cut, strip, shorten, dock, pare, lop, scythe, scissor, snip, barber. **2** touch, graze, brush, scrape, flick, skim, sweep, sideswipe.

sheaf n. bundle, collection, batch, pile, stack, packet, bale, dossier, bunch, shock, quantity, package.

shear v. **1** clip, cut, trim, mow, scissor, scythe, razor, crop, shave, barber, strip, shorten, pare, lop, snip. **2** divest, denude, deprive, strip, rob, fleece, impoverish, despoil, dispossess, swindle, mulct, filch, pauperize.

sheath n. envelope, case, cover, scabbard, container, covering, quiver, wrapper, protection, integument, skin, casing, receptacle.

sheathe v. encase, envelop, enclose, cover, conceal, protect, wrap, insert, hide, swathe, shroud, swaddle, shield, screen.
ant. uncover, reveal, draw, expose.

sheave v. COLLECT.

shebang n. Slang AFFAIR.

shed[1] v. **1** pour, trickle, drop, rain, cry, emit, flow, ooze, sweat, run, exude, secrete, leak, stream, spill. **2** radiate, beam, afford, throw, give, diffuse, spread, distribute, broadcast, disseminate, strew, scatter, transmit. **3** throw off, repel, cast off, molt, peel, disencumber, eliminate, disburden, slough, repulse, drop, discard, desquamate, exfoliate, flake.

shed[2] n. shack, lean-to, outbuilding, storehouse, outhouse, hut, toolshed, toolhouse, hovel, shelter, shanty.

sheen n. gleam, shimmer, glare, glitter, brightness, glisten, radiance, sparkle, luster, gloss, glint, glossiness, polish, veneer, glimmer, highlights, burnish, slickness, glister. —v. SHINE.
ant. dullness, matte, tarnish.

sheep n. MILKSOP.

sheepish adj. embarrassed, chagrined, shamefaced, blushing, self-conscious, apologetic, abashed, ashamed, hangdog, uncomfortable, discomfited, dismayed, disconcerted, crestfallen, abject.
ant. bold, defiant, brassy, assertive.

sheer[1] v. swerve, veer, turn aside, deviate, skew, twist, angle, shift, change course, list, tack, slant, careen, lurch, career.

sheer[2] adj. **1** absolute, total, utter, unmitigated, very, unrelieved, unqualified, pure, unalloyed, unmixed, complete, consummate, downright, out-and-out, stark, perfect. **2** diaphanous, filmy, gauzy, thin, fine, transparent, gossamer, delicate, see-through, flimsy, insubstantial. **3** perpendicular, steep, precipitous, bluff, headlong, upright, vertical, plumb, sharp, craggy.
ant. 1 partial, qualified, limited, restricted. **2** thick, opaque, substantial.

sheet n. **1** layer, lamina, laminate, lamination, leaf, pane, membrane, film, top, topping, overlay, cover, covering, ply, coat, coating. **2** expanse, surface, area, mass, extent, sweep, spread, reach, field.

shelf n. REEF.

shell n. **1** carapace, covering, shuck, case, capsule, exterior, horn, pod. **2** framework, frame, hull, scull, skeleton, cavity, mold, hollow, shape, chassis. **3** projectile, cartridge, bullet, bomb, missile, grenade, mortar, shot, ammunition, explosive, case, casing. —v. **1** hull, open, crack, remove, husk, shuck, strip, peel, split. **2** bombard, bomb, strafe, pepper, torpedo, besiege, attack, fire at, cannonade, fusillade.

shellac v. *Slang* **1** BEAT. **2** DEFEAT.

shellacking n. *Slang* **1** BEATING. **2** DEFEAT.

shelter n. **1** refuge, cover, roof, house, housing, hole, lair, den, retreat, sanctuary, asylum, hide-out, hideaway, preserve, home, harbor, stronghold, hermitage. **2** safety, protection, security, safekeeping, seclusion, privacy, comfort, warmth, concealment, hiding, conservation, preservation, immunity, custody, well-being. —v. protect, shield, cover, harbor, safeguard, preserve, conceal, house, lodge, screen, care for, look after, take in, provide for.
ant. n. **2** peril, danger, hazard, exposure, discomfort, vulnerability. —v. expose, imperil, endanger, jeopardize.

shelve v. postpone, defer, put off, set aside, table, pigeonhole, suspend, put on ice, put on the back burner (*Slang*).
ant. expedite, handle, attend to, dispose of, deal with.

shenanigans n. mischief, tomfoolery, monkeyshines, hijinks, sport, horseplay, nonsense, antics, pranks, silliness, sportiveness, clownery, buffoonery, deviltry, roguishness.

shepherd v. herd, guide, protect, direct, gather in, supervise, pilot, lead, oversee, steer, tend, escort, minister to, shield.

shibboleth n. SLOGAN.

shield n. **1** armor, buckler, mail, cuirass. **2** protection, defense, safeguard, aegis, cover, protector, patron, guardian, defender, buffer, mantle, comforter, bulwark, champion, savior. —v. **1** protect, defend, armor, guard, safeguard, secure, comfort, bulwark, arm, fortify, shelter, cherish, care for. **2** conceal, cover, hide, screen, shade, shroud, ambush, camouflage, disguise, cloak, wrap, veil, secrete, envelop, sheathe.

ant. v. **1** endanger, imperil, jeopardize. **2** expose, bare, uncover, reveal.

shift v. move, reposition, replace, displace, change, permute, transpose, transfer, rearrange, dislodge, transplant, transport, reverse, invert. —n. change, deviation, reversal, permutation, modification, alteration, metamorphosis, replacement, rearrangement, transformation, variation, difference, turnabout, move, about-face, displacement, digression, divagation.

shiftless adj. lazy, inefficient, indolent, incompetent, unskilled, inept, sluggish, unambitious, aimless, purposeless, idle, ne'er-do-well, good-for-nothing, unreliable, undependable.
ant. competent, ambitious, purposeful, energetic, industrious, assiduous, hard-working.

shifty adj. deceitful, shady, unscrupulous, slippery, unprincipled, untrustworthy, dishonest, fly-by-night, sneaky, wily, scheming, devious, cunning, treacherous, underhand, two-faced.
ant. straightforward, reliable, honest, reputable, trustworthy.

shilly-shally v. vacillate, stall, waver, hem and haw, fluctuate, dillydally. seesaw, straddle, dawdle, procrastinate, hesitate, flounder. —adj. HESITANT.
ant. decide, act, take a stand, confront, cope with.

shimmer v. gleam, glisten, shine, glimmer, twinkle, sparkle, phosphoresce, flicker, coruscate, glow, burn, light up, scintillate, reflect. —n. GLIMMER.

shindig n. *Slang* PARTY.

shine v. **1** beam, glow, sheen, glisten, glimmer, twinkle, glare, sparkle, phosphoresce, glow, scintillate, reflect, radiate, glitter, flash. **2** excel, star, lead, stand out, outdo, tower above, outclass, outrank, eclipse, surpass. —n. radiance, luster, gloss, polish, sheen, shimmer, glow, glaze, brightness, effulgence, lambency, brilliance, luminosity, burnish, veneer.

ant. *n.* dullness, matte, cloudiness, film.

shining *adj.* **1** excellent, outstanding, conspicuous, starring, leading, brilliant, preeminent, champion, spotlighted, noteworthy, prominent, illustrious, celebrated, splendid, glorious, famous, notable. **2** SHINY.

ant. dull, inconspicuous, mediocre, routine, everyday, trite.

shiny *adj.* shining, gleaming, glossy, polished, glaring, glary, glistening, lustrous, bright, sunny, radiant, sunlit, sparkling, shimmering, glowing, effulgent, luminous.

ant. dull, cloudy, foggy, matte, misty.

ship *n.* vessel, craft, watercraft. —*v.* send, transport, mail, dispatch, transmit, move, transfer, convey, carry, consign, express, export.

shipmate *n.* SAILOR.

shipshape *adj.* trim, orderly, neat, tidy, uncluttered, compact, streamlined, businesslike, unencumbered, meticulous, well-ordered, trig, immaculate.

ant. messy, cluttered, chaotic, disordered, topsy-turvy.

shipwreck *v.* DESTROY.

shirk *v.* malinger, soldier, duck, dodge, avoid, sidestep, goldbrick (*Slang*), goof off (*Slang*).

ant. shoulder, help, cooperate, take on, volunteer.

shirker *n.* slacker, idler, malingerer, do-nothing, quitter, absentee, dropout, truant, dodger, deserter, coward, goldbrick (*Slang*), goof-off (*Slang*), deserter.

shiver[1] *v.* tremble, quiver, shake, quaver, shudder, pulsate, palpitate, flutter, chatter, quake, flinch, quail. —*n.* tremor, quake, shudder, quaver, flutter, pulsation, thrill, tremulousness, trembling, quaking, tingle, quiver, throb, *frisson*.

shiver[2] *v.* SHATTER.

shlock *n.* JUNK.

shlocky *adj.* JUNKY.

shoal[1] *n.* sandbar, shallow, sandbank, bar, flat, reef, shelf, ledge.

shoal[2] *n.* throng, group, school, collection, swarm, multitude, pack, number.

shock[1] *n.* **1** collision, concussion, impact, blow, crash, smash. **2** trauma, jolt, daze, start, thrill, stupefaction, consternation, faint, faintness, wonder, horror, outrage, amazement, breakdown, crackup. —*v.* **1** horrify, outrage, amaze, stun, electrify, astound, bowl over, traumatize, daze, numb, thrill, paralyze, immobilize, overwhelm, flabbergast. **2** shake, jar, jolt, crush, shiver, rattle, buffet, joggle, jog, bump, jostle, vibrate, jounce.

shock[2] *n.* mane, bush, mass, thatch, mat, shag, crop. —*adj.* SHAGGY.

shocked *adj.* DAZED.

shocking *adj.* astounding, horrifying, stunning, overwhelming, breathtaking, scandalous, scandalizing, numbing, appalling, jolting, outrageous, hideous, ghastly, horrible, stupefying.

ant. reassuring, comforting, calming, soothing.

shoddy *adj.* inferior, second-rate, tacky, cheap, poor, vulgar, tawdry, flashy, showy, fake, meretricious, junky, cheesy (*Slang*), schlocky (*Slang*).

ant. fine, choice, tasteful, elegant, authentic, classy (*Slang*).

shoot *v.* **1** wound, hit, kill, execute, strike, fell, pelt, dispatch, plug (*Slang*), knock off (*Slang*). **2** fire, discharge, let off, eject, let fly, impel, hurl, catapult. **3** emit, send forth, project, dart, launch, spew, toss, fling. **4** flick, thrust out, protrude, extend, jut, dart, stick out, put forth. —*n.* branch, growth, offshoot, scion, outgrowth, sprout, twig, bough, sucker, limb, excrescence.

shop *n.* store, market, mart, bazaar, boutique, salon, emporium, stall, booth, supermarket, five-and-dime.

—*v.* market, purchase, sample, look, windowshop, examine, seek, procure, buy.

shopkeeper *n.* storekeeper, retailer, dealer, tradesman, tradeswoman, merchant, merchandiser, trader, monger, distributor.

shopworn *adj.* stale, trite, hackneyed, banal, overworked, musty, threadbare, moth-eaten, stereotyped, outmoded, commonplace, tired, superannuated, overused, antiquated, effete, jejune.

ant. fresh, original, imaginative, new, ingenious, unconventional.

shore[1] *n.* coast, beach, bank, strand, land, waterside, brink, littoral, margin, seaboard, seashore, verge, brim.

shore[2] *v.* prop, support, underpin, reinforce, brace, buttress, stay, sustain, hold up, strengthen.

ant. topple, overturn, tumble, level, weaken.

short *adj.* **1** abridged, truncated, stunted, small, low, brief, minimal. **2** brief, abrupt, fleeting, momentary, concise, instantaneous, instant. **3** scanty, few, laconic, terse, succinct, concise. **4** inadequate, shy, failing, insufficient, deficient, lacking, substandard. **5** curt, petulant, sharp, uncivil, testy, rude, impatient, irascible, cantankerous, quarrelsome.

ant. 1 long, tall, extensive, elongated, lengthy. **2** extended, lingering, prolonged, interminable, lengthy. **3** profuse, verbose, wordy, prolix, replete. **4** adequate, sufficient, satisfactory, excessive, lavish. **5** agreeable, genial, polite, civil, urbane.

shortage *n.* deficiency, shortfall, deficit, insufficiency, inadequacy, lack, scarcity, dearth, want, poverty, famine, need, failure.

ant. excess, superfluity, overage, glut, plethora, redundancy.

shortchange *v.* CHEAT.

shortcoming *n.* defect, imperfection, frailty, fault, flaw, drawback, infirmity, inadequacy, weakness, fail-

ing, deficiency, deficit, lack, peccadillo.

ant. strength, extra, virtue, bonus, endowment, excellence.

shorten *v.* reduce, lessen, curtail, diminish, abridge, abbreviate, condense, contract, restrict, retrench, limit, lop, trim, bob, retract, decrease.

ant. lengthen, prolong, extend, protract, stretch, increase.

shortening *n.* ABBREVIATION.

shortfall *n.* SHORTAGE.

short-lived *adj.* ephemeral, fleeting, transitory, evanescent, brief, impermanent, transient, temporary, fugitive, momentary, passing, perishable, hurried.

ant. long-lived, lasting, perdurable, permanent, eternal, agelong.

shortly *adv.* soon, directly, anon, presently, promptly, early, quickly, forthwith, speedily, straightway, betimes, immediately, momentarily.

ant. ultimately, later, eventually, finally, belatedly.

shortness *n.* **1** smallness, littleness, dwarfishness, slightness, diminutiveness, compactness, petiteness. **2** transience, brevity, ephemerality, quickness, temporariness, impermanence, abruptness, perishability. **3** scantiness, poverty, shortage, scarcity, lack, inadequacy, deficit, want.

ant. 1. length, tallness, greatness, elongation, extension. **2** permanence, endurance, lastingness, continuance, immortality. **3** plenty, excess, sufficiency, richness, adequacy.

shortsighted *adj.* thoughtless, imprudent, myopic, improvident, impulsive, inconsiderate, unthinking, heedless, indiscreet, rash, unwise, careless, reckless.

ant. foresighted, prudent, thoughtful, circumspect, cautious.

short-tempered *adj.* irascible, irritable, testy, fiery, abrupt, ill-humored, cantankerous, choleric, cranky, hot-tempered, volatile, peevish, waspish, splenetic, sharp, snappish, impatient.

ant. placid, easygoing, imperturbable, indulgent, patient, long-suffering.

shot *n.* **1** blast, discharge, detonation, explosion, firing, crack, pop. **2** taunt, criticism, shaft, crack, witticism, barb, thrust, slur. **3** missile, pellet, bullet, slug, projectile, ball, ammunition. **4** effort, attempt, try, guess, conjecture, turn, chance, opportunity, crack. —*adj.* **1** variegated, changeable, versicolor, iridescent, opalescent, moiré, shimmery. **2** exhausted, ruined, washed-up, prostrate, useless, effete, enervated, vitiated, etiolated.

ant. *adj.* **2** vigorous, fresh, energetic, robust, blooming.

shoulder *v.* **1** assume, endure, accept, take on, answer for, acknowledge, admit, put up with, own. **2** carry, bear, haul, pack, tote, uphold, lift, sustain. **3** SHOVE.

ant. **1** disown, shun, eschew, disclaim, disavow, repudiate.

shout *n.* outcry, yell, scream, call, cry, hail, halloo, hoot, bellow, whoop, roar, holler, caterwaul, bray, exclamation. —*v.* cry out, yell, call, cry, roar, scream, halloo, hail, whoop, vociferate, bellow, bawl, holler.

ant. *n.* whisper, murmur, breath, sigh, hum. *v.* whisper, murmur, mumble, breathe.

shove *v.* **1** push, propel, drive, impel, move, thrust. **2** jostle, elbow, jolt, push aside, shoulder, joggle, press, hustle. —*n.* push, thrust, impulse, impetus, boost, jog, nudge, start, propulsion, impulsion, bunt, jostle.

shovel *n.* scoop, spade, trowel, dredge, spoon. —*v.* lade, ladle, spade, scoop, heap, toss, shift, remove, move, bail, dip, trowel, spoon.

show *v.* **1** reveal, exhibit, evidence, demonstrate, display, express, manifest, disclose, evince. **2** explain, prove, establish, verify, inform, expound, elucidate, instruct, demonstrate, corroborate. **3** confer, bestow, endow, impart, dispense, lavish, accord, grant. —*n.* **1** presentation, showing, viewing, performance, entertainment, exhibition, play, production. **2** curiosity, wonder, spectacle, scene, sight, caution, exhibition, oddity. **3** display, manifestation, demonstration, revelation, indication, parade, mark, sign, example. **4** pretense, semblance, illusion, mask, trappings, color, ostentation.

ant. *v.* **1** conceal, hide, disguise, cover, screen. **2** confuse, obfuscate, confound, mystify, becloud. **3** deny, withhold, suppress, restrict, hold back.

shower *n.* fall, rain, drizzle, sprinkle, sprinkling, gush, downpour, flood, rush, surge, deluge, volley, profusion. —*v.* **1** sprinkle, rain, spatter, splash, spray, spit, drizzle, pour, fall. **2** lavish, bestow, overwhelm, deluge, heap, flood, load, rain.

showing *n.* **1** display, airing, exposure, presentation, exhibition, viewing, staging, disclosure, unveiling, premiere. **2** record, effect, performance, impression, achievement, mark, track record, appearance, the bottom line (*Slang*).

showman *n.* entertainer, spellbinder, performer, magician, impresario, master of ceremonies, emcee.

showoff *n.* braggart, exhibitionist, swaggerer, boaster, cock of the walk, braggadocio, egotist, brag, blusterer, windbag, peacock, name-dropper.

show off flaunt, parade, boast, brag, flourish, blazon, brandish, advertise, strut, swagger, puff, air, display.

ant. hide, bury, cloak, conceal, disguise, withdraw.

showy *adj.* **1** striking, splendid, brilliant, magnificent, radiant, vivid, gorgeous, conspicuous, fine. **2** gaudy, meretricious, garish, flashy, tawdry, ostentatious, loud, glaring.

ant. **1** dull, gloomy, dingy, drab, dismal, withered. **2** modest, sober, quiet, plain, low-key, unassuming.

shred *n.* strip, piece, tatter, ribbon, particle, fragment, scrap, rag, snippet, morsel, bit. —*v.* rip, frazzle, fray, slit, slice, tear, tatter.

shrew *n.* scold, fury, nag, termagant, virago, harridan, hag, spitfire, vixen, fishwife, battle-ax (*Slang*).

shrewd *adj.* keen, artful, clever, able, sly, astute, sharp, cunning, sagacious, perspicacious, canny, perceptive, discerning, long-headed, sharp, crafty, wily, sensible, savvy (*Slang*). **ant.** simple, ignorant, foolish, naive, stupid, dense.

shrewdness *n.* ACUMEN.

shrewish *adj.* ill-tempered, peevish, petulant, snappish, contentious, intractable, quarrelsome, scolding, crabby, nagging, fractious, vexatious. **ant.** placid, peaceful, pleasant, tranquil, calm.

shriek *n.* screech, scream, squawk, yell, squeal, yelp, squeak, cry, yip, yap, wail, holler. —*v.* screech, scream, shrill, squeal, yell, cry, squall, squawk, yelp, wail, holler.

shrill *adj.* 1 high-pitched, piercing, sharp, penetrating, piping, high, squeaky, treble. 2 harsh, immoderate, strident, intemperate, hysterical, bitter, rasping, complaining. **ant.** 1 low, rumbling, growling, humming, bass. 2 temperate, moderate, gentle, calm, mild.

shrimp *n.* runt, peewee, midget, mite, dwarf, pygmy, bantam, Lilliputian, Tom Thumb, half pint (*Slang*). **ant.** giant, colossus, titan, tower, Brobdingnagian.

shrine *n.* reliquary, altar, temple, landmark, memorial, monument, cradle, sanctum, sanctuary.

shrink *v.* 1 contract, shrivel, deflate, compress, condense, draw up, constrict, huddle, wither, sear. 2 diminish, lessen, decrease, dwindle, reduce, decline, wane, ebb, peter out. **ant.** 1 swell, stretch, expand, inflate, infuse. 2 grow, increase, enlarge, augment, magnify.

shrivel *v.* wither, waste away, vitiate, degenerate, deteriorate, flag, droop, fade, fail, crumble, dry up, wizen, shrink. **ant.** regenerate, recover, blossom, rejuvenate, recoup.

shriveled *adj.* shrunken, withered, sere, wizened, puckered, wasted, dried-up, crumbled, decayed, wrinkled. **ant.** burgeoning, swollen, smooth, firm, flourishing, tumescent.

shroud *n.* 1 winding sheet, cerements, pall. 2 cover, enclosure, housing, covering, screen, sheath, jacket, blanket, shield, capsule, pod. —*v.* envelop, conceal, protect, enclose, overlay, cover, screen, seclude, closet, hood. **ant.** *v.* reveal, uncover, expose, lay bare, unveil.

shrubbery *n.* bushes, planting, thicket, copse, greenery, hedge, bosk, bosket, grove, brush, undergrowth.

shrunken *adj.* SHRIVELED.

shuck *n.* husk, shell, hull, pod, shard. —*v.* cast, doff, peel off, strip off, shed, slough, take off, remove, throw away, chuck. **ant.** *v.* don, wrap, put on, assume, fit out, take on.

shudder *v.* tremble, shake, quake, rock, vibrate, quiver, shiver, twitch, jerk. —*n.* tremor, shiver, trembling, twitching, shaking, quake, spasm, paroxysm, quiver, vibration, jerk, twitch, convulsion, tic.

shuffle *v.* 1 intermix, muddle, jumble, mix, disorder, confuse, shift, interchange. 2 scuff, scuffle, shamble, hobble, slouch, limp, chug, drag. —*n.* scuffling, dragging, scraping, sliding, toddle, hobble, scuffle, shambling, limping.

shun *v.* avoid, keep clear of, eschew, evade, escape, elude, ignore, refuse, disdain, scorn, bypass, circumvent, cold-shoulder, snub. **ant.** seek, confront, face, encounter, brave, meet.

shunt *v.* turn aside, switch, divert, sidetrack, deviate, deflect, shift, swerve, veer, swing, displace, bypass.

shush *v.* HUSH.

shut *v.* **1** close, occlude, stop up, stopper, obstruct, block, clog, plug, dam, bar, cover, cork, bottle up. **2** fasten, secure, lock, bolt, seal, close, catch, latch, slam.

ant. 1 open, uncover, clear, unclog, dilate. **2** loosen, unlock, unfasten, release, open, free.

shutdown *n.* stoppage, cessation, suspension, closure, idling, closing, halt, lockout, recess, windup, phaseout.

ant. start-up, opening, resumption, installation, tooling up.

shut-eye *n. Slang* SLEEP.

shuttle *v.* alternate, wigwag, oscillate, seesaw, ply.

shy *adj.* **1** timid, bashful, diffident, modest, coy, reserved, sheepish, retiring. **2** circumspect, watchful, wary, suspicious, cautious, chary, distrustful, fearful. **3** short, insufficient, missing, deficient, under, scanty, inadequate, lacking. —*v.* startle, recoil, start, duck, flinch, swerve, draw back, jump, veer.

ant. *adj.* **1** pushing, obtrusive, bold, aggressive, forward. **2** trustful, confident, secure, reckless, fearless. **3** ample, adequate, plenty, enough, sufficient.

shyness *n.* timidity, bashfulness, reserve, diffidence, coyness, reticence, hesitancy, constraint, timorousness, demureness, skittishness, fearfulness.

ant. self-confidence, aggressiveness, boldness, assurance, forwardness, self-assertion.

shyster *n.* CROOK.

sibilant *adj.* hissing, buzzing, sibilating, whistling, susurrous.

sick *adj.* **1** ill, sickly, unhealthy, indisposed, ailing, weak, unwell. **2** nauseated, queasy, squeamish, qualmish, delicate. **3** fed up, bored, jaded, sick and tired, tired, satiated, weary, disgusted.

ant. 1 vigorous, healthy, well, in the pink, strong. **3** sanguine, eager, ardent, zestful, fresh.

sicken *v.* DISGUST.

sickening *adj.* disgusting, nauseating, sickly, revolting, loathsome, offensive, unsavory, foul, repulsive, distasteful, noisome.

ant. salutary, tonic, palatable, invigorating, restorative, healthful.

sickly *adj.* **1** ailing, weakly, unhealthy, languishing, valetudinarian, diseased, infirm, feeble, invalid. **2** pallid, peaked, haggard, dull, anemic, delicate, jaundiced. **3** unconvincing, flimsy, paltry, lame, inadequate, poor, feeble, weak, unpersuasive. **4** SICKENING.

ant. 1 robust, healthy, sound, rugged, strong. **2** rosy, sunny, plump, blooming, bright. **3** plausible, convincing, cogent, pithy, sound.

sickness *n.* **1** illness, unhealthiness, feebleness, debility, infirmity, suffering, pain, weakness, indisposition, malaise. **2** nausea, queasiness, qualmishness, squeamishness, motion sickness, seasickness. **3** disease, malady, complaint, ailment, disorder, illness, infection, affliction, infirmity, condition.

ant. 1 health, vigor, well-being, strength, vitality, robustness.

side *n.* **1** boundary, edge, margin, border, verge, limit, rim, brink. **2** face, wall, flank, surface, slope. **3** division, segment, sector, part, half, section, aspect. **4** opinion, angle, viewpoint, view, point of view, position, slant, version, aspect, stance. **5** adversary, contestant, opposition, team, faction. —*adj.* incidental, secondary, marginal, subordinate, subsidiary, ancillary, auxiliary, minor, contingent, parenthetical, irrelevant, immaterial, indirect.

ant. *adj.* main, major, germane, important, significant, material.

side effect BYPRODUCT.

sidekick *n. Slang* SUBORDINATE.

sideline *n.* avocation, hobby, pastime, diversion, amusement, relaxation, distraction, recreation, extra, interest.

ant. profession, occupation, business, work, career, preoccupation.

sidelong *adj.* OBLIQUE.

sidesplitting *adj.* HILARIOUS.

sidestep *v.* dodge, sidetrack, evade, avoid, shun, parry, duck, shuffle, shrink from, bypass, shift ground, ignore.

    ant. face up to, confront, brazen out, answer to, meet, brave.

sidetrack *v.* SIDESTEP.

siege *n.* **1** drive, campaign, pursuit, attempt, crusade, offensive, effort. **2** attack, session, stretch, spell, bout course, turn, term.

    ant. 2 let-up, lull, remission, respite, pause.

siesta *n.* NAP.

sieve *v.* SIFT.

sift *v.* **1** sieve, screen, strain, bolt, winnow, filter, pan, osmose, permeate. **2** analyze, examine, scrutinize, inspect, probe, pore over, bolt. **3** separate, distinguish, cull, set apart, eliminate, discriminate, screen.

sigh *v., n.* MURMUR.

sight *n.* **1** vision, eyesight, seeing, perception, eye. **2** spectacle, picture, scene, image, prospect, show, vista. **3** glimpse, look, glance, view, impression, scrutiny, stare, gaze. —*v.* espy, discern, make out, behold, distinguish, descry, catch sight of, perceive, see, recognize, view, ken.

sightless *adj.* BLIND.

sightly *adj.* COMELY.

sign *n.* **1** indication, intimation, suggestion, gesture, token, clue, evidence, signal, nod, mark, trace, spoor, blaze, brand, vestige, omen, harbinger, giveaway. **2** symbol, token, emblem, cipher, character, brand, mark, device, trademark, hallmark, X. —*v.* write, endorse, attest, subscribe, inscribe, countersign, autograph.

signal *n.* sign, cue, go-ahead, password, watchword, indication, notice, shibboleth, token, clue. —*adj.* notable, distinguished, extraordinary, eminent, outstanding, remarkable, arresting, striking, conspicuous, prominent, salient. —*v.* semaphore, gesticulate, pantomime, motion, flag, wigwag, wave, beckon, flash, nod, nudge, salute.

    ant. *adj.* unremarkable, humdrum, obscure, shadowy, ill-defined, feeble.

signature *n.* **1** autograph, name, hand, John Hancock, endorsement, subscription, holograph, signing. **2** imprimatur, cachet, stamp, seal, signet, mark, sign, trademark, identification, refrain, tag line, theme song.

significance *n.* **1** importance, consequence, weight, cogency, relevance, import, moment, force, signification, gravity, interest, priority. **2** SIGNIFICATION.

    ant. insignificance, triviality, irrelevance, inconsequence, frivolity.

significant *adj.* **1** meaningful, pregnant, profound, suggestive, significative, telling, indicative, expressive. **2** important, momentous, weighty, portentous, crucial, vital, consequential, material, signal.

    ant. 1 meaningless, ambiguous, idle, unrevealing, blank. **2** insignificant, trivial, trifling, paltry, picayune.

signification *n.* meaning, sense, import, significance, drift, gist, thrust, intent, effect, force, implication, denotation, connotation, acceptation, purport, intention, definition, definiens.

significative *adj.* SIGNIFICANT.

signify *v.* **1** represent, mean, suggest, denote, indicate, betoken, stand for, connote, import, show, portend, imply. **2** express, communicate, name, announce, declare, make known, reveal, say, utter, indicate, suggest.

sign up enlist, enroll, register, volunteer, join, enter, undertake, subscribe, pledge, covenant.

    ant. opt out, withdraw, cancel, repudiate, desert, drop out.

silence *n.* **1** stillness, hush, noiselessness, soundlessness, still, quiet, quietude, lull, muteness, calm. **2** secrecy, reticence, taciturnity, reserve, closeness, obscurity, oblivion. —*v.* **1** quiet, still, stifle, deaden, hush, muffle, mute, muzzle. **2** quell, suppress, put down, extinguish, crush, restrain, subdue.

ant. *n.* **1** noise, disturbance, sound, clamor, activity. **2** effusiveness, confession, garrulity, conversation, explanation. *v.* **2** inflame, agitate, instigate, stir up.

silent *adj.* **1** noiseless, soundless, hushed, inaudible, quiet, still, muted, muffled. **2** speechless, mute, dumb, close-mouthed, unresponsive, reticent, taciturn, secretive, quiet, mum.

ant. **1** noisy, clamorous, deafening, loud, audible. **2** voluble, talkative, vocal, garrulous, vociferous.

silken *adj.* SUAVE.

silky *adj.* SMOOTH.

silly *adj.* **1** foolish, witless, fatuous, empty-headed, dim-witted, dull, weak-minded, brainless, senseless, stupid, simple, thoughtless, dumb, sappy (*Slang*). **2** frivolous, clownish, slap-happy (*Slang*), absurd, ridiculous, nonsensical, idiotic, asinine, ludicrous, preposterous, zany, childish, puerile, jejune, immature, scatterbrained, spacey (*Slang*). **3** stunned, dazed, confused, addled, addlebrained, stupefied, dizzy, groggy, muddled, zonked (*Slang*), spacedout (*Slang*), slap-happy (*Slang*).

ant. **1** wise, astute, clever, sage, sapient, prudent. **2** serious, sensible, mature, sedate, thoughtful. **3** clearheaded, steady, alert, rational, conscious.

silt *n.* sediment, deposit, alluvium, ooze, settlings, diluvium, sludge, mud, dregs, guck (*Slang*).

similar *adj.* like, kindred, akin, analogous, comparable, corresponding, resembling, matching, allied, homologous, congruent, twin, duplicate, parallel, identical, alike, fungible.

ant. dissimilar, unlike, different, contrary, antithetic, disparate, alien.

similarity *n.* resemblance, correspondence, similitude, analogy, likeness, semblance, parity, parallelism, agreement, sameness, oneness, congru-

ence, homology, affinity, comparability.

ant. dissimilarity, unlikeness, disparity, difference, dissimilitude, divergence.

similitude *n.* SIMILARITY.

simmer *v.* **1** seethe, bubble, cook, stew, boil. **2** fret, chafe, brood, smart, writhe, seethe, fume, boil.

Simon Legree TYRANT.

simon-pure *adj.* AUTHENTIC.

simp *n.* *Slang* SIMPLETON.

simper *v., n.* SMIRK.

simple *adj.* **1** easy, understandable, straightforward, clear, uncomplicated, unmistakable, transparent, obvious, lucid. **2** unadorned, plain, severe, neat, natural, spare, classic. **3** mere, bald, bare, sheer, utter, unmitigated, naked, pure, unadulterated. **4** ordinary, humble, artless, unassuming, common, guileless, unpretentious, down-to-earth, basic. **5** unitary, single, undivided, whole, one, uniform, integral, monolithic. **6** SIMPLE-MINDED.

ant. **1** complex, complicated, involved, difficult, confused. **2** fussy, ornate, fancy, embellished, artificial. **3** qualified, conditional, limited, contingent, mitigated. **4** pretentious, disingenuous, luxurious, elaborate, artful. **5** composite, multiple, compound, complex, divided, various.

simple-minded *adj.* foolish, fatuous, asinine, stupid, idiotic, silly, empty-headed, dim-witted, dull, slow, dense, thick, simple, muddle-headed, scatterbrained, senseless, thoughtless, witless, half-witted, feebleminded, addlebrained, addlepated, dumb.

ant. wise, judicious, thoughtful, astute, clear-headed, sensible.

simpleton *n.* fool, nincompoop, idiot, imbecile, numskull, naif, gull, blockhead, ninny, natural, dolt, oaf, dullard, dupe, moron, jerk (*Slang*), boob (*Slang*), simp (*Slang*), klutz (*Slang*).

ant. intellect, brain, sage, savant, genius, intellectual.

simply *adv.* merely, only, just, purely, solely, but, at most, alone, barely, exclusively.

simulacrum *n.* SIMULATION.

simulate *v.* imitate, pretend, put on, affect, feign, counterfeit, dissemble, assume, sham, disguise, fabricate, invent, misrepresent, play.

simulated *adj.* ARTIFICIAL.

simulation *n.* model, mockup, imitation, reproduction, counterfeit, facsimile, copy, likeness, simulacrum, fake, dummy, pretense, dry run.

simultaneous *adj.* concurrent, contemporaneous, synchronous, synchronic, coincident, coexistent, contemporary, coeval, concomitant, attendant, accompanying.

ant. diachronous, diachronic, staggered, distant.

sin *n.* **1** *sinful act:* transgression, offense, wrong, wrongdoing, trespass, iniquity, vice, crime. **2** *sinful condition:* wickedness, unrighteousness, depravity, immorality, evil, guilt, dishonor, disgrace, infamy, opprobrium, shame, delinquency, damnation. —*v.* err, transgress, trespass, stray, fall, offend.

ant. *n.* **1** virtue, good deed, *mitzvah.* **2** righteousness, piety, rectitude, redemption, absolution, innocence, grace.

sincere *adj.* honest, genuine, single-hearted, earnest, heartfelt, unaffected, wholehearted, unfeigned, candid, straightforward, open, true, trustworthy, real, hearty.

ant. hypocritical, insincere, two-faced, deceitful, Janus-faced, simulated, counterfeit.

sincerity *n.* honesty, genuineness, candor, probity, truthfulness, frankness, openness, ingenuousness, guilelessness, artlessness, earnestness.

ant. hypocrisy, dishonesty, insincerity, duplicity, double-dealing, disingenuousness.

sinew *n.* STRENGTH.

sinewy *adj.* **1** stringy, fibrous, tough, elastic, thready, springy. **2** strong, brawny, powerful, strapping, sturdy, muscular, vigorous, robust, wiry.

ant. **1** tender, soft, pulpy, juicy, mushy. **2** weak, flabby, soft, delicate, flaccid.

sinful *adj.* wicked, bad, immoral, miscreant, evil, peccant, mischievous, vicious, corrupt, depraved, unholy, ungodly, heinous, iniquitous, unrighteous.

ant. good, moral, saintly, spotless, righteous, pure.

sing *v.* carol, trill, warble, lilt, chant, intone, hum, yodel.

singe *v.* scorch, sear, burn, char, brand, toast, grill, parch, cauterize.

singer *n.* songster, caroler, crooner, chorister, soloist, minstrel, vocalist, cantor, chanteuse, lark, nightingale, diva.

single *adj.* **1** unitary, individual, whole, simple, singular, unmixed, particular, one, only. **2** solitary, lone, alone, separate, isolated, sole, only, unique, discrete. **3** unmarried, unwed, unattached, bachelor, maiden, celibate, maidenly, spinsterish. —*n.* SINGLETON.

ant. **1** composite, mixed, conglomerate, blended, manifold. **2** accompanied, attended, many, numerous, surrounded. **3** wed, married, coupled, mated, espoused.

single-hearted *adj.* SINCERE.

single-minded *adj.* determined, resolved, faithful, unswerving, inflexible, steadfast, zealous, dogged, monomaniacal, unwavering, implacable, tireless, adamant, stubborn, firm, intense, devoted, obdurate.

ant. irresolute, inconstant, indecisive, vacillating, fickle.

single out choose, select, decide on, fix on, prefer, fancy, pick, distinguish, signalize, spotlight, separate, extricate, co-opt, cull, winnow.

ant. ignore, slight, overlook, disregard, pass over, neglect.

singleton *n.* single, unit, one, ace, loner,

integer, individual, entity, monad, unity.

ant. group, crowd, multitude, many, multiple, myriad.

singular *adj.* **1** unique, separate, individual, unparalleled, single, exceptional, distinctive, peculiar, discrete. **2** extraordinary, remarkable, uncommon, odd, unusual, curious, bizarre, fantastic, strange, conspicuous, noticeable, outré, out-of-the-way.

ant. 1 common, plentiful, nondescript, universal, multiple, numerous, fungible. **2** ordinary, everyday, familiar, normal, usual, commonplace.

sinister *adj.* malevolent, evil, inauspicious, malign, pernicious, noxious, baleful, disastrous, ominous, threatening, menacing, unlucky, corrupt, miscreant.

ant. fortunate, auspicious, promising, benign, salutary, good.

sink *v.* **1** submerge, immerse, drown, permeate, penetrate. **2** *go down or become less:* decrease, dwindle, lessen, dip, de-escalate, fall, depreciate, plummet, plunge. **3** *pass into a specified state:* lapse, subside, slump, decline, recede, fade, settle. **4** *decline in quality or condition:* retrogress, degenerate, deteriorate, descend, lose ground, disintegrate, debase, degrade. **5** defeat, ruin, overwhelm, founder, fail, collapse, finish. —*n.* **1** basin, washstand, bowl, lavatory, washbowl, drain. **2** dive, den, pit, joint (*Slang*), skid row (*Slang*).

ant. *v.* **1** float, surface, rise, sail, glide. **2** increase, grow, soar, rise, appreciate. **3** emerge, come out of, issue, escape, recover. **4** improve, reform, gain ground, elevate, ameliorate. **5** rescue, raise, help, extricate, save.

sinless *adj.* GUILTLESS.

sinner *n.* evildoer, wrongdoer, reprobate, transgressor, backslider, miscreant, delinquent, offender, malefactor, apostate.

ant. saint, model, exemplar.

sinuate *adj.* SINUOUS. —*v.* WIND.[2]

sinuous *adj.* **1** winding, undulating, tortuous, serpentine, sinuate, meandering, curved, wavy, twisted, labyrinthine, mazelike, mazy. **2** devious, indirect, roundabout, ellliptical, intricate, convoluted, erratic, oblique, complex.

ant. 1 straight, rigid, jagged, unbending, angular. **2** straightforward, foursquare, undeviating, direct, unswerving, bluff.

sip *v.* nip, tipple, sup, imbibe, taste, savor, lap, slurp (*Slang*), sample, suck.

sire *v.* beget, procreate, breed, get, engender, generate, father, propagate, multiply, spawn, inseminate.

siren *n.* charmer, seductress, temptress, witch, vampire, sexpot (*Slang*), vamp (*Slang*), Circe, Lorelei. —*adj.* SEDUCTIVE.

sissy *n.* milksop, mollycoddle, weakling, coward, milquetoast, softy, mama's boy, chicken (*Slang*), pantywaist (*Slang*), pansy (*Slang*). —*adj.* cowardly, weak, timid, effeminate, pusillanimous, soft, unmanly, effete, chicken (*Slang*).

ant. *n.* macho, he-man, buck, bull, jock (*Slang*). *adj.* manly, aggressive, tough, macho, red-blooded, plucky.

sit *v.* **1** crouch, perch, roost, rest, settle, squat. **2** meet, convene, assemble, deliberate, gather, congregate.

site *n.* place, spot, scene, location, locale, position, station, post, point, locus, whereabouts, area, arena, locality, lot.

sit in on join, participate, attend, take part, cooperate, have a hand in, observe, listen, visit.

ant. eschew, avoid, keep one's distance, disdain.

sitting duck TARGET.

situate *v.* locate, place, install, establish, put, plant, set, post, lodge, settle, house, billet.

ant. vacate, remove, depart, withdraw, retire, decamp.

situated *adj.* located, set, established,

sited, positioned, installed, founded, perched, placed, planted, nestling.

situation *n.* **1** position, location, whereabouts, bearings, lay, arrangement, disposition, orientation. **2** place, spot, locality, site, locale, point, area. **3** predicament, plight, dilemma, condition, state of affairs, station, status, ball game, circumstances, spot, fix, hole. **4** employment, post, position, appointment, office, job, station, place.

sixth sense INTUITION.

sizable *adj.* considerable, substantial, ample, generous, goodly, tidy, biggish, largish, respectable, tolerable, decent, reasonable, economy-sized, king-size.
ant. small, inconsequential, paltry, trifling, piddling, miserable.

size *n.* **1** magnitude, dimensions, extent, bulk, proportions, mass, scope, volume, range, area. **2** bigness, largeness, immensity, vastness, greatness, massiveness, ampleness, enormousness, substantiality. —*v.* rank, range, calibrate, graduate, gauge, measure, classify, catalog, sort.
ant. *n.* **2** smallness, tininess, dwarfism, littleness, slightness.

size up EVALUATE.

sizzle *v.* hiss, frizzle, fry, fizzle, crackle, sputter, splutter, spit.

skedaddle *v.* bolt, flee, scamper, skitter, scoot, sprint, skip, scurry, scuttle, scud, rush, hasten, hie, hurry, scat, get lost (*Slang*), bug out (*Slang*).
ant. loiter, delay, lag, dawdle, creep, idle.

skein *n.* coil, hank, twist, braid, plait, strand, tress, rope, clump, tangle, knot.

skeleton *n.* **1** framework, chassis, scaffolding, scaffold, husk, support, basis, frame, shell. **2** sketch, outline, diagram, draft, design, summary, essentials, basics, fundamentals.

skeptic *n.* doubter, agnostic, sceptic, freethinker, unbeliever, rationalist, atheist, infidel, apostate, pagan, heathen.

ant. believer, devotee, follower, adherent, zealot.

skeptical *adj.* doubtful, suspicious, incredulous, cynical, questioning, disbelieving, unbelieving, dubious, quizzical, agnostic, unconvinced.
ant. confident, credulous, gullible, believing, sure, certain.

sketch *n.* **1** design, draft, drawing, cartoon, outline, profile, delineation. **2** outline, summary, plan, description, brief, compendium, paragraph, skeleton, note. —*v.* draw, draft, outline, delineate, rough, block out, trace, depict, design, portray, represent, limn.

sketchy *adj.* crude, rough, brief, perfunctory, superficial, unfinished, unpolished, slight, incomplete, hasty, cursory, slipshod, meager, inadequate, imperfect, rough, makeshift, skeletal.
ant. careful, thorough, exhaustive, comprehensive, full, complete.

skew *v.* misrepresent, distort, slant, warp, bias, twist, weight, garble, exaggerate, incline, predispose.

skid *v.* slide, slip, skitter, sideslip, glide, skim, glissade, toboggan, coast, skate, shoot, glance. —*n.* PLATFORM.

skid row *Slang* SLUM.

skill *n.* **1** *ability or proficiency in general:* ability, aptitude, expertise, proficiency, address, cleverness, elegance, sophistication, dexterity, competence, knack. **2** *specific ability or job:* art, craft, job, métier, trade, calling, handicraft, forte, vocation.

skilled *adj.* SKILLFUL.

skillful *adj.* expert, adept, skilled, competent, masterly, practiced, drilled, versed, proficient, adroit, deft, able, sophisticated, capable, polished, dexterous, ambidextrous, cunning, clever.
ant. unskilled, clumsy, bungling, inept, awkward, unqualified.

skim *v.* **1** top, cream, scrape, sweep, separate, brush off. **2** skip, bounce, ricochet, skid, graze, scoot, glance. **3**

scan, glance at, dip into, flip through, leaf, read.

ant. 3 peruse, scrutinize, pour over.

skimp *v.* SCRIMP.

skimpy *adj.* scanty, insufficient, scrimpy, meager, scant, inadequate, exiguous, paltry, deficient, sparse, spare, small, thin.

ant. ample, copious, abundant, profuse, adequate, plentiful.

skin *n.* **1** integument, pelt, hide, coat, slough, dermis, corium, epidermis. **2** rind, covering, husk, pellicle, veneer, crust, integument, hull, coating, membrane. —*v.* **1** peel, flay, decorticate, exoriate, bark, husk, pare, strip, scrape, uncover. **2** CHEAT.

skin-deep *adj.* SUPERFICIAL.

skinflint *v.* miser, niggard, scrooge, curmudgeon, moneybags (*Slang*), usurer, hoarder, tightwad (*Slang*), loan shark, Shylock.

ant. spendthrift, wastrel, prodigal, philanthropist, altruist, donor.

skinny *adj.* thin, lean, underweight, emaciated, gaunt, lanky, spare, lank, rawboned, scrawny, shrunken, shriveled, slight, wiry.

ant. fleshy, obese, plump, stout, heavy, fat.

skip *v.* **1** hop, jump, caper, prance, frisk, leap, bound, gambol. **2** ricochet, skitter, flip, bounce, skim, skid, glance. **3** decamp, bolt, skedaddle, scamper, scoot, quit, sprint, flee, leave, get away, bug out (*Slang*). —*n.* hop, bound, leap, spring, gambol, caper, jump, step, trip, prance, frisk.

ant. *v.* **3** lag, delay, stay, hesitate, dawdle, loiter, hang around.

skipper *n.* MASTER.

skirmish *n.* scrimmage, disagreement, set-to, dispute, encounter, scuffle, brush, tussle, clash, argument, spat, incident, contretemps, bout, collision. —*v.* scuffle, tussle, encounter, dispute, brush, collide, scrimmage, clash, conflict, engage, combat, contest, struggle, contend.

skirt *n.* margin, border, edge, rim,

verge, periphery, perimeter, fringe, purlieu, limit, confine. —*v.* avoid, detour, bypass, go around, evade, circumvent, duck, dodge, feint.

ant. *v.* embrace, seek out, meet, welcome, challenge, confront.

skit *n.* sketch, travesty, take-off, parody, burlesque, farce, lampoon, curtain raiser, act, turn.

skitter *v.* SKID.

skittish *adj.* edgy, nervous, tense, jittery, jumpy, fidgety, on edge, restless, anxious, uneasy, restive, shy, timid, timorous, uptight (*Slang*).

ant. relaxed, calm, sedate, confident, stolid, phlegmatic.

skulduggery *n.* dishonesty, trickery, underhandedness, flimflam, deception, treachery, fraud, fraudulence, mischief, duplicity, swindle, machination, craft, thievery, robbery.

ant. rectitude, honesty, square shooting, probity, honor, integrity.

skulk *v.* sneak, slink, lurk, prowl, pussyfoot, steal, loiter, ambush, shadow, hover, hide.

skunk *n.* blackguard, scoundrel, bounder, rotter, cur, rat (*Slang*), louse (*Slang*), swine, cad, stinker, rascal, knave, rogue.

skyrocket *v.* shoot up, zoom, vault, rocket, mushroom, catapult, leap, ascend, mount, soar, explode, take off, spiral.

ant. plummet, dive, drop, plunge, dip, fall.

slab *n.* slice, plank, plinth, block, hunk, chunk, board, puncheon, panel, plate.

slack *adj.* **1** loose, limp, relaxed, listless, flabby, flaccid, lax, untied. **2** careless, negligent, neglectful, heedless, remiss, slovenly, slow, lax, permissive. **3** *not busy:* sluggish, slow, idle, dull, quiet, dormant, quiescent, dilatory. —*n.* **1** give, leeway, play, stretch, latitude, scope, room, looseness, excess. **2** inactivity, dormancy, quiescence, ebb tide, slowdown, cessation, indolence, laziness.

ant. *adj.* **1** tense, tight, taut, inflexible, rigid. **2** careful, strict, conscientious, attentive, rigorous. **3** brisk, busy, active, bustling, pressing. *n.* **1** tension, tightness, tautness, pull, traction. **2** activity, bustle, rush, exertion, liveliness.

slacken *v.* slow up, relax, abate, let up, lessen, flag, diminish, delay, retard, detain, brake, moderate, modify. **ant.** quicken, hasten, intensify, expedite, pick up.

slacker *n.* SHIRKER.

slake *v.* quench, allay, abate, extinguish, assuage, moderate, satisfy, sate, satiate, appease, decrease, lessen, slacken. **ant.** inflame, excite, stimulate, arouse, exacerbate, increase.

slam *v.* **1** shut, clap, bang, push, dash, crash. **2** *Slang* punch, wallop, smack, whack, swat, thwack, bang, strike, sock (*Slang*), crack. **3** CRITICIZE.

slander *n.* denigration, disparagement, vilification, obloquy, calumny, scurrility, libel, aspersion, detraction, smear, defamation, scandal, backbiting, odium. —*v.* defame, injure, libel, denigrate, calumniate, malign, discredit, backbite, smear, traduce, vilify, revile, disparage, asperse, detract. **ant.** *n.* eulogy, commendation, praise, defense, approval, applause. *v.* praise, commend, extol, laud, eulogize, defend.

slanderous *adj.* calumnious, defamatory, libelous, malicious, vituperative, scandalous, scurrilous, disparaging, maligning, aspersive, detractive, denigratory, depreciatory, deprecatory, damaging. **ant.** commendatory, eulogistic, laudatory, complimentary, flattering.

slang *n.* argot, jargon, cant, patois, lingo, patter, jive (*Slang*), lingua franca, pidgin English, gobbedygook.

slant *v.* **1** slope, incline, tilt, tip, list, pitch, bend, lean, skew, cant. **2** color, bias, prejudice, angle, distort, influence, twist, weight, lean, tend. —*n.*

1 incline, pitch, grade, inclination, slope, rise, ramp, tilt, diagonal, angle, gradient. **2** attitude, bias, viewpoint, point of view, opinion, judgment, leaning, reaction, view, emphasis, angle, tilt. **ant.** *n.* **1** level, flat, plane, horizontal.

slanting *adj.* sloping, oblique, diagonal, slantwise, atilt, askew, inclined, canted, skewed, listing, aslant. **ant.** straight, normal, perpendicular, vertical, square, foursquare.

slantwise *adj.* SLANTING.

slap *n.* **1** blow, cuff, whack, thwack, smack, clap, pat. **2** insult, rebuff, snub, crack, thrust, cut, criticism, rebuke, reprimand, put-down (*Slang*). —*v.* strike, smack, spank, swat, smite, clap, pat, hit, paddle, tap.

slap-dash *adj.* CARELESS.

slap-happy *adj. Slang* SILLY.

slash *v.* **1** cut, gash, slice, slit, lacerate, mutilate, lash, sever, sunder, cleave, rive. **2** reduce, decrease, pare, drop, lower, abridge, cut, abbreviate, curtail, diminish. —*n.* cut, gash, slit, slice, tear, swath, incision, jag, cleft, hack, rip, nick, snip, blaze. **ant.** *v.* **2** increase, raise, enlarge, augment, magnify.

slat *n.* lath, strip, scantling, stave, rib, strut, timber, paling, picket, board, slab.

slate *n.* ballot, list, ticket, roster, register, catalog, roll.

slattern *n.* drab, sloven, frump, trollop, dowdy, slut, draggle-tail, slob (*Slang*). **ant.** fashion plate, belle, clotheshorse (*Slang*).

slatternly *adj.* untidy, dowdy, frowzy, sluttish, sloppy, messy, slovenly, slipshod, dirty, careless, lax, disorderly. **ant.** tidy, immaculate, spruce, smart, well-groomed, trim.

slaughter *n.* massacre, carnage, murder, bloodshed, pogrom, holocaust, genocide, butchery, killing, homicide, slaying, liquidation, blood bath. —*v.* **1** *of animals:* butcher, kill, destroy, put away, sacrifice. **2** *of* *humans:* massacre, butcher, decimate, liquidate, cut down, immolate, annihilate, exterminate, slay, kill, assassinate, waste (*Slang*).

slaughterhouse *n.* shambles, abattoir, butchery.

slave *n.* **1** bondman, thrall, serf, bondservant, peon, vassal, helot, chattel. **2** addict, fiend, prey, captive, victim. **3** drudge, menial, toiler, servitor, workhorse, hack, servant. —*v.* toil, drudge, work, sweat, labor, travail, plod, grind, moil, overwork.

ant. *v.* rest, idle, dally, laze, loaf, shirk.

slaver *v.* DROOL. —*n.* SALIVA.

slavery *n.* toil, drudgery, sweat, labor, travail, work, grind, hardship, struggle, treadmill, moil, exploitation.

ant. freedom, ease, idleness, leisure, rest, relaxation.

slavey *n. Brit.* DRUDGE.

slavish *adj.* **1** servile, subservient, menial, submissive, obsequious, fawning, abject, cringing, sycophantic. **2** imitative, unoriginal, unimaginative, emulative, literal, derivative.

ant. **1** free, overbearing, domineering, exalted, independent. **2** original, independent, creative, ingenious, unique.

slay *v.* slaughter, murder, kill, massacre, butcher, assassinate, dispatch, execute, exterminate, do away with, do in (*Slang*), rub out (*Slang*), knock off (*Slang*).

sleazy *adj.* shoddy, shabby, cheap, pinchbeck, third-rate, trashy, inferior, meretricious, flimsy, gimcrack, schlock (*Slang*).

ant. superior, first-rate, choice, expensive, genuine.

sleek *adj.* **1** smooth, glossy, silky, velvety, satiny, shiny, oily. **2** smooth-spoken, polished, suave, ingratiating, unctuous, slick, glib, urbane. —*v.* GLOSS OVER.

ant. **1** rough, dull, lackluster, coarse, drab. **2** blunt, clumsy, loutish, gauche, outspoken.

sleep *n.* slumber, dormancy, hibernation, repose, nap, siesta, snooze, doze, shut-eye (*Slang*), rest, unconsciousness, narcosis. —*v.* slumber, doze, drowse, nap, snooze, rest, repose, hibernate, turn in, nod, snore.

ant. *n.* sleeplessness, wakefulness, insomnia, restlessness.

sleepless *adj.* wakeful, insomniac, wide-awake, restless, astir, alert, vigilant.

ant. sleepy, drowsy, tired, somnolent, slumberous.

sleepwalker *n.* somnambulist, noctambulist.

sleepy *adj.* **1** drowsy, nodding, somnolent, tired, weary, slumberous, yawning. **2** lethargic, slumberous, inactive, torpid, languid, indolent, sluggish, dull, costive.

ant. **1** wakeful, open-eyed, alert, keyed up, wide-awake. **2** active, alert, energetic, awake, swift.

sleight of hand prestidigitation, legerdemain, jugglery, conjuring, trickery, palming, hocus-pocus, deception, magic.

slender *adj.* **1** narrow, thin, spindly, light, small, lank, tenuous, fine. **2** rangy, slim, skinny, thin, lean, slight, wiry, spare, meager. **3** SLIM.

ant. **1** thick, broad, bulky, wide, solid, large. **2** stocky, stout, squat, dumpy, pudgy, roly-poly.

sleuth *n.* detective, private eye, private investigator, operative, undercover agent, plainclothesman, G-man, snoop, shadow, dick (*Slang*), Sherlock Holmes.

slice *n.* **1** piece, collop, cut, rasher, shaving, chop, chip, slab. **2** share, portion, segment, section, part, percentage, cut, dividend, divvy (*Slang*). —*v.* cut off, sever, skive, pare, divide, section, part, segment, shave, shred, whittle, subdivide.

slick *adj.* **1** slippery, smooth, sleek, glossy, shiny, unctuous, oily. **2** facile, superficial, plausible, glib, shallow, pat, specious, sophistical. **3** clever, deft, adept, skillful, professional, sophisticated, smart, foxy, sharp, wily. **ant. 1** rough, scaly, coarse, abrasive, wrinkled. **2** genuine, deep-seated, authentic, essential, intrinsic. **3** clumsy, backward, naive, dull, innocent.

slide *v.* **1** slip, glide, skid, toboggan, slither, coast, shoot. **2** drift, pass, lapse, elapse, slip away, go. —*n.* **1** glissade, glide, skid, slither, slip, skim, sweep, flow. **2** transparency.

slight *adj.* **1** minor, unimportant, paltry, trifling, trivial, fleeting, insignificant, modest. **2** slender, wispy, slim, spare, petite, thin, meager. **3** frail, fragile, flimsy, rickety, weak, ramshackle, unstable, delicate. —*v.* **1** snub, insult, slur, reject, affront, rebuff, high-hat, scorn, disdain, cold-shoulder, disregard, neglect, condescend. **2** shirk, slur over, scamp, neglect, skimp. —*n.* snub, insult, neglect, disregard, slur, affront, disrespect, indignity, rebuff, discourtesy, incivility, cut. **ant.** *adj.* **1** major, serious, important, considerable, severe. **2** big, stout, ponderous, massive, hulking, hefty. **3** substantial, solid, stable, sturdy, strong. *v.* **1** cherish, court, acclaim, greet, esteem. **2** heed, attend, take pains. *n.* compliment, courtesy, attention, greeting, civility, favor.

slim *adj.* **1** narrow, thin, slender, thready, filamentous, skinny, spare, slight, attenuated. **2** trivial, slight, negligible, small, meager, modest, slender, tenuous, poor, minuscule. —*v.* slenderize, reduce, lose, attenuate, narrow, contract, taper. **ant.** *adj.* **1** stout, chunky, thick, broad, wide. **2** abundant, large, substantial, liberal, copious. *v.* fatten, broaden, gain, swell.

slime *n.* muck, ooze, gumbo, mire, sludge, mud, silt, seepage, leakage, gunk, clay, guck (*Slang*).

slimy *adj.* **1** oozy, slippery, viscous, mucky, mucous, gooey, ropy, sludgy.

2 filthy, foul, vile, loathsome, nasty, offensive, obnoxious, repulsive, disgusting. **ant. 1** dry, powdery, gritty, sandy, solid. **2** pure, wholesome, attractive, clean.

sling *v.* fling, hurl, throw, heave, toss, pitch, cast, shy, chuck, catapult, hurtle, put.

slink *v.* creep, steal, sneak, skulk, prowl, lurk, pussyfoot, tiptoe.

slinky *adj.* **1** sneaking, stealthy, furtive, skulking, sly, secretive, covert, surreptitious, conspiratorial. **2** *Slang* sinuous, feline, sleek, fluid, smooth, velvety, gliding, flowing, undulating. **ant. 1** open, frank, candid, aboveboard, straightforward.

slip *v.* **1** slide, push, slither, glide. **2** fall, trip, spin, sideslip, tumble, lurch, skid, take a spill, lose one's footing, take a header. **3** slip up, err, trip, mistake, blunder, go wrong, fluff, nod. **4** steal, sidle, creep, slink, skulk, insinuate oneself.

slippery *adj.* **1** smooth, glassy, slick, lubricious, icy, oily, greasy. **2** unreliable, elusive, tricky, fickle, capricious, deceitful, devious, crafty, wily, unpredictable. **ant. 2** reliable, dependable, constant, straightforward, steadfast.

slipshod *adj.* slovenly, sloppy, careless, untidy, messy, unkempt, slatternly, haphazard, negligent, hit-or-miss, makeshift, heedless, remiss, lax. **ant.** neat, careful, well-groomed, tidy, immaculate, spruce.

slip-up *n.* MISTAKE.
slip up BLUNDER.

slit *n.* opening, slash, tear, cut, gash, cleft, fissure, crack, split, crevice, chink, trench, incision. —*v.* slash, gash, cut, incise, rive, sever, rend, cleave, divide, sunder, split, slice, snip. **ant.** *v.* join, close, mend, splice, knit, stitch.

slither *v.* glide, slink, slip, slide, wriggle, writhe, twist, snake.

sliver *n.* splinter, slip, fragment, splint, flake, chip, snippet, shard, shred, shaving.

slob *n. Slang* sloven, slattern, lout, pig, litterer, litterbug, tatterdemalion, boor, dowdy, oaf.

slobber *v.* drivel, drool, slabber, slaver, slop, dribble, salivate.

slog *v.* PLOD.

slogan *n.* catchword, motto, shibboleth, watchword, battle cry, saying, war cry, byword, tag line, trademark, jingle, chant.

slop *v.* splash, spill, spatter, splatter, slosh, spray, overflow. —*n.* slush, mush, slosh, sludge, mire, mud, muck, goo, ooze, slime.

slope *v.* slant, incline, lean, cant, list, tip, tilt, skew, pitch, angle, bend. —*n.* incline, ramp, slant, inclination, tilt, cant, gradient, bevel, diagonal, bias, grade, declivity, rise, scarp, bank, hillside.
   ant. *n.* horizontal, level, plane, flat, plain.

sloping *adj.* SLANTING.

sloppy *adj.* **1** slushy, splashy, wet, watery, spattered, splashed, pulpy, sludgy, squashy. **2** *of appearance:* messy, slovenly, careless, frowzy, dowdy, tacky, smeary, dirty, untidy. **3** *of quality:* slipshod, third-rate, careless, poor, hit-or-miss, subpar, remiss, substandard.
   ant. 1 dry, drained, clear, clean, firm. **2** tidy, careful, trim, immaculate, neat. **3** up to snuff, first-rate, meticulous, painstaking.

slosh *v.* SPLASH. —*n.* SLUSH.

slot *n.* **1** slit, aperture, orifice, opening, passage, socket, groove, trench, recess, notch, chink. **2** position, place, niche, space, line, opening, vacancy.

sloth *n.* laziness, indolence, idleness, inactivity, inertia, languor, lassitude, listlessness, lethargy, sluggishness, torpor, passivity, slackness.
   ant. activity, exertion, eagerness, liveliness, industry, energy.

slothful *adj.* lazy, indolent, sluggish, shiftless, idle, slack, torpid, inert, in-active, listless, passive, languid, supine, lax, drowsy, costive.
   ant. industrious, busy, active, strenuous, energetic, lively.

slouch *v.* stoop, shamble, slump, hunch, droop, bend, shuffle, lumber, hobble, drag, lean. —*n.* **1** stoop, crouch, slump, hunch, droop, sag. **2** lout, bungler, clod, incompetent, good-for-nothing, ne'er-do-well, sluggard, drone, bumbler, stumblebum.

slough[1] *n.* swamp, marsh, bog, fen, mire, bottoms, backwater, moor, pond, sump, slue.

slough[2] *v.* **1** *by natural development:* shed, molt, cast off, doff, throw off, desquamate. **2** *by choice:* discard, junk, scrap, throw away, doff, forsake, jettison, break, kick (*Slang*).
   ant. 2 keep, retain, conserve, reuse, save, continue.

sloven *n.* slattern, slob (*Slang*), frump, drab, draggle-tail, slut, ragamuffin, pig, tatterdemalion, trollop.

slovenly *adj.* untidy, careless, sloppy, unkempt, slatternly, slipshod, frowzy, sluttish, messy, unclean, dowdy, disorderly, lax, undisciplined, slipshod.
   ant. neat, tidy, careful, fastidious, spruce, trim.

slow *adj.* **1** tardy, belated, late, overdue, delayed, laggard, behindhand, in arrears. **2** deliberate, measured, leisurely, gradual, unhurried, moderate, prolonged, lingering. **3** dull, stupid, retarded, backward, obtuse, simple, simple-minded, dense, thick, slow-witted, dimwitted, obtuse, fatuous, dumb. **4** inactive, slack, sluggish, faltering, hesitant, lagging, dull, declining. —*v.* delay, detain, slacken, moderate, check, inhibit, impede, hold back, retard, brake, decelerate, obstruct, restrain, arrest, hinder.
   ant. *adj.* **1** fast, early, punctual, beforehand, premature. **2** hasty, speedy, swift, hurried, rapid. **3** quick, bright, smart, alert, intelligent. **4** brisk, animated, busy, lively,

active. *v.* speed up, hasten, hurry, expedite, advance, accelerate.

sludge *n.* mire, ooze, mud, goo, muck, slush, sediment, residuum, alluvium, slop, slime, gumbo.

slue *n.* SLOUGH.¹

slug *v.* smite, wallop, pommel, lay into, clout, pound, ram, batter, thrash, smash, belt, punch, strike, sock (*Slang*).

sluggard *n.* lazybones, drone, do-nothing, slug, loafer, snail, idler, lounger, slugabed, goldbrick (*Slang*). —*adj.* SLUGGISH.

ant. go-getter, live wire, hustler, doer, worker.

sluggish *adj.* torpid, inactive, sluggard, lazy, slothful, indolent, slack, inert, languid, costive, passive, listless, lax, idle, unresponsive.

ant. active, brisk, industrious, lively, busy, energetic.

slum *n.* skid row, warren, ghetto, inner city, shanty town, depressed area.

slumber *v., n.* SLEEP.

slumberous *adj.* SLEEPY.

slump *v.* **1** fail, fall, crash, collapse, sink, cave in, crumple, drop, subside, sag. **2** slouch, stoop, droop, hunch, crouch, bend, lean, hump. —*n.* decline, collapse, depression, recession, plunge, tumble, drop, dip, low, trough, failure.

slur *v.* **1** slight, disparage, depreciate, calumniate, slander, deprecate, asperse, traduce, reproach, put down (*Slang*). **2** skimp, slight, scamp, skip, ignore, scant, disregard, overlook. **3** mumble, mutter, mouth, garble, mispronounce. —*n.* disparagement, detraction, innuendo, slight, smear, slander, insinuation, belittling, reproach, affront, insult, put-down (*Slang*).

ant. *v.* **1** command, praise, eulogize, laud, compliment. **2** take care, attend to, stress, emphasize, assert. *n.* compliment, commendation, praise, eulogy, homage, honor.

slush *n.* slosh, slop, sludge, mire, ooze, mush, muck, goo, mud, slime, snow, alluvium.

slut *n.* **1** slattern, sloven, frump, draggle-tail, dowdy, slob (*Slang*). **2** whore, prostitute, harlot, call girl, doxy, strumpet, trollop, cocotte, courtesan, demimondaine, street walker, Paphian, floozy (*Slang*).

sly *adj.* **1** secret, artful, stealthy, dissembling, covert, surreptitious, underhand, evasive, veiled, sneaky. **2** crafty, foxy, disingenuous, tricky, artful, clever, roguish, wily, cunning, Machiavellian.

ant. **1** open, candid, frank, aboveboard, sincere. **2** naive, ingenuous, guileless, artless, innocent, honest.

smack¹ *n.* slap, clap, crack, blow, stroke, hit, rap, cuff, whack, thwack, sock (*Slang*), fillip, buffet, biff (*Slang*), box, whack. —*v.* **1** *deliver a sounding blow:* slap, crack, slam, plop, clap, plunk, crash, hit, whack, biff (*Slang*), sock (*Slang*), strike, snap. **2** *make a smacking noise:* sip, kiss, slap, squish, pop, snap, slurp (*Slang*), suck, lap, crackle. —*adv.* directly, exactly, pointblank, plump, spang, smack-dab, precisely, squarely, right, straight, plainly.

smack² *v.* savor, taste, smell, betoken, suggest, betray, reveal, resemble, approximate, approach, embody, imply, manifest, testify to, evince.

smacking *adj.* BRISK.

small *adj.* **1** little, diminutive, tiny, miniature, minute, wee, petite, Lilliputian, dwarfish, pocket-sized, vest-pocket, mini. **2** unimportant, minor, light, insignificant, modest, slight, trifling, trivial, inconsiderable, inconsequential, secondary. **3** small-minded, ignoble, mean, sordid, petty, stingy, narrow, narrow-minded, selfish, niggardly, bigoted.

ant. **1** large, big, huge, great, grand. **2** major, important, weighty, considerable, capital. **3** lofty, high-minded, generous, noble, elevated.

small-minded *adj.* petty, intolerant, ungenerous, mean, narrow, bigoted, narrow-minded, opinionated, rigid, limited, paltry, provincial, small. **ant.** generous, lofty, tolerant, magnanimous, high-minded, benevolent.

small potatoes TRIVIA.

small talk GOSSIP.

small-time *adj. Slang* PETTY.

smart *v.* sting, hurt, pain, pierce, prickle, prick, ache, burn, bite, nip. —*adj.* **1** quick, clever, keen, sharp, shrewd, quick-witted, heads-up (*Slang*), alert, intelligent, bright, adroit, adept, canny, prudent, wise, sensible, brainy. **2** harsh, severe, stinging, painful, sharp, keen, pricking. **3** brisk, lively, spry, nimble, vigorous, energetic, active, spirited. **4** fashionable, chic, spruce, trim, dapper, stylish, trig, natty. —*n.* sting, pang, prick, twinge, pain, anguish, affliction, vexation, distress, wound, hurt, affront, insult. **ant.** *v.* soothe, relieve, ease, palliate, comfort. *adj.* **1** stupid, dull, slow, obtuse, simple-minded. **2** mild, gentle, soft, bland, moderate. **3** slow, weak, awkward, halt, handicapped. **4** unkempt, shabby, frowzy, dowdy, untidy. *n.* balm, comfort, anodyne, solace, easement, salve.

smash *v.* **1** shatter, splinter, crash, dash, fling, break, batter, pulverize. **2** flatten, crush, squash, mash, pound, squeeze, tread on, stamp, level. **3** strike, bash, bat, whack, bang, wallop, smack, hit. **4** ruin, wreck, overthrow, devastate, raze, destroy, demolish, lay waste. —*n.* disaster, collapse, ruin, disintegration, downfall, demolition, shattering, obliteration, extinction, havoc, finish. —*adj.* SMASHING. **ant.** *n.* salvation, preservation, restoration, conservation, establishment.

smashing *adj.* impressive, great, outstanding, extraordinary, stupendous, prodigious, matchless, superb, excellent, magnificent, wonderful, overwhelming, smash, undreamt-of. **ant.** wretched, contemptible, worthless, execrable, pitiful, despicable.

smash-up *n.* COLLISION.

smatter *n.* SMATTERING.

smattering *n.* sprinkling, smatter, smidgen, snatch, snippet, scrap, rudiment, dab, trace. **ant.** wealth, depth, breadth, abundance, fund.

smear *v.* **1** smudge, blotch, soil, stain, blot, smirch, dirty, befoul, daub, spread, rub. **2** slander, vilify, denigrate, slur, discredit, besmirch, sully, revile, traduce, blacken, defame. —*n.* **1** spot, stain, daub, splotch, blotch, blot, smudge, smirch, blur. **2** defamation, slander, whispering campaign, mudslinging, character assassination, slur, backbiting, detraction.

smell *v.* stink, reek. —*n.* **1** olfaction, nose. **2** odor, aroma, scent, fragrance, perfume, stench, reek, stink. **3** hint, suggestion, aura, trace, suspicion, whiff, breath, whisper, touch.

smidgen *n.* BIT.

smile *n.* grin, smirk, simper, beam, sneer, rictus. —*v.* grin, smirk, simper, beam. **ant.** *n.* frown, glare, grimace, scowl, lower. *v.* frown, glare, scowl, lower, grimace.

smirch *v.* BESMIRCH. —*n.* STAIN.

smirk *v.* simper, smile, grin, grimace, fleer, ogle, leer. —*n.* simper, grin, ogle, smile, leer. **ant.** *v.* frown, glower, lower, glare, scowl. *n.* frown, glare, scowl.

smite *v.* **1** strike, wallop, slug, slam, hit, buffet, beat, swat, box, punch, hammer, bash. **2** afflict, chasten, scourge, punish, beset, oppress, attack, infest. **ant.** **2** spare, reprieve, let off, forbear, pardon.

smock *n.* duster, coverall, housecoat, overall (*Brit.*), pinafore, apron, overalls.

smooch *v. Slang* KISS.

smooth *adj.* **1** even, level, flat, plane, polished, sleek, unwrinkled, glossy, silky, silken, velvety. **2** unruffled, tranquil, unobstructed, open, gentle, mellifluous, mellifluent, peaceful, un-

troubled, serene, clear, calm. **3** suave, ingratiating, urbane, flattering, insinuating, oily, unctuous, glib, facile, silky, diplomatic, politic. **4** *pleasant-tasting:* bland, mild, soothing, mellow, soft, neutral, gentle, delicate. —*v.* **1** level, flatten, plane, scrape, polish, unwrinkle, sand, iron, press, roll. **2** clear, ease, expedite, facilitate, open, help, promote. **3** calm, mollify, soothe, assuage, alleviate, palliate, tranquilize.
ant. *adj.* **1** wrinkled, gritty, abrasive, uneven, serrated, ridged, corrugated, lumpy. **2** rough, turbulent, stormy, agitated, troubled, uneasy, blocked. **3** stammering, halting, awkward, lame, stumbling. *v.* **1** roughen, rumple, crinkle, furrow, wrinkle, corrugate, serrate, ridge. **2** obstruct, encumber, prevent, hinder, block. **3** aggravate, provoke, annoy, irritate, torment.

smother *v.* **1** suffocate, stifle, asphyxiate, strangle, choke. **2** suppress, disguise, gloss over, mask, muffle, repress, hide, cover up, veil, whitewash.

smudge *v.* smear, soil, smutch, mess up, daub, blot, stain, spot, dirty, mark, blacken. —*n.* smutch, smear, stain, spot, blot, daub, blur, streak, splotch, smirch, mark.

smug *adj.* self-satisfied, complacent, conceited, self-important, self-assured, cocksure, cocky, triumphant, imperturbable, placid, serene.
ant. self-doubting, apologetic, modest, hesitant, sheepish, diffident.

smut *n.* obscenity, pornography, filth, indecency, scatology, ribaldry, prurience, lewdness, suggestiveness, salaciousness, porn (*Slang*).

smutch *v.*, *n.* SMUDGE.

smutty *adj.* OBSCENE.

snack *n.* refreshment, pick-me-up, collation, nosh, tidbit, bite, tea (*Brit.*), coffee break, morsel, mouthful, lunch.

snafu *adj. Slang* confused, muddled, chaotic, anarchic, topsy-turvy, tumultuous, uproarious, disorganized, jumbled, awry, at sixes and sevens.
ant. controlled, efficient, orderly, regulated, organized, manageable.

snag *n.* **1** protuberance, projection, stump, knot, knob, knurl, overhang. **2** obstacle, difficulty, stumblingblock, bottleneck, hindrance, hold-up, barrier, block, catch, trouble.

snail *n.* SLUGGARD.

snake *n.* **1** serpent, reptile, viper, ophidian. **2** traitor, turncoat, Judas, snake in the grass, serpent, sneak, apostate, seducer, evildoer, miscreant, rascal, reptile, double-crosser. —*v.* slither, wriggle, slide, slink, crawl, twist, writhe, glide, creep, wind, meander.
ant. *n.* **2** loyalist, adherent, partyliner.

snaky *adj.* SERPENTINE.

snap *v.* **1** crack, click, pop, split, clink, splinter, crepitate, crackle. **2** snatch, gobble, bite, gnash, nip, lunge, seize, grab. **3** bark, scold, growl, snarl, curse, yell, yap, scream, howl, rap out. **4** collapse, break down, break, crack, give way, fail, go under, sink, come apart, disintegrate, sunder. —*n.* **1** crackling, pop, smack, flip, fillip, crack, crepitation, flick, crackle, susurration, susurrus. **2** lapse, lacuna, fracture, break, crack, slip, gap. **3** zest, vim, zip, energy, vivacity, verve, dash, vigor, ginger, pizzazz (*Slang*). **4** *easy task:* child's play, sinecure, breeze, lark, cinch (*Slang*), picnic (*Slang*), pushover (*Slang*).
ant. *n.* **3** slackness, languor, ennui, stupor, sloth, lassitude. **4** labor, grind, drudgery, toil, burden.

snappish *adj.* surly, captious, censorious, peevish, querulous, touchy, waspish, acrimonious, carping, critical, irascible, testy, tart, splenetic, cross, bilious, ill-natured.
ant. amiable, pleasant, affable, bland, tolerant, good-humored.

snappy *adj.* **1** brisk, energetic, animated, keen, smart, curt, crisp, quick, lively, short. **2** smart, spruce, stylish, chic, natty, jaunty, dapper, trig, modish, fashionable, *à la mode*.

ant. 1 languid, lazy, slow, torpid, dull. **2** shabby, seedy, fusty, threadbare, dowdy.

snare *n*. **1** trap, noose, gin, net, pitfall, seine, springe. **2** ruse, wile, stratagem, trick, catch, subterfuge, come-on (*Slang*). —*v*. ENSNARE.

snarl[1] *n*. growl, grumble, threat, snap, bark, gnash. —*v*. growl, grumble, threaten, menace, gnash, snap, lash out, bark.

snarl[2] *n*. **1** tangle, knot, ravel, muss, kink, tuft, snag. **2** complication, snag, entanglement, fix, difficulty, tie-up, bottleneck, jam, predicament, quandary. —*v*. ENTANGLE.

snatch *v*. seize, clutch, grasp, pluck, reach, tug, lunge, catch, wrest, pull, grab. —*n*. grab, clutch, pounce, grasp, pass, catch, reach, tug, lunge.

sneak *v*. slink, skulk, steal, lurk, prowl, creep, slip. —*n*. snake in the grass, double-dealer, skulker, lurker, dastard, wretch, worm, sneaker, slinker, coward, miscreant, cur. —*adj*. STEALTHY.

sneaky *adj*. sly, cowardly, underhand, stealthy, secretive, surreptitious, furtive, covert, unmanly, dishonorable, yellow, slippery, insidious, double-dealing, disingenuous.

ant. honest, aboveboard, frank, open, reliable, square-shooting.

sneer *n*. grimace, leer, fleer, face, smirk, grin, ogle, scoff. —*v*. jeer, scoff, scorn, deride, ridicule, flout, fleer, taunt, belittle, rail, mock, gibe, contemn.

ant. *v*. flatter, uphold, applaud, approve, defend, support.

snicker *n*. snigger, giggle, smirk, snort, titter, cackle, mock, chuckle, ridicule, laugh. —*v*. snigger, giggle, smirk, cackle, chuckle, snort, titter, laugh, mock.

snide *adj*. malicious, sarcastic, insinuating, disparaging, nasty, mean, low, derisive, derogatory, sneaky, devi-

ous, disingenuous, underhand, slanderous, two-faced.

ant. well-disposed, friendly, sincere, complimentary, candid, favorable.

sniff *v*. **1** sniffle, snuff, snuffle, snort. **2** inhale, breathe, snuff, inspire. —*n*. inhalation, sniffle, snuff, snuffle, gasp, snort.

sniffle *v*., *n*. SNIFF.

snigger *v*., *n*. SNICKER.

snip *v*. clip, cut, shear, scissor, shorten, crop, dock, bob, trim, pare, prune, remove, nip.

snippy *adj*. impertinent, insolent, impudent, flippant, cheeky, saucy, sassy, rude, ill-mannered, presumptuous, smart-alecky, snotty (*Slang*).

ant. polite, deferential, respectful, civil, mannerly.

snit *n*. pique, petulance, pettishness, annoyance, exasperation, agitation, aggravation, frustration, irritation, crankiness, testiness, bad temper.

snitch *Slang v*. **1** STEAL. **2** TATTLE.

snivel *v*. whine, whimper, pule, snuffle, blubber, mewl, fret, kvetch (*Slang*).

snobbish *adj*. patronizing, self-important, haughty, arrogant, pretentious, supercilious, condescending, parvenu, uppity, uppish, hoity-toity, high-hat, smug, cliquish, stuck-up, snotty (*Slang*), snooty.

ant. modest, unpretentious, unassuming, unostentatious.

snoop *v*. PRY.[1] —*n*. BUSYBODY.

snooty *adj*. SNOBBISH.

snooze *v*., *n*. SLEEP.

snort *v*. snuffle, snuff, grunt, honk, puff, huff and puff, whiffle, wheeze, whiff. —*n*. wheeze, snuffle, grunt, honk, snuff, puff, whiff.

snotty *adj*. *Slang* **1** NASTY. **2** SNOBBISH.

snow job *Slang* FLATTERY.

snub *v*. ignore, neglect, disregard, slight, spurn, disdain, cold-shoulder, cut, scorn, ostracize, rebuff, upstage, high-hat, snoot (*Slang*). —*n*. cut, neglect, disregard, slight, rebuff, brush-off, cold shoulder, slap, ostracism, insult, discourtesy.

snuff *v*., *n*. SNIFF.

snuffle v., n. SNIFF.

snuff out put out, extinguish, douse, quench, destroy, terminate, cut short, put an end to.

snug adj. cozy, comfortable, trim, neat, tidy, homey, homelike, comfy, safe, secure, sheltered, private.

snuggle v. nestle, cuddle, curl up, nuzzle, caress, embrace, hug, enfold.

soak v. saturate, steep, wet, drench, douse, immerse, ret, marinate, irrigate, imbue, infuse, wash, dunk, bathe. —n. bath, drenching, dousing, immersion, irrigation, wash, washing, soaking.

soak up take in, absorb, drink in, be receptive to, assimilate, imbibe, devour, be immersed in, be engrossed by, learn, acquire.

soapy adj. lathery, sudsy, foamy, bubbly, saponaceous, frothy, foamy, lathered.

soar v. go aloft, fly, take wing, rise, float, glide, sail, take flight, ascend, wing.

sob v. weep, cry, wail, keen, lament, blubber, boo-hoo, snivel, shed tears, howl, bawl. —n. cry, wail, lament, lamentation, wailing, blubbering, sniveling, bawling, keening.

sober adj. **1** temperate, rational, reasonable, calm, clear-headed, lucid, composed, self-controlled, deliberate, self-possessed, level-headed, circumspect, imperturbable, matter-of-fact. **2** dignified, sedate, staid, prim, subdued, quiet, earnest, proper, correct, straightforward. **3** thoughtful, pensive, solemn, serious, severe, grave, somber, mournful, unsmiling. **ant. 1** intemperate, besotted, muddled, befuddled, crazed. **2** noisy, wanton, undignified, jazzy (*Slang*), boisterous. **3** frivolous, gay, carefree, lighthearted, flighty.

sobriety n. RESTRAINT.

sobriquet n. NAME.

sociable adj. social, outgoing, gregarious, friendly, warm, affable, congenial, neighborly, folksy, clubbable, companionable, amiable, jolly, hospitable, extroverted. **ant.** antisocial, unfriendly, unapproachable, forbidding, misanthropic, introverted.

social adj. **1** group, organizational, communal, common, organized, worldly, societal, sociological, public, popular, mutual, collective, joint, interconnected, interdependent. **2** SOCIABLE.

society n. **1** community, group, populace, people, population, grouping, culture, tribe, country, commonality, commonwealth, folk. **2** *beau monde*, Social Register, upper crust, bluebloods, Four Hundred, the rich, the highborn, plutocracy, elite, upper class, *crème de la crème, haut monde*. **3** organization, association, club, league, alliance, fellowship, fraternity, sorority, circle, company, affiliation, federation, union, guild, gang. **4** comradeship, friendship, companionship, intimacy, amity, fellow-feeling, neighborliness, sociability, social intercourse, companionability, cordiality.

sock v., n. *Slang* SMACK.[1]

socket n. hole, chamber, cavity, recess, hollow, pocket, pit, cup, antrum.

socks n. hose, hosiery, footwear, anklets, knee-highs, half hose, argyles.

sod n. turf, lawn, sward, greensward, green, divot, clod, soil, earth.

sodden adj. drenched, soaked, saturated, wet, soggy, doughy, pasty, sopping, dripping, soft, spongy, boggy, marshy, miry, squashy, lumpy. **ant.** dry, dehydrated, desiccated, crisp, crunchy.

sofa n. couch, divan, davenport, settee, lounge, love seat, day bed, sofa bed, convertible.

soft adj. **1** malleable, pliable, flexible, spongy, doughy, ductile, plastic, supple, yielding, tractable. **2** smooth, silken, delicate, velvety, fleecy, wooly, furry, fuzzy, downy, feathery, satin. **3** gentle, mild, subdued, low, pastel, whispery, modulated, dulcet, caressing, restrained, muffled, murmurous, sweet. **4** sympathetic, tender, compassionate, warmhearted, kind, considerate, humane, softhearted, sentimental, tenderhearted, sensitive, responsive, charitable. **5** flabby, flaccid, unfit, weak, frail, feeble, debilitated, fat, pudgy, untrim, limp, lax, languid. **6** permissive, lenient, lax, indulgent, liberal, overindulgent, forgiving, laissez-faire.

ant. 1 rigid, stiff, hard, fixed, set. **2** rough, coarse, bristly, chapped. **3** fierce, loud, strident, sharp. **4** unfeeling, insensitive, hardhearted, cold. **5** muscular, fit, strong, trim. **6** strict, tough, punitive, disciplinary.

soften v. **1** enervate, enfeeble, debilitate, weaken, impair, exhaust, unnerve, emasculate, unman. **2** mitigate, assuage, temper, moderate, ameliorate, lessen, abate, appease, mollify.

ant. 1 toughen, strengthen, harden, energize, invigorate. **2** irritate, exacerbate, aggravate, intensify, increase.

softhearted adj. compassionate, sympathetic, kind, tender, generous, humane, lenient, indulgent, charitable, sentimental, forgiving, warmhearted.

ant. hardhearted, cold, dispassionate, unfeeling, unsympathetic.

soft-soap v. FLATTER.

soft soap FLATTERY.

soft touch DUPE.

softy n. DUPE.

soggy adj. sodden, drenched, soaked, saturated, wet, sopping, dripping, damp, muggy, clammy, humid.

ant. dry, crisp, moisture-free, dehydrated.

soil[1] n. earth, land, ground, loam, turf, humus, loess, sod, topsoil, subsoil, silt, clay.

soil[2] v. **1** dirty, smudge, begrime, muddy, stain, splotch, smear, mess, bespatter, spot, smutch, tarnish, blacken. **2** disgrace, defile, dishonor, sully, shame, belittle, cheapen, debase, discredit, stain, malign, dam-

age, blacken, besmirch, bespatter, tarnish. —n. spot, stain, smudge, smear, splotch, taint, spatter, splash, blot.

ant. v. **1** clean, cleanse, wash, launder, whiten, polish. **2** purify, restore, glorify, honor.

soirée n. PARTY.

sojourn v. visit, stop at, stop over, stay at, tour, vacation, holiday, weekend, summer, winter. —n. stopover, visit, vacation, holiday, rest, tour, stay, layover.

solace v. comfort, console, alleviate, soothe, condole with, ease, mitigate, ameliorate, soften, calm, reassure, relieve, assuage, cheer, restore, encourage, bolster. —n. comfort, blessing, consolation, reassurance, help, encouragement, boost, support, anodyne, relief, alleviation, mitigation, amelioration, moderation, assuagement.

ant. v. irritate, depress, undermine aggravate. n. irritation, burden, anxiety, worry, setback.

solder v. BIND.

soldier n. **1** serviceman, enlisted man, draftee, recruit, fighter, combatant, warrior, conscript, G.I. **2** follower, loyalist, adherent, partisan, scout, veteran, activist, campaigner, war horse. —v. SHIRK.

sole adj. only, lone, exclusive, separate, particular, single, one, singular, isolated, solitary.

solecism n. BARBARISM.

solemn adj. **1** majestic, awesome, powerful, awe-inspiring, splendid, sobering, sacred, holy, sanctified, grand, sublime, momentous, formidable. **2** serious, earnest, somber, grave, dignified, formal, sincere, thoughtful, melancholy, severe, funereal, sober, grave, staid, sedate.

ant. 2 joyful, light, frivolous, flippant.

solicit v. beg, entreat, ask, plead, clamor, appeal, importune, petition, beseech, supplicate, implore, sue, seek.

solicitation *n.* APPEAL.

solicitous *adj.* **1** concerned, caring, anxious, nervous, regardful, mindful, fearful, apprehensive, watchful, vigilant, uneasy, troubled. **2** eager, avid, interested, desirous, longing, hopeful, impatient, intent, yearning, keen, zealous.

ant. 1 carefree, relaxed, untroubled, nonchalant, unruffled. **2** uninterested, indifferent, undesirous, cool, apathetic.

solid *adj.* **1** firm, hard, fixed, formed, shaped, set, solidified, hardened, rigid, unyielding, inflexible, stiff. **2** well-built, sturdy, sound, secure, stable, substantial, rooted, established, safe, durable, solid, rugged, lasting. **3** serious, reliable, trustworthy, upstanding, honorable, upright, decent, sober, scrupulous, worthy, estimable, honest.

ant. 1 amorphous, soft, fluid, flexible. **2** unsubstantial, insecure, unsound, flimsy, shaky. **3** shady, unreliable, slippery, untrustworthy.

solidify *v.* HARDEN.

solitary *adj.* **1** apart, alone, cloistered, separate, monastic, solo, companionless, hermitic, withdrawn, reclusive, unattended, unaccompanied. **2** lonesome, lonely, forlorn, lorn, abandoned, deserted, friendless, outcast, unloved, desolate, forsaken, unpopular, excluded. **3** single, sole, one, unique, separate, special, only, one and only, exclusive, unmatched, unparalleled, singular. —*n.* HERMIT.

ant. *adj.* **1** social, sociable, gregarious, accompanied. **2** popular, befriended, cherished, included. **3** several, many, multiple.

solitude *n.* seclusion, privacy, retirement, quiet, peace, withdrawal, sequestration, unsociability, aloneness, reclusiveness, solitariness.

ant. sociability, participation, conviviality, gregariousness, companionship.

solo *adj.* unassisted, unaccompanied, unaided, alone, independent, unabet-ted, unsupported, single-handed, one-man, one-woman.

ant. joint, group, communal, shared.

solution *n.* **1** mixture, mix, combination, compound, blend, brew, emulsion, concoction, infusion. **2** explanation, explication, untangling, clarification, interpretation, elucidation, revelation, answer, key.

solve *v.* work out, unravel, unriddle, figure out, analyze, get an answer, see the light, understand, resolve, decipher, riddle, disentangle, penetrate, fathom.

solvent *adj.* SOUND.

somatic *adj.* CORPOREAL.

somber *adj.* dark, gloomy, funereal, depressing, dismal, melancholy, joyless, sepulchral, grim, doleful, mournful, dreary, dolorous, gray, sad.

ant. cheerful, joyous, bright, festive, gay.

somebody *n.* personage, name, V.I.P., notable, bigwig, headliner, heavyweight, celebrity, dignitary, luminary, big wheel (*Slang*), big shot (*Slang*).

ant. nobody, cipher, nothing, nonentity, zero.

sometimes *adv.* occasionally, now and then, from time to time, at times, on and off, once in a while, intermittently, unpredictably, every so often, sporadically, periodically, irregularly.

somnambulist *n.* SLEEPWALKER.

somniferous *adj.* SOPORIFIC.

somnolent *adj.* drowsy, heavy-lidded, sleepy, half-asleep, dozy, droopy, slumberous, torpid, half-awake, semiconscious, in a fog, drugged, soporific, dopey (*Slang*), out of it (*Slang*), yawning, oscitant.

ant. wide-awake, alert, lively, with it (*Slang*), on the qui vive.

song *n.* **1** chanting, lilting, caroling, chirping, vocalizing, warbling, crooning, intoning, singing. **2** melody, lilt, chant, carol, tune, air, refrain, aria, serenade, ballad, lullaby.

soon *adv.* shortly, presently, anon, in a while, before long, ere long, by and by, in a little while, betimes, directly, early on, without delay.

soot *n.* ASHES.

sooth *n.* TRUTH.

soothe *v.* **1** calm, quiet, compose, pacify, tranquilize, lull, settle, placate, relax, reassure, console, solace. **2** allay, lessen, alleviate, reduce, mitigate, ease, soften, temper, moderate, smooth, mollify.
ant. 1 agitate, roil up, stir up, anger, excite. **2** intensify, heighten, exacerbate, aggravate.

soothing *adj.* palliative, lenitive, relieving, alleviative, sedative, assuasive, balmy, emollient, demulcent, healing, helpful, easeful, calming, restful, relaxing.
ant. irritating, exacerbating, hurtful, painful, unnerving.

soothsayer *n.* PROPHET.

sooty *adj.* BLACK.

sop *v.* soak, absorb, sponge, mop, dunk, dip, immerse, wet, drench, wash, drink, douse, saturate, souse, steep. —*n.* concession, bribe, pacifier, indulgence, allowance, compromise, accommodation, relief, balm, hush money (*Slang*).

sophism *n.* FALLACY.

sophisticated *adj.* **1** worldly-wise, worldly, experienced, knowledgeable, cosmopolitan, aware, cultured, urbane, seasoned, blasé, self-assured, knowing. **2** complex, complicated, advanced, intricate, elaborate, involved, subtle, fine, delicate, sensitive, refined.
ant. 1 naive, ingenuous, provincial, inexperienced, sophomoric. **2** obvious, primitive, simple, uncomplicated.

sophomoric *adj.* **1** inane, foolish, silly, pointless, shallow, superficial, infantile, pretentious, self-important, brash, ridiculous. **2** callow, green, immature, inexperienced, unsophisticated, uninformed, juvenile, naive, innocent, fatuous, ingenuous.

ant. 1 sensible, prudent, wise, sound, thoughtful. **2** mature, experienced, worldly, seasoned, sophisticated.

soporific *adj.* **1** sleep-inducing, narcotic, opiate, somniferous, sedative, calming, soothing, tranquilizing, hypnotic, lulling, boring, dull. **2** drowsy, sleepy, somnolent, dozy, heavy-lidded, sedated, slumberous, torpid, narcotized, in a fog, doped up (*Slang*).
ant. 1 stimulating, energizing, invigorating, rousing, exciting. **2** alert, awake, clear-headed, lively, with it (*Slang*).

sopping *adj.* drenched, soaked, dripping, sodden, saturated, soggy, wringing-wet, inundated, soppy.
ant. dry, crisp, moisture-free, dehydrated.

soppy *adj.* SOPPING.

sorcerer *n.* wizard, magician, enchanter, necromancer, exorcist, shaman, medicine man, warlock, witch doctor, miracle worker, mage, magus, spellbinder, Merlin.

sorceress *n.* witch, magician, siren, enchantress, exorcist, miracle worker, fairy, fairy godmother, hex, spellbinder, Circe, Lorelei, Lilith.

sorcery *n.* wizardry, magic, witchcraft, necromancy, diabolism, exorcism, shamanism, spellbinding, enchantment, supernaturalism, alchemy, voodoo.

sordid *adj.* **1** degraded, debauched, vile, base, wicked, evil, impure, immoral, profligate, abandoned, wanton, disreputable, depraved, degenerate, vicious. **2** rundown, squalid, slummy, dirty, ramshackle, grimy, unwashed, unclean, shabby, slovenly, uncared-for, filthy. **3** selfish, mercenary, venal, corrupt, unprincipled, self-seeking, self-serving, mean, shady, avaricious, covetous, grasping, greedy.
ant. 1 pure, decent, moral, respectable. **2** clean, tidy, well-kept, fresh. **3** high-minded, altruistic, generous, unselfish.

sore *n.* **1** lesion, inflammation, irritation, bruise, cut, scrape, ulcer, boil, blister, carbuncle, pustule, pimple. **2** trouble, nuisance, affliction, annoyance, tribulation, curse, vexation, blight, burden, hurt, grief, sting, canker, visitation, plague. —*adj.* **1** painful, irritated, inflamed, infected, tender, feverish, abscessed, festering, red, ulcerous, swollen, bruised, chafed, sensitive, achy, raw. **2** distressed, pained, grieved, put out, put upon, sorrowful, aggrieved, hurt, troubled, unhappy, sad. **3** irritating, distressing, annoying, difficult, troubling, irksome, vexing, touchy, problematic, disagreeable, unpleasant. **4** extreme, crucial, desperate, great, enormous, critical, profound, grievous, severe, grave, acute, imperative, pressing, urgent, decisive. **5** angry, offended, resentful, seething, indignant, hurt, galled, stung, affronted, irate, boiling, mad, miffed, seething.
ant. *n.* **2** joy, pleasure, delight, boon. *adj.* **2, 5** pleased, delighted, happy, relaxed. **3** pleasant, agreeable, delightful. **4** minor, unimportant, ordinary.

sorehead *n.* CRANK.

sorrow *n.* **1** grief, distress, pain, sadness, woe, lamentation, dolor, mourning, misery, anguish, remorse, regret, melancholy, depression, heartbreak, wretchedness. **2** loss, deprivation, misfortune, affliction, shock, blow, disaster, tribulation, curse, plague, adversity, setback, mischance, calamity. —*v.* grieve, lament, mourn, weep, sob, regret, wail, bewail, bemoan, brood, despair, despond, agonize, cry.
ant. *n.* **1** joy, elation, gladness, happiness. **2** blessing, boon, benefit, bonanza. *v.* rejoice, celebrate, laugh, smile.

sorrowful *adj.* miserable, sad, woeful, sorry, regretful, anguished, melancholy, depressed, mournful, wretched, doleful, tearful, disheartened, *triste*, blue.

ant. joyful, happy, elated, glad, up (*Slang*).

sorry *adj.* **1** regretful, remorseful, repentant, apologetic, contrite, penitent, self-reproachful, conscience-stricken, guilt-ridden, penitential. **2** mournful, somber, melancholy, funereal, sad, depressing, distressing, lugubrious, piteous, wretched, sorrowful, pathetic, moving, pitiable. **3** paltry, worthless, picayune, piddling, meager, mean, cheap, vulgar, contemptible, low, poor, petty, meretricious.
ant. **1** glad, happy, delighted, pleased, self-congratulatory. **2** amusing, entertaining, lightsome, jolly. **3** generous, ample, plentiful, noble.

sort *n.* **1** kind, category, class, group, ilk, grouping, collection, aggregation, congeries, species, genus, classification. **2** character, nature, essence, stripe, quality, disposition, breed, stamp, description, strain, aspect. **3** way, manner, style, mode, method, fashion, wise. —*v.* class, group, classify, assort, arrange, separate, categorize, list, distinguish, differentiate, type, label, grade.
ant. *v.* jumble, mix up, scramble.

sortie *n.* attack, foray, raid, charge, sally, onslaught, drive, incursion, invasion.

SOS *n.* ALARM.

so-so *adj.* passable, mediocre, adequate, fair, tolerable, commonplace, average, bearable, undistinguished, run-of-the-mill, ordinary, humdrum, second-rate.

sot *n.* drunkard, alcoholic, drinker, drunk, tippler, toper, guzzler, inebriate, dipsomaniac, barfly, boozer, lush (*Slang*), boozehound (*Slang*), soak (*Slang*), souse (*Slang*), rummy (*Slang*).
ant. teetotaler, nondrinker, dry.

sough *v., n.* MURMUR.

soul *n.* **1** psyche, spirit, numen, anima, essence. **2** basis, core, cornerstone, spirit, essence, quintessence, heart, foundation, pith, lifeblood, marrow, center, keynote, root, *sine qua non*. **3** person, being, human, individual, entity, creature, mortal, man, woman.

soulful *adj.* profound, heartfelt, deep, meaningful, moving, emotional, expressive, poetic, eloquent, mystical, spiritual, sensitive.

sound¹ *v.* seem, appear, look, come off as, give the impression of, strike one as.

sound² *adj.* **1** healthy, unimpaired, fit, working, unflawed, intact, perfect, undamaged, unmarred, strong, sturdy. **2** correct, logical, sensible, rational, cogent, convincing, right-minded, right-thinking, well-reasoned, level-headed, intelligent, reasonable, incontrovertible. **3** established, accepted, standard, recognized, traditional, tried-and-true, preferred, orthodox, proven, authentic. **4** solvent, stable, safe, reliable, firm, solid, substantial, durable, trustworthy, reputable, responsible. **5** thorough, complete, thoroughgoing, out-and-out, strenuous, vigorous, all-out, efficacious, effective, powerful.

ant. 1 weak, feeble, damaged, unusable, out of order, out of commission. **2** foolish, silly, senseless, crazy. **3** unorthodox, untried, unproven, theoretical. **4** shaky, unreliable, risky, unstable. **5** partial, inconclusive, ineffectual.

soundless *adj.* SILENT.

sound out probe, plumb, test, try out, question, examine, grill, look into, inquire into, pump.

soupçon *n.* TRACE.

soupy *adj.* **1** FOGGY. **2** SENTIMENTAL.

sour *adj.* **1** sharp, acid, tart, lemony, vinegary, unripened, green, fermented, rancid, spoiled, bad, curdled. **2** cross, morose, acidulous, dour, cranky, crabby, irritable, grouchy, nasty, petulant, waspish, ill-natured, surly, bad-tempered, sullen. —*v.* disenchant, disabuse, disillusion, embitter.

ant. *adj.* **1** sweet, sugary, fresh, unspoiled. **2** cheerful, affable, agreeable, pleasant, good-natured.

source *n.* origin, seed, font, fountainhead, wellspring, root, basis, base, spring, derivation, home, cradle, birthplace, genesis, beginning, provenance, provenience, nucleus, germ.

sourpuss *n. Slang* CRANK.

souse *v.* steep, ret, saturate, drench, immerse, dip, brine, pickle, marinate, preserve. —*n. Slang* SOT.

souvenir *n.* memento, remembrance, relic, memory, reminder, scar, keepsake, token, trophy, emblem, symbol.

sovereign *adj.* **1** ruling, reigning, regnant, empowered, enthroned, almighty, imperial, governing, authorized, sanctioned, authoritative. **2** free, independent, autonomous, self-governing, self-ruling. **3** excellent, exalted, dominant, paramount, supreme, capital, foremost, chief, unexcelled, principal, unparalleled, transcendent, superlative, peerless. —*n.* ruler, monarch, king, majesty, queen, emperor, empress, czar, czarina, chieftain, chief, sultan, shah, autocrat, potentate, dictator.

ant. *adj.* **1** powerless, dethroned, unauthorized. **2** subservient, dependent, satellite. **3** minor, unimportant, petty, secondary.

sow *v.* **1** seed, plant, raise, grow, imbed, inseminate, impregnate, strew, scatter. **2** distribute, dispense, disseminate, implant, disperse, broadcast, lodge, inject, circulate.

space *n.* **1** area, range, distance, amplitude, locality, place, room, extent, expanse, spread, scope, volume, capacity, spaciousness, elbow room. **2** interval, recess, period, term, stretch, duration, span, age, while, cycle, season, tenure.

spacious *adj.* roomy, capacious, commodious, large, extensive, uncrowded, ample, sizable, comfortable, broad, voluminous.

ant. cramped, crowded, small, uncomfortable.

span v. **1** continue, extend into, reach into, endure, last, range over, remain, live. **2** bridge, link, join, connect, go across, traverse, stretch across, reach across. —n. extent, extension, stretch, distance, spread, width, length, height, depth, breadth, measurement, reach, range, scope.

spangle n. sequin, paillette, glitter, tinsel, rhinestone, bauble, bead, trinket, gaud, gewgaw.

spank v. slap, hit, strike, wallop, wham, flog, beat, tan, paddle, cane, thrash, whip.

spanking adj. SWIFT.

spar[1] n. BEAM.

spar[2] v. match wits, bandy words, wrangle, debate, dispute, bicker, haggle, cavil, contest, split hairs, squabble.

spare v. **1** free, relieve, liberate, pardon, deliver, rescue, reprieve, acquit, exonerate, let off. **2** give, donate, contribute, part with, afford, yield, turn over, surrender, lend. —adj. **1** extra, additional, unused, supplementary, another, excess, emergency, surplus, unoccupied, further, remaining, auxiliary, unfilled, extraneous, unnecessary. **2** thin, lean, bony, skinny, lanky, rangy, scrawny, scraggy, skeletal, undernourished, underfed. **3** sparse, scanty, modest, frugal, skimpy, stinted, unadorned, unembellished, functional, minimal, understated, restrained, ascetic.
—n. duplicate, extra, supplement, leftover, auxiliary.

ant. adj. **2** plump, fleshy, round, well-fed. **3** plentiful, abundant, elaborate, ornate.

sparing adj. **1** scanty, slight, bare, meager, skimpy, scant, spare, sparse, exiguous, inadequate. **2** economical, frugal, thrifty, saving, prudent, careful, restrained, chary, cautious, close, penurious, parsimonious, stingy.

ant. **1** abundant, plentiful, ample, plenteous, profuse. **2** generous, open-

handed, liberal, extravagant, prodigal.

spark n. **1** sparkle, scintilla, ray, flash, gleam, glimmer, glitter, glow, blink, flicker, twinkle, shimmer, coruscation. **2** trace, vestige, jot, ember, particle, remainder, reminder, scrap, speck, shadow, memory, relic, indication, sign, spoor. **3** impulse, stimulus, force, inspiration, activator, energizer, provocation, motivation, catalyst, spur, encouragement, impetus, incitement, inducement. —v. **1** sparkle, scintillate, glitter, coruscate, shimmer, flash, twinkle, glint, spangle, dazzle. **2** activate, cause, lead to, energize, stimulate, provoke, set off, inspire, incite, induce, encourage, touch off, generate, instigate, fire.

ant. n. **3** deterrent, discouragement, restraint, damper. v. **2** deter, discourage, quell, extinguish.

sparkle v. flash, scintillate, glitter, spark, effervesce, twinkle, coruscate, dazzle, bedazzle, bubble, shine. —n. **1** SPARK. **2** brilliance, wit, liveliness, vivacity, éclat, dazzle, effervescence, verve, animation, panache, flash, radiance, warmth, charisma.

sparse adj. thin, scant, scattered, spotty, uncrowded, meager, skimpy, scant, scanty, spare.

ant. dense, crowded, thick, plentiful, ample.

Spartan adj. self-disciplined, rigorous, austere, simple, severe, demanding, exacting, self-denying, strict, stringent, abstemious, spare, ascetic.

ant. self-indulgent, soft, sybaritic, luxurious.

spasm n. twitch, tic, contraction, seizure, paroxysm, fit, spell, convulsion, cramp, knot, crick.

spasmodic adj. intermittent, irregular, fitful, sporadic, erratic, transient, changeable, occasional, unanticipated, sudden, recurrent, transitory, convulsive, jerky.

ant. regular, continuous, uninterrupted, lasting.

spat *n.* quarrel, tiff, argument, dispute, squabble, difference, scrap, bicker, row, run-in, fight, wrangle. —*v.* ARGUE.

spate *n.* flood, overflow, outpouring, inundation, spill, cascade, eruption, superfluity, redundance, excess, stream, deluge, outburst, torrent, Niagara.

ant. trickle, drop, paucity, scarcity.

spatter *v.* splash, bespatter, splatter, sprinkle, spray, muddy, wet, dirty, spot, shower, plash, spritz.

spawn *v.* generate, produce, cause, engender, beget, create, lead to, bring forth, bring about, initiate, occasion.

speak *v.* 1 say, utter, verbalize, communicate, talk, articulate, enunciate, vocalize, voice. 2 lecture, orate, speechify, harangue, sermonize, expound, exhort, preach, declaim, expatiate, go on, spout, harp on.

speaker *n.* orator, lecturer, preacher, spokesman, spokeswoman, discourser, talker, voice, advocate, declaimer, speechifier, speechmaker, mouthpiece, spellbinder.

spear *n.* lance, javelin, harpoon, pike, trident, dart, assegai, shaft, spike. —*v.* pierce, impale, puncture, stick, stab, lance, shaft, harpoon, gore, run through, thrust into, capture, catch.

special *adj.* 1 uncommon, different, unique, extraordinary, rare, unfamiliar, unusual, peculiar, individual, atypical, odd, singular, unprecedented, *sui generis.* 2 specific, definite, specified, designated, precise, express, restricted, defined, delimited, limited, particular, concrete, specialized. 3 memorable, important, esteemed, notable, red-letter, distinguished, momentous, cherished, beloved, significant, gala, festive, striking.

ant. 1 standard, common, typical, usual, normal. 2 general, unlimited, unrestricted, undefined, unspecified. 3 everyday, unimportant, casual, unmemorable, insignificant.

specialist *n.* expert, professional, master, connoisseur, technician, buff, authority, trouble-shooter, adept, past master, maven.

ant. jack of all trades, dilettante, amateur, dabbler, nonprofessional.

speciality *n.* SPECIALTY.

specialize *v.* concentrate on, major in, focus on, go in for, be into (*Slang*).

specialty *n.* feature, mainstay, distinction, attraction, strength, characteristic, mark, brand, hallmark, speciality, *spécialité,* shtick (*Slang*), number (*Slang*).

species *n.* variety, sort, kind, type, form, ilk, breed, category, genre, class, classification, mold, stripe, designation, description.

specific *adj.* explicit, plain, clear, designated, specified, exact, clear-cut, precise, determinate, particularized, pointed, detailed, unmistakable, unambiguous, unequivocal, special, relevant, particular, express, distinct, definite, concrete.

ant. vague, ambiguous, indefinite, abstract, theoretical, general.

specifically *adv.* ESPECIALLY.

specification *n.* detail, condition, stipulation, particular, item, specific, fact, statement, aspect, feature, point, element, particularity.

specify *v.* particularize, detail, designate, name, stipulate, itemize, cite, enumerate, focus on, note, point out.

specimen *n.* sample, example, exemplar, representative, exemplification, instance, case, embodiment, prototype.

specious *adj.* misleading, faulty, casuistic, deceptive, sophistical, tricky, slippery, questionable, fallacious, unfounded, unsubstantiated, false, invalid, dubious.

ant. undeniable, inescapable, valid, conclusive, logical.

speck *n.* spot, particle, iota, stain, mote, scintilla, fleck, flyspeck, speckle, dot, drop, bit, pinch, jot, whit.

speckle *n.* SPECK.

spectacle *n.* 1 pageant, display, parade, performance, happening, event, vision, marvel, panorama, wonder, exposition, attraction, extravaganza. **2** scene, display, foolishness, carryings-on, exhibition, disturbance, fool, laughingstock, ass, jackass.

spectacular *adj.* marvelous, wonderful, exciting, breathtaking, stunning, dazzling, extraordinary, fantastic, awesome, striking, fabulous, theatrical, thrilling, gorgeous, magnificent. **ant.** dull, tame, boring, uninteresting, so-so.

spectator *n.* onlooker, viewer, witness, eyewitness, beholder, bystander, theatergoer, ticket-holder, sightseer, sidewalk superintendent (*Slang*), kibitzer (*Slang*), rubberneck (*Slang*).

specter *n.* phantom, apparition, ghost, shade, vision, spook, spirit, phantasm, illusion, wraith, image, fantasy, revenant, eidolon, dream.

spectral *adj.* ghostly, shadowy, spooky, wraithlike, eerie, ghastly, phantasmal, incorporeal, illusionary, insubstantial, supernatural, uncanny, weird. **ant.** corporeal, material, palpable, real, tangible.

spectrum *n.* range, spread, band, sequence, scope, assortment, variety, extent, compass, sweep, diversity.

speculate *v.* ponder, conjecture, reflect, meditate, muse, mull over, think, consider, contemplate, imagine, guess, surmise, wonder, theorize, infer, presume, suppose.

speculation *n.* **1** theorizing, rumination, contemplation, consideration, deliberation, reasoning, cogitation, ideation, thinking, guesswork. **2** theory, conjecture, hypothesis, guess, idea, thought, inference, assumption, suspicion, opinion, conclusion, surmise, supposition, impression.

speculative *adj.* **1** conjectural, theoretical, contemplative, thoughtful, hypothetical, assumed, presumed, suppositional, impractical, untried, untested, philosophical, experimental, academic, abstract. **2** risky, hazard-

ous, doubtful, dubious, uncertain, chancy, iffy, rash, insecure, unreliable, blue-sky, ticklish, uninsured, unsafe, unpredictable, problematical. **ant. 1** practical, tested, proven, validated. **2** safe, sure, guaranteed, reliable.

speech *n.* **1** speaking, communication, verbalization, articulation, expression, talk, utterance, declaration, statement, dialogue, conversation, chat, colloquy, discussion, parlance, parley, conference, debate, oratory. **2** lecture, address, sermon, talk, discourse, harangue, oration, diatribe, exhortation, pronouncement, eulogy, tirade, soliloquy. **3** idiom, language, parlance, dialect, jargon, vocabulary, locution, regionalism, localism, lingo.

speechify *v.* ORATE.

speechless *adj.* inarticulate, dumb, mute, wordless, tongue-tied, silent, choked up, dumbstruck, aphasic, mum. **ant.** articulate, communicative, talkative.

speed *n.* rapidity, swiftness, velocity, quickness, celerity, haste, alacrity, hurry, rush, promptness, nimbleness, agility. —*v.* hurry, dash, fly, race, zip, rush, run, spurt, sprint, tear, shoot, course, step on it. **ant.** *n.* slowness, sluggishness, inertia, laziness. *v.* dawdle, creep, crawl, inch, loiter, lag.

speedup *n.* acceleration, push, rush, spurt, thrust, step-up. **ant.** slowdown, stoppage, lag.

speed up accelerate, step up, hasten, precipitate, promote, expedite, advance, quicken, push, spur, propel. **ant.** slow down, decelerate, hamper, hinder, brake.

speedy *adj.* SWIFT.

spell[1] *n.* **1** incantation, conjuration, abracadabra, charm, voodoo, hex, hoodoo, jinx, invocation. **2** enchantment, bewitchment, thralldom, fascination, infatuation, charm, trance, magic, sorcery, hypnotism, allure, allurement, seductiveness.

spell[2] *n.* **1** interval, period, piece, while, term, course, turn, span, stretch, interlude. **2** siege, bout, outbreak, seizure, attack, paroxysm, incident, episode, stroke, spasm, fit. —*v.* relieve, help out, substitute for, take turns with, fill in for, pinch-hit for, cover for, alternate with.

spellbind *v.* enthrall, enchant, bewitch, charm, seduce, enslave, hypnotize, entrance, transfix, enrapture, fascinate, mesmerize, overpower.

spellbound *adj.* enthralled, enchanted, fascinated, bewitched, entranced, overpowered, charmed, mesmerized, transfixed, hypnotized, magnetized, overcome, dazzled, bemused, infatuated.

spelling *n.* orthography.

spell out detail, explain, explicate, elucidate, clarify, simplify, specify, particularize, describe, interpret.

spend *v.* **1** pay out, disburse, expend, lay out, shell out (*Slang*), fork up (*Slang*), cough up (*Slang*). **2** use up, exhaust, deplete, drain, run through, dissipate, fritter, squander, waste. **3** employ, apply, devote, use, put to use, utilize, lavish.

spendthrift *n.* big spender, wastrel, waster, prodigal, profligate, squanderer, scattergood, sport, showoff. —*adj.* wasteful, prodigal, profligate, improvident, extravagant, lavish, openhanded, overgenerous.
ant. *n.* miser, hoarder, tightwad, money-grubber. *adj.* stingy, miserly, cautious, provident, tight.

spent *adj.* exhausted, worn out, fagged out, tired, done in, weary, enervated, debilitated, wearied, beat, bushed, knocked out.
ant. lively, energetic, dynamic, peppy, vigorous.

spew *v.* **1** come forth, issue, erupt, emerge, gush, flood, burst, stream, spill, flow. **2** VOMIT.

sphere *n.* **1** globe, ball, orb, spheroid, globule, bubble, bulb. **2** scope, prov-

ince, range, compass, circle, domain, reach, field, zone, region, orbit, territory, bailiwick. **3** position, rank, status, place, standing, station, class, caste.

spherical *adj.* spheroid, globular, global, orbicular, orbiculate, round, circular.

spheroid *adj.* SPHERICAL.

sphinx *n.* mystery, enigma, riddle, question mark, closed book, problem, puzzle, conundrum.

spice *n.* flavor, color, excitement, savor, zest, tang, piquancy, raciness, taste, pungency, interest, relish, mystery, zip, pizzazz (*Slang*). —*v.* flavor, accent, color, dramatize, step up (*Slang*), jazz up (*Slang*).

spick-and-span *adj.* NEAT.

spicule *n.* SPIKE.

spiculum *n.* SPIKE.

spicy *adj.* **1** PIQUANT. **2** RACY.

spike *n.* **1** nail, stake. **2** point, needle, spine, spikelet, spicule, spiculum, projection, barb, prong, hobnail, thorn, tine.

spile *n.* STAKE.

spill *v.* **1** pour, run over, overflow, shed, flow, rain, spurt, drip, drop, dribble, stream, spray, slop over, slosh, shower. **2** divulge, reveal, tattle, make known, betray, disclose, make public, inform, blab, leak, rat (*Slang*), squeal (*Slang*). —*n.* fall, tumble, plunge, plummet, flop.

spin *v.* whirl, rotate, gyrate, turn, twist, twirl, wheel, reel, revolve, go around. —*n.* rotation, rotating, gyration, gyrating, twist, twisting, twirl, twirling, whirl, whirling, swirl, swirling, reel, reeling.

spinal column SPINE.

spindle *n.* shaft, rod, pin, axis, pivot, pole, bar, stem, arbor, mandrel.

spindling *adj.* SPINDLY.

spindly *adj.* lanky, spindling, scrawny, skinny, gangling, gangly, gawky, stringy, spindle-legged, spindle-shanked.
ant. squat, stubby, stumpy, dumpy, pudgy, squab.

spine *n.* **1** spinal column, backbone, vertebrae, vertebral column, rachis, chine. **2** ridge, spur, crest, eminence, projection, arête, hogback, horseback, chine.

spineless *adj.* weak-willed, irresolute, passive, soft, flabby, vacillating, indecisive, cowardly, chicken (*Slang*). **ant.** resolute, willful, strong, bold, tough, gutsy (*Slang*).

spin-off *n.* BYPRODUCT.

spiral *adj.* **1** helical, whorled, winding, tortile, volute, voluted, curled, coiled, twisting, corkscrew, cochlear. **2** escalating, climbing, rising, increasing, developing, dynamic, progressive, advancing. **ant.** **2** descending, downward, sinking, declining.

spire *n.* steeple, belfry, tower, bell tower, campanile, turret, minaret, peak, pinnacle, flèche.

spirit *n.* **1** soul, anima, life force, *élan vital*. **2** psyche, mind, ego, personality, self, selfhood, humanness. **3** ghost, specter, shade, wraith, spook, banshee, eidolon, apparition, revenant, phantom, phantasm. **4** mood, disposition, temper, temperament, frame of mind, humor, tendency, proclivity, bent, warp, pulse, tenor. **5** vivacity, liveliness, life, energy, courage, mettle, grit, élan, guts (*Slang*), nerve, verve, animation, esprit, enterprise, valor, bravery. **6** characteristic, attitude, feeling, motivation, quality, essence, intent, meaning, purpose, aim, goal, quintessence, substance.

spirited *adj.* vivacious, mettlesome, frisky, lively, responsive, alert, animated, enterprising, daring, dashing, perky, peppery, adventurous, dynamic, plucky, dauntless, feisty, gutty (*Slang*). **ant.** sluggish, inert, lifeless, timid, fearful, spiritless.

spiritless *adj.* lethargic, sluggish, unenthusiastic, discouraged, disheartened, listless, slow, poky, debilitated, spent, apathetic, indifferent, torpid, phlegmatic, dispirited. **ant.** lively, energetic, spirited, responsive, animated, dynamic.

spirits *n.* LIQUOR.

spiritual *adj.* **1** soulful, incorporeal, disembodied, moral, ethical, intellectual, psychic, metaphysical, philosophical, ethereal, mystical, intuitive, godly, holy, eternal, otherworldly, imponderable. **2** sacred, religious, impalpable, intangible, divine, transcendent. **ant.** **1** corporeal, material, earthly, fleshly. **2** worldly, secular, lay, mundane, temporal.

spirt *n.*, *v.* SPURT.

spit *v.* expectorate, spew, salivate, slaver, dribble, drool, slobber, foam, froth. —*n.* spittle, saliva, sputum, drool, dribble, slaver, froth, foam.

spite *n.* spitefulness, resentment, bitterness, nastiness, meanness, cattiness, malice, despite, ill will, rancor, malevolence, hostility, grudge, spleen, animosity, bitchiness (*Slang*). —*v.* harass, vex, persecute, annoy, thwart, begrudge, frustrate, hurt, wound, aggrieve, discomfit, sting, nettle, put out. **ant.** *n.* good will, charity, forgiveness, understanding, benevolence.

spitting image LIKENESS.

spittle *n.* SPIT.

spiv *n. Brit.* CHEAT.

splash *v.* **1** splatter, spatter, slosh, swash, wet, bespatter, dash, sprinkle, besprinkle, strew, plash, spray, squirt, splotch, spritz. **2** display, plaster, paint, tout, broadcast, publicize, flaunt, feature, advertise, trumpet, blazon, promote, ballyhoo, plug (*Slang*). —*n.* **1** splatter, spatter, plash, swash, swish, splotch. **2** drop, dash, splash, touch, bit, soupçon, tinge, tinct, tincture, sprinkling, trace, spot, dab. **3** spectacle, show, flourish, effect, exhibition, showiness, display, sight, production, sensation.

splatter *n., v.* SPLASH.

splay *adj.* UNGAINLY. —*v.* SPREAD.

spleen *n.* anger, resentment, rancor, spite, spitefulness, hostility, bitterness, ill will, animus, animosity, bile, malice, malevolence, venom, irritability, bitchiness (*Slang*).

ant. friendliness, warmth, good will, sympathy.

spleenful *adj.* SPLENETIC.

splendid *adj.* excellent, great, wonderful, marvelous, terrific, superb, exceptional, incredible, fantastic, fabulous, irresistible, gorgeous, topnotch, splendiferous, smashing, ripping (*Brit. Slang*).

ant. terrible, rotten, awful, dreadful, lousy (*Slang*).

splendiferous *adj.* SPLENDID.

splendor *n.* magnificence, grandeur, greatness, glory, resplendence, sumptuousness, majesty, flourish, brilliance, éclat, nobility, pomp, solemnity, impressiveness, pageantry.

ant. drabness, shabbiness, dullness, dreariness, lackluster.

splenetic *adj.* spiteful, irritable, rancorous, sour, crabby, spleenful, touchy, nasty, malicious, ill-tempered, quarrelsome, grouchy, grumpy, cranky, bitchy (*Slang*).

ant. affable, agreeable, pleasant, even-tempered, amiable.

splice *v.* unite, intertwine, join, connect, braid, interconnect, interweave, dovetail, interlace, rabbet, mortise, overlap, twine, entwine, miter, plait. —*n.* joining, joint, splicing, braid, plait, overlap, twist, miter joint, bevel, mortise, connection, attachment, dovetail, rabbet.

ant. *v.* separate, take apart, disjoint, disconnect, undo.

splinter *v.* fragment, shatter, shiver, split, fracture, break, chip, crumble, smash, crack, explode.

split *v.* 1 break, separate, divide, fragment, rive, rift, shatter, rupture, cleave, sever, pull apart, crack, splinter, open, shiver, burst, pulverize, polarize. 2 divide, distribute, allot, allocate, apportion, dole out, share, parcel, subdivide, partition, divvy up (*Slang*). 3 *Slang* QUIT. —*n.* 1 crack, rupture, fracture, rent, tear, cleft, hole, opening, fissure, break, breakage, damage, imperfection. 2 schism, division, rift, separation, disaffection, disaffiliation, breakup, breach, polarization, dissension, deviation, defection, detachment, secession, withdrawal, feud, divorce. 3 share, portion, cut, piece, subdivision, allotment, dividend, percentage, ration.

ant. *n.* 2 unity, harmony, agreement, solidarity.

split up separate, divide, divorce, go separate ways, live apart, disband, disaffiliate, break up, part company, disintegrate, dissolve, bust up (*Slang*).

splotch *n.* SPOT. —*v.* SOIL.

splutter *v.* stammer, mumble, seethe, sputter, hem and haw, stutter, rant, babble, stumble, jabber, gabble, rave, bluster.

spoil *v.* 1 impair, damage, devalue, debase, despoil, pollute, weaken, mar, deface, disfigure, deform, undo, ruin, injure, blemish. 2 overindulge, baby, cosset, spoonfeed, pamper, coddle, overprotect, smother, humor, cater to, mollycoddle, kill with kindness. 3 rot, decay, sour, putrefy, putresce, deteriorate, go bad, curdle, mildew, turn.

ant. 1 mend, repair, purify, fix, strengthen, cleanse. 2 discipline, restrain, guide, civilize.

spoilage *n.* WASTE.

spoils *n.* loot, booty, plunder, pillage, winnings, takings, quarry, pickings, graft, swag (*Slang*), take (*Slang*), haul (*Slang*), boodle (*Slang*), gravy (*Slang*).

spoilsport *n.* wet blanket, killjoy, complainer, censor, prig, malcontent, prude, sourpuss (*Slang*), party pooper (*Slang*), bluenose.

ant. good sport, boon companion, life of the party, live wire.

spoken *adj.* uttered, said, verbal, verbalized, articulated, announced, expressed, proclaimed, voiced, enunciated, intoned, sounded, oral.

sponge *v.* **1** impose on, exploit, live on, leech on, take advantage of, panhandle, cadge, scrounge (*Slang*), mooch (*Slang*), bum (*Slang*), freeload (*Slang*). **2** EXPUNGE. —*n.* SPONGER.

sponger *n.* parasite, leech, hanger-on, poor relation, cadger, drone, freeloader, loafer, sponge, bum, scrounger (*Slang*), moocher (*Slang*), deadbeat (*Slang*), panhandler (*Slang*), gold-digger (*Slang*).

sponsor *n.* patron, patroness, supporter, angel, promoter, backer, benefactor, well-wisher, champion, booster, philanthropist, Maecenas, meal-ticket (*Slang*). —*v.* back, finance, support, promote, invest in, patronize, stake, set up, answer for, guarantee, fund.

spontaneous *adj.* natural, unconstrained, uninhibited, impulsive, uncontrived, improvisational, unrehearsed, unplanned, free, extemporaneous, unpremeditated, instinctive, intuitive, unstudied, irrepressible, uncontrollable.
ant. contrived, artificial, unnatural, controlled, planned.

spoof *v.* lampoon, burlesque, satirize, parody, travesty, tease, mimic, caricature, take off, josh (*Slang*), kid (*Slang*), twit. —*n.* parody, joke, satire, burlesque, comedy, travesty, takeoff, imitation, caricature, mimicry, exaggeration, ribbing (*Slang*), joshing (*Slang*), kidding (*Slang*).

spook *n.* ghost, apparition, specter, spirit, phantom, phantasm, shade, wraith, banshee. —*v.* frighten, disturb, annoy, disquiet, unsettle, unnerve, unhinge, scare, upset, alarm, haunt, intimidate, daunt, agitate, obsess, bug (*Slang*).

spooky *adj.* **1** ghostly, eerie, weird, uncanny, supernatural, preternatural, fantastic, frightening, scary, creepy.

2 frightened, nervous, anxious, scared, jittery, skittish, unsettled, upset, unhinged, agitated, shaky, apprehensive, fearful, unstrung.
ant. 2 calm, relaxed, cool, untroubled, serene.

spool *n.* cylinder, reel, bobbin, spindle, axle, windlass, winch, winder, ball, roll.

spoon *n.* ladle, scoop, dipper, bail, crater, dip, bowl, concavity, depression, hollow.

spoonfeed *v.* SPOIL.

spoony *adj.* SENTIMENTAL.

spoor *n.* trail, track, footprints, droppings, scent, trace, mark, indication, sign, clue, hint, vestige, evidence, remainder.

sporadic *adj.* **1** infrequent, occasional, irregular, fitful, spasmodic, intermittent, discontinuous, rare, uncommon, unexpected, unscheduled. **2** localized, isolated, singular, contained, spotty, single, confined, limited, concentrated.
ant. 1 frequent, regular, uninterrupted, continuous, scheduled. **2** general, widespread, unlimited, extensive, epidemic.

sport *n.* **1** diversion, pastime, recreation, amusement, entertainment, distraction, divertissement, game, play, romp, lark. **2** jest, fun, raillery, teasing, ridicule, derision, mockery, joking, mirth, merriment, badinage, banter, joshing (*Slang*), ribbing (*Slang*). **3** mutant, mutation, monster, freak, monstrosity, aberration, oddity, deviate. —*v.* **1** play, frolic, caper, romp, cavort, horse around, gambol, disport, lark, revel. **2** trifle, toy, dally, flirt, tease, fool, make fun of, pull one's leg (*Slang*).

sporting *adj.* fair, sportsmanlike, on the square, equitable, even, honorable, gentlemanly.
ant. unfair, cheating, dishonest, inequitable, dishonorable.

sportive *adj.* playful, frolicsome, frisky, coltish, lively, jaunty, roguish, rollicking, prankish, sprightly, merry.

ant. serious, somber, grave, staid, decorous.

sporty *adj.* casual, informal, gay, loud, colorful, flashy, rakish, jaunty, showy, jazzy (*Slang*), splashy.

ant. somber, conservative, formal, subdued, quiet.

spot *n.* **1** place, location, locality, point, area, position, site, region, bearings, whereabouts. **2** splotch, stain, mark, speck, blotch, blemish, blot, fleck, mote, dot, macula, patch, dapple, freckle, mottle, daub. **3** fault, shortcoming, defect, taint, stigma, disrepute, discredit, stain, blemish, blot, black eye. **4** place, opening, slot, position, room, space, time. —*v.* **1** stain, mark, soil, bespatter, spatter, speckle, mottle, dot, splotch, blot, stud. **2** sight, locate, see, eye, espy, recognize, detect, identify, pinpoint, perceive. **3** sully, disgrace, mar, tarnish, taint, stigmatize, discredit, smear, slander, defame, blacken.

spotless *adj.* **1** clean, immaculate, scrubbed, scoured, flawless, unsoiled, unblemished, undefaced, stainless, shining. **2** pure, unsullied, exemplary, innocent, blameless, faultless, irreproachable, unimpeachable, uncorrupted, untainted, sinless, guiltless.

ant. **1** dirty, filthy, grimy, spattered, spotted, soiled, stained. **2** corrupt, tarnished, fallen, depraved, faulty, tainted.

spotlight *v.* highlight, illuminate, emphasize, accent, sharpen, heighten, enhance, feature.

ant. *v.* obscure, hide, conceal, blur, dim, eclipse.

spotty *adj.* uneven, irregular, variable, intermittent, sporadic, episodic, fitful, random, haphazard, patchy, desultory, disjointed, erratic, fluctuating.

ant. even, consistent, steady, systematic, uniform, regular, constant.

spousal *n.* MARRIAGE.

spouse *n.* mate, consort, partner, husband, wife, groom, bride, helpmate, companion, better half.

spout *v.* **1** flow, stream, pour, spew, spurt, gush, squirt, jet, discharge, surge, issue, eject, erupt. **2** bluster, harangue, rant, declaim, gush, rattle, chatter, mouth, ramble, orate. —*n.* tap, spigot, faucet, nozzle, jet, outlet, waterspout, gargoyle, conduit, pipe, tube, trough, hose.

sprawl *v.* loll, lounge, slouch, flop, recline, lean, spread out, spread-eagle, stretch out, relax, slump.

spray[1] *n.* shower, mist, cloud, sprinkle, drizzle, spritz, spindrift, foam, spume. —*v.* shower, spit, spout, sprinkle, scatter, drizzle, squirt, spurt, jet, gush, shoot.

spray[2] *n.* SPRIG.

spread *v.* **1** expand, unfold, open, unfurl, unwind, stretch, extend, inflate, dilate, widen, broaden, enlarge, sprawl. **2** part, splay, separate, flare, open, pry, diverge, divide, cleave, split. **3** apportion, dole out, parcel out, distribute, dispense, share, mete, allot, allocate, assign. **4** diffuse, broadcast, disseminate, publish, circulate, distribute, propagate, sow, hand out, promulgate, announce, divulge, advertise, air, transmit. **5** scatter, spread out, radiate, disperse, diffuse, permeate, outspread, dissipate, overrun, strew, cover. —*n.* **1** span, extent, range, dissemination, diffusion, reach, scope, compass, stretch, breadth, area. **2** feast, banquet, repast, meal, table, board, buffet.

ant. *v.* **1** contract, shrink, narrow, curl, condense, fold. **2** converge, meet, press, join, close. **5** assemble, gather, compact, cluster.

spree *n.* binge, bout, fit, spell, tear (*Slang*), drunk, bender (*Slang*), revel, debauch, orgy, carousal, bacchanalia, saturnalia, wassail, toot (*Slang*).

sprig *n.* shoot, sprout, spray, twig, slip, offshoot, branch, slip, scion, bouquet, nosegay, wreath, garland, corsage.

sprightly *adj.* lively, animated, vivacious, spry, brisk, bustling, cheerful, spirited, energetic, nimble, agile, quick, jaunty, chipper, buoyant.

ant. lethargic, spiritless, depressed, gloomy, tired, torpid, sluggish, phlegmatic.

spring v. **1** leap, jump, dart, shoot, start, buck, bound, hop, vault, leap-frog, skip, hurdle. **2** emerge, arise, procede, crop up, appear, originate, issue, stem, derive, emanate, flow, develop, grow, sprout, blossom, wax, thrive. —n. **1** elasticity, bounce, resilience, stretchiness, flexibility, buoyancy, suppleness. **2** cause, motive, stimulus, impetus, reason, spur, source, springboard, origin, beginning, wellspring, fountainhead, fount.

ant. v. **2** wither, fade, recede, decline, wane. n. **1** rigidity, brittleness, stiffness, inflexibility. **2** consequence, end, goal, result, effect, outcome.

springboard n. SPUR.

springiness n. RESILIENCE.

springy adj. ELASTIC.

sprinkle v. shower, spray, scatter, strew, rain, spatter, pepper, spread, dust, squirt, powder, moisten. —n. showering, scattering, sprinkling, smattering, spraying, dash, bit, trace, hint, pinch, drop, scrap, modicum.

ant. n. plenty, heaps, loads, a lot, mass.

sprinkling n. SMATTERING.

sprite n. fairy, elf, goblin, hobgoblin, puck, pixie, leprechaun, brownie, gnome, gremlin.

sprout v. germinate, bud, shoot, burgeon, bloom, vegetate, burst forth, spring, emerge, grow, mushroom, boom, flourish, thrive, wax.

ant. wither, shrivel, die, decay, waste away, wane.

spruce adj. neat, trim, well-groomed, clean, tidy, trig, smart, dapper, natty, chic, spiffy (*Slang*), sleek.

ant. sloppy, messy, untidy, disheveled, slovenly, unkempt.

spruce up tidy, groom, trig, arrange,

straighten up, clean up, preen, plume, dress up, doll up (*Slang*).

spry adj. active, lively, brisk, agile, limber, supple, nimble, sprightly, quick, vigorous, energetic, vivacious, peppy (*Slang*), bustling.

ant. lethargic, sluggish, inert, inactive.

spume n. froth, foam, scum, spray, fizz, effervescence, surf, suds, lather.

spunk n. mettle, pluck, courage, spirit, heart, nerve, gameness, bravery, daring, boldness, backbone, grit, guts (*Slang*), feistiness, fight, pugnacity.

ant. cowardice, timidity, fearfulness, reluctance.

spunky adj. PLUCKY.

spur n. incentive, motive, stimulus, springboard, impetus, provocation, inducement, impulse, fillip, prod, goad. —v. urge, prod, goad, prick, press, drive, stimulate, nag, encourage, exhort, incite, provoke, rouse, egg, instigate.

ant. n. deterrent, hindrance, discouragement, obstacle. v. hinder, slow, prevent, discourage, thwart, suppress.

spurious adj. false, counterfeit, fake, bogus, sham, mock, artificial, imitation, feigned, pretended, fictitious, erroneous, fraudulent, apocryphal, ungenuine.

ant. genuine, real, authentic, true, actual, veritable.

spurn v. reject, repudiate, scorn, dismiss, snub, slight, rebuff, refuse, repel, repulse, disdain, contemn.

ant. accept, admit, welcome, receive, honor.

spurt n. **1** gush, spout, spray, jet, spirt, outpour, eruption, geyser, fountain, spring. **2** outbreak, explosion, outburst, surge, flurry, rush, fit, spell, spate, flare-up, attack, wave, upsurge, groundswell. —v. gush, spew, spirt, squirt, stream, spout, jet, well, pour, surge, burst.

sputter v. **1** spatter, spit, sprinkle, splutter, crackle, sizzle, flicker, pop. **2**

stammer, stutter, splutter, jabber, babble, gibber.

spy *n.* agent, scout, investigator, operative, secret agent, undercover agent, double agent, emissary. —*v.* **1** scout, reconnoiter, watch, follow, shadow, trail, stalk, eavesdrop, oversee. **2** snoop, pry, poke, search, investigate, explore, examine, inspect, scrutinize, study, delve.

squab *adj.* SQUAT.

squabble *v.* quarrel, argue, bicker, wrangle, feud, scrap, fight, brawl, spat, contend, conflict, clash. —*n.* quarrel, argument, tiff, spat, fight, wrangle, scrap, dispute, disagreement, altercation, set-to, feud. **ant.** *v.* agree, concur, cooperate, collaborate, side with. *n.* agreement, accord, harmony, concord, peace, amity, cooperation.

squad *n.* crew, team, gang, force, task force, band, group, company.

squalid *adj.* **1** foul, filthy, wretched, untidy, unkempt, grubby, dilapidated, dirty, poor, shabby, ramshackle, grimy, dingy, slummy. **2** sordid, base, low, vile, ignoble, mean, petty, despicable, vulgar, contemptible. **ant.** **1** clean, tidy, neat, attractive, presentable. **2** noble, decent, honorable, respectable, upright.

squall[1] *n.* cry, scream, yell, yelp, outcry, wail, howl, bawl, shriek, squawk, squeal. —*v.* cry, scream, howl, bawl, yell, wail, blubber, squawk, squeal, yowl.

squall[2] *n.* storm, gale, gust, tempest, flurry, blast, bluster, cyclone, hurricane, blizzard, wind.

squalor *n.* poverty, seediness, filth, wretchedness, foulness, decay, blight, shabbiness, dinginess, sordidness, grubbiness. **ant.** wealth, comfort, elegance, luxury.

squama *n.* SCALE[1].

squander *v.* dissipate, waste, lavish, run through, throw away, fritter away, deplete, consume, expend, exhaust, spend, misspend. **ant.** save, hoard, store, accumulate, conserve, stash, keep.

square *n.* piazza, plaza, quadrangle, quad, green, park, common. —*adj.* **1** honest, fair, just, sporting, upright, equitable, impartial, conscientious, trustworthy, aboveboard, scrupulous, ethical, evenhanded. **2** *Slang* prim, conventional, conservative, corny, old-fashioned, old-fogyish, straight (*Slang*), bourgeois, conformist. —*v.* even, adjust, regulate, straighten, settle, equalize, adapt, attune, fit, reconcile, harmonize, balance, conciliate, accommodate. **ant.** *adj.* **1** cheating, dishonest, unfair, biased, partial. **2** hip (*Slang*), aware, worldly, unconventional, Bohemian, with-it (*Slang*).

squarely *adv.* directly, square, straight, straightforwardly, pointblank, exactly, right, smack, spang, smackdab.

squash *v.* **1** squeeze, press, crush, squish, mash, squelch, smash, pound, pulp, masticate, knead. **2** SQUELCH. —*n.* pulp, mush, mash, blob, heap, lump.

squat *adj.* stocky, squab, squatty, dumpy, chunky, thickset, pudgy, stubby, stumpy, blocky. **ant.** lanky, lean, gangling, spindly.

squatty *adj.* SQUAT.

squawk *v.* **1** squall, scream, shriek, howl, hoot, bray, croak, screech, squeal, cry, whoop. **2** *Slang* COMPLAIN. —*n.* **1** croak, screech, squeal, shriek, caterwaul, cry, yelp. **2** *Slang* COMPLAINT.

squeak *n.* squeal, screech, creak, shriek, chirp, cheep, tweet, peep. —*v.* squeal, grate, creak, pipe, chirp, peep, cheep, tweet, stridulate. **ant.** *n.* grunt, thud, boom, thunder.

squeal *v.* **1** cry, yell, yelp, whine, wail, bawl, squawk, scream, squeak, shrill, screech, shriek. **2** BETRAY. —*n.* squeak, yelp, cry, yell, scream, whine, wail, bark, howl, screech, shriek, bawl.

squeamish *adj.* delicate, fastidious, sensitive, finicky, fussy, dainty, queasy, precious, overnice, prim, prissy.

ant. tough, hard-boiled, callous, insensitive, stolid.

squeeze *v.* **1** press, compress, grip, pinch, tighten, constrict, nip, crush, compact, pack, crowd. **2** embrace, hug, clutch, cuddle, press, clasp, hold, enfold. —*n.* **1** pressure, compression, weight, constriction, grip, crushing, tightening. **2** crisis, difficulty, straits, jam, pinch, extremity, emergency, predicament, crunch (*Slang*), mess, rainy day.

squelch *v.* **1** crush, squash, smash, mash, stamp on, fall on, trample on, compress, flatten, compact. **2** silence, subdue, still, hush, muzzle, deflate, squash, put down (*Slang*), quell, suppress. —*n.* retort, ripost, barb, put-down (*Slang*), comeback, rejoinder.

ant. *v.* **2** encourage, boost, applaud, praise, acclaim, appreciate.

squib *n., v.* LAMPOON.

squire *n.* **1** attendant, valet, manservant, page, armor-bearer, lacky, servant, esquire, retainer. **2** escort, companion, gigolo, attendant, gallant, cavalier. —*v.* escort, accompany, usher, attend, go with, conduct.

squirm *v.* writhe, wriggle, twist, twitch, toss, jerk, fidget, flounder, shift, wiggle.

squirrel away hoard, stash, hide, store, cache, save, keep, stockpile, stow away, lay away, salt away, put aside, reserve.

ant. spend, use, consume, throw away, discard.

squirt *v.* spurt, jet, stream, gush, spray, eject, shoot, spout, sprinkle, discharge, splash, shower.

squish *v.* SQUASH.

stab *v.* pierce, jab, stick, impale, spike, spear, knife, lance, gore, wound, cut, puncture, prick, perforate, penetrate.

—*n.* **1** perforation, prick, gash, wound, cut, incision, injury, tear, laceration. **2** pang, twinge, pain, prick, ache, sting, wrench. **3** effort, attempt, try, shot, crack, go, essay, venture.

stabile *adj.* STABLE.

stability *n.* steadiness, equilibrium, balance, poise, sturdiness, firmness, soundness, solidity, constancy, durability, strength.

ant. shakiness, instability, weakness, vacillation, fluctuation.

stabilize *v.* secure, brace, anchor, settle, moor, fix, ground, root, firm, steady, reinforce.

ant. loosen, undermine, weaken, destabilize, shake.

stable[1] *adj.* **1** fixed, firm, steady, sturdy, solid, stationary, immovable, immobile, secure, entrenched, fast, strong, stabile. **2** steadfast, resolute, firm, strong-willed, staunch, constant, unswerving, persevering, persistent, abiding, durable, permanent, enduring, lasting.

ant. **1** rickety, wobbly, unsteady, shaky. **2** irresolute, vacillating, hesitant, wavering, fluctuating, precarious, delicate, tenuous.

stable[2] *n.* STAFF.

stack *n.* bundle, pile, heap, sheaf, pack, mound, mass, bank, packet. —*v.* gather, pile up, group, amass, heap up, load.

stadium *n.* coliseum, arena, amphitheater, bowl, ballpark, hippodrome, circus, gymnasium, lists, palaestra.

staff *n.* **1** scepter, mace, cane, cudgel, club, wand, baton, stave, stick, rod, pole, shaft, shillelagh, walking stick. **2** team, stable, cadre, help, force, personnel, crew, cabinet, retinue, group.

stage *n.* **1** rostrum, platform, dais, proscenium, the boards, bandstand, podium. **2** the theater, acting, drama, dramaturgy, show business, show biz (*Slang*), the footlights. **3** landing, story, floor, level, tier, deck. **4** period, phase, state, step, point, station,

plane, level, grade, degree, position.
—*v.* **1** present, produce, arrange, exhibit, show, perform, air, put on, dramatize. **2** stage-manage, orchestrate, contrive, manage, engineer, manipulate, program, prearrange, hoke up (*Slang*).

stage-manage *v.* STAGE.

stagger *v.* **1** totter, reel, sway, stumble, lurch, waver, rock, lumber, flounder, wobble, shamble, falter. **2** stun, stupefy, astound, shock, dumbfound, overwhelm, surprise, flabbergast, bewilder, confound, appall, astonish, perplex, baffle, nonplus.

staggering *adj.* ASTOUNDING.

stagnant *adj.* **1** still, standing, stationary, idle, motionless, quiet, inactive, calm, dormant, quiescent, inert, static. **2** foul, brackish, rank, stale, putrid, polluted, stinky, dirty, fetid, musty.
ant. 1 flowing, churning, moving, running, turbulent, agitated. **2** fresh, sweet, clean, clear.

stagnate *v.* vegetate, stand, idle, languish, decline, wane, deteriorate, slumber, go to seed, decay.
ant. grow, develop, evolve, move, progress.

stagy *adj.* theatrical, mannered, artificial, pretentious, over-blown, histrionic, melodramatic, hammy (*Slang*), overdone, unnatural, affected, campy.
ant. genuine, natural, unaffected, understated, played down.

staid *adj.* sedate, proper, decorous, sober, solemn, quiet, subdued, grave, serious, settled, prudent, conservative, demure, moderate, standpat.
ant. frivolous, playful, extravagant, wild, capricious, fanciful, flighty.

stain *n.* **1** spot, blemish, blot, mark, smirch, discoloration, blotch, smudge, smear, patch. **2** taint, disgrace, stigma, fault, flaw, tarnish, smirch, blot, dishonor, discredit, blemish, spot, reproach. —*v.* **1** discolor, soil, blemish, spot, spatter, dirty, smear, tarnish, begrime,

blotch, splotch. **2** dishonor, blemish, corrupt, sully, degrade, defile, debase, discredit, pollute, poison, besmirch, tarnish, taint.
ant. *n.* **2** credit, honor, glory, esteem, repute, innocence, purity. *v.* **1** clean, scrub, wipe, wash, scour, erase. **2** redeem, purge, uplift, dignify, honor, elevate.

stake *n.* **1** stick, post, spile, pole, pillar, pile, picket, pale, standard. **2** jackpot, winnings, purse, prize, ante, kitty, pool, bet. —*v.* **1** demarcate, delimit, outline, delineate, bound, mark, limit, circumscribe. **2** wager, bet, risk, hazard, venture, chance, gamble, ante. **3** back, finance, fund, treat, stand, sponsor, subsidize, support, grubstake.

stale *adj.* **1** old, musty, dry, moldy, deteriorated, spoiled, rancid, stuffy, flat, sour, crumbling, wilted, vapid. **2** trite, hackneyed, threadbare, motheaten, tired, worn, insipid, cliché, commonplace, banal, vapid, stock, stereotyped, conventional. **3** washed-up, rusty, stiff, dull, stodgy, listless, lifeless, exhausted, spent, aged, withered, over the hill, worn-out, useless.
ant. 1 fresh, new, unspoiled, green. **2** original, novel, innovative, fresh, imaginative, creative. **3** vigorous, spontaneous, dynamic, effective.

stalemate *n.* tie, draw, standstill, standoff, dead heat, halt, stop, deadlock, impasse, dead end, blind alley, corner, cul-de-sac.
ant. progress, solution, resolution, development.

stalk[1] *n.* **1** stem, axis, pedicel, peduncle, stock, petiole. **2** STEM.

stalk[2] *v.* **1** sneak, steal, shadow, tail, follow, hunt, trail, pursue, creep, slink. **2** swagger, strut, prance, stride, march, parade.

stall *n.* **1** stable, pen, fold, cubicle, compartment, cell, booth, stand, kiosk. **2** evasion, pretext, maneuver, bluff, subterfuge, ruse, device, ploy, pretense, stratagem, tactic. —*v.* arrest, halt, stop, block, obstruct, impede, clog, bog down, paralyze, hinder, interrupt, stay, still.

ant. *v.* start, spur, help, facilitate, expedite.

stalwart *adj.* **1** strong, hardy, robust, rugged, vigorous, sturdy, strapping, powerful, hale, able-bodied, stout, brawny, sinewy, muscular. **2** resolute, determined, steadfast, firm, staunch, stouthearted, indomitable, brave, bold, fearless, courageous, intrepid, plucky, spunky, mettlesome.

ant. **1** weak, puny, fragile, delicate, feeble. **2** timid, hesitant, wavering, cowardly, fearful, vacillating.

stamina *n.* strength, robustness, hardiness, endurance, toughness, sturdiness, ruggedness, vigor, vitality, energy, staying power, fortitude.

ant. weakness, delicacy, frailty, fragility, infirmity.

stamp *v.* **1** stomp, clump, trample, tramp, plod, step. **2** imprint, mark, print, brand, inscribe, impress. **3** embed, etch, engrave, imprint, impress, ingrain, fix, brand. **4** characterize, label, mark, brand, categorize, classify, pronounce, adjudge, tag, type. —*n.* **1** imprint, mark, design, sign, character, seal, trace, hallmark, signature, impress. **2** cast, kind, variety, sort, type, class, species, nature, breed, stripe.

stampede *n.* flight, race, retreat, rout, rush, dash. —*v.* flee, race, charge, bolt, retreat, rout, rush, dash.

stamping ground HAUNT.

stamp out squash, extinguish, wipe out, rub out, snuff, crush, quench, stifle, quash, eradicate, eliminate, destroy.

stance *n.* **1** pose, posture, attitude, carriage, position, bearing, manner, mien. **2** stand, standpoint, point of view, position, policy, opinion, attitude, belief, conviction, bias, posture.

stanch *v.* stop, stem, dam up, seal, close, plug, clot, halt, arrest, inhibit, check, stay, staunch. —*adj.* STAUNCH.

stanchion *n.* pillar, upright, post, support, prop, stay, brace, beam, standard, timber, stilt.

stand *v.* endure, submit to, suffer, abide, put up with, tolerate, take, face, stomach, bear, brook, sustain, weather, withstand. —*n.* **1** position, locus, spot, place, station, post, site, ground, placement, location. **2** policy, position, posture, platform, stance, point of view, standpoint, attitude, conviction, credo.

ant. *v.* reject, oppose, fight, resist, avoid.

standard *n.* **1** flag, ensign, streamer, banner, pennant, colors, emblem, sign, icon, image, insignia. **2** criterion, yardstick, guide, measure, gauge, test, touchstone, example, model, exemplar, norm, pattern, canon, rule, principle. **3** post, stake, pillar, upright, stanchion, stud, beam. —*adj.* **1** conventional, correct, accepted, established, conforming, official, authoritative, orthodox, basic, canonical. **2** average, ordinary, common, typical, regular, prevailing, usual, normal, everyday.

ant. *adj.* **1** nonstandard, unorthodox, irregular, unconventional, out of line, offbeat (*Slang*). **2** extraordinary, unusual, special, exceptional, unique, different.

standardize *v.* regulate, conform, homogenize, equalize, adjust, even, level, normalize, regularize.

standby *n.* **1** supporter, aid, aide, assistant, partisan, friend, champion, follower, disciple. **2** stand-in, substitute, replacement, alternate, understudy, proxy, pinch hitter, double.

stand-in *n.* STANDBY.

standing *n.* **1** rank, status, footing, place, position, state, grade, caliber, classification, situation, placement. **2** prestige, repute, reputation, status, eminence, importance, significance, regard, esteem, respect.

ant. **2** notoriety, disrepute, lowliness, insignificance.

standoff *n.* tie, draw, standstill, stalemate, deadlock.

standoffish *adj*. aloof, cool, remote, withdrawn, detached, distant, unfriendly, reticent, unsociable, reserved, taciturn, uncommunicative. **ant.** approachable, accessible, friendly, sociable, affable, extroverted.

standout *n*. ace, champion, topnotcher, star, expert, authority, master, sensation, winner, crackerjack (*Slang*).

standpat *adj*. CONSERVATIVE.

stand pat stay put, resist, hold on, stick to one's guns, persist, sit tight, hold out.

standpoint *n*. point of view, position, stance, posture, stand, attitude, inclination, belief, bias, outlook, opinion.

standstill *n*. halt, stop, stopping, cessation, breakdown, impasse, blockage, blind alley, cul-de-sac, dead end, stalemate, draw, deadlock. **ant.** progress, solution, continuation, development, growth.

stand up for side with, support, back, defend, protect, champion, uphold, justify, vindicate, plump for, stick up for. **ant.** oppose, reject, defy, resist, combat.

staple *n*. **1** commodity, resource, raw material, product, basic, essential, core, base. **2** storehouse, depository, repository, source, mine, center. —*adj*. main, chief, primary, principle, prime, fundamental, basic, major, predominant, essential, key. **ant.** *adj*. minor, subordinate, accessory, secondary.

star *n*. **1** asterisk, pentacle. **2** celebrity, luminary, superstar, name, heavyweight, notable, sensation. **3** protagonist, principal, lead, hero, heroine, co-star, prima donna, headliner. —*v*. lead, stand out, shine, excel, dominate, predominate, surpass. —*adj*. prominent, important, major, brilliant, outstanding, distinguished, illustrious, eminent. **ant.** *n*. **2** nonentity, nobody, zero, ci-

pher. *adj*. average, ordinary, obscure, minor, mediocre.

starch *n*. **1** formality, primness, preciseness, stiffness, rigidity, stiltedness, punctiliousness, starchiness, ceremoniousness. **2** energy, pep, vigor, drive, spirit, animation, liveliness, vim, zip, zest, verve, *élan*. **ant.** **1** casualness, informality, unceremoniousness, offhandedness, flexibility. **2** sluggishness, torpor, lethargy, lassitude, feebleness, weariness.

starchy *adj*. prim, stiff, formal, punctilious, mannered, rigid, stilted, precise, ceremonious, wooden, stuffy. **ant.** relaxed, casual, informal, easygoing, flexible.

star-crossed *adj*. doomed, unlucky, ill-fated, unfortunate, hapless, condemned, hopeless, jinxed, foredoomed, ill-starred. **ant.** auspicious, lucky, favorable, fortunate, promising, hopeful.

stare *v*. gaze, glare, glower, eye, gape, gawk, peer, rubberneck (*Slang*), eyeball (*Slang*), goggle, ogle. —*n*. gaze, look, glower, regard, glare, ogle, gape.

stargazing *n*. DAYDREAM.

stark *adj*. **1** deserted, barren, bleak, austere, plain, simple, bare, bald, naked, unadorned, unvarnished, stripped. **2** severe, harsh, difficult, firm, unbending, extreme, stern, strict, unrelenting, hard, stiff, inflexible, rigorous. **3** grim, blunt, harsh, unmitigated, pitiless, absolute, pure, plain, utter, complete. **ant.** **1** adorned, padded, embellished, ornate, fancy. **2** easy, moderate, gentle, comfortable.

starry-eyed *adj*. ROMANTIC.

start *v*. **1** jump, jerk, recoil, shrink, twitch, flinch, wince, shy, buck, bound, leap, spring. **2** begin, commence, depart, set out, inaugurate, strike up, initiate, launch, undertake, embark, enter. **3** found, establish, set up, institute, create, erect, form, organize, open. —*n*. **1** jerk, reflex, recoil, twitch, spasm, jump, jolt, convulsion. **2** beginning, commencement, inception, outset, onset, initiation, takeoff, inauguration, opening, kickoff.

ant. *v.* **2** end, conclude, terminate, stop, finish. **3** dissolve, break up, destroy, close. *n.* **2** ending, termination, windup, conclusion, outcome, culmination.

starter *n.* catalyst, initiator, precipitator, spur, impetus, incitement, springboard, stimulus, push, boost, shove, fillip, provocation, shot in the arm.

startle *v.* alarm, shock, stun, surprise, frighten, scare, jolt, shake, unnerve, unsettle, faze, consternate, agitate, astound.

startling *adj.* AMAZING.

starve *v.* waste away, wither, perish, die, famish, hunger, fast.

ant. gorge, eat, feast, fatten.

stash *v.* hide, conceal, secrete, hoard, store, salt away, squirrel away, save, stow away, lay away, cache, amass, stockpile. —*n. Slang* cache, loot, stockpile, hoard, savings, store, supply, pile, accumulation, reserve.

ant. *v.* spend, deplete, use, exhaust, dissipate.

state *n.* **1** condition, situation, circumstances, status, posture, mode, stage, phase, form, shape. **2** mood, frame, emotion, feeling, attitude, disposition, humor, temper. **3** nation, country, government, commonwealth, republic, dominion, sovereignty, community, body politic. **4** STATUS. —*v.* declare, set forth, say, express, voice, avow, claim, tell, utter, speak, recite, report, recount, articulate.

stately *adj.* **1** majestic, imposing, grand, awesome, impressive, elegant, lordly, lofty, princely, august, magnificent, noble, pompous. **2** slow, measured, deliberate, unhurried, formal, dignified.

ant. **1** lowly, base, petty, grubby, squalid, poor, mean, meek, humble. **2** lively, brisk, bouncy.

statement *n.* assertion, pronouncement, announcement, remark, utterance, declaration, allegation, proposition, comment, profession, articulation.

static *adj.* stationary, still, inert, inactive, motionless, fixed, quiescent, dormant, stagnant, at rest.

ant. dynamic, active, changing, moving, working.

station *n.* **1** post, position, spot, place, seat, location, locus, base. **2** rank, status, standing, footing, rating, state, level, position, class, caste. —*v.* place, position, post, plant, set, assign, appoint, put, fix, locate, install, establish, ensconce.

stationary *adj.* still, static, standing, fixed, immovable, permanent, rooted, anchored, secured, immobile, stuck, fastened, sedentary.

ant. portable, movable, moving, mobile, migratory.

statistic *n.* FACT.

statue *n.* sculpture, carving, statuette, figure, figurine, bust, bronze, effigy, idol, monument.

statuesque *adj.* stately, majestic, dignified, imposing, grand, regal, proud, noble, graceful, comely, shapely, handsome.

statuette *n.* STATUE.

stature *n.* **1** height, tallness, elevation, size, altitude. **2** prestige, recognition, reputation, growth, achievement, regard, eminence, distinction, quality, accomplishment.

status *n.* rank, standing, state, grade, caliber, level, position, degree, footing, station, condition, stage, situation.

statute *n.* law, ordinance, regulation, prescript, rule, decree, act, edict, legislation, bylaw.

staunch *adj.* firm, resolute, constant, trustworthy, stanch, faithful, loyal, true, devoted, steadfast, stalwart, true-blue, reliable. —*v.* STANCH.

ant. faithless, vacillating, ambivalent, questionable, unreliable.

stave *n.* rod, cudgel, staff, stick, cane, club, rung, step, spoke, shaft, rib, bar. —v. break, crush, smash, burst, pound, split, tear, splinter, rupture, crack, puncture.

stave off ward off, prevent, curb, impede, intercept, foil, repel, fend off, parry, preclude, stay, block, avoid, evade.

stay[1] v. **1** stop, halt, freeze, stall, discontinue, quit. **2** remain, continue, persist, keep, rest, lodge, reside, inhabit, live, dwell, abide, hang around, tarry, wait, linger. **3** last, keep, endure, abide, persist, persevere, remain, stand. **4** hinder, delay, impede, check, curb, stem, hamper, retard, detain, postpone, waive, put off, defer, suspend. —n. **1** sojourn, stopover, visit, holiday, vacation, rest, stop. **2** deferment, suspension, delay, postponement, reprieve, respite, interruption, break, moratorium, hiatus.

ant. v. **1** continue, press on, progress. **2** depart, leave, move on, pass through. **3** perish, collapse, expire, disintegrate. **4** hasten, speed, expedite, facilitate.

stay[2] v., n. PROP.

staying power ENDURANCE.

steadfast adj. loyal, devoted, dedicated, persevering, dutiful, faithful, dependable, reliable, trusty, steady, unwavering, resolute, stalwart, trustworthy, stedfast.

ant. disloyal, wavering, fickle, fairweather, unreliable.

steady adj. **1** firm, stable, fixed, secure, solid, constant, consistent, unfaltering, uniform, regular, permanent. **2** calm, unruffled, equable, poised, cool, even, level-headed, composed, serene, collected, patient. **3** constant, consistent, inveterate, regular, established, habitual, routine. —v. brace, balance, stabilize, fix, fasten, secure, firm, stiffen, support.

ant. adj. **1** shaky, flickering, wavering, sporadic, irregular, uneven. **2** excitable, temperamental, nervous, edgy, jittery, agitated, high-strung. **3** irregular, inconsistent, variable, erratic, intermittent.

steal v. **1** thieve, embezzle, peculate, defalcate, pilfer, lift, pocket, pinch (Slang), plunder, filch, purloin, swipe, snitch (Slang), loot, heist (Slang), cop (Slang). **2** creep, sneak, skulk, slink, slip.

stealth n. furtiveness, subterfuge, secrecy, covertness, slyness, sneakiness, surreptitiousness, concealment, unobtrusiveness.

ant. openness, publicity, overtness, fanfare.

stealthy adj. covert, sneaky, clandestine, furtive, sly, sneak, underhand, shady, devious, surreptitious, unobtrusive, secretive, private, huggermugger.

ant. aboveboard, open, overt, obvious, forthright.

steam n. **1** vapor, mist, cloud, fog, fume, effluvium, exhalation, gas, miasma. **2** energy, power, vigor, force, speed, pep, drive, starch, vim, vitality.

ant. 2 weakness, lethargy, lassitude, fragility.

stedfast adj. STEADFAST.

steep[1] adj. **1** precipitous, sheer, abrupt, high, sharp, upright, vertical. **2** expensive, exorbitant, high, dear, costly, stiff, inflated, excessive. —n. CLIFF.

ant. 1 gentle, gradual, graded, rolling, low, gradient. **2** cheap, moderate, low, inexpensive.

steep[2] v. **1** soak, bathe, saturate, drench, immerse, macerate, sop, brew, souse, douse, submerge, seethe, marinate. **2** imbue, infuse, instill, inculcate, indoctrinate, involve, saturate, impregnate, immerse, permeate.

steer v. pilot, conduct, lead, chart, direct, guide, control, operate, manage, oversee, supervise, govern.

steer clear of avoid, shun, evade, dodge, duck, elude, give a wide berth to, sidestep, bypass, circumvent.

ant. welcome, meet, seek, face, accept.

stellar *adj.* **1** astral, celestial, sidereal, starry, heavenly, astronomic, empyrean. **2** chief, principal, main, foremost, star, prime, major, leading, prominent, featured, top.

ant. 2 minor, lesser, secondary, auxiliary, assistant, supporting.

stem[1] *n.* **1** stalk, axis, pedicel, peduncle, trunk, stock, petiole. **2** stalk, shaft, rod, axis, spindle, peg, pin, rib, support.

stem[2] *v.* stop, stay, check, plug, dam, obstruct, oppose, resist, buck, overcome, breast, counter, clear, weather, withstand.

stench *n.* fetidness, miasma, reek, stink, fetor, mephitis, effluvium, noisomeness.

ant. fragrance, perfume, aroma, sweetness, freshness.

stentorian *adj.* LOUD.

step *n.* **1** pace, stride, gait, walk, footstep, tread. **2** stair, stile, riser, tread, rung, stave, round, foothold. **3** action, measure, proceeding, means, method, maneuver, expedient, device, act, deed. **4** grade, degree, level, notch, stage, interval, position, gradation, point. **5** footprint, track, trail, trace, spoor, mark, vestige, —*v.* walk, pace, tread, stride, ambulate, pad, foot, saunter, tramp, traipse, stroll, perambulate, march, strut.

step down 1 phase out, decrease, tone down, cut, lower, wind down, curtail, reduce, diminish, scale down, de-escalate. **2** resign, abdicate, quit, retire, bow out.

ant. 1 step up, increase, escalate, raise.

step on it HURRY.

steppingstone *n.* means, way, method, foothold, pathway, lift, aid, boost, bridge, instrument, opportunity, advantage, entrée, passport, channel.

ant. obstacle, impediment, stumblingblock, hindrance.

step-up *n.* increase, intensification,

escalation, boost, rise, lift, acceleration, speedup, gain, pickup, advance.

ant. decrease, de-escalation, reduction, curtailment.

step up increase, raise, intensify, escalate, boost, up, accelerate, expand, enlarge, build up.

ant. decrease, curtail, reduce, lower, step down.

stereotyped *adj.* stock, hackneyed, conventional, set, routine, commonplace, trite, banal, stale, threadbare, shopworn, platitudinous.

ant. original, fresh, novel, innovative, imaginative, creative.

sterile *adj.* **1** barren, infertile, arid, impotent, unfruitful, infecund, unproductive, aseptic, antiseptic, disinfected, sterilized, uninfected, uncontaminated. **2** dull, insipid, flat, arid, jejune, lifeless, dry, tedious, dreary, monotonous, humdrum. **3** futile, vain, useless, abortive, fruitless, profitless, pointless, otiose, ineffectual, unavailing, stillborn.

ant. 1 fertile, fruitful, fecund, rich, prolific, teeming. **2** interesting, exciting, lively, imaginative. **3** useful, productive, successful, effective, efficacious.

sterilize *v.* sanitize, purify, clean, cleanse, decontaminate, disinfect, fumigate, autoclave, depurate.

ant. contaminate, pollute, infect, foul.

sterling *adj.* valuable, precious, excellent, superior, superb, admirable, first-rate, exquisite, meritorious, superlative, invaluable.

ant. shoddy, shabby, second-rate, inferior.

stern *adj.* **1** harsh, hard, severe, strict, tough, rigorous, exacting, demanding, authoritarian, stringent, rigid, unrelenting, austere, forbidding, grim, relentless. **2** resolute, firm, strict, adamant, steadfast, fixed, steely, determined, immovable, constant, sturdy, stout.

ant. 1 lenient, gentle, merciful, easy, sympathetic, comforting, compassionate. **2** hesitant, faltering, wavering, equivocal, flexible, changeable.

stew *v.* **1** boil, cook, simmer, seethe, fricassee, pot. **2** fret, worry, brood, mope, pout, grumble, chafe, fume, rage, seethe.

steward *n.* manager, custodian, agent, administrator, caretaker, director, representative, proxy, factor, commission merchant.

stewed *adj.* DRUNK.

stick *n.* **1** twig, branch, switch, cane, club, baton, rod, shaft, staff, bar, stave, pole, stake, cudgel. **2** poke, stab, thrust, puncture, prod, jab, lunge. —*v.* **1** pierce, puncture, penetrate, stab, spear, bore, impale, prick, spike, transfix, gore, perforate. **2** fasten, attach, affix, pin, nail, tack, fuse, cement, glue. **3** put, place, thrust, poke, stuff, insert, set, lay, deposit, install.

stick at persevere, stick to, stick it out, persist, plug, plod, hang in (*Slang*), hold on, continue.
ant. oppose, criticize, knock off.

stick it out STICK AT.

stick to STICK AT.

stick-to-itiveness *n.* PERSEVERANCE.

stick-up *n. Slang* ROBBERY.

stick up for defend, support, side with, back, protect, champion, stand up for, uphold, stand by, go to bat for.
ant. oppose, criticize, knock (*Slang*), repudiate.

sticky *adj.* **1** adhesive, tenacious, gluey, glutinous, mucilaginous, gummy, tacky, viscid, syrupy. **2** humid, muggy, clammy, dank, soggy, steamy, sweaty, sultry, close. **3** awkward, embarrassing, tricky, difficult, complicated, delicate, thorny, perplexing, disconcerting, discomforting, painful.
ant. 2 dry, cool, refreshing, breezy.

stiff *adj.* **1** rigid, hard, firm, solid, brittle, unbending, inflexible, tight, tense, taut. **2** strong, powerful, steady, brisk, vigorous, violent, heavy, sturdy, heady, forceful, intense. **3** harsh, severe, tough, strict, stern, hard, stringent, exacting, demanding, rigorous, difficult, trying, arduous, laborious. **4** awkward, graceless, clumsy, ungainly, stilted, cramped, forced, wooden, mannered, formal, starchy, prim, constrained, ceremonious. —*n. Slang* **1** prig, pedant, stuffed shirt, snob, prude. **2** CORPSE.

ant. *adj.* **1** flexible, pliable, soft, elastic, workable, supple, flowing. **2** mild, weak, gentle, soft. **3** easy, mild, soft, gentle, lenient, lax. **4** relaxed, casual, informal, at ease, smooth, graceful.

stiffen *v.* harden, solidify, firm, gel, set, reinforce, petrify, ossify, congeal, thicken.
ant. soften, loosen, melt, liquefy.

stiff-necked *adj.* STUBBORN.

stifle *v.* **1** choke, suffocate, throttle, strangle, smother, asphyxiate. **2** repress, suppress, subdue, squelch, restrain, inhibit, arrest, stem, check, still, silence, muffle, dampen.
ant. 2 encourage, facilitate, allow, permit, condone.

stigma *n.* blemish, blot, spot, taint, stain, mark, brand, smirch, reproach, disgrace, dishonor, tarnish, flaw, shame.

stile *n.* STEP.

still *adj.* **1** motionless, inert, stockstill, immobile, static, stationary, resting, idle, dormant, abeyant, inactive, quiescent, passive. **2** calm, tranquil, quiet, stilly, peaceful, undisturbed, placid, pacific, serene, restful. **3** silent, hushed, low, muted, muffled, subdued, soft, gentle, inaudible. **4** dead, lifeless, inanimate, inert, extinct. —*n.* SILENCE —*adv.* nevertheless, anyhow, in any case, at any rate, on the other hand, however, notwithstanding, yet, regardless. — *v.* **1** silence, hush, quiet, muffle, muzzle, mute, gag, stifle, subdue, suppress. **2** allay, soothe, quiet, calm, tranquilize, appease, assuage, relieve, ease, mollify, mitigate, alleviate, smooth over.

ant. *adj.* **1** moving, dynamic, running, active. **2** agitated, ruffled, excited, turbulent. **3** loud, noisy, blaring. **4** living, animate, alive. *v.* **2** aggravate, exacerbate, intensify, sharpen, excite.

stilly *adj.* STILL.

stilted *adj.* formal, stuffy, stiff, pompous, pedantic, labored, wooden, awkward, mannered, studied.

ant. natural, casual, free, spontaneous.

stimulate *v.* **1** rouse, spur, arouse, incite, foment, animate, activate, stir, whet, galvanize, spark, provoke, awaken, enkindle, urge. **2** rev up, pep up (*Slang*), invigorate, energize, animate, excite, quicken, accelerate, step up.

ant. 1 suppress, squash, dampen, discourage, prevent, deaden. **2** slacken, slow, retard, abate.

stimulating *adj.* STIRRING.

stimulus *n.* stimulant, bracer, tonic, intoxicant, pick-me-up, upper (*Slang*), provocation, motive, incentive, spur, impetus, fillip, inspiration, goad, impulse, inducement.

ant. depressant, inhibitor, retardant, downer (*Slang*).

sting *v.* **1** pierce, prick, nettle, stab, stick, bite, hurt, wound, irritate, pinch, burn, chafe. **2** distress, trouble, grieve, hurt, prick, afflict, cut, wound, torment, vex, wrench. **3** stimulate, goad, rouse, spur, needle, arouse, incite, whip, urge, provoke, prompt, press. —*n.* **1** biting, pinching, smarting, irritation, prickle, burning, tingling, soreness. **2** pang, twinge, ache, pain, pinch, bite, stab, stitch, nip.

stingy *adj.* **1** penurious, miserly, avaricious, parsimonious, niggardly, tightfisted, closefisted, ungenerous, tight, close, greedy, sparing, penny-pinching, grudging, stinting, mean. **2**

scanty, meager, skimpy, thin, lean, inadequate, small, sparing.

ant. 1 generous, open-handed, lavish, liberal, charitable. **2** bountiful, plentiful, abundant, handsome, profuse.

stink *n.* stench, malodor, fetor, miasma, foulness, rankness, reek, effluvium, mephitis —*v.* reek, smell, offend.

ant. *n.* perfume, aroma, fragrance, bouquet, scent.

stint *v.* limit, restrict, bound, confine, straiten, skimp, pinch, scrape, scrimp, economize —*n.* task, assignment, mission, duty, job, chore, spell, hitch.

ant. *v.* squander, lavish, dissipate, misspend, deplete.

stipend *n.* allowance, pay, salary, fee, wages, hire, income, emolument, remuneration, compensation, honorarium.

stipulate *v.* specify, require, condition, provide, agree, designate, indicate, demand, insist, offer, negotiate.

stipulation *n.* specification, provision, item, requirement, consideration, restriction, proviso, condition, term, article, clause.

stir[1] *v.* **1** mix, mingle, blend, beat, whip, whisk, scramble, combine, toss, agitate. **2** budge, disturb, agitate, nudge, propel, dislodge, shift, move, toss, wiggle, rustle, shake. **3** bestir, waken, awaken, rouse, animate, spark, stoke, prod, excite, incite, fan, provoke, spur, instigate, prompt, stimulate. **4** affect, move, touch, excite, upset, shake, impress, disturb, perturb, provoke, jar, trouble. —*n.* excitement, commotion, bustle, flurry, fuss, ado, to-do, pother, disturbance, uproar, tumult, ferment.

ant. *v.* **2** rest, stand, stagnate. **3** calm, lull, suppress, still, dampen, prevent, stifle.

stir[2] *n. Slang* JAIL.

stirring *adj.* stimulating, exciting, animated, lively, spirited, rousing, inspiring, emotional, provocative, impassioned, thrilling, galvanic.

ant. dull, boring, uninspiring, numbing, soporific.

stitch *n.* PANG.

stock *n.* **1** merchandise, goods, commodities, inventory, line. **2** supply, stockpile, store, pile, accumulation, arsenal, hoard, fund, reserve, reservoir. **3** lineage, ancestry, family, background, extraction, descent, pedigree, line, strain, clan, house, race, species, heritage, tribe. —*v.* supply, load, fill, furnish, replenish, provision, store, equip, stock up, fit out. —*adj.* banal, commonplace, trite, everyday, run-of-the-mill, routine, ordinary, standard, stereotyped, hackneyed, worn, set.

ant. *v.* deplete, exhaust, expend, use up, remove. —*adj.* original, novel, fresh, new, exceptional, unusual, extraordinary.

stockade *n.* **1** barricade, palisade, paling, fence, barrier, bulwark, breastwork, parapet. **2** JAIL.

stockpile *v.* store, stock, amass, accumulate, save, hoard, reserve, lay aside, lay up, lay in, lay by, gather, garner, pile up. —*n.* STOCK.

ant. deplete, spend, use, exhaust, squander.

stockstill *adj.* STILL.

stocky *adj.* squat, pudgy, dumpy, thickset, chunky, blocky, stout, plump, stubby, stumpy, squatty.

ant. lean, lanky, thin, skinny, spindly.

stodgy *adj.* dull, boring, tedious, uninteresting, wearisome, monotonous, dreary, tiresome, humdrum, ponderous, stuffy.

ant. lively, entertaining, interesting, stimulating, exciting, sprightly.

stoical *adj.* impassive, resigned, philosophical, imperturbable, patient, forbearing, long-suffering, stolid, indifferent, detached, dispassionate.

stoke *v.* STIR.

stolid *adj.* insensitive, impassive, sedate, sluggish, apathetic, phlegmatic, lethargic, dull, bovine, unemotional.

ant. passionate, ardent, emotional, animated, excitable, sensitive, anxious.

stomach *v.* endure, put up with, submit to, stand, tolerate, suffer, abide, countenance, brook, swallow, take. —*n.* INCLINATION.

stomp *v.* STAMP.

stone *n.* **1** rock, concrete, masonry, marble, granite, flint, pebble, gravel. **2** jewel, gem, birthstone, bijou, rock (*Slang*).

stone-blind *adj.* BLIND.

stone-broke *adj.* DESTITUTE.

stoned *adj.* DRUNK.

stony *adj.* heartless, icy, unfeeling, pitiless, callous, merciless, austere, chilly, cold, stern, unrelenting, hardhearted, harsh, coldblooded, ruthless.

ant. compassionate, tender, kind, gentle, merciful.

stooge *n.* dupe, puppet, pawn, tool, henchman, accomplice, lacky, flunky.

stool *n.* **1** seat, footstool, footrest, camp stool, hassock, ottoman. **2** feces, excrement, excreta, dung, droppings, ordure, waste.

stool pigeon *Slang* INFORMER.

stoop *v.* **1** bend, nod, bow, kneel, squat, crouch, lean, slump, slouch, hunch, sag, droop. **2** sink, debase, descend, lower, demean, degrade, abase, submit, condescend, deign, grovel, humiliate, kowtow. —*n.* bow, droop, slouch, squat, slump, bend.

stop *v.* **1** halt, arrest, suspend, interrupt, stall, still, turn off, shut off. **2** suppress, crush, deter, quash, bar, stifle, end, terminate, impede, squelch, restrain, prevent, block, hinder, thwart. **3** withhold, suspend, cut off, block, check, plug, stem, stay, stop up, occlude, cork, close, seal, dam, clog. **4** cease, desist, discontinue, halt, quit, refrain, drop, end, suspend, cut off. —*n.* cessation,

abeyance, halt, suspension, stoppage, pause, rest, let-up, end, termination, discontinuance.
ant. *v.* **1** begin, start, turn on, run, drive, initiate, strike up. **2** encourage, aid, help, facilitate. **3** unplug, open, clear. **4** commence, continue, persist, carry on. —*n.* start, beginning, commencement, running, continuance.

stopgap *adj.* makeshift, alternate, substitute, provisional, temporary, tentative, emergency, improvised, contrived, impromptu.

stopover *n.* SOJOURN.

stoppage *n.* obstruction, impediment, hindrance, blockage, obstacle, interruption, cutoff, curtailment, stricture.

stopper *n., v.* PLUG.

stopple *n., v.* PLUG.

storage *n.* saving, hoarding, stockpiling, safekeeping, keeping, collection, stowage, accumulation, storing.

store *v.* **1** stockpile, reserve, stow away, hoard, save, deposit, accumulate, reserve, gather, squirrel away, salt away, stash, garner, collect. **2** furnish, equip, stock, supply, provide, provision, outfit. —*n.* **1** stockpile, stock, supply, reserve, accumulation, nest egg, cache, stash (*Slang*). **2** shop, emporium, market, mart, boutique, business.
ant. *v.* **1** deplete, spend, distribute, disburse.

storehouse *n.* WAREHOUSE.

storekeeper *n.* SHOPKEEPER.

storeroom *n.* WAREHOUSE.

store up SALT AWAY.

storied *adj.* NOTABLE.

storm *n.* barrage, rain, avalanche, bombardment, flood, deluge, tumult, convulsion, upheaval, tempest, commotion, outburst, explosion, eruption, flurry. —*v.* **1** rage, fume, rant, rampage, fulminate, run amok, blow up, rave, bluster, raise Cain (*Slang*), go berserk. **2** attack, assault, charge, invade, strike, lay siege to, raid, rush, besiege, assail.

stormy *adj.* **1** turbulent, blustery, tempestuous, inclement, gusty, rough, squally. **2** violent, rough, disturbed, agitated, heated, passionate, vehement, frenzied, wild, fiery, tempestuous, explosive, volcanic, tumultuous.
ant. **1** fair, balmy, mild, clement. **2** calm, smooth, tranquil, halcyon, serene, peaceful, pacific.

story *n.* narrative, anecdote, tale, yarn, fable, account, sketch, record, description, article, chronicle, history.

storyteller *n.* narrator, author, raconteur, anecdotist, fabulist, chronicler.

stout *adj.* **1** fat, pudgy, portly, plump, corpulent, obese, thickset, rotund, chubby, fleshy, tubby, heavy. **2** firm, strong, sturdy, vigorous, sound, hardy, durable, robust, stalwart, able-bodied, muscular, hefty, strapping, brawny, tough. **3** STOUTHEARTED.
ant. **1** slim, thin, lean, bony, skinny, slender. **2** puny, scrawny, frail, weak, fragile, delicate.

stouthearted *adj.* brave, courageous, stout, hardy, bold, intrepid, heroic, dauntless, fearless, valiant, spunky, plucky, unflinching, spirited, lionhearted.
ant. cowardly, craven, cringing, timid, afraid, fearful, hesitant.

stow *v.* pack, wedge, cram, crowd, stuff, tuck, jam, squeeze, compact, place.

straggle *v.* stray, deviate, meander, drift, digress, wander, ramble, roam, rove, range.

straight *adj.* **1** linear, rectilinear, even, plumb, vertical, horizontal, unbent, taut, extended, drawn. **2** honest, honorable, trustworthy, legitimate, reliable, direct, forthright, fair, equitable, straightforward, just, upright. **3** uninterrupted, continuous, unbroken, nonstop, sustained, constant, serial, consecutive. **4** ordered, neat, correct, proper, arranged, balanced, organized, aligned, accurate, right. **5** *Slang* conventional, bourgeois, middleclass, square (*Slang*), orthodox, traditional.

ant. 1 crooked, bent, twisted, curved, wavy, curly. **2** dishonest, devious, shifty, underhand, crooked, tricky, artful. **3** broken, intermittent, discontinuous, irregular, sporadic, fitful. **4** disordered, scrambled, mixed up, confused, wrong. **5** offbeat, unconventional, Bohemian, unorthodox.

straightaway *adv.* immediately, directly, at once, promptly, quickly, speedily, instantly, summarily, *tout de suite*, forthwith, pronto (*Slang*), straightway.

ant. gradually, slowly, hesitantly, tardily.

straighten out rectify, correct, settle, disentangle, adjust, regulate, reconcile, square, order, resolve.

ant. disrupt, upset, complicate, mess up, disorder.

straighten up tidy, trig, spruce up, clean up, clear up, fix up, arrange.

ant. mess, upset, jumble.

straightforward *adj.* candid, honest, sincere, aboveboard, frank, blunt, open, truthful, forthright, outspoken, direct, plain-spoken, ingenuous.

ant. dissembling, devious, hedging, oblique, deceitful, disingenuous.

straightway *adj.* STRAIGHTAWAY.

strain[1] *v.* **1** pull, draw, stretch, tighten, tense. **2** exert, struggle, strive, work, toil, drive, tax, labor, overexert, rack, force. **3** sprain, pull, wrench, twist, injure. **4** exaggerate, stretch, overwork, overdo, pervert, abuse, overstate, magnify, embellish, elaborate. —*n.* **1** pulling, tug, stretching, tension, tautness, tightness. **2** pressure, stress, burden, tension, force, effort, press, struggle, exertion. **3** injury, sprain, wrench, cramp, crick.

ant. *v.* **1** release, loosen, ease, slacken.

strain[2] *n.* **1** stock, extraction, lineage, ancestry, descent, family, progeny, genealogy, breed, species, subspecies, race. **2** tendency, disposition,

quality, streak, trace, inclination, nature, character, trait. **3** tone, style, manner, burden, air, vein, timbre, tenor, cast, note, accent.

strained *adj.* UNEASY.

straitened *adj.* embarrassed, distressed, destitute, restricted, constrained, strapped, pinched, needy, broke, bankrupt, poverty-stricken.

ant. comfortable, flush, solvent, well-off, affluent.

straitjacket *v.* CONFINE.

strait-laced *adj.* PRUDISH.

strand[1] *v.* abandon, desert, forsake, maroon, leave in the lurch, reject, quit, drop, walk out on, cast off. —*n.* SHORE.

ant. help, accompany, escort, protect, stand by.

strand[2] *n.* **1** thread, filament, wire, fiber, string, cord, yarn, lock, tress. **2** component, element, ingredient, theme, thread, motif, part, loose end, fragment, piece.

strange *adj.* **1** unfamiliar, unusual, new, novel, unknown, anomalous, extraordinary, peculiar, queer, odd, funny, bizarre, outlandish, extraordinary, curious, irregular, unheard-of. **2** foreign, alien, exotic, distant, external, remote, outlandish, outside, extraneous. **3** unaccustomed, unfamiliar, uncomfortable, disoriented, lost, awkward, bewildered, ill at ease, uneasy, discombobulated.

ant. 1 familiar, usual, everyday, commonplace, ordinary, expected, regular. **2** native, indigenous. **3** at home, habituated, comfortable, easy, at ease.

stranger *n.* **1** newcomer, interloper, unknown, outsider, intruder, visitor, guest, caller. **2** foreigner, alien, outlander, immigrant.

ant. 1 friend, acquaintance, chum, pal, intimate. **2** native, resident, inhabitant.

strangle *v.* **1** choke, throttle, garrote, hang, smother, suffocate, strangulate. **2** stifle, suppress, quash, quell, repress, crush, squash, hush, quiet, subdue, squelch, drown, snuff out, check, extinguish, restrain.

strangulate *v.* STRANGLE.

strap *n.* thong, band, ribbon, leash, cord, belt, strip, tape. —*v.* fasten, tie, bind, lash, truss, tether, attach. **ant.** loosen, untie, unstrap, free, detach.

strapped *adj.* DESTITUTE.

strapping *adj.* robust, muscular, athletic, sturdy, burly, able-bodied, strong, stout, powerful, brawny, bouncing. **ant.** weak, puny, frail, sickly, feeble.

stratagem *n.* maneuver, artifice, machination, tactic, deception, ruse, trick, device, pretext, strategy, contrivance, scheme, stall, play, subterfuge.

strategic *adj.* significant, major, consequential, important, decisive, crucial, key, critical, vital, signal, cardinal. **ant.** minor, insignificant, unimportant, inconsequential.

strategy *n.* **1** tactics, logistics, planning, plotting, gamesmanship, intrigue, maneuvering, machination. **2** plan, maneuver, policy, program, blueprint, game plan, scheme, plot.

stratum *n.* **1** layer, level, stratification, seam, belt, vein, zone, horizon, course, tier, stage, bed, sheet, streak, veneer. **2** class, group, caste, bracket, level, standing, position, stage, gradation, category, division, sphere, order, degree, rank, status, echelon.

straw in the wind omen, portent, harbinger, sign, augury, presentiment, foretoken, foretaste, indication, suggestion, intimation, hint, clue, promise.

stray *v.* **1** rove, roam, wander, range, ramble, drift, straggle, meander, gad, jaunt, tour, go. **2** deviate, drift, digress, diverge, divert, deflect, lose one's way, go astray, turn, bend, slip up, err, lapse, go amiss.

streak *n.* **1** stripe, band, mark, stroke, strip, bar, dash, line, belt, striping, striation, beam, ray, stream, scratch,

core, layer, vein, stratum. **2** trace, quality, nature, property, trait, tendency, touch, characteristic, stamp, tenor, tone, grain, vein, habit, makeup, constitution, temper.

stream *n.* **1** brook, creek, rivulet, river, branch, fork, feeder, tributary, watercourse, current, flow, course, rill, runnel, freshet, streamlet, kill. **2** outpouring, outburst, surge, rush, torrent, burst, eruption, onrush, discharge, deluge, flood, eruption. —*v.* flow, issue, pour forth, course, run, roll, proceed, progress, rush, surge, gush, flood, overflow, spill, cascade.

street *n.* road, avenue, lane, boulevard, alley, passageway, passage, track, trail, artery, channel, thoroughfare, roadway, highway, thruway, expressway, turnpike.

street Arab WAIF.

streetwalker *n.* PROSTITUTE.

strength *n.* **1** power, force, vigor, energy, might, puissance, sinew, muscle, thews, punch, dash, drive, vim, verve, vitality, life, spirit, fire. **2** willpower, determination, will, fortitude, endurance, persistence, toughness, tenacity, stoutness, durability, resistance, stick-to-itiveness, backbone, stamina, guts (*Slang*). **3** potency, effectiveness, effectuality, capability, capacity, competence, adequacy, intensity, concentration, forcefulness, potentiality, caliber, kick, punch, bite. **ant. 1** frailty, weakness, fragility, delicacy, puniness, infirmity. **2** cowardice, vulnerability, timidity, pusillanimity. **3** impotence, powerlessness, incapacity, futility.

strengthen *v.* fortify, reinforce, brace, prop up, support, buttress, bolster, stiffen, harden, toughen, heighten, deepen, intensify, aggravate, enhance, increase, energize, animate, activate. **ant.** weaken, enfeeble, impair, undermine, sap, soften, cripple, diminish, lessen.

strenuous *adj.* arduous, demanding,

difficult, laborious, wearisome, toilsome, hard, tough, rough, rugged, punishing, uphill, troublesome, Herculean.

ant. easy, effortless, light, mild, slight, simple.

stress *n.* **1** emphasis, importance, significance, concern, moment, weight, gravity, force, import, note, accent, brunt, crux, insistence. **2** tension, tautness, strain, pressure, anxiety, frustration, press, pinch, struggle, trauma, shock, angst. —*v.* emphasize, accentuate, accent, feature, highlight, underline, punctuate, mark, insist, demand, harp on, maintain.

ant. *v.* minimize, belittle, play down, understate, soft-pedal, overlook.

stretch *v.* **1** draw out, extend, pull, enlarge, expand, amplify, magnify, widen, broaden, distend, dilate, swell, inflate, prolong, protract, reach, spread, run, go, cover, range. **2** hold out, put forth, extend, reach out, stick out, thrust out. **3** strain, stress, draw, drag out, pull, rack, force, exert, tense, tighten. —*n.* **1** extension, stretching, prolongation, lengthening, elongation, elasticity, give, flexibility, ductility. **2** distance, length, extent, measure, reach, way, piece, expanse, range, course, compass, scope, scale, gamut. **3** time, term, period, interval, span, spell, hitch (*Slang*), season, hour, duration, tenure.

ant. *v.* **1** compress, squeeze, condense, concentrate, curtail, contract. **2** withdraw, pull back, retract, curb, arrest.

strew *v.* scatter, sprinkle, bestrew, disperse, sow, broadcast, distribute, disseminate, spatter, speckle, pepper, powder.

stricken *adj.* crippled, hurt, shaken, impaired, damaged, injured, struck down, crushed, dashed, shot, spoiled, ruined, undone, demoralized, unnerved, tormented.

strict *adj.* **1** exacting, meticulous, devout, orthodox, particular, fastidious, fussy, finicky, nice, scrupulous, conscientious, literal, close, verbatim, faithful. **2** stern, severe, harsh, tough, exacting, demanding, unsparing, firm, authoritarian, rigid, hard, inflexible, no-nonsense (*Slang*).

ant. **1** slipshod, careless, sloppy, negligent, loose. **2** relaxed, easygoing, lax, tolerant, forbearing, indulgent, permissive.

stride *n.* step, pace, footstep, lope, gait, tread, straddle, walk, march, saunter. —*v.* walk, step, pace, tread, bestride, stroll, march, saunter, lope, trudge, plod, slog, tramp, hike.

strident *adj.* grating, shrill, piercing, penetrating, harsh, screeching, high-pitched, jangling, jarring, rasping, squeaky, hoarse, guttural, raucous, stridulant, stridulous, cacophonous.

ant. soothing, gentle, mellifluous, dulcet, harmonious, euphonious, sweet, smooth.

strife *n.* contention, discord, fighting, conflict, struggle, battle, war, clash, rivalry, competition, altercation, wrangling, bickering, squabbling, quarreling, controversy, disputation.

ant. peace, harmony, concord, tranquillity, conciliation, amity, reconciliation, cooperation.

strike *v.* **1** hit, smack, knock, punch, whack, thwack, box, pound, cuff, beat, slap, pommel, hammer, thrash, trounce, clout, wallop, crack, swat, poke, jab, rap, bat, belt, smite, sock (*Slang*), lambaste (*Slang*), clobber (*Slang*), wham, bang, slam, whomp (*Slang*), paste (*Slang*). **2** collide, crash, bump, smash, graze, sideswipe, contact. **3** attack, assault, raid, charge, rush at, pitch into, invade, advance, assail, besiege, beleaguer. —*n.* **1** blow, hit, punch, smack, knock, box, clout, cuff, stroke, crack, swat, whack, rap, slap, slam, smash, poke, wallop. **2** attack, assault, thrust, raid, air raid, air strike, bombardment, onslaught, invasion, intrusion.

strike dumb ASTONISH.

strike up START.

striking *adj.* noteworthy, notable, outstanding, remarkable, unmistakable, conspicuous, impressive, pronounced, bold, prominent, signal, pointed, telling, marked, significant. **ant.** unimpressive, indifferent, mediocre, pedestrian, ineffectual, minor, commonplace.

string *n.* **1** twine, cord, strand, binding, ribbon, tie, band, strip, line, thread, thong, fiber, braid, twist, filament, rope, wire, cable, ligature. **2** series, succession, run, progression, row, set, sequence, bunch, pack, batch, train, suite, thread, line, list, accumulation, continuity.

string along *Slang* **1** cooperate, collaborate, go along, join, follow, pursue, side, team up. **2** deceive, cheat, mislead, misguide, misdirect, beguile, delude, fool, dupe, trick, hoodwink, hoax.

stringent *adj.* strict, severe, exacting, demanding, difficult, hard, rigorous, tough, exigent, rigid, unbending, firm, relentless, stiff, tight, harsh, inflexible. **ant.** moderate, lenient, convenient, soft, easy, compliant, flexible.

string up HANG.

stringy *adj.* **1** threadlike, thready, wiry, fibrous, fibroid, capillary. **2** viscous, viscose, viscid, gluey, ropy, gummy, glutinous, mucilaginous, gelatinous, thick, sticky, tacky.

strip[1] *n.* length, measure, span, stretch, piece, portion, band, ribbon, bar, belt, stripe, swath, swatch.

strip[2] *v.* **1** lay bare, uncover, expose, bare, remove, divest, take off, denude, scrape, scale, peel, pare, flake, skim, husk. **2** rob, plunder, loot, pillage, sack, ransack, despoil, spoil, ravage, forage, raid, rifle, milk, fleece, bleed, exhaust, drain. **3** divest, empty, remove, take out, pull out, extract, withdraw, deprive. **ant.** **1** cover, surface, overlay, face, varnish, paint, conceal, cloak. **2** fill,

furnish, lay in, stock, load, pack, supply, store.

stripe[1] *n.* **1** band, belt, bar, strip, stroke, dash, mark, swath, streak, line, gash, path, scratch, trail, striation, stratum. **2** quality, kind, type, ilk, make, cast, mold, stamp, grain, vein, makeup, disposition, mood, humor, temperament, temper, tendency, persuasion, nature.

stripe[2] *n.* WELT.

stripling *n.* LAD.

strive *v.* try, apply, oneself, attempt, endeavor, seek, aim, strain, labor, hustle, struggle, vie, push.

stroke *n.* **1** blow, hit, smack, knock, whack, thwack, box, cuff, strike, stripe, lash, switch, slap, slam, bang, poke, crack, swat, rap, pound, sock (*Slang*), clout, spank. **2** caress, touch, contact, feel, brush, graze, rub. —*v.* caress, fondle, touch, pat, pet, rub, brush, massage, knead, nuzzle.

stroll *v.* saunter, ramble, perambulate, traipse, meander, poke along, mosey, toddle, walk. —*n.* saunter, walk, ramble, tramp, jaunt, stretch, turn, airing, constitutional, perambulation.

strong *adj.* **1** powerful, mighty, stalwart, vigorous, robust, energetic, hearty, strapping, athletic, brawny, muscular, sturdy, stout, rugged, solid, durable, healthy, sound. **2** strong-willed, resolute, determined, tenacious, firm, unyielding, staunch, courageous, self-assertive, aggressive, forceful, dynamic, energetic, intense, fervid. **3** astute, keen, sagacious, trenchant, cogent, profound, sound, sensible, reasonable, levelheaded, competent, able. **4** *of a rival or opponent:* formidable, impressive, redoubtable, powerful, challenging, major, mighty. **5** *powerful in effect:* potent, forceful, effective, efficacious, undiluted, harsh, heady. **6** extreme, emphatic, excessive, immoderate, intemperate, severe,

harsh, inordinate, unusual, drastic, extraordinary, Draconian, radical.
ant. 1 feeble, frail, weak, fragile, shaky, infirm, decrepit. **2** weak-willed, indecisive, cowardly, wavering, irresolute, vacillating. **3** incompetent, obtuse, incapable, muddle-headed. **4** weak, slight, easy, minor, paltry, puny. **5** diluted, watered-down, impotent, fruitless, inefficacious. **6** moderate, temperate, middle-of-the-road, bland, ordinary.

strong-arm *v.* COERCE.

stronghold *n.* fort, fortress, bastion, citadel, tower, castle, fortification, battlement, fastness, keep, blockhouse, bunker, bulwark, rampart, barricade.

strong-minded *adj.* STRONG-WILLED.

strong-willed *adj.* resolute, determined, staunch, firm, strong-minded, self-possessed, self-assertive, self-controlled, fixed, unyielding, inflexible, dogged, tenacious, stubborn, willful, obstinate, obdurate.
ant. indecisive, vacillating, irresolute, erratic, halfhearted, compromising, inconstant.

structure *n.* **1** building, construction, edifice, framework, erection. **2** organization, plan, arrangement, composition, constitution, make-up, design, form, anatomy, fabric, shape, apparatus, *apparat*, policy, program, blueprint, pattern, scheme, recipe, pattern, plot, formula. —*v.* conceptualize, organize, plan, think of, consider, objectify, project, analyze, contemplate, conceive, envisage, visualize, picture.

struggle *n.* **1** exertion, effort, strain, striving, endeavor, stress, trouble, labor, pains, pursuit, scramble. **2** conflict, strife, contention, discord, altercation, contest, competition, duel, set-to, rivalry, combat, battle, war. —*v.* **1** fight, contend, contest, compete, clash, battle, combat, scrap, scuffle, vie with, tussle, joust, tilt. **2** strive, strain, exert oneself,

toil, work, grind, labor, drudge, persevere, carry on, hold out.
ant. *v.* **1** cooperate, collaborate, coexist, join forces, unite. **2** surrender, give up, resign.

strumpet *n.* WHORE.

strut *n.* **1** swagger, flounce, prance. **2** support, brace, bolster, prop, rib, stay, angle, guy, splint, shoring. —*v.* swagger, prance, flounce, parade.

stub *n.* end, tip, remainder, leftover, point, nib, tail, tag, dock, butt, fag end, roach (*Slang*).

stubbly *adj.* STUBBY.

stubborn *adj.* **1** opinionated, contentious, dogmatic, narrow-minded, narrow, unreasoning, irrational, bigoted, stiff-necked, unbending, rigid, inflexible, argumentative, strong-minded, cross-grained, bull-headed, pig-headed, mulish. **2** determined, resolute, unshakable, set, obstinate, strong-willed, persistent, pertinacious, headstrong, unyielding, adamant, obdurate, intractable.
ant. 1 open-minded, broad-minded, reasonable, flexible. **2** uncertain, vacillating, indecisive, weak-willed.

stubbornness *n.* OBSTINACY.

stubby *adj.* **1** stubbly, stiff, bristly, stubbled, rough, hairy, bearded, whiskery, fuzzy, frizzy, hirsute, hispid, barbellate, setaceous. **2** short, stumpy, stocky, chubby, pudgy, tubby, squat, chunky, squab, stunted, thickset, dwarfish.
ant. 1 smooth, polished, glassy, velvety, sleek, glossy. **2** tall, lanky, gangling, slim, slender.

stuck-up *adj.* conceited, snobbish, vain, swell-headed, egotistic, arrogant, puffed-up, proud, haughty, lofty, condescending, uppish, uppity, self-important, snooty, high-hat, hoity-toity.
ant. humble, modest, plain, simple.

student *n.* pupil, learner, trainee, beginner, novice, tyro, follower, disciple, apostle, proselyte, scholar, undergraduate, collegian.

studied *adj.* calculated, planned, deliberate, measured, weighed, premeditated, predetermined, willful, conscious, purposeful, intended.

ant. unpremeditated, spontaneous, natural, extemporaneous, impulsive, unguarded, instinctive.

studious *adj.* **1** bookish, well-read, learned, erudite, cultivated, literate, educated, lettered, highbrow, intellectual, pedantic, academic, scholarly. **2** diligent, attentive, careful, assiduous, thorough, rigorous, painstaking, considerate, industrious, sedulous, scrupulous, exacting.

ant. **1** illiterate, uneducated, ignorant, unschooled, uninformed. **2** careless, negligent, hit-or-miss, offhand, lackadaisical.

study *v.* **1** learn, read, master. **2** examine, investigate, inspect, search into, analyze, scrutinize, query, review, peruse, consider, observe, contemplate, ponder, weigh, deliberate, mull over, ruminate, meditate. —*n.* **1** learning, schooling, instruction, training, education, tutelage, pedagogy, edification, tuition, erudition, scholarship, cultivation, enlightenment, lucubration, reading, exercise, drill. **2** subject, course, branch, discipline, curriculum. **3** examination, investigation, overview, report, white paper, inspection, exploration, scrutiny, inquiry, analysis, research, perusal, survey, review.

stuff *v.* **1** fill, pack, load, charge, heap, pad, line, wad, plug, obstruct, stop up, clog, block, close, choke, jam, dam, cork, congest, occlude. **2** cram, gorge, jam, crowd, satiate, cloy, surfeit, sate, glut, gluttonize, gormandize. —*n.* **1** material, matter, things, objects, substance, contents, staple, stock, rubbish, rubble, trash, debris, scrap, junk, flotsam, jetsam. **2** essence, heart, core, basis, element, principle, essential, substance, quintessence, nucleus, gist, nub, pith. **3** nonsense, foolishness, baloney (*Slang*), balderdash, bunk (*Slang*), bosh, hogwash, humbug, malarky

(*Slang*), falderal, trumpery, rot, bosh, tripe, poppycock.

stuffed shirt PRIG.

stuffy *adj.* **1** airless, stifling, close, choking, suffocating, oppressive, stagnant, humid, sultry, muggy, sweaty, languid, breezeless, becalmed. **2** pompous, stodgy, strait-laced, old-fogyish, formal, stilted, staid, dull, uninspired, unimaginative, uninteresting, boring, tedious.

ant. **1** ventilated, airy, breezy, fresh, invigorating. **2** informal, casual, natural, colloquial, relaxed, at ease.

stultify *v.* frustrate, thwart, hinder, obstruct, impede, inhibit, balk, check, trammel, neutralize, invalidate, vitiate, negate, nullify, veto.

ant. advance, promote, improve, foster, facilitate, expedite, boost.

stumble *v.* **1** trip, topple, tumble, founder, totter, teeter, stagger, falter, lurch, sprawl, rock, reel, pitch, fall, take a header. **2** blunder, err, slip, bungle, boggle, fumble, muff, fudge, miscalculate. **3** *come upon by chance:* happen, chance, come, run, hit, encounter, discover, find.

stumblingblock *n.* OBSTACLE.

stun *v.* **1** stupefy, daze, benumb, stagger, shock, dull, blunt, paralyze, knock out, deaden, anesthetize, drug, dope, narcotize. **2** astound, astonish, amaze, startle, surprise, stagger, overwhelm, stupefy, dazzle, confound, awe, dumbfound, flabbergast.

stung *adj.* AGGRIEVED.

stunned *adj.* DAZED.

stunning *adj.* astounding, astonishing, amazing, bewildering, overwhelming, staggering, confounding, awesome, indescribable.

ant. prosaic, ordinary, commonplace, unexciting, dull, routine.

stunt[1] *v.* cramp, impede, check, curtail, suppress, muffle, restrain, cut, nip, throttle, choke, stifle, minimize, abbreviate, shorten, dwarf.

ant. stimulate, encourage, force.

stunt[2] *n.* feat, exploit, deed, act, trick, performance, sensation, maneuver, execution, adventure, enterprise, achievement, operation, action.

stunted *adj.* short, puny, scrubby, stubby, stumpy, runty, undersized, dwarf, pygmy.

ant. tall, towering, lofty, elevated, gigantic, rangy.

stupefaction *n.* AMAZEMENT.

stupefied *adj.* DAZED.

stupefy *v.* STUN.

stupendous *adj.* prodigious, gigantic, colossal, mammoth, jumbo, enormous, elephantine, gargantuan, monstrous, huge, monumental, titanic, phenomenal, voluminous.

ant. small, tiny, puny, slight, diminutive, minuscule, dainty.

stupid *adj.* **1** unintelligent, dull-witted, slow-witted, dull, dopey (*Slang*), slow, dense, thick, obtuse, blank, vacant, vacuous, empty-headed, mindless, blockheaded, witless, blockish, senseless, brainless, foolish, simple, simple-minded, puerile, doltish, thickheaded, thick-witted, lumpish, dumb, asinine, half-witted, deficient, subnormal, retarded, feebleminded, idiotic, imbecile, moronic. **2** stupefied, insensate, dazed, benumbed, numb, dull, sluggish, groggy, punch-drunk, punchy, muddled, muddle-headed, soporific, lethargic, comatose, phlegmatic, listless, languorous, apathetic, unfeeling, semiconscious, spiritless. **3** futile, profitless, vain, fruitless, pointless, ineffectual, empty, inane, fatuous, foolish, unreasonable, silly.

ant. 1 intelligent, bright, smart, brilliant, wise, clever, quick-witted, sharp. **2** alert, keen, lively, sprightly, wide-awake, vigilant. **3** sensible, reasonable, practical, purposeful, effective.

stupidity *n.* dull-wittedness, unintelligence, dumbness, dullness, obtuseness, blockheadedness, vacuity, slowness, denseness, sluggishness, oafishness, doltishness, simple-mindedness, incapacity, feeble-mindedness, idiocy, imbecility, retardation.

ant. intelligence, acumen, discernment, brightness, smartness, keenness.

stupor *n.* insensibility, stupefaction, numbness, dullness, faint, coma, blackout, anesthesia, semiconsciousness, unconsciousness, lethargy, languor, sluggishness, torpor, lassitude, grogginess, muddleheadedness, ischemia, swoon.

sturdy *adj.* **1** hardy, healthy, robust, vigorous, rugged, hearty, hale, lusty, strong, stalwart, stout, able-bodied, husky, brawny, substantial, solid, rugged, firm, durable. **2** resolute, determined, unyielding, firm, staunch, steadfast, strong, invulnerable, enduring, persistent, plucky, tough, redoubtable, formidable, mettlesome.

ant. 1 weak, ailing, sickly, frail, feeble, puny, flimsy. **2** faltering, vacillating, indecisive, frivolous, capricious, fickle.

style *n.* **1** fashion, vogue, taste, mode, *bon ton,* chic, smartness, fad, craze, rage, custom, cast, cut, stamp, set, mold. **2** manner, mode, way, fashion, genre, form, shape, variety, kind, type, category, character, treatment.

stylish *adj.* fashionable, chic, modish, voguish, elegant, smart, spruce, sporty, swank, ritzy (*Slang*), chichi, dapper, natty, faddish, doggish, *à la mode.*

ant. unfashionable, passé, shabby, tacky, stale, old-fashioned, obsolete.

stymie *v.* baffle, thwart, frustrate, foil, balk, obstruct, hamper, impede, block, check, stump, stall, scotch, spike, checkmate, confound, perplex, nonplus.

suasion *n.* PERSUASION.

suave *adj.* slick, smooth, glib, silken, facile, smooth-tongued, unctuous, oily, ingratiating, flattering, fulsome, oleaginous, charming, urbane, sophisticated, diplomatic.

ant. brusque, gruff, blunt, uncouth, boorish, tongue-tied, vulgar, coarse.

sub *n.* SUBSTITUTE.

subaltern *n.* SUBORDINATE.

subdue *v.* **1** conquer, defeat, overcome, overpower, overwhelm, vanquish, subjugate, suppress, triumph over, crush, humble, worst, best, quell, quash, control, master, tame. **2** lessen, reduce, soften, mute, muffle, dampen, dull, mollify, mellow, tone down, moderate, modulate, temper, chasten.
ant. **1** lose, succumb, capitulate, fail, surrender, give in to. **2** increase, intensify, augment, raise, boost, inflate.

subject *adj.* **1** subordinate, subservient, dependent, subdued, captive, enslaved, subjugated. **2** exposed, liable, open, susceptible, prone, vulnerable, disposed. —*n.* **1** citizen, national, compatriot, countryman, native, inhabitant, occupant, dweller, denizen, civilian, vassal, liege, servant. **2** patient, client, participant, victim, guinea pig. **3** theme, topic, motif, thesis, statement, proposition, issue, point, lesson, matter, moral, problem, question, consideration, affair, business. —*v.* **1** expose to, put through, undergo, experience, endure, suffer. **2** SUBJUGATE.
ant. *adj.* **1** superior, ruling, dominant, leading, controlling. **2** exempt, excepted, privileged, immune. *v.* **1** shield, protect, spare, spoil.

subjective *adj.* **1** personal, introspective, individual, private, idiosyncratic, mental, felt. **2** biased, emotional, prejudiced, partial, interested, partisan, nonobjective.
ant. **1** objective, impersonal, factual, verifiable. **2** impartial, disinterested, detached, unbiased, neutral.

subjugate *v.* conquer, vanquish, overwhelm, subject, overpower, crush, humble, subdue, quell, rout, suppress, put down, harness, enslave.

sublimate *v.* PURIFY.

sublime *adj.* magnificent, grand, great, exalted, lofty, elevated, ethereal, inspiring, moving, glorious, noble, majestic, stately, handsome, august, solemn.
ant. frivolous, inane, ridiculous, absurd, ludicrous.

submerge *v.* immerse, submerse, sink, plunge, duck, immerge, inundate, drown, engulf, overwhelm, bury, douse, souse, dip, dunk, dive, founder, whelm.

submerse *v.* SUBMERGE.

submission *n.* **1** surrender, capitulation, subservience, subjection, subjugation, subordination, abandonment, bondage, thralldom, servitude, captivity. **2** compliance, acquiescence, obedience, deference, subjection, dutifulness, dependence, complaisance, docility, humbleness, resignation, passivity.
ant. **1** victory, triumph, ascendancy, mastery, advantage. **2** resistance, revolt, rejection, defiance, disobedience.

submissive *adj.* docile, obedient, yielding, acquiescent, compliant, manageable, meek, gentle, mild, resigned, passive, unassertive, deferential, humble.
ant. self-assertive, domineering, forceful, aggressive, bumptious.

submit *v.* **1** surrender, yield, succumb, give up, capitulate, cede, back down, give way, resign, accede, comply, acquiesce, defer. **2** present, offer, propose, proffer, tender, extend, hold out, introduce, volunteer, suggest, put forward, advance, propound, state, pose.
ant. **1** resist, hold out, defy, hold fast.

subnormal *adj.* SUBSTANDARD.

subordinate *adj.* **1** secondary, minor, second, supplementary, subsidiary, ancillary, marginal, contingent, subaltern. **2** subservient, subject, dependent, inferior, lesser, junior, under. —*n.* underling, assistant, aide, inferior, subaltern, second, subsidiary, junior, attendant, follower, dependent, servant, retainer, sidekick (*Slang*). —*v.* subject, control, restrain, check, subdue, inhibit, belittle, repress, suppress, downgrade, depreciate, reduce, diminish, lessen, minimize, lower.

ant. *adj.* **1** primary, initial, superior, first, beginning, premier. **2** ruling, sovereign, commanding, controlling, governing.

suborn *v.* BRIBE.

subpoena *v.* SUMMON. —*n.* SUMMONS.

subscribe *v.* assent, agree, concur, consent, accept, acknowledge, approve, support, endorse, allow, admit, grant, warrant, comply, concede, acquiesce.

ant. reject, abstain, disapprove, dissent.

subsequent *adj.* following, succeeding, ensuing, successive, next, proximate, latter, later, after, posterior, sequent, consequent.

ant. preceding, previous, antecedent, prior, foregoing, precursory.

subservient *adj.* servile, obsequious, slavish, abject, sycophantic, truckling, fawning, toadying, groveling, bootlicking.

ant. insolent, arrogant, haughty, disdainful, swaggering, imperious, presumptuous.

subside *v.* **1** sink, settle, decline, go down, lower, descend, slip, slide, slump, droop, sag, fall. **2** abate, quiet down, level off, quieten (*Brit.*), ease, calm down.

ant. **1** rise, ascend, advance, climb, mount. **2** agitate, roil, stir up, aggravate.

subsidiary *adj.* auxiliary, assisting, supplementary, ancillary, accessory, serving, assistant, helping, contributing, contingent, dependent.

subsist *v.* live, exist, be, occur, endure, survive, remain, prevail, stand, continue, abide, last, run.

ant. die, expire, perish, cease.

subsistence *n.* **1** life, existence, being, presence, occurrence, endurance, continuance, duration, extension, permanence. **2** SUSTENANCE.

substance *n.* **1** matter, material, stuff,

elements, constituents, content. **2** essence, essentials, fundamentals, quintessence, gist, nucleus, core, nub, meat, pith, heart, spirit, sense, purport, import, effect, basis, force, drift, tenor. **3** wealth, means, resources, assets, funds, finances, riches, fortune, treasure, property, possessions, prosperity, affluence. **4** cogency, force, solidity, strength, weight, power, potency, impact, effect, soundness, sense.

substandard *adj.* inferior, subnormal, second-rate, poor, subpar, mediocre, inadequate, deficient.

ant. standard, up to snuff, adequate.

substantial *adj.* **1** solid, strong, firm, sturdy, sound, stable, steady, rugged, stout, durable, well-made. **2** generous, ample, considerable, sizable, large, hefty, big, goodly, grand. **3** wealthy, rich, well-to-do, affluent, prosperous, moneyed, solvent, sound, solid, well-fixed.

ant. **1** flimsy, fragile, frail, weak, unsubstantial. **2** trifling, petty, skimpy, niggling, meager, mean. **3** poor, needy, impoverished, pinched, destitute.

substantiate *v.* confirm, verify, establish, corroborate, affirm, support, demonstrate, uphold, sustain, authenticate, document, validate, certify, attest.

ant. disprove, dispute, refute, confute, controvert, expose.

substitute *v.* supplant, replace, put in place of, displace, switch, exchange, supersede, relieve, spell, succeed, act for, represent, deputize, surrogate. —*n.* replacement, substitution, exchange, alternate, deputy, agent, representative, secondary, surrogate, ersatz, sub, relief, backup, fill-in, stand-in, proxy, understudy, standby, extra, irregular, bench warmer, ringer (*Slang*), pinch hitter. —*adj.* alternate, alternative, sub, equivalent, dummy, proxy, ersatz, makeshift, backup, second-string.

ant. *adj.* original, first, primary, earliest, basic, actual, real.

subterfuge *n.* ruse, stratagem, alibi, pretext, excuse, trick, artifice, deception.

subterranean *adj.* UNDERGROUND.

subtile *adj.* SUBTLE.

subtle *adj.* **1** delicate, fine, gentle, dainty, nice, refined, rarefied, airy, tender, thin, slender, subtile, finespun, elusive, shadowy, ethereal, illusory. **2** sensitive, acute, keen, astute, discerning, discriminating, perceptive, selective, discreet, critical, quick, sharp, precise, refined. **3** skillful, ingenious, versatile, adroit, deft, agile, dexterous, artful, clever, shrewd, wily, sophisticated, crafty, cunning, subtile, slick, sly, suave, foxy.

ant. **1** gross, coarse, rough, earthy, crude. **2** insensitive, obtuse, dense, uncritical, mindless. **3** awkward, bumbling, inept, naive, ingenuous, artless.

subversion *n.* overthow, overturn, upset, inversion, subverting, reversal, fall, downfall, ruin, destruction, demolition, waste, ravage.

subvert *v.* **1** overthrow, overturn, upset, overwhelm, demolish, destroy, ruin, wreck, devastate. **2** corrupt, debase, degrade, defile, deprave, contaminate, poison, taint, undermine, warp, spoil, ruin, mar.

ant. **1** erect, establish, found, build, construct.

succeed *v.* **1** accomplish, achieve, attain, fulfill, consummate, effect, bring off, triumph, win, gain, realize, complete, perfect, finish, execute, come off, perform, engineer, produce, make, make good, do. **2** follow, come after, ensue, supersede, result, replace, supplant, substitute for, relieve.

ant. **1** fail, disappoint, founder, default, abort. **2** precede, forerun, antedate, preface, introduce, prevene.

success *n.* **1** achievement, accomplishment, fulfillment, completion, attainment, realization, satisfaction, victory, consummation, triumph, conquest, outcome, issue, windup, conclusion, execution. **2** eminence, status, station, prestige, fame, prosperity, wealth, well-being, comfort, fortune, luck.

ant. **1** loss, defeat, breakdown, collapse, ruination, debacle, frustration. **2** disfavor, disgrace, poverty, failure, decline.

successful *adj.* **1** complete, perfect, accomplished, consummate, victorious, triumphant, winning, effective, unbeatable, efficient, eficacious, workable, functioning, ongoing. **2** prosperous, well-off, well-to-do, thriving, flourishing, booming, comfortable, fortunate, lucky, affluent, rich.

ant. **1** unworkable, inefficient, faulty, deficient. **2** unfortunate, penurious, needy, miserable, disadvantaged.

succession *n.* **1** continuation, following, accession, progression, consecutiveness, prolongation, extension, rotation. **2** series, sequence, order, run, row, progression, course, file, line, train, thread.

successive *adj.* consecutive, succeeding, continuous, following, ensuing, sequent, sequential, subsequent, serial.

succinct *adj.* concise, terse, short, brief, curt, laconic, pithy, trenchant, pointed, crisp, neat, compact, summary, condensed, shortened, abbreviated, compressed.

ant. verbose, prolix, loquacious, long-winded, garrulous.

succor *n.* help, aid, assistance, relief, support, rescue, lift, boost, backing, service, benefit, ministration. —*v.* help, aid, assist, relieve, support, rescue, abet, bolster, comfort, back, uphold, foster, nurture, promote, encourage, favor, befriend.

ant. *v.* injure, harm, ill-use, obstruct, hinder, thwart, impede, frustrate.

succulent *adj.* juicy, moist, fleshy, pulpy, mushy, sappy.

ant. dry, juiceless, desiccated.

succumb *v.* **1** submit, yield, give way, comply, accede, acquiesce, defer to, obey, resign, give up, give in, surrender, capitulate, go under, fall, relent. **2** DIE.
ant. 1 hold out, persist, persevere, endure, continue, carry on.

such *adj.* similar, like, corresponding, comparable, suchlike, allied, matching, duplicate, twin, analogous.
ant. dissimilar, unlike, different, disparate, divergent, various.

suchlike *adj.* SUCH.

suck *v.* draw in, sip, imbibe, swallow, gulp, lap up, siphon, ingest, inspire, drain, sponge, soak up, absorb, admit.

sucker *n. Slang* dupe, gull, chump, fool, cat's-paw, sitting duck, easy mark, butt, pushover (*Slang*), pigeon (*Slang*), boob (*Slang*) fair game, *naïf*, butt, tool, victim.

suckle *v.* breast-feed, nurse, wet-nurse, feed, nurture, nourish.

sudden *adj.* **1** quick, swift, rapid, speedy, abrupt, brief, short-lived, meteoric, brisk, fleet, express, prompt, expeditious, instant, immediate, instantaneous. **2** surprising, unexpected, unanticipated, unforeseen, unpredictable, startling, astonishing. **3** hasty, hurried, rushed, precipitous, headlong, impetuous, impulsive, rash.
ant. 1 prolonged, long-lasting, protracted, extended, drawn-out, long, slow. **2** anticipated, expected, predictable. **3** cautious, careful, prudent, considered, thoughtful.

suddenly *adv.* quickly, swiftly, speedily, instantly, instanter, fast, immediately, hurriedly, instantaneously, at once, presently, now, abruptly, hastily, precipitously, rashly, impulsively.
ant. slowly, sluggishly, leisurely, unhurriedly, hesitantly, deliberately, carefully.

sue *v.* ASK

suffer *v.* **1** hurt, ache, ail, grieve, agonize, despair. **2** sustain, undergo, put up with, support, experience, encounter, go through, endure, bear, tolerate, accept, stand. **3** permit, allow, let, condone, countenance, tolerate, admit, accord, grant, authorize, empower, sanction, license, warrant.
ant. 2 reject, repudiate, eliminate, banish, relegate, deny. **3** refuse, disallow, deny, rebuff, bar, oppose.

sufferance *n.* PERMISSION.

suffering *n.* **1** anguish, agony, distress, misery, pain, grief, torment, woe, heartache, affliction, trial, ordeal, burden, torture, *Weltschmerz*. **2** injury, wound, hurt, pain, ache, aching, pang, stab, sting, smart, twinge, twitch.
ant. 1 comfort, tranquillity, peace, satisfaction, *Gemütlichkeit*.

suffice *v.* satisfy, serve, do, avail, fulfill, answer, meet, qualify, fill the bill, pass muster, measure up.
ant. fail, fall short, disappoint.

sufficient *adj.* adequate, enough, ample, plentiful, abundant, plenteous, copious, liberal, satisfactory.
ant. scanty, meager, deficient, lacking, incomplete.

suffocate *v.* strangle, choke, gag, throttle, garrote, stifle, smother, asphyxiate, extinguish, snuff out, deaden, quench.

suffuse *v.* spread, pervade, permeate, diffuse, infiltrate, saturate, overrun, fill, penetrate, infuse, steep, imbue, transfuse, impregnate, tinge, leaven.

sugar *v.* SWEETEN.

sugar-coat *v.* SWEETEN.

sugary *adj.* saccharine, sweet, complaisant, agreeable, honeyed, sentimental, gushing, mushy, cloying, mawkish, goody-goody, fulsome.
ant. acid, acerbic, crusty, sarcastic.

suggest *n.* **1** propose, set forth, put forward, advise, recommend, advocate, counsel, urge, entreat. **2** imply, intimate, hint, insinuate, signify, indicate, denote, mean, betoken, promise, portend, herald, foretoken, adumbrate, presage, augur.

suggestion *n.* **1** proposal, proposition, statement, expression, position, stipulation, motion, charge, presentation, opinion, thought, recommendation, advice, counsel, admonition, entreaty. **2** implication, intimation, indication, insinuation, suspicion, hint, tip, clue, lead, scent, tinge, vestige, shade, shadow, trace, touch, inkling, glimmer.

suggestive *adj.* **1** stimulating, meaningful, provocative, significant, stimulative, provoking, constructive, expressive, eloquent, pregnant. **2** improper, indecent, indelicate, unseemly, unbecoming, immodest, off-color, risqué, spicy, racy, salty, ribald, blue, bawdy.
ant. **1** unproductive, meaningless, empty, void, irrelevant. **2** decorous, modest, polite, proper, genteel, polished, refined.

suicide *n.* self-murder, self-destruction, hara-kiri, suttee, self-immolation.

suit *n.* **1** set, group, collection, ensemble, combination, assembly, series, suite. **2** lawsuit, case, proceeding, action, litigation, prosecution, charge, indictment, arraignment, cause. —*v.* **1** fit, accommodate, comply with, agree with, correspond, meet, serve, do, answer, accord, observe, follow, comport with, reconcile, adapt, adjust, shape, tailor. **2** please, satisfy, gratify, agree with, like, appease, delight, enchant, enthrall.
ant. *v.* **2** clash with, upset, displease, dissatisfy.

suitable *adj.* appropriate, proper, fitting, fit, meet, seemly, becoming, satisfactory, adequate, tailor-made, acceptable, commensurate, convenient, opportune.
ant. inappropriate, ill-advised, awkward, irrelevant, unbecoming, unseemly, inapplicable.

suite *n.* **1** attendants, retinue, company, following, escort, entourage, association, companions, convoy, train, court, cortege. **2** APARTMENT.

suitor *n.* boy friend, young man, fellow, man, lover, admirer, date, courter, wooer, pursuer, steady (*Slang*), beau, gallant, squire, inamorato, swain.

sulk *v.* brood, mope, pout, fret, grump, grouch, crab, grouse, glower, fume.

sulky *adj.* moody, brooding, melancholy, depressed, blue, sullen, grumpy, grouchy, mopish, glum, morose, cranky, temperamental, in the dumps.
ant. cheerful, animated, gay, sprightly, merry, lively.

sullen *adj.* morose, glum, ill-humored, sulky, melancholy, depressed, mopish, moody, peevish, petulant, bilious, brooding, cross, testy, crabbed, mean, sour, cantankerous.
ant. animated, vivacious, enthusiastic, buoyant, jovial, breezy, joyous.

sully *v.* soil, dirty, defile, stain, spot, blacken, darken, blot, smirch, smudge, smutch, begrime, tarnish, taint, mar, spoil, befoul, pollute, contaminate, corrupt.
ant. purify, cleanse, polish.

sultry *adj.* **1** stifling, oppressive, humid, close, suffocating, stuffy, still, sticky, muggy, moist, sweltering, torrid, tropical, burning, hot. **2** passionate, inflamed, impassioned, ardent, torrid, hot, flushed, fiery, hot-blooded, amorous, erotic, sensual, sexy, enticing, suggestive, alluring, come-hither (*Slang*).
ant. **1** cool, cold, chilly, bracing, breezy, brisk, tonic, invigorating.

sum *n.* **1** money, cash, funds, capital, assets, amount, means, resources. **2** summation, total, whole, reckoning, score, tally, aggregate, count, number, amount. **3** essence, core, substance, heart, nub, capsule, brief, digest, summary, recapitulation, bottom line (*Slang*).

summarize *v.* condense, abridge, digest, abbreviate, abstract, outline, synopsize, epitomize, capsulize, recapitulate, review, sum up.
ant. expand, enlarge on, expatiate, embroider, flesh out.

summary *n.* précis, compendium, synopsis, digest, brief, encapsulation, condensation, abridgment, abstract, résumé, outline, syllabus, survey, review, rundown, wrap-up, substance, schema, epitome. —*adj.* peremptory, prompt, speedy, quick, swift, immediate, instant, hasty, expeditious, precipitate.

summation *n.* conclusion, recapitulation, summing up, peroration, summary, review, run-through, restatement, brief, digest.

summit *n.* **1** top, peak, apex, crown, crest, height, vertex, acme, zenith, cap, tip, brow, climax, culmination. **2** maximum, ultimate, limit, consummation, *ne plus ultra*, climax, culmination, acme, zenith, height.

summon *v.* **1** send for, call, bid, page, order, ask, demand, invite, seek, solicit, canvass, evoke, invoke, conjure, muster. **2** convene, convoke, assemble, call together, gather, rally, mobilize, muster, recruit, conscript, draft. **3** subpoena, cite, call, serve.

summons *n.* call, subpoena, bid, notification, invitation, solicitation, writ, warrant.

sumptuous *adj.* lavish, extravagant, exorbitant, luxurious, rich, fancy, elaborate, posh, magnificent, splendid, grand, plush (*Slang*).
  ant. spare, plain, simple, austere.

sum up conclude, finish, close, consummate, recapitulate, recount, restate, reiterate, go over, review, summarize.

sun *n.* center, hub, heart, focus, light, core, nucleus, navel, kernel, pivot, daystar. —*v.* sun-bathe, bask, bake, fry, tan.

sun-bathe *v.* SUN.

sunder *v.* break apart, sever, spilt, cleave, tear, rend, crack, splinter, rive, fracture, rupture, divorce.
  ant. unite, join, seal, bring together, conjoin.

sundown *n.* SUNSET.

sundry *adj.* various, several, divers, numerous, many, manifold, myriad, miscellaneous, diverse, assorted, heterogeneous, motley.
  ant. uniform, homogeneous, single, one, exclusive, select, distinct.

sunken *adj.* **1** lower, under, inferior, down, subordinate, retreating, recessed, subjacent, sub, nether. **2** *deeply depressed or fallen in:* depressed, hollow, concave, hollowed, indented, dented, dimpled.
  ant. **1** higher, upper, elevated, outstanding. **2** protruding, prominent, swelling, convex, bulging.

sunless *adj.* dark, cheerless, gloomy, dreary, dismal, bleak, dim, black, hopeless, pessimistic.

sunny *adj.* **1** bright, light, radiant, shiny, glowing, aglow, gleaming, luminous, brilliant, dazzling, lustrous, refulgent, resplendent. **2** cheerful, genial, friendly, pleasing, pleasant, winsome, bright, attractive, radiant, sparkling, beaming, optimistic.
  ant. **1** dark, shadowy, sunless, dim, murky. **2** dour, gloomy, sullen, melancholy, pessimistic.

sunrise *n.* dawn, sunup, daybreak, daylight, dawning, dayspring, break of day, twilight, east, cockcrow, aurora.

sunset *n.* dusk, sundown, evening, nightfall, twilight, night, eventide, even, gloaming, crepuscule.

sunup *n.* SUNRISE.

sup *v.* SIP.

super *adj.* outstanding, extraordinary, incomparable, excellent, great, matchless, peerless, superior, prime, prize, nonpareil, unexcelled, champion. —*n.* SUPERINTENDENT.
  ant. *adj.* commonplace, prosaic, unimpressive, undistinguished, pedestrian, hackneyed.

superabundant *adj.* ABUNDANT.

superannuated *adj.* **1** retired, pensioned, dismissed. **2** obsolete, antiquated, passé, outmoded, outworn, musty, rusty, old, ancient, retired, discarded, antique, archaic, extinct, fossil.
  ant. **2** modern, progressive, contem-

porary, up-to-date, advanced, new-fangled.

superb *adj.* **1** excellent, extraordinary, exquisite, fine, marvelous, wonderful, super. **2** magnificent, impressive, grand, imposing, splendid, majestic, stately, luxurious, sumptuous, elaborate, elegant.

ant. 1 poor, inferior, second-rate, indifferent, worthless. **2** modest, unpretentious, humble, homely, mean, commonplace.

supercilious *adj.* haughty, snobbish, patronizing, condescending, cavalier, offhand, aloof, remote, lofty, toplofty, lordly, imperious, disdainful, contemptuous, arrogant, snooty, stuck-up.

ant. unpretentious, unassuming, humble, diffident, self-deprecating.

supererogatory *adj.* SUPERFLUOUS.

superficial *adj.* **1** exterior, surface, external, outer, outside, outermost, cover, peripheral. **2** *not profound:* shallow, skin-deep, slight, obvious, commonplace, patent, surface. **3** hasty, cursory, hurried, quick, snap, passing, slap-dash, fast, feverish. **4** apparent, seeming, evident, ostensible, outward.

ant. 1 interior, internal, inside, inmost. **2** profound, deep, in-depth, complex. **3** considered, careful, thoughtful, thoroughgoing, painstaking. **4** genuine, authentic, real, valid, veritable.

superfluity *n.* REDUNDANCY.

superfluous *adj.* redundant, unnecessary, inessential, supererogatory, supernumerary, extra, pleonastic, excessive, surplus, excess.

ant. vital, necessary, required, essential, indispensable, minimal.

superfluousness *n.* REDUNDANCY.

superintend *v.* SUPERVISE.

superintendent *n.* **1** supervisor, head, manager, foreman, chief, overseer, director, boss, leader, steward, inspector. **2** janitor, custodian, super, caretaker, keeper, doorman, door-keeper, porter, guardian, warden, concierge.

superior *adj.* **1** better, peerless, distinguished, extraordinary, notable, eminent, excellent, uppermost, first-rate, first-class, high-grade, top-notch, high-caliber, sterling, top-drawer, super, crack, tops (*Slang*). **2** greater, more, larger, bigger, grander. **3** disdainful, haughty, airy, indifferent, lofty, supercilious, patronizing, snobbish, condescending, highfalutin, stuck-up. —*n.* higher-up, chief, boss, head, senior, director, leader, master, principal, commander, captain, commandant, kingpin (*Slang*). VIP, brass (*Slang*), honcho (*Slang*).

ant. *adj.* **1** inferior, second-rate, low-grade, poor, imperfect, bad. **2** smaller, lesser, slighter, less, shorter. **3** humble, ingenuous, respectful, unaffected. —*n.* inferior, subordinate, assistant, underling.

superlative *adj.* finest, highest, superior, best, supreme, surpassing, peerless, nonpareil, matchless, preeminent, paramount, principal, primary, magnificent, utmost, topmost, top-notch, maximum.

ant. worst, lowest, pedestrian, undistinguished, indifferent.

supernal *adj.* CELESTIAL.

supernatural *adj.* **1** metaphysical, otherworldly, supranatural, preternatural, unearthly, unworldly, transcendental, unaccountable, incomprehensible, marvelous, wonderful, incredible, inexplicable, fantastic, bizarre, strange, prodigious, superhuman, ghostly, weird, uncanny, eerie, spooky. **2** miraculous, divine, otherworldly, mystical, thaumaturgic.

ant. 1 physical, tangible, earthly, real, actual, material.

supernumerary *adj.* SUPERFLUOUS.

supersede *v.* replace, supplant, displace, succeed, substitute for, surrogate, set aside, discard, reject.

superstar *n.* STAR.

superstition *n.* **1** credulity, gullibility,

fallacy, delusion, illusion, misapprehension, black magic, moonshine, old wives' tale, hocus-pocus, mumbo-jumbo. **2** notion, belief, lore, myth, fable, tradition, custom.

superstitious *adj.* gullible, credulous, naive, ingenuous.
ant. skeptical, rational, doubting.

supervise *v.* direct, manage, oversee, run, administer, superintend, boss, head, regulate, govern, conduct, guide, lead, steer, engineer, mastermind, control, command, rule.

supervision *n.* direction, management, administration, government, regulation, conduct, control, guidance, superintendence, governance, leadership, jurisdiction, charge, care, surveillance, auspices, umbrella.

supervisor *n.* manager, head, director, chief, leader, overseer, superintendent, boss, foreman, steward, inspector, governor.

supervisory *adj.* managerial, administrative, supervising, executive, overseeing, superintendent, managing, regulative, governing, leading, directorial, directing, officiating, head, chief.

supine *adj.* abject, spineless, cowardly, listless, lifeless, spiritless, weak, weak-kneed, pusillanimous, wishy-washy, soulless, feeble, jejune, unresisting.
ant. resolute, defiant, tough, strong, tough-minded, unyielding.

supplant *v.* replace, displace, supersede, succeed, substitute for, act for, spell.

supple *adj.* **1** *easily bent:* flexible, pliant, pliable, elastic, plastic, resilient, ductile, tractile, malleable, rubbery, limp. **2** *able to move easily:* agile, limber, lithe, nimble, loose, relaxed, lithesome, willowy, deft. **3** compliant, acquiescent, complaisant, yielding, willing, unresisting, flexible, adaptable, agreeable, resigned, docile, passive. **4** *quick to respond or adjust:* responsive, receptive, sensitive, adaptable, quick, alert, ready,

susceptible, impressionable, malleable, game.
ant. 1 rigid, stiff, hard, taut, inflexible, inelastic. **2** ungainly, clumsy, stiff, awkward, cramped, tight. **3** stubborn, obstinate, steadfast, unwavering, intransigent, uncompromising. **4** insensitive, unresponsive, rigid, inflexible, arbitrary, hidebound, conventional.

supplement *n.* postscript, rider, addition, attachment, addendum, complement, appendix, codicil. —*v.* complete, fill out, complement, add.

supplemental *adj.* SUPPLEMENTARY.

supplementary *adj.* additional, extra, auxiliary, supplemental, added, surplus, further, more, other, spare, new, fresh, ancillary, collateral, accessory, supernumerary, adventitious, incidental.
ant. prime, essential, basic, fundamental, root, minimum.

suppliant *n.* SUPPLICANT.

supplicant *n.* petitioner, entreater, suppliant, suitor, solicitor, seeker, claimant, applicant, beggar, aspirant, candidate.

supplicate *v.* entreat, petition, appeal, plead, implore, beg, beseech, crave, pray, invoke, adjure, request.

supplication *n.* entreaty, appeal, petition, request, application, call, demand, plea, cry, solicitation, beseechment, invocation.

supplies *n.* provisions, stores, rations, food, larder, provender, groceries, comestibles, victuals, edibles, reserves, stockpile.

supply *v.* **1** provide, furnish, give, contribute, present, accommodate, assign, consign, replenish, satisfy, stock, provision, provender, purvey, store, fund, equip, outfit, accouter. **2** compensate for, make up for, balance, cover, offset, counterbalance. —*n.* store, stock, reserve, provision, replenishment, quantity, amount, inventory, merchandise.

support *v.* **1** hold up, bear, sustain, carry, keep up, prop up, buttress, bolster, shore up. **2** provide for, maintain, sustain, assist, fund, attend to, keep. **3** encourage, bolster, champion, back up, fortify, strengthen, abet, endorse, advocate, assist, help, aid, approve, uphold, countenance. **4** corroborate, substantiate, uphold, bear out, verify, authenticate, testify to, document, evidence, show, prove. **5** endure, tolerate, bear, stand, abide, put up with, accept, condone, countenance, suffer, entertain. —*n.* **1** subsistence, maintenance, keep, livelihood, living, sustenance. **2** supporter, mainstay, backbone, upholder, champion, advocate, backer, promoter, backing, reinforcement, buttress, bulwark, brace, stay, prop, crutch, shoring.

supportive *adj.* sustaining, stabilizing, bolstering, strengthening, supporting, salutary, restorative, curative, invigorating.

suppose *v.* presume, believe, think, expect, imagine, guess, suspect, surmise, conjecture, assume, reckon, understand, gather, infer, conclude, judge, opine, deduce.

supposed *adj.* assumed, believed, presumed, understood, deemed, accepted, presupposed, postulated, presumptive, ostensible, given, putative, intimated, insinuated, tacit, implied, implicit.

supposedly *adv.* seemingly, ostensibly, purportedly, allegedly, avowedly, professedly, presumably, presumptively, presumedly.

supposition *n.* conjecture, hypothesis, assumption, presumption, presupposition, inference, surmise, guess, thesis, theorem, postulate, proposition, axiom, given.

suppress *v.* **1** quash, subdue, repress, put down, crush, squash, squelch, strangle, stop, end, prohibit, quench, extinguish, silence. **2** withhold, censor, curb, repress, restrain, check, constrain, inhibit, limit, cramp, confine, block, interdict, muzzle, gag, tame, still, muffle, mute.

ant. 1 encourage, inflame, feed, fuel, fire. **2** free, unloose, let go, release, express.

suppression *n.* crushing, restraint, interdiction, check, curb, stay, arrest, repression, prohibition, deterrence, inhibition, blocking, quashing.

suppurate *v.* fester, ooze, secrete, discharge, seep, exude, run, weep.

supremacy *n.* primacy, predominance, priority, precedence, superiority, preeminence, championship, ascendancy, sovereignty, paramountcy, dominance, sway, leadership, dominion, mastery.

supreme *adj.* dominant, leading, ranking, paramount, preeminent, principal, chief, main, topmost, crowning, foremost, stellar, capital, first, unsurpassed, peerless, par excellence, incomparable, greatest, utmost, tops (*Slang*).

surcease *n.,v.* END.

surcingle *n.* GIRDLE.

sure *adj.* **1** certain, indisputable, unquestionable, unmistakable, clear, definite, decided, absolute, positive, confident, firm, secure, irrevocable, inescapable, inevitable, assured, cocksure, guaranteed, warranted, certified. **2** reliable, dependable, sound, unfailing, firm, faithful, true, solid, secure, established, steadfast, trustworthy, trusty, predictable.

ant. 1 doubtful, uncertain, unconfirmed, questionable, shaky, vulnerable, insecure. **2** undependable, unreliable, fallible, false, disappointing.

surely *adv.* **1** certainly, positively, doubtless, absolutely, definitely, undoubtedly, indubitably, clearly, unmistakably, unquestionably, irrefutably, precisely, exactly, unequivocally. **2** indeed, truly, really, doubtless. certainly, assuredly, of course, by all means.

surface *n.* **1** outside, face, facade, top, exterior, skin, shell, superficies, covering. **2** appearance, facade, veneer. —*v.* **1** smooth, even, level, plane, coat. **2** ascend, rise, emerge, crest, break water. **3** *come to public notice:* transpire, come out, come to light, emerge, leak out.

surfeit *v.* overeat, satiate, glut, cram, cloy, overindulge, gorge, stuff, overload, overfeed, overfill, pack. —*n.* **1** glut, satiety, fill, overindulgence, satiation, saturation, congestion, gluttony. **2** excess, surplus, superfluity, redundancy, plethora, extravagance, exorbitance, inordinacy, fulsomeness, intemperance.

surge *v.* swell, heave, undulate, flood, upsurge, rise, roll, eddy, swirl, billow, toss, gush. —*n.* **1** wave, billow, swell, heave, undulation, roller, comber, gush, rush, gurge, flood, torrent. **2** increase, rise, jump, climb, leap, step-up, explosion, hike, ascent. **ant.** *n.* **2** plunge, decline, nose-dive, dive, descent, crash.

surly *adj.* rude, insolent, gruff, brusque, churlish, impertinent, cheeky, pert, discourteous, sullen, fresh (*Slang*). **ant.** courteous, polite, civil, gracious, amiable.

surmise *v.* infer, guess, hypothesize, conjecture, presume, assume, deduce, theorize, gather, judge, suppose, estimate, reckon, conclude, deem. —*n.* conjecture, supposition, assumption, presumption, presupposition, inference, deduction, guess, speculation, opinion, assessment, appraisal, theory, hypothesis, postulate, guesstimate (*Slang*).

surmount *v.* overcome, prevail, overwhelm, defeat, best, worst, conquer, vanquish, subdue, overpower, overthrow.

surpass *v.* exceed, better, outdo, excel, overpass, overmatch, overrun, top, overtop, beat, distance, outdistance, pass, trump, eclipse, outshine, outstrip, transcend.

surpassing *adj.* EXCELLENT.

surplus *n.* excess, overage, leftover, extra, remainder, store, residue, reserve, reservoir, spare, oversupply, overload, superfluity, plethora, glut,

surfeit. —*adj.* extra, superfluous, spare, leftover, remaining, residual, supernumerary, excessive. **ant.** *n.* shortage, shortfall, undersupply, lack. —*adj.* wanting, scant, lacking, short, shy.

surprise *v.* **1** astonish, amaze, startle, astound, confound, flabbergast, dumbfound, nonplus, shock, electrify. **2** take unawares, catch off-guard, encounter, chance upon. **3** attack, assault, assail, go at, charge, raid, rush at, pitch into, fall on. —*n.* **1** astonishment, amazement, bewilderment, admiration, wonder, wonderment, shock, awe, incredulity. **2** blow, jolt, jar, shock, start, stunner, bombshell, thunderbolt, sensation, eye-opener, marvel, wonder, miracle, phenomenon, curiosity, kicker (*Slang*).

surprising *adj.* amazing, astonishing, startling, astounding, unexpected, unanticipated, unforeseen, shocking, electrifying, stunning, confounding. **ant.** expected, routine, commonplace, predictable.

surrender *v.* yield, give up, capitulate, submit, cede, quit, succumb, accede, resign, abandon, knuckle under, relinquish, waive. —*n.* capitulation, submission, yielding, relinquishment, cession, abandonment, acquiescence, resignation, compliance, renunciation, release, withdrawal, forsaking. **ant.** *v.* hold out, hold on, stay, hang in (*Slang*).

surreptitious *adj.* furtive, stealthy, sly, sneaky, shifty, underhanded, clandestine, secret, covert, hidden, undercover, hush-hush. **ant.** open, exposed, public, undisguised, candid, aboveboard, overt.

surrogate *n., v.* SUBSTITUTE.

surround *v.* encircle, enclose, encompass, circle, envelop, circumscribe, environ, enfold, girdle, wrap, hem, hedge in, sheathe, bound.

surroundings *n.* environment, environs, ambiance, milieu, setting, context, background, atmosphere, vicinity, precincts, purlieu, neighborhood, community.

surveillance *n.* observance, watch, lookout, vigil, scrutiny, guard, vigilance, charge, care, supervision, tracking, tailing, trailing, bugging, eavesdropping.

survey *v.* **1** reconnoiter, observe, look over, contemplate, regard, watch, view, descry, behold, take in. **2** scrutinize, inspect, examine, study, search, trace, track. —*n.* study, review, overview, investigation, examination, inquiry, search, scrutiny, analysis, probe, canvass, poll, questionnaire, quiz.

survive *v.* outlive, outlast, outwear, persist, remain, prevail, endure, last, abide, live, stay, continue, exist.

susceptible *adj.* **1** vulnerable, sensitive, responsive, unresistant, subject, liable. **2** emotional, sensitive, tender, approachable, thin-skinned, tenderhearted, soft.
ant. 1 resistant, protective, hardened, obdurate. **2** distant, hard, aloof, unemotional, thick-skinned.

suspect *v.* **1** distrust, mistrust, doubt, misdoubt, question, challenge, query. **2** believe, think, imagine, surmise, judge, suppose, assume, presume, deem, reckon, infer, consider, regard, feel, expect. —*adj.* suspicious, suspected, distrusted, mistrusted, doubtful. —*n.* accused, defendant, prisoner.
ant. *v.* **1** trust, rely on, accept, credit, believe. —*adj.* trustworthy, honest, reliable, believable, trusted.

suspend *v.* **1** bar, banish, exclude, ban, exile, force out, dismiss. **2** interrupt, delay, defer, break, postpone, put off, adjourn, prorogue. **3** hang, depend, dangle, swing.
ant. 1 instate, reinstate, invest, confirm.

suspense *n.* anticipation, apprehension, tension, strain, stress, anxiety, nervousness, edginess.

suspension *n.* **1** dismissal, removal,

ejection, disbarment, liquidation, purge, banishment. **2** interruption, cessation, discontinuation, break, pause, remission, respite, postponement, deferral, adjournment, delay, moratorium. **3** hanging, dangling, dependence.

suspicion *n.* **1** distrust, doubt, mistrust, qualm, uncertainty, skepticism, premonition, intimation, hunch, feeling, impression. **2** trace, touch, suggestion, hint, dash, inkling, tinge, shade, glimmer, clue, scent, soupçon, intimation.
ant. 1 trust, confidence, faith, security, belief.

suspicious *adj.* **1** *arousing suspicion:* questionable, doubtful, suspect, ambiguous. **2** *having suspicions:* dubious, doubting, skeptical, mistrustful, questioning, disbelieving, incredulous, leery, wary, distrustful, cynical.
ant. 1 trustworthy, aboveboard, reliable, respectable, reputable. **2** trustful, gullible, credulous, unquestioning, naive.

sustain *v.* **1** carry on, keep up, maintain, continue, keep, hold, retain, uphold, protract, extend, prolong, lengthen, last, remain, persevere, survive, persist, prevail. **2** nurture, nourish, feed, supply, furnish, foster, nurse, support. **3** suffer, undergo, endure, bear, stand, support, tolerate, abide, withstand, put up with, accept, condone, countenance, brook, brave. **4** corroborate, endorse, prove, uphold, confirm, establish, affirm, verify, attest, substantiate, validate.

sustenance *n.* **1** nourishment, food, nutriments, edibles, victuals, groceries, rations, provisions, refreshment, provender, bread, nurture, comestibles, refection. **2** livelihood, support, subsistence, maintenance, means, keep, upkeep, living, sustainment. **3** SUBSISTENCE.

svelte *adj.* slender, slim, willowy, trim, neat, lean, slight, spare, thin.
ant. stocky, dumpy, rotund, pudgy, obese.

swaddle *v.* SWATHE.

swag *n.* **1** carving, ornament, stonework, decoration, tracery, festoon, garland. **2** *Slang* loot, plunder, booty, spoils, pillage, boodle (*Slang*), haul, take (*Slang*), goods, pickings.

swagger *v.* **1** strut, stride, parade, swashbuckle, prance, flounce, bounce, saunter, amble. **2** bluster, boast, brag, swank, flaunt, display, show off, grandstand, flourish, roister, gasconade. —*n.* bravado, bluster, braggadocio, boastfulness, brag, rodomontade, gasconade, fanfaronade.

swain *n.* lover, boy friend, sweetheart, young man, beau, admirer, suitor, wooer, fiancé, squire, gallant, cavalier, paramour, inamorato.

swallow *v.* **1** eat, drink, consume, devour, gulp, ingest, imbibe, down, guzzle, digest, ingurgitate, bolt. **2** tolerate, suffer, endure, stomach, put up with, take, bear with, accept, abide, stand for.

swallow up engulf, absorb, devour, consume, envelop, use up, deplete, expend, waste, drain, exhaust.

swamp *n.* bog, mire, quagmire, morass, slough, quicksand, sump, marsh, everglade, fen, bottoms. —*v.* **1** drench, soak, saturate, steep, waterlog, flood, deluge, inundate, submerge, submerse, sink, drown. **2** overwhelm, tax, overtax, overwork, strain, extend, exceed, overload, overdose, glut, gorge, stuff, congest, flood, deluge, inundate.

swank *n.* **1** ostentation, showiness, display, gaudiness, flashiness, show, exhibitionism, swagger, bravado, pretension, pretense, airs. **2** stylishness, chic, fashion, style, smartness, elegance, *bon ton*, class (*Slang*), cool (*Slang*), dressiness, nattiness, dapperness. —*adj.* SWANKY.

swanky *adj.* showy, flashy, smart, swank, fancy, ritzy (*Slang*), jazzy (*Slang*), dressy, natty, dashing, sharp (*Slang*), sporty, ostentatious.

ant. conservative, restrained, austere, subtle.

swan song farewell, good-bye, denouement, finale, *au revoir*, last hurrah, last gasp.

swap *v.* trade, barter, exchange, switch, dicker, bargain, swop. —*n.* barter, trade, exchange, trade-off, switch, deal, horse-trade, bargain, traffic, transaction.

sward *n.* TURF.

swarm *n.* throng, mass, horde, crowd, bunch, scores, host, legion, army, flock, hive, press, crush, mob, multitude. —*v.* cluster, horde, mass, bunch, throng, crowd, teem, clump, steam, surge.

swart *adj.* SWARTHY.

swarthy *adj.* dark, tawny, dark-skinned, dark-complexioned, olive-skinned, dusky, swart.
ant. light, fair, pale.

swash *v., n.* SPLASH.

swat *v.* smack, whack, slap, strike, smite, swot, hit, knock, belt, bang, crack, tap, clout, thump, buffet, wallop.

swath *n.* strip, band, path, trail, track, clearing, aisle, corridor, stripe, bar, mark, row.

swathe *v.* swaddle, blanket, bundle, wrap, cloak, mantle, clothe, dress, garb, sheathe, shroud, bandage, envelop, enwrap, cover.

sway *v.* **1** teeter, totter, alternate, oscillate, swing, fluctuate, shift, wobble, reel, seesaw. **2** influence, affect, tend, incline, lean toward, tilt, tip, bend, prompt, predispose, dispose, induce, persuade, guide, determine. —*n.* power, dominion, authority, command, control, mastery, jurisdiction, grasp, grip, force, weight, influence, hegemony, suzerainty.

swear *v.* **1** avow, vow, adjure, aver, depose, depone, attest, vouch, give one's word, affirm, guarantee, warrant. **2** curse, imprecate, cuss. **3** declare, assert, affirm, aver, state, allege, claim, pronounce, maintain, announce, contend, say.

swear off abjure, renounce, give up, forswear, abandon, forgo, shun, avoid, abstain.

swearword *n.* curse, profanity, obscenity, oath, cuss, dirty word, four-letter word, expletive, epithet.

sweat *v.* **1** perspire, excrete, exude, moisten. **2** drudge, toil, slave, grind, grub, struggle, strive, strain, plod, plug away, hustle, labor, work, moil. **3** worry, fret, chafe, fuss, stew, suffer. —*n.* **1** perspiration, moisture, water, wetness, excretion, exudation. **2** distress, worry, anxiety, concern, agitation, strain, stress, apprehension, uneasiness, fretfulness, nervousness, impatience, jitters, edginess, panic, funk, flap (*Slang*).

sweep *v.* **1** brush, broom, clean, tidy up. **2** graze, brush, touch, glance, skim, pass over, glide. —*n.* **1** stroke, motion, movement, gesture, pass. **2** length, extent, stretch, span, reach, measure, range, distance, area, scope, compass.

sweeping *adj.* extensive, comprehensive, far-reaching, wide-ranging, all-inclusive, out-and-out, blanket, omnibus, thoroughgoing, exhaustive, extreme, radical.
ant. limited, modest, qualified, narrow, superficial.

sweet *adj.* **1** sugary, saccharine, sweetish, sweetened, candied, honied, syrupy. **2** delightful, pleasant, gratifying, pleasing, pleasurable, enjoyable, agreeable, delectable. **3** amiable, genial, congenial, likable, lovable, sympathetic, winning, charming, nice, pleasant, agreeable, gentle, good, fine, angelic.
ant. **1** sour, tart, sharp, acerbic, acrid. **2** unpleasant, offensive, unsavory, distasteful, repulsive, offensive. **3** nasty, crabby, choleric, caustic, grouchy, acrimonious, dour.

sweeten *v.* **1** sugar, honey, candy, dulcify. **2** ease, lighten, alleviate, lessen, relieve, moderate, soften, temper, buoy, assuage, subdue, palliate. **3** sugar-coat, sugar, gild, gild the lily.

sweetheart *n.* lover, girl friend, boy friend, darling, dear, truelove, valentine, flame (*Slang*), beau, swain, admirer, steady (*Slang*).

sweet-talk *v.* FLATTER.

sweet talk FLATTERY.

swell *v.* **1** increase, enlarge, expand, grow, dilate, distend, rise, wax, gain, advance, multiply, tumefy, accumulate, appreciate, accrue, strengthen, intensify. **2** bulge, blow up, balloon, inflate, fill out, billow, rise, puff, protrude. **3** flaunt, puff up, show off, give oneself airs, put on airs, swank (*Slang*), swagger. —*n.* **1** expansion, increase, growth, swelling, inflation, enlargement, augmentation, rise, upsurge, upturn, accrual, appreciation. **2** projection, rise, swelling, bulge, protuberance, bump, hump, lump, knob, boss, knoll, spine, hillock, convexity. **3** dandy, fop, sport, dude, blade, spark, beau, playboy, gallant, coxcomb. —*adj. Slang* EXCELLENT.
ant. *v.* **1** decrease, sink, lower, diminish, wane, shrink. **2** deflate, collapse, flatten, constrict, puncture. **3** shrink, demur, cringe, skulk, cower, retire, quail.

swelling *n.* enlargement, distention, protuberance, bulge, lump, bump, dilation.

sweltering *adj.* torrid, hot, oppressive, scorching, boiling, burning, sizzling, baking, blistering, sultry, stifling, suffocating.

swerve *v.* veer, dodge, deflect, turn, sheer off, career, tack, jib, shy, bend, shift, avoid, detour, deviate, digress, diverge.

swift *adj.* **1** quick, rapid, fast, fleet, speedy, sudden, hasty, spanking, headlong, abrupt, precipitant. **2** brief, fleeting, passing, short, short-lived, transient, transitory, temporary, impermanent, ephemeral, momentary, fugitive, evanescent, meteoric. **3** alert, responsive, prompt, sensitive, smart, quick, agile, nimble, ready, heads-up (*Slang*).
ant. **1** slow, sluggish, drawn-out,

plodding, lagging. **2** enduring, permanent, continuous, imperishable, persistent, immutable. **3** dull, stolid, slow-witted, dull-witted.

swig *n.* gulp, mouthful, drink, draft, swill, guzzle, quaff, drain, sip. —*v.* SWILL.

swill *v.* swig, gulp, guzzle, quaff, imbibe, drink, chugalug (*Slang*), suck, tipple, booze, nip, tope. —*n.* **1** garbage, slops, scrapings, leavings, scourings, scraps, waste, refuse, offal, hogwash, dregs, slime, scum, muck, scratch, grub (*Slang*), chow (*Slang*), fodder. **2** SWIG.

swimming *adj.* dizzy, giddy, reeling, dazed, groggy, light-headed, vertiginous, punch-drunk, dopey, befuddled, muddled, addled, silly.

swindle *v.* cheat, defraud, trick, bilk, gyp, con (*Slang*), dupe, fleece, deceive, chisel, gouge, finagle, rook, gull, hoodwink, hornswoggle (*Slang*), bamboozle, rip off (*Slang*).

swindler *n.* con man (*Slang*), cheat, chiseler, cheater, sharp, sharper, shark, gyp, bilker, flimflammer, charlatan, fraud, faker, quack, mountebank, blackleg.

swine *n.* **1** hog, pig, sow, porker, boar, shoat, piggy. **2** scoundrel, wretch, rogue, knave, villain, skunk, cad, bounder (*Brit.*), rotter (*Brit.*), heel (*Slang*), rat (*Slang*), louse (*Slang*).

swing *v.* **1** sway, wave, fluctuate, alternate, oscillate, reciprocate, pendulate, wag, waver, seesaw, reel, roll, wobble, shift, vary. **2** turn, pivot, swivel, about-face, rotate, revolve, spin, wheel, twist, whirl, pirouette. **3** hang, suspend, dangle, depend, droop, flutter, sag. **4** brandish, flourish, wave, wield, shake, wag, flaunt. —*n.* **1** thrust, poke, jab, roundhouse, hook, uppercut, slice, stroke, motion, follow-through. **2** tour, trip, excursion, jaunt, junket, circuit, loop, turn, whirl, spin, journey, passage.

swinge *v.* FLAG.

swinging *adj. Slang* WITH-IT.

swinish *adj.* gross, greedy, vile, gluttonous, piggish, hoggish, sensual, beastly, bestial, coarse, repulsive, filthy, foul, nasty, base.

swipe *v.* **1** smack, strike, slap, hit, smite, whack, swat, knock, jab, cuff, thwack, poke, punch. **2** *Slang* pilfer, purloin, filch, steal, rob, thieve, make off with, snatch, lift, pinch (*Slang*), cop (*Slang*). —*n.* smack, blow, slap, thwack, swat, strike, hit, whack, stroke, clip.

swirl *v., n.* WHIRL.

switch *n.* stick, twig, branch, stalk, shoot, spear, sprig, rod, cane, birch, whip, ruler, club, paddle, ferule. —*v.* **1** shift, change, divert, turn aside, deflect. **2** exchange, trade, barter, change, swap, interchange. **3** WHIP.

swivel *v.* pivot, swing, rotate, revolve, turn, spin, whirl, swirl, round, reel, wheel, twist, about-face, pirouette.

swoon *v., n.* FAINT.

swoop *v.* dive, plunge, plummet, drop, lunge, pitch, fall, descend, nose-dive, plop, pounce, snatch, seize, take.

swop *v.* SWAP.

sword *n.* blade, saber, broadsword, bayonet, machete, cutlass, rapier, foil, epée.

swot *v.* SWAT.

sybarite *n.* hedonist, epicurean, *bon vivant*, sensualist, voluptuary.
    ant. Spartan, ascetic, abstainer, teetotaler.

sycophancy *n.* FLATTERY.

sycophant *n.* flatterer, bootlicker, toady, fawner, lackey, flunky, apple polisher (*Slang*), backslapper, courtier, lickspittle, yes-man, jackal, cat's-paw.

syllabus *n.* synopsis, summary, abstract, epitome, outline, digest, abridgment, condensation, brief, abbreviation, draft, survey, capsule, sketch, précis, compendium, conspectus.

symbol *n.* emblem, token, example, representative, exponent, exemplification, model, sample, specimen, sign, mark, signal, badge, prototype, archetype.

symbolic *adj.* emblematic, figurative, symbolistic, allegorical, metaphorical, allusive, referential, ideographic, illustrative, exemplary.

symbolistic *adj.* SYMBOLIC.

symbolize *v.* represent, stand for, exemplify, emblematize, allegorize, embody, personify, illustrate.

symmetry *n.* correspondence, congruity, proportion, balance, equilibrium, parallelism, parity, regularity, uniformity, evenness, proportionality.

ant. asymmetry, imbalance, irregularity, disparity, unevenness, disproportion.

sympathetic *adj.* **1** compassionate, tenderhearted, kind, kindly, kindhearted, open-hearted, understanding, feeling, concerned, charitable, generous, warm. **2** congenial, compatible, like-minded, agreeable, fraternal, harmonious, amiable, friendly.

ant. 1 unfeeling, hard-hearted, indifferent, unmoved, cold. **2** uncongenial, discordant, inharmonious, conflicting, clashing.

sympathize *v.* commiserate, condole, feel for, pity, empathize, understand.

sympathy *n.* **1** harmony, congeniality, compatibility, concord, unity, affinity, rapport, unanimity, empathy. **2** compassion, commiseration, pity, mercy, condolence, consolation, tolerance, generosity, sensitivity, sentiment, understanding. **3** agreement, accord, concurrence, assent, compliance, consent, acquiescence, endorsement, acknowledgment, approval, acceptance.

ant. 1 friction, discord, antagonism, animosity, strife, division, conflict. **2** malice, spite, ill will, aversion, abhorrence. **3** disagreement, variance, difference, opposition, dissent.

symphony *n.* **1** *of sounds:* harmony, consonance, euphony, concord, chorus, unison. **2** *any agreeable blend-*

ing: unison, harmony, unity, concord, compatibility, affinity, congruity, accord, agreement, conformity, consistency.

ant. 1 dissonance, cacophony, discord. **2** discord, dissonance, conflict.

symposium *n.* discussion, forum, conference, panel, round table, seminar, meeting, parley, session, deliberation, assembly, committee, debate, rap session (*Slang*), bull session.

symptom *n.* **1** *of a disease:* condition, sign, prodrome, complaint, prognostic. **2** sign, mark, token, telltale, signal, trait, characteristic, earmark, index, indication, promise, omen, portent, intimation, augury, foreshadowing, warning, alarm.

synch *v. Slang* SYNCHRONIZE.

synchronize *v.* coincide, concur, accord, harmonize, coordinate, synch (*Slang*).

synchronous *adj.* SIMULTANEOUS.

syndicate *n.* association, consortium, conglomerate, alliance, coalition, amalgamation, affiliation, union, merger, consolidation, federation, cartel, trust, monopoly.

synod *n.* council, conclave, convocation, consistory, congregation, gathering, concourse, presbytery, assembly, conference, convention, session, congress, parliament, tribunal, soviet.

synopsis *n.* summary, abstract, abridgment, précis, digest, epitome, résumé, rundown, sketch, brief, capsule, condensation, abbreviation, syllabus, skeleton, outline, review, recapitulation, compendium, conspectus.

synthesis *n.* **1** combining, assembling, combination, arranging, composition, mixing, blending, fusion, melding, coalescence, amalgamation, formation. **2** compound, mixture, amalgam, combination, composite, complex, union, blend, fusion, alloy, admixture.

synthesize *v.* compound, amalgamate, admix, constitute, concoct, mix, merge, blend, fuse, meld, coalesce, combine, unite.

ant. separate, analyze, dissect, decompose, resolve, disintegrate, separate.

synthetic *adj.* artificial, unnatural, man-made, manufactured, synthesized, counterfeit, mock, quasi, pseudo, fake, unreal, ungenuine, spurious, sham, bogus, phony (*Slang*).

ant. natural, original, pure, genuine, authentic.

syrupy *adj.* SENTIMENTAL.

system *n.* arrangement, organization, order, plan, program, method, pattern, setup, lay-out, disposition, sequence, group, unit, schema, blueprint, procedure, scheme, design,

way, process, practice, routine, *modus operandi.*

systematic *adj.* **1** taxonomic, classified, categorized, classificatory, catalogued, assorted, grouped, pigeonholed, graded, typed. **2** methodical, orderly, organized, procedural, uniform, regular, balanced, measured, steady, constant, consistent, exacting, scrupulous, punctilious, precise.

ant. 2 untidy, disorganized, disorderly, sloppy, erratic, inconsistent.

systematize *v.* classify, arrange, order, categorize, catalog, codify, class, methodize, rank, rate, grade, sort, place, group, tabulate, index, program, organize, regulate, coordinate.

ant. disarrange, scramble, upset, confuse, scatter, jumble, pi.

T

tab¹ *n.* flap, strip, tongue, lip, projection, tag, fastening, label, closing, loop, frog, tally.

tab² *n.* BILL.¹

tabernacle *n.* TENT.

table *n.* **1** tabulation, itemization, schedule, agenda, list, chart, canon, index, column, listing, catalog, contents. **2** PLATEAU. —*v.* postpone, pigeonhole, shelve, delay, lay over, put off, stay, lay aside, defer, put on the back burner (*Slang*).

ant. *v.* deal with, settle, dispose of.

tableau *n.* scene, setting, picture, spectacle, representation, grouping, study, arrangement, still life.

tableland *n.* PLATEAU.

tablet *n.* **1** pad, notebook, sketchbook. **2** wafer, pill, pellet, lozenge, drop, capsule, troche, disk, cake.

taboo *n.* prohibition, ban, forbiddance, restriction, limitation, proscription, repression, interdict, interdiction, no-no (*Slang*). —*adj.* prohibited,

forbidden, proscribed, outlawed, banned, illicit, impermissible, unaccepted, frowned on, unacceptable, *verboten,* out-of-bounds, off-limits.

ant. *adj.* permitted, accepted, allowed, sanctioned.

tacit *adj.* implied, inferred, unspoken, implicit, understood, taken for granted, assumed, acknowledged.

ant. spoken, explicit, spelled-out.

taciturn *adj.* reserved, silent, uncommunicative, reticent, quiet, diffident, laconic, closemouthed, withdrawn, aloof.

ant. chatty, informative, outgoing, talkative.

tack *n.* **1** nail, brad, thumbtack, carpet tack, pin, pushpin. **2** course, direction, policy, line, tactic, strategy, plan, path, procedure, design, program, way, method, scenario. —*v.* fasten, attach, secure, pin, nail, clip, staple.

tackle *v.* **1** undertake, try, attack, work

on, attempt, take on, take up, essay, engage in. **2** seize, grab, intercept, take hold of, clutch, grip, pounce on, capture, stop.

ant. 1 avoid, evade, set aside, shelve.

tack on append, add, supplement, attach, affix, annex, enlarge, amplify, combine, augment, extend, lengthen.

ant. remove, delete, shorten, take out, take off.

tacky[1] *adj.* sticky, gummy, gluey, gooey, mucilaginous, gelatinous.

tacky[2] *adj.* unfashionable, tasteless, shabby, cheap, chintzy, vulgar, tawdry, unstylish, mangy, pretentious, blowzy, frumpy, schlocky (*Slang*), tatty (*Brit.*).

ant. fashionable, smart, elegant, stylish, chic.

tact *n.* savoir faire, diplomacy, discretion, thoughtfulness, delicacy, circumspection, sensibility, sensitivity, politesse, politeness, consideration, discernment, insight, prudence, subtlety, polish, urbanity.

ant. boorishness, insensitivity, grossness, bluntness, gaucherie.

tactful *adj.* diplomatic, discreet, polite, mannerly, politic, considerate, discerning, sensitive, thoughtful, astute, circumspect, urbane, prudent, judicious.

ant. gauche, clumsy, indiscreet, thoughtless.

tactic *n.* scheme, strategem, plan, ploy, device, technique, tack, maneuver, contrivance, game, machination, line, course, dodge, trick.

tactical *adj.* adroit, clever, shrewd, cunning, flexible, foxy, expert, proficient, strategic, Machiavellian, deft, artful.

ant. clumsy, inept, blundering, bungling, gauche.

tactless *adj.* rude, undiplomatic, gauche, indiscreet, impolitic, impolite, thoughtless, boorish, stupid, insensitive, inconsiderate, clumsy, tasteless, untactful, heavy-handed, ill-mannered.

ant. tactful, discreet, diplomatic, polite.

taffy *n.* FLATTERY.

tag *n.* label, identification, classification, description, ticket, tab, slip, stub, marker, name, monicker (*Slang*), dog tag, I.D. (*Slang*). —*v.* **1** label, mark, ticket, identify, classify, tab, size, name, title, docket, earmark. **2** follow, dog, tail, trail, hound, shadow, heel, pursue, stalk.

tail *n.* back, backside, rear, end, posterior, hindquarters, butt, rump, behind, bottom, breech, extremity, rear end, croup, *derrière*. —*v.* shadow, follow, trail, trace, tag, stalk, track, pursue, hound, dog, spy on. —*adj.* rearmost, hindmost, final, bottom, last, concluding, ultimate.

ant. *n.* head, front, top, anterior, face. *adj.* front, first, beginning, opening, head, topmost.

tailor *v.* adapt, shape, fit, adjust, cut, modify, transform, fashion, convert, redo, mold, suit, temper, coordinate, regulate.

tailor-made *adj.* SUITABLE.

taint *v.* contaminate, corrupt, debase, spoil, pollute, infect, besmirch, sully, vitiate, defile, poison, debauch, adulterate, blight, dirty, stain. —*n.* contamination, corruption, pollution, defilement, decay, putrescence, putrefaction, rot, poison, adulteration, impurity, blight, debasement.

ant. *v.* purify, cleanse, disinfect, clean.

take *v.* **1** grasp, seize, grab, clutch, snatch, capture, catch, collar, apprehend, hook, tackle, pounce on, arrest, nab, entrap, snare, bag. **2** choose, select, buy, pick, pick out, opt for, purchase, prefer, favor, single out, abstract, settle on. **3** put up with, tolerate, endure, suffer, bear, submit to, swallow, stomach, brook, abide, go through, undergo, withstand, brave, weather. **4** carry, bring, tote, pick up, lug, haul, cart, fetch, drag, schlep (*Slang*). **5** require, demand, need, want, necessitate, call for. **6** *Slang* CHEAT. —*n.* **1** *Slang* receipts, profits, gate, proceeds, return, loot, net, gross, earnings, yield, swag (*Slang*), boodle (*Slang*), rake-off (*Slang*), gravy (*Slang*). **2** catch, collection, haul, bag, pickings, crop, mess, heap, batch, stack, accumulation.

ant. *v.* **1** release, let go, free. **2** reject, refuse, turn down, discard.

take after resemble, look like, favor, recall, evoke, suggest.

take back retract, recant, go back on, renounce, back down, disclaim, eat one's words, renege.

ant. maintain, insist, reaffirm.

take in DECEIVE.

take note of ACKNOWLEDGE.

takeoff *n.* parody, caricature, imitation, spoof, satire, burlesque, travesty, mimicry, lampoon, exaggeration.

take off 1 leave, go, set out, exit, embark, withdraw, abandon, entrain, emplane, disappear, vanish, hit the road, quit, split (*Slang*), bug off (*Slang*). **2** accelerate, speed up, spurt, soar, zoom, leap ahead, skyrocket, shoot ahead, zip, race, surge, escalate, step on it (*Slang*).

ant. 1 return, come back, reappear, land. **2** slow down, decelerate, fall behind, lose ground, lag.

take on HIRE.

takeover *n.* usurpation, confiscation, displacement, coup, revolution, expropriation, *coup d'état*, *putsch*, merger, incorporation, conglomeration.

take place happen, occur, befall, betide, come to pass, eventuate, come up, crop up, arrive, arise, come about, transpire.

tale *n.* **1** story, narrative, narration, report, saga, account, yarn, anecdote, recital, legend, fable, description, *conte*, novella. **2** gossip, rumor, fabrication, falsehood, fiction, untruth, hearsay, fib, tall story, scuttlebutt (*Slang*).

talebearer *n.* gossip, rumormonger, taleteller, tattler, telltale, tattletale,

scandalmonger, newsmonger, busybody, troublemaker, informer, yenta (*Slang*).

talent *n.* aptitude, gift, genius, forte, ability, endowment, capability, faculty, skill, strength, bent.

taleteller *n.* TALEBEARER.

talisman *n.* amulet, charm, fetish.

talk *v.* **1** converse, chat, chatter, confer, consult, discuss, gab, gossip, prattle, prate, rap (*Slang*), natter (*Brit.*). **2** utter, speak, say, articulate, voice, pronounce, enunciate, express, verbalize. **3** inform, reveal, divulge, disclose, air, publicize, broadcast, apprise, intimate, betray, leak, confess, snitch (*Slang*), spill (*Slang*), rat (*Slang*), sing (*Slang*). —*n.* **1** speech, conversation, verbalization, expression, articulation. **2** lecture, discourse, oration, sermon, address, recitation, speech, declamation, homily, eulogy, tirade. **3** report, rumor, hearsay, tidings, news, insinuations, hints, gossip, publicity, stories, accounts, scuttlebutt (*Slang*). **4** conference, discussion, chat, parley, round table, seminar, interview, consultation, meeting, conclave, dialogue, tête-à-tête, symposium, session, causerie, talkathon, gabfest (*Slang*), rap session (*Slang*). **5** babble, prattle, blather, verbiage, chatter, bombast, cant, rant, twaddle, balderdash, nonsense, drivel, gobbledygook, hot air (*Slang*), yak (*Slang*).

talkative *adj.* garrulous, loquacious, voluble, gabby, chatty, talky, effusive, mouthy, windy, bombastic, verbose, gossipy, long-winded, prolix, wordy.

ant. taciturn, quiet, laconic, mum.

talkativeness *n.* GARRULITY.

talking-to *n.* REPRIMAND.

talky *adj.* TALKATIVE.

tall *adj.* high, lofty, towering, soaring, elevated, elongated, imposing, extended, giant, gigantic.

ant. short, low, small, abbreviated, dwarfish.

tally *n.* **1** score, mark, number, scratch, tick, entry, listing, recording, check, fact, figure, statistic, inscription. **2** count, reckoning, account, addition, enumeration, total, sum, computation, calculation, statistics, record, census. —*v.* **1** score, register, enter, mark, inscribe, record, tick off, check, docket, catalog, inventory, scratch, inscribe, list, tabulate. **2** count, reckon, add, total, tote, compute, sum up, calculate. **3** agree, jibe, coincide, match, accord, fit, dovetail, parallel, check, correspond. **ant.** *v.* **3** disagree, contradict, clash.

talon *n.* CLAW.

tame *adj.* **1** tamed, domesticated, broken, domestic, domiciled, leashed, trained, broken in, subdued, busted (*Slang*). **2** docile, gentle, tractable, submissive, manageable, obedient, controllable, meek, compliant, willing, adaptable. **3** dull, unexciting, tepid, humdrum, bland, safe, insipid, vapid, everyday, unchallenging, lifeless, spiritless, boring, commonplace, prosaic. —*v.* **1** domesticate, train, break in, discipline, subjugate, master, control, harness, leash, yoke, conquer, curb, bust (*Slang*). **2** soften, tone down, subdue, moderate, water down, dull, soft-pedal, temper, calm, mute. **ant.** *adj.* **1** wild, feral, undomesticated. **2** balky, unmanageable, willful, disobedient, refractory. **3** exciting, thrilling, spirited, lively, adventurous. *v.* **2** heighten, intensify, sharpen, spice.

tamp *v.* pack down, press, stuff, cram, ram, poke, pound.

tamper *v.* meddle, interfere, fiddle, mess, fool, tinker, monkey, mix, obtrude, pry, butt in, horn in (*Slang*).

tan *v.* THRASH.

tang *n.* **1** bite, piquancy, nip, zest, zip, sharpness, spiciness, tartness, sting, pungency, spice, punch. **2** flavor, taste, quality, trace, hint, whiff, pinch, aroma, scent, smell, smack, odor, savor, touch, reminder.

tangent *adj.* TANGENTIAL.

tangential *adj.* **1** marginal, subordinate, ancillary, secondary, supplementary, tangent, minor, contingent, subsidiary, incidental, side. **2** variable, divergent, digressive, erratic, unfixed, unsettled, deviant, shifting, aberrant, divagating, inconstant, inconsistent. **ant.** **1** central, essential, pivotal, crucial, focal. **2** invariable, immutable, fixed, constant, undeviating.

tangible *adj.* concrete, real, material, palpable, objective, solid, substantial, manifest, plain, actual, clearcut, veritable, precise, specific, factual. **ant.** elusive, imaginary, vague, flimsy.

tangle *v.* twist, snarl, mess, ensnare, entangle, trap, entrap, enmesh, clog, clot, knot, embroil, implicate, seduce. —*n.* snarl, knot, confusion, clot, web, maze, jam, trap, mess, complication, problem, disorder, foul-up (*Slang*), snafu (*Slang*). **ant.** *v.* straighten out, untangle, free.

tangy *adj.* sharp, tart, spicy, pungent, piquant, acrid, zesty, peppery, biting, seasoned, hot. **ant.** bland, insipid, tasteless, mild, flat.

tank *n.* vessel, basin, cistern, receptacle, jug, vat, container, pit, boiler, reservoir, sump, pool, well, cask, tub.

tantalize *v.* tease, bait, torment, frustrate, thwart, titillate, stimulate, provoke, foil, baffle, withhold, beckon, bewitch, lead on.

tantalizing *adj.* TEMPTING.

tantamount *adj.* equivalent, equal, comparable, indistinguishable, same, selfsame, synonymous, identical, interchangeable, convertible. **ant.** different, disparate, unequal.

tantrum *n.* fit, seizure, rampage, outburst, scene, storm, flare-up, snit, conniption, flap (*Slang*).

tap[1] *n.* faucet, spout, cock, nozzle, spigot, bunghole, valve, conduit. —*v.* draw on, use, exploit, utilize, turn to account, profit from, work, milk, mine, resort to, take advantage of.

tap² *v.* touch, tip, pat, rap, drum, palpate, peck, beat, strike, hammer. —*n.* pat, peck, touch, caress, tip, beat, bang, smack, stroke, knock, blow, buffet, strike.

tape *n.* strip, band, ribbon, binding, bandage, fillet, roll, reel, spool, filament, braid. —*v.* bind, tie, bandage, close, seal, secure, wrap, package, swaddle.

taper off dwindle, wane, lessen, decrease, thin out, end, decline, slacken, weaken, abate, reduce, contract, narrow, subside, fade, wind down, de-escalate, phase out.

ant. increase, grow, strengthen, intensify, step up.

tardy *adj.* **1** late, behindhand, delayed, dilatory, belated, overdue, unpunctual. **2** slow, sluggish, leisurely, torpid, slow-moving, creeping, crawling, dawdling, languishing.

ant. 1 prompt, punctual, on time. **2** quick, swift, speedy, fleet, rapid.

target *n.* **1** bull's-eye, mark. **2** butt, victim, sitting duck, scapegoat, fall guy (*Slang*), patsy (*Slang*), easy mark (*Slang*), pigeon (*Slang*). **3** goal, objective, purpose, aim, end, ambition, object, intention, hope, dream, wish.

tarnish *v.* dim, dull, darken, oxidize, discolor, debase, sully, mar, blacken, stain, spoil, soil, besmirch, blot, taint, dishonor. —*n.* discoloration, darkening, blemish, stain, dullness, debasement, taint, blackening, blot, defacement, disgrace, dishonor, degradation, stigma.

ant. *v.* shine, gleam, sparkle, brighten, uplift. *n.* brightness, luster, glory, honor.

tarry *v.* remain, linger, dawdle, procrastinate, dally, dillydally, stay, wait, loiter, stall, delay, temporize, hang around, cool one's heels.

ant. move on, hasten, rush, keep up.

tart *adj.* **1** sharp, sour, acid, vinegary, tangy, astringent, acetic, acerbic, strong, spicy, piquant, acidulous. **2** severe, caustic, biting, nasty, cutting, wounding, sharp, barbed, acerbic, acidulous, critical, unkind, catty, curt, trenchant, brusque.

ant. 1 sweet, sugary, honeyed, ripe. **2** agreeable, pleasant, gentle, kind, soothing.

task *n.* assignment, responsibility, obligation, job, chore, onus, burden, trouble, work, stint, duty, errand, concern, charge, undertaking, load.

taskmaster *n.* overseer, boss, foreman, slave-driver, martinet, tyrant, supervisor, stickler, disciplinarian, Simon Legree, honcho (*Slang*).

taste *v.* **1** savor, relish. **2** experience, feel, undergo, endure, have, perceive, understand, sense, partake of, participate in, know. —*n.* **1** flavor, savor, aroma, tastiness, essence, tang, relish, smack, sapor, sapidity. **2** sample, bit, sip, drop, little, mouthful, morsel, tidbit, bite, swallow, sprinkle, crumb, slice, spoonful. **3** fondness, liking, appreciation, preference, inclination, penchant, bent, weakness, leaning, cultivation, palate, predisposition.

tasteful *adj.* elegant, artistic, graceful, aesthetic, fine, well-chosen, becoming, suitable, discriminating, felicitous, choice, fastidious, refined, chic, smart.

ant. vulgar, offensive, unbecoming, tasteless.

tasteless *adj.* **1** insipid, bland, vapid, dull, uninteresting, unexciting, tame, mild, flat, boring, uninspired, stale, watered-down, flavorless, weak. **2** vulgar, crude, tactless, improper, unsuitable, out of place, crass, graceless, boorish, offensive, coarse, tacky.

ant. 1 tasty, savory, delicious, piquant, zesty. **2** elegant, tasteful, graceful, becoming, refined.

tasty *adj.* delicious, savory, appetizing, aromatic, piquant, delectable, luscious, toothsome, tangy, refreshing, tempting, palatable, sapid, tasteful, well-seasoned.

ant. tasteless, flavorless, unsavory, stale, unappetizing.

tatter *n.* rag, shred, tear, rip, rent, damage.

tattle *v.* **1** chatter, babble, tittle-tattle, chitchat, prattle, jabber, gabble, blather, prate, chin, jaw (*Slang*), yak (*Slang*), natter (*Brit.*). **2** blab, tell on, inform, divulge, reveal, disclose, leak, gossip, tip off, let fall, betray, snitch (*Slang*), squeal (*Slang*), peach (*Slang*), spill (*Slang*). —*n.* gossip, chatter, blather, tittle-tattle, rumormongering, prattle, twaddle, babble, hearsay, small talk, tongue-wagging, loose talk, mudslinging.

tattletale *n.* TALEBEARER.

taunt *n.* jibe, cut, barb, insult, slap, sneer, sarcasm, jeer, provocation, insinuation, dig. —*v.* provoke, challenge, jeer, deride, insult, cut, sting, put down, twit, scoff, sneer, mock, ridicule, rag (*Slang*).

taut *adj.* **1** tight, tense, flexed, stretched, rigid, drawn, extended, stiff, hard. **2** trim, tidy, shipshape, snug, spruce, neat, trig. **3** ANXIOUS.
ant. **1** slack, loose, relaxed. **2** disorderly, messy, sloppy.

tautology *n.* REDUNDANCY.

tavern *n.* inn, saloon, roadhouse, public house, pub (*Brit.*), bistro, bar, lodge, taproom, restaurant, cabaret, ginmill (*Slang*).

tawdry *adj.* gaudy, vulgar, tacky, showy, pretentious, raffish, cheap, tasteless, flashy, meretricious, loud, sordid, shabby, garish, tinsel, tatty (*Brit.*).
ant. subdued, tasteful, elegant, classic, understated.

tax *n.* **1** levy, tithe, assessment, tribute, impost, toll, excise, custom, tariff, duty, capitation, taxation, exaction, rate (*Brit.*). **2** burden, demand, imposition, onus, responsibility, pressure, chore, strain, weight, load, drain, hardship, stress, obligation, trial. —*v.* **1** assess, tithe, levy, rate (*Brit.*). **2** burden, impose, charge, inflict, task, weigh down, load down,

strain, oblige, push, overwork, overburden, exhaust, drain, weaken, sap. **3** blame, accuse, charge, incriminate, lay, impeach, inculpate, condemn, indict, convict, attribute to, impute, arraign, impugn, attack, sue.
ant. *v.* **3** exonerate, clear, exculpate, acquit.

taxing *adj.* demanding.

teach *v.* **1** instruct, edify, tutor, enlighten, inculcate, lecture, indoctrinate, inform, impart, profess, expound. **2** guide, discipline, educate, school, nurture, cultivate, civilize, illuminate, coach, drill, exercise, preach, counsel, train, groom.
ant. **1** learn, absorb. **2** follow, obey.

teacher *n.* educator, schoolteacher, instructor, scholar, tutor, preceptor, mentor, trainer, coach, lecturer, professor, pedagogue, docent, schoolmaster, schoolmistress, don (*Brit.*).
ant. pupil, student, learner, scholar.

teaching *n.* education, pedagogy, schooling, training, tutoring, coaching, instruction, preparation, edification, nurture, inculcation, indoctrination, acculturation, guidance, cultivation.

team *n.* crew, unit, group, gang, force, workers, side, opposition, band, clique, squad, club, body, faction, bunch.

teamwork *n.* cooperation, coordination, community, collaboration, unity, *esprit de corps,* common cause, alliance, fellowship, concert, collusion, unanimity, harmony.

tear *v.* **1** rip, shred, tatter, pull apart, rend, slash. **2** injure, lacerate, rupture, mangle, gash, wound, bruise, dismember, maim, break, mutilate, claw, scratch. **3** disrupt, divide, split, splinter, break up, wrack, wreck, disunite.

tear down demolish, raze, level, dismantle, pull down, knock down, fell, destroy, devastate, wreck, flatten.
ant. build, erect, construct, renovate.

tearful *adj.* weeping, crying, sobbing, blubbering, weepy, teary, lachrymose, mourning, wailing, lamenting, whimpering, sniveling.

tear into ATTACK.

tease *v.* **1** annoy, harass, bother, twit, pester, irritate, josh, taunt, vex, bedevil, rally, hector, rag (*Slang*), rib (*Slang*). **2** coax, beg, importune, plead, nag, wheedle, press, ply, badger, cajole, insist.

teat *n.* nipple, tit, papilla, pap.

technical *adj.* skilled, specialized, scientific, vocational, professional, occupational, technological, qualified, expert, trained, functional, particularized, arcane, esoteric.

technicality *n.* formality, nicety, detail, particular, distinction, specification, red tape, punctilio, trifle, triviality, convention, ritual.

technician *n.* specialist, expert, adept, craftsman.

technique *n.* style, craft, method, formula, pattern, *modus operandi,* device, practice, craftsmanship, skill, art.

tedious *adj.* boring, tiresome, monotonous, wearisome, dull, dreary, humdrum, repetitious, uninteresting, bothersome, prosaic, routine, unvaried.

ant. exciting, challenging, interesting, stimulating.

teeming *adj.* overflowing, abounding, swarming, humming, full, crowded, packed, brimming, dense, thick, buzzing, chockful, overrun, glutted, jammed, crawling.

ant. empty, unoccupied, vacant, bare.

teen-age *adj.* adolescent, pre-adult, pubescent, juvenile, youthful.

teeny *adj.* TINY.

teeter *v.* **1** vacillate, waver, seesaw, dilly-dally, fluctuate, hesitate, sit on the fence, hem and haw. **2** TOTTER.

teetotal *adj.* TOTAL.

telescope *v.* shorten, compress, condense, abridge, abbreviate, reduce, contract, curtail, cut, trim, shrink, summarize, epitomize, lessen.

ant. extend, lengthen, amplify, draw out, flesh out.

tell *v.* **1** relate, narrate, describe, detail, say, speak, write, express, articulate, communicate, verbalize, state, utter, recount, recite, chronicle. **2** divulge, reveal, disclose, report, inform, broadcast, publicize, acquaint, tattle, apprise, hint, confess, disseminate, educate, leak, spill, bruit. **3** ascertain, distinguish, discriminate, recognize, decide, discern, perceive, make out, verify, estimate, establish, detect, differentiate, find, specify. **4** order, command, direct, oblige, charge, bid, instruct, require, enjoin, authorize, ask, call upon, summon.

teller *n.* narrator, raconteur, chronicler, reporter, storyteller.

telling *adj.* effective, striking, impressive, cogent, forceful, effectual, potent, substantial, considerable, trenchant, weighty, decisive, momentous, signal, powerful, influential.

ant. negligible, vain, minor, ineffectual, slight, insignificant.

tell off REPRIMAND.

tell on TATTLE.

telltale *adj.* betraying, revealing, informative, tattletale, indicative, suggestive, significant, symptomatic, meaningful, emblematic.

temerity *n.* boldness, rashness, foolhardiness, intrepidity, nerve, grit, gall, audacity, effrontery, heedlessness, recklessness, presumption, venturesomeness, *sangfroid,* guts (*Slang*), chutzpah (*Slang*).

ant. timidity, cowardice, bashfulness, fear, shyness.

temper *n.* **1** rage, tantrum, outburst, flare-up, fit, snit, explosion, pique, passion, rampage, agitation, tempest, storm, fury. **2** mood, attitude, feeling, frame of mind, pulse, tenor. **3** TEMPERAMENT. —*v.* moderate, mitigate, soften, modify, tame, adapt, adjust, proportion, admix, attenuate, weaken, palliate, tone down, reduce, diminish.

temperament *n.* nature, disposition, temper, makeup, constitution, spirit, personality, humor, quality, stamp, kind.

temperamental *adj.* volatile, mercurial, moody, unstable, capricious, unpredictable, erratic, dramatic, histrionic, emotional, impetuous, tempestuous, turbulent, unreliable, changeable, chameleonic.
ant. calm, even-tempered, stable, stolid, phlegmatic.

temperance *n.* **1** moderation, self-control, self-discipline, judiciousness, restraint, abstemiousness, frugality, measure, discretion, prudence. **2** teetotaling, abstinence, prohibition.
ant. **1** self-indulgence, wantonness, abandon, dissoluteness. **2** overindulgence, crapulence, intemperance.

temperate *adj.* **1** mild, pleasant, moderate, agreeable, balmy, breezy, soft, clement. **2** restrained, prudent, measured, moderate, judicious, reasonable, sensible, conservative, controlled, middle-of-the-road. **3** calm, self-controlled, stable, equable, even-tempered, cool-headed, unexcited, unexcitable, self-possessed, sane, levelheaded.
ant. **2** extreme, immoderate, excessive, prodigal. **3** excitable, intense, passionate, temperamental, impetuous.

tempest *n.* commotion, storm, uproar, outbreak, explosion, upheaval, clamor, tumult, excitement, ferment, to-do, eruption, hubbub, cataclysm.
ant. peace, quiet, calm, serenity, tranquillity.

tempestuous *adj.* stormy, turbulent, violent, tumultuous, dramatic, temperamental, passionate, raging, furious, agitated, importunate, hysterical, frenzied, uncontrolled, uncontrollable, impetuous.
ant. smooth, serene, calm unruffled, even, quiet.

tempo *n.* pace, speed, time, timing, pacing, beat, rapidity, velocity, measure, rate.

temporal *adj.* **1** mundane, finite, material, worldly, secular, lay, earthly, terrestrial, mortal, civil, political. **2** transitory, ephemeral, transient, fleeting, evanescent, impermanent, passing, short-lived, fugitive, momentary.
ant. **1** spiritual, godly, religious, heavenly, ecclesiastical. **2** lingering, lasting, long-lasting, durable, permanent.

temporary *adj.* transient, transitory, provisional, impermanent, momentary, brief, fleeting, short-lived, transitional, provisory, standby, fill-in, stopgap, substitute, *pro tempore, pro tem.*
ant. settled, fixed, tenured, lasting, permanent.

temporize *v.* stall, filibuster, delay, tarry, tergiversate, equivocate, hang fire, hedge, fudge, hem and haw, straddle, maneuver, see how the wind blows.
ant. decide, act, confront, settle on, expedite, execute.

tempt *v.* lure, entice, lead on, seduce, attract, invite, captivate, appeal to, inveigle, bait, intrigue, bewitch, magnetize, draw, charm.

temptation *n.* lure, bait, attraction, magnet, invitation, enticement, decoy, inducement, stimulus, persuasion, provocation, urge, allurement, snare, bribe.

tempting *adj.* attractive, alluring, enticing, seductive, inviting, provocative, magnetic, fascinating, charming, appetizing, irresistible, desirable, tantalizing, engaging.
ant. repulsive, unattractive, off-putting, uninviting.

tenability *n.* CREDIBILITY.

tenable *adj.* defensible, justifiable, arguable, cogent, correct, workable, practical, practicable, rational, reasonable, viable, sensible.
ant. unjustifiable, indefensible, impractical, untenable, impossible.

tenacious *adj.* **1** cohesive, tough, firm, agglutinate, agglutinant, clinging, retentive, strong. **2** stubborn, obstinate, persistent, unyielding, resolute, dogged, mulish, intransigent, determined, unwavering, willful, constant, unremitting, steadfast, inflexible, perseverant.

ant. 1 stringy, grainy, loose, friable. **2** changeable, tractable, yielding, lax, wavering.

tenant *n.* leaseholder, lessee, occupant, dweller, householder, resident.

tend[1] *v.* **1** incline, lean, dispose, verge, gravitate. **2** lead, conduce, contribute, predispose, guide, direct.

tend[2] *v.* look after, attend, take care of, minister to, watch over, manage, mind, supervise, shepherd, guide, see to, protect, wait on, cater to, help.

ant. neglect, ignore, disregard, shirk.

tendency *n.* **1** inclination, leaning, propensity, bent, penchant, impulse, disposition, predisposition, partiality, proclivity, mind. **2** drift, movement, trend, path, direction, course, tenor, bias, current, flow, intention, design, drive, sweep.

tender[1] *adj.* **1** delicate, fragile, breakable, frail, weak, soft, flimsy, insubstantial. **2** gentle, considerate, compassionate, sympathetic, caring, thoughtful, kind, affectionate, sentimental, loving, demonstrative, sweet, solicitous, warm-hearted. **3** *arousing sensitive feelings:* touching, moving, poignant, evocative, memorable, meaningful, intimate, personal. **4** sore, irritated, bruised, inflamed, swollen, uncomfortable, painful, aching, throbbing, raw, chafed. **5** touchy, ticklish, difficult, troublesome, awkward, complicated, delicate, unpleasant, knotty, sticky, fraught.

ant. 1 sturdy, tough, strong, hard, thick, unbreakable. **2** harsh, cruel, cold, heartless, insensitive, unfeeling.

tender[2] *v.* offer, present, proffer, hand in, hand over, volunteer, give, suggest, submit, advance, propound, place, propose. —*n.* offer, proposal,

proposition, suggestion, bid, presentation, overture, advance.

ant. *v.* withdraw, withhold.

tenderfoot *n.* BEGINNER.

tenderhearted *adj.* compassionate, sympathetic, warm-hearted, softhearted, kind, sensitive, responsive, affectionate, understanding, gentle, merciful, benign, altruistic, tolerant, humane, sentimental.

ant. hardhearted, unfeeling, ruthless, cold.

tenet *n.* opinion, belief, principle, creed, dogma, doctrine, credo, view, position, platform, gospel, catechism, conclusion, theory, conviction, ideology.

tenor *n.* **1** intent, purport, drift, meaning, sense, import, intention, implication, argument, substance. **2** tendency, course, evolution, drift, character, kind, nature, style, essence, direction, flow, design, path, route, progress, stamp, quality, vein.

tense *adj.* **1** taut, stretched, tight, extended, rigid, braced, strained, pulled, tensed, flexed, drawn. **2** anxious, fearful, apprehensive, nervous, jittery, on edge, uneasy, disturbed, taut, distressed, worried, edgy, short, keyed-up, uptight (*Slang*).

ant. 1 loose, sagging, relaxed. **2** calm, cool, relaxed, placid, easy.

tensility *n.* RESILIENCE.

tension *n.* **1** tautness, tightness, stretch, stress, extension, rigidity, stiffness, pull, strain, tensility, traction, pressure. **2** anxiety, nervousness, strain, stress, pressure, apprehension, distress, worry, uneasiness, *angst.*

ant. 1 looseness, flexibility, sag. **2** peace of mind, calm, serenity, relaxation, tranquillity.

tent *n.* tepee, wigwam, yurt, wickiup, tabernacle, booth, pavilion, canvas, big top.

tentative *adj.* **1** conditional, contingent, trial, unconfirmed, probationary, hypothetical, proposed, indefinite, unauthenticated, dependent, possible, iffy. **2** hesitant, timid, uncertain, anxious, unsure, faltering, diffident, shy, constrained, doubtful, insecure, wavering, dubious, shaky.

ant. 1 definite, settled, unconditional, final, resolved. **2** direct, bold, assured, confident, unhesitating.

tenuous *adj.* **1** slight, weak, insubstantial, far-fetched, paltry, flimsy, shaky, shallow, trivial, makeshift. **2** slender, thin, attenuated, lean, delicate, airy, frail, fine, gossamer, fragile.

ant. 1 sound, solid, hard-and-fast, firm. **2** thick, heavy, sturdy, chunky, strong, dense.

tenure *n.* term, time, incumbency, reign, rule, administration, regime, hold, occupancy, tenancy, proprietorship, possession, right, election, entitlement.

tepee *n.* TENT.

tepid *adj.* **1** lukewarm, warmish, temperate, mild. **2** unenthusiastic, indifferent, so-so, cool, uninterested, apathetic, unconcerned, distant, reserved, bored, unexcited, ho-hum, lukewarm, unimpressed.

ant. 1 hot, boiling, scalding. **2** enthusiastic, excited, passionate, heated.

tergiversate *v.* EQUIVOCATE.

term *n.* **1** word, expression, phrase, locution, idiom, concept, verbalization, idea, thought, name, appellation, designation, usage, epithet. **2** duration, time, tenure, spell, era, incumbency, administration, course, interlude, reign, epoch, age, interval, semester. **3** end, conclusion, termination, fruition, limit, finish, completion, boundary, close, windup, ending, culmination. —*v.* name, call, designate, style, dub, entitle, title, tag, label, define, specify.

termagant *n.* shrew, virago, nag, scold, fishwife, hellion, terror, vixen, harridan, witch, fury, spitfire, Xanthippe, bitch (*Slang*).

terminal *adj.* ultimate, final, end, last, terminating, concluding, extreme,

outside, bounding, utmost, farthest, definitive. —*n.* TERMINATION.

ant. initial, beginning, first, foremost, opening, introductory, prefatory.

terminate *v.* **1** stop, end, finish, conclude, cut off, discontinue, cease, complete, culminate, wind up. **2** bound, limit, edge, border, confine, delimit, circumscribe, encompass, bracket, enclose.

ant. 1 start, begin, introduce, inaugurate, open.

termination *n.* **1** cessation, discontinuation, pause, interval, rest, intermission, halt, completion, stoppage, recess, discontinuance, phaseout. **2** terminal, terminus, boundary, limit, close, end, edge, finish, finale, ending, border, extremity, frontier. **3** outcome, upshot, conclusion, result, consequence, effect, issue, denouement, payoff, windup, fruition.

ant. 3 beginning, start, opening.

terminology *n.* vocabulary, terms, lexicon, nomenclature, phraseology, lingo, vocabulary, names, cant, argot, language, jargon.

terminus *n.* TERMINATION.

terms *n.* conditions, stipulations, specifications, items, itemization, contract, agreement, understanding, footing, relationship, provisos, provisions, rapprochement, entente, protocol.

terrace *n.* slope, lawn, bank, embankment, court, courtyard.

terrain *n.* TERRITORY.

terrestrial *adj.* earthly, worldly, mundane, terrene.

terrible *adj.* **1** awesome, terrifying, frightening, intimidating, appalling, dread, awe-inspiring, formidable, alarming, fearsome, horrifying, overwhelming, portentous, terrific, scary. **2** severe, extreme, acute, awful, dreadful, painful, beastly, frightful, fierce, excruciating, distressing, shameful, scandalous.

terrific *adj.* **1** great, extraordinary, marvelous, magnificent, wonderful, stunning, powerful, tremendous, breath-taking, amazing, excellent, super (*Slang*). **2** TERRIBLE.

ant. 1 unimpressive, mediocre, so-so, poor.

terrify *v.* scare, frighten, petrify, terrorize, shock, horrify, appall, panic, affright, cow, paralyze, alarm, intimidate, harrow.

territory *n.* **1** terrain, region, district, tract, land, acreage, holding, expanse, area, locale. **2** specialty, province, realm, sphere, department, activity, job, sector, domain, field, turf (*Slang*), bailiwick, forte, function, expertise.

terror *n.* **1** fear, panic, fright, dread, alarm, apprehension, intimidation, immobilization, shock, horror, awe. **2** brat, pest, horror, hellion, devil, fiend, imp, nuisance, mischief-maker, pain, problem child, trouble-maker, spitfire, hellcat, rogue.

terrorize *v.* TERRIFY.

terse *adj.* succinct, brief, curt, short, to the point, concise, clipped, pithy, compact, trenchant, neat, summary, epigrammatic, crisp, laconic.

ant. wordy, verbose, long-winded, prolix, talky.

test *v.* examine, try, prove, analyze, investigate, assess, check, quiz, validate, verify, look into, probe, grade, sound, check up on, assay. —*n.* **1** examination, observation, trial, probation, investigation, probe, assay, scrutiny, evaluation, diagnosis, analysis, inspection. **2** criterion, standard, measure, proof, guidepost, guideline, measurement. **3** ordeal, crucible, strain, battle, stress, agony, contest, competition, struggle.

testament *n.* credo, avowal, statement, assertion, testimony, belief, declaration, affirmation, profession, deposition, manifesto, doctrine, tenet, attestation.

tested *adj.* PROVEN.

testify *v.* **1** bear witness, give testimony, affirm, declare, attest, depose, swear, vouch, aver, avouch, profess.

2 show, exemplify, indicate, demonstrate, prove, validate, confirm, argue, document, uphold, substantiate, support, vindicate, verify, corroborate.

ant. 2 contradict, disprove, gainsay, controvert.

testimony *n.* declaration, statement, acknowledgment, assertion, proof, evidence, deposition, attestation, substantiation, validation, verification, corroboration, admission, avowal.

testy *adj.* irritable, crotchety, disagreeable, irascible, cranky, cross, waspish, petulant, crabby, peevish, touchy, tetchy, crusty, huffy, nasty, choleric, impatient, short-tempered, bilious, curmudgeonly, short, snappish.

ant. affable, genial, patient, good-humored, kindly, cheerful.

tetchy *adj.* TESTY.

tête-à-tête *adj.* CONFIDENTIAL.

tether *n.* restraint, check, rein, bridle, rope, leash, cord, constraint, halter, tie, restriction, limitation, hamper, hindrance, control.

text *n.* TEXTBOOK.

textbook *n.* schoolbook, text, manual, primer, reference, source.

textile *n.* fabric, cloth, material, goods, yard goods, yarn, fiber, piece goods.

textual *adj.* LITERAL.

texture *n.* **1** *of a physical thing:* surface, feel, consistency, touch. **2** structure, organization, nature, character, feel, sense, composition, make-up, substance, quality, experience, impression.

thankful *adj.* grateful, appreciative, gratified, pleased, beholden, obliged, indebted.

ant. ungrateful, resentful, thankless.

thankless *adj.* **1** ungrateful, unappreciative, rude, insolent, inconsiderate. **2** unappreciated, unrewarded, unrewarding, futile, fruitless, unprofitable, profitless, wasted, unrequited.

ant. 1 thankful, grateful, appreciative. **2** rewarding, fruitful, profitable, appreciated.

thaumaturgy *n.* MAGIC.

thaw *v.* **1** melt, dissolve, liquefy, deliquesce, defrost. **2** relax, soften, unbend, warm up, yield, unwind, mellow, relent, succumb, accede, let one's hair down.
ant. 1 freeze, solidify. **2** stiffen, harden, tense up, tauten.

theater *n.* **1** playhouse, cinema, opera house, amphitheater, drive-in, music hall, odeon, lyceum. **2** auditorium, hall, lecture hall, assembly hall, exhibition hall. **3** stage, drama, dramatics, dramaturgy, plays, theatricals, show biz (*Slang*). **4** site, arena, field, locus, locale, setting, sector, zone, scene, place, background, terrain.

theatrical *adj.* **1** dramatic, thespian, legitimate, live, staged, histrionic, dramaturgic, compelling, moving, artful, memorable. **2** pretentious, showy, stagy, overdone, artificial, camp, campy, exaggerated, affected, mannered, corny, hammy, melodramatic, maudlin, sentimental, tearjerking (*Slang*).
ant. 2 natural, unaffected, straightforward, unexaggerated.

theft *n.* stealing, larceny, robbery, thievery, burglary, looting, shoplifting, pilfering, purloining, filching.

theme *n.* subject, topic, thread, motif, focus, keynote, crux, point, motive, refrain, signature.

theorem *n.* axiom, principle, fundamental, basic, ABC, dictum, assumption, construct, truism, rule.

theoretical *adj.* speculative, hypothetical, abstract, untested, untried, conjectural, suppositional, deductive, assumed, presumed, academic, pure, presumptive, abstruse, postulatory, ideological.
ant. practical, pragmatic, experiential, inductive.

theorize *v.* speculate, imagine, suppose, hypothesize, hypothecate, conjecture, construct, assume, presume, infer, propound, posit, think, formulate, propose.

theory *n.* **1** plan, thesis, scheme, idea, explanation, hypothesis, proposition, procedure, assumption, formulation, formula, construct, postulate, concept, system. **2** guess, conjecture, guesswork, supposition, inference, deduction, speculation, intuition, stab, surmise, suspicion, fancy, notion, opinion, inkling.

therapeutic *adj.* curative, healing, beneficial, sanative, restorative, healthful, salubrious, corrective, remedial, recuperative, salutary, constructive.
ant. detrimental, harmful, damaging, destructive.

therapy *n.* treatment, cure, remedy, corrective, restorative, regime, regimen, medicine.

thereabouts *adv.* approximately, roughly, somewhat, near, generally, close, nigh.

thereafter *adv.* thence, thenceforth, afterward, afterwards, later, subsequently.
ant. previously, before, until.

therefore *adv.* consequently, so, accordingly, ergo, thus, as a result.

thereupon *adv.* presently, promptly, without delay, forthwith, immediately, then, directly, straightway, straightaway, suddenly.

thermal *adj.* HOT.

thesis *n.* **1** treatise, dissertation, monograph, paper, disquisition, research, investigation, essay. **2** THEORY.

thespian *adj.* THEATRICAL. —*n.* ACTOR.

thews *n.* STRENGTH.

thick *adj.* **1** broad, deep, wide, massive, large, hefty, voluminous, solid, bulky, capacious, substantial, ample. **2** viscous, soupy, creamy, coagulated, gelatinous, clotted, condensed, thickened, viscid, jellied. **3** dense, impenetrable, heavy, impermeable, impervious, compact. **4** dull, stupid, insensitive, vapid, thickheaded, slow, obtuse, dimwitted, simple, dumb, retarded, brainless, simple-minded, doltish, oafish, moronic.
ant. 1 thin, narrow, slender, shapely.

2 liquid, liquefied, watery. **3** sparse, thinned out, penetrable. **4** bright, quick, brainy, perceptive, smart, sharp, keen.

thicken v. intensify, deepen, solidify, compact, condense, congeal, curdle, jell, clabber, clot, harden, set, concentrate, compact.

ant. rarefy, attenuate, thin, liquefy, weaken.

thicket n. underbrush, shrubbery, bosket, copse, brush, bush, bosk, hedge, undergrowth, covert, brake, wood, grove.

thickhead n. DUNCE.

thickheaded adj. STUPID.

thick-skinned adj. insensitive, callous, stolid, dull, obtuse, unresponsive, impervious, dense, thickheaded, stupid, hardened.

ant. sensitive, thin-skinned, impressionable, responsive, feeling, tender, touchy.

thick-witted adj. STUIPD.

thief n. filcher, robber, burglar, pilferer, purloiner, kleptomaniac, larcenist, swindler, embezzler, confidence man, con man (*Slang*), mugger, pickpocket, yegg (*Slang*).

thieve v. purloin, steal, pilfer, filch, snatch, seize, lift, loot, take, crib, finger, peculate, embezzle, misappropriate, swipe (*Slang*).

thievery n. theft, thieving, robbery, stealing, embezzlement, filching, pilfering, plunder, burglary, kleptomania, rustling, swindling, looting, larceny.

thin adj. **1** narrow, flimsy, insubstantial, slight, gossamer, translucent, filmy. **2** slender, lean, emaciated, bony, gaunt, spare, skinny, scrawny. **3** rarefied, tenuous, diffuse, wispy, rare, fluid, dilute, attenuated. **4** scanty, deficient, scant, meager, sparse, limited, poor, skimpy. **5** superficial, slight, shallow, feeble, faint, lame, weak, poor. —v. water down, dilute, attenuate, rarefy, lessen, weaken, adulterate, diminish, reduce, decrease, weed out, diffuse.

ant. adj. **1** thick, opaque, wide, solid, massive. **2** fat, plump, stout, heavy, corpulent, obese. **3** dense, thick, viscous, compact, condensed. **4** abundant, sufficient, large, plenty, profuse. **5** ponderous, vigorous, forceful, substantial, deep. v. concentrate, strengthen, thicken, compact, condense, increase.

thing n. **1** entity, object, article, body, being, something, mass, shape, form, figure. **2** matter, circumstance, condition, feature, situation, factor, incidental, contingency. **3** act, deed, event, occurrence, incident, process, performance, phenomenon. **4** procedure, step, item, particular, detail, feature, aspect, consideration. **5** quality, attribute, characteristic, feature, property, peculiarity, endowment, adjunct. **6** issue, case, point, to-do, cause célèbre, fuss, crisis, problem. **7** THINGAMAJIG.

ant. **1** illusion, figment, nothing, phantom, vacuum, hallucination.

thingamabob n. THINGAMAJIG.

thingamajig n. thingamabob, gew-gaw, doodad, doohickey, gimmick, whatnot, something, thing, gismo (*Slang*), widget (*Slang*), what-do-you-call-it, what's-its-name, what-you-call-it, what-you-may-call-it.

things n. possessions, belongings, effects, paraphernalia, impedimenta, trappings, gear, equipment, goods, baggage, supplies, furnishings, apparatus.

think v. **1** conceive, imagine, reason, remember, recollect, reflect, call to mind, consider, contemplate, cogitate, ponder, mull over, meditate, speculate, ruminate, cerebrate. **2** believe, suppose, deem, judge, reckon, regard, consider, count, opine, surmise, conclude.

thinking n. THOUGHT.

think over reflect upon, ponder, weigh, mull, ruminate, peruse, study, deliberate, cogitate, meditate, contemplate, consider, muse.

thin-skinned adj. sensitive, touchy, irritable, impressionable, responsive, susceptible, delicate, tender, excitable, volatile, petulant, irascible, temperamental.

ant. thick-skinned, insensitive, callous, stolid, imperturbable, tough.

third-rate *adj.* SECOND-CLASS.

thirst *n.* longing, craving, yearning, pining, appetite, desire, hunger, yen, lust, itch, hankering, eagerness. —*v.* crave, desire, yearn, long, hunger, pine, covet, hanker, pant.

ant. *n.* distaste, antipathy, aversion, dislike, disinclination, apathy.

thong *n.* strip, strap, latchet, leash, lace, lashing, line, string.

thorn *n.* **1** spine, prickle, barb, bristle, spur. **2** vexation, annoyance, nuisance, irritant, affliction, scourge, cross, bane, curse, plague.

ant. 2 blessing, balm, comfort, manna, benefaction.

thorny *adj.* painful, vexatious, difficult, controversial, complicated, perplexing, troublesome, ticklish, annoying, irritating, unmanageable, distressing, trying, sore, volatile.

ant. easy, simple, pleasant, uncomplicated, manageable.

thorough *adj.* **1** complete, exhaustive, comprehensive, full, sweeping, out-and-out, total, entire, thoroughgoing, radical. **2** painstaking, assiduous, meticulous, careful, conscientious, diligent, exact, precise, sedulous, efficient.

ant. 1 incomplete, partial, sketchy, perfunctory, inadequate. **2** careless, crude, inefficient, frivolous, cursory.

thoroughbred *adj.* **1** pedigreed, purebred, blooded, full-blooded, pureblood. **2** first-class, excellent, courtly, elegant, polished, first-rate, refined, cultivated, accomplished, aristocratic, handsome.

ant. 1 half-breed, crossbred, hybrid, mongrel, crossed. **2** second-rate, crude, coarse, rude, unpolished, rough.

thoroughfare *n.* highroad, highway, avenue, street, road, roadway, boule-

vard, artery, mainline, turnpike, parkway, expressway, thruway.

thoroughgoing *adj.* **1** painstaking, careful, assiduous, thorough, efficient, exhaustive, sweeping, conscientious, meticulous, total. **2** out-and-out, unmitigated, sheer, flagrant, blatant, unqualified, egregious, extreme, arrant, utter, complete.

ant. 1 cursory, slap-dash, careless, hasty, superficial. **2** tentative, partial, rudimentary, undeclared, undeveloped.

thoroughly *adv.* QUITE.

thought *n.* **1** meditation, lucubration, cogitation, ideation, reasoning, contemplation, speculation, reflection, thinking, rumination, calculation. **2** idea, concept, conclusion, judgment, opinion, notion, conception, impression, fancy, supposition. **3** attention, heed, consideration, care, regard, concern, worry, caution, anxiety, solicitude. **4** intention, plan, design, expectation, anticipation, hope, purpose, dream, aim, object.

thoughtful *adj.* **1** meditative, deliberative, ruminant, reflective, thinking, intellectual, conceptual, contemplative, pensive, musing, speculative. **2** attentive, careful, considerate, unselfish, kind, helpful, solicitous, tactful, neighborly, discreet.

ant. 1 unthinking, stupid, unreflective, unreasoning, thoughtless. **2** inconsiderate, selfish, indifferent, unkind, self-centered.

thoughtless *adj.* inconsiderate, selfish, self-centered, indifferent, heedless, inattentive, unmindful, careless, unthinking, negligent, remiss, unconcerned.

ant. considerate, unselfish, solicitous, thoughtful, kind, concerned.

thrall *n.* **1** SLAVE. **2** THRALLDOM.

thralldom *n.* bondage, servitude, enslavement, enthrallment, subjection, subjugation, vassalage, peonage, oppression, domination, slavery, serfdom, thrall, indenture.

ant. freedom, liberty, liberation,

emancipation, manumission, independence.

thrash v. **1** flog, beat, thresh, flail, whip, lash, tan, strike, strap, pommel. **2** defeat, rout, drub, trounce, best, beat, conquer, vanquish, overwhelm, worst.

thrash out kick around, thresh out, get to the bottom of, mull over, debate, rehash, discuss, exhaust, have out, delve into, investigate, probe, settle.

thread n. **1** filament, fiber, string, cord, line, tendril, yarn, staple, strand, wire, wisp. **2** drift, strain, theme, course, tenor, motif, matter, subject, nexus, gist.

threadbare adj. **1** worn, ragged, shabby, frayed, seedy, napless, tacky, pilled, worn-out. **2** commonplace, hackneyed, stale, common, stereotyped, trite, moth-eaten, banal, humdrum, jejune.

ant. 1 brand-new, unused, fresh, well-preserved, good, virgin. **2** original, new, novel, fresh, unfamiliar, unusual.

threat n. menace, danger, peril, risk, hazard, jeopardy, foreboding, sword of Damocles, cloud, portent, warning, omen, caveat, caution, intimidation.

ant. reassurance, protection, deliverance, solace, encouragement.

threaten v. menace, imperil, terrorize, portend, forebode, impend, endanger, augur, intimidate, loom, fulminate, warn, caution, forewarn, bully.

ant. protect, defend, hearten, embolden, reassure, lull.

threatening adj. menacing, dangerous, sinister, foreboding, minatory, dark, lowering, portentous, ominous, forbidding, warning.

ant. auspicious, reassuring, encouraging, bright, promising, lulling.

threesome n. TRIO.

threshold n. beginning, dawn, vanguard, frontier, commencement, inception, opening, start, brink, verge, outset, entrance, debut.

ant. close, decline, twilight, end, dissolution, finish.

thresh out THRASH OUT.

thrift n. frugality, economy, prudence, husbandry, providence, conservation, thriftiness, saving, carefulness, management, cheeseparing, parsimony.

ant. waste, extravagance, prodigality, improvidence, thriftlessness, carelessness.

thrifty adj. frugal, economical, provident, prudent, forehanded, saving, sparing, careful, Spartan, parsimonious, penny-wise, chary, penurious.

ant. wasteful, extravagant, prodigal, open-handed, lavish, free.

thrill v. excite, electrify, arouse, titillate, move, affect, please, agitate, enrapture, enchant, ravish, touch, pierce, stimulate, stir, galvanize, tickle. —n. **1** excitement, titillation, pleasure, stimulation, ferment, sensation, frenzy, intoxication, agitation, kick (Slang). **2** pulsation, twinge, shock, tingling, pulse, fluttering, tremor, surge, quiver, gooseflesh.

ant. v. calm, lull, tranquilize, becalm, quiet, sedate. n. **1** boredom, ennui, languor, tedium, slackness, serenity.

thrive v. prosper, flourish, succeed, get ahead, make a bundle (Slang), advance, improve, bloom, burgeon, luxuriate, increase, grow, boom, batten, wax.

ant. languish, fail, die, wane, droop, wither.

throb v. pulsate, palpitate, oscillate, beat, vibrate, heave, shake, quaver, tremble, flutter. —n. pulsation, tremor, palpitation, paroxysm, spasm, stab, heartthrob, surge, impulse, wave, thrill.

throe n. PANG.

throng n. **1** crowd, multitude, host, jam, mass, press, horde, group, gang, herd, band, assemblage, congregation. **2** swarm, myriad, array, concentration, deluge, host, galaxy, bevy, bunch, congress. —*v.* crowd, jam, collect, flock, mass, press, push, swarm, congregate, assemble, troop, pack, jostle, herd.

ant. *v.* scatter, spread out, disperse, disband, separate, depart.

throttle *v.* **1** strangle, choke, suffocate, stifle, smother, asphyxiate, garrote, burke. **2** silence, suppress, check, stop, squelch, smother, gag, obstruct, repress, inhibit, arrest.

through and through thoroughly, completely, altogether, wholly, totally, entirely, fundamentally, radically, utterly, throughout, everywhere.

ant. partially, somewhat, more or less, moderately, sporadically, superficially.

throw *v.* propel, hurl, fling, heave, cast, toss, pitch, sling, lob, shy, chuck, let fly. —*n.* propulsion, projection, toss, fling, hurl, lob, pitch, sling, heave, cast, chuck, shy, shot.

throw away discard, throw out, cast off, dispose of, dispense with, get rid of, junk, scrap, jettison, dump, reject, eliminate, unload.

ant. keep, retain, save, put by, conserve, hold.

throw out THROW AWAY.

throw over JILT.

throw up vomit, disgorge, puke, regurgitate, upchuck, be sick, bring up, eject, retch, heave, gag.

thrust *v.* **1** push, shove, force, propel, lunge, jab, poke, stab, ram, impel, drive, plunge, stick, jam. **2** interpose, introduce, interject, intrude, insinuate, insert, intercalate, inject, interpolate. —*n.* **1** shove, blow, dig, push, lunge, plunge, jab, poke, stab, pass. **2** attack, assault, onset, charge, raid, sally, onslaught, sortie, incursion, drive, foray. **3** gist, import, significance, sense, intention, intent, substance, meaning, tenor, burden, pith, essence.

thud *n., v.* THUMP.

thug *n.* assassin, ruffian, killer, gangster, mobster, gunman, hoodlum, mugger, hooligan, hit man (*Slang*),

hood (*Slang*), mafioso, cutthroat, murderer, butcher.

thumbnail *adj.* BRIEF.

thump *n.* thud, slam, bang, plunk, clump, clout, stroke, thwack, knock, blow, throb. —*v.* **1** *strike a sounding blow:* bang, bump, knock, slam, thud, thwack, plump, clump. **2** *strike with a heavy object:* drub, thud, pound, cudgel, bludgeon, lambaste, hammer, thwack, whack, punch.

thunder *v.* roar, fulminate, bluster, growl, bark, boom, clamor, shout, rumble, roll, resound, crash, crack, reverberate.

thwack *v.* smack, paddle, slap, whale, belabor, whack, slam, strike, beat, thump, clout, rap, bash. —*n.* blow, smack, slap, clout, bash, stroke, whack, box, buffet, pat, blow, thump, rap, slam, hit.

thwart *v.* frustrate, obstruct, hinder, baffle, cross, circumvent, foil, balk, contravene, prevent, oppose, defeat, outwit.

ant. abet, facilitate, assist, support, help, cooperate.

tic *n.* SPASM.

ticket *n.* **1** voucher, coupon, card, pass, permit, slip, token, certificate, twofer (*Slang*), freebie (*Slang*). **2** label, tag, docket, sticker, tab, slip. **3** ballot, slate, list, roster, catalog, roll, register. —*v.* label, tag, mark, docket, identify, characterize, brand, earmark.

tickle *v.* please, amuse, divert, titillate, stimulate, excite, entertain, delight, interest, intrigue, tantalize, fascinate, rejoice.

ant. irritate, annoy, pester, vex, bore.

ticklish *adj.* delicate, touchy, difficult, awkward, trying, uncertain, dicey, chancy, risky, critical, unstable, sensitive.

tidbit *n.* morsel, treat, delicacy, dainty, goody, snack, titbit, nosh, mouthful.

tide *n.* flood, burst, avalanche, wave, outpouring, outburst, flow, stream, current, trend, tendency, drift, direction.

tidings *n.* information, news, announcement, intelligence, declaration, advice, word, communication, report, message.

tidy *adj.* **1** neat, orderly, well-ordered, shipshape, trig, trim, well-kept, well-groomed, spruce, systematic. **2** goodly, substantial, considerable, generous, large, ample, adequate, handsome, respectable. —*v.* put right, set in order, neaten, set right, arrange, redd, straighten, spruce up, clean, pick up.

ant. *adj.* **1** untidy, unkempt, sloppy, messy, slovenly. **2** small, scanty, insignificant, paltry, niggardly. *v.* disarrange, mess up, upset, litter, jumble.

tie *v.* **1** fasten, attach, bind, join, unite, couple, connect, ligate, link, knot, yoke, knit, hold. **2** restrict, bind, check, tether, rein, leash, hobble, manacle, shackle, restrain. —*n.* **1** fastening, ligature, cord, rope, string, leash, band, ribbon, thong, coupling. **2** obligation, bond, affiliation, allegiance, nexus, connection, link, attachment, association, constraint.

ant. *v.* **1** separate, disconnect, loosen, untie, sever. **2** free, loose, release, untie, liberate.

tie-in *n.* association, connection, liaison, linkage, tie-up, relationship, hookup, coalition, combination, affiliation, alliance.

tier *n.* rank, row, stratum, layer, level, course, bank, step.

tie-up *n.* **1** snarl, snag, bottleneck, block, jam, hitch, snafu (*Slang*), blockage, stoppage, failure, interruption, blackout, breakdown, malfunction. **2** TIE-IN.

tiff *n.* quarrel, spat, clash, words, row, tussle, misunderstanding, dispute, scrap, altercation, wrangle, squabble, difference.

ant. harmony, peace, amity, calm, reconciliation.

tight *adj.* **1** fixed, secure, firm, fast, safe, immovable. **2** taut, stretched, pulled, tense, strained, inflexible,

rigid, stiff. **3** snug, small, close, narrow, strait, form-fitting, skintight, tapered, constrictive. **4** full, heavy, busy, strict, stringent, demanding, exacting. **5** TIGHT-FISTED. **6** *Slang* DRUNK.

ant. **1** insecure, unsafe, slack, loose, lax. **2** slack, loose, flexible, pliant, lax. **3** loose, roomy, large, ample, commodious. **4** easy, undemanding, leisurely, light.

tighten *v.* stretch, tauten, tense, strain, pull, lace up, stiffen, draw, screw, twist.

ant. slacken, relax, loosen, unbind, loose, let go.

tight-fisted *adj.* stingy, miserly, close, mean, greedy, avaricious, usurious, rapacious, grasping, parsimonious, penny-wise, niggardly, cheap, small, illiberal.

ant. generous, open-handed, ungrudging, philanthropic, liberal, munificent.

tightwad *n. Slang* MISER.

tilt *v.* **1** slant, incline, slope, tip, list, lean, cant, heel, pitch. **2** aim, thrust, propel, lunge, charge, point, drive. **3** argue, debate, disagree, compete, skirmish, encounter, contend, join issue, clash, joust. — *n.* slant, slope, tip, grade, gradient, incline, inclination, steep, bevel, acclivity, dip, rise.

ant. *n.* level, flat, plain, horizontal, plane.

timber *n.* **1** wood, lumber. **2** puncheon, rafter, beam, board, upright, cross beam, lath, joist, scantling, truss, rib, two-by-four. **3** FOREST.

timberland *n.* FOREST.

time *n.* **1** epoch, era, period, age, day, year, season, date, cycle. **2** interval, duration, term, period, space, spell, slot, span. **3** occasion, juncture, opportunity, term, point, season, place, climax, heyday, flowering.

time-honored *adj.* VENERABLE.

timeless *adj.* eternal, unending, immortal, lasting, everlasting, immemorial, infinite, perpetual, unlimited, endless, ceaseless, imperishable, unchanging.

ant. mortal, transitory, ephemeral, evanescent, temporary, temporal.

timely *adj.* seasonable, convenient, fitting, opportune, suitable, providential, appropriate, well-timed, felicitous, fortunate, proper, happy, welcome.

ant. untimely, awkward, inappropriate, ill-timed, unfortunate, inopportune.

timid *adj.* fearful, timorous, shrinking, shy, skittish, nervous, diffident, coy, retiring, bashful, modest, irresolute, faint-hearted, apprehensive, milky.

ant. aggressive, self-assured, resolute, adventurous, forward, spirited.

timorous *adj.* TIMID.

tincture *n.* TINT.

tinge *v.* tint, color, wash, stain, tincture, lace, flavor, season, suffuse, instill, imbue, infuse, impregnate infiltrate. —*n.* trace, dash, hint, soupçon, tincture, touch, tint, cast, smack, dollop, quality, suggestion, redolence.

tingle *v.* tinkle, jingle, ring, ping, chime, plink, ting, prickle, tickle, quiver, shiver, bite, sting. —*n.* prickle, sting, shiver, thrill, quiver, chill, itch, tickle, numbness, throb.

tinker *v.* putter, fumble, dabble, fiddle, dawdle, potter, fuss, boondoggle, dally, mess around, bungle, botch.

tinkle *v.* jingle, ping, ring, plink, chime, tingle, ting, clink, chink, ding, dingdong. —*n.* tintinnabulation, chime, ring, tingle, plink, clink, ping, jingle, dingdong, ding, chink, ting.

tinsel *n.* veneer, paste, ormolu, fool's gold, bauble, gilt, glitter, spangle, rhinestone, gimcrack, plastic, show, finery, brummagen, pinchbeck, deception, illusion. —*adj.* gaudy, meretricious, tawdry, specious, garish, flashy, superficial, bespangled, glittering, showy, trashy, cheap, gimcrack.

ant. *adj.* tasteful, genuine, low-key, understated, conservative, precious.

tint *n.* tinge, hue, shade, rinse, wash, color, tincture, cast, tone, dye, stain. —*v.* tinge, rinse, color, dye, wash, tincture, stain, imbue, tone, shade.

tintinnabulation *n.* TINKLE.

tiny *adj.* minute, diminutive, minuscule, miniature, insignificant, peewee, teeny, wee, petite, dwarfish, Lilliputian, microscopic, infinitesimal.

ant. huge, immense, colossal, elephantine, vast, large.

tip[1] *v.* tilt, slant, cant, incline, bend, pitch, heel, angle, slope, lean, put askew. —*n.* TILT.

tip[2] *n.* **1** gratuity, gift, present, perquisite, fee, donation, cumshaw, pourboire, douceur, bonus, consideration. **2** hint, cue, information, pointer, suggestion, warning, tip-off, inkling, intimation, signal, dope (*Slang*). —*v.* give, donate, requite, reward, recompense, pay, remunerate.

tip[3] *n.* **1** point, end, nib, extremity, cusp, vertex, edge, angle. **2** crown, crest, pinnacle, cap, peak, summit, apex, top, tip-top, head.

tip[4] *n., v.* TAP.

tip-off *n.* warning, tip, alert, alarm, signal, sign, inkling, cue, low-down (*Slang*), indication, exposition, key, revelation.

tip off divulge, disclose, reveal, leak, inform, let on, confide, initiate, notify, warn, alert, signal, caution.

tipple *v.* drink, booze, tope, guzzle, sip, quaff, nip, imbibe, swig, swill, fuddle, bend an elbow.

ant. abstain, go on the wagon, teetotal.

tipsy *adj.* drunk, boozy, intoxicated, inebriated, fuddled, befuddled, dizzy, shaky, unsteady, confused, staggering, reeling, drunken.

ant. sober, temperate, abstemious.

tip-top *adj.* FIRST-RATE.

tirade *n.* outpouring, outburst, screed, phillipic, diatribe, denunciation, declamation, harangue, speech, lecture, dressing-down, scolding, jeremiad.

tire[1] *v.* **1** exhaust, weary, wear out, fatigue, fag, flag, enervate, jade. **2** irk, bore, bother, exasperate, weary.

ant. 1 refresh, revive, energize, restore, recuperate. **2** arouse, stimulate, interest, alert, pique.

tire[2] *n.* rim, hoop, felly, tread.

tired *adj.* weary, fatigued, exhausted, enervated, worn-out, wearied, jaded, toilworn, fagged, spent, strained, all in, pooped (*Slang*).

ant. rested, refreshed, energetic, tireless, fresh, eager.

tireless *adj.* untiring, unflagging, energetic, active, industrious, inexhaustible, indefatigable, unwearying, enduring, tough, untired, vigorous.

ant. tired, wearied, exhausted, fatigued, flagging.

tiresome *adj.* tedious, wearisome, irksome, monotonous, humdrum, dull, exhausting, uphill, fatiguing, difficult, arduous, troublesome.

ant. refreshing, stimulating, exciting, rousing, restful, restorative.

tiro *n.* TYRO.

tissue *n.* **1** fabric, gauze, mesh, gossamer, film, stuff, cloth, webbing. **2** network, chain, nexus, structure, web, collection, mass, set.

tit *n.* TEAT.

titan *n.* giant, colossus, superman, powerhouse (*Slang*), Goliath, Amazon, Samson, Brobdingnagian, mammoth, monster, ogre, leviathan.

ant. dwarf, elf, pygmy, Lilliputian, peewee, half pint (*Slang*).

titbit *n.* TIDBIT.

tithe *n., v.* TAX.

titillate *v.* TICKLE.

titivate *v.* DRESS.

title *n.* **1** name, heading, inscription, caption, head, legend. **2** epithet, designation, cognomen, term, name, sobriquet, denomination, nickname, moniker (*Slang*), characterization, appellation. **3** championship, crown, banner, badge, laurels, flag, cup, emblem.

titter *v.* giggle, snigger, snicker, chuckle, chortle, twitter, cackle, snort, laugh, smirk, simper. —*n.* gig-

gle, snicker, snigger, twitter, chuckle, chortle, cackle, simper, snort, smirk, laugh.

tittle *n.* jot, mote, speck, bit, mite, scrap, shred, scintilla, particle, iota, dash, whit, drop, grain, atom.

ant. mass, chunk, block, lump, hunk, mountain.

tittle-tattle *n., v.* TATTLE.

titular *adj.* nominal, purported, so-called, titulary, honorary, ostensible, professed, supposed, reputed, quasi, putative.

ant. real, actual, true, effective, functioning, full-fledged.

toad *n.* miscreant, monster, rascal, villain, cur, swine, cad, snake, reptile, monstrosity, freak.

toady *n.* sycophant, flatterer, yes-man, flunky, bootlicker, lackey, tool, timeserver, fawner, courtier, stooge, truckler, parasite, lickspittle, myrmidon. —*v.* fawn, truckle, flatter, crawl, cringe, grovel, kowtow, bootlick, crouch, cower, bow, kneel.

ant. *v.* defy, rebel, stand up to, resist, outface, confront.

to-and-fro *adj.* alternating, oscillating, shuttling, rocking, pitching, undulatory, fluctuating, back-and-forth, zigzag, wobbly.

ant. stationary, immobile, fixed, unwavering, straight, direct.

toast *n.* drink, pledge, salute, obeisance, celebration, compliment, salutation, commemoration, homage. —*v.* drink to, hail, salute, celebrate, compliment, glorify, extol, commemorate, honor.

toboggan *v.* PLUNGE.

tocsin *n.* ALARM.

today *adv.* now, at present, at this time, at once, promptly, pronto (*Slang*), straightaway, immediately, presently, currently, contemporaneously, nowadays.

toddle *v.* totter, waddle, stumble, hobble, shamble, wobble, trip, shuffle.

toddy *n.* DRINK.

to-do *n.* stir, fuss, bustle, ado, disturbance, tumult, turmoil, commotion, confusion, noise, flurry, bother, excitement, racket.

ant. calm, quiet, peacefulness, serenity, tranquillity.

toe v. kick, tap, tip, boot, strike, touch, punt.

toehold n. footing, foothold, purchase, beachhead, bridgehead, wedge, opening, access, opportunity, advantage.

toga n. ROBE.

together adv. **1** collectively, hand in hand, unanimously, in tandem, side by side, as a whole, as one, en masse, unitedly, conjointly, mutually, in common. **2** simultaneously, in unison, at the same time, concurrently, in chorus, with one accord, as one.

ant. **1** singly, separately, individually, alone, only, exclusively. **2** alternately, serially, separately, alone.

toggery n. CLOTHING.

togs n. CLOTHING.

toil n. labor, drudgery, travail, grind, exertion, moil, pains, task, struggle, sweat, effort, work. —v. drudge, travail, moil, sweat, grind, grub, struggle, labor, slave, strain, strive, plod, work.

ant. n. indolence, sloth, leisure, relaxation, ease, repose. v. rest, relax, repose, loll, pause, slacken.

toilet n. **1** bathroom, washroom, rest room, powder room, lavatory, john (*Slang*), privy, loo (*Brit.*), water closet, WC, closet, commode, latrine, head, urinal. **2** grooming, dressing, makeup, maquillage, toilette, sprucing up, ablutions.

toilsome adj. laborious, difficult, burdensome, oppressive, wearisome, fatiguing, arduous, heavy, onerous, demanding, uphill, strenuous, tiring, tedious, hard.

ant. simple, slight, easy, soft, leisurely, light.

toilworn adj. TIRED.

token n. **1** sign, indication, evidence, manifestation, signal, expression, proof, badge, symbol, mark, emblem. **2** souvenir, memento, keep-

sake, memorial, reminder, relic, handsel, remembrance, symbol. **3** characteristic, feature, trait, attribute, aspect, indicator, index, clue, mark. —adj. nominal, symbolic, partial, small, minimal, professed, pretended, equivalent, substitute, perfunctory, formal, hollow.

ant. adj. thoroughgoing, genuine, wholehearted, veritable, out-and-out, bona fide.

tolerable adj. **1** endurable, bearable, sufferable, supportable, admissible, excusable, allowable, defensible, passable. **2** fair, middling, so-so, indifferent, mediocre, passable, medium, innocuous, ordinary, adequate, respectable.

ant. **1** insupportable, outrageous, insufferable, unbearable, inexcusable. **2** extraordinary, exceptional, outstanding, unusual, singular.

tolerance n. **1** open-mindedness, liberality, broad-mindedness, reasonableness, magnanimity, impartiality, universality, catholicism, receptivity, benevolence. **2** stamina, endurance, toughness, resilience, staying power, fortitude, resistance, buoyancy, hardiness, robustness.

ant. **1** prejudice, intolerance, narrowness, bigotry, chauvinism. **2** weakness, fragility, frailty, infirmity, vulnerability.

tolerant adj. indulgent, broad-minded, lenient, easygoing, reasonable, open-minded, unprejudiced, liberal, magnanimous, benevolent, receptive, complaisant, catholic, permissive, forbearing, patient, long-suffering.

ant. discriminating, prejudiced, bigoted, chauvinistic, unreasonable, unreceptive.

tolerate v. **1** allow, permit, let, warrant, accord, admit, authorize, approve, suffer, indulge, concede, sanction, license. **2** bear, endure, abide, put up with, suffer, stand, submit to, sustain, stomach, swallow.

ant. **1** prohibit, forbid, disapprove,

ban, outlaw, veto. **2** reject, repel, protest, fight, refuse.

toll[1] *n.* tax, charge, tariff, fee, levy, rate, assessment, impost, fare, rental, tribute, exaction, duty, tithe.

toll[2] *v.* sound, ring, clang, knell, peal, strike, chime, call, summon, signal, command, announce.

tomb *n.* grave, mausoleum, crypt, sepulcher, vault, sepulture, monument, catacomb, charnel house, memorial, cenotaph.

tomfool *n.* FOOL. —*adj.* FOOLISH.

tomfoolery *n.* nonsense, silliness, foolishness, merriment, drollery, buffoonery, absurdity, high jinks, folly, trifling, jape, antic, lark, escapade, monkeyshines (*Slang*).
ant. sobriety, seriousness, gravity, solemnity, heaviness.

ton *n. any large amount*: mass, load, abundance, much, great deal, weight, lot, pile, glut, profusion, deluge, avalanche, tidal wave.

tone *n.* **1** sound, pitch, modulation, overtone, harmonic, partial, note, inflection, intonation, cadence, accent, emphasis. **2** mood, tenor, style, spirit, disposition, note, burden, humor, bent, tendency, temper, manner. **3** character, trend, pecularity, tendency, quality, nature, trait, style, complexion, idiosyncrasy.

toneless *adj.* MONOTONOUS.

tongs *n.* pincers, grapnel, forceps, pliers, nippers, tweezers, clamp, claw, hook, grapple.

tongue *n.* **1** utterance, articulation, speech, talk, discourse, expression, verbalization, enunciation, articulateness, gift of gab. **2** language, lingo, dialect, vernacular, patois, jargon, idiom, cant, argot, slang.

tongue-in-cheek *adj.* facetious, playful, quizzical, ironic, satirical, pretending, teasing, insincere, mocking, exaggerated, sly.
ant. serious, forthright, candid, sincere, straightforward, matter-of-fact.

tongue-tied *adj.* speechless, mute, dumb, inarticulate, mum, gagged, taciturn, laconic, silent, reticent.
ant. articulate, wordy, talkative, verbose, prolix.

tonic *adj.* bracing, invigorating, healthful, restorative, energizing, stimulating, salubrious, strengthening, salutary, curative, remedial, analeptic.
ant. deleterious, enervating, harmful, debilitating, enfeebling, weakening.

tony *adj.* FASHIONABLE.

too *adv.* also, besides, in addition, yet, furthermore, plus, to boot, likewise, further, moreover, additionally, as well, else, along with, by the same token.

tool *n.* **1** implement, appliance, contrivance, instrument, apparatus, utensil, device, machine, equipment, gear, mechanism. **2** wherewithal, means, apparatus, appurtenance, medium, vehicle, agency, instrument, mechanism, equipment, gear.

toot *v.* tootle, sound, blow, blare, wind, tweedle, honk, blast, trumpet, pipe. —*n.* **1** blast, tootle, peep, note, honk, blare, beep, snort, blow, sound. **2** *Slang* SPREE.

tooth *n.* tine, snag, jag, projection, process, prong, point, barb, spur, hook, cog, sprocket.

toothsome *adj.* delicious, appetizing, flavorful, savory, tasty, palatable, luscious, tempting, delectable, pleasing, sweet, mouthwatering, yummy.
ant. unpalatable, distasteful, disagreeable, unsavory, revolting, nauseating.

tootle *v., n.* TOOT.

top *n.* **1** summit, culmination, pinnacle, apex, head, crown, peak, crest, tip, height, acme, zenith, vertex. **2** lid, cover, cap, stopper, ceiling, roof, canopy, awning. —*adj.* chief, key, leading, main, principal, dominant, eminent, important, talented, paramount, foremost, outstanding, top-drawer, first-rate, elite. —*v.* **1** cap, crown, cover, tip, roof. **2** surpass, outdo, excel, exceed, lead, best, beat, eclipse, transcend, outshine.

ant. *n.* **1** bottom, root, foot, nadir, depth. *adj.* worst, talentless, unknown, incompetent, lousy (*Slang*).

top-drawer *adj.* FIRST-RATE.

topflight *adj.* FIRST-RATE.

topic *n.* subject, theme, motif, issue, matter, point, question, text, thesis, subject matter, argument, problem, business, proposition, field.

topical *adj.* **1** local, parochial, current, passing, present-day, immediate, timely, temporary, restricted, limited. **2** thematic, texual, germane, pertinent, particular, apropos, relevant.

top-level *adj.* CHIEF.

top-lofty *adj.* HAUGHTY.

top-notch *adj.* FIRST-RATE.

topping *adj.* **1** EMINENT. **2** EXCELLENT (*Brit.*).

topple *v.* fall, tumble, collapse, totter, sink, crumble, dissolve, founder, overthrow, overturn, bring low, knock down.
ant. rise, ascend, tower, construct, put together, build.

tops *adj. Slang* FIRST-RATE.

topsy-turvy *adj.* **1** disordered, messy, confused, untidy, jumbled, disorderly, cluttered, disarrayed, upset, disarranged, unsystematic, upsidedown. **2** upended, overturned, upside-down, inverted, upset, reversed, capsized, wrong side up.
ant. **1** orderly, systematic, well-ordered, neat, tidy. **2** upright, erect, righted, normal, perpendicular.

torch *n.* taper, light, link, illumination, lamp, beacon, flambeau, flashlight spotlight, cresset.

torchbearer *n.* LEADER.

torment *n.* **1** pain, anguish, agony, suffering, pang, throe, discomfort, distress, misery. **2** annoyance, affliction, worry, plague, distress, torture, rack, martyrdom, trial, scourge, tribulation. —*v.* **1** torture, afflict, distress, pain, wound, harry, agonize, plague, hurt, excruciate. **2** tease, goad, annoy, tantalize, provoke, pester, harry, plague, worry, vex, harass.

ant. *n.* **1** pleasure, joy, comfort, delight, ease. —*v.* **1** relieve, assuage, alleviate, mitigate, soothe. **2** satisfy, please, mollify, amuse.

torpedo *v.* destroy, demolish, wreck, queer, quash, stamp out, sabotage, nullify, abort, kill, screw up (*Slang*), put the kibosh on (*Slang*), mess up, ruin, spoil.
ant. salvage, spare, rehabilitate, aid, facilitate, further.

torpid *adj.* **1** dormant, numb, sluggish, motionless, inert, inactive, slow, slack, lethargic, comatose. **2** apathetic, spiritless, dull, indifferent, phlegmatic, listless, languorous, lethargic, spiritless, lackadaisical, passive, unconcerned, languid.
ant. **1** alert, active, keyed up, stimulated, energetic. **2** spirited, enthusiastic, lively, keen, mettlesome.

torpor *n.* **1** stupor, dormancy, inertia, apathy, coma, numbness, inactivity, sluggishness, lethargy, insensibility. **2** listlessness, apathy, indifference, languor, dullness, lassitude, lethargy, weariness, unconcern, phlegm.
ant. **1** consciousness, awareness, activity, reactivity, mobility. **2** enthusiasm, spirit, alertness, mettle, interest.

torrent *n.* **1** stream, spate, freshet, rapid, river, waterfall, cascade, cataract, flood, eddy. **2** outburst, rush, gush, spate, flux, storm, flood, deluge, avalanche, tide.

torrid *adj.* **1** parched, hot, scorching, burning, fiery, broiling, baking, suffocating, tropical, stifling. **2** passionate, fervent, desirous, ardent, amorous, erotic, impassioned, lustful, amatory, perfervid.
ant. **1** temperate, cool, cold, frigid, arctic. **2** dispassionate, indifferent, cool, frigid, phlegmatic.

tortuous *adj.* **1** winding, sinuous, twisted, crooked, circuitous, curved, labyrinthine, mazy, meandering, serpentine, sinuate. **2** devious, tricky, crooked, dishonest, deceitful, deceptive, evasive, perverse, misleading, circuitous, indirect, ambiguous.

ant. 1 straight, plumb, direct, rectilinear, inflexible. **2** straightforward, candid, upright, honest, reliable, direct.

torture *n.* agony, suffering, pain, punishment, anguish, torment, martyrdom, dolor, inquisition, rack, pang, crucifixion, Gethsemane. —*v.* torment, afflict, agonize, harrow, punish, maltreat, savage, distress, agitate, martyr, rack, crucify, impale.

ant. *n.* enjoyment, pleasure, bliss, comfort, well-being, welfare. *v.* comfort, relieve, please, ease, soothe, solace.

toss *v.* throw, pitch, fling, hurl, cast, flip, chuck, shy, propel, project, dump, fork. —*n.* throw, fling, pitch, cast, heave, hurl, chuck, shy, flip, put.

tot *n.* CHILD.

total *n.* sum, sum total, totality, aggregate, mass, lump, amount, gross, whole, all, entirety. —*adj.* complete, teetotal, entire, whole, full, gross, utter, thoroughgoing, consummate, absolute, out-and-out, unqualified, thorough, unmitigated, outright. —*v.* **1** add, tot up, compute, sum up, reckon, calculate, number, amount to, reach, come to. **2** *Slang* DEMOLISH.

ant. *adj.* partial, part, limited, restricted, conditional, qualified, incomplete.

totalitarian *adj.* monolithic, autocratic, absolute, tyrannical, despotic, tyrannous, authoritarian, dictatorial.

totality *n.* total, entirety, aggregate, sum total, everything, all, whole, sum, gross, summation, aggregation.

tote *v.* carry, drag, lug, haul, move, transfer, transport, convey, pull, pack, bear, wear, schlep (*Slang*).

totter *v.* teeter, waver, wobble, shake, sway, stumble, toddle, stagger, falter, oscillate, tremble, rock, reel, trip, quaver.

tot up TOTAL.

touch *v.* **1** feel, handle, contact, finger, palpate, paw, probe, massage, rub, press, grope. **2** tap, hit, strike, impinge, glance, graze, rap, pat, slap, tip. **3** abut, border on, adjoin, come to, reach, join, contact, neighbor, meet. **4** affect, move, impress, influence, sway, strike, inspire, thrill, stir, melt. **5** concern, interest, relate to, affect, pertain to, bear on, apply to, have to do with. —*n.* **1** handling, contact, manipulation, impact, impingement, communication, juncture, contiguity, pressure. **2** feeling, feel, sensation, taction, tactility, palpability. **3** feel, texture, quality, character, nature, property, feeling, attribute. **4** flair, sensibility, approach, style, manner, quality, appreciation, understanding, mark. **5** trace, dash, hint, shade, breath, soupçon, twinge, drop, whiff, jot, spot.

ant. *n.* **5** lot, much, plenty, mass, deal, heaps.

touched *adj.* CRAZY.

touching *adj.* affecting, appealing, moving, poignant, pathetic, sad, heartbreaking, melting, pitiable, lamentable, mournful.

touchstone *n.* STANDARD.

touch upon relate to, concern, bear on, pertain to, belong to, connect with, speak of, hint at, impinge on, allude to, discuss, treat, mention.

touchy *adj.* **1** thin-skinned, sensitive, impressionable, cranky, cross, susceptible, testy, irritable, temperamental, hypersensitive, suspicious, irascible, petulant, paranoid, splenetic, choleric. **2** controversial, sensitive, polemical, debatable, questionable, controvertible, delicate, explosive, divisive.

ant. 1 thick-skinned, callous, stolid, insensitive, imperturbable, serene, cool (*Slang*). **2** safe, uncontroversial, academic, philosophic, settled.

tough *adj.* **1** resilient, dense, fibrous, cohesive, firm, strong, wiry. **2** hardy, vigorous, strong, sturdy, stout, invincible, indomitable, hard, tenacious, resilient. **3** difficult, arduous, demanding, troublesome, punishing, challenging, baffling, intractable, complicated, formidable. **4** resolute, unyielding, inflexible, hard-nosed (*Slang*), stiff-necked, uncompromising, hard-bitten, hard-boiled, stubborn, rigid, intransigent. **5** severe, exacting, stiff, merciless, harsh, stringent, rough, stern, Draconian, bitter. **6** unfortunate, regrettable, lamentable, unlucky, disastrous, sorry, unhappy, ill-omened, bad. —*n.* ruffian, rowdy, rascal, hooligan, bully, roughneck, blackguard, brute, mugger, hoodlum, bruiser, thug, gangster.

ant. *adj.* **1** brittle, fragile, friable, crumbly, soft. **2** weak, puny, frail, weakly, fragile, soft. **3** easy, simple, effortless, pleasant, undemanding, cushy (*Slang*). **4** irresolute, indecisive, weak, yielding, vacillating. **5** lenient, mild, soft, easy, gentle. **6** fortunate, good, lucky, happy, cheerful.

toughen *v.* harden, inure, accustom, habituate, acclimate, become used to, season, temper, anneal, caseharden, strengthen, discipline.

ant. enfeeble, weaken, sap, soften, enervate, exhaust.

tour *n.* **1** excursion, journey, trip, jaunt, outing, expedition, voyage, pilgrimage, peregrination, wanderings. **2** turn, shift, term, period, circuit, stint, round, assignment. —*v.* travel, circle, cover, traverse, peregrinate, roam, journey, visit, rove, take in, see, explore, voyage.

tourist *n.* traveler, journeyer, voyager, tripper (*Brit.*), rubberneck (*Slang*), sightseer, excursionist, globe-trotter, pilgrim, wayfarer, vagabond, wanderer.

tousle *v.* disarrange, dishevel, rumple, muss, tangle, disorder, disarray, ruffle, knot, mat, entangle.

ant. tidy, arrange, groom, primp, neaten, comb.

tout *v.* **1** solicit, peddle, canvass, seek, drum up, sell, vend, hawk, importune, beseech, entreat. **2** publicize, puff, vaunt, praise, ballyhoo, advertise, celebrate, exalt, extol, promote, plug (*Slang*).

ant. 2 denigrate, depreciate, belittle, malign, run down, ridicule.

tout de suite IMMEDIATELY.

tow *v.* pull, drag, tug, draw, haul, lug, trawl, trail, entrain, take in tow.

tower *n.* **1** spire, belfry, campanile, minaret, turret, pylon, skyscraper, monument, needle, steeple, obelisk. **2** citadel, stronghold, fort, defense, refuge, blockhouse, fortress, castle, martello tower, bulwark.

towering *adj.* imposing, lofty, great, gigantic, impressive, colossal, heroic, magnificent, sky-high, high, tall, elevated.

ant. insignificant, lowly, inferior, prostrate, humble, low.

town *n.* settlement, village, center, urban area, city, metropolis, suburb, cosmopolis, borough, burg, community, burgh, municipality, hamlet.

toxic *adj.* poisonous, noxious, virulent, venomous, harmful, injurious, septic, pernicious, unhealthy, pestilential.

ant. nontoxic, harmless, nonpoisonous, healthful, salutary, medicinal.

toxin *n.* POISON.

toy *n.* **1** plaything, pastime, game, amusement, recreation. **2** trifle, bauble, trinket, bagatelle, gew-gaw, conceit, gimcrack, knickknack, kickshaw, plaything. —*v.* **1** trifle, twiddle, putter, play, sport, dabble, fiddle, romp, dally, amuse oneself. **2** flirt, tantalize, fondle, caress, bill and coo, trifle, philander, tease, coquet, dally.

trace *n.* **1** vestige, mark, remnant, sign, aftermath, token, clue, hint, suggestion, breath, whiff, soupçon, taste, shade, drop, **2** TRACK. **3** TRAIL. —*v.* **1** track, trail, follow, dog, shadow, hound, chase, pursue, stalk, hunt. **2**

investigate, analyze, scrutinize, discern, ferret out, search out, ascertain, discover, find. **3** copy, draw, sketch, outline, mark out, delineate, describe.

track *n.* **1** mark, trail, trace, footprint, spoor, blaze, vestige, telltale, indication, clue. **2** course, path, orbit, trail, wake, way, pathway. **3** succession, round, train, series, sequence, cycle, progression. —*v.* TRAIL.

track down ferret out, fathom, bottom, discover, find, expose, bring to light, catch, apprehend, unearth, untangle, solve.

track record RECORD.

tract[1] *n.* expanse, stretch, area, acreage, parcel, district, territory, domain, region, terrain, extent, space, estate, quarter.

tract[2] *n.* pamphlet, treatise, broadside, leaflet, booklet, monograph, sermon, homily, commentary, brochure, dissertation, essay, thesis.

tractable *adj.* docile, manageable, biddable, amenable, compliant, obedient, willing, submissive, governable, teachable, placable, pliant, complaisant.

ant. defiant, unruly, contumacious, disobedient, stubborn, intractable.

traction *n.* friction, pull, haulage, adhesion, resistance, opposition, tension, pulling, dragging.

trade *n.* **1** occupation, business, profession, vocation, job, position, employment, pursuit, calling, craft. **2** clientele, customers, custom, public, patrons, patronage, shoppers. **3** exchange, swap, interchange, barter, deal, dealing, trade-off, traffic, truck. —*v.* **1** exchange, swap, traffic, interchange, truck, barter. **2** deal, do business, patronize, frequent, shop, buy, transact.

trademark *n.* **1** colophon, logotype, logo, trade name, brand name, brand. **2** identification, cachet, hallmark, emblem, mark, insignia, seal, stamp, signature, monogram.

trade name TRADEMARK.

trade-off *n.* **1** TRADE. **2** COMPROMISE.

trade off cancel out, balance, offset, match, exchange, counterbalance, compensate for, countervail, eliminate.

tradition *n.* ritual, custom, usage, myth, legend, observance, rite, practice, folklore, superstition, convention, prescription, imperative, standard, belief, attitude, doctrine, information, opinion, knowledge, institution.

traditional *adj.* conventional, usual, ritual, customary, familiar, habitual, accustomed, common, normal, routine, prescriptive, unwritten.

ant. unconventional, unusual, unfamiliar, uncommon, rare.

traduce *v.* defame, slander, malign, disparage, depreciate, revile, abuse, decry, vilify, asperse, calumniate, run down, bad-mouth (*Slang*).

ant. defend, praise, honor, support, extol, respect.

traffic *n.* **1** trade, commerce, merchandising, business, buying, selling, marketing, exchange, interchange, barter. **2** communication, contact, intercourse, dealings, business, truck, connection, meeting, interaction, give-and-take. —*v.* buy, sell, market, truck, deal, bootleg, trade, barter, exchange, hustle (*Slang*).

tragedy *n.* misfortune, disaster, catastrophe, calamity, adversity, affliction, cataclysm, blow, reverse, woe, grief.

ant. fortune, prosperity, happiness, joy, merriment.

tragic *adj.* sorrowful, lamentable, pathetic, pitiful, deplorable, mournful, grievous, disastrous, calamitous, shocking, dire, dreadful, desolate, dark, heavy.

ant. happy, bright, cheerful, fortunate, comic, amusing.

trail *v.* **1** drag, tow, entrain, draw, pull, train. **2** track, pursue, trace, follow, stalk, hunt. **3** spy on, shadow, watch, follow, chase, pursue, keep tabs on. **4** droop, hang, dangle, draggle, drag. **5**

lag, straggle, dawdle, loiter, fall behind. —*n.* **1** impress, track, spoor,
scent, mark, telltale, wake. **2** path,
runway, trace, track, byway, footpath, road. **3** TRAIN.

ant. *v.* **5** lead, head, front, win, be
foremost.

train *n.* **1** trail, tail, wake, appendage,
tag end. **2** procession, queue, following, retinue, cortege, suite, line, entourage. **3** sequence, series, succession, chain, line, set, string. **4**
aftermath, residue, sequel, consequence, result, trail. —*v.* **1** teach, instruct, discipline, educate, drill, rehearse, practice, habituate, prepare,
prime, groom. **2** aim, point, level, direct, line up, position, slant.

traipse *v.* gad, roam, wander, walk
about, saunter, tramp, stroll, trip,
promenade, skip, flit, meander, rove,
ramble, trek.

trait *n.* feature, quality, characteristic,
idiosyncrasy, particularity, attribute,
peculiarity, earmark, quirk, mannerism, stigma, mark, lineament.

traitor *n.* turncoat, renegade, quisling,
recreant, betrayer, deserter, double-
dealer, snake in the grass, conspirator, mutineer, plotter, apostate, informer, Judas, rat (*Slang*), ratter
(*Slang*), defector.

traitorous *adj.* treasonable, treacherous, false, faithless, perfidious,
two-faced, double-dealing, unfaithful, seditious, mutinous, recreant,
apostate.

ant. loyal, true, constant, steadfast,
reliable, faithful.

trajectory *n.* flight path, orbit, curve,
route, course, track, path, line.

trammel *n.* hindrance, fetter, hobble,
shackle, restraint, impediment, curb,
clog, yoke, bond, check, chain,
tether, rein. —*v.* hinder, obstruct, restrict, encumber, hem in, hobble,
confine, hamper, clog, fetter,
shackle, prevent.

ant. *v.* assist, further, promote, support, advance, expedite.

tramp *v.* **1** wander, roam, trek, gad,

stray, range, ramble, saunter, peregrinate, hike, rove, march, journey,
tour, travel. **2** TRUDGE. —*n.* **1** hobo,
vagrant, bum, derelict, beggar, vagabond, panhandler, wanderer, beachcomber. **2** hike, walk, stroll, jaunt,
excursion, saunter, ramble, march. **3**
Slang WHORE.

trample *v.* stomp, squash, tramp, tread,
tread on, stamp, crush, tread under-
foot, step on, stump.

trample on oppress, injure, encroach
upon, crush, quash, do violence to,
humiliate, debase, prostrate, violate,
subvert, infringe on, deny.

trance *n.* daze, dream, daydream, reverie, spell, vision, concentration,
absorption, abstraction, brown study,
pipe dream, sleepwalking, coma,
hypnosis.

tranquil *adj.* **1** calm, relaxed, serene,
placid, unruffled, peaceful, com-
posed, unperturbed, equable, philosophical, sedate. **2** quiet, motionless,
peaceful, hushed, calm, still, placid,
smooth, even, restful, halcyon.

ant. **1** agitated, excited, troubled, disturbed, fuming. **2** noisy, tumultuous,
stormy, uproarious, disturbing.

tranquillity *n.* peacefulness, serenity,
placidity, quietude, calm, hush, repose, stillness, calmness, peace,
quiet, composure, restfulness, concord, harmony.

ant. uproar, commotion, disorder,
tumult, disturbance, trouble, noise,
agitation, excitement.

transact *v.* accomplish, carry through,
do, conduct, dispatch, prosecute, operate, execute, manage, carry out,
perform, negotiate, enact.

transaction *n.* deal, bargain, contract,
agreement, arrangement, settlement,
undertaking, affair, matter, negotiation, exchange, business, accommodation.

transcend *v.* **1** exceed, go beyond, overleap, surpass, pass beyond, overstep,
overpass, surmount, rise above. **2**
beat, outdo, outstrip, overshadow,

overtop, outrank, outdistance, outvie, outrival, eclipse.

transcendent *adj.* TRANSCENDENTAL.

transcendental *adj.* **1** consummate, transcendent, incomparable, sublime, supreme, matchless, surpassing, unequalled. **2** supernatural, noumenal, unknowable, preternatural, otherworldly, ineffable, occult.

ant. 1 ordinary, commonplace, everyday, common, indifferent, mediocre. **2** material, mundane, terrestrial, phenomenal, empirical.

transcribe *v.* copy, take down, record, set down, write, note, paraphrase, summarize, rewrite, duplicate, reproduce.

transcript *n.* TRANSCRIPTION.

transcription *n.* **1** copying, transcribing, duplication, reproduction, rewriting, recording, replication, writing, paraphrasing, summarizing. **2** copy, transcript, version, replica, reproduction, facsimile, duplicate, paraphrase, restatement, summary.

transfer *v.* **1** transplant, transpose, change, pass, dispatch, give, transport, transmit, consign, send, carry. **2** deed, make over, sign over, convey, devise, assign, donate, grant, deliver, give, alienate. —*n.* transference, transferal, transmittal, translocation, assignment, relocation, transplantation, removal, transposition, transposal, transition, transmission, replacement, displacement, transportation.

transferal *n.* transplantation, transplant, removal, translocation, relocation, transference, displacement, replacement, reassignment, transport, transportation, transmittal, transposition, transposal.

transfigure *v.* transform, alter, make over, metamorphose, disguise, modify, change, transmute, transmogrify, reconstruct, convert, translate.

transfix *v.* **1** impale, spear, pierce, puncture, skewer, pin, perforate, spike, gore, stake, run through. **2** stun, spellbind, petrify, galvanize,

hypnotize, amaze, confound, fascinate, mesmerize, astound.

transform *v.* transmute, convert, change, alter, modify, remake, reconstruct, make over, translate, transfigure, transmogrify, metamorphose.

transformation *n.* transmutation, alteration, modification, metamorphosis, change, conversion, transfiguration, reconstruction, reformation, translation, transmogrification, transubstantiation.

transfuse *v.* PERMEATE.

transgress *v.* **1** sin, go astray, fall from grace, err, violate, disobey, break, ignore, defy, lapse, run wild, rebel, misbehave, break the law, trespass. **2** exceed, overstep, encroach, trespass, go too far, infringe, invade, impinge, overpass, transcend, intrude.

transgression *n.* sin, lapse, evildoing, sinfulness, wickedness, misbehavior, immorality, encroachment, trespass, infringement, invasion, intrusion, impingement, disobedience, violation, offense, infraction, vice, crime, criminality.

transient *adj.* **1** temporary, impermanent, transitory, passing, brief, fleeting, momentary, ephemeral, short-lived, fugitive, provisional, temporal, inconstant. **2** vagrant, casual, migratory, migrating, on the wing, footloose, unrooted, vagabond, peripatetic, unsettled, nomadic, transitional, pro tem, on the move.

ant. 1 permanent, enduring, constant, continuing, lasting. **2** settled, installed, tethered, established, resident.

transit *n.* **1** TRANSITION. **2** TRANSPORTATION.

transition *n.* **1** transformation, change, flux, conversion, progress, alteration, variation, passage, transit, shift, modification, movement, transmutation, graduation, transmogrification. **2** bridge, connection, step, phase, gradation, upheaval, disturbance, hiatus, gap, dislocation, link, tie, thread.

transitory *adj.* ephemeral, impermanent, fleeting, brief, transitional, transient, evanescent, passing, fugitive, short-lived, momentary, temporary, mortal, perishable, unlasting, vanishing.

ant. permanent, eternal, long-lasting, continuous, imperishable.

translate *v.* **1** render, construe, paraphrase, interpret, explain, spell out, simplify, reword, rephrase, elucidate, decipher, decode, clarify, define, gloss. **2** change, alter, modify, transmute, transform, transmogrify, redo, rework, refashion, convert, recast, reconstruct, metamorphose, transpose, transplant.

translation *n.* interpretation, revision, rewording, paraphrase, gloss, transformation, reconstruction, rendering, rendition, alteration, change, modification, transmutation, conversion, transposition, explanation, simplification, clarification, metamorphosis, transposition.

transmission *n.* conveyance, passage, transfer, conduction, dispatch, consignment, sending, shipment, transference, forwarding, relocation, delivery, broadcast, dispersion, radiation, transmittal, transportation.

transmit *v.* send, convey, conduct, transfer, carry, transport, relocate, dispatch, ship, forward, pass on, conduct, deliver, consign, mail, post, discharge, disperse, radiate, broadcast.

transmogrify *v.* TRANSFORM.

transmute *v.* TRANSFORM.

transparent *adj.* **1** diaphanous, filmy, sheer, see-through, lacy, cobwebby, glassy, translucent, gauzy, porous, thin, vitreous, clear, crystalline, porous, peekaboo. **2** obvious, plain, unambiguous, simple, unequivocal, understandable, overt, visible, detectable, explicit, blatant, patent, unmistakable, apparent, glaring. **3** guileless, frank, open, ingenuous, naive, candid, forthright, direct, unaffected, unpretentious, artless, honest, simple, childlike.

ant. **1** opaque, murky, clouded, filmy, painted, coated. **2** covert, complex, hidden, profound. **3** subtle, devious, wily, underhand.

transpire *v.* come to light, emerge, appear, arise, come about, occur, happen, evolve, take place, eventuate, come to pass.

transplant *v.* TRANSFER.

transport *v.* carry, convey, ship, truck, take, move, transfer, conduct, cart, bear, bring, deliver, haul, run, express. —*n.* **1** TRANSPORTATION. **2** rapture, euphoria, ecstasy, elation, bliss, happiness, delight, enchantment, felicity, beatitude, paradise, heaven, seventh heaven, cloud nine (*Slang*).

ant. **2** depression, melancholy, tailspin, the dumps, funk, the blues.

transportation *n.* **1** conveyance, transport, shipment, delivery, removal, transference, conduction, movement, transmission, dispatch, consignment. **2** shipping, moving, trucking, hauling, cartage, delivery, express, freight, transit, transport.

transported *adj.* euphoric, enchanted, blissful, enraptured, ecstatic, rapturous, exultant, elated, beatific, rhapsodic, thrilled, manic, in seventh heaven, on cloud nine (*Slang*).

ant. miserable, unhappy, depressed, blue, in a tailspin, in the dumps, in a funk.

transpose *v.* reverse, switch, shift, exchange, transfer, interchange, substitute, invert, alternate, transplant, change places, swap places.

transverse *adj.* crosswise, diagonal, athwart, oblique, crossed, cater-cornered, cross.

trap *n.* **1** snare, net, pit, pitfall, toil, noose, deadfall, gin, decoy, springe. **2** enticement, pitfall, booby trap, deception, lure, stratagem, ruse, maneuver, come-on (*Slang*), blind, plant, decoy, ploy, web, artifice, strategy, gimmick. **3** *Slang* MOUTH. —*v.* snare, catch, enmesh, ensnare, waylay, corner, inveigle, hook, trick, deceive, capture, take, bag, take in, dupe, fool.

trappings *n.* adornments, embellishments, trimmings, signs, symbols, emblems, marks, perquisities, superficialities, appearances, show, fittings, indications, finery.

trash *n.* **1** rubbish, garbage, dross, leavings, oddments, waste, debris, rubble, dregs, rejects, refuse, junk, scourings, residue, sweepings, dust (*Brit.*). **2** nonsense, drivel, foolishness, prattle, jabber, gibberish, tripe, eyewash (*Slang*), inanity, asininity, hot air (*Slang*), malarky (*Slang*), crap (*Slang*).
ant. 1 treasure, valuables, substance, assets. **2** sense, logic, meaning, significance.

trauma *n.* shock, jolt, wound, upset, upheaval, blow, breakdown, disturbance, ordeal, reversal, disorientation, strain.

traumatic *adj.* shocking, wounding, upsetting, disorienting, disturbing, disabling, crippling, scarring, painful, disordering, confusing, bewildering.
ant. healing, helpful, therapeutic, wholesome, calming.

travail *n.* **1** pain, agony, distress, anguish, anxiety, torture, torment, misery, unhappiness, suffering, discomfort, ache, trial, ordeal, wretchedness. **2** toil, labor, sweat, drudgery, exertion, slavery, effort, strain, work, grind, struggle, strife, servility, bondage, rat race (*Slang*). —*v.* TOIL.
ant. 1 pleasure, joy, happiness. **2** relaxation, repose, rest.

travel *v.* **1** journey, wander, roam, tour, cruise, sail, peregrinate, rove, trek, trip, voyage, jaunt, commute. **2** proceed, advance, pass, move, progress, go. —*n.* **1** traveling, touring, cruising, commuting, peregrinating, wayfaring, progress, advancement, passage, movement, transportation. **2** tour, trek, journey, expedition, passage, transport, crossing, itinerary, trip, excursion, voyage, safari, pilgrimage, jaunt, junket.

ant. 1 remain, stay, stay put, hibernate, hole up.

traverse *v.* **1** cross, go across, pass through, overpass, pass over, go over, cut across, intersect, bisect, penetrate, travel across, march over, cover, bridge, cut through. **2** scan, examine, scrutinize, pore over, investigate, eye, look over, look into, review, run through, inspect, dissect, study, explore, plumb. **3** thwart, frustrate, oppose, deny, counteract, rebut, counter, cross, gainsay, foil, contravene, balk, hinder, outmaneuver, check.

travesty *n.* mockery, joke, caricature, farce, parody, burlesque, distortion, poor imitation, misrepresentation, lampoon, falsification, counterfeit, mimicry. —*v.* mock, burlesque, lampoon, ridicule, parody, make fun of, misrepresent, exaggerate, satirize, ape, counterfeit, deride, distort, twit, jeer at.

tray *n.* salver, server, container, holder, receptacle, coaster, platter, trencher, waiter.

treacherous *adj.* **1** disloyal, duplicitous, treasonous, perfidious, untrustworthy, unfaithful, double-dealing, two-faced, deceitful, unscrupulous, unprincipled, opportunist, Machiavellian, sly, devious. **2** misleading, insecure, unsafe, tricky, deceptive, unreliable, unstable, precarious, unsteady, dangerous, slippery, undependable, ramshackle, unsound, hazardous.
ant. 1 faithful, loyal, true. **2** safe, secure, sound.

treachery *n.* disloyalty, perfidy, treason, duplicity, untrustworthiness, faithlessness, double-dealing, deceit, deceitfulness, betrayal, opportunism, infidelity, deception, trickery, subversion, mutiny.
ant. loyalty, fidelity, allegiance, fealty.

tread *v.* **1** step on, walk along, step over, walk over, pace, walk, stride, plod, march, tramp, amble, hike, trudge. **2** crush, oppress, bear down on, trample, subdue, subjugate, enslave, exploit, extirpate, wipe out, quell, suppress, persecute, browbeat, stomp. **3** TRAMPLE.

treason *n.* betrayal, subversion, disloyalty, mutiny, revolution, lawlessness, perfidy, duplicity, deceit, lese-majesty, sedition, insurrection, collaborationism, insubordination, conspiracy.

ant. loyalty, patriotism, allegiance, faithfulness, fealty.

treasonous *adj.* TREACHEROUS.

treasure *n.* **1** riches, treasury, treasure house, gold mine, treasure-trove, nest egg, mint, fortune, savings, capital, wealth, hoard, resources, fortune. **2** jewel, pearl, diamond, dear one, darling, beloved, precious, gem, prize, idol, angel, bijou, rarity, nonpareil, paragon. —*v.* cherish, hold dear, esteem, value, venerate, prize, safeguard, appreciate, love, protect, dote on, adore, regard, revere.

treasure-trove *n.* TREASURE.

treasury *n.* TREASURE.

treat *v.* **1** behave, conduct oneself, regard, react, look upon, deal with, handle, act toward, manage, cope, use, utilize, manipulate, include, cover, express. **2** medicate, doctor, nurse, dose, prescribe for, operate, relieve, cure, remedy, palliate. —*n.* delight, joy, pleasure, relaxation, fun, entertainment, refreshment, lift, change, break, windfall, blessing, relief, boon.

ant. *n.* pain, nuisance, bore, burden, drag (*Slang*).

treatise *n.* monograph, thesis, dissertation, study, exposition, textbook, text, tract, essay, commentary, critique, disquisition, explanation, exegesis.

treatment *n.* **1** handling, procedure, conduct, behavior, reaction, management, attitude, point of view, use, dissection, explanation, exposition, process, analysis, style. **2** therapy, therapeutics, medication, doctoring,

prescription, regimen, recommendation, cure, remedy, rehabilitation, method, prophylaxis.

treaty *n.* pact, compact, agreement, entente, understanding, arrangement, concordat, convention, covenant, bargain, contract, bond, deal.

trek *v.* **1** slog, trudge, drag, tramp, hike, wade, plod, shamble, straggle, lumber, limp, hobble, slog, schlep (*Slang*). **2** journey, travel, tour, migrate, peregrinate, wander, traverse, roam, rove, range, jaunt, junket, meander, sightsee. —*n.* journey, trip, tour, safari, hike, migration, peregrination, excursion, expedition, sightseeing, pilgrimage, emigration, crossing, schlep (*Slang*).

tremble *v.* **1** shake, quiver, quake, shiver, palpitate, shudder, quaver, throb, flutter, quail, pulsate. **2** wobble, teeter, totter, rock, vibrate, oscillate, rattle, move, sway, seesaw, flounder, dodder.

tremendous *adj.* **1** enormous, monumental, huge, vast, extensive, great, mammoth, giant, oversize, colossal, immense, mountainous, gigantic, titanic, whopping. **2** wonderful, marvelous, prodigious, stupendous, extraordinary, miraculous, fabulous, exceptional, excellent, stunning, divine, super (*Slang*), swell (*Slang*), out of this world (*Slang*).

ant. 1 small, tiny, little, puny, runty. **2** terrible, awful, rotten, lousy (*Slang*).

tremor *n.* quiver, tremble, trembling, palpitation, quake, shiver, spasm, quaver, flutter, pulsation, throb, throbbing, vibration, beating, shaking.

tremulous *adj.* **1** quavering, quaky, trembling, shaking, quivery, spasmodic, shaky, fluttery, shivering, convulsive, throbbing, palpitating. **2** fearful, faltering, hesitant, irresolute, timid, uncertain, wobbly, wavering, weak, cowardly, flinching, quailing, scared, cowering, cringing. **3** excited, agog, atremble, aquiver, aflutter, keyed-up, stimulated, stirred, agitated, restless, restive, impatient, worked-up, flustered, on tenterhooks.

ant. 1 still, motionless, immobile. **2** firm, fixed, resolute, brave, heroic. **3** calm, relaxed, phlegmatic, apathetic, unmoved.

trench *n.* ditch, dugout, entrenchment, earthwork, fortification, moat, excavation, trough, channel, fosse, gutter, breastwork.

trenchant *adj.* **1** vigorous, effective, effectual, clear, strong, emphatic, potent, forceful, explicit, unequivocal, salient, impressive, meaningful, powerful, viable. **2** cutting, hurtful, sarcastic, acidulous, keen, sharp, incisive, biting, pointed, caustic, piercing, curt, acerbic, destructive, nasty.

ant. 1 weak, ineffectual, vague, foolish, meaningless. **2** soothing, flattering, mollifying, kind.

trend *n.* **1** tendency, drift, movement, current, flow, course, direction, prevalence, predominance, tenor, tone, mood, tack, route, fashion. **2** preference, inclination, choice, partiality, predisposition, penchant, tone, bias, notion. —*v.* tend, run, move, course, go, incline, extend, turn, bend, gravitate, verge, drift, lean.

trendy *adj. Slang* stylish, voguish, *en vogue,* popular, modish, fashionable, now, current, latest, in (*Slang*).

ant. old-fashioned, obsolete, dated, passé, old hat (*Slang*).

trepidation *n.* apprehension, anxiety, fear, trembling, foreboding, misgiving, agitation, panic, perturbation, nervousness, nerves, jitters, dread, alarm, cold sweat.

ant. confidence, composure, hope, optimism, pleasure.

trespass *v.* **1** encroach, poach, intrude, infringe, violate, obtrude, overstep, invade. **2** misbehave, transgress, stray, fall, go astray, sin, offend, disobey, err, fall from grace, break the law, go too far. —*n.* **1** misbehavior, misconduct, transgression, infringe-

ment, breach, wrong, crime, malfeasance, sin, offense, error, disobedience, infraction, violation. **2** encroachment, intrusion, infringement, poaching, invasion, inroad, incursion, aggression, violation, obtrusion.

tress *n.* lock, curl, plait, switch, ringlet, hank, loop, coil.

triad *n.* TRIO.

trial *n.* **1** tryout, test, experiment, try, check, whirl, probe, experimentation, dry run, use, examination, scrutiny, application, analysis, assay. **2** ordeal, hardship, difficulty, travail, pain, trouble, tribulation, affliction, torment, vexation, grief, misery, sorrow, anguish, adversity, misfortune. —*adj.* experimental, test, tentative, heuristic, investigative, probational, speculative, unverified, unsubstantiated, analytical, interrogatory, preparatory, empirical, provisional, contingent.

tribe *n.* **1** group, clan, family, sept, gens, caste, stirps, stock, race, country. **2** coterie, clique, club, set, faction, circle, gang, bunch, ring, crowd.

tribulation *n.* suffering, ordeal, misery, trial, oppression, sorrow, trouble, hardship, affliction, adversity, misfortune, curse, distress, depression, pain.

ant. joy, happiness, pleasure, ease, blessing.

tribunal *n.* court, tribune, judges, arbitrators, adjudicators, decision-makers, law court, bench, bar, judiciary, referees.

tribute *n.* **1** accolade, compliment, applause, acclaim, prize, gift, testimonial, eulogy, memorial, commendation, award, medal, recognition, panegyric, kudos, bouquet. **2** TAX.

ant. 1 condemnation, derision, obloquy, brickbat.

trice *n.* INSTANT.

trick *n.* **1** deception, ruse, artifice, ploy, scheme, trap, snare, plot, subterfuge, stratagem, expedient, pretense, swindle, hoax. **2** prank, joke, lark,

caper, antic, mischief, gambol, frolic, romp, monkey business, monkeyshine, jape, pleasantry, horseplay. **3** knack, skill, talent, legerdemain, expertise, finesse, facility, competence, handiness, cleverness, ingenuity, adroitness. —*v.* deceive, cheat, dupe, delude, seduce, trap, swindle, victimize, shortchange, take in, gull, bamboozle, mislead, outwit, hoax.

trickery *n.* deception, dupery, subterfuge, artifice, craftiness, wiles, seduction, entrapment, pretense, lies, dissimulation, guile, quackery, charlatanry, chicanery, cunning.

ant. honesty, fairness, forthrightness, square dealing, truth, truthfulness.

trickle *v.* dribble, drop, leak, ooze, drip, squirt, seep. —*n.* drop, droplet, dribble, leak, drip, squirt, seepage.

tricky *adj.* **1** crafty, deceitful, slippery, devious, wily, conniving, scheming, underhand, untrustworthy, sly, cunning, treacherous, foxy, insidious, stealthy. **2** intricate, complex, complicated, delicate, subtle, ticklish, difficult, knotty, perplexing, debatable, disputable, risky, sticky.

ant. 1 honest, direct, truthful, aboveboard, artless, ingenuous. **2** obvious, simple, easy.

tried *adj.* TRUSTWORTHY.

tried and true TRUSTWORTHY.

trifle *v.* fool with, play, toy, dabble, palter, philander, flirt, coquet, dally, dawdle, piddle, putter, fiddle. —*n.* triviality, toy, nothing, bagatelle, knickknack, trinket, bauble, tempest in a teapot, plaything, child's play.

trifling *adj.* insignificant, inconsequential, picayune, petty, small, unimportant, trivial, minor, paltry, worthless, meager, inappreciable, irrelevant, meaningless, measly.

ant. major, vital, crucial, weighty, significant.

trig *adj.* TRIM.

trigger *v.* set off, cause, provoke, produce, generate, effectuate, spark, lead to, bring about, elicit, touch off, prompt, motivate, activate.

ant. inhibit, prevent, stop, repress, block.

trill *n.* warble, quaver, chirp, song, ornament, embellishment, *fioritura,* tremolo.

trim *v.* **1** prune, clip, cut, crop, neaten, dock, shorten, barber, tidy, lop, even, bob, truncate, pare, shear. **2** decorate, ornament, adorn, dress, beautify, brighten, embellish, bedizen, deck, bedeck, garnish, array, trick out, jazz up (*Slang*). —*n.* condition, fitness, shape, fettle, health, preparation, adjustment, training, constitution, form, circumstance, tone. —*adj.* spruce, sprucedup, dapper, neat, trig, smart, groomed, tailored, fit, *soigné,* shipshape, orderly, tidy, uncluttered.

ant. *v.* **2** divest, denude, simplify, functionalize. *adj.* messy, untidy, cluttered, sloppy, frumpy.

trimmings *n.* extras, finishing touches, fixings, accessories, ornaments, embellishments, adornments, decorations, garnish, adjuncts, appurtenances, furbelows, fripperies, accents.

trinity *n.* TRIO.

trinket *n.* bauble, ornament, trifle, knickknack, gew-gaw, bead, charm, bagatelle, bibelot, *petit rien,* token, memento, souvenir, keepsake.

trio *n.* trinity, threesome, triad, triple, triplet, triumvirate, triangle, trilogy, trine, triune, triplex, triptych.

trip *n.* **1** journey, tour, excursion, outing, run, junket, commute, trek, expedition, voyage, pilgrimage, cruise, hike, ramble, schlep (*Slang*). **2** misstep, stumble, fall, lurch, tumble, spill, sprawl, topple, pitch. **3** false move, blunder, error, mistake, slip, miscalculation, oversight, lapse, fumble, gaucherie, slip-up, indiscretion, folly, boner (*Slang*), faux pas. —*v.* **1** stumble, tumble, slip, fall, sprawl, topple, pitch, flop. **2** dance, gambol, skip, cavort, canter, prance, frolic, spring, leap, frisk, caper, bob, hop, flit, dart. **3** blunder, botch, slip,

slip up, err, bungle, miscalculate, misjudge, fumble, bumble, mess up (*Slang*), muff (*Slang*), flub (*Slang*), fluff (*Slang*), louse up (*Slang*), blow it (*Slang*).

ant. *v.* **2** plod, trudge, lumber, shuffle, slog.

tripe *n.* rubbish, nonsense, garbage. tommyrot, poppycock, drivel, gibberish, trash, bilge, claptrap, bunk (*Slang*), baloney (*Slang*), hot air (*Slang*).

triple *n.* TRIO.

triplet *n.* TRIO.

tripper *n. Brit.* TOURIST.

triste *adj.* SAD.

trite *adj.* hackneyed, stereotyped, stale, cliché, overused, worn-out, motheaten, tired, threadbare, stock, unoriginal, unimaginative, platitudinous, banal, bromidic.

ant. fresh, new, original, unexpected, unfamiliar.

triturate *v.* PULVERIZE.

triumph *v.* **1** outdo, best, succeed, win, conquer, overcome, come through, subdue, worst, master, defeat, vanquish, outwit, prevail, overpower, surpass. **2** rejoice, exult, jubilate, celebrate, crow, brag, show off, boast, swagger, glory, congratulate oneself, gloat, take a bow, pat oneself on the back. —*n.* **1** victory, conquest, success, mastery, hit, coup, accomplishment, achievement, masterstroke, feat, ascendancy, hit, smash, killing. **2** rejoicing, exultation, jubilation, celebration, congratulations, elation, pride, acclaim, recognition, applause, accolade, ovation, glorification, tribute, honor.

ant. *v.* **1** fail, lose, succumb, flop, miss the boat. **2** fret, regret, sorrow, bewail. *n.* **1** failure, defeat, flop, fiasco. **2** humiliation, dishonor, ignominy, shame.

triumphal *adj.* TRIUMPHANT.

triumphant *adj.* **1** exultant, triumphal, elated, proud, rejoicing, celebrating, crowing, joyful, exhilarated, boastful, smug, self-satisfied. **2** victorious,

successful, crowned, acclaimed, undefeated, champion, preeminent, ascendant, masterful, winning.

ant. **1** humbled, shamed, embarrassed, abashed, humiliated. **2** beaten, conquered, defeated, unsuccessful, failed.

triumvirate *n.* TRIO.

trivia *n.* trifles, trivialities, minutiae, details, niceties, nonsense, busywork, red tape, pettiness, paltriness, irrelevancies, small potatoes, side issues, inessentials.

ant. basics, essentials, fundamentals, vitals.

trivial *adj.* insignificant, unimportant, trifling, petty, paltry, picayune, piddling, slight, inconsequential, inconsiderable, meaningless, nit-picking, measly, mingy, frivolous, worthless.

ant. vital, essential, basic, crucial, momentous.

triviality *n.* trifle, detail, nicety, nothing, inessential, bagatelle, toy, mote, jot, particle, pin, iota, speck.

troglodyte *n.* **1** BRUTE. **2** HERMIT.

troll *v.* **1** sing, carol, intone, chant, bellow, blast, shout, yodel, jubilate. **2** roll, turn, rotate, revolve, spin, trundle, twirl, wheel, gyrate.

trollop *n.* **1** PROSTITUTE. **2** SLATTERN.

troop *n.* gathering, muster, group, flock, herd, congregation, company, assemblage, gang, crowd, throng, multitude, cluster, swarm, bevy, bunch. —*v.* march, go, tramp, proceed, advance, move, file, parade, step, stride, invade, swarm, flock, traipse, tread.

troops *n.* soldiers, soldiery, men, enlisted men, G.I.s, NCOs, doughboys, armed forces, militia, troopers, draftees, recruits, rank and file, dogfaces (*Slang*), tommies (*Brit.*), poilus.

ant. civilians, citizens, citizenry.

trope *n.* METAPHOR.

trophy *n.* prize, cup, award, guerdon, medal, blue ribbon, memento, remembrance, spoils, honor, wreath, crown, testimonial, decoration, souvenir, token.

tropical *adj.* humid, sweltering, muggy, steamy, stifling, close, sultry, lush, overgrown, sun-drenched, hot, torrid.

ant. cold, dry, snowbound, frosty, frigid.

trot *n.* lope, jog, canter, run, gait, pace. —*v.* lope, jog, canter, hurry, gallop, run, scamper, rush, bustle, get going, get moving, hie, move along, speed, dart, hasten, sprint, scoot, step on it.

troth *n.* FAITH.

trouble *n.* **1** distress, worry, disquiet, affliction, hardship, anxiety, nervousness, sorrow, grief, misery, torment, vexation, discomfort, pain, agony. **2** illness, plague, ailment, pest, burden, nuisance, headache, responsibility, catastrophe, accident, disaster, misfortune, bad luck, bad news, blow. **3** dilemma, problem, embarrassment, difficulty, mess, spot, hole, blind alley, predicament, quandary, squeeze, bind, jam, muddle, mix-up. **4** labor, sweat, exertion, pains, bother, muscle, care, thought, effort, toil, inconvenience. **5** agitation, unrest, commotion, clamor, ferment, discord, lawlessness, discontent, dissatisfaction, rumbling, grumbling, rebellion, rumpus, fracas, crime. —*v.* **1** distress, worry, annoy, discomfit, agitate, afflict, sadden, hurt, vex, pester, upset, move, anger, irritate, irk. **2** inconvenience, incommode, discommode, put out, disturb, bother, encumber, hinder, impose on, burden.

ant. *n.* **1** joy, pleasure, gratification. **2** delight, treat, blessing. **5** peace, order, calm. *v.* **1** soothe, please, delight, elate.

troublemaker *n.* mischief-maker, agitator, *agent provocateur*, imp, demon, devil, delinquent, firebrand, scaremonger, rumormonger, gossip, incendiary, rebel, ruffian, scamp, Pandora.

ant. angel, goody-goody, peacemaker, arbiter, saint.

troublesome *adj.* **1** irritating, annoying, irksome, pesky, trying, vexing, provoking, harassing, disturbing, distressing, onerous, burdensome, besetting, galling, plaguy. **2** difficult, complicated, complex, tricky, arduous, wearisome, heavy, severe, demanding, thorny, toilsome, tough.

ant. **1** pleasant, agreeable, cooperative, relaxing. **2** undemanding, simple, light, easy.

troublous *adj.* uneasy, restless, restive, troubled, agitated, disquieted, disturbed, disorderly, explosive, tumultuous, turbulent, perturbed.

ant. serene, peaceful, quiet, relaxed.

trough *n.* trench, hollow, furrow, gutter, depression, channel, manger, crib, canal, duct, ditch, moat, course.

trounce *v.* **1** thrash, punish, beat, whip, cane, lash, flog, stomp, birch, switch, thwack, whack, pommel. **2** defeat, lick, best, beat, drub, outdo, outplay, rout, overwhelm, upset, trim, wipe out.

ant. **2** lose, take a beating, take a drubbing, be defeated.

troupe *n.* company, cast, troupers, actors, performers, thespians, entertainers, players, band.

trouper *n.* ACTOR.

trousseau *n.* OUTFIT.

truant *n.* absentee, delinquent, ne'er-do-well, hooky-player, loafer, drifter, deserter, vagrant, vagabond, shirker, malingerer, dodger, goldbrick (*Slang*), goof-off (*Slang*), good-for-nothing. —*adj.* ABSENT.

truce *n.* **1** armistice, cessation of hostilities, cease-fire, white flag, suspension of hostilities. **2** respite, lull, recess, intermission, breathing spell, reprieve, interval, abeyance, break, pause, delay, time out, cessation, breather, suspension.

truck[1] *v.* TRANSPORT.

truck[2] *n.* **1** dealings, business, communication, doings, negotiations, contact, relations, relationship, commerce, traffic, transactions, connection, association. **2** TRADE. —v. TRADE.

truckle v. yield, submit, defer, grovel, please, bow, take orders, knuckle under, bend, fawn, court, bootlick, pander, flatter, ingratiate oneself.

ant. oppose, resist, disagree, criticize, stand up to.

truculent adj. cruel, savage, ferocious, fierce, brutal, barbarous, ruthless, vicious, inhumane, uncivilized, bloodthirsty, rapacious, murderous, pugnacious, bellicose.

ant. gentle, peaceable, kind, civil, civilized.

trudge v. tramp, hike, trek, climb, lumber, plod, march, slog, drag, hobble, shamble, shuffle, limp, flag, clump, clomp, schlep (*Slang*). —n. tramp, hike, trek, climb, march, schlep (*Slang*).

true adj. **1** factual, exact, valid, sure, accurate, incontrovertible, correct, clear-cut, literal, orderly, plumb, symmetrical, straight, even. **2** real, genuine, pure, actual, unadulterated, veritable, authentic, authoritative, unmixed, unalloyed, unpolluted, natural. **3** loyal, trustworthy, faithful, reliable, unswerving, constant, staunch, devoted, firm, steadfast, tried and true, true-blue. **4** just, rightful, legitimate, bona fide, lawful, official, recognized, accepted, approved, licit, sanctioned, authorized, ordained, warranted. **5** honest, truthful, upright, righteous, straightforward, honorable, principled, reputable, ethical, high-minded, veracious, unbiased, unprejudiced, scrupulous, impartial.

ant. **1** imaginary, unreal, fictitious, vague. **2** counterfeit, adulterated, fake, phony (*Slang*). **3** treacherous, inconstant, double-dealing, disloyal. **4** illegitimate, illicit, unlawful, unauthorized. **5** slippery, bigoted, lying, dishonest.

true-blue adj. FAITHFUL.

truelove n. SWEETHEART.

truism n. platitude, bromide, cliché, saw, banality, commonplace, chestnut, proverb, adage, axiom, byword, precept.

trull n. PROSTITUTE.

truly adv. really, actually, in fact, factually, verily, indeed, honestly, truthfully, precisely, accurately, rightfully, correctly, literally, in truth, frankly, as a matter of fact.

ant. maybe, perhaps, doubtfully, mistakenly.

trump v. SURPASS.

trumpery n. RUBBISH.

trumpet n. blast, fanfare, flourish, bray, toot, blare, din, trumpeting, clarion call, alarm, alarum, tucket. —v. noise about, noise abroad, announce, broadcast, publish, proclaim, herald, blazon, bruit about, promulgate, disseminate, spread the word, advertise, publicize, tout.

ant. v. conceal, hide, hush up, softpedal, play down.

truncate v. shorten, prune, trim, lop, dock, pare, abbreviate, cut short, clip, curtail.

truncheon n. club, billy, cane, cudgel, bat, stick, bludgeon, blackjack, shillelagh. —v. BEAT.

trunk n. **1** torso, body. **2** box, chest, case, footlocker, container, coffer, caisson, bin, hamper, crate, carryall, basket, pannier.

truss n. framework, prop, underpinning, shoring, girder, strut, brace, buttress. —v. bind, tie, fasten, support, brace, shore up, bolster, prop, corset, cradle, sustain.

trust n. **1** confidence, reliance, faith, credence, reassurance, belief, credulity, hope, acceptance, expectation, dependency, certainty, credit, hopefulness, certitude, optimism. **2** trusteeship, responsibility, obligation, charge, liability, duty, commission, accountability, office, answerableness. —v. **1** rely, depend, have faith, count, believe, lean, bank, credit, accredit, swear by, turn to, look to. **2** expect, hope, believe, look forward

to, anticipate, contemplate, calculate, imagine, foresee, await, think likely, reckon, envisage, presume, suppose. **3** ENTRUST.
ant. *n.* **1** distrust, suspicion, uncertainty, doubt. —*v.* **1** disbelieve, distrust, be wary of, doubt, suspect.

trustful *adj.* TRUSTING.

trusting *adj.* trustful, credulous, ingenuous, gullible, unsuspecting, unwary, innocent, naive, optimistic, simple, unguarded, dependent, unworldly, childlike.
ant. suspicious, wary, on guard, cautious, vigilant.

trustworthiness *n.* CREDIBILITY.

trustworthy *adj.* reliable, dependable, upright, honorable, truthful, tried, tried and true, tested, substantiated, unimpeachable, validated, proven, responsible, scrupulous, credible, incontrovertible.
ant. dubious, shady, questionable, slippery, crooked.

trusty *adj.* trustworthy, faithful, dependable, loyal, responsible, solid, steadfast, aboveboard, unwavering, true, honorable, conscientious, principled, incorruptible, devoted, staunch.
ant. irresponsible, undependable, dishonorable, treacherous, irresolute.

truth *n.* **1** truthfulness, reality, trueness, sooth, verity, veracity, fact, authenticity, actuality, verisimilitude. **2** fact, axiom, truism, gospel, certainty, the case, principle, law, proof, verity, troth, low-down (*Slang*). **3** realism, genuineness, verisimilitude, fidelity, faithfulness, accuracy, correctness, validity, naturalism, honesty, frankness, candor, exactness, precision.
ant. **1** illusion, fiction, imagination, unreality. **2** falsehood, lie, uncertainty. **3** inaccuracy, erroneousness, dishonesty, incorrectness, invalidity.

truthful *adj.* **1** accurate, true, axiomatic, correct, factual, real, certain, genuine, actual, authentic, verifiable, veritable, irrefutable, valid. **2** honest,

frank, candid, straightforward, veracious, meticulous, trustworthy, sincere, scrupulous, reliable, dependable, straight, aboveboard.
ant. **1** false, imaginary, unreal, counterfeit. **2** lying, mendacious, dishonest, devious.

try *v.* **1** attempt, essay, endeavor, strive, venture, aim, undertake, make an effort, exert oneself, tackle, take a crack at, have a go at, make a stab at, take pains. **2** test, try out, experiment with, use, judge, evaluate, apply, examine, analyze, taste, sample, appraise, assess, assay. **3** tax, strain, trouble, inconvenience, upset, unnerve, irritate, annoy, plague, bother, burden, overload, impose on, bug (*Slang*). —*n.* TRIAL.

trying *adj.* taxing, burdensome, arduous, troublesome, irksome, irritating, difficult, exhausting, bothersome, pesty, unnerving, tiresome, onerous, exasperating, aggravating.
ant. soothing, undemanding, comforting, simple, easy.

tryout *n.* test, audition, dry run, experiment, trial, check, essay, hearing, chance, whack (*Slang*), attempt, trial balloon, crack.

try out TRY.

tryst *n.* appointment, rendezvous, date, assignation, meeting, tête-à-tête, vis-à-vis, engagement.

tsar *n.* CZAR.

tub *n.* vat, vessel, washtub, basin, sink, bowl, keg, tun, cask, bucket, barrel, bathtub, bath.

tubby *adj.* CHUBBY.

tube *n.* pipe, passage, channel, duct, catheter, cannula, conductor, conduit, canal, fistula, cylinder, tunnel.

tubercle *n.* nodule, node, lump, tumor, growth, protuberance, swelling, neoplasm.

tubular *adj.* cylindrical, hollow, tubulous, cannular, tubulate, columnar, fistular, fistulous.

tuck *v.* **1** wrap, cover, swathe, blanket, bed down, put to bed, enfold, swaddle. **2** cram, stuff, press, contract, pinch, seam, furrow, fold, stitch, tighten, narrow, pleat.

tuckered out WEARY.

tuft *n.* bunch, clump, knot, tassel, tussock, shock, sheaf, cluster, ruff, cowlick, forelock, crest, plume, bangs, frizz.

tug *v.* tow, drag, haul, pull, heave, draw, yank, strain, wrench, jerk, lug, schlep (*Slang*). —*n.* pull, wrench, yank, jerk, lug, strain, heave, hitch, draft, traction.

tumble *v.* **1** roll, toss, somersault, roll over, toss about, pitch, reel. **2** fall, topple, trip, sprawl, stumble, slip, take a spill, lurch, lose one's footing, flop. —*n.* **1** fall, spill, sprawl, descent, drop, somersault, acrobatics, flop, pratfall (*Slang*). **2** jumble, mess, disorder, disarray, chaos, confusion, dishevelment, tangle, hodgepodge, muddle, mélange, heap, stew, litter, disarrangement.

ant. *n.* **2** neatness, order, tidiness.

tumbledown *adj.* dilapidated, rickety, falling, coming apart, disintegrating, shaky, jerry-built, unsteady, decrepit, ramshackle, insecure, tottering, crumbling, broken-down.

ant. sturdy, solid, substantial, rugged.

tumbrel *n.* CART.

tumefy *v.* SWELL.

tumescent *adj.* TURGID.

tumid *adj.* TURGID.

tumor *n.* swelling, growth, cyst, sarcoma, carcinoma, cancer, lump, node, nodule, tubercle, polyp, neoplasm, malignancy.

tumult *n.* **1** uproar, commotion, disturbance, furor, hubbub, trouble, clamor, demonstration, upheaval, ferment, racket, turbulence, tumultuousness, turmoil, uprising, vociferation, pandemonium. **2** hysteria, hysterics, panic, agitation, frenzy, passion, desperation, disorientation, tantrum, paroxysm, derangement, flap (*Slang*), screaming meemies (*Slang*).

tumultuous *adj.* **1** disorderly, violent,

raging, tempestuous, stormy, furious, turbulent, vociferous, riotous, mutinous, clamorous, uncontrollable, unruly, chaotic. **2** agitated, hysterical, disturbed, frantic, frenzied, manic, excited, seething, temperamental, unstable, passionate, volcanic, hectic, mercurial.

ant. **1** orderly, quiet, reasonable, obedient. **2** phlegmatic, self-controlled, even-tempered, cool.

tune *n.* **1** melody, air, refrain, song, strain, aria, theme, lilt, motif, ditty, carol, descant. **2** approach, attitude, mood, manner, mode, demeanor, mind, behavior, opinion. **3** concord, agreement, harmony, conformity, concert, unison, accord, accordance, sympathy, congeniality, compatibility, affinity, consonance, concurrence, correlation.

ant. **3** discord, antipathy, friction, aversion.

tuned in *Slang* AWARE.

tuned out *Slang* ABSENT.

tuneful *adj.* melodious, musical, lilting, catchy, singable, sweet-sounding, lyrical, euphonious, harmonious, consonant, ariose.

ant. tuneless, cacophonous, discordant, jangly, dissonant.

tunic *n.* COAT.

tunnel *n.* passageway, subway, burrow, underground (*Brit.*), tube, underpass, shaft, adit, pit, mine, drift, crosscut. —*v.* dig, burrow, excavate, scoop out, penetrate, furrow, blast through, mine.

turbid *adj.* **1** muddy, opaque, murky, dark, dim, roiled, thick, blurry, smudgy, cloudy, foul, unclear. **2** confused, addled, addlebrained, foggy, mixed-up, vague, disturbed, unsettled, muddled, messy, disoriented, incoherent, muddle-headed, rattled.

ant. **1** crystal, clear, fresh. **2** lucid, coherent, clear-headed.

turbulent *adj.* **1** disturbed, agitated, stirred up, restless, windswept, violent, stormy, tempestuous, raging, rough, tumultuous, blustery, rugged.

2 insubordinate, rebellious, mutinous, riotous, disorderly, unruly, chaotic, anarchic, undisciplined, wild, insurgent, restless, lawless, ungovernable.

ant. 1 smooth, glassy, unruffled. **2** submissive, obedient, tractable.

turf *n.* sod, sward, grass, green, divot, greensward, lawn, grassland, meadow, meadowland, lea, pasture, verdure.

turgescent *adj.* TURGID.

turgid *adj.* **1** distended, swollen, tumid, tumescent, turgescent, swelled, puffy, inflated, edematous, dropsical, bloated, protuberant. **2** bombastic, inflated, tumid, wordy, orotund, pompous, grandiose, florid, declamatory, showy, overdone, flatulent.

ant. 1 detumescent, deflated, shrunken. **2** succinct, terse, crisp, concise, understated.

turkey *v. Slang* FLOP.

turmoil *n.* tumult, agitation, turbulence, disturbance, unrest, disorder, chaos, strife, commotion, trouble, furor, upheaval, confusion, excitement.

ant. order, tranquillity, peace, quiet.

turn *v.* **1** rotate, revolve, reverse, transpose, upend, flip, flop, upset, overturn, spin, invert, go around, wheel, gyrate, circle, whirl, switch. **2** bend, curve, fold, twist, arc, flex, swivel, warp, deform, zigzag, snake, coil, curl, spiral. **3** transform, change, transmute, transmogrify, alter, reform, reshape, transfigure, metamorphose, vary, differ, convert, reconstruct, recast, mutate. **4** ferment, curdle, spoil, sour, acidify, acidulate, clot, putresce, putrefy, taint, decompose, mold, deteriorate, go bad. **5** deflect, divert, diverge, redirect, return, digress, divagate, swerve, shift, veer, tack, skid, sidetrack, fork, change course, put about, turn off, swing around. **6** distract, persuade, alter, prevail upon, bring round, prejudice, rethink, reconsider, withdraw, change one's mind, defect, renege,

retract, revise. **7** reel, whirl, spin, lurch, stagger, swirl, twirl, rotate, swim. —*n.* **1** rotation, revolution, spin, gyration, reversal, inversion, twist, coil, loop, pirouette, twirl, wheel, flip, whirl, eddy. **2** deflection, bend, curve, warp, arc, zigzag, variation, digression, divagation, swerve, shift, divergence, tack, deviation, swing. **3** chance, attempt, try, succession, time, opportunity, place, occasion, moment, bout, round, go. **4** style, manner, way, characteristic, disposition, tendency, bent, inclination, idiosyncrasy, temperament, mode, humor, makeup. **5** deed, act, action, gesture, office, reaction, reciprocation, doing, response, course, step, conduct. **6** walk, drive, outing, excursion, tour, circuit, promenade, exercise, airing, stroll, jaunt, jog, run, amble, constitutional.

turnabout *n.* about-face, *volte-face*, reversal, switch, recantation, retraction, defection, repeal, repudiation, tergiversation, apostasy, disavowal, renunciation.

turncoat *n.* renegade, traitor, defector, apostate, betrayer, deserter, opportunist, Judas, recreant, double-dealer, informer, squealer, rat (*Slang*), collaborationist, quisling.

turndown *n.* **1** rejection, no, refusal, rebuff, dismissal, repulse, objection, gate, demurrer, noncompliance, nonfulfillment, snub, disinclination, unwillingness, disapproval, noncooperation. **2** decline, fall, falling-off, drop, plunge, slump, descent, dip, depression, tailspin, downswing, downtrend.

ant. 1 acceptance, acquiescence, agreement, approval, yes. **2** upswing, uptrend, increase, step-up.

turn down reject, refuse, turn away, decline, rebuff, deny, disdain, dismiss, repulse, demur, object to, scorn, frown on, spurn.

ant. accept, accede, grant, yield, acquiesce.

turning point crisis, crux, point of no

return, high-water mark, moment of truth, crossroads, apex, climax, apogee, zenith, zero hour, transition.

turn off 1 STOP. **2** TURN. **3** *Slang* bore, weary, tire, jade, irk, wear on, displease, irritate, alienate, repel, disgust, offend, sicken, nauseate.

turn on 1 hinge, depend, be contingent, be affected, result from, follow from, arise from, flow from, issue from, be conditional, hang, be subject to. **2** set in motion, start, ignite, light, power, energize, fire, open, pull the switch, plug in. **3** *Slang* excite, titillate, please, stimulate, elate, attract, captivate, transport, enchant, amuse, delight, enrapture, ravish, entrance. **ant. 2** turn off, close, switch off. **3** turn off, bore, depress, weary, tire.

turnout *n.* **1** assemblage, crowd, muster, group, congregation, throng, multitude, body, gathering, forgathering, audience, congress, accumulation, crew, pack. **2** output, production, productivity, results, product, yield, achievement, crop, harvest, outturn.

turn out 1 eject, expel, banish, throw out, oust, drive out, force out, evict, dispossess, dislodge, unseat, deport, discharge, dismiss, cast out. **2** become, develop, evolve, prove to be, end up as, happen, occur, grow into, work out, emerge, transpire, result.

turn over 1 upset, overturn, reverse, topple, up-end, knock over, overthrow, tip over, keel, capsize. **2** hand over, transfer, transmit, relegate, give, render, assign, commission, pass, deliver, surrender, convey, consign, pass along. **ant. 2** keep, hold, retain, hold on to, withhold.

turn up unearth, dig up, expose, come up, come up with, reveal, appear, exhume, disinter, find, discover, uncover, bare, disclose, bring to light, arrive. **ant.** conceal, hide, bury, cover, disappear.

turpitude *n.* depravity, wickedness, baseness, immorality, corruption, degeneracy, vileness, rottenness, evil, criminality, viciousness, villainy, perfidy, wrongdoing, sinfulness. **ant.** virtue, goodness, high-mindedness, incorruptibility.

turret *n.* tower, steeple, cupola, lookout, observatory, watchtower, belvedere, minaret, spire, belfry.

tussle *v.* scuffle, struggle, grapple, wrestle, contest, fight, battle, vie, scrap, spar, exchange blows. —*n.* **1** scuffle, struggle, contest, fight, melee, bout, sparring, wrestling, battle, brawl, scrimmage, fray, skirmish, scrap, set-to. **2** debate, argument, disagreement, quarrel, squabble, spat, wrangle, row, clash, dispute, controversy, falling-out, difference, tiff, words, rhubarb (*Slang*).

tussock *n.* TUFT.

tutelage *n.* **1** guardianship, care, protection, management, guidance, custody, wardship, safekeeping, auspices, aegis, patronage, trusteeship, benefaction, superintendence. **2** instruction, education, teaching, tutoring, coaching, enlightenment, training, preparation, cramming, schooling.

tutelary *adj.* PROTECTIVE.

tutor *n.* instructor, teacher, coach, trainer, educator, docent, pedagogue, crammer (*Brit.*), lecturer, guide, guru. —*v.* train, prepare, educate, teach, coach, cram, lecture, instruct, enlighten, explain, correct, inform, drill.

twaddle *n.* prattle, jabber, nonsense, silliness, foolishness, piffle, tittle-tattle, gibberish, garbage, tripe, drivel, chatter, tommyrot, verbiage, idle talk. —*v.* PRATTLE.

tweak *v.* pinch, twist, jerk, pull, squeeze, yank, nip. —*n.* pinch, twist, jerk, pull, squeeze, yank, nip, twinge, spasm.

tweet *v., n.* TWITTER.

twiddle *v.* twirl, fiddle, toy, handle, monkey with, fidget, wiggle, jiggle, spin, finger, fuss with, fool with, potter, fritter, fribble.

twig *n.* branch, shoot, stick, sprig, switch, bough, offshoot, stem, withe.

twilight *n.* **1** sundown, dusk, evening, sunset, gloaming, crepuscule, nightfall, eventide. **2** last gasp, swan song, decline, fall, finale, last act, end, downfall, collapse.

   ant. 1 sunrise, dawn, sunup, morning. **2** birth, rise, beginning.

twin *n.* duplicate, mate, double, likeness, simulacrum, facsimile, look-alike, counterpart, alter ego, match, fellow, imitation, copy, equivalent, replica, ringer (*Slang*), carbon copy.

twine *v.* twist, entwine, coil, spiral, braid, loop, wrap, interweave, plait, splice, interlace. —*n.* string, rope, yarn, cord, cordage, sisal, hemp, packthread.

twinge *n.* pang, pain, stab, stitch, throe, ache, bite, gnaw, cramp, spasm, tic, malaise, throb, discomfort.

twinkle *v.* **1** sparkle, shine, glitter, flash, coruscate, glow, glisten, glimmer, light up, brighten, scintillate, shimmer. **2** blink, wink, flicker, glint, dance, shift, shuffle, quiver, flutter, dart. —*n.* **1** glimmer, flicker, flash, glint, scintillation, spark, glow, shimmer, glimmering, scintilla. **2** TWINKLING.

twinkling *n.* instant, trice, second, wink, moment, flash, jiffy, jiff, breath, twinkle.

twirl *v.* spin, whirl, rotate, twist, pirouette, turn, wheel, revolve, gyrate, eddy, twiddle.

twist *v.* **1** wind, entwine, coil, wreathe, wrap, twine, swaddle, swathe, interlace, splice, braid, interweave, plait. **2** deform, distort, misshape, contort, warp, disfigure, wring, buckle, wrench, strain, sprain. **3** confuse, mix up, obscure, pervert, misinterpret, misrepresent, garble, falsify, misconstrue, misstate, color, change. **4** rotate, revolve, spin, turn, screw, roll, whirl, twirl, wheel. **5** squirm, writhe, wriggle, fidget, shimmy, un-

dulate, snake, jiggle, twitch, wiggle, joggle. —*n.* **1** curve, turn, bend, zigzag, snake, ess, deflection, warp, curl, spiral, coil, undulation. **2** bent, turn of mind, inclination, attitude, proclivity, quirk, bias, idiosyncrasy, foible, eccentricity, caprice, aberration, vagary, oddity. **3** variation, variant, novelty, stunt, trick, improvisation, invention, gimmick (*Slang*), shtick (*Slang*), number (*Slang*).

twit *n.* reproach, cut, dig, gibe, taunt, sting, jeer, slur, disparagement, charge, rebuke, accusation, reprimand, aspersion, knock, put-down (*Slang*), scoff.

twitch *v.* jerk, pull, quaver, tremble, palpitate, quiver, throb, blink, flutter, shiver, shake, contract. —*n.* spasm, tic, jerk, contraction, pull, throb, quiver, palpitation, shake, tremor, shiver, blink.

twitter *v.* chirp, warble, tweet, trill, chirrup, sing, cheep, peep. —*n.* **1** tweet, warble, song, chirrup, cheep, trill, peep, chirp, twee. **2** excitement, flurry, stir, bustle, flutter, to-do, agitation, ado, hubbub, disquiet, perturbation, anxiety, tizzy (*Slang*).

two-bit *adj. Slang* CHEAP.

two-edged *adj.* AMBIGUOUS.

two-faced *adj.* hypocritical, insincere, double-dealing, treacherous, disloyal, devious, perfidious, untrustworthy, opportunist, lying, unscrupulous, unprincipled, dissembling, mealy-mouthed, deceitful, cunning, misleading, disingenuous, sly, artful, tricky, wily.

   ant. honest, sincere, straightforward, artless, ingenuous.

two-time *v. Slang* BETRAY.

tycoon *n.* magnate, financier, capitalist, industrialist, millionaire, captain of industry, plutocrat, power, VIP, *haut bourgeois,* bigwig, big shot (*Slang*), big wheel (*Slang*).

tyke *n.* imp, devil, urchin, hell-raiser, mischiefmaker, pixy, rascal, brat, street Arab, gamin, ragamuffin, hellion, whippersnapper.

type *n.* **1** group, class, category, sort, kind, genus, species, ilk, caste, breed, strain, stamp, order, clan, classification. **2** model, standard, example, archetype, quintessence, embodiment, specimen, representative, rule, criterion, symbol, personification, essence. **ant. 2** exception, oddity, freak, mutation, aberration.

typical *adj.* average, normal, characteristic, representative, standard, quintessential, regular, usual, stock, ordinary, orthodox, conventional, common, run-of-the-mill, expected. **ant.** odd, unusual, abnormal, irregular, atypical.

typify *v.* represent, sum up, exemplify, characterize, symbolize, embody, incarnate, personify, illustrate, epitomize, signify, stand for, indicate, betoken.

tyrannical *adj.* despotic, arbitrary, tyrannous, dictatorial, autocratic, oppressive, ruthless, inhumane, high-handed, ironfisted, overbearing, authoritarian, coercive, bloody, cruel. **ant.** democratic, easygoing, humane, reasonable, understanding.

tyrannize *v.* dictate to, oppress, coerce, victimize, punish, bully, threaten, subjugate, dehumanize, brutalize, persecute, overpower, crush, brainwash, squelch.

tyrannous *adj.* TYRANNICAL.

tyranny *n.* **1** despotism, absolutism, dictatorship, autocracy, authoritarianism, czarism. **2** severity, stringency, rigidity, sternness, rigor, harshness, rigorousness, austerity, strictness, oppression, brutality, coercion, cruelty, inhumanity, dehumanization, terrorism, heartlessness, sadism, savagery, ferocity. **ant. 2** ease, relaxation, laxity, laissez-faire, humaneness, gentleness, mercy, understanding.

tyrant *n.* despot, dictator, autocrat, absolutist, authoritarian, fascist, sadist, czar, bully, brow-beater, inquisitor, Simon Legree, overlord.

tyro *n.* novice, beginner, novitiate, student, apprentice, neophyte, greenhorn, freshman, pupil, amateur, tenderfoot, rookie (*Slang*). **ant.** veteran, master, professional, expert, pro.

tzar *n.* CZAR.

U

ubiquitous *adj.* omnipresent, universal, widespread, pervasive, prevalent, pervading, interfused, unavoidable, worldwide. **ant.** nonexistent, absent, wanting, missing.

ugly *adj.* **1** unsightly, plain, homely, unattractive, ill-favored, repulsive, unprepossessing, hideous, grotesque, unlovely. **2** shocking, heinous, despicable, revolting, repugnant, abhorrent, depraved, corrupt, disgusting, repulsive. **3** harmful, damaging, pernicious, dangerous, sinister, malignant, baneful, malevolent, injurious, wicked, ruinous. **4** quarrelsome, querulous, ill-tempered, baleful, testy, irascible, malevolent, threatening, evil, dark, malefic. **ant. 1** pretty, comely, attractive, handsome, beautiful. **2** virtuous, good, irreproachable, praiseworthy, high-minded. **3** slight, trivial, harmless, benign, insignificant. **4** agreeable, pleasant, good-humored, sunny, compliant.

ukase *n.* DECREE.

ulcer *n.* SORE.

ulcerous *adj.* SORE.

ulterior *adj.* secondary, indirect, supplemental, extraneous, unavowed, undisclosed, undeclared, covert, hidden, unrevealed, unexpressed, remote, additional.
ant. primary, declared, overt, direct, immediate, manifest.

ultimate *adj.* **1** utmost, uttermost, extreme, maximum, superlative, supreme, greatest, highest, preeminent, maximal. **2** last, final, terminal, concluding, culminating, eventual, closing, farthest, remotest, utmost, extreme, furthest, outermost, uttermost. —*n.* perfection, quintessence, culmination, nonpareil, summit, last word, *ne plus ultra,* seventh heaven, nirvana, paragon, greatest.

ultimately *adv.* at last, finally, in the end, eventually, after all, lastly, fundamentally, basically.

ultra *adj.* EXTREME.

ultramodern *adj.* MODERN.

ululate *v.* HOWL.

umbrage *n.* resentment, pique, anger, offense, displeasure, dudgeon, grudge, rancor, antipathy, bitterness, animosity, dissatisfaction, indignation.
ant. amity, good will, cordiality, harmony, sympathy.

umbrella *n.* canopy, shade, shield, parasol, tarp, tarpaulin, tent, awning, bubble, screen, gamp (*Brit.*), sunshade, bumbershoot.

unable *adj.* helpless, ineffectual, unfit, inadequate, ineffective, inept, impotent, incapable, powerless, weak, defenseless, useless.
ant. able, fit, capable, strong, effective, potent.

unadorned *adj.* PLAIN.

unadulterated *adj.* PURE.

unafraid *adj.* FEARLESS.

unaligned *adj.* NEUTRAL.

unalterable *adj.* immutable, unchangeable, fixed, invariable, unchanging, permanent, steadfast, fated, irreversible, inflexible, ironclad, irrevocable, irreparable.

ant. changeable, revocable, impermanent, variable, reversible.

unanimity *n.* ACCORD.

unanimous *adj.* agreeing, concordant, like-minded, united, undivided, harmonious, concerted, common, unified, universal, solid, of one mind.
ant. differing, split, dissident, schismatic, divided.

unappetizing *adj.* uninviting, unappealing, unpalatable, uninteresting, distasteful, insipid, vapid, stale, unattractive, off-putting, unsavory, unpleasant.
ant. toothsome, agreeable, appealing, attractive, interesting, pleasant.

unapproachable *adj.* ALOOF.

unassailable *adj.* **1** incontrovertible, certain, undeniable, indubitable, unquestionable, indisputable, irrefutable, proven, conclusive, sound, incontestable, established, undoubted. **2** IMPREGNABLE.
ant. 1 dubious, uncertain, doubtful, debatable, unfounded, shaky.

unassuming *adj.* modest, unpretentious, self-effacing, humble, diffident, reserved, simple, meek, retiring, unobtrusive, submissive, unassertive.
ant. pretentious, arrogant, bumptious, conceited, presumptuous, obtrusive.

unattached *adj.* independent, neutral, nonaligned, uncommitted, uninvolved, disinterested, indifferent, impartial, nonpartisan, detached, free.
ant. involved, committed, aligned, implicated, partial, entangled.

unattractive *adj.* UGLY.

unavailing *adj.* futile, ineffective, unproductive, vain, empty, idle, useless, fruitless, ineffectual, nugatory, inadequate, worthless, inept, weak, bootless, otiose.
ant. effective, worthwhile, rewarding, fruitful, useful, valid.

unavoidable *adj.* inevitable, ineluctable, fated, inexorable, inescapable, unpreventable, irresistible, sure, compulsory, obligatory, necessary, certain, undeniable.

ant. avoidable, uncertain, preventable, escapable, optional.

unawares *adv.* unexpectedly, by surprise, abruptly, all at once, suddenly, off guard, without warning, with one's guard down.

unbalanced *adj.* unsound, erratic, deranged, unhinged, disordered, disturbed, abnormal, irrational, insane, daft, crazy, eccentric, off, non compos, nutty (*Slang*), kinky (*Slang*).
ant. sane, sound, steady, self-possessed, level-headed.

unbearable *adj.* intolerable, insufferable, insupportable, oppressive, unendurable, unsustainable, unacceptable, inadmissible, too much (*Slang*).
ant. bearable, tolerable, supportable, endurable, acceptable.

unbecoming *adj.* **1** unattractive, unflattering, inappropriate, uncomely, incongruous, unsuitable, out of keeping, ill-fitting, plain, homely, drab. **2** improper, offensive, indecent, reprehensible, discreditable, indecorous, gross, ignoble, unseemly, indelicate.
ant. **1** pretty, neat, chic, suited, graceful, smart. **2** proper, admirable, decorous, upright, decent.

unbelievable *adj.* incredible, inconceivable, untenable, staggering, improbable, outlandish, far-fetched, unthinkable, preposterous, suspicious, unconvincing, apocryphal, questionable, irrational, absurd.
ant. obvious, credible, persuasive, convincing, conceivable, believable.

unbeliever *n.* skeptic, doubter, infidel, scoffer, disbeliever, Pyrrhonist, questioner, independent, agnostic, doubting Thomas, iconoclast.
ant. believer, follower, adherent, disciple, dupe, gull, party-liner.

unbelieving *adj.* SKEPTICAL.

unbend *v.* relax, ease up, let up, melt, warm, loosen up, be diverted, enjoy, play, unwind, slow down, let it all hang out (*Slang*).
ant. strain, fidget, stiffen, tense up.

unbending *adj.* stiff, tense, reserved, distant, aloof, haughty, wooden, formal, unsociable, rigid, inflexible, uneasy, uptight (*Slang*).
ant. relaxed, at ease, sociable, friendly, outgoing.

unbiased *adj.* unprejudiced, impartial, fair, just, evenhanded, objective, equitable, disinterested, detached, nonpartisan, neutral, balanced.
ant. biased, unfair, slanted, bigoted, unjust, prejudiced.

unblemished *adj.* PERFECT.

unblushing *adj.* SHAMELESS.

unbosom *v.* confide, confess, disclose, lay bare, unburden, unfold, admit, divulge, reveal, communicate, tell, come clean (*Slang*).
ant. veil, cover up, conceal, guard, hide, hold out (*Slang*).

unbounded *adj.* BOUNDLESS.

unbridled *adj.* unrestrained, unruly, intemperate, ungovernable, intractable, uncontrolled, unchecked, ungoverned, excessive, intemperate, licentious, riotous, uncurbed, rampant.
ant. restrained, controlled, suppressed, checked, limited, inhibited.

unburden *v.* **1** divest, unload, relieve, free, disencumber, clear, disburden, rid, purge, extricate, disentangle. **2** cast off, get rid of, relieve oneself of, admit, reveal, disclose, confess, own up to, make a clean breast of.

uncalled-for *adj.* **1** unnecessary, superfluous, nonessential, excessive, surplus, unneeded, needless, supererogatory, redundant. **2** unjustified, unwarranted, gratuitous, unprovoked, supererogatory, out-of-bounds, inappropriate, wanton, unwelcome, improper.
ant. **1** needed, necessary, essential, required, indispensable, vital. **2** justified, appropriate, acceptable, proper, fitting, welcome.

uncanny *adj.* **1** weird, supernatural, eerie, eldritch, mysterious, spooky, preternatural, unearthly, strange, unnatural. **2** remarkable, incredible, miraculous, astonishing, exceptional, fantastic, unbelievable, unusual, singular.

ant. 1 commonplace, ordinary, natural, explicable, everyday. **2** normal, ordinary, common, usual, unexceptional.

uncaring *adj.* INDIFFERENT.

unceasing *adj.* CEASELESS.

unceremonious *adj.* ABRUPT.

uncertain *adj.* **1** indefinite, undecided, iffy, open, indeterminate, problematic, moot, unfixed, unsure, questionable, vague. **2** unpredictable, changeable, chancy, surprising, fitful, inconstant, undependable, unreliable, erratic, irresolute, wavering. **3** dubious, doubtful, skeptical, unsure, suspicious, unconvinced, incredulous, distrustful, undecided, hesitant, in a quandary.

ant. 1 decided, fixed, definite, closed, pinpointed. **2** predictable, unfailing, steady, reliable, constant. **3** assured, convinced, confident, certain, positive.

uncertainty *n.* doubt, indecision, dubiety, insecurity, hesitation, skepticism, suspicion, misgiving, vagueness, mistrust, ambiguity, vacillation, qualm.

ant. certainty, confidence, trust, assurance, belief, sureness.

unchanging *adj.* CONTINUOUS.

uncharted *adj.* UNKNOWN.

unchaste *adj.* IMPURE.

uncivil *adj.* DISCOURTEOUS.

uncivilized *adj.* **1** barbarian, savage, primitive, barbaric, wild, uncouth, barbarous, brutish, brutal, ferocious. **2** churlish, coarse, uncivil, gross, crude, boorish, vulgar, rude, unmannered, uncultivated.

ant. 1 civilized, socialized, cultured, advanced. **2** civil, refined, polished, suave, urbane.

unclad *adj.* NAKED.

unclear *adj.* CONFUSING.

uncloak *v.* UNMASK.

uncomfortable *adj.* uneasy, embarrassed, troubled, self-conscious, edgy, ill at ease, unhappy, cheerless,

miserable, discomfited, disquieted, nervous, abashed, puzzled.

ant. comfortable, snug, relaxed, unworried, untroubled, serene.

uncommitted *adj.* NEUTRAL.

uncommon *adj.* **1** unusual, rare, infrequent, occasional, sparse, scarce, sporadic, few, isolated, unfamiliar, strange, peculiar, odd, queer. **2** remarkable, extraordinary, exceptional, singular, special, noteworthy, striking, superior, notable, impressive, inimitable, incomparable.

ant. 1 common, familiar, many, numerous, frequent. **2** ordinary, commonplace, matter-of-fact, humdrum, banal.

uncommunicative *adj.* reserved, taciturn, laconic, closemouthed, reticent, secretive, tight-lipped, evasive, unresponsive, guarded, mum, curt, short, silent.

ant. talkative, communicative, voluble, garrulous, loquacious, blabbermouthed.

uncomplicated *adj.* SIMPLE.

uncomprehending *adj.* IGNORANT.

uncompromising *adj.* inflexible, strict, resolute, steadfast, firm, rigid, indomitable, inexorable, tenacious, obstinate, stubborn, intransigent, immovable, unyielding.

ant. accommodating, agreeable, flexible, conciliatory, pliable, yielding.

unconcerned *adj.* **1** relaxed, composed, careless, cool, unruffled, unworried, nonchalant, casual, imperturbable, untroubled, serene, collected, easy. **2** uninterested, indifferent, uninvolved, aloof, detached, apathetic, dispassionate, listless, cool, incurious, distant, disinterested.

ant. 1 anxious, agitated, worried, perturbed, ardent. **2** interested, avid, curious, eager, involved.

unconditional *adj.* absolute, unqualified, full, total, complete, entire, unreserved, positive, unlimited, unrestricted, categorical.

ant. conditional, limited, qualified, contingent, restricted, partial.

unconscionable *adj.* **1** preposterous, prodigious, extravagant, inordinate, unreasonable, excessive, immense, exorbitant. **2** unscrupulous, monstrous, wanton, unprincipled, conscienceless, unjust, unfair, unethical, immoral, amoral.

ant. 1 reasonable, limited, moderate. **2** scrupulous, honorable, just, fair.

unconscious *adj.* **1** insensible, comatose, lethargic, senseless, insensate, asleep, stunned, narcotized, numb, stoned (*Slang*). **2** ignorant, unaware, heedless, unsuspecting, unmindful, unwitting, incognizant, uninformed, unacquainted, unheeding. **3** accidental, unwitting, inadvertent, unpremeditated, unintentional, unintended, unplanned, involuntary, chance, stray, fortuitous.

ant. 1 conscious, awake, sensible, alert, aware. **2** cognizant, alive to, familiar, acquainted, knowing. **3** deliberate, calculated, studied, intentional, planned.

unconventional *adj.* informal, unorthodox, nonconformist, unceremonious, free and easy, erratic, unusual, bizarre, odd, original, avant-garde, bohemian, free, swinging (*Slang*), with-it (*Slang*).

ant. strait-laced, conventional, proper, smug, bourgeois, formal, square (*Slang*).

unconvincing *adj.* implausible, dubious, inconclusive, indecisive, questionable, unpersuasive, doubtful, improbable, weak, flimsy, suspect, specious.

ant. convincing, persuasive, credible, believable, incontrovertible, undeniable.

uncounted *adj.* COUNTLESS.

uncouple *v.* UNFASTEN.

uncouth *adj.* **1** outlandish, odd, bizarre, outré, strange, unusual, freakish, unfamiliar, unconventional, unknown, fantastic. **2** boorish, coarse, unrefined, awkward, oafish, rough, vulgar, loutish, gawky, graceless, ill-mannered, rude.

ant. 1 usual, natural, ordinary, familiar, home-grown. **2** courteous, refined, elegant, graceful, well-mannered.

uncover *v.* unearth, lay bare, dig up, expose, reveal, disclose, set forth, discover, make known, show, open, unfold, unmask.

ant. hide, conceal, disguise, screen, mask.

unctuous *adj.* ingratiating, obsequious, mealy-mouthed, fawning, servile, slick, sanctimonious, insinuating, sycophantic, kowtowing, smooth-spoken, glib, bland, smooth, smarmy.

ant. sincere, independent, candid, straightforward, brash, impudent.

undaunted *adj.* fearless, intrepid, stouthearted, unafraid, doughty, resolute, brave, courageous, audacious, bold, plucky, undismayed, undiscouraged, unfaltering.

ant. cowardly, awed, dismayed, terrified, daunted, discouraged.

undecided *adj.* irresolute, wavering, uncertain, hesitant, tentative, unresolved, undetermined, openminded, unconvinced, indecisive, uncommitted, doubtful, dubious.

ant. decided, determined, committed, resolved, settled, sure.

undefined *adj.* AMORPHOUS.

undeniable *adj.* incontrovertible, indisputable, incontestable, unquestionable, indubitable, irrefutable, irrefragable, obvious, evident, conclusive, certain, unimpeachable, unanswerable.

ant. deniable, doubtful, uncertain, untenable, controversial, debatable.

undependable *adj.* unreliable, untrustworthy, unstable, changeable, variable, fickle, wavering, vacillating, shifty, uncertain, capricious, irresponsible, unsure, treacherous.

ant. dependable, trustworthy, unfailing, certain, stable, invariable.

under *adv.* below, beneath, down, downward, underneath, lower, down under. —*adj.* **1** subordinate, inferior, underling, dependent, lower, lesser, subaltern, ancillary, subsidiary, junior, subject. **2** lower, lesser, smaller, worse, deficient, substandard, defective, faulty, inferior, minus, short, bottom.

ant. *adv.* over, up, aloft, higher, above. *adj.* **1** superior, higher, ranking, over, upper, independent. **2** greater, larger, bigger, superior, better.

undercover *adj.* UNDERGROUND.

undercurrent *n.* overtone, atmosphere, aura, suggestion, feeling, connotation, hint, murmur, flavor, trend, tendency, counterpoint, implication, drift.

undercut *v.* UNDERMINE.

undergo *v.* experience, go through, encounter, be exposed to, meet with, pass through, endure, submit to, suffer, bear, weather, withstand, stomach, tolerate, sustain.

ant. miss, skip, forego, avoid, refuse, reject.

underground *adj.* **1** subterranean, nether, subterraneous, plutonic, plutonian, buried, sunken, hypogeal, hypogeous, hypogean, hypogeic. **2** undercover, clandestine, secret, covert, surreptitious, concealed, hidden, privy, hush-hush, stealthy, disguised, hugger-mugger.

ant. **1** surface, aboveground, exposed. **2** public, overt, revealed, aboveboard, open.

underhand *adj.* sly, furtive, undercover, crafty, surreptitious, hidden, stealthy, clandestine, secret, concealed, deceitful, disingenuous, dishonorable, underhanded.

ant. aboveboard, open, candid, direct, outright, frank.

underhanded *adj.* UNDERHAND.

underline *v.* EMPHASIZE.

underling *n.* subordinate, inferior, helper, servant, menial, hireling, attendant, retainer, minion, stooge, nonentity, flunky, gal Friday, man, boy, girl.

ant. superior, leader, higher-up, boss, overlord, master.

underlying *adj.* basic, fundamental, essential, intrinsic, rudimentary, basal, elementary, substantive, material, primary, prime, major, vital, cardinal.

ant. peripheral, subsidiary, extraneous, nonessential, attendant, minor.

undermine *v.* weaken, sap, undercut, subvert, demoralize, erode, sabotage, disable, debilitate, enfeeble, cripple, foil, thwart.

ant. reinforce, strengthen, buttress, sustain, promote, shore up.

underneath *adv.* under, beneath, below, down, downward, down under, lower.

ant. over, atop, above, up, aloft, higher.

underpinning *n.* **1** footing, foundation, groundwork, base, support, substructure, understructure, bed, basis. **2** foundation, basis, support, ground, groundwork, rudiment, backbone, keystone, center, nucleus, core, essence, seedbed, root, cradle.

understand *v.* **1** appreciate, apprehend, see through, interpret, penetrate, catch on, dig (*Slang*), psych out (*Slang*), intuit, make out. **2** master, know, grasp, take in, fathom, command, excel at, dig (*Slang*), follow, savvy (*Slang*), get the hang of. **3** realize, gather, feel, discern, recognize, grasp, perceive, see, conceive, comprehend.

understanding *n.* **1** comprehension, uptake, grasp, insight, discernment, cognizance, awareness, penetration, judgment, intelligence, perception, reason. **2** agreement, compact, settlement, bargain, pact, deal, accord, entente, covenant, pledge, promise. **3** view, viewpoint, point of view, opinion, estimation, belief, notion, idea, interpretation, judgment. **4** compassion, sympathy, indulgence, sensitivity, humanity, kindness, tenderness, pity, concern, commiseration, empathy, ruth.

ant. 1 stupidity, density, inanity, folly, dullness. **4** severity, harshness, cruelty, antipathy, inhumanity.

understood *adj.* assumed, axiomatic, granted, implicit, presumed, reputed, implied, tacit, inferential, accepted, unsaid, putative.

ant. dubious, questionable, debatable, unsure.

undertake *v.* attempt, take on, contract, covenant, promise, pledge, assume, set about, engage in, enter upon, take up, try, begin.

ant. abstain, avoid, desist, balk, refuse, demur.

undertaking *n.* enterprise, task, project, attempt, endeavor, venture, engagement, business, essay, effort, affair, adventure.

undesirable *adj.* objectionable, unwelcome, distasteful, unpleasant, unpleasing, obnoxious, displeasing, exceptionable, unsatisfactory, unacceptable, unappealing, uninviting, repugnant.

ant. desirable, inviting, engaging, attractive, agreeable, appealing.

undeveloped *adj.* IMMATURE.

undiplomatic *adj.* TACTLESS.

undisturbed *adj.* CALM.

undivided *adj.* WHOLE.

undo *v.* **1** reverse, annul, cancel, nullify, invalidate, veto, offset, neutralize, frustrate, stultify, abrogate, obviate. **2** UNFASTEN.

ant. ratify, validate, affirm, uphold, reinforce.

undoing *n.* destruction, ruin, disgrace, downfall, blow, affliction, fall, misadventure, mischance, defeat, failure, calamity, comeuppance.

ant. triumph, ascendancy, success, fortune, prosperity.

undoubted *adj.* CERTAIN.

undoubting *adj.* CERTAIN.

undreamed-of *adj.* unsuspected, unforeseen, astonishing, unheard-of, unimagined, unexpected, unconsidered, incredible, inconceivable, miraculous.

ant. commonplace, routine, customary, well-known, wonted, everyday.

undress *v.* strip, disrobe, doff, unclothe, uncover, unrobe, divest, dismantle, peel. —*n.* nudity, nakedness, dishabille, divestment, negligée, disarray.

ant. *v.* dress, don, put on, clothe, robe.

undue *adj.* excessive, immoderate, overmuch, disproportionate, superfluous, needless, extravagant, intemperate, extreme, inordinate, undeserved, unsuitable.

ant. moderate, temperate, suitable, mild, proportionate, condign.

undulate *v.* fluctuate, swing, heave, wave, billow, sway, pulsate, surge, swell, roll, vibrate, oscillate, throb, waver.

undulation *n.* waviness, billowing, pulsation, fluctuation, surging, beat, pulse, ripple, surge, heave, billow, sinuosity, oscillation.

unduly *adv.* excessively, improperly, unjustly, overmuch, inordinately, unnecessarily, unsuitably, disproportionately, unreasonably, unusually, abnormally.

ant. duly, properly, justly, moderately, appropriately, reasonably.

undying *adj.* immortal, eternal, deathless, imperishable, unceasing, never-ending, perpetual, infinite, endless, everlasting, indestructible.

ant. mortal, fleeting, impermanent, ephemeral, short-lived, momentary.

unearth *v.* UNCOVER.

unearthly *adj.* **1** extraterrestrial, extramundane, lunar, stellar, astral, heavenly, interstellar, galactic, supernatural, preternatural. **2** fearsome, baleful, terrible, loathsome, nightmarish, terrifying, Satanic, weird, eerie, uncanny.

ant. 1 earthly, terrestrial, sublunar, familiar, mundane. **2** natural, ordinary, pleasant, accustomed, benign.

uneasiness *n.* APPREHENSION.

uneasy *adj.* **1** disturbed, unquiet, agitated, restless, upset, on edge, edgy, roiled, troubled, nervous. **2** strained, embarrassed, ill at ease, discomposed, uncomfortable, self-conscious, shy, chagrined, constrained, perplexed, nonplused. **3** precarious, unstable, insecure, unsettled, shaky, risky, unsteady, volatile, unsafe, vulnerable, perilous.

ant. 1 peaceful, calm, serene, quiet, restful. **2** confident, easy, self-possessed, cheerful, cool (*Slang*). **3** safe, settled, secure, solid, firm.

unemotional *adj.* PHLEGMATIC.

unendangered *adj.* SAFE.

unendurable *adj.* INSUFFERABLE.

unenlightened *adj.* IGNORANT.

unenviable *adj.* regrettable, unfortunate, uneasy, uncomfortable, disagreeable, painful, unfavorable, undesirable, hapless, disadvantageous, unattractive, unlucky.

ant. enviable, agreeable, coveted, attractive, fortunate, advantageous.

unequal *adj.* **1** unmatched, different, mismated, dissimilar, opposite, diverse, disparate, unlike, unsuited, various. **2** variable, irregular, unbalanced, uneven, asymmetric, fitful, topheavy, lop-sided, askew, skewed.

ant. 1 equal, similar, matched, equivalent, like. **2** balanced, regular, uniform, steady, constant.

unequaled *adj.* PEERLESS.

unequivocal *adj.* unmistakable, plain, clear, explicit, unambiguous, definite, certain, straight, distinct, incontrovertible.

ant. ambiguous, equivocal, enigmatic, obscure, noncommittal.

unerring *adj.* certain, accurate, infallible, unfailing, sure, reliable, correct, exact, faultless, precise, perfect, right.

ant. mistaken, errant, failing, fallible, faulty, incorrect.

unessential *adj., n.* INESSENTIAL.

unethical *adj.* shady, dishonorable, unscrupulous, improper, unprincipled, corrupt, unjust, unfair, immoral, wrong, unworthy, unbecoming, conniving, suspect.

ant. upright, ethical, scrupulous, honorable, worthy, moral.

uneven *adj.* **1** rough, lumpy, bumpy, irregular, gnarled, jagged, unsmooth, unlevel, rugged, craggy. **2** unequal, disparate, lop-sided, dissimilar, unbalanced, mismatched, odd, topheavy, askew. **3** variable, fluctuating, fitful, spasmodic, unsteady, unstable, shifting, changeable.

ant. 1 smooth, level, even, flat, plane. **2** balanced, symmetrical, well-matched, equal, even. **3** uniform, constant, stable, steady, unvarying.

uneventful *adj.* quiet, placid, dull, monotonous, humdrum, uninteresting, insignificant, inconsequential, unmemorable, routine, tedious, ordinary, wonted, unremarkable.

ant. memorable, momentous, eventful, epochal, historic, remarkable.

unexampled *adj.* UNIQUE.

unexcelled *adj.* EXCELLENT.

unexceptional *adj.* commonplace, ordinary, humdrum, unremarkable, insignificant, unimpressive, trivial, undistinguished, mediocre, pedestrian, stereotyped, banal, customary, usual.

ant. exceptional, outstanding, noteworthy, remarkable, unusual, significant.

unexciting *adj.* BORING.

unexpected *adj.* unforeseen, unanticipated, sudden, unlooked-for, undreamed-of, unthought-of, unwonted, fortuitous, accidental, chance, surprising, astonishing.

ant. expected, awaited, foreseen, anticipated, planned.

unexplainable *adj.* INEXPLICABLE.

unfailing *adj.* inexhaustible, sure, dependable, reliable, endless, bottomless, steady, persistent, unflagging, unerring, infallible, constant, steadfast.

ant. unreliable, erratic, spotty, spasmodic, fitful, untrustworthy.

unfair *adj.* unjust, dishonest, deceptive, prejudiced, biased, unethical, unprincipled, unscrupulous, exploitative, bigoted, intolerant, discriminatory, arbitrary.

ant. honest, fair, evenhanded, just, scrupulous, ethical.

unfaithful *adj.* **1** disloyal, delinquent, faithless, negligent, deceitful, fickle, inconstant, capricious, mercurial, untrue, changeable, perfidious, treacherous. **2** imperfect, inaccurate, erroneous, careless, unreliable, inexact, faulty, defective, spurious, distorted, imprecise.

ant. **1** loyal, steadfast, faithful, unchanging, true. **2** accurate, exact, careful, true, scrupulous.

unfamiliar *adj.* **1** unacquainted, inconversant, incognizant, unversed, unskilled, unaware, unaccustomed, unhabituated, uninformed, unconscious. **2** strange, new, unknown, unusual, uncommon, novel, extraordinary, unaccustomed, foreign, curious.

ant. **1** acquainted, conversant, familiar, cognizant, aware. **2** familiar, old, accustomed, wonted, usual.

unfashionable *adj.* OLD-FASHIONED.

unfasten *v.* uncouple, unfix, undo, disconnect, detach, unhitch, untie, unbind, unloose, unlace, unclasp, loosen.

ant. fasten, close, attach, hitch, connect, fix.

unfathomable *adj.* INSCRUTABLE.

unfavorable *adj.* adverse, negative, derogatory, disparaging, contrary, opposed, inimical, hostile, antagonistic, antipathetic, poor, low.

ant. favorable, approving, well-disposed, positive, warm.

unfearing *adj.* FEARLESS.

unfeeling *adj.* hard, callous, unsympathetic, insensitive, hardhearted, cold, heartless, inhumane, stony, pitiless, cruel.

ant. humane, sympathetic, sensitive, soft, kind, benevolent.

unfeigned *adj.* SINCERE.

unfettered *adj.* FREE.

unfinished *adj.* INCOMPLETE.

unfit *adj.* **1** unsuitable, unqualified, inadequate, incompetent, unequipped, incapable, ineligible, unsuited, unacceptable, unprepared, useless. **2** unhealthy, flabby, feeble, weak, debilitated, puny, soft, sick, sickly, devitalized, decrepit.

ant. **1** suitable, qualified, competent, able, acceptable. **2** vigorous, conditioned, fit, rugged, robust.

unfix *v.* UNFASTEN.

unflagging *adj.* tireless, unremitting, unceasing, constant, steady, indefatigable, unwearied, unfaltering, unfailing, persevering, persistent, relentless, inexhaustible.

ant. failing, tiring, weakening, diminishing, languishing, declining.

unflappable *adj.* imperturbable, composed, level-headed, impassive, self-contained, unexcitable, nonchalant, insouciant, cool, patient, collected.

ant. excitable, hotheaded, choleric, turbulent, impatient.

unflattering *adj.* CRITICAL.

unfledged *adj.* IMMATURE.

unfold *v.* **1** open, spread out, unfurl, undo, unwrap, straighten out, expand, unroll, unravel, separate. **2** disclose, explain, reveal, clarify, emerge, tell, make clear, make known, publish, relate, show, bare, expose.

ant. **1** furl, fold, roll up, double over, crease. **2** conceal, withhold, cover, suppress, hide.

unforeseeable *adj.* UNPREDICTABLE.

unforeseen *adj.* unexpected, surprising, unplanned, unlooked-for, unanticipated, unintended, accidental, fortuitous, irregular, anomalous, startling.

ant. foreseen, anticipated, expected, routine, regular, intended.

unforgettable *adj.* MEMORABLE.

unfortunate *adj.* **1** ill-starred, ill-fated, disastrous, calamitous, ruinous, catastrophic, unlucky, unhappy, doomed, star-crossed. **2** regrettable, unsuitable, deplorable, inappropriate, infelicitous, ill-advised, improper, bad, reprehensible, hapless,

shocking. —*n.* underdog, victim, loser, failure, outcast, pariah, derelict, vagrant, beggar, bum.
ant. *adj.* **1** fortunate, blessed, lucky, affluent, successful. **2** suitable, praiseworthy, commendable, proper, good.

unfounded *adj.* groundless, baseless, unjustified, fallacious, unsubstantiated, illogical, trumped-up, false, spurious, ill-founded, erroneous, vain, idle, fabricated, invented.
ant. factual, substantiated, confirmed, proven, verified, attested.

unfriendly *adj.* unsociable, aloof, haughty, uncongenial, disagreeable, snobbish, unsympathetic, hostile, cold, distant, chilly, ill-disposed, inhospitable, reclusive, withdrawn.
ant. sociable, affable, friendly, congenial, forthcoming, warm.

unfruitful *adj.* FRUITLESS.

ungainly *adj.* awkward, clumsy, gangling, gawky, splay, ungraceful, inelegant, uncouth, clownish, loutish, lumbering, hulking, unwieldy.
ant. attractive, graceful, comely, elegant, neat, trim.

ungenerous *adj.* STINGY.

ungentle *adj.* ROUGH.

ungenuine *adj.* SPURIOUS.

ungodly *adj.* SINFUL.

ungovernable *adj.* UNRULY.

ungraceful *adj.* GRACELESS.

ungracious *adj.* unmannerly, discourteous, impolite, gauche, rude, uncivil, churlish, boorish, uncouth, illbred, ill-mannered, indelicate.
ant. mannerly, polite, well-bred, affable, urbane, courteous.

ungrateful *adj.* thankless, unthankful, unappreciative, unmindful, unaware, heedless, forgetful, unthinking, selfish.
ant. grateful, thankful, appreciative, mindful, aware.

unguarded *adj.* **1** thoughtless, unthinking, careless, rash, foolhardy, unwary, indiscreet, imprudent, incautious, heedless. **2** guileless, open, aboveboard, straightforward, frank,

candid, direct, ingenuous, artless, innocent.
ant. **1** cautious, wary, careful, discreet, prudent. **2** guarded, indirect, veiled, hedging, secretive.

unguent *n.* OINTMENT.

unguis *n.* CLAW.

unhandy *adj.* CLUMSY.

unhappy *adj.* **1** sad, depressed, melancholy, disturbed, mournful, sorrowful, dissatisfied, miserable, wretched, pained, distressed. **2** unfortunate, ill-omened, unlucky, unpropitious, cursed, sinister, infelicitous, malign, ominous, inauspicious. **3** inappropriate, untactful, inept, inopportune, awkward, infelicitous, unsuitable, gauche, ill-timed, clumsy, awkward, malapropos.
ant. **1** cheerful, happy, glad, joyous, jolly. **2** propitious, fortunate, lucky, flourishing, benign. **3** timely, apt, appropriate, suitable, apropos.

unharmed *adj.* SAFE.

unhealthy *adj.* **1** sick, sickly, unwholesome, diseased, unwell, ailing, ill, poorly, morbid, invalid, infirm, frail. **2** noxious, virulent, poisonous, harmful, unhealthful, unsalutary, detrimental, infective, toxic, septic.
ant. **1** healthy, vigorous, robust, wholesome, sound. **2** healthful, salubrious, curative, hygienic, beneficial.

unheard-of *adj.* outrageous, unbelievable, unreasonable, outlandish, preposterous, inconceivable, astonishing, fantastic, outré, extravagant, extreme.
ant. believable, reasonable, ordinary, common, moderate.

unheedful *adj.* CARELESS.

unheeding *adj.* CARELESS.

unhinge *v.* unsettle, confuse, dismay, upset, unbalance, unnerve, agitate, shatter, derange, disorder, madden, craze, convulse.
ant. compose, soothe, pacify, appease, restore, tranquilize.

unhitch *v.* UNFASTEN.

unholy *adj.* SINFUL.

unhurt *adj.* SAFE.

uniform *adj.* **1** unvarying, homogeneous, similar, same, regular, constant, undeviating, undiversified, symmetrical, alike. **2** unchanging, consistent, undeviating, persistent, constant, identical, selfsame, universal, general, unvarying. —*n.* livery, habit, costume, silks, regimentals, regalia.

ant. *adj.* **1** irregular, uneven, dissimilar, diverse, different. **2** inconsistent, changeable, variable, haphazard. —*n.* mufti, civvies (*Slang*).

unify *v.* unite, bind, consolidate, fuse, blend, link, combine, join, connect, associate, coalesce, coordinate.

ant. divide, alienate, separate, disunite, disconnect.

unimpaired *adj.* SOUND².

unimportant *adj.* insignificant, minor, immaterial, second-rate, one-horse, inconsequential, paltry, trivial, indifferent, mediocre, picayune, petty, small-time (*Slang*), bush-league (*Slang*).

ant. important, significant, major, eminent, key, big-time (*Slang*).

uninhibited *adj.* unrepressed, liberated, free, open, untrammeled, unrestrained, unsuppressed, loose, unbridled, intemperate, licentious.

ant. repressed, constrained, formal, tense, stiff, suppressed.

unintelligent *adj.* STUPID.

unintelligible *adj.* incomprehensible, obscure, enigmatic, inscrutable, garbled, indistinct, undecipherable, illegible, meaningless, inexplicable, baffling, mysterious.

ant. understandable, intelligible, comprehensible, obvious, distinct.

uninterested *adj.* indifferent, unconcerned, incurious, unmindful, heedless, apathetic, languid, listless, weary, bored, blasé, uninvolved.

ant. interested, curious, alert, concerned, involved, alive.

uninteresting *adj.* BORING.

uninterrupted *adj.* CONTINUOUS.

uninviting *adj.* UNAPPETIZING.

uninvolved *adj.* ALIENATED.

union *n.* **1** combination, consolidation, amalgamation, annexation, incorporation, appropriation, unification, junction, confederation, coalition, federation, meeting. **2** unison, junction, accord, convergence, concurrence, conjunction, agreement, accordance, unity, harmony. **3** whole, group, compound, amalgam, unit, bloc, couple, association, alliance, guild, team, confederation, coalition, league. **3** MARRIAGE.

ant. **1** separation, divergence, dissolution, segregation, disruption. **2** disagreement, discord, dissonance, split, hiatus.

unique *adj.* **1** unexampled, unprecedented, sui generis, single, sole, lone, singular, only, one and only. **2** exceptional, extraordinary, peerless, incomparable, nonpareil, unparalleled, remarkable, unusual, outstanding, unequaled.

ant. **1** fungible, numerous, many, abundant, multiple, plentiful. **2** common, everyday, usual, ordinary, familiar.

unison *n.* harmony, accord, concord, consonance, compatibility, affinity, concurrence, accordance, unanimity, agreement, unity, union, concert.

ant. discord, disagreement, dissonance, dissidence, strife, dissension.

unit *n.* measure, part, portion, quantity, piece, element, member, constituent, component, item. —*adj.* UNITARY.

unitary *adj.* **1** unit, one, singular, sole, individual, unaccompanied, lone. **2** undivided, whole, entire, intact, indiscrete, indivisible, unbroken, complete, integral.

ant. **1** plural, multiple, paired, binary, accompanied. **2** divided, discrete, incomplete, dissected, split.

unite *v.* **1** combine, merge, fuse, join, cement, mix, connect, couple, amalgamate, attach, coalesce. **2** associate, cooperate, coordinate, connect, marry, unify, ally, join, reconcile, centralize.

ant. 1 separate, part, break, sever, detach. **2** disengage, segregate, disband, divorce, part.

unity *n.* **1** oneness, singularity, identity, singleness, undividedness, wholeness, integrity, integrality, entirety. **2** harmony, consensus, mutality, concord, agreement, single-mindedness, solidarity, union, unison.

ant. 1 multiplicity, plurality, division, disunity. **2** disharmony, disunion, discord, disagreement.

universal *adj.* all-inclusive, unlimited, catholic, ecumenical, comprehensive, boundless, prevalent, common, general, pandemic, worldwide, total, entire.

ant. limited, exclusive, unique, particular, rare.

universe *n.* creation, cosmos, macrocosm, nature, infinity.

unjoined *adj.* SEPARATE.

unjust *adj.* wrongful, inequitable, unfair, partial, iniquitous, injurious, biased, prejudiced, unmerited, unjustified, undeserved, wrong, wicked.

ant. just, fair, ethical, good, impartial.

unjustifiable *adj.* INEXCUSABLE.

unkempt *adj.* untidy, slovenly, shaggy, rumpled, sloppy, careless, slatternly, messy, frowzy, neglected, disheveled, dowdy, bedraggled.

ant. tidy, neat, spruce, trim, well-groomed, presentable.

unkind *adj.* unsympathetic, harsh, cruel, inhuman, unmerciful, unfeeling, inconsiderate, hardhearted, brutal, merciless, ungracious, disobliging.

ant. kind, amiable, considerate, congenial, softhearted, sympathetic.

unknowing *adj.* IGNORANT.

unknown *adj.* **1** unrecognized, uncharted, hidden, dark, mysterious, strange, unfamiliar, unplumbed, unusual, unperceived, ignored. **2** unidentified, anonymous, nameless, undefined, indeterminate, undiscov-

ered, undesignated, unnamed, undetermined, undisclosed.

ant. 1 known, recognized, understood, familiar. **2** identified, defined, labeled, tagged, revealed.

unlace *v.* UNFASTEN.

unlasting *adj.* TRANSITORY.

unlawful *adj.* illicit, illegal, prohibited, lawless, forbidden, illegitimate, unauthorized, actionable, unlicensed, unconstitutional.

ant. legal, lawful, licit, legitimate, permitted, authorized.

unleash *v.* FREE.

unless *prep.* save, except, excepting, if not, aside from, leaving out, bar, barring, excluding, with the exception of.

unlettered *adj.* illiterate, uneducated, ignorant, untaught, unschooled, unlearned, uninstructed, unversed, untutored, inerudite.

ant. literate, educated, informed, schooled, learned.

unlike *adj.* different, unrelated, diametrical, opposite, dissimilar, unequal, diverse, assorted, miscellaneous, variant, heterogeneous, diversified, incongruous, discordant.

ant. like, similar, identical, twin, equal, same.

unlikely *adj.* improbable, doubtful, implausible, questionable, incredible, fishy, unbelievable, unreasonable, unimaginable, inconceivable, rare.

ant. likely, probable, conceivable, credible, believable.

unlimited *adj.* LIMITLESS.

unlooked-for *adj.* UNEXPECTED.

unloose *v.* **1** FREE. **2** UNFASTEN.

unlucky *adj.* inauspicious, ill-fated, disastrous, hapless, unsuccessful, unfortunate, unprosperous, baleful, ill-omened, cursed, unhappy, miserable.

ant. lucky, auspicious, fortunate, blessed, prosperous, happy.

unman *v.* UNNERVE.

unmanageable *adj.* INTRACTABLE.

unmask *v.* expose, uncloak, unveil, lay open, uncover, reveal, betray, lay bare, unwrap, undo, uncurtain, show up.

ant. conceal, disguise, cover up, veil, hide.

unmerciful *adj.* MERCILESS.

unmistakable *adj.* evident, obvious, clear, unambiguous, manifest, certain, distinct, plain, patent, sure, palpable, visible, decided.

ant. unclear, dim, doubtful, uncertain, obscure, hidden.

unmistaken *adj.* CORRECT.

unmitigated *adj.* absolute, thoroughgoing, out-and-out, arrant, utter, sheer, unrelieved, unredeemed, unqualified, veritable, outright, rank.

ant. partial, qualified, occasional, conditional, restricted, sometime.

unmodish *adj.* OLD-FASHIONED.

unnatural *adj.* **1** monstrous, inhuman, brutal, savage, coldblooded, heinous, diabolical, horrendous, unspeakable, fiendish, evil. **2** contrived, artificial, stilted, forced, affected, theatrical, factitious, insincere, labored, strained, self-conscious.

ant. 1 humane, merciful, benign, pitiful, good. **2** natural, artless, unaffected, unstudied, simple.

unnecessary *adj.* unneeded, unrequired, inessential, needless, useless, uncalled-for, superfluous, redundant, excess, supererogatory, dispensable.

ant. necessary, needed, essential, useful, indispensable.

unneeded *adj.* UNNECESSARY.

unnerve *v.* unman, enervate, disconcert, upset, confound, fluster, shake, disarm, discourage, enfeeble, weaken, emasculate.

ant. steel, support, strengthen, arm, encourage.

unnumbered *adj.* NUMBERLESS.

unobtrusive *adj.* INCONSPICUOUS.

unoccupied *adj.* EMPTY.

unparalleled *adj.* unmatched, unprecedented, unrivaled, unequaled, unique, exceptional, unheard-of, matchless, peerless, incomparable,

inimitable, rare, unparagoned, singular, sui generis.

ant. ordinary, usual, commonplace, matched, equaled, surpassed.

unperturbed *adj.* CALM.

unpitying *adj.* CRUEL.

unpleasant *adj.* disagreeable, objectionable, distasteful, displeasing, ill-natured, rude, unwelcome, unpleasing, unacceptable, offensive, obnoxious, repulsive, unappetizing, repellent, noisome.

ant. pleasant, agreeable, attractive, compliant, gracious, amiable.

unplumbed *adj.* UNKNOWN.

unpolished *adj.* ROUGH.

unprecedented *adj.* novel, new, unexampled, exceptional, unequaled, unparalleled, unrivaled, unique, sui generis, unheard-of, extraordinary, remarkable, singular.

ant. common, run-of-the-mill, ordinary, everyday, usual, frequent.

unpredictable *adj.* unforeseeable, uncertain, incalculable, indeterminate, aberrant, random, chance, unsure, desultory, erratic, changeable, mercurial, fickle, inconstant, unreliable, volatile, frivolous, flighty.

ant. foreseeable, regular, predictable, calculable, certain, steady, dependable, stable.

unprejudiced *adj.* UNBIASED.

unpretentious *adj.* HUMBLE.

unprincipled *adj.* UNSCRUPULOUS.

unproductive *adj.* unprofitable, useless, fruitless, unavailing, ineffective, vain, futile, otiose, idle, worthless, inefficient, nonproductive, counterproductive.

ant. effective, productive, useful, rewarding, efficient, worthwhile.

unprofessional *adj.* amateur, amateurish, inept, inexpert, unskilled, undisciplined, unworkmanlike, inefficient, incompetent, inexperienced, green.

ant. professional, expert, adept, skilled, disciplined, efficient.

unprotected *adj.* VULNERABLE.

unquestionable *adj.* indisputable, certain, indubitable, incontrovertible, undeniable, conclusive, unmistakable, doubtless, sure, unexceptionable, irrefutable, unimpeachable.

ant. questionable, uncertain, dubious, doubtful, ambiguous, inconclusive.

unquiet *adj.* RESTLESS.

unravel *v.* EXPLAIN.

unreal *adj.* **1** hypothetical, insubstantial, incorporeal, immaterial, intangible, mythical, impalpable, ideal, illusory, insensible, supposed. **2** false, imitation, untruthful, spurious, counterfeit, sham, seeming, ersatz, mock, pretended. **3** imaginary, chimerical, phantasmagoric, visionary, fanciful, fictitious, vain, illusory, fabulous, hallucinatory.

ant. **1** palpable, substantive, material, physical, sensible. **2** authentic, genuine, true, real, bona fide. **3** real, objective, veritable, realistic, factual.

unreasonable *adj.* **1** unreasoning, irrational, illogical, silly, absurd, insane, unwise, brainless, idiotic, foolish, senseless. **2** immoderate, exorbitant, preposterous, excessive, extravagant, unheard-of, unjust, unfair, unthinkable, impossible.

ant. **1** logical, sane, intelligent, rational, wise, sensible. **2** reasonable, moderate, limited, fair, equitable.

unreasoning *adj.* UNREASONABLE.

unregenerate *adj.* **1** unrepentant, impious, unconverted, wicked, unholy, godless, sinful, hardened, unhallowed, blasphemous. **2** stubborn, obstinate, contrary, recalcitrant, inflexible, obdurate, refractory, intractable, self-willed, perverse.

ant. **1** repentant, converted, virtuous, blessed, pious. **2** flexible, submissive, obliging, docile, amiable.

unrehearsed *adj.* SPONTANEOUS.

unrelenting *adj.* ADAMANT.

unreliable *adj.* UNDEPENDABLE.

unremarkable *adj.* UNEXCEPTIONAL.

unremitting *adj.* incessant, constant, indefatigable, unwearied, continual, unceasing, persistent, relentless, una-

bated, tenacious, assiduous, unrelenting, sedulous, persevering.

ant. desultory, fitful, spasmodic, irregular, inconstant, unsteady.

unremorseful *adj.* REMORSELESS.

unreserved *adj.* unrestricted, unqualified, wholehearted, complete, unlimited, entire, absolute, unstinting, total, full, all-out, unrestrained.

ant. qualified, incomplete, reserved, grudging, partial, limited.

unresisting *adj.* PLIABLE.

unrespectful *adj.* IRREVERENT.

unresponsive *adj.* PHLEGMATIC.

unrest *n.* dissatisfaction, turmoil, rebellion, protest, sedition, turbulence, defiance, animosity, dissension, disaffection, agitation, restlessness.

ant. calm, peace, order, serenity, quiet, tranquillity.

unrestrained *adj.* unconstrained, abandoned, uncontrolled, immoderate, unbridled, unconfined, licentious, wanton, unreserved, inordinate, unchecked, lax, dissolute.

ant. inhibited, austere, controlled, repressed, disciplined, checked.

unrestricted *adj.* FREE.

unriddle *v.* SOLVE.

unrivaled *adj.* PEERLESS.

unruffled *adj.* calm, serene, tranquil, peaceful, placid, composed, collected, undisturbed, imperturbable, phlegmatic, cool, sedate, nonchalant, philosophical.

ant. disturbed, agitated, ruffled, excited, ardent, bothered.

unruly *adj.* ungovernable, recalcitrant, intractable, refractory, headstrong, insubordinate, willful, uncontrollable, unmanageable, disobedient, disorderly, lawless, turbulent, hyperactive.

ant. amenable, tractable, docile, governable, obedient, biddable.

unsafe *adj.* hazardous, dangerous, risky, perilous, precarious, insecure, uncertain, menacing, treacherous, threatening, ominous, unprotected, unsound, unstable.

ant. safe, secure, harmless, sure, snug, protective.

unsanitary *adj.* unhygienic, unclean, insanitary, squalid, filthy, dirty, disease-ridden, unhealthful, infested, sordid, polluted, contaminated, fusty, moldy, septic.
ant. sanitary, hygienic, clean, spotless, healthful, antiseptic.

unsatisfactory *adj.* unacceptable, disappointing, inadequate, insufficient, deficient, faulty, poor, dissatisfactory, unworthy, weak, short, inappropriate, unsuitable, unpleasing.
ant. satisfactory, adequate, sufficient, suitable, pleasing, appropriate.

unsavory *adj.* **1** unappetizing, unpalatable, disagreeable, distasteful, inedible, smelly, rancid, rank, sickening, nauseating. **2** shady, infamous, repugnant, raffish, disreputable, notorious, scandalous, offensive, monstrous, despicable, revolting, contemptible.
ant. **1** savory, tasty, appetizing, palatable, pleasing, good. **2** worthy, blameless, virtuous, moral, upright.

unscrupulous *adj.* unprincipled, unethical, dishonest, immoral, dishonorable, ruthless, exploitative, manipulative, corrupt, fraudulent, unjust, conscienceless, unrestrained, wanton, crooked, underhand.
ant. high-minded, ethical, honorable, scrupulous, public-spirited, principled.

unseat *v.* depose, oust, dismiss, discharge, displace, replace, turn out, divest, dispossess, fire, debar, defeat, break.
ant. seat, invest, inaugurate, institute, install, elect.

unseeing *adj.* BLIND.

unseemly *adj.* unbecoming, unattractive, inappropriate, improper, indecorous, unseasonable, unsuitable, unfitting, indecent, objectionable, unsightly, indelicate, vulgar, gross.
ant. seemly, decorous, proper, becoming, fitting, acceptable.

unseen *adj.* HIDDEN.

unselective *adj.* PROMISCUOUS.

unselfish *adj.* altruistic, liberal, generous, disinterested, open-handed, charitable, unstinting, munificent, lavish, bountiful, selfless, self-sacrificing, devoted, magnanimous.
ant. egotistical, greedy, tight-fisted, stingy, miserly, mean.

unsettle *adj.* confuse, upset, disturb, discompose, disconcert, startle, perturb, fluster, agitate, bother, unhinge, unnerve, bewilder, worry.
ant. calm, soothe, pacify, lull, quiet, tranquilize.

unshackle *v.* FREE.

unshaken *adj.* CALM.

unsighted *adj.* BLIND.

unsightly *adj.* ugly, unattractive, ill-favored, unlovely, unprepossessing, unpleasant, homely, plain, repellent, repulsive, hideous.
ant. pretty, comely, attractive, agreeable, handsome, beautiful.

unskeptical *adj.* GULLIBLE.

unskilled *adj.* INEPT.

unskillful *adj.* awkward, unpracticed, inexpert, bungling, incompetent, inept, amateurish, untrained, inexperienced, inapt, maladroit, clumsy, green, unprofessional, unworkmanlike.
ant. skillful, adept, dexterous, masterly, able, habile.

unsociable *adj.* UNFRIENDLY.

unsophisticated *adj.* **1** unworldly, ingenuous, naive, inexperienced, sincere, unaffected, natural, simple, artless, straightforward, direct. **2** simple, plain, unadorned, uncomplex, uncomplicated, unembellished, uninvolved.
ant. **1** worldly, worldly-wise, disingenuous, knowing, affected. **2** complicated, esoteric, advanced, ingenious, elegant, complex.

unsound *adj.* **1** flimsy, defective, rickety, faulty, imperfect, fragile, decayed, tumbledown, frail, infirm. **2** unhealthy, frail, delicate, diseased, ill, ailing, sickly, feeble, unwell, invalid. **3** irrational, fallacious, invalid, senseless, groundless, specious, un-reasonable, sophistic, nonsensical, il-logical, false, implausible.

ant. 1 strong, solid, sturdy, well-made, substantial. **2** healthy, robust, sound, well, strong. **3** rational, logi-cal, valid, reasonable, plausible.

unspeakable *adj.* heinous, horrendous, atrocious, flagitious, monstrous, abominable, outrageous, dreadful, vicious, pernicious, vile, nefarious.

unspecialized *adj.* GENERAL.

unstable *adj.* **1** fluctuating, unsteady, variable, insecure, instable, unsafe, precarious, tottering, teetering, swaying, rickety, shaky, infirm. **2** vacillating, inconstant, weak, capri-cious, fickle, mercurial, infirm, un-steady, untrustworthy, deranged, er-ratic, volatile, irresolute.

ant. 1 stable, firm, steady, solid, se-cure. **2** level-headed, reliable, steady, sound, stable.

unsteady *adj.* UNSTABLE.

unsterile *adj.* DIRTY.

unsterilized *adj.* DIRTY.

unsubstantial *adj.* INSUBSTANTIAL.

unsubtle *adj.* GROSS.

unsuccessful *adj.* fruitless, unavailing, ineffectual, unprosperous, manqué, would-be, failed, ill-starred, useless, stultified, nugatory, bootless, futile, vain, losing.

ant. successful, prosperous, auspi-cious, thriving, winning, victorious.

unsuitable *adj.* unfitting, unsatisfac-tory, ineligible, inappropriate, inap-plicable, unbefitting, unbecoming, inapt, inexpedient, improper, incon-gruous, disqualified.

ant. fitting, eligible, suitable, befit-ting, satisfactory, qualified.

unsure *adj.* UNCERTAIN.

unsurpassed *adj.* EXCELLENT.

unsuspecting *adj.* TRUSTING.

unsuspicious *adj.* GULLIBLE.

unswerving *adj.* steadfast, unwavering, steady, consistent, true, constant, stable, unfaltering, uncompromising, determined, firm, resolute, stanch, devoted.

ant. irresolute, vacillating, unsteady, wavering, indecisive, inconsistent.

untactful *adj.* TACTLESS.

untainted *adj.* PURE.

untamed *adj.* WILD.

untangle *adj.* disentangle, unravel, un-weave, straighten out, clear up, ex-plain, explicate, unsnarl, solve, ex-tricate, ravel, disencumber, disem-barrass.

ant. confuse, entangle, complicate, enmesh, snarl, tangle.

untenable *adj.* indefensible, unsound, weak, vulnerable, unprotected, dis-jointed, defective, shaky, insecure, groundless, unreasonable, fallacious, illogical, irrational.

ant. impregnable, invulnerable, strong, unassailable, secure, water-tight.

unthankful *adj.* UNGRATEFUL.

unthinking *adj.* THOUGHTLESS.

unthrifty *adj.* PROFLIGATE.

untidy *adj.* messy, disorderly, unkempt, slatternly, slovenly, mussy, shaggy, sloppy, upside-down, neglected, di-sheveled, careless, dowdy.

ant. tidy, neat, well-kept, spruce, presentable, orderly.

untie *v.* UNFASTEN.

untimely *adj.* premature, inopportune, unseasonable, inconvenient, inap-propriate, inauspicious, ill-timed, un-suitable, malapropos, inapt, mis-timed.

ant. timely, welcome, opportune, well-timed, fortunate, auspicious.

untiring *adj.* TIRELESS.

untold *adj.* INNUMERABLE.

untoward *adj.* **1** unfavorable, adverse, contrary, unfortunate, unlucky, troublesome, disadvantageous, un-propitious, inopportune, difficult. **2** indecorous, improper, gross, un-seemly, wrong, objectionable, unbe-coming, untasteful, embarrassing, unsuitable, unwelcome, distasteful.

ant. 1 favorable, timely, lucky, fortu-nate, happy. **2** seemly, proper, suita-ble, becoming, fitting.

untrue *adj.* false, fake, incorrect, inaccurate, mistaken, erroneous, deceptive, misleading, apocryphal, spurious, fictitious, wrong, invalid, lying, fraudulent, dishonest.

ant. true, accurate, veracious, factual, correct, valid.

untrustworthy *adj.* unreliable, disloyal, treacherous, undependable, shifty, dishonest, false, doubtful, questionable, unsound, fallible, inaccurate, tricky, slippery, deceitful, fairweather.

ant. reliable, honest, loyal, steadfast, accurate, true.

untruth *n.* LIE.

untruthful *adj.* lying, mendacious, false, dishonest, disingenuous, deceitful, dissembling, deceptive, fraudulent, hypocritical, meretricious, inaccurate.

ant. truthful, honest, candid, true, veracious, accurate.

untutored *adj.* IGNORANT.

untypical *adj.* UNUSUAL.

unusual *adj.* odd, rare, extraordinary, atypical, unwonted, irregular, abnormal, anomalous, unnatural, unfamiliar, alien, strange, bizarre, uncommon, untypical, infrequent.

ant. common, familiar, wonted, normal, ordinary, usual.

unvarying *adj.* SAME.

unversed *adj.* IGNORANT.

unwarlike *adj.* PEACEFUL

unwarrantable *adj.* INEXCUSABLE.

unwarranted *adj.* UNCALLED-FOR.

unwary *adj.* incautious, careless, reckless, hasty, heedless, imprudent, unguarded, indiscreet, rash, headlong, precipitate, remiss, precipitous.

ant. wary, circumspect, chary, cautious, guarded, discreet.

unwavering *adj.* STEADFAST.

unwearying *adj.* TIRELESS.

unwell *adj.* sick, ailing, sickly, ill, indisposed, upset, disordered, unhealthy, out of sorts, diseased, poorly, delicate, weak, valetudinarian, morbid, frail, feeble, invalid.

ant. well, healthy, fine, sound, vigorous, robust.

unwholesome *adj.* unhealthful, unhealthy, baneful, detrimental, pernicious, insalubrious, harmful, noxious, deleterious, poisonous, injurious, unsound, corrupting, demoralizing, contaminating, ruinous, destructive, immoral, evil.

ant. healthful, wholesome, beneficial, edifying.

unwieldy *adj.* awkward, cumbersome, hulking, unmanageable, clumsy, unhandy, inconvenient, massive, massy, bulky, ponderous, cumbrous.

ant. maneuverable, manageable, handy, convenient, yare.

unwilling *adj.* reluctant, loath, averse, indisposed, disinclined, laggard, opposed, grudging, slow, recalcitrant, balky, restive, contrary, negative.

ant. willing, amenable, inclined, eager, voluntary, compliant.

unwind *v.* RELAX.

unwise *adj.* imprudent, injudicious, ill-advised, indiscreet, shortsighted, impolitic, irresponsible, foolhardy, foolish, stupid, senseless, silly, dumb, ill-considered, unintelligent, unreasonable.

ant. wise, prudent, judicious, discreet, sensible, smart.

unwonted *adj.* UNUSUAL.

unworkable *adj.* IMPRACTICAL.

unworldly *adj.* UNSOPHISTICATED.

unworthy *adj.* undeserving, unfit, wanting, defective, inferior, inadequate, worthless, meritless, unqualified, unsuited, ineligible.

ant. worthy, deserving, suited, eligible, adequate, fit.

unwrinkled *adj.* SMOOTH.

unwritten *adj.* TRADITIONAL.

unyielding *adj.* inexorable, immovable, relentless, obdurate, inflexible, determined, irresistible, adamant, resolute, intractable, stubborn, steadfast, stanch, firm, uncooperative.

ant. flexible, compliant, cooperative, yielding, tractable, adaptable.

unyoke *v.* SEPARATE.

up *adj.* alert, ready, prepared, primed, aware, fit, set, all set, equal, psyched up (*Slang*). —*v.* increase, raise, boost, jack, lift, step up, heighten, augment, intensify, add to.

ant. *adj.* unprepared, unaware, unprimed, unfit, unequal. —*v.* lower, decrease, reduce, cut, slash, down.

up-and-coming *adj.* enterprising, energetic, promising, aggressive, ambitious, dynamic, pushing, sedulous, diligent, determined, eager, on the make, go-getting, hustling.

ant. languid, lazy, apathetic, lackadaisical, slothful, nonchalant.

upbeat *adj.* OPTIMISTIC.

upbraid *v.* reproach, scold, rebuke, berate, admonish, reprimand, revile, vituperate, rail, chastise, chide, blame, censure, reprove.

ant. praise, applaud, approve, reward, puff, laud.

upbringing *n.* rearing, breeding, nurture, training, raising, tending, care, cultivation, education, schooling, acculturation.

upchuck *v.* VOMIT.

update *v.* revise, modernize, streamline, rejuvenate, renovate, refurbish, amend, recast, renew, reorganize, revamp, rework.

upgrade *v.* promote, elevate, advance, raise, push, forward, dignify, glorify, improve, enhance, exalt, ennoble.

ant. downgrade, demote, degrade, disrate, cut, declass.

upheaval *n.* revolution, convulsion, cataclysm, misrule, anarchy, breakdown, devastation, overthrow, disorder, destruction, rapine, riot.

ant. order, law, tranquillity, rule, peace, harmony.

uphold *v.* **1** hold up, prop, support, shore up, brace, buttress, underpin, keep up, sustain, bear. **2** aid, encourage, sustain, defend, support, back, confirm, vindicate, champion, advocate.

ant. 1 let down, pull down, let fall. **2** attack, belittle, denigrate, fail, abandon.

upkeep *n.* maintenance, repair, management, conservation, preservation, running, housekeeping, sustenance, subsistence, expense, overhead, cost.

uplift *v.* **1** ELEVATE. **2** raise, improve, upraise, edify, cultivate, inspire, stimulate, refine, better, advance, ameliorate, hearten, encourage. —*n.* elevation, advancement, betterment, improvement, amelioration, aggrandizement, preferment, promotion, edification, enrichment, exaltation, exhilaration, cultivation.

ant. *v.* **2** downgrade, worsen, lower, damage, discourage. —*n.* degradation, fall, depression, demotion, impoverishment, descent.

upper *adj.* UPPERMOST.

upper hand advantage, control, mastery, rule, dominion, supremacy, ascendancy, superiority, preeminence, driver's seat, whip hand, catbird seat.

ant. disadvantage, back seat, second fiddle.

uppermost *adj.* highest, top, foremost, predominant, preeminent, topmost, supreme, loftiest, leading, dominant, paramount, greatest, principal, utmost, upper.

ant. lowest, least, slightest, humblest, lowliest, lowermost.

uppish *adj.* UPPITY.

uppity *adj.* arrogant, overweening, haughty, snippy, proud, uppish, presumptuous, impertinent, self-important, conceited, snobbish, stuck-up.

ant. humble, meek, servile, lowly, unassuming, obsequious.

upraise *v.* ELEVATE.

upright *adj.* **1** vertical, erect, perpendicular, upstanding, on end, stand-up, plumb. **2** righteous, just, honest, upstanding, virtuous, scrupulous, honorable, true, trustworthy, aboveboard, straightforward, veracious.

ant. 1 horizontal, prone, recumbent, prostrate, lying. **2** dishonest, dishonorable, corrupt, devious, wicked.

uprising *n.* revolt, insurrection, mutiny, insurgence, riot, upheaval, rebellion, revolution, putsch, disturbance, outbreak, coup d'état, takeover.

uproar *n.* **1** chaos, disturbance, mayhem, commotion, turmoil, turbulence, riot, confusion, upheaval, hubbub, fracas, violence, conflict, pandemonium, damage. **2** din, noise, clangor, tumult, clamor, hubbub, hurly-burly, outcry, hullabaloo, racket.

ant. 1 serenity, tranquillity, peace, order, calm. **2** quiet, stillness, silence, peace, calm.

uproarious *adj.* **1** loud, noisy, clamorous, clangorous, tumultuous, boisterous, rowdy, stentorian, obstreperous, deafening, raging, brazen. **2** hilarious, ludicrous, sidesplitting, absurd, rollicking, convulsing, gleeful, comical, funny, rib-tickling.

ant. 1 quiet, inaudible, low-key, still. **2** sad, morose, serious, mournful, sorrowful.

uproot *v.* extirpate, extract, pluck out, pull up, root up, root out, grub, weed out, dig up, unearth, deracinate, exile, displace.

ups and downs vicissitudes, fluctuations, changes, ebb and flow, the breaks.

upset *v.* **1** overturn, overthrow, capsize, tip over, topple, upturn, overset, upend, invert. **2** confuse, disturb, agitate, disquiet, bewilder, fluster, unnerve, derange, perturb, disconcert, ruffle, dismay. —*n.* disorder, disturbance, derangement, perturbation, indisposition, illness, complaint, malady, disease, prostration, disquiet, agitation, discomposure, turbulence. —*adj.* **1** overturned, overthrown, capsized, toppled, upturned, overset, upended, inverted, upside-down. **2** confused, disturbed, agitated, disquieted, bewildered, flustered, unnerved, deranged, perturbed, disconcerted, ruffled, dismayed, overwrought.

ant. *v.* **1** erect, pick up, set right, reinstate, steady. **2** soothe, quiet, lull, calm, comfort, pacify. *adj.* **1** upright, standing, erect, vertical, perpendicular. **2** calm, quiet, pacified, unperturbed, unruffled.

upshot *n.* outcome, result, eventuality, denouement, conclusion, termination, consummation, finale, effect, payoff, climax, development, product, sequel, end.

upstage *adj.* HAUGHTY.

upstanding *adj.* UPRIGHT.

upstart *n.* parvenu, arriviste, social climber, vulgarian, pretender, nouveau riche.

upswing *n.* upturn, improvement, upsurge, revival, recovery, betterment, amelioration, rise, advance, lift, increase, headway.

ant. downturn, decline, dip, slump, depression.

uptake *n.* UNDERSTANDING.

uptight *adj. Slang* uneasy, anxious, nervous, disconcerted, tense, bothered, on edge, jittery, restive, rattled, worried, distressed, concerned, perturbed, paranoid.

ant. relaxed, easy, lighthearted, resilient, carefree, nonchalant.

up-to-date *adj.* **1** recent, current, latest, new, neoteric, prevailing, up-to-the-minute, contemporary, late, modern, present. **2** fashionable, new, modish, avant-garde, new-fangled, current, modern, up-to-the-minute, now, newest, latest, in, contemporary, trendy (*Slang*).

ant. 1 old, obsolete, former, once, historic, out-of-date. **2** old-fashioned, passé, out-of-date, antiquated, dated.

upturn *n.* UPSWING.

upward *adv.* aloft, high, higher, overhead, above, up, over, atop, upstairs, skyward, skywards, unhill, upwards.

ant. down, downward, lower, under, below.

urban *adj.* citified, metropolitan, municipal, civic, burghal, oppidan.

ant. rural, countrified, rustic, bucolic, pastoral.

urbane *adj.* polite, courteous, suave, diplomatic, polished, sophisticated, smooth, politic, civil, mannerly, refined, well-bred, elegant.

ant. rude, bluff, discourteous, clownish, impolite, bucolic.

urchin *n.* **1** child, lad, shaver, kid, scamp, imp, brat. **2** guttersnipe, street Arab, gamin.

urge *v.* **1** force, drive, goad, spur, hasten, speed, push, impel, incite, stimulate, propel, press. **2** plead, beg, exhort, implore, advocate, entreat, press, egg on, beseech, encourage, solicit. —*n.* drive, yen, longing, yearning, itch, impulse, tendency, wish, desire, motivation, urgency.

ant. *v.* **1** deter, restrain, rein, check, hold back. **2** discourage, caution, dissuade, remonstrate, warn. —*n.* reluctance, distaste, repugnance, aversion, indisposition, antipathy.

urgency *n.* insistence, importunity, exigency, immediacy, entreaty, pressure, stress, necessity, seriousness, gravity, importance, tenacity, solicitousness, positiveness, perseverance, pertinacity.

ant. irresolution, vacillation, slackness, negligence, unimportance.

urgent *adj.* pressing, exigent, compelling, important, imperative, crucial, demanding, critical, momentous, immediate, grave, weighty.

ant. unimportant, frivolous, trifling, insignificant, unessential, unnecessary.

urinate *v.* micturate, pass water, make water, wet, void, eliminate, pee, piss, wee-wee, pee-pee, tinkle.

urn *n.* **1** vase, jar, container, jardiniere, receptacle, cachepot, amphora, ossuary, crock, cruse, pot. **2** samovar, coffee maker, pot.

usage *n.* **1** treatment, utilization, employment, use, application, procedure, disposition, operation, manipulation, regulation, conduct, handling. **2** custom, use, practice, habit, mode, method, fashion, way, wont, convention, vogue, tradition, routine, regime, pattern, groove, rut.

use *v.* **1** utilize, employ, make use of, operate, wield, turn to account, have recourse to, take advantage of, ply,

put to use. **2** treat, behave toward, handle, act toward, care for, deal with, manage, supervise, control, boss. **3** exploit, take advantage of, misuse, milk, manipulate, maneuver. —*n.* **1** utilization, employment, disposition, exercise, application, exploitation, service, function, action, practice. **2** function, enjoyment, support, instrumentality, service, help, assistance, usefulness, advantage, benefit, avail, utility, help, good, convenience. **3** purpose, object, point, end, service, function, utility, value, significance, import. **4** USAGE.

used *adj.* secondhand, worn, timeworn, hand-me-down, shopworn, threadbare, tattered, stale, shabby, ragged, old, worn-out, outworn.

ant. unused, brand-new, virgin, fresh, new.

used to accustomed to, habituated to, familiar with, given to, wont to, inured to, addicted to, attuned to, conversant with, at home in, tolerant of.

ant. unused to, unaccustomed to, intolerant of, unfamiliar with, strange to.

useful *adj.* serviceable, helpful, profitable, beneficial, useable, workable, practicable, utilitarian, instrumental, advantageous, effectual, applicable, fruitful, conducive, salutary.

ant. useless, worthless, inapplicable, unprofitable, vain, fruitless.

useless *adj.* futile, unavailing, ineffectual, unserviceable, worthless, fruitless, valueless, inept, vain, idle, profitless, bootless, feckless, unusable, hopeless.

ant. useful, worthwhile, workable, profitable, practical, fruitful.

use up expend, exhaust, consume, devour, absorb, deplete, wear out, burn up, run through, finish, dissipate, squander, fritter away, swallow up, waste, drain.

ant. save, spare, husband, conserve, hoard, stint.

usher *n.* guide, attendant, escort, conductor, porter, doorkeeper, ostiary, gatekeeper, guard. —*v.* **1** accompany, escort, conduct, squire, show, guide, lead, direct, convoy, marshal. **2** introduce, herald, launch, inaugurate, ring in, precede, induct, initiate, originate, open the door to, pave the way for.

usual *adj.* customary, common, everyday, general, ordinary, prevalent, accustomed, wonted, habitual, familiar, normal, regular, frequent, expected.
ant. uncommon, rare, unusual, unexpected, infrequent, sparse.

usurp *v.* take, take over, seize, commandeer, lay hold of, possess, appropriate, wrest, encroach, arrogate, exact, claim, assume, infringe upon, trespass, steal.

utensil *n.* vessel, tool, implement, instrument, receptacle, container, holder, device, apparatus, gadget.

utilitarian *adj.* practical, pragmatic, functional, realistic, down-to-earth, sensible, efficacious, useful, helpful, handy, serviceable, convenient.
ant. impractical, visionary, utopian, fanciful, worthless.

utility *n.* usefulness, fitness, practicality, functionality, avail, use, benefit, convenience, advantage, point, profit, efficacy, service, serviceableness.

utilize *v.* USE.

utmost *adj.* **1** maximal, maximum, extreme, greatest, largest, highest, most, supreme, sovereign, best, uttermost. **2** remotest, outermost, ultimate, extreme, final, end, terminal, top, uppermost, uttermost, last, farthest. *n.* most, best, greatest, highest, last word, perfection, zenith, acme, tops (*Slang*), *ne plus ultra.*
ant. **1** minimal, least, poorest, minimum, smallest. **2** immediate, neighboring, nearest, next, adjoining, adjacent.

utopia *n.* Eden, Elysian fields, New Jerusalem, satori, nirvana, salvation, paradise, bliss, golden age, perfection, Shangri-la.
ant. hell, inferno, the abyss, Tartarus, Hades, purgatory.

utter[1] *v.* say, express, give out, vocalize, articulate, enunciate, talk, sound, speak, voice, pronounce, announce, declare, divulge, reveal.

utter[2] *adj.* extreme, quintessential, utmost, veriest, complete, total, thorough, overwhelming, absolute, arrant, maximal, unqualified, unconditional.

utterance *n.* **1** vocalization, expression, speech, talk, pronunciation, enunciation, articulation, delivery, accent. **2** pronouncement, words, locution, expression, statement, declaration, announcement, speech, remark, disclosure, account, story.

uttermost *adj.* UTMOST.

V

vacancy *n.* emptiness, void, vacuum, vacuity, vacuousness, hollowness, depletion, blankness, nothingness, space, hole, gap.
ant. fullness, plenitude, completeness, profusion.

vacant *adj.* **1** empty, depleted, used up, hollow, vacuous, blank, void, bare, unfilled, devoid. **2** unoccupied, untenanted, unrented, unlived-in, unused, available, to let, rentable, tenantless, unleased, uninhabited, idle, forsaken, abandoned. **3** emptyheaded, foolish, stupid, stupefied, meaningless, senseless, inane, glassy-eyed, vacuous, blank, absent-

minded, inattentive, bemused, dead-pan (*Slang*), oblivious, withdrawn.
ant. 1 full, filled, replete, packed, stuffed. **2** occupied, lived-in, rented. **3** attentive, intelligent, alert, knowing, aware.

vacate *v.* ANNUL.

vacation *n.* holiday, rest, relaxation, ease, furlough, respite, repose, leisure, sabbatical, leave, breathing-spell, breather, break.
ant. work, labor, daily grind, routine, rat race (*Slang*).

vacillate *v.* waver, wobble, totter, see-saw, shift, oscillate, fluctuate, shilly-shally, flounder, hem and haw, back and fill, blow hot and cold, alternate.

vacuity *n.* **1** void, vacuum, vacuous-ness, emptiness, space, blankness, nothingness, vacancy, gap, hole, hiatus, interruption, interval, blank. **2** ignorance, stupidity, unawareness, unresponsiveness, foolishness, brain-lessness, inanity, senselessness, insensibility, mindlessness, imbecility, idiocy, incomprehension. **3** nonsense, absurdity, chatter, prattle, froth, trash, hogwash, bunk (*Slang*), hot air (*Slang*).
ant. 1 fullness, substance, matter, content. **2** intelligence, brains, gray matter, knowledge.

vacuous *adj.* blank, stupid, un-comprehending, vacant, dull, inane, mindless, empty-headed, imbecilic, dimwitted (*Slang*), unintelligent, fatuous, foolish, besotted, bovine, dumb, unaware, thoughtless, inatten-tive, distracted, distrait, absent-minded.
ant. alert, responsive, intelligent, bright, knowledgeable, attentive, aware.

vacuum *n.* emptiness, void, gap, blank, hollow, chasm, vacancy, vacuity, nothingness, abyss, hole.

vagabond *adj.* **1** wandering, nomadic, footloose, peripatetic, roving, migra-tory, gadabout, unsettled, wayfaring, itinerant, transient, vagrant, drift-ing. **2** homeless, rootless, irrespon-

sible, shiftless, aimless, ne'er-do-well, good-for-nothing, truant, fly-by-night, harum-scarum, improvident, disreputable, happy-go-lucky, beg-garly. —*n.* VAGRANT.
ant. 1 established, installed, an-chored, rooted. **2** responsible, hard-working, ambitious, reliable.

vagary *n.* whim, notion, fancy, caprice, quirk, daydream, crotchet, fantasy, impulse, conceit, chimera, whimsy, kink.

vagrant *n.* drifter, tramp, vagabond, beggar, bum, parasite, freeloader, beachcomber, hobo, good-for-noth-ing, ne'er-do-well, cadge, sponger, outcast, pilferer. —*adj.* aimless, way-ward, unsettled, irresponsible, vaga-bond, shiftless, unemployed, jobless.
ant. *adj.* settled, rooted, employed, purposeful, ambitious.

vague *adj.* **1** indefinite, unspecified, un-certain, unfixed, intangible, mysteri-ous, confusing, casual, random, un-specific, doubtful, inconclusive, problematic. **2** blurry, misty, foggy, blurred, shadowy, fuzzy, unfocused, impalpable, hazy, cloudy, nebulous, dreamlike, filmy, dim, beclouded. **3** ambiguous, muddled, muddle-headed, unclear, obscure, abstruse, enigmatic, cryptic, equivocal, in-comprehensible, absent-minded, be-fuddled, perplexed.
ant. 1 specific, definite, certain, specified, spelled out. **2** sharp, out-lined, contoured, distinct. **3** obvious, comprehensible, practical, unambig-uous.

vain *adj.* **1** conceited, haughty, af-fected, proud, self-important, smug, self-righteous, self-satisfied, preen-ing, narcissistic, egotistical, arro-gant, complacent, boastful, super-cilious, cocky, stuck-up, swaggering, swell-headed. **2** futile, useless, worth-less, sterile, unproductive, ineffec-tual, unprofitable, unavailing, ineffective, unyielding, unrewarding, barren, empty, unreal, fanciful, un-founded, imaginary.

ant. 1 humble, self-effacing, modest, diffident. **2** effective, rewarding, realistic, practical, productive.

vainglory *n.* VANITY.

vale *n.* VALLEY.

valentine *n.* SWEETHEART.

valet *n.* manservant, body servant, dresser, man, groom, attendant, man Friday, flunky, gentleman's gentleman.

valiant *adj.* valorous, courageous, intrepid, heroic, powerful, strong, unflinching, brave, daring, stalwart, bold, undaunted, gallant, gutsy (*Slang*).

ant. cowardly, weak, timid, craven, fearful.

valid *adj.* **1** proven, sound, cogent, conclusive, well-grounded, validated, effective, potent, substantial, substantiated, undeniable, logical, inescapable, weighty, viable, sufficient, justifiable. **2** authentic, incontestable, bona fide, legitimate, genuine, enforceable, official, undisputed, irrefutable, binding, legal, lawful.

ant. 1 unconvincing, unproved, unsound, vague, ineffective. **2** invalid, null, void.

validate *v.* substantiate, corroborate, authenticate, confirm, support, uphold, prove, authorize, sanction, certify, bear out, vindicate, sustain, verify, warrant.

ant. contradict, disprove, negate, cancel.

validation *n.* APPROVAL.

valise *n.* suitcase, travel case, satchel, grip, bag, carryall, carrying case, luggage, baggage, attaché case.

valley *n.* dell, dale, glen, vale, lowland, hollow, gully, basin, chasm, gorge, concavity, gulch, ravine, bowl, crater.

ant. hill, highland, headland, upland, rise.

valor *n.* bravery, heroism, intrepidity, boldness, stamina, courage, dauntlessness, fearlessness, fortitude, gallantry, mettle, nerve, spunk, toughness, guts (*Slang*), grit.

ant. cowardice, fear, timidity, cold feet.

valuable *adj.* **1** costly, expensive, high-priced, dear, extravagant, exorbitant, luxurious, luxury, deluxe, lavish, sumptuous. **2** valued, estimable, precious, worthy, irreplaceable, cherished, worthwhile, meritorious, treasured, esteemed, invaluable, admirable, choice, special, praiseworthy.

ant. 1 cheap, shoddy, trifling, schlocky (*Slang*). **2** disdained, worthless, detestable, contemptible.

valuation *n.* ESTIMATE.

value *n.* **1** merit, worth, desirability, purpose, use, good, benefit, advantage, profit, usefulness, worthiness, importance, avail, efficacy, significance. **2** ideal, standard, ethic, credo, belief, yardstick, model, criterion, guide, example, precept, tenet, goal, purpose. **3** market price, purchasing power, buying power, face value, real value, evaluation, estimation, worth, quotation, equivalent. —*v.* **1** evaluate, assess, appraise, weigh, price, balance, judge, rate, measure, size up, compute, determine, reckon, calculate. **2** prize, cherish, hold dear, love, guard, safeguard, protect, esteem, treasure, appreciate, admire, respect.

ant. *v.* **2** disdain, disregard, despise, scorn, spurn.

valueless *adj.* WORTHLESS.

vamoose *v. Slang* LEAVE.

vamp[1] *v.* PATCH.

vamp[2] *n.* siren, *femme fatale*, flirt, temptress, seductress, enchantress, coquette, Circe, Lorelei, sorceress, vampire.

van *n.* truck, wagon, transport, cart, dray, trailer, lorry (*Brit.*).

vandal *n.* wrecker, saboteur, hooligan, delinquent, plunderer, looter, destroyer, pillager, barbarian, savage, iconoclast, marauder, arsonist, housebreaker, Hun.

vanguard *n.* **1** front, lead, van, head, spearhead, forefront, front line, leadership, fore. **2** leaders, trendsetters, tastemakers, avant-garde, pioneers, pacemakers, pacesetters, harbingers, heralds, precursors, forerunners, experimenters, unorthodox, modernists, innovators, bellwethers, leadership.

ant. 1 rear, back, rearguard. **2** conservatives, orthodox, standpatters.

vanish *v.* disappear, fade away, evanesce, sink, melt, dissolve, die, die out, go, depart, leave, be gone, perish, evaporate, end, withdraw, exit.

ant. appear, arrive, enter, remain.

vanity *n.* vainglory, conceit, narcissism, egotism, self-admiration, self-conceit, self-praise, self-glorification, smugness, bragging, arrogance, hauteur, boastfulness.

ant. humility, self-effacement, modesty, diffidence.

vanquish *v.* **1** conquer, defeat, best, outdo, defeat, overwhelm, subjugate, crush, humble, rout, overthrow, triumph, drub, surpass, lick. **2** transcend, control, surmount, overcome, master, overpower, prevail, suppress, subdue, eliminate, eradicate, extirpate, wipe out, blot out.

vantage *n.* advantage, superiority, dominance, authority, ascendancy, leadership, purchase, footing, pull, influence, power, clout (*Slang*), in.

ant. handicap, hindrance, vulnerability, disadvantage, drawback.

vapid *adj.* **1** tasteless, flat, insipid, flavorless, stale, weak, wishy-washy, watery, unpalatable, unsavory. **2** boring, dull, uninteresting, pointless, jejune, insipid, lifeless, sterile, inane, meaningless, vacuous, monotonous, tedious, tiresome, senseless, blah (*Slang*).

ant. 1 sparkling, bubbly, zesty, tasty, savory. **2** exciting, colorful, lively, provocative, zingy (*Slang*).

vapor *n.* moisture, mist, fog, haze, steam, cloud, smoke, dew, smog, exhalation, miasma, emanation, film, spray, dampness, humidity.

vaporize *v.* humidify, mist, steam, reek, evaporate, distill, fume, exhale, gasify, spray, atomize, volatilize.

ant. dehydrate, dehumidify, dry, desiccate.

vaporous *adj.* misty, foggy, damp, humid, befogged, dewy, hazy, smoggy, steamy, cloudy, miasmic, moist, murky, muggy, nebulous.

ant. dry, clear, bright.

variable *adj.* **1** alterable, modifiable, changeable, flexible, elastic, unfixed, mutable, transformable, versatile, protean, adjustable, convertible, reversible. **2** unsteady, unstable, volatile, mercurial, unreliable, undependable, fluctuating, inconstant, wayward, fickle, capricious, contingent. —*n.* uncertainty, contingency, unknown, possibility, risk, fortuity, happenstance.

ant. *adj.* **1** immutable, unchangeable, fixed, rigid. **2** steady, stable, predictable, regular, reliable. *n.* certainty, sure thing, constant.

variance *n.* **1** VARIATION. **2** discrepancy, difference, variation, modulation, divergence, deviation, incongruity, distinction, dissimilarity, inconsistency. **3** dispute, disagreement, altercation, misunderstanding, quarrel, argument, controversy, schism, division, breach, dissension, incompatibility, contention, squabble.

ant. 2 similarity, equivalence, correspondence, congruity. **3** accord, unison, agreement.

variant *adj.* VARYING.

variation *n.* **1** modification, variance, change, alteration, modulation, mutation, aberration, transformation, variegation, assortment, diversification, transfiguration, transmogrification, metamorphosis. **2** VARIANCE.

varicolored *adj.* VARIEGATED.

varied *adj.* assorted, diversified, heterogeneous, diverse, variegated, various, miscellaneous, different, differing, sundry, mixed, motley, dissimilar.

ant. homogeneous, monotonous, uniform, duplicate.

variegate *v.* DIVERSIFY.

variegated *adj.* streaked, pied, mottled, dappled, varicolored, rainbow, iridescent, multicolor, checkered, kaleidoscopic, opalescent, marbled, speckled, brindled, striped. **ant.** uniform, monotone, monochromatic, unvarying.

variety *n.* **1** diversity, variation, difference, dissimilarity, change, nuance, variegation, heterogeneity, nonconformity, multiplicity. **2** sort, kind, type, brand, make, class, description, category, grade, classification, genre, species, ilk, strain, kidney. **3** collection, assortment, mixture, potpourri, farrago, melange, miscellany, hodgepodge, medley, olio, salmagundi. **ant. 1** monotony, sameness, similarity, homogeneity, invariability.

various *adj.* **1** varying, diverse, assorted, differing, several, sundry, mixed, miscellaneous, heterogeneous, manifold. **2** particular, identifiable, individual, different, classifiable, specific, respective, separate, special. **3** unlike, dissimilar, changing, disparate, divergent, incongruous, distinct, distinguishable, unmatched, discrepant, unrelated. **ant. 3** similar, equivalent, matching, alike.

varmint *n.* VERMIN.

vary *v.* **1** change, modify, alter, transform, modulate, transmute, transmogrify, reshape, reform, redo, refashion, temper, metamorphose, transfigure. **2** assort, diversify, mix, intermix, variegate, scramble, contrast, jumble, mottle, shade, deviate, depart, diverge.

varying *adj.* differing, changing, shifting, fluctuating, different, distinct, variable, variant, flexible, distinguishable, alternating, unfixed, unpredictable. **ant.** unvarying, monotonous, settled, regular, fixed.

vase *n.* urn, pot, flower-holder, vessel, jar, jug, amphora, jardiniere.

vassal *n.* underling, hireling, subordinate, minion, flunkey, serf, henchman, myrmidon, yes-man, satrap, puppet, satellite, subject, slave, dependent, gofer (*Slang*). **ant.** boss, ruler, overlord, top dog, master.

vast *adj.* immense, enormous, extensive, tremendous, significant, substantial, huge, weighty, consequential, limitless, boundless, immeasurable, widespread, great. **ant.** small, limited, narrow, paltry, tiny.

vat *n.* tub, tank, cistern, bath, vessel, carboy, caldron, cask, keg, bucket, tun, boiler.

vault *v.* leap, spring, jump, hurdle, clear, bound, leapfrog, pole-vault, hop. —*n.* leap, spring, jump, bound, long jump, broad jump, pole vault, hop.

vaunt *v.* boast, brag, swagger, strut, show off, vapor, triumph, parade, gloat, jubilate, exaggerate, crow, talk big (*Slang*), blow one's own horn (*Slang*).

veer *v.* **1** shift, turn, swerve, tack, swing, zigzag, deviate, depart, diverge, curve, dodge, drift. **2** deviate, tergiversate, switch, defect, desert, apostatize, secede, differ, divagate, diverge.

vegetable *n.* cipher, nullity, blob, cretin, simpleton, zombie (*Slang*), imbecile, idiot, moron, natural, defective, dotard. —*adj.* IDLE.

vegetarian *adj.* herbivorous.

vegetate *v.* stagnate, languish, aestivate, molder, idle, deteriorate, go to seed, mope, laze, loaf, droop, mark time, waste away, twiddle one's thumbs. **ant.** participate, respond, react, develop, accomplish, bustle, grow, bloom.

vegetation *n.* verdure, flora, plants, greenery, plant life.

vegetative *adj.* IDLE.

vehemence *n.* PASSION.

vehement *adj.* forceful, impassioned, violent, ardent, fervent, zealous, fierce, intense, powerful, energetic, fiery, inflamed, heated, excited, furious. **ant.** mild, weak, tame, timid, apathetic, cool.

vehicle *n.* means, medium, agency, instrument, tool, channel, mechanism, agent, wherewithal, device, apparatus, intermediary, instrumentality.

veil *n.* cover, protection, screen, mask, camouflage, disguise, blind, curtain, covering, shade, shield, shroud. —*v.* screen, cover, conceal, hide, mask, cloak, camouflage, disguise, protect, shelter, shroud, dissemble. **ant.** *v.* reveal, uncover, expose, display, disclose.

vein *n.* manner, style, attitude, strain, spirit, note, thread, quality, tenor, course, mood, tendency, disposition.

velocity *n.* speed, pace, tempo, rapidity, swiftness, celerity, fleetness, quickness.

velvety *adj.* SMOOTH.

venal *ad.* corrupt, bribable, mercenary, corruptible, unprincipled, rotten, untrustworthy, dishonest, disreputable, shady, crooked, unscrupulous, criminal. **ant.** honest, upright, incorruptible, law-abiding.

vend *v.* SELL.

vendible *adj.* COMMERCIAL.

vendor *n.* seller, purveyor, tradesman, shopkeeper, retailer, merchant, trader, marketer, marketeer, dealer, huckster, peddler, monger. **ant.** buyer, customer, purchaser, client, patron.

veneer *n.* pretense, facade, false front, cover-up, appearance, guise, show, semblance, dissimulation, exterior, camouflage, surface, affectation, air. —*v.* cover up, whitewash, camouflage, varnish, gloss over, disguise, conceal, mask, screen, hide, launder, misrepresent, falsify, dissimulate, dissemble.

venerable *ad.* august, revered, worthy, time-honored, respectable, honorable, time-tested, reverend, holy, sacrosanct, esteemed, estimable, hallowed, illustrious. **ant.** unknown, undeserving, unworthy, disreputable, worthless.

venerate *v.* revere, respect, worship, look up to, adore, honor, hallow, glorify, esteem, exalt, saint, canonize, deify, idolize, apotheosize. **ant.** scorn, spurn, execrate, deride, mock.

veneration *n.* reverence, awe, respect, worship, adoration, deference, esteem, homage, devotion, glorification, obeisance, admiration, regard. **ant.** scorn, contempt, disrespect, derision.

venery *n.* LUST.

vengeance *n.* retribution, revenge, requital, wrath, fury, retaliation, reprisal, counterblow, counterattack, vindictiveness, nemesis, *lex talionis*. **ant.** mercy, pity, forbearance, benevolence, tolerance.

vengeful *adj.* vindictive, retaliative, wrathful, punitive, avenging, furious, spiteful, unforgiving, merciless, pitiless, ruthless, bloodthirsty, rancorous, truculent, savage. **ant.** merciful, forgiving, forbearing, humane, indulgent, lenient.

venial *adj.* forgivable, pardonable, excusable, trivial, slight, understandable, minor, petty, picayune, allowable, justifiable, paltry, unimportant, inconsequential. **ant.** inexcusable, unpardonable, egregious, unforgivable, grievous, grave.

venom *n.* **1** rancor, ill will, spite, spitefulness, malevolence, malice, hate, hatred, truculence, vindictiveness, bile, hostility, animosity, rage, spleen. **2** POISON. **ant. 1** good will, charity, kindness, mercy, pity.

venomous *adj.* **1** toxic, poisonous, envenomed, deadly, virulent, lethal,

noxious, malefic, dangerous, harmful, baneful. **2** malicious, spiteful, vindictive, caustic, truculent, cruel, hostile, vicious, savage, rancorous, acrimonious, feral, destructive.
ant. 1 harmless, nontoxic, nonpoisonous. **2** forbearing, charitable, humane, tolerant, forgiving.

vent *n.* **1** expression, airing, utterance, exposure, revelation, disclosure, representation, articulation, announcement, proclamation. **2** outlet, passage, opening, hole, duct, hatch, escape, escape hatch, escape valve, safety valve, avenue, slit, slot, pipe, spout, flue. —*v.* express, air, let out, verbalize, communicate, utter, tell, make known, let on, reveal.
ant. *v.* repress, bottle up, squelch, stifle, inhibit.

ventilate *v.* expose, air, discuss, examine, inspect, look into, dig up, uncover, bring to light, review, criticize, analyze, scrutinize, go into.
ant. bury, conceal, cover, repress, hide, suppress.

venture *v.* **1** dare, risk, gamble, chance, stake, bet, wager, hazard, lay odds, take a flyer, jeopardize, endanger, imperil, speculate, plunge. **2** dare say, proffer, think likely, put forward, hazard, opine, assume, presume, conjecture, broach, advance, bet. —*n.* risk, hazard, chance, speculation, flyer, wager, gamble, trial balloon, bet, plunge, dare, enterprise, undertaking, deal, adventure, endeavor.

venturesome *adj.* **1** bold, daring, adventurous, enterprising, ambitious, energetic, aggressive, brave, confident, hopeful, courageous, optimistic, dynamic, purposeful, venturous. **2** risky, dangerous, hazardous, uncertain, speculative, chancy, tricky, unsure, problematical, ticklish, shaky, precarious, insecure, debatable, rash, venturous.
ant. 1 timid, cowardly, lazy, aimless. **2** safe, sure, certain, secure, guaranteed.

venturous *adj.* VENTURESOME.

Venus *n.* beauty, goddess, glamour girl, Juno, belle, model, charmer, dazzler, dream girl, vision, beauty queen, eyeful (*Slang*), looker (*Slang*), knockout (*Slang*).

veracious *adj.* truthful, factual, honest, trustworthy, reliable, dependable, frank, candid, aboveboard, straightforward, genuine, scrupulous.
ant. lying, false, mendacious, deceitful, dishonest.

veracity *n.* honesty, truthfulness, candor, frankness, integrity, reliability, trustworthiness, dependability, sincerity, uprightness, rectitude, impeccability, conscientiousness, meticulousness.
ant. mendacity, dishonesty, deceitfulness, lying, duplicity.

veranda *n.* porch, gallery, balcony, terrace, deck, sunporch, lanai, piazza, loggia, portico, stoop.

verbal *adj.* **1** oral, spoken, stated, expressed, declared, voiced, unwritten, informal, nuncupative, parol. **2** VERBATIM.
ant. 1 written, formal, documented.

verbalism *n.* **1** LOCUTION. **2** VERBIAGE.

verbalize *v.* say, express, articulate, communicate, put into words, make known, speak, air, announce, pronounce, voice, utter, vent, convey, come out with.
ant. repress, contain, suppress, hide, inhibit.

verbatim *adj.* word-for-word, literal, exact, precise, verbal, scrupulous, factual, truthful, meticulous, faithful, true.
ant. garbled, inexact, misquoted, distorted.

verbiage *n.* wordiness, prolixity, verbalism, long-windedness, circumlocution, diffuseness, rigmarole, bombast, blather, loquacity, logorrhea, verbosity, garrulity, hot air (*Slang*).
ant. terseness, precision, pithiness, laconism, concision.

verbose *adj.* wordy, prolix, long-winded, diffuse, circumlocutory, bombastic, garrulous, gabby, voluble, repetitious, redundant, discursive, drawn-out.

ant. concise, laconic, direct, terse, pithy.

verbosity *n.* REDUNDANCY.

verdant *adj.* green, fresh, springlike, leafy, shady, grassy, blooming, flourishing, luxuriant, lush, verdured.

ant. fading, dying, withering, autumnal, bare.

verdict *n.* **1** decision, finding, judgment, decree, ruling, award, sentence, adjudication, determination, conclusion. **2** assertion, opinion, say-so, consensus, estimation, sentiment, inference, diagnosis, answer, response, reaction, feeling, evaluation, reading.

verdure *n.* VEGETATION.

verge[1] *n.* edge, brink, threshold, boundary, limit, border, hem, frontier, outskirts, fringe, margin, brim, extremity, curb, perimeter.

verge[2] *v.* approach, incline toward, border, tend, trend, near, come close, skirt, gravitate toward, draw near, converge, touch.

verification *n.* PROOF.

verify *v.* test, try, assay, weigh, look into, analyze, prove, probe, examine, sound, evaluate, judge, determine, estimate, ascertain.

verily *adv.* CERTAINLY.

verisimilar *adj.* PROBABLE.

verisimilitude *n.* CREDIBILITY.

veritable *adj.* genuine, true, real, actual, authentic, regular, bona fide, legitimate, sound, unquestionable, authenticated, demonstrable, incontestable, certified.

ant. false, fake, counterfeit, fictitious, fraudulent.

verity *n.* **1** truthfulness, correctness, accuracy, precision, veracity, reliability, legitimacy, authenticity, unimpeachability, fidelity, exactness, rigor, rightness, faithfulness. **2** fact,

actuality, reality, certitude, certainty, truth, axiom, truism, gospel.

ant. **1** inaccuracy, imprecision, incorrectness, untruthfulness, irregularity, mendacity. **2** lie, error, fiction, falsehood, mistake.

vermin *n.* **1** pests, varmints. **2** scum, dregs, parasite, varmint, rascal, rat, louse, snake, outcast, pariah, riffraff, trash, rabble.

vernacular *n.* jargon, lingo, shoptalk, idiom, slang, patois, argot, cant, parlance. —*adj.* popular, demotic, vulgar, common, local, folk, informal, colloquial, idiomatic, indigenous, native, dialectical, ordinary, plebeian.

vernal *adj.* YOUTHFUL.

versatile *adj.* **1** clever, ingenious, handy, gifted, resourceful, talented, many-sided, all-around, multi-faceted, adroit, inventive, competent, bright. **2** practical, useful, flexible, adaptable, convertible, convenient, handy, functional, serviceable, adjustable, all-purpose.

ant. **1** specialized, limited, one-sided. **2** impractical, useless, unfunctional.

verse *n.* **1** stanza, strophe, canto, stave, stich, versicle, jingle. **2** poetry, poesy, versification, metrics, prosody, rhyme, doggerel.

versed *adj.* proficient, trained, skilled, experienced, schooled, practiced, seasoned, educated, qualified, competent, accomplished, well-informed, conversant, able, expert.

ant. ignorant, inexperienced, unskilled, green, unfamiliar.

version *n.* rendition, rendering, translation, adaptation, description, paraphrase, reading, viewpoint, construction, understanding, interpretation, depiction, opinion, estimate, assessment.

vertex *n.* APEX.

vertical *adj.* perpendicular, upright, orthogonal, plumb.

ant. horizontal, level, prone, flat.

vertiginous *adj.* DIZZY.

verve *n.* animation, spirit, enthusiasm,

energy, élan, liveliness, dash, sparkle, zip, vivacity, eagerness, vitality, zing.

ant. dullness, sluggishness, apathy, inertia, laziness.

very *adv.* **1** extremely, unusually, uncommonly, greatly, immensely, inordinately, exceedingly, highly, intensely, deeply, especially, enormously, profoundly, hugely. **2** exactly, precisely, identically, truly, really, unquestionably, actually, literally, positively, strictly. —*adj.* **1** absolute, downright, complete, whole, utter, unmitigated, unqualified, total, out-and-out, unvarnished, plain, obvious, visible, entire, unbounded, supreme. **2** suitable, right, correct, proper, wanted, desired, desirable, appropriate, fitting, fit, applicable, perfect, relevant, necessary, requisite, essential, needed, called for.

ant. *adv.* **1** slightly, barely, hardly. *adj.* **1** more or less, partial, approximate. **2** inappropriate, wrong, unsuitable, useless.

vesicate *v.* BLISTER.

vesicle *n.* BLADDER.

vessel *n.* **1** receptacle, container, bottle, vial, pitcher, pot, pan, vase, tub, vat, cask, keg, ewer, basin. **2** ship, craft, boat.

vest *v.* entrust, delegate, empower, endow, consign, confer, bequeath, devise, invest, deputize, turn over, hand over, authorize, entitle, assign.

vestal *n.* VIRGIN.

vested *adj.* inalienable, absolute, fixed, immutable, independent, noncontingent, nontransferable, statutory, established, sanctioned, guaranteed, inviolable.

ant. provisional, contingent, variable, occasional.

vestibule *n.* entrance hall, entrance way, foyer, antechamber, hall, hallway, passage, passageway, lobby, entry, corridor, waiting room, reception room.

vestige *n.* trace, remnant, tinge, touch, remains, hint, glimmer, shadow, relic, token, record, memento, scent, scar, memory, spoor, telltale.

vestigial *adj.* rudimentary, undeveloped, imperfect, incomplete, obsolescent, useless, nonfunctional, purposeless.

ant. functional, useful, practical, developed, perfect.

vestment *n.* GARMENT.

vest-pocket *adj.* SMALL.

vesture *n.* CLOTHING.

vet *n.* VETERAN.

veteran *n.* old hand, master, professional, adept, crackerjack, past master, pro, expert, authority, old-timer, vet. —*adj.* experienced, adept, practiced, seasoned, battle-scarred, conversant, versed, proficient, professional, masterly, knowledgeable, knowing, crackerjack.

ant. *n.* beginner, tyro, neophyte, apprentice. *adj.* green, inexperienced, raw, unschooled.

veto *v.* disapprove, negate, forbid, discountenance, turn down, reject, prohibit, bar, ban, restrain, disallow, taboo, interdict, nix (*Slang*), put the kibosh on (*Slang*). —*n.* disapproval, cancellation, prohibition, rejection, disallowance, restraint, ban, refusal, turndown, no, thumbs down, taboo.

ant. *v.* approve, consent, uphold, support, ratify. *n.* approval, support, consent, permission, ratification.

vex *v.* irritate, annoy, trouble, plague, irk, pester, pique, chagrin, bother, disturb, rile, grate, provoke, distress, bug (*Slang*).

ant. comfort, soothe, please, mollify, gratify.

vexation *n.* trouble, irritation, annoyance, bother, distress, provocation, aggravation, burden, affliction, sorrow, worry, grievance, distress, harassment.

ant. comfort, balm, pleasure, blessing, gratification.

vexatious *adj.* annoying, harassing, troublesome, irritating, irksome, bothersome, disturbing, burden-

some, provoking, plaguy, chafing, galling, exasperating, nerve-racking, nettlesome.
ant. soothing, pleasant, relaxing, agreeable, comforting, balmy.

viable *adj.* **1** alive, living, vital, sprouting, developing, growing. **2** workable, practicable, effectual, practical, operative, feasible, useful, doable, possible, promising.
ant. 2 ineffectual, impracticable, futile, unworkable.

viands *n.* VICTUALS.

vibrant *adj.* **1** vibrating, pulsing, pulsating, throbbing, resonating, resonant, sonorous, reverberating, reverberant, resounding, ringing. **2** vigorous, strong, alive, vital, energetic, sound, spirited, active, animated, lively, sparkling, powerful, potent, forceful, eager, ardent.
ant. 2 weak, thin, feeble, sluggish, inactive.

vibrate *v.* **1** oscillate, waver, beat, pulse, pulsate, sway, fluctuate, throb, undulate, swing, pendulate. **2** resound, resonate, echo, reecho, reverberate, ring, peal, clang, boom, rumble.

vicarious *adj.* surrogate, sympathetic, indirect, empathetic, at one remove, secondhand, by proxy.
ant. direct, personal, firsthand, own, proper.

vice *n.* **1** depravity, evil, wickedness, sinfulness, profligacy, wantonness, corruption, venality, dissoluteness, degeneracy, debauchery, immorality, licentiousness, evildoing, brutality. **2** weakness, frailty, sin, transgression, trespass, lapse, delinquency, wrong, violation, misdeed, dereliction, outrage, crime, bad habit, compulsion.

vicinity *n.* **1** nearness, proximity, closeness, propinquity, adjacence, contiguity, juxtaposition, apposition, affinity, juncture. **2** neighborhood, surroundings, bounds, confines, precincts, environs, purlieus.

vicious *adj.* **1** depraved, debauched, evil, wicked, sinful, immoral, wanton,

profligate, rotten, corrupt, venal, debased, dissolute, degenerate, vile, villainous, miscreant. **2** spiteful, malicious, nasty, cutting, hurtful, cruel, venomous, hostile, mean-spirited, vindictive, slanderous, merciless, unprovoked, unforgivable, bitchy (*Slang*).
ant. 1 upright, decent, virtuous, moral, righteous, puritanical. **2** kind, gentle, good-natured, sympathetic, friendly.

vicissitudes *n.* ups and downs, changes, variations, chance, shifts, fortune, fate, lot, destiny, luck, adventures.

victim *n.* **1** casualty, sufferer, martyr, prey, fatality, patient, invalid, case. **2** dupe, easy mark, gull, scapegoat, butt, target, innocent, lamb, patsy (*Slang*), pigeon (*Slang*), sitting duck (*Slang*), sucker (*Slang*), fall guy (*Slang*).

victimize *v.* **1** abuse, prey on, exploit, maltreat, injure, persecute, oppress, enslave, wrong, brutalize, attack, martyrize, assault. **2** dupe, cheat, fool, gull, swindle, defraud, mislead, seduce, betray, delude, take in, trick, bamboozle, outwit, double-cross (*Slang*).

victor *n.* winner, master, champion, conqueror, ace, hero, medalist, vanquisher, world-beater, number 1, champ (*Slang*), top dog (*Slang*). —*adj.* VICTORIOUS.
ant. *n.* loser, also-ran, failure, flop.

Victorian *adj.* proper, prudish, prim, puritanical, stuffy, conventional, self-satisfied, self-righteous, smug, hypocritical, philistine, illiberal, intolerant, priggish, narrow, bigoted, sanctimonious, pietistic, pharisaic, provincial, insular.
ant. liberal, broad-minded, unconventional, bohemian.

victorious *adj.* triumphant, victor, winning, successful, conquering, top, first, ascendant, prime, unbeaten, undefeated, jubilant, exultant.
ant. losing, unsuccessful, beaten, bested, defeated, humbled.

victory *n.* success, triumph, mastery, ascendancy, conquest, supremacy, masterstroke, coup, win, landslide, domination, primacy.
ant. defeat, failure, loss, downfall.

victuals *n.* **1** meals, nourishment, eats, diet, food, viands, vittles, meat, edibles, comestibles, fare, substance, cooking, cuisine, grub (*Slang*). **2** supplies, provisions, rations, provender, larder, commissary, groceries, stores, stock.

vie *v.* compete, contend, strive, emulate, rival, contest, challenge, tilt, run against, oppose, wrestle, grapple, tussle.

view *n.* **1** examination, survey, inspection, consideration, attention, glance, once-over, eye, look, observation, contemplation, scrutiny, scanning, investigation, reconnaissance. **2** vista, scene, setting, landscape, prospect, panorama, outlook, spectacle, image, sight, vision. **3** purpose, prospect, goal, aim, ambition, object, objective, target, intention, hope, desideratum. **4** opinion, judgment, perspective, point of view, viewpoint, attitude, belief, impression, concept, reaction, inference, verdict, finding, advice, diagnosis. —*v.* **1** see, behold, look at, notice, witness, observe, perceive, glimpse, note, discern, gaze, stare. **2** examine, scrutinize, scan, inspect, survey, investigate, study, analyze, explore, reconnoiter, look into, pore over. **3** deem, regard, consider, reflect, review, react, think, contemplate, gauge, envisage, judge, reason, fancy, cogitate, believe, suppose.

viewpoint *n.* POINT OF VIEW.

vigilance *n.* CAUTION.

vigilant *adj.* watchful, wary, alert, cautious, circumspect, heedful, on guard, guarded, wide-awake, careful, attentive, observant, canny, on the qui vive, on the lookout.
ant. dozing, unwary, careless, preoccupied, unconcerned, blind, trusting.

vignette *n.* sketch, profile, anecdote,

characterization, slice of life, study, tale, word picture, depiction, portrayal, thumbnail sketch.

vigor *n.* **1** strength, prowess, might, vim, fitness, sturdiness, energy, soundness, vitality, robustness, stamina, zip, muscle. **2** power, potency, effectiveness, intensity, force, fervor, vehemence, zeal, gusto, spirit, verve, ardor, forcefulness, impact, passion.
ant. **1** weakness, debility, feebleness, infirmity, fragility. **2** apathy, coolness, ineffectuality, indifference, lukewarmness.

vigorous *adj.* strong, sturdy, energetic, mighty, red-blooded, robust, lusty, forceful, intense, powerful, fervid, spirited, hardy, vehement, zealous, peppy, forceful, ardent, passionate.
ant. weak, flabby, slack, feeble, apathetic.

vile *adj.* **1** corrupt, evil, wicked, vicious, dishonorable, venal, sinful, debauched, debased, immoral, villainous, profligate, contemptible, base. **2** disgusting, awful, terrible, rotten, miserable, loathsome, nauseating, filthy, foul, wretched, scandalous, revolting, repulsive, dreadful, lousy (*Slang*).
ant. **1** righteous, moral, honorable, upright, virtuous. **2** appealing, attractive, appetizing, wonderful, excellent.

vilification *n.* slander, libel, defamation, mudslinging, smear, slur, denigration, character assassination, abuse, ridicule, disparagement, invective, calumny, accusation, name-calling.
ant. praise, accolade, commendation, acclaim, approbation.

village *n.* municipality, hamlet, town, suburb, crossroads.

villain *n.* scoundrel, fiend, brute, rotter, rascal, knave, libertine, cur, swindler, blackguard, evildoer, snake-in-the-grass, rogue, reprobate, miscreant.
ant. hero, prince, nice guy, idol.

villainous *adj.* wicked, evil, sinful,

fiendish, immoral, criminal, satanic, vile, vicious, infamous, detestable, hateful, diabolical, cruel, inhuman, inhumane, miscreant. **ant.** virtuous, heroic, saintly, righteous, moral, humane.

villainy *n.* CRIME.

vim *n.* VIGOR.

vincible *adj.* VULNERABLE.

vindicable *adj.* JUSTIFIABLE.

vindicate *v.* clear, exonerate, excuse, exculpate, reprieve, acquit, absolve, pardon, discharge, free, whitewash. **ant.** accuse, blame, inculpate, punish, blacken.

vindictive *adj.* vengeful, spiteful, malicious, retaliatory, unforgiving, unmerciful, merciless, revengeful, bitter, rancorous, implacable, inexorable, pitiless, hardhearted, retributive. **ant.** forgiving, charitable, merciful, clement, lenient.

vinegary *adj.* ACID.

vintage *n.* crop, yield, return, output, produce, production, harvest, ingathering, collection, achievement.

violate *v.* **1** break, infringe, transgress, trespass, shirk, disobey, disregard, defy, oppose, resist, overlook, contravene. **2** profane, desecrate, offend, disdain, disrespect, dishonor, outrage, blaspheme, repudiate, mock, scorn, revile, deride, maltreat, defile, sully. **3** interfere, impinge, impose, intrude, interrupt, encroach, invade, usurp, overstep, appropriate, disturb, obtrude, break in. **4** ravish, rape, deflower, take by force, abuse, assault, molest. **ant. 1** comply, observe, obey, heed, uphold. **2** respect, honor, esteem, venerate, cherish.

violence *n.* **1** destructiveness, brutality, force, fury, rage, savagery, passion, frenzy, truculence, ferocity, explosiveness, madness, bloodthirstiness, murderousness. **2** intensity, severity, turbulence, power, tumult, wildness, roughness, extremity, magnitude, harshness, unrestraint, abandon.

violent *adj.* **1** destructive, brutal, explosive, eruptive, volcanic, stormy, turbulent, tumultuous, fierce, savage, seething, bursting, boiling, surging. **2** impassioned, frenzied, passionate, fiery, rabid, manic, psychopathic, murderous, demonic, berserk, maddened, crazed, irrational, insane, wild, ungovernable. **3** intense, extreme, severe, unbearable, killing, intolerable, grave, acute, inordinate, outrageous, undue, unremitting, dire, unrestrained. **ant. 1** serene, calm, unruffled, quiescent, tranquil. **2** reasonable, rational, controlled, cool. **3** mild, moderate, normal, usual.

viper *n.* villain, traitor, devil, menace, cutthroat, beast, scoundrel, troublemaker, snake-in-the-grass, rat, swine, vulture. **ant.** lamb, dove, innocent, peacemaker, Good Samaritan.

viperous *adj.* MALICIOUS.

virago *n.* VIXEN.

virgin *n.* celibate, vestal, maid, maiden. —*adj.* **1** pure, pristine, virginal, unsullied, unspoiled, untouched, clean, uncorrupted, undefiled, immaculate, unpolluted, unblemished, spotless. **2** VIRGINAL. **ant.** *adj.* **1** spoiled, polluted, defiled, contaminated, dirty, used.

virginal *adj.* **1** maidenly, vestal, chaste, pure, celibate, continent. **2** VIRGIN.

virile *adj.* masculine, manly, male, manful, potent, lusty, strong, forceful, muscular, strapping, vigorous, stalwart, macho. **ant.** unmanly, effeminate, impotent, spineless, weak.

virtually *adv.* essentially, practically, effectively, to all intents and purposes, in effect, in essence, for all practical purposes, substantially, in the main, basically, fundamentally, intrinsically, in principle.

virtue *n.* **1** incorruptibility, rectitude, uprightness, righteousness, highmindedness, integrity, honor, nobility, morality, worthiness, goodness. **2**

merit, good, asset, blessing, value, credit, strength, boon, gift, help, plus.
ant. 1 sinfulness, venality, baseness, immorality. **2** sin, error, weakness, curse, disadvantage, handicap.

virtuosity *n.* mastery, finish, polish, artistry, éclat, brilliance, bravura, accomplishment, genius, skill, panache, expertise, flair, verve.
ant. ineptness, amateurishness, dullness, monotony, mediocrity.

virtuoso *n.* master, artist, genius, technician, wizard, magician, artiste, star.

virtuous *adj.* righteous, upright, dutiful, admirable, conscientious, honorable, high-minded, noble, moral, incorruptible, ethical, principled, good, exemplary.
ant. base, dishonorable, disreputable, venal, corrupt.

virulent *adj.* **1** noxious, harmful, poisonous, lethal, deadly, septic, toxic, unhealthy, unwholesome, pernicious, deleterious, destructive. **2** acute, severe, terminal, fatal, mortal, killing, tragic, incurable, irremediable, malignant, hopeless. **3** bitter, hostile, envenomed, embittered, malicious, spiteful, vindictive, murderous, savage, truculent, vicious, rancorous.
ant. 1 harmless, nontoxic, nonpoisonous. **2** superficial, mild, benign, curable. **3** well-disposed, friendly, gentle, charitable, kind.

visage *n.* **1** appearance, aspect, look, mien, expression, comportment, demeanor, air, presence, conduct, features, cast, guise, countenance, bearing. **2** FACE.

visceral *adj.* instinctive, emotional, intuitive, gut (*Slang*), spontaneous, involuntary, reflex, inner, natural, subconscious, automatic.
ant. rationalized, intellectual, intellectualized, reasoned, thought-out.

viscid *adj.* VISCOUS.
viscose *adj.* VISCOUS.

viscous *adj.* semiliquid, semisolid, thick, gummy, syrupy, viscid, dense, sticky, tacky, gluey, viscose, glutinous, adhesive, mucilaginous, slimy.

visible *adj.* perceptible, observable, discernible, perceivable, seeable, discoverable, detectable, noticeable, recognizable, evident, conspicuous, prominent, obvious, clear, manifest, arresting, unconcealed, unmistakable.
ant. imperceptible, undetectable, unclear, concealed, hidden.

vision *n.* **1** sight, eyesight, seeing, eye, perception. **2** spectacle, view, eyeful, sight, scene, prospect, outlook. **3** illusion, dream, fantasy, phantasm, specter, mirage, appearance, conception, idea, daydream, concept, image, fancy, ideal. **4** discernment, foresight, imagination, prescience, awareness, foreknowledge, intuition, penetration, perspective, farsightedness, wisdom, sagacity, sense, providence, perspicuity.

visionary *adj.* **1** imaginary, disembodied, unreal, idealized, incorporeal, fancied, illusory, transcendental, fictitious, spectral, ghostly, fantasized, dreamed-up, intangible, phantom. **2** impractical, romantic, daydreaming, dreamy, mystical, utopian, speculative, clairvoyant, prescient, imaginative, prophetic, idealistic, quixotic, unrealistic, fanciful, extrasensory. —*n.* utopian, dreamer, romantic, idealist, theorizer, romanticist, Don Quixote, daydreamer, prophet, poet, illusionist.
ant. *adj.* **1** real, actual, palpable, material. **2** realistic, hardheaded, pragmatic, mundane. *n.* realist, pragmatist, pessimist, cynic.

visit *v.* **1** go see, call on, come to see, look at, tour, inspect, drop in on, stop by, pay a call, look in on, look up, travel to. **2** stay at, stay with, stop at, stop over, sojourn, winter, summer, weekend, tarry, vacation. —*n.*

stop, stay, call, trip, tour, stopover, sojourn, sightseeing, get-together, weekend, sojourn, visitation.

visitant *n.* VISITOR.

visitor *n.* guest, caller, visitant, sojourner, houseguest, tourist, sightseer, traveler, inspector, frequenter, habitué, denizen.

vista *n.* view, outlook, scene, panorama, sight, landscape, seascape, scenery, prospect, picture, spectacle.

visual *adj.* **1** optic, optical, ocular, ophthalmic. **2** visible, observable, discernible, noticeable, perceptible, seeable, clear, apparent, manifest, plain.

ant. 2 invisible, imperceptible, unnoticeable, hidden, covered, concealed.

visualize *v.* imagine, picture, conceive, envisage, dream, fantasize, evoke, conjure up, see in the mind's eye, invent, call to mind.

vital *adj.* **1** animate, living, existing, alive, live, viable, palpable, breathing, quick, functioning, biological, generative, life. **2** essential, basic, crucial, indispensable, important, critical, imperative, decisive, elementary, fundamental, requisite, material, prime, primary, mortal. **3** vivacious, animated, vibrant, vigorous, dynamic, lively, spirited, energetic, strong, exuberant, aggressive, active, high-powered, peppy.

ant. 1 inanimate, dead, lifeless. **2** superficial, unimportant, irrelevant. **3** inert, passive, weak, phlegmatic.

vitality *n.* animation, exuberance, vigor, strength, robustness, dynamism, verve, vivacity, liveliness, responsiveness, ebullience, pep, vim, pizzazz (*Slang*).

ant. weakness, inertia, apathy, unresponsiveness, sluggishness.

vitalize *v.* ANIMATE.

vitiate *v.* **1** impair, weaken, devalue, adulterate, spoil, corrupt, pollute, water down, devitalize, thin, invalidate, injure, undermine, sabotage, undo, obliterate, contaminate, depre-

ciate. **2** corrupt, taint, blemish, debase, defile, despoil, mar, deprave, pervert, blight, poison, infect, sully.

ant. 1 strengthen, buttress, improve, invigorate. **2** purify, exalt, uplift, elevate.

vitriol *n.* SARCASM.

vitriolic *adj.* cutting, acidulous, caustic, sharp, nasty, biting, hurtful, sarcastic, corrosive, destructive, acrimonious, acerbic, bitchy (*Slang*).

ant. gentle, soothing, agreeable, complimentary.

vittles *n.* VICTUALS.

vituperate *v.* BERATE.

vituperation *n.* faultfinding, denunciation, criticism, abuse, censure, scolding, tongue-lashing, invective, obloquy, billingsgate, condemnation, castigation, tirade, scurrility, calumniation.

ant. praise, flattery, approval, acclaim.

vivacious *adj.* lively, animated, spirited, vital, exuberant, ebullient, sparkling, cheerful, bubbling, blithe, effervescent, irrepressible, scintillating.

ant. listless, lifeless, melancholy, dull, boring.

vivid *adj.* **1** lively, spirited, animated, vital, bright, vivacious, dynamic, energetic, vigorous, live, brisk, forceful, ardent, fiery. **2** strong, intense, potent, memorable, impressive, warm, distinct, sharp, powerful, unforgettable, expressive, brilliant, striking, colorful, graphic, pictorial, telling.

ant. 1 dispirited, quiet, lifeless, weak, withdrawn. **2** pale, hazy, unclear, dull, colorless.

vivify *v.* ANIMATE.

vixen *n.* shrew, termagant, virago, hellion, hellcat, spitfire, witch, fury, scold, fishwife, harridan, bitch (*Slang*).

vocabulary *n.* **1** lexicon, glossary, dictionary, thesaurus, wordbook, phrasebook. **2** language, verbiage, terminology, phraseology, lingo, idiom, parlance, dialect, patois, tongue, slang, jargon, cant.

vocal *adj.* **1** voiced, spoken, articulated, verbalized, oral, verbal, sonant, said, uttered, sung, intoned. **2** expressive, articulate, communicative, clamorous, vociferous, demanding, audible, outspoken, talkative, noisy. **ant. 1** speechless, mute, dumb. **2** silent, inarticulate, uncommunicative, quiet.

vocation *n.* **1** occupation, employment, job, trade, business, profession, work, livelihood, living, specialty, field, line. **2** calling, call, pursuit, career, life's work, métier, consecration, dedication, cause, forte, aptitude, genius, devotion.

vociferant *adj.* VOCIFEROUS.

vociferous *adj.* clamorous, noisy, vociferant, demanding, shouting, loud, riotous, vocal, vehement, loudmouthed, importunate, rackety, deafening, uproarious, turbulent. **ant.** hushed, muted, quiet, silent, still.

vogue *n.* fashion, style, trend, *dernier cri,* mode, fad, craze, rage.

voguish *adj.* MODISH.

voice *n.* opinion, expression, tongue, vote, choice, articulation, communication, utterance, option, wish, participation, say, say-so, suffrage, demand. —*v.* articulate, say, express, verbalize, state, announce, utter, communicate, proclaim, pronounce, speak, hold forth.

void *adj.* **1** empty, devoid, vacuous, barren, hollow, lacking, destitute, wanting, vacant, unoccupied, unfilled. **2** invalid, useless, futile, vain, nonviable, unproductive, powerless, ineffectual, unenforceable, inoperative, annulled, canceled, null, nil, dead. —*n.* vacuum, emptiness, abyss, nothingness, vacuity, pit, chasm, vacancy, nullity, hole, oblivion. —*v.* **1** nullify, cancel, veto, invalidate, annul, revoke, abrogate, wipe out, abolish, repeal, rescind,

undo, repudiate, negate. **2** eliminate, empty, cleanse, evacuate, urinate, defecate, drain, clear, pass water, discharge, emit, eject, micturate, excrete. **ant.** *adj.* **1** full, replete, abounding, complete, occupied. **2** valid, binding, viable, productive, useful. *v.* **1** uphold, enforce, validate, establish, support. **2** fill, ingest, digest.

volant *adj.* AGILE.

volatile *adj.* mercurial, inconstant, unstable, changeable, fickle, temperamental, excitable, up and down, capricious, moody, erratic, unpredictable, variable, flighty, impetuous. **ant.** steady, unchanging, regular, even-tempered.

volatilize *v.* EVAPORATE.

volcanic *adj.* VIOLENT.

volition *n.* WILLPOWER.

volley *n.* discharge, stream, flow, barrage, broadside, rain, outpouring, downpour, flight, fusillade, shower, storm, salvo.

volubility *n.* GARRULITY.

voluble *adj.* talkative, verbal, fluent, articulate, loquacious, smoothtongued, fast-talking, verbose, glib, facile, garrulous, eloquent, effusive, chatty, long-winded, discursive. **ant.** taciturn, terse, hesitant, succinct, reticent, tongue-tied.

volume *n.* **1** book, tome, edition, printing, publication, paperback, hardback, folio, quarto, octavo, album. **2** amount, quantity, output, aggregate, measure, total, sum, bulk, mass, magnitude, capacity.

voluminous *adj.* **1** abundant, prolific, plentiful, extensive, copious, opulent, lavish, bulky, extended, profuse. **2** ample, capacious, massive, huge, large, enormous, commodious, mammoth, cumbersome, sizable, weighty. **ant. 1** deficient, scant, insufficient. **2** small, tiny, slight.

voluntary *adj.* optional, volunteer, unforced, free, volitional, uncompelled, conscious, willing, spontaneous, unconstrained, deliberate, gratuitous, chosen, intended, intentional, willful. **ant.** involuntary, forced, compelled, compulsory.

volunteer *v.* offer, give, provide, proffer, donate, tender, present, submit, suggest, propose, contribute, furnish, supply, bestow. —*adj.* VOLUNTARY. **ant.** *v.* withhold, withdraw, refuse, deny.

voluptuary *n.* hedonist, sensualist, sybarite, bon vivant, pleasure-seeker, libertine, epicure, worldling, thrill-seeker, pleasure-lover. **ant.** ascetic, self-denier.

voluptuous *adj.* sensuous, sensual, sexual, erotic, pleasure-loving, luxurious, fleshly, hedonistic, carnal, epicurean, sexy, sybaritic, self-indulgent, profligate, delicious, thrilling, enjoyable, pleasurable. **ant.** ascetic, monkish, self-denying, inhibited.

volute *adj.* SPIRAL.

voluted *adj.* SPIRAL.

vomit *v.* **1** throw up, puke, retch, regurgitate, spit up, spew, upchuck, heave, disgorge, regorge, barf (*Slang*). **2** erupt, belch, expel, discharge, eject, burst forth, gush, surge forth, disgorge, eruct, eructate, stream forth, jet, spurt.

voracious *adj.* **1** ravenous, greedy, ravening, gluttonous, edacious, crapulous, hungry, starved, famished, hoggish, piggish. **2** insatiable, unquenchable, bottomless, grasping, rapacious, omnivorous, covetous, insatiate, avaricious, unappeasable, avid. **3** immoderate, intemperate, excessive, uncontrolled, inordinate, unbridled, unrestrained, unlimited, undue, gross, wanton, prodigious. **ant. 1** picky, fussy, delicate. **2** sated, slaked, satisfied, undemanding. **3** moderate, temperate, self-controlled, judicious.

voracity *n.* GREED.

vortex *n.* **1** whirlpool, whirlwind, eddy, maelstrom, twister, cyclone. **2** pre-

dicament, involvement, entanglement, quicksand, trap, quagmire, tailspin, merry-go-round, hornet's nest, imbroglio, bind, tight squeeze, rat race (*Slang*).

votary *n.* devotee, student, follower, admirer, enthusiast, fan, disciple, partisan, adherent, aficionado, nut (*Slang*), freak (*Slang*), groupie (*Slang*).

vote *n.* franchise, ballot, say, option, choice, preference, election, selection, suffrage, poll, plebiscite, voice, show of hands, referendum.

vouch for guarantee, underwrite, assure, warrant, attest, avouch, testify, prove, corroborate, substantiate, support, certify, endorse, sponsor, confirm, verify.

vouchsafe *v.* condescend, deign, grant, permit, allow, suffer, acquiesce, humor, cosset, indulge, concede, tolerate, accord, stoop to, yield, accommodate.

vow *n.* pledge, oath, affirmation, promise, assurance, engagement, plight, avowal, parole, word of honor, guarantee, troth. —*v.* swear, pledge, affirm, promise, warrant, guarantee, vouch, assure, contract, certify, plight, undertake.

voyage *n.* cruise, sail, crossing, traverse, traversal, sailing, trip, journey, flight, passage, transport. —*v.* cruise, sail, travel, journey, cross, traverse, fly, go, navigate.

voyeur *n.* PEEPING TOM.

vulgar *adj.* **1** coarse, unrefined, ill-mannered, low-minded, low-bred, boorish, crude, tasteless, uncouth, loud-mouthed, brassy, trashy, gaudy, sleazy, raffish, tawdry. **2** obscene, offensive, off-color, smutty, dirty, foul, risqué, filthy, indecent, scurrilous, indelicate, ribald, blue. **3** popular, general, ordinary, everyday, plebeian, demotic, common, folk, informal, mass, commonplace, lowbrow, non-U (*Slang*). **4** VERNACULAR.

ant. 1 polished, elegant, cultivated, tasteful, refined. **2** acceptable, standard, clean, inoffensive. **3** elite, aristocratic, upper-class, privileged.

vulgarian *n.* boor, barbarian, showoff, roughneck, redneck, lout, churl, upstart, philistine, arriviste, social climber, parvenu, nouveau riche, Babbitt.

vulgarism *n.* BARBARISM.

vulgarity *n.* **1** coarseness, baseness, tawdriness, tastelessness, philistinism, grossness, crudeness, indecency, impropriety, rudeness, crassness, ill-breeding, indelicacy, showiness, meretriciousness, shabbiness. **2** obscenity, filth, smut, dirt, scurrility, rib-aldry, indecency, pornography, license.

ant. 1 elegance, refinement, polish, taste, tact, sensibility, savoir faire.

vulnerable *adj.* unprotected, weak, exposed, delicate, sensitive, unguarded, pregnable, insecure, unresistant, undefended, unarmed, assailable, conquerable, accessible, destructible, susceptible.

ant. invincible, unconquerable, indestructible, unassailable, impregnable.

vulture *n.* parasite, bloodsucker, jackal, sadist, con man, predator, exploiter, extortionist, harpy, shark.

ant. victim, prey, pigeon, sitting duck, target.

W

wabble *v.* WOBBLE.

wacky *adj. Slang* zany, crazy, irrational, unpredictable, peculiar, strange, erratic, odd, eccentric, kinky (*Slang*), goofy (*Slang*), nutty (*Slang*), screwy (*Slang*), screwball (*Slang*).

ant. rational, sane, sober, predictable.

wad *n.* gob, lump, mass, clump, hunk, chunk, packing, lining, filler, wadding, stuffing.

waddle *v.* wobble, toddle, totter, rock, sway, hobble, roll, stagger, swing, waver, weave, reel.

wafer *n.* cooky, cracker, biscuit, snap, chip, lozenge.

waffle *v.* **1** *Brit.* JABBER. **2** HEDGE. —*n.* *Brit.* NONSENSE.

waft *v.* float, glide, drift, sail, fly, breeze, transport, transmit, carry, bear, convey. —*n.* breath, current, flow, breeze, whiff, puff, gust, wind.

wag *v.* shake, swing, waggle, wiggle, jiggle, sway, wave, oscillate, bob, nod, quiver. —*n.* waggle, shake, bob, nod, swing, toss, wave, oscillation, wiggle, jiggle.

wage *n.* wages, pay, payment, salary, compensation, hire, fee, earnings, remuneration, stipend, income, emolument. —*v.* undertake, carry on, pursue, engage in, practice, conduct, commit, perpetrate, maintain, proceed with, manage.

wager *v.* bet, gamble, stake, speculate, risk, take a flier, plunge, chance, lay, play for, hazard. —*n.* bet, risk, gamble, chance, stakes.

wages *n.* **1** WAGE. **2** REWARD.

waggish *adj.* humorous, droll, facetious, funny, jocose, comical, sportive, jocular, witty, jesting, frolicsome, mischievous, puckish, prankish.

ant. serious, grim, sober, staid, prim, morose, sullen, humorless.

waggle *v., n.* WAG.

wagon *n.* cart, wain, lorry, surrey, buggy, dray, van, tumbrel, carriage, coach, stagecoach.

waif *n.* urchin, gamin, street Arab,

stray, guttersnipe, mudlark (*Brit.*), foundling, ragamuffin, vagabond, tramp, vagrant.

wail *v.* grieve, mourn, lament, cry, moan, weep, sob, bemoan, bewail, sorrow, beat one's breast. —*n.* lament, lamentation, cry, moan, jeremiad, plaint.

wait *v.* abide, linger, remain, tarry, stay, pause, rest, dawdle, dally, mark time, bide one's time, expect, await, look for, anticipate. —*n.* delay, pause, procrastination, interval, halt, lull, recess, suspension, stay, deferment, adjournment, respite, intermission.

ant. *v.* begin, start, commence, resume, recommence.

wait on administer to, serve, tend, attend, help, assist, aid, look after, work for, minister to, take care of.

waive *v.* relinquish, remit, forswear, abjure, renounce, drop, disclaim, yield, forgo, surrender, give up.

ant. press, claim, demand, insist, pursue.

wake[1] *n.* vigil, watch, deathwatch, session, funeral, post-mortem.

wake[2] *n.* aftermath, trail, path, course, track, train, backwash, spoor, vestige.

wakeful *adj.* awake, wide-awake, sleepless, restless, alert, watchful, cautious, vigilant, wary, on guard.

ant. asleep, dozing, incautious, unwary, off guard.

waken *v.* WAKE UP.

wake up waken, awaken, awake, rise, get up, stir, bestir, rouse.

ant. sleep, doze, nap, slumber, snooze.

walk *v.* stride, step, stroll, saunter, amble, ambulate, tread, hike, march, pace, perambulate, tramp, strut, traipse, hoof it. —*n.* **1** stroll, hike, ramble, promenade, trek, constitutional, gait, pace, stride, tread. **2** sidewalk, pathway, promenade, esplanade, lane, footpath, trail, passageway, catwalk, crosswalk, aisle.

walkaway *n.* pushover (*Slang*), snap,

cinch (*Slang*), walkover, setup, picnic (*Slang*), runaway, child's play.

ant. struggle, grind, strain, trial, ordeal.

walking papers DISMISSAL.

walk out on desert, forsake, abandon, quit, strand, jilt, leave in the lurch, back out of.

ant. stay, stand by, stick to.

walkover *n.* WALKAWAY.

walk over patronize, despise, scorn, spit on, use, exploit, trample on, bully, insult, abuse.

ant. respect, consider, honor, appreciate.

wall *n.* partition, barrier, divider, panel, screen, obstruction, fence, hedge, barricade, parapet, breastwork, stockade, palisade, railing, balustrade.

wallop *v.* beat, thrash, batter, punch, pound, slug, clobber (*Slang*), trounce, drub, lambaste (*Slang*), pommel, lick, whip. —*n.* strike, blow, swat, bash, smack, whack, clout, cuff, box, belt, slug, lick, punch, haymaker (*Slang*).

walloping *adj.* WHOPPING.

wallow *v.* **1** roll, slosh, flounder, toss, welter, grovel, pitch, plunge, tumble, lurch. **2** indulge, luxuriate, revel, bask, delight, savor, feast, relish, grovel.

ant. 2 abstain, refrain, forbear, eschew.

wampum *n.* MONEY.

wan *adj.* **1** pale, ashen, livid, pallid, ghostly, colorless, pasty, anemic, waxen, careworn, peaked, haggard, gaunt, emaciated, drawn. **2** faint, feeble, dim, languid, weak, thin, gentle, vapid, spiritless.

ant. 1 flushed, blooming, glowing, ruddy, rosy. **2** hearty, robust, vivid, strong, spirited.

wand *n.* rod, stick, staff, baton, scepter, mace, truncheon.

wander *v.* **1** roam, range, rove, cruise, gad, drift, ramble, peregrinate, straggle, meander, prowl, gallivant. **2** stroll, saunter, amble, meander, wind, weave. **3** stray, swerve, veer, deviate, digress, diverge, deflect, err, shift, lapse.

ant. 3 conform, follow, toe the mark.

wanderlust *n.* restlessness, adventurousness, nomadism, dromomania, vagabondage.

wane *v.* **1** ebb, diminish, decrease, subside, abate, dwindle, shrivel, atrophy, wither, weaken, fade, dim. **2** decline, recede, decrease, expire, age, terminate, lapse, fail, die, disappear, run its course. —*n.* decrease, decay, decline, lessening, ebb, abatement, fading.

ant. *v.* **1** wax, grow, intensify, expand, increase. **2** wax, develop, advance. *n.* increase, step-up, strengthening, intensification.

wangle *v.* finagle, wheedle, worm, angle, engineer, jockey, wheel and deal (*Slang*), machinate, manipulate, scheme, make a pitch for (*Slang*).

want *v.* **1** desire, crave, yearn, hanker, pine, hunger, thirst, wish, covet, fancy. **2** lack, fall short, miss, need, require, demand, call for. —*n.* **1** lack, scarcity, shortage, dearth, deficiency, insufficiency, meagerness, paucity, inadequacy, exiguity, absence. **2** poverty, destitution, indigence, need, pennilessness, privation, penury, straits, insolvency, pauperism. **3** necessity, need, requisite, requirement, yearning, longing, craving, desire, wish, hunger, thirst, passion, desideratum.

ant. *v.* **1** reject, despise, spurn, scorn. **2** satisfy, fulfill, meet. *n.* **1** abundancy, plenitude, plenty, sufficiency, adequacy. **2** affluence, prosperity, plenty, wealth, comfort, luxury. **3** revulsion, aversion, dislike.

wanting *adj.* **1** missing, lacking, short, shy, minus, scant, less, without, absent, incomplete. **2** substandard, under par, subpar, deficient, poor, inadequate, defective, faulty, imperfect, shoddy.

ant. 1 full, replete, saturated, complete. **2** adequate, satisfactory, acceptable, good, perfect.

wanton *adj.* **1** licentious, lewd, lustful, lascivious, salacious, dissolute, lecherous, carnal, prurient, immoral, loose, fast, lickerish. **2** senseless, unprovoked, gratuitous, groundless, uncalled-for, willful, perverse, irresponsible, wayward, impulsive, arbitrary, capricious. **3** extravagant, wild, unrestrained, lavish, rash, freewheeling, loose, reckless, outrageous, intemperate, immoderate. —*n.* libertine, profligate, debauchee, rake, lecher, satyr, slut, hussy, bawd, whore, tart, jade.

ant. *adj.* **1** puritanical, prudish, priggish, Victorian. **2** justified, provoked, called-for, excusable. **3** restrained, circumspect, cautious, reserved, inhibited, guarded, prudent. *n.* prude, prig, Victorian, puritan.

wantonness *n.* ABANDON.

war *n.* warfare, strife, conflict, hostilities, arms, bloodshed, struggle, battle, crusade, campaign, engagement, contention, contest, discord. —*v.* fight, battle, combat, contend, crusade, clash, vie, struggle, oppose, contest, attack.

ant. *n.* peace, harmony, accord, cooperation, friendship, alliance, concord.

warble *v.* trill, chirp, chirrup, sing, twitter, quaver.

ward *n.* **1** hall, dormitory, wing, section, annex, pavilion. **2** precinct, district, bailiwick, quarter, zone, borough, *arrondissement*, department, barrio, ghetto.

warden *n.* custodian, guardian, keeper, protector, curator, ranger, gamekeeper, supervisor, manager, superintendent.

warder *n.* GUARD.

ward off parry, stave off, fend off, foil, repel, avert, repulse, thwart, deter, forestall, preclude, prevent, deflect, block, check.

ant. receive, accept, permit, allow, welcome.

wardrobe *n.* **1** armoire, closet, clothespress, locker, chest, chiffonier, bureau. **2** attire, raiment, clothes, clothing, garb, trousseau, outfit, costume, ensemble, togs, get-up, duds, apparel, dress.

warehouse *n.* storehouse, store, storeroom, stockroom, depository, depot, repository, vault, loft, armory, arsenal.

wares *n.* goods, merchandise, commodities, products, staples, inventory, line, stock, vendibles.

warfare *n.* WAR.

wariness *n.* CAUTION.

warlike *n.* **1** bellicose, belligerent, combative, aggressive, pugnacious, warmongering, militaristic, militant, trigger-happy, hostile, antagonistic. **2** martial, military, tactical, strategic, logistic.
ant. **1** pacifistic, nonviolent, peaceful, conciliatory, friendly, accommodating.

warlock *n.* sorcerer, wizard, witch, magician, conjurer, necromancer, shaman, witch doctor, medicine man, voodoo.

warm *adj.* **1** heated, tepid, lukewarm, hot, muggy, close, stifling, sultry, stuffy, oppressive. **2** ardent, enthusiastic, fervent, fervid, zealous, eager, warm-blooded, earnest, effusive, cordial, friendly, heartfelt, passionate, amorous, loving. **3** lively, agitated, vehement, heated, animated, passionate, violent, excitable, fiery, emotional, stormy, volcanic, furious. —*v.* **1** interest, awaken, waken, arouse, stir, stimulate, turn on (*Slang*), inspire, excite, incite, enkindle, provoke. **2** cheer, please, comfort, gladden, delight, console, content.
ant. *adj.* **1** cold, cool, icy, frigid, chilly, glacial. **2** lethargic, apathetic, indifferent, cool, stolid, unemotional. **3** calm, dispassionate, tranquil, serene, collected, low-key. *v.* **1** discourage, inhibit, dampen, suppress, stifle,

subdue. **2** depress, distress, alienate, antagonize, disaffect.

warm-blooded *adj.* ARDENT.

warm-hearted *adj.* kind, affectionate, generous, kindly, loving, tender, compassionate, sympathetic, soft-hearted, considerate.
ant. mean, coldblooded, selfish, heartless, stern, hardhearted, unfeeling.

warmongering *adj.* WARLIKE.

warmth *n.* **1** heat, temperature, glow, flush, fever, hotness, warmness, radiance. **2** ardor, zeal, enthusiasm, passion, excitement, intensity, eagerness, fervor, zest, earnestness, spirit. **3** compassion, affection, empathy, sympathy, understanding, friendliness, cordiality, graciousness, amiability, generosity, hospitality, openness.
ant. **1** chill, coldness, coolness, frigidity. **2** apathy, indifference, lethargy, torpor, halfheartedness. **3** selfishness, coldness, aloofness, remoteness, callousness.

warn *v.* caution, forewarn, alert, alarm, threaten, forebode, advise, counsel, admonish, recommend, exhort, urge, notify, inform, signal.

warning *n.* admonition, monition, advice, recommendation, caution, notification, alarm, caveat, threat, signal, sign.

warp *v.* corrupt, pervert, deprave, twist, distort, infect, poison, misguide, prejudice, bias, jaundice.
ant. edify, ennoble, straighten out, rehabilitate, correct.

warrant *n.* warranty, authorization, guarantee, sanction, justification, license, mandate, credential, certification, security, assurance, surety, permit, right, permission. —*v.* **1** assure, guarantee, vouch, pledge, plight, attest, certify, answer for, underwrite, back, endorse. **2** justify, legitimate, validate, support, sustain, uphold, vindicate, confirm, establish, substantiate, authenticate. **3** AUTHORIZE.

ant. *v.* **2** discredit, refute, belie, undermine.

warranty *n.* GUARANTEE.

warrior *n.* soldier, fighter, fighting man, combatant, mercenary, commando, legionnaire, guerrilla, brave, veteran, campaigner.

wary *adj.* **1** alert, vigilant, watchful, on guard, cautious, careful, wide-awake, prudent, heedful, mindful, guarded, chary, suspicious, leery. **2** shrewd, wily, clever, sly, crafty, wise, foxy, cagey, artful, slick, sharp.
ant. **1** off guard, unwary, reckless, napping, foolhardy, heedless. **2** naive, gullible, guileless, artless.

wash *v.* cleanse, clean, launder, scrub, bathe, tub, shower, rinse, shampoo, scour, swab, mop, lave, wet, hose. —*n.* bath, shower, cleaning, scrubbing, ablution, soaking, rinsing, washing, shampoo, tubbing.

washed-out *adj.* **1** faded, pale, colorless, faint, dim, bleached, blanched, pallid, dull, discolored. **2** exhausted, spent, tired, fatigued, worn-out, pooped (*Slang*), weary, all in, beat, bushed, tuckered out, played out.
ant. **1** vivid, bright, shining, intense, deep. **2** refreshed, vigorous, energetic, lively, spry.

washed-up *adj.* finished, through, all over, ended, over the hill, done for, kaput (*Slang*), ruined, on the rocks, on the skids (*Slang*).

washout *n.* *Slang* FAILURE.

washy *adj.* WATERY.

waspish *adj.* irritable, irate, bad-tempered, irascible, peevish, cranky, grumpy, testy, churlish, snappish, surly, cross, cantankerous, crabby, petulant.
ant. genial, good-humored, good-natured, pleasant, agreeable, cheerful.

wassail *n.* carousal, revel, debauch, orgy, binge, spree, bacchanalia, saturnalia, festivity, merrymaking, celebration, party, bash (*Slang*). —*v.* carouse, debauch, revel, celebrate, frolic, make merry, feast, drink, booze.

wastage *n.* WASTE.

waste *v.* **1** squander, dissipate, lavish, scatter, misspend, abuse, fritter away, trifle, throw away, run through, pass up, miss, lose. **2** weaken, debilitate, enfeeble, emaciate, erode, sap, wear out, corrode, eat away, gnaw, atrophy, disable, undermine. **3** consume, use up, deplete, exhaust, ravage, drain, empty, strip, dissipate. **4** DEVASTATE. —*n.* **1** consumption, dissipation, extravagance, squandering, misuse, lavishness, prodigality, wastage, wastefulness, excessiveness. **2** spoilage, scraps, remainders, debris, detritus, rubble, dregs, discards, remnants, chaff, leavings, spillage. **3** garbage, rubbish, trash, refuse, junk, litter, leavings, dross, swill, offal, pollutant. **4** excrement, excreta, urine, feces, stool, droppings. **5** WASTELAND.
ant. *v.* **1** conserve, economize, husband, stint, seize, take advantage, capitalize on. **2** strengthen, build up, fortify, reinforce. **3** save, preserve, conserve, keep, maintain. *n.* **1** conservation, frugality, thrift, economy.

wasteful *adj.* extravagant, lavish, profligate, improvident, spendthrift, prodigal, wanton, thriftless, destructive, ruinous, costly, nonproductive.
ant. thrifty, economical, provident, useful, productive.

wasteland *n.* waste, desert, wilderness, wilds, steppe, badlands, barrens, tundra, veld.

watch *v.* look, observe, view, examine, inspect, contemplate, regard, scan, scrutinize, survey, oversee, gaze, eye, expect, await, anticipate. —*n.* attention, observation, surveillance, oversight, scrutiny, inspection, vigil, notice, lookout.

watchdog *n.* sentry, guard, lookout, sentinel, warder, monitor, overseer, inspector.

watchful *adj.* alert, vigilant, open-eyed, on guard, wary, wide-awake, observant, cautious, guarded, attentive, on the lookout, on the *qui vive*.

ant. inattentive, heedless, caught napping, absent-minded, off guard.

watchfulness *n.* CAUTION.

watchword *n.* SLOGAN.

water down ADULTERATE.

waterfall *n.* cascade, cataract, falls, rapids, chute, shoot.

watering place *Brit.* RESORT.

Waterloo *n.* DEFEAT.

watershed *n.* milestone, landmark, turning point, pivot, juncture, climax, crisis, zero hour.

watertight *adj.* foolproof, firm, airtight, solid, flawless, impregnable, incontrovertible, tight, unassailable, invulnerable, unshakable, unarguable. **ant.** shaky, uncertain, untenable, questionable, tenuous.

watery *adj.* **1** diluted, thin, washy, wishy-washy, weak, feeble, reduced, watered-down, attenuated, cut. **2** vapid, insipid, tame, mild, flat, dull, flavorless, bland, tasteless, jejune, lifeless, namby-pamby. **ant.** **1** condensed, concentrated, thick, fortified, dense. **2** exciting, strong, powerful, pungent, stimulating.

wattle *v.* weave, interweave, mat, twist, intertwist, braid, plait, twine, intertwine, interlace.

wave *v.* **1** undulate, sway, wag, flutter, flap, vibrate, swing, ripple, oscillate, fluctuate, rock. **2** flourish, brandish, wield, flaunt, shake, swing. —*n.* **1** undulation, ripple, swell, billow, ridge, surf, breaker, chop, roller. **2** *type of hair:* curl, twirl, twist, ringlet, frizz, coil, curve. **3** surge, upsurge, rise, groundswell, upwelling, flood, deluge, outpouring, sweep, storm, stampede, epidemic, rash, outbreak.

waver *v.* **1** sway, weave, totter, reel, wobble, stagger, falter, stumble, careen, lurch. **2** vacillate, hesitate, pause, falter, shift, dilly-dally, shilly-shally, blow hot and cold, balk, demur, hang back, shrink, flinch. **ant.** **2** decide, resolve, persist, stick to one's guns.

wavy *adj.* curved, undulating, rolling, rippling, curly, coiled, twisted, serpentine, winding, curvilinear, sinuate.

wax *v.* grow, increase, enlarge, magnify, expand, balloon, dilate, stretch, spread, inflate, fill out, swell, widen, develop, sprout. **ant.** wane, decrease, narrow, diminish, dwindle, shrink, contract.

waxen *adj.* PALE^2.

waxy *adj.* PALE^2.

way *n.* **1** direction, region, route, course, bearing, line, path, tack, vector. **2** path, course, road, avenue, passage, lane, channel, track, access, trail, journey, transit, progress, itinerary, trip. **3** distance, interval, extent, stretch, length, space, span. **4** practice, manner, style, mode, procedure, method, approach, means, technique, system, fashion, usage, habit, wont, custom. **5** aspect, point, particular, detail, respect, part, item, feature. **6** desire, wish, will, fancy, ambition, demand, pleasure, preference, choice.

waylay *v.* ambush, attack, set upon, pounce, swoop, entrap, surprise, accost, buttonhole, intercept.

way-out *adj. Slang* FAR-OUT.

wayward *adj.* **1** willful, headstrong, disobedient, perverse, refractory, stubborn, intractable, contrary, obstinate, unruly, disorderly, rebellious, recalcitrant, froward. **2** erratic, capricious, irregular, fitful, changeable, inconsistent, inconstant, variable, fickle, mutable, unstable, unpredictable. **ant.** **1** compliant, malleable, obedient, accommodating, submissive, tractable, obliging. **2** reliable, predictable, regular, consistent, constant, steady.

weak *adj.* **1** feeble, weakly, frail, fragile, enervated, infirm, faint, delicate, flabby, limp, powerless, ineffectual, impotent, vulnerable, helpless. **2** spineless, weak-kneed, wishy-washy, wavering, vacillating, hesitant, spiritless, faint-hearted, chicken-hearted, milk-and-water, timorous, irresolute, weak-minded. **3** deficient, defective, ineffectual, poor, inadequate, substandard, lacking, inefficient, incapable, ineffective, unable, lame. **4** diluted, cut, reduced, understrength, watery, thin, attenuated, vapid, insipid, flimsy, insubstantial.

ant. 1 strong, vigorous, robust, sturdy, energetic, powerful. **2** courageous, strong-willed, resolute, decisive, determined, staunch. **3** adequate, effective, forceful, capable. **4** strong, stiff, fortified, thick, concentrated.

weaken *v.* debilitate, enervate, enfeeble, sap, flag, exhaust, cripple, disable, undermine, devitalize, paralyze.

ant. strengthen, toughen, invigorate, energize, revitalize.

weak-kneed *adj.* WEAK.

weakling *n.* sissy, jellyfish, mollycoddle, mouse, namby-pamby, milquetoast, baby, milksop, weak sister.

weakly *adj.* WEAK.

weak-minded *adj.* irresolute, indecisive, wavering, spineless, weak-kneed, pusillanimous, vacillating, faint-hearted, timid, timorous.

ant. firm, headstrong, resolute, determined, strong-minded, stalwart, courageous.

weakness *n.* **1** frailty, fragility, delicacy, feebleness, infirmity, debility, impotence, enervation, decrepitude, vulnerability. **2** failing, fault, foible, lapse, peccadillo, shortcoming, flaw, blemish, defect, spot. **3** fondness, liking, penchant, bent, taste, appetite, disposition, attraction, inclination, predilection, proclivity, propensity, affinity, partiality.

ant. 1 strength, power, vigor, vitality, robustness. **3** repugnance, aversion, dislike, antipathy, distaste, revulsion.

weal[1] *n.* WELL-BEING.

weal[2] *n.* WELT.

wealth *n.* **1** capital, money, assets, estate, property, pelf, lucre. **2** opulence, affluence, riches, means, resources, fortune, substance. **3**

abundance, plenitude, profusion, bounty, bounteousness, copiousness, ampleness, plenty, fullness.

ant. 2 poverty, indigence, destitution, need, want, penury. **3** scarcity, spareness, lack, insufficiency, shortage, paucity, dearth.

wealthy *adj.* affluent, rich, prosperous, well-to-do, well-off, moneyed, successful, well-heeled (*Slang*), flush, loaded (*Slang*).

ant. poor, needy, destitute, indigent, poverty-stricken, penniless, broke.

weapon *n. any means to be used against an adversary:* deterrent, defense, means, stratagem, device, trick, scheme, barb, shaft, shot, ammunition, resort.

weaponry *n.* ARMS.

wear *v.* **1** have on, put on, don, bear, sport, dress in. **2** exhibit, show, display, affect, assume, manifest. **3** grind, erode, scuff, abrade, rub, fret, frazzle, fray, tatter, impair. —*n.* **1** apparel, clothes, clothing, garb, attire, gear, rig, dress, outfit. **2** impairment, wear-and-tear, attrition, disintegration, deterioration, corrosion, erosion, decay, depreciation, dilapidation, destruction.

ant. *n.* **2** maintenance, preservation, upkeep, repair.

wearing *adj.* fatiguing, exhausting, punishing, demanding, strenuous, exacting, hard, rigorous, laborious, grinding, taxing, arduous, onerous.

ant. easy, light, effortless.

wearing apparel CLOTHES.

wearisome *adj.* tiresome, tedious, annoying, trying, irksome, vexatious, boring, monotonous, dull, dreary, bothersome, burdensome, oppressive.

ant. enjoyable, interesting, stimulating, exhilarating, refreshing, agreeable, pleasurable.

wear off diminish, fade, wane, dissipate, abate, slacken, disappear, peter out, subside, blow over, decline, ebb.

ant. intensify, step up, grow,

strengthen, endure, stay, remain, persist.

wear out 1 waste, use up, consume, exhaust, sap, drain, deplete, erode, grind, gnaw, rub. **2** tire, exhaust, fatigue, weary, harass, overwork, strain, fag, overtax, fret.
ant. 1 save, preserve, restore, replenish. **2** refresh, invigorate, energize, revitalize, pep up (*Slang*).

weary *adj.* **1** worn out, tired, fatigued, exhausted, tuckered out, pooped (*Slang*), spent, fagged, all in, bushed, beat, run down. **2** bored, tired, jaded, discontented, dissatisfied, impatient, disgusted, sick, annoyed, dispirited, fed up. —*v.* tire, exhaust, fatigue, wear out, enervate, fag, sap, fret, strain, burden, tax, jade, bother, vex, harass, plague, annoy.
ant. *adj.* **1** energetic, bouncy, spry, animated, lively, vivacious. **2** excited, rapt, engrossed, interested, fascinated. *v.* enliven, invigorate, awaken, refresh, revive, animate.

weasel *n.* sneak, cheat, rat (*Slang*), snake, double-dealer, double-crosser (*Slang*), betrayer, fink (*Slang*), traitor, welsher (*Slang*). —*v.* equivocate, hedge, fudge, evade, dodge, straddle, quibble, shuffle, palter, fence, trim, beat around the bush.

weasel out renege, fudge, back out, cop out (*Slang*), pull out, chicken out (*Slang*), welsh, turn one's back, fink out (*Slang*).

weather *n.* climate, atmosphere, clime, temperature, elements. —*v.* survive, endure, overcome, withstand, suffer, pull through, ride out, surmount, bear, tide over, stand, resist.
ant. *v.* succumb, collapse, cave in, fall, fail.

weave *v.* **1** interlace, intertwine, mat, knit, braid, plait, wattle, crochet, twine, twist, spin, loop, thread, insert. **2** make up, compose, fashion, invent, fabricate, construct, design, create, produce, contrive, build.

web *n.* **1** trap, snare, booby trap, entanglement, mesh, net. **2** network, tangle, snarl, labyrinth, criss-cross, jumble, maze. —*v.* ENTANGLE.

wed *v.* **1** marry, espouse, tie, tie the knot, mate, couple, hitch. **2** unite, attach, devote, dedicate, join, bind, stick, tie, marry, link.
ant. 1 divorce, separate. **2** separate, sever, divide, split.

wedding *n.* marriage, nuptials, vows, espousal, bridal.

wedge *n.* **1** chock, keystone, key, voussoir, quoin, V, cuneus, cleat, cotter, shim. **2** gambit, ploy, device, tactic, stratagem, opening, access, step, opportunity, foot in the door. —*v.* crowd, squeeze, jam, stuff, cram, lodge, thrust, force, ram, press, elbow.

wedlock *n.* matrimony, marriage, union, connubiality.

wee *adj.* tiny, minute, minuscule, little, small, diminutive, petite, miniature, microscopic, Lilliputian, pint-size, teeny, itsy-bitsy.
ant. large, huge, gigantic, enormous, jumbo, mammoth.

weed *v.* clear, hoe, uproot, extirpate, extract, pull, pick, pluck.

weed out get rid of, remove, discard, eliminate, dispense with, throw away, shed, exclude, reject, extirpate.

weedy *adj.* LANKY.

ween *v.* SUPPOSE.

weep *v.* **1** cry, sob, bawl, wail, snivel, blubber, shed tears, whimper, keen, boohoo. **2** mourn, lament, grieve, bewail, fret, regret, bemoan, sorrow, beat one's breast, deplore.

weepy *adj.* TEARFUL.

weft *n.* FABRIC.

weigh *v.* consider, ponder, judge, evaluate, estimate, study, measure, contemplate, meditate, reflect, deliberate.

weigh down weigh upon, burden, overburden, oppress, trouble, depress, bear down upon, pressure, load, overload, lade, encumber.
ant. relieve, lighten, help, lift, support, comfort, succor.

weight *n.* **1** mass, heaviness, poundage, tonnage, gravity, heft, avoirdupois. **2** burden, pressure, strain, anxiety, load, encumbrance, onus, millstone, responsibility, nuisance, cross, albatross. **3** influence, importance, impact, consequence, seriousness, gravity, import, moment, significance, authority. —*v.* freight, load, overload, encumber, lade, ballast, burden, overburden, weigh down.

weighty *adj.* **1** important, serious, solemn, grave, far-reaching, momentous, significant, critical, crucial, vital, consequential. **2** cogent, influential, powerful, potent, impressive, authoritative, compelling, persuasive, assuring, forceful, solid, convincing.

ant. 1 trivial, frivolous, insignificant, petty, inconsequential. **2** dubious, unconvincing, weak.

weigh upon WEIGH DOWN.

weird *adj.* unearthly, unnatural, uncanny, eerie, spooky, mysterious, odd, bizarre, fantastic, queer, strange, peculiar, eldritch.

ant. normal, natural, unexceptional, mundane, ordinary.

weirdo *n. Slang* ECCENTRIC.

welch *v. Slang* WELSH.

welcome *adj.* acceptable, pleasant, pleasurable, agreeable, pleasing, gratifying, satisfying, desirable, amiable, charming, delightful, enjoyable, appreciated. —*n.* greeting, reception, salutation, applause, glad hand (*Slang*), hospitality, acceptance, red carpet, welcome mat, open arms. —*v.* greet, hail, receive, admit, accept, embrace, salute, roll out the red carpet.

ant. *adj.* unwelcome, disagreeable, undesirable, disliked, unpleasant. *n.* rebuff, slight, snub, cold shoulder, ostracism, rejection, exclusion. *v.* spurn, snub, rebuff, turn away.

weld *v.* **1** fuse, solder, braze, bond, seam. **2** connect, attach, join, cement, bind, merge, bond, coalesce,

link, unite, combine, conjoin. —*n.* joint, juncture, seam.

ant. *v.* **2** detach, separate, part, divide, sever.

welfare *n.* well-being, weal, happiness, health, prosperity, success, interest, advantage, behalf, benefit, fortune, profit.

well[1] *n.* **1** shaft, pit, hole, bore, line, pipe, pump. **2** WELLSPRING. —*v.* **1** pour, surge, spring, flow, spout, jet, gush, flood, issue, stream, bubble, spurt. **2** gush, pour, discharge, rain, shower, shed, exude, effuse, emit, emanate.

well[2] *adv.* **1** satisfactorily, favorably, agreeably, nicely, acceptably, happily, pleasantly, smoothly, comfortably, luxuriously. **2** correctly, expertly, proficiently, ably, properly, excellently, admirably, superbly, skillfully, competently, adeptly, effectively, smoothly. **3** intimately, closely, personally, considerably, thoroughly, completely, fully, extensively, deeply, profoundly, sufficiently. **4** kindly, graciously, favorably, agreeably, glowingly, highly, warmly, complimentarily, approvingly, commendingly.

ant. 1 badly, poorly, unsatisfactorily, amiss, wrong. **2** ineptly, clumsily, awkwardly, poorly. **3** superficially, barely, hardly, scarcely. **4** ill, disparagingly, maliciously, critically.

well-appointed *adj.* well-furnished, well-equipped, elegant, comfortable, well-fitted, well-provided, luxurious, plush, posh (*Slang*).

ant. shabby, inadequate, run-down, bare, austere.

well-balanced *adj.* stable, sound, sensible, rational, well-adjusted, self-possessed, level-headed, reasonable, sober.

ant. unstable, neurotic, irrational, unbalanced.

well-being *n.* weal, welfare, good, health, happiness, comfort, ease, prosperity, success, fortune, advantage, Gemütlichkeit.

ant. hardship, adversity, distress, ill-being.

well-bred *adj.* polite, polished, civilized, refined, cultivated, courteous, genteel, cultured, urbane, well-mannered.

ant. uncouth, coarse, rude, vulgar, base.

well-done *adj.* satisfactory, acceptable, skillful, proficient, masterful, adept, expert, adroit, excellent, superb.

ant. poor, inadequate, unsatisfactory, inept, bungled.

well-favored *adj.* ATTRACTIVE.

well-fed *adj.* PLUMP.

well-fixed *adj.* WELL-TO-DO.

well-founded *adj.* solid, sound, firm, well-grounded, authoritative, authenticated, valid, reliable, established, factual, proven, confirmed, substantiated, verified.

ant. spurious, dubious, questionable, unreliable, unfounded, groundless.

well-grounded *adj.* WELL-FOUNDED.

wellspring *n.* well, fount, source, origin, fountainhead, spring, reservoir, fund, mine, reserve, lode, vein.

well-to-do *adj.* affluent, prosperous, wealthy, rich, well-fixed, well-off, well-heeled (*Slang*), flush, moneyed, successful, flourishing, thriving.

ant. poor, insolvent, indigent, destitute, needy, hard up.

well-turned *adj.* **1** well-chosen, elegant, clever, felicitous, well-thought-out, crafted, skillful, well-done, exquisite, graceful, well-wrought, polished, excellent, classic. **2** SHAPELY.

ant. 1 clumsy, awkward, inappropriate, ungraceful, inapt.

welsh *v. Slang* renege, back down, weasel out, back out, welch (*Slang*), shirk, evade, avoid, duck, dodge, fink out (*Slang*).

ant. carry out, fulfill, complete, discharge, execute.

welt *n.* stripe, weal, wale, bruise, sore, mark, ridge, lump, swelling, scar. —*v.* FLOG.

welter *n.* turmoil, commotion, fuss, fury, to-do, ado, storm, frenzy, bustle, tumult, hubbub, uproar, riot. —*v.* WALLOW.

Weltschmerz *n.* melancholy, world-weariness, discontent, gloom, depression, pessimism, despair, sadness, despondency, dejection, hopelessness, apathy.

ant. optimism, cheerfulness, joy, hopefulness.

wench *n.* **1** girl, maid, maiden, damsel, miss, lass, chick (*Slang*), minx, hussy. **2** prostitute, slut, strumpet, harlot, tramp (*Slang*), tart (*Slang*), trollop, whore, floozy (*Slang*), chippy (*Slang*), hooker (*Slang*).

wend *v.* proceed, go, progress, continue, pass, move, travel, advance, walk, step.

wet *adj.* moist, moistened, damp, dampened, sodden, dank, clammy, humid, dewy, bedewed, soaked, waterlogged, drenched, soggy, saturated. —*v.* dampen, moisten, soak, water, humidify, drench, douse, wash, irrigate, souse, saturate, steep. —*n.* WETNESS.

ant. *adj.* dry, arid, parched, desiccated, dehydrated, waterless. *v.* dehumidify, dry, dehydrate, desiccate.

wet blanket KILLJOY.

wetness *n.* moisture, humidity, wet, damp, dampness, dew, mist, dankness, sogginess, clamminess, mugginess.

ant. dryness, aridity.

whack *v., n.* SMACK.

whacking *adj. Brit.* WHOPPING.

whale *v.* BEAT.

whammy *n. Slang* jinx, hex, spell, curse, charm, evil eye, bewitchment, voodoo, hoodoo.

wharf *n.* pier, dock, jetty, quay, landing, marina, berth, port, harbor, mooring.

wheal *n.* PIMPLE.

wheedle *v.* cajole, coax, persuade, flatter, worm, blandish, inveigle, entice, lure, draw, induce, influence.

wheel *n.* disk, hoop, ring, circle, annulus, annulet, roller, cylinder, caster. —*v.* **1** turn, pivot, swivel, revolve, rotate, gyrate, spin, whirl, swing, pirouette, twirl, swirl, roll, circle, orbit. **2** deflect, stray, shift, deviate, diverge, veer, swerve, digress, wander, reverse, recant, rethink, reconsider.

wheel and deal *Slang* finagle, connive, scheme, wangle, maneuver, intrigue, conspire, angle, machinate, engineer, plot.

wheeze *v.* gasp, pant, murmur, puff, snuff, sniff, sniffle, snuffle, whiffle, whine.

whelm *v.* **1** SUBMERGE. **2** OVERWHELM.

wherewithal *n.* MEANS.

whet *v.* **1** hone, sharpen, grind, file, edge, strop. **2** excite, stimulate, arouse, intensify, sharpen, stir, prompt, provoke, pique, quicken, awaken, spur, inflame.

ant. 1 dull, blunt, wear down, abrade. **2** deaden, depress, numb, dampen, subdue, stifle.

whiff *n.* puff, gust, breath, waft, breeze, wind, flurry.

whip *v.* **1** beat, switch, lash, strike, scourge, flog, wallop, thrash, horsewhip, flagellate, flail, trounce, bastinado, knout, spank. **2** buffet, lash, batter, seize, snatch, grab, whisk, flick, jerk, yank, throw, toss, fling. **3** defeat, overcome, vanquish, conquer, beat, lick, drub, overpower, best, shellac (*Slang*), upset, rout, trounce. —*n.* switch, scourge, bullwhip, knout, strap, lash, crop, cat-o'-nine-tails, cane, rod, cudgel, birch, rawhide, truncheon.

whipping *n.* beating, thrashing, flogging, licking, spanking, caning, birching, flagellation, strapping, scourging.

whipping boy SCAPEGOAT.

whip up AROUSE.

whirl *v.* swirl, purl, spin, twirl, eddy, gyre, spiral, twist, reel, revolve, rotate, turn, wheel, gyrate. —*n.* **1** swirl, twirl, spin, gyration, revolution, rotation, wheeling, coil, roll, eddy, twisting, vortex, pirouette. **2** rush, bustle, tumult, uproar, stir, turbulence, confusion, commotion, agitation, whirlwind. **3** TRIAL.

whirlpool *n.* eddy, maelstrom, vortex, swirl, gulf, whirl, gurge.

whirlwind *n.* **1** tornado, cyclone, twister, typhoon, windstorm, dust storm, dust devil, waterspout, baguio. **2** WHIRL.

whish *v., n.* WHIZ.

whisk *v.* **1** brush, sweep, wipe, swish, whip, flick. **2** beat, mix, foam, whip, fluff up, cream, aerate.

whisker *n.* bristle, hair, vibrissa, seta, setula, awn, striga, arista.

whiskers *n.* beard, sideburns, burnsides, side-whiskers, stubble, goatee, Vandyke, imperial.

whiskey *n.* spirits, alcohol, liquor, drink, firewater, moonshine, strong drink, hard liquor, distilled liquor.

whisper *n.* **1** hint, inkling, insinuation, innuendo, implication, intimation, suggestion, allusion, rumor. **2** rustle, susurrus, sigh, swish, murmur, sough, buzz, hiss. —*v.* rustle, susurrate, swish, sough, buzz, sigh, hiss, murmur.

whistle *v.* trill, pipe, siffle, skirl, tweedle, shrill, sing, tweet, twitter, sigh, screech, scream, hiss, whoosh.

whit *n.* bit, grain, iota, jot, shred, speck, particle, smidgen, mote, mite, tittle, atom, scintilla, scrap.

white *adj.* **1** light, colorless, pallid, pale, ashen, whitish, chalky, ivory, milky, marmoreal. **2** silvery, gray, hoary, grizzled, frosty, rimed, snowy, snow-white, faded. **3** innocent, pure, immaculate, chaste, unsullied, unblemished, unstained, spotless, clean. —*v.* WHITEN.

ant. 1 black, blackish, dark, dusky. **3** impure, tarnished, dirty, soiled, guilty.

white elephant burden, millstone, encumbrance, extravagance, onus, imposition, care, drain, incubus, albatross.

white-hot *adj.* HOT.

whiten *v.* blanch, bleach, white, fade,

pale, blench, lighten, silver, frost, rime, whitewash, etiolate.

ant. darken, color, blacken, shadow, shade.

whitewash *n.* cover-up, gilding, camouflage, glossing over, extenuation, exoneration, justification, dissimulation, excuse, snow job (*Slang*). —*v.* gloss over, cover up, exonerate, exculpate, palliate, mitigate, extenuate, excuse, clear, acquit, justify, absolve. **ant.** *n.* exposé, disclosure, incrimination, exposure, muckraking. *v.* expose, inculpate, incriminate, involve, implicate.

whitish *adj.* WHITE.

whittle *v.* cut, shave, carve, trim, pare, slice, hack, slash, sculpt, shape, snip, hew.

whiz *v.* hiss, whish, swish, rustle, whir, whoosh, hum, buzz. —*n.* 1 hum, whir, whish, buzz, hiss, whoosh, rustle, swish. 2 *Slang* wizard, genius, expert, sensation, prodigy, marvel, champion, master, brain, mastermind, whiz kid (*Slang*).

whole *adj.* 1 entire, complete, undivided, integral, full, aggregate, gross, total, undiminished, unabridged, uncut. 2 sound, intact, in one piece, unhurt, unbroken, undamaged, perfect, mint, unimpaired, inviolate. 3 hale, healthy, vigorous, robust, well, better, healed, recovered, strong, sound. —*n.* 1 entirety, aggregate, totality, sum total, bulk, mass, gross, all, sum. 2 entity, system, ensemble, unity, integral, assemblage, totality, coalition, universe.

ant. *adj.* 1 incomplete, partial, diminished, lessened, lacking. 2 broken, injured, defective, damaged, shattered. 3 ill, maimed, unhealthy, lame, sick. *n.* 1 part, element, particle, piece, fraction, portion.

wholehearted *adj.* undivided, unstinting, dedicated, unreserved, zealous, enthusiastic, hearty, sincere, single-hearted, unlimited, unqualified, undisguised, complete, warm.

ant. grudging, half-hearted, insincere, tepid, partial.

wholesale *adj.* large-scale, indiscriminate, far-reaching, comprehensive, sweeping, broad, inclusive, extensive, diffuse, mass.

ant. discriminate, limited, piecemeal, selective.

wholesome *adj.* healthful, healthy, salutary, beneficial, invigorating, nutritious, salubrious, helpful, improving, good, fresh, sound, normal, sane, rational.

ant. harmful, unwholesome, unhealthy, sickly, morbid.

wholly *adv.* 1 completely, totally, thoroughly, altogether, fully, entirely, outright, all, utterly, absolutely. 2 exclusively, only, solely, alone, entirely, completely, totally.

ant. 1, 2 partially, partly, comparatively, somewhat, relatively, in part.

whoop *v.* yell, shout, cry out, bellow, roar, halloo, holler, clamor, howl, shriek, hoot, call, cry. —*n.* shout, yell, roar, huzza, hurrah, cheer, howl, hoot, clamor, uproar, hullabaloo.

whopper *n.* 1 giant, colossus, monster, mammoth, jumbo, wonder, miracle, rarity, prodigy, marvel. 2 lie, tall story, fish story, fabrication, falsehood, invention, fable, untruth, prevarication, canard.

whopping *adj.* extraordinary, walloping, striking, unusual, whacking (*Brit.*), extravagant, mammoth, overwhelming, stunning, monstrous, huge, enormous, outstanding.

ant. unremarkable, obscure, inconspicuous, imperceptible, unnoticeable.

whore *n.* prostitute, streetwalker, call girl, courtesan, harlot, strumpet, trollop, slut, trull, floozy (*Slang*), tramp (*Slang*), wanton, wench, hooker (*Slang*).

why *n.* cause, reason, motive, rationale, basis, ground, foundation, purpose, excuse, occasion, inspiration, provocation.

wicked *adj.* **1** evil, depraved, malevolent, sinful, bad, vicious, unjust, nefarious, flagitious, unprincipled. **2** mischievous, roguish, sly, arch, impish, devilish, naughty, rascally, contrary, perverse. **3** troublesome, painful, bothersome, refractory, onerous, complicated, distressing, challenging, difficult, trying. **ant.** **1** good, upright, just, virtuous, meritorious. **2** well-behaved, proper, good. **3** easy, trifling, simple, painless, trivial.

wide *adj.* **1** broad, ample, extended, outspread, extensive, spacious, capacious, roomy, large, vast. **2** far, distant, apart, removed, remote, off, far-off, detached, isolated, separate. **3** catholic, inclusive, all-inclusive, all-embracing, comprehensive, general, liberal, ecumenical, limitless, eclectic. **4** open, unclosed, extended, expanded, distended, dilated, ajar, wide-open. **ant.** **1** small, narrow, restricted, scant, strait. **2** close, near, in, inside, central. **3** exclusive, limited, narrow, specific, preclusive. **4** closed, shut, sealed, narrow, stenotic.

wide-awake *adj.* **1** AWAKE. **2** alert, vigilant, watchful, keen, attentive, observant, aware, informed, shrewd, astute, careful, wary, cautious, heedful. **ant.** **2** inattentive, dull-witted, listless, slow, obtuse, heedless.

wide-eyed *adj.* uninformed, unsophisticated, naive, credulous, uncritical, receptive, innocent, impressionable, agog, agape, astonished. **ant.** blasé, jaded, sophisticated, worldly-wise, knowing.

widen *v.* broaden, expand, extend, enlarge, stretch, spread, distend, dilate, magnify, amplify, augment, spread out, increase, unfurl, open. **ant.** narrow, constrain, concentrate, focus, constrict, squeeze.

wideness *n.* WIDTH.

widespread *adj.* **1** pervasive, extensive, far-flung, comprehensive, disseminated, sweeping, wholesale, far-reaching, worldwide, nation-wide, dispersed. **2** common, rife, popular, regnant, general, public, catholic, prevalent, epidemic, universal. **ant.** **1** limited, narrow, local, sporadic, circumscribed, confined. **2** uncommon, exclusive, limited, rare, special, esoteric.

widget *n.* gadget, device, contrivance, thing, object, whatnot, doodad, doohickey, gew-gaw, thingamajig, thingamabob.

width *n.* wideness, breadth, girth, broadness, scope, reach, extent, amplitude, span, spaciousness, bore, diameter.

wield *v.* **1** handle, brandish, use, flourish, ply, manipulate, shake, swing, work, utilize, employ, operate. **2** command, exercise, control, manage, make use of, exert, apply, use, utilize, avail oneself of, put to use.

wife *n.* spouse, helpmate, consort, mate, partner, woman, squaw, lady, rib, bride.

wig *n.* hairpiece, toupee, peruke, periwig, fall, transformation, front, switch.

wiggle *v.* wriggle, twist, twitch, waggle, jiggle, wag, shake, flutter, squirm, writhe, zigzag, quiver, jerk, tremble. —*n.* twitch, wriggle, twist, waggle, wag, jiggle, tremble, shake, quiver, flutter, shiver, squirm.

wild *adj.* **1** natural, native, undomesticated, untamed, feral, desert, waste, uncultivated, unrefined, uncared-for, unbroken, indigenous. **2** uncivilized, unrefined, primitive, barbarous, barbaric, savage, rude, rough, ferocious, fierce. **3** undisciplined, unruly, erratic, reckless, unwise, imprudent, thoughtless, madcap, flighty, giddy. **4** dissolute, profligate, dissipated, fast, loose, lewd, licentious, corrupt, debauched, lax. **5** violent, turbulent, stormy, frenzied, crazed, raving, raging, furious, mad, distracted. **6** odd, strange, bizarre, extravagant, grotesque, visionary, extreme, untraditional, unconventional, fantastic, far-out (*Slang*).

ant. 1 tamed, cultivated, cared-for, domesticated, acclimated. **2** cultured, civilized, enlightened, advanced, cultivated. **3** disciplined, steady, composed, thoughtful, wise. **4** proper, strict, prim, virtuous, moral. **5** calm, sane, sober, lucid, rational. **6** ordinary, conventional, humdrum, down-to-earth, realistic.

wilderness *n.* **1** wasteland, wilds, desert, barrens, wild, bush, tundra, outback, steppe. **2** confusion, profusion, welter, congeries, multitude, host, mass, clutter.

wildlife *n.* fauna, game, animals, animal kingdom, creation, creatures.

wile *n.* trick, artifice, ruse, maneuver, stratagem, deception, trap, craft, device, fraud, cheat, snare, contrivance, machination. —*v.* lure, beguile, mislead, entice, attract, seduce, lead astray, delude, fascinate, charm, bewitch, decoy, dupe, bamboozle.

wilful *adj.* WILLFUL.

will *n.* **1** choice, order, decision, judgment, intent, volition, bidding, behest, discretion, direction. **2** purpose, wish, desire, mind, intention, inclination, pleasure, preference, decree, disposition. **3** volition, self-control, forcefulness, willpower, resoluteness, steadfastness, persistence, determination, resolution, decision. —*v.* decide, choose, resolve, intend, determine, see fit, purpose, elect, prefer, list, want, opt, bid.

willful *adj.* **1** deliberate, intentional, contemplated, planned, designed, premeditated, voluntary, intended, willed, volitional. **2** stubborn, headstrong, inflexible, unruly, obstinate, recalcitrant, ungovernable, intractable, refractory, pigheaded.

ant. 1 accidental, involuntary, unwitting, unintentional, instinctive. **2** tractable, submissive, biddable, obedient, docile.

willing *adj.* agreeable, obliging, responsive, acquiescent, accommodating, compliant, ready, inclined, disposed, amenable, content, eager, fain, prompt.

ant. unwilling, reluctant, averse, loath, disinclined, resistant.

willowy *adj.* svelte, slender, lissome, graceful, long-legged, lithe, flexible, supple, limber, pliant.

ant. dumpy, thickset, stocky, stiff, rigid, inflexible.

willpower *n.* volition, determination, will, persistence, steadfastness, firmness, resoluteness, perseverance, stubbornness, insistence, inflexibility, grit, drive, strength.

ant. apathy, languor, indecision, impotence, weakness.

willy-nilly *adv.* unavoidably, compulsively, inevitably, perforce, irresistibly, involuntarily, inadvertently, necessarily, of necessity, inescapably, helplessly, uncontrollably, come what may.

ant. voluntarily, purposely, by design, deliberately, intentionally.

wily *adj.* sly, cunning, shrewd, foxy, designing, artful, crafty, calculating, scheming, shifty, slick, tricky, sharp.

ant. simple, naive, dull, fatuous, foolish, stupid.

win *v.* **1** triumph, conquer, prevail, succeed, surpass, defeat, beat, best, worst, vanquish, lead. **2** get, achieve, attain, earn, obtain, procure, acquire, reach, secure, gain. —*n.* victory, success, triumph, conquest, killing, achievement, hit, coup, winning, accomplishment, feat.

ant. *v.* **1, 2** fail, miss, lose, fall. *n.* loss, defeat, beating, upset, failure, washout (*Slang*).

wince *v.* flinch, shrink, cringe, recoil, draw back, quail, start, tremble, quake, falter, hesitate, blench, shy.

wind[1] *n.* **1** breeze, draft, air, breath, gust, blast, zephyr. **2** breath, breathing, respiration, pant, gasp, expiration, sigh. **3** chatter, twaddle, gabble, small talk, prattle, tittle-tattle, hot air

(*Slang*), drivel, nattering (*Brit.*), gab. **4** bragging, conceit, self-importance, braggadocio, bluster, swagger, boastfulness, vanity, gasconade, fanfaronade.

ant. 4 self-effacement, self-deprecation, modesty, humility, diffidence, reserve.

wind² *v.* **1** coil, twine, wrap, twist, spiral, furl, encircle, entwine, turn, screw. **2** meander, zigzag, pivot, veer, sinuate, slither, crank, curve, bend, slue. —*n.* bend, turn, twist, circuit, loop, curl, convolution, twirl, fold, quirk, zigzag, circle.

windbag *n.* chatterbox, babbler, blatherer, monologist, blabber, braggadocio, braggart, gossip, prattler, rattler, yakker (*Slang*).

wind down taper off, de-escalate, slacken, decrease, cool off, lessen, diminish, dwindle, subside, decline, decelerate, reduce.

ant. accelerate, intensify, escalate, exacerbate, heat up, rev up.

windfall *n.* luck, fortune, manna, fluke, godsend, boon, stroke of luck, find, strike, jackpot.

ant. mischance, misfortune, accident, loss, mishap.

winding *adj.* spiral, twisting, serpentine, crooked, curved, sinuous, writhing, bending, turning, tortuous, coiling, reeling.

ant. straight, direct, undeviating, true, right, plumb.

window *n.* opening, gap, aperture, portal, slot, orifice, viewer, avenue, eyepiece, passage, channel, entrance.

windup *n.* conclusion, culmination, end, finale, denouement, finish, wrap-up, completion, termination, eventuality, postscript.

ant. onset, beginning, conception, outbreak, start.

wind up conclude, settle, terminate, liquidate, complete, wrap up, finalize, close, finish, end, dispose, discharge, disentangle.

ant. begin, start, commence, initiate, undertake.

windy *adj.* **1** stormy, tempestuous, blowy, gusty, blustery, breezy, squally, blustering. **2** boastful, talkative, wordy, verbose, conceited, bombastic, glib, pompous, idle, empty.

ant. 1 calm, still, windless, becalmed, close. **2** reticent, taciturn, reserved, modest, quiet.

wing *n.* annex, ell, extension, addition, arm, flank, appendage, branch, section, sector. —*v.* **1** fly, aviate, plane, soar, take wing, sail, drift, glide, zoom, hover. **2** speed, hasten, fly, hurry, rush, zoom, dart, flit, buzz, whisk.

wing it *Slang* IMPROVISE.

wink *v.* **1** blink, nictitate, nictate, squint, bat. **2** twinkle, glimmer, gleam, sparkle, winkle, glitter, flash. —*n.* blink, nictitation, squint, twinkle, winking, bat.

wink at OVERLOOK.

winner *n.* champion, victor, laureate, champ (*Slang*), master, conqueror, leader, medalist, best, top, ace.

ant. loser, also-ran, underdog, failure, washout (*Slang*).

winning *adj.* attractive, winsome, charming, engaging, delightful, amiable, fascinating, captivating, bewitching, endearing, sweet, lovely, alluring, enchanting, fetching, becoming, disarming.

ant. unattractive, unpleasant, offensive, irksome, uncongenial, repellent.

winnow *v.* separate, cull, divide, strain, sieve, sift, screen, select, part, glean, pick, weed out.

wino *n.* DRUNKARD.

win over persuade, influence, sway, entice, move, attract, inveigle, convince, convert, prevail on.

winsome *adj.* charming, attractive, winning, comely, appealing, amiable, alluring, bewitching, endearing, debonair, engaging, lovable, fascinating, pleasant.

ant. repulsive, disagreeable, unpleasant, repellent, distasteful, ugly.

wintry *adj.* cold, bleak, cheerless, chilly, frosty, harsh, stormy, boreal, polar, arctic, icy, frozen, ice-bound, brumal.

ant. summery, pleasant, sunny, genial, bright, mild.

wipe *v.* rub, brush, swipe, mop, towel, clean, dry, clear, cleanse, burnish, polish, swab, erase, sponge. —*n.* rub, stroke, lick, pass, swab, mop, scrub, toweling, sponging, cleansing, drying.

wipe out kill, murder, annihilate, destroy, exterminate, eradicate, obliterate, raze, extirpate, efface, rub out (*Slang*), waste (*Slang*), liquidate.

wiretap *v.* EAVESDROP.

wiry *adj.* tough, lean, strong, stringy, slender, sinewy.

ant. pudgy, flabby, flaccid, fat.

wisdom *n.* discernment, judgment, insight, wit, common sense, rationality, sapience, sagacity, profundity, enlightenment, erudition, knowledge, intelligence, learning, prudence, intuition.

ant. stupidity, fatuity, ignorance, insanity, folly, idiocy.

wise *adj.* **1** discerning, sapient, farseeing, sage, intuitive, judicious, sensible, prudent, sane, learned. **2** shrewd, calculating, cunning, crafty, artful, foxy, keen, sharp, politic, wary. **3** aware, alert to, alive to, mindful, cognizant, informed, acquainted with, knowing, *au courant*, hip (*Slang*). **4** *Slang* arrogant, impertinent, flippant, flip, self-assured, audacious, impudent, fresh (*Slang*), smart, smart-alecky.

ant. **1** simple, foolish, ignorant, obtuse, dull. **2** open, sincere, straightforward, upright, direct. **3** unaware, ignorant, unmindful, naive, stupid. **4** humble, modest, meek, unpretentious, respectful.

wisecrack *n. Slang* witticism, joke, quip, squib, jibe, gag, jest, pleasantry, spoof, *bon mot*, taunt, sneer, epigram.

wish *n.* **1** desire, longing, hankering, inclination, yearning, craving, want, will, liking, pleasure. **2** petition, request, appeal, application, entreaty, plea, suit, behest, proposal, invocation. —*v.* **1** desire, yearn, long for, crave, covet, fancy, care for, need, lack, want. **2** request, command, entreat, ask, order, direct, beg, plead, beseech, implore.

ant. *n.* **1** distaste, aversion, dislike, revulsion, disinclination.

wishful *adj.* wistful, desirous, yearning, longing, hopeful, optimistic, dreamy, unrealistic, fanciful.

wishy-washy *adj.* **1** thin, diluted, watery, flat, insipid, weak, flavorless, tasteless, attenuated, adulterated. **2** weak, ineffective, purposeless, indecisive, namby-pamby, feeble, effeminate, ineffectual, irresolute, soft, languid.

ant. **1** tangy, tasty, strong, flavorful. **2** aggressive, active, decisive, effective.

wisp *n.* **1** tuft, shred, snippet, bunch, tatter, strip, clutch, clump. **2** trace, streak, touch, shred, shade, hint, bit, film, jot, speck, iota, whit.

wistful *adj.* **1** wishful, yearning, desirous, craving, athirst, aspiring, longing, desirous, unsatisfied, unfulfilled. **2** musing, pensive, reflective, introspective, contemplative, sad, thoughtful, dreamy, meditative, melancholy.

ant. **1** sated, replete, satisfied, satiated, full. **2** giddy, frivolous, thoughtless, flighty, gay.

wit *n.* **1** intelligence, cleverness, intellect, reason, common sense, mind, gray matter, sense, brains, brainpower. **2** humorist, wag, funnyman, jester, wisecracker (*Slang*), jokesmith, comedian, funster, punster, banterer. **3** repartee, humor, irony, drollery, satire, sarcasm, wordplay, witticisms, gags, jokes, puns, quips, wisecracks (*Slang*).

ant. **1** stupidity, foolishness, idiocy, folly, fatuity, insanity.

witch *n.* **1** magician, sorceress, enchantress, pythoness, sibyl. **2** hag, crone, harridan, beldam.

witchcraft *n.* black magic, sorcery, enchantment, witchery, necromancy, black art, diabolism, wizardry, voodooism, obeah, shamanism, the occult.

witch doctor shaman, medicine man, faith healer, exorcist, magician, sorcerer, witch, warlock, wizard, hex, voodoo.

witchery *n.* WITCHCRAFT.

witching *adj.* BEWITCHING.

withal *adv.* notwithstanding, nevertheless, nonetheless, however, still, yet, all the same, at all events, on the other hand, for all that, in spite of that.

withdraw *v.* **1** remove, draw away, take away, draw back, draw out, take out, take back, retract. **2** retire, depart, resign, vacate, leave, abdicate, quit, relinquish, go, secede, retreat.

withdrawal *n.* recession, retreat, secession, flight, separation, desertion, retirement, exodus, abdication, exit, departure, leave, evacuation.

withdrawn *adj.* aloof, unsociable, reclusive, introverted, unresponsive, unfriendly, distant, solitary, retiring, secluded, detached, uninvolved. **ant.** outgoing, sociable, responsive, involved, genial, friendly.

wither *v.* **1** dry out, shrink, shrivel, droop, wilt, fade, decay, brown, wrinkle, wizen, waste away. **2** languish, decline, decay, fade, fail, deteriorate, degenerate, molder, worsen, retrograde. **ant.** **1** freshen, revive, renew, recover, straighten. **2** flourish, thrive, prosper, recover, improve.

withhold *v.* **1** hold back, restrain, keep back, check, curb, repress, suppress, delay, hinder, inhibit, detain. **2** refuse, deny, hold, keep, hold back, reserve, retain, keep back, maintain, suppress, conceal, hide. **ant.** **1** promote, expedite, advance, hasten. **2** give, grant, release, relinquish, reveal.

with-it *adj.* *Slang* up-to-date, in the swim, up-to-the-minute, modern,

swinging (*Slang*), fashionable, advanced, avant-garde, current, *au courant*, trendy (*Slang*). **ant.** old-fashioned, old-fogyish, out-of-date, passé, obsolete, dated.

withstand *v.* resist, oppose, endure, face up to, strive against, combat, confront, hold out against, weather, breast, face, brave, defy, antagonize, stand up to. **ant.** falter, retreat, fail, give way, weaken, fall back.

witless *adj.* foolish, silly, stupid, slow, daft, dull-witted, dumb, shallow, obtuse, feeble-minded, half-witted, addle-brained. **ant.** sharp, quick, clever, intelligent, alert.

witness *n.* **1** bystander, viewer, onlooker, spectator, observer, eyewitness, beholder, deponent, corroborator, testifier. **2** evidence, testimony, corroboration, attestation, confirmation, deposition, declaration, proof, affirmation. —*v.* see, experience, observe, look on, note, notice, perceive, behold, view, watch, sight, observe. **ant.** *v.* ignore, miss, disregard, overlook.

witticism *n.* *bon mot*, epigram, quip, jest, conceit, riposte, pleasantry, sally, squib, joke, pun, gag, quirk, paradox, wisecrack (*Slang*).

witty *adj.* humorous, facetious, jocular, clever, ingenious, original, sharp, quick, alert, funny, droll, waggish, laughable, jocose. **ant.** stupid, dull, slow, obtuse, fatuous, witless.

wizard *n.* **1** magician, sorcerer, necromancer, diviner, soothsayer, conjurer, enchanter, wonder-worker. **2** genius, prodigy, mastermind, expert, wonder, adept, specialist, virtuoso, master, pro. **ant.** **2** dolt, imbecile, incompetent, clod, amateur.

wizardry *n.* magic, sorcery, witchery, enchantment, black art, conjuration, diabolism, necromancy, witchcraft, occultism, alchemy, voodooism, obeah.

wizened *adj.* shriveled, dried up, withered, sere, faded, wilted, desiccated, cramped, shrunken, puckered, gnarled, wizen.
ant. turgid, plump, rounded, swollen.

wobble *v.* **1** stagger, dodder, wabble, sway, totter, waver, rock, waggle, vibrate, oscillate, shimmy, roll, reel. **2** VACILLATE.

woe *n.* **1** sorrow, anguish, grief, regret, suffering, agony, misery, wretchedness, distress, pain. **2** affliction, calamity, disaster, catastrophe, tribulation, adversity, trial, hardship, trouble, misfortune.
ant. **1** joy, happiness, bliss, pleasure, felicity. **2** blessing, benefit, luck, fortune, prosperity.

woebegone *adj.* MOURNFUL.

woeful *adj.* **1** direful, baneful, unfortunate, grievous, distressing, lamentable, disastrous, calamitous, catastrophic, tragic. **2** sorrowful, mournful, distressed, doleful, woebegone, sad, unhappy, anguished, wretched, grieved. **3** paltry, mean, shabby, wretched, miserable, deplorable, sorry, pitiful, inadequate, worthless.
ant. **1** fortunate, propitious, providential, auspicious, beneficial. **2** happy, glad, carefree, contented, cheerful. **3** generous, ample, luxurious, prosperous, enviable.

wolf *n.* **1** savage, fiend, shark, ruffian, brute, sadist, tiger, sharper, cheat, swindler. **2** *Slang* libertine, philanderer, profligate, rake, roué, womanizer, lady-killer, ladies' man, Don Juan, Casanova, masher (*Slang*).
ant. **1** lamb, innocent, Samaritan, philanthropist, benefactor.

wolf down gulp, bolt, devour, raven, cram, gobble, gorge, gluttonize, swallow whole, attack.
ant. pick up, nibble, peck at, nip, sniff, sample.

wolfish *adj.* rapacious, savage, fierce, voracious, predatory, insatiable,

greedy, ravenous, avaricious, bloodthirsty, ferocious, merciless, pitiless.
ant. gentle, mild, compassionate, harmless, generous, benevolent.

womanizer *n.* lecher, libertine, profligate, sensualist, rake, roué, wolf (*Slang*), debauchee, satyr, goat, rip, fornicator, Don Juan, Casanova.
ant. ascetic, celibate, puritan, monogamist, family man, monk.

womanly *adj.* feminine, matronly, ladylike, motherly, gentle, sympathetic, nurturing, tender, compassionate, unaggressive.

wonder *n.* **1** astonishment, surprise, wonderment, stupefaction, fascination, puzzlement, awe, admiration, bewilderment, amazement. **2** miracle, marvel, sensation, prodigy, eye-opener, portent, rarity, bombshell, corker (*Slang*), dynamite, dynamo, curiosity, surprise. —*v.* **1** doubt, puzzle, ponder, question, query, conjecture, speculate, meditate. **2** marvel, boggle, start, admire, gape, stare, hold one's breath.
ant. *n.* **1** stolidity, boredom, coolness, sang-froid, calm, composure. **2** commonplace, stereotype, triviality, bore, trifle.

wonderful *adj.* astonishing, wondrous, awesome, miraculous, marvelous, prodigious, spectacular, fabulous, awe-inspiring, striking, surprising, singular, unusual.
ant. common, banal, everyday, normal, wonted, nondescript.

wonderment *n.* surprise, wonder, astonishment, amazement, fascination, awe, incredulity, bewilderment, confusion, excitement, transport.

wondrous *adj.* WONDERFUL.

wont *n.* habit, custom, practice, use, rule, way, habitude, usage, fashion, manner, mode, vogue.

woo *v.* **1** court, pay suit, make love to, make advances, chase, pursue, set one's cap for, address. **2** court, pursue, cajole, flatter, jolly, wheedle, coax, influence, persuade.

wooden *adj.* **1** *of physical movement:*

stiff, awkward, rigid, ungainly, gauche, gawky, graceless, clumsy, inept, maladroit. **2** *of manner:* unbending, stiff, pompous, formal, stilted, awkward, rigid, tense, taut, correct, artificial, cold, ceremonious, distant, off-putting, uptight (*Slang*). **ant. 1** graceful, lissome, agile, pliable, flexible, flowing. **2** relaxed, warm, informal, welcoming, disarming.

woodenhead *n.* BLOCKHEAD.

woodland *n.* timberland, forest, bush, woods, brush, grove, thicket, copse, covert, shrubbery, parkland.

wooer *n.* suitor, gallant, beau, lover, admirer, sweetheart, fiancé, boy friend, inamorato, cavalier, steady (*Slang*), flame (*Slang*).

woolgathering *n.* daydreaming, absentmindedness, preoccupation, reverie, musing, abstraction, wandering, brown study, inattention, vagary. **ant.** attention, concentration, vigilance, alertness, heed.

woolly *adj.* fuzzy, vague, blurred, nebulous, obscure, hazy, clouded, foggy, murky, unfocused. **ant.** sharp, clear, clear-cut, well-defined, definite.

woozy *adj. Slang* befuddled, confused, hazy, addled, inebriated, muddled, bemused, fuddled, dizzy, tipsy, punch-drunk, punchy. **ant.** clear-headed, steady, lucid, composed, sober.

word *n.* **1** lexeme, graph, phone, name, vocable, term. **2** speech, talk, utterance, discourse, expression, idiom, locution, remark, comment, words. **3** message, news, report, gossip, rumor, communication, account, information, tidings, advice. **4** promise, pledge, assurance, assertion, avowal, word of honor, engagement, warrant, troth, declaration. —*v.* phrase, express, style, set forth, voice, utter, put, enunciate, couch, give voice to, frame, formulate.

wordage *n.* WORDINESS.

wordbook *n.* thesaurus, vocabulary,

lexicon, dictionary, glossary, gloss, gradus, speller.

word for word verbatim, literally, to the letter, strictly, completely, faithfully, exactly, precisely, fully, totally, truly. **ant.** figuratively, loosely, approximately, in other words, paraphrastically.

wordiness *n.* verbiage, verbosity, prolixity, grandiloquence, bombast, redundancy, tautology, circumlocution, indirection, long-windedness, wordage. **ant.** shortness, brevity, conciseness, economy, simplicity.

wording *n.* phrasing, phraseology, diction, style, syntax, verbiage, locution, language, idiom, parlance, collocation.

wordless *adj.* dumb, silent, inarticulate, voiceless, mute, speechless, mum, tongue-tied, taciturn, soundless. **ant.** garrulous, voluble, talkative, prolix, wordy.

wordy *adj.* verbose, prolix, long-winded, diffuse, rambling, talkative, loquacious, redundant, garrulous, inflated, periphrastic, circumlocutory, tautological, roundabout. **ant.** concise, brief, terse, succinct, pithy, trenchant.

work *n.* **1** labor, toil, exertion, effort, travail, moil, drudgery, industry, grind, slavery. **2** job, occupation, calling, employment, profession, vocation, metier, industry, business, trade. **3** task, job, chore, undertaking, project, stint, deed, feat, enterprise, performance, achievement. **4** WORKMANSHIP. —*v.* **1** labor, hire out, toil, drudge, moil, sweat, grub, strive, slave, grind, travail. **2** function, operate, run, go, act, perform. **3** succeed, prosper, prevail, influence, achieve, triumph, flourish. **4** cause, bring about, produce, create, make, effect, generate, accomplish, perform, do. **5** drive, handle, wield, control, operate, manage, ply, use. **6** manipulate, knead, process, shape, prepare, carve, treat, chisel. **7** solve, figure out, work out, untangle, explain, answer, crack, decipher.

ant. *n.* **1** play, leisure, idleness, ease, sloth, rest. **2** unemployment, inactivity, stoppage, cessation, halt. *v.* **1** idle, rest, laze, play. **2** stop, stall, balk, fail. **3** fizzle, misfire, lose out, fail, collapse.

workable *adj.* practical, practicable, feasible, doable, possible, attainable, useful, achievable, serviceable, operative, effective, effectual, viable.

ant. impossible, impractical, unattainable, unworkable, useless.

workaday *adj.* everyday, commonplace, prosaic, wonted, humdrum, accustomed, familiar, usual, ordinary, common, routine, regular, habitual.

ant. unusual, gala, red-letter, extraordinary, special, eventful.

worker *n.* workman, workingman, workingwoman, workwoman, employee, hand, helper, wage earner, toiler, laborer, doer, agent, drudge, slave, producer, breadwinner.

workingman *n.* WORKER.

workings *n.* WORKS.

workingwoman *n.* WORKER.

workman *n.* WORKER.

workmanlike *adj.* masterly, expert, skillful, competent, thorough, proficient, capable, careful, meticulous, precise, accurate, neat, adept, professional, tidy.

ant. amateurish, incompetent, botchy, slap-dash, clumsy, unskillful.

workmanship *n.* skill, craftsmanship, expertise, execution, handiwork, work, construction, manufacture, texture, technique, proficiency, competence, manipulation.

work of art *objet d'art, chef-d'oeuvre,* masterpiece, masterwork, classic, gem, jewel, nonpareil, treasure, museum piece, creation.

workout *n.* drill, practice, exercise, conditioning, warmup, training.

work out 1 develop, form, devise, con-

trive, elaborate, evolve, design, plan, arrange, work up. **2** succeed, prosper, flourish, work, pan out, result, conclude, terminate. **3** exercise, warm up, drill, practice, train, condition.

works *n.* machinery, workings, action, mechanism, gear, apparatus, engine, motion, movement.

workwoman *n.* WORKER.

world *n.* **1** earth, globe, orb, planet, terra firma. **2** universe, macrocosm, cosmos, creation, nature, existence. **3** system, group, division, phylum, kingdom, realm, section, set. **4** milieu, ambience, circumstances, environment, conditions, surroundings. **5** much, multitude, host, mass, heap, pile, mountain, sea, lot, many, oodles.

worldly *adj.* **1** mundane, earthly, secular, profane, temporal, terrene, worldly-minded, materialistic, terrestrial, sublunary. **2** sophisticated, knowing, shrewd, politic, worldly-wise, practical, blasé, realistic, astute, experienced, urbane, cosmopolitan.

ant. **1** spiritual, metaphysical, unworldly, unearthly. **2** naive, artless, gullible, simple, guileless.

worldly-minded *adj.* WORLDLY.

worldly-wise *adj.* WORLDLY.

world-weariness *n.* WELTSCHMERZ.

worldwide *adj.* universal, ubiquitous, omnipresent, pandemic, widespread, overall, world, global, general, all-inclusive, international, cosmopolitan, ecumenical.

ant. local, insular, national, parochial, restricted, limited.

worm *n.* **1** canker, blight, cancer, bane, scorpion, scourge, curse, plague. **2** wretch, sneak, cur, heel (*Slang*), louse (*Slang*), miscreant, scoundrel, rogue, reprobate, villain. —*v.* insinuate, ingratiate, infiltrate, penetrate, slip, creep, inch, crawl, intrude, wriggle, writhe.

worn *adj.* **1** damaged, frayed, tattered, shabby, used, threadbare, dingy,

dilapidated, abraded, exhausted. **2** hackneyed, shopworn, banal, secondhand, trite, stereotyped, jejune, vapid, inane, outworn.
ant. 1 new, undamaged, fresh, brand-new, unused. **2** original, up-to-date, novel, fresh, daring.

worn-out *adj.* exhausted, tired-out, spent, run-down, jaded, effete, prostrate, weary, dog-tired, played-out, tuckered-out, overtired.
ant. fresh, renewed, refreshed, rested, restored.

worrisome *adj.* annoying, nagging, irritating, vexatious, galling, distressing, disturbing, troublesome, vexing, irksome, bothersome, trying, provoking, rankling, carking.
ant. pleasing, heartening, encouraging, gratifying, cheering, agreeable.

worry *v.* fret, trouble, chafe, agonize, brood, bother, pester, annoy, harass, harry, tease, torment, plague. —*n.* **1** anxiety, uneasiness, apprehension, concern, care, misgiving, solicitude, fear, trepidation, vexation, agitation. **2** trouble, care, grief, plague, burden, hurt, misfortune, annoyance, difficulty, threat.
ant. *v.* soothe, reassure, pacify, lull, comfort. —*n.* **1** relief, contentment, easiness, unconcern, freedom, insouciance.

worse *adj.* inferior, lower, poorer, lesser, baser, second-rate, debased, meaner, weaker, degraded, subverted, deteriorated, deficient.
ant. better, finer, higher, purer, stronger, improved.

worsen *v.* deteriorate, decay, degenerate, spoil, decline, disintegrate, impair, debase, damage, aggravate, exacerbate, contaminate, molder.
ant. better, improve, brighten, recover, mend.

worship *n.* **1** adoration, homage, devotion, cult, reverence, admiration, love, idolatry, idolization, glorification, esteem, respect. **2** liturgy, ritual, celebration, ceremony, rite, service, oblation. —*v.* **1** venerate,

reverence, revere, glorify, honor, exalt, adore, respect. **2** dote on, adore, admire, idolize, cherish, love, adulate, treasure.
ant. *v.* **1** flout, scoff at, dishonor, mock, blaspheme. **2** detest, disdain, despise, dislike, hate.

worshipful *adj.* reverent, adoring, idolatrous, devout, reverential, fervent, pious, venerating, devotional, sanctified, prayerful, solemn, consecrated, prostrate.
ant. impious, blasphemous, irreverent, abusive, profane.

worst *v.* defeat, vanquish, best, beat, conquer, overthrow, subdue, crush, quell, overcome, overpower, master, rout, subjugate.

worth *n.* **1** value, excellence, merit, worthiness, importance, significance, usefulness, virtue, credit. **2** price, cost, expense, value, charge, estimation, appraisal. **3** wealth, riches, assets, holdings, portfolio, estate, possessions, property.
ant. 1 uselessness, unworthiness, insignificance, paltriness, triviality.

worthless *adj.* valueless, useless, futile, unimportant, profitless, vain, feckless, purposeless, unproductive, pointless, meaningless, trashy, meretricious, empty, contemptible, despicable, barren, trivial, paltry.
.**ant.** worthwhile, worthy, important, useful, essential.

worthwhile *adj.* rewarding, beneficial, serviceable, productive, profitable, useful, valuable, advantageous, gainful, lucrative, helpful, expedient, important, invaluable.
ant. profitless, useless, worthless, wasteful, vain.

worthy *adj.* deserving, estimable, excellent, commendable, worthwhile, reputable, exemplary, meritorious, reliable, dependable, good, valuable, suitable, fit. —*n.* notable, pillar of society, luminary, VIP, magnate, personage, bigwig, eminence, leader, name, decision-maker, big shot (*Slang*), big wheel (*Slang*).

ant. *adj.* worthless, useless, unworthy, bad, disreputable, valueless. —*n.* nobody, cipher, man in the street, nonentity, John Doe.

would-be *adj.* self-styled, pretended, so-called, manqué, quasi, nominal, pseudo, spurious, counterfeit, surrogate, bogus, substitute.

ant. genuine, actual, bona fide, real, true.

wound *n.* **1** injury, laceration, lesion, hurt, sore, cut, scratch, gash, abrasion, stab, trauma. **2** insult, offense, pain, hurt, trauma, grief, blow, injury, affront, loss. —*v.* **1** hurt, lacerate, injure, bruise, traumatize, cut, scratch, stab, gash, abrade. **2** insult, affront, offend, mortify, outrage, injure, pain, pique, hurt, grieve, traumatize.

wow *v. Slang* astonish, amaze, astound, bowl over, dumbfound, delight, impress, electrify, overwhelm, surprise, enchant, excite.

wrack *n.* **1** ruin, destruction, ruination, havoc, devastation, desolation, dissolution, waste, perdition, obliteration, disintegration. **2** WRECKAGE. —*v.* WRECK.

wraith *n.* ghost, specter, spook, apparition, shade, spirit, banshee, phantom, phantasm, doppelganger, eidolon, vision.

wrangle *v.* argue, quarrel, debate, dispute, bicker, scrap, spar, brawl, contend, altercate, squabble, differ, jangle, cavil, spat. —*n.* dispute, tiff, quarrel, spat, set-to, argument, altercation, scrap, fight, squabble, clash, imbroglio, fracas, row.

wrap *v.* enfold, envelop, bundle, enclose, cover, package, roll up, swathe, muffle, wind, furl, fold, conceal. —*n.* mantle, cloak, cape, shrug, shawl, jacket, wraparound, duster, coat, pelisse, capote.

ant. *v.* unwrap, open, uncover, unfold, unfurl.

wrap-up *n.* SUMMARY.

wrap up conclude, finish, complete, top off, crown, clinch, wind up, sum up, summarize, recapitulate, dispose of, finalize, terminate.

wrath *n.* rage, anger, fury, indignation, resentment, choler, exasperation, vexation, irritation, ire.

ant. pleasure, forbearance, delight, equanimity, gratification.

wrathful *adj.* angry, furious, mad, raging, incensed, outraged, wroth, enraged, irate, indignant, resentful.

ant. contented, pleased, equable, appeased, pleasant, satisfied.

wreak *v.* inflict, visit, exact, bring about, bring down on, work, commit, cause, exercise, effect.

ant. forbear, hold back, abstain from, desist from.

wreath *n.* band, circlet, spiral, ring, garland, chaplet, festoon, crown, coronet, diadem.

wreathe *v.* encircle, entwine, surround, festoon, frame, adorn, ring, wind, twist, writhe, twine, intertwine, interweave, enfold.

wreck *v.* destroy, raze, ruin, wrack, smash, demolish, spoil, ravage, blast, gut, devastate, shatter, dilapidate. —*n.* **1** wreckage, destruction, demolition, fragmentation, crash, ruin, devastation, smash, crack-up. **2** WRECKAGE. **3** basket case (*Slang*).

ant. *v.* preserve, guard, secure, conserve, protect.

wreckage *n.* detritus, debris, flotsam, relics, trash, wrack, jetsam, fragments, rubbish, rubble, junk, waste, ruins, remains, hulk, shell, wreck.

wrench *n.* **1** twist, jerk, pull, strain, sprain, cramp, crick, spasm, pang, charley horse, stitch. **2** pain, ache, twinge, pang, blow, shock, throe, spasm, anguish, dolor. —*v.* **1** twist, jerk, pull, wrest, tear, contort, wring, sprain, strain, turn. **2** rack, torment, torture, harass, wring, rend, harrow, vex.

wrest *v.* pull, twist, force, move, turn, wrench, wring, seize, take.

wrestle *v.* struggle, contend, grapple, compete, strive, contest, combat, engage, joust, fight, labor, strain.

wretch *n.* **1** ruffian, cur, good-for-nothing, rogue, villain, worm, pig, swine, scoundrel, sneak, louse (*Slang*), heel (*Slang*), rat (*Slang*). **2** unfortunate, victim, martyr, scapegoat, sufferer, pariah, outcast.

wretched *adj.* **1** dejected, depressed, unhappy, mournful, miserable, distressed, sad, forlorn, afflicted, pitiable, woeful. **2** destitute, poor, needy, indigent, deprived, poverty-stricken, squalid, pitiful, unfortunate, hopeless, miserable. **3** unsatisfactory, sleazy, shoddy, poor, cheap, inferior, trashy, worthless, bad, paltry. **4** despicable, contemptible, vile, scurvy, shameful, base, mean, bad, outrageous, ignominious. **ant. 1** happy, cheerful, glad, gay, euphoric. **2** rich, comfortable, affluent, fortunate, lucky. **3** good, satisfactory, sound, first-class, well-made. **4** noble, worthy, virtuous, estimable, admirable.

wriggle *v.* **1** wiggle, twist, twitch, squirm, writhe, waggle, crawl, zigzag, wag, jerk, jiggle. **2** inveigle, wheel and deal (*Slang*), insinuate, elbow, penetrate, infiltrate, intrude, ingratiate, crawl, sneak. —*n.* jiggle, twitch, wiggle, twist, squirm, quiver, shake, waggle, wag, tremble, flutter, shiver.

wring *v.* **1** squeeze, compress, twist, extract, obtain. **2** wrest, extort, force, wrench, exact. **3** affect, touch, move, distress, torment, melt, harrow, rend, wound, pain.

wrinkle[1] *n.* crease, crumple, pucker, fold, rumple, crinkle, furrow, ridge, groove, corrugation. —*v.* crease, crumple, pucker, purse, rumple, crinkle, furrow, corrugate, fold. **ant.** smooth, straighten, flatten, iron, level.

wrinkle[2] *n.* GIMMICK.

writ *n.* SUMMONS.

write *v.* **1** pen, pencil, scrawl, scribble, jot, scratch, inscribe. **2** describe, set down, draft, frame, record, indite, fill in, put down, note down, draw up. **3** correspond, epistolize. **4** author, create, compose, originate, invent, produce.

writer *n.* **1** author, littérateur, bookman, man of letters, penman, wordsmith, hack, potboiler. **2** calligrapher, penman, copyist, scribe, chirographer.

write-up *n.* CRITIQUE.

writhe *v.* **1** twist, contort, distort, turn, wrench, coil, twine, wiggle, wriggle, squirm, weave. **2** suffer, ail, wince, pain, agonize, struggle, thrash, anguish.

writing *n.* **1** script, handwriting, hand, penmanship, longhand, scrip, calligraphy, chirography. **2** work, composition, opus, publication, document, inscription, correspondence, letter, note, notice, jotting. **3** literature, belles-lettres, letters, authorship, journalism.

wrong *adj.* **1** incorrect, mistaken, erroneous, false, untrue, inexact, inaccurate, fallacious, imprecise, faulty. **2** unsuitable, inappropriate, unfit, inapt, inept, improper, awkward, nonstandard, unacceptable, incongruous. **3** illegal, immoral, unethical, bad, evil, felonious, sinful, improper, criminal, wicked. **4** amiss, awry, faulty, askew, imperfect, inefficient, out of order, out of commission, out of kilter, inoperative. —*n.* injury, injustice, inequity, grievance, foul play, wickedness, tyranny, misdeed, trespass, sin, evil, vice, crime, oppression. —*v.* **1** injure, abuse, maltreat, oppress, victimize, cheat, mistreat, hurt, harm, persecute. **2** defame, malign, discredit, dishonor, traduce, vilify, slander, libel, denigrate, calumniate, asperse. **ant.** *adj.* **1** right, correct, true, accurate, perfect. **2** suitable, appropriate, fitting, standard, apt. **3** good, moral, licit, legal, ethical. **4** all right, efficient, working, functional, OK.

wrongdoer *n.* miscreant, sinner, evildoer, offender, transgressor, malefactor, trespasser, law-breaker, culprit, blackguard, scoundrel, criminal.

wrongful *adj.* injurious, unjust, improper, unfair, dishonest, inequitable, unethical, undue, immoral, unmoral, underhanded, wrong.
ant. fair, just, moral, proper, rightful.

wrong-headed *adj.* fractious, pigheaded, cross-grained, perverse, opinionated, intractable, unyielding, obdurate, headstrong, difficult, mulish, dogged, stubborn, contrary, froward, crotchety.

ant. compliant, open-minded, reasonable, tractable, acquiescent.
wrong-headedness *n.* OBSTINACY.
wrought *adj.* made, fashioned, formed, worked, put together, shaped, contrived, created, constructed, built, crafted.
wrought up *adj.* OVERWROUGHT.
wry *adj.* **1** askew, distorted, warped, crooked, bent, twisted, displaced, contorted, deformed, awry. **2** ironic, sardonic, dry, quizzical, mocking, sarcastic, droll, perverse, rueful, satiric, cynical.
ant. 1 straight, unbent, normal, limber, supple.

X

X-ray *n.* roentgenogram, roentgenograph, Roentgen ray, radiograph, radiogram, skiagram, skiagraph.

Y

yahoo *n.* YOKEL.
yak *Slang v.* talk, chatter, babble, prattle, gabble, gab, jabber, gas (*Slang*), yackety-yack (*Slang*), yap (*Slang*), schmooze (*Slang*), chew the fat (*Slang*), chew the rag (*Slang*), natter (*Brit. Slang*). —*n.* **1** chat, chitchat, gossip, chatter, talk, heart-to-heart, tête-à-tête, prattle, schmooze (*Slang*), kaffeeklatsch. **2** guffaw, laugh, belly laugh, horselaugh, howl, scream, roar, yuk (*Slang*), yuck (*Slang*), yock (*Slang*).
yammer *v.* whine, whimper, fret, complain, grumble, wail, pule, snivel,

bleat, grouse, blubber, bawl, clamor, nag, kvetsch (*Slang*).
yank *v.* jerk, pull, grab, wrest, snatch, twist, nab, tug, twitch, wring, pluck, extract, uproot. —*n.* jerk, twist, pull, extraction, uprooting, grab, pluck, tug.
yap *n.* **1** *Slang* JABBER. **2** YELP. **3** *Slang* MOUTH. —*v.* **1** *Slang* JABBER. **2** YELP.
yard *n.* enclosure, courtyard, compound, pale, close, pound, pen, backyard, patio, lawn, garden, grounds.
yardstick *n.* criterion, standard, measure, norm, example, touchstone,

measuring rod, gauge, rule, test, canon, basis, guide, guideline, exemplar, rule of thumb.

yarn *n.* tale, story, anecdote, fabrication, narrative, fiction, reminiscence, adventure, myth, whodunit, thriller, romance, cliffhanger.

yaw *v.* pitch, roll, toss, turn, bend, lean, swerve, veer, tack, curve, deviate, zigzag, change course.

yawp *v., n.* YELP.

yearly *adj.* annual.

yearn for desire, want, ache for, hope for, crave, pine for, wish, hunger for, covet, dream about, long for, thirst for, hanker after, aspire to.

yearning *n.* craving, desire, hunger, ache, thirst, hankering, longing, itch, yen, hope, aspiration, ambition, sadness.

years *n.* era, time, period, epoch, decade, days, span, age, dynasty, reign, administration, generation.

yeasty *adj.* frothy, foamy, bubbly, spumy, scummy, lathery, spumous, barmy, sudsy.

yegg *n. Slang* THIEF.

yell *v.* shout, scream, yowl, howl, holler, clamor, vociferate, yammer, screech, roar, bark, bellow, bawl, yelp, shriek. —*n.* shout, shriek, scream, howl, yowl, holler, clamor, screech, bellow, yelp, bark, yammer.

yellow *adj.* **1** sensational, lurid, muckraking, melodramatic, dirty, cheap, sordid, overemotional, rabble-rousing. **2** cowardly, craven, mean, dishonorable, untrustworthy, contemptible, weak, sneaky, unreliable, fearful, apprehensive, scared, frightened, chicken (*Slang*). **ant. 2** bold, rash, daring, intrepid, courageous.

yelp *v.* yip, yap, yawp, squeak, squeal, shriek, bark, howl, screech, cry out. —*n.* yip, yap, yawp, bark, shriek, squeak, squeal, cry, screech, howl, complaint.

yen *n.* appetite, craving, itch, taste, desire, longing, hunger, thirst, fancy, yearning, concupiscence, lust, letch (*Slang*).

yenta *n.* GOSSIP.

yeomanly *adj.* brave, rugged, stout, intrepid, trusty, valiant, courageous, stouthearted, gallant, valorous, tough, dashing, spunky, heroic, gutsy (*Slang*).

yes-man *n.* sycophant, toady, bootlicker, fawner, stooge, flunky, henchman, vassal, flatterer, tool, cat's-paw, hanger-on.

yet *adv.* in addition, additionally, besides, moreover, also, to boot, over and above, as well.

yield *v.* **1** produce, furnish, bring forth, provide, bear, give, offer, afford, shed, pay, beget, engender, confer, supply. **2** relinquish, surrender, give in, give up, give way, submit, accede, assent, grant, consent, comply, agree, succumb, admit, acquiesce. —*n.* product, output, result, accrual, profit, production, harvest, crop, gain, proceeds, bounty, revenue, interest, income. **ant.** *v.* **2** resist, refuse, refute, oppose, stand up to.

yip *n., v.* YELP.

yock *n. Slang* YAK.

yoke *n.* **1** bond, tie, tether, coupling, leash, link, connection, union, halter, collar, frame, crossbar, linkage, chain, halter. **2** bondage, servitude, serfdom, slavery, peonage, enslavement, duress, subjugation, confinement, coercion, burden, weight. —*v.* join, unite, combine, link, connect, couple, mate, marry, hitch, splice, fasten.

yokel *n.* bumpkin, oaf, hick, provincial, rustic, clodhopper, gawker, innocent, peasant, lout, hayseed, yahoo, ignoramus, rube (*Slang*). **ant.** cosmopolite, sophisticate, city slicker, bon vivant.

yon *adj.* YONDER.

yond *adj.* YONDER.

yonder *adj.* yon, yond, distant, faraway, faroff, thither, remote. **ant.** near, nearby, close.

young *adj.* **1** growing, youthful, youngish, pubescent, preadolescent, preteen, teen-age, adolescent, juvenile, underage, minor, junior, immature, girlish, boyish. **2** new, recent, undeveloped, untried, youngish, underdeveloped, newborn, tentative, unexplored, untested, unfulfilled. **3** vigorous, fresh, energetic, sprightly, modern, current, up-to-date, contemporary, forward-looking, active, dynamic, lively, spirited, bold, enterprising. **4** inexperienced, naive, callow, green, childish, childlike, infantile, immature, sophomoric, unsophisticated, puerile, awkward. —*n.* offspring, brood, progeny, litter, spawn, fledglings, nestlings, descendants, issue, stock, family, small fry. **ant.** *adj.* **1** mature, grown, full-grown, adult. **2** completed, developed, tested, tried and true. **3** tired, weary, ancient, aged, old-fashioned. **4** experienced, knowing, knowledgeable, weathered, sophisticated. *n.* progenitors, ancestors, parents.

youngish *adj.* YOUNG.

youngster *n.* child, tot, sapling, fledgling, youth, girl, boy, teen-ager, adolescent, preadolescent, kid, minor, junior, colt, sprout.

youth *n.* **1** childhood, boyhood, girlhood, adolescence, teens, puberty, pubescence, youthfulness, juvenility, nonage, minority, salad days, heyday. **2** infancy, beginnings, commencement, outset, start, starting point, inception, inauguration, emergence, incipience. **3** young man, juvenile, young adult, stripling, boy, lad, preadolescent, adolescent, youngster, teen-ager, minor, kid, pup.

youthful *adj.* **1** young, juvenile, inexperienced, immature, childlike, adolescent, pubescent, growing, developing, maturing, ripening, boyish, girlish. **2** energetic, robust, active, fresh, buoyant, optimistic, vernal, vigorous, burgeoning, dynamic, peppy, lighthearted, carefree, happy-go-lucky. **ant.** **1** aging, declining, waning, old. **2** tired, weary, careworn, burdened.

yowl *v., n.* YELL.

yuck *n. Slang* YAK.

yuk *n. Slang* YAK.

yummy *adj.* delicious, delightful, attractive, zesty, appetizing, tempting, satisfying, delectable, pleasing, enjoyable, savory, luscious, ambrosial, scrumptious (*Slang*). **ant.** unsavory, unappetizing, unattractive, unsatisfying.

Z

zany *adj.* ludicrous, clownish, funny, hilarious, absurd, uproarious, nonsensical, foolish, mad, crazy, wild, goofy (*Slang*), loony (*Slang*), nutty (*Slang*). —*n.* clown, fool, comic, jester, buffoon, entertainer, mime, stooge, screwball (*Slang*), comedian, comedienne.

zap *Slang n.* push, drive, muscle, vigor, energy, aggressiveness, punch, determination, thrust, vim, strength, vitality, pep, impetus. —*v.* **1** KILL. **2** ATTACK. **ant.** *n.* sloth, laziness, inertia, sluggishness.

zeal *n.* ardor, enthusiasm, spirit, fire, fervor, eagerness, devotion, passion, verve, heart, fanaticism, single-mindedness, fervency, zest, drive, ambition. **ant.** apathy, coolness, detachment, aimlessness.

zealot *n.* fanatic, monomaniac, partisan, enthusiast, champion, bigot, crank, dogmatist, doctrinaire, ideologue, witch-hunter, crank, eager beaver (*Slang*), freak (*Slang*)..

zealous *adj.* enthusiastic, fervent, overeager, devoted, sedulous, impassioned, irrational, single-minded, monomaniacal, hard-working, fanatic, fervid, undeviating, unremitting, ardent.
ant. apathetic, cool, uninterested, lazy, bored.

zenith *n.* summit, acme, top, pinnacle, tip, apogee, *ne plus ultra,* climax, peak, maximum, optimum, crest, height, culmination, consummation.
ant. bottom, nadir, depths.

zero *n.* **1** naught, cipher, 0. **2** nothing, nadir, bottom, nonexistence, none, nil, nothingness, insignificance, smoke, bubble, thin air, zilch (*Slang*), goose egg (*Slang*).

zero hour crisis, turning point, moment of truth, emergency, juncture, confrontation, test, trial, ordeal, extremity, pinch, plight, dilemma, crunch (*Slang*), squeeze.

zero in on concentrate, focus, pinpoint, converge, close in, aim, center, be on target, come to the point, hit the nail on the head.

zest *n.* pleasure, enjoyment, thrill, excitement, enthusiasm, relish, gusto, eagerness, appetite, satisfaction, delight, exhilaration, life.

ant. distaste, apathy, boredom, ennui.

zestful *adj.* exciting, thrilling, piquant, enjoyable, pleasurable, stimulating, provocative, delightful, gratifying, vivacious, animated, zippy, zingy.
ant. dull, insipid, flat, boring, listless.

zilch *n. Slang* ZERO.

zing *n.* ZIP.

zip *n.* energy, vitality, animation, vivacity, dash, sparkle, zest, verve, high spirits, get-up-and-go, zing, élan, punch, drive, pep. —*v.* dash, hurry, bustle, fly, rush, bolt, speed, dart, scurry, scamper, hasten, sprint, charge, scoot, hustle, career, skedaddle.
ant. *n.* sloth, lethargy, apathy, laziness, debility. —*v.* dawdle, idle, fritter, drag, bumble.

zippy *adj.* ENERGETIC.

zombie *n.* CORPSE.

zone *n.* sector, region, belt, locale, area, district, site, section, neighborhood, territory, terrain, sphere, precinct, province, borough, turf (*Slang*).

zonked *adj. Slang* INTOXICATED.

zoo *n.* menagerie, zoological garden, animal farm, vivarium.

zoom *v.* **1** roar, buzz, race, speed, vroom, streak, flare, flash, fly, whiz, take off, tear. **2** climb, soar, rise, ascend, escalate, skyrocket, mount, spiral, advance, increase, grow.
ant. 2 drop, descend, plummet, decrease, fall.

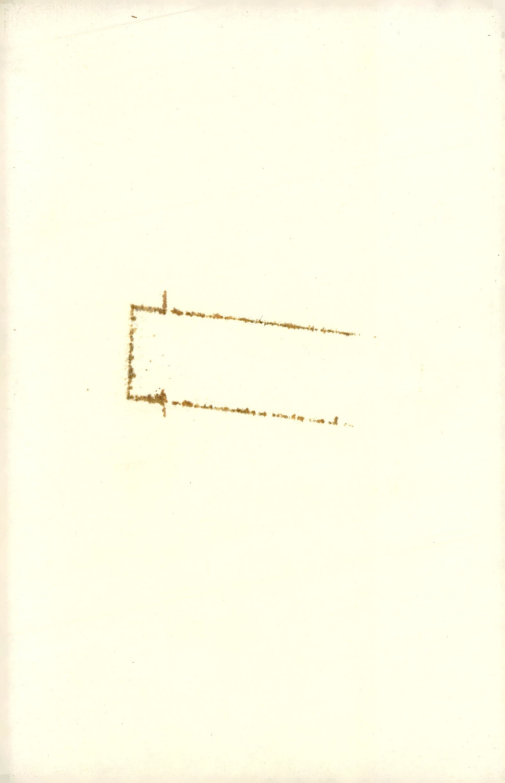